Introduction to Conflict Resolution

Introduction to Conflict Resolution

Discourses and Dynamics

Edited by
Sara Cobb, Sarah Federman,
and Alison Castel

ROWMAN & LITTLEFIELD
INTERNATIONAL

London • New York

Published by Rowman & Littlefield International Ltd
Unit A, Whitacre Mews, 26–34 Stannary Street, London SE11 4AB

www.rowmaninternational.com

Rowman & Littlefield International Ltd.is an affiliate of Rowman & Littlefield
4501 Forbes Boulevard, Suite 200, Lanham, Maryland 20706, USA
With additional offices in Boulder, New York, Toronto (Canada), and Plymouth (UK)
www.rowman.com

British Library Cataloguing in Publication Data

A catalogue record for this book is available from the British Library

ISBN: HB 978-1-7866-0851-2
       PB 978-1-7866-0852-9

Library of Congress Cataloging-in-Publication Data

Names: Cobb, Sara B., editor. | Frederman, Sarah, editor. | Castel, Alison, editor.
Title: Introduction to conflict resolution : discourses and dynamics / edited by Sara Cobb,
   Sarah Frederman, and Alison Castel.
Description: Lanham, Maryland : Rowman & Littlefield International, 2019. | Includes
   bibliographical references and index.
Identifiers: LCCN 2018046342 (print) | LCCN 2018057757 (ebook) | ISBN 9781786608536
   (Electronic) | ISBN 9781786608512 (cloth : alk. paper) | ISBN 9781786608529 (pbk. : alk.
   paper)
Subjects: LCSH: Peace-building. | Conflict management. | World politics—1945–1989. |
   World politics—1989–
Classification: LCC JZ5538 (ebook) | LCC JZ5538 .I578 2019 (print) | DDC 303.6/9—dc23
LC record available at https://lccn.loc.gov/2018046342

Contents

PART II: Epoch Two: Coexistence as Peace, 1991–2000

EPOCH TWO—TOPICS

EPOCH TWO—APPROACHES

PART III: Epoch Three: Transboundary Conflicts, 2001–Present

Preface

As the saying goes, "Every generation demands its own translation of . . ." Virgil, Marx, *Madame Bovary*, you fill in the blank. The same can be said about anthologies or any intentional collection of previously published pieces; the difference is that "generations" in the latter case tend to be very short, with different anthologies, driven by different editorial intentions, seeming to appear within years or months of one another, sometimes in virtual simultaneity. Thus, the current anthology joins several contemporary collections of important readings in Conflict Analysis and Resolution (or in Peace and Conflict Studies). What sets this one apart is the approach taken by the editors: a combination of method and sensibility, of the "voice" they bring, in organizing and contextualizing their material.

This voice and sensibility both arise from within a particular history and culture of pedagogy, that of the School for Conflict Analysis and Resolution (S-CAR) at George Mason University. In 1981, in the first academic program of its kind in the world, ICAR (as it was then called, an *Institute* not a School), the program matriculated its first postgraduate (MSc) class in Conflict Resolution. In 1988 ("Analysis" having been added to the degree), the PhD followed, and in 2004 (reversing the usual trajectory of degree evolutions in higher education), BA and BS degrees were offered. In the beginning, while relying on whatever material then existed in the emerging field—in behavioral economics, game theory, the social psychology of prejudice, Kantian (and Gandhian) peace theory—being the first university program of its kind meant that faculty faced the task of conceptualizing and tying together, into some sort of teachable coherence, what were often disparate islands of extant research, scholarship, and modalities of practice. Sometimes we argued against the limitations of existing work as we saw them, or pointed to gaps or lacunae; for example, we looked at the lack of attention to culture or gender. In all cases, we who helped teach and write the field into existence were responding to events outside the academy, to the zeitgeist and to the dominant ways of thinking (and doing) that characterized the different periods of time during which the field—reactively—developed.

This is how the editors organized their approach to the field: in terms of three broad "Epochs," each anchored in time and the major events that drive the way Conflict Analysis and Resolution scholars and practitioners conceive their projects. In each Epoch, there is a dominant discourse that sets the parameters for how Conflict Analysis and Resolution is conceived—and, equally important, what is left out and what is, in a discursive sense, "inconceivable." The editors choose selections to illuminate exemplars of theory, research, and practice that characterize each Epoch. The movement through time is from models based on rational choice and positivism, to ethnographic and interpretivist notions of culture, identity, and difference to, in Epoch Three, narratives of power, reflexivity, and as practice, participatory action research. As it turns out, this movement also charts changes in the dominant pedagogies of S-CAR and our field in general.

The main "voice" in this book is Foucauldian, and Foucault is a good choice. As frustrating as he can be, if one tries to extract clear and stable definitions of key terms ("power") or consistent statements of "theory" (something rejected outrightly), Foucault has nevertheless taught us how to employ (his preferred terms) an "analytic" (*discourse*) and a "method" (*genealogy*) that are persuasive less in the abstract than when he uses them to take on a case, as in his studies of criminality and the prison, of medicine, and sexuality. Foucault is strongest when deployed and not deconstructed. This is how the editors use him.

The genealogical method is a good way to organize important readings in Conflict Analysis and Resolution because first, like all the social or human sciences, Peace and Conflict Studies are pre-paradigmatic in the sense that Thomas Kuhn invoked "paradigm." This is because there was never a period, or Epoch, as the editors employ the term, when one could identify a "normal" science of Peace and Conflict Studies. To be sure, as the editors persuasively argue, there were dominant discourses, but they were never without contemporaneous alternative or counter-discourses. In true, "normalized" science, by contrast, almost everyone works within the same epistemological paradigm until mounting anomalies make it impossible (though resistance by working scientists to shifting paradigms might be fierce!).

As an example of pre-paradigmatic, take the main theorists of Epoch One. While it is the case that rational choice theory, positivist formal modeling (game theory), and negotiation discursively dominated writing and thinking in the field, at the very same time, John Burton (a powerful intellectual influence at S-CAR) pushed for the importance of "basic human needs," not empirically quantifiable, observable, or scalable: not at all verifiable in the positivist's sense of the term. Moreover, such needs drove or impelled patently nonrational (if not irrational) behavior on the part of actors whose needs were suppressed. They are willing to engage in struggle up to and including all-out and self-destructive "deviance, terrorism, and war." Also at the same time, in Epoch One, Johan Galtung was proposing a structural theory of conflict that was diametrically opposed to the implicit methodological individualism of the rational choice theorists and not really in sympathy with Burton's sociobiology or ontology of basic human needs. Genealogy is a much better way of notating the "slippage" from the near total discursive dominance that characterizes normal *science*, to the heteroglossia (dominant and sub- and counter-discourses) of Epochal Conflict Analysis and Resolution. Genealogy abjures any hint of historical causality or necessity in favor of a kind of openness to alternative paths to the present and to "outcomes" that are contested or contestable. At home with conflict and power, genealogy is a perfect way to organize readings in conflict and power!

Genealogy is better suited than simple chronology ("history") to tell a contentious story. Some articles, written and published in later time periods, rightly appear as representative of earlier Epochs; for example, in Epoch One, Paul Collier's work on "greed vs. grievance," or the Global Peace Index. The genealogical presentation allows students to see the "family resemblances" that link theory to research and practice within and across all three Epochs. It also explains why (unlike in the physical or natural sciences) old theories and practices in Conflict Analysis and Resolution never entirely go away but live on as alternative discourses. (Compare theories of phlogiston, ether, or homunculi.) With genealogy, the past is never truly left behind. As Foucault taught, and the editors exemplify as they narrate the story of our field, what genealogy gives us is, inevitably, a "history of the present." It allows earlier Epochs to be critically "read" from the perspective of later ones.

The second reason why genealogy and discourse are good ways of organizing this story is that Conflict Analysis and Resolution or Peace and Conflict Studies are, more so than other social sciences, hyperreactive to the changing social and political events of the times. This is because, from the outset, the field made commitments to *practice*, to action in the world that responds to deep and destructive conflict. (This is also why, in the face of rapid and disruptive social change from Epoch One onward, generations of thinking and practice in our field seem so short.) Different crises and challenges characterized each Epoch. These challenges include, from the end of World War II to the breakup of the Soviet Union, to 9/11 and Iraq-Afghanistan, such shifts as wars between states or state superpowers (Epoch One); wars carried on inside states—genocides and ethnic cleansings (Epoch Two); wars between states and non-state, or trans-state, actors (e.g., Taliban, FARC, or ISIS), which is Epoch Three's "conflicts without borders." How conflict analysis and resolution responded—conceptually, methodologically, and practically—in each Epoch is the story this book tells.

One critical point the editors make as they move the story from Epoch to Epoch is that older theories, methodologies, and practices may often prove ill-suited or worse in addressing new manifestations of conflict. Recognizing this dilemma in theory and practice, in fact, is as close as our field gets to identifying the "anomalies" that lead eventually to genuine paradigm shifts in the physical or natural sciences. For example, "You can't bomb your way to peace." *It would be akin to anomalies that shift our paradigms decisively if, in fact, they were ever recognized as anomalies.* Regrettably, they are not. We do our work against a different power/knowledge nexus. This is why we as a nation keep trying to "resolve" conflicts by bombing our way through them. (This is also why Evolution may be the dominant discourse of Biology but is only contentiously so in the discursive regime of "science" textbooks in Kansas or Texas.) We have a long way to go before *ours* can lay claim to being a dominant discourse.

Kevin Avruch,
Dean, School for Conflict Analysis and Resolution, George Mason University

Introduction
UNDERSTANDING UNDERSTANDING

This is no ordinary textbook. It is different, perhaps even *extra*-ordinary, because you will see that "we" (first person plural) are present, as writers, rather than hiding behind the ubiquitous third person authoritative voice. Even though this is an anthology, "we" authors have a perspective; as such, "we" have a responsibility to name it so that you, as a reader, can critically evaluate it. Our job as authors is to present our perspective as a framework, a story, to help you make sense of the development of the field of conflict resolution. We believe that this story will enable you to be critical, as a reader, in your effort to understand how the field of conflict resolution understood itself as it developed. So we will, in this text, offer you a way of making sense of how pioneers in the field of conflict resolution made sense of violent conflict and its resolution over time.

We could begin our story about violent conflict in prehistory, as anthropologists of war have done, documenting the nature of the weapons, and the numbers of deaths, across time and around the world. However, this approach, as Brian Ferguson has noted,[1] often problematically framed some groups as culturally prone to conflict. Considerable research seeks to address the question as to whether human beings are driven by natural Darwinian impulses to compete for resources (both food and reproductive).[2] However, Ferguson has argued, in our view rightly so, that conflicts are historically situated and grounded in the local conditions. Therefore, he moves us away from the Darwinian explanations of violence toward an effort to understand the cultural and political systems that underlie violent conflict. We follow Ferguson, focusing on the development in the West of the theories that have been used to assess and intervene in conflicts.

While we might wish it to be different, the West has been ground zero for the emergence of conflict resolution as a discipline. The main academic centers that anchored conflict resolution research have been in the United States and Europe: these include the universities of Harvard, George Mason, Georgetown, Bradford, as well as the Peace Research Institute in Oslo and the Uppsala Conflict Data Program, and so on. Therefore, the field emerged largely in response to changes in Western contexts but has, in fact, expanded well beyond. Degree programs and conflict research centers proliferate across the world. Students can now choose from more than a hundred graduate programs and more than fifty undergraduate programs globally. The ideas espoused in these programs carried forward by their graduates and through publications shape thinking in government, business, and within civil society. In this book, we choose not to display the multitudinous and multicultural approaches to the field of conflict resolution. *We tell a story about how the field developed.*

1

Because the field of conflict resolution developed in the West, our story will be limited to Western approaches. Of course, every society throughout human history developed means for addressing conflict. To say that the discipline of conflict resolution *developed* in the West does not mean the West created all approaches to conflict. For example, we credit Mahavira (599 BCE–527 BCE) with introducing nonviolence to humanity; Mahatma Gandhi and Martin Luther King Jr. demonstrated the power of this approach in the face of oppression. In the field of conflict resolution, however, Gene Sharp became the approach's largest promoter. Therefore, we consider how Sharp's work shaped the field not because he matters more than the others; in fact, he acknowledges being influenced by their ideas. However, it was his work that moved this idea more centrally into our discipline.

Similarly, to say that the West started working with truth and reconciliation models in the wake of genocide seeks not to undervalue or ignore the cultures that have long used similar approaches. Native Americans and the Māori people, for example, employed restorative models upon which these Western models draw. Despite these acknowledgments, we also know how focusing on the Western appropriations of these approaches has and continues to hamper the ability of the field to address conflicts effectively in non-Western settings. This text will provide you, as a reader and a student, an opportunity to critically reflect on those limitations. We also cannot deny the influence of Western approaches to conflict on global institutions such as the United Nations, international courts, the World Bank, and regional organizations such as the European Union and regional banks, as well as nation-states all over the world. To focus on them reflects not their perfection but rather their dominance—warranted or unwarranted.

Focusing on Western theories of conflict and resolution developed in the last hundred years cannot provide all the "truths" or approaches but rather offers a framework to trace how people understand and respond to conflict. From this perspective, *this book offers more than an introductory understanding of conflict; this book helps us understand our understanding of conflict.* Students learn to understand conflict by "standing under" the theories, research methodologies, and practices that are core to the field. This standing under allows students to trace the consequences of these practices on the dynamics of conflict itself.

We believe competency requires more than the ability to use the frameworks for analysis or resolution, such as the ability to assess and critique the frameworks themselves. This text extends beyond listing and describing a set of analytic tools used to understand conflict, choosing instead to educate students to understand these tools as *a set of discourses;* then, as practitioners, they can more skillfully choose among them. For this reason, we made this book an anthology. We expose students to the most dominant frameworks in the field through the voices of those who anchored them. Students will read the foundational concepts from the foundational thinkers and then reflect upon them as discourses that both responded to world events and then went on to frame the field. In this way, the book develops critical thinking skills as well as an understanding of the field.

"Discourse" as a Frame for Analysis

A discourse exists as a system of meaning that, as a unit, extends beyond a sentence.[3] Discourse operates as a set of words functioning together to describe or explain something, or to tell a set of stories about something. For example, allopathic medical discourse describes diseases as well as pharmaceutical and surgical treatment processes; however, a naturopathic doctor uses a different discourse, one that centers on "imbalances" and natural remedies supporting the body's ability to heal itself. Most disciplines have discourses, and similar to the example above, each discourse has within it sub-discourses. We also have discourses for child-rearing, for example, wherein "spare the rod, and spoil the child" promotes strict discipline. We also have an entirely different discourse about child-raising that is focused on "exploration and discovery." In this parallel discourse, the parent encourages the child to move at their own pace and to engage in their own interests and curiosities. In the spare-the-rod discourse, the natural interests of the child may not exist. Thus, each discourse, no matter the domain, carries with it *ways of being, associated sets of practices*, and *accounts/explanations* that all fit together coherently and offer a framework for both understanding and action. Nonexistence for a discourse means no one discusses or speaks of it.

As such, "discourse" refers to the system of words used as a form of speaking and sense-making that is associated with a set of practices (Foucault 1982). Fields and disciplines do not simply have their distinct discourses; *they are shaped by them*. So, for example, medical discourse shapes the functioning of hospitals and clinics; educational discourse shapes schools and the educational process; parenting discourse shapes how we raise children. Each broad discourse helps form and regulates the associated institutions that practice the discourse. Michel Foucault, a famous philosopher of discourse, studied the development of the prison system as a function of the development of a new, technical discourse of punishment. "Criminals" become items in the justice system, almost similar to widgets on a conveyer belt in a factory—mandatory sentencing laws set prison terms no matter the context of the crime. This reinforces discourses of uniformity and robs the accused of a unique self. This thinking still shapes prisons today.

Discourses also shape how we view and what we do with our bodies. In addition to prisons, Foucault also studied sexuality and published his insights as *The History of Sexuality* in 1978. Foucault considered how the repression of discourse about sexuality and the body led by religious institutions and practices, along with the Victorian culture, separated people from their experience of themselves as having bodies and as sexual beings. However, today, we see the LGBTQIA communities challenging discourses that deny or control the experience of the body, or seek to regulate the expression of sexual preferences. The development of the discourse in relation to gay people evolved from a discourse about promiscuous sexual behavior (in the 1980s) to a discourse that now includes relationships, love, commitment, and marriage.

Foucault also studied how the rise of the medical "clinic" or the medicalization of illness and pain framed the body. In this discourse, bodies are spoken about as disconnected from the spirit, the heart, or social relationships. The language of medical practice takes for granted that doctors and nurses have the privilege and the authority to regulate the bodies of patients—their knowledge is power to structure and regulate. From this perspective, "power" in conflict resolution lies not with certain individuals or groups that can impose their will on others, but in the discourse that shapes how we account for human nature, how we define conflicts, and how we describe peace or conflict resolution. Moreover, these discourses are not static—they can and do change over time in response to world events and in relation to changing social norms.

For example, consider the invention of the birth control pill in the 1950s. As the pill became more widely available, the social norms surrounding sex began to change. Prior to the pill, there were not excellent ways to prevent pregnancy, so social norms (more or less) regulated who could have sex and under what circumstances. Discourse emphasized the importance of marriage and positioned sex outside of marriage illicit. However, women's newfound freedom gave birth to the "women's liberation movement"—women now controlled their own bodies and spoke more openly and directly about their oppression and the need for equality. The Pill, as an event, contributed to the emergence of feminism, a discourse about the capacity of women to be the architects of their own lives and deserving of equal rights. Note, during the 1950s and 60s in the United States, the discourse of "rights" came to the fore more generally. Vibrant national discussions about equality, segregation, injustice, civil rights, and the women's movement drew on these discourse streams. Together we see these streams constituting a period of time where the discourse of equality in the United States shaped, and was shaped by, the civil rights movement and the women's liberation movement as well as anti-war protests and social justice movements across the Americas and Europe. Using this "discourse" optic, we see how important events or world conditions shape how we make sense of ourselves and conflicts. We can also see the ways that discourses themselves recursively shape how we see these events.

EPOCHS: DESCRIBING DOMINANT DISCOURSES

Without fretting about causality—how and whether events give rise to a discourse—we can say certain discourses become, for a variety of reasons, dominant in a given time frame. We refer to these time frames that reflect a dominant discourse as "Epochs." Of course, within an Epoch the dominant discourses shaping our understandings of ourselves and our lives intertwine with other discourses in other sectors of society. For example, the equality discourse in the 1960s in the United States supported legislation for equal rights that also intertwined with discourses in the peace movement, which was connected via themes of social justice. The injustice of the Vietnam War and discourses around this injustice expanded beyond peace as the absence of war or violence. These discourses of equality, peace, and social justice demanded a new social order whereby governments treat people as human beings worthy of dignity. People deserve to have their needs met and be equal before the law. In sum, every Epoch's dominant discourse is comprised of a set of discursive streams that flow into it, also intersecting with one another. In spite of the separate domains of practice (legal domains, university classrooms, and newsrooms, in the case of "equality"), each having their own distinct discourses associated with those practices, we argue that certain notions (equality, peace, etc.) often connect to dominant discourse associated with a given Epoch in time.

More than notions, words, or thoughts, discourses eventually become material; they allow us to see and do some things while also governing and regulating what we see and what we do. For example, medical discourse enables doctors to conduct diagnosis and design treatments while this same discourse hampers doctors from attending to the patient as a human being or helping families address grief. Likewise, some educational discourses enable teachers to promote reading skills while at the same time discouraging creativity. The current push for educational testing pulls attention away from, for instance, developing the social skills needed to live happily and productively. Discourses about equality provided the foundation for changing legislation in the courts. This improved equality before the law, but also sidelined the wonderful differences that make groups special and unique. We see similar dynamics at play in the field of conflict resolution. Each set of discourses around conflict, its causes and effects, facilitate some action and understanding while disregarding or not completely acknowledging others. In the long term, understanding how each discourse shapes understanding and action proves more powerful than mastering any one approach.

These examples of discursive regimes highlight several important points: first, discourses are institutionalized and anchored in practices and organizations; second, discourses regulate what we can say and do, what we notice, and what we take for granted—they structure what we know and what we *can* know; third, social change always alters our discourse and our way of making sense of something; finally, we see how any large discourse adopted as a practice, institutionalized via policy and organizations, will have offshoots, *streams* that draw on it, while remaining associated with a particular set of associated practices. In sum, a discourses approach offers us a window into how we understand the world and provides an excellent method for systematic, scientific inquiry—no matter what the field.

> The Implicit Association Test, developed by Project Implicit at Harvard aims to reveal implicit attitudes. Take a test at https://implicit.harvard. edu/implicit/.

Understanding the world through the examination of discourse might seem to be problematic, *if* we presume scientific observation occurs undistorted by the meaning or frames we have prior to observation. However, we know assumptions shape "observations," and the vast majority of these assumptions are anchored in implicit attitudes or stereotypes. Assumptions shape how we know the world. The discourse approach of this book helps make assumptions visible because stereotypes live not in the minds of individuals but rather in the discourses and the systems for sense-making. Therefore, "bias" can be as understood as social phenomena, anchored in institutions and part of accepted knowledge. We seek not individual perpetrators (or wrongdoers), but rather we make visible belief systems that frame our world. Therefore, we examine accepted knowledge not to increase our approximation of the truth, but to make explicit the implicit. We explore conflict resolution as a set of discourse streams not to "get the facts" about conflicts, but to liberate us of assumptions handed down to us, over time, as theories about the sources of conflicts, its dynamics, and the pathways to peace.

When addressing violent conflict, how we work with and respond to these assumptions can have life-and-death consequences. We, the authors, argue for a relationship between descriptions of the world, the language used in those descriptions, and how we can mitigate violent conflict. We think understanding anything requires understanding how it is being understood; this second-order level of understanding allows us not just to reflect on the observed phenomenon, but also to reflect on the process of observing itself. We resemble both the athlete on the field as well as the commentator looking down from above; we are in the game and reflecting upon it.

This allows us to use the meaning systems and associated discourses used to observe/frame violence as well as examine them. As such, this anthology makes sense for our discursive approach to study; through a wide selection of articles, we can present the voices and frameworks that most consistently define and circulate in our field.

DISCOURSE AND CONFLICT RESOLUTION

Looking with a discursive "eye" at the development of conflict resolution, we propose three broad discourse streams that emerged, sequentially, over time. Each stream is associated with a set of world events to which the conflict resolution discourse responded. Even after the era that bore them past, these streams remained viable, legitimate sources of discourse anchored in institutions and mobilized by policymakers. In the sections that follow, we offer a description of each discourse stream, setting the stage for the organization of the book, which is divided into three sections, each one addressing a given discourse stream. In each of these sections, we explore the use of this discourse in conflict resolution theory, as well as in forms of conflict resolution practice (praxis) and in the research methods. This textbook's point of difference is that we do not "teach" conflict resolution as a static set of theories and practices; instead we pull back the curtain on the discourses that structure and regulate what we know about conflict and how we practice conflict resolution. In the section that follows, we introduce you to the three discourse streams pertinent to our story, shaping the development of the field of conflict resolution.

Three Discourse Streams: The Genealogy of Conflict Resolution Theory and Practice

Ideas, like individuals, cultures, nations, and institutions, have histories—they have genealogies. Responses to conflict also have genealogies. A genealogical approach asks, how do we know what we know? Where did these ideas come from, and what are the limits of our knowledge? Applied to conflict analysis and resolution, we can ask how we know about the nature of conflict as well as its possibilities for resolution. Answers to these questions help us see the ancestry of our field.

In the West over the past seventy-five years the nature of conflict has shifted dramatically from wars between states, such as the Cold War, to intrastate wars, and from intrastate wars to "transboundary wars" where violent groups join together across regions of the world to enact violence. These shifts became three distinct discourse streams, each one reflecting its own "rules of the game" for the analysis and practice of conflict resolution. Rules of the game govern each stream's way of talking about the nature of conflict, about how it works, and about how it can and should be resolved or addressed. While designed to solve problems, discourses can colonize the conflict resolution landscape. This book traces the nature of these discourses that shape our understanding of conflict to help us work with ideas without being colonized by them. This is a challenging task. We must recognize ideas that we take as true and explore their evolution over the past hundred years. During this short time period, tectonic shifts have dramatically changed how we make sense of conflict, which has, in turn, shaped the nature of how we intervene in conflict.

While the field of conflict resolution has had many iterations since the end of World War II, the field has not developed in a vacuum. All of the conflict theories emerged, in part, as a response to world events and were then framed and defined by the policy community, largely in the United States, as well as by scholars, largely in the West. Furthermore, these theories have also emerged in the context of certain scientific traditions, each with its own set of assumptions about the nature of knowledge, how it is created, and for what purpose. So these two contexts, the actual world events as well as the specific scientific methods used to research violent conflict, have both influenced the nature of the theories and the practical solutions that have developed over time.

To be clear, each of the three streams addressed in this book *remain in use today*—none of them are obsolete, and all remain in operation in different institutional settings and associate with different policy frameworks.

U.S. State Department policies and initiatives rely on discourses of the danger and threat posed by extremists portrayed as violent automatons, bent on killing others to promote their radical ideology.[4] Unsurprisingly, related policies and practices focus on blocking, countering, and destabilizing terrorist groups and partnering with others in that effort. We see "terrorists" framed as non-people, as

Figure Int.1.   Discourse Approaches

groups without a history (the recognition that the label "terrorists" frames groups as non-people resembles Foucault's recognition of how the penal system treated criminals as objects as non-people). A personal narrative of this "terrorist"—were he allowed to tell it—might include accounts of oppression and marginalization, not to mention the negative impact of the wars that the United States has initiated or perpetrated on them. No counter discourse exists to engage or build relationships with the people policymakers and others frame as "terrorists." Indeed, once framed this way, the only options are to kill or contain them. We see in this example how the system of meaning, the discourse stream, fits a given set of practices and policies anchored in and by particular institutions.

THREE EPOCHS OF CONFLICT RESOLUTION DISCOURSE

There are, we posit, three basic discourses used to describe or account for violent conflict. Each of these discourses emerged in a given time frame, an Epoch, associated with a set of world events and an approach to science itself. While the emergence of each of these discourses is tied to a given time frame, each one of these continues today.

We have named these discourse streams Epoch One, Epoch Two, and Epoch Three. Across these three discourses, the field of conflict resolution has accumulated theories for understanding conflict, practices for intervention, and research methods for assessment (of both conflicts and interventions). Each Epoch has a dominant discourse stream. Each Epoch enriched the set of resources available for addressing and redressing conflict. Each Epoch has its own *signature* visible in the way it made sense of conflict. All three Epochs provided much-needed frameworks for understanding and research. All three anchored critically important tools for resolving conflicts. Examining the contributions of each Epoch allows us to generate a story that highlights the strengths and limitations of the approaches associated with a given Epoch. Even though the Epochs are delineated by a particular time frame, the approaches that emerged during that period continue well beyond the end of the Epoch. So, for example, discourses that emerged in the wake of World War II are still used and often useful today, as are those that emerged in the wake of the genocide in Rwanda and now those in the wake of 9/11. Careful readers will notice that selected readings do not always chronologically match the era about which we are writing. A theory or approach need not be written in a particular time frame to reflect its values and governing frameworks.

The following introduces the three Epochs and their emergence in response to global events. Each Epoch will be described more fully within the book through an introduction to each era.

Epoch One (1945–1990) developed after World War II in response to the threat of nuclear annihilation and the shadow of nuclear war. During the Cold War, leaders in the West focused on how to deter the Soviet Union from building nuclear arsenals, all while negotiating treaties and "gaming" strategies to win. Epoch One begins as World War II ends and comes to a close when the Cold War ends. In Epoch One discourse, people are seen as "rational actors" that make "choices" in line with their "interests." Conflict arises, according to this era of thinking, when competition exists over resources. Actors seek to maximize their gain in the context of a zero-sum game. The world was framed as a fixed pie: if I win, you lose. Preventing conflict meant addressing issues of scarcity. In Epoch One tactics and strategies, participants often speak of "good guys" and "bad guys" or "us" and "them" with middle or overlapping positions ignored or sidelined. The rise of social media, especially Twitter which promotes simplistic language, facilitates the binary framing of events and actors.

Epoch One approaches say that people can become violent if and when their basic human needs are not met (John Burton). The cause of violence was less focused on rational choices of individuals and more focused on the structures (public and private) that contributed to marginalized people (Johan Galtung). During this Epoch, we see the emergence of controversies about the determinants of conflict such as greed versus grievance that are often grounded in economic frameworks for understanding conflict (Paul Collier). These models situate individual behavior as a central factor in understanding conflict and operate under contested assumptions that individuals are inherently aggressive or violent (David Barash and Charles Webel). Today, those interested in individual behavior as a source of conflict and healing increasingly draw on advances in neuroscience. Neuroscientist Daniel Reisel (2013), for example, studies stimulating growth in the brain's amygdala through restorative justice practices.[5]

Both of these discourse streams (one of negotiation, one on "structural violence") populate and regulate the early stages of the development of conflict resolution. These discourses are still dominant today. The post-2016 rise of fascist and nationalist discourses in the United States and Europe that promote racial and national boundaries reflect an Epoch One insider/outsider approach to conflict. These current discourses also reflect Epoch One's discursive dominance even though, as we will show, the field has and continues to advance others. Research in Epoch One centers on causality and studies focused on the factors that contributed to violence or to peace by identifying variables useful for predicting outcomes. As a result, researchers produced predictive models to provide early-warning indicators, with examples that include the Global Peace Index and the Failed States Report.

Baltimore Neighborhood Indicators Alliance uses similar models to help understand local challenges and ongoing structural inequalities. Artificial Intelligence (AI), through more sophisticated algorithms based on increasingly complex data inputs, makes these models increasingly useful while also replicating some of their fallibilities. In June 2017, for example, at the Good Global Summit in Geneva, Amnesty International's Secretary General Salil Shetty highlighted the potential of artificial intelligence for peacebuilding. But there are challenges. These systems, now able to code themselves through learning algorithms, make it increasingly difficult to understand how computers generate output. This becomes a crucial question, for example, when militaries use these outputs to determine targets and a group's likely links to insurgencies.

The rise of transnational corporations and their increasing role in conflicts provides yet another example of how Epoch One discourses continue to operate. Corporations are increasingly recognized as legitimate, rational actors on the world stage as they focus on the interests of profits and shareholders. Their actions are often studied using Epoch One theories and methods. Transnational corporations continue to expand. Some are larger in revenue than the GDP of the countries in which they operate. Engagement with these powerful actors requires understanding of their motivations and needs. This "rational actor" or "structural violence" discourse center on negotiation and mediation framed as processes for developing win-win solutions, introducing cooperation into otherwise competitive environments (Edward Wertheim). William Ury's highly referenced book, *Getting to Yes,* tried to shift the conversation—via the field of negotiation—from win-lose to win-win. This approach to conflict moved toward more positive engagement between parties but still treated people as rational actors motivated by interests.

Epoch Two (1991–2000) is the largest part of the book because the discourses of this era are still prolific in our field today. This new discourse stream appeared in the wake of the fall of the Berlin Wall. When the Soviet Union collapsed, signaling the ending of the Cold War, the West expected a prolonged period of peace. Instead, inter-ethnic conflicts, perhaps held in place by large state actors, emerged. A horrific genocide erupted in Bosnia and another in Rwanda. People were being slaughtered for their supposed ethnic or tribal affiliation. While this occurred in World War II during the Holocaust, during the Cold War period the dominant form of conflict seemed to be a struggle for power and world dominance. The turn toward ethnic cleansing seemingly from an inability to coexist with difference gave rise to Epoch Two discourse.

In response to the war in Bosnia and the genocide in Rwanda, identity and culture became central to our understanding of violent conflict. These events were accompanied by developments in research, or scientific methods, as well as the emergence of new forms of practice in the field of conflict resolution. In this discourse, conflicts were described as a function of *identity—culture, religion, gender, and ethnic differences* became the source of violent conflict. Students access these discourses through foundational articles by Kevin Avruch (culture), Marc Gopin (religion), Louis Kriesberg (identity), and Sandra Cheldelin (gender). Barnett Pearce and Stephen Littlejohn saw these identity clashes as moral conflicts, which Peter Coleman believed contributed to the intractability (insolubility) in certain contexts. In these discourses, people are not just "*motivated*" (a word used in Epoch One discourse to account for actors' "*behavior*"), they are prone to violence when their foundational identity is threatened or violated. In this discourse, psychological processes such as "trauma" become central, as well as core emotions such as *fear, anger, hatred,* and *humiliation*.

Epoch Two approaches to conflict become practices rather than strategies. We explore the worlds of others—their meaning-making systems. So rather than seeing those with whom we are in conflict within a two-dimensional frame, we now approach them and amplify our shared humanity. We see *dialogue and reconciliation processes* developed in an effort to redress core cultural differences and "heal" from conflict. Unlike Epoch One where Track One (formal diplomacy) controlled practice and policies, Epoch Two practices were institutionalized in nongovernmental organizations (NGOs) which emerged on the conflict resolution scene as central actors that contributed to policy development. The practices emergent within these sets of discourses work with core emotions (Daniel Shapiro and Roger Fisher). The meditation practices of this era also help groups find reconciliation in the face of blinding emotions (Adam Curle). Peacebuilding (John Paul Lederach) and Truth and Reconciliation processes (Robert Irwin Rotberg and Dennis Thompson) also sought healthy ways to bring together groups with differing religions, cultures, and identities with the hopes of creating peaceful coexistence (Antonia Handler Chayes). Gene Sharp promoted nonviolence as a means of facing these vitriolic conflicts without perpetuating the violence that decimates communities.

The methods anchored in anthropology (Brian Hoey; Carolyn Nordstrom), rather than the quantitative approaches central to Epoch One, use "participant observation" and "interpretation" to make sense of cultural processes. This is a radical departure from the focus on causality in Epoch One. Ethnographic approaches helped researchers embed themselves in the local contexts and appreciate the complex webs of identity informed by gender roles, culture, ethnic differences, and religion. Grounded theory (Demola Akinyoade), an inductive research methodology, orients scholars to first find data "on the ground" and then use rigorous qualitative and/or quantitative methods of analysis rather than deductive methods that require developing theories first. This shifts the orientation to local contexts. Case studies (Sarah Federman), rather than sweeping global studies, become important in this Epoch because they help scholars and practitioners describe the topography of conflicts in local contexts. The field remained situated in Epoch One and Epoch Two approaches until the September 11 attacks rattled the West and much of the world.

Epoch Three (2001–today) emerged in the wake of the September 11 attacks on the United States. No longer was the enemy of the West knowable and identifiable. As such, strategies for coexistence and cultural sensitivity became unviable. This enemy operated in the shadows; they were faceless and dispersed, without geographical boundaries to delineate their groups. Negotiation and mediation would not be possible with actors who, it appeared, simply wanted our annihilation and would even take their own lives in the process.

While there were certainly Epoch One responses to the September 11 attacks ("What are the strategic interests of terrorists, and how can we win?") and Epoch Two responses ("What are the cultural and identity roots of Wahhabism?") in the discourse stream associated with Epoch Three, conflict is described as function of not just who *they* are but who *we* are in relation to them. Here we see the emergence of Epoch Three discourses that emphasize reflexivity. By "reflexivity" we mean a recognition of the circular relationship between the world "out there" and our beliefs and/or actions. In this framework, all parties consider how they (or the histories of their group) might contribute to the social structure holding the conflict in place. Conflict, in this more reflexive discourse, must also account for the moral boundaries we have crossed, for the inequalities we have generated, and for the marginalization we have perpetrated. Geographically, conflicts are seen as transboundary. In the prior Epochs, conflict analysis did not include an examination of those conducting research (the "Observer") or designing interventions. The approaches of Epoch Three turn the lens on researchers back on the observers, the analysts, our culture, and our nations. We must account for our role, our actions, and our politics. Epoch Three is a discourse of moral responsibility; and to be morally responsible, one must make explicit and transparent the values used to engage in "critical reflection." We see the emergence of power, marginalization, and voice as lenses for understanding and approaching this moral responsibility. In Epoch Three, this means that even victims, including the United States, are not automatically expunged from responsibility. Whereas victims often had a privileged seat in Epoch Two, Epoch Three explores the politics of victimhood (Diane Enns).

Coexistence, the hallmark of Epoch Two, seems less likely and less peaceful. Leigh Payne contemplates a more "contentious coexistence." We now strive to live in the tensions, rather than unravel them all. Conflict resolution practice now becomes *praxis*—critical self-reflection that leads to new actions designed to transform inequality. This praxis places discourse centrally (Vivienne Jabri, Sara Cobb, Hilde Lindemann Nelson, and John Winslade). Intervention is performed at the discursive or narrative (story) level. Nelson offers examples for how to work with and transform "damaged identities." Winslade helps mediators learn to transform stories about self and other.

Related feminist research methods speak about the importance of "standpoints"—the location from which we know (Enloe). In Epoch Three, knowing is entirely a function of building awareness about where one stands and how one sees. Epoch Three builds on strategies from narrative and reflective practice to decrease marginalization, as well as help uncover pragmatic "solutions." Reducing marginalization requires adding additional voices to the discussion and assessing how our participation in conflict affects our understanding and intervention. Chris Argyris and Donald Schön (1973) have long pointed to the gap between "theories of action" and "theories in use." Colloquially known as the gap between what we say and what we do, Epoch Three works to reduce this gap. In doing so, we unmask our role as intervener, acknowledging that we play a role in conflicts even if we prefer to see ourselves as "resolvers." Epoch Three considers the politics of the role the intervenor plays in order to help address power imbalances and marginalization. Future imagines and creativity are harnessed for solutions as well as to help individuals re-story themselves, others, the culture, relevant institutions, and stories about the past which all contribute to the conflict. John Paul Lederach's *Moral Imagination* talks about the vision we must inspire and nourish to transform our world.

This Epoch's discourse stream has become mainstream, in many NGOs, social movements, and even in the "local" movement to engage communities in the design of solutions to their own problems, practiced in governmental agencies, as well as international development institutions. As part of the wave of reflexivity, foundational assumptions are questioned in Epoch Three: victimhood (Enns), speaking/silence (Leslie Dwyer), and trauma all get a second look. Approaches to conflict that promote identity shifts of both the practitioner and conflict party take hold. Transformation requires not just a system or behavior change, but also a radical embeddedness in conflict contexts (Shawn Ginwright) and its discourses (Cobb). Research in Epoch Three includes the participation of those being studied, and *participatory action research* (PAR) emerges as a means of enhancing reflexivity and refusing the "othering" of those being studied. In this way, Epoch Three research also reflects on Epoch Two approaches that intellectually colonized those being studied. This book is written from an Epoch Three perspective and reflects on some of the earlier readings from this standpoint.

Engagement with market actors (corporations) will increase in the years ahead. Transnational corporations increasingly dwarf the countries in which they operate. The largest entities in the world are increasingly corporations, not nations. To ignore the roles of corporations in conflict marginalizes the field, not the powerful role corporations will continue to play in conflict (Federman 2017). These entities frame much of our new world order. Conflict scholars and practitioners will need to find ways to engage with and hold accountable these growing entities. As readers can see, the field continues to unfold. We hope that readers will become key players in the field's development.

As noted earlier, while each of these discourses emerged in a given time frame, they all remain as resources for both analysts and practitioners—the diagram below demonstrates the overlapping and ongoing nature of this discourse. Therefore, students will see articles written later than the Epoch in which they are classified. This demonstrates how discourses continue long after the events that gave rise to them have fallen out of the forefront of contemporary discourses. The more that students understand the contexts that bore the approach, the better they can apply them to the proper contexts. In doing so, students will also observe phenomena from each of the Epochs in their exploration of historical conflict contexts.

COMMUNITIES OF PRACTICE WITHIN THE EPOCHS

There are "communities of practice" (Wenger 1998) for each of these discourses. A "community of practice" (CoP) is the name for the group of people that *use* a given practice. For example, much of the diplomatic community operates in Epoch One discourse; they assess the interests of other states, design policy choices/options, and engage in negotiation. Formal diplomacy is an Epoch One CoP. Many peacebuilding organizations use Epoch Two discourse, as they describe their peacebuilding efforts to bring two different identity groups together, and to bridge their differences. For example, the Middle East Peace Initiative (MEPI)[6] seeks to promote peace through "people to people" and "citizen diplomacy" programs that intend to engage the population in a conflict rather than convince the leaders to change their policies. The CoP for Epoch Two discourses are often NGOs and a growing number of formal governmental institutions, such as the Bureau of Conflict and Stabilization Operations with the U.S. State Department increasingly recognizes the importance of fostering "civilian power."[7] This shift in focus to locals is emblematic of Epoch Two. Increasing numbers of activist groups work as allies in Epoch Three discourses to reduce the marginalization of certain groups, while being mindful of their own politics in the process. These practitioners work on changing conflict dynamics, including their own role in that conflict system. For example, Black Lives Matter is a CoP that seeks to foster dialogues between the Black community and its allies, fostering discussion of how race, gender, and class intersect.[8] Allies are explicitly encouraged to reflect on

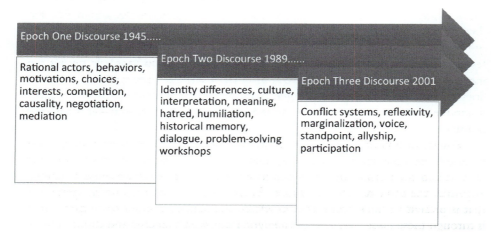

Figure Int.2.   Overlapping Epoch Discourse

racism and how it is perpetuated and, more specifically, how they, even as allies, may have participated in racial prejudice, all with the goal of generating reflective awareness such that they, as allies, do not fall into traps and perpetuate their own racial privilege. The group, Showing Up for Racial Justice (SURJ), encourages just that. SURJ organizes "white people to act as part of a multiracial majority for justice with passion and accountability." The group partners with African American groups, but members do their own self-reflective work.

In this book, tracing the development of these discourses is a form of genealogical analysis that exposes the lineage of language and its role in the development of theory, practice, and research. Exploring the genealogy of conflict resolution disrupts entrenched patterns of power, revealing the way that language shapes and governs our understanding of those patterns.

Exposing Power

Following Foucault's study of discourse, we adopt his method of a "genealogical approach" to the study of the relationship between discourse and history.[9] In his method, Foucault posited that events unfold and institutions develop in direct relation to the nature of the language and discourse. So instead of understanding history as a sequence of events, he described history as the development of given discourse, tracing the way it structured our understanding, our practices, and our institutions. For example, in *Discipline and Punish*, Foucault describes the birth of the prison system as a function of what he calls "disciplinary power," which, in turn, is a way of talking about the microstrategies and institutionalized technologies for forcing people to conform to the social rules and norms. This disciplinary power is manifest in schools, where children's bodies are regulated and their natural impulses are curbed; they are manifest in hospitals, via the centralized nursing stations, where the biological processes of patients are monitored and visiting hours regulated. They are manifest in our streets—there are a growing number of CCTV cameras in the streets of Washington, DC, for example, and which are predominantly located in African American communities.[10] This discourse of the need for surveillance and the regulation of people pervades our airports, where security instructs us to remove portions of our clothing so that our bodies are more clearly seen; they inspect all of our bags. While the government, of course, does this to protect innocent people from terrorist acts, these airport practices discipline all people. Moreover, we have all grown accustomed to it—it is the new normal.

Power, as Foucault has described it, is a function of the capacity of a given discourse for organizing, structuring, and shaping the set of practices that flow from it and the norms and standards that people use to evaluate those practices. Together, the three domains examined in this book expose the knowledge/power that is present in the discourses used within the field of conflict resolution, for it is through these discourses that the analytic frameworks emerge and through these discourses that the resolution practices are developed and implemented. Our story of the development of the field of conflict resolution is anchored in the story of recent wars, for it is here that we can see the roots of the emergence of different discourse and the Epochs within which they developed—a three-act drama where the nature of violence itself evolves. In our discursive analysis of this evolution, the drama that unfolds diverges from how the field has traditionally been organized. In our telling of the story of the evolution of these discourses, relationships of power become critical. We must understand the dynamics of the field including legitimized and central discourses as well marginalized approaches still working to gain traction. Epoch One discourses predominate our social and political landscapes as people gravitate toward rigid narratives that create certainty in today's chaotic world. Models of control and deterrence make possible border walls and harsh punishments. In the face of these hardliner tactics, Epoch Three discourse works to contest, resist, and reimagine social relations of power. The goal is to decrease polarization and increase complexity in our descriptions of "Self," "Other," and the conflict. However, these discourses struggle to gain traction. Epoch Three approaches often must fend for themselves in a hostile environment still dominated by Epoch One frameworks. One advocating complexity in a polarized environment can be labeled an apologist. Challenging victim discourses that do damage can be labeled racist or sexist. The integration of new discourses is not always easy or comfortable. This book helps prepare readers for the discursive environments they encounter in their professional lives as well as their lives as global citizens.

COLLAPSING TRADITIONAL DIVISIONS

Traditionally, conflict resolution has been taught as a field divided into three sections: international conflict, organizational conflict, and interpersonal conflict. These divisions reflect a "levels of analysis" approach that distinguished the macro level from the mezzo level from the micro level. This division was useful as indeed each one has its own domains of practice and methods of intervention. The proliferation of globalization challenged these divisions. The "local" no longer exists separately from the global, but rather is itself an instance of the global. A family conflict over religion may replicate a religious conflict between two large groups at a global level, just as the dissatisfaction and alienation of youth in a given high school sets up a dynamic that replicates the same conflict between youth and established government forces across a set of nations. Likewise, how a family or small group talks about conflict is never isolated from the larger global landscape or the norms circulating in mass and social media. The stories (at times in the form of analogies) that people draw upon to understand and resolve their conflict come from the broader culture. The fight between a Hispanic youth and his parents, for example, is often penetrated by the same dilemmas, moral values, and tensions that circulate in the city as a whole, as well as the state and the nation. Additionally, the pressure to join gangs is compounded and affected by drug cartels, government sanctions, and so on. Little is separate. The local is now global, and the global is now local. Because "micro" conflicts are framed and understood using the stories and memes that circulate at the global level, the distinction between micro and macro breaks down. Furthermore, we argue that all conflict is "inter-personal" in that it is between (inter) people. Even diplomatic efforts involve personality struggles as well as state interests (e.g., North Korean leader Kim Jong-un and U.S. president Donald Trump over North Korea's nuclear threats). For these reasons, we eschew the levels approach to conflict analysis and have instead used "discourse" as a tool for developing a description of the field, one that operates as a story about how the field evolved over time.

UNDERSTANDING IN CONCLUSION

As we have mentioned, this book tells a story about the development of the field of conflict resolution by framing it as a three-act play: Epoch One, Epoch Two, and Epoch Three. Therefore, the book is divided into these three Epochs; each one is described regarding the world events that were critical to shaping the discourse, as well as the associated discourses that emerged in response to those events. In each Epoch, we offer readings that discuss the theories used in conflict resolution that were deployed using the dominant discourse stream associated with that Epoch. We do the same for conflict practices, as well as research methods associated with the Epoch's dominant discourse. Within each Epoch, each reading is associated with the three sections (Topics, Responses to Conflict, and Research Methodologies). Each reading also has a headnote, to help readers make the connection between the article and the Epoch. Each Epoch closes with a set of discussion questions that can help readers explore the strengths and weaknesses of the associated theories, practices, and research methodologies from within the discourse that is in use in that Epoch.

As authors, we have chosen articles for each Epoch's readings that exemplify the discourse in use within that Epoch. We also chose articles on the basis of the contribution it has made to the field, so that this book is also a tour of the seminal scholars and practitioners in the field. We have also chosen some works by emerging scholars and others whose work properly reflects certain discourses.

The Value for Students and the Field

Looking at conflict and its resolution as a history of changing discourses enables readers to understand the relationship between world events, meaning systems, and the analytic tools we have for both conflict analysis and resolution. Until students can identify the conflict out of which a solution or approach was born, they will be limited in their ability to see if such an approach makes sense for a given context. Clearly, a tit-for-tat Cold War strategy will not work in response to airport terrorism, nor will diversity discussion groups make sense in ISIS dominated regions. Each solution responded to certain problems, and while elements may apply in given contexts, many do not. Misapplying a solution can worsen conflicts and delay more meaningful and lasting responses. As MIT's Peter Senge often warns, "today's problems come from yesterday's 'solutions'" (1990, 57). By this, he means that many problems we face are borne from solutions employed in the past. Cars help us move, but they pollute, for example. Residential schools in Canada aimed to "assimilate" indigenous children into Canadian culture, but this resulted in a traumatized generation that suffered much abuse. Today, the schools are considered a tool of genocide designed to kill indigenous culture. A simpler example could be drug use by an individual in response to emotional pain; the drug addiction becomes a new problem that was employed to solve the problem of depression.

We began by introducing Foucault's definition of power as those discourses that have the ability to inspire actions and create norms in a given context. By showing the readers the origins of conflict-related discourse, you will better understand whether a framework is applied because of relevance or simply because it has power. Interrupting dominant discourses that further entrench conflict requires an appreciation of the contexts out of which they emerged. Introducing complementary discourse will be more successful if it can be presented as an extension to, rather than a replacement of, contemporary normative approaches.

Beyond the classroom, this approach provides the field of conflict resolution with an innovative opportunity to draw on paradigms within the field without being dominated by them. Approaches applied ought to be chosen for their salience rather than power. Otherwise, the field risks applying solutions that amplify and create problems rather than speak to emerging conundrums. We have many cautionary tales that demonstrate this point. For example, strategic force, such as drones, aims to limit the power of extremists. However, extremists can use video footage of the civilian death caused by these attacks to recruit new members to their cause. This mismatch of problem/solution sets limits on how our own actions will be understood by others. Understanding what impact our actions may have on others enables us to design interventions that resolve, rather than reproduce, the conflicts they intended to impact.

In closing, this book seeks not the truth but rather what Argyris (1996) has called "actionable knowledge," which is knowledge that would help us be effective in practice. We are less concerned with whether something is true than whether it has power. Since the days of Aristotle and through to the Enlightenment, knowledge has been tied to "truth." This truth emerged as a function of accurate, empirical observations. The rational deductions derived from these observations presumably lead to accurate knowledge, making possible both prediction *about* the world and control *of* the world. Indeed, much of the research in conflict studies has aimed at generating "accurate" accounts of the causes of violent conflict precisely so that we could either predict it or control it. However, as Argyris and others have argued, we rarely can control for all the variables necessary to identify the causes of conflicts. Worse, if we try, our efforts to control these variables have unintended consequences. For example, if we assume that conflicts arise from identity differences, then we must, logically, try to reduce those differences to resolve the conflict. However, this would likely threaten people who already experience their identity as being under siege. Looking for "common ground" could backfire if it generates a framework that erases or sidelines core differences. Likewise, deterrence strategies characteristic of Epoch One that treat others as "rational actors" may disable us from understanding the role of emotions in violent conflict and examining the role of storytelling in conflict resolution.

As such, this textbook is not the usual anthology of critical contributors to the field but an exploration of these discourses that enabled, as well as constrained, our approaches to conflict resolution. Such an exploration generates what philosopher and educational reformer John Dewey called "critical intelligence," or the capacity to critically reflect on problems, with others, toward the design of an ethical and creative solution. It is our hope that students of conflict resolution are thus engaged not only in a retrospective understanding of the history of the field but are also able to hone the skills needed to design the next generation of theory, research, and practice in the field.

Note to the Reader

This book was designed to be used in both graduate and undergraduate conflict courses. For the newer student, the headnotes will be especially helpful in guiding understanding of the major points of the article and connecting the framework to the Epoch. We suggest that readers try to avoid getting too caught up in all of the details of the articles and focus instead on understanding the frameworks being employed. That said, should you find certain passages resonant or are particularly problematic, we hope you will make a note for yourself. Your notes will provide clues as to the aspects of the field that are most important to you.

References

Argyris, Chris. "Actionable Knowledge: Intent versus Actuality." *Journal of Applied Behavioral Science*. 32, no. 4. December 1996, pp. 441–44.

Argyris, Chris and Donald Schon. *Theory in Practice: Increasing Professional Effectiveness*. San Francisco: Jossey-Bass, 1974.

Borofsky, Rob and Bruce Albert. *Yanomami: The Fierce Controversy and What We Can Learn from It*. Berkeley: University of California Press, 2005.

Federman, Sarah. "Genocide Studies and Corporate Social Responsibility: The Contemporary Case of the French National Railways (SNCF)," *Genocide Studies and Prevention: An International Journal* 11, no. 2 (October 2017): 13–35.

Foucault, Michel. *The Archaeology of Knowledge: And the Discourse on Language*. New York: Vintage, 1982.

———. *The History of Sexuality: An Introduction*. New York: Knopf Doubleday Publishing Group, 2012.

Gutting, Gary. *Foucault: A Very Short Introduction*. New York: Oxford University Press, 2005.

Senge, Peter M. *The Fifth Discipline: The Art and Practice of the Learning Organization.* New York: Doubleday/Currency, 1990, 57.

Wenger, Etienne. *Communities of Practice: Learning, Meaning, and Identity.* New York: Cambridge University Press, 1998.

Notes

1. Brian Ferguson is an anthropologist who has studied the intersection of culture and history in his studies of warfare, particularly between tribal communities. See https://www.youtube.com/watch?v=Nu72eMyQy_o for his discussion of the role of colonial powers in accelerating violent conflict between indigenous groups.

2. See Borofsky (2005) for a discussion of Napoleon Chagnon's thesis that males fight each other for reproductive privilege. Rob Borofsky and Bruce Albert, *Yanomami: The Fierce Controversy and What We Can Learn from It* (Berkeley: University of California Press, 2005).

3. See http://www.merriam-webster.com/dictionary/discourse.

4. See https://www.state.gov/j/ct/programs/.

5. Restorative justice practices bring those harmed and those who harmed in conversation to find ways to heal, respond to damage, and prevent future occurrences.

6. See http://www.mepnetwork.org/.

7. See https://www.state.gov/j/cso/resources/.

8. See http://blacklivesmatter.com/getinvolved/.

9. For primary readings, consider Foucault's early description of genealogical methods in *The Archaeology of Knowledge.* For secondary resources on Foucault, consider Gary Gutting's 2005 *Foucault: A Very Short Introduction.*

10. See the 2012 report of CCTV cameras in DC at https://publicintelligence.net/washington-dc-cameras/ and likely the number has grown since then. More recently, the police in DC offered funding to encourage residents to install CCTV cameras on their property, enlisting residents in the work of surveillance.

PART 1

EPOCH ONE: THE COLD WAR TO THE FALL OF THE BERLIN WALL, 1945–1990

From the Cold War to the Fall of the Berlin Wall

Root Causes of Conflict and Deterrence

Epoch One emerged between the end of World War II and the fall of the Berlin Wall, a time period characterized by a deep desire to develop predictive models to deter nuclear war, as well as to strive for peace between conflicting nation-states, as indeed, the world wars had been conflicts between nations. Both of these strategies were part of the overall effort to promote international peace and security.

The wars to end all wars (World War I and World War II) were terribly costly regarding human life and economic loss. While 500 years have passed between the Chinese discovery of gunpowder and the production of firearms, technologies of destruction advanced rapidly in the twentieth century. Within less than a century, the world saw the introduction of aerial bombing, the development of gas chambers, the birth of the machine gun, the manufacturing of chlorine and mustard gas, and the creation of tanks and submarines—all of which facilitated mass killing. However, it was the invention and use of nuclear weapons that truly changed the rules of the game—such a weapon not only ensured the annihilation and total destruction of everything and everyone in its target zone, but it also poisoned the environment as well as future generations with radioactive waste.

Dropping the Atomic Bomb

August 6, 1945, Hiroshima, Japan, became the first country hit with an atomic bomb. And the United States became the first (and still only) country to deploy an atomic bomb in an inhabited region. The bomb destroyed the city upon impact and immediately killed just under a hundred thousand people, with tens of thousands of others dying of related conditions in the weeks, years, and decades that followed. Rebuilding only commenced five years after the detonation. August 9, 1945, Nagasaki became the second—and as of now—the last city struck with an atomic bomb. Within a moment of landing, the bomb reduced the population of roughly 260,000 to less than 200,000.

In an effort to end World War II, the United States dropped atomic bombs on Hiroshima and Nagasaki. The bombs killed roughly 200,000 people within a month of detonation, most of whom were civilians, not soldiers on a battlefield. Survivors were often severely burned or were, later in life, subjected to terrible cancers; subsequent generations suffered birth defects. The cities themselves were annihilated.[1]

While there are different opinions as to whether the use of nuclear weapons was ethical, it clearly set off an arms race, with multiple countries acquiring nuclear weapons. This process continues today, despite the presence of international laws, most notably the Treaty on the Non-Proliferation of Nuclear Weapons (NPT)—made by those that have the weapon. While the NPT prohibits the development of nuclear weapons by those that do not have them, the treaty itself has failed to block several countries from becoming nuclear states (e.g., Israel, India, Pakistan, and North Korea). Nonetheless, these international treaties were intended to reduce and regulate weapon stockpiles. The threat of a "nuclear winter" following detonation forced countries to restrain from using the atomic weapons they possessed.[2] The threat remains; the 2017 nuclear threats issued by North Korea's leader Kim Jong-un, as well as U.S. President Donald Trump's threat to use military force to disarm North Korea, demonstrate the ongoing risk and instability that nuclear weapons pose to international peace security. Tensions between India and Pakistan are also heating up again.

The Birth of the United Nations

The successor to the League of Nations, the United Nations officially launched October 24, 1945, just months after the official close of World War II. The majority of fifty-one member countries ratified the charter along with the five permanent members of the Security Council (United States, France, Britain, Soviet Union, Republic of China).

U.S. Secretary of State James F. Byrnes reminded people at the time that while the creation of the UN provides a chance for peace, ultimately the people's will would determine whether peace prevailed.

While many countries sought to acquire the bomb after the US detonation in World War II, others (including those working in conflict resolution) focused on "mutual deterrence," an approach at the foundation of the Cold War between the United States and the Soviet Union.

From the ashes of these destructive world wars, a broad and deep international discussion emerged about regulation to ensure these wars would never occur again. Out of these discussions, the United Nations was born.[3] Although there continues to be legitimate critique of the UN as an effective institution for global peace, it was an innovation and a substantial contribution to international governance.

While human rights as a concept has earlier origins in France, Eleanor Roosevelt was the force behind the United Nation's Universal Declaration of Human Rights. Her work helped human rights become a moral and legal framework for the West, rising powerfully out of the ashes of the Holocaust. Post-World War II, the Nuremberg Trials placed Nazi leaders on trial for "crimes against humanity," a new legal category. The trials also served to document and judge the crimes committed by the Nazi regime. However, while this was ongoing, there was also a massive effort to rebuild Germany—the Marshall Plan recognized that the peace and security of all nations required an investment in Germany to ensure they did not, once again, seek to claim world dominance.[4] The Marshall Plan set a critically important precedent—victors helped the vanquished rebuild, rather than leaving them to struggle to reconstitute their societies by themselves. However, even with the Marshall Plan, the establishment of the United Nations, and the birth of human rights, global peace would not hold.

Carving Up the World

These world wars had also lead to colonization, by the victors, of the Ottoman Empire (via the Sykes–Picot Agreement).[5] We now know that this division of territories did not respect cultural or religious boundaries, setting the stage for more violent conflict as colonized people fought to regain control over their own territories. As in the aftermath of World War I, the victors (France, Britain, the Soviet Union, and the United States) carved up the world; these "mandates" (Article 22 of the League of Nations) legitimized colonization of the vanquished. Additionally, the Soviets imposed the Iron Curtain, dividing post-war Europe into Soviet-dominated and non-Soviet-dominated regions. These divisions, which prohibited travel between regions, would last the duration of the Cold War. Moreover, these divisions have played a central role in restricting development and suppressing self-rule, freedom of religion, and economic growth. Finally, Israel came into being following the UN allocated portions of Palestine to the Jews, as a homeland, following the devastation and death brought about by the Holocaust. While this provided the foundation for a Jewish state, it marginalized thousands of Arabs in refugee camps and instantiated the conflict between Jews and Arabs across the Middle East. In all of these cases of "partition," there were losers, people who lived under oppressive regimes.

The United States responded to these partitions by drawing its own moral boundaries through which it contrasted the "free" world (a democratic, free market society) with the "Communist" world in which the state limited freedom and controlled information as well as economic exchange. These moral boundaries between worlds justified the U.S. backing of Israel even when at the expense of Palestinians and the Arab world more broadly. The competitions between communism and capitalism (liberal democracy) and between the Arab and Western world were born, anchored in and through the descriptions each side made about the Other. These descriptions clearly delineated the binary construction of "Us versus Them" that characterized the period of time when democracy and capitalism fought to dominate over communism, as well as the struggle between the Arab world and the West. These divisions provided the foundation for a struggle for dominance anchored by the "proxy wars" that emerged over the next fifty years.

A "proxy war" is a war between two or more groups of people that stand in for the conflict between the countries that back or support them. During the Cold War, a host of proxy wars mushroomed where the United States and the Soviet Union supported one of the conflicting groups or parties. The Korean War was a conflict between a communist North Korea and a democratic South Korea. The "Banana Wars" occurred between groups framed as communists by the United States which feared that attempts to unionize agricultural workers in Central and South America and the U.S.-based agricultural companies (Dole, Chiquita, and Fresh Del Monte) operating in this region. The Vietnam War involved the United States in an effort to "protect" Vietnam, as well as Southeast Asia, more broadly, from communism. The West, namely the United States, argued that if Vietnam fell, it would have a domino effect[6] and lead to the entrenchment of communism in that part of the world. The political goal became "containment" of communism—a failed premise that led to the death of over a million people. The U.S. Central Intelligence Agency functioned over many years, post–World War II, to unseat other governments with socialist or populist tendencies, even preferring autocratic or military rulers who would promote capitalism. This policy of "containment" contributed to conflict (and genocides) in Indonesia and Cambodia, where coups overthrew governments and murdered millions in the process. Engagement in these proxy wars remains one of the United States' darker chapters.

The United States and the West feared nuclear warfare most of all, so taking on the Soviet Union directly to oppose communism would be impossible; proxy wars were the strategy of choice. In this fear of the Soviet Union, the world—including the United States—turned a blind eye to Joseph Stalin's purges. While he was leader of the Soviet Union, Stalin was responsible for the murder of millions of his own people, and roughly fourteen million people passed through forced labor camps, called gulags. Estimates suggest that Stalin's purges led to the assassination of twenty-five million, equal to the amount of all people killed in World War II, including the Holocaust. However, fear of nuclear war with the USSR led no one to intervene directly. The systematic executions ended only when Stalin died in 1951. Nuclear war may have been averted, but millions were murdered all the same.

Epoch One Discourses

In this context, governments were focused on *competition* between *nation-states* where each nation was trying to *win*, not as a clear permanent victory as a single outcome, but as a *strategic advantage* in an ongoing struggle for dominance across the globe. The struggle for dominance in this context of the Cold War was understood using game theory. Conflict resolution emerged as a framework anchored by game theory, which is defined as "the study of mathematical models of conflict and cooperation between intelligent, rational decision-makers."[7] Game theory presumed that people are rational actors "choosing" their moves based on their assessment of their needs and interests, as well as their assessment of the rational actions of others. When game theory was developed, neither emotion nor culture figured into game theory's explanatory model. In fact, people were assumed to be predictable, just like the mathematical models. Deterrence theory, which became dominant during the Cold War, was based on the idea that no rational being would use nuclear weapons if there was a credible threat of mutually assured destruction. In 1960, Thomas Schelling wrote *The Strategy of Conflict,*[8] where he advanced our understanding of both everyday as well as large-scale conflicts, presuming that all conflicts are "games" where parties make strategic moves to gain an advantage. The discourse of "game" fit hand and glove with the development of negotiation as the process for allowing both parties to have their needs and interests met. Again, rational actors calculated possible strategies, and made their moves on the global stage, presuming that the other parties were doing the same.

Negotiation was itself a global breakthrough—it enables parties to navigate differences in ways that would lead to "mutual gain." Moreover, there was recognition that, in a nuclearized world, states were forced to deal with their adversaries over and over again, on multiple and overlapping issues. The fact that parties could rely on their other's making rational choices generated not only many excellent international treaties (the Treaty on the Nonproliferation of Nuclear Weapons [NPT], UN Charter on Human Rights, and the UN itself), but it also established a culture of diplomacy in which negotiated settlements were both possible and preferable. However, the agreements often had little "ground truth," as they were created by diplomats who were removed from the local conditions or lived experience of a given population. Moreover, as we shall see in Epoch Two, this would limit the durability of any given peace agreement.

There is another dimension reflected in the discourse of game theory—these were scientific, mathematical models. The scientific approach to conflict was premised on the belief that we could study the social world using the same statistical models used to study the natural world. The idea was that people and their cultures and history were invariant beings that could be understood as objects, rather than beings strongly impacted by culture, identity, and emotions. Statistical studies, such as the research on "failed" or "fragile' states, were efforts to distill the presence of variables that could both predict, as well as control, violence. Additionally, these studies became foundational to the emergence of development strategies, such as the UN Millennium Goals.[9] The world wars had brought home the message that the world could not be complacent about the conditions that contributed to conflict and much of these development efforts since World War II have been efforts to reduce global instability by reducing the risk of violence.

These two discourses are interrelated. The discourse of quantitative science overlapped with the discourse of game theory—both relied on mathematical models of human beings. Both were often focused on the deep structure of people (their invariant psychological processes, such as aggression) or their rational processes. Both were concerned to avoid bias that would reduce objectivity of the scientific process, as well as the analysis of the "game" by the players involved. We see, in the sections that follow, how these discourses anchored theories of conflict, tactics, and strategies for addressing conflict, and the research methods used to study conflict, in Epoch One.

THEORIES IN EPOCH ONE

The palpable threat of nuclear war made new theories and strategies in conflict analysis and resolution paramount. Experts in the fields of international relations, political science, psychology, military strategy, economics, and other fields set about finding root causes and creating predictive models. The solutions they sought would focus on individual behavior in order to provide universalist understandings about the "root causes" of conflict. The world was seen as dangerous and harsh. As such, our field drew on the *realist* approaches in political science and international relations, which held that nation-states pursue interests. Therefore, our job in conflict resolution was to understand our interests and theirs and devise a way for the needs of both to be met without the use of violence. Few scholars and practitioners operating in our field at this time considered local contexts or different players. (Anthropologists and sociologists had long situated themselves locally, but it took time for the field of conflict resolution to adopt them.) Epoch One theorists grappled with whether aggression was inherent in all humans and, therefore, the root of violence (David Barash). Others considered violence not only as physical violence but also as "structural violence" (Johan Galtung) whereby people's basic human needs were unmet and they became violent (John Burton). Galtung urged his contemporaries not to believe an absence of violence signified safety. He distinguished positive peace and negative peace—even a wealthy and nonviolent one could be repressive.

Economists and political scientists considered alternative theories, claiming that economic stability promoted peace. This followed the same thinking as the Marshall Plan—build up weaker states so they do not seek violent means to meet their needs. Paul Collier, for example, examined the contexts of economic instability that make greed, and then grabs for power, likely. Rebel groups, he found, formed when they perceived opportunities for economic gain. They would then create a list of grievances to justify their claims to power. His work anchored the "greed versus grievance" debate still prevalent today.

CIVIL RIGHTS AND OTHER MOVEMENTS

Prior to Galtung, Martin Luther King Jr. spoke about the difference between negative and positive peace in his Letter from a Birmingham Jail. King underscores how the white moderate perpetuates systems of oppression through inaction. King also challenges pacification as a strategy for long-term peace for healthy societies. Through King and, more generally, civil rights (as well as women's rights and environmental activism in the 1960s), we see a growing awareness of the systemic inequities that either led to violent conflict or perpetuated peace for a privileged few. In Epoch One, civil rights began just as a small offshoot of the field of conflict resolution, becoming more prominent in Epoch Two. Human rights, a more global application of civil rights, built off this same offshoot. Even though the prevention of war and violence dominated the conflict resolution field during Epoch One, those working in civil rights and human rights sought positive peace. Peace studies began during this time, as did the peace movement—catalyzed by the Vietnam War. Their approaches move more centrally into the field in Epoch Two.

TACTICS AND STRATEGIES IN EPOCH ONE

We refer to Epoch One practices as *Tactics and Strategies* because they aim to outthink or outplay an opponent; rational choice theory, game theory, negotiation, factor analysis, and other models developed to anticipate and respond to nuclear threats. The idea that groups had interests and these interests needed to be met for successful negotiation dominated the field. In simulations using these models, full collaboration led to fewer gains than pseudo-collaboration. In other words, those who collaborated and then defected (e.g., reneged on promises) at the end did better than those who collaborated fully. This discouraged working

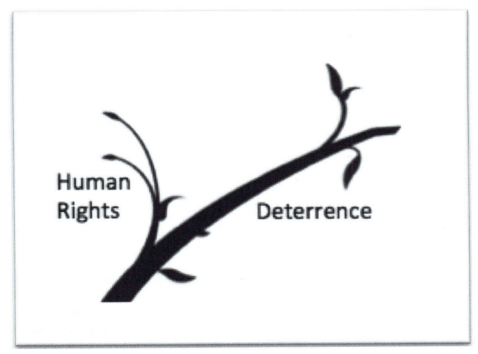

Figure E1.1.   Civil Right and Human Rights, an offshoot in Epoch One, became more central in the field in Epoch Two

together and emphasized competition and deception. In these simulations, emotions were considered distractions to be overcome. Jennifer Learner at Harvard—a leader in decision science—argued that decision-making was actually "clouded by emotion." Emotions polluted rational decisions. Rationally determining one's interests and then rationally pursuing them became the hallmark of the Epoch One approach.

Epoch One theories and models all sought universal answers to address the root causes of conflict. These top-down models aimed at creating predictive models also aimed at preventing chaos and global destruction. Each of these theories had significant policy implications. If humans are aggressive by nature, for example, then laws and conflict programs must seek to control and limit people's natural urges. Because emotions were seen as the enemy of rational decisions, people's emotional reactions to various situations would be discounted and/or subdued. The elite, with presumably more distance with which to view conflict rationally, were better positioned to develop violence prevention programs and policies for peace.

Their approaches and predictive models, however, were based on assumptions that would soon be tested and toppled. People and states did *not* always act in their own best interest; furthermore, they could not always identify the exact nature of their interests. Strategies and tactics emerging from their model of the world focus on loss aversion—preventing war rather than creating peace. The issue of power—retaining or gaining it—was not addressed as a central component of interests. Some states worked to maintain the status quo as a means of retaining power; others worked to acquire more power. What was meant by *power* was explored or measured only by military prowess. Those producing scholarship in Epoch One did not yet fully consider how their own power interests influenced (past and present) the conflicts they studied and in which they tried to intervene.

RESEARCH IN EPOCH ONE

Research in Epoch One reflected the empirical approaches that dominated the field. Just as the world appears to operate according to consistent laws of physics, positivists believe the social world also operates according to consistent social laws. Researchers operating in this Epoch see themselves as objective observers of phenomena that must be studied from a distance. Researchers cannot include intuitive interpretations of the world. Said another way, only the hard sciences count. So those doing research in an Epoch One frame use quantitative methodologies—only factors that can be objectively measured count.

While *positivism* developed outside of the field of conflict resolution, it framed our field during Epoch One. The hope was that if we can study societies objectively, we can predict conflict and find and identify the ideal site of intervention. In this way, the approach to conflict resembled the approach of Western medicine to illness; research focuses on finding the cause of illness and intervening. The idea of creating a healthy body or healthy societies for long-term well-being are seen as soft, ineffective approaches. Martin Luther King Jr. as well as Galtung called this *negative peace* because these methods defined peace only as the absence of violence and not as a healthy flourishing society. A society with no physical violence that enslaves people, for example, cannot be considered truly peaceful (having positive peace). These studies, however, did not seek out structural inequalities. Instead, Epoch One research approaches and sought out answers for the following types of questions:

- What **causes conflict?**
- **How** does one stave off people's natural urges toward violence?
- What **factors** contribute to conflict escalation?
- What are the **stages of development** in a conflict?
- **Why** do peace negotiations fail?
- When and where will violence erupt again?

Researchers explored these questions in a culture of empiricism. Studies sought to find *truths* that teach us about causality, root causes, and stages of development to help us control the circumstances that lead to conflict. People believed truth could be accessed through observation. Primary methods of research during this time included survey research, factor analysis, and experimental design.

Epoch One Strengths and Limitations

Epoch One made significant contributions to our explanatory models of conflict, as well as to our strategies for intervention. The large-scale quantitative studies enable global institutions, such as the World Bank and the UN, to identify a set of variables predictively associated with violent conflict and these were in turn all associated with poverty. The alleviation of poverty was the foundation for the UN Millennium Goals, and later, they morphed into the Sustainable Development Goals. Statistical analysis of the indicators of poverty and its relation to conflict was critical to international development efforts.[10]

However, perhaps the most significant contribution of Epoch One to conflict analysis and resolution was the development of "principled" negotiation in Roger Fisher, William Ury, and Bruce Patton's *Getting to Yes*.[11] First published in 1981, the book shifted the field from "hard bargaining" where each party struggled to gain advantage over their adversary to "principled negotiation." In principled negotiation, parties focus on developing a relationship with the Other that would enable those involved to identify their needs and interests and mutually respect those interests and needs while moving towards an agreement. This became known as the "win-win" solution. It offered an alternative to more contentious (hard) or acquiescent (soft) approaches. This approach to negotiation changed the world. This process enabled collaborative solutions to conflicts in private, corporate settings, as well as in public sector settings. It was very widely read, widely adopted, and continues today to provide a strategy for working through "difficult conversations."[12] Principled negotiation has enabled us, as a species, to move away from "tit-for-tat" games where parties would be punished by each other, to win-win processes, contributing greatly to the local, national, and international solutions to conflict.

Epoch One, like any paradigm, has its limitations. The scientific methods focused on *why* things happened but did not consider the dynamics of *how* they happened. Interest in the *how* would increase in Epochs Two and Three once the *why* failed to predict outbreaks. The Epoch One approach to research also omitted questions of culture and context, such as the idea that what we know about the world depends on *how* we know it. For example, if we survey people during a social dinner, we may receive different answers than if we survey them at work. Epoch One also ignores the identity of the researcher, the social construction of identity, and how identities change over time—all central questions in Epoch Two. However, the limitations of any given discourse often set up the conditions for the evolution of that discourse, as it struggles to address its own limitations. In this case, there would be a series of global events that would enable us to explore the limits of Epoch One, as Epoch Two discourses were mobilized.

While Epoch One is only the first of three discourses addressed in the book, it remains the predominant framework through which the western world approaches conflict. Epoch One, focused on strategic moves and predictions, promotes either/or thinking. The post-2016 resurgence of nationalist and fascist discourse in the United States and parts of Europe and Latin America calls into question how far reaching the more collaborative approaches of Epoch Two have really traveled. In the United States, election discourse and subsequent governmental policies dehumanize others and remain anchored in "Us" versus "Them" discourse. Game theory and other similar models often rely on this binary construction of the world.

Keywords for Epoch One: root causes, human needs, aggression, greed, grievances, prediction and control, principled negotiation, rational choice, game theory, structural violence, mutual deterrance, tactics, tit for tat

References

Fisher, Roger, William L. Ury, and Bruce Patton. *Getting to Yes: Negotiating Agreement Without Giving In.* New York: Penguin, 2011.

King Jr., Martin Luther. "Letter from Birmingham Jail." April 16, 1963. Accessed online January 16, 2018.

The Learning Network. "Oct. 24, 1945 United Nations Is Born." *The New York Times*, October 24, 2011. http://learning.blogs.nytimes.com/2011/10/24/oct-24-1945-united-nations-is-born/.

Lerner, J. S., D. A. Small, and G. Loewenstein. "Heart Strings and Purse Strings: Carry-over Effects of Emotions on Economic Decisions." *Psychological Science* 15, no 5 (2004): 337–41.

McArthur, J. "The Origins of the Millennium Development Goals." *SAIS Review* XXXIV no. 2, (2014): 5–24.

Simon, Reeva S., and Eleanor Harvey Tejirian. *The Creation of Iraq, 1914–1921*. New York: Columbia University Press, 2004.

Notes

1. For a "backward glance" of the bombing of Hiroshima and Nagasaki, see http://www.bbc.co.uk/guides/zq7yg82.

2. "Nuclear winter" refers to the alleged cooling that can occur on Earth after a nuclear war. The bombs can lead to firestorms that block direct sunlight for prolonged periods of time.

3. The Learning Network. "Oct. 24, 1945: United Nations Is Born." *The New York Times*, October 24, 2011. http://learning.blogs.nytimes.com/2011/10/24/oct-24-1945-united-nations-is-born/.

4. The Marshall Plan, initiated by the United States, funneled billions into Western Europe to rebuild the region.

5. The Sykes–Picot Agreement of 1916 enabled the United Kingdom and France, with the support of Russia, to divide up the world into areas of influence. This was a secret agreement. See Reeva S. Simon, and Eleanor Harvey Tejirian. *The Creation of Iraq, 1914–1921*. New York: Columbia University Press, 2004.

6. "The Cold War 'containment' notion was born of the Domino Theory, which held that if one country fell under communist influence or control, its neighboring countries would soon follow." http://www.u-s-history.com/pages/h1965.html.

7. See Myerson, R. (1991). *Game Theory: Analysis of Conflict*. Boston, MA: Harvard University Press, p.1. This work built on that of John Von Neumann, who developed the mathematical models underlying game theory itself in 1948.

8. See Schelling, Thomas C. (1960). *The Strategy of Conflict*. Boston, MA: Harvard University Press.

9. See http://www.worldbank.org/en/news/press-release/2013/05/01/twenty-fragile-states-make-progress-on-millennium-development-goals.

10. See McArthur, J. (2014). "The Origins of the Millennium Development Goals." *SAIS Review* XXXIV, no. 2: 5–24. http://johnmcarthur.com/wp-content/uploads/2015/01/SAISreview2014mcarthur.pdf.

11. Fisher, Roger, William L. Ury, and Bruce Patton. *Getting to Yes: Negotiating Agreement Without Giving In*. New York: Penguin, 2011.

12. The book *Getting to Yes* spawned the creation of the Program on Negotiation at Harvard Law School, as well as a host of additional books, including Douglas Stone et al's *Difficult Conversations*. The Program on Negotiation has anchored negotiation training and research since the early 1980s and has tremendous influence teaching negotiation in law and business schools across the United States and globally.

Aggression

David Barash and Charles Webel

David Barash received his PhD in zoology from the University of Madison–Wisconsin and now serves as professor of psychology at the University of Washington. His studies in zoology exposed him to Darwinian theories, which he applies to peace studies. His coauthor, Charles Webel, is a professor of peace studies at Chapman University in California. Webel continues to write with Barash while publishing other works about terrorism, civil resistance, and nonviolence.

Barash and Webel raise the question of biological fatalism: Does human biology and instinct make violence an unavoidable part of human destiny? "Wars begin in the minds of men" says the United Nations Educational, Scientific and Cultural Organization (UNESCO). Even though theorists have claimed that human ability to enact harm exceeds its ability to safely manage the harm it can enact, the authors argue war is not in our genes. Their concern is less about whether theories of human aggression are true and more concerned that accepting biology as destiny absolves humans from taking responsibility for their actions. Believing war is in our genes, they believe, can be used to justify violence. They push back against what they call *biological pessimism*, even though renowned psychoanalysts, including Sigmund Freud, carried such pessimism.

The article describes and then critiques these human nature theories. They warn against applying theories of individual human psychology to group behavior. They also point out counterarguments, such as those cultures that have never engaged in war, and they highlight periods of peace during human history as well as war resistors. Ultimately, however, their argument is not so much that the theorists were wrong about human aggression, but that fear is a self-fulfilling prophecy. If we believe that war is inevitable, we allow it. We must believe peace is possible, hold societies responsible for their behavior, and surrender the emotional appeal of war.

This article reflects Epoch One in its concern for whether or not the root causes of violence are located in and can be discovered by examining the thoughts and behaviors of individuals and its search for the reasons of war that transcend cultural differences. The authors also concur with Paul Collier that even though war can evoke great passion, it is not always prompted by passion. Instead, it can be prompted by the careful calculations of a group of individuals, who are seeking resources or power.

Questions to consider: Do you think humans are destined to be violent? If so, how do we explain nonviolent people and war resistors? If not, then what accounts for the amount of violence still occurring?

The Individual Level

A weapon is an enemy even to its owner.

—Turkish proverb

Wars require the organized activity of large numbers of people. But even the facts of complex organization and massive numbers do not eliminate the personal involvement and responsibility of individuals. To some degree, individual people acquiesce to war, prepare for it, and often participate in it, either passively (by permitting it to occur) or actively (by providing material assistance or actually doing the fighting). If many individuals didn't allow, encourage, or engage in them, wars wouldn't happen. Hence, without denying the importance of other dimensions—which we shall explore in subsequent chapters—our search for the reasons for wars might commence by looking to the inclinations and behavior of individual people.

The preamble to the constitution of the United Nations Educational, Scientific, and Cultural Organization (UNESCO) states that "wars begin in the minds of men" (and we must add, women as well, although possibly to a somewhat lesser extent). It takes no great stretch of imagination to charge the human psyche with prime responsibility for the initiation of war. Former senator J. William Fulbright emphasized the personal dimension of war making (and thus, war preventing) when he wrote:

> The first, indispensable step toward the realization of a new concept of community in the world is the acquisition of a new dimension of self-understanding. We have got to understand . . . why it is, psychologically and biologically, that men and nations fight; why it is . . . , that they always find *something* to fight about.[1]

When we concern ourselves with peace and war, we normally talk about the actions of large social units, often entire countries. But at least in part, when we say that a social unit "acts" in a particular way, what we really mean is that many individuals within those units act in such a manner. Thus, we say that the state acts, often meaning that the people within it—especially decision makers in the government—act.

First, we examine four major perspectives on the reasons for wars by focusing on the level of the individual person: instinct theory, sociobiology (and evolutionary psychology), Freudian and post-Freudian psychoanalysis, and the postulation of innate human depravity. These perspectives, while differing in significant ways, share an emphasis on the role of inborn, biological factors. Then, after considering some criticisms of these "human nature" approaches, we consider a variety of other factors believed to operate at the individual level, all of which involve greater attention to the role of learning and other social experiences.

Aggression, Drives, and Instincts

Many thinkers have assumed human beings to be instinctively aggressive. A particularly influential version of instinctivist theory has developed around presumed biological traits of the human species. Thus, one of the most influential U.S. textbooks on international relations begins as follows: "The drives to live, to propagate, and to dominate are common to all men."[2]

According to such notions, human warfare can be traced to our biological heritage, attributable directly to genetic, hormonal, neurobiological, and/or evolutionary mechanisms, including a tendency to form dominance hierarchies, to defend territories, and to behave aggressively toward others. Much emphasis is placed on the existence of comparable behavior patterns among certain animals, and the presumption that the behavior of animals reflects underlying principles that hold for the human species as well.

The Lorenzian Approach

Perhaps the most influential exponent of this perspective was the Nobel Prize-winning Austrian ethologist (student of the biology of animal behavior), Konrad Lorenz. Lorenz helped conceptualize a view of instinctive behavior according to which animals are endowed with certain behaviors, called "fixed action patterns," whose actual physical performance is genetically fixed and unvarying from one individual to another. In his book *On Aggression*, Lorenz argued that certain "species preserving" aspects of aggression applied to human beings as well. They include the following:

1. Providing an opportunity for competition within a species, after which the most fit will emerge to produce the next generation.
2. Achieving spacing and population control, to minimize the disadvantages of overpopulation.
3. Establishing a means whereby the pair-bond can be strengthened, as by shared aggression of a mated pair against competitors.

Lorenz was not concerned with extolling human aggression, but with understanding it. He noted that, in moderate amounts, aggression may well be functional and healthy, but at the same time, he deplored its occurrence in excess, especially when combined with what he called "militant enthusiasm," the tendency of people to lose their normal inhibitions against violence when united with others similarly motivated. Lorenz also emphasized that animals that have lethal natural weapons, such as wolves or hawks, also tend to possess innate inhibitions against employing such weapons against members of the same species. By contrast, animals such as rabbits, doves, or human beings—not naturally equipped with lethal weapons—lack such inhibitions. According to this line of thought, the human condition is especially perilous because while we have developed the ability, by technological means, to kill our fellow humans, quickly, easily, and in great numbers, our biological evolution remains far behind our technological progress. We continue to lack genetically based mechanisms to keep our newfound lethality in check.

The Lorenzian approach, which tends to "extrapolate war from human instinct," is in some ways a caricature of biological (ethological) views. According what might be called the *classical ethological approach,* aggression is genetically controlled behavior, such that the actual behavior patterns are rigidly stereotyped, invariant, and independent of learning. In this perspective, aggression can also emerge spontaneously; that is, individuals have a *need* to discharge this drive by behaving aggressively.

Lorenz suggests that one way to deal with our instinctive penchant for aggression and militant enthusiasm is by rechanneling this biological energy in socially useful (or at least, nondestructive) forms of competition, such as athletics, the exploration of space, or medical research. Nonetheless, Lorenz is led to a pessimistic assessment of the human future:

> An unprejudiced observer from another planet, looking down on man as he is today, in his hand the atom bomb, the product of his intelligence, in his heart the aggressive drive inherited from his anthropoid ancestors, which this same intelligence cannot control, would not prophesy long life for the species.[3]

Other members of the "war in our genes" school have also contributed to the instinctivist approach. "Was my response to Pearl Harbor innate or conditioned?" asked the writer Robert Ardrey:

> Was it something I had been born with or something I had been taught? Was it truly a command of genetic origin, an inheritance from the experience and natural selection of thousands of generations of my human and hominid ancestors?[4]

In this book and in his earlier work, *African Genesis,* Ardrey clearly associates himself with the Lorenzian view, arguing that since human beings evolved from anthropoid apes that hunted at least occasionally, and were probably at least somewhat carnivorous, then we must be genetically aggressive as well.

Is War in Our Genes?

Although biology may well provide valuable insights into the current human condition, such simplistic extrapolations from animal to human can also be dangerously misleading. For example, it is no more valid to argue that human beings are naturally murderous because baboons sometimes kill other baboons than it is to conclude that human beings are naturally vegetarians because gorillas exclusively eat plants or that humans can fly because birds have wings.

There is a danger that by accepting war as part of "human nature," one thereby justifies war itself, in part by diminishing the human responsibility to behave more peacefully. If war is "in our genes," then presumably we cannot act otherwise, so we should not be blamed for what we do; maybe, then, we shouldn't even bother trying to do anything about our warlike inclinations. At minimum—and perhaps, at its most pernicious—such biological fatalism supports a pessimistic perspective on the human condition, one that provides an excuse for the maintenance of large military forces and leads to profound distrust of others, especially those who look different from ourselves. There is, indeed, evidence that people who are generally promilitary tend to be disproportionate believers in the doctrine that war is somehow etched in our DNA.

To address (and scientifically to refute) biological determinism, a group of prominent behavioral scientists from 12 nations met in 1986 in Seville, Spain, and agreed on the "Seville Statement," which has since been endorsed by the American Psychological Association and the American Anthropological Association, and other scholarly organizations. Some excerpts from this statement are as follows:

- It is scientifically incorrect to say that we have inherited a tendency to make war from our animal ancestors. Warfare is a peculiarly human phenomenon and does not occur in other animals. War is biologically possible but it is not inevitable, as evidenced by its variation in occurrence and nature over time and space.
- It is scientifically incorrect that war or any other violent behavior is genetically programmed into our human nature. Except for rare pathologies, the genes do not produce individuals necessarily predisposed to violence. Neither do they determine the opposite.
- It is scientifically incorrect to say that in the course of human evolution there has been a selection for aggressive behavior more than for other kinds of behavior. In all well-studied species, status within the group is achieved by the ability to cooperate and to fulfill social functions relevant to the structure of that group.
- It is scientifically incorrect to say that humans have a "violent brain." While we do have a neural apparatus to act violently, there is nothing in our neurophysiology that compels us to.
- It is scientifically incorrect to say that war is caused by "instinct" or any single motivation. The technology of modern war has exaggerated traits associated with violence both in the training of actual combatants and in the preparation of support for war in the general population.
- We conclude that biology does not condemn humanity to war, and that humanity can be freed from the bondage of biological pessimism. Violence is neither in our evolutionary legacy nor in our genes. The same species . . . [that] invented war is capable of inventing peace.

Sociobiology and Evolutionary Psychology

A more sophisticated version of instinctivism is associated with the discipline of sociobiology, whose best-known practitioner has been the entomologist Edward O. Wilson. The mainstream sociobiological approach, which in the 1990s was somewhat superseded by an even more recent discipline known as evolutionary psychology, differs from instinctivism in that it places new emphasis on evolution as a process rather than a historical event. That is, sociobiologists and evolutionary psychologists are particularly concerned with the *adaptive significance* of behavior, or the way in which particular behavior patterns are maintained and promoted in a population because they contribute to the reproductive success of individuals (not species) that possess these traits.

A sociobiological or evolutionary psychological view of human war examines such phenomena as ecological competition (for food, nesting sites, etc.), male-male competition (for dominance in the pecking order and for mates), and the role of kinship patterns in directing aggressive behavior in particular ways. Among many species, for example, males tend to be larger, showier, and more aggressive than females. In addition, biological differences between males and females mean, among other things, one male can successfully fertilize many females. Sexual differences of this sort, in turn, convey a reproductive payoff (enhanced evolutionary fitness) to individuals—especially males—who succeed in defeating their rivals, whether in symbolic display or outright combat. Consistent with this theory, men tend to be more aggressive than women (especially outside the family), and more likely to be involved in public violence of all sorts, including war. Another important tenet of sociobiological theory is the role of genetic relatedness: Individuals who share genes probably will behave benevolently (altruistically) toward each other, because such behavior tends to contribute to the success of genes predisposing toward such behavior; conversely, a low probability of genetic relatedness is likely to be associated with aggressiveness. Consistent with this theory, appeals to patriotism often involve what anthropologists call *fictive kinship,* calling on citizens to stand up for the motherland, fatherland, Uncle Sam, "brothers and sisters," and so forth.

As for competition, it has been defined by Wilson as "the active demand by two or more individuals . . . for a common resource or requirement that is actually or potentially limiting."[5] Many studies have pointed to the role of primitive war in gaining access to mates, animal protein, and social prestige, such that warfare among preindustrial or nontechnological peoples, which in the past appeared to be irrational and nonadaptive, is now increasingly seen to possess an internal logic of its own—although not necessarily a logic that is consciously appreciated by the participants.

Sociobiologists and evolutionary psychologists tend to back away from the simplistic "either/or" dichotomy of instinctivism, on the one hand, or social constructionism, on the other hand. It is misleading to ask, as Robert Ardrey has done, whether a given behavior is instinctive or learned, since all behavior results from the interaction of genetic potential with experience, both nature and nurture. "In order to be adaptive," writes Wilson, it is enough that aggressive patterns be evoked only under certain conditions of stress such as those that might arise during food shortages and periodic high population densities. It also does not matter whether the aggression is wholly innate or is acquired part or wholly by learning. We are now sophisticated enough to know that the capacity to learn certain behaviors is itself a genetically controlled and therefore evolved trait.[6]

Finally, another important evolutionary perspective, represented notably by anthropologist Robert Bigelow, considers war to have had a prominent role in the early evolution of the human species. Conceivably, proto-human warrior bands were a major selective force in our own early evolution, with successful bands killing off those that were less successful. Large brains could well have contributed to success in violent intergroup conflict by promoting relatively sophisticated communication, formation of social alliances, and effective use of weapons. Those enjoying such success would presumably have left more descendants, who in turn were likely to possess these favored traits and capacities.

Freudian and Post-Freudian Psychoanalytic Theory

Sigmund Freud was the creator of psychoanalysis and in many ways the founder of modern psychiatry. He is particularly noteworthy for his emphasis on the role of the unconscious in human behavior. Freud himself was a pacifist, and he especially deplored what he saw as a vicious, lethal streak among human beings. In his later work, Freud attributed much of humanity's more "inhumane" behavior to the operation of *Thanatos,* or the death instinct, which he saw as opposed to *Eros,* the life instinct. In a famous letter to Albert Einstein, he noted, "We are led to conclude that this [death] instinct functions in every living being, striving to work its ruin and to reduce life to its primal state of inert matter."[7] When Thanatos is thwarted by Eros, its energy is displaced outward onto subjects other than oneself, resulting in aggression between individuals or among groups.

The notion of a death instinct remains associated with Freud's thought, and this idea was extended by one of his followers, Melanie Klein (the founder of object-relations psychoanalysis). But Freud also argued that, regardless of whether Thanatos exists within the human psyche or if we are "simply" aggressive by nature, civilization demands that people repress their primitive tendencies toward destructive and aggressive behavior if they are to live together with a minimum of violent conflict. Parents must provide discipline for their children, society must restrict its citizens, and ultimately, some form of supranational authority will be necessary to enforce a system of world government over individual states that would otherwise function anarchically, argued Freud. Hence, civilization demands the repression of both Eros and Thanatos, which in turn necessarily produces discontent (and neurosis) among its populace.

Another important Freudian concept especially relevant to war is that of *narcissistic injury*. Narcissism involves infatuation with one's self, and in moderation it is considered a normal stage in personality development. But when the individual associates himself or herself with a larger group, especially with the nation-state, slights or injuries to the group are easy to perceive as injuries to one's self. The resulting "narcissistic rage" may involve an unrelenting compulsion to undo the hurt; in the pursuit of this vengeful justice, great violence may be self-righteously employed. Many of the most destructive wars in the 20th century were perpetrated by people seeking to retake territory that had been wrested from them by others (e.g., the French yearning to recapture the provinces of Alsace and Lorraine from Germany which was a major reason for World War I, or the Vietcong and North Vietnamese, who sought during the Vietnam War to reunite their country). Other wars have been instigated by ethnic groups seeking to secede from a central governmental authority, only to precipitate intervention by armed forces from the nation-state from which they hoped to disconnect (as in Nigeria, Ethiopia, Indonesia, the former Yugoslavia, and Russia).

Like the Lorenzian and (to a lesser extent) the sociobiological and evolutionary psychological approaches, the orthodox Freudian perspective tends to be pessimistic about the prospects for ameliorating, much less eliminating, "this ineradicable defect in human nature." Thus, Freud maintained, for example, that we really shouldn't be so disillusioned about atrocities during wartime, because the notion that humankind was fundamentally civilized is itself illusory.

Furthermore, according to Melanie Klein and some of her followers, human aggression is ultimately rooted in the earliest "primitive" states of human existence, before there is an ego or language to modulate, rechannel, or defuse it. Human destructiveness manifests itself, among other things, in the "paranoid-schizoid" anxieties and defenses (such as splitting and projection) initially used by infants to ward off feelings of abandonment (by the mother or other caregivers) and fears of annihilation and disintegration. According to Kleinian theory, therefore, human aggression is implicit even in the womb; it emerges full-blown during the first years of life (when the infant quite literally bites the mother's hand and breast that feed it); and persists throughout the entire life span, either as unconscious sadomasochistic fantasies or overtly in self- and other-destructive behaviors. The goal of psychoanalytic therapy from a Kleinian perspective is accordingly to induce the "malignant" (destructive and disowned) parts of the self to become "reintegrated" within a "whole-object" psyche, not to seek in vain to eradicate aggression from either the individual or from the human species.

Some students of human behavior have concluded that much human misery, including even the penchant for war itself, derives in part from the consequences of being mistreated as children. It is further argued that many acts of violence toward children—whether overt, such as beating or sexual abuse, or more subtle, such as severe criticism and belittling by significant others in a child's early environment—have in turn been buttressed by the view that human beings are inherently sinful and depraved. From a more secular perspective, the neo-Kleinian psychoanalytic theorist and pediatrician D. W. Winnicott claimed that with "good enough mothering," the infant's proclivities toward aggression could be mollified;

conversely, without a nurturing environment, babies and young children who are deprived of maternal love and positive reinforcement are at risk for developing pathological character structures and for engaging in self- and other-destructive behaviors.

Other prominent psychoanalysts have not been as pessimistic as most Kleinians and have in fact rejected the very notion of a death drive. Wilhelm Reich, for example, argued that the unprecedented violence and destructiveness unleashed on Europe during the first part of the 20th century were and not simply the latest manifestation of the eternal battle between Eros and Thanatos, but could instead be better explained in terms of the historical development of character pathologies ("armor") and socially induced aggression under modern capitalism. And more contemporary schools of psychoanalytic theory and therapy—notably the ego, self, relational, and critical psychologists—have also stressed the roles of environment, culture, social interaction, and socialization in eliciting and reinforcing aggressive and destructive behaviors.

"Innate Depravity" and "Human Nature"

Some thoughtful people have long maintained that human beings are innately depraved, nasty, and evil, basing this claim on a loosely argued blend of biology, moral outrage, and on occasion, theology. Looking over the blood-letting of the English civil war (1642–1649), Thomas Hobbes concluded that there was "a general inclination of all mankind, a perpetual and restless desire for power after power that ceaseth only in death."[8] To some extent, Hobbes's pessimism can be traced to a Biblical—especially to a conservative Christian—tradition that teaches that human nature is inherently flawed. Suffused with original sin, humans are deemed to be inherently incapable of becoming good. Consider these sentiments from the 16th-century theologian John Calvin, perhaps the most influential advocate of this perspective:

> Even infants themselves, as they bring their condemnation into the world with them, are rendered subject to punishment of their own sinfulness. . . . For though they have not yet produced the fruits of their iniquity, yet they have had the seed of it in them. Their whole nature is, as it were, a seed of sin and therefore cannot but be . . . abominable to God.[9]

In Calvinist theology, because of our allegedly innate human sinfulness, we were cast out of the Garden of Eden, doomed to death. We therefore deserve—indeed, we require—to be treated sternly and punished vigorously. In any event, according to this pessimistic Christian view, a true state of personal peace can be achieved only by grace, just as a state of political peace squires the Second Coming of Christ. And until then, war is inevitable.

This attitude is not limited to conservative Christians, however. Another approach, rarely articulated, emphasizes that human beings have not only a capacity for violence but also a deep-seated love of bloodletting, hatred, and destruction. In his letter to Albert Einstein, Freud observed that "man has within him a lust for hatred and destruction. . . . It is comparatively easy task to call this into play and raise it to the level of a collective psychosis."[10] And in the 17th century, John Milton wrote that even if our species were rendered somehow impervious to injury from all outside forces, yet the perverseness of our folly is so bent, that we should never cease hammering out of our own hearts, as it were out of a flint, the seeds and sparkles of new misery to ourselves, till all were in a blaze again.[11]

From this perspective, especially endorsed by theologians such as Luther, St. Augustine, John Calvin, and Reinhold Niebuhr, as well as by religiously motivated political leaders such as Oliver Cromwell or satirists like Jonathan Swift, war is an evil unique to humanity. Niebuhr argued that it was the "sinful character of man" that necessitated "the balancing of power with power."[12] The philosophers Spinoza and Kant located the evils of human violence in the fact that our rational faculties are regularly overwhelmed by our irrational and untamed emotions.

This is only a very limited sampling of a widespread notion. Although it is quite difficult to prove, the idea of innate human weakness and depravity remains very popular, especially among the lay public. It has also been especially influential among those who are sympathetic to military force, if not to war itself. Thus, if human nature is inherently nasty and warlike, then we can never have any confidence in morality, law, or anything else to deliver us from war, since these are only frail, artificial institutions constructed by fundamentally flawed human beings. Because human nature presumably cannot be changed, the only recourse to safeguard personal or national security—regrettably—is to arms.

Criticisms of Human Nature Theories

The various human nature theories about the reasons for human violence all contain flaws. For example, human beings undoubtedly have the biological capacity to kill one another—proven by the fact that they have often done so. The danger is that such a broad generalization may be useless in analyzing the past or predicting the future. Other, more specific problems m these theories exist as well. For example, consider the following:

1. Although war is a widespread human trait, it is not a universal one; certain cultures, such as the Tasaday of the Philippine Islands, the South African bushmen (or San), the Semai (in Southeast Asia), and the Inuit, apparently never engaged in war, although interpersonal violence was not unknown. Explanations based on human nature should apply to these peoples no less than to others. Although some societies are clearly more war prone than others, there is also no evidence whatever that such difference reflect inherent differences in human nature.

2. Even among war-prone cultures, there have been many years of peace. If human nature caused World War II or the Vietnam War, then what about the peace that preceded and followed these wars? If human nature causes war, then it must also cause peace—the neutrality of Sweden, the demilitarized U.S.-Canadian border, Gandhi's nonviolence. Any explanation that is so broad becomes useless. To paraphrase a military metaphor of Karl von Clausewitz, he who seeks to explain everything, explains nothing.

3. Even within war-prone cultures, there have been war resisters, peace advocates, and long-time nonviolent traditions such as the Mennonites and the Quakers; are they less "human," or less "natural," than their more violent fellow citizens?

4. The fact that animals behave in certain ways does not necessarily mean that human beings do so; we seem to be unique in our capacity for complex, abstract, and symbolic thought, which gives us the opportunity to reason, to analyze, and to rise above our unpleasant or dangerous inclinations.

5. If war is a result of a fixed human nature, then it is predestined and unavoidable, since we cannot—by definition—behave counter to our own nature. There is a special danger in the belief that war is inevitable, because it is likely to discourage people from seeking to end war and to promote peace. Moreover, it can also serve to *justify* war by making it appear somehow "good" because it is natural.

The above criticisms are all valid to a degree, especially when applied to naive or crude instinctivism. But they also oversimplify the more sophisticated human nature arguments. Thus, most biologically inclined theorists recognize that genetic factors do not irrevocably commit a person, or a society, to a given course of action. Rather, they create predispositions for behaving aggressively or violently when circumstances are appropriate; similarly, nothing in sociobiological or evolutionary psychological thought suggests at such predispositions could not be overridden by religious beliefs, historical circumstances, collective social action, and so on. There is nothing inconsistent with the proponents of such theories suggesting that human beings can say "No" to their genes, neurons, and/or hormones.

Human Nature and Genetic Determinism

There is a great difference between a possible genetic *influence* on war proneness and the doctrine of genetic *determinism*. The former implies the existence of tendencies, likely to be subtle and capable of being overridden, whereas the latter implies rigid, ironclad automatic responses. There may well be genetic and neurobiological influences that human beings, if they are to be peaceful, must overcome or sublimate; this is not to say that our genes, neurons, and/or hormones predetermine our behavior, condemning us to violence.

As to morality, advocates—and critics—of biologically based arguments should be wary of what the philosopher David Hume first identified—and later labeled by the 20th-century British philosopher G. E. Moore—as the *naturalistic fallacy,* the mistaken belief that "is implies *ought.*" In other words, whatever insights biological and neurosciences might provide regarding how the natural world and the human brain work, these are distinct from ethical guidance as to what is good and what right conduct entails. Typhoid is natural; this does not mean that it is good. War may or may not be natural; whether it is good, however, is an entirely different question. In any event, if typhoid, or war, is to be prevented or cured, we must understand its causation, whether or not we are pleased by what we find.

Frustration-Aggression

Among explanations for war that do not depend on explicit assumptions about human nature, one of the most influential has been the frustration-aggression hypothesis, which was developed to explain individual aggressiveness as well. According to this theory, first proposed by psychiatrist John Dollard and his colleagues, aggressiveness is produced by frustration, which in turn is defined as "an interference with the occurrence of an instigated goal-response at its proper time in the behavior sequence."[13] Thus, if a hungry rat is presented with food, after which a glass wall is interposed between the animal and its desire, the rat is likely to become aggressive. A similar thing happens with frustrated human beings, people who have been seeking something unsuccessfully—food, political freedoms, access to a disputed territory, union with others who practice the same customs—or who have obtained partial success only to be prevented from achieving their ultimate goals.

In its initial formulation, frustration theory was presented rather dogmatically. "The occurrence of aggressive behavior always presupposes the existence of frustration, and contrariwise, the existence of frustration always leads to some form of aggression."[14] This rigidity led to problems comparable to those encountered with some human nature theories: The argument can become circular if all cases of aggression are defined as involving preexisting frustration, and vice versa, if any behavior that follows frustration is defined to be aggression.

Frustration theory has subsequently been modified to recognize that frustration creates a predisposition or readiness for aggression, by producing an intervening emotional state: anger. In addition, environmental stimuli—targets and/or cues—are necessary for aggression to be produced. Finally, an individual's learning experiences and society's expectations exert a powerful influence on the connection between frustration and aggression. Of course, other responses to frustration are also possible, namely, submission, resignation alienation, withdrawal, avoidance, or even acceptance, but this does not in itself argue against the strength of the frustration-aggression link.

Frustration can also result in resentment, which (like the above responses) may or may not subsequently produce aggressive behavior. Frustration may be especially high when there is a discrepancy between expectations and realities: Bad social conditions, such as poverty or political repression, are made to seem even worse by high expectations that conflict with unpleasant realities. Accordingly, the "revolution of rising expectations," particularly in the less advanced economies, has been associated with frustration and violence.

Political and military authorities often respond to collective efforts to promote social change with increased repression, but the forceful repression of strongly felt needs (such as the yearning for Palestinian self-determination, and before that, of Zionists for a Jewish state) can in itself be highly frustrating and thereby ultimately increase hostility and aggression. In some cases, frustration finds its outlet in aggressive behavior against others who are not actually the perceived frustrating agent.

There is another possible twist to the connection between frustration and war, namely, boredom. It has been suggested that war is especially appealing to those whose lives are lacking in excitement and interest. "The absence of delight in daily living," wrote the historian John Nef, "has helped to leave many lives empty and sterile and so, fair game for any excitement, including the most terrific of worldly excitements, that of war."[15] Furthermore, once a society has elevated military values, has trained men and boys (and increasingly, women and girls) to be warriors, and has institutionalized and mythologized the war experience, people may be especially prone to be frustrated and bored with peace. Of course, warfare itself actually involves prolonged periods of boredom and monotony. The endless repetition, drill, and "hurry up and wait" behavior that characterize military routine are hardly antidotes for civilian ennui. Military boredom may lead, however, to frustration, which in turn leads to greater willingness to go to war, if only to "see action" and thereby finally to break the suspense.

Social Learning

Clearly, human beings are strongly influenced by their experiences—those that occur early in development and that also characterize later socialization—as well as society's norms and expectations. Most psychologists and sociologists maintain that human violence arises in response to experiences, rather than bubbling up out of our genetic constitution. "The important fact," wrote psychologist John Paul Scott, "is that the chain of causation in every case eventually traces back to the outside. There is no physiological evidence of any spontaneous stimulation for fighting arising within the body."[16] Scott has emphasized that individuals are particularly likely to fight if they have fought successfully in the past and that aggression often results from a breakdown in social structures. (It is also noteworthy, on the other hand, that some of the most aggressive societies have been highly structured: Nazi Germany and Fascist Italy, for example.)

Conditioning

One of the most important developments in 20th-century psychology revolved around the learning phenomenon known as *conditioning,* especially associated with the work of B. F. Skinner. The basic idea is that behavior will be influenced by its consequences for the individual: Certain behaviors tend to be *reinforcing,* that is, they make it more likely that the individual will repeat the previous behavior. Some authorities employ the phrase "instrumental aggression" to refer to aggressive behavior that is oriented primarily toward attaining some goal, such as winning a war or recovering territory, rather than causing injury as such.

Conditioning theory applied to human aggressiveness suggests that people will behave aggressively when such behavior leads to reinforcing (i.e., positive) results and, conversely, that the likelihood of aggression will be reduced if it leads to negative results. By extrapolation, members of whole societies can presumably be influenced similarly, making war more probable if their behavior has been positively reinforced (rewarded) or negatively reinforced (punished). For example, the international aggressiveness of Nazi Germany was positively reinforced during most of the 1930s by the appeasement policies of the West; by contrast, it can be argued that international adventuring on the part of the United States was negatively reinforced by its divisive and ultimately unsuccessful involvement in Southeast Asia (resulting in a subsequent reluctance to commit American ground troops to foreign combat, the so-called Vietnam syndrome).

Socialization to Aggressiveness

Some societies actively encourage aggressiveness from early childhood. For example, consider the Fulani people of northern Nigeria, among whom most males seek to embody the ideals of "aggressive dominance." As boys, young Fulani males are taught to beat their cattle to prevent them from wandering off and to fight back unhesitatingly whenever they have been attacked. If they refrain from retaliation, they are mocked as cowards. They show virtually no emotion when struck with sticks during increasingly serious fights, and by the time they are young men, the Fulani are proud of their battle scars. Not surprisingly, they are also prone to personal fighting as well as warfare.

Mark May, an influential social psychologist, summed up the dominant American view of the 1940s when he wrote that "men not only lean when it is best to fight or not to fight, whom to fight and whom to appease, how to fight and how not to; but they also learn whom, when, and how to hate." May went on to discuss the phenomenon of social learning for group aggressiveness:

> Learning to fight and to hate involves much more than learning to box, to duel, or to participate in other forms of group violence. Systematic education for aggressive warfare in ancient Sparta or in modern Germany includes, besides physical education in games and contests, universal compulsory military training; the inculcation of certain attitudes, prejudices, beliefs; and devotion to leaders and ideals. The whole purpose and direction of such education is toward group aggression.

Similar processes of socialization can also produce a group characterized by peace rather than by aggression. In such a group, according to May, there is the minimum amount of physical violence among the members. Antagonism, hostilities, and conflicts are held in check by customs, laws, and rules which are enforced in part by duly constituted authorities and in part by inner compulsions of loyalties and the sense of social responsibility. Peace between groups as well as within a group is maintained by the joint action of external authority and social attitudes of tolerance and good will.[17]

Also important in this context is the phenomenon of "imitative learning," whereby individuals are prone to do something if they witness others doing the same thing. Thus, aggressiveness and hostility—or alternatively, an inclination to settle disputes peacefully—can become part of the ethos of a society.

Self-Fulfilling Behaviors

An important sociological concept is what Robert Merton has called the *self-fulfilling prophecy*, according to which a belief becomes true if enough people believe that it is true. In the realm of aggressive behavior, hostility often begets hostility on the part of others, which in turn not only reinforces the initial hostility but also intensifies it. People may create their own inter-personal environments simply by behaving with a certain expectation: If someone is suspicious, secretive, and blameful, he or she is likely to elicit comparable behavior. This pattern has the makings of a vicious circle, in which hostility becomes self-reinforcing in a kind of positive feedback. A similar pattern can apply to international relations as well. For example, if country A, convinced of the hostility of country B, increases its armaments, then B may well respond in kind. This in turn reinforces the "enemy image" already present, leading to further militarily oriented actions, each of which may truly be intended to be "defensive" but that, taken as a whole, diminish the security of all participants. Such a process characterizes much of the history of arms races.

Redirected Aggression

Other patterns in behavioral development also take place, often without the explicit intent of producing aggressiveness. In James Joyce's short story "Counterparts," a man who is browbeaten by his boss, and who then stops at a pub after work and is defeated at arm wrestling, finally goes home—and beats up his young son. This phenomenon is known as *displaced* or *redirected* aggression, whereby anger—often generated by other sources—is displaced or redirected to different targets. The Bible describes how the ancient Israelites would designate one animal as a *scapegoat*, which would be abused and driven from the herd, ostensibly taking with it the sins and anger of those who remained behind, uninjured, and purified.

Frequently, the victims of redirected aggression are smaller, weaker, or already the subjects of social abuse: a religious or racial minority, advocates of unpopular political doctrines, and so on. Blacks, communists in the United States, Arab immigrants in France, religious and ethnic minorities (especially those with dark skin, such as the Roma) in Russia and the countries spawned by the collapse of the former Soviet Union and Yugoslavia, all have borne the brunt of redirected aggression by people who have been themselves deprived or disadvantaged. Although local minorities provide convenient "targets of opportunity," foreign nationals are particularly targeted as objects of redirected group anger.

The Authoritarian Personality

Following World War II and the Holocaust in which six million of Europe's Jews (as well as millions of pacifists, gays, Roma, war resisters, mentally disabled people, political dissidents, and civilian noncombatants) were murdered, researchers led by the German philosopher Theodor Adorno and the American social psychologist Nevitt Sanford sought to identify those personal traits and experiences that predispose people toward anti-Semitism and related authoritarian and antidemocratic ideologies and practices. Their work resulted in the F-Scale (for Fascist), which gave a rough measure of an individual's tendency toward authoritarianism. The *authoritarian personality* was found to be positively correlated with a rigidly hierarchical family structure: the husband dominant over the wife, and parents (especially fathers) demanding unquestioned obedience and respect from their children. This moralistic and disciplinarian style of child rearing was often combined with a strongly nationalistic outlook, ready submission to powerful external authority, and fear of weakness and of moral "contamination" by "aliens and other outsiders."

The resulting *authoritarian personality structure* can engender an autocratic, xenophobic, and militaristic approach to social problems, both domestically and in foreign relations. Such people often (unconsciously) have a relatively poor self-image that makes them especially prone to following orders blindly, even if these orders involve inflicting injury on one's self or others and even if the behaviors involved go counter to fundamental precepts of traditional morality, such as "thou shalt not kill."

Closely connected with the notion of an authoritarian personality is the concept of *identification with the aggressor,* in which the victim tends to adopt the attributes of a powerful punishing agent (parent, government), in order to alleviate anxiety; in the process, the victim is transformed into an aggressor, either directly or indirectly by supporting aggression on the part of others. It may be significant that comparatively permissive societies seem to be less warlike than those with high levels of physical punishment of children and of sexual repression.

Alienation and Totalism

Psychoanalysts Erich Fromm and Erik Erikson have emphasized, more than their drive-oriented colleagues, the influences of culture, society, and the environment on people's propensity for engaging in violent and other antisocial conduct. They have also focused on the role of painful, or traumatic, experiences operating through nonrational psychic processes. Fromm distinguished between *defensive aggression* and *malignant aggression,* with the latter involving a passionate drive to hurt others (sadism) or one-self (masochism). But unlike the human nature theorists, he attributes malignant aggression to social conditions rather than to innate human traits. In particular, Fromm blames *alienation,* an acute loneliness and disconnectedness from others, for the inclination by very alienated people to avenge their pain by acts of extreme destruction; they are also ripe candidates for inclusion in violent organizations, where they can lose themselves in a group that is united by their hatred of others. This might include the Ku Klux Klan and other neo-Nazis in the United States, skinheads in Great Britain as well as other "terrorist" and hate groups worldwide. It must also be noted, however, that feelings of social and political alienation might also motivate psychologically healthy personalities to participate in social movements to *oppose* injustices and wars.

In similar vein, Erikson has pointed out that, especially when it is changing rapidly, a society may generate ambiguities and unresolved stresses that combine with the individual's developmental problems to produce *totalism,* a susceptibility to all-or-nothing simplifications: us versus them, good versus evil, God versus the devil. Given the sacrifices that war demands—not only economic and political but also the willingness to sacrifice one's life and to go against the standard societal prohibition against taking another's life—it is not surprising that totalistic thinking and war should go hand in hand.

The Attractions of War

In *Notes from the Underground,* Dostoyevsky wrote, "In former days we saw justice in bloodshed and with our conscience at peace exterminated those we thought proper to kill. Now we do think bloodshed abominable and yet we engage in this abomination, and with more energy than ever."[18] This energy derives at least in part from the fact that some people at least find war a positive experience. Many combatants have extolled the sheer intensity of confronting the basic phenomena of life and death, and in the process, exploring the boundaries of one's capacities. For some soldiers, especially young men, there is something exhilarating about meeting death face to face, perhaps even heroically and for a noble cause, rather than to be overtaken alone in the night. Teilhard de Chardin (who served in World War I) wrote, "The front cannot but attract us, because it is . . . the extreme boundary between what you are already aware of, and what is still in the process of formation. Not only do you see there things that you experience nowhere else, but you also see emerge from within yourself an underlying stream of clarity, energy, and freedom that is to be found hardly anywhere else in ordinary life. . . . This exaltation is accompanied by a certain pain. Nonetheless it is indeed an exaltation. And that is why one likes the front in spite of everything, and misses it."[19]

For others, there may be a compelling sexual component, as revealed in this passage from Norman Mailer:

> All the deep, dark urges of man, the sacrifices on the hilltops, the churning lusts of night and sleep, weren't all of them contained in the shattering, screaming burst of a shell? The phallus-like shell that rides through a shining vagina of steel. The curve of sexual excitement and discharge, which is, after all, the physical core of life.[20]

And most significant of all, perhaps, is the satisfaction of "belonging" and companionship, particularly a kind of male bonding, that most men do not experience during civilian life. Shakespeare's Henry V rhapsodizes about the pleasure the forthcoming battle holds for

> We few, we happy few, we band of brothers;
> For he to-day that sheds his blood with me
> Shall be my brother. *(Henry V*, IV, iii)

Or consider this commentary, from a combat veteran of World War II:

> We are liberated from our individual impotence and are drunk with the power that union with our fellows brings. In moments like these many have a vague awareness of how isolated and separate their lives have hitherto been. . . . With the boundaries of the self expanded, they sense a kinship never known before. Their "I" passes insensibly into a "we." . . . At its height, this sense of comradeship is an ecstasy.[21]

The American philosopher and psychologist William James (1842–1910) believed that the raw emotional appeal of war constituted one of the greatest difficulties in overcoming it. In a renowned essay, James presented the case for war's attractiveness:

> The war against war is going to be no holiday excursion or camping party. The military feelings are too deeply grounded to abdicate their place among our ideals until better substitutes are offered. . . . Modern war is so expensive that we felt trade to be a better avenue to plunder, but modern man inherits all the innate pugnacity and all the love of glory of his ancestors. Showing war's irrationality and horror is of no effect upon him. The horrors make the fascination. War is the *strong* life; it is life *in extremis*. . . . Inordinate ambitions are the soul of every patriotism, and the possibility of violent death the soul of all romance. . . . If war had ever stopped, we should have to reinvent it . . . to redeem life from flat degeneration. . . . Its "horrors" are a cheap price to pay for rescue from the only alternative supposed, of a world of clerks and teachers, of . . . consumer's leagues and associated chanties, of industrialism unlimited, and feminism unabashed. . . . Militarism is the great preserver of our ideals of hardihood, and human life with no use for hardihood would be contemptible. Without risks or prizes for the darer, history would be insipid indeed.

James then suggested that these attractions could be overcome only be substituting another crusade, which he called "the moral equivalent of war":

> A conscription of the whole youthful population to form for a certain number of years a part of the army enlisted against Nature . . . would preserve in the midst of a pacific civilization the manly virtues which military party is so afraid of seeing disappear in peace. . . . So far, war has been the only force that can discipline a whole community, and until an equivalent discipline is organized, I believe that war must have its way.[22]

None of these selections should be seen as reflecting enthusiasm for war, but rather a grudging recognition that *even* war has not only its horrors but also its attractions. A famous *bushido* tract from ancient Japan advises that "when all things in life are false, there is only one thing true, death."[23] The most war-prone ideologies generally claim that their long-term goal, however, is to eliminate war. But there is a notable modern exception: Fascism. Fascism has tended to glorify war, and (judging by its success in the 20th century), it struck a favorable chord in many people. "War alone," wrote Italian dictator Benito Mussolini,

> brings up to their highest tension all human energies and puts a stamp of nobility upon the people who have the courage to meet it. All other trials are substitutes, which never really put a man in front of himself in the alternative of life and death. A doctrine, therefore, which begins with a prejudice in favor of peace is foreign to Fascism.[24]

Of course, the fact that someone may be a fascist does not itself contribute a satisfactory explanation for his or her inclinations toward war. Rather, one must also consider those factors that presumably have led him or her to embrace such a war-prone ideology: frustration, authoritarian personality structure, inadequate nurturance during childhood, social an biological influences, and so on.

A final contributing reason for war, working at the individual level, may well be a kind of sanitized romanticizing of battle, found in many children's cartoons and toys, movies (such as the *Star Wars* films), music, art, and literature. For example, consider the following verse, by English poet A. E. Housman:

> I did not lose my heart in summer's eve,
> When roses to the moonrise burst apart:
> When plumes were under heel and lead was flying,
> In blood and smoke and flame I lost my heart.
> I lost it to a soldier and a foeman,
> A chap that did not kill me, but he tried;
> That took the sabre straight and took it striking
> And laughed and kissed his hand to me and died.[25]

To be sure, there also exists a rich catalog of antiwar songs, stories, movies, and poems, ranging from the delicate and plaintive (as in the song "Where Have All the Flowers Gone?") to the unrelentingly realistic and grotesque (as in *All Quiet on the Western Front, Johnny Got His Gun, Catch-22,* and *Saving Private Ryan*). Opponents of war, however, are obliged to recognize those aspects of war that have long exercised a positive appeal for many humans.

Inhibitions Against War

The history of warfare shows that people are capable of the most heinous acts of brutality. From American history alone, consider the massacre of Sioux Indians at Wounded Knee in South Dakota in the late 19th century, or the massacre at My Lai in Vietnam about 100 years later: In both cases, hundreds of men, women, and children were slaughtered wantonly. Indeed, the preceding sections may leave the impression that war exerts a virtually irresistible attraction to human beings at the individual level, whether through our innate characteristics, our experiences, or via the lure of excitement, camaraderie, and ideology. But in fact, even beyond ethical and religious strictures, there are many inhibitions that serve to check the personal propensity for war.

One of these inhibiting factors is fear for one's own life. In Euripedes' *The Suppliants,* the Theban herald points out that "if death had been before their own eyes when they were giving their votes, Hellas [Greece] would never have rushed to her doom in mad desire for battle." There are, in fact, very few heroes during a war; most soldiers seek to do the minimum necessary to save themselves and their close colleagues.

As to alleged bloodlust and war fever, consider that during World War II rarely did more than 25% of American soldiers fire their guns in battle; even during intense firefights, about 15% opened fire. And this applied to intensely trained combat infantrymen. A study sponsored by the U.S. Army concluded that "it is therefore reasonable to believe that the average and healthy individual—the man who can endure the mental and physical healthy of combat—still has such an inner and usually unrealized resistance towards killing a fellow man that he will not of his own volition take life if is possible to turn away from that responsibility."[26] It can even be argued that, in many wars before 1950, fear of killing, rather than fear of being killed, is the largest cause of battle failure.

By the Korean and Vietnam wars, however, the percentage of soldiers willing to fire their weapons appears to have gone up significantly, largely because of improved training and greater emphasis on establishing within-group solidarity among individual combat unit. Army discipline has long been recognized as crucially important, largely because the side that broke and ran has historically been the one that was butchered. A major part of military training (especially in boot camp) seeks to countermand the basic moral teaching—not limited, incidentally, to Western tradition—"Thou shalt not kill." The goal of basic training, in the armed forces of most countries, has not so much been the teaching of new techniques and skills as the inculcation of new attitudes: unquestioning obedience to military superiors and an increased willingness to kill. Despite some resistance, most people can in fact learn these things, usually in just a few weeks. This should not be surprising, since a profound asymmetry of power exists between the recruit and the officers who train them: "Recruits usually have no more than twenty years' experience of the world, most of it as children, while the armies have had all of history to practice and perfect their techniques."[27]

Actual killing during combat is widely considered the role of enlisted men or, at most, junior officers. By 1914, for example, lieutenants and captains in the British Army led men into battle carrying only a swagger-stick or, at most, a pistol. "Officers do not kill," was the common understanding at that time, and there is reason to believe that, if they had the choice, most enlisted men would not have done so either. George Orwell, for example, who fought as an anti-Fascist volunteer on the Loyalist side during the Spanish Civil War, recounted that he was unable to shoot an enemy soldier whom he observed "half-dressed and . . . holding up his trousers with both hands. . . . I did not shoot partly because of that detail about his trousers. . . . A man who is holding up his trousers isn't a 'Fascist,' he is visibly a fellow creature, similar to yourself, and you don't feel like shooting him."[28]

Some Issues in Nuclear Psychology

Because of its special features, nuclear war also merits special consideration at the level of individual psychology. Many aspects of nuclear psychology operate at the level of decision makers. Other factors, however, affect the psychological functioning of all human beings.

When it comes to nuclear war, feelings of attraction and revulsion are particularly intense. Some people evince a strange love for weapons of such all-encompassing power (hence, the title of the famous satirical movie *Dr. Strangelove, or How I Learned to Stop Worrying and Love the Bomb*). Others, by contrast, are especially repelled by the grisly prospect of ending war on so massive a scale. And yet, because a full-fledged nuclear conflict has not yet occurred, and because, in addition, the effects of nuclear explosions have difficulty focusing their minds and energies on such a topic, which is at once horrifying and yet strangely unreal.

When confronted with deeply unpleasant information, for example, people often respond with *denial*, a refusal to confront an unpleasant reality. This process is particularly well-known with respect to personal death: Virtually every cognitively unimpaired adult recognizes that eventually he or she will die; however, most of us go about over lives as though our own death holds little reality. When confronted with the facts, we concur; if not, we often practice denial. Something similar can be identified with respect to the nuclear danger: Most of us go about our daily lives as though the prospect of instantaneous nuclear holocaust does not hang over us, simply because such an overwhelming threat is too painful and emotionally disruptive to admit into our moment-by-moment consciousness.

This behavior, although presumably adaptive for the individual, also has unintended and potentially dangerous consequences. By refusing to confront unpleasant realities, people who might otherwise become mobilized in opposition to nuclear weapons are likely to place their attention and energy elsewhere. Moreover, they abandon the field to those who have insulated themselves from the negative consequences of their activities, and who, by virtue of career advancement and/or ideology, have committed themselves to a more pronuclear, and possibly prowar, orientation.

Denial is encouraged by the fact that nuclear weapons tend to lack psychological reality: They are kept in secret, restricted installations, and in the United States, the Department of Defense refuses, as a matter of policy, either to "confirm or deny" their presence (even in other countries allied to the United States). This policy has ostensibly been adopted so as to keep information from would-be nuclear terrorists. Regardless, one important effect of official secrecy clearly is to keep the American public uninformed and, to some extent, to facilitate denial. Hence, for most people, nuclear weapons cannot be seen, touched, smelled, or heard, and so it requires a conscious effort to consider that they exist at all.

Closely related to denial is another personal, psychological phenomenon of the nuclear age, often called *psychic numbing*. This phrase was originally applied by psychiatrist Robert J. Lifton to the *hibakusha*, the victims of the atomic bombing of Hiroshima and Nagasaki. Psychic numbing refers to a loss of emotional sensitivity and awareness that appeared to result from the survivors' immersion in the mass death that characterized those events. It can be argued that to some extent, we are all victims of Hiroshima and Nagasaki, in that all of us suffer from some degree of psychic numbing, as the nuclear menace pervades our unconscious.

Another important psychological mechanism of the nuclear age has been called the "more is better syndrome." In some ways, it appears to be a vestige of prenuclear times, when security was obtained (at least in some cases) by accumulating more weapons than one's opponent. In a world bristling with nuclear overkill, it seems unlikely that "more" is even meaningful, let alone and yet the tendency persists for many people to think in this way.

A Final Note on Individual-Level Explanations of Wars

Approximately 1% to 2% of human deaths during the 20th century were inflicted by other human beings. In other words, 98% to 99% of recent human deaths were not caused directly by intentional, individually inflicted violence. Moreover, of those deaths that are caused by other people, the majority are due to collective violence rather than to individual aggression.

Many social scientists have insisted that war is a human invention, not a biological necessity. They cite the high level of social organization and structuring involved in any military enterprise and the fact that different societies make war, if they do so at all, in very different ways, depending on the social structures and technological options. Different societies also make war for different reasons, including pride, prestige, revenge, and the quest for resources. It can also be argued that decisions regarding war, especially in large, modern societies, are not made at the individual level, or at least not at the level of the average citizen. Certainly, such decisions do not involve the simple summation of all individual inclinations within the population, nor do they follow the results of plebiscites or referenda submitted to the citizenry to vote for or against a particular war. Rather, war is decided by political (and often military, economic, and strategic) elites, after which the populace generally goes along, sometimes eagerly, but usually only after considerable manipulation or even outright coercion. And sometimes, war isn't really deliberatively "decided" at all; it just seems to "happen," often by mistake or misjudgment.

In addition, although war typically *arouses* great passions, it is not always true that war is the *result* of such passions. In some cases, wars appear to have been chosen by intelligent, instrumentally rational individuals, after carefully calculating the costs and benefits of alternative courses of action. According to military historian Michael Howard:

> In general men have fought during the past two hundred years neither because they are aggressive nor because they are acquisitive animals, but because they are reasoning ones: because they discern, or believe they can discern dangers before they become immediate, the possibility of threats before they are made.[29]

Humans also fight when they can perceive—whether accurately or not—that they will gain substantially by doing so.

One influential view, then, is that, rather than being a result of some wild, instinctive human nature, war can be the consequence of our coolest, most cerebral faculties. Individuals may fight with passion when placed in warlike situations, but throughout history, authorities have often had to resort to force to induce their supposedly vicious, hot-headed, and war-loving citizens to fight at all. Traditionally, many soldiers have been forced into battle with guns at their backs, hating and fearing their officers and discipline dodgers than the "enemy." There have been many more draft dodgers and deserters than people protesting on the streets that they have been provided with sufficient opportunity to go to war.

In any event, any serious effort to prevent war—and to establish a just and lasting peace—must take into account the inclinations and behavior of individual people, especially people with wealth and power. However, the "war against war" should not limit itself to the level of individual psychology, since, as we shall soon see, the behavior of organized groups may differ significantly from that predicted by a study of personal motivation and/or biology.

Notes

1. J. William Fulbright. Preface to Jerome D. Frank. 1967. *Sanity and Survival.* New York: Random House.

2. Hans Morgenthau. 1967. *Politics Among Nations.* New York: Knopf.

3. Konrad Lorenz. 1966. *On Aggression.* New York: Harcourt, Brace & World.

4. Robert Ardrey. 1966. *The Territorial Imperative.* New York: Atheneum.

5. Edward O. Wilson. 1971. In J. Eisenberg and W. Dillon, eds., *Man and Beast: Comparative Social Behavior.* Washington, DC: Smithsonian Institution Press.

6. Edward O. Wilson. 1975. *Sociobiology: The New Synthesis.* Cambridge, MA: Harvard University Press.

7. Sigmund Freud. 1964. Reprinted in J. Strachey, ed. and trans., *The Standard Edition of the Complete Psychological Works of Sigmund Freud.* London: Hogarth.

8. Thomas Hobbes. 1930. *Selections.* F. J. E. Woodbridge, ed. New York: Scribner.

9. John Calvin. 1956. *On God and Man.* F. W. Strothmann, ed. New York: Frederick Ungar.

10. Freud, The Standard Edition.

11. John Milton. 1953–1982. "The Doctrine and Discipline of Divorce." In *Complete Prose Works.* New Haven, CT: Yale University Press.

12. Reinhold Niebuhr. 1940. *Christianity and Power Politics.* New York: Scribner.

13. John Dollard et al. 1939. *Frustration and Aggression.* New Haven, CT: Yale University Press.

14. Ibid.

15. John Nef. 1950. *War and Human Progress.* Cambridge, MA: Harvard University Press.

16. John Paul Scott. 1975. *Aggression.* Chicago: University of Chicago Press.

17. Mark May. 1943. *A Social Psychology of War & Peace.* New Haven, CT: Yale University Press.

18. Fyodor Dostoyevsky. *1960. Notes from the Underground.* New York: E. P. Dutton.

19. Pierre Teilhard de Chardin. 1965. The Making of a Mind: Letters from a Soldier-Priest, 1914–1919. New York: Harper & Row.

20. Norman Mailer. 1968. *The Armies of the Night,* New York: New American Library.

21. J. Glen Gray. 1967. *The Warriors: Reflections on Men in Battle.* New York: Harper & Row.

22. William James. 1911. "The Moral Equivalent of War." In *Memories and Studies.* New York: Longmans, Green.

23. Z. Tamotsu. 1937. *Cultural Nippon.* Iwado, ed. and trans. Tokyo: Nippon Cultural Foundation.

24. Benito Mussolini. Quoted in Seyom Brown. 1987. *The Causes and Prevention of War.* New York: St. Martin's.

25. From A. E. Housman. 1936. *More Poems.* New York: Knopf.

26. S. L. A. Marshall. 1947. *Men against Fire.* New York: William Morrow.

27. Gwynn Dyer. 1987. *War.* New York: Crown.

28. George Orwell. 1968. *Homage to Catalonia.* New York: Harcourt Brace Jovanovich.

29. Michael Howard. 1984. *The Causes of War.* Cambridge, MA: Harvard University Press.

Human Needs

John Burton

Born in Australia, John Burton received his doctorate from the London School of Economics. In his early thirties, he held various senior positions in the Australian government. However, it was Burton's theories that made him a foundational figure in the field of conflict resolution. In part thanks to Burton, Australia remains an academic center for the field.

An outgrowth of Abraham Maslow's hierarchy of needs articulated in *Towards a Psychology of Being*, Burton claims individuals have universal human needs such as food, shelter, identity, security, and recognition. Unlike Maslow, Burton argues the need for identity and recognition can be as strong as physical needs. When denied access for sustained periods, people may fight to the death for both. Burton's interest is not in defining these needs so much as determining if whether unmet needs are a root cause of violence. Therefore, he considers the mechanisms within organizations and communities that facilitate or challenge both physical and psychological need fulfillment. Challenges could include limited job opportunities and, in more extreme cases, limited access to food or safety resulting in starvation or attack. While sometimes weather and other external conditions make meeting basic human needs difficult, administrative policies also often adversely affect people.

Burton's theory of conflict is that humans will pursue their needs regardless of obstacles. When faced with tremendous challenges, people may use forms of resistance and, in some cases, violence to fulfill their needs. Burton's article encourages conflict practitioners to learn how to distinguish between negotiable interests and nonnegotiable needs. To address these needs, he suggests societies need to shift from top down to bottom up, meaning that the focus needs to turn to the concerns of the local peoples. Note, Burton makes the distinction between *human rights*, which he says are culturally defined, and *human needs*, which he defines as universal.

This article reflects Epoch One thinking in its efforts to identify universal human behaviors, root causes, and structural forms of violence. *Needs theory* became a way to articulate the problems caused by the structural violence articulated in Galtung's article.

Questions to consider: Do you think people turn to violence because of unmet needs? Do you think needs are universal? If so, would all cultures and people within those cultures be likely to meet their needs in the same way? Would all people be willing to go to war to meet those needs?

Needs Theory

John Burton

Deprivations and "Structural Violence"

Circumstances sometimes impose deprivations on people and communities about which little can be done by those affected. Sometimes such deprivations are due to conditions over which there can be no control, such as accidents and unavoidable weather and environmental conditions. It is in such circumstances that others contribute assistance.

"Structural violence," by contrast, is a term used to describe damaging deprivations caused by the nature of social institutions and policies. As such it is, by definition, an avoidable, perhaps a deliberate violence against the person or community. Structural violence is sometimes associated with some specific acts, such as economic sanctions and discriminations imposed on people. More generally, structural violence results from compliance processes, perceived injustices, and deprivations such as an absence of job opportunities. There are also much more damaging instances, such as starvation and deprivations experienced in civil wars. The origins of structural violence are, therefore, the policy and administrative decisions that are made by some and which adversely affect others.

Societies and institutions within them have degrees of structural violence which are endemic. In a complex social organization, be it a society or a large factory, there is frequently limited face-to-face contact. For organizational reasons there must be those who have leadership roles and those over whom they exercise authority. The former do not know the latter as personalities: they are units within a system. The latter, like the machines they operate, are required to observe behavioral norms and practices determined by those in authority. Unless the organization is democratic in the widest participatory sense, these norms inevitably tend to accommodate institutional or organizational interests, with insufficient knowledge or consideration of those affected, giving rise to structural violence.

All industrial societies, as they have evolved, have this feature, stemming from the physical separation of those who are in authority and those who are required to conform. The system being administered, whether it be the political and social system as a whole or a particular enterprise, is administered in the belief that it is the appropriate one, and conformity is expected. Furthermore, whether the system has known defects or not, the belief is that required behaviors can be enforced if necessary.

At a political level apathy and withdrawal are interpreted as a willingness to accept systems, even though alienation—an emotional response to structural violence—is experienced. When 50 per cent or so of citizens do not take part in an electoral process, as in the United States where voting is not compulsory, it is likely that this is not acceptance, but a sense of alienation. Such alienation is frequently accompanied by protest forms of behavior, such as the formation of alternative groups with which to identify.

A false interpretation of apathy leads those who achieve leadership and elite status to assume that, subject to some negotiation, they can exercise control. The belief that law and order in a society can be enforced is a belief that is deeply ingrained in the thinking of societies that have evolved within a power frame. That compliance can be enforced, that deterrence deters, is a proposition that has had wide acceptance.

The human-needs frame of analysis is based on the proposition that, while structural violence is a reality, while, that is, there is a large degree of forced compliance, there are situations and conditions which are beyond the capability of the person or identity group to accommodate. There are human needs that *will* be pursued. In response to structural violence there will be resistance to the imposed conditions, violent resistance if necessary.

The concept of structural deprivation and violence is relevant to institutions throughout systems, including not only the workplace, but importantly the family. The family is a social institution in which in most cultures the male spouse has had traditionally, a dominant role, and in which parents, usually untutored in parenting, frequently impose compliance measures upon their children which are destructive of development and a sense of identity. Domestic violence, the sexual abuse of children and physical abuse even within the frame of learning and obedience, are all examples of structural violence. In Part Two it will be argued that responses include, in the longer term, many forms of anti-social behaviors in society, in the workplace and in political activities, even in important leadership roles.

Structures and Human Needs

If there are fundamental drives that the individual and identity group cannot voluntarily contain, then it cannot be assumed that law and order can be enforced except in conditions in which protest behaviors are physically impossible—as in slavery. The whole basis of law and order and organizational control are threatened in any circumstances in which such drives are frustrated.

This is, therefore, the fundamental question to pose: are there some human needs that *will* be pursued, regardless of consequences—that destroy the major premise of civilizations—that deterrence deters? If the answer is yes, then there must be a challenging paradigm shift in thinking and in decision making at all system levels.

Experience suggests that this is the case: there are clear limits to abilities willingly to conform. The young person leaving school can expect and accept problems in finding employment for the first time. But continuing unemployment, leading to a sense of being a nobody and to experiencing alienation, is unacceptable. Under such circumstances adjustment within the norms of society is not possible in the absence of extensive family and social support. Suicide, theft, street gangs, violence against migrants and competitive ethnic groups, are understandable responses. The member of an ethnic minority who experiences discrimination, in addition to other threats to identity and recognition as a person, may be even more likely to act recklessly, to follow terrorist leaderships and to seek achievement in anti-social and subversive ways. Most damaging of all is the transfer of anger by those who feel deprived, not against those responsible, for they are not accessible, but against others within a community also suffering, such as other minorities, and even others who live in the same locality.

Remote we-they authority relationships are a common feature of modern societies as they have evolved. We-they relationships dominate legislatures, legal systems and the workplace. The norms of such relationships inevitably extend even to face-to-face relationships, as in the home, where frequently a parent, having been brought up in a tense relationship or having lost opportunities for identity at the workplace, seeks to gain it by dominating behaviors. Dominating behaviors come to be admired. Political leaders score points with their electorates if they are seen to be tough on foreign nations when they do not conform with demands made to them. Examples of collaborative activities, such as small community organizations with agreed goals as in volunteer fire-fighting, or employee ownership of enterprises, exist and are popular, but they are by no means dominant.

The Evolution of Needs Theory

In structural violence there is no identifiable culprit, but there are victims. In the 1960s Johan Galtung posed the question, who are the "criminals" behind this violence? He wrote extensively seeking to identify those who cause structural violence.[1]

Soon after Galtung's contribution, conflict resolution processes were developed initially at the international level. *Needs theory* became a short-hand way of describing the problems created by structural violence and pointed more directly to ways in which they could be tackled. The onus of responsibility for dealing with problems of structural violence was on those who had the greatest influence within the system. They, too, would suffer in the longer term if the problems were not resolved. Thirty years later the exponential increase in conflict, violence and crime universally, at levels from the family to the inter-ethnic and the international, is leaving the real "criminals" with no constructive option but in their own interests, to become involved in problem-solving through conflict resolution processes in which all parties affected must play a part.

What needs theory did was to direct attention to a distinction between *negotiable interests* and *non-negotiable needs,* between disputes and conflicts. The former could be dealt with by legal and bargaining processes. Non-negotiable needs, on the other hand, required processes that would lead to altered perceptions by the parties concerned, and in some cases agreed structural change.

Clarity is required on the term "human needs." It should not be confused with "human rights." The U.S. government in the 1990s tried to force China to observe certain human rights, such as the right to protest, threatening to limit trading opportunities if this were not done. "Rights" in the United States do not include the right of a job or the right to have a living, or the practical, as distinct from the legal, right not to suffer discriminations. In democracies claims are made for the right of assembly, of expression, of choice. There could be societies which did not include these opportunities for political and social participation, but which, nevertheless, were acceptable to their members in given developmental circumstances. Even in democracies such rights are curbed in times of an emergency, such as war. "Rights" have a cultural connotation, usually associated with particular systems of government.

The distinctive feature of "needs," on the other hand, is that they are assumed to be inherent in human beings and in other species also and, therefore, universal and not just cultural. It is for this reason that those working within *needs theory* (see below) consider it appropriate to generalize across cultures and across societal levels from the interpersonal and family to the international.

Such needs have long been recognized. Abraham Maslow, in his *Towards a Psychology of Being,* had a list of needs ranging from the physical, such as food and shelter, to relationship needs.[2] He implied that it was the physical needs that were sought first. But more recent studies suggest that relationship needs are sometimes sought at the sacrifice of physical needs and even of life itself.

There are other writers, such as Renshon, whose concern is far more with psychological needs being met in political systems.[3] Renshon stresses the need for personal control, a useful broad concept, and makes an analysis of political behaviors. He comes up with a series of realistic propositions that deal with behavior at all social levels from the family to the political. They are based on replies to questionnaires sent to relevant groups. The impact of experience at all social levels is examined, leading to important insights into political attitudes and behaviors. Davies makes an extensive review of needs theorists, especially those whose views have a relevance to political participation and apathy.[4]

The Power of Human Needs

An early recognition of the power of human needs was expressed in 1973, when Paul Sites wrote a book titled *Control: The Basis of Social Order.*[5] The control to which he was referring was not control by authorities, but the control that persons exercise by reason of their inherent drives. Subsequently he referred to "Needs as Analogues of Emotions."[6]

At an international conference, held in Berlin in 1979, consideration was given to human needs by a group of scholars drawn from various disciplines, seeking a better understanding of human relationships. Their papers, *Human*

Needs, edited by Katrin Lederer, were published in 1980.[7] Many of these same scholars met in 1989 with others interested in the nature of conflict and its resolution. Within this conflict frame there was no idealism attached to the desirability of observing human needs. It was a straightforward costing orientation: if needs were not satisfied there would be costly conflicts. Inherent needs for recognition, identity and security (more a psychological security than a physical one) were emphasized in their papers.

It was interesting that the initial human needs scholars, while searching for a theoretical frame for their sociological interests, did not directly relate their thinking to the issue of conflict. Nor had those in the conflict resolution field previously considered the human needs frame as that which would enable them to develop their thinking from immediate conflict resolution thinking to future problem prevention by appropriate policies which took account of needs. The experience made possible a "Conflict Series" of four books, published in 1990, one of which included the papers of the 1989 conference referred to above.[8]

These experiences suggest that terms such as identity and recognition require far more definition than concepts and language presently make possible. Nevertheless, the conceptual frame is there. The implications are far-reaching. If *a need for recognition* and identity is inherent, or deeply ingrained in human nature, then obviously there will be every endeavor, by whatever means are available, to achieve it. The inherent human needs concept explains why persons identify with ethnic groups that seek their separate autonomies and why they denigrate peoples of other cultures. By reference to them, one can explain the source of street gangs and their claims for territory. Light is thrown *on some* aggressive leadership behaviors. One can understand why threat and coercion will not in all circumstances curb behaviors, even in the short term, and why they could further stimulate violent responses.

Malleable or Compelling?

This literature, however, does not deal with the question posed above, whether needs can be controlled in ways that allow for social conformity, or whether coercion and deterrence must fail in some circumstances. For the purposes of this analysis, just how needs are defined is not a major issue. Some summary notion such as personal control, or recognition and identity, is probably adequate for our purposes. The issue of concern is whether such needs can be suppressed and whether, therefore, citizens can become subject to control by authorities, or whether needs remain a power unto themselves, not subject to control by the individual, placing the individual outside the control of authorities. It is this nature of needs that is of concern rather than a precise definition and listing of them.

By inherent or basic, terms used interchangeably in many writings, is meant deep-rooted—nothing will change such a need. It will be pursued regardless of cost. Whether this is due to a natural instinct, or to a very early acquisition in some species, is a difficult biological question to answer. It is not an issue that need concern us. Our concern is whether there are some aspirations or needs that *will* be pursued, regardless of consequences, at least when basic physical needs have been met so that total apathy does not exist.

The empirical evidence seems to be clear: there are so many examples of needs of identity leading to tremendous outpourings of time and energy in the pursuit of some social or interest goal, and so many examples of frustrated needs leading to alienation or revenge-type behaviors. Religious and ethnic conflicts arc examples of the pursuit of such needs. Perhaps the most convincing empirical evidence comes, however, from doctors who deal with cases of violence and have the opportunity to explore, not only the nature of human needs, but why it is that they are compelling. In *Deadly Consequences: How Violence Is Destroying Our Teenage Population and a Plan to Begin Solving the Problem*, Dr. Deborah Prothrow-Smith reviews her research into the chemical responses to frustration and violence.[9] This is a complex subject and further research is called for; but it does seem that the deductive hypothesis of the needs theorists has support in studies of the chemistry of the brain.

Needs Theory and Organizational Problems

An issue of concern in an analysis of social problems at all system levels, from the family to the international, is not just the existence of these human needs. It is important to determine whether people in their adult lives, and in their social and political responses in the family, in the workplace, and in leadership roles nationally and internationally, are responding to the same needs. Is it possible to generalize across social levels, from person to person, nation to nation, assuming the same needs, even though the circumstances and responses seem so different? Should separate disciplines, dealing with social interactions at different social levels, assume the same human needs? If human needs were satisfied, would serious violence at all social levels then be avoided?

As has been observed, disciplines have been separated out from the total body of knowledge by reference to social levels: the person (Psychology), societies (Sociology), political groupings (Politics) and global relationships (International Relations). Those identifying with these separate fields tend to have their own special frames. They claim that separate studies are justified because behavior at different social levels is different. But this may be a mistake. The need for identity may find expression in person-to-person relationships in ways different from those in group relationships, but while forms will differ, the drives for identity are experienced regardless of social level.

The conclusion to which we are coming is that seemingly different and separate social problems, from street violence to industrial frictions, to ethnic and international conflicts, are symptoms of the same cause: institutional denial of needs of recognition and identity, and the sense of security provided when they are satisfied, despite losses though violent conflict.

This conclusion may not relate to the personal experience of many of those who take an intellectual interest in these problems. Professionally they have their identity and their security. They can cross cultural and ethnic boundary lines without feeling threatened. They are not subject to discriminations. This probably explains why such people take a "liberal" view on the integration of ethnic minorities by one-person-one-vote processes, as was the case in South Africa in 1994. If they suffered acutely from the frustration of human needs that touches the identity and security of the person, then they might adopt a different analytical approach. It would be one that sought to get to the roots of the problem. In an ethnic conflict situation the "liberal" view would then be to provide some form of separate autonomies, especially in cases in which communities were in separate regions. Such communities would then feel more secure and would make close functional relationships with others.

Needs and Problem-Solving

This chapter has been concerned with the behavioral component—human needs—of the analysis of conflict, violence and crime. The behavioral component has been introduced, not for any value or idealistic reason, but for practical cost reasons. It may be that the theoretical frame is still incomplete; but what seems clear is that compliance strategies and deterrence measures can no longer be claimed as an effective means by which to control behaviors. They are, therefore, costly in their consequences. Recognizing the costs of not accommodating this behavioral component provides a motivation for change.

The alternative to authoritative compliance and to structural violence is, in the specific case, the bringing together in an analytical frame the offenders and those who represent the economic-political-social structures and norms with which offenders seem to be in conflict. This analytical problem-solving approach to problems in relationships is still at an early stage of development. It has not made an impact yet in politics, industrial relations or law. It is only in recent years that problem-solving conflict resolution has become a taught subject, and even now it is usually confined to a post-graduate level.

To go one step further and to eliminate structures and policies which generate conflict, violence and crime it would be necessary to go back to face-to-face societies in which there was no separation of those who determined the social norms and those who were required to observe them. Societies would need to be transformed from centralized systems, top-down administrations, to decentralized, bottom-up decision-making, if more face-to-face relationships were to be introduced. The views put forward by writers such as John Dryzek in his *Discursive Democracy* and Jane Mansbridge in her *Beyond Adversary Democracy,* and others referred to in the previous chapter, cannot be brushed aside. But a return to face-to-face societies is no longer possible. There have to be central authorities and perhaps even global authorities. However, the two are not necessarily incompatible. Bottom-up decision-making, reflecting human needs, is possible at a community level to deal with problems which occur at that level. From representatives at that level there can be an important input into central decision-making to bring macro decision-making into line with human needs.

Civilizations are now being forced to make a major decision. The evolution of the industrialized nation-state and trends towards a global economy with policies determined by the relatively powerful have tended to eliminate an important input from community levels. Deregulation trends in developed capitalist economies are still moving in that direction. Societies must now decide whether to allow natural evolution based on competition and relative power to determine the future, leading to more highly organized conflict, violence and crime, or to take control of evolution and to accommodate the basic drives and needs of the human race. In practice, this means a decision whether to shift from the traditional power politics frame of decision-making, and from the management control of institutions, to a more consultative problem-solving one. It means moving towards democracies that are not based on power or majorities, but which are participatory throughout all institutions.

Notes

1. J. Galtung, "A Structural Theory of Aggression," *Journal of Peace Research*, 1 (1964).

2. A. Maslow, *Towards a Psychology of Being* (Princeton, NJ: Princeton Press, 1962).

3. S. Renshon, *Psychological Needs and Political Behavior: A Theory of Personality and Political Efficacy* (New York: Free Press, 1974).

4. J. Davies, *Human Nature in Politics: The Dynamics of Political Behavior* (New York: John Wiley, 1963).

5. P. Sites, *Control: The Basis of Social Order* (New York: Dunellen Publishers, 1973).

6. P. Sites, "Needs as Analogues of Emotions," in John Burton, ed., *Conflict: Human Needs Theory* (New York: St. Martin's Press, 1990).

7. K. Lederer, ed., *Human Needs* (Cambridge MA: Oelgeschlager, Gunn and Hain, 1980).

8. The four books in the Conflict Series are John Burton, *Conflict: Resolution and Provention*; John Burton, ed., *Conflict: Human Needs Theory*; John Burton and Frank Dukes, eds., *Conflict: Readings in Management and Resolution*; and John Burton and Frank Dukes, *Conflict: Practices in Management, Settlement and Resolution* (New York, St Martin's Press, 1990).

9. D. Prothrow-Smith with M. Weissman, *Deadly Consequences: How Violence Is Destroying Our Teenage Population and a Plan to Begin Solving the Problem* (New York: HarperPerennial, 1991).

Greed and Grievance

Paul Collier

Paul Collier is a professor of economics and policy at Oxford University. From 1998–2003, he served as the director of the Development Research Group at the World Bank. In 2010, *Foreign Policy* magazine named Collier a top global thinker. In this foundational article, Collier based his argument for the economic causes of civil war on a statistical analysis of civil wars occurring during the time frame of 1956–1999 across 161 countries. He found it was not those countries with the greatest levels of inequality that erupted into war, but rather in those places where rebellion was economically feasible. In doing so, he challenges a popular perception of his time that civil wars occur in response to great injustices. Rather, Collier claims, civil wars occur when rebel groups observe a viable way to fund a grab for power. Only then do they contrive a list of complaints (grievances such as inequality, lack of democracy, and ethnic divisions) to justify their rebellion. In other words, civil wars exist when groups see money lying on the table. They grab the money and make a dash for power. Collier hypothesizes that the feasibility of war leads to war; predators hunt only when predators can kill.

These groups use the rhetoric of injustice to galvanize support for their attempts to overthrow the government. Collier claims some rebels may deeply believe their own grievances but would not fight for them had the funds not been available. His indicators for an economically viable context for the rise of rebel groups include low national incomes and dependence on primary commodity exports (such as bananas, coffee, oil, etc.). His study also considers the importance of geography (dispersion of the population), history (regency of civil war), and the ethnic composition of the country.

He urges those studying and responding to conflict not to be seduced by the discourses of grievance emerging from rebel groups, especially when greed and opportunity may be the root cause of the uprising. Misunderstanding the cause of the violence could lead to those intervening to respond only to the list of injustices, ignoring the factors that may lead to yet another uprising—available funds. Collier pushes his readers to consider rebellion not as a social justice revolution but the result of organized crime.

> The article represents an Epoch One approach to conflict because of its search for root causes and for its effort to identify indicators (geography, history, diversity, primary commodities, and income) useful for predicting possible outbreaks of civil war. A study seeking applicability across all cultures is also characteristic of Epoch One approaches.
>
> Questions to consider: Do you think rebellions only happen when they are financially viable? What complaints have people used to legitimize their civil conflict? Do you think those complaints were justified?

Economic Causes of Civil Conflict and Their Implications for Policy

Paul Collier

This chapter presents an economic perspective on the causes of civil war, based on global empirical patterns over the period 1965–1999. During this period, the risk of civil war has been systematically related to a few economic conditions, such as dependence on primary commodity exports and low national income. Conversely, and astonishingly, objective measures of social grievance, such as inequality, a lack of democracy, and ethnic and religious divisions, have had little systematic effect on risk. I argue that this is because civil wars occur where rebel organizations are financially viable. The Michigan Militia, which briefly threatened to menace peace in the United States, was unable to grow beyond a handful of part-time volunteers, whereas the Revolutionary Armed Forces of Colombia (FARC) has grown to employ about twelve thousand people. The factors that account for this difference between failure and success are to be found not in the "causes" that these two rebel organizations claimed to espouse, but in their radically different opportunities to raise revenue. The FARC earns around $700 million per year from drugs and kidnapping, whereas the Michigan Militia was probably broke.

The central importance of the financial viability of the rebel organization as the cause of civil war is why civil wars are so unlike international wars. Governments can always finance an army out of taxation, and so governments can always fight one another. The circumstances in which a rebel organization can finance an army are quite unusual. This is why my analysis is entirely confined to civil war: what I have to say has little or no bearing on intergovernment war. Because the results are so counterintuitive, I start by arguing why social scientists should be distrustful of the loud public discourse on conflict. I then turn to the evidence, describing each of the risk factors in civil war. I try to explain the observed pattern, focusing on the circumstances in which rebel organizations are viable. Finally, I turn to the policy implications. I argue that because the economic dimensions of civil war have been largely neglected, both governments and the international community have missed substantial opportunities for promoting peace.

Greed or Grievance? Why We Can't Trust the Discourse

There is a profound gap between popular perceptions of the causes of conflict and the results from recent economic analysis. Popular perceptions see rebellion as a protest motivated by genuine and extreme grievance; rebels are public-spirited heroes fighting against injustice. Economic analysis sees rebellion more as a form of organized crime or, more radically, something that is better understood from the distinctive circumstances in which it is feasible, rather than worrying about what might motivate its participants. Either economists are being excessively cynical or popular perceptions are badly misled. I first want to suggest why perceptions might indeed be wrong.

Popular perceptions are shaped by the discourse that conflicts themselves generate. The parties to a civil war do not stay silent: they are not white mice observed by scientists. They offer explanations for their actions. Indeed, both parties to a conflict will make a major effort to have good public relations. The larger rebel organizations will hire professional public relations firms to promote their explanation, and the governments that they are opposing will routinely hire rival public relations firms. Imagine, for a moment, that you are the leader of a rebel organization, needing to offer an explanation of your goals. What are the likely elements? Most surely, they roll be a litany of grievances against the government, for its oppression, unfairness, and perhaps victimization of some part of the population that your organization claims to represent. That is, your language will be the language of protest. You will style your rebellion as a protest movement, driven to the extremity of violence by the extremity of the conditions that "your" people face. Almost certainly, the government will have responded to your insurgency with an incompetent counterinsurgency campaign. "Almost certainly" because counterinsurgency is extremely difficult.

The most obvious difficulty that a government faces in counterinsurgency is getting its army to fight. People prefer not to risk getting killed. Governments try various economic incentives to overcome this problem. For example, in one recent African conflict the government decided to pay its soldiers a premium if they were in a combat zone. Shortly after this incentive was introduced, the war appeared to spread alarmingly. In previously safe areas rebel groups set off explosions near barracks. It turned out that government soldiers were probably planting these explosions themselves. However, the more serious problems occur when the government succeeds in persuading its army to fight but then lacks the means to control the behavior of soldiers on the ground. From Vietnam onward, the result has been atrocities. Rebel groups may even hope for government atrocities because the atrocities then fuel the grievances. This discourse of grievance is how most people understand the causes of conflict. A "thorough" analysis of the causes of a conflict then becomes a matter of tracing back the grievances and counter grievances in the history of protest.

An economist views conflict rather differently. Economists who have studied rebellions tend to think of them not as the ultimate protest movements but as the ultimate manifestation of organized crime. As Herschel I. Grossman states, "in such insurrections the insurgents are indistinguishable from bandits or pirates."[1] Rebellion is large-scale predation of productive economic activities. I will shortly set out why economists see rebellion in this way and the rather powerful evidence for it. However, this view is so at odds with the popular discourse on conflict that there is a temptation to dismiss it as fanciful. The techniques of economics don't help its arguments: compared with the compelling historical detail produced by histories of protest, the economist's approach seems arcane and technocratic. So, before I explain why economists see rebellion as they do, I want to show why the discourse on conflict cannot be taken at face value.

For a few moments, suspend disbelief and suppose that most rebel movements are pretty close to being large-scale variants of organized crime. *The discourse would be exactly the same as if they were protest movements.* Unlike organized crime, rebel movements need good international public relations and they need to motivate their recruits to kill. They need good international public relations because most of them are partially dependent on international financial support. They need to motivate their recruits to kill, because, unlike a mafia, a predatory rebel organization is periodically going to have to fight for its survival against government forces. A rebel organization simply cannot afford to be regarded as criminal: it is not good publicity and it is not sufficiently motivating. Rebel organizations have to develop a discourse of grievance in order to function. Grievance is to a rebel organization what image is to a business. In each case the organization will devote advertising resources to promote it. In the economist's view of conflict, grievance will turn out to be neither a cause of conflict nor an accidental by-product of it. Rather, a sense of grievance is deliberately generated by rebel organizations. The sense of grievance may be based on some objective grounds for complaint, or it may be conjured up by massaging prejudices. However, while this distinction is morally interesting to observers—is the cause *just?*—it is of no practical importance. The organization simply needs to generate a sense of grievance; otherwise, it will fail as an organization and so tend to fade away.

This interpretation of conflict is obviously not shared by rebel organizations or by the people who honestly support them: the justice of the struggle seems central to success. In contrast, the economic theory of conflict argues that the motivation of conflict is unimportant; what matters is whether the organization can sustain itself financially. It is this, rather than any objective grounds for grievance, that determines whether a country will experience civil war. The rebel organization can be motivated by a whole range of considerations. It might be motivated by perceived grievances, or it might simply want the power conferred by becoming the government. Regardless of why the organization is fighting, it can fight only if it is financially viable during the conflict. War cannot be fought just on hopes or hatreds. Predatory behavior during the conflict may not be the objective of the rebel organization, but it is its means of financing the conflict. By predatory behavior I mean the use of force to extort money or goods from their legitimate owners.

The economic theory of conflict then assumes that perceived grievances and the lust for power are found more or less equally in all societies. Groups are capable of perceiving that they have grievances more or less regardless of their objective circumstances, a social phenomenon known as relative deprivation. Some people will have a lust for power more or less regardless of the objective benefits conferred by power. In this case, *it is the feasibility of predation that determines the risk of conflict.* Predation may be just a regrettable necessity on the road to perceived justice or power, but it is the conditions for predation that are decisive. Whether conflict is motivated by predation, or simply made possible by it, these two accounts come to the same conclusion: rebellion is unrelated to objective circumstances of grievance while being caused by the feasibility of predation.

On the most cynical variant of the theory, rebellion is motivated by greed, so that it occurs when rebels can do well out of war. On the power-seeking variant of the predation theory, rebels are motivated by a lust for power, but rebellion occurs only when rebels can do well out of war. On the subjective grievance variant of the predation theory, rebels are motivated by grievances, imagined or real, but rebellion occurs only when rebels can do well out of war. These three variants have in common the implications that rebels are not necessarily heroes struggling for a particularly worthwhile cause and that the feasibility of predation explains conflict. They can thus be grouped together in contrast to the objective grievance theory of conflict, in which rebels are indeed heroes struggling for a worthwhile cause, with the intensity of objective grievances explaining the occurrence of conflict.

Economists would argue that it is not really necessary to distinguish among the three variants of the predation theory. It does not really matter whether rebels are motivated by greed, by a lust for power, or by grievance, as long as what causes conflict is the feasibility of predation. Indeed, economists tend to attach little credence to the explanations that people give for their behavior, preferring to work by "revealed preference": people gradually reveal their true motivation by the pattern of their behavior, even if they choose to disguise the painful truth from themselves. Rebel leaders may much of the time come to believe their own propaganda, but if their words are decried by their behavior, then their words have little explanatory power.

There is less reason to doubt that those who support rebellion from afar are genuinely committed to the cause of grievance redressal. However, such supporters may simply have been duped. Rebel leaders have always sought outside supporters—"useful idiots" in Lenin's telling phrase. Among the people who are most susceptible to the discourse of grievance are those who care most passionately about oppression, inequality, and injustice. In short, if rebellion presents itself as the ultimate protest movement, it will attract as noncombatant supporters those who normally support protest movements. The economic theory of conflict argues that these people have been taken in by accepting the discourse at face value. As a proposition in social science this theory of conflict is a case of modern economics meeting old Marxism. As in Marx, the underlying cause of conflict is economic: in this case, the rebel organization is predatory on certain parts of the economy. As in Marx, the "superstructure" is a set of beliefs that are false. The difference is simply that it is the *rebel* supporters who have the "false consciousness": they are gulled into believing the discourse that self-interested rebel leaders promote.

So, "greed or grievance"?—we can't tell from the discourse. Occasionally, the discourse is rather blatantly at variance with the behavior. Take the recently settled conflict in Sierra Leone. A rebel organization built itself into around twenty thousand recruits and opposed the government. The rebel organization produced the usual litany of grievances, and its very scale suggested that it had widespread support. Sierra Leone is, however, a major exporter of diamonds, and there was considerable evidence that the rebel organization was involved in this business on a large scale. During peace negotiations the rebel leader was offered and accepted the vice presidency of the country. This, we might imagine, would be a good basis from which to address rebel grievances. However, this was not sufficient to persuade the rebel leader to accept the peace settlement. He had one further demand, which, once conceded, produced (temporary) settlement. His demand was to be the minister of mining. Cases such as this are at least suggestive that something other than grievance may be going on beneath the surface of the discourse. It is to this hidden structure of rebellion that I now turn.

The Evidence

Modern economics has two powerful tools: statistics and theory. People who are not economists are seldom convinced simply by economic theory so I will begin with the statistical evidence. Together with Anke Hoeffler, I have analyzed the pattern of conflict using a large new database on civil wars during the period 1965–1999.[2] Completely independently, two political scientists, James Fearon and David Laitin, followed the same approach, and their results are very similar.[3] I will focus on my own work, simply because I am more familiar with its limitations.

A civil war is classified as an internal conflict with at least one thousand battle-related deaths. During this period there were seventy-three civil wars globally, and, in principle, we analyze the pattern as to why these wars occurred among the 161 countries in our sample. We divide the period into eight five-year subperiods and attempt to predict the occurrence of war during a subperiod by the characteristics at its start. The statistical techniques we use are logit and probit regressions. In practice, some civil wars occur in situations where there is virtually no other data about the country. We know that it had a war, but we do not know enough of its other characteristics to include it in our analysis. This reduces our sample to forty-seven civil wars. However, this is still sufficient to find some strong patterns. While our published results do not use data beyond 1999, in our more recent work we have revisited our analysis, including data through the end of 2004. The core results remain the same.

In order to get some feel for how important different risk factors are, it is useful to think of a baseline country. I will take as a baseline a country whose characteristics were all at the mean of our sample. By construction, then, this is an extraordinarily ordinary country. These characteristics give it a risk of civil conflict of about 14 percent in any particular five-year period. Now, one by one, I will vary some of the more important risk factors.

One important factor is that countries that have a substantial share of their income (GDP) coming from the export of primary commodities are radically more at risk for conflict. The most dangerous level of primary commodity dependence is 26 percent of GDP. At this level the otherwise ordinary country has a risk of conflict of 23 percent. In contrast, if it had no primary commodity exports (but was otherwise the same), its risk would fall to only one- half of 1 percent. Thus, without primary commodity exports, ordinary countries are pretty safe from internal conflict, while when such exports are substantial the society is highly dangerous. Primary commodities are thus a major part of our conflict story. Recently, a number of scholars have revisited the issue: the August 2005 issue of the *Journal of Conflict Resolution* was devoted to it. Fearon may be correct in arguing that what we took for an inverted-U relationship between primary commodities and the risk of conflict is no such thing: there is no downturn. Fearon thinks that the risk is largely confined to oil, but other scholars disagree on this point. Rather, beyond a certain point the risk simply levels off. In our current work, Anke and I have updated our analysis by five years to December 2004 and incorporated the latest revisions from political scientists on which events were and were not civil wars. With these new data we still find the same results, but at the time of writing our work is not yet completed. By the time of publication it should be on my website.

What else matters? Both geography and history matter. Geography matters because if the population is highly geographically dispersed, then the country is harder for the government to control than if everyone lives in the same small area. The geography of the Democratic Republic of the Congo (the former Zaire) makes the country unusually hard for government forces to control because the population lives around the fringes of a huge area, with the three main cities in the extreme west, extreme southeast, and extreme north. In comparison, Singapore would be a nightmare for a rebellion. In this city-state there is nowhere to hide and government forces could be anywhere in the country within an hour. With Congo-like geographic dispersion our otherwise ordinary country has a risk of conflict of about 50 percent, whereas with Singapore-like concentration its risk falls to about 3 percent. There is also some evidence that mountainous terrain increases the risk, presumably because it offers greater possibilities of safe haven for rebel forces.

History matters because if a country has recently had a civil war, its risk of further war is much higher. Immediately after the end of hostilities there is a 40 percent chance of further conflict. This risk then falls at around one percentage point for each year of peace. However, how much history matters depends on the size of the diaspora. For example, some countries have very large diasporas in the United States relative to their remaining resident population, whereas others do not. Suppose that our otherwise ordinary country has ended a civil war five years ago and now wants to know what its chances of peace are during the next five years. If the country has an unusually large American diaspora, its chances of conflict are 36 percent. If it has an unusually small diaspora, its chances of conflict are only 6 percent. We focus on diasporas living in the United States because the data are not available for most other countries. Anecdotal evidence points to diasporas based in other countries being a similar problem. For example, finance for explosives used in massacres committed by the Tamil Tigers has been traced to a bank in Canada, and the Albanian diasporas in Europe financed the Kosovo Liberation Army. So, diasporas appear to make life for those left behind much more dangerous in postconflict situations.

Economic opportunities also matter. Conflict is concentrated in countries whose populations have little education. The average country in our sample had only 45 percent of its young males in secondary education. If a country that had 45 percent of its youths in school increased that percentage by 10 percentage points to 55, it would cut its risk of conflict from 14 percent to about 10 percent. Conflict is more likely in countries with fast population growth: each percentage point on the rate of population growth raises the risk of conflict by about 2.5 percentage points. Conflict is also more likely in countries in economic decline. Each percentage point off the growth rate of per capita income raises the risk of conflict by around 1 percentage point. Conceivably, the apparently adverse effect of slow growth might be spurious, owing to reverse causation. If there was a high risk of civil war, investment might decline and hence growth would slow: the slow growth would appear to cause subsequent conflict, but actually causality would be the other way around. This problem was recently addressed in a valuable contribution by Edward Miguel, Shanker Satyanath, and Ernest Sergenti.[4] They manage to isolate variations in the growth rate that are completely unrelated to the risk of civil war by studying the impact of rainfall shocks on growth, using longtime series on rainfall, country by country, across Africa. Essentially, in a year when rainfall is above its normal level for a given country, growth is also atypically high, and conversely when rainfall is below normal. They show that the growth shocks predicted from rainfall shocks powerfully affect the risk of civil war. By design, these growth shocks are uncontaminated by the risk of war and so the direction of causality is unambiguous; rapid growth really does reduce the risk of civil war.

The ethnic and religious composition of the country matters. If there is one dominant ethnic group that constitutes between 45 percent and 90 percent of the population—enough to give it control but not enough to make discrimination against a minority pointless—the risk of conflict doubles. For example, in Sri Lanka the Tamils are a minority of about 12 percent of the population, and in Rwanda and Burundi the Tutsi are around 10 percent to 15 percent of the population. Of course, in Sri Lanka the Tamils are a weak minority, whereas in Rwanda the Tutsi are a strong minority, controlling the government. However, clearly, in Rwanda the Tutsi minority is too scared of being subject to ethnic dominance to hand over power. While ethnic dominance is a problem, ethnic and religious diversity does not make a society more dangerous—in fact, it makes it safer. A country that is ethnically and religiously homogeneous is surprisingly dangerous—the risk is 23 percent. In comparison, a country with ethnic and religious diversity equal to the maximum we find in our sample has a risk of only about 3 percent. Other than in the fairly unusual case of dominance, diversity makes a society much safer.

Finally, some good news. Since 1990 the world has been significantly safer from civil conflict. If we add a dummy variable for the period since the end of the Cold War, it is statistically significant with quite a large effect. If we hold these causes of conflict constant at the average, the risk of conflict was only half as great during the 1990s as during the Cold War. Of course, some of the other causes of conflict also changed during the 1990s—on average, per capita incomes rose faster than during the 1980s, which also reduced the risk of conflict. However, some countries became more dependent on primary commodity exports or their economies collapsed, and these countries became more prone to conflict. As of 1995, the country with the highest risk of civil conflict according to our analysis was Zaire, with a three-in-four chance of conflict within the ensuing five years. Sadly, our model "predicted" this all too accurately. I should stress, however, that our analysis in not well suited to prediction: firefighters have to look elsewhere. To predict a civil war, it is surely more useful to focus on near-term indicators such as political incidents and rising violence. Rather, our model is useful in pointing to the typical structural risks and so provides some guidance on longer-term policies for prevention.

This has been the statistical pattern of civil conflict since 1960. It is interesting both for what is important and for what is not. Clearly, there are some powerful dangers coming from primary commodities and diasporas, and there used to be risks from the Cold War. However, equally striking is what does *not* appear to affect conflict risk. Inequality, whether of incomes or of assets, has no discernible effect. Unequal societies are not more prone to conflict, although conflicts in unequal societies do seem to last longer.[5] A lack of democratic rights appears to have no significant effect. Ethnic and religious diversity, as noted, far from increasing the risk of conflict, actually reduces it. These are all obvious proxies for objective grievances. Unequal, ethnically divided societies with few political rights might sound like exactly the sorts of places that would be most prone to rebellion. They are surely the sorts of places most in need of protest. And yet such places, as far as we can tell, have no higher risk of violent conflict than anywhere else—indeed, thanks to their ethnic diversity, they are somewhat safer. The only protest-type variable that matters is ethnic dominance. This may be because we are not measuring objective grievances well enough. However, we have made an honest effort to utilize all the available comparable indices of objective grievance, of which there are now a number. At least as a working hypothesis, civil war is much more strongly related to the economic and geographic variables discussed earlier than it is to objective grievances.

There are thus two surprises to be explained: why rebellion is so unrelated to the objective need for protest, and why it is so strongly related to primary commodities and diasporas.

Why Is Rebellion Not Like Protest?

Economists have studied the dynamics of protest.[6] The first problem with getting a protest going is that it is a "public good." That is, if the protest succeeds in securing justice, everyone will benefit, whether or not they bother to take part in the protest. Public goods always face collective-action problems: it makes more individual sense to free-ride on the efforts of others, and if everyone free-rides, nothing happens. This is a problem in a protest because the government might punish people who take part, unless there are so many people that there is safety in numbers. Further, in order to protest, most people must lose a day of income. This is one reason why such a high proportion of protesters are often students. The temptation to free-ride on a justice-seeking *rebellion* is very much stronger than the temptation to free-ride on a justice-seeking *protest*. A protest costs little, risks little, and offers a sense of citizenship. In effect, protesters are forcing an open election on an issue. Rebellion is a full-time commitment, and it is dangerous. Economists would predict that the collective action problem for a justice-seeking rebellion would usually be insuperable.

Timur Kuran's insight in analyzing the dynamics of protest was to see that a successful protest would be one that escalated, and that this depended on a cascade of participation, drawing in increasingly lukewarm supporters. Suppose the potential supporters of a protest are ranked in order of their willingness to take personal risk. The most ardent supporters join the protest first, at the stage when it is small, because it is easy for the government to victimize participants. Each time an additional supporter joins the protest the risks of punishment for participation go down. The cascade depends on the reduction in this risk inducing enough people to change their minds and join the protest that the risk falls further, inducing another group of people to change their minds. If the cascade works, then when a few committed people create an initial spark it turns into a prairie fire. Could the rebellions we observe be failed protest movements, cases in which a brave few hundred created the spark, but the rest of the society failed to ignite, leaving the brave core to turn into guerrilla fighters against the government? Are rebels just heroes who have been let down by the mass of cowards and so driven into more violent actions to protect themselves? Well, if they are, we should observe a clear pattern in rebellion.

Kuran suggests that the cascade is more likely to work in fairly homogeneous societies, where there is a dense continuum of opinion. Many people will be on the margin of changing their minds and so will be swung into action as the risks of government punishment start to fall. In contrast, if the society is split up into many different groups who see the concerns of other groups as irrelevant to their own, instead of a continuum of opinion there are clusters broken by gaps. As soon as the cascade reaches the first gap it stops. One implication of this insight is that the societies in which protest will get stuck are those that are diverse. That is, if rebellions are the stuff of heroes let down by cowards, we should expect to find more of them in diverse societies. Recall that in fact we find precisely the opposite.

Diverse societies have a much lower risk of rebellion than homogeneous societies. Of course, if we scour history sufficiently thoroughly, we will find examples of protest movements that aborted into rebellion. If we scour history, we can find anything. However, the image of the rebel band as that part of the population that is the most dedicated and self-sacrificing is difficult to reconcile with the facts. Rebellion is not generally linked to the objective grievances—such as inequality and political repression—that are repeatedly used in rebel discourse. Nor is its incidence high in societies where we would expect protest movements to face the most difficulties. The sole exception to this is that in situations of ethnic dominance—with or without democracy—minorities (or majorities) may take to the gun. Other than this, the modern rebel appears truly to have been a "rebel without a cause."

A recent analysis of rebel recruitment by Jeremy Weinstein adds an important insight into how rebel motivations may evolve over time.[7] Initially, the rebellion may be motivated by a desire to rectify perceived grievances. However, if there are prospects of gaining control of lucrative revenues, for example, through natural resources or kidnapping, this will gradually affect the composition of recruitment. The volunteers who seek to join the movement will increasingly be drawn from those with criminal rather than altruistic intent, and even an altruistic rebel leader will have difficulties in screening out the criminals. Whatever characteristics the leader demands will be mimicked by criminals wishing to join. Hence, the rebel organization will gradually evolve from being altruistic to being criminal. This may well describe the evolution of the FARC from its origins as a rural protest movement to its present reality as a massive drug operation. Even when rebel recruits are truly dedicated and self-sacrificing, this devotion to a cause is not a reliable indicator that the cause is worthwhile. Probably the largest collective self-sacrificing organization in history was Hitler's SS: toward the end of World War II thousands of men were prepared to die hopelessly for a cause that was despicable beyond measure. Suicide bombers and billionaires who abandon their wealth for the fugitive life are evidently devoted. This does not make their cause remotely worthy of respect. Most societies have a small minority of people seeking meaning in a cause, whatever that might be.

What Conditions Make Predatory Rebellions Profitable?

Empirically, the risk of rebellion is strongly linked to three economic conditions: dependence on primary commodity exports, low average income of the country, and slow growth. I now suggest why this is the case.

Primary commodity exports are the most lootable of all economic activities. An economy that is dependent on them thus offers plenty of opportunities for predatory rebellion.[8] One indication that primary commodity exports are highly lootable is that they are also the most heavily taxed activity—the same characteristics that make it easy for governments to tax them make it easy for rebels to loot them. Indeed, rebel predation is just illegal taxation. Conversely, in some countries government has been described as legalized predation in which primary commodities are heavily taxed in order to finance the government elite. In the worst cases, those who are the victims of such predation may not discriminate much between the behavior of the rebel organization and that of the government. This does not, however, mean that the rebels are "no worse" than the government. The presence of a rebel organization plunges the society from peace into civil war, and the costs of war are likely to outweigh the costs of government predation.

Primary commodity exports are especially vulnerable to looting and taxation because their production relies heavily on assets that are long-lasting and immobile. Once a mine shaft has been sunk, it is worth exploiting, even if many of the anticipated profits are lost to rebels. Once coffee trees have been planted, they are worth harvesting, even if much of the coffee has to be surrendered. Thus, rebel predation does not kill off the activity or shift it elsewhere, as would happen were manufacturing the target. Further, because the produce is exported, it has to be transported to the port. Along the way there are many geographic "choke points" at which rebels can extract a tribute if they can control them, even if only sporadically. The government can be presumed to control the best choke point of all—the port itself. This behavior makes a rebel group somewhat like organized crime. However, it is organized crime with a difference. The government will try to defend the choke points from rebel attacks—it is, after all, defending its own revenue. Hence, unlike a mafia, the rebel group must expect sometimes to confront substantial government forces and so will need to protect itself. Rebel groups therefore need to be much larger than mafias. Typically, rebel organizations have in the range of five hundred to five thousand fighters, whereas mafia membership is generally in the range of twenty to five hundred. It is because rebel organizations need to be large and to confront government forces in order to function as predators that conflicts can produce cumulative mortality in excess of one thousand and so qualify empirically as civil wars.

Why is the risk of conflict much higher in countries where incomes are low? The explanation that jumps to mind is that when people are poor they have little to lose from joining a rebel group, so that rebel organizations find recruitment cheap. There may be something in this, but if young men can be recruited cheaply for the rebel organization, they can also be recruited cheaply by the government. Hence, low income does not automatically give rebellion an advantage. However, low income does indirectly advantage the rebels. Around the world, the share of income that accrues to the government as tax revenue rises with income. For example, most OECD governments (that is, the rich countries) get about 40 percent of national income as tax revenue. In the really poor economies, the percentage is much lower. For example, in Ghana and Uganda in the early 1980s, the government was raising only about 6 percent of national income as taxation. This reduces die capacity of the government to spend on defense and so makes rebel predation easier. Indeed, in low-income economies, governments will typically derive about half of their revenue from taxes on primary commodity exports (directly or indirectly), so that their revenue base is quite similar to that of the rebels. At higher income levels the government supplements these revenues with revenues from taxes on other economic activities. Thus, poor countries have a high incidence of conflict because governments cannot defend. Of course, there might be other reasons why poverty makes it easier for rebels. Poverty might make people desperate or angry. However, if this was an important effect we would expect to find that inequality made conflict more likely: for a given level of average income, the more unequal income distribution is, the more severe the poverty of the poorest. In fact, inequality does not seem to affect the risk of conflict. Rebellion seems not to be the rage of the poor.

Indeed, if anything, rebellion seems to be the rage of the rich. One way in which rebel groups can lock into predation of primary commodity exports is to secede with the land on which the primary commodities are produced. Such attempted secessions by rich regions are quite common: Katanga, which sought to secede from Zaire, was a copper-mining region; Biafra, which fought to secede from Nigeria, was an oil-producing region; Eritrea, which succeeded in its secessionist ambitions, was a region with double the per capita income of the rest of Ethiopia; and Aceh in Indonesia is an oil-producing region with per capita GDP three times the national average. To the extent that the rebel group is not just benefiting itself through predation but is fighting a political cause, that cause is the grievance of a rich minority at paying taxes to the poor majority. Such rebellions may have more in common with the politics of Staten Island (where a rich suburb tried to secede from the tax jurisdiction of New York) than of Robin Hood. Slow economic growth and rapid population growth both make rebellion more likely. Presumably, both of these assist rebel recruitment. The rebel organization needs to build itself up fairly fast in order to survive against the army. Hence, for a given level of income, the rebel organization has an easier task if there are few job opportunities, few schooling opportunities, and many young people needing work.

So, the observed pattern of rebellion is quite intelligible. High primary commodity exports, low income, and slow growth are a cocktail that makes predatory rebellions more financially viable. In such circumstances rebels can do well out of war.

Why Might Diversity Make a Society Safer Rather than More Dangerous?

One of the most surprising empirical regularities is that societies that are diverse in terms of both ethnicity and religion seem to be significantly safer than societies that are homogeneous. A standard measure of ethnic diversity proxies ethnicity by language and calculates the probability that two people drawn randomly from the country's population will be from different linguistic groups. As part of our work Anke and I constructed an equivalent measure of religious diversity. Unfortunately, there are no global data that combine ethnicity and religion showing us the mosaic, country by country, of ethnoreligious combinations. We approximate such a concept by combining the ethnic diversity and religious diversity measures, investigating the combination both by addition and by multiplication. It is this measure that is significantly negatively related to the risk of conflict. If ethnic and religious hatreds were an important cause of conflict, it might be expected that the pattern would be the reverse, since in homogeneous societies there would be no other group to hate. Conflict seems not to be generated by such hatreds. Indeed, Fearon and Laitin actually investigate a measure of the intensity of intergroup hatred and find it unrelated to the risk of civil war. However, it is less evident why diversity makes a society considerably safer, instead of simply having no effect.

I think that diversity may make a society safer because it can make rebellion more difficult. This is because, first and foremost, a rebel organization is neither a mafia nor a protest movement, but an army. Armies face huge problems of organizational cohesion and motivation. To fight effectively, soldiers must overcome their individual instincts to avoid danger and must take risks to help other members of their team. Military history abounds in stories of small groups defeating larger groups because they were better fighting units. The government army also faces these problems, but it has the advantage of already having had a long time to deal with them. In contrast, the rebel organization cannot usually afford to take years to build up morale before it starts operations: it must recruit from scratch and start fighting as soon as possible. One simple principle is to keep the recruits as alike as possible. The more social ties there are within the organization—the same kin group, or at least the same ethnic group, language group, and religion—the easier it will be to build a fighting force. This may be especially true of the officer corps. The easiest way for a government to defeat a rebellion may be to buy off some of the officers. The more "social capital" there is within the group, the more cohesive it is likely to be.

This principle implies that in ethnically diverse societies rebellions will tend to be ethnically particular. This has two important corollaries. First, the more that the society is divided into a patchwork of different ethnic and religious groups, the more difficult it will be to recruit a force of a sufficient scale to be viable. For example, in Africa the average ethnolinguistic group has only about 250,000 people, of whom about 25,000 will be young males. Thus, even before we allow for any further divisions of religion, an organization of 5,000 fighters will need to recruit 20 percent of the age group. Diversity in the society thus makes the rebel task more difficult and so makes rebellion less likely.

The second corollary is that where conflict does take place in ethnically diverse societies, it will take the form of some particular ethnic group rebelling against the government. As in any army, recruits will be motivated to kill the enemy by basic indoctrination as to why the enemy deserves to be killed. Indeed, the simple Leninist theory of the rebel organization, which many rebel movements adopt even if they do not adopt Marxist ideology, is that people are initially so oppressed that they do not realize they are oppressed. *It is a key task of the rebel organization to make people realize that they are the victims of injustice.* The economic theory of rebellion accepts this proposition and makes one simple but reasonable extension:

the rebel organization can inculcate a subjective sense of injustice whether or not this is objectively justified. The astounding self-sacrifice displayed by SS troops in their loyalty to Hitler is a disturbing indication that passionate commitment to a cause can be inculcated by effective propaganda regardless of the underlying merits of the cause. The rebel organization needs to inculcate a sense of injustice and will work to create it. From this follows a hatred of the enemy and a willingness to fight.

The inculcation of grievance is not a frivolous activity; it is vital for an effective fighting force. Take, for example, the Eritrean Peoples Liberation Front (EPLF), which was probably the most effective rebellion in recent history. Its recruitment base was barely two million people and it had little foreign government support, yet it defeated an Ethiopian army of more than four hundred thousand men that was supported by Russia. Its success obviously depended on having its much smaller army well motivated. The EPLF deliberately built this motivation by routinely withdrawing its recruits from the front for six months to send them to indoctrination courses. If the society in which the rebellion occurs is ethnically diverse, the rebel organization will nevertheless be ethnically homogeneous to assist cohesion. Since the rebels will therefore be ethnically different from most of the rest of society, the obvious discourse for the rebel leadership to adopt with its recruits is that of ethnic grievance. Hence, ethnic grievance is actively manufactured by the rebel organization as a necessary way of motivating its forces. As a result, where conflicts occur in ethnically diverse societies, they will look and sound as though they were caused by ethnic hatreds.

A more remarkable example is the conflict in Somalia. Somalia is one of the most ethnically homogeneous societies in the world, although, as in all traditional societies, within the single ethnic group are many lineage or kin groups. In the initial postindependence period, political power had been shared reasonably comfortably among these clan groups. However, in the instability following a dictatorship, a political opportunist, Mohammed Farah Aideed, induced the group living around the national arsenal to seize its considerable contents. The group then proceeded to build an army around these armaments. Building an army fast, Aideed based recruitment on his clan and its proximate lineage groups—in the absence of ethnic distinctions, clan membership was the only basis for creating cohesion in a fighting force. The excluded clans naturally felt threatened by this bid for power and so armed themselves in response. The resulting violent conflict in effect turned what had been a patchwork of closely related clusters of people into large rival groupings that hated each other. The conflict created the equivalent of interethnic hatred in an ethnically unified society.

A surprisingly similar example is the conflict in the Democratic Republic of the Congo. Congo is at the opposite end of the spectrum from Somalia, a society that is highly ethnically diverse. When President Kabila the First fell out with his Tutsi military support, he needed to build an army to oppose them. Because Congo was so ethnically divided, this was difficult. Kabila needed to recruit across ethnic boundaries in order to build a sufficient fighting force. He therefore manufactured an encompassing ethnic grouping, of which all groups other than the Tutsi were members, namely, the Bantu. Just as Aideed had forged several clans in Somalia into a common fighting group distinct from the excluded clans, so Kabila hoped to forge several ethnic groups into a common fighting group. In both cases, the conflict created a need to manufacture intergroup hatred, but the basic conditions for it—a society divided into two large groups—did not exist. In both cases military necessity led to the invention not just of the grievances but of the groupings themselves. Even if conflict is not caused by divisions, it actively needs to create them.

When such conflicts are viewed during or after the event, the observer sees ethnic hatred. The parties to the conflict have used the discourse of group hatred to build fighting organizations, so it is natural for observers to interpret such conflicts as being caused by ethnic hatred. Instead, the conflicts have caused the intergroup hatred and may even, as in Somalia, have created the groups.

If the rebel organization succeeds in generating group grievance, perhaps by manufacturing both the grievance and the group, the resulting civil war becomes defined in terms of political conflict. However, it is the military needs of the rebel organization that have created this political conflict rather than objective grievances. Analysts often reason back from the political discourse during conflict and deduce that the war is the consequence of particularly intense political conflict, based in turn on particularly strong reasons for grievance. Yet the intensity of objective grievance does not predict civil war. Many societies sustain intense political conflict for many years without war developing. Political conflict is universal, whereas civil war is rare. My argument is that where rebellions happen to be financially viable, wars will occur. As part of the process of war, the rebel organization must generate group grievance for military effectiveness. The generation of group grievance politicizes the war. Thus, the war produces the intense political conflict, not the intense political conflict the war.

If Diversity Increases Safety, Why Is Ethnic Dominance So Dangerous?

The one exception to the rule that homogeneous societies are more dangerous than societies with more than one ethnic group is a society characterized by ethnic dominance. By ethnic dominance I mean a society in which the largest single ethnic group has somewhere between 45 percent and 90 percent of the population. It is not difficult to see why such societies are dangerous. Having 45 percent or more of the population is sufficient in a democracy to give the group permanent control: what political scientists call a stable winning coalition. Having less than 90 percent of the population suggests that it might be worth exploiting this power by transferring resources from the minority. If the minority is much smaller than 10 percent of the population, there is normally so little to be gained by exploiting it that the gain may be more than swallowed up in the costs of the transfer system.

Thus, in societies characterized by ethnic dominance, the majority probably has both the power to exploit the minority and an interest in doing so. The minority may become sufficiently fearful of permanent exploitation that it decides to fight. This is the exception to the absence-of-objective-grievance effects, and a reason for it may be that democracy can offer no prospect of redress. In diverse societies not characterized by ethnic dominance, small groups that are excluded from power can hope at some stage to bid themselves into a winning coalition. Even dictators do not last forever. Thus, for example, in Kenya, where no tribe has close to a majority, the fifteen years of President Jomo Kenyatta's rule strongly favored his own large tribe, the Kikuyu. However, Kenyatta had chosen as his vice president someone from a very minor tribe. On the death of Kenyatta, the vice president, Daniel arap Moi, succeeded to the presidency and for twenty-five years held together a winning coalition of small tribes, excluding both the Kikuyu and the Luo, the two largest tribal groups. The small tribes in Kenyatta's Kenya were thus right to hope for eventual redress through the political rather than the military process. In contrast, in societies characterized by ethnic dominance, the minority has little to hope for from the political process. Thus, it is possible that rebellion in societies with ethnic dominance is the behavior of despair. Note that it makes little difference whether it is the majority or the minority that is in power. Even if the minority is in power, it dare not trust democracy because it does not trust the majority. This is perhaps the case with the Tutsi-dominated governments of Rwanda and Burundi, and perhaps even of the minority Tigrean-dominated government of Ethiopia. The current acute difficulties in Iraq are thus consistent with what might be expected in a society characterized by ethnic dominance.[9]

Why Are Diasporas So Dangerous?

Recall that, empirically, if a country that has recently ended a conflict has a large diaspora, its risk that the conflict will resume is sharply increased.

There is little mystery about this effect. Diasporas sometimes harbor rather romanticized attachments to their group of origin and may nurse grievances as a form of asserting continued belonging. They are much richer than the people in their country of origin and so can afford to finance vengeance. Above all, they do not have to suffer any of the awful consequences of renewed conflict because they are not living in the country. Hence, they are a ready market for rebel groups touting vengeance and so are a source of finance for renewed conflict. They are also a source of pressure for secession. For example, the (peaceful) secession of Slovakia from the then Czechoslovakia was initiated not in Czechoslovakia itself but in the Czechoslovak diaspora organizations in North America. City by city, the diaspora organization divorced.[10] The reductio ad absurdum of such a trend would be for immigrant populations of the United States and the European Union to split their countries of origin into tiny "ethnic theme parks" while themselves enjoying the advantages of living in nations with scale and diversity.

Another source of foreign finance is governments that are enemies of the incumbent government. During the Cold War each of the superpowers offered inducements for Third World governments to align with them. Once a government had done this, it became the potential target of destabilization efforts from the other superpower. One means of destabilization was to fund rebel groups. Once the Cold War ended, the need for such destabilization ended, and so the external finance for rebel organizations declined, which perhaps explains why the risk of civil conflict was lower during the 1990s. Many governments of low-income countries are on bad terms with their neighbors. Because the international community strongly discourages international war, notably through reductions in aid, warfare with neighbors usually has to be covert. The most straightforward means of such warfare is to arm and finance a rebel group that fights the neighbor. For many years, the government of Uganda covertly supported the Sudan People's Liberation Army, and in response the government of Sudan supported the Lord's Resistance Army in northern Uganda. One problem with such support is that, because the support is covert, it is very difficult to verify if it has ceased, and so it is correspondingly difficult to conclude an effective peace agreement between the two governments: each party has an incentive to sign an agreement but not abide by it.

The Costs of Civil War

A typical civil war inflicts an immense amount of damage: death, disease, and poverty. Anke and I have attempted to put a cost on this damage and to determine how the cost is divided among different groups of victims.[11] Estimating the cost of conflict is an essential step toward cost-benefit analysis. In turn, cost- benefit analysis has two important applications. The first is to give some broad sense of whether civil war is "worthwhile": is it usually a reasonable "investment" for those societies that embark on it? The second is to guide policies for reducing the incidence of civil war. Most policies cost money, and some cost lives. Are such expenditures warranted in terms of their likely savings?

The costs of civil war are partly directly economic and partly social. By the end of the typical war, the economy is about 15 percent poorer than it would otherwise have been, and mortality is much higher, mainly due to disease triggered by movements of refugees and the collapse of public health systems, rather than to combat deaths. These effects are highly persistent after the end of the war: the typical war lasts about seven years, but it takes over a decade to recover. Hence, much of the cost of a civil war, about half, occurs *after it is over.* Further, a lot of the costs accrue to neighboring countries: both economic decline and disease spread across borders. Because the typical country has about three neighbors, all of whom are affected, the total cost to neighbors is about as large as the cost to the country itself. One implication is that most of the costs of a war accrue either to the future or to neighbors and so are not taken into account by those who start them. Even where rebels initiate conflict with some sense of future benefits to society outweighing future costs, they omit key costs and so their decisions are biased in favor of conflict. Taking all the costs together, we estimate that the typical civil war costs about $60 billion. This is a huge sum, more than double the annual income of the typical civil war country. It dwarfs any likely benefits: most civil wars are terrible investments. It also suggests that it is worth spending large sums to reduce their incidence as long as we can find interventions that are effective.

So What Can Be Done?

I have spent a long time on the diagnosis of the problem because different diagnoses lead to radically different policy solutions.

If you accept the conventional grievance account of conflict, then the appropriate policy interventions are to address the possible objective causes of grievance. On this account, countries should reduce inequality and increase political rights. These noble objectives are desirable on many grounds, but if the objective is civil peace, then by my analysis they will be ineffective.

A further policy, if you accept the grievance account, might be to redraw borders, split countries, and even move populations so as to achieve greater ethnic homogeneity. In contrast, if you accept that diversity makes countries safer, then this is the road to increased civil conflict and presumably also to increased international conflict. Perhaps an example of such an eventuality is the breakup of Yugoslavia. In the old Yugoslavia there was a sufficiently high degree of diversity that no one group constituted a majority—the society was not characterized by ethnic dominance. First, Slovenia, the richest region of Yugoslavia, seceded in what could be interpreted as an instance of the "rage of the rich," although there were almost surely other motivations. Then Croatia, the next-richest region, also seceded. Owing to these two secessions, the residual Yugoslavia *was* characterized by ethnic dominance. Civil and international war followed.

Hence, the policies that follow from the grievance diagnosis are variously ineffective and counterproductive if you accept the predation diagnosis. What policies will work if this alternative interpretation of conflict is in fact correct? First, we need to distinguish between conflict prevention and postconflict situations. Before conflict, the approach implied by the predation analysis is to work through the major risk factors, identifying how to reduce them. Note that this approach is radically different from the more traditional approach that attempts to identify grievances and redress them. The new approach is basically one of making it harder for rebel organizations to get established, and addressing objective grievances is not usually an effective way of achieving this objective. Postconflict, the problem is rather different. Rebel organizations have forced themselves onto the political landscape and have generated group grievance. Although both the grievances and the groups may be manufactured, they now exist and postconflict policy must address them. Hence, whereas conflict prevention should not be built around the reduction of objective grievances, the construction of sustainable peace in postconflict societies will have to address the subjective grievances of the parties to the conflict. I therefore consider the problems of conflict prevention and postconflict peacebuilding separately.[12]

Policies for Conflict Prevention

Each society is different. The overall risk of conflict in a society is built up from a series of risk factors, and the balance of risk factors will differ from one country to another. Hence, the first step in conflict prevention is to decompose the overall risk into its constituent components and then put the most effort into reducing those risks that are the most important and the most amenable to policy. I take the potential risk factors in turn.

Economies with about a quarter of GDP coming from natural resource exports are acutely at risk for civil conflict. There are four strategies that might reduce this risk. First, the government can facilitate diversification of the economy away from dependence on primary commodities. Better economic policy promotes diversification. In a really poor policy environment, the only export activities that survive are those with high location-specific rents. The World Bank's annual measure of policy (the Country Policy and Institutional Assessment) is significant in explaining the extent of primary commodity dependence. Policy improvement, sustained over a five-year period, reduces dependence in the next five-year period.[13]

Second, a government can try to make loot- seeking rebels unpopular by transparently using the revenue from primary commodity exports to fund effective basic service delivery. If the money is seen to be funding primary education and rural health centers, then the population is going to be more hostile to rebels than if they believe that the money is sent off to Swiss banks. There are, however, limits to the effectiveness of this policy. For example, many of the youths who fought for the rebel movement in Sierra Leone are so unpopular that they dare not return to their communities, but this unpopularity did not stop them from joining a rebellion. The rebels deliberately targeted drug addicts and children for recruitment and so had an unusually dependent labor force.

Third, the international community can make it more difficult for rebel groups to sell the commodities that they loot. Most of the international markets in commodities are, at some point along the marketing chain, fairly narrow, in the sense that there are not many market participants. Although primary commodities are more difficult to identify than branded manufactured goods, they differ in quality, and so markets can usually identify the origin of the commodity in the process of determining its quality. For example, at the stage at which diamonds are cut, their provenance can be established with reasonable accuracy, and diamond cutting is a highly skilled activity that can potentially be subject to a degree of international regulation. Of course, it will never be possible to drive illegal supplies out of the market, but it should be possible to drive them to the fringes of the market, where the goods can be sold only at a deep discount. Rebel preda-tion would then become less lucrative. The Kimberley Process, which is a recent initiative to keep looted diamonds off the market, not only is important for the diamonds trade but also provides a model for other lootable commodities, such as timber and oil.

Low income and economic decline are further risk factors. There is no quick fix to low income. However, within a single generation it is now possible for most poverty-stricken societies to lift themselves out of poverty. In a single generation South Korea managed to grow its per capita income from $300 a year to $10,000 a year. Most very poor countries have poor economic policies. Changing these policies is often politically difficult because in the short term vested interests lose, but many societies have faced down these interests and transformed themselves. In such situations international aid has been shown to be effective in accelerating growth. For example, during the 1990s Uganda transformed its economic policies, and with the help of the international donor community it sustained a 7 percent annual growth rate. It is on track to realize the government objective of overcom-ing poverty within a generation. Within Uganda, a rebel group called the AFL recruited by offering the unemployed 200,000 shillings per month (about US$150). Rapid growth will gradually make recruitment harder.

A further risk factor is ethnic dominance. If a society has a single ethnic group that is large enough to dominate democratic institutions, then democracy itself is not sufficient to reassure minorities. Ethnic dominance is a difficult problem. The most realistic approach is to entrench minority rights into the constitution. This can be done either by explicitly legislating group rights or through strong individ-ual rights. If all individuals are secure from discrimination, then individuals in minority groups are secure. The scope for this approach depends on the credibility of the checks and balances that the state can erect on government power. Usually, state institutions are not strong enough for this degree of trust, and so they can usefully be reinforced by international or regional commitments. For example, the European Union is requiring that the many Eastern European countries hoping to join it treat their minorities equally. Latvia moderated its policies toward its Russian minority in response to this requirement.

If governments and the international community can defuse the risk from its primary commodity exports, generate rapid growth, and provide credible guaran-tees to minorities, then the risk of conflict can be radically reduced. Conflict prevention can be achieved through large efforts on a few risk factors.

Policies for Postconflict Peacebuilding

All the policies that are appropriate for conflict prevention are also appropriate for postconflict peacebuilding. However, they are unlikely to be sufficient. In the first decade of postconflict peace, societies face roughly double the risk of conflict that the preconflict risk factors would predict. Postconflict societies are thus at substantial additional risk because of what has happened to them during conflict.

Several factors may account for this increase in risk. A rebel organization has built an effective military capability, in part by the manufacture of group grievance and in part by the accumulation of armaments, money, and military skills. People have gotten used to violence, so the norms that inhibit political violence in most societies will have been eroded. People's political allegiance may have polarized, so that, as in Somalia, ethnic dominance has been created by the conflict even if the society was initially either diverse or homogeneous.

Many societies have severe objective group grievances that sustain intense political conflict without getting close to civil war. Group grievance and intense political conflict are not in themselves dangerous: they are indeed the normal stuff of democratic politics. However, in postconflict societies, civil war has first built intense political conflict and then conducted that conflict through violence. Whereas most of the societies that have group grievances have no tradition of conducting their political conflict by means of violence, postconflict societies may have no tradition of conducting their political conflict nonviolently.

The rebel organization usually maintains its effectiveness during the postconflict period. Compared with a preconflict society with the same risk factors, the postconflict society is therefore much better prepared for war. The rebel organization has already recruited, motivated, armed, and saved. For example, Jonas Savimbi, the head of the Angolan rebel organization UNITA, was reputed to have accumulated over $4 billion in financial assets during the first war, some of which he then used to finance the start of the second.

Peace requires either that the intense political conflict continue but that the military option of conducting it be made infeasible, or that the political conflict itself be resolved. Each of these is difficult. Removing the military option requires demilitarizing the rebel organization, turning it into a conventional political party. This can happen. For example, Renamo, once a rebel military organization in Mozambique, is now a successful political party. Renamo was willing to demobilize, whereas UNITA was not. Mozambique was a post-conflict success, whereas Angola was a failure, partly because Angola had diamonds, whereas Mozambique did not. Aid donors were able to come up with a moderate financial package for Renamo, which made peaceful political contest an attractive option. Diamonds had made UNITA so rich that nothing donors could offer would matter, while renewed predation offered massive rewards. UNITA is believed to have earned about $2 billion from diamond mining in the first two years of renewed war. The extreme importance of aid donors to the Mozambique economy may also have made the maintenance of a democratic system in which Renamo would have a fair chance more credible. In Angola the government did not need the donors and so had no means of reassuring UNITA that democratic rights of political contest would be maintained. Even when the rebel group demobilizes, the precedent of violent conflict is fresh in people's minds. This is perhaps why time itself improves the prospects of peace: the habits of peaceful conflict replace those of violent conflict.

The alternative to continuing the political contest but making the military option infeasible is to resolve the political contest itself. This requires at a minimum that grievances be addressed, even though on average they are not objectively any more serious than those in peaceful societies. If, indeed, group grievance has been manufactured by rebel indoctrination, it can potentially be deflated by political gestures. While grievances may need to be addressed objectively, the main purpose of addressing them is probably to change people s perceptions.

The task of dealing with conflict that lacks proper boundaries between the political and the violent is difficult whether the approach is to restore boundaries or to resolve the political conflict. However, the attitudes of the domestic population appear not to be the main reason why postconflict societies have a risk of further conflict that is so much greater than implied by their inherited risk factors. Recall that the main risk comes from diasporas living in rich countries. What can be done to reduce this risk? One approach is to build the diaspora into the peace process. For example, in the conflict in Northern Ireland it is evident that the Irish American diaspora played a major part in financing violence. Both the Protestant and Catholic rebel military organizations actively raised funds in North America, and a number of the guns used in shootings turned out to have come (hopefully indirectly) from the Boston police department. When the peace faction within the IRA initiated the peace process, its leader went to Boston, and the British and Irish governments chose an American senator to head the peace negotiations.

An extension of this approach is to target campaigns at the diaspora that emphasize that the domestic population wants to maintain peace because the costs of violence are so high. Diasporas bear none of these costs, and so they need to be reminded that others do. Governments can go much further. Diasporas are potentially major assets for the development process, with skills and business connections. The diaspora organizations can be given explicit tasks in promoting economic recovery, facing them with a choice between a constructive and a destructive role. A complementary policy is for the governments of the countries in which these diasporas are resident to put clear limits on the activities of the diaspora organizations. Political support for violent rebel organizations is legitimate, but supplying material aid is not. For example, U.S. efforts to prevent countries such as Libya, Sudan, and Afghanistan from harboring terrorists who have killed U.S. citizens would have greater prospects of success were they to be set in the context of an international policy to set limits on the conduct of diasporas.

Dependence on primary commodity exports turns out to be even more important as a risk factor in postconflict societies than in preconflict societies: the same level of dependence generates a significantly higher risk. In mitigating the risks from primary commodities, one policy is open to postconflict governments that is not available preconflict: the government might decide to share the revenues peacefully and legally with the rebel organization. The rebels then do not need to fight in order to get what they want. This is, perhaps, what the government of Sierra Leone decided to do by bringing the rebel leader into government as minister of mining. Such a policy attempts to give rebels a greater interest in peace.

There are, however, limits to this policy. If it is profitable for one rebel group to be predatory on primary commodity exports, once that group has been bought off, it will probably be profitable for another group to replace it.

While a postconflict government has more options for dealing with primary commodity dependence, it has fewer options for dealing with ethnic dominance. The provision of constitutional guarantees for ethnic minorities is unlikely to cut much ice in the low-trust environment that follows years of mutual hatred and killing. In such situations one option is for the international community to provide reassurance through an extended phase of military presence and its own guarantees. This is the solution currently being attempted in Bosnia and Kosovo. A further possibility is to determine that the country as constituted is unviable. However, rather than ethnic cleansing, a better solution may be federation with a neighboring country in which no ethnic group is dominant.

As in conflict prevention, rapid growth will assist peace. However, the task of achieving rapid growth requires somewhat different policies in postconflict societies. After a long war, economies tend to bounce back; they are so far below their productive potential. For example, in the first five years of peace after a fifteen-year war, economies grow on average at 6 percent a year.[14] Mozambique suffered an even longer war than this and recovered even more rapidly. One of the casualties of civil war is trust. Because life is so uncertain, people shorten their time horizons and are less concerned with building a reputation for honesty. Some people find it more profitable to behave opportunistically. As this behavior becomes more commonplace, the society switches into a low-level equilibrium of mutual suspicion and widespread opportunism. This raises the cost of all sorts of business transactions. For example, in Kampala, Uganda, a manufacturer of mattresses sold them wholesale on credit to agents who went up-country to sell them retail. One of the agents claimed that his entire consignment had been stolen by northern rebels. The manufacturer had to accept this alibi and forfeit the money. On the grapevine, he heard that the agent had invented the story, but he could not be sure what to believe.

Once a society has suffered a collapse into low trust, it takes concerted action to change expectations, and, meanwhile, many functions that other governments rely on simply don't work. The tax collection system, the courts, accountants, and doctors may all have been corrupted by opportunistic behavior. Of course, it is not only societies that have suffered civil war that can experience a breakdown of trust. However, in postconflict situations it is the norm. The government can respond to this problem by creating coordinated changes in expectations, institution by institution. For example, one quite common approach has been to close the old revenue-collecting part of the civil service and establish a new, independent institution to which people are freshly recruited.

In return for better pay they are subjected to more rigorous checks for honest conduct. Being a new institution, it is to some extent able to shed the burden of bad expectations that the old institutions carry.

The combination of primary commodity predation and opportunism implies that some people do well out of war.[15] Although most people lose, others have an interest in war restarting. Hence, when wars do restart, it is not necessarily simply an outpouring of irrational hatred or deep fears. Indeed, both hatreds and fears can be played on by those who expect to gain materially. One way in which a postconflict government can defend the peace against such manipulation is to publicize self-interest for what it is. Society at large needs to recognize that some groups have an interest in a return to conflict.

A corollary of this analysis is that rebel organizations, existing or prospective, can be viewed as rational economic agents. This has both a hopeful and a cautionary implication. The hopeful implication is that rebel organizations are likely to respond to incentives. For example, were the UN Security Council to introduce sanctions that made the economic and military circumstances of rebellion more difficult, the incidence of rebellion would decline. The cautionary implication is that it may be of little avail to buy rebel groups off. In countries where the objective conditions make rebellion financially feasible, if one group is bought off, others are likely to occupy the "market" opportunity for the generation of grievance.

Conclusion

Popular perceptions of the causes of civil conflict take at face value the discourse of the rebel organization. Civil war appears to be an intense political contest, fueled by grievances that are so severe as to have burst the banks of normal political channels. Rebellions are thus interpreted as the ultimate protest movements, their cadres being self-sacrificing heroes struggling against oppression. In fact, most rebellions cannot be like this. When the main grievances—inequality political repression, and ethnic and religious divisions—are measured objectively, they provide little or no explanatory power in predicting rebellion. In most income societies there are many reasons for grievance, but usually these do not give rise to rebellion. Objective grievances and hatreds simply cannot usually be the cause of such a distinctive phenomenon as violent conflict. They may well generate intense *political* conflict, but such conflict does not usually escalate to violent conflict.

In contrast, economic characteristics—depend*ence on prim*ary commodity exports, low average incomes, slow growth, and large diasporas—are all significant and powerful predictors of civil war. These characteristics all make rebellion more materially feasible: they enable rebel leaders to buy the guns and feed the soldiers, and furthermore to perpetrate large-scale killing without themselves being killed in the process. A viable private army, which is the distinguishing feature of a civil war, is extremely expensive to maintain over the long periods that such wars typically last. Where a private army is viable, the agenda of its leadership could potentially be anything. It maybe a public-spirited demand for improved governance. It maybe a megalomaniacs agenda of sadism. It may be a mafia-style grab for loot. It may be little more than insanity: Jonestown or Waco with the violence turned outward instead of inward on the devotees. Over the years of a conflict the agenda is likely to evolve, with any political objectives eroding and eliding into rebellion-as-business. Hence, it is these factors that determine viability, rather than objective grievances, that are the true "root causes," which conflict prevention must address if it is to be successful. Since conflict prevention to date has paid scant attention to these causes of conflict, there is probably considerable scope for policy, both domestic and international, to prevent civil conflict more effectively.

While objective grievances do not generate violent conflict, violent conflict generates subjective grievances. This is not just a by-product of conflict but an essential activity of a rebel organization. Rebel military success depends on motivating its soldiers to kill the enemy, and this—as in the classic Leninist theory of rebel organizations—requires indoctrination. Hence, by the end of a civil war, there is intense intergroup hatred based on perceived grievances. A conflict has been generated that has no boundaries between political and violent actions. The task in postconflict societies is partly, as in preconflict societies, to reduce the objective risk factors. However, postconflict societies are much more at risk than is implied by the inherited risk factors, because of this legacy of induced polarizing grievance. Either boundaries must be reestablished between the political contest and violence or the political contest must be resolved. Neither of these is easy, which is why, once a civil war has occurred, the chances of further conflict are so high.

Notes

1. Herschel I. Grossman, "Kleptocracy and Revolutions," *Oxford Economic Papers* 51 (1999): 269.

2. Paul Collier and Anke Hoefiler, "Greed and Grievance in Civil War," *Oxford Economic Papers* 56 (2004): 563–595.

3. James Fearon and David Laitin, "Ethnicity, Insurgency and Civil War," *American Political Science Review 97* (2003): 75–90.

4. Edward Miguel, Shanker Satyanath, and Ernest Sergenti, "Economic Shocks and Civil Conflict: An Instrumental Variables Approach," *Journal of Political Economy* 112 (2004): 725–754.

5. Paul Collier, Anke Hoeffler, and Mans Soderbom, "On the Duration of Civil War?" *Journal of Peace Research* 41 (2004): 253–273.

6. Timur Kuran, "Sparks and Prairie Fires: A Theory of Unanticipated Political Revolution," *Public Choice* 61 (1989): 41–74.

7. Jeremy Weinstein, "Resources and the Information Problem in Rebel Recruitment," *Journal of Conflict Resolution* 49 (2005): 598–624.

8. For a formal model of loot-seeking rebellion, see Paul Collier, "Rebellion as a Quasi-Criminal Activity," *Journal of Conflict Resolution* 44 (2000): 839–854.

9. Paul Collier, "Iraq: A Perspective from the Economic Analysis of Civil War," *Turkish Political Quarterly 4* (2005): 71–80.

10. I would like to thank Professor Frederick Prior of Swarthmore College for this information.

11. Paul Collier and Anke Hoefiler, "Conflict," in *Global Crises: Global Solutions*, ed. E. Lomborg (Cambridge: Cambridge University Press, 2004).

12. For a fuller review of policy options, see Paul Collier, Lani Elliot, Harvard Hegre, Anke Hoeffler, Marta Reynol-Querol, and Nicholas Sambanis, *Breaking the Conflict Trap* (New York: Oxford University Press, 2003).

13. Paul Collier and Anke Hoeffler, "Aid, Policy and Peace," *Defence and Peace Economics* 13 (2002): 435–450.

14. Paul Collier, "On the Economic Consequences of Civil War," *Oxford Economic Papers* 51 (1999): 168–183; and Collier and Anke Hoeffler, "Aid, Policy and Growth in Post-Conflict Societies," *European Economic Review* 48 (2004): 1125–1145.

15. Paul Collier, "Doing Well Out of War," in *Greed and Grievance: Economic Agendas in Civil Wars*, ed. Mats Berdal and David Malone (Boulder, CO: Lynne Rienner, 2000).

Structural Violence

Johan Galtung

Like John Burton, Johan Galtung is often considered a founder of the field of peace and conflict studies, though he began with a PhD in mathematics from the University of Oslo. He later pursued a PhD in sociology, and after a short stint at Columbia University, he returned to Oslo to found the Peace Research Institute Oslo (PRIO). The switch from mathematics to peace studies might be surprising until one learns that a twelve-year-old Galtung watched as Nazis arrested his father. With over 1,000 articles and over a hundred books, he remains one of the most prolific writers in our field.

In this article, Galtung examines the field's working definitions of "peace" and "violence," concepts he claims are inextricably linked. He offers a typology of violence, arguing that "violence is present when human beings are being influenced so that their actual somatic and mental realizations are below their potential realizations." This definition diverged from the commonly held belief at the time of the article's publication, which defined violence as a solely somatic, or bodily, event. If the field defined violence only as a physical violence, he feared grossly unjust societies would be permitted to operate uninterrupted. His definition of violence as "the distance between the potential and the actual" encourages the field to seek *psychological* violence that impedes individuals and communities from flourishing. Psychological, or soul, violations can include brainwashing, threats, or other means of use intimidation used to influence behavior.

One of the significant contributions of Galtung's work is his promotion of the idea of *structural violence*. He argues that violence can be enacted not simply by individuals, but also by systems institutionalizing inequality, discrimination, bias, or in other ways thwarting individual self or community-actualization. This structural violence can be latent, meaning that it is not visible or active, yet destructive nonetheless. Communities experiencing this kind of latent violence can be defined as experiencing a *negative peace* as opposed to a *positive peace* defined by the presence of social justice. Galtung urges peace research to embrace both aspects of peace: those working to reduce bodily harm and those addressing structural violence.

Galtung's work advanced the field of conflict resolution by pushing scholars and practitioners to look beyond nuclear threat as the primary source of potential violence and consider other forms of violence existing within societies. The piece here reflects Epoch One in its positioning victims of violence as being acted upon by outside forces, namely, institutions and structures; they are rarely articulated as active agents in their experience.

Questions to consider: Is peace simply the absence of violence? Can violence be psychological? Is the destruction of "things" violence, or only the harm of bodies? In what ways is defining peace and violence important to peace research?

Violence, Peace, and Peace Research*

Johan Galtung

1. Introduction

In the present paper we shall be using the word "peace" very many times. Few words are so often used and abused—perhaps, it seems, because "peace" serves as a means of obtaining verbal consensus—it is hard to be all-out against peace.[1] Thus, when efforts are made to plead almost any kind of policy—say technical assistance, increased trade, tourism, new forms of education, irrigation, industrialization, etc.—then it is often asserted that that policy, in addition to other merits, will also serve the cause of peace. This is done regardless of how tenuous the relation has been in the past or how dubious the theory justifying this as a reasonable expectation for the future. Such difficulties are avoided by excluding any reference to data from the past or to theories about the future.

This practice is not necessarily harmful. The use of the term "peace" may in itself be peace-productive, producing a common basis, a feeling of communality in purpose that may pave the ground for deeper ties later on. The use of more precise terms drawn from the vocabulary of one conflict group, and excluded from the vocabulary of the opponent group, may in itself cause dissent and lead to manifest conflict precisely because the term is so clearly understood. By projecting an image of harmony of interests the term "peace" may also help bring about such a harmony. It provides opponents with a one-word language in which to express values of concern and togetherness because peace is on anybody's agenda.[2]

One may object that frequent use of the word "peace" gives an unrealistic image of the world. Expressions like "violence," "strife," "exploitation" or at least "conflict," "revolution," and war should gain much higher frequency to mirror semantically a basically non-harmonious world. But leaving this major argument aside for the moment, it is obvious that some level of precision is necessary for the term to serve as a cognitive tool. At this point, of course, nobody has any monopoly on defining "peace." But those who use the term frequently in a research context, as peace researchers (will) do, will at least have gained some experience when it comes to definitions that should be *avoided* for one reason or another.

To discuss the idea of peace we shall start from three simple principles:

1. The term "peace" shall be used for social goals at least verbally agreed to by many, if not necessarily by most.
2. These social goals may be complex and difficult, but not impossible, to attain.
3. The statement peace is absence of violence shall be retained as valid.

The third principle is not a definition, since it is a clear case of *obscurum per obscurius*. What we intend is only that the terms "peace" and "violence" be linked to each other such that "peace" can be regarded as "absence of violence." The reasons at this early point in our semantical excursion, are twofold: the statement is simple and in agreement with common usage, *and* defines a peaceful social order not as a point but as region—as the vast region of social orders from which violence is absent. Within this region a tremendous amount of variation is still possible, making an orientation in favor of peace compatible with a number of ideologies outlining other aspects of social orders.

Everything now hinges on making a definition of "violence." This is a highly unenviable task, and the suggestions will hardly be satisfactory to many readers. However, it is not so important to arrive at anything like *the* definition, or *the* typology—for there are obviously many types of violence. More important is to indicate theoretically significant dimensions of violence that can lead thinking, research and, potentially, action, toward the most important problems. If peace action is to be regarded highly because it is action against violence, then the concept of violence must be broad enough to include the most significant varieties, yet specific enough to serve as a basis for concrete action.

Thus, the definition of "peace" becomes a major part of a scientific strategy. It may depart from common usage by not being agreed to "by most" (consensus not required), yet should not be entirely subjectivistic ("agreed to by many"). It should depict a state of affairs the realization of which is not utopian ("not impossible to obtain"), yet not on the immediate political agenda ("complex and difficult"). And it should immediately steer one's attention toward problems that are on the political, intellectual, and scientific agenda of today, and tomorrow.[2]

2. On the Definition and Dimensions of "Violence"

As a point of departure, let us say that *violence is present when human beings are being influenced so that their actual somatic and mental realizations are below their potential realizations.* This statement may lead to more problems than it solves. However, it will soon be clear why we are rejecting the narrow concept of violence—according to which violence is *somatic* incapacitation, or deprivation of health, alone (with killing as the extreme form), at the hands of an *actor* who *intends* this to be the consequence. If this were all violence is about, and peace is seen as its negation, then too little is rejected when peace is held up as an ideal. Highly unacceptable social orders would still be compatible with peace. Hence, *an extended concept of violence is indispensable* but that concept should be a logical extension, not merely a list of undesirables.

The definition points to at least six important dimensions of violence. But first some remarks about the use of the key words above, "actual" and "potential." *Violence is here defined as the cause of the difference between the potential and the actual,* between what could have been and what is. Violence is that which increases the distance between the potential and the actual, and that which impedes the decrease of this distance. Thus, if a person died from tuberculosis in the eighteenth century it would be hard to conceive of this as violence since it might have been quite unavoidable, but if he dies from it today, despite all the medical resources in the world, then violence is present according to our definition. Correspondingly, the case of people dying from earthquakes today would not warrant an analysis in terms of violence,[3] but the day after tomorrow, when earthquakes may become avoidable, such deaths may be seen as the result of violence. In other words, when the potential is higher than the actual is by definition *avoidable* and when it is avoidable, then violence is present.

When the actual is unavoidable, then violence is not present even if the actual is at a very low level. A life expectancy of thirty years only, during the neolithic period, was not an expression of violence, but the same life-expectancy today (whether due to wars, or social injustice, or both) would be seen as violence according to our definition.

Thus, the potential level of realization is that which is possible with a given level of insight and resources. If insight and/or resources are *monopolized* by a group or class or are *used for other purposes*, then the actual level falls below the potential level, and violence is present in the system. In addition to these types of *indirect* violence there is also the *direct* violence where means of realization are not withheld, but directly destroyed. Thus, when a war is fought there is direct violence since killing or hurting a person certainly puts his "actual somatic realization" below his "potential somatic realization." But there is also indirect violence insofar as insight and resources are channeled away from constructive efforts to bring the actual closer to the potential.[4]

The meaning of "potential realizations" is highly problematic, especially when we move from somatic aspects of human life, where consensus is more readily obtained,[5] to mental aspects. Our guide here would probably often have to be whether the value to be realized is fairly consensual or not, although this is by no means satisfactory. For example, literacy is held in high regard almost everywhere, whereas the value of being Christian is highly controversial. Hence, we would talk about violence if the level of literacy is lower than what it could have been, not if the level of Christianity is lower than what it could have been. We shall not try to explore this difficult point further in this context, but turn to the dimensions of violence.

To discuss them, it is useful to conceive of violence in terms of influence, as indicated in the statement we used as a point of departure above. A complete influence relation presupposes an influence, an influencee, and a mode of influencing.[6] In the case of persons, we can put it very simply: a *subject*, an *object*, and an *action*. But this conception of violence in terms of a *complete* interpersonal influence relation will lead us astray by focusing on a very special type of violence only; also *truncated* versions where either subject or object or both are absent are highly significant. To approach this we shall start with two dimensions characterizing the violent action itself, or the mode of influence.

The *first distinction* to be made is between *physical* and *psychological* violence. The distinction is trite but important mainly because the narrow concept of violence mentioned above concentrates on physical violence only. Under physical violence human beings are hurt somatically, to the point of killing. It is useful to distinguish further between "biological violence," which reduces somatic capability (below what is potentially possible), and "physical violence as such," which increases the constraint on human movements[7]—as when a person is imprisoned or put in chains, but also when access to transportation is very unevenly distributed, keeping large segments of a population at the same place with mobility a monopoly of the selected few. But that distinction is less important than the basic distinction between violence that works on the body, and violence that works on the soul; where the latter would include lies, brainwashing, indoctrination of various kinds, threats, etc. that serve to decrease mental potentialities. (Incidentally, it is interesting that such English words as "hurt" and "hit" can be used to express psychological and physical violence: this doubleness is already built into the language.)

The *second distinction* is between the *negative* and *positive* approach to influence.[8] Thus, a person can be influenced not only by punishing him when he does what the influencer considers wrong, but also by rewarding him when he does what the influencer considers right. Instead of increasing the constraints on his movements the constraints may be decreased instead of increased, and somatic capabilities extended instead of reduced. This may be readily agreed to, but does it have anything to do with violence? Yes, because the net result may still be that human beings are effectively prevented from realizing their potentialities. Thus, many contemporary thinkers[9] emphasize that the consumer's society rewards amply he who goes in for consumption, while not positively punishing him who does not. The system is reward-oriented, based on promises of euphoria, but in so being also narrows down the ranges of action. It may be disputed whether this is better or worse than a system that limits the range of action because of the dysphoric consequences of staying outside the permitted range. It is perhaps better in terms of giving pleasure rather than pain, worse in terms of being more manipulatory, less overt. But the important point is, the awareness of the concept of violence can be extended in this direction, since it yields a much richer basis for discussion.

The *third distinction* to be made is on the object side: *whether or not there is an object that is hurt.* Can we talk about violence when no physical or biological object is hurt? This would be a case of what is referred to above as truncated violence, but nevertheless highly meaningful. When a person, a group, a nation is displaying the means of physical violence, whether throwing stones around or testing nuclear arms, there may not be violence in the sense that anyone is hit or hurt, but there is nevertheless the *threat of physical violence* and indirect threat of mental violence that may even be characterized as some type of psychological violence since it constrains human action. Indeed, this is also the intention: the famous balance of power doctrine is based on efforts to obtain precisely this effect. And correspondingly with psychological violence that does not reach any object: a lie does not become more of a truth because nobody believes in the lie. Untruthfulness is violence according to this kind of thinking under any condition, which does not mean that it cannot be the least evil under some widely discussed circumstances.

Is destruction of things violence? Again, it would not be violence according to the complete definition above, but possibly some "degenerate" form. But in at least two senses it can be seen as psychological violence: the destruction of things as a foreboding or threat of possible destruction of persons,[10] and the destruction of things as destruction of something very dear to persons referred to as consumers or *owners.*[11]

The *fourth distinction* to be made and the most important one is on the subject side: *whether or not there is a subject (person) who acts.* Again it may be asked: can we talk about violence when nobody is committing direct violence, is acting? This would also be a case of what is referred to above as truncated violence, but again highly meaningful. We shall refer to the type of violence where there is an actor that commits the violence as *personal* or *direct*, and to violence where there is no such actor as *structural* or *indirect.*[12] In both cases individuals may be killed or mutilated, hit or hurt in both senses of these words, and manipulated by means of stick or carrot strategies. But whereas in the first case these consequences can be traced back to concrete persons as actors, in the second case this is no longer meaningful. There may not be any person who directly harms another person in the structure. The violence is built into the structure and shows up as unequal power and consequently as unequal life chances.[13]

Resources are unevenly distributed, as when income distributions are heavily skewed, literacy/education unevenly distributed, medical services existent in some districts and for some groups only, and so on.[14] Above all the *power to decide over the distribution of resources* is unevenly distributed.[15] The situation is aggravated further if the persons low on income are also low in education, low on health, and low on power—as is frequently the case because these rank dimensions tend to be heavily correlated due to the way they are tied together in the social structure.[16] Marxist criticism of capitalist society emphasizes how the power to decide over the surplus from the production process is reserved for the owners of the means of production, who then can buy themselves into top positions on all other rank dimensions because money is highly convertible in a capitalist society—if you have money to convert, that is. Liberal criticism of socialist society similarly emphasizes how power to decide is monopolized by a small group who convert power in one field into power in another field simply because the opposition cannot reach the stage of effective articulation.

The important point here is that if people are starving when this is objectively avoidable, then violence is committed, regardless of whether there is a clear subject-action-object relation, as during a siege yesterday or no such clear relation, as in the way world economic relations are organized today.[17] We have baptized the distinction in two different ways, using the word-pairs personal-structural and direct-indirect respectively.

Violence with a clear subject-object relation is manifest because it is visible as *action*. It corresponds to our ideas of what *drama* is, and it is personal because there are persons committing the violence. It is easily captured and expressed verbally since it has the same structure as elementary sentences in (at least Indo-European) *languages*: subject-verb-object, with both subject and object being persons. Violence without this relation is structural, built into structure. Thus, when one husband beats his wife there is a clear case of personal violence, but when one million husbands keep one million wives in ignorance there is structural violence. Correspondingly, in a society where life expectancy is twice as high in the upper as in the lower classes, violence is exercised even if there are no concrete actors one can point to directly attacking others, as when one person kills another.

In order not to overwork the word violence we shall sometimes refer to the condition of structural violence as *social injustice*.[18] The term "exploitation" will not be used, for several reasons. First, it belongs to a political vocabulary, and has so many political and emotional overtones that the use of this term will hardly facilitate communication. Second, the term lends itself too easily to expressions involving the verb exploit, which in turn may lead attention away from the structural as opposed to the personal nature of this phenomenon—and even lead to often unfounded accusations about intended structural violence.[19]

The *fifth distinction* to be made is between violence that is *intended* or *unintended*. This distinction is important when *guilt* is to be decided, since the concept of guilt has been tied more to *intention*, both in Judaeo-Christian ethics and in Roman jurisprudence, than to *consequence* (whereas the present definition of violence is entirely located on the consequence side). This connection is important because it brings into focus a bias present in so much thinking about violence, peace, and related concepts: ethical systems directed against *intended* violence will easily fail to capture structural violence in their nets—and may hence be catching the small fry and letting the big fish loose. From this fallacy it does not follow, in our mind, that the opposite fallacy of directing all attention against structural violence is elevated into wisdom. If the concern is with peace, and peace is absence of violence, then action should be directed against personal as well as structural violence; a point to be developed below.

Sixth, there is the traditional distinction between two levels of violence, the *manifest* and the *latent*.[20] Manifest violence, whether personal or structural, is observable; although not directly since the theoretical entity of "potential realization" also enters the picture. Latent violence is something which is not there, yet might easily come about. Since violence by definition is the cause of the difference (or of maintaining the non-decrease) between actual and potential realization, increased violence may come about by increases in the potential as well as by decreases in the actual levels. However, we shall limit ourselves to the latter and say that there is latent violence when the situation is so unstable that the actual realization level "easily" decreases. For personal violence this would mean a situation where a little challenge would trigger considerable killing and atrocity, as is often the case in connection with racial fights. In such cases we need a way of expressing that the personal violence is also there the day, hour, minute, second before the first bomb, shot, fist-fight, cry—and this is what the concept of latent, personal violence does for us. It indicates a situation of unstable equilibrium, where the level of actual realization is not sufficiently protected against deterioration by upholding mechanisms.

Similarly with structural violence: we could imagine a relatively egalitarian structure insufficiently protected against sudden feudalization, against crystallization into a much more stable, even petrified, hierarchical structure. A revolution brought about by means of a highly hierarchical military organization may after a brilliant period of egaliatarianism, and after major challenge, revert to a hierarchical structure. One way of avoiding this, of course, is to avoid hierarchical group struggle organizations in the first run, and use nonviolent nonhierarchical guerrilla organizations in the fight so as to let the means be a preview of the egalitarian goal.[21]

That concludes our list of dimensions of violence, although many more could be included. One question that immediately arises is whether any combinations from these six dichotomies can be ruled out *a priori*, but there seems to be no such case. Structural violence without objects is also meaningful; truncation of the complete violence relation can go so far as to eliminate both subjects and objects. Personal violence is meaningful as a threat, a demonstration even when nobody is hit, and structural violence is also meaningful as a blueprint, as an abstract form without social life, used to threaten people into subordination: if you do not behave, we shall have to reintroduce all the disagreeable structures we had before.

Disregarding the negative-positive distinction as less important in this context, we end up, essentially, with the typology illustrated in Figure 1.

If peace now is regarded as absence of violence, then thinking about peace (and consequently peace research and peace action) will be structured the same way as thinking about violence. And the violence cake can evidently be cut a number of ways. Tradition has been to think about violence as personal violence only, with one important subdivision in terms of "violence versus the threat of violence," another in terms of "physical versus psychological war," still another (important in ethical and legal thinking) about "intended versus unintended," and

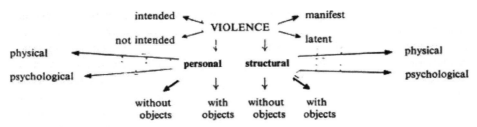

Figure 1. *A Typology of Violence*

so on. The choice is here to make the distinction between personal and structural violence the basic one; justification has been presented (1) in terms of a unifying perspective (the cause of the difference between potential and actual realization) and (2) by indicating that there is no reason to assume that structural violence amounts to less suffering than personal violence.

On the other hand, it is not strange that attention has been focused more on personal than on structural violence. Personal violence *shows*.[22] The object of personal violence perceives the violence, usually, and may complain—the object of structural violence may be persuaded not to perceive this at all. Personal violence represents change and dynamism—not only ripples on waves, but waves on otherwise tranquil waters. Structural violence is silent, it does not show—it is essentially static, it *is* the tranquil waters. In a *static* society, personal violence will be registered, whereas structural violence may be seen as about as natural as the air around us. Conversely: in a highly *dynamic* society, personal violence may be seen as wrong and harmful but still somehow congruent with the order of things, whereas structural violence becomes apparent because it stands out like an enormous rock in a creek, impeding the free flow, creating all kinds of eddies and turbulences. Thus, perhaps it is not so strange that the thinking about personal violence (in the Judaeo-Christian-Roman tradition) took on much of its present form in what we today would regard as essentially static social orders, whereas thinking about structural violence (in the Marxist tradition) was formulated in highly dynamic northwest-European societies.

In other words, we conceive of structural violence as something that shows a certain stability, whereas personal violence (e.g., as measured by the tolls caused by group conflict in general and war in particular) shows tremendous fluctuations over time. This is illustrated in Figure 2.

Figure 2. *Time and the Two Types of Violence*

This is to a large extent tautological. A type of violence built into the social structure should exhibit a certain stability: social structures may perhaps sometimes be changed overnight, but they may not very often be changed that quickly. Personal violence, which to a larger extent is seen as subject to the whims and wishes of individuals, should show less stability. Hence personal violence may more easily be noticed, even though the "tranquil waters" of structural violence may contain much more violence. For this reason we would expect a focus or personal violence in after-war periods lest they should become between-war periods; and if the periods protracts sufficiently for the major outburst of personal violence to be partly forgotten, we would expect a concentration on structural violence, provided the societies are dynamic enough to make any stability stand out as somehow unnatural.[23]

3. *The Means of Personal and Structural Violence*

To make this distinction less abstract, let us now explore how personal and structural violence, are, in fact, carried out. Starting with personal violence, concentration on "actual somatic realization": how can it be reduced or kept low at the hands of somebody else? The question is simple, as are the answers since they suggest an instrumental approach to the problem of violence. There is a well-specified task to be done, that of doing bodily harm unto others, and there are persons available to do it. But this is a production relation, suggesting a "development" much like in the economic sector of society, with the introduction of increasingly refined tools and differentiated social organization—only that the tools in this case are referred to as weapons or arms, and the organization is not called a workshop or a factory, but a gang or an army.

A typology of personal, physical violence can now be developed focussing on the *tools* used, starting with the human body itself (in the elementary forms of fist fights and the more advanced forms, such as *Karate* and *Aikido*), proceeding towards all kinds of arms culminating, so far, with ABC weapons. Another approach would use the form of *organization*, starting with the lone individual, proceeding via mobs and crowds ending up with the organizations of modern guerrilla or army warfare. These two approaches are related: just as in economic organizations the means and mode of production (here direct bodily violence) depend on each other, and if one is lagging behind a conflict will arise. Together these two approaches would yield the history of military warfare as a special case, since much bodily violence is not military. The approach would be cumulative for a weapon or technique, and a form of organization once developed may become obsolete but not erased; hence this typology would not be systematic, but always open to record new developments.

A more systematic approach can be obtained by looking at the target: the human being. He is relatively known anatomically (structurally) and physiologically (functionally), so typologies can be developed on that basis. One primitive typology might be as shown in Table 1. The basic distinction is not water-tight, but nevertheless useful: for one thing is to try to destroy the machine (the human body) itself, another to try to prevent the machine from functioning. The latter can be done in two ways: denial of *input* (sources of energy in general, air, water, and food in the case of the body), and denial of *output* (movement). The human output can be *somatic*, recorded by the outside as movement (with standstill as a limiting case) or *mental* not recorded directly from the outside (only by indicators in the form of movements, including movements of vocal chords). The borderline between physical and psychological personal violence is not very clear, since it is possible to influence physical movements by means of psychological techniques, and vice versa: physical constraints certainly have mental implications.

In Table 1 some of the techniques have been indicated in parenthesis. A note should be added here about *explosions*. In principle they are of two kinds: to propel some missile, and to work directly on human bodies. Explosions are much used for the latter purpose because they combine the anatomical methods: a standard bomb would combine 1 and 2; add some shrapnel and 3 is also taken care of; add some simple chemicals so as to make it a fire bomb and 4 is taken into account; some gases would include 5 and if in addition the contraption is made nuclear the crowning achievement, 6, is there—presumably for ever, at least in principle, since it is difficult systematically to unmake an invention, it can only be suppressed. New weapons can always be invented, based on one or any combination of the principles in the Table. But there is also room for the more basic innovation: the introduction of a new principle.

Is it now possible to construct a corresponding typology for structural violence? If we accept that the general formula behind structural violence is inequality, above all in the distribution of power, then this can be measured; and inequality seems to have a high survival capacity despite tremendous changes elsewhere.[24] But if inequality persists, then we may ask: which factors, apart from personal violence and the threat of personal violence, tend to uphold inequality? Obviously, just as military science and related subjects would be indispensable for the understanding of personal violence, so is the science of social structure, and particularly of stratification, indispensable for the understanding of structural violence.

Table GT.1.   A Typology of Personal Somatic Violence

Focussed on the anatomy	*Focussed on the physiology*
1. crushing (fist fight, catapults)	1. *denial of air* (choking, strangulation)
2. *tearing* (hanging, stretching, cutting)	2. *denial of water* (dehydration)
3. *piercing* (knives, spears, bullets)	3. *denial of food* (starvation due to siege, embargo)
4. *burning* (arson, flame, thrower)	4. *denial of movement*
5. poisoning *(in water and food, in gases)*	a. by body constraint (chains, gas)
6. *evaporation* (as in nuclear explosion)	b. by space constraint (prison, detention, exile)
	c. by brain control (nerve gases, "brainwashing")

This is not the occasion to develop general theories of social structure, but some ideas are necessary to arrive at some of the mechanisms. Most fundamental are the ideas of *actor, system, structure, rank* and *level*. Actors seek goals, and are organized in systems in the sense that they interact with each other. But two actors, e.g., two nations, can usually be seen as interacting in more than one system; they not only cooperate politically, e.g., by trading votes in the UN, but also economically by trading goods, and culturally by trading ideas. The set of all such systems of interaction, for a given set of actors, can then be referred to as a structure. And in a structure an actor may have high rank in one system, low in the next, and then high in the third one; or actors may have either consistently high ranks or consistently low ranks.

However, if we look more closely at an actor, e. g. a nation, we shall very often be able to see it as a structure in its own right, but an integrated structure since it is able to appear as an actor. This "Chinese boxes" view of actors is very important, and leads to the concept of level of actors. There are three major interpretations:[25]

- in terms of *territories:* a nation can be seen as a set of districts, in turn seen as a set of municipalities, and these are then seen as a set of individuals;
- in terms of *organizations:* a factory can often be seen as an assembly line with sub-factories feeding into the assembly-line with their products, finally coming down to the individual worker.
- in terms of *associations:* they can often be seen as consisting of local chapters, ending up with individual members.

Thus, the image of the social order or disorder can be presented as in Figure 3.

In all these systems there is interaction, and where there is interaction, value is somehow exchanged. It then makes very much sense to study what the value-distribution is after the system has been operating for some time, and the gross distinction has been made between egalitarian and inegalitarian distributions.

We can now mention six factors that serve to maintain inegalitarian distributions, and consequently can be seen as mechanisms of structural violence:

Linear ranking order—the ranking is complete, leaving no doubt as to who is higher in any pair of actors;

Acyclical interaction pattern—all actors are connected, but only one way—there is only one "correct" path of interaction;

Correlation between rank and centrality—the higher the rank of the actor in the system, the more central his position in the interaction network;

Congruence between the systems—the interaction networks are structurally similar.

Concordance between the ranks—if an actor is high in one system then he also tends to be high in another system where he participates and

High rank coupling between levels—so that the actor at level n-1 are represented at level n through the highest ranking actor at level n-1.

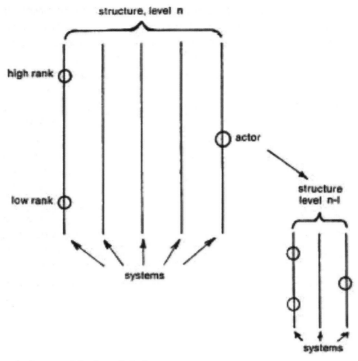

Figure 3.   *An Image of the Social Order*

The factors can best be understood by examining to some extent their negation, starting with the last one.

Thus, imagine that a nation is dominated by an economic and cultural capital, but has a much smaller political capital through which most political interaction in the international system is carried out. This would tend to distribute the power at the level of cities since the coupling is not at the highest point. Similarly, we could imagine that the major road from the capital to a district did not connect directly with the district point of gravity but with some peripheral point; as when a government is represented abroad not by the president or prime minister but by the foreign minister—or a sub-factory not by the manager but by his deputy. But very often the top actor at level n-1 is made the representative at level n—with a number of implications.[26]

Similarly, imagine there is considerable rank discordance, even to the point where the summated rankings of the actors tend to be relatively equal. In that case, patterns of inequality would be less consistent and less reinforcing, and the amount of disequilibrium in the system would also tend to upset any stability. Moreover, if the systems are not congruent but differ in structure, actors will not so easily generalize interaction patterns but be more flexible, less frozen into one way of acting (for instance servility). And if the actor with highest rank did not necessarily have the most central position in the network this would diminish his power, which would also be diminished if actors with lower ranks were to a larger extent permitted direct interaction (not only interaction mediated through the actors with high rank). Finally: nonlinear, pyramidal (also known as partial) ranking order permits more leeway, more flexibility in the system.[27]

Many propositions can now be developed about this, a basic one being that social systems will have a tendency to develop all six mechanisms unless deliberately *and persistently* prevented from doing so. Thus the pattern is set for an aggravation of inequality, in some structures so much so that the lowest-ranking actors are deprived not only relative to the potential, but indeed below subsistence minimum. Inequality then shows up in differential morbidity and mortality rates, between individuals in a district, between districts in a nation, and between nations in the international system—in a chain of interlocking feudal relationships. They are deprived because the structure deprives them of chances to organize and bring their power to bear against the topdogs, as voting power, bargaining power, striking power, violent power—partly because they are atomized and disintegrated, partly because they are overawed by all the authority the topdogs present.

Thus, the net result may be bodily harm in both cases, but structural violence will probably just as often be recorded as psychological violence. Hence, highly different means may lead to highly similar results—a conclusion to be explored later.

4. *The Relation between Personal and Structural Violence*

In this section some comments will be offered on this relationship, following this outline:

> Is there really a distinction between personal and structural violence at all?
> If there is, does not one type of violence presuppose the manifest presence of the other?
> If pure types exist, could it not nevertheless be said that they have a prehistory of the other type?
> If this is not generally the case, could it not be that one type of violence presupposes the latent presence of the other?
> If this is not the case, could it not be that one is the price we have to pay for the absence of the other?
> If this is not generally the case, could it not be that one type is much more important in its consequences than the other?

Let us start with the first question.

It may be argued that this distinction is not clear at all: it disregards slights of the structural element in personal violence and the personal element in structural violence. These important perspectives are regained if a person is seen as making his decision to act violently not only on the basis of individual deliberations but (also) on the basis of expectations impinging on him as norms contained in roles contained in statuses through which he enacts his social self; *and*, if one sees a violent structure as something that is a mere abstraction unless upheld by the actions, expected from the social environment or not, of individuals. But then: does not this mean that there is no real distinction at all? Cannot a person engaging in personal violence always use expectations from the structure as an excuse, and does not a person upholding an exploitative social structure have responsibility for this?

The distinction that nevertheless remains is between violence that hits human beings as a *direct* result of Figure 4 type actions of others, and violence that hits them *indirectly* because repressive structures (as analyzed in preceding section) are upheld by the summated and concerted action of human beings. The qualitative difference between these actions is the answer. The question of guilt is certainly not a metaphysical question; guilt is as real as any other feeling, but a less interesting one. The question is rather whether violence is structured in such a way that it constitutes a direct, personal link between a subject and an object, or an indirect structural one, not how this link is perceived by the persons at either end of the violence channel. The objective consequences, not the subjective intentions are the primary concern.

But are personal and structural violence empirically, not only logically, independent of each other? Granted that there may be a corrrelation so that structures richly endowed with structural violence often may also display above average incidence of personal violence, it is possible to have them in pure forms, to have one without the other? Are there *structures where violence is person-invariant* in the sense that structural violence persists regardless of changes in persons? And conversely, are there *persons where violence is structure-invariant* in the sense that personal violence persists regardless of changes in structural context?

The answer seems to be yes in either case. The typical feudal structure, with a succession of incapsulating hierarchies of metropole-satellite relationships is clearly structurally violent regardless of who staffs it and regardless of the level of awareness of the participants: the violence is built into the structures. No personal violence or threat of personal violence are needed. And there are persons who seem to be violent in (almost) any setting—often referred to as "bullies." Characteristic of them is precisely that they carry their violent propensity with them far outside any structural context deemed reasonable by society at large, for which reason they will often be institutionalized (in prison or mental hospital, depending on which basic norms they infract first and most clearly). Hence, we may conclude that the two forms of violence are empirically independent: the one does not presuppose the other.

But from this alone it cannot be concluded that there is no necessary (not only sufficient) *causal relationship* between the two types of violence, or that the even stronger condition of *one-way reductionism* is not fulfilled. One may argue that all cases of structural violence can, by closer scrutiny, be traced back to personal violence in their *pre-history*. An exploitative caste system or race society would be seen as the consequence of a large-scale invasion leaving a thin, but powerful top layer of the victorious group after the noise of fighting is over. A

bully would be seen as the inevitable product of socialization into a violent structure: he is the rebel, systematically untrained in other ways of coping with his
conflicts and frustrations because the structure leaves him with no alternatives.
That structural violence often breeds structural violence, and personal violence
often breeds personal violence nobody would dispute—but the point here would
be the cross-breeding between the two. In other words: pure cases are only pure
as long as the pre-history of the case or even the structural context are conveniently
forgotten.

Far from denying that these may be fruitful perspectives both for research into
the past and the etiology of violence as well as for search into the future and
therapy for violence we would tend to reject the position that violence presupposes
a pre-history of violence of the same or opposite kinds. This view is a breeding
theory, and like all breeding theories it fails to answer two questions: how did the
process come into being at all? And is spontaneous generation of violence impossible, or are all cases of violence the legitimate offspring of other cases of violence—
handed down through some kind of apostolic succession, the content being more
like "original sin" though?

Take the case of structural violence first. Here it may be argued we will never
get the perfect test-case. Imagine we based our thinking on something like this:
people, when left to themselves in isolation (in a discussion group, stranded on an
isolated island, etc.) will tend to form systems where rank, or differential evaluation of relatively stable interaction patterns referred to as status, will emerge; high
ranks tend to cluster on persons who already have some high ranks, and interaction tends to flow in their direction—hence the net result is sooner or later a
feudal structure. One might then object: yes, because these persons are already
socialized into such structures, and all they do is to project their experiences and
their habits so as to give life to an embryonic structure. And there is no way
around it: human beings, to be human, have to be rated by humans, hence there
will always be an element of succession.

Maybe, but, we also suspect that the reasoning above holds true even under
tabula rasa conditions because it probably is connected with the fact (1) that
individuals are different and (2) that these differences somehow are relevant for
their interaction behavior. Hence, special measures are needed to prevent the formation of feudal structures: structural violence seems to be more "natural" than
structural peace. And similarly with personal violence: it is difficult to see how
even the most egalitarian structure would be sufficient to prevent cases of violence,
whether they result from conflicts or not. Personal violence is perhaps more "natural" than personal peace. It could also be argued that an inegalitarian structure is
a built-in mechanism of conflict control, precisely because it is hierarchical, and
that an egalitarian structure would bring out in the open many new conflicts that
are kept latent in a feudal structure.

One could now proceed by saying that even if one type of violence does
not presuppose the manifest presence of the other, neither synchronically, nor
diachronically, there is nevertheless the possibility that manifest structural violence
presupposes latent personal violence. When the structure is threatened, those who
benefit from structural violence, above all those who are at the top, will try to

preserve the status quo so well geared to protect their interests. By observing the activities of various groups and persons when a structure is threatened, and more particularly by noticing who comes to the rescue of the structure, an operational test is introduced that can be used to rank the members of the structure in terms of their interest in maintaining the structure. The involvement that does not show clearly in times of unimpeded persistence is brought up to the surface when there is turbulence. But one has to observe carefully, for those most interested in the maintenance of status quo may not come openly to the defence of the structure: they may push their mercenaries in front of them.[28] In other words, they may mobilize the police, the army, the thugs, the general social underbrush against the sources of the disturbance, and remain themselves in more discrete, remote seclusion from the turmoil of personal violence. And they can do this as an extrapolation of the structural violence: the violence committed by the police is personal by our definition, yet they are called into action by expectations deeply rooted in the structure—there is no need to assume an intervening variable of intention. They simply do their job.

This view is probably generally very valid, even if it may underestimate the significance of a number of factors:

1. the extent to which the "tools of oppression" may have internalized the repressive structure so that their personal violence is an expression of internalized, not only institutionalized norms;
2. the extent to which those who benefit from the structural violence may themselves have severe and sincere doubts about that structure and prefer to see it changed, even at their own expense;
3. the extent to which the "challenge of the structure" may be a personal confrontation with the police etc. more than with the structure, and reveal more about the dynamics of interpersonal relations than about the structure.[29]
4. the extent to which all members in a violent structure, not only the top dogs, contribute to its operation and hence are all responsible as they can all shake it through their non-cooperation.

But these are minor points; social affairs always refuse to be captured in simplistic formulations. More important is whether one can also turn the proposition around and gain some insight by saying that manifest personal violence presupposes latent structural violence—which is not the same as saying that it presupposes manifest structural violence. The idea would be that of an egalitarian structure maintained by means of personal violence, so that when this pattern of violence is challenged to the point of abolition there will be an emergence of structural violence.

The proposition is interesting because it may open for some possible insights in structures yet unknown to us. It does not seem *a priori* unreasonable to state that if the absence of personal violence is combined with a pattern of structural violence, then personal violence is nevertheless around the corner—and correspondingly that if absence of structural violence is combined with personal violence, then structural violence is also around the corner. All we are saying is only that the sum of violence is constant, only that one has to take into account the latent variety of the type of violence "abolished" to see more clearly how that type is in a standby position, ready to step in once the other type crumbles. Absence of one type of violence is bought at the expense of the threat of the other.

But, however insight-stimulating this may be in certain situations we refuse to accept this pessimistic view for two reasons. First, the two propositions seem simply not to be true. It is not at all difficult to imagine a structure so purely structural in its violence that all means of personal violence have been abolished, so that when the structure is threatened there is no second trench defense by mobilizing latent personal violence. Similarly, a structure may be completely unprepared for freezing the released forces stemming from a reduction of personal violence into a hierarchical order. Empirically such cases may be rare, but yet significant.

Second, the assumption would be that human beings somehow need violence to be kept in line; if not of the personal type, then of the structural variety. The argument would be that if there is no personal violence or threat of personal violence then a very strong hierarchical order is needed to maintain order and to control conflict; and if there is no structural violence or threat of structural violence, then personal violence will easily serve as a substitute. But even if this may be a reasonable theory to explain possible empirical regularities, that in itself is not sufficient argument for reifying a regularity into a principle supposedly eternally valid. On the contrary, this would be a highly pessimistic view of the human condition, and to accept it fully would even be a capitulationist view.

From the problem of whether one type of violence is necessary to *obtain* or *sustain* the other type, whether at the manifest or the latent levels, it is not far to the opposite problem; is one type of violence necessary or sufficient to *abolish* the other type? The question, which actually splits into four questions, brings us directly into the center of contemporary political debate. Let us examine briefly some of the arguments.

1. *Structural violence is sufficient to abolish personal violence.* This thesis seems to have a certain limited and short-term validity. If all the methods mentioned above for sustaining structural violence are implemented, then it seems quite possible that personal violence *between the groups segregated by the structure* is abolished. The underdogs are too isolated and too awed by the topdogs, the topdogs have nothing to fear. But this only holds between those groups; within the groups the feudal structure is not practised. And although the structure probably is among the most stable social structures imaginable, it is not stable in perpetuity. There are many ways in which it may be upset, and result in tremendous outbursts of personal violence. Hence, it may perhaps be said to be a structure that serves to compartmentalize personal violence in time, leading to successions of periods of absence and presence of personal violence.

2. *Structural violence is necessary to abolish personal violence.* This is obviously not true, since personal violence will cease the moment the decision not to practise it is taken. But this is of course begging the question: under what condition is that decision made and really sustained? That structural violence represents an alternative in the sense that much of the "order" obtained by means of (the threat of)

personal violence can also be obtained by (the threat of) structural violence is clear enough. But to state a relation of **necessity** is to go far outside our limited empirical experience.

3. *Personal violence is sufficient to abolish structural violence.* Again, this thesis seems to have a certain limited short-term validity. Personal violence directed against the topdogs in a feudal structure incapacitating them bodily by means of the techniques in Table GT.1, used singly or combined. When the topdogs are no longer there to exercise their roles the feudal structure can clearly no longer function. Hence, just as under 1 above *between*-group structural violence *may* be abolished by this process. But to abolish the *topdogs* in a violent structure is one thing, to abolish the violent *structure* quite another, and it is this *fallacy of misplaced concreteness* that is one of the strongest arguments against the proposition. The new power group may immediately fill the vacancies, retaining the structure, only changing the names of the incumbents and possibly the rationalization of the structure, in which case the structural violence is not even abolished for a short term. Or the structure may re-emerge after some time, because of internal dynamism or because it has after all been firmly imprinted on the minds of the new power-holders and has thus been present all the time in latent form.

4. *Personal violence is necessary to abolish structural violence.* This is, of course, a famous revolutionary proposition with a certain currency. One may argue against it on three grounds: empirically, theoretically and axiologically. *Empirically* one would point to all the cases of structural change decreasing structural violence that seem to take place without personal violence. The counter-argument will be that there were cases with no basic change of the structure, for if there had been a fundamental threat to the power-holders then they would have resorted to personal violence. *Theoretically* one would point to the qualitative difference between the means of personal and structural violence and ask: even if personal violence *may* lead to the abolition of structural violence, is it not likely that some, and possibly also more effective means of changing a structure would be structural, for instance systematic changes of interaction networks, rank profiles etc.? In other words, the belief in the *indispensability of personal violence* could be said, on theoretical grounds, to be a case of *fetishization* of personal violence. And then there is the *axiological* argument: even if personal violence could be seen as indispensable up till today, on empirical and/or theoretical grounds, this would be one more good reason for a systematic search for the conditions under which this indispensability would disappear.

Again our search seems to fail to uncover any absolutes. It is hard to sustain a belief in sufficiency or necessity one way or the other. The two types of violence simply do not seem to be more tightly connected empirically than logically—and as to the latter, the whole exercise is an effort to show that they may be seen as logically independent even though they are continuous with each other: one shades into the other.

But even if one now rejects reduction- ism one way or the other there would still be good reason for focussing research attention more on one kind of violence than on the other: it may always be argued than one is much more important in its consequences than the other. Thus, imagine we were able to calculate the losses incurred by the two forms of violence, or the gains that would accrue to mankind if they could be eliminated. In principle this should not be quite impossible, at least not for the simpler physical forms of violence that show up in terms of mortality, and possibly also in terms of morbidity. Mortality and morbidity rates under the condition of absence of war can usually be calculated relatively well by extrapolation from pre-war and postwar data. It is more difficult for the case of absence of exploitation, but not impossible: we could calculate the levels attained if all available resources were used for the purpose of extending and improving the biological life-span and in addition were distributed in an egalitarian fashion in social space. The costs incurred by violence of one form or the other would then appear as the difference between the potential and the actual, as the definition requires, and the costs can then be compared. One could also imagine calculations of the costs of the joint operation of the two forms of violence.

One significant feature of such calculations, that definitely should have a high priority on the research program of peace research institutes, is that the door would be opened for answers to questions such as whether the costs in terms of personal violence were higher or lower than the gains in reduction of structural violence in, say, the Cuban revolution. The present author would say that they were definitely lower, using comparable Latin American countries as a basis for evaluating the costs of the structural violence under Batista, but in the equation one would of course also have to include the personal violence under Batista and the structural violence under Castro, e.g., in the form of almost complete alienation of the former bourgeoisie, not only as status holders, but as persons. Such statements are impressionistic however, they should be backed up empirically.

But however attractive such calculations may be—for reasons of intellectual curiosity about the dynamics of violence, structural and personal, even to develop much higher levels of theoretical insights in these phenomena than we possess today—this is not the same as accepting cost-benefit analysis in this field as a basis for political action. The point here is not so much that one may have objections to projecting the mathematical "one human life-year = one human life-year," regardless how it is lost or gained, on to the stage of political action, but rather that this type of analysis leads to much too modest goals for political action. Imagine that the general norm were formulated "you shall act politically so as to decrease violence, taking into account both before and after levels of personal and structural violence." A norm of that kind would be blind to possible differences in structural and personal violence when it comes to their potential for getting more violence in the future. But it would also condone action as long as there is any decrease, and only steer political action *downwards* on the violence surface, not lead to a systematic search for the *steepest* gradient possible, even for a descent route hitherto unknown to man.

But equally important is to recall that it is hardly possible to arrive at any general judgment, independent of time and space, as to which type of violence is more important. In space, today, it may certainly be argued that research in the Americas should focus on structural violence, between nations as well as between individuals, and that peace research in Europe should have a similar focus on personal violence. Latent personal violence in Europe may erupt into nuclear war, but the manifest structural violence in the Americas (and not only there) already causes an annual toll of nuclear magnitudes. In saying this, we are of course not neglecting the structural components of the European situation (such as the big power dominance and the traditional exploitation of Eastern Europe by Western Europe) nor are we forgetful of the high level of personal violence in the Americas even though it does not take the form of international warfare (but sometimes the form of interventionist aggression).

5. On the Definition of "Peace" and "Peace Research"

With the distinction between personal and structural violence as basic, violence becomes two-sided, and so does peace conceived of as the absence of violence. *An extended concept of violence leads to an extended concept of peace.* Just as a coin has two sides, one side alone being only one aspect of the coin, not the complete coin, peace also has two sides: *absence of personal violence*, and *absence of structural violence*.[30] We shall refer to them as *negative peace* and *positive peace* respectively.[31]

For brevity the formulations "absence of violence" and "social justice" may perhaps be preferred, using one negative and one positive formulation. The reason for the use of the terms "negative" and "positive" is easily seen: the absence of personal violence does not lead to a positively defined condition, whereas the absence of structural violence is what we have referred to as social justice, which is a positively defined condition (egalitarian distribution of power and resources). Thus, peace conceived this way is not only a matter of control and reduction of the overt use of violence, but of what we have elsewhere referred to as "vertical development."[32] And this means that peace theory is intimately connected not only with conflict theory, but equally with development theory. And peace research, defined as research into the conditions—past, present, and future—of realizing peace, will be equally intimately connected with conflict research and development research; the former often more relevant for negative peace and the latter more relevant for positive peace, but with highly important overlaps.

To justify this way of looking at peace and peace research, let us see where the many efforts to conceive of peace in terms of only *one* of these "sides" or aspects leads us. Such efforts are likely to bring into focus, in theory and indeed in practice, the onesidedness on which they are based and to highlight the need for richer concepts of peace. Here only a very sketchy outline of this type of analysis will be presented, particularly since relations between personal and structural violence were to some extent explored in the preceding section.

Thus, a research emphasis on the reduction of personal violence at the expense of a tacit or open neglect of research on structural violence leads, very easily, to acceptance of "law and order" societies.[33] Personal violence is built into the system as work is built into a compressed spring in a mattress: it only shows when the mattress is disintegrating. And on the other hand there may be a research emphasis

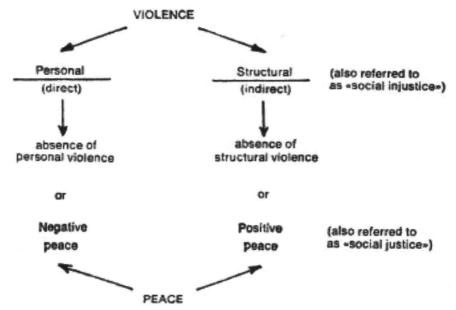

Figure 4.   *"The Extended Concepts of Violence and Peace"*

on righting social wrongs on obtaining social justice at the expense of a tacit or open acceptance and use of personal violence. The short-term costs of personal violence appear as small relative to the costs of continued structural violence. But personal violence tends to breed manifest physical violence, not only from the opponent but also inside one's own group—and the aftermath of violent revolutions generally seems to testify to this.

We may summarize by saying that too much research emphasis on one aspect of peace tends to rationalize extremism to the right or extremism to the left, depending on whether one-sided emphasis is put on "absence of personal violence" or on "social justice." And these two types of extremism are of course not only formally, but also socially closely related and in a dialectic manner: one is often a reaction to the other. When put into practice both may easily develop into well-known social orders where neither of the two aspects of peace are realized: gross social injustice is maintained *by means of* highly manifest personal violence. The regime usually tries to maintain a *status quo*, whether it means forceful maintenance of traditional social injustice that may have lasted for generations, or the forceful maintenance of some new type of injustice brought in by an attempt to overthrow the old system.

If "peace" now is to be interpreted as an effort to play on both, one may ask: does this not simply mean some kind of "moderate" course, some effort to appear "objective" by steering carefully between the two types of extremism outlined above? There is no doubt a danger in this direction. Efforts to avoid both personal and structural violence may easily lead to accept one of them, or even both. Thus, if the choice is between righting a social wrong by means of personal violence or doing nothing, the latter may in fact mean that one supports the forces behind social injustice. And conversely: the use of personal violence may easily mean that one gets neither long-term absence of violence nor justice.

Or, we can put the argument in a slightly different framework. If we are interested in e.g., social justice but also in the avoidance of personal violence, does this not constrain our choice of means so much that it becomes meaningful only in certain societies? And particularly in societies that have already realized many social-liberal values, so that there is considerable freedom of speech and assembly, and organizations for effective articulation of political interests? Whereas we are literally immobilized in highly repressive societies, or "more openly repressive societies" as modern critics of liberalism might say? Thus, if our choice of means in the fight against structural violence is so limited by the non-use of personal violence that we are left without anything to do in highly repressive societies, whether the repression is latent or manifest, then how valuable is this recipe for peace?

To this we may answer along many lines.

One answer would be to reject the definition given above of peace, because we want "peace" to refer to something attainable and also in fact attained, not to something as Utopian as *both* absence of personal violence *and* social justice. We may then slant the definition of "peace" in the direction of absence of personal violence, *or* absence of structural violence, depending on where our priorities are. In our definition above we have suggested that the two enter in a completely symmetrial manner: there is no temporal, logical or evaluative preference given to one or the other. Social justice is not seen as an adornment to peace as absence of personal violence, nor is absence of personal violence seen as an adornment to peace as social justice. Unfortunately, on the printed page, one has to appear before the other or above the other, and this is often interpreted as priority (compare the recent debate on whether a certain group's political slogan should be "peace and freedom" or "freedom and peace"). Actually, somebody should invent some way of printing so that absolutely no connotation of priority is implied.

This approach presupposes that we somehow are attracted by the term "peace" and would like to let that word express our goal rather than some other word. But another answer would be to give up the word "peace" and simply state our interest in one or both of the two values and then try to do our best along both dimensions, so to speak. This appears less satisfactory, because of the generally widespread use of the term "peace"—so widespread and so generally acknowledged that it possibly presents some kind of substitute in this secular age for feelings of devotion and community that in former ages were invoked by reference to religious concepts. In fact, "peace" has indeed religious overtones to many, and that this probably contributes to the use of the word "peace" as a carrier of feelings of universal love and brotherhood in our days. Hence, in spite of the many possibilities for semantic confusion, we would argue in favor of retaining the term "peace."

A third answer would be to combine the first two approaches, to talk little or at least not very loudly about peace—for fear of blushing, among other reasons—and to give up one of the two goals, absence of violence and social justice. This attitude, found today in several circles, may be commended for its honesty and lack of hypocrisy. Neither the "law and order" racist or primitive capitalist society, nor the openly repressive post-revolutionary society is presented as realizations of "peace," but as social orders where one made a choice between two evils, direct violence or social injustice, using what was seen as the lesser evil to drive out the greater evil (possibly ending up with both).

And then there is a fourth approach which will be preferred in this context. It may be expressed as follows:

Both values, *both* goals are significant, and it is probably a disservice to man to try, in any abstract way, to say that one is more important than the other. As mentioned, it is difficult to compare the amount of suffering and harm that has been caused by personal or structural violence; they are *both* of such an order of magnitude that comparisons appear meaningless. Moreover, they *seem* often to be coupled in such a way that it is very difficult to get rid of both evils; more likely the Devil is driven out with Beelzebub. In view of this difficulty, so amply testified through human history, we should be very careful in passing moral judgments too readily on those who fail to realize both goals. To realize one of them is no mean achievement either, particularly if we consider the number of social orders and regimes that realize neither.

But the view that one cannot meaningfully work for both absence of personal violence and for social justice can also be seen as essentially pessimistic, as some sort of intellectual and moral capitulationism.[34] First of all, there are many forms of social action available today that combine both in a highly meaningful way. We are thinking of the tremendously rapid growth in the field of nonviolent action, both in dissociative nonviolence that serves to keep parties apart so that the weaker part can establish autonomy and identity of its own, and associative nonviolence that can serve to bring them together when a basis for equal non-exploitative partnership exists.[35] We are thinking of all that is known about the theories of symmetric, egalitarian organization in general.[36] We are thinking of the expanding theory of vertical development, of participation, decentralization, codecision. And we are thinking of the various approaches to arms control and disarmament issues, although they are perhaps of more marginal significance.[37] This is not the place to develop these themes; that will be done in other contexts. But secondly, once the double goal has been stated—that peace research is concerned with the conditions for promoting both aspects of peace—there is no reason to believe that the future will not bring us richer concepts and more forms of social action that combine absence of personal violence with fight against social injustice once sufficient activity is put into research and practice.[38] There are more than enough people willing to sacrifice one for the other—it is by aiming for both that peace research can make a real contribution.

Notes

*The present article (PRIO-publication No. 23–9—is a revised version of talks originally presented by the author at the Oslo Conference on the plan for a peacemaker's academy, organized jointly by the Peacemakers' Academy Committee, Vermont and the International Peace Research Institute, Oslo, 14–17 November 1968; at the peace research seminar organized by the Gandhian Institute of Studies, Varanasi, 8–9 March 1969; at the meeting of the Japan Peace Research Group Tokyo, 27 March 1969; at a seminar organized by the Seminar for Peace and Conflict Research, Lund, 26 April 1969, and at the international seminar organized by the Centro Studi e Iniziative, Partinico, 3–4 May 1969. I am indebted to the organizers of these meetings, Randolph Major, Sugata Dasgupta, Hisako Ukita, Håkan Wiberg and Danilo Dolci and to many participants for highly stimulating comments and criticism. But special gratitude should be expressed to Herman Schmid, Lund University, Sweden, for his lucid and important criticism of some concepts of peace research, in *Journal of Peace Research*, 1968, pp. 217–232. Although I agree neither with his critique nor with his proposals, and feel that his way of presenting my own views is misleading, there are certainly few persons who have stimulated discussion and rethinking in this fundamental field so much. However, the present article is not a systematic answer to his arguments, but rather an effort, partly stimulated by him, to indicate what to the present author seems to be a fruitful way of thinking about violence, peace and peace research.

1. This point is elaborated further in *Theories of Peace* (forthcoming), Chapter 1.1.

2. This, of course, is not strictly true. It was not on Fascist or Nazi agendas, nor is it on the agenda of contemporary revolutionary thinking. However, even for these cases violence is not an end, but rather a means to overcome obstacles impeding the realization of a future order, the millennium, the communist society, etc.; these future orders do not seem to contain violence. But this is hardly a universal human invariant. The Viking paradise looks violent, and warlike tribes/societies like the Pathans would probably put complete absence of violence last on the agenda, if at all.

3. But what if a social order is such that some people live well in solid, concrete houses and others in shacks that crumble under the first quake, killing the inhabitants? In other words, even if the natural disaster is unavoidable, differential social impact may have been avoidable. This may certainly justify the use of the term "structural violence" for such differential housing standards, not only because of differential exposure to earthquakes (as in the earthquake zone in Western Sicily), but because of implications for differential health standards in general, educational possibilities, and so on and so forth. Whether it justifies the use of such epithets as "violent" or "assassin" to the people sustaining such social structures, or (which is not quite the same) to the people on top of such social structures, is another matter.

4. Since the potential level depends not only on the use and distribution of available resources, but also on insight, a crucial person in this picture is the scientist or anyone who opens for new insights into how old, or new, resources may be utilized. In other words, anyone who makes possible what was formerly not feasible raises the level of potentiality. But the level may also be lowered, perhaps not so often because insight is forgotten (although history is full of such cases too) as because resources become more scarce—for instance due to pollution, hoarding, over-utilization, etc. In short, we make no assumption about the shape of the potential realization curve through time, nor do we make any assumption about the corresponding curve for actual realization. In particular we reject the optimistic assumption according to which both curves are monotonously increasing and with a decreasing gap so that there is asymptotic convergence of the actual to the potential, "until the potentialities of man are fully realized." This is an ideology, usually in the form of an underlying assumption, not a description or reality. As Bertrand Russell writes (*Autobiography*, Vol. III, p. 221): "When I was young, Victorian optimism was taken for granted. It was thought that freedom and prosperity would spread gradually throughout the world by an orderly process, and it was hoped that cruelty, tyranny and injustice would continually diminish. Hardly anyone was haunted by the fear of great wars. Hardly anyone thought of the nineteenth century as à brief interlude between past

and future barbarism." In short, let us make no assumptions, but focus on the causes for a discrepancy between the curves, admitting for a lag in the application and distribution of new insights; whether they are called technological or social.

5. However, it is by no means obvious how potential life-span should be defined. One cannot use the age at death of the oldest person dying today or this year; this may be too low because he does not benefit from possible advances in hygiene etc. made too late to have an impact on him, or not yet made, and it may be too high because he is specially advantaged genetically. But the average of the p% of the social order benefiting fully from insight and resources already available should at least yield a basis for an estimate of what is possible today.

6. In an article "On the Meaning of Nonviolence," *Journal of Peace Research*, 1965, pp. 228–257 the concept of influence is basic in an effort to analyze the difference between violence and nonviolence, and positive and negative versions of the latter. In the present article the focus is on a typology of violence, not on a typology of nonviolence.

7. Ibid., pp. 230–234.

8. Loc. cit.

9. This is a recurrent theme in Herbert Marcsue, *One-dimensional Man* (Boston Press, 1968), especially Part I, "One-dimensional Society."

10. This is a recurrent theme in much of the analysis of violence in the United States. Violence against property is seen as training, the first window-pane crushed to pieces is also a blow against the bourgeois in oneself, a liberation from former constraints, an act of communication signalling to either camp a new belongingness and above all a rejection of tacit rules of the game. "If they can do that to property, what can they do to persons."

11. It was pointed out by Herman Kahn (at a seminar at PRIO, May 1969) that middle class students and lower class police may have highly different relations to property: as something highly replaceable for the middle class student in an affluent society, as something difficult to attain for a lower class Irish cop. What to one is a relatively unproblematic act of communication may to the other be sacriligeous, particularly since students probably aspire to mobility and freedom unfettered by property ties.

12. The term "institutional violence" is often sometimes used, but we have preferred "structural" since it is often of a more abstract nature and not anything that can be traced down to a particular institution. Thus, if the police are highly biased the term "institutionalized violence" may be appropriate, but this is a highly concrete case. There may be violence built into a structure without any police institution at all, as will be developed in the next section.

13. This is clearly expressed by Stokeley Carmichael in "Black Power" (*The Dialectics of Liberation*, David Cooper ed., London Penguin, p. 151, 1968): "It is important to this discussion of racism to make a distinction between the two types: individual racism and institutional racism. The first type consists of overt acts by individuals, with usually immediate results of the death of victims, or the traumatic and violent destruction of property. This type can be recorded on TV cameras and can frequently be observed in the process of commission.

"The second type is less overt, far more subtle, less identifiable in terms of specific individuals committing the acts, but is no less destructive of human life. The second type is more the overall operation of established and respected forces in the society and thus does not receive the condemnation that the first type receives. His distinction individual/institutional is the same as our personal/structural. But we prefer the term 'personal' because the person sometimes acts on behalf of groups, whereas 'individual' may be interpreted as the opposite of 'group.' But particularly in the context Carmichael discusses group violence is immensely important—the mob lynching as opposed to the individual murderer—but that does not make the violence institutional. It still satisfies all the other criteria, e.g., it consists of 'overt acts by individuals,' 'can be recorded on TV-cameras' (as in a war), etc."

14. The difficulty here, as often pointed out, is that international statistics usually reflect averages and not dispersions, ranking nations in order of average achievement, not in terms of degree of equality achieved in distribution. One reason is of course that such data are not readily available, but that is only begging the question *why* they are not available. One reason for that again may be that it upsets ranking orders and reveals less positive aspects of social orders used to define themselves as world leaders, but that is hardly a sufficient explanation. Another reason might be that the problem is simply not sufficiently clearly defined, nor is it regarded as sufficiently feasible or indeed desirable to decrease dispersions. When this becomes sufficiently crystallized it will also find expressions in international statistics.

15. The remark in the preceding note holds *a fortiori* here: not only is it difficult to present any measure of dispersion of power, it is difficult enough to measure power at all, except in the purely formal sense of voting rights. He who comes up with a really meaningful measure in this field will contribute greatly to crystallization of political fighting as well as administrative endeavors.

16. Again the same: the publications of these correlations would contribute significantly to increased awareness, since the current ideology is precisely that correlations between achieved and ascribed ranks should be as low as possible, preferably zero.

17. Economic sanctions occupy interesting middle position here. They are clearly violent in their ultimate consequences, which are starvation etc., but the hope is of course that they are slow enough to permit capitulation much before that. At the same time they are clearly also built into the structure, for the most vulnerable countries are also the countries that tend to be at the bottom of the international stratification in general: high in dependence on trade, low in commodity dispersion and low on trade partner dispersion. See Johan Galtung, "On the Effects of International Economic Sanctions, With Examples from the Case of Rhodesia," *World Politics*, 1967, pp. 387–416.

18. One expression of what is meant by social justice is found in declarations of human rights, where a number of norms about equality are stated. However, they very often suffer from the deficiency that they are personal more than structural. They refer to what individuals can do or can have, not to whom or what decides what they can do or have; they refer to distribution of resources, not to power over the distribution of resources. In other words, human rights as usually conceived of are quite compatible with paternalism whereby power-holders distribute anything but ultimate power over the distributions, so that equalization without any change in the power structure is obtained. It is almost painful to see how few seem to realize that much of the current anti-establishment anti-authority revolt is precisely about this: concessions are not enough, not even equality is enough, it is the way in which decisions about distribution are arrived at and implemented that is basic. But there is little reason to believe that this will not also in due time crystallize into some kind of human right and be added to that list of philosophical and political battlefields.

19. Exploitation also has an ambiguity which we actually have exploited in this section. There seems to be a liberal interpretation in terms of distribution and inequality, and a Marxist interpretation in terms of power, particularly over the use of the surplus produced by others (in a capitalist economy). Clearly one can have one type of exploitation without the other.

20. I am indebted to Hans Rieger and other participants in the seminar at the Gandhian Institute of Studies for pointing out the possibility of using the manifest-latent distinction in connection with both personal and structural violence.

21. This is a point where Gandhi and Mao Tse-Tung would agree in theory, although in practice they are both so dominant in their organizations that it probably was not too meaningful to speak of real egalitarianism.

22. See Note 13 for Carmichael's analysis. The basic point in our communication structure is of course that personal violence much more easily "can be recorded on TV cameras," although this is not correct strictly speaking. There is no intrinsic reason why structural violence should not be registered on TV cameras; in fact, really good cameramen delight in doing exactly this. But the concept of *news* is against its prominent display; that concept is in itself geared to personal rather than structural violence. For an analysis, see Johan Galtung and Mari Holmboe Ruge, "The Structure of Foreign News," *Journal of Peace Research*, 1965, pp. 64–91, especially on person versus structure-oriented news.

23. Herman Schmid seems to be very correct when he points out (op. cit., p. 217) that peace research grew out of a certain historical condition and the basic concepts were colored by that condition. No doubt this explains some of the emphasis on *symmetric conflict*, and we would add, on personal violence both because of war memories and war threats. However, the threats of a major war in the North Atlantic area failed to materialize, economic growth continued, but exploitation remained constant or increased. So, towards the end of the "sixties the focus changes;" for some persons to a completely new focus (as when Schmid and others would argue in favor of conflict creation research, of polarization and revolution research), for others (as the present author) to an extension of focus, as argued in the present article.

24. Thus, it is almost unbelievable how little the gap between rich and poor seems to be affected by the general increase, within nations and between nations.

25. This is the general theme in Johan Galtung, "A Structural Theory of Integration," *Journal of Peace Research*, 1968, pp. 375–395.

26. One of these implications is of course that it enhances his power: he monopolizes information from the level above and can convert this into power at his own level. Another implication is that he is very often untrained for or unfit for the task to be performed at the higher level since his frame of reference all the time has been level n-1. The manager of a certain type of products suddenly finds himself on the board of a big business corporation doing quite different things; the leading nation in a regional alliance suddenly finds itself responsible for world affairs and forced to think within a completely new frame of reference, and so on.

27. We have not discussed the possibility of denying rank differences completely by making everybody equal, since there seem always to be some differences that elude equalization attempts and these differences tend to become significant. Make everybody citizens with equal voting rights, and differences in style of life become overwhelming, abolish class differences on trains and the upper classes go by plane, and so on.

28. Few have expressed this image as well as Eldridge Cleaver in *Soul on Ice* (London: Cape, 1969, p. 92):

"Both police and the armed forces follow orders. Orders. Orders flow from the top down. Up there, behind closed doors, in antechambers, in conference rooms, gavels bang on the tables, the tinkling of silver decanters can be heard as ice water is poured by well fed, conservatively dressed men in horn-rimmed glasses, fashionably dressed American widows with rejuvenated faces and tinted hair, the air permeated with the square humor of Bob Hope jokes. Here all the talking is done, all the thinking, all the deciding.

Gray rabbits of men scurry forth from the conference room to spread decisions throughout the city, as News. Carrying out orders is a job, a way of meeting the payments on the house, a way of providing for one's kiddies. In the armed forces it is also a duty, patriotism. "Not to do so is treason."

29. See Note 11 for Kahn's analysis, where he added that fighting with fists would be about as natural for the Irish cops as it is unnatural for the upper middle class student, and fighting with words as natural for that student as it is unnatural for the cop. Hence, when the student destroys property and heaps abuse on the police he challenges the police much beyond the tolerance level, and the police respond with the reaction they know, violence; a reaction for which the students are untrained. One does not need structural explanations to account for an outburst of violence in such cases. But one could ask why such people are in the police department, and one explanation can supplement rather than supersede another.

30. This coin metaphor, of course, is not to suggest that one side excludes the other. Indeed, as pointed out so many times in the preceding section: a given social order may exhibit both, one or (perhaps) neither of them. The metaphor applies to the conceptualization of peace, not to the empirical world.

31. Of course, I am very much aware of changes in my own presentation of these concepts, just as I am confident that new formulations will follow in the wake of those presented here. Whereas "negative peace" remains fairly constant, meaning "absence of violence," I think it gains from the precision given to "violence" in that context, a "personal violence." But "positive peace" is constantly changing (as is "positive health" in medical science). I used to see it in terms of integration and cooperation ("An Editorial," *JPR*, 1964, pp. 1–4), but now agree fully with Herman Schmid that this expresses a much too integrated and symmetric view of conflict groups, and probably reflects the East-West conflict or a certain ideology in connection with that conflict. I would now identify "positive peace" mainly with "social justice," the latter taken in the double sense of this article— but I think one could also be open to other candidates for inclusion since the definition given of violence is broad enough also to point in other directions. This is to some extent attempted in section 1.3 of *Theories of Peace*. Moreover, I think Schmid is basically right (op. cit. p. 221) in saying that there is a tendency to focus on negative peace because consensus is more easily obtained—but I share his rejection of that tendency. To reveal and unmask the subtle mechanisms of structural violence and explore the conditions for their removal or neutralization is at least as important, although comparisons of the two types of violence in terms of priorities seems a little bit like discussing whether medical research should focus on cancer or heart diseases. And to this should be added, emphatically, that a discipline fully satisfied with its own foundations and definition is probably a dead discipline. Fundamental debate and debate over fundamentals are the signs of health, not of disease. These issues are difficult, and we shall make progress only through more practice in analyzing them and more praxis in working with them.

32. In *Theories of Development*, forthcoming.

33. Thus, there is little doubt that in general peace research (Schmid, op. cit., p. 222) in this decade that has passed since it was launched has met with more approval from the north-western establishment in the world than from other quarters, but so has cancer research. From this it does not follow that peace research is meaningless to the third world and to revolutionary forces. The same skewed distribution can be found almost anywhere, due to the skewed distribution of world resources and the generally feudal structure of the world. But Schmid is certainly right in setting peace research in a social setting: "who will pay for it," and "who will be able to implement advice from peace researcher" are basic questions. I only fail to see that there should be any implicit reason why peace research should fall into the arms of the establishment more than into other arms not to mention be able to retain considerable autonomy in its pursuits. This presupposes an academic structure that does not steer all research into the arms of the power-holders, left or right,

but leaves the road open for pursuits of insights into the mechanisms behind any kind of violence, any kind of obstacle to human self-realization.

34. Thus, peace research is seen here as an effort to promote the realization of *values*. To what extent these values coincide or not with the interests of certain *groups* is another matter. Hence, peace research could not be identified with the ideology of a group unless that group professed the same values. It ia also an open question whether group identification with these values will in fact serve to promote these values.

35. Some of this is explored in "On the Meaning of Nonviolence," and infinitely much more can be done in this direction. However, the important thing seems to be that there is no reason whatsoever why peace research should be tied to study of symmetric conflict only, and to integrative, or as we prefer to say, "associative" (integrative being too strong a term) approaches. Any effort to explore structural violence will lead to awareness of asymmetric conflict, between parties highly unequal in capabilities—and I think it is unfair to state that this is neglected in the type of peace research carried out at the International Peace Research Institute in Oslo. The terms "top dog" and "underdog" may be unfamiliar and even be resented by those who prefer to do this research in a Marxist tradition and jargon, but it is nevertheless an effort. More precisely, the effort has been to understand better the *structure* of structural violence, one little indication of which is given in section 3 of this article. And there is no implicit reason why the remedy should be in associative policies only. On the contrary, I tend to feel in general that associative policies are for equals, i.e. for symmetric conflict, whereas polarization and dissociative policies are much better strategies for exploited groups. This is also reflected in the doubleness of nonviolent strategies, all themes to be more fully developed in *Theories of Conflict* (forthcoming). When Schmid says (op. cit., p. 219) that peace research "should explain . . . how latent conflicts are manifested—/and/how the present international ystem is seriously challenged or even broken down" he seems to betray the same type of onesidedness that he accuses peace research of—interest in controlling manifest conflicts only, in bringing about integration, in formulating problems in terms meaningful to international and supranational institutions. But this onesidedness will almost inevitably result if research shall be geared to serve the interests of specific groups, high or low, instead of the promotion of values. It is as hard to believe that disintegration, polarization, dissociation is always the best strategy as it is to believe the opposite.

But this seems to be closely related to Schmid's conflictology (op. cit., pp. 224–228), where he seems to believe that I have a subjectivistic conception of conflict. If there is anything the conflict triangle purports to achieve it is exactly the opposite: the definition of conflict independently of attitudes and behavior, and also independently of perceptions of the situation held by the parties (as different from their attitudes to each other). To me, conflict is incompatibility of goals, but how these goals are established is a quite different matter. To ask the parties for their perception of what they pursue and what, if anything, stands in the way is one, but only one approach. I have nothing against definitions in terms of "interests" the concept of "goal" is wide enough to encompass. The difficulty is, as Schmid readily and frankly admits (op. cit. p. 227) to "decide what the interests are" and I share with him the idea that "this is a challenge rather than a reason to abandon the idea of an interest definition of conflict." But I feel these interests have to be postulated, as I think Marx to a large extent did, and then one has to explore the implications. I also think they can be seen as expressions of values, but not necessarily held by the actor, nor necessarily held by the investigator, just as postulated values. Thus, if one feels it is contrary to the interests of children, as autonomous human beings, to accept the tie as the children *of* their biological parents, then there is certainly an incompatibility in the present family system: parents have interests as owners incompatible with the children's interests as self-owners. The only difference between this example and Schmid's master-slave example is that he gives a paradigm for a conflict of the past, I a paradigm for a conflict of the future, and moreover for a conflict I think will be manifested fairly soon, in line with the general wave towards defeudalization of the social order. And I certainly agree with Schmid that polarization will here be a part of the solution.

36. For an effort in this direction, see Johan Galtung, *Cooperation in Europe* (Strasbourg: Council of Europe, 1968).

37. An effort to give some reasons why are found in "Two Approaches to Disarmament: The Legalist and the Structuralist," *Journal of Peace Research* 1967, pp. 161–195.

38. And it is of course not necessary that all or most or much of this sails under the flag of "peace research" or any other flag for that matter—only the slightly totalitarian minded would be inclined to feel so. What is important is that it is done, and that there is contact between different approaches so that they and others can benefit from ideological and institutional pluralism.

Negotiation

Edward Wertheim

Edward Wertheim received his PhD in Organizational Behavior at Yeshiva University in New York. He now works as an Associate Professor within Northeastern University's School of Business. He teaches negotiation, organizational behavior, and mediation. Outside of the United States, Wertheim has taught in Vietnam, France, Singapore, Hungary, Egypt, and Belgium. Wertheim also works as a professional mediator.

Wertheim's piece offers a comprehensive look at negotiation as a strategy to approach conflicts. He makes sure to point out that conflicts are not just snapshots but an ongoing part of life. The two types of negotiation that are foundational to understanding the practice are the *distributive approach* and the *integrative approach*. The distributive approach assumes that there is a fixed amount, number, or "pie" that is being negotiated and that when one person gains in the process, the other person inherently loses (i.e., win-lose). In the integrative approach, it is assumed that the interests of both parties will be considered and that compromise will lead to a mutually beneficial outcome (i.e., win-win). The model of negotiation asks that practitioners understand the goals of each side, moving away from strong "positions" or stances and move to negotiating each parties' underlying "interests" or that which they value.

Negotiation is a strategy that was largely employed as the conflict resolution field emerged, exemplified by Cold War–era strategies to avoid nuclear annihilation. Because conflict during this time was characterized by interstate conflict, negotiations remained at the level of state leaders, taking into account state interests. In considering Epoch One, this kind of top-down strategy to approaching conflict proliferated; however, the outcomes did not necessarily produce sustained peace. The model as it was used during that time was not the idealized version described by Wertheim; rather, it was used to ensure the legitimacy of self-interest and dominance at all cost. Historical approaches to negotiation were anchored in myths that over time have been proven ineffective but still operate as foundational ideas widely accepted in society. One of those myths is that in order to get the most optimal outcome, one needs to be hard-hitting, unwavering, and self-interested.

Questions to consider: Where do you negotiate in your daily life? Where, if you could negotiate better, might you dramatically improve your situation or the situation of your organization? In what kind of conflict might negotiations *not* prove useful or might even provoke greater unrest?

Negotiations and Resolving Conflict

Edward Wertheim

In a successful negotiation, everyone wins. The objective should be agreement, not victory.

Every desire that demands satisfaction and every need to be met is at least potentially an occasion for negotiation; whenever people exchange ideas with the intention of changing relationships, whenever they confer for agreement, they are negotiating.

Introduction

(Suggestion: This guide will be easier to follow if you think about a specific negotiation or conflict situation you have recently been involved in.)

In the course of a week, we are all involved in numerous situations that need to be dealt with through negotiation; this occurs at work, at home, and at recreation. A conflict or negotiation situation is one in which there is a conflict of interests or what one wants isn't necessarily what the other wants and where both sides prefer to search for solutions, rather than giving in or breaking-off contact.

Few of us enjoy dealing with conflicts—either with bosses, peers, subordinates, friends, or strangers. This is particularly true when the conflict becomes hostile and when strong feelings become involved. Resolving conflict can be mentally exhausting and emotionally draining.

But it is important to realize that conflict that requires resolution is neither good nor bad. There can be positive and negative outcomes as seen in the box below. It can be destructive but can also play a productive role for you personally and for your relationships—both personal and professional. The important point is to manage the conflict, not to suppress conflict and not to let conflict escalate out of control. Many of us seek to avoid conflict when it arises but there are many times when we should use conflict as a critical aspect of creativity and motivation.

Table WE.1.   Outcomes of Conflict

Potential Positive Outcomes of Conflict	Potential Negative Outcomes of Conflict
• can motivate us to try harder—to "win" • can increase commitment, enhance group loyalty • increased clarity about the problem • can lead to innovative breakthroughs and new approaches • conflict can clarify underlying problems, facilitate change • can focus attention on basic issues and lead to solution • increased energy level; making visible key values • involvement in conflict can sharpen our approaches to bargaining, influencing, competing	• can lead to anger, avoidance, sniping, shouting, frustration, fear of failure, sense of personal inadequacy • withholding of critical information • lower productivity from wasteful conflict • careers can be sidetracked; relationships ruinied • disrupted patterns of work • consume huge amount of time-loss of productivity

You will be constantly negotiating and resolving conflict throughout all of your professional and personal life. Given that organizations are becoming less hierarchical, less based on positional authority, less based on clear boundaries of responsibility and authority, it is likely that conflict will be an even greater component of organizations in the future. Studies have shown that negotiation skills are among the most significant determinants of career success. While negotiation is an art form to some degree, there are specific techniques that anyone can learn. Understanding these techniques and developing your skills will be a critical component of your career success and personal success.

Major Causes of Conflict

Opposing interests (or what we think are opposing interests) are at the core of most conflicts. In a modern complex society, we confront these situations many times a day. The modern organization adds a whole new group of potential causes of conflict that are already present:

- competition over scarce resources, time
- ambiguity over responsibility and authority
- differences in perceptions, work styles, attitudes, communication problems, individual differences
- increasing interdependence as boundaries between individuals and groups become increasingly blurred
- reward systems: we work in situations with complex and often contradictory incentive systems
- differentiation: division of labor which is the basis for any organization causes people and groups to see situations differently and have different goals

- equity versus equality: continuous tension exists between equity (the belief that we should be rewarded relative to our relative contributions) and equality (belief that everyone should receive the same or similar outcomes).

The Five Modes of Responding to Conflict

It is useful to categorize the various responses we have to conflict in terms of two dimensions:

1. How important or unimportant it is to satisfy our needs and
2. How important or unimportant it is to satisfy the other person's needs.

Answering this questions results in the following five modes of conflict resolution. None is these is "right" or "wrong." There are situations where any would be appropriate. For example, if we are cut off driving to work, we may decide "avoidance" is the best option. Other times "avoidance" may be a poor alternative. Similarly, collaboration may be appropriate sometimes but not at other times.

COMPETITION: DISTRIBUTIVE (WIN-LOSE) BARGAINING

Satisfying your needs is important; satisfying the other's needs isn't important to you

COLLABORATION: INTEGRATIVE (WIN-WIN)

Satisfying both your needs and the other's needs is important

COMPROMISING:

Satisfying both your needs and the other's are moderately important

AVOIDING:

You are indifferent about satisfying either your needs or the other's needs: no action is likely

ACCOMMODATING:

Simply yield (it doesn't matter to you and it matters to the other person)

In general, most successful negotiators start off assuming *collaborative (integrative)* or win-win negotiation. Most good negotiators will try for a win-win or aim at a situation where both sides feel they won. Negotiations tend to go much better if both sides perceive they are in a win-win situation or both sides approach the negotiation wanting to "create value" or satisfy both their own needs and the other's needs.

We will focus on the two most problematic types: *collaborative* (integrative) and *Competitive* (distributive).

Of the two the more important is *collaborative* since most of your negotiation and conflict resolution in your personal and professional life will (or should) be of this nature. This is because most negotiation involves situations where we want or need an ongoing relationship with the other person. While it is important to develop skills in "competitive" bargaining (e.g., when buying a car), or skills that allow us to satisfy our concerns while ignoring the other's goals, this approach has many negative consequences for both our personal lives and for our professional careers especially if we are to have an ongoing relationship with the other person . . .

> *The key to successful negotiation is to shift the situation to a "win-win" even if it looks like a "win-lose" situation. Almost all negotiation have at least some elements of win-win. Successful negotiations often depend on finding the win-win aspects in any situation. Only shift to a win-lose mode if all else fails.*

Reducing Conflict that Already Exists

Organizations also take steps to reduce conflict. The following list suggests some of these ways:

- physical separation
- hierarchy (the boss decides)
- bureaucratic approaches (rules, procedures)
- integrators and third-party intervention
- negotiation
- rotating members
- interdependent tasks and superordinate goals ("We are all in this together . . .")
- intergroup and interpersonal training

Rational versus The Emotional Components of Negotiation

All negotiations involve two levels: *a rational decision making* (substantive) process and a *psychological* (emotional) process. The outcome of a negotiation is as likely to be a result of the psychological elements as it is the rational element. In most cases, the failure of two people to reach the "optimal" resolution or best alternative stems from intangible factors such as:

Psychological Factors that will Affect Negotiations

- how comfortable each feels about conflict
- how each perceives or mis-perceives the other

- the assumptions each makes about the other and the problem
- the attitudes and expectations about the other
- the decisions each makes about trust, about how important "winning" is, how important it is to avoid conflict, how much one likes or dislikes the other; how important it is to "not look foolish."

Understanding the "rational" part of the negotiation is relatively easy. Understanding the "psychological" part is more difficult. We need to understand ourselves and our opponents psychologically. Failure to understand these psychological needs and issues is at the root of most unsuccessful negotiations.

This is made more difficult because norms in most organizations discourage open expression of negative personal feelings. Thus intense emotional conflicts are often expressed and rationalized as substantive issues. People often drum up disagreements on trivial issues to provide justification for an emotional conflict with another individual (Ware and Barnes).

BASIC ISSUES IN CONFLICT MANAGEMENT

- what are the personal and organizational consequences of the conflict
- what are the behavioral patterns that characterize the conflict
- substantive issues versus emotional issues
- apparent underlying and background conditions leading to the conflict welcome. . . .

The Two Most Important Kinds of Bargaining: Distributive (win-lose) versus Integrative (win-win)

All bargaining situations can be divided into two categories:

DISTRIBUTIVE (ALSO CALLED COMPETITIVE, ZERO SUM, WIN-LOSE, OR CLAIMING VALUE).

In this kind of bargaining, one side "wins" and one side "loses." In this situation there are fixed resources to be divided so that the more one gets, the less the other gets. In this situation, one person's interests oppose the others. In many "buying" situations, the more the other person gets of your money, the less you have left. The dominant concern in this type of bargaining is usually maximizing one's own interests. Dominant strategies in this mode include manipulation, forcing, and withholding information. This version is also called "claiming value" since the goal in this type of situation is to increase your own value and decrease your opponent's.

Integrative (collaborative, win-win or creating value).

In this kind of bargaining, there is a variable amount of resources to be divided and both sides can "win." The dominant concern here is to maximize joint outcomes. An example is resolving a different opinion about where you and a friend want to go to dinner. Another example is a performance appraisal situation with a subordinate or resolving a situation of a subordinate who keeps coming in late to work. Dominant strategies in this mode include cooperation, sharing information, and mutual problem solving. This type is also called "creating value" since the goal here is to have both sides leave the negotiating feeling they had greater value than before.

It needs to be emphasized that many situations contain elements of *both distributive and integrative bargaining.* For example, in negotiating a price with a customer, to some degree your interests oppose the customer (you want a higher price; he wants a lower one) but to some degree you want your interests to coincide (you want both your customer and you to satisfy both of your interests—you want to be happy; you want your customer to be happy). The options can be seen in the table below:

Integrative or Win-Win Bargaining: The Critical Points

- Plan and have a *concrete strategy:* Be clear on what is important to you
- Separate *people* from the problem
- Emphasize *win-win* solutions
- Focus on *interests,* not positions
- *Create Options* for Mutual Gain: Generate a variety of possibilities before deciding what to do
- Aim for an outcome be based on some *objective standard*
- Consider the other party's *situation*
- Know your *BATNA* (Best Alternative to a Negotiated Alternative)
- Pay a lot of attention to the *flow* of negotiation
- Take the *Intangibles* into account
- Use *Active Listening* Skills

Do some thinking ahead of time:

Planning for the Negotiation

Before the negotiation it is helpful to plan. Know whether you are in a win-win or win-lose situation.

Be sure of your goals, positions, and underlying interests. Try to figure out the best resolution you can expect, what is a fair and reasonable deal and what is a minimally acceptable deal. What information do you have and what do you need. What are your competitive advantages and disadvantages? What are the other's advantages and disadvantages? Give some thought to your strategy.

It is very important to be clear on what is important to you. Be clear about your real goals and real issues and try to figure out the other person's real goals and issues. Too many negotiations fail because people are so worried about being taken advantage of that they forget their needs. People who lose track of their own goals will break off negotiations even if they have achieved their needs because they become more concerned with whether the other side "won."

It is helpful to have a min-max strategy. Have a "walk-away" position. When entering a negotiation or conflict resolution, make sure you have already thought about answers to these questions: *Planning for the negotiation: The min-max approach*

- What is the minimum I can accept to resolve the conflict?
- What is the maximum I can ask for without appearing outrageous?
- What is the maximum I can give away?
- What is the least I can offer without appearing outrageous?
- Try to predict the answers the other person will have to these questions

It is important to know your competitive advantage—your strongest points. Also you need to know the advantages to the other's argument. Similarly, know your weaknesses and the other's weaknesses.

In most conflict resolution or negotiation situations you will have a continuing relationship with the other person so it is important to leave the situation with both sides feeling they have "won." It is very important that the other person doesn't feel that he or she "lost." When the other person loses, the results are often lack of commitment to the agreement or even worse, retaliation. *The most common failure is the failure of negotiating parties to recognize (or search for) the integrative potential in a negotiating problem; beneath hardened positions are often common or shared interests.*

Separate people from the problem

Address problems, not personalities: Avoid the tendency to attack your opponent personally; if the other person feels threatened, he defends his self-esteem and makes attacking the real problem more difficult; separate the people issues from the problem.

Maintain a rational, goal oriented frame of mind: If your opponent attacks you personally, don't let him hook you into an emotional reaction; let the other blow off steam without taking it personally; try to understand the problem behind the aggression.

Emphasize win-win solutions

Even in what appears to be win-lose situations, there are often win-win solutions; look for an integrative solution; create additional alternatives, such as low cost concessions that might have high value to the other person; frame options in terms of the other person's interests; look for alternatives that allow your opponent to declare victory.

Find underlying interests

A key to success is finding the "integrative" issues—often they can be found in underlying interests.

We are used to identifying our own interests, but a critical element in negotiation is to come to understanding the other person's underlying interests and underlying needs. With probing and exchanging information we can find the commonalities between us and minimize the differences that seem to be evident. Understanding these interests is the key to "integrative bargaining." The biggest source of failure in negotiation is the failure to see the "integrative" element of most negotiation. Too often we think a situation is win-lose when it is actually a win-win situation. This mistaken view causes us to often use the wrong strategy. Consider a situation where your boss rates you lower on a performance appraisal than you think you deserve. We often tend to see this as win-lose-either he/she gives in or I give in. There is probably a much higher chance of a successful negotiation if you can turn this to a win-win negotiation.

A key part in finding common interests is the *problem identification.* It is important to define the problem in a way that is mutually acceptable to both sides. This involves depersonalizing the problem so as not to raise the defensiveness of the other person. Thus the student negotiating a problem with a professor is likely to be more effective by defining the problem as "I need to understand this material better" or "I don't understand this" rather than "You're not teaching the material very well."

Use an Objective Standard

Try to have the result be based on some objective standard. Make your negotiated decision based on principles and results, not emotions or pressure; try to find objective criteria that both parties can use to evaluate alternatives; don't succumb to emotional please, assertiveness, or stubborness.

Try to understand the other person: Know his/her situation

Often we tend to focus on our needs, our goals, and our positions. To successfully resolve conflict, it is important to focus also on the other person. We need to figure out what the other's goals, needs, and positions are as well as their underlying interests. We need to think about the personality of the other person, how far we can push, how open or concealed we should make our positions.

Acquire as much information about the other's interests and goals; what are the real needs versus wants; what constituencies must he or she appease? What is her strategy? Be prepared to frame solutions in terms of her interests.

An important part of this is to recognize that people place very different values on issues than ourselves. For example, a clean room may be much more important to you than it is to your roommate. We must understand how the other person sees reality, not just how we see reality.

If through pressure, deception or sheer aggressiveness, we push people to the point where they see themselves as likely to lose, this creates problems. The opponent will retaliate and fight back; losers often lose commitment to their bargain. Also negotiators get reputations that can backfire. Remember that settlements which are most satisfactory and durable are the ones that address the needs of both parties.

Know Your Best Alternative

Try to explore the other side's BATNA and certainly be aware of your own. See if you can change the other person's BATNA. If the other person's BATNA is poor (the alternatives to reaching an agreement with you are unattractive), you are in a better position.

PAYING ATTENTION TO THE FLOW OF NEGOTIATION

Negotiation is a sequence of events

There is a tendency to think about conflict or the negotiating situation as an isolated incident. It is probably more useful to think about conflict as a process, or a complex series of events over time involving both external factors and internal social and psychological factors. Conflict episodes typically are affected by proceeding and in turn produce results and outcomes that affect the conflict dynamics.

A negotiation usually involves a number of steps including the exchange of proposals and counter proposals. In good-faith negotiation, both sides are expected to make offers and concessions. Your goal here is not only to try to solve the problem, but to gain information—information that will enable you to get a clearer notion of what the true issues might be and how your "opponent" sees reality. Through offers and counter offers there should be a goal of a lot of information exchange that might yield a common definition of the problem.

Such an approach suggests the importance of perception—conflict is in the eye of the beholder. Thus, situations which to an outside observer should produce conflict may not if the parties either ignore or choose to ignore the conflict situation. Conversely, people can perceive a conflict situation when in reality there is none.

Next, once aware of the conflict, both parties experience emotional reactions to it and think about it in various ways. These emotions and thoughts are crucial to the course of the developing conflict. For example, a negotiation can be greatly affected if people react in anger perhaps resulting from past conflict.

Then based on the thoughts and emotions that arise in the process of conflict resolution, we formulate specific intentions about the strategies we will use in the negotiation. These may be quite general (e.g., plan to use a cooperative approach) or quite specific (e.g., use a specific negotiating tactic).

Finally, these intentions are translated into behavior. These behaviors in turn elicit some response from the other person and the process recycles.

This approach suggests we pay particular attention to these generalizations:

- Conflict is an ongoing process that occurs against a backdrop of continuing relationships and events;
- Such conflict involves the thoughts, perceptions, memories, and emotions of the people involved; these must be considered.

- Negotiations are like a chess match: have a strategy; anticipate how the other will respond; how strong is your position, and situation; how important is the issue; how important will it be to stick to a hardened position.
- Begin with a positive approach: Try to establish rapport and mutual trust before starting; try for a small concession early.
- Pay little attention to initial offers: these are points of departure; they tend to be extreme and idealistic; focus on the other person's interests and your own goals and principles, while you generate other possibilities.

The Intangibles:

Other elements that affect negotiation

Intangibles are often the key factors in many negotiations. Some of these intangibles are:

- *Personalities:* Be conscious of aspects of your personality such of your own needs and interpersonal style as well as the other person's personality; these factors will play a key role and understanding yourself will be an important factor.
- *Your own personality and style:* How much you trust the person; how free with your emotions; how much you want to conceal or reveal;
- *Physical space:* Sometimes where the negotiation takes place can be important; are we negotiating in a space we are uncomfortable and other is comfortable?
- *Past interaction:* If there is a history of conflict resolution with this person, think about how this history might affect the upcoming negotiation.
- *Time pressure:* Think about whether time pressure will affect the negotiation and whether you need to try to change this variable.
- *Subjective utilities:* Be aware that people place very different values on elements of a negotiation. For example, in negotiating for a job, you may place a high value on location and relatively lower on salary; it is important to be aware of your subjective utilities and try to ascertain the other person's subjective utilities; it is difficult to know in advance or even during the negotiation what a particular outcome will mean to the other party. Finding out what is "valued" is one of the key parts of negotiation.
- *Understand the Context for the Conflict*

What are the important personal and organizational consequences of the conflict? What are possible future consequences?
What behavior patterns characterize the conflict?
What are the substantive issues? Are the issues biased by each side's perceptions and feelings?
What are the underlying or background factors that have lead to the situation and the related feelings, perceptions, and behaviors?

Be an Active Listener

Good communication skills are critical although it is easy to forget them in the "heat of battle." Try to separate the problem from the person. Focus on the problem (e.g., "this accounting concept is unclear to me") not the person (e.g., "you did a lousy job explaining this"). When we tie the person to the problem, the other person gets defensive and communication tends to become very difficult.

Don't: Talk at the other side, focus on the past, blame the other person.

Do: Be an active listener.

> This involves continuously checking to see if you are understanding the other person. Restate the other's position to make sure you are hearing him or her correctly. Focus on the future; talk about what is to be done; tackle the problem jointly.

How can I change what seems like a "win-lose" situation to a "win-win" (or what if the other person doesn't play by these rules?)

There are many advantages to trying to shift a win/lose situation to a win/win. Yet we will be in situations where the other person either doesn't wish to reach a "win-win" or doesn't realize it is in his or her best interest to achieve a collaborative solution. In these situations it is necessary for us to open lines of communication, increasing trust and cooperativeness.

Sometimes conflicts escalate, the atmosphere becomes charged with anger, frustration, resentment, mistrust, hostility, and a sense of futility. Communication channels close down or are used to criticize and blame the other. We focus on our next assault. The original issues become blurred and ill-defined and new issues are added as the conflict becomes personalized. Even if one side is willing to make concessions often hostility prevents agreements. In such a conflict, perceived differences become magnified, each side gets locked into their initial positions and each side resorts to lies, threats, distortions, and other attempts to force the other party to comply with demands.

It is not easy to shift this situation to a win-win but the following lists some techniques that you might use:

- reduce tension through humor, let the other "vent," acknowledge the other's views, listen actively, make a small concession as a signal of good faith
- increase the accuracy of communication; listen hard in the middle of conflict; rephrase the other's comments to make sure you hear them; mirror the other's views
- control issues: search for ways to slice the large issue into smaller pieces; depersonalize the conflict-separate the issues from the people
- establish commonalities: since conflict tends to magnify perceived differences and minimize similarities, look for greater common goals (we are in this together); find a common enemy; focus on what you have in common
- focus less on your position and more on a clear understanding of the other's needs and figure out ways to move toward them

- make a "yesable" proposal; refine their demand; reformulate; repackage; sweeten the offer; emphasize the positives
- find a legitimate or objective criteria to evaluate the solution (e.g., the blue book value of a car)

Some Tricks that Skilled Negotiators Use

We constantly trade-off in negotiations. An example is when a union negotiation trades wage gains for job security. An important ingredient of negotiation is assessing the tradeoffs. In general, we start by identifying the best and worst possible outcomes, and then specify possible increments that trade-offs can reflect, and finally, consider how the increments relate to the key issues.

If we pursue "integrative bargaining," we try to create gains for both parties. An example is offering something less valuable to us but more valuable to the other person (e.g., the other person may highly value payment in cash rather than through financing whereas we may be indifferent to this). The following are ways of creating joint gains.

When to reveal your position: This depends on the other person. It is not a good idea to reveal your minimum position if the other person needs to feel he has worked hard to reach it; the other person may need to feel he or she has worked very hard to move you to your position.

Case from a Workshop on Negotiation

We had to sell a training program to Sue, a former member of our law firm. We knew she needed to purchase a program and she also held a grudge against our firm. Mary heaped abuse on us. I wanted to punch her, but Chuck (my partner) just smiled and began applying some standard negotiating principles.

First, he identified our interests as the selling of a program at a decent price and the maintenance of a good relationship with Mary and her law firm (focus on interests, not positions). Next, he completely ignored Mary's obnoxious personality (separate people from problems). And he offered to sell Mary only the latest program, with a price break for a quick sale (options for mutual gain).

But his most effective technique was the "jujitsu." When the other side pushes, don't push back. When they attack, don't counterattack; rethink their attack as an attack on mutual problems. Two tools are used—ask questions instead of making statements, and respond with prolonged silence in the face of unreason. Chuck used them both, and we completed the sale and got a better price than we had hoped for. Other techniques you can use:

- Broadening the Pie: Create additional resources so that both sides can obtain their major goals
- Nonspecific Compensation: One side gets what it wants and the other is compensated on another issue

- Logrolling: Each party makes concessions on low-priority issues in exchange for concessions on issues that it values more highly
- Cost Cutting: one party gets what it wants; the costs to the other are reduced or eliminated
- Bridging: Neither party gets its initial demands but a new option that satisfies the major interests of both sides are developed

What if I want "to win" and I don't care about the other person's interests (Distributive or win-lose Bargaining)

In this situation, strategy is different than in integrative bargaining. In this mode, one seeks to gain advantage through concealing information, misleading, or using manipulative actions. Of course, these methods have serious potential for negative consequences. Yet even in this type of negotiation, both sides must feel that at the end the outcome was the best that they could achieve and that it is worth accepting and supporting.

Most critical in this mode is to set one's own opening target and resistance points and to learn what the other's starting points, target points, and resistance points are. Typically, the resistance point (the point beyond which a party will not go) is usually unknown until late in negotiation and is often jealously concealed by the other party. This is what you need to find out.

The range between resistance points is typically the bargaining range; if this number is negative, successful negotiation is usually impossible. For example, if you are willing to pay up to $3,000 and the seller is willing to go as low as $2,800, there is a $200 positive spread or bargaining range if the negotiators are skillful enough to figure it out. The goal of a competitive bargaining situation is to get the final settlement to be as close to the other party's resistance point as possible. The basic techniques open to the negotiator to accomplish this include

- influence the other person's belief in what is possible (e.g., a car dealer telling you what your used car is worth)
- learn as much as possible about the other person's position especially with regard to resistance points
- try to convince the other to change his/her mind about their ability to achieve their own goals
- promote your own objectives as desirable, necessary, ethical, or even inevitable.

Is it Ethical to "Lie or Bluff" in Negotiations?

The answer to this question depends on one's values, one's culture, and the situation. What might be acceptable in poker would probably not be acceptable in most business situations. What might be acceptable in Cairo might not be acceptable in Boston. Different cultures and different situations contain inherent "rules" about the degree to which bluffing or misrepresentation is deemed acceptable.

In poker and in general negotiations one is not expected to reveal strength or intentions prematurely. But discretion in making claims and statements should not be confused with misrepresentation. In general, in our culture, our "rules" forbid and should penalize outright lying, false claims, bribing an opponent, stealing secrets, or threatening an opponent. While there may be a fine line between legitimate and illegitimate withholding of facts, there is a line and again we are distinguishing between the careful planning of when and how to reveal facts versus outright lying.

Bluffing, while it may be ethical, does entail risk. The bluffer who is called loses credibility and it can get out of hand. Also remember, that most negotiations are carried out with people with whom you will have a continuing relationship. Again, while our culture supports and encourages those who are careful about how and when to disclose facts, out culture does not condone outright lying.

An old British Diplomat Service manual stated the following and it still might be useful.

Nothing may be said which is not true, but it is as unnecessary as it is sometimes undesirable to say everything relevant which is true; and the facts given may be arranged in any convenient order. The perfect reply to an embarrassing question is one that is brief, appears to answer the question completely (if challenged it can be proved to be accurate in every word), gives no opening for awkward follow-up questions, and discloses really nothing.

Skilled negotiators develop techniques to do this. A favorite one is to answer a question with a question to deflect the first question.

Final Advice

> Be unconditionally constructive. Approach a negotiation with this—"I accept you as an equal negotiating partner; I respect your right to differ; I will be receptive." Some criticize my approach as being too soft. But negotiating by these principles is a sign of strength.
>
> Nierenberg, *The Art of Negotiating*

All of us engage in many negotiations during a week but that doesn't mean we become better at it. To become better we need to become aware of the structure and dynamics of negotiation and we need to think systematically, objectively, and critically about our own negotiations. After engaging in a negotiation, reflect on what happened and figure out what you did effectively and what you need to do better.

There is no one "best" style; each of us has to find a style that is comfortable for us. Yet, everyone can negotiate successfully; everyone can reach agreements where all sides feel at least some of their needs have been satisfied. This involves a lot of alertness, active listening, good communication skills, great flexibility, good preparation, and above all it involves a sharing of responsibility for solving the problem, not a view that this is "their" problem.

To summarize the most important keys to successful conflict resolution:

- bargain over interests, not predetermined positions
- de-personalize the problem (separate the person from the problem)
- separate the problem definition from the search for solutions
- try to generate alternative solutions; try to use objective criteria as much as possible
- reflect on your negotiations; learn from your successes and mistakes

> Have unlimited patience. Never corner an opponent and always assist the other person to save his face. Put yourself in his shoes—so as to see things through his eyes. Avoid self-righteousness like the devil—nothing is so self-blinding.
>
> —B. H. Liddell Hart, historian

Appendix 1: Some Types of Negotiators

The Aggressive

Opener negotiator unsettle the other side by making cutting remarks about their previous performance, unreasonabless, or anything that can imply the opponent is worth little

The Long Pauser

List to the other side but don't answer immediately; appear to give it considerable thought with long silences; hope the silence will get the other side to reveal information you need.

The Mocking Negotiator

Mock and sneer your opposition's proposals to get the other side so upset that they will say something they may regret later.

The Interrogator

Meet all proposals with searching questions that will imply the opponents haven't done their homework; challenge any answers in a confronting manner and ask the opposition to explain further what they mean.

The Cloak of Reasonableness

Appear to be reasonable while making impossible demands for the purpose of winning the friendship and confidence of the others.

Divide and Conquer

Produce dissension among opposition so they have to pay more attention to their own internal disagreements rather than the disagreements with the opposition; ally with one member of the team and try to play him or her off against the other members of the team.

The "Act Dumb" Negotiator

Pretend to be particularly dense and by doing so exasperate the opposition in hopes that at least one member of the opposing team will reveal information as he tries to find increasingly simple ways to describe proposals with each proposal being elaborated and amplified so anyone can understand it.

Appendix 2: Three Styles: Soft, Hard, and Principles Negotiation

Dealing with Difficult People Hostile Aggressive
- Stand up for yourself; use self-assertive language
- Give them time to run down . . . avoid a direct confrontation

Complainers
- Listen attentively; acknowledge their feelings; avoid complaining with them
- State the facts without apology . . . use a problem solving mode

Claims:
- Keep asking open ended questions; be patient in waiting for a response
- If no response occurs, tell them what you plan to do, because no discussion has taken place

Superaggreables:
- In a non-threatening manner, work hard to find out why they will not take action
- Let them know you value them as people
- Be ready to compromise and negotiate, and don't allow them to make unrealistic commitments
- Try to discern the hidden meaning in their humor

Negativists:
- Do not be dragged into their despair. . . . Do not try to cajole them out of their negativism
- Discuss the problems thoroughly, without offering solutions

Table WE.2.   Three Styles: Soft, Hard, and Principled Negotiation

Soft	Hard	Principled
friends	adversaries	problem solvers
goals: agreement	victory	wise outcome
make concessions	demand concessions	separate people from problem
be soft on people and problems	be hard on problem and people	be soft on people, hard on problems
trust others	distrust others	proceed independent of trust
change position easily	dig in	focus on interests not positions
make offers	make threats	explore interests
disclose bottom line	mislead	avoid having bottom line
accept one sided loss	demand one sided gain	invent options for mutual gain
search for acceptable answer	search for one answer you will accept	develop multiple options
insist on agreement	insist on your position	insist on objective criteria
try to avoid contest of wills	try to win context of wills	try to reach result based on standards
yield to pressure	apply pressure	yield to principle not pressure

- When alternatives are discussed, bring up the negatives yourself
- Be ready to take action alone, without their agreement

Know-it-Alls
- Bulldozers: Prepare yourself; listen and paraphrase their main points; question to raise problems
- Balloons: State facts or opinions as your own perception of reality; find a way for balloons to safe face; confront in private

Indecisive Stallers
- Raise the issue of why they are hesitant. . . . Possibly remove the staller from the situation
- If you are the problem, ask for help. . . . Keep the action steps in your own hands

(from *Coping with Difficult People*, R. M. Bramson, Doubleday, 1981)

SOME PRINCIPLES OF THIRD PERSON MEDIATION
- Acknowledge that you know the conflict exists and propose an approach for resolving it
- Try to maintain a neutral position regarding the people in the dispute
- Make sure the discussion focuses on issues, not on personalities
- Try to get the people to focus on areas where they might agree

- Try to separate the issues and deal with them one at the time, starting with those where agreement might be easiest
- You are not a judge, but rather a facilitator; judges deal with problems; you deal with solutions—your focus is not on who is right and who is wrong
- Make sure people agree on the solutions that are agreed upon

From Negotiation to Win

If your approach is a win-lose or distributive bargaining approach, you might prefer these ideas: The Critical Rules
- no free gifts; trade every concession; use the big IF
- start high, make small concessions, especially in the end; try to have the other side make the first offer on the issues being negotiated
- be patient; remember to nibble at the end
- keep looking for creative concessions to trade

The Important but Obvious Rules
- do your homework; start slowly; set a complete agenda
- keep the climate positive; discuss small things first
- remember that everything is negotiable
- never accept their first offer; settle everything at the end
- leave the other side feeling it has done well
- consider using the good guy-bad guy approach
- try to have the other

Krunchlist

This is a brief list and I encourage you to add your own suggestions:

Sweet Gentle Krunches
- Where do we go from here. . . . What are we really talking about here. . . . What can we do about this? This doesn't work for us.
- I've got a problem with this; Where can you help me cut this? That really isn't what I expected; I know we can do better
- Take another look at the numbers; Budgets are tight; That would be really tough for us
- I hope we have room to negotiate; Can we talk? Work with me on this. . . .

Middle of the Road Krunches
- You've got to do better on this; That's not acceptable; I'm a bit disappointed in your offer; You're too expensive
- Run that by me again; I can't afford that; That won't do; Pass, No sale; That's a pretty big bite
- Be reasonable; I don't think we're communicating
- You're not giving me anything on this; That doesn't turn me on; Perhaps we have a misunderstanding here

- I'm looking for a much better number; They'll never buy that; We're still not there; No can do
- You're not speaking my language; It'll never fly; How much???? What???

REGIONAL AND ETHNIC KRUNCHES
- (heard in NYC) Talk to me; You're bustin my chops; I can't hear you; You're killin' me; Do you want my children to starve?
- (in the South) Say what?? There's not enough juice in that for us; That's not a big enough work; That bug won't boil; That dog won't hunt/pig won't fly; you're in the right church but the wrong pew; we're within huggin' distance, but we're not ready to kiss yet; which end of the horse do you think you're talking to?

MORE AGGRESSIVE KRUNCHES
- Ouch; Yeah right; Time out; That's below my cost; Do you want my business or what? You want me to lose my job?
- No way; I thought we were friends; I'm not a tourist, I live here; We're not the Salvation Army; We must have a bad connection
- What's your real offer? That really hurts; I don't want the gold plating; Would you like my arm and leg too; Gimme a break
- You're not even close; I've got a family to feed; The decimal point must be off; I love your humor; Be serious
- At that price, we can't even talk; You're gonna kill us; You're really squeezing me; Where's the fat?
- What's the bottom line—is that your target or bottom line?

INFLAMMATORY KRUNCHES (BE SURE TO SMILE)
- You're insulting my intelligence; I was born at night, not last night
- Over my dead body; Who do you think you are? Do you have a bridge you'd like to sell me?
- Is that in dollars or pesos? Are we in Oz? Is this April Fools Day?
- You ought to be in comedy; 50,000 comedians out of work and you're trying to be funny
- Go ahead and shoot me; Go ahead and call 911; Get outta here; Go rub a lamp
- Is it on loan from a museum? You're dreaming; Is this a negotiation or a burial?
- (for a job offer) I didn't know it was part-time
- When donkeys fly; What planet are you from? My mama didn't raise no fool
- Not in my lifetime; You call that an offer? Did you drink your lunch? I thought I had a drinking problem
- What are you smoking? Did you take your medication? Let's wait til your 'ludes wear off
- Don't let the door slam on the way out; Have a nice flight home
- That's your competition in the lobby

NONVERBAL KRUNCHES
- feigned heart attack, choking, rolling eyes, looking at ceiling
- caucus; pulling necktie over head (noose)

RESPONSES TO KRUNCHES
- Make me an offer; What are you looking for? What could you live with? What do you need?
- Do you have a figure in mind? Give me a number; What's your budget? What is fair?
- What is the problem? What were you thinking about?
- If you were in my shoes, what would you do?

EVALUATING YOUR NEGOTIATION SKILLS

Negotiation Exercise:_____My Name_____Partner
Fill this out after the interaction/negotiation; you are encouraged to discuss your critique directly with your partner. You can learn a lot from each other. What are your key impressions of the other person?

What techniques did the other person use in dealing with the conflict/negotiation in the interaction, did you . . . win, lose, deadlock, both win, both lose?

RANK FROM 1 (NOT TRUE AT ALL) TO 5 (VERY TRUE)

The negotiation was very effective_____
  I left the negotiation satisfied_____
  He/she created a cooperative climate_____
  My "opponent" was easy to understand_____
  What style of interaction was used?_____
  She/he made me feel comfortable_____
  She/he listened well_____
  She/he was credible_____

RANK THE OTHER PERSON (YOUR "OPPONENT") ON THESE VARIABLES:

Look at these Overall Guidelines for Effective Negotiation and rank how well you did (5 = excellent); rank your "opponent"
Me_____Opponent_____

Consider the other party's situation

Acquire as much information about the other's interests and goals; What are the real needs versus wants; What constituencies must he or she appease? What is her strategy? Be prepared to frame solutions in terms of her interests.

Have a concrete strategy

Negotiations are like a chess match; Have a strategy; Anticipate how the other will respond; How strong is your position, and situation? How important is the issue? How important will it will be to stick to a hardened position?

Table WE.3.   **Rank the other person (your "opponent") on these variables**

Cooperative	1	2	3	4	5	Competitive
Judgmental	1	2	3	4	5	Empathetic
Controlling	1	2	3	4	5	Problem oriented
Supportive	1	2	3	4	5	Defensive
Comfortable	1	2	3	4	5	Suspicious
Cautious	1	2	3	4	5	Open/trusting
Credible	1	2	3	4	5	Not credible
Listened	1	2	3	4	5	Tuned out
Honest	1	2	3	4	5	Dishonest
Interested in me	1	2	3	4	5	Not interested
Easy to understand	1	2	3	4	5	Hard to understand

Begin with a positive approach

Try to establish rapport and mutual trust before starting; try for a small concession early.

Address problems, not personalities

Avoid the tendency to attack your opponent personally; if the other person feels threatened, he defends his self-esteem and makes attacking the real problem more difficult; separate the people issues from the problem.

Maintain a rational, goal oriented frame of mind

If your opponent attacks you personally, don't let him hook you into an emotional reaction; let the other blow off steam without taking it personally; try to understand the problem behind the aggression.

Pay little attention to initial offers

These are points of departure; they tend to be extreme and idealistic; focus on the other person's interests and your own goals and principles, while you generate other possibilities.

Emphasize win-win solutions

Even in what appears to be win-lose situations, there are often win-win solutions; look for an integrative solution; create additional alternatives, such as low cost concessions that might have high value to the other person; frame options in terms of the other person's interests; look for alternatives that allow your opponent to declare victory.

Insist on using objective criteria

Make your negotiated decision based on principles and results, not emotions or pressure; try to find objective criteria that both parties can use to evaluate alternatives; don't succumb to emotional pleasure, assertiveness, or stubbornness (on the back). What *specific suggestions* can you give the other person to help him or her be more effective in negotiations.

References

Gourlay, R. "Negotiations and Bargaining," *Management Decision* 25(3) (1987):23.

Lax, D. A. and J. K. Sebenius, *The Manager as Negotiator* (New York: Free Press, 1986).

Nierenberg, Gerard *The Art of Negotiating: Psychological Strategies for Gaining Advantageous Bargains* (New York: Barnes & Noble Press, 1995).

Nierenberg, Gerard, *Fundamentals of Negotiation.*

Pruitt, D. G. "Strategic Choice in Negotiation," *American Behavioral Scientist* 27 (November-December 1983): 167–94.

Savage, G. T., J. D. Blair, and R. L. Sorenson, "Consider Both the Relationships and Substance When Negotiating Strategically," *Academy of Management Executive* 3(1) (1989): 40.

Ware, James and Louis B. Barnes, "Managing Interpersonal Conflict," *HBR*, 1978.

Game Theory

Steven J. Brams

Steven J. Brams is a social theorist and professor of politics at New York University, where he has taught since 1969. He is the author or co-author of eleven books that involve applications of game theory or social choice theory to voting and elections, international relations, the Bible, and theology. Brams completed his PhD in Political Science at Northwestern University. Before turning to academia, Brams worked for the Institute for Defense Analysis. Between 1990 and 1991, he served as president of the Peace Science Society (International). He was also a Guggenheim Fellow.

Game theory—via mathematical models—studies how conflict plays out between rational actors. Sometimes known as the theory of social situations, game theory models approach conflict as if those engaged in the issues will respond rationally when faced with choices. Though biologists, computer scientists, psychologists, and others work with game theory in this article, Brams considers game theory in relation to conflict resolution. He opens first with a discussion of the Cuban Missile Crisis. This crisis, which occurred in 1962, represented the kinds of issues the field of conflict resolution dealt with between World War II and the end of the Cold War. The Missile Crisis was a strategy game played out between the United States and the Soviet Union. Brams also considers the Iran hostage crisis through the lens of game theory. Brams explains how that in crises such as these each player makes a move trying to calculate how that move will influence the countermove by an opponent.

The game theory that developed to help politicians and others "win" these strategy games became a highly sophisticated field of study that continues to develop today. Readers will understand how the interplay between moves and countermoves can be thought through in logical, mathematical ways. Brams also addresses the risks of these games—one cannot control how one interprets the meaning of one's action.

Questions to consider: What might an understanding of game theory offer someone working in conflict? What happens if the opponent responds in a way that seems irrational? What might be the consequences of one group misinterpreting the move of the other side?

Game Theory
Theory of Moves

Steven J. Brams

During the Cuban missile crisis in October 1962, the Kennedy administration demanded that the Soviet Union remove its missile bases from Cuba. The Soviets acquiesced, but only after the world teetered for days between peace and disaster. Theodore C. Sorenson, special counsel to President Kennedy, later recalled, "We discussed what the Soviet reaction would be to any possible move by the United States, what our reaction with them would have to be to that Soviet reaction, and so on, trying to follow each of those roads to their ultimate conclusion."

The Cuban missile crisis is a classic, albeit high-stakes, example of strategic game-playing. Like chess players, world leaders in conflict situations make carefully considered moves and countermoves. But the outcomes are not always what the players or onlookers expect; in particular, it is sometimes hard to understand why players choose conflict over cooperation.

A body of theory, called game theory, has been developed and applied over the past half-century to analyze mathematically the strategic behavior of people in situations of conflict. The theory facilitates reconstruction of past situations and modeling of possible future ones, which can explain how rational decision makers arrive at outcomes that are often puzzling at first glance.

Game theory approaches conflicts by asking a question as old as games themselves: How do people make "optimal" choices when these are contingent on what other people do? The seminal work was done in the 1940s by mathematician John von Neumann and economist Oskar Morgenstern, both of Princeton University, who discovered that they held similar ideas about strategies in games. They realized, first, that strategies are interdependent: Players cannot make unilaterally optimal decisions, because one player's best choice depends on the choices of other players. Von Neumann was responsible for most of their theoretical work, whereas Morgenstern pushed the applications toward economic questions.

Their collaboration led to a monumental and difficult treatise. *Theory of Games and Economic Behavior* (1944), which was revised in 1947 and then again in 1953. Over the next several decades investigators applied game theory to strategic situations ranging from the evolution of animal behavior to the rationality of believing in God.

According to the classical theory, players choose strategies, or courses of action, that determine an outcome. Von Neumann and Morgenstern called their theory "thoroughly static" because it says little about the dynamic processes by which players' choices unfold to yield an outcome.

I have developed what I call the "theory of moves" to add a dynamic dimension to classical game theory. Like the classical theory, the theory of moves focuses on interdependent strategic situations in which the outcome depends on the choices that all players make, But it radically alters the rules of play, enabling players to look ahead—sometimes several steps—before making a move.

These modifications lead to different stable outcomes, or equilibria, from those of classical game theory and new concepts of power. In this article, I shall describe informally ideas underlying the theory of moves and illustrate some of its concepts in several games—the last being one that models the Iran hostage crisis that began in 1979.

Making Moves

Before considering the theory of moves, it is worth noting some basic elements of classical game theory. Von Neumann and Morgenstern defined a game as "the totality of rules of play which describe it," which includes a starting point and a list of legal moves that players can make. The game of tic-tac-toe, for example, begins when one player makes a mark on a three-by-three board. The rules state that a player can mark either an X or an O, but only in an unmarked block. After the first player makes a mark, the second player does, with the players then alternating in making marks on the board. The game ends when one player gets three marks in a row or all the blocks are filled.

Most games can be described in two different ways. The "extensive form" is given by a game tree, with play beginning at the first fork in the tree. One player selects one side of this fork, which moves the game to another fork. Then the other player selects a side of that fork, and so on until the game ends. This form of a game provides a full description of its sequential moves.

By contrast, the "normal form" is given by a payoff matrix, in which players choose strategies simultaneously or, if not, at least independently of each other. (A strategy gives a complete plan of possibly contingent choices—if you do this, I will do that, etc.) Thus, if a game *has two players, each with two possible strategies, it can be represented by a two-by-two payoff matrix. One player's strategy choices are given by the two rows; the other's are given by the two columns. Each row-and-column intersection defines an outcome, where payoffs are assigned to the two players.*

The theory of moves combines the extensive and normal forms of classical game theory. A theory-of-moves game is played on a payoff matrix, like a normal-form game. The players, however, can move from one outcome in a payoff matrix to another, so the sequential moves of an extensive-form game are built into the more economical normal form. In large part, I shall concentrate on two-player games in which each player has two strategies; more complicated *games become quite intractable after just a few moves, although in principle the theory of moves is applicable to* n-*person games in which each of the a players has a finite number of strategies.*

Beyond the structure of a game (normal or extensive form), one can make other modifications in the definition of what constitutes a rational choice. A rational choice depends on, among other things, how far players look ahead as they contemplate each other's possible moves and countermoves. In addition, moves are influenced by the capabilities of the players and their information about each other.

The theory of moves incorporates all these features. It is dynamic because players do not make choices *de novo*. Instead, their choices depend on the past and present as well as the future, which players can anticipate at least in part and about which I assume they can make rational calculations.

In the theory of moves, I assume that players can rank the possible outcomes from best to worst These payoffs, however, are only ordinal: They indicate an order of preference, but not the degree to which a player prefers one outcome over

Figure 1.   Game theory evaluates behavior in conflict situations. During the Cuban missile crisis, President Kennedy demanded that the Soviet Union remove its missiles from Cuba. Kennedy and his advisors, shown here in an Excom (Executive Committee) meeting, considered all their possible moves, the possible countermoves by the Soviets and the possible counter-countermoves by the United States. U.S. decision makers used their knowledge of the past and predicted future moves, which classical game theory tends to treat myopically. The author's theory of moves adds a dynamic component to classical game theory, enabling players to look ahead and select strategies that yield "nonmyopic equilibria." Photograph courtesy of the John F. Kennedy Library

another. (Although other forms of decision-making theory indicate the degree of preference in payoffs, I have chosen ordinal payoffs to simplify the analysis and make it more applicable to real-life strategic situations.) In addition, the theory allows for power differences among players by assuming, for example, that one player may have the ability to carry out threats when necessary. Finally, the theory is information-dependent, meaning that players do not always share the same information, making misperception and deception possible.

The theory of moves includes six basic rules. Rule 1 states that a game starts at an "initial state," which is a row-and- column intersection of a payoff matrix. Rule 2 says that either player can switch to a new strategy, thereby generating a new outcome; the first player to move is called Player 1. According to Rule 3, the other player, Player 2, can then move. A game's end is determined by Rule 4: The players respond alternately until neither switches strategies. The resulting outcome is the "final state," which is the only point at which the players accrue payoffs.

The remaining rules, which I call rationality rules, explain the reasons for moving or not moving. Rule 5 states that a player will not make a move unless it

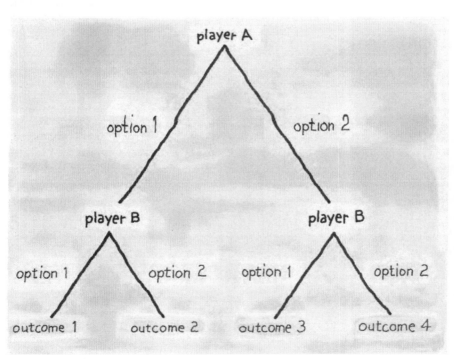

Figure 2.   Extensive forms of classical game theory are given by a game tree. This game involves two players, with each player able to choose one of two options. The game begins when Player A selects an option. Then Player B selects an option, which leads to one of four possible outcomes. This form highlights the sequential nature of moves.

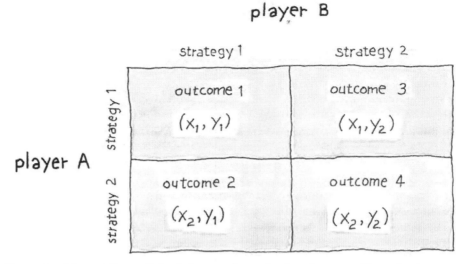

Figure 3. Normal form of classical game theory is given by a payoff matrix. In a two-player game in which each player has two strategies, the matrix is two-by-two. Player A's strategies are represented by the two rows, and Player B's are represented by the two columns. Players independently select strategies that lead to an outcome. Each outcome is assigned payoffs, which arc given in x-y combinations such that xi is the payoff to the row player (Player A) and yi is the payoff to the column player (Player B), where i and j are given by the players' strategies (either 1 or 2).

leads to a preferred outcome, based on his or her anticipation of the final state. Rule 6, which I call the two-sidedness rule, says that a player considers the rational calculations of the other players before moving, taking into account their possible moves, the possible countermoves of the other players, their own counter-countermoves, and so on. Thus, a player may do immediately better by moving first according to Rule 5; but if this player can do even better by letting the other player move first, and it is rational for that player to do so, then the first player will await this move, according to Rule 6.

Truels

Some of the differences between classical game theory and the theory of moves arise in an imaginary confrontation situation called a truel. A truel is like a duel, except there are three players. It illustrates nicely the applicability of the theory of moves to games with more than two players.

In the truel I posit, a player has two choices: either to fire or not to fire at one of the other two players. Each player has one bullet and is a perfect shot. The players cannot communicate, which prevents the selection of a common target. I assume that a player's primary goal is to survive, and his or her secondary goal is to survive with as few other players as possible.

In this rather gruesome situation, the theory of moves suggests a different outcome than does classical game theory. In fact, the theory of moves provides a resolution that is more satisfactory for all the players.

If the players must make simultaneous strategy choices, they will all fire at each other according to classical game theory. They do so because their own survival does not depend one iota on what they do. Since they cannot affect what happens to themselves but can affect only how many others survive (the fewer the better, according to the postulated secondary goal), they should all fire at each other.

Such a scenario generates two possible results: Either one player survives or no players survive. Players A and B might both fire at Player C, who fires at one of them, say Player A. This leaves a single survivor, Player B. On the other hand, each player may fire at a different player, leaving all players dead.

If each player has an equal probability of firing at one of the other two players, there is only a 25 percent chance that any player will survive. The reason is that Player A will be killed if fired at by Player B, Player C or both (three cases); the only case in which Player A will survive is if Players B and C fire at each other, which gives Player A one chance in four of surviving. Although this calculation implies a 75 percent chance that some player will survive, an individual player will be more concerned with his or her own low chance (25 percent) of survival.

The theory of moves offers a different perspective. Instead of assuming simultaneous strategy choices, it asks each player: Given your present situation and the situation that you anticipate will ensue if you fire first, should you fire? At the start of a truel, all the players are alive, which satisfies their primary goal of survival but not their secondary goal of surviving with as few others as possible. Player A now contemplates shooting Player B to reduce the number of survivors. By looking ahead, however, Player A realizes that firing at Player C will cause Player C subsequently to fire at him or her (Player A). This would be in Player C's interest, because it would make C the sole survivor.

Instead of firing, therefore, Player A will, thinking ahead, not shoot at anybody. By symmetry, the other players will choose the same strategy, so all will survive. This longer-term perspective leads to a better outcome than that provided by classical game theory, in which each player's primary goal is satisfied only 25 percent of the time when players make simultaneous strategy choices without looking ahead.

The purpose of the theory of moves, however, is not to generate a better outcome but to provide a more plausible model of a strategic situation that mimics what people might think and do. The players in a truel, artificial as such a shoot-out might be, would be motivated to look ahead, given the dire consequences of their actions. To be sure, classical game theory can also provide this outcome if one player (say, A) were designated to move first. Then Player A would rationally choose not to fire, lest he or she be killed subsequently by the sole surviving player (either B or C).

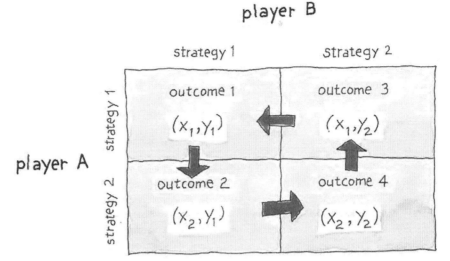

Figure 4. Theory of moves embeds a game tree in a payoff matrix. Players can move from an initial outcome or state to another one by either moving vertically (Player A) or horizontally (Player B). The matrix shows the strategies of the players and their payoffs at various outcomes. The arrows within the matrix reveal how players might move—in this case counterclockwise—between different outcomes through a sequence of moves.

What classical game theory does not ask is whether it is rational for one player, if afforded the opportunity, to move first. This is specified by the rules in the classical theory instead of being made endogenous—that is, incorporated into the theory as a question to be answered—as in the theory of moves.

Changing the rules of play may generate still different outcomes. For example, permit the players of a truel the additional option of firing in the air, thereby disarming themselves, and specify the order of play, such as Player A goes first, followed by Players B and C going simultaneously. Given these rules, Player A will fire in the air, and then Players B and C will shoot each other. The disarmed Player A is, after all, no threat, so he or she would not be shot by Player B or Player C. On the other hand, Players B and C will fire immediately at each other; otherwise, they will have no chance of surviving to get in the last shot. In the end, Player A will be tire sole survivor under these rules that give a player the option of firing in the air.

Prisoners' Dilemma

Game theory's most famous game is called Prisoners' Dilemma. It starts with the following scenario: Two persons, suspected of being partners in a crime, are arrested and placed in separate cells so that they cannot communicate with each other. Although they are in fact guilty, without a confession from at least one suspect, the district attorney does not have sufficient evidence to convict them of the crime.

In an attempt to extract a confession, the district attorney explains to each suspect the following consequences of their joint actions. If one suspect confesses and the other does not, the one who confesses can go free for cooperating with the state, but the other gets a 10-year sentence. If both suspects confess, they get reduced sentences of five years. If both remain silent, each goes to prison for one year on a lesser charge of carrying a concealed weapon.

Prisoners' Dilemma can be reduced to a two-by-two payoff matrix, in which 4 is the best payoff, 3 is the next-best, 2 the next-worst, and 1 the worst. Each prisoner has a choice of two strategies, confession or silence, giving four possible outcomes for each prisoner: no sentence (4), a one-year sentence (3), a five-year sentence (2), and a 10-year sentence (1). The four possible outcomes that may result are compromise (both remain silent, giving each prisoner a payoff of 3), conflict (both confess, giving each prisoner a payoff of 2) and one or the other "wins" (one confesses and gets a payoff of 4, and the other remains silent and gets a payoff of 1).

The silence-silence outcome is a compromise, because it requires that both players forgo their best payoffs and instead get their next-best payoffs at (3, 3). The confession-confession outcome is a conflict, because if both players try for

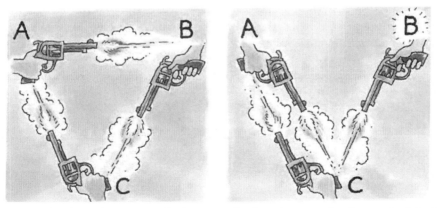

Figure 5.   Truel is a three-person duel. Here each player is assumed to have a single bullet and be a perfect shot. A player's primary goal is surviving, and the secondary goal is surviving with as few others as possible. If the players must make simultaneous choices, a player cannot affect his or her own survival but can affect how many others survive; consequently, each player is motivated to shoot another. Classical game theory indicates two possible outcomes: either no one survives (left), or one player—Player B in this case—survives (right).

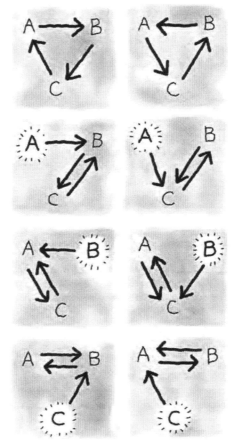

Figure 6.   Truel, according to classical game theory, produces a single survivor in 75 percent of the cases. There are eight different firing combinations, and the arrows above reflect who shoots at whom. In two cases (top row), no one survives. The other six combinations leave either Player A, Player B, or Player C as the sole survivor.

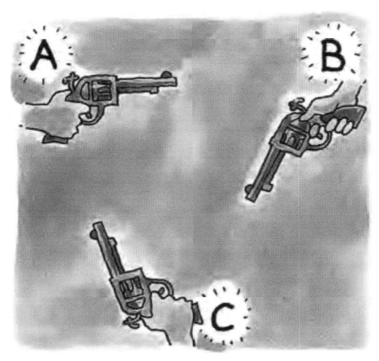

Figure 7.   Truel, according to the theory of moves, leaves three survivors. The theory of moves has each player ask: What will happen if I shoot first? If Player A shoots at Player B, Player C will subsequently shoot at Player A, so Player A decides not to shoot. The other players reach the same decision, and they all hold their fire.

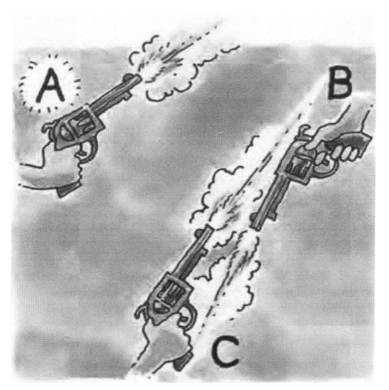

Figure 8.   Third option of shooting in the air modifies the results of a truel under both classical game theory and the theory of moves. If Player A goes first and shoots in the air, thereby being disarmed, Players B and C must shoot at each other if they want any chance of survival. That leaves Player A as the sole survivor.

their best payoffs at (4, 1) or (1, 4) by confessing when the other stays silent, they both get their next-worst payoffs at (2, 2).

The outcome depends on the choices of both players. If both remain silent, they get the compromise, or (3, 3), outcome. Nevertheless, each prisoner has an incentive to defect from that outcome to obtain his or her best payoff at (4, 1) or (1, 4) by confessing when the other remains silent. But if both choose to confess, they bring upon themselves the conflict, or (2, 2), outcome, which is obviously worse for both than (3, 3).

The dilemma, according to classical game theory, is that both players have dominant strategies of confessing, because these choices give each suspect a better payoff regardless of the other suspect's strategy choice. But if both suspects confess, they receive the conflict outcome, which gives them their next-worst payoffs at (2, 2). Moreover, conflict is the unique equilibrium outcome: Neither suspect has an incentive to depart unilaterally from confession, because switching to silence would give that player its worst payoff of 1.

What should the suspects do to save their skins, assuming that neither has any compunction about squealing on the other? If either suspect confesses, it is advantageous for the other to confess as well to avoid the worst payoff, a 10-year sentence. The rub is that confessing when the other suspect does, and receiving a five-year sentence, is not all that appealing, even though neither suspect can ensure a better outcome. Finally, if one suspect remains silent, it is better for the other to turn state's evidence and go free.

There have been many attempts to justify the compromise outcome in which both suspects keep silent. Most of these attempts involve changing the rules of play to allow for repetition. Then, the argument goes, the suspects would recognize the folly of suffering the conflict outcome again and again, come to their senses and both choose silence. In *The Evolution of Cooperation* (1984), however, Robert Axelrod of the University of Michigan argues that the best route to this end will not generally be the unconditional choice of silence. Instead, it will be a tit-for-tat strategy, wherein each player chooses silence conditional on the other's choice of silence in the previous round.

The theory of moves gives the same result, but in a one-shot play of Prisoners' Dilemma, if the players are sufficiently farsighted to look ahead more than one step and do not start at the conflict outcome. Assume that both suspects are initially silent, which gives the compromise outcome. If one suspect changes from silence to confession, that player also recognizes that the other suspect will, according to the theory of moves, respond by confessing as well. Such a move and countermove would induce the conflict outcome. Therefore, the players will remain silent and stay at the compromise outcome, making this what I call a "nonmyopic equilibrium."

Proceeding from an initial state at which one or the other suspects wins (one suspect remains silent and the other confesses) requires more subtle reasoning. If Suspect 1 remains silent and Suspect 2 confesses, they would get payoffs of 1 and 4, respectively, at (1, 4). Although at this point Suspect 1 would have an immediate incentive to confess, both players would realize only payoffs of 2 from this action at (2, 2). On the other hand, both would realize that if Suspect 2 instead selected silence, they would achieve the compromise outcome at (3, 3). Thus, from the initial states of (3, 3), (4, 1) and (1, 4), the players, thinking ahead, will be motivated to stay at (3, 3) (if already there) or to move to that outcome from (4, 1) or (1, 4). Regrettably, even the theory of moves does not enable the players to escape from (2, 2), so this conflict outcome is also a nonmyopic equilibrium.

Prisoners' Dilemma has been used to model a great variety of strategic situations, from arms races to price wars to the overpopulation problem. The players in such situations—countries, companies, or couples—would prefer that no one buy more arms, reduce prices or have more children. Nevertheless, each of these players does better, whatever the other players do, by engaging in such noncooperative behavior. The consequence is that they all end up worse off than if they had cooperated.

The theory of moves shows that cooperation does not depend necessarily on signing an enforceable contract or playing a repeated game. Instead, cooperation depends on calculating that compromise is the nonmyopic equilibrium, or rational outcome, starting from any state except (2, 2).

Iran Hostage Crisis

Although a rational player should look ahead before acting, that advice works well only if the players have complete information about their opponents. The United States apparently lacked such information about Iran in November 1979, when Iranian militants seized personnel at the U.S. embassy. By analyzing the news reports of the time and the later writings of some government officials, Walter Mattli of the University of Chicago and I reconstructed the strategic thinking of decision makers in this crisis. As I shall show, it explains well why the crisis took so long to resolve.

During the crisis, the military capabilities of the two opponents were almost irrelevant. In April 1980 the United States attempted a rescue that cost eight American lives and freed no hostages, but the conflict was never really a military one. The crisis can be best represented as a game in which President Jimmy Carter misperceived the preferences of Ayatollah Ruholla Khomeini. In desperation, Carter sought a solution in the wrong game.

Why did Khomeini sanction the takeover of the American embassy by militant students? Doing so provided two advantages. First, by creating a confrontation with the United States, Khomeini was able to sever the many links that remained between Iran and the "Great Satan" from the days of the shah. Second, the takeover mobilized support for extremist revolutionary objectives just at the moment when secular elements in Iran were challenging the principles of the theocratic state that Khomeini had installed.

Carter's primary goal was immediate release of the hostages. His secondary goal was holding discussions with Iranian religious authorities about resolving the differences that had strained relations between the United States and Iran. Of

Figure 9.   Prisoners' Dilemma involves two suspected criminals. The suspects face the following consequences: If one confesses and the other remains silent, the confessor goes free (the best payoff of 4) and the silent suspect gets a 10-year sentence (the worst payoff of 1); if both confess, they get five-year sentences (the next-worst payoff of 2); and if both remain silent, they get one-year sentences (the next-best payoff of 3). The payoff matrix reveals four possible outcomes: compromise, conflict and one or the other suspect "wins." In classical game theory, both suspects have dominant strategies of confessing. That produces the conflict outcome, which is an equilibrium outcome (blue) because neither suspect would move unilaterally from it. The theory of moves can induce the compromise outcome. If the dilemma begins at this outcome (silence), both suspects can look ahead and see that confessing will induce the other suspect to confess as well, so both suspects remain silent. If the dilemma begins with one or the other suspect winning, the winning suspect would move from confession to silence—generating the compromise outcome—to prevent the conflict outcome from occurring when the losing suspect, to do better, decides to confess as well. If the dilemma begins at the conflict outcome, the theory of moves provides no reason to move from it.

course, if the hostages were killed, the United States would likely defend its honor, probably through a military strike on Iran.

Carter considered two strategies: negotiation and military intervention. Because the seizure of the embassy had led to a severing of diplomatic relations, negotiation could be pursued only through the United Nations Security Council, the World Court or informal diplomatic channels. Military intervention could

Figure 10.   Iranian militants seized U.S. embassy personnel in November 1979, initiating the Iran hostage crisis. Iranian students assembled outside the embassy for an anti-American protest on November 5, 1979. By assessing the news reports of that time amid later writings of government officials, the author and Walter Mattli recreated the possible moves of that "game." President Carter considered two strategies: negotiation or military intervention. Khomeini also had two strategies: negotiation or obstruction.

have taken the form of a rescue mission, as it did, or punitive strikes against selected targets, such as refineries, rail facilities or power stations.

Khomeini also had two strategies: negotiation or obstruction. His negotiating demands included a return of the shah's assets and ending U.S. interference in Iran's affairs. On the other hand, a refusal to negotiate was sure to block a resolution of the crisis.

The two players and their two strategies generate a two-by-two payoff matrix. Each cell in the matrix has an associated payoff for each player. As in Prisoners' Dilemma, 1 assumes that Carter and Khomeini can rank the four outcomes from best (4) to worst (1).

Carter obtains a better payoff by choosing negotiation, which would save him from the overwhelming difficulties of military intervention, whatever Khomeini does. In December 1979 those difficulties were compounded by the Soviet invasion of Afghanistan, which eliminated the Soviet Union as a possible ally in seeking concerted action for the release of the hostages. Moreover, the Soviet troops

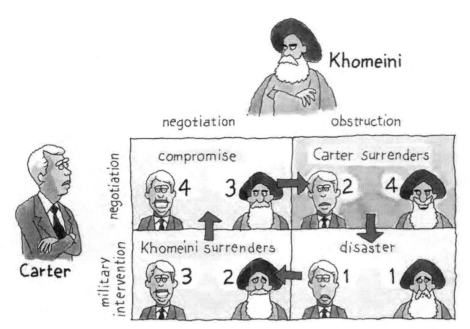

Figure 11.   Carter apparently misperceived the structure of the Iran hostage crisis by believing that Khomeini preferred compromise to a confrontation that Carter thought might end in a disaster. Carter's misperceived payoff matrix shows that he gets a better payoff by selecting negotiation, regardless of Khomeini's choice. According to this payoff matrix, Khomeini's best strategy depends on Carter's selection. If Carter selects military intervention, Khomeini should select negotiation. If Carter selects negotiation, Khomeini should select obstruction, resulting in the outcome called "Carter surrenders," which is the equilibrium outcome (blue). If the players moved and countermoved around the matrix, the moves would be clockwise, because in that direction no player ever moves from his best payoff.

next door in Afghanistan made the strategic environment for military intervention anything but favorable.

Carter initially believed that his selection of negotiation would appeal to Khomeini as well. The president perceived that Khomeini faced serious problems in Iran, such as demonstrations by the unemployed and Iraqi incursions across Iran's western border. In Carter's 1982 memoir, *Keeping Faith,* he reported his belief that a U.S. choice of negotiation would give Khomeini a dignified way out of the impasse.

The president also believed that Khomeini preferred a U.S. surrender that would result from the obstruction of negotiations. That result, Carter thought, would give Khomeini his best payoff of 4, whereas Khomeini would get his next best payoff of 3 if both sides selected negotiation. And finally Carter saw Khomeini

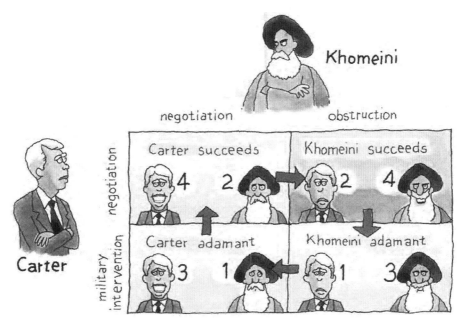

Figure 12.   Real-game payoff matrix, taking into account Iran's internal politics as revealed by events and analysis, shows that Khomeini has a dominant strategy of selecting obstruction, which is better for him regardless of Carter's strategy. Like the misperceived-game payoff matrix (Figure 11), Carter has a dominant strategy of selecting negotiation. These strategies lead again to a negotiation-obstruction outcome, which is an equilibrium outcome (blue), now called "Khomeini succeeds" because Khomeini ranks the other outcomes differently than in the misperceived-game payoff matrix. Cycling in this matrix would be clockwise.

getting inferior payoffs of 2 and 1 if the United States selected military intervention.

Carter's Miscalculations

Unfortunately for Carter, he misperceived the strategic situation and, hence, played the wrong game. Khomeini wanted the total Islamization of Iranian society; he viewed the United States as "a global Shah—a personification of evil" that had to be cut off from any contact with Iran. Khomeini abjured his nation never to "compromise with any power . . . [and] to topple from the position of power anyone in any position who is inclined to compromise with the East and West."

For Khomeini to have selected negotiation would have weakened his uncompromising position. Iranian leaders who tried negotiating, including President

Abolhassan Bani-Sadr and Foreign Minister Sagdegh Ghotbzadeh, lost in the power struggle. Bani-Sadr was forced to flee for his life to Paris, and Ghotbzadeh was arrested and later executed.

In the "real game"—the actual strategic situation—Khomeini most preferred obstruction (4 and 3), regardless of the U.S. strategy choice. Doubtless, he preferred that the United States choose negotiation (4) over military intervention (3).

What does classical game theory say about the rational choices of the players in the misperceived game and the real game? In both games, Carter's dominant, or unconditionally best, strategy is negotiation. Regardless of what Khomeini chooses, Carter's payoff from negotiation is better than his payoff from military intervention. In the misperceived game, for example, if Khomeini chooses negotiation, Carter gets a *payoff of 4* by *choosing negotiation* and a payoff of 3 by choosing military intervention; if Khomeini chooses obstruc*tion,* Carter receives a payoff of 2 by *choosing negotiation* and a payoff of 1 *by choosing military* intervention.

Although Carter's dominant strategy in both games is independent of Khomeini's choice, Khomeini's best choice in the misperceived game depends on what Carter selects. If Carter chooses negotiation, which he should because it is dominant, Khomeini, anticipating this, does better by choosing obstruction, which gives him a payoff of 4, rather than choosing negotiation, which gives him a payoff of 3. So in the misperceived game, Khomeini should choose obstruction, leading to the negotiation-obstruction outcome. That outcome, which 1 call "Carter surrenders," gives Carter a payoff of 2 and Khomeini a payoff of 4.

Game theory calls this outcome—Carter chooses negotiation and Khomeini chooses obstruction—rational in the real game as well, because both players have dominant strategies associated with it. in the real game, I call this outcome "Khomeini succeeds." (The other three outcomes in the real game are ranked differently by Khomeini from those in the misperceived game, which is why I give them different shorthand descriptions.) In the real game, the rationality of the (2, 4) outcome is reinforced by Khomeini's dominant strategy of obstruction associated with it; obstruction is not dominant in the real game but, instead, Khomeini's best response if Carter chooses his own dominant strategy of negotiation.

Given that Carter does better in both games by choosing negotiation, why would he consider, much less try, military intervention? Classical game theory does not give a reason, but the theory of moves suggests the basis for his miscalculation. Carter might have thought—with some justification in the misperceived game—that by threatening Khomeini with military intervention he would induce him to choose negotiation, giving Carter the opportunity, by choosing negotiation himself, to obtain his best payoff.

The reasoning underlying this calculation goes as follows: In the misperceived game, a negotiation-negotiation outcome gives Carter his best payoff of 4 and gives Khomeini his next-best payoff of 3. A threat by Carter to choose military intervention, if carried out, would inflict upon Khomeini his two worst outcomes in the misperceived game: a payoff of 2 if he chose negotiation and a payoff of 1 if he chose obstruction. Since Khomeini would prefer a payoff of 2 over 1, he would choose negotiation, given Carter's threat were credible. However, because both players do better by choosing "compromise" at (4, 3) rather than "Khomeini

Figure 13.   Carter tried military intervention even though negotiation was his dominant strategy in both games. The attempted rescue mission left one U.S. helicopter destroyed and another abandoned. Classical game theory makes such a strategy appear irrational in both game matrices, whereas the theory of moves offers a rational explanation for Carter's action. In the misperceived-game matrix (Figure 11), Carter believes that selecting military intervention—or threatening its use—will force Khomeini to select negotiation in order to improve his payoff, at which point Carter can also choose negotiation to obtain his best payoff at the "compromise" outcome, which is also better for Khomeini. In the real-game payoff matrix (Figure 12), Khomeini cannot be swayed from obstruction. The crisis, in fact, remained at a negotiation-obstruction outcome until the hostages were released on January 20, 1981.

surrenders" at (3, 2), Khomeini should choose negotiation when Carter does, assuming that he takes seriously Carter's threat of military intervention.

There are two problems with this reasoning. First, it is not clear that Carter had what I call the "threat power" needed to induce a compromise outcome in the misperceived game. More important, that was not the game being played. In the real game, Khomeini had no reason to accede to a threat from Carter, because his political position was stronger if he refused to compromise. Regardless of Carter's choice, Khomeini does better by selecting obstruction in the real game.

Nonetheless, Carter tried threats. He dispatched the aircraft carrier USS *Kitty Hawk* and its supporting battle group from the Pacific to the Arabian Sea. The carrier USS *Midway* and its battle group were already in the area. Those two battle groups created the largest U.S. naval force in the Indian Ocean since World War

II. But this vast array of firepower proved useless, at least for the purpose of inducing Khomeini to select negotiation.

The failed rescue operation in April 1980 kept the situation at the negotiation-obstruction outcome for another nine months. This was so despite the fact that Iranian leaders had concluded in August 1980—after the installation of an Islamic government consistent with Khomeini's theocratic vision—that keeping the hostages was a net liability.

Further complicating Iran's position was the attack by Iraqi forces in September 1980. It was surely no accident that the hostages were set free on the day of Carter's departure from the White House on January 20, 1981. Although Gary Sick claims in *October Surprise* (1991) that the hostages were not released before the November 1980 presidential election because of a secret deal that Iran made with Ronald Reagan's supporters, later congressional investigations disputed Sick's claim, at least regarding the involvement of George Bush.

Perhaps Carter should not be judged too harshly for misperceiving the strategic situation. If he had correctly foreseen the real game from the start, both game theory and the theory of moves agree that he could not have moved away from an outcome that gave him a payoff of 2 and Khomeini a payoff of 4. What the theory of moves explains, and game theory does not, is why Carter might have thought that he could implement the compromise outcome through the exercise of threats.

The theory of moves also shows how a series of moves and countermoves in the misperceived game can induce this outcome if Carter has what is called "moving power." Assume that the players move and countermove in a clockwise direction on the misperceived game payoff matrix. In that direction, neither player ever moves from his best outcome (Carter vertically or Khomeini horizontally). In a counterclockwise direction, by contrast, players do move from their best outcomes: Khomeini moves from a payoff of 4 at (2, 4) when he switches from obstruction to negotiation, and Carter moves from a payoff of 4 at (4,3) when he switches from negotiation to military intervention. So, if there is cycling, it must be in a clock*wise* direction.

If Carter believed that he had moving power—the ability to force Khomeini to stop in the move-countermove process—Carter could force Khomeini to stop at the negotiation-negotiation outcome or the military intervention-obstruction outcome, which are the two outcomes where Khomeini has the next move. Khomeini would prefer the former, which gives him a payoff of 3, rather than the latter, which gives him a payoff of 1. In the real game, however, these outcomes give Khomeini payoffs of 2 and 3 respectively, so he would choose to stay at the military intervention-obstruction outcome. As a consequence, Carter's hoped-for negotiation-negotiation outcome in the misperceived game became, in April 1980, a military intervention-obstruction outcome in the real game.

The theory of moves formally incorporates into the framework of game theory an initial state in a payoff matrix, possible moves and countermoves from it to try to reach a nonmyopic equilibrium, and threat and cycling to wear down an opponent. It also allows for the possibility that players possess only incomplete information, as I illustrated in the case of the Iran hostage crisis, which can lead to misperception. As a theory that assumes that players can rank outcomes but not necessarily attach utilities to them, it is eminently applicable to the way we contemplate the strategic choices of others as we try to make our own best choices in a dynamic environment.

Bibliography

Axelrod, Robert. (1984). *The Evolution cf Cooperation.* New York: Basic Books.

Brams, Steven J. *Negotiation Games: Applying Game Theory to Bargaining and Arbitration.* New York: Routledge.

Brams, Steven J. (forthcoming). *Theory of Moves.* Cambridge, UK: Cambridge University Press.

Brams, Steven J., and Walter Mattli. (1993). Theory of moves: overview and examples. *Conflict Management and Peace Science* 12(2): 1–39.

Carter, Jimmy. (1982). *Keeping Faith: Memoirs of a President,* New York: Bantam Books.

Christopher, Warren (ed.). (1985). *American Hostages in Iran: The Conduct of a Crisis.* New Haven, CT: Yale University Press.

Sick, Gary. (1991). *October Surprise: America's Hostages in Iran and the Election of Ronald Reagan.* New York: Random House.

Von Neumann, John, and Oskar Morgenstern. (1953). *Theory of Games and Economic Behavior.* 3rd ed. Princeton, NJ: Princeton University Press.

Alternative Dispute Resolution (ADR)

Frank E. A. Sander

Frank E. A. Sander, professor emeritus of Harvard Law School, began his academic career first with a mathematics degree from Harvard followed by a law degree. While an expert on taxation, his works on alternative dispute resolution (ADR) earned him the status of a founder of the field. Before joining the law faculty at Harvard, he worked as a clerk for a judge of the U.S. Court of Appeals and as a clerk at the U.S. Supreme Court for Justice Felix Frankfurter. Sander lectured around the world and served as a legal arbitrator for almost fifty years.

In this article, Sander outlines and describes ADR approaches. ADR approaches are methods of negotiation and resolution occurring outside of courts. He says roughly 95 percent of all cases filed in the courts are ultimately resolved outside using one ADR approach or another. While interest in ADR was on the rise when this article was published in 1985, the need for ADR emerged when courts found themselves inundated with claims during the Civil Rights and anti-Vietnam movements in the 1960s. ADR approaches originally emerged to:

- Relieve court congestion,
- Enhance community involvement,
- Facilitate access to justice, and
- Provide more "effective" resolutions

The article reviews how negotiation, mediation, and arbitration were developed to facilitate disputes between individuals and also between individuals and businesses, as well as within and between governments and other institutions. While the article does not directly apply these approaches to international or intranational violence, the methods developed in this context influenced the field of conflict resolution.

The critiques of ADR echoed the early critiques of conflict resolution; both fields found themselves critiqued for attempts to mediate away or assuage the true grievances of poor or marginalized populations. Sander responded that courts proved no better in their ability to upend the variety structural violence articulated by Johan Galtung and John Burton. Epoch Two scholars address these critiques more fully, though Sander does offer an early nod to the critique that unaddressed power differentials in mediations can do harm.

Questions to consider: ADR was created in response to the overwhelming of the court system, but it is often touted as good for the parties in conflict. If they can leave traditional power dynamics entrenched, who is ADR designed to serve? The state, the individuals in conflict, or both?

Alternative Dispute Resolution
Alternative Methods of Dispute Resolution

Frank E. A. Sander

I. Introduction**

Beginning in the late sixties, American society witnessed an extraordinary flowering of interest in alternative forms of dispute settlement. This interest emanated from a wide variety of sources ranging from the Chief Justice of the United States Supreme Court to corporate general counsel, the organized bar and various lay groups.[1] Following a decade or so of virtually unabashed enthusiasm, serious questions and doubts are now being raised. Additionally, we are slowly accumulating limited data concerning viable models and empirical effects. Hence, this may be an opportune time for evaluating and exploring promising future directions.

Perhaps a good place to begin is with some definitions. What exactly do we mean by "alternative dispute resolution mechanisms" (ADRMs)? Alternative to what? Presumably "alternative" is used as a substitute for the traditional dispute resolution mechanism, the court. Interestingly enough, however, courts do not resolve most disputes. The literature on dispute processing and dispute transformation has delineated ways in which grievances may be turned into ongoing disputes, and the myriad ways in which disputes may be resolved by means other than court adjudication.[2] In fact, disputes that cannot be readily adjusted may be presented initially to a whole host of dispute processors such as arbitrators, mediators, fact-finders or ombudsmen. If the dispute is ultimately filed in court, approximately 90–95 percent of these disputes are settled by negotiation, with little or no court litigation. Hence, the argument for "alternatives" is not based on the need to find a substitute for court adjudiciation. Rather, it is based on the need to gain a better understanding of the functioning of these alternative mechanisms and processes.

Alternatives to courts are not a new phenomenon.[3] Yet, the current resurgence of alternative dispute resolution seems to have a freshness about it. The movement appears to have a much broader theoretical and practical base. It might therefore be useful briefly to speculate on the confluence of events that have led to the current renewal of interest in alternatives.

The sixties were characterized by considerable strife and conflict, emanating in part from the civil rights struggles and the Vietnam War protests. An apparent legacy of those times was a lessened tolerance and a greater tendency to turn grievances into disputes. Also relevant was a significant increase in the statutory creation of new causes of action.

A noteworthy development from these events was that courts found themselves inundated with new filings, triggering cries of alarm from the judicial administration establishment. This judicial congestion led to claims that equal access to justice had been denied.[4] Spurred in part by these conditions, parties attempted to resolve some of these disputes through alternative dispute resolution mechanisms. In the 1964 Civil Rights Act Congress established the Community Relations Service in the United States Department of Justice to aid courts and others in settling intractable racial and community disputes. The Ford Foundation established the National Center for Dispute Settlement and the Institute of Mediation and Conflict Resolution to study dispute settlement mechanisms.[5]

Any attempt to isolate the roots of a complex and ill-understood movement is bound to suffer from oversimplification. One can readily identify a number of other social forces that contributed to the recent flowering of the alternatives movement. One contributor is the waning role of some of society's traditional mediating institutions such as the family, the church, and the ward healer. A second influence is the discernible recent mood of anti-professionalism.[6] Both these conditions point toward the creation of alternative indigenous mechanisms such as community mediation centers and family dispute settlement tribunals.[7] Of course, need alone does not always lead to constructive solutions. Fortunately, for the alternatives movement, the Law Enforcement Assistance Administration (LEAA) took a firm interest in developing and testing ADRMs, even if the required nexus with the criminal law system at times distorted the proper emphasis.

Certain intellectual developments paralleled these social forces. Over the past 15–20 years some cultural anthropologists have attempted to apply their study of foreign dispute settlement to the local scene.[8] Contemporaneous with that effort has been the work of other legal scholars, most notably the late Lon Fuller, who have attempted to analyze characteristics of various dispute processes such as mediation and arbitration. These scholars proposed some useful conclusions about, the strengths and limitations of particular processes for particular types of. disputes.[9]

From this brief and fragmentary history, four goals of the alternatives movement emerge:

1) to relieve court congestion, as well as undue cost and delay;
2) to enhance community involvement in the dispute resolution process;

3) to facilitate access to justice;
4) to provide more "effective" dispute resolution.[10]

These goals might overlap and conflict. Consider, for example, the problem of "excessive" access. If society is too ready to provide access for all kinds of disputes, this will lengthen the queue and aggravate the congestion problem. Similarly, measures aimed at relieving court congestion would take a very different form from measures designed to enhance community control over dispute settlement. Hence, it is essential to think clearly and precisely about the reasons for pursuing ADRMs.

Considering the complex social conditions that have led to court congestion and concomitant delay,[11] it seems specious to assume an appropriate use of alternatives can significantly affect court case loads. This is not to say that a cautious and informed use of ancillary mechanisms to screen court cases is not worth undertaking. On the contrary, such a program holds considerable promise. But the notion that a pervasive use of arbitration and mediation will solve "the court crisis" seems misguided. The principal promise of alternatives stems from the third and fourth goals set forth above. Our primary efforts should be directed toward these two goals. And since the access goal can only be fulfilled by providing access to an ADRM that is appropriate for the particular dispute, the third and fourth goals in effect coalesce.

II. Current Types of Disputes and Programs

This section presents a brief overview of the rich variety of ADRMs presently in use. Of necessity the picture will be somewhat fragmentary and conclusory.[12] Because many mechanisms involve a blend or sequence of different dispute processes, it might be useful first to provide a brief restatement of the basic processes.

The most common and familiar form of dispute settlement between two parties is bargaining or negotiation. Negotiation offers the great advantage of allowing the parties themselves to control the process and the solution. Sometimes, however, disputants are unable to settle the dispute, and a third party must be engaged. If a third party joins the negotiations, the parties must determine whether he or she has power to impose a solution on the parties, or whether the third party is simply to help the disputants arrive at their own solution. The latter role is commonly referred to as conciliation or mediation. The former might entail some form of adjudication, by a court, an administrative agency, or a private adjudicator, also known as an arbitrator.[13]

A. LABOR MEDIATION AND ARBITRATION

The model for many of the current mechanisms is the system developed during World War II for handling grievances arising under collective bargaining agreements. Typically, such agreements provide for a series of steps whereby an employee with a grievance first complains to his foreman. Next a meeting occurs between the Union Committee and the Plant Committee. Finally, if the matter cannot be resolved within the plant by negotiation, the parties select an outside arbitrator, often with the assistance of the American Arbitration Association or the Federal Mediation and Conciliation Service. This procedure is comparatively expeditious and inexpensive, even though recent complaints suggest it is becoming more formal, costly, and time-consuming. In short, it is too much like the court system it was originally designed to circumvent.[14]

This procedure for dealing with disputes arising under collective bargaining agreements should be contrasted with disputes which arise in reaching such agreements. With collective bargaining, negotiation and mediation are the principal dispute settlement tools, because economic terms of employment are rarely externally imposed on the parties. Hence, if an agreement cannot be achieved by these means, the principal economic weapon, the strike, might be deemed necessary. However, in certain public sector industries where strikes cannot be tolerated fire departments, police departments and schools, compulsory arbitration is sometimes utilized.[15]

Troublesome questions have also been raised when employees present claims arising under recent enactments guaranteeing non-discrimination on account of sex, race or age. Such cases have often created bitter contests, with sharply differing factual assertions. Therefore, some commentators, have suggested that adjudication is unsuitable because of its "win-lose" nature and have argued for resolving some of these cases by a process of mediation.[16]

B. COMMERCIAL ARBITRATION

Long before the rise of labor arbitration, commercial contract disputes were submitted to arbitration by a panel of experts in the industry. This mechanism works particularly well in industries where a continuing relationship exists between the parties. Such cases necessitate an expeditious and amicable method, by which one or more individuals familiar with the trade practices can resolve the disputes. The American Arbitration Association now handles close to 10,000 of these disputes each year. In addition, an untold number are handled similarly under private industry agreements.

C. CONSUMER DISPUTES

In a sense, consumer disputes could be subsumed under the category of commercial arbitration. Consumer disputes, however, typically involve smaller claims. Additionally, consumer contract agreements rarely provide for arbitration of disputes.[17]

In recent years several mechanisms have been developed for extra-judicial handling of consumer disputes. Some states have created consumer protection divisions within the attorney general's office, where such claims are sought-to be mediated, often by volunteers.[18] Likewise, some industry groups, such as the Better Business Bureaus, have established procedures for arbitrating such claims. Some industries (e.g., automobiles and major appliances) even set up panels providing free arbitration of the consumer's claim.[19] Of course, consumer claims also can be presented in small claims court[20] and, where available, to media action programs such as Call for Action, where the service provided is not really dispute resolution but information and referral. Because of the clout wielded by these latter groups, they sometimes act in effect like mediators or ombudsmen in adjusting consumer grievances. A recent study, however, suggests the effectiveness and accessibility of some of these mechanisms may be suspect.[21]

D. INTERPERSONAL DISPUTES

One of the best examples of the need for new dispute resolution mechanisms can be seen with respect to various types of interpersonal disputes. Here, the tendency of courts to look backwards and produce winners and losers is least responsive to the needs of the parties, who usually are seeking to resolve present controversies and avoid future disputes. Mediation, which helps the parties settle their problems jointly, is far more suited to this task than adjudication.[22]

1. Neighborhood Justice Centers

In the past decade well over two hundred community dispute centers have been created.[23] These are known by various names, ranging from "citizen complaint center" to "neighborhood justice center." These centers are either freestanding institutions or are affiliated with the court.[24] Center referrals are received from the court, prosecutor, police or other community agencies; some disputants also come on a walk-in basis. The kinds of cases handled varies widely, from landlord-tenant disputes to domestic and neighbor quarrels.[25]

Although dispute centers vary greatly, two differing prototypes deserve exploration. One, commonly attached to a prosecutor's office, features rapid screening of a large number of cases to determine whether quick settlement might be possible and desirable. These programs involve high-volume processing in very short sessions, which law students often conduct. Whether this process should be viewed as true mediation is open to question.

In contrast to this approach is the more typical mediation, conducted by a professionally trained mediator or by a person drawn from the neighborhood who has received mediation training. Two or three mediators often conduct these mediations, which typically last three to four hours. These meetings allow disputants a full opportunity to present their views, and permit the mediators to meet with each of the disputants separately before attempting to reach agreement.

On the whole, the experience with these projects has been encouraging, although further public education is needed to stimulate greater resort to these unfamiliar institutions. Americans appear too prone to presume that anyone engaged in a dispute should take it to a lawyer or court. Ironically, the individuals who do use the new projects find them helpful and satisfying, and the agreements reached appear to endure.[26] New York recently became the first state to recognize the value of these agencies by providing public funding for them.[27]

2. Divorce Mediation

Although some neighborhood justice centers handle divorces, these cases often present more challenging problems of dispute settlement because complex legal and tax issues arise, as well as difficult questions of child custody. In 1981, California became the first state to require mediation to resolve all child custody disputes. In a number of other jurisdictions, mediation services are available in court-connected agencies. The principal development in divorce mediation, however, has occurred outside the courts, as lawyers and mental health professionals perform mediation as a private service. Although public interest in this alternative to the traditional legal process is widespread, the institution of divorce mediation remains in a state of infancy. Questions yet to be resolved include: Who should be the mediators? What kind of training should they receive? How should their services be compensated? How, if at all, will representative lawyers fit into this process? Should a new form of regulation be developed for this newly emerging profession?[28]

3. Parent/Child Disputes

Another subcategory of cases that might be heard in neighborhood justice centers, but is sometimes handled in separate projects, involves various types of parent/child disputes. A recent study attempted to inventory such projects.[29] One such project is the Children's Hearing Project in Cambridge, Massachusetts, which is patterned on a similar proceeding in Scotland. Both projects utilize citizens from the community to help parents and children settle their disputes.[30]

E. INTRA-INSTITUTIONAL DISPUTES

Some institutions have recently applied the grievance machinery model of the labor sector to their intra-institutional settings. For example, a California prison established a grievance committee comprising prisoners and supervisory personnel to air prisoner complaints. If the case could not be resolved internally, it would be submitted, at least in an advisory capacity, to an outside arbitrator. This process features initial consideration by a group with representation from both sides, and the possibility of ultimate submission to an outside authority.[31] This process has been replicated in other correctional facilities[32] and other institutional settings, such as schools.[33]

Despite the analogy to the collective bargaining context, there are obvious differences between labor and prison contexts. In the prison all power is on one side, and that side is often reluctant to surrender any power, even to an outside arbiter's advisory review. Hence, the success of grievance mechanisms in the more complex prison setting has been questioned.[34] Alternative ways of resolving prisoner disputes, which make up a very large proportion of the recent caseload growth in the federal courts, are voluntary mediation of prisoner grievances, and ombudsman mechanisms.[35] The latter method involves a third party of great ability and integrity who is empowered to investigate complaints or grievances. Following completion of the inquiry, the ombudsman makes recommendations to the individual in charge of the institution. Usually an ombudsman has no coercive power, but if he is highly regarded, his judgment is given considerable respect. It would be difficult for the institution's presiding authority wholly to ignore a prestigious ombudsman's report that a meritorious grievance had been unfairly ignored. Therein, of course, lies a principal reason for institutional resistance to this mechanism.

F. CLAIMS AGAINST THE GOVERNMENT

The ombudsman institution first arose in Scandinavia in response to citizen's complaints against the government. A number of American states and municipalities now have ombudsmen.[36] An analogue of the ombudsman concept has been the development of media action lines such as Call for Action on television.[37]

G. PUBLIC DISPUTES

Most of the controversies considered previously involve two disputants, with relatively concrete, defined concerns. In recent years, however, more large-scale disputes have arisen involving a multiplicity of parties and interests. Examples of such disputes are community conflicts over whether a facility should be built in the area, certain racial controversies, major claims to land holdings by native Americans, and environmental disputes.[38] Such cases have proved to be far more intractable, and have often required a combination of litigation and mediation. A number of organizations, most of them privately sponsored, have sought to develop special expertise in the handling of such cases.[39]

H. COURT-ANNEXED MECHANISMS

Most of the mechanisms discussed thus far are primarily found in the private dispute resolution sector and are not a part of the formal court structure. In an attempt to make courts more responsive to the emerging alternatives movement, ADRMs have been incorporated in one way or another into the court system. In that respect, these developments represent a partial foreshadowing of the "multi-door courthouse" notion more fully explored in Section III below.

1. Small Claims Adjudication and Mediation

Over fifty years ago courts were recognized as too elaborate and expensive for simple cases involving only small claims. This led to the creation of small claims court, where litigants themselves, without lawyers, can present their disputes. These actions normally involve claims of not more than $1,000 and result in a type of quick, rough justice. Some scholars have recently raised serious questions about the efficacy of small claims courts.[40] Nevertheless, the institution appears to be an essentially durable one that has carved a place in the catalog of useful dispute settlement mechanisms. An interesting recent variant has been utilization of mediation in small claims court.[41]

2. Compulsory Arbitration

Following a 1950s experiment in Philadelphia a number of jurisdictions have recently passed legislation requiring all monetary claims cases up to a certain limit (generally around $10,000–$15,000) to be initially processed by arbitration. In view of the prevailing right to trial by jury, a right to *de novo* review must then be accorded in the courts. However, such recourse to the courts might be subjected to cost sanctions if the petitioner does not prevail in court. Absent such a sanction, the net result might be to substitute two proceedings for the previous one. A similar program was begun on an experimental basis in three federal district courts.[42] Preliminary data from these experiments are encouraging, and show that even where a sizeable percentage of the cases are appealed to court, very few proceed to trial.[43]

3. Malpractice Screening

Following the malpractice "crisis" in the mid-seventies, a number of states set up special procedures for malpractice actions. Often the parties are initially required to arbitrate their differences. In other jurisdictions, such as Massachusetts, a screening panel is established, consisting of a doctor, lawyer and judge. The panel determines whether a *prima facie* case is established. If not, the plaintiff may proceed only by putting up a bond for the defendant's costs.[44]

The success of these experiments has varied. In some states, the special procedures have been abandoned or declared unconstitutional. In others, the mechanisms have worked well to screen out spurious claims.

4. Large Litigation

Many of the devices discussed above are applicable only to what has sometimes been referred to as "minor disputes." Some devices have also been developed to deal specifically with large and complex litigation.

a. Rent-a-Judge

Arbitration often employs experienced individuals such as retired judges to arbitrate difficult cases. Such use of arbitration, by consent of the parties, is quite different from that discussed in Section 2 above, where reference to arbitration is compulsory rather than consensual.

A variant of this practice has developed in some jurisdictions, notably California. It calls for parties to select a retired judge to hear the case, much as an arbitrator would. The procedures applied are the same as those that would apply in court, except as otherwise modified by the parties. Most notably, the judge's decision has the same force and effect as a judgment entered by a regular court.

The Rent-a-Judge procedure raises important policy questions. For example, should parties be able to hire the best available judges under circumstances where their decision has the full force of law, just as if the case had been decided in court? How does this practice square with the notion of equal access to the courts regardless of means? What will be the impact of such a practice on the regular judiciary? These questions and others deserve more discussion than they have received thus far.[45]

b. Mini-Trial

Ten years ago some imaginative litigants in the federal district court in California developed an innovative extrajudicial mechanism to aid in the settlement of complex and protracted litigation.[46] The procedure calls for the parties to select an experienced individual to preside at a two-day information exchange. Each party has one day to present its case in any form it desires, including questions for the opposing side. The highest official of each party, assuming a corporate litigant, must attend this hearing. At the end of the proceeding, the two top officials confer, without their lawyers, to evaluate the case. In the seminal case utilizing this innovative procedure, the parties promptly settled.[47] If an agreement is not reached, then the presiding official will give his view concerning how the case would be resolved in court. The parties then use this additional information to discuss settlement. If settlement is not achieved, the procedure has no evidentiary effect and the case returns to court. In virtually all cases which have utilized this procedure, however, settlement has been achieved.[48] The procedure has the additional virtue that it can be readily adapted to different situations (e.g., the presider can be dispensed with, more or less time can be allowed for the presentations).

III. Problems and Prospects

As noted earlier, the recent resurgence of the alternatives movement has now passed through several phases. After the initial period of exuberant expansionism, a more critical and reflective phase has ensued, and a number of difficult and fundamental questions are emerging. The remainder of this paper will attempt to address some of these questions.

A. RELATION OF ADRMS TO EACH OTHER AND TO THE COURT SYSTEM

Implicit in the preceding discussion is the notion that dispute resolution mechanisms are dispersed throughout the social fabric. The mechanisms are either public or private, mandatory or optional. Wherever disputes arise among individuals or organizations, a complex network of possible grievance mechanisms appears to be available for the venting of these grievances.[49] The question which naturally arises is what, if any, relationship should exist among the different types of mechanisms. This question assumes importance not only for the disputant who might benefit from some guidance concerning where to take any particular dispute, but also for a society seeking to provide a coherent response to these grievances.

One can envision a system possessing a hierarchy, and structure within the formal public dispute resolution system, complemented by a vast and ill-understood network of indigenous dispute mechanisms. In essence, that is our present system. Disputants might first try to utilize the array of informal mechanisms provided in the particular arena where the dispute arises. Then, as a last resort, disputants might take the controversy to the public forum, the court.[50] That is the paradigm but in fact, informal private mechanisms, are frequently not available, or if they are, they are not resorted to. The result is often the typically American tendency to take the case immediately to court. The net effect is that many disputes presented to court are not appropriate for court adjudication and could be better handled by some other mechanism.[51]

This situation led me to suggest, in a paper delivered at the Pound Conference in 1976, a more comprehensive and diverse mechanism known as a Dispute Resolution Center.[52] This center would provide a variety of dispute resolution processes, according to the needs of the particular dispute. This concept was later termed "the multi-door courthouse" (MDC).[53]

What would such an institution look like? A provisional first-step type of MDC could consist essentially of a screening and referral clerk who would seek to diagnose incoming cases and refer them to the most suitable ADRMs. Depending on the available mechanisms in the particular community, referrals might be made to mediation, arbitration, court adjudication, fact finding, malpractice screening, media action lines or an ombudsman. Such a model would be subject to all the familiar deficiencies of a referred scheme. For example, slippage often occurs between the act of referral and the receiving agency's actual handling of the case.

A more ideal model would contain all the "doors" under one roof, as part of an integrated dispute resolution center. Such a mansion might feature the following doors:

(1) effective and accessible small claims adjudication;
(2) services for family, landlord/tenant, and other continuing relations cases;
(3) ombudsmen for the processing of disputes between citizens and large bureaucracies;
(4) social service agencies providing mental health counseling and treatment of alcohol and drug related problems;
(5) trial court of general jurisdiction for novel statutory and constitutional claims, as well as major criminal cases; and
(6) compulsory arbitration for small monetary claims.

Additional dispute processing forums might include those mediating or arbitrating juvenile matters and those handling ordinance violations such as bad checks and health code and building code violations.[54]

Recently, under the auspices of the American Bar Association, three cities, Tulsa, Houston and Washington, D.C., have been selected for experimental multi-door courthouse projects. These programs are now in their initial eighteen month pilot phase. At the end of that period mid-course corrections will be made in the structure of the referral scheme to take account of malfunctioning or missing "doors." In a final six month phase, the ABA hopes to draw on the learning of these experiments to develop a nationally replicable model.

An integrated multi-door courthouse would have a number of benefits as well as potential pitfalls. First, such a full-service MDC would provide an efficient way of availing a wide range of dispute processes. It could also serve as a major source of information and referral, transcending the particular "doors" that are available. Second, bringing such diverse ADRMs under the court umbrella would solve the increasingly difficult question of how to fund alternative mechanisms. Likewise, it would avoid the pro-court adjudication bias inherent in the present system where the state pays the costs of court adjudication but not those of other, often more suitable, mechanisms.

Third, because of the predominant emphasis on courts in our society, most alternatives are seldom used. This caseload drought is ironic in light of the generally high satisfaction rate among those parties using alternative mechanisms.[55] Thus, a major difficulty appears to be popular unfamiliarity with these mechanisms. This requires additional public education, but it also argues for building ARDMs into an expanded court system.[56]

These are some of the substantial benefits that might be derived from such an ADRM experiment. However, major obstacles exist as well. A critical feature would be the initial screening which would require a highly skilled intake worker rather than a bureaucratic court functionary. Accordingly, a crucial question is whether ADRM specialists presently have sufficient knowledge of the particular characteristics of various dispute processes and mechanisms. This knowledge is necessary to confidently refer particular types of cases to one or another mechanism. While this science is at a primitive stage, one could posit a number of plausible criteria for determining the suitability of various dispute mechanisms.[57]

1. Nature of Case

ADRMs should be designed to handle a novel claim challenging the constitutionality of a statute quite differently from a claim applying established principles to a specific set of facts. Only the former merits the unique skills and resources of a court. The latter can be more expeditiously and inexpensively dealt with by arbitration.

2. Relationship of Disputants

Adjudication typically seeks to make a definitive determination with respect to past events, while mediation attempts to restructure the relationship of the disputants.[58] Thus, mediation best resolves cases involving long-term relationships extending into the future. For example, a mediator is more likely to resolve effectively a mid-contract dispute between a landlord and tenant, or even a divorce, than is a judge. Not only will a mediator be better equipped to restructure future relationships, but the open-ended and non-coercive process of mediation is also more likely to teach the parties to recognize and resolve future controversies. Mediation thus gives maximum durability to the settlement the parties have crafted.

A significant qualification, however, is presented in the case where the two disputants have substantially disparate bargaining power. In such a case, mediation is either pointless, or worse yet, threatens to take undue and unfair advantage of the weaker party. ADRM specialists must learn far more about the optional combination of formal adjudicative and informal mediation processes for this type of case.[59]

3. Size and Complexity of Claim

Society has already taken some account of the size and complexity criterion in establishing, on an optional basis, small claims courts for the processing of minor disputes. Some states have even experimented with the use of different tracks for cases of different complexity.[60] Generally, however, transaction costs in processing disputes have largely been ignored. To be sure, certain cases (e.g., a serious crime or a major constitutional challenge) should not be measured by the amount in controversy. Beyond those cases and others raising similar considerations, however, should not we lawyers be more attuned to the immense public cost every time a lawsuit is processed in court? If a case involves only $1000 and does not raise larger issues of public policy, should society not *require* such a case to be processed in small claims court or its functional equivalent? The counterargument, of course, is that for the low-income consumer a claim of $1000 over his defective refrigerator is as important as a multi-million dollar claim is for General Motors. That argument, however, misses the point. If the larger claim is also a straightforward collection action, it also does not deserve access to the deluxe adjudication model. These factors and others need further exploration. Indeed, one of the potential benefits of such a tentative typology is that it will permit the acquisition of significant additional data to test some of the stated hypotheses.

In addition to the cited general criteria, certain programmatic channels might also be proposed. For example, medical malpractice claims would be directed to the appropriate screening tribunal. Prisoners' claims might be sent to an internal grievance mechanism to be initially processed.[61] And if the jurisdiction had an ombudsman, claims against the government would be directed there.

As appealing and efficient as such a scheme might be, it would undoubtedly have its costs. First, intelligent central referral presumes the intake official is completely aware of all the facts. However, disputants are often notoriously inarticulate in voicing their real grievances. In such a case, the true complaint does not surface until much later in the proceeding. Second, any new institution also runs the risk of sinking to the lowest bureaucratic level, and thereby eliminating the benefits that emanate from decentralized, indigenous dispute resolution. A related bureaucratic nightmare has the MDC simply shunting difficult and undesirable cases to an endless series of "alternatives" from which the disputants emerge dissatisfied and disillusioned.

A final question is whether the referral process should be optional or compulsory. A system of mandatory referral raises different questions of law and policy than would a merely advisory reference. No single uniform answer to this question is required. At the outset, referral should undoubtedly be voluntary, while necessary information is obtained about the workings of the system. But once that level of experience and understanding is attained with respect to a particular class of cases, that particular referral process might become mandatory. For example, sufficient data now exist to warrant the initial compulsory referral of small monetary claims to arbitration.[62] However, ADRM specialists must first learn more about what types of cases are particularly suitable for such treatment, and what types of cases are not.[63]

B. DATA DROUGHT

Despite all of the recent developments in alternative modes of dispute settlement, relatively little is known about the critical questions of ADRMs.[64] For example, ADRM specialists have essentially no sophisticated data concerning the relative time and cost of alternative dispute settlement mechanisms such as arbitration and mediation. No doubt this problem is due to the difficult questions that would be posed by such an inquiry. What, for example, are the appropriate ingredients of cost? What is the aggregate cost to the system? What is the cost to the parties? And how does one determine the comparative cost of a case in court? Should cost be determined on a marginal or an average basis? What is the appropriate time frame?

Suppose, for example, that a particular court case cost $462, while a mediated solution cost $597. Does this show that mediation is more costly, even if the effect of the mediation were not only to settle the present dispute but to prevent future ones? This question suggests the difficulty of measuring potential benefits to be derived from particular forms of dispute settlement. Perhaps these questions explain why so little sophisticated research has been published.

Nevertheless, reliable data now exist confirming one's intuitive assumption that mediation leads to higher disputant satisfaction—even where no settlement is reached—and concomitantly to greater compliance with the terms of the settlement. Although such results might be suspect in situations where the mediated cases resulted from self-selection, some of the studies involve a process akin to random assignment.[65] Hence, these results are extremely important and encouraging, particularly in fields like child support enforcement where noncompliance is a significant problem.[66]

C. CRITIQUES

In recent years the alternatives movement has been severely attacked from a number of quarters. Perhaps the most pervasive of these has emanated from the political left. The argument suggests that providing ADRMs for the poor and powerless constitutes the establishment's attempt to "cool out" legitimate grievances by negotiating or mediating away poor people's legal rights.[67]

To the extent that this argument rests on implicit premises of distributive justice, it goes well beyond the issues of formal versus informal justice. In fact, little evidence suggests that the courts can, barring very exceptional situations, bring about major redistributions of wealth and power. Indeed, given the existing constraints of restricted access to the courts and the summary treatment accorded many litigants, it is far from clear that disputants fare less well in the informal system.[68] Moreover, the limited empirical evidence supports the conclusion that disputants prefer the informal system.[69] Perhaps, from a radical perspective, this only proves that the courts themselves are an instrument of capitalist domination. However, that argument takes us considerably beyond the issue of formal versus informal justice.

If the focus is narrowed to the actual operation of the informal system, a number of legitimate issues arise. Particularly where alternatives are considered for minor criminal cases, questions arise concerning the availability of various procedural and constitutional protections.[70] Perhaps this question becomes essentially one of fair notice and free choice. If the "defendant" prefers the informal process after having been fully apprised of the protections and consequences in each system, there can be little complaint. This goal, however, might be difficult to achieve in practice. In fact, some programs fail to fully disclose the different procedures and consequences of each system. Occasionally, those programs effectively push the complainee into the informal system, for example, by sending him a letter on District Attorney stationary so "suggesting."[71] Where the program is overtly compulsory, in court-annexed arbitration, different types of issues arise, such as whether the legally required right of access to the courts, following exhaustion of the alternative mechanism, can be significantly burdened, as by imposing various "costs" on the judicial petitioner.

Other problems stem from inadequate conceptualization of ADRM processes. For example, if a substantial power disparity exists between disputants then mediation will be inappropriate because it threatens to exploit the apparent powerlessness of one disputant.[72] Perhaps here again it is largely a question of full information coupled with free choice.[73] Or, as noted with respect to a comparable situation in an environmental dispute, we need to learn more about the optimal interrelationship between the formal and the informal legal processes. ADRM specialists should strive to combine the court's power-equalizing role with the greater participation, flexibility and range of choices offered by the meditative process.[74]

D. ROLE OF LAWYERS IN ADRMS

What is the proper role of attorneys in alternative dispute resolution mechanisms? First, ADRMs must distinguish between a lawyer's role as a representative of the disputants, and a lawyer's role as a dispute resolver. With respect to the former, much turns on the nature of the proceeding. If, for example, the dispute is a low-key squabble between two neighbors, lawyers might not be needed. However, if the dispute is a complex divorce case involving technical issues in a zero sum context, the argument for legal representation becomes much more compelling. In short, the issue of legal representation in ADRMs is not unlike that in court. The mere fact that the alternative process is nonadversary does not necessarily indicate that lawyers have no legitimate role.[75]

When the lawyer's role as dispute resolver is considered, the lawyer's claimed expertise must rest on a different footing. Unfortunately, much of a law student's training is in adversary dispute settlement rather than accommodative problem-solving. This situation is rapidly changing, however. Increasingly, legal education encompasses mediation and other ADRM training.[76] Hence, lawyers should be neither specially qualified nor disqualified for alternative dispute resolution. Depending on the case in question, lawyers with appropriate training might often possess excellent credentials for alternative dispute resolution.

The new roles outlined above present an exciting challenge to the legal community. If it is to be successfully met, the new system will require

1) the continued support of the legal education community (include the continuing legal education establishment);
2) an open mind on the part of the legal ethics committees who will be asked to sanction the work done by these newly created professionals;
3) some institutional mechanisms capable of providing training and possibly financial support to aid traditional lawyers in making appropriate vocational changes; and
4) possible regulation and certification of the new professionals.

IV. Conclusion

The alternative dispute resolution movement is at a critical turn in the road. Too often in the past, hopes of a coordinated program of experimentation and research have been dashed as the dispute resolution program fell victim to the budgetary ax. The establishment of the National Institute of Dispute Resolution may represent the final opportunity for the sound development of this promising movement.

Successful ADRMs require a broad effort to expand our presently limited understanding of the field. Progress will require continued experimentation and research, as well as further attempts to conceptualize the field. Enhanced public education about the benefits to be derived from alternative modes of dispute settlement will be necessary. Above all, the ADR movement will require the broadened involvement and support not only of the legal and legal education establishments, but also of the political and social orders and the public at large.

Notes

1. J. Marks, E. Johnson Jr. & P. Szanton, *Dispute Resolution in America: Processes in Evolution* (Nat'l Inst, for Dispute Resolution 1984).

2. Felstiner, Abel & Sarat, *The Emergence & Transformation of Disputes: Naming, Blaming, Claiming*, 15 L. & Soc'y Rev. 631 (1980–1981); Galanter, *Justice in Many Rooms*, 19 J. of Legal Pluralism 1 (1981).

3. *See* J. Auerbach, *Justice Without Law? Resolving Disputes Without Lawyers* (1983).

4. *See* Access to Justice and the Welfare State 147 (M. Cappelletti ed. 1981).

5. Ford Foundation, New Approaches to Conflict Resolution 25 (1978).

6. Compare the return to midwives in medicine. *See* Smith, *A Warmer Way of Disputing: Mediation & Conciliation*, 26 Am. J. of Comp. L. 205 (Supp. 1978).

7. *See* J. Marks, E. Johnson, Jr. & Szanton, *supra* note 1.

8. *See*, e.g., Nader, *Disputing Without the Force of Law*, 88 Yale L.J. 998 (1979).

9. *See*, e.g., Fuller, *The Forms and Limits of Adjudication*, 92 Harv. L. Rev. 353 (1979) [hereinafter cited as Fuller, *Adjudication*] Fuller, Mediation,—*Its Forms and Functions*, 44 S. Cal. L. Rev. 305 (1971) [hereinafter cited as Fuller, *Mediation*]; Fuller, Collective Bargaining and the Arbitrator, 1963 Wis. L. Rev. 1 [hereinafter cited as Fuller, *Collective Bargaining*].

10. Although no definitive work has been done with respect to how to measure "effectiveness," presumably to be taken into account are such factors as cost, speed, satisfaction (to the public and the parties) and compliance. *Cf.* Getman, *Labor Arbitration and Dispute Resolution*, 88 Yale L.J. 916 (1979).

11. *See* J. Lieberman, The Litigious Society (1981); Manning, *Hyperlexis, Our National Disease*, 71 Nw. U.L. Rev. 767 (1977); *see also* Council on the Role of Courts, The Role of Courts in American Society (J. Lieberman ed. 1984) [hereinafter cited as CORC].

12. For further elaboration, see E. Green, S. Goldberg & F. Sander, Dispute Resolution (1985); J, Marks, E. Johnson & P. Szanton, Dispute Resolution in America: Processes in Evolution (1984) (National Institute for Dispute Resolution pamphlet); Singer, *Non-Judicial Dispute Resolution Mechanisms: The Effects on Justice for the Poor*, 1979 Clearinghouse Rev. 569. E. Johnson, V. Kanter & E. Schwartz, Outside the Courts: A Survey of Diversion Alternatives in Civil Cases (1977).

13. There are of course a host of hybrid processes, such as fact finding, inquiry and final offer selection. E. Green, S. Goldberg & F. Sander, *supra* note 12.

14. *See generally* E. Teple & R. Moberly, Arbitration and Conflict Resolution (1979); Getman, supra note 10.

15. Occasionally in these situations final offer arbitration is used. Here the arbitrator can select only one side's or the other's best offer, nothing in between. An obvious effect of this mechanism is to induce more serious bargaining. E. Green, S. Goldberg & F. Sander, *supra* note 13.

16. *See*, e.g., Meacham, *The Use of Mediation to Resolve Employment Discrimination Complaints*, 28 Bost. Bar J. 21 (May–June 1984); A. Westin, Corporate Programs for Handling Employee Discrimination Complaints: An Analysis of Current Mechanisms to Resolve EEO Disputes Through Internal or Voluntary Mechanisms (1983) (unpublished mimeo by the Educational Fund for Individual Rights, Columbia University Law School).

17. One exception is medical care agreements that provide for the handling of malpractice claims by an arbitration tribunal. *See* Henderson, *Contractual Problems in the Enforcement of Agreements to Arbitrate Medical Malpractice*, 58 Va. L. Rev. 947 (1972).

18. E. Johnson, V. Kantor & E. Schwartz, supra note 12, at 67.

19. F. Sander, American Bar Association Report on the National Conference on Minor Disputes Resolution, May 1977 (1978). Manufacturers of automobiles and major appliances are among the industries utilizing free arbitration panels. *Id.*

20. *See infra* notes 40–41 and accompanying text.

21. No Access to Law: Alternatives to the American Judicial System (L. Nader ed. 1980].

22. Fuller, *Mediation, supra* note 9.

23. American Bar Association Special Committee on Alternative Dispute Resolution, Dispute Resolution Directory (1983).

24. Recently, a number of church groups have also sponsored such programs. *See, e.g.*, R. Kraybill, Repairing the Breach, Ministering in Community Conflict (1982).

25. *See* Neighborhood Justice: Assessment of an Emerging Idea (R. Tomasic & M. Feeley eds. 1982).

26. R. Cook, J. Roehl & D. Sheppard, Neighborhood Justice Field Test: Final Evaluation Report (1980).

27. *See* 1981 N.Y. Laws, ch. 847.

28. *See* ABA, Alternative Means of Family Dispute Resolution (1982); ABA, Divorce Mediation: Readings (1985); J. Haynes, Divorce Mediation: A Practical Guide for Therapists and Counselors (1981); Winks, *Divorce Mediation: A Nonadversary Procedure No-Fault Divorce*, 19 J. Fam. L. 615 (1981); J. Lemmon, Family Mediation Practice (1985).

29. E. Vorenberg, State of the Art Survey of Dispute Resolution Programs Involving Juveniles, (A.B.A. Special Committee 1982).

30. *See, e.g.*, Children's Hearings (F. Martin & K. Murray eds. 1976).

31. For elaboration of other essential aspects of such a grievance mechanism, see Keating & Kolze, *An Inmate Grievance Mechanism: From Design to Practice*, 39 Fed. Probation 42 (1975).

32. *See, e.g.*, G. Cole, R. Hansen & J. Silbert, Alternative Dispute Resolution Mechanisms for Prisoner Grievances (Nat'l Inst. Corrections 1984).

33. *See* Resolving Conflict in Higher Education (J. McCarthy ed. 1980).

34. *See* G. Cole, R. Hansen & J. Silbert, *supra* note 32.

35. *See id.*

36. *See* W. Gellhorn, When Americans Complain (1966); Frank, *Stale Ombudsman Legislation in the United States*, 29 U. Miami L. Rev. 397 (1975).

37. *See* Palen, *Media Ombudsmen: A Critical View*, 13 L. & Soc'y Rev. 799 (1979)

38. *See* Roundtable Justice: Case Studies in Conflict Resolution (R. Goldmann ed. 1980).

39. *See, e.g.*, G. Bingham, Resolving Environmental Disputes: A Decade of Experience (1985).

40. *See, e.g.*, J. Ruhnka & S. Weller, Small Claims Courts: A National Examination (1978); F. Sander, *supra* note 19; Ynguesson & Hennessey, *Small Claims, Complex Disputes: A Review of the Small Claims Literature*, 9 L. & Soc'y Rev. 219 (1975).

41. McEwen & Maiman, *Small Claims Mediation in Maine: An Empirical Assessment*, 33 Me. L. Rev. 237 (1981).

42. *See* Lind & Shapard, *Evaluation of Court-Annexed Arbitration in Three Federal District Courts*, Fed. Jud. Center (1981); Levin, Alternative Dispute Resolution in the Federal Courts, 37 U. Fla. L. Rev. 29 (1985).

43. *See, e.g.*, J. Adler, D. Hensler & C. Nelson, Simple Justice: How Liticants Fare in the Pittsburgh Arbitration Program (1983) (published by Rand Corp.).

44. *See* Note, *Recent Medical Malpractice Legislation—A First Checkup*, 50 Tul. L. Rev. 655 (1976); Comment, *An Analysis of State Legislative Reponses to the Medical Malpractice Crisis*, 1975 Duke L.J. 1417.

45. *See* E. Green, Avoiding the Legal Logjam—Private Justice California Style, 1982 Corporate Dispute Management, Note, *The California Rent-A-Judge Experiment: Constitutional and Policy Considerations of Pay-As-You-Go Courts*, 94 Harv. L. Rev. 1592 (1981).

46. Green, Marks & Olson, *Settling Large Case Litigation: An Alternative Approach*, 11 Loy. L.A.L. Rev. 493 (1978).

47. *Id.*

48. E. Green, The C.P.R. Mini-Trial Handbook, 1982 Corporate Dispute Management.

49. *See* Galanter, *supra* note 2.

50. At present, it is almost accidental if community members find their way to an appropriate forum other than the regular courts. Several other modes of dispute resolution already are available in many communities. Still, since they are operated by a hodge–podge of local government agencies, neighborhood organizations, and trade associations, citizens must be very knowledgeable about community resources to locate the right forum for their particular dispute. Johnson, Toward a Responsive Justice System, State Courts: A Blueprint for the Future 107, 122 (1978) (publication of National Center for State Courts).

51. *See* Sander, *Varieties of Dispute Processing*, 70 F.R.D. Ill (1976).

52. *Id.*

53. *See* E. Green, S. Goldberg & F. Sander, *supra* note 13, at 514.

54. *See* McGillis, *Minor Dispute Processing: A Review of Recent Developments*, in Neighborhood Justice, *supra* note 25, at 60.

55. *Cf.* Cook, Roehl & Sheppard, *supra* note 26; Pearson, *How Child Custody Mediation Works in Practice*, 20 Judges J. 11 [hereinafter cited as *Child Custody Medialion*]; Pearson, *An Evaluation of Alternatives to Court Adjudication*, 7 Just. Sys. J. 420 (1982) [hereinafter cited as *An Evaluation of Alternatives*]; McEwen & Maiman, *supra* note 41.

56. Cratsley, *Community Courts: Offering Alternative Dispute Resolution Within the Judicial System*, 3 Vt. L. Rev. 1 (1978).

57. *See* E. Green, S. Goldberg, & F. Sander, supra note 12; CORC, supra note 11.

58. *See* Fuller, *Mediation, supra* note 9.

59.   For example in an environmental dispute where the situational power resides predominantly in the polluter, an initial adjudication might be required to more nearly equalize the power relationship and bring the more powerful respondent to the bargaining table.

60. *See* Action Commission to Reduce Court Cost and Delay, Attacking Litigation Cost and Delay 7 (ABA 1984).

61. *Cf.* 42 U.S.C. 1997e (1932), authorizing stay of a federal civil rights action up to 90 days to permit exhaustion of an internal grievance mechanism, provided such remedy has been found to be "plain, speedy, and effective." This statute suggests the desirability of developing procedures for certifying certain ADRMs as meeting minimal requirements of fairness and efficacy—a kind of "Good Dispute Processing Seal of Approval." Such ADRMs might be given priority in funding and referrals. *Id.*

62. *See* J. Adler, D. Hensler & C. Nelson, *supra* note 43, at 524.

63. *See* An Evaluation of Alternatives, *supra* note 55.

64. *See* E. Green, S. Goldberg & F. Sander, *supra* note 13, at .

65. *See Child Custody Mediation, supra* note 55. *See also* W. Felstiner & L. Williams, Community Mediation in Dorchester, Massachusetts (1979, 1980); Cook, Roehl & Sheppard, *supra* note 26; McEwen & Maiman, *supra* note 41.

66. *See* J. Cassetty, *Child Support and Public Policy: Securing Support from Absent Fathers* (1978); *but cf.* D. Chambers, Making Fathers Pay: The Enforcement of Child Support (1979).

67. *See The Politics of Informal Justice* (R. Abel ed. 1982); R. Hofrichter, *Justice Centers Raise Basic Questions*, in Neighboring Justice, *supra* note 25.

68. *See* Rosenberg, *Civil Justice and Civil Reform*, 15 Law & Soc. Rev 473 (1980–1981); Johnson, *supra* note 50.

69. *See, e.g.*, R. Cook, J. Roehl & D. Sheppard, *supra* note 26. It is also somewhat puzzling that the communitarians who share many of the goals of the radical critics seek precisely the opposite result (i.e., delegalization and community-controlled dispute settlement). *See* R. Shonholtz, Neighborhood Justice Systems: Work, Structure, and Guiding Principles, 5 Mediation Q 3 (1984).

70. *See* Snyder, *Crime and Community Mediation—The Boston Experience A Preliminary Report on the Dorchester Urban Court Program*, 1978 Wis. L. Rev. 737; Rice, *Mediation and Arbitration as a Civil Alternative to the Criminal Justice System—An Overview and Legal Analysis*, 29 Am. U.L. Rev. 17 (1979).

71. *See* F. Sander, *supra* note 19.

72. Consider the power inequity between an overweaning husband, with access to professional resources, and a meek, subservient wife. See M. Levine, Power Imbalances in Vermont Law School Dispute Resolution Project, A Study of Barriers to the Use of Alternative Methods of Dispute Resolution 137 (1984).

73. For example, in the marital example in the previous footnote, the wife would first have to receive competent legal advice concerning her "rights" in court. If she then, for her own good reasons, knowingly opts for the informal system that should be no cuase for objection.

74. The individually tailored quality of most mediative solutions, however, might prove to be a disadvantage when dealing with recurring violations. For example, if a vendor has committed various consumer regulation violations, and settlement by mediation is considered for each claim, the underlying issues are never likely to be rectified. What is needed here is some form of "aggregate" remedy, akin to the "pattern and practice" litigation the Massachusetts Attorney General sometimes brings as a result of repeated complaints to the mediation branch of the Consumer Protection Division. See also the operation of the Swedish Consumer Complaint Board described in M. Eisenstein, *The Swedish Public Complaints Board: Its Vital Role in a System of Consumer Protection*, in 2 Access to Justice 491 (Cappelletti & Weisner eds. 19). This is another task that might be better fulfilled in the Multi-Door Courthouse central screening intake. Of course that could not deal with the problem of multi-jurisdictional violations; other techniques would be needed there. *Cf.* T. Ehrlich & J. Frank, Planning for Justice (1977) (published by Aspen Institute).

75. Consider, for example, the varying possible roles for representative lawyers in divorce mediation. *See* J. Folberc, & A. Taylor, Mediation (1984); Silberman, *Professional Responsibility Problems of Divorce Mediation*, 16 Fam. L.Q. 107 (1982). A lawyer might act simply as adviser to the mediator. *See, e.g.*, O. Coogler, Structured Mediation in Divorce Settlements (1978). Alternatively, each spouse could be urged to consult an attorney after a tentative agreement has been reached, or even at the outset of the entire process. *See* Samuels & Shawn, *The Role of the Lawyer Outside the Mediation Process*, 2 Med. Q. 13 (1983).

76. *See, e.g.*, Riskin, *Mediation and Lawyers*, 43 Ohio L.J. 29 (1982). A 1982 conference for law teachers engaged in or interested in dispute settlement drew well over 100 participants, and questionnaires sent out to all ABA-accredited law schools showed a sizeable proportion having some curricular and/or extra-curricular program in alternative dispute settlement.

¨This paper is a revision of a draft paper prepared for a conference on the lawyer's changing role in dispute settlement, held at Harvard Law School in October 1982. The paper differs somewhat from that delivered at the University of Florida College of Law in Fall 1984.

Global Peace Index and Global Terrorism Index

Visions of Humanity, Institute for Economics and Peace

The Global Peace Index (GPI), initiated by the Institute for Economics and Peace, first launched in 2007. The GPI became the first report to rank countries according to peacefulness. Entrepreneur Steve Killelea is credited with developing the idea for the index, which has since been endorsed by respected leaders from the Dalai Lama to economist Jeffrey Sachs to former UN Secretary-General Kofi Annan.

The research approach used to produce the GPI represents a mode of research that informs policy and often receives significant funding. Consistent with the aims of Epoch One, this study looks for indicators for peace to both predict and control outbreaks of global violence. Researchers want to know how states fail. Once identified, these indicators are analyzed regarding large amounts of data to conduct a causal analysis. The validity of studies are proven through large data sets, quality indicators (factors), and strong statistical methodology. This particular GPI defines peace as the absence of active violence. Negative peace or structural violence is not included.

While the GPI does tell a story, many conflict resolution professionals note how this form of research overlooks systemic relations between parts and the biases of researchers weighing indicators. Researchers decide what indicators matter; they do not seek the advice of affected parties to find out what they see as important.

In 2012, the same institute launched the Global Terrorism Index (GTI) to rank changes in terrorist activity. The GTI ranks 163 countries and is based on over 150,000 cases of terrorism collected by the Global Terrorism Database. The hope is that by finding trends, we can anticipate and interrupt terrorist outbreaks.

Visit the Indexes online:

Global Peace Index: http://visionofhumanity.org/indexes/global-peace-index/

Global Terrorism Index: http://visionofhumanity.org/indexes/terrorism-index/

Questions to consider: When reading the GPI, try to locate the United States. What kind of view of the world is this index painting? Can you understand how peace is being measured?

Failed States

Daniel C. Esty, Jack Goldstone, Ted Robert Gurr, Barbara Harff, Pamela T. Surko, Alan N. Unger, and Robert Chen

The authors of this piece were part of the State Failure Project. The project, commissioned by the Central Intelligence Agency's Directorate of Intelligence, was formed in response to Vice President Al Gore's request. The task force consisted of academic, data, and management specialists. The co-authors listed were the senior consultants to the Task Force. They worked to assist U.S. government policy-makers who wanted to anticipate which states might erupt into violence. Such violence often leads to widespread humanitarian crises.

The Task Force reviewed state failures occurring from 1955–1994, the majority of the Epoch One period. They sorted the conflicts into categories and then identified demographic, political, social, environmental, and economic variables. The article discusses the variables and the task forces' recommendations for the next steps. The idea of this approach to conflict is that if we can predict where the failures will be, we can intervene in advance. As mentioned throughout Epoch One, prediction dominated the field during this period. The article considers the strengths and limitations of the methodology but does not address bias or the need to solicit feedback from local populations about what they believe brings stability.

Questions to consider: What kind of research is used to collect this kind of data? What kinds of policies or state actions do you think these findings might support? Do you think knowing about potential violence is enough to prevent it?

"Failed States and International Security: Causes, Prospects, and Consequences"

Purdue University, West Lafayette
Feburary 25-27, 1998

The State Failure Project
Early Warning Research for U.S. Foreign Policy
Planning

*by Daniel C. Esty, Jack Goldstone, Ted Robert Gurr,
Barbara Harff, Pamela T. Surko, Alan N. Unger, and
Robert Chen*

State failure and state collapse are new labels for a type of severe political crisis exemplified by events of the early 1990s in Somalia, Bosnia, Liberia, and Afghanistan. In these instances the institutions of the central state were so weakened that they could no longer maintain authority or political order beyond the capital city, and sometimes not even there. Such state failures usually occur in circumstances of widespread and violent civil conflict, often accompanied by severe humanitarian crises. These conditions may precede or follow the institutional collapse of the state; sometimes they are instrumental in causing it. In a general sense they are all part of a syndrome of serious political crisis which, in the extreme case, leads to the collapse of governance.[1]

The international consequences of state failures are profound. Failed states often threaten regional security and require major inputs of humanitarian assistance. And they pose long-term and costly challenges of rebuilding shattered governments and societies. A vital policy question is whether failures can be diagnosed far enough in advance to facilitate effective international efforts at prevention or peaceful transformation. The State Failure Task Force was established in response to a 1994 request from the office of the Vice President of the United States to design and carry out a data-driven study on the correlates of state failure. The ultimate objective is to develop a methodology to identify key factors and critical thresholds signaling a high risk of political crisis in countries some two years in advance. This chapter describes the approach taken in the first phase of the Task

Force's work, outlines some general findings, and identifies research issues to be dealt with in future work.[2]

Identifying State Failures and Control Cases

No more than a dozen complete collapses of state authority have occurred during the last 40 years, too few for meaningful generalization. Therefore the Task Force broadened its focus to include partial state failures. This is consistent with distinctions that other researchers have made between states that have collapsed completely and those in the process of failing. Zartman (1995:9) observes that "State collapse is a long-term degenerative disease . . . an extreme case of governance problems." Helman and Ratner (1992–93:5) identify states whose survival was threatened in the early 1990s, among them Ethiopia, Georgia, and Congo/Zaire. In Africa, states were said to be in serious danger of collapse in Mozambique, Angola, Rwanda, Burundi, Chad, and Sierra Leone (Nellier, 1993; cited in Zartman, 1995:3, 11). Whereas all these states experienced very serious problems of violent challenges and ineffective governance in the early 1990s, by early 1997 some had pulled back from the brink—examples are Georgia and Mozambique—whereas others had collapsed and then were reconstituted under new leadership —as in Ethiopia and Rwanda.

The first challenge facing the Task Force was to identify systematically all occurrences of partial or complete state failure that began between 1955 and 1994. We began from existing compilations of revolutionary and ethnic conflicts, regime crises, and massive human rights violations that are typically associated with state breakdown. The problem set of state failures thus includes four categories of serious political conflicts and crises that have been identified in specialized studies and data collections. Within each category, events are scaled by magnitude to permit analysis of the conditions associated with the extent of state failure.[3]

Revolutionary wars are sustained military conflicts between insurgents and central governments, aimed at displacing the regime[4] (n = 40). They include:

- Large-scale and intense guerrilla wars with more than 250,000 deaths; for example, mujahidin warfare against the Khalq regime in Afghanistan, 1978–1992.
- Large-scale and intense guerrilla and civil wars with 10,000 to 250,000 deaths; for example, the Sandinista guerrilla war against the Somoza regime in Nicaragua, 1978–1979.
- Small-scale guerrilla wars and rebellions that result in 1,000 to 10,000 deaths; for example, left-wing guerrilla warfare against the Colombian government, 1984 to the present.

Ethnic wars are secessionist civil wars, rebellions, protracted communal warfare, and sustained episodes of mass protest by politically organized communal groups[5] (n = 75). They include:

- Large-scale and intense ethnic wars with more than 250,000 deaths; for example, the rebellion by southern Sudanese, 1983 to the present.
- Large-scale and intense wars with between 10,000 and 250,000 deaths; for example, the Kurdish rebellion against the Khomeini regime in Iran, 1979–1984.
- Small-scale communal wars and rebellions with 1,000 to 10,000 deaths; for example, the Intifadah campaign in the Israeli-occupied territories, 1988–1994.
- Protracted episodes of violent communal rioting, clashes, and terrorism; for example, violent protest by Azerbaijanis against Soviet policies, 1987–1991.

Genocides and politicides (geno/politicides) are defined as sustained policies by states or their agents and, in civil wars, by contending authorities that result in the deaths of a substantial portion of members of communal or political groups. In genocides the victimized groups are targeted primarily because of their communal (ethnic, religious) characteristics. In politicides, by contrast, victims are targeted mainly because of their political opposition to the state or dominant group[6] (n = 46). They include:

- Episodes involving more than 250,000 deaths; for example, the Khmer Rouge killings and starvation deaths in Cambodia, 1975–1979.
- Episodes involving between 100,000 and 250,000 deaths; for example, the civilian death toll from massacres and starvation during RENAMO's rebellion against the government of Mozambique, 1976–1992.
- Events involving between 10,000 and 100,000 deaths; for example, Tutsi army massacres of Hutus in Burundi, 1993.
- Events involving fewer than 10,000 deaths; for example, the victims of the military's "dirty war" against the left in Argentina, 1976–1980.

Adverse or disruptive regime transitions are major, abrupt shifts in patterns of governance, including state collapse, periods of severe regime instability, and shifts toward authoritarian rule[7] (n = 82). They include:

- Collapse of central state authority for two or more years; for example, the collapse of central government in Somalia, 1989 to the present.
- Transition toward autocratic rule by revolution or coup; for example, the military coup against the Allende regime in Chile, 1973.
- Abrupt transitions toward autocratic rule by nonviolent means; for example, the replacement of democratic institutions by one-party rule in Sierra Leone in 1978.
- Violent regime instability accompanied by revolution or coup, with no increase in autocracy; for example, north-south rivalry and civil war after the attempted merger of North and South Yemen in 1990.

These 243 conflicts and crises are the basis of the problem set, that is, the study's dependent variable. It includes almost all serious events of these types that began between 1955 and mid-1994 in all states in the international system with populations greater than 500,000.[8] Area specialists subsequently have proposed some additions to and deletions from the set, mostly events of low magnitude, which will be taken into account in a future revision of the problem set. The analyses reported below are based on the initial problem set.

The four kinds of conflicts and crises in the problem set often coincide or occur sequentially in the same country. The Iraqi Kurds, for example, fought four successive rebellions between 1961 and 1992; and in 1988–1989 the Iraqi government responded with the murderous al Anfal campaign, a case of politicide against a politically-organized communal group. Where conflicts or crises overlapped or came in quick succession, these were combined into consolidated cases. The 113 consolidated cases include 62 single events of the four kinds plus 51 complex cases consisting of linked sequences of events (of any kind) in which less than five years elapsed between the beginning and end of successive events.

The next research task was to match the 113 consolidated cases of state failure with a random sample of control cases three times as large. For each year in which a consolidated case began, three cases were selected at random from countries in which no such events of any type or magnitude were under way or about to begin in the next two years. The question for all statistical analyses was to identify those independent variables, and sets of variables, that discriminated most significantly and efficiently between the problem set and the control set.

Explaining State Failure: The Independent Variables

A very large number of independent variables were considered for inclusion, ranging from indicators of democracy and ethnic cleavages to the size of the youth age bulge, and from income inequality to the presence of IMF standby agreements. Candidate variables were identified in Task Force brainstorming sessions based on theoretical arguments, observed empirical regularities, and observations from policy makers. Cross-national data on important variables often proved to be limited or missing, especially data for the global South and for the 1950s and 1960s. Nonetheless it was possible to acquire a great many existing datasets; and to code or collect some new data, especially on political variables. No classified data sources were used, though the Task Force did ask whether comprehensive data might be available from intelligence sources on such variables as leadership traits and traffic in small arms; no usable comparative data on these variables could be identified. A team from the Consortium for International Earth Science Information Network (CIESIN) assembled an initial matrix of 617 measures for each country for each year it was in the study. The maintenance and updating of this dataset was and continues to be a major task of the project.

Expert assessments of the potential significance, quality, and coverage of the 617 measures were made by the analytic team from Science Applications International Corporation and led to a Task Force decision to concentrate statistical analysis on 75 high priority measures. Of the high priority variables 21 were demographic and social, 24 political, and 30 environmental and economic. The first cut was to conduct t-tests or chi-square tests to determine their capacity to differentiate between the states that had a regime crisis and the control cases that did not. This univariate analysis identified 31 powerful variables, listed in Table 2.1, that discriminated at a statistically significant level between the problem and control set.

The next step was to subject these 31 variables to two kinds of multivariate analysis: logistic regression analysis and neural network clustering. Regression analysis is a technique familiar to early warning researchers, neural network analysis is not. Neural network clustering provides a non-linear modeling technique, and can be used on datasets where the values for some variables are missing, a property that can become important when additional variables are added to the analysis. Combinations of two, three, five and up to 14 variables contained in the 31-variable set were examined together in an inductive approach to specifying the most accurate analysis or model. Regression analysis was used first, then neural net analysis was applied to the variables found to be significant in regressions. Several models approached 70 percent accuracy in identifying which states would fail between 1955 and mid-1994. The two techniques used gave similar results.[9] The single best model, according to both regression and neural net analyses, included three variables: openness to international trade, infant mortality, and democracy.

Table 2.1.   Independent Variables that Discriminate between State Failures and Control Cases (statistically significant using a t or x^2 test with P < .05).

Demographic/Societal
Calories/capita/day
Military personnel/physicians ratio
Civil liberties index
Infant mortality
Life expectancy
Extended longevity
Percent of children in primary school
Percent of teens in secondary school
Girls/boys ratio in secondary school
Youth bulge
Labor force/population

Political/Leadership
Party legitimacy
Party fractionalization
Executive dependence on
legislature
Separatist activity
Years since major regime change
Ethnic character of ruling elite
Religious character of ruling elite
Political rights index
Maximum ethnic cleavage
Democracy

Economic/Environmental
Defense expenditures/total government expenditures
Government revenues/GDP

Investment share of GDP
Trade openness (imports plus exports/GDP)
Real GDP/capita
Cropland area
Land burden (farmers/cropland) x (farmers/labor force)
Reports of famine

1. *Openness to international trade* is the sum of imports + exports as a percent of GDP; high openness is associated with a low risk of state failure. There are several reinforcing theoretical explanations for this finding. Trade serves as a measure of a country's integration into the global economy and the international community. One consequence of economic and political interdependence is that regimes are more inclined to adhere to international norms of good governance, and more sensitive to external encouragement to observe those norms and to censure for violating them. In domestic politics, a large volume of trade is dependent on a stable rule of law and fair enforcement of contract and property rights. Where trade is less significant to the economy, regimes may have more latitude for arbitrary, unpredictable, or corrupt behavior that offends key political groups and prompts them to revolutionary challenges.

2. *Infant mortality* is the ratio of reported deaths of infants under one year old per thousand live births: infant mortality rates above the international median for a given year are associated with a high risk of state failure. Infant mortality is indicative of the quality of life in a society. It tends to be lower in countries with high GDP per capita, but also is relatively low in some poorer countries whose governments devote substantial public resources to health, education, and welfare services. Its importance as an indicator of stability is likely due to its inverse association with popular discontent. Regimes that are unwilling or unable to raise the quality of life to international standards are at risk of popularly-based challenges. This relationship is likely to be more pronounced in democratic countries where discontented publics have greater opportunities to organize opposition.

3. *Democracy* is indexed by reference to competitive political participation, election of chief executives, and institutionalized checks on executives' exercise of power. Regimes above a middling threshold of democracy (5 or above on the 10-point Polity III scale; Jaggers and Gurr 1995:472) have a low risk of state failure. The finding is consistent with a large body of theory and observation about the conflict-inhibiting effects of democratic governance. Since democratic elites are dependent on popular support to gain and retain office, they are more responsive to popular discontents and more likely to accommodate potentially dissident political and ethnic challengers. They also are likely to have strong normative and institutional inhibitions against committing or tolerating massive human rights violations.

Two of the three variables in the general model correlate with a number of others used in the study. *Infant mortality* is a marker indicator that represents a basket of interdependent conditions. It performs slightly better in most of the models estimated than do other quality-of-life indicators such as per capita caloric intake, access to clean water, and GDP per capita. Depending on the availability of data, one could substitute some of these other variables for infant mortality without a major reduction in the predictive power of the models. *Democracy* is not a marker or surrogate indicator but rather a summary measure of open political institutions. It correlates strongly with indices of political rights, civil liberties, party legitimacy, and more weakly with some quality of life indicators. The indicator of *trade openness* has few close correlates either conceptually or empirically. Of the 75 key variables analyzed in the study, it correlates closely only with the density of roads—generally accepted as an indicator of economic development—and population size.

An important interaction effect was observed between democracy and the other two variables in the basic model. Among more democratic countries, the risk of failure was greater when infant mortality—which we interpret as a broad measure of living standards and quality of life—was high and when trade openness was low. Among less democratic countries, by contrast, the risk of failure was greater when trade openness was low, regardless of the level of infant mortality. Reference to specific groups of countries helps clarify these findings.

- Among less democratic countries with trade openness above the world median (countries whose total imports + exports exceeded three-quarters of their GDP), risks of state failure were very low, irrespective of levels of infant mortality. Gabon and Zimbabwe are countries that in 1994 fitted this profile.
- Among less democratic countries with lower levels of trade openness, risks of failure were substantial but levels of infant mortality do not help differentiate among levels of risk. Cuba and North Korea are examples of nondemocratic countries with low trade openness in the early 1990s.
- Among more democratic countries, the study found that the higher the infant mortality rate, the greater the risk of state failure. All other things being equal, more democratic countries with high infant mortality faced a greater risk of failure than did less-democratic countries. In an effort to probe this relationship, a cluster analysis was done of cases in the study with high (5 +) democracy, GDP per capita below the world mean (used here as a surrogate indicator of quality of life) and openness below 60 percent. About 40 percent of the democracies in this situation prior to 1992 failed. Democratic countries where infant mortality substantially exceeded the 1994 world median of 45 deaths per thousand live births include Bangladesh, Benin, Bolivia, Kyrghizia, Nepal, and Paraguay. Several countries in this group, including Kyrghizia, had state failures between 1994 and mid-1997.
- A significant risk of state failure was observed in democracies where infant mortality rates ranged between the median and one-half the median. Democracies where infant mortality were in this range in 1994—between 10 and 45 deaths per thousand live births—include Armenia and Romania. Examples of quasi-democratic states in this range in 1994 include Jordan, Mexico, and Thailand.[10]

- A very low risk of failure was observed in countries where infant mortality rates fell below one-quarter of the median. In 1994 this included the advanced industrial democracies and, among others, Greece, Portugal, and South Korea.

The Task Force recognized the need for models that are specific to each of the four types of state failures included in the problem set. Such analyses were done for the two most numerous types: violent or abrupt regime change and ethnic war, with results that dovetailed closely with the general model.

1. Regime crisis: Stepwise logistic regression identified two strong variables, infant mortality and number of years since the previous major regime change. The model's predictive power was improved by the addition of trade openness. These three variables together correctly estimated violent or abrupt regime transitions in 69 percent of cases. Neural net analysis achieved 70 percent accuracy using infant mortality and trade openness alone.

2. Ethnic war: Stepwise regression identified three strong variables that jointly provided 78 percent accuracy. As in the general model, trade openness reduced the risk. Two other variables, not in the general model, increased the risk of ethnic war: the ethnic character of the ruling elite, if it represents only one group in an ethnically divided society; and a youth age bulge, i.e., a large proportion of the adult population concentrated in the young adult years. Neural net analysis achieved 72 percent accuracy with the three variables from the general model plus youth bulge and years since last major regime change.

Strengths and Limitations of the State Failure Project

The State Failure Project is the most broadly conceived empirical effort we know of to identify the correlates of political crises globally and across a long span of time. It makes use of a wider range of data than previous studies in conflict and crisis analysis and is one of the few studies of its genre to employ two different analytic methods. The dataset compiled for the study is unique in depth and coverage, though many gaps remain. The initial models are parsimonious, internally consistent, and have important implications for researchers' theoretical understanding of the preconditions of state failure and for long-range policy planning.[11] And the project has gained substantial visibility and credibility among those responsible for the analysis of global security and for planning U.S. foreign policy. The first phase of the State Failure project thus strengthens the case for a systematic approach to risk assessment and early warning of political crises.

Having said this, some important cautions are in order.

- The study has been largely inductive. It was not designed to test existing theoretical arguments about the causes of specific kinds of political crises.

- The models classify correctly about 70 percent of historical cases. A model with 70 percent accuracy two years in advance would correctly identify about two out of three failures and two out of three stable countries. Given historical failure rates of about three per year, this translates into approximately one missed regime crisis per year. The number of false positives states classified at high risk of failure that did not fail in a given year is roughly 50 out of the 166 countries in the analysis.
- The models are based on historical analysis. It remains to be demonstrated that they will be equally accurate in identifying prospective cases of state failures.
- Models have not yet been identified that help to account for the type or degree of state failure or the sequential relations among them. Researchers and analysts also need to learn more about the conditions that keep partial state failures from escalating, and that contribute to the reconstruction of collapsed states.
- Many variables of theoretical and policy interest were not included in the initial analyses because suitable broad-coverage indicators did not exist. Others were used despite significant data gaps and irregularities. The limits are particularly serious with respect to international and domestic political factors and environmental variables.
- Most variables in the models refer to background or structural conditions that are relatively slow to change. In the terminology used elsewhere in this volume, the models are (at best) suitable for long-term risk assessment. If they are to be used for early warning, they must be complemented by the analysis of potential accelerators and triggers.

Conclusion

Most of the limitations enumerated above can be overcome, at least in part, through future work. Members of the Task Force expect that most of these issues will be addressed, if not by the Task Force itself then by other researchers and agencies.

IMPROVING THE QUALITY AND COVERAGE OF DATA

The initial results suggest priorities for future data gathering and coding on background variables. High priority should be given to identifying more precise and time-sensitive indicators of quality of life, international economic linkages, and ethnic polarization especially at the leadership level. Longer-run efforts are needed to improve the coverage and reliability of ecological and environmental indicators. All indicators that contribute significantly to the models, including revised models that may be identified in future research, should be kept as close to current as possible.

TYPES, MAGNITUDE, AND DURATION OF STATE FAILURE

Policy planning and risk assessment will be improved once we are able to say something about which type of state failure is most likely to occur in high-risk countries, and with what magnitude. One way to do this is to use an expanded set of background variables to identify the probability of occurrence of each type of state failure. Regression analysis also can be used to estimate models of magnitudes and duration. A more innovative approach to the problem of duration also can be suggested: to model the conditions associated with the ending dates of state failure. Indicators of regime capacity, economic productivity, and international assistance are likely to figure in such models. The authors suggest that some such models should be estimated.

ACCELERATORS AND TRIGGERS

Researchers want to understand the political and social dynamics that link the background conditions to the onset or avoidance of state failure. Policy makers and analysts need more than watch lists: they want to know about the signals that suggest a state failure is imminent. There are several research approaches to this problem. One is to use theory and comparative evidence to identify accelerators of various types of conflict and crisis. Barbara Harff (chapter five in this volume) lays out the rationale for this approach and sketches suggestive evidence from four cases. The approach only works if causal models have already been specified: "accelerators" are, in effect, variables outside the parameters of a static or systems model whose effects depend in whole or part on their interaction with conflict-disposing background conditions. This approach is recommended for future work by early warning researchers. An inductive alternative is to search for patterns in "events" that are observed to cluster prior to the onset of historical instances of state failure. Examples of this approach are represented in this volume by Philip Schrodt and Deborah Gerner (chapter 7 in this volume) and Peter Brecke (chapter 9 in this volume).

CONFLICT MANAGEMENT

Foreign policy makers have for a long time relied on foreign assistance and preventive diplomacy to reduce the risks of state failure, or alternatively to help regimes recover from crises (see Lund, 1996). An innovative complement to the analysis of accelerators is to specify and study the effects of "de-accelerators," i.e., the events and interventions that contribute to conflict resolution and recovery. The inductive approach to this research task is to look for evidence of cooperative interactions in the flow of conflict events. A stronger argument can be made for a deductive approach: the impact of conflict-management interventions surely depends on the context in which they are employed. This implies that we should begin with empirically plausible theories or models about the conditions that increase or decrease different types of political crises and conflicts.

MODEL-BUILDING AND EXPERT ASSESSMENTS

The 70 percent accuracy of the Task Force's initial models in accounting for failure or non-failure of states suggests how wide the gap is between general risk assessment and early warning of specific crises. Econometric models of national and global economic processes have similar indeterminacy but nonetheless have proven to be extremely useful for policy makers. Moreover the indeterminacy is a spur to building more refined and accurate models. Early warning researchers should be able to close part of the gap by identifying and analyzing the accelerators and triggering events of political crises. At the end of the process, though, all evidence on a country situation—data on background conditions and the stream of events—needs to be interpreted through substantive as well as theoretical lenses. The quantitative modeling and theoretical analysis of the dynamics of political crises is not designed to replace expert assessments. The two kinds of analysis are complementary. If risk assessment and early warning are to be put on a systematic footing, it will be done by teams of generalists and country specialists working with shared information within a shared perspective.

Notes

1. The terms *state failure* and *state collapse* are analogous to but broader than well-established analytic terms like political instability and internal war. Helman and Ratner (1992–93) discuss implications of state failure for international policy. Zartman (1995) gives the term state collapse more precise analytic content and uses it in comparative case studies. Also see Kaplan (1994) and Ayoob (1996). The State Failure Task Force is the first effort to identify a comprehensive list of instances of state failures.

2. The study was commissioned by the Central Intelligence Agency's Directorate of Intelligence in response to Vice President Gore's request and was carried out by a Task Force consisting of academic experts, data collection and management specialists from the Consortium for International Earth Science Information Network (CIESIN), and analytic methods professionals from Science Applications International Corporation (SAIC). The co-authors of this chapter are senior consultants to the Task Force. The views expressed in this chapter are those of the authors and do not represent the official view of the U.S. government, the U.S. intelligence community, or the Central Intelligence Agency.

3. The magnitudes of state failure were not analyzed in the first phase of the Task Force's work.

4. The primary source is Small and Singer 1982, with an update through 1993 provided by Professor Singer. Civil wars by communal groups are included under ethnic wars.

5. From the Minorities at Risk project's profiles of conflicts involving all politically active communal groups from 1946 to 1989, updated and annotated for the State Failure Project. See Gurr 1993a, 1994, and chapter 1 in this volume.

6. The general definition and distinctions are developed by Harff (1992: 27–30). The primary data source is her inventory of episodes of gross human rights violations since 1945 (Table 3.1 in Harff 1992), updated and annotated by Barbara Harff and Michael Dravis for the State Failure project.

7. Interruptions and abrupt shifts in regime authority patterns were identified from the Polity III data set (Jaggers and Gurr 1995), which includes annual codings of the authority traits of all regimes since 1800. The data set was updated and annotated by Keith Jaggers for the State Failure project. Note that nonviolent transitions from autocracy to democracy are not considered state failures and thus are not included in the problem set.

8. The United States was excluded from the study. If it had been included, 1960s racial violence in the South and urban riots and rebellions in the North would have entered in the problem set as low-magnitude ethnic war.

9. The accuracy with which cases are classified can be adjusted depending on whether the analysts care more about the number of "false positives" or "missed failures." For example, models can be estimated that accurately classify all failures, but at the cost of vastly increasing the number of false positives. The accuracy rates reported here are based on a study design that divides errors evenly between "false positives" and "missed failures."

10. The governments of these countries have some democratic features but as of 1994 were below the 5 threshold on the Democracy indicator.

11. Some theoretical and policy implications of the study are dealt with in the State Failure Task Force Report for official U.S. government use dated 30 November 1995.

Negotiation Outcomes

Cynthia Irmer and Daniel Druckman

Cynthia Irmer, a conflict resolution expert and lawyer, has worked within the U.S. Department of State on human rights focusing on strategic planning, gender equality, religion, foreign policy and more. She has also provided conflict resolution training to everyone from government ministers to armed rebel groups to civilians interested in peace. Her work has carried her throughout Africa, Asia, Europe, and North and Central America. Daniel Druckman is now professor emeritus of the School of Policy, Government, and International Affairs at George Mason University. He received his PhD at Northwestern University where he studied social psychology, sociology, and international relations. Beyond academia, he trained United Nations diplomats in mediation and negotiation, leading similar workshops in India, Peru, the Philippines, Bolivia, Crimea in Ukraine, and beyond. His consulting work brought him in contact with numerous organizations and government agencies to work on trade, security, and environmental issues.

This research uses a mixed-methods approach to analyze data from the conflicts between Armenia and Azerbaijan over Nagorno-Karabakh and between Georgia and South Ossetia to examine the comparative influences of international relations (IR) and conflict resolution (CR) perspectives on negotiation outcomes by testing a set of hypotheses about the relative influence of negotiating processes (CR) and contexts (IR) on outcomes. The researchers conclude that there is a stronger correlation between negotiation process and outcome where more attention is paid to ongoing relationships between parties. Resolutions emerge from mutual interests rather than basic bargaining. This conclusion is partly drawn from the relationship between the variable of trust and the process, which together are shown to result in better negotiation outcomes. The authors note that changing some of the contextual variables used in the study could produce different outcomes, but they believe that this model ACE (association, causation, and explanation) is replicable for measuring negotiation outcomes more broadly.

Using quantitative methods and factor analysis is characteristic of Epoch One approaches to conflict research. While the scope of data for this project is grand and adheres to researcher objectivity, research of this type is later critiqued for the absence of the researcher's accountability for using variables that are most reflective of the researcher's decision-making, or what some refer to as a top-down analysis. Also aligning with Epoch One, this research is attempting to provide a causal analysis of root causes to create a predictive model for controlling negotiation outcomes.

Questions to consider: What kind of research is used to collect this kind of data? Who designs the research and the questions? From where is the research carried out? Whose "interests" does this type of research support?

Explaining Negotiation Outcomes

Process or Context?

Cynthia Irmer[1] and Daniel Druckman[2]

Two substantial traditions of negotiation scholarship provide different perspectives on the factors that generate outcomes. One of these traditions is found in the work of conflict resolution (CR) theorists. They place their bets on the role played by the negotiation process. Another is found in the work of many international relations (IR) researchers. They prefer studying the role played by the larger contexts surrounding negotiation. This clash of perspectives is due, at least in part, to a prevailing focus on either micro (CR) or macro (IR) level variables. We confront these perspectives in this article by pitting them against each other as competing hypotheses. The central question of the research is whether process or context has a stronger impact on the outcomes of negotiations intended to end violence.

We provide background on the competing arguments along with hypotheses. Three sets of hypotheses are presented in an attempt to capture the issue; they emphasize either process or context. The hypotheses are evaluated in sequence, with both a large and small number of cases, proceeding from statistical analyses that demonstrate association (A) to qualitative investigations that ascertain causation (C) to plausibility probes that identify explanatory mechanisms (E). The ACE methodology is a contribution to the analysis of comparative case studies. By employing the logic of experimentation, we go beyond the discovery of statistical relationships. The methodology allows us to probe both for causation and explanation. This is an innovation for case-based research, which has been primarily descriptive or correlational.

Conflict Resolution: Process

A fundamental question asked by many CR researchers is: To what extent are outcomes the result of negotiating processes? A number of the early conceptual frameworks posit that outcomes derive directly from negotiating processes (Sawyer & Guetzkow, 1965 Randolph, 1966; Druckman, 1973). Walton and McKersie (1965) introduced the distinction between two types of processes, distributive and integrative bargaining. Better, more lasting outcomes were thought to derive from integrative than from distributive processes. Support for this hypothesis has come from a variety of laboratory studies (see Pruitt, 1981, and Pruitt & Carnevale, 1993, for reviews), computer simulations (Bartos, 1995), and field studies (Kressel, Fontera, Forlenza, Butler, & Fish, 1994). These studies have identified the factors that increase the chances of discovering an integrative solution: They include logrolling skills, attractiveness of alternatives, information exchange processes, low time pressure, and privacy (see Druckman & Robinson, 1998, for a review of the factors). Emphasized in particular is the importance of problem solving—as contrasted to bargaining—processes. An attempt is made in this study to investigate the role of problem solving in negotiations intended to achieve peace agreements between countries in conflict or at war.

Many of the earlier frameworks suggest that problem-solving processes increase the chances of obtaining more comprehensive outcomes. This usually means that more issues are resolved, more attention is paid to ongoing relationships, and attempts are made to address the sources of the conflict. In contrast, less comprehensive (more partial) outcomes consist of fewer issues settled and less attention paid to long-term matters such as relationships and sources of conflict. A similar distinction is made between resolutions and settlements. The former deal with the parties' needs and values as well as interests; the latter is limited to an efficient agreement that may primarily handle the distributive issues (see Druckman, 2002, for more on this distinction). A key element in problem solving is the willingness by negotiating parties to explore together a variety of possible options that can be evaluated in terms of satisfying their underlying interests and needs. This element is often missing when parties engage in an exchange of concessions that occur in bargaining. At the heart of this argument is the assumption that different kinds of negotiation processes produce different outcomes. This assumption takes the form of a hypothesis to be explored in this study.

With regard to international negotiation, Hopmann (1995) connects the distinction between bargaining and problem solving to the prevailing perspectives on IR. The customary competitive bargaining engaged in by diplomats reflects a realist approach to foreign policy. The emphasis is placed on achieving relative gains—correlated to relative power—both inside and outside of negotiating venues. This approach has produced inflexibility on the part of negotiators and impasses as the outcome of many intergovernmental talks. The less-often used problem-solving approach corresponds to a liberal approach to foreign policy. The emphasis is placed on attaining absolute gains that refer to joint (rather than relative) benefits. This approach should produce negotiator flexibility and more satisfactory negotiation outcomes. Indeed, evidence for these relationships was obtained by Wagner (2008). Her content analyses of 13 historical cases of bilateral and multilateral negotiations showed that problem-solving behaviors correlated significantly with the extent to which outcomes were integrative or comprehensive. Processes that are more likely to lead to integrative agreements included frequent problem-solving behaviors, a sustained use of these behaviors through the middle phases of negotiation, a framing of the issues in terms of shared values, and the creation of formulae. These processes were found to occur less often in negotiations over security issues.

Similar findings were obtained from the Druckman and Lyons (2005) comparative study of peace processes. They found that frequent problem-solving behaviors with an emphasis on joint gains led to more integrative outcomes than frequent distributive behaviors with an emphasis on relative gains. The former were displayed by parties negotiating the 1992 Rome agreement that resolved the conflict in Mozambique; the latter were displayed by the parties negotiating the 1994 cease fire between Armenia and Azerbaijan over Negorno-Karabakh. The authors note that problem-solving behaviors are more likely to occur when parties enter talks with cooperative orientations. Liberal approaches to foreign policy are more likely to encourage these orientations, which, in turn, set into motion a process sequence that results in sustained political agreements. Those agreements are closer to a resolution (as in Mozambique) than to a settlement (as in Nagorno-Karabakh) of the conflict.

Our analysis examines the relationship between process and outcome. At the same time, however, our approach accounts for the evidence upon which these conclusions (i.e., problem-solving or distributive bargaining process and more or less comprehensive outcomes) are made. We accomplish this by organizing the component parts of process and outcome identified in the earlier studies on negotiation into a series of continua, measuring each case on eight separate aspects of process and five features of outcome. With regard to process, we distinguish between competitive, mixed, and cooperative processes. These approaches are defined in several ways: whether the negotiators emphasize relative or absolute joint gains (Hopmann, 1995); whether they employ distributive or integrative strategies (Walton & McKersie, 1965); whether they promote their own positions or focus on their underlying interests (Fisher & Ury, 1981), and whether they primarily exchange concessions or share information about their interests and needs (Kressel et al., 1994). These distinctions resemble the aggregated categories of hard versus soft bargaining derived from the categories of the bargaining process analysis coding system (Walcott & Hopmann, 1978). The other process variables include the difference between concealing and sharing information (Groom, 1986; Kressel et al., 1994), threatening or advising/questioning (Fisher, 1997), ambiguous or clear language (Walton & McKersie, 1965; Kelman, 1965), and the distinction among types of conflict behaviors (competing, avoiding, accommodating, cooperating, collaborating) (Fisher, 1997; Groom, 1986).

An attempt was also made to unpack the concept of negotiating outcomes, particularly the distinction between comprehensive and partial or unresolved outcomes. The earlier studies emphasize contrasting outcomes: those that consider implementation and those that do not (Groom, 1986; Kressel et al., 1994; Druck-man, Martin, Allen Nan, & Yagcioglu, 1999); those that include joint projects versus those that only reflect the parties' claims (Fisher, 1997); and those that resolve underlying issues versus those that do not (Fisher, 1997; Azar & Burton, 1986). In addition, outcomes of peace negotiations address the extent to which demobilization of troops or demilitarization has occurred (Lyons, 2002) and the extent to which constitutional reform was instituted (Groom, 1986; Hume, 1994).[1]

The review suggests that processes and outcomes are correlated. Many of the earlier studies also suggest that processes cause outcomes. Thus, two general hypotheses are offered:

Hypothesis la: Cooperative or problem-solving (competitive/distributive) nego-tiation processes co-vary with more (less) comprehensive negotiating outcomes.

Hypothesis lb: Cooperative or problem-solving (competitive/distributive) negotiation processes lead to more (less) comprehensive negotiation outcomes.

These hypotheses do not, however, suggest reasons why the relationship between processes and outcomes occur. Questions that arise are: What accounts for the relationship between negotiating processes and outcomes and why do cooperative (competitive) processes result in comprehensive (partial) outcomes? The experimental literature offers some clues. Trust has been shown to be key to negotiation strategies and outcomes as both an antecedent and consequence (Lewicki & Bunker, 1996). High and low trusts distinguish between integrative and distributive strategies (Rotter, 1971; Kramer, 1994; Lewicki, Litterer, Min-ton, & Sanders, 1994). Trusting negotiators have been shown to use more integra-tive or cooperative strategies than those who do not trust their opponents (see also Parks & Rumble, 2001). In these experiments, trust was assessed prior to negotia-tion. This is difficult to do with historical case studies. The cases can however be analyzed for the way trust develops during the course of a negotiation. Moving from initial low levels to higher levels of trust should coincide with more coopera-tive processes leading to better joint outcomes. This stage-like concept progresses from mistrust to calculus-based, knowledge-based, and identity-based trust (Lew-icki & Stevenson, 1997). An attempt is made in this study to assess the progression of trust in several cases. The relationship posited is that the development of trust and cooperative (problem-solving) behavior are mutually reinforcing processes that lead to more comprehensive outcomes. Two hypotheses are suggested:

Hypothesis 2a: Cooperative (competitive) negotiation processes co-vary with increased (decreased) trust between the parties.

Hypothesis 2b: Increased (decreased) levels of trust—going from calculus (identity) to identity (calculus)-based trust—lead to more (less) comprehensive negotiating outcomes.

International Relations: Context

An emphasis on context rather than process is found in the work of many IR researchers. Results obtained in several negotiation studies suggest that context may be important. In a study of base-rights negotiations, Druckman (1986) showed that the final agreement was primarily the result of an external event, in that case the death of a head of state. Similar findings were obtained from an analysis of 23 cases of bilateral and multilateral international negotiations. Outcomes did not derive from processes. They were influenced more by outside influences, political relations, and features of the negotiating situation (Druckman, 1997). Those analyses also found that the set of cases could be distinguished in terms of conference size and issue complexity. One difference is that treaties were the more likely outcome of bilateral than multilateral talks. These studies call attention to the importance of factors outside of the process, in the negotiating situation. The factors are aspects of the proximal situation confronting negotiators.

While calling attention to the importance of these factors, the studies do not probe the broader contexts in which the negotiations occurred. That context includes the more distal features of regional and international structures including geography. Those are the types of factors emphasized more generally by macro-level perspectives on negotiation in IR (e.g., Simmons, 2002; Werner, 1999).

Information about these more distal features of the negotiating context can be found in the democratic peace, militarized interstate conflict, and alliance literatures. The previous research on these topics shows that four variables are particularly relevant to relationships among negotiating parties before, during, and after conflict. They are regime type, geographic proximity, alliances, and regional stability. Similar regimes, particularly if they are democracies, have been shown to avoid going to war against each other, preferring instead to resolve their differences through negotiation (Maoz & Russett, 1993). Conflicts between neighboring states have been found to be more intense than those between distant states, due in part to the need to protect their borders or the desire to expand those borders (Magstadt, 1994; Harbour, 2003). Members of the same international alliance are more likely than nonallied states to resolve disputes between them peacefully, particularly if the states are members of small alliances (Oren, 1990). Mousseau (1998) has argued that alliance bureaucratic structures provide mechanisms for internal dispute resolution.

Regional stability has also been shown to contribute to peaceful relations among states. Referred to as "spillover effects," conflict in one country can destabilize another country in the same region (Singer & Wildavsky, 1996). The settlements of violent conflicts are more difficult to negotiate in less stable regions. These variables are aspects of the broad context thought to account for negotiating outcomes. The discussion above suggests a third set of hypotheses:

Hypothesis 3a: More (less) comprehensive outcomes result from negotiations between similar (different) regimes, particularly if the similar regimes are democracies.

Hypothesis 3b: More (less) comprehensive outcomes result from negotiations between distant (neighboring) states.

Hypothesis 3c: More (less) comprehensive outcomes result from negotiations between members of the same (different) relatively small international alliance.

Hypothesis 3d: More (less) comprehensive outcomes result from negotiations between members of stable (unstable) regions.

The three sets of hypotheses confront competing explanations for negotiation outcomes. Are outcomes accounted for primarily by negotiating processes or more by the context within which negotiation occurs? Conceivably, both process and context may influence outcomes, as noted by Druckman (1983, 2007). The issue addressed by this study concerns the relative strength of these types of factors. This issue addresses independent influences. But, more complex interactions between process and context may also occur, as when trust develops more easily between parties who are members of the same alliance or have similar regimes. Thus, contextual factors may have indirect influences on outcomes through processes. Processes may intervene between contextual factors and outcomes. We return to this issue in the discussion section.

This study is significant in several ways. It contributes a systematic approach for comparative research with cases. The hypotheses are evaluated by a sequence of analyses referred to as association, causation, and explanation (ACE). It provides insights into an important theoretical issue that divides those conflict researchers who focus their attention on process and the IR scholars who study context. Going beyond statistical relationships, the analyses suggest a possible mechanism for the findings. Further, the diverse set of cases analyzed strengthens the argument for external validity. In the sections to follow, we discuss the logic of this sequence, the methods used for analysis, the results, implications for the issues that are addressed, and ideas for further research.

The Approach

The multi-method approach taken in this study is shown in Table IR.1. A large-N statistical analysis precedes the small focused comparisons and process tracing. These analyses are sequential. Each question asked follows from the results obtained from the analyses performed on the prior question. For example, a non-spurious relationship obtained between processes and outcomes leads to an investigation of causality. Hypothesized results are also shown in the table. The first question addresses hypothesis 1a: What is the relationship between negotiating processes and outcomes? This hypothesis is addressed with 26 cases of negotiations to end violent international conflicts.[2] Spearman rank-order correlations were computed among the various process and outcome variables as well as between an aggregated process and outcome index.

The second question addresses hypotheses 3a-d. It asks whether the obtained co-variance between process and outcome is genuine or a reflection of several aspects of the larger context surrounding the negotiations. Partial rank-order correlations were computed to ascertain the relationship between process and outcome controlling for the influences of the four context variables. As well, the relationship between context and outcome was assessed controlling for the influence of the process variables.

Next, we address hypothesis 1b by probing the direction of the relationship between processes and outcomes. This probe consists of a structured focused-comparison that matches cases for similarities and differences. The logic was developed originally by John Stuart Mill and is referred to as the method of difference

Table IR.1.   Methods, Hypothesized Relationships, and Cases

Method of analysis	Process variable	Outcome variable	Case(s)
Large-N studies			
Correlation/partial correlation	Problem solving Distributive bargaining	More comprehensive Less comprehensive	Sampling of 26 cases
Small-n studies			
Most similar (Mills' method of difference)	Problem solving Distributive bargaining	More comprehensive Less comprehensive	Georgia/South Ossetia Nagorno-Karabakh
Most different (Mills' method of agreement)	Problem solving Problem solving	More comprehensive More comprehensive	Ecuador/Peru Mozambique
Plausibility probe— trust develops	Problem solving	More comprehensive	Ecuador/Peru Mozambique Georgia/South Ossetia
Plausibility probe— trust diminishes	Distributive bargaining	Less comprehensive	Nagorno-Karabakh

and the method of agreement (see Faure, 1994). His "method of difference" consists of examining the most similar cases for differences on the independent and dependent variables. His "method of agreement" consists of examining the least similar cases for similarities on the independent and dependent variables. These experimental-like comparisons bolster an interpretation that the independent variables caused the dependent variable because other variables were "held constant" (most similar cases) or differed in ways that only the similar independent variable under study—namely, the negotiation process—would have been responsible for the values on the dependent variable (least similar cases).

The conflicts between Armenia and Azerbaijan over Nagorno-Karabakh and between Georgia and South Ossetia were selected for the most similar comparisons. These cases were similar in terms of geographic location, population size, variety and distribution of ethnic groups, religion, literacy rate, type of government, and labor force demographics. They differed however on the process variables. The question asked is whether they differed also on the dependent outcome variables. The conflicts within Mozambique and between Ecuador and Peru were selected for the least similar comparisons. These cases differed on the nonprocess variables but were similar on the process variables. The question asked is whether similar outcomes occurred. For both analyses, we asked—following hypothesis 1b—whether problem-solving (distributive) processes lead to comprehensive (partial or impasse) outcomes (see Table 1). These four cases were not included in the larger set used for the statistical analyses.

Further evidence that bears on causality was provided by the results of a process-tracing analysis of the four cases used in the focused comparison. Referred to by George and Bennett (2005) as process verification, we asked whether the observed relationships between process and outcome correspond to theoretical predictions. Affirmative evidence is provided by an unbroken chain of events from processes to outcomes. This is indicated by a continuously high or increasing level of problem-solving behaviors exhibited during the process culminating in comprehensive outcomes. It is also indicated by a continuing low or decreasing level of problem-solving behaviors exhibited during the process culminating in less comprehensive outcomes.[3]

The fourth question addresses hypotheses 2a and 2b on the mechanism that explains the process-outcome relationship. This question was addressed by performing a plausibility probe on each of the four cases selected for the focused comparisons. Referred to by George and Bennett (2005) as process induction, we asked whether the relationship between process and outcome is mediated by trust. This is indicated by movement during the process from lower (mistrust or calculus-based trust) to higher levels (knowledge or identity-based trust) of trust for the problem-solving cases, as suggested by hypothesis 2b. It is also indicated by decreasing levels of trust for cases with distributive processes, also suggested by hypothesis 2b.[4] Trust levels were monitored throughout the process following Trochim's pattern matching technique.[5] The result is a chronological path that shows variation as well as central tendencies. The paths for problem-solving and distributive cases are compared. A chain of expected changes (variation) or of expected average levels of trust would support the hypothesis that this variable moderates the process-outcome relationship.

In the next section we describe the criteria used for case selection. This is followed by a discussion of the way that the various process, outcome, and context variables were measured.

Cases

The criteria used to select cases for the large-N analyses were: (a) a settled violent international conflict, (b) a violent conflict between a governing regime and an insurgency that was settled, or (c) the settlement process consisted primarily of negotiation. An extensive search resulted in 55 cases of post-World War II negotiated settlements of conflicts widely dispersed around the world from the 1940s to the 1990s. However, many of these cases were not sufficiently documented to permit coding on many of our variables. Using documentation as another criterion for selection, 26 cases were chosen for analysis. Most cases were located through the Pew Case Studies on International Affairs at Georgetown's Institute for the Study of Diplomacy, the Harvard Law School Program on Negotiation, books of case studies (e.g., Greenberg et al., 2000) and some internet sources. The cases ranged between 20 and 75 pages in length.

Additional cases were selected for the qualitative analyses. Since these cases were to be used for more detailed process tracing, book length documentation was desired. With the assistance of knowledgeable scholars, we selected four cases not used in the large-*N* analyses. As shown in Table 1, the two most similar cases were the conflicts in Georgia/ South Ossetia (Gluskin, 1997) and in Nagorno-Karabakh (Mooradian, 1996). The two most different cases were the conflict between Ecuador and Peru (Marcella & Downes, 1999) and within Mozambique (Hume,

1994). These cases were used also for the plausibility probes designed to identify a mechanism responsible for the relationship between negotiating process and outcome.

Measuring Processes, Outcomes, and Context

The variables consisted of eight indicators of negotiating process, five outcome variables, four context indicators, and a trust scale for the plausibility probe. Sources for each variable were discussed above. The process and outcome variables were scaled in terms of four steps, ranging from most competitive (least comprehensive) to most cooperative (most comprehensive). The decision to use four steps was made in conjunction with our reading of the case documentation. A key decision was the distinction between the two mixed categories: It was possible to distinguish between a moderate amount of competition (some agreements) and a moderate amount of cooperation (a larger number of agreements). These steps seemed to capture the range of variation found in the case documentation. An example of a process scale is as follows:

(1) *Commitment to positions:* A party has "dug in its heels" and become unwilling to change a negotiating position, especially due to a belief in perceived power or superiority over the other party.
(2) *Mixed:* A party is attempting to strengthen its position, wanting to stick with it, but recognizing that it may not have capabilities to stand firm.
(3) *Mixed:* A party may be willing to abandon or alter its position, but only because it feels it does not have the capacity to stand firm.
(4) *Identify interests:* A party has begun to discard some of its inaccurate preconceptions of the other and to develop an understanding of the parties' interests underlying the conflict.

The other process variables include the extent to which parties exchanged information, a focus on maximizing own versus joint interests, relative or absolute (joint) gains, threatening or empathizing with the other party, demanding or brainstorming, using ambiguous or clear language, and being competitive or cooperative. Each of these variables captured the distinction among being competitive (1), accommodative (2), cooperative (3), or collaborative (4).

A negotiation was an incident within which codeable events occurred. Events consisted of the actions or behaviors shown by parties (or representatives) as documented during the course of negotiations. An event occurred during formal sessions as well as during more informal meetings around the negotiation. An example of an event coded in each of the categories of the continuum shown above follows.

The five outcome variables consisted of a consideration of implementation issues, extent to which joint projects were considered, the extent to which underlying issues were addressed, the extent of demilitarization, and the extent to which

Table IR.2.   Codeable Events

(1) Commitment to positions	(2) Mixed	(3) Mixed	(4) Identify interests
However, the U.S. did not attempt to improve its own BATNA, for two reasons. First, American policy makers generally viewed military power as roughly equivalent to negotiating power—neither side could be expected to give up at the conference table what had not been conceded on the battlefield. (Greenberg, 1992; 14)	The second meeting consisted of two phases: a private meeting between the heads of delegation Guebuza and Dommingos, and a plenary session. The result was a total failure and the parties decided to stop the talks for a month to reflect on their different statements. (Martinelli, 1999; 5)	The agreement and the oil concessions themselves needed the approval of the Iranian Majlis; Majlis elections were contingent upon the withdrawal of foreign forces from Iranian territory. Hence, the Soviets were tied to their commitment to withdraw in order to reap the benefits of their agreement, and they did accordingly (Maloney, 1991; 7)	Fortunately, for the outcome of the negotiations, the players slowly discarded inaccurate preconceptions as personal relationships developed. The negotiations lasted for over a year, long enough to test attributional/situational assumptions (Oppenheimer, 1990; 14)

constitutional reforms were undertaken. An aggregated outcome variable combines these criteria, resulting in varying degrees of comprehensive outcomes. The implementation variable scale is as follows:

(1) *Outcomes do not consider implementation:* The agreement does not mention or discuss difficulties with or options for addressing implementation issues that may arise. For example, "The deal failed to hold because the most fundamental prerequisite for agreement—values on both sides must be changed—was never achieved" (Maloney, 1991, 33).

(2) *Mixed:* Parties acknowledge possible difficulties implementing the agreement but do not mention them in the agreement.

(3) *Mixed:* Parties may have considered difficulties with or options for implementing the agreement but have not addressed this in the agreement.

(5) *Outcomes consider implementation:* Parties have identified potential difficulties with implementing the agreement and made some provision for or statement about addressing such difficulties in the agreement. For example, "Even with a substantive compromise in place, there was still a perceived need to develop independent institutions in order to guide the transition process. One useful precedent in the South African context was the Commission of Inquiry into Public Violence" (Bouckaert, 2000; 254).

The four context variables were regime type, geographic proximity, alliances, and regional stability. Categories for regime type were derived from Mousseau's (1998) modification of the Polity IV data set. Each negotiating case was categorized as "all parties have autocratic regimes," "mixed" (autocratic parties negotiating with democratic parties), and "all parties are democratic." The 1994 National Geographic World Political Map[6] was used to define the geographic proximity variable. Each case was judged as "the parties were within the boundaries of the same sovereign state" (an example of intra-state conflict), "at least two parties shared a common border" (contiguous states), and "none of the parties shared a common border" (noncontiguous states). Oren's (1990) data set was used to define alliances: the parties in each case were judged as "not aligned," "members of the same multilateral alliance," or "members of the same small alliance." Singer and Wildavsky's (1996) distinction between zones of turmoil and zones of peace was used to define the regional stability variable. Each case was categorized in terms of the locus of conflict: "within a zone of turmoil" (instability), "neither type of zone" (somewhat stable), or "within a zone of peace" (stability). These distinctions apply both to the Cold War and post-Cold War periods. Definitions of each category of the regime type variable with examples are the following:

(1) *Autocracy:* At the time of the conflict, no party had a democratic form of government. An example is the Beagle Channel conflict between Argentina and Chile.
(2) *Mixed:* At the time of the conflict, fewer than all parties had democratic forms of government. An example is the 1972 Simla Agreement between India and Pakistan.
(3) *Democracy:* At the time of the conflict, all parties to the conflict had a democratic form of government. An example is the 1993 negotiation about the islands dispute between Japan and Russia.

The development of trust among the parties is hypothesized as an intervening variable that explains process-outcome relationships. Several stages of trust development have been proposed including calculus, knowledge, and identity-based trust. These categories can be arranged on a scale that preserves an ordering from less to more trusting relationships: Calculus-based trust is a more conditional form than identity-based trust. The order is as follows:

(1) *No trust:* The text indicates that parties did not trust each other. For example, "When the Chairman refused their advice, the Karabakh leadership perceived that he was making a political statement in support of Azerbaijan" (Mooradian, 1996; 398).
(2) *Calculus-based trust:* The text indicates that parties perceived the others as being consistent in their behavior, acting as though they believed the other would do what it said it would, or witnessed that the other kept its promises. For example, "One participant attributed this to the fact that the South Ossetian issue was very low priority in high Georgian political circles at the time" (Gluskin, 1997; 35)
(3) *Knowledge-based trust:* The text indicates that there was increased interaction among the parties, increased information sharing among parties, or that parties could accurately predict the other's behavior. For example: "At the next round of negotiations, the parties agreed that they would begin discussing the impasses, that neither would veto the proposals of the other, and that all problems would be discussed in summarized accounts. This meant that Peru and Ecuador would at least listen to each others' positions" (Marcella & Downes, 1999; 77–78).
(4) *Identity-based trust:* The text indicates that the parties began recognizing they had shared interests and similar motivations, goals, and objectives, that they had

shared reactions in a common situation, or that they stood for the same values and principles. For example, "Just before the start of the second brainstorming session in Norway, the sides took an important step towards a resolution of the conflict . . . the parties signed a Memorandum outlining confidence building measures to be enacted to ensure security in the region" (Gluskin, 1997; 36).

These categories were used to code each of the events. Sequential events were organized by time of occurrence, enabling us to perform a time series analysis.

Steps were taken during the coding process to avoid possible biases. First, the set of cases was placed in two random orders. Second, the process coding, on the eight variables, was performed on the first random order. Third, the outcome coding, on the five variables, was done on the second random order. And finally, process and outcome scores were aggregated for each case in preparation for the statistical analyses.

Reliabilities

Two additional coders, working independently, were given randomly selected case studies and asked to: (a) identify codeable process events, (b) place each on the most relevant process scale, and (c) assign the event a score of 1–4 on the continuum selected. Two analyses of these data were performed. One compared the decisions made by each coder with those made by the first author. With regard to identification of codeable events, average agreement for one rater was 88%, for the other rater, 85%. With regard to selection of the specific scaled continuum for each event, one rater agreed on 73% of the events while the other showed agreement on only 50% of the events. For placement on the scale selected, agreements of 88% and 100% were obtained. Only one of these agreement percentages is problematic. A possible explanation is that, unlike the first rater, the second was not in the field of conflict analysis. The discrepancy (73% versus 50%) may have reflected a difference between them in content-relevant knowledge. However, when asked to assign a level to the event on the selected continuum, these raters agreed all of the time.

A second analysis compared the coding results obtained by the first author with the results obtained by the first coder using Cohen's Kappa statistic and the averaging method (see Robson, 2002; see also Vanbelle and Albert, 2009, on the averaging method). It should be noted that this statistic is sensitive to any deviation from complete agreement. Thus, the estimates are conservative. With regard to scale choice, the unweighted kappa coefficient is 0.71 $(SE = .04)$. The frequencies and proportions of agreement are shown in Table 2. The observed agreements deviate substantially from those expected by chance with only one exception. Coders disagreed on scale G (ambiguous or clear language): three of the six disagreements were between the G and H (type of conflict) scales. With regard to choices on the scales, the unweighted kappa coefficient is also 0.71 $(SE = .07)$. The 40 of 47 possible agreements on the problem-solving choices deviates substantially from the 22 agreements expected by chance. The proportion of agreement is 0.73

(maximum possible is 0.97) which also deviates substantially from the proportion expected by chance, which is 0.30. Similarly, the 47 agreements on distributive categories deviate substantially from the 29 expected by chance. The proportion of agreement is 0.76 (maximum possible is 0.98), which also deviates substantially from the chance proportion of 0.37. From these results, we conclude that the process scales are reliable.

The first author's outcome judgments were then compared with those generated by another independent coder. With regard to outcomes, the unweighted kappa coefficient is 0.66 (maximum possible is 0.77). The observed agreements between these two independent coders on each of the five outcome scales deviated substantially from chance: 0.47 (observed; maximum possible is 0.67) versus 0.13 (chance expected); 0.55 (maximum possible is 0.67) versus 0.13; 0.53 (maximum possible is 0.93) versus 0.16; 0.78 (maximum possible is 1) versus 0.08, and 0.08 (maximum possible is 0.8) versus 0.04, respectively. These results indicate that the outcome scales are reliable.[7]

Reliability statistics for the trust scale were calculated on comparable negotiation data reported in three recent studies. In one study, we assessed trust on the statements made by leaders surrounding the talks at Oslo I (Donohue & Druckman, 2009). Independent judgments made by two coders were aggregated across the types of trust. The kappa coefficient was 0.82. In another study, we assessed reliability for each scale based on reports from negotiators in a simulated international negotiation (Druckman, Olekalns, & Smith, 2009). The Cronbach alphas were 0.49 (calculus-based trust), 0.62 (knowledge-based trust), and 0.79 (identity-based trust). In a third study, we assessed reliability for each scale based on reports from negotiators in a simulated business negotiation (Druckman et al., 2009). The alphas were 0.45 (calculus-based trust), 0.64 (knowledge-based trust), and 0.72 (identity-based trust). These results indicate that the trust ratings are generally reliable. Less agreement on calculus-based trust suggests that this is a more challenging category to code.

Table IR.3.   Frequencies and Proportions of Agreement on the Process Variables

Variable*	Frequency		Proportion	
	Chance	Observed	Chance	Observed
A	9	32	.14	.76
B	2	14	.06	.78
C	2	13	.07	.50
D	1	7	.04	.35
E	5	22	.10	.69
F	1	10	.04	.63
G	.03	0	.01	0
H	4	18	.16	.75

Note. *Process scales: A, maintain positions/discuss interests; B, conceal information/free exchange of information; C, maximize individual interests/jointly explore common problems; D, seek relative gains/seek absolute gains; E, violence, threatening/questioning, reassuring; F, concession-making, retracting/brainstorming; G, ambiguous language/clear language; H, competitive/accommodative/co-operative/collaborative.

Results

The results are presented in four parts following the order described above in the section "The Approach." First, the findings obtained from the statistical analyses of 26 cases are shown. These include both the process-outcome and context variable correlations. Second, the focused-comparison findings are described for both the most and least similar comparisons. Third, the process-tracing results are presented for each of the four cases used in the focused-comparisons. A final section displays the time-series tracings, referred to as plausibility probes, for each case.

STATISTICAL FINDINGS

Average scores on each process and outcome variable were calculated for each case. These averages were then aggregated across the eight process and five outcome variables for summary indices. The aggregated scores are shown in the Appendix by case. Overall, the mean process score across the cases is 2.15, with a range from 1.09 to 3.21. On average, negotiators in these cases used a distributive more than a problem-solving approach. The mean outcome score is 2.06, with a range from 1.33 to 3.30. Thus, many of the cases concluded with less comprehensive or more partial outcomes.

Correlations between the process and outcome variables are shown in Tables 3 and 4. The Spearman correlation between the aggregated process and outcome indices is 0.81 ($p < .001$).[8] This correlation indicates that type of negotiation process is strongly related to type of outcome, with 64% of the variation in one variable explained by the other. The more distributive the process, the less comprehensive the outcome. Further, the correlations between each of the process variables and aggregated outcome is substantial, ranging from a low of 0.39 (ambiguous versus clear language) to 0.79 (concession-making/retracting versus brainstorming). Similarly, the outcome variables are highly correlated with aggregated process with correlations ranging from 0.46 (consideration of implementation) to 0.76 (individual versus joint claims). These results support hypothesis 1a.

The process-outcome correlations do not take context into account. Correlations between each of the context variables and the aggregated process variable is generally low: -.37 (regime type), -.45 (geographic proximity), .06 (alliances), and .03 (regional stability) (see Table 5). Similarly, correlations with the aggregated outcome variable are quite modest -0.22, -0.51, 0.05, and 0.23, respectively. Only the geographic proximity variable is significant. Closer parties, such as those engaged in civil wars, are more likely to engage in distributive bargaining resulting in less comprehensive outcomes. But, these findings do not confront the possibility of a spurious relationship between process and outcome. That issue is addressed with partial correlations.

Correlations between process and outcome remain high when each context variable is controlled: 0.79 (controlling for regime type); 0.75 (for geographic

Table IR.4.   Correlations Among Process Variables*

	AGPRO	A	B	C	D	E	F	G	H
AGOUT	.81	.67	.78	.65	.75	.49	.79	.39	.66
AGPRO		.92	.72	.88	.86	.83	.90	.44	.87
A			.56	.85	.78	.84	.78	.30	.79
B				.55	.65	.52	.68	.36	.60
C					.80	.74	.86	.39	.82
D						.64	.85	.31	.74
E							.69	.30	.71
F								.39	.80
G									.59

Note. *AGOUT, aggregate outcome; AGPRO, aggregate process; A, maintain positions/discuss interests; B, conceal information/free exchange of information; C, maximize individual interests/jointly explore common problems; D, seek relative gains/seek absolute gains; E, violence, threatening/questioning, reassuring; F, concession-making, retracting/brainstorming; G, ambiguous language/clear language; H, competitive/accommodative/co-operative/collaborative.

Table IR.5.   Correlations Among Outcome Variables*

	AGPRO	I	J	K	L	M
AGOUT	.81	.75	.81	.63	.47	.82
AGPRO		.46	.76	.58	.60	.64
I			.52	.29	.30	.52
J				.49	.38	.60
K					.10	.60
L						.45

Note. *I, outcome does/does not consider implementation; J, outcome restates original claims/undertakes joint project; K, underlying issues resurface/are addressed (e.g., relationships return to status quo/are transformed); L, ceasefire/demobilization/disarmament/demilitarization; M, no change in government structure/ transitional government (e.g., elections, constitutional reforms).

Table IR.6.   Correlations Among Context Variables

	AGOUT	Regime type	Geographic proximity	Alliances	Regional stability
AGPRO	.81	-.34	-.45	.06	.03
AGOUT		-.22	-.51	.05	.23
Regime type			.41	.14	.32
Geographic proximity				.13	.48
Alliances					.43

proximity); 0.80 (for alliances); and 0.81 (for regional stability). Thus, the outcomes obtained in this set of cases are strongly associated with the type of process used. This result applies as well to disputing parties in close proximity. If these parties can be encouraged to engage in a problem-solving process, their talks are likely to conclude with more comprehensive agreements. These results do not support hypotheses 3a-d.

STRUCTURED FOCUSED COMPARISONS

The correlation analyses reported in the previous section do not establish a causal relationship between process and outcome, as suggested by hypothesis 1b. A different kind of analysis is needed to assess the direction of the relationship between these variables. As described in the section "The Approach," structured focused comparisons were used to compare processes and outcomes in sets of both matched and mismatched cases. As shown in Table 1, the matched cases are Georgia/South Ossetia and Nagorno-Karabakh. As noted above, these cases are similar on most of categories used for comparison: geographic location, population size, distribution of ethnic groups (one dominant group), distribution of religions (one dominant religion), official language, literacy, date of independence, type of government, and distribution of labor force. The mismatched cases are Mozambique and Ecuador/Peru. These cases are dissimilar on most of the nine categories used for comparison. The procedure consisted of comparing each pair of cases on the aggregated process and outcome scores.

With regard to the matched cases, the aggregated process scores were 3.5 (Georgia/ South Ossetia) and 1.5 (Nagorno-Karabakh). The aggregated outcomes were 3.5 and 1.2, respectively. The problem-solving process used by negotiators to settle the Georgia/ South Ossetia conflict resulted in comprehensive outcomes. The distributive process used in the cease fire negotiations between Armenia and Azerbaijan resulted in a much less comprehensive agreement. The similarity of these cases on a variety of other variables bolsters the inference that outcomes are caused by the approach taken to negotiate the parties' differences.

On the mismatched cases, the process scores were 2.6 (Mozambique) and 2.8 (Ecuador/Peru). The outcomes were identical, 3.5 for each case. In both cases, a process that was more like problem solving than distributive led to a comprehensive outcome. This finding of very similar processes and identical outcomes for cases that differ on a variety of other variables further reinforces the likelihood of a causal relationship between process and outcome, as posited by hypothesis 1b. Indeed, this finding for mismatched cases provides evidence for a robust relationship. A next step is to probe the negotiating process in more detail with process-tracing techniques.

PROCESS TRACING

The aggregate measures described do not capture the way the negotiation process unfolds through time. These are summary measures of problem-solving and distributive codes across the phases of negotiation. It is necessary also to know whether these behaviors increased or decreased from earlier to later phases. This is assessed by comparing the aggregated process measure for the first and last third of the negotiation conducted in each of the four cases. The comparisons are made for the number of codes assigned in each of the four categories, including distributive (1), mixed/distributive (2), mixed/ problem-solving (3), and problem-solving (4) behaviors. The results are reported for each case in Table IR.8.

Considerably more problem-solving behaviors were coded during the last third of the talks than during the earlier phase of the negotiations about the conflict in Mozambique (32 versus 3 problem-solving codes). There were fewer mixed and distributive codes during the later phases. Similarly, for the Ecuador/Peru and Georgia/South Ossetia cases, more problem-solving (and fewer distributive) codes were assigned during the last than first third of the negotiation. The Nagorno-Karabakh case presents a different picture. Although there is a trend toward more problem-solving behaviors from the first to the last phase, the bulk of the codes occur in the distributive categories: 89% in the first and 65% in the third phase. Further, no category four problem-solving behaviors were recorded in either the early or late phases. These data show clear trends toward increased problem-solving behavior for the three cases that concluded with comprehensive outcomes. They also show less distributive behavior from the beginning to the end of the Nagorno-Karabakh talks, a case that resulted in a less comprehensive outcome. The shift from distributive to problem-solving was not sufficient to produce a comprehensive agreement. Overall, the process tracings buttress support for the causal relationship between negotiating processes and outcomes suggested by hypothesis 1b.

PLAUSIBILITY PROBE

The second set of hypotheses suggests that the relationship between process and outcome can be explained by trust. These hypotheses are addressed with a time-series analysis or plausibility probe described in "The Approach" section. The analysis is performed in steps. First, we advanced a concept—trust—that is hypothesized to explain the relationship between process and outcome. Second, we developed a scale designed to measure the concept. Third, events were coded for each case on the scale. And fourth, the events arranged in a time series to discern patterns in the way the measure varies through the course of the negotiation process. This probe generates a plausible explanation for why different processes lead to different outcomes.

Hypothesis 2a suggests that trust co-varies with process: trust encourages problem-solving behavior, which, in turn, enhances trust between the parties. The

Table IR.7.   Early and Late Processes by Coding Categories and Cases

Category	Mozambique		Peru/Ecuador		Georgia/South Ossetia		Nagorno-Karabakh	
	Last third	First third	Last third	First third	Last third	First third	Last third	First third
Problem solving (4)	32	3	16	1	29	0	0	0
Mixed/problem solving (3)	75	84	28	16	15	4	39	12
Mixed/distributive (2)	44	50	15	15	9	18	47	49
Distributive (1)	4	13	9	9	1	3	24	48

mutually reinforcing effects of trust and problem solving increase the chances for a more comprehensive agreement. The scale, drawn from Lewicki and Stevenson (1997) and shown above in the section on "Cases," captures the idea of levels of trust. Starting with no trust, the scale progresses from less (calculus-based) to more (knowledge and identity-based) trust. The coded levels are plotted against time for each of the four cases used in the focused-comparison analysis. A different number of events were coded for each case: 98 codes for Mozambique, 40 for Peru/Ecuador, 15 for Georgia/South Ossetia, and 53 for Nagorno-Karabakh. The results are shown in Figure 1.

The patterns displayed in the figures demonstrate that trust is an important variable. For three of the four cases, low levels of trust are evident at the beginning, increasing through the course of the negotiations, and concluding at relatively high levels. Evidently, the parties moved back and forth between higher and lower levels but gravitated toward identity-based trust (level 4) at the end. It is as though they were tentative in their expression of trust or hesitant to be fully trusting until later in the talks. The key here is that they came around before settling on an agreement. Not so for the case of Nagorno-Karabakh. Although these negotiating delegations got off to a good start, showing knowledge-based trust in early time periods, they did not sustain this optimistic appraisal. At the end, they evinced a calculus-based trust (level 2). This low level of trust is coincident with the large number of distributive behaviors shown by these negotiators.

These results indicate that increased (decreased) levels of trust co-vary with more (less) comprehensive outcomes. This finding supports hypothesis 2a, which suggests mutually reinforcing effects of trust and problem-solving behaviors: Higher levels of trust were obtained for cases with more comprehensive outcomes. Less clear is the direction of the relationship between trust and process: Does trust (problem-solving) drive problem solving (trust)? This leader-lagger pattern remains to be evaluated. Thus, a verdict on hypothesis 2b awaits the results of research that examines the time lag between these variables. These and other issues are discussed in the section to follow.

Discussion

The literature reviewed in the opening section of this article suggests that relationships between negotiating processes and outcomes should not be taken for granted. Results obtained from earlier studies are mixed, with some calling attention to the role played by external factors as influences on outcomes. These then became contending explanations that correspond generally to the different perspectives of CR and IR theorists: Do outcomes result primarily from the way the process unfolds (CR) or are they influenced more strongly by the broader context surrounding the negotiation (IR)? Our results are clear. Outcomes correlate with process, not with context, as these variables were defined in the analysis. Further analyses lend support to a causal relationship between process and outcome. Thus,

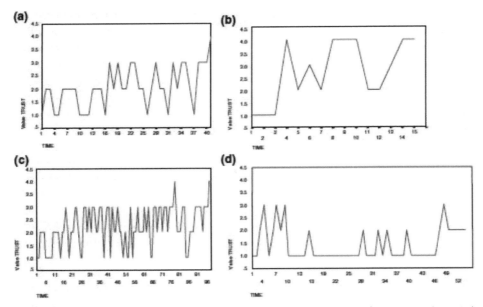

Figure 1.   (a) Trust Development—Ecuador/Peru. (b) Trust Development—Georgia/South Ossetia. (c) Trust Development—Mozambique. (d) Trust Development—Nagorno-Karabakh.

hypotheses 1a and 1b are supported; hypotheses 3a-d are not supported. Confidence in these findings is bolstered by the robust sampling of cases analyzed, the step-by-step probes of causation and explanation, and the multiple indicators of both processes and outcomes. Thus, the CR perspective garners more support from these findings than the IR perspective.

The plausibility probe highlights the role played by trust in these talks. This demonstration shows that trust co-varies with process as specified by hypothesis 2a. An evaluation of causal influence entails separating trust from negotiating behavior. Although this is difficult to do with case studies, it is not beyond the realm of possibility. For example, cases can be selected for the four combinations of high/low trust and high/low problem-solving behavior. Using outcome as the dependent variable, this focused comparison would isolate the relative effects of the two independent variables. The other issue concerning trust, raised in the introduction, is about complex interactions. Levels of trust may be influenced by such contextual variables as alliances or regional stability. These levels may then encourage or discourage cooperative behaviors leading to more or less comprehensive outcomes. This suggests a path model where contextual factors set in motion processes that lead to certain outcomes. It can be investigated with such tools as structural equation modeling (Byrne, 2001).

The results of this study are important both for theory and practice. With regard to theory, the findings support those CR frameworks that emphasize the importance of process. Particularly notable are the early frameworks of Sawyer and

Guetzkow (1965) and Walton and McKersie (1965). The former highlighted a causal relationship between process and outcome. The latter offered the distinction between distributive and integrative (problem-solving) models of negotiation. These conceptual contributions are linked by our findings. Distributive processes led to less comprehensive outcomes. Integrative (problem-solving) processes produced more comprehensive outcomes. The findings also address the long-standing debate between the macro-level theorists of IR and the process-oriented researchers in the field of CR. The former tend to black-box the negotiation process in favor of explanations that rely on policy or systemic variables (examples are found in the work of Simmons, 2002; Walter, 2002; and Werner, 1999). The latter focuses on the interactions and conversations held among the negotiators themselves (see also Donohue & Hoobler, 2002, and Donohue, 2003, for further empirical examples of interaction analysis).

Although the results lend support to the process-oriented approach, it is conceivable that other contextual variables may prove to be stronger influences on outcomes than those included in our analyses. While the variables chosen for analysis in this study were derived from earlier empirical work, they do not exhaust the list of potentially relevant contextual factors. For example, such aspects of the conflict environment as intervention by regional neighbors, border permeability, or disposable natural resources may come into play. These variables have been shown to influence the implementation of peace agreements (Downs & Stedman, 2002). Further, as noted earlier, process and context may interact. Impacts of context on process are likely when conflicts between other nations escalate during the negotiations, when changes occur in related (or linked) negotiations, or when policy changes within either or both parties' governments occur (see Druckman et al., 2009, for an experimental example of impacts from the social climate). These relationships remain to be investigated.

With regard to practice, the findings can be used to support various third-party initiatives ranging from traditional mediation within the context of formal talks (referred to as Track I) to unofficial activities (referred to as Track II) often initiated by nongovernmental organizations. Each type of initiative is based on the assumption that help with the process will produce more satisfactory outcomes. A particularly strong case has been made for the value of problem-solving workshops in IR. By creating an atmosphere conducive to problem-solving discussions, these practitioners claim that members of disputing groups will develop a more complex, less stereotyped view of each other. This, in turn, is presumed to lead to more amiable relationships between their groups (Rouhana, 2000). By showing that problem-solving processes produce better outcomes, our findings bolster these claims. They reinforce the value of interventions—whether Track I or II—intended to encourage problem-solving processes or to discourage distributive approaches to the resolution of conflict. They also offer the optimistic appraisal that opportunities for change are provided by tampering with a more malleable process than with a less malleable context surrounding negotiation.

Another important contribution of this study is to methodology. A multi-method approach to investigation is rare in case studies of negotiation and peace processes. This is not surprising given the demands on data collection and analysis.

Both a large number of cases for statistical analysis and sufficient documentation of details for qualitative inquiry are needed. These challenges were met in this study. A sufficiently large data set was complemented by rich descriptions of processes in the cases selected for the microscopic probes.

Further, the logical progression of analyses performed may be a model for future research. It is an inductive progression guided by hypotheses. The next step depends on findings obtained from the previous analysis. Nonspurious association (A) between variables must be demonstrated before causality (C) can be assessed. Evidence for causality precedes the search for a plausible explanation (E). This sequence, referred to by the acronym ACE, corresponds to the way that laboratory experiments are conducted. It captures the control, time-lagged, and intervening variable features of experimental design with retrospective case-based material. The control feature is addressed with partial correlations; an analog to the time-lagged feature is structured focused comparisons, and the intervening variable search is set in motion with a plausibility probe. The result is a real-world demonstration of negotiation processes causing outcomes through the development of trust.

A number of ideas are suggested for further research. These include exploring the effects of other variables and sampling other types of cases, including those assisted by third parties. As noted above, the four contextual variables chosen for analysis in this study do not exhaust the domain. Although the plausibility probe highlights trust development as an explanation for the causal relationship between process and outcome, the analysis did not compare trust with other possible explanations. Other hypothesized mechanisms include the development of affiliative perceptions, trends toward symmetry in perceived power, and an increased (decreased) number of forward (backward)-looking statements through the course of the talks. However, these variables have been shown to correlate with trust (Donohue & Druckman, 2009). Thus, it will be necessary to evaluate their independent effects either by using statistical controls or by conducting experiments.

Of course the results are based on the particular sampling of cases used for analysis. The cases share the features of being settled violent conflicts, negotiations conducted primarily between parties representing different countries, and having adequate documentation for coding. Other kinds of negotiated conflicts can be sampled. Examples include nonviolent territorial disputes, extending previous treaties such as those over base rights, and arms control or nonproliferation talks. Considerable documentation is also available for a variety of bilateral, trilateral, and multilateral trade talks (such as NAFTA), multilateral regime negotiations (such as those intended to establish cooperative relations among regional neighbors), and conference diplomacy in the areas of environmental regulation (such as the Rio and Kyoto agreements) and security (such as the United Nations conference on disarmament). Extending the sampling further, we could code process and context variables for cases of assisted, third-party negotiations such as those included in the Bercovitch and Trappl (2006) data set. The question of interest is whether the causal relationship between negotiation processes and outcomes, obtained in this study with a broad sampling of violent conflicts, is found also with other types of negotiated conflicts. This question, along with the others mentioned above, provides an interesting agenda for further research.

Notes

1. Office of the Coordinator for Reconstruction and Stabilization, U.S. Department of State, Washington, DC.

2. Department of Public and International Affairs, George Mason University, Fairfax, Virginia, and Australian Centre for Peace and Conflict Studies, University of Queensland, Brisbane, Australia.

3. All the cases chosen for analysis resulted in settlements. Although the settlements varied in degree of comprehensiveness (the dependent variable), there were no stalemates. Thus, we did not consider cases where problem-solving behaviors did not culminate in agreements.

4. Continuous high (low) levels of trust for the problem-solving (distributive) cases also suggest that trust is a plausible explanation for the process-outcome relationship.

5. See Trochim's web site at: http://www.socialresearchmethods.net/kb/pmconval .htm.

6. This map can be found on the following web page: http://www.maps.com/ map.aspx?pid = 15622.

7. Blind coding of outcomes—as was done here—may in fact underestimate agreement. It is likely that proper understanding of the cases and their context would produce near-complete agreement on outcomes for practically all of the cases. Further, it should be noted that the quadratic weighted kappa was an impressive 0.76.

8. The correlation increases to 0.86 when the four cases used in the small-n analyses are added to the data set. To avoid a selection bias that could influence the small-n results, the correlation with the additional cases was computed (N = 30) only after those analyses were completed.

References

Azar, E., & Burton, J. W. (Eds.) (1986). *International conflict resolution: Theory and practice.* Boulder, CO: Lynne Rienner.

Bartos, O. J. (1995). Modeling distributive and integrative negotiations. *Annals of the American Academy of Political and Social Science, 542,* 48–60.

Bercovitch, J., & Trappl, R. (2006). The Confman.2002 data set. In R. Trappl (Ed.), *Programming for peace: Computer-aided methods for international conflict resolution and prevention. Advances in group decision and negotiation* (Vol. 2, pp. 115–144). Dordrecht, The Netherlands: Springer.

Bouckaert, P. (2000). South Africa: The negotiated transition from apartheid to nonracial democracy. In M. Greenberg, J. H. Barton, & M. E. McGuinness (Eds.), *Words over war: Mediation and arbitration to prevent deadly conflict* (pp. 237–260). Lanham, MD: Rowman & Littlefield.

Byrne, B. (2001). *Structural equation modeling with AMOS: Basic concepts, applications, and programming.* Hillsdale, NJ: Lawrence Erlbaum.

Donohue, W. A. (2003). The promise of an interaction-based approach to negotiation. *The International Journal of Conflict Management, 3–4,* 167–176.

Donohue, W. A., & Druckman, D. (2009). Message framing surrounding the Oslo I accords. *Journal of Conflict Resolution, 53,* 119–145.

Donohue, W. A., & Hoobler, G. D. (2002). Relational frames and their ethical implications in international negotiation: An analysis based on the Oslo II negotiations. *International Negotiation, 7,* 143–167.

Downs, G., & Stedman, S. J. (2002). Evaluation issues in peace implementation. In S. Stedman, D. Rothchild, & E. Cousens (Eds.), *Ending civil wars: The implementation of peace agreements* (pp. 43–69). Boulder, CO: Lynne Rienner.

Druckman, D. (1973). *Human factors in international negotiations: Social-psychological aspects of international conflict.* Sage Professional Papers in International Studies, Number 02–020. Beverly Hills, CA: Sage.

Druckman, D. (1983). Social psychology and international negotiations: Processes and influences. In R. F. Kidd & M. J. Saks (Eds.), *Advances in applied social psychology* (Vol. 2, pp. 51–81). Hillsdale, NJ: Lawrence Erlbaum.

Druckman, D. (1986). Stages, turning points, and crises: Negotiating military base rights, Spain and the United States. *Journal of Conflict Resolution, 30,* 327–360.

Druckman, D. (1997). Dimensions of international negotiations: Structures, processes, and outcomes. *Group Decision and Negotiation, 6,* 395–420.

Druckman, D. (2002). Settlements and resolutions: Consequences of negotiation processes in the laboratory and in the field. *International Negotiation, 7,* 313–338.

Druckman, D. (2007). Negotiating in the international context. In I. W. Zartman (Ed.), *Peacemaking in international conflict: Methods & techniques* (pp. 111–162). Washington, DC: United States Institute of Peace.

Druckman, D., & Lyons, T. (2005). Negotiation processes and postsettlement relationships: Comparing Nagorno-Karabakh with Mozambique. In I. W. Zartman & V. Kremenyuk (Eds.), *Peace versus justice: Negotiating forward- and backward-looking outcomes* (pp. 265–286). Lanham, MD: Rowman & Littlefield.

Druckman, D., Martin, J., Allen Nan, S., & Yagcioglu, D. (1999). Dimensions of international negotiation: A test of Ikle's typology. *Group Decision and Negotiation, 8,* 89–108.

Druckman, D., Olekalns, M., & Smith, P. L. (2009). Interpretive filters: Social cognition and the impact of turning points in negotiation. *Negotiation Journal, 25,* 13–40.

Druckman, D., & Robinson, V. (1998). From research to application: Utilizing research findings in negotiation training programs. *International Negotiation, 3,* 7–38.

Faure, A. M. (1994). Some methodological problems in comparative politics. *Journal of Theoretical Politics, 6,* 307–322.

Fisher, R. J. (1997). *Interactive conflict resolution.* Syracuse, NY: Syracuse University Press.

Fisher, R., & Ury, W. (1981). *Getting to yes.* Boston: Houghton Mifflin.

George, A. L., & Bennett, A. (2005). *Case studies and theory development in the social sciences.* Cambridge, MA: MIT Press.

Gluskin, M. (1997). Facilitated joint brainstorming in the Georgia-South Ossetia conflict: A preliminary evaluation. Working paper. Cambridge, MA: Conflict Management Group. Greenberg, D. (1992). *The American use of force in Vietnam: An unconventional approach to negotiation.* Cambridge, MA: Harvard Law School.

Greenberg, M., Barton, J. H., & McGuinness, M. E. (2000). *Words over war: Mediation and arbitration to prevent deadly conflict.* Lanham, MD: Rowman & Littlefield.

Groom, A. J. R. (1986). Problem solving in international relations. In E. Azar & J. W. Burton (Eds.), *International conflict resolution: Theory and practice* (pp. 85–116). Boulder CO: Lynne Rienner. Harbour, F. (2003). Collective moral agency and the political process. In T. Erskine (Ed.), *Can institutions have responsibilities? Collective moral agency and international relations* (pp. 6983). London: Palgrave.

Hopmann, P. T. (1995). Two paradigms of negotiation; Bargaining and problem solving. *Annals of the American Academy of Political and Social Science, 542,* 24–47.

Hume, C. (1994). *Ending Mozambique's war: The role of mediation and good offices.* Washington, DC: United States Institute of Peace Press.

Kelman, H. C. (Ed.) (1965). *International behavior: A social-psychological analysis.* New York: Holt.

Kramer, R. M. (1994). The sinister attribution error: Paranoid cognition and collective distrust in organizations. *Motivation & Emotion, 18,* 9–22.

Kressel, K. A., Fontera, S., Forlenza, S., Butler, F., & Fish, L. (1994). The settlement orientation versus the problem-solving style in custody mediation. *Journal of Social Issues, 50,* 67–84.

Lewicki, R. J., & Bunker, B. B. (1996). Developing and maintaining trust in work relationships. In R. M. Kramer & T. R. Tyler (Eds.), *Trust in organizations: Frontiers of theory and research* (pp. 114–139). Thousand Oaks, CA: Sage.

Lewicki, R. J., Litterer, J. A., Minton, J. W., & Sanders, D. M. (1994). *Negotiations* (2nd ed.) Burr Ridge, IL: Irwin.

Lewicki, R., & Stevenson, M. A. (1997). *Trust development in negotiation: Proposed actions and a research agenda.* Paper presented at a conference on Trust and Business: Barriers and Bridges. Chicago, IL: DePaul University.

Lyons, T. (2002). *Post-conflict elections: War termination, democratization, and demilitarizing politics.* Working Paper No. 20, Institute for Conflict Analysis and Resolution. Fairfax, VA: George Mason University.

Magstadt, T. (1994). *Nations and governments: Comparative politics in regional perspectives.* New York: St. Martin's Press.

Maloney, S. (1991). *Outwitting a superpower: Iranian-Soviet negotiations, 1945.* Working Paper Series 91–94. Cambridge, MA: Program on Negotiation at the Harvard Law School.

Maoz, Z., & Russett, B. (1993). Normative and structural causes of democratic peace: 19461986. *American Political Science Review, 87,* 624–638.

Marcella, G., & Downes, R. (1999). *Security cooperation in the western hemisphere: Resolving the Ecuador-Peru conflict.* Miami, FL: North-South Center Press (University of Miami).

Martinelli, M. (1999). *Mediation activities by non-State actors: An account of St. Egidio's initiatives.* Copenhagen, Denmark: Copenhagen Peace Institute. Retrieved June 1, 2009, through Columbia International Affairs Online (www.ciaonet.org/abs/wps/mamol.html).

Mooradian, M. (1996). Third party mediation and missed opportunities. In "Nagorno-Karabakh: A design for a possible solution." Unpublished doctoral dissertation. Fairfax, VA: George Mason University.

Mousseau, M. (1998). Democracy and compromise in militarized interstate conflicts, 19161992. *Journal of Conflict Resolution, 42,* 210–230.

Oppenheimer, P. (1990). *A process analysis of the 1971 Quadripartite agreement on Berlin.* Working Paper Series 90–5. Cambridge, MA: Program on Negotiation at the Harvard Law School.

Oren, I. (1990). The war proneness of alliances. *Journal of Conflict Resolution, 34,* 203–233.

Parks, C. D., & Rumble, A. C. (2001). Elements of reciprocity and social value orientation. *Personality and Social Psychology Bulletin, 27,* 1301–1309.

Pruitt, D. G. (1981). *Negotiation behavior.* New York: Academic Press.

Pruitt, D. G., & Carnevale, P. J. (1993). *Negotiation in social conflict.* Pacific Grove, CA: Brooks/Cole.

Randolph, L. (1966). A suggested model of international negotiation. *Journal of Conflict Resolution, 10,* 344–353.

Robson, C. (2002). *Real world research* (2nd ed.). Oxford, England: Blackwell.

Rotter, J. B. (1971). Generalized expectancies for interpersonal trust. *American Psychologist, 26,* 443–452.

Rouhana, N. N. (2000). Interactive conflict resolution: Issues in theory, methodology, and evaluation. In P. C. Stern & D. Druckman (Eds.), *International conflict resolution after the Cold War* (pp. 294–337). Washington, DC: National Academy Press.

Sawyer, J., & Guetzkow, H. (1965). Bargaining and negotiation in international relations. In H. C. Kelman (Ed.), *International behavior: A social-psychological analysis* (pp. 58–111). New York: Holt.

Simmons, B. A. (2002). Capacity, commitment, and compliance: International institutions and territorial disputes. *Journal of Conflict Resolution, 46,* 829–856.

Singer, M., & Wildavsky, A. (1996). *The real world order: Zones of peace, zones of turmoil.* Chatham, NJ: Chatham House Publishers.

Vanbelle, S., & Albert, A. (2009). A note on the linearly weighted Kappa coefficient for ordinal scales. *Statistical Methodology, 6,* 157–163.

Wagner, L. M. (2008). *Problem-solving and bargaining in international negotiations.* Leiden, The Netherlands: Martinus Nijhoff.

Walcott, C., & Hopmann, P. T. (1978). Interaction process analysis and bargaining behavior. In R. T. Golembiewski (Ed.), *The small group in political science: The last two decades of discovery* (pp. 251–261). Athens, GA: University of Georgia Press.

Walter, B. F. (2002). Re-conceptualizing conflict resolution as a three-stage process. *International Negotiation, 7,* 299–311.

Walton, R. E., & McKersie, R. B. (1965). *A behavioral theory of labor negotiations: An analysis of a social interaction system.* New York: McGraw-Hill.

Werner, S. (1999). The precarious nature of peace: Resolving the issues, enforcing the settlement, and renegotiating the terms. *American Journal of Political Science, 43,* 912–934.

Table IR.8.   Cases, Parties, and Indices

Title of case study	Parties	Scores Process	Outcome
"The Geneva Accords on Afghanistan: A Case Study of the United Nations as a Third Party Mediator" (1988)	Afghanistan Soviet Union	2.11	1.33
"A Process Analysis of the 1971 Quadripartite Agreement on Berlin" Federal Republic of Germany France German Democratic Republic Great Britain Soviet Union United States		2.22	2.00
"The Vatican Mediation of the Beagle Channel Dispute: Crisis Intervention and Forum Building" (1984)	Argentina Chile	2.50	2.75
"From Lisbon to Dayton: International Mediation and the Bosnia Crisis" (1995)	Bosnia Croatia Serbia	1.53	1.77
"Settlement for Cambodia: The Khmer Rouge Dilemma" (1990)	Democratic Kampuchea Khmer Rouge China Vietnam	2.29	3.13
"The Camp David Accords: A Case of International Bargaining" (1978)	Egypt Israel	2.31	2.00
"Outwitting a Superpower: Iranian-Soviet Negotiations, 1945"	Iran Soviet Union	2.38	1.60
"Israel's Armistice Agreements: Analysis of Negotiation Processes Leading up to and Concluding in Armistice Accords with Egypt, Lebanon, Syria, and Transjordan in 1949"	Egypt Israel Jordan Lebanon Syria	2.15	1.43
"Negotiation on the Periphery: The Islands Dispute Between Japan and Russia" (1993)	Japan Russia	2.63	2.60
"Kilometer 101: Oasis or Mirage? An Analysis of Third-Party Self-Interest in International Mediation" (1973)	Egypt Israel	1.04	1.40
"The Madrid Conference: Baker's Enticing Diplomacy" (1996)	Egypt Israel Jordan Palestine Saudi Arabia Syria	1.52	1.60
"One Step Towards Peace: The 'Final Peace Agreement' in Mindanao" (1996)	Moro National Liberation Front Republic of the Philippines	2.90	2.88

Table IR.8.   (Continued)

Title of case study	Parties	Scores Process	Outcome
"Striking a Balance: The Northern Ireland Peace Process" (1998)	Democratic Unions Party Great Britain Irish Republican Army Sinn Fein Ulster Unionist Party United Kingdom Unionist Party	2.48	2.79
"The Oslo Channel"	Israel Palestine Liberation Organization	2.54	2.52
"The Panama Canal Negotiations" (1978)	Panama United States	1.81	2.20
"The Partition of Poland" (1772)	Austria Poland Prussia Russia	2.46	2.00
"Paying the Price: The Sierra Leone Peace Process" (1996)	National Provincial Ruling Council (NPRC) Revolutionary United Front (RUF)	2.40	2.00
"The 1972 Simla Agreement: An Asymmetrical Negotiation"	India Pakistan	2.01	1.63
"Report on Peacemaking Initiative in Somaliland" (1997)	Garhajis Republic of Somaliland	3.21	2.80
"South Africa: The Negotiated Transition from Apartheid to Nonracial Democracy" (1994)	African National Congress Congress of South African Trade Unions South Africa United Democratic Front	2.89	3.30
"The Tamil-Sinhalese Ethnic Conflict in Sri Lanka: A Case Study in Efforts to Negotiate A Settlement, 1983–1988"	India Sinhalese people Tamil people Sri Lanka	1.65	1.64
"The Suez Crisis, 1956"	Egypt Israel	1.70	1.20
"Politics of Compromise: The Tajikistan Peace Process" (1994)	Tajikistan United Tajik Opposition	2.94	3.06
"The American Use of Force in Vietnam: An Unconventional Approach to Negotiation" (1973)	North Vietnam U.S.	1.09	1.00

Table IR.8.   (Continued)

Title of case study	Parties	Scores Process	Outcome
Zarko Affair (1970)	Israel	1.51	1.40
"Releasing the Hostages at Revolutionary Airstrip: The Failure of Negotiation by Design"	Jordan Germany Palestine Switzerland		
"The May 1983 Agreement over Lebanon"	Israel Lebanon Palestine Liberation Organization	1.80	1.40

Notes

1. Other aspects of processes (e.g., tactics and issues) and outcomes (e.g., durability) may also be relevant. Our focus on extent of problem-solving processes and comprehensive outcomes derives from the earlier literature reviewed above.

2. Twenty-two of the 26 cases used in the analysis were inter-state conflicts.

3. All the cases chosen for analysis resulted in settlements. Although the settlements varied in degree of comprehensiveness (the dependent variable), there were no stalemates. Thus, we did not consider cases where problem-solving behaviors did not culminate in agreements.

4. Continuous high (low) levels of trust for the problem-solving (distributive) cases also suggest that trust is a plausible explanation for the process-outcome relationship.

5. See Trochim's web site at: http://www.socialresearchmethods.net/kb/pmconval .htm.

6. This map can be found on the following web page: http://www.maps.com/map.aspx?pid = 15622.

7. Blind coding of outcomes—as was done here—may in fact underestimate agreement. It is likely that proper understanding of the cases and their context would produce near-complete agreement on outcomes for practically all of the cases. Further, it should be noted that the quadratic weighted kappa was an impressive 0.76.

8. The correlation increases to 0.86 when the four cases used in the small-n analyses are added to the data set. To avoid a selection bias that could influence the small-n results, the correlation with the additional cases was computed (N = 30) only after those analyses were completed.

End of Epoch Questions

Questions for Discussion

- What were the primary concerns of those studying conflict during the events that launched Epoch One?
- What kinds of problem-solving did Epoch One approaches help facilitate?
- What methodologies and/or approaches to knowledge are favored in Epoch One?
- Which disciplines were most involved in the field at this time?
- What might be some of the concerns if the field had stayed only in Epoch One?

Activities:

Golden Balls is a British game show available on YouTube. Watch a clip of the show, and see if you can describe how it is indicative of Epoch One.

PART II

EPOCH TWO: COEXISTENCE AS PEACE, 1991–2000

Epoch Two (1991–2000)

Coexistence as Peace

On November 9, 1989, Germans shocked the world when, in the middle of the night, some citizens began to dismantle the Berlin Wall. The Wall, the physical symbol of the four-decade Cold War, soon collapsed, and within just a year, Germany reunified. Families and loved ones who had been long-separated by this wall found one another again. This catalyzed a tectonic shift in world politics because within one more year, on Christmas day in 1991, Soviet leader Mikhail Gorbachev would resign, and the Soviet Union would collapse. Boris Yeltsin took his place as the leader of Russia and invested billions in economic reform while reducing Russia's nuclear arsenal. The world breathed a sigh of relief; the threat of nuclear warfare that dominated the world stage for almost half a century had seemed to have dissolved in just a few years.

The world anticipated a period of peace when the two enormous foes that had dominated global politics shifted relationships. Political discourse foretold an anticipated "Peace Dividend," referring to the billions of dollars the United States and the former Soviet Union (now Russia) had directed into the nuclear arms race that could now support peace around the world. However, peace did not reign, and instead, conflicts *within* nations erupted, leading to the slaughter of innocent civilians, killed not because of their political ideology, but because of their ethnic and/or religious identity.

The large-scale violence immediately following the Cold War seemed motivated by hatred between groups, not motivated by a struggle over resources. The Epoch One tactics focused on the cold calculations of the other side proved less useful when addressing group hatreds anchored in historical memories of trauma (Volkan 2006). While Germany, Western Europe, the United States, and the former Soviet Union began building new bonds, other groups fractured. In the 1980s, Yugoslavia—formally made up of Bosnia and Herzegovina, Croatia, Macedonia, Montenegro, Serbia, and Slovenia—broke up. Soon after, between the years of 1992 and 1995, an estimated 200,000 people had been massacred over ethnic divisions—the Bosnian War. Ethnic cleansing became a tool for winning the war. In addition to murder, we see the systematic use of rape as a weapon of war.[1] This would lead to an increased interest in gender—how war affects men and women differently (Cheldelin and Eliatamby 2011). It would also lead to a shift in the women's rights movement; in 1993, the United Nations acknowledged women's rights as *human* rights, making crimes against women more visible and thereby more punishable.

War in Epoch Two looked bloody and barbaric, unlike distant game theoretic strategies of the Cold War. The resolution of the Bosnian War, via the Dayton

Accord, preserved the peace, but it also preserved the ethnic divisions between people. Before the agreement designed to bring peace in Bosnia and Herzegovina had even been signed, another genocide erupted more than 5,000 miles away. In just a hundred days in 1994, roughly one million Rwandans had been slaughtered by other Rwandans. Ethnic divisions between the Hutu and Tutsi tribes had led to one of the bloodiest civil wars, with rape again being used as a tool for ethnic cleansing. With an estimated 70 percent of the Tutsi population slaughtered and thousands of others infected with HIV due to rape, the country was crippled. Two million Hutus fled into neighboring countries, causing a refugee crisis in surrounding nations. The Rwandan genocide shocked the world with pictures of hundreds of thousands of bodies, bearing the mark of machetes, dumped into mass graves. With over a million people accountable for genocide, the remaining Rwandan justice system struggled. Could they really incarcerate all of those responsible? To deal with this juridical overload, they created community, participatory courts called Gacaca courts, designed to bring peace if not justice.

In the 1990s, ethnic conflict was not limited to the Balkans and Rwanda; the Algerian Civil War, fought between the government and Islamic rebel groups, endured from 1991–2002. The United States intervened in Iraq in what became the Gulf War (1990–1991). While positioned as a US response to Iraqi aggression, the war also raised a question posed by Samuel Huntington: Are we moving into an era of an unavoidable clash of civilizations?

Amidst these conflicts, other regions facing long protracted conflicts moved toward peace. On April 6, 1994, literally one day before the genocide in Rwanda began, the leaders of Northern Ireland made joint statements about how to end the violence in their region. The talks had begun in the 1980s and did not officially result in an agreement until 1998. However, violence erupted periodically, leading to yet another peace process in 2007, demonstrating that peace was not just an agreement, but as a long process of building bridges that cross identity divisions, opening up new spaces for rebuilding relationships of trust and respect. The Palestinian–Israeli conflict also made hopeful steps; the Oslo Accords were heralded as a breakthrough in 1993. The agreement did not hold, but provided a foundation for the 2000 Camp David Summit with US President Bill Clinton, Palestinian leader Yasser Arafat, and Israeli Prime Minister Ehud Barak. While this summit did not lead to an agreement, the often-circulated photographed handshake between the leaders inspired hope for the possibility of a negotiated settlement, even if peace remained elusive.

Those interested in peace had to address ethnic conflicts, and to do that, they had to develop new theories and new approaches, as well as new research methods, for indeed, the Epoch One tools did not enable them to address ethnic conflict. They found the deterrence policies and the strategic and predictive models of the Cold War insufficient. The causal, predictive linear models and the focus on individual motivations from Epoch One could not address the emerging complexity and attention to systems and groups rather than individuals that characterize Epoch Two discourses. Instead, systems theories looked at conflicts as composed of interrelated parts (Vallacher et al. 2010) and identity-group dynamics were interrogated.

Increasingly, the field of conflict resolution focused on identity differences; these were differences in how people saw themselves as people, differences regarding their identification with specific cultural markers and historical "truths." However, these differences disabled "rational" or strategic responses to conflict—they did not stop and consider their needs and interests but rather, in the white-hot environment of hatred, solved their conflicts by brutal killing sprees and genocide.

As identity differences became central to explaining and intervening in conflict, the role of emotion became more central. As negotiation, an Epoch One tactic assumed that people were rational actors. It was not a useful process for addressing ethnic conflict. Indeed, new strategies, including reconciliation and dialogue (Rotberg and Thompson 2010), came to the fore. The field began to promote discourses of coexistence (Chayes 2003), tolerance, and appreciation in an effort to redress the intense feelings that were the foundation of intergroup conflict. The Epoch One focus on understanding a party's needs and interests evolved toward understanding the "moral frameworks" of conflict parties (Pearce and Littlejohn 1997), which required a better understanding of how identity, culture (Avruch 1998), and religious beliefs (Gopin 2003) functioned in conflict. Some analysts believed that conflicts could become entrenched precisely because "identity" was itself understood as fixed, contributing to the intractability of identity-based conflicts.

The field also turned its attention towards local populations, not just the interests expressed by the leaders or governments. The discourses of conflict analysis and resolution in Epoch Two recognize societal differences that were previously repressed by leaders. For example, when Tito, the leader of the communist state of Yugoslavia, died in 1980, the religious and ethnic differences between groups came roaring back, leading to the Bosnian War. Indeed, Tito is credited for uniting Yugoslavia, but what he really did was suppress, not address, the differences between groups. As former Soviet states became more open, they were threatened, in turn, by the rise in ethnic tensions.

As identity became the explanatory framework for understanding conflict, the "causes" of conflict moved beyond the interests of the political elite and there was an increased attention to the *experiences* of the general population, including innocent victims of violence. At this point, the field of conflict analysis and resolution considered how identity, culture, and religion influence conflict dynamics. During the 1990s, those working on conflict-related issues focused less on individual motivations for violence and more on how conflict manifests in groups. Specifically, scholars and practitioners sought to understand how adherence to particular group identities contributed to conflict by denigrating out-group members. A paradoxical relationship became visible: while group membership enhanced feelings of belonging and safety, they simultaneously provided groundwork for future conflict and sometimes violence. Group boundaries can create dangerous and contentious borders.

Approaches in Epoch Two

In Epoch Two, we call responses to violence *approaches* rather than tactics or strategies—words that reflect the mindset of Epoch One. Epoch One discourses of coexistence proliferate as practitioners explore how can we live together in close geographical proximity, especially in the aftermath of the violence that severed communities and entire nations. They asked: What methods can bring people together across cultural, ethnic, and racial divides to reconcile their differences and move forward toward peaceful coexistence? And indeed, "peace" itself was understood as not just the absence of war, but also the presence of the skills needed to live alongside their differences with Others.

The practices that emerged in response to these questions relied heavily on the theory that bringing people into *contact* with one another would break through long-held stereotypes and that exposure to the "Other" would permeate barriers and lead to mutual understanding (Everett 2013). This was known as the "contact hypothesis" (Allport 1979), and it was a central tenant of Epoch Two theory (even though it was first developed in the 1950s). It assumed that contact between people, under certain conditions, can promote mutual understanding and tolerance. "Facing History, Facing Ourselves" is an excellent example of a conflict resolution NGO that uses the contact hypothesis in their efforts to provide tolerance. However, they also recognize the conditions that enable or inhibit the move toward tolerance.[2] This is an excellent example of an Epoch Two framework for understanding and redressing violent conflict.

In efforts to promote tolerance and understanding, Epoch Two practitioners believe that neutral, third-party interveners were critical to facilitating the interactions between conflicting groups. Rather than relying on top-down strategies employed during Epoch One, it was now necessary to integrate a new set of practitioner skills grounded in concepts such as dialogue, recognition, reconciliation, understanding, active listening, appreciative inquiry, and neutrality. While some critiqued these practices' abilities to decrease violence, they remain essential tenets of peacebuilding and conflict resolution processes at the time and today.

Within these approaches, attention to context, which had previously been ignored, became critical for developing processes to address conflicts. In some cases, participants in dialogue and reconciliation processes were selected based on their sphere of influence. Herbert Kelman (2002) brought together Israeli and Palestinian academics, journalists, and NGO leaders, for example, in his problem-solving workshops with the hope that strides made toward reconciliation behind closed doors would reverberate once participants reintegrated their experiences and elaborated them back into their communities. Problem-solving workshops continue today, and they have provided a format for conflict mitigation and conflict resolution between groups. For example, Susan Allen (Nan 2011)[3] describes the use of problem-solving workshops in the context of the conflict between Georgia and South Ossetia. In the post-communist era, they struggled with practical resource issues as well as identity-related ones.

Another Epoch Two development, advanced by Adam Curle (1986), conceptualized a form of mediation that enabled groups to come together to speak about their conflicts, if they were "primed" to do so. If primed, the promise of mediation was that groups (and individuals) could work through their differences and find common ground. The third-party was critically important, as a neutral facilitator, that could function as the keeper of the process. Unlike arbitration (part of alternative dispute resolution from Epoch One), a mediator's role was not to determine the outcome and adjudicate innocence or guilt. Instead, a mediator served as a neutral observer and provided a container or a space for contentious conversations to emerge and evolve with their guidance.

In general, "Epoch Two" practitioners are more concerned with the quality of the relationship, long-term, between the parties, than a focus on agreements or outcomes. As attention shifted to the relationships between parties, another new approach emerged: Appreciative Inquiry (AI) (Cooperrider and Whitney 2005).[4] This approach is premised on the idea that issues, when framed as problems, are then concretized as problems. Alternatively, when we focus on issues as reflecting our strengths and capacities, the issues become platforms for change, rather than problems that constrain or limit creative solutions. While AI emerged in organizational conflict settings, it has been widely used across many conflict contexts as an approach that enables parties to learn together about each other and their context. It has been used particularly in community settings to enable groups to deal with differences in dialogue processes.

Indeed, dialogue has been a critically important approach to conflict in Epoch Two. Dialogues are often designed to bring together diverse groups and ensure that all participants have an opportunity to be heard. The proliferation of conflicts on the intrastate level challenged practitioners to think on grander scales for how to heal and reconcile entire populations. Whereas in the past direct victims of violent conflict had largely been ignored by states and left out of peace agreements and reconciliation processes, concern for repairing relationships and including victims deepened in Epoch Two.

The move to include populations in peace processes was critically important to yet another approach in Epoch Two: restorative justice, as exemplified in South Africa's truth and reconciliation process. After apartheid, which lasted about the duration of the Cold War, in 1994, the South African government held over 1,000 public hearings. This Truth and Reconciliation Commission (TRC), conceptualized by Reverend Desmond Tutu in response to apartheid in South Africa, became emblematic in this new era of restorative practices. While the South African commission became the most well-known, Truth Commissions actually began largely in Latin America to hold governments accountable for violent atrocities committed there. These commissions enabled those involved with the violence to confess in exchange for legal impunity. As forums for voices rather than punishment, legal discourse became a less dominant force. Building on the alternative dispute resolution mechanisms introduced in Epoch One, truth commissions expanded what could be considered appropriate mechanisms of justice, reconceptualized in the face of new conflict dimensions. TRCs were soon used around the world, despite being widely criticized for failing to do more than give lip service to reconciliation between ethnic groups. Those who told their stories in these public forums often questioned the value of the experience. In the case of South

Africa, the racial differences, institutionalized during apartheid, reflected deep wounds and a history of oppression that could not be treated by traditional justice processes but had to be addressed as a wound in the social fabric, one that required healing.

During this era, the United States had its own wounds to address. These became visible in the aftermath of the 1991 video documenting the beating of an African American, Rodney King, in Los Angeles.[5] Shockwaves swept across LA and, eventually, the nation. When an all-white jury acquitted the officers identified on the scene on all charges, riots broke out in Los Angeles—people were outraged over the mistreatment of African Americans by police officers. In a speech by Rodney King, he asked, "Can't we all just get along?"—a hallmark of the discourse of coexistence in Epoch Two and, therefore, practices of peacebuilding and conflict resolution. Of course, the United States has become witness to ongoing shooting deaths and beatings of African Americans by white police officers, giving rise to advocacy groups such as Black Lives Matter. However, unlike the Epoch Two approaches to reconciliation or restorative processes, these more recent advocacy groups seek equality and justice, not just understanding differences.

Within the United States, Epoch Two discourses question how to work with people from different racial, ethnic, and cultural backgrounds also greatly impacted the development of approaches to conflict in workplace settings. Diversity training emerged as a critical aspect of managing employee relationships. The programs emphasized finding similarities between people despite different skin colors or historical backgrounds. Political correctness amplified; people strived to say the "right thing" while the implicit biases that anchored prejudice remained intact. However, as with South Africa's TRC and other peacebuilding mechanisms, the diversity-promoting spaces created to reconcile differences pushed toward sameness and often failed to acknowledge the marginalization of particular groups or to move past "differences" to important conversations about the politics of oppression. This often further silenced and marginalized these groups. Consensus models of conflict resolution seem to promote inclusiveness, but often, they just pressure dissenters into silent resignation or inner rebellion.

Acknowledging marginalization challenges the role of neutrality in Epoch Two approaches. If parties of unequal status engage in a conflict resolution process and the third-party intervener must be neutral, how then can the outcome favor the marginalized group? If we "equalize" the playing field during processes of reconciliation but the power inequity still exists outside of the formulated context, will reconciliation hold once the process ends? The mediator's neutrality can also perpetuate the power differential between parties. These questions of power differentials between parties were not properly addressed by the approaches in Epoch Two, a critique that receives considerable attention in Epoch Three.

Research in Epoch Two

Research methodologies introduced at this time shifted from Epoch One assumptions that humans are rational thinkers in favor of understanding emotion, culture, and identity and their influence on conflict dynamics. As researchers attempted to understand such subjectivity, linear, statistical approaches could not capture the nuance of human behavior that was now seen to be influenced by a more complex set of dynamics associated with how people understood themselves, how they understood Others, and how these descriptions of Self and Other contributed to the conflict dynamics.

As researchers worked to understand identity and the interpretative processes contributing to conflict and resolution, qualitative research on conflict gained prominence and significance. These research approaches recognized that culture and history played critically important roles in conflict as well as reconciliation processes. Those conducting research in Epoch Two also started to consider dynamics at the local level. Rather than looking for universal truths, as predominated in Epoch One, many started to consider truth as something socially constructed and mutable over time. Research methods reliant on factor analysis and rational choice theory, prevalent in Epoch One, were seen as limited in their ability to capture the complexity that emerged during Epoch Two, in the face of the proliferation of intrastate conflict. As the "subjectivity" of populations became more salient for researchers trying to understand conflict dynamics, the focus shifted to interpretative and situated methodologies such as ethnography. In Epoch Two, reality itself was considered to be a subjective phenomenon that needed to be examined to understand larger meaning systems and how people were making sense of conflict within their particular contexts.

Examining meaning systems required that research move away from large data sets and macro-level statistical analysis, turning instead toward understanding cultures, ethnicities, and identities, which meant that they needed to engage with people's lived experiences of themselves and others in particular conflict contexts. The introduction of ethnography (Hoey 2014; Nordstrom 2004), which was borrowed from anthropology and case study methodology, allowed conflict researchers to engage with in-depth analysis of one particular context and to explore the complexity embedded within that one particular conflict (Federman 2017). While these sites for analyses might be focused on particular cases, they enabled researchers to develop theories about the role of culture and religion as both causing conflict and being a resource for conflict resolution. Ethnographers prioritized the voices of differing cultures and incorporated a focus on the historical influences on the evolution of conflict. The hope was that the understanding that emerged from this research would help lead to an appreciation of differences that would, in and of itself, reduce the outbreak and duration of the conflict. Coexistence as a practice means not just living alongside one another, but cooperating in spite of differences and historical divisions. Coexistence, as an approach to conflict resolution, challenges parties to come together and work through misunderstanding and even violence that threatens to separate them. Coexistence recognizes destinies as intertwined. We cannot just live in our separate spaces and advance society. However, coexistence has its challenges. Looking at the Israeli–Palestinian conflict, for example, we have many peacemakers working towards a shared future, but violence on both sides consistently thwarts peacemaking efforts, causing parties to withdraw back into their own groups. Coexistence means staying committed to peace even in the face of violence. People committed to peace can be considered traitors especially when they continue talking to the "other side" in the wake of violent outbreaks. This might be the biggest challenge for the field—continuing to work towards peace even when people lose hope.

Epoch Two: Contributions and Limitations

In Epoch Two, we see the field of conflict analysis and resolution responding to the intrastate conflict that more prominently emerged after the fall of the Berlin Wall and the collapse of the Soviet Union. No longer did the theories and practices of Epoch One suffice to address the new dynamics whereby conflicts emerged along cultural, ethnic, racial, and religious identity lines. Epoch Two practitioners responded with a new set of theories and practices that worked to enhance our understanding of group formation and how they operate to entrench people in or possibly loosen the grips of violent conflict. The discourse in this Epoch centers on coexistence as peace, intergroup dialogue, and living side by side. In today's parlance, it would translate into "people-to-people" programs that include victimized populations in the conversations across affected communities. The theoretical frameworks, approaches, and the research methodologies associated to Epoch Two, all advanced our understanding of ethnic conflicts and enabled the field to begin to address identity differences and the central role of emotions and culture, as well as provided approaches for engaging local populations in healing the wounds of conflict.

While Epoch Two served the field tremendously, it still left some questions unanswered. Most notably, these approaches and theories did not interrogate the notion of power and how it operates, not only in conflicts themselves but in the creation and implementation of peacebuilding programs. Likewise, Epoch Two emphasizes speaking between and within groups, assuming a cathartic relationship between sharing one's side of a story or speaking pain to heal and transform violent relationships. Those participating in these processes did not uniformly find such experiences cathartic or beneficial in the long term. Diversity and coexistence programs that emphasized sameness and political correctness began to police or regulate speech rather than transform prejudice. In Epoch Three, scholars and practitioners will take heart to these critiques and push the field to expose and explore the more complex relationships between victims and perpetrators. Notions of power and voice also become central in Epoch Three.

Keywords for Epoch Two: intrastate conflict, interethnic conflict, identity, culture, gender, religion, coexistence, peacebuilding, dialogue groups, mediation, nonviolence, diversity training, ethnography, case studies.

References

Allport, Gordon W. *The Nature of Prejudice*. Unabridged, 25th anniversary ed. Reading, MA: Addison-Wesley, 1979.

Avruch, Kevin. "Frames for Culture and Conflict Resolution." In *Culture and Conflict Resolution*, 52–57. Washington, DC: United States Institute of Peace, 1998.

Chayes, Antonia Handler, and the Program on Negotiation at Harvard Law School. "Introduction." In *Imagine Coexistence: Restoring Humanity after Violent Ethnic Conflict*, xviii-xxii. San Francisco: Jossey-Bass, 2003.

Cheldelin, Sandra I., and Maneshka Eliatamby. *Women Waging War and Peace: International Perspectives of Women's Roles in Conflict and Post-Conflict Reconstruction*. New York: Bloomsbury, 2011. Challenging the Dominant Narrative (Conclusion)

Cooperrider, David L., and Diana Kaplin Whitney. *Appreciative Inquiry*. Oakland, CA: Berrett-Koehler Publishers. 2005.

Curle, Adam. "Mediation." In *In the Middle: Non-Official Mediation in Violent Situations*, 9–20. New York: St. Martin's Press, 1986.

Everett, Jim A. C. "Intergroup Contact Theory: Past, Present, and Future," In *The Inquisitive Mind* 17. Last modified 2013. http://www.in-mind.org/article/intergroup-contact-theory-past-present-and-future.

Gopin, Marc. "Religion as an Aid and a Hindrance to Postconflict Coexistence Work." In *Imagine Coexistence: Restoring Humanity After Violent Ethnic Conflict*, edited by Antonia Chayes and Martha L. Minow, 252–66. San Francisco: Jossey-Bass, 2003.

Hoey, Brian A. "A Simple Introduction to the Practice of Ethnography and Guide to Ethnographic Fieldnotes." *Marshall University Digital Scholar* (2014). Available at: http://works.bepress.com/brian_hoey/12/.

Jones, Joshua A. "Addressing the Use of Sexual Violence as a Strategic Weapon of War." *Inquiries Journal/Student Pulse* 5 (04) 2013. Retrieved from http://www.inquiriesjournal.com/a?id=732.

Kelman, Herbert C. "Interactive Problem Solving as a Tool for Second Track Diplomacy." In *Second Track Citizens Diplomacy: Concepts and Techniques for Conflict*, edited by John L. Davies and Edward Kaufman (Editor), 81–106. Lanham, MD: Rowman & Littlefield, 2002.

Nan, Susan Allen. "Adapting Interactive Conflict Resolution for Catalytic Roles in Context: The Georgian-South Ossetian Point of View Process." SSRN Scholarly Paper ID 1872646. Rochester, NY: Social Science Research Network, 2011. https://papers.ssrn.com/abstract=1872646.

Nordstrom, Carolyn. *Shadows of War: Violence, Power, and International Profiteering in the Twenty-First Century*. 1st ed. Berkeley, CA: University of California Press, 2004.

Pearce, Barnette and Stephen Littlejohn. "The Problem of Moral Conflict." In *Moral Conflict When Social Worlds Collide*, 48–81. Thousand Oaks, CA: SAGE Publishing, 1997.

Rotberg, Robert I., and Dennis Thompson. "Truth v. Justice: The Morality of Truth Commissions." Princeton University Press, 2010. Truth Commissions and the Provision of Truth, Justice, and Reconciliation 3–21.

Sander, Frank E. A. "Alternative Methods of Dispute Resolution: An Overview." *University of Florida Law Review* 37 (1985): 1–18.

Sharp, Gene. *Waging Nonviolent Struggle: 20th Century Practice and 21st Century Potential*. Manchester, NH: Extended Horizons, 2005: 13–24.

Vallacher, Robin R., Peter T. Coleman, Andrzej Nowak, Lan Bui-Wrzosinska. "Rethinking Intractable Conflict: The Perspective of Dynamical Systems." *American Psychologist* 65, no. 4 (2010): 262–78.

Volkan, Vamik D. "Large-Group Psychodynamics and Massive Violence."*Ciência & Saúde Coletiva* 11, no. 2 (2006): 303–14.

Notes

1. Rape had been historically seen as a consequence or prize of war and violence, but it is at the time of the Bosnian and Rwandan wars that the field begins to consider it a strategic method (Jones, 2013).

2. See the Facing History and Facing Ourselves website where they address the contact hypothesis at https://www.facinghistory.org/sounds-change/gordon-allports-contact -hypothesis.

3. Susan Allen, formerly Susan Allen Nan, describes her work using "interactive conflict resolution" in Nan, Susan Allen (2011). "Adapting Interactive Conflict Resolution for Catalytic Roles in Context: The Georgian-South Ossetian Point of View Process (June 25, 2011)." IACM 24th Annual Conference Paper. Available at SSRN: https://ssrn.com/ abstract = 1872646 or http://dx.doi.org/10.2139/ssrn.1872646.

4. Please note that Appreciative Inquiry emerged in the 1990s, but many publications describing AI continue to be published much later.

5. See the footage of the beating here: http://abcnews.go.com/Archives/video/march -1991-rodney-king-videotape-9758031.

Coexistence

Antonia Handler Chayes

Antonia Handler Chayes is a professor of Practice of International Politics and Law at Tuft University's Fletcher School. Prior to teaching at Tufts, Chayes taught at the Harvard Kennedy School and was vice chair of Conflict Management Group, an international nonprofit dedicated to dispute resolution. During the Carter Administration, she served as the under-secretary of the U.S. Air Force. She received her BA from Harvard (Radcliffe) and received her law degree from George Washington University.

In Epoch Two, there is increased attention paid to peacebuilding in the aftermath of conflict. Conflicts erupt with regularity even after peace treaties are signed, suggesting that a cease-fire and signed settlement are not enough to ensure lasting, positive peace. Chayes frames the discussion of peacebuilding using the framework of coexistence. Many NGOs and international organizations arrive in the aftermath of conflict with food and supplies designed to meet the basic needs of individuals, doing little to address the "simmering hatred" and "devastated relationships." Without addressing these lingering tensions, even the most generous contributions can exacerbate distrust, especially if they suggest a perceived bias in favor of one group. The emotional wake of war is often considered secondary to meeting primary needs. Chayes argues, however, that "ruptured relationships cannot wait, and that addressing them in terms of coexistence involves a goal that is both feasible and honest."

By coexistence, she means finding small ways opposing parties can work together to rebuild their communities. The reconciliation observing parties often hope for often proves too great a challenge. The smaller goal of productive coexistence is often more feasible and can provide a stepping stone to future reconciliation.

This article represents an Epoch Two approach in its concern with and attention to ongoing tensions between groups. Chayes recognizes the amount of intergroup tensions often held in place by autocratic regimes. The Bosnian War after the end of the Cold War is one such example. A growing concern for the underlying tensions that fuels and refuels conflict also demonstrates Epoch Two's growing consideration of local groups and group dynamics. No longer is it enough to achieve a masterful negotiation at the level of leadership. The community dynamics now matter as much as governmental policies.

Questions to consider: Is coexistence enough? What might coexistence look like in a post-war context? How is coexistence similar or different to the notion of tolerance?

Imagine Coexistence

Antonia Handler Chayes

How can people build peace after violent ethnic conflict? This extraordinary challenge, familiar across the globe, is heightened when displaced persons and refugees return home or move to regions where their very presence risks reopening the conflict. The challenge begins at the moment when international organizations and nongovernmental organizations (NGOs) enter the scenes of carnage. These organizations often emphasize expectations of reconciliation and reinforce local voices toward that end soon after conflict ends. The actions of these helping agencies too often ignore the simmering hatred that often persists after the gunfire has subsided. The distrust and tensions that linger call for immediate action in refugee camps and other places where fleeing people need food, shelter, and medicine. From the beginning, the choice of priorities by international and nongovernmental groups intending to help should reflect an understanding of the ongoing tensions so that even the most basic repairs to infrastructure and the most basic humanitarian assistance are immediately sensitive to the question of rebuilding a peaceful society.

Intercommunal tensions held in check by autocratic regimes during the Cold War exploded once the authority of those regimes began to crumble. Ambitious, corrupt, and greedy leaders preyed on distrust and fear by manipulating economic resentments and separating people and communities along crude ethnic or religious lines that can come to feel long-standing and authentic. Similar dynamics have occurred in Eastern Europe, in Africa, and in South Asia. Understanding this process of transforming genuine distrust into deeply believed myths of ethnic division is essential for any effort to repair the fabric of a war-torn society. Hatred, once stirred, has given rise to widespread violence and led to enduring nationalism and separatism, even after the violence has subsided.

Although each context of internal conflict is unique, certain recurring problems seem common to all and can be planned for and dealt with to help overcome the hatreds and tensions that fueled the conflict in the first place:

- New patterns of refugee movement are part of the ongoing ethnic conflicts that seek to expel or return people of a given group as the very means of expressing power. After basic peace is announced, these displaced people need food, shelter, protection, and resettlement.

- The country is likely to be devastated, without sewers, water, or electricity. Its communications and transportation infrastructure needs immediate repair and reconstruction or in some instances initial construction.
- Returning peoples need assistance to rebuild homes and lives; they also often need medical care and social services.
- Food, shelter, jobs, and health care may be lacking for displaced people and for many who remained in their home areas. Houses, schools, and hospitals are likely to have been destroyed.
- All residents need an assurance of safety and the restoration of law and order.
- The restoration of self-governance based on the rule of law and international human rights principles is likely to be a commitment demanded by the international community, along with efforts to disarm and demobilize combatants.
- The economy is likely to be devastated, with facilities and resources destroyed or impaired and prospects for international investment reduced or nonexistent.

These are just some of the recurring problems encountered in every internal conflict of the past dozen years. Each of them has demanded planning and urgent action on the part of the international community. Because of what are fairly described as urgent needs to meet basic human needs, those seeking to help seldom address systematically the devastated relationships between people who fell on opposite sides of the conflict. Yet if the methods of assistance, physical restoration, and governance do not also address these relationships, the prospects for restoring lasting peace are minimal. Indeed, it may be more satisfying emotionally for former combatants and victims to maintain hostile attitudes and pursue separation than to imagine the difficulties faced by others and to take the hard initial steps toward cooperation and collaboration. If helping agencies are inattentive to these dynamics, they may make matters worse. By handing out blankets and food or roofing materials and permits for vehicles without attention to the continuing tensions across groups, helping agencies may feed perceptions of unfairness and bias and therefore exacerbate resentment and mistrust. Through inattention, agencies can miss the chance to restore civility and begin the long journey to peace. The subject of intergroup relationships deserves as much priority as the efforts to ensure housing, food, medical care, and security.

Too often, issues such as reconciliation and the punishment of war criminals are treated as separate from rebuilding infrastructure, providing food and shelter, and ensuring security and the rule of law. Typically, reconciliation and accountability are deferred until after these initial steps of reconstruction have been taken. Yet whether addressed explicitly or not, the relationships across the lines of division will be profoundly affected by these initial stages of reconstruction. It is understandable to postpone formal processes of accountability, like war crimes trials or truth and reconciliation inquiries, yet inattention to the smoldering anger and resentments risks creating circumstances for new conflict or barriers to the basic steps of reconstructing the physical environment.

The argument embodied in this book is that the ruptured relationships cannot wait and that addressing them in terms of coexistence involves a goal that is both feasible and honest. Coexistence lends itself to immediate consideration. It also reflects an honest assessment of what is both possible and necessary immediately after conflict. It remains a difficult and complex challenge to bring civility and peace to a society at war with itself. Rebuilding homes and electrical grids looks more achievable—and such efforts, if pursued thoughtfully, may even strengthen the chances for civility and peace. Yet, pursued without attention to the remaining lines of conflict, even these basic steps may exacerbate the conflict and render prospects for long-term peace more remote. One of the major points of this book is that the concept of coexistence must infuse every effort to rebuild a society after conflict, both physically and institutionally. It cannot be postponed and thus must not be separated from other steps to help after ethnic conflict.

Another major point here is that coexistence may seem too small an aspiration in the face of calls for reconciliation; yet precisely because it is more modest, coexistence may be achieved while reconciliation may remain elusive or even an insulting notion to people still reeling from the murder of their loved ones or their own torture or rape. Reconciliation is certainly a worthy ultimate goal, but as Sadako Ogata points out in the Preface, she and her colleagues concluded that first "to help refugees return to . . . devastated communities, the fabric of the society would have to be stitched back together."

Under Ogata's courageous leadership, UNHCR, together with a group of academics and practitioners represented in this book, developed a cooperative project that this group called Imagine Coexistence. We chose the word *imagine* because in the early stages of recovery from intense violence, any attempt to bring parties together takes a leap of imagination. Promoting coexistence may seem a less ambitious goal than promoting reconciliation after interethnic conflict. But to be effective, it must pervade all areas of assistance, not merely those that focus on relationships, and in that respect, it is a tall ambition indeed.

Coexistence means more than simple peaceful living side by side. As we have conceived it, coexistence involves at least some degree of interaction and cooperation across the lines of ethnic division. International and nongovernmental initiatives can facilitate interactions and cooperation, but only by working assiduously to improve postconflict conditions while simultaneously working to restore communication and to avoid misunderstandings or work them through as they arise.

It has become clear that some efforts at assistance and restoration may make matters worse. Clumsy, premature attempts at reconciliation may do more harm than good. By contrast, strategically selected projects that build on shared interests rather than dividing people along the lines of prior conflicts may promote coexistence. The authors of this book seek to foster coexistence as a vital dimension of humanitarian practice and theory after intense ethnic conflict. Initiatives in the arts, dispute resolution, sports, new technologies, education, interfaith dialogue, and business can serve as such projects. Creating occasions for people from previously warring groups to work side by side or in parallel efforts toward common goals can be effective starting points for fostering coexistence. They may provide a better setting than dialogue alone in building trusting relationships, as several chapters based on field observations illustrate. It may often be more effective to promote coexistence indirectly, not by talking about it or by directly tackling intergroup tension but by building shared experiences, addressing pressing needs in ways that involve people from different groups, or enhancing the daily quality of life in ways to enlarge hope for the future. But these efforts cannot be isolated from either dialogue or community and national politics.

This volume represents an unusual effort to marry theory and practice in fostering coexistence. Our team includes scholars from many fields, NGO practitioners, and evaluators. They focus on approaches that will begin the process of rebuilding a peaceful society with the very first brick that is laid. Several authors explore antecedents in field practice for UNHCR's Imagine Coexistence project. The first chapters grow from field efforts of international organizations and NGOs in regions marked by violent ethnic conflict, including Bosnia and Herzegovina and Rwanda, the areas chosen for pilot projects by UNHCR. Some chapters reflect direct involvement with the Imagine Coexistence project. Like that initiative, these chapters invite people to imagine the possibility of coexistence and treat imagination as the first and essential ingredient for peaceful coexistence after conflict. They illustrate the scope of actual efforts undertaken over a large range of activities.

UNHCR wisely sought to evaluate the effectiveness of coexistence efforts, and UNHCR staff involved have worked with scholars to draw up an approach that will permit field personnel to assess the relative values of various projects as coexistence becomes a counterpoint theme in building peace. This is especially challenging as there are as yet no established evaluation tools in this area. Chapters in this volume synthesize and assess the bodies of potentially relevant evaluation approaches while also providing narrative accounts and case studies of coexistence efforts.

The very importance of coexistence has made it imperative to understand some of the obstacles that are thrown up to thwart such efforts. Some of the case studies describe the actual frustrations encountered. Three chapters examine in detail how widespread "state machinery" corruption is after conflict and how barriers to economic development are heightened by the very forces that have fanned the conflict, driven by economic greed. Efforts to mainstream coexistence are further frustrated by bureaucratic rigidities in the very agencies that aim to help, because it may deviate from standard operating procedures and interfere with carefully guarded organizational prerogatives. These problems persist and must be anticipated in the design and operation of coexistence initiatives.

The concrete areas addressed in-depth, such as arts, education, and economic development, are illustrative of how coexistence efforts might be mainstreamed in rebuilding a war-torn society. The positive and negative role of religion is addressed. Other areas could have been be subjected to the same approaches— mental and physical health programs, sports, building a civil police force, disarmament, and civil society generally.

The theoretical approaches reflect research into some of the emotional and social dynamics of ethnic conflict that can build conditions for coexistence: narrative, myth, and identity are addressed both theoretically and in the context of cases. The human drive for repair itself provides hope, as one chapter explores.

All the contributors to this book hope that the experiences and ideas found in this collection will open fresh avenues for experiments in coexistence that increase the chances of success. In seeking to inform practice and research, the authors also express deep gratitude to the people at UNHCR and elsewhere in the field who have undertaken or enabled the work examined here and to the United States Institute of Peace for supporting this effort. It is a project of imagination that could kindle new hope after ethnic conflict.

Identity

Louis Kriesberg

Louis Kriesberg was the founding director of the Program on the Analysis and Resolution of Conflicts at Syracuse University, where he also taught in the sociology department. He has written over 160 book chapters as well as many books on constructive conflicts and conflict transformation. He trained hundreds of graduate students and professionals in non-violent approaches to conflict. He received his PhD from the University of Chicago.

Kriesberg's article provides an overview of how identity relates to conflict. Identities, he writes, can relate to race, ethnicity, gender, or religion, for example, and can be as particular as in the identification with family or have a broader more collective nature, as in the case of national identity. There is some debate as to how identities are formed. While some say that identities are formed as a result of particular physical traits or lived experiences, others argue that identity is innate. However, as is reflected in this essay, Kriesberg considers ethnicity to be largely a social construct and not always easily transformed. He argues that intergroup conflicts occur when groups develop an "us vs. them" mentality.

It is important to examine what people hold onto about their identities and what aspects of their identity they feel is most salient (significant), that they might be unable to compromise. How do people in different identity groups view one another, and who is included or not? Along with these questions, examining context relations (i.e., internal factors in each group) with adversarial groups, as well as the social context of the group's interaction, is essential for understanding how identity groups operate in conflict.

Kriesberg argues that individuals can hold multiple identities in conflict and during conflict people cling to the most significant identity. One might cling more tightly to a national identity if that identity is being challenged. These ideas were critical at the time of Epoch Two when global conflict faced new challenges in the wake of the fall of the Berlin Wall. Kriesberg demonstrates how the once primary Yugoslavian identity eventually shifted once Serbs, Croats, and Bosnians began to adhere more strongly to their more particular religious and ethnic identities.

Understanding that identity adherence depends on context is important, and it is a critical shift from Epoch One, which largely overlooked the role of identity and context in conflict. Identity theory focused a new lens on conflict that has captivated researchers and practitioners and theoretically underpins many approaches. Critics of identity theory would argue that identity is not as fixed as it is often portrayed. Not only is there a great deal of intra-group variance, but also the general categorization of people into particular groups may be overly rigid and fixed: it does not recognize that identity is shifting all the time. Additionally, it is offered that great attention is needed to create an understanding of how power operates in identity construction and conflict. Critical thinking on identity argues for understanding intersectionality and the way that our multiple identities are constantly interacting and cannot necessarily be segmented and grouped.

Questions to consider: What are your most salient identities? Why are identities so important? What role does identity play in the emergence of conflict? Do you believe that identity is a central consideration for how conflicts develop?

" 'Us' versus 'Them' "

Louis Kriesberg

Israelis and Palestinians, India and Pakistan, governments and insurgents, Protestants and Catholics, whites and blacks, labor and management . . . these are all examples of identities that have at some times and some places resulted in intractable conflicts.

For an intergroup (e.g., racial, ethnic, or religious) conflict to occur, the opponents must have a sense of collective identity about themselves and about their adversary, each side believing the fight is between "us" and "them." Some of those conflicts become intractable, persisting destructively for a very long time, despite efforts to resolve them. In some such conflicts the antagonists seem to be fighting each other about the identities that they hold about themselves and those they attribute to the other side. Such conflicts are sometimes called identity-based conflicts and regarded as particularly prone to becoming intractable.

This essay examines: (1) the characteristics of various kinds of identities, (2) how particular qualities of collective identities contribute to a conflict becoming intractable, (3) what shapes collective identities, and (4) how such identities can be modified to help transform and resolve intractable conflicts.

Developing a sense of self is an essential part of every individual becoming a mature person. Each person's self-conception is a unique combination of many identifications, identifications as broad as woman or man, Catholic or Muslim, or as narrow as being a member of one particular family. Although self-identity may seem to coincide with a particular human being, identities are actually much wider than that. They are also collective—identities extend to countries and ethnic communities, so that people feel injured when other persons sharing their identity are injured or killed. Sometimes people are even willing to sacrifice their individual lives to preserve their identity group(s). Palestinian suicide bombers are a well-publicized example.

For the large, intergroup struggles discussed in this essay and much of this Web site, collective identities are necessary.[1] People who share the same collective identity think of themselves as having a common interest and a common fate.

Some of the many identities people have are nested within each other, usually compatibly, as is the case for geographic identities within a country. For example, I can identity both with New York (my state) and the United States (my country). However, some identities may compete with each other, as occurs in wars of secession. For example, in the 1950s and 1960s many people living in what was then Yugoslavia felt pride in having stood up to the Soviet Union in 1948 and in creating a new economic system. Yet in the 1990s, most people in Yugoslavia felt that their identities as Serbs, Croats, Slovenes, Muslims, or Bosnians were more salient than their identity as Yugoslavs.

Sources of Identity

Identities are constructed on the basis of various traits and experiences. Many of those characteristics are open to different interpretations. Race is a good example. Skin color is an important marker of identity in many societies, but in others it is of minimal importance. Many people in the United States assign relatively great importance to skin color; furthermore, they tend to dichotomize color into black and white, claiming that having any African ancestry, even over several generations, may make a person identify with being black. But in other countries race is partly defined by traits that may be acquired later in life. For example, in Mexico, "Indians" can become "Mestizos" by wearing Western clothing and speaking Spanish.

Similarly, some analysts speak of ethnicity as a primordial phenomenon, relatively ancient and unchanging. Other analysts stress that ethnicity is socially constructed, with people choosing a history and common ancestry and creating, as much as discovering, differences from others.[2] In this essay, I consider ethnicity to be largely socially constructed, while I recognize that some traits of ethnicity are not easily modified by social processes.

For instance, some traits are fixed at birth, such as parental ethnicity and religion, place of birth, and skin color. Other traits may be acquired or modified later, such as language spoken, religion practiced, clothing worn, or food eaten. Insofar as the traits chosen to define membership in an ethnicity are determined at birth, ethnic status is ascribed; and insofar as they are modified or acquired in later life, ethnic status is achieved.

Many identities, then, are not based on ascribed traits but on shared values, beliefs, or concerns, which are varyingly open to acquisition by choice. This includes shared religious adherence—indeed, members of many religious communities proselytize to win converts to their faith. This is also true for political ideologies, attachment to particular pieces of land, or practicing a particular way of life.

Identities vary in many other ways. They are self-designations and also attributions made about other persons. They can endure for generations or change with shifting situations. They can exclude or include. And since everyone has multiple identities, their relative importance and compatibility differs in various times and circumstances.

Identity Effects on Intractability

Additional insights into identity issues are offered by Beyond Intractability project participants.

Collective identities are inherent in social life, whether part of a conflict or not. When and how identities contribute to intractable conflicts depends greatly on the content of the identities held. Certain qualities of identities contribute significantly to the intractability of conflicts, and whether those conflicts are constructive or destructive.

Persistent Identities: Protracted conflicts are made possible by enduring identities, often based on ascribed characteristics. Thus, the protracted nature of many ethnic conflicts depends on the persistence of the ethnic groups, deriving from socialization within the group and from suffering resulting from discrimination and exclusion by other ethnic groups. For example, the survival of Jews as an ethnic group, even without a single territorial base, has derived from socialization within the community about Jewish religious and cultural qualities and from external anti-Semitism.

Primary Identities: The primacy or importance of an identity is another quality that affects its contribution to the persistence of a conflict. Persons and groups have multiple identities, but the identities are not all equally significant to them. Conflicts related to highly significant identities have a tendency to persist, since threats to those identities are not easily put aside.[3] For instance, particular pieces of land can be key elements of identity, whether they are the village, region, or country of birth and ancestral attachment. When land is a key focus of identity, struggles over that land can become protracted. This is often the case for aboriginal peoples in territories controlled by later settlers.

Non-Compromising Identities: The nature of the collective identities also affects the difficulty in reaching an accommodation between conflicting groups. Members of groups with identities that place a high priority on being honored and being treated with deference may have difficulty making compromises for or respecting other groups. Furthermore, some self-conceptions relating to ideas of sovereignty, authority, and legitimacy constitute barriers to successful settlement of a conflict.

Views of the "Other": Many other attributes of identities affect the way conflicts are conducted. Certainly, the character attributed to the adversary is often related to the destructiveness of a conflict. If people in the enemy collectivity are viewed as subhuman, even denigrated as vermin, they are more easily subjected to gross human rights violations and even extermination attempts. If enemy people are regarded as evil, then extreme methods are justified to destroy them. Obviously, the targets of such characterizations will reject them and may subsequently reciprocate them.

Even less extreme characterizations of the other group can contribute to a conflict's intractability. This may occur when one group's identity is fashioned in opposition to another. For example, during the Cold War, an important aspect of American identity for many people in the United States was to be anti-Communist.

Inclusivity: In addition, identities vary in their exclusiveness or inclusiveness, the degree to which people who do not yet share the identity may be welcomed to do so or be excluded. Inclusive identities are less prone to foster intractable conflict.

Nationalism: Considerable attention for many years has been given to nationalism as a source of intractable conflicts. Nationalism as an ideology asserts that nations or groups of people who share a common history and destiny have the right to have a territory or state of their own. Given the movement and intermingling of people on earth and the changing political systems of the world, such a right for everyone is not realizable. Furthermore, nationalist sentiments often are a variant of ethnocentrism, the tendency to see one's own group as superior and more deserving of respect than all others.[4] This is particularly evident when nationalist sentiments are shaped by ethnic identities. They are less evident in civic nationalism, which affirms citizenship in a country as obtainable by all who choose to live there.[5] Furthermore, it is indeed possible for people to be patriotic, celebrating their own people or country, without denigrating or dominating other peoples or countries.

Victimhood: Another important characteristic of identities is the degree to which people hold identities that incorporate their sense that they have generally been victims of oppression and domination by others. Such conceptions tend to make people feel threatened and mistrustful. Fearing attacks, they may act to prevent them, but in ways that the other side likewise experiences as threats. The result can be self-perpetuating destructive struggles.

Adversarial Identities: Finally, a conflict's intractability depends upon the identities of the adversary. Identities can mesh with each other in ways that are more or less destructive. Two groups with ethno-nationalist identities and with attachment to some of the same land are prone to engage in an intractable conflict. However, a group with an ethno-nationalist identity and even a high sense of superiority may avoid an intractable conflict with a group that has identities emphasizing other-worldly religious concerns.

Shapers of Identity

Three settings shape collective identities: (1) internal factors within each group, (2) relations with adversary groups, and (3) the social context of the groups' interaction. Each setting is discussed in turn.

(1) INTERNAL FACTORS AND PROCESSES

Certain characteristics of group members affect their identities and their views of the groups with which they are in opposition.

Universal Human Needs: Some conflict resolution analysts and practitioners argue that all people and groups are driven to attain certain basic and universal human needs. Among these, they say, are recognition, security, and identity.[6] Human needs theorists and practitioners believe that the frustration of these needs underlies many social conflicts. Since such needs are non-negotiable, they argue, an inability to attain these needs often leads to intractable conflict. Other theorists and practitioners, however, stress the cultural variability in the way needs are understood and certainly in the ways in which they are satisfied.[7] This is the approach taken in this essay.

Past Experience: Past experience, for example, is an important influence on a conflict's intractability. Groups may pass on the heritage of suffering and of enmities arising from historical traumatic events.[8] Of course, if those events are to shape contemporary identities, they must be kept alive in families, schools, and religious institutions, and sometimes aroused and amplified by political leaders, intellectuals, or other influential persons. If that occurs, identities tend to form that foster intractable conflicts.

Adversarial Attitudes: Various cultural patterns prevalent within a society, group, or organization contribute to a conflict's intractability.[9] These patterns include a predilection, for example, not to trust members of other groups, to denigrate them, or to act with hostility toward them. Specific ideologies and ways of thinking also contribute to conflict intractability. Thus, people in a group with a collective identity significantly based on racism would tend to denigrate others they regard as inherently inferior and feel free to act in destructive ways against the inferior beings. This is likely to result in determined resistance and protracted destructive struggle.

Leadership: Finally, it should be recognized that political and religious leaders play important roles in shaping identities. Leaders put forward identities that include some people while excluding others. They may expect to benefit from the construction and strengthening of exclusive identities, privileging their own language or religion and gaining power by arousing emotions against other groups and peoples. For example, Hitler and the Nazis helped create an extreme racist German identity that contributed greatly to the destructiveness of the wars Germany undertook.

(2) RELATIONS WITH ADVERSARIES

Identities are profoundly shaped by interactions molded in conflict, and in turn influence the course of a conflict.[10]

Violence and Coercion: Antagonistic interactions with large components of violence and other forms of coercion tend to produce identities incorporating toughness in resisting coercion and in imposing it on others. Members of the group who act tough are then celebrated by other members of their group and held up as models to be emulated as exemplars to people in their camp. At the same time, members of the opposing side are likely to be seen as cruel and vicious and bearing hatred. Such views hamper transformation of an intractable conflict, since people in the other camp will tend to reciprocate the hostile behavior and ways of characterizing people.

Negative Characterizations: Such interactions are never wholly symmetrical. If a group is relatively powerful, it will try to impose its definitions on other groups. The Nazis' violent imposition of their characterization of who and what Jews were stands as a grotesque example of that tendency. In most instances, the imposition of a definition and characterization is less organized and violent; but some degree of imposition is discernable in many relationships.

Positive Relationships: Not all interactions between adversaries, however, are adversarial; usually some members of the opposing sides engage in particular inter-actions that are mutually desired and even cooperative. Some people may be engaged in profitable economic transactions with the other side or they may col-laborate in cultural or research activities. Having a large proportion of mutually gratifying interactions tends to mitigate and counter the destructive consequences of contentious interactions.

(3) SOCIAL CONTEXT

The social setting within which conflict groups contend with each other also greatly affects the adversaries' identities.

Ways of Thinking: The prevailing ways of thinking in every period of history profoundly influence how people characterize themselves and each other. Identi-fications in terms of religious beliefs, class relations, ethnicity, or lifestyles are more or less striking in different times and places. For example, racist ways of thinking have been more pervasive in some eras than in others and class-consciousness has been more prevalent in European societies than in the United States.

Self-Determination: Thus too, in an age sympathetic to nationalism, ethnic group members tend to claim the right of collective self-determination, and they find support for such claims from nonmembers. The collapse of the Soviet Union undermined the appeal of the secular and universalistic communist ideology, while the rapid changes of the modern world created new sources of discontents. Funda-mentalist interpretations of the world in Islam, Christianity, Judaism, and Hindu-ism are in part responses to the resulting unsatisfied needs for meaning, community, and hope.

Modeling: The social context provides a repertoire of possible identities to assume. Identities that others have constructed and used to advance their interests serve as models, and similar identities then become attractive. Thus, in the United States, African Americans in the 1960s' civil rights struggle stressed their identity as blacks and served as models for other disadvantaged peoples.

External Influences: Moreover, some external actors (that is, people outside the identity group) actively promote particular interpretations of history, economic relations, or God. They promulgate their views and transform social relations, as has happened with secular and religious revolutions and social movements. They also influence everyone's sense of identity, if only in opposition to the spreading of new world-views.

Changing Identities and Transforming Intractable Conflicts

Although many aspects of identity contribute to a conflict's intractability, there are also ways to modify identities so as to reduce the intractability of a conflict. In parallel with the preceding section, policies in three settings are discussed: (1) within each group, (2) in the relations between the groups, and (3) in their social context.

Policies vary in their appropriateness at different phases of conflict intractability. Six phases are particularly significant:

conflict emergence,
conflict escalation,
failed peacemaking efforts,
institutionalization of destructive conflict,
de-escalation leading to transformation, and
termination of the intractable character of the conflict.

These six phases are only loosely sequential, since some occur simultaneously and conflicts often return to an earlier phase. For each setting, one can identify policies that

help prevent conflicts from becoming intractable,
help stop the prolongation and escalation of intractable conflicts, and
help transform and resolve intractable conflicts.

Internal Policies: Policies that may help modify identities so as to reduce conflict intractability may be conducted by a great variety of persons within each adversary camp, differing in rank and in arena of activity.

Preventive Policies: All may be engaged in preventive policies, which help to prevent conflicts from becoming intractable. Within all communities and countries, being peaceful and loving is part of people's identities. Parents, schoolteachers, religious leaders, artists, entertainers, and many others can foster those qualities in their children, students, congregants, and audiences. Furthermore, school texts, films, and news reports can convey the humanity and perspectives of groups with whom conflicts have occurred.

Interruptive Policies: The modified conceptions of themselves and of other groups and peoples can support additional actions that reduce the likelihood of destructive conflicts arising. These actions may be initiatives to reduce grievances felt by adversaries or reciprocations of peaceful gestures by the other side. The growth of organized dissent from the uncompromising policies of the dominant leadership is also helpful in interrupting intractable conflicts. Rival leadership factions, middle-level leaders (e.g. community or organizational leaders), or grass roots organizations may undertake dissent, as sometimes occurs in peace movement mobilizations. The dissenters may appeal to aspects of the prevailing identity that pertain to relations within the group rather than antagonisms with outsiders.

Transformational Policies: Many other internal policies are relevant for the fundamental transformation of an intractable conflict. One approach is acting to change the ideologies and belief systems that sustain the conflict. For example, in 1986, the general synod of the Dutch Reformed Church, the major church of the Afrikaners of South Africa, resolved that the forced separation of peoples could not be considered a biblical imperative. The removal of religious support for apartheid contributed greatly to the negotiated end of the entire apartheid system in South Africa.

Much public and scholarly attention is now given to revealing the truth about past injustices and human rights violations in order to build a secure peace. Knowledge of past and ongoing oppression by people within the oppressor community or country can alter their self-identity. They may come to see themselves as being complicit in wrongly harming others. Once they accept that responsibility, they would be more likely to apologize and to offer some degree of compensation for past injuries. This has been the case for Germans after World War II, for example.

RELATIONS BETWEEN ADVERSARIES

How adversaries interact with each other is particularly important in transforming collective identities and conceptions each adversary has about itself and about the other. Neither side in a conflict is hapless. Policies may be undertaken by either side to foster joint actions that prevent, interrupt, and transform intractable conflicts.

Preventive Policies: Many policies can help prevent intractable conflicts from emerging and becoming entrenched. For example, if one side is forthcoming about providing compensatory benefits for past injustices or providing assurances that past injustices will end, the other side tends to pursue limited and non-vindictive goals. There is a risk, however, that the compensations and assurances will be seen as signs of weakness, and the goals raised higher. Attribution theory suggests another possibility.[11] It holds that people tend to believe that members of their own group are good by nature, while members of another group act well only due to their circumstances. It follows that if those others have done some good deed, it is only because they were forced to do so and more coercion will yield even greater benefits. Negotiating shared understandings about conciliatory moves can help reduce such misunderstandings.

The way each adversary resists oppression and injustice in turn affects that group's self-identity and conception of the other. For example, in the case of African Americans and European Americans in the 1950s and early 1960s, the nonviolent way the civil rights struggle was waged and the way the country as a whole responded affected both parties: it helped change the collective identities of both African and European Americans, increasing the civic character of American identity rather than its ethnic character. Furthermore, American identity went from being characterized as a melting pot within which "foreign" elements assimilated to an enduring multicultural society.

Interruptive Policies: Many other policies help interrupt or stop destructive escalation. These are policies that regulate strife and/or provide assurances that the vital interests of the other side will not be attacked. In many ways, the Cold War between the United States and the Soviet Union managed to limit the threat each posed the other. The arms control agreements helped channel and manage the arms race. The Helsinki Accords, signed in 1975, assured the Soviet Union that the borders established in Europe after World War II were inviolable, including the shift of Soviet borders westward and the division of Germany. Thus assured, the Soviet Union eased the barriers to Western influence.

Transformative Policies: Adversaries can act in ways that help transform the intractable conflict between them, by contributing to a fundamental transformation of one or both opponents. For example, during the Cold War, cultural, educational, and other social exchanges between the United States and the Soviet Union were conducted at official and non-official levels. They contributed to changes in the way many members of the Soviet elites saw themselves and viewed Americans, and people on each side developed new perceptions of the other side. The changes in both identities and conceptions contributed to a transformation in the Soviet Union and the end of the Cold War.[12]

Other confidence-building measures between adversaries include agreements to inform each other of military maneuvers and establish mechanisms to be more transparent about actions that otherwise might seem threatening. Confidence-building measures tend to reduce denigrating views of the other side and reduce the inclination to characterize oneself in terms of opposition to the other side.

Reconciliatory actions are increasingly common in order to achieve peace. They may not only promote regard for the other side, but also transform the identity of those undertaking the actions. Taking such actions reduces the likelihood of holding onto sentiments that people sharing one's collective identity are superior to other peoples and more wholly human. Certainly, such reconciliatory actions reduce the grievances of those who previously suffered the indignities of low regard, increasing the likelihood of ending an intractable conflict.

Finally, the adversaries can pursue policies that support shared overarching identities. Thus, new institutional arrangements can better highlight broad identities, such as being European. In addition, an old identity may be modified to be more inclusive, as occurred in South Africa with its political transformation and as is occurring in the United States as its multicultural character is increasingly stressed.

Social Context

Actors who are not members of the adversarial camps can carry out policies that help to prevent, interrupt, and end intractable conflicts; only a few strategies are briefly noted here.

Preventive Policies: Official and nonofficial agencies may help alleviate deteriorating living conditions that otherwise might exacerbate ethnic antagonisms and ignite fights that become intractable. This may include alerting people inside and outside the areas affected about the risks of pursuing conflicts destructively, further imperiling lives.

Outside actors can also foster norms and institutions that help develop nondestructive ways of handling the inevitable disputes of social life. A wide variety of organizations engage in training and consultations to support such methods. Indeed, the world climate may be more or less supportive of various methods of struggle, whether it be armed struggle, democratic elections, terrorism, or nonviolent resistance. Groups resorting to one of these methods may get assistance from particular allies or face external opposition for doing so.

Interruptive Policies: Once a conflict has already become protracted and destructive, intermediaries are particularly needed to stop further deterioration. Domestically, this is often recognized as a primary obligation of the central government, which tries to manage internal conflicts rather than exacerbate them as a party in the fight. Internationally, the U.N. and regional intergovernmental organizations (IGOs) increasingly undertake intermediary interventions. Outside intervention sometimes may even use force to stop violence, as done by U.N. peacekeeping or other multilateral forces.

External actors may also halt further deterioration by constraining one or both sides in a conflict. One such constraint is economic sanctions, directed to stop gross violations of human rights. Sanctions can affect the self-conceptions of some parties to an intractable conflict. The widespread condemnation of South African white minority's treatment of non-whites under apartheid contributed to changes in the way white South Africans saw themselves and their opponents.

Transformative Policies: Outside actors may also undertake a variety of mediating roles to help stop and even transform an intractable conflict. Mediation generally entails according some legitimacy to the antagonistic sides in a conflict and treating the representatives with human regard, even when the parties themselves do not. In such circumstances, participating in the mediation may prompt each side to modify its conception of the other and also of itself.

The social context also affects the long-term transformation of intractable conflicts and the establishment of enduring peaceful accommodations. External actors can be important agents in ensuring compliance to agreements, which helps build trust between former adversaries. Experiences providing grounds for mutual trust affect self-identities and also conceptions of the other side that help transform intractable conflicts.

External actors may also contribute resources that help fulfill the terms of agreements and overcome threats to the conflict's transformation and enduring resolution. The resources may include emergency food, assistance in rebuilding infrastructure, aid in training and education, and protection against violent acts by opponents of stability.[13]

Conclusions

Identities can greatly contribute to conflict intractability. How adversaries think about who they are and who and what their enemies are profoundly influences the course of any conflict between them. Their sense of identity and conceptions of each other contribute to their conflict's destructive quality as well as to its long duration. Whether and how identities contribute to intractable conflicts depends on their particular qualities. Of course, identities alone do not determine a conflict's intractability; many other factors are discussed in many other essays in this web site. Identities can and do change in ways that help prevent, limit, and end intractable conflicts. These changes are brought about by groups within each adversary camp, by the way the adversaries interact, and by the conduct of persons and groups who intervene or otherwise affect the primary adversaries. In addition, adversaries are not unchanging, unitary groups; each has many kinds of members with their own interactions with each other and with persons and groups in and outside the adversary camps. All this complicates but also offers opportunities to avert, interrupt, and end intractable conflicts.

Notes

1. Louis Kriesberg, *Constructive Conflicts: From Escalation to Resolution*. 4th ed. (New York: Rowman & Littlefield, 2011), <http://books.google.com/books?id = rrCIgtn S1MYC>.

2. Benedict Anderson, *Imagined Communities: Reflections on the Origin and Spread of Nationalism* (London: Verso, 2006), <http://books.google.com/books?id = 8YlMLi UzaEcC>.

3. Terrell A Northrup, "The Dynamic of Identity in Personal and Social Conflict," in *Intractable Conflicts and Their Transformation*, eds. L. Kriesberg, T.A. Northrup, and

S.J. Thorson (Syracuse, NY: Syracuse University Press, 1989), 55–82. <http://books .google.com/books?id = Lj2vg3xMHO8C>.

4. Robert A. Levine and Donald T. Campbell, *Ethnocentrism: Theories of Conflict, Ethnic Attitudes, and Group Behavior* (New York: John Wiley & Sons, 1972), <http:// books.google.com/books?id = pB5qAAAAIAAJ>.

5. Anthony Smith, *National Identity* (Reno: University of Nevada Press, 1991), <http://books.google.com/books?id = bEAJbHBlXR8C>.

6. John Burton, *Conflict: Resolution and Prevention* (New York: Macmillan, 1990). <http://books.google.com/books?id = P_gsAQAAIAAJ>.

7. Kevin Avurch, *Culture & Conflict Resolution* (Washington, DC: United States Institute of Peace, 1998), <http://books.google.com/books/about?id = OofmUhey GJAC>.

8. Vamik Volkan, *The Need to Have Enemies and Allies: From Clinical Practice to International Relationships* (New York: Jason Aronson, 1994). <http://books.google.com/ books?id = QAwIAQAAMAAJ>.

9. Marc H. Ross, *The Management of Conflict: Interpretations and Interests in Comparative Perspective* (New Haven, CT: Yale University Press, 1996), <http://books.goo gle.com/books?id = I_ClCy8APxgC>.

10. Patrick G. Coy and Lynne M. Woehrle, *Social Conflicts and Collective Identities* (New York: Rowman & Littlefield, 2000), <http://books.google.com/books?id = L_ALolUT2WsC>.

11. Harold H. Kelley, "The Process of Causal Attribution," *American Psychologist* 28, no. 2 (1973), 107–128.

12. Louis Kriesberg, *International Conflict Resolution: The U.S.-USSR and Middle East Cases* (New Haven, CT: Yale University Press, 1992), <http://www.amazon.com/Inter national-Conflict-Resolution-U-S-USSR-Middle/dp/0300051751>.

13. Arie M. Kacowicz and others, eds., *Stable Peace Among Nations* (New York: Rowman & Littlefield, 2000), <http://books.google.com/books?id = M6XxILmLs90C>. Social Media Photo Credit: http://maxpixel.freegreatpicture.com/Self-Personality-Per sona-Identity-Facade-Mask-1306181. Public Domain.

Culture

Kevin Avruch

Anthropologist and sociologist Kevin Avruch currently serves as Dean for the School for Conflict Analysis and Resolution at George Mason University, where he has taught since 1980. Avruch wrote the preface to this book because of his long-standing relationship with the field, and his seminal work championing the importance of culture in understanding and responding to conflict. While an almost assumed component of the field today, when Avruch began, his work challenged the Epoch One grand theories of human behavior that ignored local contexts. As such, Avruch was one of the first scholars to bring culture into the conflict resolution discourse.

Avruch's work continues to help professionals improve their understanding of cultural differences in negotiation styles. Culture, he claims, becomes visible when there is a difference. When two people operate according to the same schema, culture remains invisible. A shared worldview can make it seem as if one has no worldview. He urges those interested in improving their understanding of culture not to think of norms as homogenous or static but instead as fluid. An individual will likely operate according to a variety of cultural norms. Even individuals within the same group will carry multiple cultural identities. The shifting and multidimensional nature of culture can make it difficult to study. To help those developing cultural training for negotiators and others, Avruch introduces two anthropological approaches to the study of culture. They are called *etic* and *emic* approaches.

Etic approaches make broad-level statements about cultures. The findings are often gathered from secondary sources about the culture in question. The aim of etic research is to report findings transferrable to all cultures. In emic approaches, by contrast, researchers embed themselves in contexts to understand cultural nuances. Emic approaches are more time-consuming and are context-rich. Because they closely describe a local site, the findings are not always transferrable. He uses Israeli-Palestinian negotiations to demonstrate the advantage of using a combination of both approaches.

The introduction of culture is an important factor for consideration of the characteristic of Epoch Two. In Epoch One, negotiation training and game theory exercises usually occurred without consideration for cultural differences, assuming that reason was universal.

Questions to consider: If you wanted to study someone's culture, how might you design your research? If you had to develop a training program for conflict resolution professionals about your own culture, what considerations would be most important to you?

Frames for Culture and Conflict Resolution

Kevin Avruch

The focus of this part, which brings culture and conflict resolution into the same frame of reference, is mainly a methodological one. Concentrating again on international negotiations, particularly Arab-Israeli ones, we present two different strategies for making sense of cultural differences in "negotiation styles." One strategy is based on an actor-centered, thickly described, and context-rich—an emic—way of looking at culture. The other strategy is based on an analyst-centered, "objective," and transcultural—an etic—way of looking at culture. Both strategies bring with them benefits for conceptualizing cultural differences and intercultural negotiations, but in the end we make the case for not neglecting context, the heart of a cultural account.

Conceptualizing Cultural Difference

Earlier we outlined two different conceptions of conflict, one centered on scarcity and power, the other on perception or belief. It was easy to see that when culture is understood as ideational codes, schemas, metaphors, or cognitive models, there is an affinity between the perception/belief—the cognitivist—model of conflict and cultural approaches to conflict resolution, but that scarcity or power—broadly speaking, materialist—understandings of conflict would be less hospitable to such approaches. The epitome of such materialist and power-based understandings of conflict, we argued, could be seen in the classical realist approach to international relations and the state system. Our critique of the realist approach, and specifically of its use of the notion of power, was meant to question the deep divide drawn between cognitivist and materialist approaches to conflict (and by extension, to conflict resolution). One approach ought not preclude the other; but perhaps it is more important to argue specifically that even such seemingly "brute facts" as scarcity or power are not exempt from the interpretive lenses placed by culture between actors and the world. Or—if the sin of reification hangs too heavily over putting culture's role in that way (and it does)—we can say that actors think about their worlds, and problems in it such as power discrepancy, coercion, or social harmony, in terms of cognitive models passed on to them by others who have encountered these problems before. When two actors meet who have different models for recognizing and dealing with these sorts of problems, and when their respective models are backed up in their eyes by some special authority, authenticity, or feeling of lightness that may range all the way from ecclesiastical or sacred morality to self-evident common sense, then we may begin to speak of cultural difference.

Notice that culture appears as a sort of optical or perceptual illusion here: Although always a presence, it can best be seen when thrown into relief by the quality of difference. For if two actors meet who share the same model or schema for dealing with, say, the power asymmetry evident between them, then culture is invisible, part of and buried in the deepest, and in this case shared, context of their encounter: Of course a Harijan stands when a Brahmin enters the room. It takes an outsider, one who does not share the same schema of millennium-old social and ritual hierarchy we gloss as "caste," to literally see (Hindu) culture, here. For Hindus, culture is invisible in this encounter because it is simply the way the world is. If the Harijan political activist refuses to stand (and increasingly, many do), or if the Brahmin reformer gently urges him not to (less frequently the case), then it is because either or both of them have imagined another, alternative world.

One reason culture seems to have infiltrated the study of international relations around the issue of negotiation is that international negotiations are where actors from different worlds encounter one another as interlocutors, and their differences become visible as the encounter throws them into relief. This is often more than a matter of difference in mere conversational styles, as Zartman argues. It is a matter of difference in respective definitions of what constitutes a conversation. To return momentarily to the domain of diplomacy, it is one thing to have a model of the ideal diplomatic encounter based on the schema of the British commercial transaction—"credit, confidence, consideration, and compromise." And it is quite another to model one on the image of a harmonious interpersonal relationship, a socially expansive notion of friendship, and a complexly manipulable set of dependencies and obligations implied by the first two—that is, the rich, embedded, and widely ramifying schema called in Chinese guanxi and analyzed in depth by Richard Solomon.[1]

But a very real problem arises when one tries to find a way to talk about these cultural differences, especially if the aim is to educate, train, or prepare individuals from one culture to work in another. The place to start is by avoiding from the outset the several inadequate ideas of culture that were discussed earlier on: culture as homogenous, reified, uniformly distributed, customary, and timeless. Instead, we should see culture from a situated actor's perspective. And we should see process over pattern. Now culture becomes less monolithic and more frangible, subject, that is, to the exigencies of change in a changeable world. An actor carries multiple cultures—national, confessional, ethnic, organizational, or occupational, to name a few—whose behavioral or motivational relevance also is situational and changeable. Not all actors, even in ostensibly the same social group or institution, necessarily carry the same array of multiple cultures (cultures are socially distributed); nor for any one actor is the psychological or motivational salience of a given subculture the same as for any, or all, other actors (cultures are psychologically distributed). This newer orientation to culture roots the concept more closely to the domains of ongoing social practice and experiential learning, where real folk live their lives. But it also has the effect of decentering or destabilizing the notion of culture by complexifying or "thickening" it. It makes it harder to use the idea to train or prepare individuals on what to expect in a new sociocultural setting, especially if the trainers are expected to explain what's out there in terms of independent/dependent variables, linearly arrayed in a monocausal and deterministic theory, or if training demands are strongly oriented toward the confidence-interval free prediction of a specific actor's behavior—something cultural analysis is not capable of.

Broadly speaking, there have been two main strategies for talking about culture—or cultural differences, to be precise—both of which can be found in the training- or practitioner-oriented literature. The strategies correspond generally to a distinction made in anthropology between emic and etic approaches to sociocultural phenomena. An emic approach is one that privileges an actor-centered understanding, what used to be called, in times less concerned with political correctness, "the native's point of view." An emic analysis identifies, systematizes (where possible or appropriate), and utilizes native categories, terms, and propositions about the world, culture, or the domain under study. By contrast, an etic approach privileges the analyst's understanding (or explanation) of these things. Native categories or thinking are of course collected and analyzed, but as data in aid of etic theorizing and explanation and not, as in emic studies, as ends in themselves. By definition, the aim of an etic analysis is to systematize data from different (emic) domains in order to construct (or discover—the verbs lead to different epistemologies) categories that work trans-emically. Over a couple of decades much ink has been spilled in academic debate and controversy within anthropology over the merits and defects of these approaches, a debate that continues today even if the terms themselves are less often encountered. For our purposes, the terms are useful as a shorthand, pointing to different ways of conceptualizing an approach to culture that has relevance for training negotiators or conflict resolutionists.

Emic Approaches

One hallmark of an emic approach is the identification and use of a native term or institution as the key organizing concept for description and analysis. A good example is Solomon's use of the Chinese notion of guanxi (ways of constructing interpersonal relationships) or you-yi (a sense of "friendship" that relies heavily on ideas of mutual obligation), referred to earlier. Another example can be found in the very large literature on Japanese culture, from Ruth Benedict onward, where the related ideas of wa ("balance" or "harmony," especially in a working team) and amae (an affect characterizing and binding individuals in an asymmetrical, dependency relationship) are often highlighted.[2] In a brief study of negotiating in the Middle East, William Quandt identifies two different indigenous models, each appropriate in different settings and with different actors. These are, respectively, the suq (marketplace) model and the bedu (bedouin) model.[3] Within anthropology, perhaps the most famous example of this sort of analysis is one that deconstructed not a word or phrase, but a rather curious institution: Clifford Geertz's "thick description" of the phenomenology and varied sociocultural entailments of the Balinese cockfight.[4]

The great advantage to the emic approach is that it roots the analyst more deeply (Solomon or Geertz) or less deeply (Quandt) in the relevant cultural context. It brings with it all of the strengths of ethnography: the attention to context and detail and nuanced translation. By focusing on the Chinese notion of "friendship" (you-yi), for example, Solomon is able to show how it differs from American understandings of the same term and, equally important, how these different understandings carry with them very different social or behavioral implications. Because his research was conducted (and disseminated) in a forthrightly political and policy-oriented setting, moreover, Solomon addresses explicitly how the notion plays out in official negotiations between Chinese and American interlocutors. He shows how it can thus be used in interparty manipulations of each other deployed and countered in a series of moves Solomon calls "the games of guanxi." (By contrast, the more classical ethnographic uses of emic, thick description eschew—and probably disfavor—such manipulative strategizing.) The advantages of the emic approach for teaching or training purposes are self-evident, and especially so if used by individuals who will be posted to, or otherwise functioning in, that particular cultural setting. Moreover, much of this sort of description is amenable, if recast and analyzed further, to the sort of metaphor, cognitive model, or schema approaches we have been advocating.

The major disadvantage of this approach is that, in the proverbial wrong hands, it can slip all too easily back into thinking about culture in categories that we have labeled inadequate. At the very least, we need to have some sense of the sociological distribution of these key ideas in the relevant population, as well as their psychological salience for relevant individual actors. We need to be sensitive to the fact that there are undoubtedly always other, competing and perhaps even contradictory, models or schémas that interact complexly to "produce" behavior. We need to be cautious about imputing a timeless changelessness to these ideas. In sum, we need to be very careful not to think we have found the key that unlocks all the mysteries of American, Balinese, Chinese, or Japanese culture. The Balinese are not their cockfight in some metaphysical distillation (as Geertz would be the first to argue). Wa or amae are not all, or even most, of what there is to being Japanese.[5] These terms need to be properly circumscribed—kept fairly close to their main domain of relevance and rooted constantly in close dialectical examination of ongoing social practice, of texts or behavior (as Solomon does for guanxi and negotiations). When this is done, the emic approach is literally indispensable for a cultural understanding of conflict and its management or resolution. One version of this approach emphasizes the elucidation of the natives' own understandings and theories of conflict, and their own techniques or processes for managing or resolving it, what Avruch and Black call respectively ethnoconflict theories and praxis.[6]

In the eyes of many, however, a strength of the approach, its close connectedness to a particular cultural context, is also its major drawback. What good does it do to know all about wa if you are heading off to negotiate with the French? More generally, does a concentration on emics prevent us from making comparisons and generalizations that are valid across cultural contexts? Finally, isn't a concentration on emics in the end merely "descriptive" (a damning word in the positivist's lexicon) and thus of limited usefulness in the grand nomothetic task of theory building? The answers to all of these questions depend in part on where one stands with regard to larger epistemological issues in the social or human sciences; but among many who raise them a search for another, etic, vocabulary for speaking of cultural differences is a reasonable one. In the section that follows we will briefly discuss a few of the schemes that have been related specifically to negotiation or conflict resolution.

Etic Approaches

The hallmark of the etic approach is the identification of underlying, structurally deep, and transcultural forms, expressed in terms of certain descriptors that are putatively capable of characterizing domains across all cultures. These approaches vary greatly in their derivation and the sorts of data their authors feel they need to support them. Some of them seem to have been derived almost intuitively, after an analyst's wide experience of different cultures (an example is Edward T. Hall's high-context/low-context distinction). Others appear to have been derived deductively, by virtue of devotion to a particular theoretical orientation (Mary Douglas's grid/group is an example). Still others were derived inductively, after subjecting large numbers of responses collected across different cultures to aggregating techniques (factor or cluster analyses) designed to reduce them and reveal their underlying structure (an example is Geert Hofstede's work on national cultural differences). All of them claim to present the analyst with a seemingly universal scale or set of dimensions upon which all cultures can be placed and thus to present a vocabulary for encapsulating and comparing cultures across the board.

Perhaps the most widely used is Hall's high-context/low-context distinction.[7] The core of this distinction is a linguistic or paralinguistic one. A high-context communicational style (or individual message, for that matter) is one in which most of the information, or meaning, is "in the person" or the physical context within which communication takes place; relatively little is in the explicit and coded message itself. By contrast, a low-context style or message is one wherein most of the information or meaning is to be found explicitly in the coded message.

In high-context communication, language use is expressive; in low-context communication, it is instrumental. High-context styles are rich paralinguistically (in kinesics, gestures, and so on); low-context styles are paralinguistically impoverished. In low-contrast interactions what you hear is what you get; there is a directness—often a rather assertive one—to communication. In high-contrast interactions, what is in the explicit message is rarely the entire story; much is implied and indirect and is to be found, as Hall puts it, in the receiver and the setting.

Hall is quite clear that high context and low context define two ends of a communicational continuum and also that styles may differ within a social group, so that, for example, all other things being equal, communication within a family will tend toward being high context, and communication in instrumental, secondary, or task-oriented groups, toward low context.[8] But Hall also uses the terms as virtual dichotomies and assigns them to entire cultures: American culture, for example, is on the low end (but not so low as Swiss-German or Scandinavian); Chinese culture is on the high. Not surprisingly, the most interesting interactions occur when high-context styles—read "cultures"—meet low-context ones. Here the chances for miscommunication, misperception, and thus conflict increase. Moreover, if the interaction occurs specifically within a setting designed to limit or ease conflict—international diplomatic negotiations, for instance—then the effects of high-context/low-context miscommunication are exacerbated. Nowhere is this dimension explored more productively and convincingly than in the work of Raymond Cohen, both in his focused study of Egyptian-Israeli diplomacy (where such communication resulted in a "dialogue of the deaf") and in his more general work on diplomatic negotiating "across cultures."[9]

Hall's high-context/low-context distinction is not the only etic model available. In fact, by limiting itself to a single continuum or dimension, it is among the more simple ones. Several use two orthogonal scales. The social anthropologist Mary Douglas looks to sociological dimensions (rather than communicational ones) in her grid/group theory of cultural "bias," as she once called it: "group" refers to the boundedness of social units, and "grid" to the prescriptive forces that limit individual choice with respect to social role enactments.[10] Grid/group has been applied to explain a number of conflict situations, especially environmental ones.[11] The management consultant Wendy Hall, borrowing from earlier work by R. R. Blake and J. S. Mouton on the so-called managerial grid, identifies two behavioral dimensions that express all possible styles of negotiation: assertiveness and responsiveness (the degree of emotional expression or reserve).

Combining them yields four basic "cultural styles," which she calls the Compass Model, assigning to each a cardinal point.[12] Stephen Weiss (like Wendy Hall, concerned mainly with business settings but linked more explicitly in his case to national differences as well) identifies twelve cultural characteristics of negotiations, mostly on behavioral (rather than cognitive or sociological) grounds. He groups the characteristics into five main categories: the actors' basic conception of negotiation, their orientation toward time, their willingness to take risks, their protocol, and their decision-making style.[13] Finally, at the far end of the categories proliferation scale, some researchers in intercultural communication have come up with more than sixty etic characteristics, a veritable smorgasbord on which we can find just about any dichotomous distinction any theorist ever came up with: high and low context, shame and guilt, urban and rural, doing and being, and even the venerable and Benedictine Apollonian and Dionysian.[14]

Of all of these etic schemes, the one with the most methodological authority has been that developed by Geert Hofstede.[15] Hofstede did a large-scale survey for the multinational corporation IBM in which he examined work-related values.[16] He found that the values clustered into four major underlying dimensions or indices: power distance (the degree of inequality in a society, from small to large); collectivism versus individualism; masculinity versus femininity (his gloss for assertiveness and its opposite, say, modesty); and uncertainty avoidance (weak to strong).[17] In his more recent work a fifth dimension was added: long-term orientation to life versus short-term. He noted that this fifth dimension did not emerge from his initial analysis of the data because of

> a cultural bias in the minds of the various scholars studying culture, including myself. We all shared a "Western" way of thinking. The new dimension was discovered when . . . [a different researcher resident in the Far East used a different] questionnaire composed by "Eastern," in this case Chinese, minds.[18]

The descriptive or heuristic advantage of a dimensional model like Hofstede's, located somewhere between the single continuum of high context versus low context and the categorical profligacy of the sixty-plus schemes, is obvious: it is a very good way to make a "first cut" at aggregating and categorizing cultural data, including those that may bear on such aspects of conflict analysis as the perception of uncertainty and on such aspects of conflict resolution as negotiating styles. In general, the advantage of etic schemes is that they permit comparison across cases and thus the possibility for building theory. They provide for us a shared vocabulary for talking about cultural variation and diversity. For purposes of training or educating practitioners, providing such a comparative and generalizing vocabulary is a very good thing. Nevertheless, some cautions are in order, first, about Hofstede's work, and second, about the promise of etic approaches in general.

Hofstede's dimensional model is impressive as a way of talking about cultural difference; when he turns to examining some of the root causes of the dimensions—of social inequality or "masculine" cultures, for example—the work falters, moving uneasily between ahistoricist generalizing and mild environmental or climatic determinisms. However, cultural analyses have always been vulnerable to causalist mishandling. Perhaps more important—especially since Hofstede's model is the most methodologically rigorous of all the etic ones we have examined thus far, and such rigor allows Hofstede himself to raise this point—we must ask just how much cultural variation and diversity his four or five dimensions really, account for. Here is Hofstede's answer.

> The four [dimensions] together account for 49 percent of the country [national culture] differences in the data, just about half. The remaining

half is country [national culture] specific: *it cannot be associated with any worldwide factor*, at least not in the data I had. [Emphasis added.]

Charmingly answering the obvious follow-up question, Hofstede continues:

Whether explaining half of the difference is a lot or not depends on one's degree of optimism. An optimist will call a bottle half full while a pessimist will call it half empty.[19]

Methodologists will of course argue whether explaining 49 percent of the variance is a lot or a little—and it does, in a real sense, "depend." But we can also suggest, in a rough-and-ready way, that in the world out there any analyst who can adequately explain an admittedly complex phenomenon slightly less than half the time (or, at about the same level of confidence as flipping the proverbial coin) would not inspire much confidence in his clients.

Combining Emic and Etic Approaches

We cautioned earlier against proclaiming a particular indigenous notion or institution—wa, suq, guanxi, or the cockfight—as the open-everything key to any specific culture. If this is the besetting sin of emic approaches, then the limitations exposed in Hofstede's work should alert us to the waiting seductions of etic models: that we have found the even greater key for explaining (or certainly for predicting the behavior of actors in) all cultures everywhere. In some sense, the tension between emic and etic is related to the one we identified earlier as between local and generic understandings of culture itself. Emic approaches provide "thick description" and rich context. Etic models offer cross- cultural categories or discretely arrayed variables that, being scalable, are amenable to codings in databases and statistical manipulations; they seem to be able to reduce tremendous cultural diversity onto a few manageable dimensions.

But it is in their very power to reduce diversity that we find their greatest limitation. (This leaves aside the methodological question of how much diversity they are really explaining.) When the continuums are turned into dichotomies (as they usually are, despite the cautions of their authors), these schemes become very crude instruments for measuring rather fine aspects of culture. Moreover, if they lapse, shorthandlike, into reified essentialisms—for instance, "Egypt is high context, Israel low context"—then one may entirely lose sight of all the corrections to the inadequate ideas of culture we have put forward. To review these corrections, first, cultures are mixes of all the dimensions—as are individuals!—and the dimensions are likely to be differentially distributed among individuals. Second, different domains, institutions, or social practices even within the same sociocultural setting are likely to differ in their dimensional profiles. Third, dimensional profiles may not be all that stable even within particular social groups or institutions. Fourth, and perhaps most profoundly, the very concepts that constitute the defining attributes of the scales—concepts such as "risk" or "individualism" or "authority"—are themselves subject to cultural definitions.[20] Finally, we must be very careful about attributing a specious causality to etic constructions, a sort of spurious prescriptiveness. If we have characterized an observable complex of, say, Egyptian or Israeli negotiating behavior as high or low context, it is logically questionable to then turn the argument around and say that some quality we now call high (or low) "contextedness" causes this behavior or that.

However, although we must always be careful about imputing causality, it is the case that a well-put-together typology or dimensional profile can help us to look for, even to probabilistically expect, elements of a cultural complex to hang together. For instance, having characterized Egyptian negotiating behavior as high context on the basis, say, of an expressive use of language, a rich paralinguistic repertoire, and a proclivity toward indirection—Egyptian negotiators hate to say "no" too directly—one is justified in looking for, and even expecting to find, an orientation toward negotiating that holds, in effect, that rudeness to one's interlocutor is a bad thing and ought to be avoided, even at the cost of what the interlocutor, say, an Israeli, may interpret as "insincerity." By contrast, low-context Israeli negotiators, for whom language is instrumental and unadorned with paralinguistics, and for whom facticity rather than rhetorical flourish is to be extolled, can be expected to—and do—demonstrate a certain directness and assertiveness in their communicational style (what Israeli Hebrew refers to as dugri speech).[21] Moreover, however much Israelis expect and appreciate dugri among themselves, dugri is perceived as rudeness in interaction with Egyptians, even if, as Cohen points out, the Egyptians are sophisticated and experienced diplomats. Conversely, the high-context Egyptians come across to Israelis (even to the sophisticated and experienced diplomats among them) as insincere or duplicitous.[22]

What then are the uses of etic schemes? First, they allow comparison, even for instruction across cases, and they enable efficient, retrievable handling of large amounts of cultural data. They can give us a good idea of what elements of a cultural complex tend to hang with other elements and, contrariwise, what elements we would be likely not to encounter. Etic schemes are thus a way to get at "first cuts," albeit potentially very rough cuts, of a cultural domain. But context ought never be sacrificed to the (false) efficiencies of aggregated data or one-size-fits-all theorizing. As an example, take the quality called "individualism" (typically arrayed in these schemes against something called "collectivism"). Nowhere does individualism exist as a monodimensional, undifferentiated quality—nor is the variation or heterogeneity simply a matter of more or less intensity on a scale. A complex quality such as individualism is always part of a dense cultural matrix of networked and interconnected schemas for cognitive understanding and motivated social action in the world. Within American culture, we can, for instance, speak about the "individualism" of the deeply believing or born-again Christian, for whom individualism parses because the individual is the ultimate locus of salvation and grace but for whom a crucial instrumentality of grace is the reaching out, the witnessing of the faith, to other individuals.[23] Compare this sense of individualism to the Adam Smith construction of it, the individual as a rationally selfish utilities maximizer, or the even more emphatic Hobbesian construction of the individual as an entity engaged in perpetual zero-sum struggles against other individuals in a nasty, brutish, and resource-poor world. All may be legitimately glossed by "individualism," and arguably all may share what Wittgenstein called a "family resemblance." But resemblance aside, they also are constitutive of different worlds as phenomenologically experienced and socially constructed by actors. To code all of these variations in a database as representing an instance of scalable "individualism" is to miss the richness and meaning that only a strong attention to context, to culture in the local sense, is able to convey.

Clearly, with respect to what we have called emics and etics, we need some nonmutually exclusive approach to linking culture with conflict analysis and resolution, the more so if we are to include cultural factors in the education and training of practitioners. To envision some combination of the two, let us take one more example, again from the Middle East.

Anyone who has observed Arab-Israeli negotiations has remarked on the almost obsessive concern of Israelis over the details of any agreement, and on their desire to have all possible contingencies accounted for in the final text (along with a general distrust of verbal contracts in favor of strongly written ones). This is related to the overwhelming emphasis that Israelis put on security. If we consult Hofstede's "uncertainty avoidance index," Israel does appear as a strong avoidance country. It ranks above aggregated Arab countries—and expectedly so if we have observed their respective negotiating styles and concerns.[24] Taking into account Hofstede's insightful distinction between uncertainty avoidance and risk avoidance—that sometimes we will take large (focused) risks to avoid more diffused uncertainties—we can even explain the Israeli tendency to take on such risks when they think their security is at stake. (Examples are the surprise attack of June 1967, the Entebbe raid of 1976, and the bombing of Iraq's Osirak nuclear reactor in 1981.) Now, clearly we have learned something from Hofstede's index, and a neophyte to the world of Arab-Israeli conflict or negotiations would do well to consult it.[25]

But it is only by careful attention to the Israeli context—to an understanding of history, symbolism, and psychocultural dynamics—that we get a real sense of what "security" means to Israelis. Security is connected to—instantiated in—a number of related schemas about the world that in effect enable Israelis to deal both with recurring situations and with unexpected ones. For some Israelis, typically the Orthodox, schemas may derive from a Judaic tradition that preaches "a people who dwells alone in the world" surrounded by implacably hostile nations.[26] For other Israelis, schemas derive from Zionist interpretations of such historical events as Masada or Tel Hai.[27] And for many, many Israelis, it is the European Holocaust that searingly defines the costs of inattention to national security. To understand the place of the Holocaust in Israeli political culture or political psychology demands a monograph in itself.[28] Our point here is more modest: to argue that any understanding of such etic a measure as "uncertainty avoidance" for Israeli society or polity ultimately demands the thick description and emic understanding of Israeli culture. And this, by the way, is not only a requirement for foreign analysts of Israel or third-party mediators to the Arab-Israeli conflict, but also for the various Arab interlocutors in negotiation with Israel[29] (most crucially the Palestinians) and, finally and not least, for the Israelis themselves.[30]

Put into the broader framework of Middle East conflict resolution, the purpose of such a deep, contextual—cultural—understanding of Israel's obsession with security is of course only part of the task. Another part would demand that now the Israelis undertake the same thick description and analysis of, say, the Palestinian concern with peoplehood and sovereignty.

Notes

1. The British ideal is taken once again from Nicholson's *Diplomacy*, 77. The "games of *guanxi*" are explored in Solomon's *Chinese Political Negotiating Behavior*, esp. 17–29.

2. See, for example, T. Rohlen, *For Harmony and Strength* (Berkeley: University of California Press, 1974), 47.

3. W. B. Quandt, "Egypt: A Strong Sense of National Identity," in Binnendijk, ed., *National Negotiating Styles*, 105–123. A neat comparison, showing subtle but consequential differences even within a shared (commercial-transaction) schema, can be made of Nicholson's British shopkeeper with Quandt's bazaar merchant.

4. Geertz, *Interpretation of Cultures*.

5. See S. Reed, *Making Common Sense of Japan* (Pittsburgh: University of Pittsburgh Press, 1993), 34–39.

6. In K. Avruch P. W. Black, "The Culture Question and Conflict Resolution," *Peace and Change* 16, no. 1 (1991): 22–45; the approach is exemplified in most of the articles found in K. Avruch, P. W. Black, and J. Scimecca, eds., *Conflict Resolution: Cross-Cultural Perspectives* (New York: Greenwood Press, 1991). It parallels the work of John Paul Lederach, who has developed it further for training purposes.

7. Presented most fully in E. T. Hall, *Beyond Culture* (New York: Anchor Books, 1976); but also see his classic *The Silent Language* (New York: Doubleday, 1959).

8. Aspects of high and low context are reproduced in Basil Bernstein's more narrowly sociolinguistic notion of "restricted" (high-context: closed and status-oriented) codes and "elaborated" (low-context: open-ended and person-oriented) codes, a notion much used in education-research, especially in ethnographies of ethnic and class conflict in the classroom setting. See B. Bernstein, "Elaborated and Restricted Codes: Their Social Origins and Consequences," in J. Gumperz and D. Hymes, eds., "The Ethnography of Communication," *American Anthropologist* 66, no. 6, part 2 (1964): 55–69.

9. Cohen, *Culture and Conflict in Egyptian-Israeli Relations and Negotiating across Cultures*.

10. Mary Douglas, *Natural Symbols: Explorations in Cosmology*, 2d ed. (London: Routledge, 1996).

11. See, for example, M. Douglas and A. Wildavsky, *Risk and Culture: An Essay on the Selection of Technological and Environmental Dangers* (Berkeley: University of California Press, 1982).

12. North: Low-assertive, low-responsive; South: high-assertive, high-responsive; East: low-assertive, high-responsive; and West: high-assertive, low-responsive. See W. Hall, *Managing Cultures: Making Strategic Relationships Work* (New York: Wiley, 1995). 5Off. Hall is more interested in organizational cultures than in national ones (though she claims her model is perfectly adequate for national ones, too), and her treatment, as are many in the business or management literature—and, one suspects, in the classified government or

intelligence literature on national negotiating styles—is very instrumental in tone and aim: how to know the other so as to better manipulate the other (and resist being manipulated in turn). On the managerial grid, see R. R. Blake and J. S. Mouton, *The Managerial Grid* (Houston: Gulf Publishing, 1964).

13. A. Weiss, "Negotiating with Romans, Part I," *Sloan Management Reviews* 35, no. 2 (1994): 51–61. Weiss's scheme has been used in the business-oriented literature, for instance in the popular handbook aimed at intercultural managers, P. Harris and R. Moran, *Managing Cultural Differences*, 4th ed. (Houston: Gulf Publishing, 1996), 45–46.

14. G. Weaver, *Culture, Communication, and Conflict* (Needham Heights, MA: Ginn Press, 1994), 45–47.

15. First, in G. Hofstede, *Cultures' Consequences: International Differences in Work-Related Values* (Beverly Hills, Calif.: Sage, 1980); more recently in G. Hofstede, *Cultures and Organizations: Software of the Mind* (New York: McGraw-Hill, 1991).

16. Two surveys were done, one in 1968 and the other in 1972. According to Hofstede, the database comprised about 116,000 questionnaires from employees in 72 IBM subsidiaries, across 38 different occupations and 20 languages, from more than 50 countries.

17. Hofstede makes a point of differentiating "uncertainty" from "risk" (cf. Weiss). Uncertainty is a free-floating and diffuse anxiety about the world in general; risk is focused fear about the probability of occurrence of a specific (and negative) event. Uncertainty avoidance is directed mostly toward the reduction of ambiguity or ambiguous situations; Hofstede argues (correctly) that individuals may in fact engage in highly risky behavior—such as picking a fight with a powerful opponent—if they think it will reduce ambiguity.

18. Hofstede, *Cultures and Organizations*, 14–15.

19. Ibid., 252.

20. This is why, Hofstede insightfully tells us, he missed the fifth dimension, the length-of-term orientation toward life, in his initial reduction of the voluminous values data; the dimension was not "inside" his "Western" mind, to begin with.

21. See T. Katriel, *Talking Straight: "Dugri" Speech in Israeli Sabra Culture* (Cambridge: Cambridge University Press, 1986).

22. A caveat about the different typologies or models is in order here. Although Hall's high-context/low-context model "predicts" that Israelis will be perceived as rude, assertive, and less concerned about the maintenance of social relationships than their high-concept Egyptian interlocutors, in Hofstede's model Arab countries (lumped together, including Egypt) actually rank higher than Israel does on the "masculinity index," which measures degree of assertiveness, concern with relationships, and so on. (Out of fifty-three ranked countries, Israel ranked twenty-ninth, Arab countries twenty-third.) Despite a sense, strong in Hofstede's later work, that most of these etic schemes are getting at different parts of the same elephant—as do E. Hall's and Basil Bernstein's—the question of intertypology reliability is open and unexplored.

23. For cultural unpacking of this sense of individualism, see C. Greenhouse, *Praying for Justice: Faith, Order, and Community in an American Town* (Ithaca, NY: Cornell University Press, 1986).

24. Of fifty-three ranked countries, Israel is nineteenth, Arab countries twenty-seventh.

25. Costa Rica, however, a country that has managed to do away with its army despite its tumultuous Central American surroundings, ranks higher than Israel by several notches in uncertainty avoidance. One presumes that the explanation for this apparent paradox lies in a deeper exploration of the Costa Rican context, if not in some defect in the design of Hofstede's model.

26. Although he relies on the more traditional idea of ideology rather than schema or cognitive model, Ian Lustick sets out the world view of the Nationalist Orthodox and their construal of Judaism clearly in his *For the Land and the Lord: Jewish Fundamentalism in Israel* (New York: Council on Foreign Relations, 1988).

27. See, for example, N. Ben-Yehuda, *The Masada Myth: Collective Memory and Mythmaking in Israel* (Madison: University of Wisconsin Press, 1995); and more generally, Y. Zerubavel, *Recovered Roots: Collective Memory and the Making of Israeli National Tradition* (Chicago: University of Chicago Press, 1995).

28. Start with Menachem Begin's autobiography, *The Revolt* (New York: Nash, 1977).

29. As for the Arabs, many commentators, including Cohen, have written about the Arabs' massive misunderstanding, in the weeks before the June 1967 war, of the powerful effects their ("high-context") genocidal rhetoric (especially on the radio) had on Israelis, by whom it was "schematized"—cognized and acting as a behavioral motivator—in terms of the Holocaust (and prescribing, for many Israelis, its major motivational lesson: "Never again!").

30. As for the Israelis: Masada, after all, ended in the Jewish resistors' mass suicide when facing imminent defeat by the Romans. It is not then surprising (but hardly hopeful or reassuring) that the Israeli nuclear option has been called the "Masada option." Some of the possible outcomes of using Masada as a schema for action are explored by Y. Harkabi in his *The Bar Kokhba Syndrome: Risk and Realism in International Relations* (New York: Rossel Books, 1982). (Bar Kokhba was a Zealot leader on Masada, and reputedly the organizer of the suicide.) Avner Cohen (personal communication) notes that former Prime Minister Levi Eshkol referred to Israel's bomb as the "Samson option," a biblical metaphor whose accompanying schema is at once terrifying and depressing.

Religion

Marc Gopin

Dr. Marc Gopin, the director of the Center on Religion, Diplomacy and Conflict Resolution (CDRC) at George Mason University's School for Conflict Analysis and Resolution, is truly a scholar-practitioner. He writes for the academic community as well as the public and has lectured at elite institutions around the world. He has also trained thousands worldwide in peacebuilding strategies. Gopin brings graduate students to Israel where he has worked for decades on the Arab–Israeli conflict as well as to the Turkish border to work with Syrian refugees. Gopin encourages his students to participate politically and socially.

In this article, Gopin posits the inter-ethnic warfare prevalent in Epoch Two stems not just from the end of the Cold War, which kept various other conflicts at bay. He believes these ethnic struggles were in part a response to materialistic homogenization, resulting from the expansion of Western culture worldwide. Groups sought the roots of their identity, and in doing so, they often found themselves pitted against one another. He identifies Epoch Two as a time of great uncertainty in large part due to confusion over identity.

In this context, Gopin observed a resurgence of interest in traditional religious practices. While it is a logical response to identity loss, Gopin considers this a dangerous turn. He hypothesizes that religion will be one of the greatest causes of mass violence in the coming years. Paradoxically, religion has and can "set the stage for a fully functioning global moral community." The challenge for peacemakers is to emphasize the religious values most congruent with peace, such as humility, listening, and compassion. The works of great religious peacemakers can also be emphasized; the Dalai Lama, Martin Luther King Jr., and Gandhi all saved lives by steering their religious communities away from violence.

Gopin's emphasis on creating bridges between groups based on shared values makes this an Epoch Two approach to conflict.

Questions to consider: Does religion inevitably lead to conflict? Can you think of examples where religious groups brought peace to a violent situation?

Religion as an Aid and a Hindrance to Postconflict Coexistence Work

Marc Gopin

The post–Cold War era is characterized by two countervailing trends. One trend is unprecedented economic integration and cultural homogenization, especially at the hands of materialist culture associated with the Western forms of investment, media, advertising, and entertainment. But the other trend is unprecedented cultural and religious fractionalization. People the world over are rebelling against the materialistic homogenization, searching out the roots of their identity, exploring the uniqueness of their background and its original systems of meaning. It is not an age of a new world order but one of great social, cultural, and psychological uncertainty in the context of an overwhelming and almost overpowering economic integration of the world.

Many people turn to religion now—but in divergent ways. Paradoxically, it is a time when we witness both great creativity in religious life and an unparalleled invigoration of old patterns of belief and practice. On the one hand, people engage in new explorations of religion or secular perspectives, sometimes completely independent from traditional religious authority, dogma, or law. This trend grows as diverse peoples of all faiths mix together, especially in large cosmopolitan centers; as women participate in unprecedented levels in public religious life; and as liberal states enable free religious inquiry and experimentation. Yet at the same time, partly in reaction to these trends, others express extreme enthusiasm for traditional religious practices and beliefs as ways to oppose state or secular authorities or global secular culture. The first trend of creative exploration includes multifaith communication and cooperation never equaled in human history. This, too, is transforming modern life and creating a common global culture. Thus while the fractionizing character of religious revivalism is more noticeable and sometimes more violent, a quiet revolution of integration is taking place as well.

Religion is thus one of the most salient phenomena likely to cause massive violence in this century. But religion will also play a critical role in constructing a global community of shared moral commitments and vision. Religion's visionary capacity and its inculcation of altruistic values have given birth to extraordinary leaders, such as Mahatma Gandhi, Martin Luther King Jr., the Dalai Lama, and Bishop Desmond Tutu, who have in turn had a dramatic effect on pushing the global community toward ever-greater commitments to human rights and compassion for human and nonhuman life, regardless of race or citizenship. Less well known globally, but equally revolutionary in their context, are people such as Badshah Khan, the nonviolent Islamic leader of the Pathans; Rabbi Abraham Joshua Heschel, of U.S. civil rights era fame; Dorothy Day, one of the preeminent Catholic peacemakers of the twentieth century; and many others. In other words, religion has helped set the stage for a fully functioning global moral community that may take a very long time to fully materialize, but that is unquestionably closer to fruition than it was a century ago. There have always been exclusive religious visions of a peaceful world. Never before in history, however, have so many leaders and adherents been inspired to work for a truly inclusive vision that is multicultural and panreligious.

The contraindications to this trend are painfully apparent in the murders and tortures of recent history and the religiously motivated contributions of financial support for brutal regimes. Since September 2001, no one can forget the power of radical religious zealots to kill an unprecedented number of civilians, astonishing in their willingness to commit suicide for the sake of otherworldly gains. Suicide is the most difficult of all security breaches, because it calls into question every human being one sees and what he or she may be carrying around, literally or figuratively. And let not the al-Qaida network obscure the fact that Timothy McVeigh, the Oklahoma City bomber, was deeply influenced by a paranoid and bizarre form of Christian identity. Furthermore, religious murder used to take much longer to carry out due to poor technology, but the sum total of its effects historically, in terms of the great religious wars and crusades, is well known for its massive atrocities. At the same time, there is an unmistakable level of global commitment to shared values that is being upheld and defended every day by literally hundreds of government and nongovernmental agencies globally who adhere to and legally uphold the international agreements of the United Nations. Difficult as it is to imagine, the brutal abuses in places such as Bosnia, Kosovo, Tibet, and Burma would be even worse than they have been, were it not for this global consensus.

I consider here the paradoxical contributions of religion to the social order (or disorder) when there are at least some collective efforts under way to promote coexistence between enemy groups.

Learning from History: Humility, Active Listening, and Ritual

Radical religion as a destabilizing and destructive force in human history was manifest from the earliest stages of monotheism. Biblically based monotheisms—Judaism, Christianity, and Islam—insist on the sacred nature of the Hebrew Bible, and in that book, the genocide of selected "idolatrous" nations is not only permitted but in fact commanded. Whether or not genocides actually took place after the Israelites entered the land of Canaan is hard to know, but the textual precedent for mass murder gave permission for centuries thereafter for the massacre of polytheistic natives wherever in the world they were encountered, the sad legacy of the successful Christian conquest of Europe, Africa, and the Americas. Theology was always invoked at the critical moment to justify the slaughter. It goes without saying that millions of believers abhorred this practice, but by and large, the organized hierarchy of religion was either silent or complicitous. From the crusades of the Middle Ages to turn-of-the-twentieth-century American decisions to Christianize the Philippines, the results were always the same: the deaths of hundreds of thousands of innocents fallen afoul of cynical theological constructs.

Islam's success was built on violent conquest as well, and the conquests continued well after Muhammad's death. The results were less bloody comparatively but quite intolerant by today's standards of civil rights, especially for polytheists. And there were occasional periods of extremism at the hands of radicals such as the Almohides and Almorávides, stained with the deaths of innumerable nonbelievers. Enslavement of polytheists and destruction of their own religions became the standard pattern, and some of this abuse continues to this day (in Sudan, for example).

Eastern and indigenous religions have had similar problems and by-products. Indigenous religions in and stemming from Africa were often predicated on the use of occult powers to destroy one's enemies, while wars and violence built on Buddhist or Taoist principles have been well known from Japan to Sri Lanka, especially in the twentieth century.

Religion had an important role to play in undergirding the neo-fascist and racist political movements in South Africa, Bosnia, and Rwanda. In each case, the complicity of leading religious figures or institutions was critical to the success of the oppression. Furthermore, at any number of times in the past quarter century, Israelis and Arabs came closer together, inching toward solutions, only to have religious extremists assassinate major leaders, including Sadat and Rabin, and slaughter hundreds in the most brutal fashion, creating political circumstances that stalemated all efforts. The majority of Jews now killed by Arabs in this war are being killed by heavily funded religious extremists, whereas the backbone of the settler presence in the West Bank continues to be the religious settlers and their ideological supporters in the Israeli government.

Yet it would be wrong to ignore the power of religion as a force for love and intergroup coexistence. Only the truly intolerant secularist would divorce the horrific evidence of religion's folly from the equally compelling evidence that the creative imagination of religious geniuses from Amos and Isaiah to Jesus, Rumi, and Gautama Siddharta have saved millions of people from their own worst impulses. In so doing, they made a more peaceful world than what might have been. In addition to the creation of peace-generating dogma, religion's inspiration has provided the world with political geniuses such as Gandhi, King, and the Dalai Lama, who undoubtedly saved hundreds of thousands, if not millions, of lives by steering their constituencies to nonviolent resistance and constructive ways of pursuing justice and peace.

What are the cognitive and emotional underpinnings of great religious souls? What beliefs, practices, and mental disciplines animate their extraordinary courage and creativity? And how can these be put to use in coexistence work? As I explore more fully elsewhere,[1] a series of beliefs and practices that become second nature, habits of the mind and heart to generate extraordinary paradigms of interpersonal behavior, can be of benefit to religious and nonreligious actors alike.

Across diverse religions, great leaders have developed beliefs in the connection or interrelatedness of all sentient life, the sacredness of each and every human being, and the possibility of human change and evolution for the better, or repentance. Practices include a series of mental assumptions and concentrations that lead to a habitual embrace of compassion, peace, justice, mourning as a sacred task, forgiveness, and apology. Finally, the extraordinary religious peacemakers understand the power and importance of story, mythic structure, and above all, ritual as a transformative act.

Despite the presence of such extraordinary religious figures both in history and today, the fact is that we face some unprecedented circumstances of so many millions of religious people bumping up against competitors in a crowded and confusing world. The question then becomes how to take the best of religious beliefs and practices and apply them to unprecedented levels of interaction. Here is where the intellectuals of the world, those who for centuries have been at the forefront of often courageous interreligious exploration, have done such a great disservice. They have emphasized the skills that they have—and not others—and overlooked the importance of skills that they sometimes lack. They have emphasized ideas, words, abstract discussions of theology, even comparative studies of myth, but not the single most important ingredient of coexistence: relationships and the emotional bond that is the bedrock of all moral interactions. What is needed globally is not just discussion and dialogue but building relationships, which can rest only in part on intellectual discussion and dialogue. Essential to building relationships in a world marked by conflict among groups aligned through religious identities are gestures and forms that have religious resonance.

Relationships depend on gestures of honor, shared understandings of civility, hospitality, generosity, expressions of regret, and shared defense against needless suffering. All of these characteristics of relationship building can and must be founded on religious sources, especially because extremists will bring their own readings of religious sources to deny the possibility or permissibility of relationships based on respect and equality.

Moral and religious leaders on all sides can play a crucial role in generating these relationships, but no peace process should be subverted or suffocated by leaders who are tyrannical, backward-looking, or self-serving. Creative conflict resolution, including religiously informed conflict resolution, must work with but also circumvent the kind of encrusted leadership that is part of the problem.

There is one trait that is more important than all the rest for peacemaking, and that is humility. The ability to listen to the soul of the other in silence emerges from the discipline of humility. I am reminded of the enthusiasm that Buddhist teachers receive when they come to Israel and how odd it is that these "polytheists" receive such a warm welcome, especially from Israeli youth. Young people always help us perceive what is missing in a culture, what its great weaknesses are. A young person has not yet had to buy into his or her culture or don any particular socioeconomic strait-jacket and therefore becomes an important barometer of tragic flaws in the prevailing culture. These Buddhist teachers practice silence, laugh at themselves in ways unthinkable to monotheistic hierarchies, and speak, above all and repeatedly, about humility and compassion for all living things. These leaders attract young disaffected Israelis in search of spiritual solace because of what is missing in life for many people of this region. Both Jewish and Arab youth in a tension-ridden state officially neither at war nor at peace rarely witness the gentleness, humanity, and noncombativeness displayed by these great Buddhist teachers.

It seems clear from a religious viewpoint that humility, silence, and the wisdom of compassionate listening respond to what has been wrong in the region of conflict. Ironically, these qualities have ample precedent in the monotheistic literature, both as recommended moral behavior and as deep religious experience.[2] Muslims, Jews, and Christians can find throughout Biblical and Qur'anic literature evidence that humility is a sine qua non of the human being's position before God. It is a quintessential act of faith.[3] In Judaism it is even portrayed as a divine attribute to be emulated,[4] and for all Abrahamic traditions, the great prophet of the Bible, Moses, is described as the humblest of all men.[5]

Silence may not seem as central in Judaism and Islam as it is in Buddhism, at least when it comes to prayer, and yet where do the monotheistic prophets and heroes receive their wisdom if not through silent listening in desert and wilderness?

With humility, silence, and listening, there is a happy coalescence of diverse religious traditions and the most avant-garde conflict resolution practice. The best peacemakers that I have watched work—the best social change makers in general—are people who understand silence, who value the power of orchestrating the evolution of human relationships without dominating those relationships or encounters. Such peacemakers are not afraid of open discussion and even welcome it, but they do not relish argumentation for its own sake. They do not see every conversation as a win-lose competition, and they do not mistake overall progress and success in their endeavors with the need to come out "on top" in every encounter and conversation, even in their peace efforts. This requires great personal discipline, a very long view of time and "outcomes," and a strong degree of personal inner peace. It also requires a deeply felt patience, a basic trust in humanity and the world, viewed over time, and a love of imperfect human beings as such.

The kind of silence that builds relationships is not actually total silence. The complete silence of strangers, even given in respect, may trigger suspicion or worries that behind the silence is disdain or behind the smile is hatred. Compassionate, active listening requires probing but subtle questions that indicate more to the other than mere respectful silence.

Many people I know who love peace have not internalized these values sufficiently and thus become bad peacemakers despite their best intentions. The task of evoking and inculcating these values and worldviews is something that could benefit from a fusion of spiritual values and training in conflict resolution. Till now, far too much of the emphasis of conflict resolution has been on process, replicable processes for use in all contexts, as if peacemaking were a General Motors car to be disassembled and shipped to all parts of the world and reassembled regardless of circumstances. Not only does that approach not work, but it is barbaric, for it ignores the cultural context. It is far better to offer ways to encourage the development of peacemakers in each culture and religion[6] and cultivate the peacemaking personality honored in various religious traditions. The character of the peacemaker is a major concern in religious literature, and it should be the same for conflict resolution theory and practice.

Finally, humility necessarily interlaces—as many emotive and ethical gestures do—with the bestowal of dignity and honor. Human beings, particularly those who have suffered indignity and injury, crave the dignity of being heard and understood almost as much as they need air to breathe and water to drink. In our rush to economic and geographical negotiations of conflict, we constantly forget this basic need. Leah Green's Compassionate Listening Project represents a conscious institutionalization of listening as peacemaking integrated with compassion and has specialized in bringing groups to Israel to listen compassionately to the entire spectrum of Jewish and Palestinian political and religious life.[7] This listening has proved to be transformative for many participants and should be studied further.

Some additional examples of innovative peacemaking and relationship building include shared study of sacred texts in Jerusalem, across enemy lines. The act of study becomes not only a gesture of respect and reconciliation but also the basis of relationship building, shared mourning, and constructive argumentation. Rebuilding destroyed religious sites has been an important part of reconciliation in Bosnia. The restoration of devastated or abused cemeteries has proved to be of immense value, as has been the visitation of sites of massacres, with the accompanying acknowledgment by word and deed of the pain of the other. In fact, much of the successful Christian-Jewish reconciliation work of the past thirty years has occurred at these very sites.

Such examples may seem hard to imagine in the heat of conflict. Yet in Jerusalem, just two days after Islamic extremist suicide bombers destroyed the lives of dozens of Israeli teenagers, there were shared celebrations of Ramadan and Hanukkah by those superior religious souls of the region who hold on, sometimes by a thread, to relationships and humanization of the other. The United States, Cambodia, and India have seen marching used in an opposite way as it has been in Ireland. Both for war and peace, marching is a sacred act. Marching together is a vital and ongoing means of reconciliation, from Maha Gosananda's walks to Gandhi's marches to marches retracing the path of slaves in Richmond, Virginia, and black and white members of Congress in the United States retracing the Freedom Marchers' treacherous journeys through the South. All of these marches have been deeply spiritual events, rituals of immense power and transformation for those who participated in or witnessed them.

Prayers became critical to some efforts to frame tough negotiations in Latin America, a way to make a moral space and presence in the midst of hard bargaining, a way to make an oasis of vision in the midst of the predictable and necessary tale of grievances and injuries. Increasingly, secular educational institutes, such as the Adam Institute in Israel,[8] have seen the value of overlaying their education for democracy and human rights with cultural and religious foundations that will appeal to the spiritual side of the youth who they are educating. These are just a few examples. A full documentation, a true telling of this global story, awaits.

A final example is close to my heart. That is an effort on the part of sheikhs and rabbis in Israel and Palestine to create a religious peace treaty, a symbol of peace, and a token cease-fire.[9] An Islamic concept, referred to as hudna, has had a history in the Middle East that allows for the possibility of coexistence. Hudna is a hotly debated topic because a religious cease-fire has the implication of a temporary cessation of hostilities, not true peace. Those of us who have worked on this religious treaty have believed that the power of religious symbolism as a force for even a temporary cessation of violence and hate would be enough to generate other symbolic gestures and further progress on the hard-core issues. It would give momentum to religion as a source of healing rather than hatred, which could be built on by further efforts. Most important, it would give a voice to religious leaders who have been threatened and silenced by the well-financed radicals supported by oppressive leaders around the Middle East.

We whistled in the wind for a long time. We met with as many diplomats as we could. We made the case for the wisdom of this path to politicians and seasoned diplomats. Many were persuaded but remained silent. We managed to get support in principle from a letter received from the president of the United States. We met with Palestinian Chairman Yasser Arafat on several occasions with really extraordinary results. As dubious and duplicitous a peace partner as he is, we felt that just getting the approval of the top leaders would generate new possibilities. It did and it has. The leaders are important, but the goal of their involvement should be to circumvent their intransigence and ultimately make their presence less important, historically speaking.

Despite the kneejerk skepticism of many, we have now come to a situation in which key Arab businessmen, members of the Israeli Parliament, the Palestinian Legislative Council, the attorney general of Israel, and the president of Israel have publicly expressed interest in cultural and religious symbols of reconciliation and, specifically, interest in hudna. This is rather startling, considering that this is taking place in the midst of the intifada and in the immediate aftermath of September 11, 2001.

We have argued that such gestures have no business attempting to replace security cooperation and counterterrorism measures but that counterterrorism measures have no business trying to substitute for a means to change the one thing that perpetuates all wars: fear bom of hatred. That requires trust, forgiveness, and many other treasures of the human mind that only the path of ritual and culture can truly provide.

Supporting Coexistence Through a Religious Lens

Here I will develop a series of suggestions for anyone who wants to promote coexistence among conflicting groups where religion plays a role in the conflict or where religious resources can help build peace.

1. Recognize the paradox of religious hate and love, violence and prosocial values, and face the implications. The most important step to take is to abandon naïve beliefs about religion that register it mentally as either a categorical positive or negative in terms of coexistence.

There may be political interests at work in either demonizing or lionizing religion, such as President Bush's recent attempts rhetorically to see Islam in only good terms. But for strategists of coexistence, it is critical to examine and understand how each religion involved in the conflict promotes countervailing values. One of the primary reasons that this is so important is that the adversary groups are generally very familiar with the worst and best in their religions, cleverly using both to strengthen the us-them dynamics of conflict and violence wherein the members of one's own group are the righteous victims and the others are only abusers. They will know when you are soft-pedaling religion and when you are covering up their own religious leaders' contributions to the conflict. This will not help matters. It is imperative to acknowledge fully both contributions to the war, the positive and the negative, and it is important to engage religion in a way that will be believable to inherently skeptical audiences.

2. Rein in the damage of prejudices and hatred emanating from the texts and traditions of organized religion, as well as from religious leaders and representatives. How does one contain the damage done by organized religions in the context of war? By stimulating and generating a public repudiation of the activities of some in the war, especially if and when they used particular symbols, traditions, or texts in the course of justifying or perpetrating any atrocities. Each use of religion for atrocity must be responded to hermeneutically in exactly the same fashion.

Religious leaders or representatives who were active during the war must be encouraged and, if possible, compelled to repudiate those same uses of religion during the war. They must reject and, if possible, disown actual religious perpetrators, especially those who committed atrocities in the name of religion.

If these leaders cannot or will not repudiate prior religious hermeneutics, then it is important to encourage alternative leaderships and courageous individuals who will engage in that repudiation. This is most successfully accomplished where there are third-party strategies to stimulate these reactions bilaterally and simultaneously or consecutively. These reactions should be accompanied by acknowledgments of the pain inflicted and apologies. This may take years, but the efforts must begin as soon as possible and on a small scale.

3. Understand the paradoxes of hermeneutic variation with time and place. Understand the war within each religion both in the traditional way and in the contemporary setting. If one understands in a deep way the hermeneutic variation of traditions and the war within communities over their values choices, one is in a much better position to strengthen those who are engaged in battles for the prosocial side of a religious tradition. It is important to know the substance of the debate as well as the players, because conflict resolution or coexistence third parties will then be in a better position to design appealing peace strategies that mesh nicely with each community's way of framing its choices morally and spiritually.

4. Find the peacemakers, and strengthen them within and between communities. Strengthening the peacemakers means helping them financially and spiritually. It means giving them whatever they need to persist. They should be the ones, for the most part, to explain their needs and what will make them more effective. But it is also the case that sometimes peacemakers are so far on the fringe that they are not necessarily adept at social influence. We must also keep in mind that in every corporate religious group there are peacemakers who leave the group and struggle from the outside and others who work from within. Mechanisms of support for religious peacemakers should always be so structured by third parties as to be ready for inclusion. This is particularly problematic historically for peacemakers who tend to be as exclusive as any other inbred groups. It is the job of third parties not to allow left-right or peace- violence divisions to become encrusted in religious communities. There should a highly elastic and creative process of ever-widening communication and creativity.

5. Build alliances of new hermeneutics, interpretations, and symbols to support coexistence. In the long run, with the work of local peacemakers, more possibilities of interreligious alliances can emerge and support new hermeneutics, new interpretations, and symbols of coexistence. The more varied each group's religious actors are, the more they will find their counterparts on the other side. Liberals will find liberals and conservatives will find conservatives, and out of a broadened coalition of those committed to coexistence will come a slow and steady defeat of those committed to violence.

6. Focus on deeds more than dialogue, or make dialogue contingent on or interactive with a regime of righteous bilateral deeds. Dialogue is overrated. It may make a good platform for leaders to demonstrate their political importance, but it just as often generates skepticism, especially when it is engaged too soon. It is the rage of the masses that is the critical dynamic of religion and war, and that rage is not turned off like a spigot. It is true that leaders are critical symbols of social change, and fostering their relationship with one another is crucial. But we must not overrate the contribution of dialogue. The masses of people understand, in their wisdom, the evidence of reconciliation, acknowledgment, and repentance, in the realm of deeds rather than in the rhetoric of political manipulation.

7. Understand and use the interaction of economics, psychology, power relations, and military reality, along with religious trends, to coordinate more effectively secular and religious efforts of peace, security, and development. Efforts at religious coexistence work can be hampered by bureaucratic division of efforts and poorly integrated thinking about the nature of conflict. Just as deeds are crucial to true religious trust, development and poverty relief are at the heart of serious conflict resolution. These two insights can and should be integrated in the form of creative programs and joint activities that the warring communities design with the help of others. Similarly, religious healing and psychological recovery need to work hand in hand. Each must understand the peculiar approaches of the other and attempt a cooperative or parallel set of processes. The case is the same with security concerns. Issues of public safety, crime, and justice should be framed in terms of religious values wherever possible. This suggestion does not mean surrendering the public order to religious authority. At the end of the day, there

is no peace when one religious community or another controls the military or judiciary or the public space. Most religious adherents around the world have come to understand that religion is at its best when it does not control the temporal space. Democracy and human rights ultimately depend on this principle. That having been said, there is no reason that the liberal forms of social order—judiciary, police, democracy—should not be hermeneutically framed in religious ways. Enough adherents around the world are actively engaged in this framing process—often in very deep ways—that this alliance of civil society need not be seen as the enemy of religion. This process must be aggressively funded the world over. We are engaged not in a war of religions but rather a war within religions and civilizations over the future of civil liberties, particularly the freedom of women. It is my impression that most religious adherents want human rights and democracy, but not if it is perceived to be a means of crushing their identity or civilization. We need to work harder at making the case for a culture- and religion-friendly liberal social order. And we need the international corporations and representatives of capitalism to become an asset, not a liability, in this struggle.

8. Face and focus on the tremendous psychological power of religion to stimulate mood swings, and use gestures of acknowledgment, apology, and repentance for reconciliation, but be prepared to combat the compelling contagion of righteous hatred. Religion can produce powerful and irrational symbols of hatred, such as desecrations, libels, conspiracies, or devil discoveries. These can erupt in a highly charged situation in which some unscrupulous group in search of power can provoke and capitalize on symbolic religious rage. Be prepared with alternative and liberal healing symbols of religion, such as broadly publicized and filmed interfaith ceremonies of healing or restoration of a holy site that has been destroyed or desecrated.

9. Explore and use the power of symbols to divide, unite, and reconcile. The greatest danger that we face from religion today is its tremendous power to stimulate rage in massive numbers of people. Irresponsible clerics cannot resist the opportunity to capitalize on this power to actively fight world orders with which they see themselves unable to coexist. In a poverty of vision, these clerics have not yet reached the conclusions that millions of other clergy have about the modern world: that it is possible for religion to flourish even with Coca-Cola, MTV, and absolute freedom of choice by women and men. But the free-floating rage of millions of people waits, like a ripe fruit, for power-hungry individuals and institutions to trigger and appropriate. And then the sociopaths, the fascistic leaders and terrorists, come along as the great release of the rage. This was as true in the twentieth century, under the aegis of fascism and communism, as it is today under the aegis of fundamentalism.

It is our job to undermine that rage aggressively with compassion, acknowledgment, antipoverty plans, and inherent respect for cultural and religious diversity. If there is global religious rage, then a global Marshall Plan is necessary to quell it. Respect is the ultimate way to undermine the violent potential of religion and give voice to the majority in each religious tradition who tend to abhor the abduction of their religion by rage.

Religion can serve as the language for triggering rage or as the vehicle for cultivating relationships, active listening, and rituals of respect across difference. Religions can organize people into warring factions or instead sustain coexistence and development. Religions can divide or instead build bridges to peace.

Notes

1. M. Gopin, *Between Eden and Armageddon: The Future of World Religions, Violence and Peacemaking* (New York: Oxford University Press, 2000). See also M. Gopin, Holy War, Holy Peace: How Religion Can Bring Peace to the Middle East (New York: Oxford University Press, 2002).

2. See Tractate Derekh Eretz Zuta 1 and Avot of Rabbi Nathan 15; for a representative collection of rabbinic approaches to humility, see M. C. Luzzatto, *The Path of the Just*, trans. S. Silverstein (New York: Feldheim, 1969), ch. 22. There are numerous sources on silence and its relationship to understanding. See Midrash Rabbah (Margoliot ed.), Leviticus 16:5; Midrash Tanhuma (Warsaw ed.), Va'ye'tseh.6; Otsar Midrashim Alpha Beta d'Ben Sira, para. 19; Tractate Derekh Eretz Zuta 7; and T. B. Pesahim 99a.

3. See, for example, Qur'an 7:161; 57:16.

4. See Midrash Rabbah, Deuteronomy 7:12; and Midrash Tanhuma (Warsaw ed.), Bereshit 4, Vay'erah 8, Ki Tisah 15.

5. Numbers 12:3.

6. See M. Gopin, The Religious Component of Mennonite Peacemaking and Its Global Implications," in C. Sampson and J. P. Lederach (eds.), *From the Ground Up: Mennonite Contributions to International Peacebuilding* (New York: Oxford University Press, 2000). For more information, see the Compassionate Listening Project Web site at http://www.mideastdiplomacy.org/clp.html.

7. See Adam Institute for Democracy and Peace at http://www.adaminstitute. org.il/english/index.html.

8. For the full text of at least one proposed peace treaty, as well as an extensive analysis of it, see Gopin, *Holy War, Holy Peace*.

9. For the full text of at least one proposed peace treaty, as well as an extensive analysis of it, see Gopin, *Holy War, Holy Peace*.

Gender

Sandra I. Cheldelin and Maneshka Eliatamby

Sandra Cheldelin received her EdD degree in the psychological foundations of education at the University of Florida. Cheldelin has more than
four decades' experience as a practitioner working with over 150 organizations and communities in over fourteen countries. While now professor
emeritus of conflict at George Mason University, she continues to intervene on issues of conflict, race, and gender. Her publications helped bring
gender forward as a lens for studying conflict. Maneshka Eliatamby, who
received her PhD from the School for Conflict Analysis and Resolution
(S-CAR) at George Mason University, now works as a senior associate at
the Search for Common Ground, an organization dedicated to transforming how the world addresses conflict. Her work focuses on countering
violent extremism, peacebuilding, gender, and youth.

   In Epoch Two, we see a greater curiosity about differences, whether
these be cultural, historical, or biological. The importance of a gender
lens became pronounced during this period when Bosnian rape camps
made rape no longer solely a prize of war but now also a tool of war.
Cheldelin and Eliatamby's essay reflects this increased interest in women's
susceptibility to and participation in conflict, war, violence, and peacebuilding. They also challenge long-standing assumptions about women
serving only as peacemakers or victims whereas men only serve as the
aggressors. Reflective of this belief of women's role in peacemaking, at the
2009 Vancouver Peace Summit, the Nobel Peace Prize–winning Dalai
Lama pronounced, "Western women will save the world." This inspira-
tional moment for Western women need not obscure that women do not
uniformly serve as peacemakers. Thousands of women have joined armed
groups and enter into combat. When not participating in combat, women
have supported war in many ways. Spartan women, for example, are
quoted to have said to husbands and sons, "Come back with your shield
or on it!"

   Cheldelin and Eliatamby also observe the opportunity war creates for
women to realign social structures, often creating more equality with
men. When women pick up arms and stand alongside men or serve as
suicide bombers, their social position shifts. In World War II, Rosie the
Riveter, with her rolled up sleeves, bandana, and large biceps, reflected
women's shifting roles when the men were at war. Large-scale violence
creates opportunities for shifting gender roles.

The article concludes with a call to for increasing the inclusion of women in peacebuilding not because women are nurturing, but rather because of their deep experiences of exclusion and social inferiority.

Questions to consider: What possibilities are created when we look at conflict through a gender lens? How might considering gender shift how we work to prevent and/or respond to violent conflicts? How might considering gender better support men as well as women?

Challenging the Dominant Narrative

Sandra I. Cheldelin and Maneshka Eliatamby

Introduction

There are several misconceptions about women's roles and behavior during times of conflict, violence, war, and peace building. One of the common stories about conflict and violence is that women, more than men, are the victims. While women and children are often adversely affected during times of war and natural disaster, this argument discounts two major realities that hold true in such situations; first, that men are spared of victimhood and, secondly, that women's roles are limited to that of the victim.

Another misconception about women is that they are best suited for peacemaking—some believe that women have an inherent capacity to work collaboratively and bring parties that are in conflict together in dialogue with each other. Moreover, Manchanda (2010) goes further and in stating that "the flat assumption that women are for peace (is) because they are the worst sufferers in conflict." While this book acknowledges the truth behind these claims, from our own experiences in the fields of peace building and development, we know that this is not the entire truth—not the whole story. Rita Manchanda quotes Cynthia Cockburn as stating that "if women have a distinctive angle in peace, it is not due to women being nurturing. It seems more to do with knowing oppression when we see it" (Manchanda 2001,17). Manchanda argues that women's experiences of being excluded and "inferiorized" gives them special insight into the root causes of conflict. In many cultures, women's socialization places them in inferior positions to their male counterparts. It is this disadvantaged vantage point that has shaped women's ontology and epistemology for millennia. This gender-specific paradigm has also given them the insight and ability to understand violent structures and the root causes of violence and to take actions to change the structures that give birth to and foster violence. Manchanda claims that women do not always delineate between domestic and public/political structures of violence and "are more likely to see a continuum of violence, because they experience the connected forms of domestic and political violence that stretches from the home, to the street to the battlefield" (Manchanda 2001,17).

Popular rhetoric also often ignores how women's lives change as a result of war and traumatic experiences and how they forge strategies to survive these situations. Rarely do we hear stories of women that have demonstrated their capacities for agency—voice, action, retaliation, and intervention—in times of conflict and post-conflict reconstruction and how their adoption of new roles transforms gender dynamics in the societies from which they come.

Reflecting on our own work in the academy and in the field, we have come to recognize that women play a myriad of roles in the face of war and peace, in violence and intervention, in competition and collaboration—and that their roles are hardly monolithic. The multiplicity of women's roles is too often ignored both in academic teaching and research, as well as in practice. Through the stories of women's experiences in wartime and as part of peace building, we have attempted to fill this void, shed light on this multiplicity, and force acknowledgment of the variety of roles women play.

The chapters reveal that women are not always innocent bystanders in times of conflict—neither are their voices silenced in post-conflict times. This multiplicity of roles is illustrated in the themes that emerged from the cases in this book. Five themes stand out as most important: (1) there is a strong connection between violence and gendered identity, (2) gendered identities are influenced by social movements, (3) stopping violence depends on using social movement networks committed to sustainable peace, (4) peace requires access to broad-based educational opportunities, and (5) successful post-conflict reconstruction requires a commitment to gender-based mainstreaming and social justice issues. The stories presented in this book are evidence that women have successfully navigated the labyrinth of experiencing and making war and calling for, creating, and sustaining peace.

Women Waging War

Common discourse suggests that war is gendered. Men are the dominant players, and women are either the victims or the innocent bystanders. Francis Fukuyama even goes as far as stating that "males are genetically predisposed to violence" (Bouta et al. 2005,11). Despite these mainstream views of gendered roles in violence and war, Bouta et al. (2005, 11), found that females were active participants in fighting forces and combat in 55 different conflicts. Mazurna and Carlson's review of women in the Sierra Leone conflict found that women's involvement in violence was a rather complex phenomenon, and that while they were often "captives and dependents . . . they were also involved in planning and executing the war" (Mazurana and Carlson 2004). Our book has explicated six such cases: Chechnya, Eritrea, Liberia, Nepal, Sierra Leone, and Sri Lanka.

Clearly, women do not always bear nurturing and nonviolent qualities in the face of war and peace. In such extreme cases as the Chechnyan and Sri Lankan female suicide terrorists, women were simultaneously victims and perpetrators, trapped in men's tactics of war. Strapping on explosives—becoming human bombs—in the name of their country or their group allowed them to redefine their gender role in society. When violence is experienced as a result of actions by the state, or when a country is under the control of a foreign power, it helps the propaganda efforts to recruit female suicide bombers. When there is control of a country by a foreign power, there will be increased cases of suicide terrorism, and the role of women in them will grow. One reason is the "shock effect" grounded in gendered stereotypes. Female-based aggression and violence violates cultural assumptions about women as weak and vulnerable, recasting them as violent, murderous, and destructive.

This tactic is especially enticing to women as a way to redefine who they are in society. In the chapters "Fighting for Emancipation" and "Dying for Equality," we see how women chose violence as a means of negotiating not only their wartime situation but their position in society as a whole. Women witness the elite status and privileges afforded to females in suicide cadres willing to carry out their missions. These women achieve a greater sense of equality with men and are granted heroine status with female militants. This is in stark contrast to their previous statuses and inequalities. In her chapter titled "Girls with Guns," Patricia Maulden states that "[I]n both Sierra Leone and Liberia the possession of an AK-47 or in some cases a machete produced an instant realignment of the traditional power structure" (chapter 5). This appears to be the case in numerous other instances as well. In Turshen and Twagiramariya's book *What Women Do in Wartime*, authors Goldblatt and Meintjes write on women's experiences in South Africa and state that "[w]ar also breaks down the patriarchal structures of society that confine and degrade women. In the very breakdown of morals, traditions, customs, and community, war also opens up and creates new beginnings" (Turshen 1998, 20).

Various liberation and revolutionary movements have included women's rights and equality for men and women in their programs for political change (Manchanda 2001,12–13). While these chapters shed light on glimmers of hope during dark times of war—situations sometimes providing unexpected opportunities for women to challenge the patriarchal structures that they come from—these wartime gains unfortunately do not necessarily translate into women's emancipation during post-conflict and peace times. Liberation achieved in battle is not always sustainable, and women are often required to return to prewar social norms. However, this concept is difficult to comprehend at the point when the AK-47 one is holding has begun to earn the respect of males on the battlefield and women begin to experience more freedom and emancipation than they ever had prior to taking up arms. Additionally, we recognize that while authors such as Manchanda

(2010) have begun researching and writing on how women negotiate post-conflict and postwar situations, we recognize that this is an area that is still under-researched and undertheorized.

Gendered Identity and Social Movements

Women-led social movements are different from those that are led by men. Women's experiences give them a sense of agency and gender consciousness. They believe that, as a group, they can make gender-specific demands. The many examples of women's movements in this book provide insight into how they are organized, how they work, and how they are sustained. What seems most apparent is that women conceptualize of and organize social movements differently. This is particularly evident in Zimbabwe, where Women of Zimbabwe Arize (WOZA) has maintained a strong grassroots base and has created a broad-based network of support. Members used their role as mothers to champion their cause. The leaders set ambitious but relevant goals and grounded their work in traditional notions of femininity.

By seeking to address both the practical and strategic gendered needs of men and women, WOZA members were able to capture the attention of the entire community. They presented themselves as mothers, sisters, and women—those most affected in postwar cleanup—and they engaged in a Standup for Your Child movement. Women took their children to the streets, encouraged other women to vote during the March 2008 elections, claimed their vote as a mark against the government's inefficiency and injustice, and declared their role to be protectors of the next generation's inheritance.

Often members of women's movements established a human rights narrative. Connecting women's issues with human rights forced the personal to be political and the private domain (usually female) to be considered in the public sphere of influence, making women and children's issues relevant and worthy of attention. These women created coalitions of support among civil society groups, using media as a tool for activism and a conduit for raising awareness. They exposed oppression, brutality, and harassment by the police; pressured the state to observe the rule of law; and demanded women's rights to justice and fair trials. Framing their narrative as human rights issues provided them a shared vision and therefore made it easier to mobilize supporters and recruit sympathizers, locally and globally—some of these movements got the support of such organizations as Amnesty International, Human Rights Watch, and Women Human Rights Defenders. These women-led social movements are impressive examples of navigating the labyrinth by embracing and expanding on gendered identity.

Women Waging Peace

Stopping the war and making the transition to a state of peace—the public domain—is almost always limited to men. Women are seldom players in stopping war and ending conflict. During Sri Lanka's cease-fire negotiations conducted in the early 2000s, while the country had a female president and while women actively participated as combatants on behalf of the LTTE, there were no women at the negotiating table (thè LTTE later included the female heads of the organization's political wing in one of the subcommittees overseeing an aspect of the negotiations). It was clearly the responsibility of both parties to the conflict, the Sri Lankan government and the LTTE as well as the negotiating teams made up of the Norwegian and Japanese governments, to ensure the inclusion of women, who according to statistics, makeup nearly 51 percent of the country's population. The stories of women's exclusion from these negotiations at the peace table are not endemic to Sri Lanka alone. This same story repeats itself in Nepal, Uganda, Liberia, Sierra Leone, and Guatemala, to name a few. Even in those cases where women have been included, their participation is often limited and minimized.

It is clear that steps toward including women at the negotiating table are greatly needed. This certainly was the vision and intention behind the United Nations Security Council Resolutions 1325 and its subsequent Resolution 1820, which are discussed later in this chapter.

Social Networks Committed to Sustainable Peace

Several cases presented demonstrate ways women's social networks made a commitment to peace as their dominant narrative. They employed numerous activities: (1) encouraged mobilization of women across societal divides, (2) supported and assisted women in building sustainable and effective networking mechanisms, (3) recognized the needs of local communities and promoted local initiatives, (4) took into consideration the cultural aspect of societies where the movement was developing, (5) provided support through capacity-building initiatives (many were funded and trained by international as well as domestic organizations), and (6) made long-term commitments to support the growth and development of women.

While a woman's movement may initiate a peace process, sustainable peace ultimately requires a societal shift from hostility toward and disregard of half of its population to one of partnership and respect. Unfortunately, achieving peace becomes a public domain of work, and women are usually left out, as previously noted. Rwanda, however, appears to be a success story. Its citizens have been able to sustain peace in its postgenocide war. They initiated a healing and reconciliation process—HAGURUKA, detailed in Uwineza and Brown's chapter titled "Engendering Recovery" (chapter 9). When craft-making training programs were offered, the organizers focused attention on the purpose of the training—creating economic opportunities for women and their families—and not on the different backgrounds of the attendees. In this case, both Hutu and Tutsi women learned to make marketable crafts. In the evenings, however, trainees discussed various other topics, sometimes led by outside experts, about relationships, HIV/AIDS, reconciliation experiences, and the like. These trainings became a venue for women's economic empowerment and trauma healing.

This highlights that sustainable peace movements must embrace gender as an integrated strategy so that women are better prepared and empowered to lead their families in recovery. Women must participate in both social and economic revitalization. Ambassador Swanee Hunt identifies at least ten other indicators of progress in her successful network of peace. The range of activities reflected in her movement is broad and comprehensive and could be viewed as benchmarks for other successful programmatic efforts: policy makers speak regularly about the importance of women's involvement; network members have access to the most powerful government officials in the world; women leaders address key organizations such as the United Nations, the U.S. Congress, the World Bank, and the European Union; network leaders are regularly sought after to present and discuss their issues; publications and dissemination efforts are often referenced; international conferences and organizations seek out leaders to advise; and documentary filmmakers and other media sources want to tell their stories. Creating partnerships with other organizations, human rights advocates, and conflict resolution specialists is critical to build stable communities based on mutual respect and the rule of law.

Post-Conflict Programs and Education

There are a number of lessons about post-conflict programming and the critical role of education in these chapters. An important one focuses on the reintegration of women and child soldiers and ways programmatic intentions that address boys' needs are different from the needs of girls. Youth Demobilization, Disarmament, Rehabilitation, and Reintegration (DDRR) programs in West Africa reflect a belief that boys and danger are linked, and therefore it is essential to move quickly to mitigate potential crises. That is, large numbers of male youth wandering aimlessly through their communities with little to do are likely to engage in violence. The danger element is informed by the male's behavior as a child soldier who killed or traumatized members of their own families and community members. Unfortunately girls are left out of programmatic offerings—based on the gendered assumption they were victims or that they are not, by nature, dangerous or a threat to reengage violence. As a result, these girls become further marginalized, as they are already without support from former wartime husbands and are not welcome in their families and communities. Some become violent and engage in girl-gang-related activities. The more than 17,000 girls and women who were engaged in the war in Liberia are a case in point.

This only highlights the essential task of providing educational opportunities to young women too. Teaching job skills to girls allows them a path out of poverty and powerlessness. So, too, do women need to learn of their legal rights. As noted in several situations, conflating Islamic and patriarchal values, especially in rural areas of some Islamic countries, can be particularly troubling. Women's rights groups find it challenging to separate the cultural issues from the religious ones, especially when there are parallel legal systems complicating women's access to justice. Women have demonstrated that awareness-raising programs through media campaigns are useful in informing women of their rights and ways to access their legal systems.

Support should be given to help women educate one another. The regional alliances that were formed in the women's movements in Pakistan, Egypt, and Turkey provide inspiration and offer success stories for other developing and neighboring states. As technology becomes more available, women's rights groups can access one another within their communities and countries as well as in regional and international arenas.

Our experiences in the field have also shed light on the fact that post-conflict training and education needs to go beyond the traditional DDRR processes, especially where women and girls have actively participated in warfare. Many of the traditional societies that these girls and women come from stigmatize and shun those returning from combat, especially the females who are considered to have violated social norms. For example, many women who attempted to return to their homes in Eritrea were not welcome by their families and villages and were forced to create "female-only villages." Girls attempting to return to their schools in Sri Lanka's Eastern Province were ostracized even by their teachers—some of them gave up hope of proper reintegration and education. It is clear that the formal DDRR processes must also include training and education for the local populations these women and girls are returning to.

Mainstreaming, Social Justice, and Human Security

After years of violence and conflict, it is clear that retuning communities and societies to peace and prosperity requires intentional and well-supported mainstreaming efforts. These efforts must involve all stakeholders of peace, especially women, as they are the group most invested in family and community stability and most able to reweave torn communities—essential to the psychological, social, and economic welfare of their societies. Allowing women access to all levels of decision making forces governments to recognize the need for institutional and legal reform. It cannot be limited to numerical representation in leadership positions of government. Gender mainstreaming in other critical sectors such as education, business, security, and military is the only way of ensuring sustainability for their achievements.

The international legal system has set the stage to demand equal justice for women and men, especially through the passage of UN Security Council Resolutions 1325 and 1820 that are focused on gender mainstreaming. UN Security Council Resolution 1325, which was adopted in October 2000, calls for the implementation of gender perspectives in post-conflict reconstruction, focusing on the needs of women and girls during repatriation, resettlement, rehabilitation, and reintegration. This legislation was followed by UN Security Council Resolution 1820 in June 2008—in direct response to loopholes in UN Security Council Resolution 1325 pertaining to sexual violence prevention and response. UN SCR 1820 views sexual violence now as "unacceptable and preventable" and not merely as an inevitable feature of conflict—the previously dominant narrative. However, it should be noted that this legislation, too, is limited to the discussion of sexual violence against civilians during and in the aftermath of armed conflict—it does not include acts of sexual violence committed before the start of armed conflict.

The efficacy of these two resolutions is still to be determined. Rwanda and Liberia are often cited as success stories where women have been included both in negotiations for peace as well as in post-conflict governance. Liberia boasts Africa's first female president, Ellen Johnson Sirleaf, while Rwanda's parliament is made up of more than 51 percent women. While both of these cases indicate tremendous leaps toward achieving equal participation in government, it is still to be determined whether women holding leadership positions indicates and translates into women's empowerment at the grassroots and civil society levels. In 1960, Ceylon (now Sri Lanka) became the first country to have a woman elected as its leader, and India, Pakistan, and Bangladesh have elected women to the highest level of leadership since. However, in all of these cases, the election of a female head of state has not translated to women's emancipation at the grassroots level. Manchanda (2010,1), in an article titled "Nepali Women Seize the Political Dawn," states that, while the new constitution of Nepal requires women's participation at the local and national governmental levels, in reality, much of the decision making in the country takes place among men behind closed doors. This begs the question, Have egalitarian legislations adopted by these countries' new constitutions changed women's daily lives? While it is beyond the scope of this book to evaluate the efficacy of UN Resolutions 1325 and 1820 from this standpoint, we recognize the need for such research.

While such legislations have set the stage to demand equal rights through the implementation of international laws, it is time for leaders around the world to be institutionally accountable in regard to gender crimes, providing gender equality in such social structures as education and health care and insisting on equality in social and political settings. We must work toward recognition of victims as people and not stigmatized cultural symbols and establish programs wherein women are valued beyond their reproductive capabilities. In societies where female gender identity has been limited to childbearing and rearing and where qualities gendered as "feminine" are given lower status, women likely will be the victims of violence. During wartime, when women are the victims of rape and torture, too often they are blamed for the violence. For real change to occur and be sustainable, the consequences of such violence need to be reframed and recontextualized so that women are not held responsible for their plight. Not being stigmatized would go a long way toward restoring a sense of dignity and rebuilding individual and community identity.

Again, the case of Rwanda provides an example where local laws changed the lives of the local population. Formed in 1991, HAGURUKA initially focused on the rights of women and children in Rwandan society. They began by assessing the impact of mass violence on women—many of whom were widows or whose husbands were imprisoned. One of the main issues focused on was the loss of control of family property to male relatives. However, as a result of the genocide and the lack of a functioning legal system, the organizations became involved in emergency assistance. In 1996, HAGURUKA returned its focus to its original mission, which led to the enactment of new laws pertaining to family property. The network's leadership and governance training framed gender as an issue for national development. They avoided a so-called feminist struggle with men and instead endeavored to involve men in their fight. While debating proposed bills of law to protect women's rights in parliament, leaders framed women in the affirmative as "our mothers, sisters and wives." This helped men understand the importance of supporting such bills rather than feeling confronted with disempowerment. The lesson here is not to alienate men but instead to incorporate them in gender integration efforts.

Imagining the Unimaginable

The cases we present in this book where women have participated in conflict in which they have been agents of peace clearly show how their gendered social roles are transformed as a result of trauma and violence. They have broken numerous societal barriers and changed their gendered roles and cultures. These women give the field of peace building the hope that there is room for forgiveness and positive transformation even in the most protracted conflicts. Women's stories of survival and hope also emerge in less violent, but equally troubling environments. This is reflected in the story of the Gulf of Mexico's experiences with Hurricane Katrina and the BP oil spill, and in the crime-ridden inner city of Baltimore, Maryland.

It is time to imagine what has historically been the unimaginable. For example, one way to address Schneider's (2008, 994) claim that it is particularly cruel to target women, especially when they are most often not the initial instigators of violence and war, is to hear President Nelson Mandela's call for violence against women to be recognized as a human issue—and not one limited to a woman's issue, a feminist issue, or an international development issue. There is legislation in place to provide the foundation to stop victimizing women (United Nations, 2010). It is now up to the citizens, including men, to isolate the perpetrators.

It is time to acknowledge that what women bring to the table enhances and expands the content and quality of the conversation and increases the likelihood of stopping violence and sustaining peace. Women already bridge the gap between the private and public spheres, and therefore the dominant narrative of a bifurcated private and public arena is not only a dishonest one, it also does the field of conflict resolution and the communities that we serve a disservice. It is dishonest because the stories of women's participation in the public arena—WOZA, the Gulf of Mexico, Rwanda, and the global inclusive security movement, to mention a few—demonstrate women successfully positioning themselves in both spheres. It is a disservice to the field because it limits our imagination of what is possible.

Women's position in the private and public spheres uniquely places them as true representatives, of inclusive human security.

A number of cases in the book suggest that, instead of viewing women solely as innocent bystanders of conflict, we need to acknowledge that thousands of women join armed groups and go into combat. Once we have acknowledged this and researched and comprehended the root causes of their violence, only then will we be successful in countering this trend. What we know about female suicide cadres and combatants is that the patriarchal cultures from which they come are contributing factors in their decision to adopt violence. The cases presented are about traditionally patriarchal cultures where women have lower status and where women see the adoption of extreme violence as a form of agency. When a culture has strict traditions and practices that subordinate women and ascribe their particular roles, women who do not fit into these roles are often ostracized and marginalized. When women are excluded, they are left with few options within their own societal structures. They then become more vulnerable to the option of taking up arms or joining a terrorist group.

Bouta et al. (2005, 9) state that "[k]ey development challenges are to acknowledge women's and men's participation in armies, and to target all women that joined the armies—with or without weapons—with assistance." Access to primary, secondary, and higher education for girls and women is particularly important. Similarly, educating boys and men is a critical intervention in mitigating the causes of violence. Education broadens the mind and liberates societies from the clutches of unfair and inhumane cultural traditions. Long-term benefits of universal education can address the gap in uneven development across societies, including in Egypt, Eritrea, Liberia, Nepal, Pakistan, Sierra Leone, Sri Lanka, and Turkey, to name a few.

The story of women waging war and peace can be dramatically different. But for this, we must dare to imagine what was previously unimaginable.

As President Mandela states, men, too, need to assume responsibility for altering the narrative of war and violence. We acknowledge the existence of separate male- and female-dominated domains. However, we envision the establishment and viability of a third—a human domain. The stories in this book are more than a glimmer of hope in this direction—we can imagine and work toward actualizing this human domain, where men as well as women are included in the formal and informal political, economic, and social processes in their communities, countries, regions, and around the globe. It is our intent that the stories of hope in this book serve as a launching point for imagining and establishing this new narrative and providing women and men around the world the courage to engage it.

References

Bouta, Tsjeard, George Frerks, and Ian Bannon. 2005. *Gender, Conflict, and Development.* Washington, DC: The International Bank for Reconstruction and Development/The World Bank.

Manchanda, Rita 2010. "Nepali Women Seize the New Political Dawn: Resisting Marginalisation after Ten Years of War." Center for Humanitarian Dialogue., http://peace talks.hdcentre.org/2010/08/women-in-nepal/comment-page-l/

Manchanda, Rita (ed.). 2001. *Women, War and Peace in South Asia: Beyond Victimhood to Agency.* London: Sage Publications.

Mazurana, Dyan and Khristopher Carlson. 2004. *From Combat to Community: Women and Girls of Sierra Leone.* The Policy Commission, Women Waging Peace, available http://www.peacewomen.org/assets/file/Resources/NGO/ PartPPGIssueDisp_CombatToCommunty_WomenWagePeace_2004.pdf.

Schneider, Mary Deutsch. 2008. "About Women, War, and Darfur: The Continued Quest for Gender Violence Justice." *North Dakota Law Review*, 83,915.

Turshen, Meredith. 1998. "Women's War Stories," in Meredith Turshen and Clotilde Twagiramariya (eds), *What Women Do in Wartime* (pp. 1–26). London and New York: Zed Books Ltd.

United Nations. 2010. Handbook for Legislation on Violence against Women, ASDF, Department of Economic and Social Affairs, Division for the Advancement of Women, http://www.un.org/womenwatch/daw/vaw/handbook/Handbook%20for %201egislation%20on%20violence%20against%20women.pdf.

Beyond Intractability

Heidi Burgess

Heidi Burgess is a founder and co-director of the University of Colorado Conflict Information Consortium. She received her PhD in sociology and has worked it the field of conflict resolution as a scholar and practitioner for roughly forty years. Primarily focused on intractable conflicts and public policy dispute resolution, she also dedicates significant time to making conflict resolution knowledge available on the internet. Her site, Beyond Intractability (beyondintractability.org), provides an accessible free knowledge database on conflict.

Intractability is a contested term developed to describe 5 percent of conflict in the world that is characterized by entrenched dynamics that seem impossible to resolve. These conflicts are usually grounded in morals, domination, or other high-stake, irreconcilable differences. According to the authors, one of the quintessential conflicts that falls within this category is Israel–Palestine, where one can observe that smaller subordinate conflicts are addressed within the larger conflict, but the underlying conflict itself remains intact. The concept of intractability is not to be confused with the assumption that the conflict is impossible to resolve, but rather that it has certain characteristics that make it particularly difficult to address. That perceptions play such a huge role in how conflicts are understood opens the door to shifting them to address or shift the conflict dynamics constructively.

Intractability is an Epoch Two concept because it draws on system dynamics to understand conflict relationships. Where Epoch One was grounded on stand-alone factors that failed to consider interrelationship, intractability opens up a new understanding of relationship. Often, intractability is associated with identity conflicts or moral conflicts in keeping with Epoch Two conflict theories.

Questions to consider: Do you believe there are some conflicts that can never be resolved? If so, why do you think that? What are the potential consequences of giving up on resolution?

What Are Intractable Conflicts?

Heidi Burgess

Definition

"Intractability" is a controversial concept, which means different things to different people. Some people on the initial BI (Beyond Intractability) project team intensely dislike the term, as they saw it as too negative: intractable conflicts are impossible to resolve, they say, so people think they are not worth dealing with. "Do not use a term that undermines everything we are trying to do," argued project member Andrea Strimling.[1]

Nevertheless, all BI participants that we have talked to (which includes many 100s) agree that there is a set of conflicts out there that are hard to deal with. "Protracted." "Destructive." "Deep-rooted." "Resolution-resistant." "Intransigent." "Gridlocked." "Identity-based." "Needs based." "Complex." "Difficult." "Malignant." "Enduring."

All of these words capture some of what we are trying to get at, but none capture it all. As we see it, intractable conflicts are those that lie at the frontier of the field—the conflicts that stubbornly seem to elude resolution, even when the best available techniques are applied. Examples abound: abortion, homosexual rights, and race relations in the United States; and the Israeli-Palestinian problem, Sri Lanka, and Kashmir (among many others) abroad. [2]

These conflicts are not hopeless, and they most certainly are worth dealing with. But they are very different from more tractable conflicts, such as most labor-management conflicts, some family conflicts, many workplace conflicts and even many international conflicts that can be successfully resolved through negotiation or mediation. Intractable conflicts need a different, more multi-faceted, and more prolonged approach.

Characteristics of Intractable Conflicts

Mutable Characteristics

First we should say that intractability is not a dichotomous concept. In other words, you can't have two bins—one tractable, and one intractable—and put conflicts in one bin or the other. Rather, intractability exists on a continuum, with very stubborn, apparently intractable conflicts at one end; very simple, readily resolvable conflicts at the other end and many conflicts somewhere in between the two extremes.

PRE-DISPOSING CHARACTERISTICS

Intractability is also a dynamic state. Few conflicts are intractable at the beginning; rather, they become one way or the other according to how they are handled. Conflicts that become highly escalated and involve repeated patterns of violence are likely to move toward the intractable end, sometimes quite quickly. Conflicts that are managed skillfully to limit escalation and violence are likely to move toward the tractable end.

Additional insights discussing intractable conflicts are offered by Beyond Intractability participants.

But some characteristics make conflicts more difficult to handle no matter what. One might say these conflicts are "predisposed" to become intractable. For example, conflicts that involve irreducible, high-stakes, win-lose issues that have no "zone of possible agreement" (ZOPA) often become intractable. These are conflicts from which the participants see no "Way Out" (using a Bill Zartman term),[3] because any "solution" would require giving up some very important value.[4]

Louis Kriesberg adds that the conflicts we are concerned with are especially destructive. Some conflicts go on for a long time, but if they do not do damage, and if the parties are not worried about them, he does not consider them intractable. Intractable conflicts are conflicts that are doing substantial harm, yet the parties seem unable to extricate themselves—either alone or with outside help. This is because the perceived costs of "getting out" are still seen as higher than the costs of "staying in."[5]

Yet intractability is a perception, not a firm characteristic, which can be perceived differently by different people or groups. While some people may consider Israeli-Palestinian conflict to be intractable, others may not, because they see the costs of staying in as higher than the costs of an agreement.[6]

Perception is important, because it influences action. If a conflict is perceived to be intractable, then disputants are likely to engage in desperate measures, such as suicide bombings. Yet those very measures are likely to increase the intractability of the conflict. However, if a conflict is seen to be moving beyond intractability, then more credibility is given to the peacebuilders, the people on both sides and in the middle who are trying to broker some kind of agreement.

The key, it would seem, is not in denying that intractable conflicts exist, as they clearly do, but to develop an image of a "way out," not necessarily substantive, but at least procedural. In other words, people have to have the understanding that there are positive things they can do, even while they are stuck in the morass of an intractable conflict. There are positive actions that can be taken to transform the conflict from a destructive one to a constructive one, even if a full resolution cannot soon be found.

Indeed, even in the context of long-running seemingly intractable conflicts, particular disputes or "episodes" are settled. For example, a law can be passed providing greater or diminished access to abortions, an agreement can be reached regarding the terms of a cease-fire on the West Bank and Gaza Strip, or a Supreme Court decision can clarify what types of "Affirmative Action" programs are constitutional and which are not. Understood for what they are, such settlements are helpful. They often defuse tension and anger, and provide a vehicle for people working together. But they do not solve the underlying conflict, which must be confronted with a long series of settlements to different issues over a long period of time. Only after all the issues are confronted and successfully dealt with will a true "resolution" be found.

Causes of Intractability

The causes of intractability are varied. In earlier publications, we have listed three:

> Irreconcilable Moral Differences
> High-Stakes Distributional Issues
> Domination or "pecking order" conflicts

Irreconcilable moral differences are conflicts about right and wrong, good and evil. They may be rooted in different religions, different cultures, or different worldviews. For example, most abortion foes will not negotiate about an act they consider equivalent to murder; similarly, most homosexual rights advocates will not negotiate about their rights to equal treatment under the law. Rather, they will continue to fight for what they know is right, even if they know that, over the short term, they cannot win. What is important to them is that they are engaged in a noble crusade.

High-Stakes distributional issues are conflicts over "who gets what" when the item in contention is very valuable—often impossible to do without. People are unlikely to abandon continuing struggles over land, water, employment opportunities, and wealth in general. When there isn't enough to "go around," or when distribution is highly inequitable, these fights are likely to be especially bitter and destructive.

Domination or "pecking order" conflicts are conflicts over power and status: who is on top of the social and political hierarchy, and who is not. While people with higher status tend to win the distributional conflicts, more often than not, status conflicts go beyond distributional conflicts—they involve subjective assessments of an individual's or a group's "goodness," "value" or "social worth."

The presence of one or more of these characteristics does not automatically make a conflict intractable, but it makes it more likely to be at the intractable end of the continuum. And the more of these characteristics a conflict has, the farther left on the continuum (meaning the more intractable) a conflict is likely to be. All of these issues, for example, are combined in the identity conflicts which divide the many different ethnic, religious, class, and national groups which are at the center of so many of the world's tragic and deadly trouble spots. Identity conflicts involve conflicts over social status and privilege and the distribution of scarce resources, along with a moral component, since each group tends to believe in its own moral superiority. The combination of all three of these aspects makes these conflicts especially difficult to resolve.

Other authors suggest additional causes:

Peter Coleman makes a distinction between issues, context, and conflict dynamics.

Issues: The issues of intractable conflicts are varied, he says, but there tend to be multiple, inter-related issues relating to resources, values, power, and basic human needs. Another issue Coleman highlights is time. Intractable conflicts usually have "an extensive past, a turbulent present, and a murky future."[7] The hatred, the fear, and often the history of past atrocities are hard to let go of, which makes moving into a new relationship with the former "enemy" especially difficult.

Context: Many intractable conflicts, especially at the intergroup and international levels, are embedded in a context of long-standing differences and inequalities. They are "rooted in a history of colonialism, ethnocentrism, racism, sexism, or human rights abuses" which causes a large imbalance of power and what Edward Azar called "structural victimization," or what Johann Galtung called "structural violence." Both terms suggest that the low-power groups are harmed by the basic social structure of society.

Dynamics: Intractable conflicts tend to be self-perpetuating. Guy Burgess has often argued that the enemy is not the other side, but rather the process of escalation, that takes conflicts out of the disputants' control, and pushes them to act in increasingly extreme ways that would not, under other circumstances be considered remotely acceptable.[8] Indeed, unrestrained escalation is often what takes a formerly tractable conflict and turns it into an intractable one. Like a one-way road without a road going the other way anywhere to be found, escalation is easy to fall into. It is much harder to get out of.

Human needs are stressed by many other scholars as well, among them John Burton[9] and Herbert Kelman,[10] who believe that deep-rooted conflicts are caused by the absence of the fundamental needs of security, identity, respect, safety, and control. These needs, human needs theorists argue, are non-negotiable. As such, if they are absent, the resulting conflict will remain intractable until the structure of society is changed to provide such needs to all.

Identity, in particular, is a human need that is singled out by numerous authors (most notably Jay Rothman[11] and John Paul Lederach)[12] as a fundamental driver of intractable conflict. When identities are threatened, people respond very negatively and take either defensive or often also offensive action to protect what they see as the essence of themselves. Identity conflicts in particular are not negotiable interest-based conflicts, so if they are approached with interest-based negotiation, the settlements are likely to be temporary, at best.

Complexity: The sheer complexity of these problems also contributes to intractability. There are so many issues and parties that it is often not logistically possible to do all that is required to reconcile competing interests, even when such reconciliation is theoretically possible. Even when everyone knows "the way out," complexity can make it seemingly impossible to get there. Most observers, for instance, believe that the solution to the Israeli-Palestinian problem is a two-state solution (meaning the continuation of the State of Israel and the formation of a second state of Palestine), but there are so many difficult issues involved, no one seems to know how to get from here to there.

Social-Psychological Factors: Intractable conflicts typically have conflicts within groups as well as between groups. Morton Deutsch argues that these internal conflicts actually perpetuate the external conflict, as leaders need to perpetuate the external conflict to preserve their identity as a leader and to encourage group cohesiveness.[13] Fear of losing face also keeps leaders involved in conflicts that are doing more harm than good. If they see no way out that doesn't admit that all their previous sacrifices were wrong or in vain, they are likely to continue to call for more sacrifices, rather than admitting that they made a mistake.[14]

Consequences of Intractable Conflict

The consequences of intractable conflicts are huge, most of them negative, because intractable conflicts tend to be pursued in damaging and destructive ways. The violence that is very common in intergroup and international conflicts causes widespread loss of life and damage to property. This creates massive economic costs, which are supplemented by the costs of defense. But the social and psychological costs are huge too: the fear, the hatred, the anger, the guilt are difficult to deal with while the conflict is ongoing, and are equally difficult to remedy after the conflict has supposedly been resolved. In the Rwandan conflict, for example, the Rwandan children who either watched their parents be killed, or who were forced to kill others themselves, will probably never be psychologically healthy. How can these children put their lives back together and grow into productive adults? A few will, one hopes, but most, probably, will not.

Even conflicts that occur within violence limiting institutions—such as conflicts over abortion, sexual orientation, or race relations in the U.S. have significant negative socio-economic and psychological costs. They tear apart relationships, and challenge institutions (such as churches and schools) which spend much of their time dealing with these issues rather than focusing on their primary goals of education and/or spiritual growth and healing.

Intractable conflicts can be particularly paradoxical, as they cause disputants to destroy themselves and the things they value in an effort to destroy the other. They may even realize that this is happening, but they will continue, because the goal of destroying the other is seen as supreme (even though the reason to destroy the other is because you think they are out to destroy you). Needless to say, such situations are very destructive for all sides.

Beyond Intractability

As we said at the beginning of this essay, many of the participants in this project, as well as others, have felt that we should not use the term "intractable," because it sounds too hopeless. If conflicts are intractable, they said, that means nothing can be done about them. So why would people read this website, they asked?

We have several answers to this question.

First, even though intractable conflicts may not be amenable to final, near-term resolution, they are not hopeless. The parties, with or without the help of intermediaries, can move beyond intractability to make their interactions less destructive and more constructive. Even when conflicts cannot be resolved, parties can learn to live together with less distrust, overt hostility, and violence. They can learn to work with people on the other side, and come to understand the reason for their differences, even if those differences do not go away.

People who have engaged in dialogues about abortion, for example, do not change their attitudes about abortion. But they do change their attitudes about the people on the other side: they learn they are intelligent, thoughtful, caring, humans who, for a variety of reasons, see the issue of abortion differently. But they are people who can and should be respected, people who can even become one's friends.[15]

People caught up in ethnic conflicts, too, can learn to respect people on the other side, learning that they also are intelligent, thoughtful, caring humans who are caught up in a cycle of fear and violence that nobody wants. Working together to try to figure out how to disrupt that cycle is a positive way to respond to intractable conflict, and can make those conflicts less destructive, even as they continue.

Second, sometimes, seemingly endless, hopeless intractable conflicts are resolved. The Cold War is one example; South African apartheid is another. When we started working in this field in the 1970s, both conflicts seemed firmly entrenched. No one imagined the Berlin Wall falling, much less the disintegration of the Soviet Union and the inclusion of former Warsaw Pact countries in NATO. Few imagined the end of apartheid, with Nelson Mandela serving as president and former President F. W. de Klerk as one of his two deputy presidents. These amazing transformations prove that no matter how deep-rooted, widespread, and seemingly "endless," intractable conflicts do end. And even more are transformed, as is evidenced by the fragile, but growing peace in Northern Ireland.

Third, if we just ignore intractable conflicts, very often they will just get worse. Like an untreated infection, they will spread, getting "hotter and hotter," and doing more and more damage. As with untreated infections, in destructive conflicts, people will die. So ignoring them, though perhaps tempting, is not a good option.

While our field does not know how to stop these very difficult conflicts completely, we do know a lot about violence prevention and conflict transformation. The breadth and depth of our knowledge is illustrated in this knowledge base: it has over 200 entries now, and over 100 more will be available within the next few months, all discussing what we know about how to deal with intractable conflicts effectively.

However, we still have a lot to learn. Though over 100 people contributed to this website, we could not come close to including all of their knowledge, let alone all of the knowledge of others around the world who have been dealing with these conflicts every day. We welcome contributions from other people who have ideas to add to our collection. These problems are too difficult to assume that any one group of people "knows the answer." This website is a start, but we hope readers will help us make it better.

Since the nature of intractability was a central topic of discussion as this project was developing, we are including several essays on that topic. This is one; others have been contributed by Louis Kriesberg, who wrote several early books on the subject, and Jacob Bercovitch, who has been studying the use of mediation as a means to end intractable conflicts for many years.

Current Implications

The term "intractable" was controversial when we started to use it; it still is. However, more and more of the conflicts our communities and countries seem to be embroiled in now seem to fit this definition. We stand by the assertion that "intractable does not mean impossible" but it does mean really, really difficult to resolve.

And even when resolution seems to be achieved, it can later vanish. Reading through this essay in 2017, I hiccuped on the paragraph towards the end that says "sometimes, seemingly endless, hopeless intractable conflicts are resolved." It then cites the Cold War and South Africa as examples. The Cold War seems to be coming alive again, and while South Africa has not returned to apartheid, race relations and politics are not nearly as settled there as many of us hoped or believed. The same can be said for Northern Ireland, although "the Troubles" have not re-ignited in full force.

So continued vigilance is necessary with these conflicts, even after "resolution" has apparently been achieved.

Notes

1. Statement made at the first project conference in March of 2002.
2. For intractable conflict case studies, see *Grasping the Nettle: Analyzing Cases of Intractable Conflict.* Chester A. Crocker, Fen Osler Hampson, Pamela R. Aall, eds. 2005. <http://books.google.com/books?id=fshaG2v8O-YC>.

3. The presence or absence of a "way out" is discussed in Bill Zartman's discussions of Ripeness and Promoting Ripeness in this Knowledge Base.

4. Observation made by Morton Deutschin in a project discussion on the meaning of "intractability" in March 2002.

5. Ibid.

6. For a discussion of intractability in the Israeli-Palestinian conflict, see Stephen Cohen's "Intractability and the Israeli-Palestinian Conflict" in *Grasping the Nettle: Analyzing Cases of Intractable Conflict*. Chester A. Crocker, Fen Osler Hampson, Pamela R. Aall, eds. 2005. <http://books.google.com/books?id = fshaG2v8O-YC>.

7. See Peter Coleman's "Intractable Conflict" in *Handbook of Conflict Resolution*. Morton Deutsch, Peter Coleman, eds. (San Francisco: Jossey-Bass), 2000. 432.

8. See his essays on violence breakover, personalization breakover, as well as the main essay on escalation.

9. See *Conflict: Human Needs Theory*. John Burton. (New York: St. Martin's Press). 1993. <http://books.google.com/books?id = cryZPwAACAAJ>.

10. See *International Behavior: A Social Psychological Analysis*. Herbert Kelman, ed. (New York: Ardent Media Incorporated). 1980. <http://books.google.com/books?id = 5925PQAACAAJ>.

11. See *Resolving Identity-Based Conflicts in Nations, Organizations, and Communities*. Jay Rothman. (San Francisco: Jossey-Bass). 1997. <http://unitednationstest.beyondintractability.org/bksum/rothman-resolving>.

12. See *Building Peace: Sustainable Reconciliation in Divided Societies*. John Paul Lederach. (United States Institute of Peace). 1998. <http://www.beyondintractability.org/library/external-resource?biblio = 7829>.

13. See Morton Duetsch as discussed in the Intractable Conflict Knowledge Base Conference in March of 2002.

14. See the essay on entrapment.

15. See Anne Fowler and other's "Talking with the Enemy" in *The Boston Globe* Focus Section. 28 January 2001. <http://pubpages.unh.edu/~jds/BostonGlobe.htm>.

Moral Conflict

W. Barnett Pearce and Stephen W. Littlejohn

W. Barnett Pearce, known for his contributions to communications theory, received his PhD from Ohio University. He has taught at numerous universities while spending over fifteen years facilitating meetings throughout the world. He served as a Fulbright Fellow in Argentina in 1997. He now works via Pearce Associates, which offers training, consulting, facilitation, and research to non-profits and educational institutions. Stephen Littlejohn received his PhD from the University of Utah and worked as a professional mediator and facilitator while serving as a professor of communication at Humboldt State University in California for more than twenty-six years. His publications focus on the intersection of communication, conflict, and dialogue. In 2008, he received the Paul Bartlett Peace Prize for his international work in mediation. He now lectures at the University of New Mexico.

Pearce and Littlejohn discuss moral conflicts as clashes occurring when social groups differ in beliefs, needs, and desires. These differences are anchored in language and often the result of the moral order into which one is born. When people wish to order their lives differently than the predominant social model, conflict erupts. Groups can differ not only in their specific beliefs and ways of being, but they can also differ over the methods that produce moral values. This leads to distrust on both sides, even when groups make efforts toward peace. People do not know how to move beyond the moral orders in which they find themselves; their inflexibility is not presented as a character flaw but instead as an understandable consequence of invisible, albeit constraining, social rules.

The authors make a distinction between moral differences (suppressed) and moral conflicts (expressed), a distinction that resembles Johan Galtung's distinctions of negative and positive peace. Moral conflicts may present as simply different opinions on homosexuality, for example, but actually can represent deep clashes over a sense of world order. These conflicts can become quite vitriolic because participants see that differences in values and beliefs will produce different futures, different kinds of knowledge, and can ultimately transform societies. The groups in conflict intuitively seem to understand ways of life may be at stake. One group often wants to change the cultural topography, and the other wishes to maintain the existing structure. The authors describe moral conflicts as: 1) intractable; 2) interminable; 3) morally attenuated; and 4) rhetorically attenuated. The article describes each in detail. The authors propose third parties can help create a new grammar that allows these different languages about the world to communicate and co-create. With assistance, parties can recognize the differences and then move forward.

This reading reflects an Epoch Two approach because the authors point to identity as a source of conflict. They see identity as fixed and nonnegotiable. This approach expands the interests-based approach of Epoch One by encouraging negotiators and mediators to consider moral orders as well as desires and needs.

Question to consider: How might talking about conflict as "clashes" between groups further entrench conflict? What conflict have you experienced or witnessed that seemed intractable? Did it ever shift? If so, how?

The Problems of Moral Conflict

W. Barnett Pearce and Stephen W. Littlejohn

Back in the mid-1980s, before the current rage over television talk programs, we watched an amazing spectacle. Talk show host David Fenigan pitted a group of conservative Christians against gay and lesbian activists on the topic of gays in the church.

One has to imagine the scene to get the full impact. In a small television studio, three speakers were set up on stage. On the left was the director of the Unitarian Office of Gay and Lesbian Affairs; on the right was the chair of the Massachusetts Moral Majority, a Baptist minister; in the middle was a Reformed Jewish rabbi. We had to believe that the left-to-right arrangement was purposefully metaphoric.

The room was divided by an aisle separating the two audience groups. Perhaps a naive producer had some educational goal in mind, but we think the setup was more appropriate for a fireworks display on the Fourth of July. And fireworks is what we got.

Within minutes, the "discussion" degraded to a ruckus. The Moral Majoritarian made articulately degrading and insulting comments about the gay community, while his opponents attacked him for lacking humanity and Christian love.

Anger and hurt ran deep, as the Unitarian and Baptist shot salvos across the rabbi. At one point, the Baptist "reported" that the venereal disease rate in San Francisco was 22 times the national average and concluded, "I won't shake your hand."

This television program was but a skirmish in one of the great culture wars of our time. Hunter (1991) describes the situation:

> I define cultural conflict very simply as political and social hostility rooted in different systems of moral understanding. The end to which these hostilities tend is the domination of one cultural and moral ethos over all others. Let it be clear, the principles and ideals that mark these competing systems of moral understanding are by no means trifling but always have a character of ultimacy to them. They are not merely attitudes that can change on a whim but basic commitments and beliefs that provide a source of identity, purpose and togetherness for the people who live by them. It is for precisely this reason that political action rooted in these principles and ideals tends to be so passionate. (p. 42)

The new element in the contemporary culture war, Hunter (1991) notes, is that the "divisions of political consequence" are not, as they were in the past, "theological and ecclesiastical in character" but result from the clash of "differing worldviews . . . our most fundamental and cherished assumptions about how to order our lives—our own lives and our lives together in this society" (p. 42). Culture wars are based on more than value difference; they also involve clashing methods for establishing moral values. At issue, Hunter argues, is

> the matter of moral authority . . . the basis by which people determine whether something is good or bad, right or wrong, acceptable or unacceptable, and so on. . . . It is the commitment to different and opposing bases of moral authority and the world views that derive from them that creates the deep cleavages between antagonists in the contemporary culture war. (pp. 42–43)

Matters of Definition

We call the type of conflict Hunter describes above "moral conflicts." They happen when people deeply enmeshed in incommensurate social worlds come to clash. Because their social worlds are at odds, what they want, believe, and need differs, and the actions of those wants, beliefs, and needs do not fit in the world of the opponent. Because ways of dealing with conflicts are a part of one's social world, when these conflicts do occur, they lack a common procedure for dealing with them. Actions taken by one side to be good, true, or prudent are often perceived by the other as evil, false, or foolish—perhaps even sinister and duplicitous. The intensity of moral conflicts is fueled when such actions are treated as malicious or stupid by the other side.

This description of moral conflict was constructed on the basis of our research and in the writings of others who address similar issues. Our approach, for example, focuses on some of the same features highlighted in Thorson's (1989) notion of intractable conflicts. According to Thorson, in this type of conflict, what someone does as an attempt to resolve the conflict is likely to be perceived by the other participants as a curious or surprising move intended to win the conflict. Rather than resolving the dispute, well-intentioned acts intensify and prolong it.

In the same way, our description of moral conflicts resembles Burton's (1990) notion of real conflicts as opposed to mere disputes. In such conflicts, the basic issues are deeply embedded in the participants' moral orders and are not negotiable.

Although abstract definitions of moral conflicts are useful for certain purposes, they should not be pushed too far. Matters of definition involve a necessary trade-off between abstract terms that are useful for delineating categories and more specific terms that help describe actual events.

The danger of having an overly specific definition is illustrated by Hunter's (1991) analysis of culture wars. His account depends on—and is better because it includes—a specific reading of American history in which the influence of religion is emphasized and the goal of each side in the conflict is to dominate the others. At the same time, Hunter's discussion is relatively silent about the experiences of those outside the Judeo-Christian tradition. Although this degree of specificity serves his purpose well, we must be cautious about applying his definitions to other moral conflicts, such as the political disputes between Hindus and Muslims in India, Jews and Arabs in the Middle East, or Muslims, Chinese, and Indians in Malaysia (e.g., Mess & Pearce, 1986).

So although we believe we have a pretty good definition of moral conflict, we acknowledge the need to be careful with definitions. Somewhere, sometime, someone will show us a moral conflict that has somewhat different features. This chapter is designed to outline our theoretical approach to moral conflicts, with the full recognition that this, like every theory, is partial and may ignore certain aspects of moral conflicts that prove important in the end.

In our writing, we distinguish between moral difference and moral conflict (Littlejohn, 1994a; 1995b). As explained in chapter 5, moral differences may lie beneath the surface without expression, remaining suppressed and hidden. This is the genesis of oppression. On the other hand, moral differences sometimes are expressed in an open clash, which is the genesis of repression. In chapter 5, we discuss the difficult choices people make in deciding how and whether to express perceived moral differences. We characterize the set of choices faced by activists, peacemakers, and interested others as a dialectic between expression and suppression, a dialectic that must be managed in every case of moral difference.

The Heart of the Matter

Moral difference exists when groups have incommensurate moral orders. In this section, we look more closely at these two key terms—incommensurate and moral orders. Moral difference is more than differing opinions about whether one should get an abortion, have homosexual sex, or teach creation science because it lies at a deeper level. Groups that differ morally differ in how they view being, knowledge, and values. Moral differences may tend to be expressed on surface issues such as abortion, sexual orientation, and school curriculum, but the differences that lie deep in the moral order are rarely expressed directly.

A moral order is the theory by which a group understands its experience and makes judgments about proper and improper actions. It is a set of concepts and system of rules and standards for action (Wong, 1984). It is the basis for what most people think of as common sense (Wentworth, 1989). Amoral order thus provides a tradition of truth and propriety. Stout (1988) shows that every moral tradition holds certain images of order inviolate. Any action that threatens the concept of order within the tradition will be seen as an abomination, and what is a perfectly acceptable act within one tradition can be an abomination in another.

Moral orders can be understood in a variety of ways. According to Wittgenstein (1972), a moral order is a belief system of "subjective certainty" that consists of the things we do not doubt, or as Johnson (1990) puts it, the "things upon which we can regularly depend" (p. 20). Moral orders are akin to Berger, Berger, and Kellner's (1973) idea of the life plan, which is socially created and includes a sense of the individual's identity. Sennett (1970) sees the moral order as a means for establishing purity in life, "to build an image or identity that coheres, is unified, and filters out threats in social experience" (p. 9).

Knowledge itself is constructed from within a moral tradition (e.g., Harre, 1979, 1984). Reality is social, and the moral order within which it is constructed is a product of a historical process in which stories are told and retold and a moral tradition established. McGee (1984) makes this point clearly with an example:

> People do not simply "have" beliefs. . . . Beliefs are products of inter-
> action with the total environment—which is to say that people think
> in groups, from a particular perspective or mindset, and with the
> resources of an historically-grounded pattern of expectations. . . . It is
> sufficient for marketing purposes to know that Elmer Pitt is a 24-year-
> old steelworker in Gary, Indiana with $2,000 disposable income. . . . It
> may be more significant to know that Elmer is a deacon in his church
> and translates every experience into the terms of his Christian faith—a
> faith he has both inherited from the past as a condition of his life experi-
> ence and accepted enthusiastically of his own volition. (p. 2)

The moral order cannot be separated from the discourse used to produce it because the two form a loop, each affecting the other. We like to use the term *social reality* as a label for the set of meanings a person uses to interpret and act within a situation. Social realities are learned through communication with others during a lifetime. We are therefore interested in studying the ways in which people understand facts, issues, and conflicts as a function of their communication practices.

A social reality has been described as a production in which a group's "resources," or meanings and assumptions, are tightly intertwined with its practices (Pearce, 1989). Doing and thinking cannot really be separated. Our ways of thinking (our resources) are affected by our practices, and our practices are affected by our ways of thinking. A moral order, then, which is at the root of a group's resources, is constructed and reconstructed in what that group says and does.

The tight knot between the moral order and everyday practice is best illustrated with the twin terms *grammar* and *ability*. Every social situation has a grammar of action, sometimes flexible and sometimes rigid. If the situation is to be coherent, this grammar must be followed. Like the grammar of a sentence, however, there may be many variations of acceptable ways of acting, but it is not the case that "anything goes." If the grammar is not followed, the activity is incoherent. Unlike a sentence, however, most social situations require two or more people to coordinate their actions into a coherent "grammatical" sequence.

We take the metaphor of grammar from Wittgenstein's analysis of language games, in which the meaning of an act or utterance is determined by its place in a rule-governed sequence of events. For Wittgenstein, behavior occurs within structured contexts. He did not mean that games are trivial, such as playing golf as opposed to going to work, or manipulative, such as "games people play" (Berne, 1964). His famous dictum that "meaning is in use" refers to an action being a "move" in a rule-governed sequence of events that has implications far beyond its denotation. For example, "Knight to King's 8" means far more than the movement of a piece of carved wood on a painted square; it might be utter foolishness or an astonishingly brilliant play that guarantees the fame of the player, depending on its use in the game.

In addition, Wittgenstein argued that language games have a family resemblance and are themselves "moves" in a "form of life." When Martin Luther refused to recant his theological writings, his statement, "Here I stand; I can do no other," was not just an expression of some intrapsychic state. It was a strategic move at the juncture of different grammars of epistemology, morality, and authority. It changed history by setting off a sequence of events that reconstructed the dominant "form of life" in Europe.

The term *grammar* describes the structure of these games and that which connects them to each other within forms of life. But what is the relationship among different grammars? Is it possible to understand a grammar incommensurate with one's own? Although he did not use the term, Winch (1958) suggested that each grammar is a particular way of being human and that all grammars are various ways of being human. By exploring other grammars and forms of life, we can move in other social worlds.

> Ways of speaking are not insulated from each other in mutually exclusive systems of rules. What can be said in one context by the use of a certain expression depends for its sense on the uses of that expression in other contexts (different language games). Language games are played by men who have lives to live—lives involving a wide variety of different interests, which have all kinds of different bearings on each other. Because of this, what a man says or does may make a difference not merely to the performance of the activity upon which he is at present engaged, but to his life and to the lives of other people.

What we may learn by studying other cultures are not merely possibilities of different ways of doing things, other techniques. More importantly we may learn different possibilities of making sense of human
life, different ideas about the possible importance that the carrying out
of certain activities may take on for a man, trying to contemplate his
life as a whole. (p. 318)

We understand people to be "powerful particulars" (Harré, 1984) who have
abilities to act into such situations. By using the metaphor of abilities, we deliberately frame individuals' social performance as learned, variable, and open to critique, just as the ability to perform a musical instrument or play football is. We
are specifically interested in people's abilities to perform within the grammars of
specific situations, to relate to persons who live within other grammars, and to
move among language games.

As we use the term, moral orders have (on the moral side) little to do with
codes of sins and virtues and (on the order side) little to do with orderliness. We
chose the term *moral* because we want to emphasize that people's actions are based
in what seems good and right. We chose the term *order* because we want to emphasize that in a specific situation, there are always constraints on our actions in the
form of ideas about truth and right. These ideas are not abstract but are products
of the interaction we have with other people in our social groups. Actions and
ideas are closely tied together; our actions create ideas, and ideas constrain actions.
The term moral order, then, denotes the pattern of one's compulsions and permis-
sions to act in certain ways and one's prohibitions against acting in other ways.

In a sense, then, moral orders create the boundaries of what a person is able
to do. But the notion of abilities does not lend itself to the categorization of people
or prediction of their behaviors. An ability is always contingent on circumstances.
Such unpredictability is a crucial ingredient of social life. We like anthropologist
Frake's (1980) warning that "culture" is not "a script for the production of social
occasions" but "a set of principles for creating dramas, for writing scripts, and, of
course, for recruiting players and audiences."

Culture is not simply a cognitive map that people acquire, in whole or in part,
more or less accurately, and then learn to read. People are not just map-readers;
they are map-makers. People are cast out into the imperfectly charted, continually
shifting seas of everyday life. Mapping them out is a constant process resulting not
in an individual cognitive map, but in a whole chart case of rough, improvised,
continually revised sketch maps. . . . Different cultures are like different schools
of navigation designed to cope with different terrains and seas. In this school, one
must learn not only how to map out everyday life, but also how to fix one's
position, determine a destination, and plot a course. And because people do not
voyage alone, one must recruit a crew. Maps, positions, and courses must be
communicated and sold. The last time—on a real boat in a real sea—I tried to
sell a position and course to my crew . . . , I won the argument but promptly ran
the boat aground. That's the way life is. (pp. 6–7)

In our work, then, we wish to describe ways in which people together follow
grammars, or logics, in episodes and how social worlds are created in this process.

Most forms of conflict are played out within some frame, a grammar that provides options and moves from which to choose. One person's moves are governed by rules, but they are also governed in part by the contingent responses of the other person.

Moral conflict occurs when disputants are acting within incommensurate grammars. Because they (plural) are trying to play different games simultaneously, each (singular) finds his or her own abilities to act, to think, to feel, and to relate to others reduced by the actions of the other. In moral conflicts, new types of abilities are required—not just the ability to act skillfully within the context of one's own grammar but the ability to transcend one's own grammar, to join the grammars of others, and to weave these grammars together.

Moral conflicts mark the sites in our society in which incommensurate forms of life overlap. As we unwrap this text, we hope to show that new grammars and hence new games, even new forms of life, may become possible.

Our analysis takes the perspective that particular beliefs, sayings, or doings are not well understood if taken in isolation from everything else that the person involved believes, says, and does. Each utterance is the tip of a semantic iceberg; each action is part of an ecology of significations in which the relations among the acts define the meaning of the acts themselves. Each thing that we do or say is a move in a language game, and this language game, in turn, is part of a cluster of such games that compose a form of life. We are confronted at every moment with the question "What shall we do?" and that question is embedded within a matrix of obligations, prohibitions, duties, rights, and aspirations. These overlapping webs constitute what logicians call a deontic logic of "oughtness," which, we believe, is the substance of our positions as persons in conversations with others (Pearce, 1994; Pearce & Cronen, 1980).

Although the concept of deontic logic may seem a little stuffy, it is not removed from mundane experience. Indeed, it calls into relief those things that connect one person's acts to those of other people. The conclusion we reach when we use deontic logic is not just a proposition about a state of affairs—such as Socrates's man being mortal—but a sense that one ought to act in a particular way.

This deontic logic is sometimes powerfully felt as the compulsion to act in certain ways and refrain from acting in others. People often report that they have no alternative, that they simply have to (or cannot) act. Sometimes, this deontic logic is more subtle and not prescriptive. It may permit a range of actions or allow choice. In general, here is how we reason deontically:

> When people like them do that kind of thing, in a situation like this, someone like me "must," "should," "may," or "must not" respond by taking this action, because that will make them do what they should, and I can confirm my concept of self and transform my relationship with them.

If, for example, the members of a militia believe that (a) there is an international conspiracy to take over the United States and form a one-world government, (b) this will mean an end of our cherished liberties, and (c) the only way to prevent this is to prepare to resist, then they will conclude that right-minded people should form an armed organization, go to boot camp, and have weekend drills.

People give ordinary descriptions of this deontic logic when they account for their actions or talk about their motives and intentions. Our vocabulary of passion, interest, and fear consists of various ways of connecting our actions to those of others and the world around us. One of the reasons groups in conflict have trouble breaking the pattern of interaction between them is that each is sealed into its own deontic logic, caught in the loop of its moral order.

As a case in point, consider the "beautiful choice" television commercials of the early 1990s (Littlejohn, 1993). The campaign consisted of a number of "gentle" television commercials opposing abortion. It was put together by the Arthur S. DeMoss Foundation, a Christian organization that gives money to conservative causes such as Campus Crusade for Christ, Walk Thru the Bible Ministries, the Pat Boone Foundation, and the Fellowship of Christian Athletes.

The commercials are highly professional 30-second spots. Most feature the celebration of the birth and life of children who might otherwise have been aborted. (One expresses the regrets of a mother who did choose abortion; another features a child who survived an abortion attempt.) All the commercials end with the slogan "Life. What a Beautiful Choice."

The content of the advertisements is highly emotive and features attractive people usually in happy scenes with lovely background music. They are, as one observer noted, reminiscent of Hallmark card ads (Ames, Leonard, Lewis, & Annin, 1992). We know of seven commercials in the campaign. The discourse, linguistic and visual, of the entire series of commercials provides an idea of the elements of the moral order tied to it. The moral order reflected in the DeMoss commercials is consistent with that of religious antiabortion rhetoric in general. A substantial overlap seems to exist between the moral categories in the DeMoss commercials and those found in our earlier studies of the Religious Right (Pearce, Littlejohn, & Alexander, 1987,1989), including the dimensions of simplism, moralism, monism, and preservationism, categories defined earlier by Lipset and Raab (1970).

Simplism is the notion that life's situations are not really complex. They may be problematic, but the available lines of action are few in number and easy to separate. The essential ingredients of the problem are always the same, and particular individuals and context have little to do with it. In all cases, one can and should make a clear decision in favor of one course of action over the other.

In antiabortion rhetoric, simplism requires that we view the unplanned pregnancy as a simple, if anxiety-provoking, situation. One's unique circumstances do not change the nature of the situation. There are two choices, abort or give birth, as the DeMoss commercials clearly express.

This moral tenet differs substantially from the idea commonly found in pro-abortion discourse that problematic situations are complex and that their solutions are not simple. In deciding what to do about an unwanted pregnancy, a woman must weigh several factors. The right thing to do in one set of circumstances is not the same as that in another. Furthermore, the options are several, and they are not simple. From a pro-choice perspective, any decision a woman might make entails consideration of a large number of other possibilities.

The second dimension of this system of thought is moralism. Moralism defines all action in moral terms. In other words, one's actions can always be defined as good or bad, right or wrong. This premise allows one to choose among the few possible responses to a problem on the basis of which is best. Good decisions follow the path that is morally clear and leads to the prescribed state, whereas bad decisions prevent the achievement of this goal. The DeMoss spots clearly express this tenet. One choice, birth, is good; the other, abortion, is bad. Giving birth will lead to desired ends, whereas having an abortion will lead to undesirable ones. There is no middle ground.

In contrast, pro-choice advocates are less able to judge individual choices as good or bad. A choice may be considered good and bad, involving both advantages and disadvantages. Pro-choice advocates are less able to define a single desired moral state. Instead, moral outcomes are considered highly relativistic and individual.

Moralism requires the presence of another dimension, monism, or the use of a clear set of standards for right and wrong. It is the adoption of a doctrine to guide moral choice. The standard of good and evil, usually prescribed by an authority, is clearly stated and can be applied in all situations. For the Religious Right, this standard is usually scriptural, and the states to which we aspire are defined by God. In conservative Judeo-Christian thought, only God can give and take life, making clear the conservative religious stand on abortion and euthanasia.

The pro-choice movement, of course, is based on a moral premise quite at odds with monism. People become pro-choice advocates in part because they do not believe single moral authorities can be trusted. Their rhetoric expresses a much more situational ethic, in which courses of action are decided on the basis of individual needs and situational circumstances.

The fourth dimension of the religious antiabortion moral order is preservationism, a quality of most conservative thought. Values that are perceived to be maintained through time are considered good and to be protected. Such ideas are sustained by consensus within the community because they protect the community. They are usually based on time-tested virtues or expectations for how individuals should behave (MacIntyre, 1981).

The contrast between the preservationism in antiabortion rhetoric and the individualism of pro-choice rhetoric is striking. For pro-choice advocates, *Roe v. Wade* (1973) was a moral victory because it departed from traditional arrangements that were viewed as oppressive to women.

Our analysis of the "beautiful choice" campaign shows that it is possible to learn something about a moral order by looking carefully at the discourse produced as part of it. Moral orders, however, resist precise description because they are not objects standing still for our inspection, and we do not occupy a pristine position from which to describe them.

> In every instance . . . we are partly insiders with immediate awareness
> of what it is to be, and partly outsiders looking at surfaces. The dual

role, the in-and-out movement of the mind seeking to penetrate its object, frames every experience with the irony of its own finitude. In the distractions of practical life and in the security of theorizing alike we may lose sight of that irony. (Wheelwright, 1954, p. 13)

To understand and work with a particular moral order, however, we will need to develop a language that permits us to understand it and, as we will see later, to compare it with others. Some useful concepts for making perspicuous contrasts are found in the scholarly literature.

For example, Cooper (1981) differentiated individual, social, and anchored moralities, each of which may be either monolithic (based on single premises) or polylithic (based on multiple premises). In monolithic moral orders, everything is seen as related to simple moral principles, whereas in polylithic ones, issues are seen as separated and context bound. This distinction helps to clarify one difference between the pro-life and pro-choice positions described above.

Nisbett (1966) made a distinction between moral orders built on rights and those built on virtues. A rights-oriented order is based on the individual as the independent unit of action. It assumes individual differences, and moral actions promote the dignity and choice of persons. A virtues-oriented order is based on the community as the unit of action. Individual differences are insignificant, whereas group differences are important. Proper actions conform to social expectations, promote the welfare of the community, and thereby award honor. Many of the most vexing social issues in contemporary society seem to reflect these distinctions, but in interesting ways. For example, a claim of a woman's right to control her own body leads to actions that make great sense within a rights-oriented moral order but that are incomprehensible within a virtues-oriented one.

A historian or anthropologist exploring the sediments of history in the rights- and virtues-oriented moral orders will uncover particular forms of society and ways of being human associated with each. As a structuring concept, individual rights emerge from the particular historical context of the Enlightenment and modernity; a virtues-based approach emerges from traditional society. As detailed elsewhere (Pearce, 1989), part of these moral orders have to do with ways of conducting conflict. When modernists act in ways that seem obligated and good within their moral order, these very acts offend traditionalists and "prove" the perfidy of the modernists. At the same time, when traditionalists act in ways that seem obligated and good within their own moral order, they "prove" their ignorance and intransigence to the modernists. As such, the ways in which the various sides act in the conflict themselves become the issue in the conflict.

In sum, then, moral difference is defined by differing moral orders, each constructed within a tradition of communication. But these differences are never simple. A moral difference is characterized by another term we find ourselves using frequently—incommensurate. Differing moral orders are incommensurate.

The idea of incommensurate differences is probably most commonly attributable to Kuhn, who used the term to describe different scientific paradigms. In *The Structure of Scientific Revolutions* (1970), he wrote,

The proponents of competing paradigms practice their trades in different worlds. . . . One is embedded in a flat, the other in a curved, matrix of space. Practicing in different worlds, the two groups of scientists see different things when they look from the same point in the same direction. Again, that is not to say that they can see anything they please. Both are looking at the world, and what they look at has not changed. But in some areas they see different things, and they see them in different relations one to the other. That is why a law that cannot even be demonstrated to one group of scientists may occasionally seem intuitively obvious to another. Equally it is why, before they can hope to communicate fully, one group or the other must experience the conversion that we have been calling a paradigm shift. Just because it is a transition between incommensurables, the transition between competing paradigms cannot be made a step at a time, forced by logic and neutral experience. Like the gestalt switch, it must occur all at once [though not necessarily in an instant] or not at all. (p. 150)

Scientists from incommensurate traditions may have trouble talking to one another because they use a different vocabulary and logic, but this does not mean that they cannot talk to one another at all. Incommensurate systems of thought cannot be mapped point by point onto one another, but they can be compared. Bernstein (1985) made incommensurability a key concept in his analysis of contemporary philosophy and social theory, and he focused on a type of openness that permits comparison:

What is sound in the incommensurability thesis is the clarification of just what we are doing when we do compare paradigms, theories, language games. We can compare them in multiple ways. We can recognize losses and gains. We can even see how some of our standards for comparing them conflict with each other. We can recognize—especially in cases of incommensurability in science—that our arguments and counter-arguments in support of rival paradigm theories may not be conclusive. We can appreciate how much skill, art, and imagination are required to do justice to what is distinctive about different ways of practicing science and how "in some areas" scientists "see different things." In underscoring these features, we are not showing or suggesting that such comparison is irrational but opening up the types and varieties of practical reason involved in making such rational comparisons. (pp. 92–93)

Comparing incommensurate worldviews of any sort, whether scientific theories or the moral orders of antiabortion and pro-choice activists, is not easy. It is an art and, like any art, can be learned and evaluated. Bernstein (1985) wrote,

The skill or the art here (and it is a rare art) is to do this in a manner that avoids two extremes—the extreme of mutely contemplating something without any understanding, and the extreme of too easily and facilely projecting our own well-entrenched beliefs, attitudes, classifications, and symbolic forms onto the alien phenomenon. While this is an art that requires patience, imagination, attention to detail, and insight—and cannot be completely captured by the specification of rules of procedure—it is certainly a rational activity in which we can discriminate better and worse understandings and interpretations of the phenomenon. (p. 91)

As an abstract term, incommensurate moral orders is somewhat vague but, we think, useful. These terms sensitize us to the form of conflict that seems most difficult to manage well. Our perspective as communication theorists orients us away from propositions about moral conflict and toward the real world of actions and meanings. We take as the primary data what real people in real situations actually say and do to and with each other, and our interest, ultimately, is to do something in moral conflicts that will help manage them better. By being sensitized, to the moral orders in which specific acts occur and their differences, we are challenged to intervene in ways that do not oversimplify the situation.

Special Issues in Moral Difference

As we study the dimensions of moral orders, we are struck by the importance of certain issues that have not yet been addressed in this book. We think these are important enough to bring out early on, so we address them now. Specifically, we are talking about culture, empowerment, and emotion.

CULTURAL ISSUES

Precisely because realities are socially constructed, culture is a powerful influence on the moral order. Persons are always cultural because they are always born into and live in a culture, but persons are also individuals because no two people have identical socialization histories. Some people are more or less monocultural, even traditional, and possess a rather unified worldview shared with many other members of the culture. Others are multicultural and have a more diverse, sometimes even contradictory, worldview. So we never know exactly how other people will respond, although we can always bet that the response will be in some way or another cultural.

In the natural course of events, we usually assume that the other people with whom we are engaged share a common cultural view. Often, however, this is not the case. Cultural divergence becomes painful in conflict situations when others challenge our common expectations about how to proceed (e.g., Donohue & Bresnahan, 1994). Problems arise when one party in essence says to the other, "People like us don't do it that way." Behind this feeling is a more fundamental fact: "People like us don't think about things that way." Thus, thinking itself differs from one culture to another, making cultural forms fundamentally moral.

A number of writers have reflected on the moral basis of cultural difference. Carbaugh (1985), for example, describes cultural differences as the dominant and oppositional symbols that are important to members of a group. Many Americans, for example, treat symbols of the nation such as the flag as significant and contrast these with symbols of internationalism and world government such as the United Nations. For other cultures, this national-international distinction is meaningless. Some cultures hold up symbols of the family as significant and look at symbols of individual autonomy as antithetical to that. Some cultures revere religious symbols and consider profane ones in opposition; for others, the sacred-profane distinction is not part of the moral order. For any set of symbols and oppositions that frame a culture's moral order, some other group will find the distinction insignificant.

The many ways in which cultural ideas vary are well documented (Triandis & Albert, 1987). These include, among others, broad versus narrow, abstract versus concrete, personal versus nonpersonal, and process versus product. Often these differences correspond with varying beliefs about what constitutes moral action. Different cultures have different ideas about what is appropriate and inappropriate, desirable and undesirable, behavior.

Especially important are ideas about how conflict should be handled. For example, men in "Teamsterville" (the working class in South Side Chicago) handle their differences by insults, threats, and fighting (Philipsen, 1975). In the Navajo Peacemaking Court, by contrast, a dispute is never considered an isolated incident between two individuals and is not handled by trading insults or blows. For the Navajo, the dispute always affects the families and the larger community. The peacemaker meets with the entire family, provides structure, makes suggestions, asserts Navajo values, and teaches the parties how to restore community (Fagre, 1995).

Like Teamsterville and the Navajo Nation, most cultures of the world have some form of third-party intervention in disputes (Merry, 1989). Our colleague Jonathan Shailor (1988) reviews 15 case studies of conflict resolution across cultures from the ethnographic literature, ranging from the Assadi of Iran to the Baptists of Hopewell, Georgia. Shailor notes many differences in how the peoples of the earth think about, express, and resolve their differences. As an example, consider the role of talk in conflict resolution:

> Some theorists assume that maximizing the exchange of information between disputants is an important means of developing a satisfactory compromise. In other words, "the more communication, the better." Five cases from the current corpus directly contradict this assumption. In "Teamsterville" [South Side Chicago], talk geared toward producing mutual understanding is often considered an invitation to violence. . . . In some cases of mediation in Iran, mutual misunderstanding between disputants is the goal of the mediator. In separate private sessions, the mediator attempts to convince each disputant that he/she has successfully "rubbed the nose of the opponent in the dirt." Clearly, in both Teamsterville and Iran, "mutual understanding" through "more" or "better" communication is not a culturally valued goal. Neither is it among the "Yanuyanu" or the Ilongot, or on the island of Kiriwina. (pp. 197–98)

The use of silence also varies across cultures. Fagre (1995) compared the place of silence in the Navajo Peacemaking Court on the reservation and non-Navajo mediations in the Albuquerque Metropolitan Court. The Navajos generally saw words as powerful. For them, silence was a way to protect against harming others or damaging interpersonal harmony. For the non-Navajos, silence was uncomfortable and signaled something wrong.

We live in a world in which numerous cultural groups, not all ethnic, regularly bump against one another. This is certainly the case in many communities in the United States. In the Southwest, for example, Native American, Hispanic, and Anglo cultures frequently interact, and intercultural mediations are common. One of us recently heard a Hispanic mediator say that he feels quite comfortable mediating disputes within his own group of "native" Spanish in northern New Mexico but is at a loss in handling disputes among Mexican Americans in the southern part of the state. With comments such as this, it is no wonder that mediation administrators in the Southwest, like those in many other parts of the country, are increasingly concerned about the inter-cultural problem.

EMPOWERMENT ISSUES

Another source of moral difference consists of ideas about empowerment. What does it mean to have power? A woman once declined a friend's invitation to an event because, as she said, "My husband won't let me do that." From the friend's feminist perspective, that looked like pure submission. The feminist did not realize, however, that this woman's husband got liver for dinner that night.

We cannot tell the power arrangements between two people by watching them interact for a short time because we do not know what their actions mean to them from the perspective of their own system. What may appear to be aggressive behavior by a spouse may be quite submissive when we better understand what the interaction means to the couple itself.

Empowerment can never be divorced from the context of meaning and action in which persons are operating. Before we can ask how to empower someone, we must ask other questions first: Empowerment toward what end? What counts as empowerment within the moral community? For people with communitarian ideals, empowerment does not mean learning to act in a self-determined way. For people with an expressive-emotive notion of the word, empowerment means being able to say (verbally or nonverbally) what they feel. For those whose reality is based on hierarchy, empowerment means perpetuating the system and maintaining their place of honor within it. Only in the most utilitarian and individualistic moral orders does empowerment mean the ability to maximize personal interest.

Empowerment is often important in conflict resolution settings. Most American mediators, for example, consider empowerment to mean creating a set of conditions in which each disputant can achieve self-determination (Shailor, 1994). This is a thoroughly monocultural view. To the extent that good outcomes are beneficial to both parties, this view of empowerment means that disputants are enabled to cooperate in achieving a joint solution that meets both of their interests.

Bush and Folger (1994) see this condition as a dual process in which empowerment is the twin of recognition. Empowerment occurs "when disputing parties experience a strengthened awareness of their own self-worth and their own ability to deal with whatever difficulties they face, regardless of external restraints" (p. 84), and recognition occurs when they "experience an expanded willingness to acknowledge and be responsive to other parties' situations and common human qualities" (p. 85). This idea of empowerment is appropriate in certain moral orders but not in all. Critics (e.g., Harrington, 1986; Littlejohn, 1995a) are quick to point out that ideas of power based on individualism and neutrality may actually disempower individuals from cultures that do not share this reality.

EMOTIONAL ISSUES

No discussion of conflict would be complete without addressing the role of emotion. People come to clash because of their passions. People engaged in significant conflicts "feel" strongly and experience emotion. Some say that extreme reactions in conflict situations are primarily emotional.

People normally experience emotions as raw and real. Anger, joy, and sadness are nothing more than what they are—anger, joy, and sadness. Experiencing emotions as pure and universal, disconnected from the moral order, is perfectly understandable because emotions seem to come on us as a natural state, and we feel them physiologically.

But those feelings are labeled, understood, and acted on in ways that are socially constructed. The meaning of emotions and how they should be handled, like all aspects of human action, arise in moral orders. According to Averill (1986), emotional concepts consist of rules and norms that define what certain feelings should be taken to mean, whether they should be considered positive or negative, and how they should be played out. What do anger, grief, elation, and envy look like? These emotions are "performed" and identified differently in different cultures. And they may not even exist in some cultures.

Consider, for example, what we have to presume to feel jealous. First, we must believe that individuals engage one another in relationships. Second, we must have a concept such as loyalty or exclusivity in relationships. Third, we must see ourselves as separate from others but in need of others. Many cultures of the world do not have concepts for separateness, relational loyalty, individual autonomy, or dependence, and in such cultures, jealousy would be a foreign emotion.

Some emotions are now obsolete because we no longer have the beliefs that make them possible (Harré, 1984). An example is accidie, which was commonly suffered in the Middle Ages. We have no way today accurately to define this term, but it is something like guilt arising from not having fulfilled one's spiritual obligations. Melancholy is another term we no longer use today. It was something like a state of depression, but not exactly that. It had a good dose of wistful nostalgia connected with it.

So it is not inconceivable that individuals embroiled in a conflict may understand and act on their emotions somewhat differently. Many North Americans see emotions as contained within them (Carbaugh, 1988). We hear expressions such as "bursting with joy," "full of anger," "boiling over," "letting off steam," "brimming with pride," and "holding it in." The container idea of emotion is a socially constructed one, and not all groups experience emotion in this way. For example, some people talk about emotion as "being possessed."

Some therapists and mediators encourage clients to engage in emotional venting. Virtually every mediation training in the United States teaches that disputants should be given an opportunity to vent their pent-up emotions if necessary. The idea here is that emotions will get in the way of rational negotiation and must be reduced by letting the emotions out.

Have you ever talked to emotional persons who seemed to get more and more worked up as they spoke? They don't seem to calm down with venting. With this type of person, expressing feelings is more like "rehearsing" than venting. For others, expressing feeling is more like getting the other person's attention than letting out tension. Still other people come from a tradition in which emotions are not something to be let out but something to be controlled.

As a consequence of these different ideas about different emotions, some people find venting alienating, embarrassing, or just plain inappropriate. There are people who see the expression of emotions as a private and personal thing that is never done in the presence of others, certainly not around a stranger such as a mediator. Others see the expression of feeling as a way of showing affection, concern, and caring, not venting. And some use emotional expression as a way to tell others that they really mean what they are saying.

Ideas about emotions—what they are, where they are located, and what to do about them—are deeply embedded in the moral order. For some people, "telling it like it is" is the best way to communicate with others. For other people, "controlling your emotions" is an act of adult responsibility. For still others, emotion is a resource to be used strategically to gain power and change things. Each of these modes of response is appropriate, right, and good from the perspective of the communicator's moral order, but it is appropriate, right, and good only in the context of many other related ideas that constitute the communicator's moral order. One cannot divorce the construction of emotion from the totality of a person's belief system.

Moral difference is part of the human condition. Let us turn now to a more careful examination of what happens when social worlds come to clash.

From Difference to Clash

How do you know a moral conflict when you see one? There is no formula, but certain markers (we hate to use the term "red flags') will be apparent:

1. The participants use the same vocabulary but mean different things by it. For example, honor for one means martial excellence, but for the other, economic success.

2. The participants use different vocabularies for comparable functions. For example, one uses a vocabulary of rights and the other a vocabulary of virtues to discuss morality.

3. The participants describe themselves as locked into opposition with each other. For example, they deny that they have any choices and claim that "in a situation such as this, when they do what they did, a person like me has no alternative, I must. . ."

4. Actions that one side thinks will defuse the situation or even resolve the conflict are perceived by those on the other side as demonstrating the perfidy of the first and obligating them to respond by continuing or intensifying the conflict.

5. Participants are unable to articulate the logic of the other side's social world in ways that the other side will accept.

6. The discourse between the conflicted groups contains a large number of statements about what is wrong with the other group.

7. If asked to imagine a resolution to the conflict, the participants can think only of capitulation and elimination of the other group.

Our studies have led us to expect moral conflicts to have four general characteristics. They are (1) intractable, (2) interminable, (3) morally attenuated, and (4) rhetorically attenuated.

Moral Conflicts Are Intractable

Moral conflicts tend to be intractable in two senses. They are intractable, first, because they are self-sustaining. The original issue becomes irrelevant, and new causes for conflict are generated by the actions within the conflict itself. The means by which the conflicted parties seek resolution become the provocation of continued conflict.

How do we resolve a conflict about a matter of theology when one person appeals to the definitive interpretation by a religious leader and another denies the legitimacy of that leader? How do we resolve a question of political legitimacy when one side appeals to the constitutionality of its position and the other intends to set aside or rewrite the constitution? In contemporary society, the question of how to deal with others who do not think and act like us is a difficult challenge (Pearce, 1993).

Traditional ways of dealing with conflicts assume that there should be an agreed-on way of dealing with conflicts. This agreed-on procedure may specify duels to the death, impartial judicial proceedings, or the decree of the king, but whatever their content, they provide an agreed-on context or frame within which conflicting parties may manage their conflict. In contemporary society, however, this common frame is not always present. In moral conflicts, the conflicting parties not only find themselves at loggerheads about some issue but also disagree about how to go about resolving their conflict. In many cases, each is morally repulsed by actions that the other takes as the appropriate means of resolving the conflict.

Social worlds collide when attempts to resolve even the most ordinary conflicts of mundane life (the problem of garbage removal and disposal?) reveal that we (whoever we might be) disagree with them (whoever they might be) not only about garbage but also about what means of resolving our differences are morally right, aesthetically preferred, and politically prudent. The question of which one of us is right has produced many a quarrel, but this question is much more tractable than the question of how we should go about determining which one of us is right. Should we resolve our conflict by ballot, bullet, or Bible? Should we persuade each other with good reasons, consult the entrails of a chicken, or conduct a media campaign to convince a plurality of the voters to support our side of the controversy? Should we employ the services of third-party intervention agents, or should we kill or disempower those who disagree with us (including those pesky third-party intervention agents)?

Whatever the issue or cause of conflict in contemporary society, it risks mobilizing groups with incommensurate traditions. In moral conflicts, when each group tries to act consistently with what they perceive is morally good, ethically just, and politically expedient, they "prove" to the other side that they are fools or villains. As the conflict continues, the originating issue is lost and the other side's means of dealing with the conflict is itself the force that drives the interactions among the various conflicted parties.

The originating cause of moral conflicts quickly disappears from the public discourse or is cited more as a club with which to beat one s opponent than an issue to be resolved. Public discourse often focuses on the ways in which the other side's methods of handling conflict are morally depraved.

So moral conflicts are intractable because they are self-sustaining. They are intractable, too, because, ironically, perpetuating the conflict seen is virtuous by those involved. These individuals are not always—or even usually—oriented toward finding a solution; instead, they may derive important aspects of their identity from being warriors or opponents of their enemy (Northrup, 1989). Conflicts are often treated as if they are disagreements between people who want to settle, but the continuation of conflicts offers highly desirable roles to some participants. Some moral orders even sanctify the role of combatant. If the conflict were to disappear, those most deeply enmeshed in it would miss it most. Coser (1964) noted that conflict is not just a matter of clashing ideas but "a struggle over values or claims to status, power, and scarce resources, in which the aims of the conflicting parties are not only to gain the desired values but also to neutralize, injure, or eliminate their rivals" (p. 232).

On some occasions, the continuation of a conflict is preferable to what would have to be given up if an accommodation with the other side were reached. Azar (1990) suggests that moral conflicts originate in basic human needs, such as "security, distinctive identity, social recognition of identity, and effective participation in the processes that determine conditions of security and identity, and other such developmental requirements" (p. 146). The costs of prolonged conflict might seem easily bearable if these matters were at stake. Those deeply enmeshed in a moral conflict may be unable to discern the effects of the conflict itself, even if those effects themselves threaten the basic human needs that compel the conflicted parties to continue their conflict.

Public discourse in moral conflicts contains the "power words" of the participants. Because the actions of the other side are seen as alien, the discourse seldom stays focused on specifics; it quickly moves to sweeping generalizations, oracular pronouncements, and abstract principles.

Hunter (1991) notes that the conflict between the "progressives" and the "orthodox" is "not just an expression of different 'opinions' or 'attitudes' on this or that issue, like abortion." Rather, "the culture war emerges over fundamentally different conceptions of moral authority, over different ideas and beliefs about truth, the good, obligation to one another, the nature of community, and so on" (p. 49). As a result, the proponents cite God, patriotism, sanity, freedom, the Founding Fathers, or whatever else constitutes their foundational authority.

This excerpt from an argument (quoted by Hunter, 1991) between Randall Terry, a spokesperson for the pro-life organization Operation Rescue, and Faye Wattleton, then president of Planned Parenthood, shows how the issue is fought not on specific issues of policy but on the larger issues of how one's moral order is structured.

> Terry: The bottom line is that killing children is not what America is all about. We are not here to destroy our offspring.
> Wattleton: Well, we are also not here to have the government use women's bodies as the instrument of the state, to force women into involuntary servitude.
> Terry: (laughing) Oh, come on, Faye.
> Wattleton: I think that as Americans celebrate the Fourth of July, our independence, and when we reflect on our personal liberties, this is a very, very somber time, in which the courts have said that the most private aspects of our lives are now . . . not protected by the Bill of Rights and the Constitution. And I believe that this is a time for Americans to reflect on the need to return to the fundamentals, and the fundamentals of personal privacy are really the cornerstones upon which our democracy is built.
> Terry: I think that to assume or even suggest that the founding fathers of this country risked their lives and many of them died so that we can kill our offspring is pathetic. (p. 49)

Note the power words. Terry introduces the phrase "what America is all about." Wattleton offers some portion of her understanding of the term, identifying "personal liberties" as the key, equating control over "women's bodies" with "involuntary servitude," and citing "personal privacy" as a "cornerstone" of the constitutional guarantees of liberties. Terry does not refute her attempt to articulate "what America is all about" but pronounces it "pathetic," and the by now familiar pattern of public discourse in moral conflict continues.

Moral Conflicts Are Interminable

Moral conflicts are interminable because they are intractable, but they are interminable for other reasons as well. In moral conflicts, the issues cannot be adequately described in the terms that any of the participants would supply. Because their moral orders differ, they disagree about the meaning and significance of the issues, tactics, or potential resolution. As Wittgenstein (1969) said, "When language-games change, then there is a change in concepts, and with the concepts me meanings of words change" (p. 65).

We have been told of the failure of a well-meaning negotiator who urged both sides of an international conflict to be willing to compromise. One side, valuing compromise as a necessary and virtuous means of democratic politics, readily agreed; the other, for whom compromise meant an irresponsible and immoral surrender of one's principles, was offended and broke off negotiations.

MacIntyre (1981) believes that moral conflicts have "no terminus" and thus "go on and on and on" (p. 6) because the contemporary language of morality is disordered. We inhabit, he suggests, fragments of various intellectual traditions and put them together in incompatible ways. Thus the debate about U.S. military intervention in the next Third World country selected for this honor cannot come to resolution because the disputants are, unknown to themselves, arguing from different moral positions. Even if we can get back to the original positions, we have no basis for choosing among them; thus the conflicts continue unabated.

> It is precisely because there is in our society no established way of deciding between these claims that moral argument appears to be necessarily interminable. From our rival conclusions we can argue back to our rival premises; but when we do arrive at our premises argument ceases and the invocation of one premise against another becomes a matter of pure assertion and counter-assertion. Hence perhaps the slightly shrill tone of so much moral debate. (MacIntyre, 1981, p. 8)

There is relatively little extension of arguments in moral conflict. Each side understandably becomes reticent about offering its cherished beliefs when the other side criticizes those beliefs and/or uses them as "proof" of the other's mistakes. Arguments are not extended because they go past each other by using incommensurate terms and meanings. Even if the participants in a moral conflict wanted to extend their argument, they would be frustrated.

Public discourse in moral conflict is filled with predictable misunderstandings and erroneous perceptions of the other. Key terms for one side are passed over as unimportant by the other or are defined and used differently. For example, in his analysis of culture wars, Hunter (1991) noted that both sides use the same terms—freedom and justice—but with "almost precisely inverted" meanings. "Where cultural conservatives tend to define freedom economically (as individual economic initiative) and justice socially (as righteous living), progressives tend to define freedom socially (as individual rights) and justice economically (as equity)" (p. 115).

A common pattern in moral conflict is the juxtaposition of incommensurate assertions, followed by a stunned silence or pause after which each side acts as its own moral order suggests. Each participant is surprised and offended by the other's actions and denounces it. Each takes offense at being denounced and protests its own virtue. . . and so it goes.

Public Discourse in Moral

Conflict Is Morally Attenuated

Participants in moral conflict often abandon what their own moral order values as the "best" forms of behavior. During the Cold War, for example, the West engaged in many undemocratic practices because it was "forced" to do so by the actions of its enemy, the international communist bloc.

Those who engage in conflict always run the risk of coming to resemble the other—their "enemy"—with whom they are locked in the most intimate of embraces. Gay rights activists sometimes sound awfully hateful when they accuse their opponents of being hatemongers. We can delude ourselves into thinking that "our" new weapons are good but that "their" new weapons are threats to peace. The dreadful irony is that in the very process of combating that which we despise, we become it.

Less metaphysically, conflict always privileges some tactics over others, and there is no reason to assume that the values of one's moral order fit perfectly with the winning tactics in a particular conflict. Given a discrepancy, will the ideal or pragmatic prevail? Those who prize integrity over success may preserve their integrity but lose the contest; those who prize success may win the contest but not recognize themselves when they ascend to the victor's platform.

In moral conflict, demonization of the opponent is a particularly seductive strategy. Once demonized, any other dirty trick, from simply excluding them from polite conversation to wars of extermination, seems appropriate.

Our capacity to live peaceably with each other depends upon our ability to converse intelligibly and reason coherently. But this ability is weakened by the very differences that make it necessary. The more we need it, the weaker it becomes, and we need it very badly indeed. (Stout, 1988, p. 3)

CONFLICT IS RHETORICALLY ATTENUATED

The rhetoric of moral clash contributes to a state of disarray in public discourse. We do not wish to blame anyone for this problem. We believe that the poor quality of much of contemporary public discourse is the unintended outcome of well-meaning spokespersons who are doing their best to handle difficult conflicts. As Burgess (1970) noted, however, the times are out of joint, and normal ways of dealing with conflict do not work (p. 125). Said differently: Not all conflict is alike, and the ways of managing conflict that are effective and positive in some situations may be ineffective or counterproductive in others.

Many genres of talk are possible in moral conflict. These include dialogue, interviews, appeals to precedents or maxims, elaborations of particular visions or the good and beautiful, exhortations to do good and resist evil, condemnations of the other, and research into the pragmatic effects of various policies. Given so rich an array of possibilities, MacIntyre (1981) was struck by the frequency with which statements that express disagreement are used in moral conflict and the infrequency of the other types of statements (p. 6). Perhaps MacIntyre's observations focused on more restrained people than ours; we are struck by the extent to which people in moral conflicts invidiously categorize and descriptively denounce the personalities, intelligence, social manners, personal ancestries, prospects for eternal abode, and reasoning of those with whom they disagree.

Of course, to say that a discourse is attenuated means "compared with something else." We are particularly struck by the contrast, noted in our report of the anti-CIA demonstration in chapter 1 of this volume, between the discourse that takes place when opposing sides converse with or at each other in public and that which takes place when they speak in more friendly situations, whether among themselves or to a good listener not identified with the other side. The discourse between groups is coarse, brutish shallow, and brittle compared with that within groups. To the extent that the content of public discourse resembles this between-group rhetoric, it cannot function as the site of democratic processes.

Sophisticated rhetoric consists of a shared quest for "good reasons" for believing or acting in certain ways. In moral conflict, the patterns of communication that occur more typically include ad hominem attacks, denunciations, and curses. Slogans and chants replace arguments intended to persuade and inform; various forms of denunciations and diatribes squeeze out scarcely noticed opportunities for dialogue.

In our experience, deeply enmeshed members of conflicting groups usually cannot give rich accounts of the moral orders of the other group. When they are urged to do so, their accounts end rather quickly in offensive descriptions ("they are just stupid!") or attributions ("they are evil and can't be trusted"). They are able to give rich accounts of their own moral orders, however—if we can hear them in their own terms.

Hearing another person's moral language, if that differs from our own, is difficult. In a major study of contemporary American society, Bellah, Madsen, Sullivan, Swidler, and Tipton (1985) sought to identify the moral languages of "ordinary Americans" (pp. 20, 161–63). The researchers "did not seek to impose our ideas on those with whom we talked"; however, they "did attempt to uncover assumptions, to make explicit what the person we were talking to might rather have left implicit. The interview as we employed it was active, Socratic" (p. 304).

A respondent in one of these interviews said that "lying is one of things I want to regulate." The interviewer, Ann Swidler, asked, "Why?"

> Well, it's a kind of thing that is a habit you get into. Kind of self-perpetuating. It's like digging a hole. You just keep digging and digging . . . It's just so basic. I don't want to be bothered with challenging that. It's part of me. I don't know where it came from, but it's very important. . . . Well, some things are bad because . . . I guess I feel like everybody on this planet is entitled to have a little bit of space, and things that detract from other people's space are kind of bad. (Bellah et al., 1985, pp. 304–305)

Swidler and the others interpreted this conversation as showing that this respondent lacked a sufficiently powerful moral language. When confronted by a persistent Socratic interviewer, he was quickly reduced to incoherent babbling about everybody having space and so forth. Noting that he is a middle-aged man who is successful in business, whose first marriage failed but who has remarried and is thoughtfully restructuring his life to make sure that this marriage succeeds his colleagues concluded,

> His description of his reasons for changing his life and of his current happiness seems to come down mainly to a shift in his notions of want would make him happy. His new goal—devotion to marriage and chil-dren—seems as arbitrary and unexamined as his earlier pursuit of mate-rial success. Both are justified as idiosyncratic preference rather than as representing a larger sense of the purpose of life. (p. 6)

In his commentary on this research, Stout (1988) suggested that Palmer spoke an eloquent moral language, just not the one that Swidler was prepared to hear. Palmer grounded his moral judgments in a narrative of his own life rather than attempting (until Swidler kept prompting him) to make categorical ethical pro-nouncements. When describing his own experience, Palmer used a moral vocabu-lary of reciprocity, involvement, shared goals, and mutual respect; his lame individualism was not his "first moral language" but his language of "last resort" when talking with a relentless (and relentlessly academic) interviewer (pp. 195–96). In his analysis of the interview, Stout warned that

> there are many propositions that we are justified in believing but wouldn't know how to justify. Anything we could say on behalf of such a proposition seems less certain than the proposition itself. By now it is hard to debate with flat-earthers. What real doubt do they have that can be addressed with justifying reasons? . . . We ought to I be suspicious of people who want reasons even when they can't supply reasonable doubts. (pp. 35–36)

When Brian Palmer said that the wrongness of lying is basic, Stout (1988) argued that what he means is that "he can't think of anything more certain than the wrongness of lying that might be introduced to support the idea that lying is wrong. He'd rather not be bothered with the sort of challenge that the question implies" (p. 195).

Palmer's rich moral language became rhetorically attenuated in his attempt to respond to his interviewer, and his interviewer was unable to give a well-developed analysis of his moral order because she was not attuned to hear what he said as an answer to her questions. In this way, the discourse among people with different moral orders often become rhetorically attenuated.

Is There a Better Way?

The more important issue, of course, is not whether we can recognize or even understand moral conflicts. It is whether we can do something about them. Fortu-nately, we do not have to hope or imagine that there are effective ways of improv-ing the quality of public discourse in moral conflict. Part III of this book describes several projects that demonstrate both that it can be done and some of the ways in which it can be done.

Moral conflicts can be viewed from many perspectives, of course. However else they may be seen, they may be understood as a particular form of communication. This perspective is useful in understanding how moral conflict can be managed more effectively.

Conflict Is a Precarious Pattern of Interaction

The heading of this section is deliberately designed to be provocative. If one's interest in moral conflict starts, as ours did, by observing fully grown, passionate struggles, patterns of communication seem remarkably persistent and impervious to change. But if one looks more closely at their etiology, these patterns appear far more unnecessary and fragile. Indeed, asking how conflicts begin and how they develop can be useful questions.

If we ask how people get from "here" to "there" in a conflict, then we begin to wonder, "Aren't there a number of points at which people could have handled their conflict differently?" And then the next question becomes, "What did they do to get into this sorry state of affairs?" When we address this question, we are guided by three principles of communication.

First, communication is a process of making and doing. If we want to understand communication, we must ask what is "made" and what is "done" when it occurs. So, for example, when Bob and Ellen argue about money, they may be making a personal world in which money is a defining quality of their relationship. And, depending on their own sense of what is going on, they may be doing any number of things—fighting, arguing, bantering, kidding, filling time, establishing power, or something we cannot even imagine.

Likewise, when anti-gay moralists and pro-gay advocates fight in the street, they are doing something they might call "returning to basic Values," "protecting human rights," "fighting hate," "resisting oppression," "establishing moral action," and so on. And in the process, they are making what we call moral conflict.

We can never know exactly what is being made or done m the abstract because the meanings of communication depend on its context. And that is our second principle: Communication is contextual. Just about everybody takes this general idea as a truism, but we mean something more muscular than the common idea that meanings are determined by context. For us, the context affects meaning, but meaning in turn establishes context.

Any act of communication, such as Bob and Ellen's argument or a gay rights battle, is connected to what has gone before and what will happen next. Each act we perform is both "out of" and "into" a context. What Bob and Ellen are doing and what they are making are determined in part by what they did and made before, and that in turn establishes a basis for understanding what they will do and make next.

Furthermore, we assume that there is never only one context. We are always acting out of and into contexts structured by stories of who we are, of our relations to other people (whether present or not), of what we are doing, and of what is going on around us. There is no fixed limit to the contexts of any action.

We assume further that contexts are made by the communicative acts that occur in them, just as actions themselves are formed by the contexts in which they occur. Both the text and context are aspects of unfinished, continuous patterns of communication. If one asks activists to interpret something they said during a gay rights campaign, they will answer differently, depending on the outcome. If the gay rights measure passes, proponents will describe their actions as skillful campaign practice, and opponents will say that they fought the good battle for morality. If the measure fails, proponents will say that they stood up for individual rights in the face of great adversity, and the opponents will say that they were merely expressing the moral sense of the majority. What is made and done depends on the past, but it depends on the future, too.

The third principle that guides our analysis is this: Communication is a process of coordination. Although awkward to express, the point is that an act is never completed by one party alone. A request requires the presence and response of someone who can grant the request. A promise requires another person to hear and respond favorably to an intention. A child is always disciplined by another person, and an audience does not exist without a performer. How can there be a war with only one side? How can there be a debate with only one advocate? The meaning of an act, then—what is made and done—depends in large measure on the responses it elicits. And the response elicits a response, which leads to another response, and another, and another. Communication, then, is not merely a process of transmitting information to another person; it is always a continuing process of coordinating actions.

Hope for Change

The three principles outlined in the previous section provide real hope that negative and intractable patterns can change. Because communication is contextual, people can change the pattern of conflict by telling different stories about what they are doing and making. Mediators are often successful because they do offer opportunities for changing the context of the dispute by suggesting new frames for defining what is going on.

Looking at the pattern of interaction in a new way is nothing more than restructuring the context. There are a number of practical ways in which this is done. One is to change the number of participants and the roles they play. Staub (1989), for example, notes the effect of bystanders or observers in inhibiting the worst excesses of violent behavior. Just by having others there and bearing witness to some other group, the context changes.

The context can be changed by addressing a different audience. For example, when Reagan and Gorbachev met at their first summit meeting they found that the discourse they had previously used became strikingly inappropriate when they were in one another's presence (Pearce, Johnson, & Branham, 1992). The same thing happens when people who are accustomed to yelling at each other at public rallies and street confrontations are put into a private setting. People can restructure the context too by establishing special forms of communication squiring new types of responses. Some of these are discussed in detail in Part III of this book.

If communication is created by people together as an act of coordination, then third parties can skillfully participate in making new, more productive patterns. Without a mediator, for example, a gang member's demand to meet with the mayor might well be judged as a ploy and rejected out of hand by the mayor's staff. A mediator, on the other hand, might ask just the right question to elicit a different response: "If the mayor agreed to meet with you, how would that make things different?" Here a "demand" is changed to a "prediction."

Without a third party present, a spokesperson's accusation that opponents are fools would likely be greeted with a counterinsult. A mediator, on the other hand, might reframe the comment in a way that transforms the context: "It sounds as if you would really like to discuss this issue on an intellectual level." Here a dirty "insult" is changed to a positive "challenge." These types of intervention moves can open up the opportunity for different patterns of communication to develop.

From Theory to Practice

The only (!) problem with the ways of improving the quality of public discourse outlined above is that they require us to act skillfully in ways that are not anticipated in the natural course of events. They require the development of new forms of communication and new skills, and that is hard work.

These skills do not require inordinate motor reflexes or even unusual intelligence. They do require certain unlearnings. One cannot practice these skills well if one shares Plato's distrust of the people, which leads to a single-minded reliance on expert opinion. Such a preference for expertise, coupled with the facts that experts differ in their opinions and that some of these differences are incommensurate, constitutes a recipe for moral conflict. The opposite of this preference for expertise is not the absurd belief that ignorance is best but the recognition of the difference between technical expertise and knowledge of other sorts. It is the difference between a single-minded subordination of all human interests to the technical and the enlightened recognition that even folks who do not know how to build a bridge have interests that might be best served if the bridge is not built.

In the same way, these skills in managing moral conflict cannot be practiced well by those who think of conflict as do Machiavelli and Alinsky. As Fisher and Ury (1981) taught us, the dichotomy between a hard and soft style of bargaining does not exhaust the available alternatives. If it did, there would be no difference between giving in and transforming the conflict; there would be no difference between the sensibilities of Jean-Henri Dunant, who saw something more fundamental than the question of who won and who lost, and the sensibilities of a coward with no physical courage. Yet these differences are regularly occluded in the editorial pages of our newspapers and on radio talk shows, where self-appointed savants equate openness to new solutions with a failure of nerve, inconsistency, and a backing down from one's position.

Finally, these skills cannot be practiced well by those who cannot see what is said and done in a conflict as a move in a game that is incomplete and framed within many contexts. The ability that needs to be developed is that of focusing on what one wants to create rather than responding to what other people have done. For example, several nations—including Germany, Cambodia, Japan, Argentina, Uruguay, Chile, El Salvador, Nicaragua, and Haiti—have recently been confronted with the problem of dealing with people who committed atrocities. If the issue is posed as a choice between justice or mercy, then it seems that one must decide to punish them or to grant them amnesty, and both have significant negative implications. The decision to punish them continues the cycle of state-sponsored violence; the decision to grant them amnesty undercuts the sense of justice.

Several countries have hit on a strategy that recognizes the atrocities and holds the perpetrators to account but does not punish them. The decision is to frame the issue as "truth." For example, in Argentina, a blue-ribbon committee published an exhaustive account, naming names and showing pictures, of the atrocities of the "dirty war" and presented it in a formal ceremony to the president. It was titled Nunca Más, or "Never Again." There is a sensibility here that is hard to describe. It involves taking responsibility for perpetuating patterns of social interaction, whether of war, abuse, oppression, or simply a devalued public discourse, and, without exonerating the guilty, simply declares that the pattern stops here and acts accordingly.

We can respond to moral conflicts in a number of ways. In the following section of the book, we explore several communication patterns that collectively form a response to the difficult character of contemporary times.

AUTHORS' NOTE: Excerpts from Hunter (1991) are from *Culture Wars*, by J. D. Hunter (New York: HarperCollins Publishers). Copyright © 1991 by HarperCollins Publishers. Reprinted by permission.

Chosen Trauma

Vamik D. Volkan

2001. How does this inform American politics in 2022?

Vamik Volkan, a trained doctor, is now professor emeritus of psychiatry at the University of Virginia. Volkan was born in Cyprus but found his way to the chairmanship of the American Psychiatric Association, where he worked to bring together leaders of feuding nations for unofficial negotiations. Volkan has long contributed to the peace and conflict field with accomplishments too many to list here. Volkan provided the keynote address back in 2006 in South Africa to celebrate the life of Archbishop Desmond Tutu as well as the tenth anniversary of that country's Truth and Reconciliation Commission.

Volkan's piece argues for distinctions between individual and large-group psychology. He notes that "practicing psychoanalysts, with some exceptions, have basically tended to treat their patients without much interest in or attention paid to political or diplomatic issues and the enormous public health problems that are found in massively traumatized societies. When writing about such issues, they usually apply theories of individual psychology to large-group processes without taking into consideration that once they begin, large-group processes take on their own specific directions and appear as new political, social, or ideological movements."

Volkan defined the concept of "large-group identity": a sense of sameness shared by thousands or millions of people. When this large-group identity is threatened, the large-group behavior regresses, demonstrating narcissistic and paranoid characteristics that lead to "primitive mental mechanisms."

One of Volkan's most drawn-upon concept that explains large-group identity in the aftermath of violence is "chosen trauma," which is the shared mental representation of an event in a large group's history in which the group suffered a catastrophic loss, humiliation, and helplessness at the hands of enemies. When members of a victim group are unable to mourn such losses and reverse their humiliation and helplessness, they pass on to their offspring the images of their injured selves and psychological tasks that need to be completed. This process is known as the "transgenerational transmission of trauma." These transgenerational chosen traumas are vulnerable to reactivation, which can be a strategy of political leaders for particular kinds of gains or to mobilize groups.

Identity and trauma are both concepts characteristic of Epoch Two as more attention was paid to those most affected by violence and context became tantamount to our understanding of the emergence of violence. To clarify, Volkan did not mean that groups "chose" to be traumatized. He meant that they chose to emphasize particular moments in history.

Questions to consider: What is the process by which chosen traumas are transferred between generations? What are some of the large group traumas of one of your identity groups?

Large-Group Psychodynamics and Massive Violence

Vamik D. Volkan

Since I am a psychoanalyst, I naturally approach the study of large-group psychodynamics and violence primary from a psychoanalytic angle. In 1932 Albert Einstein wrote a letter to the father of psychoanalysis, Sigmund Freud, asking if this new science could offer insights that might deliver humankind from the menace of war. In his response to Einstein, Freud[1] expressed little hope for an end to war and violence, or the role of psychoanalysis in changing human behavior beyond the individual level. Even though some analysts such as Jacob Arlow[2] have found indications of cautious optimism in some of Freud's writings, Freud's general pessimism was mirrored by many of his followers. This, I think, has played a key role in limiting the contributions psychoanalysis has made to international relations in general and in finding more peaceful solutions for conflicts between enemy groups in particular.

Another factor that has played a role in limiting such psychoanalytic contributions, I believe, was the impact of the Holocaust on psychoanalytic practice.[3] Let me explain: in his early efforts to develop psychoanalytic theories, Freud gave up the idea that the sexual seduction of children came from the external world, and instead focused on the stimuli that comes from the child's own wishes and fantasies for formation psychopathology. Since early psychoanalysts followed this tradition, classical psychoanalysis accepted this de-emphasis on actual seduction coming from the external world when considering the developing child's psyche and generalized it to include de-emphasis on the role of traumatic external events. This de-emphasis included traumatic international events as they impact the mental health of individuals affected by them. The Holocaust is a prime example. For a long time, psychological studies of the Holocaust were too painful to be carried out, and the whole topic of its psychological impact on those who were affected directly and on the human psyche in general was avoided. (Despite of some studies on this topic, in general, a "denial" of the psychological plight of Holocaust survivors strangely persisted for decades after the World War II—a defense that, astonishingly, extended even to Israel. In a November 2, 1995 story, an Israeli television station reported that even the Jewish state had long neglected the trauma undergone by Holocaust survivors. After their arrival in 1940s, survivors had been immediately treated for depression and other mental disorders in psychiatric hospitals. Incredibly, however, many of these patients' official files did not even mention that they were Holocaust victims.)

Harold Blum's[4] description of a Jewish patient who came to him for re-analysis illustrates the extent to which mutual resistances may prevail when both the analyst and the analysand belong to the same large group that has been massively traumatized by an external historical event. Blum's patient's first analyst, who was also Jewish, failed to "hear" their large group's shared trauma at the hands of the Nazis in his analysand's material. As a consequence, mutually sanctioned silence and denial pervaded the entire analytic experience, leaving unanalyzed residues of the Holocaust-related issues in the analysand's symptoms.

We can wonder how many Jewish analysts after World War II were like Blum's patient's former analyst and how many of them, without being aware of it, influenced the application of psychoanalytic treatment in a way that tended to ignore Holocaust-related external reality. I suggest that some of them who were very influential in the field of psychoanalysis, both in the United States and elsewhere, exaggerated their bias in favor of a theoretical position called "classical analysis" that focused only on the analysand's internal wishes and fantasies. We now know that in post-World War II Germany as well, there has been both German and German-Jewish analyst-supported (unconscious) resistance to exploring the intertwining of internal and external wars and the influence of Holocaust-related issues on analysands' psyches (Jokl[5]; Grubrich-Simitis[6]; Eckstaedt[7]; Streeck-Fischer[8]; and Volkan, Ast and Greer[9]).

Since Freud, many authors who are not themselves practicing psychoanalysts have referred to psychoanalysis in their attempt to understand world affairs and large-group psychology in general. They have often referred to Freud's[10,11,12,13] writings such as Totem and Taboo, Group Psychology and the Analysis of the Ego, the Future of an Illusion, Civilization and its Discontents, and his correspondence with Einstein mentioned above. The main problem with their approach, as Ivan Hendrick[14] noticed long ago, is that because of it, psychoanalysis is misused by intellectuals, who argue its validity as if it were a philosophy, an ethical system, a set of theories; such discussion [. . .] seems alien and unproductive to the analyst himself, whose primary convictions originate in what his patients have told him. This approach by these authors usually overlooked two important considerations. First, psychoanalytic theories that systematize new findings in the field have been expanded enormously in the decades since Freud's first pioneer work. To be sure, some authors who are not practicing psychoanalysts now refer to new psychoanalytic theoreticians, such as Jacques Lacan, when writing about large-group psychology. In general, however, these authors also utilize the new psychoanalytic theories as if they were a set of philosophical considerations.

Second, observations afforded by clinical psychoanalytic practice have much more to offer the study of world affairs, ethnic identity, political leader-followers interactions, the eruption of massive violence and its influence on public health. Working with children in psychoanalytic therapy or analyzing borderline or narcissistic adults, in my mind, informs us more about large-group psychology than does studying metapsychology or psychoanalytic theories of the mind. Often international relationships are dominated by the utilization of shared primitive defense mechanisms such as introjection, projection, splitting, and denial. Clinical work with children, borderline and narcissistic patients teach us a great deal about such mechanisms.

Meanwhile, practicing psychoanalysts, with some exceptions, have basically tended to treat their patients without much interest in or attention paid to political or diplomatic issues and the enormous public health problems that are found in massively traumatized societies. When writing about such issues, they usually apply theories of individual psychology to large-group processes without taking into consideration that once they begin, large-group processes take on their own specific directions and appear as new political, social or ideological movements. Recently however, especially since September 11, 2001, practicing psychoanalysts have shown more interest in large-group psychology.

My findings on large-group psychology come from actual fieldwork in various troubled spots of the world. In 1977, then-Egyptian president Anwar el-Sadat stunned the political world by visiting Israel. When he addressed the Israeli Knesset he spoke about a psychological wall between Arabs and Israelis and stated that psychological barriers constitute 70 percent of all problems existing between the Arabs and the Israelis. With the blessings of the Egyptian, Israeli and American governments, the American Psychiatric Association's (APA's) Committee on Psychiatry and Foreign Affairs followed up on Sadat's statements by bringing together influential Israelis, Egyptians and later Palestinians for a series of unofficial negotiations that took place between 1979 and 1986. My membership in this committee initiated my study of large-group psychology, enemy relationships, and interactions between political leaders and their followers, and I began contemplating strategies to tame aggression between enemy groups.

This six-year study of the Arab-Israeli conflict as seen through a psychological lens was also the opportunity that provided the beginnings of my examination of the psychology of large groups and societies in its own right. Later I observed other "enemy" representatives such as Russians and Estonians, Georgians and South Ossetians, Serbs and Croats or Turks and Greeks—in various years-long unofficial negotiation series. I also interviewed traumatized people in refugee camps where "we-ness" becomes palpable. Furthermore, I spent time with political leaders such as the former U.S. president Jimmy Carter, former Soviet leader Mikhail Gorbachev, the late Yasser Arafat, the present Estonian president Arnold Rüütel, and Northern Cyprus president Rauf Denktas as and observed aspects of leader-followers psychology through these leaders' verbalized thought processes and actions. Eventually, I was able to define the concept of "large-group identity:" a sense of sameness shared by thousands or millions of people. It is this sense of sameness which explains what people mean when they say, "We are Finnish," "We are Arabs," "We are Jews," or "We are communists."[15,16,17,18,19]

Large-Group Identity

Because of their clinical interests, psychoanalysts have focused more on small groups and the psychodynamics involved when seven to fifteen individuals gather for a series of meetings. Wilfred Bion's[20] work is among the best known of such studies. A "small group" with a definite leader, a structured task, and an awareness of time evolves as a "work group" and performs its task with an adaptation to reality. Bion describes how, when such a group's security is threatened or when it is not given a realistic and structured task, it begins to function according to certain "basic assumptions," which are very familiar to psychoanalysts.

In the psychoanalytic literature the term "large group" often refers to 30 to 150 members who meet in order to deal with a given issue. When the task given to such a "large group" is by design unstructured and vague, the "large group" regresses. At this time, observers notice increased anxiety, chaos, and panic among its members.[21,22,23,24] In order to escape the panicky atmosphere that envelopes them, regressed "large groups" exhibit narcissistic or paranoid characteristics and reorganize themselves by sharing and utilizing primitive mental mechanisms.

Otto Kernberg also refers to groups composed of 30 to 150 individuals as "large groups." He uses the term "crowds" when he refers to spectators at a big sports event or large theatrical performance. He also mentions disorganization in crowds after natural disasters and then speaks of "mass movements" and "societal and cultural processes." He primarily illustrates the emergence of aggression in "small groups," "crowds" and "societies" when regression and disorganization sets in.

In this chapter I refer to tens, hundreds of thousands, or millions of individuals (most of whom will never meet during their lifetimes) who belong to a large group from childhood on. I use the term large-group identity (i.e., an ethnic identity) to refer to a shared permanent sense of sameness.

The psychodynamics of ethnic, national, religious or ideological large groups are different from the psychodynamics of "small groups," "large groups" (composed of 30 or 150 individuals), or "crowds." For example, a "crowd" in a football stadium becomes a group and remains so just before, during, and perhaps soon after the sports event. On the other hand, let us consider an ethnic or religious large group, like Greeks or Catholics. The membership in these large groups begins in childhood. Elsewhere I illustrate how each member's core personal identity is intertwined with their large-group identity.[16,19]

When I think of the classical Freudian theory of large groups, I visualize people arranged around a gigantic maypole, which represents the group leader. Individuals in the large group dance around the pole/leader, identifying with each other and idealizing the leader. I have expanded this maypole metaphor by imagining a canvas extending from the pole out over the people, forming a huge tent.

This canvas represents the large-group identity. I have come to the conclusion that essential large-group psychodynamics center around maintaining the integrity of the large-group identity, and leader-follower interactions are just one element of this effort.

Imagine thousands or millions of persons living under this huge tent. They may get together in subgroups, they may be poor or rich or women or men and they may belong to certain clans or professional organizations, but all of them are under one huge tent. The pole of the tent is the political leadership. From an individual psychology point of view, the pole may represent an oedipal father; from a large-group psychology point of view, the pole's task is to keep the tent's canvas erect (to maintain and protect the large-group identity). Everyone under the tent's canvas wears an individual garment (personal identity), but everyone under the tent also shares the tent canvas as a second garment. Elsewhere I have identified seven threats that, when they are woven together, produce the cloth— the canvas of the large-group tent—ranging from shared identifications to "chosen traumas,"[17,19] a term I will explain later in this chapter.

In our routine lives we are not keenly aware of our shared second garment, just as we are not usually aware of our constant breathing. If we develop pneumonia or if we are in a burning building, we quickly notice each breath we take. Likewise, if our huge tent's canvas shakes or parts of it are torn apart, we become obsessed with our second garment, and our individual identity becomes secondary. (Before going any further I must explain that here I am speaking of general large-group processes, leaving out certain people such as dissenters). We become preoccupied with the large-group identity and will do anything to stabilize, repair, maintain and protect it, and when we do, we are willing to tolerate extreme sadism or masochism if we think that what we are doing will help to maintain and protect our large-group identity. In the long run, such behavior is inevitably reflected in public health issues.

Large-Group Psychodynamics

Since large groups are made up of individuals, it stands to reason that large-group processes reflect individual psychology. But a large group is not a living organism that has one brain, so once a large-group process starts within the society, it establishes a life of its own. To illustrate this I will compare the process of mourning in an individual and in a large group.

Psychoanalysts, psychiatrists and other mental health professionals know a great deal about the individualized process of mourning. Mourning is an obligatory human psychobiological response to a meaningful loss. When a loved one dies, the mourner has to go through predictable and definable phases until the mourning process comes to a practical end.[25,26] Finnish psychoanalyst Veikko Tähkä,[27] along with others going all the way back to Sigmund Freud himself, contributed greatly to our understanding of the individual mourning process during which the mourner internally reviews his or her experiences with the lost person and slowly lets this person be psychologically "buried." If everything goes in a routine fashion, the mourner also identifies with aspects and functions the dead person possessed when still living, and keeps the dead person "alive" within the mourner's psyche. This process takes a few years. Sometimes the individual mourning processes can be "infected" due to various causes, and we can predict what may happen after such "infections."

Large groups also mourn. Since a large group is not one living organism, the psychodynamics of its mourning over the loss of loved ones, lands, and prestige after a war or war-like situation will manifest as societal processes. For example, after a major shared trauma and loss at the hand of enemies, a political ideology of irredentism (a shared sense of entitlement to recover what had been lost) may emerge that reflects a complication in large-group mourning and an attempt both to deny losses and to recover them. What Greeks call the Megali Idea (Great Idea) is this kind of political ideology. Such political ideologies may last for centuries and may disappear and reappear when historical circumstances change.

The last time we very clearly witnessed the reappearance of a political ideology of entitlement was after the collapse of Yugoslavia. When the huge Yugoslav tent was gone the Serbs, the Croats, the Bosniaks and others became preoccupied with establishing themselves under their specific smaller tents. When a large group asks, "Who are we now?" it becomes preoccupied with repairing, protecting, and maintaining the canvas of its tent. In order to hold on to the large-group identity, it tries to illuminate specific symbols woven into the fabric of its tent's canvas. When ethnic, nationalistic, religious or ideological identity markers are illuminated, doing so reassures the society that their large-group identity still exists. I named one of these significant markers a chosen trauma.

A chosen trauma is the shared mental representation of an event in a large group's history in which the group suffered a catastrophic loss, humiliation, and helplessness at the hands of enemies. When members of a victim group are unable to mourn such losses and reverse their humiliation and helplessness, they pass on to their offspring the images of their injured selves and psychological tasks that need to be completed. This process is known as the "transgenerational transmission of trauma." (For a review and an examination of this concept see: Volkan, Ast and Greer[9]). All such images and tasks contain references to the same historical event, and as decades pass, the mental representation of such an event links all the individuals in the large group. Thus, the mental representation of the event emerges as a significant large-group identity marker. A chosen trauma reflects the "infection" of a large-group's mourning process, and its reactivation serves to link the members of a large group. Such reactivation can be used by the political leadership to promote new massive societal movements, some of them deadly and malignant.

Political leaders may initiate the reactivation of chosen traumas in order to fuel entitlement ideologies. The story of how Slobodan Milosevic allowed and supported the re-appearance of the Serbian chosen trauma (the mental representation of the June 28, 1389 Battle of Kosovo) is well documented.[16] According to the myth that developed among the Serbs some 70 years after the Battle of Kosovo, the event and the Serbian characters of this battle—especially the Serbian leader Prince Lazar who was killed during the battle—mingled with elements and characters of Christianity. As decades passed, Prince Lazar became associated with Jesus Christ, and icons showing Lazar's representation in fact decorated many Serbian churches throughout the six centuries following the battle. Even during the communist period when the government discouraged hero worship, Serbs were able to drink (introject) a popular red wine called "Prince Lazar."

As the six-hundredth anniversary of the Battle of Kosovo approached in 1989, with the permission and encouragement of Milosevic, Lazar's 600-year-old remains, which had been kept north of Belgrade, were placed in a coffin and taken over the course of the year to almost every Serb village and town, where they were received by huge crowds of mourners dressed in black. Again and again during this long journey, Lazar's remains were symbolically buried and reincarnated, until they were buried for good at the original battleground in Kosovo on June 28, 1989. On this day, the six-hundredth anniversary of the Battle of Kosovo, a helicopter brought Milosevic to the burial ground where a huge monument made of red stone symbolizing blood had been built. In the mythology, Prince Lazar had chosen the Kingdom of Heaven over the Kingdom of earth. By design, Milosevic descended from a helicopter, representing Prince Lazar coming to earth to find a new Kingdom, a Greater Serbia.

Thus Milosevic and his associates, by activating the mental representations of Lazar and the Battle of Kosovo, along with the peak emotions they generated, were able to create a year-long "time collapse." The perceptions, feelings, and expectations concerning a past hero and event were collapsed into the perceptions, feelings, and expectations about at a current "enemy," thus magnifying its threat. Milosevic and his associates first encouraged a shared sense of victimization followed by a shared sense of entitlement for revenge. This led to genocidal acts in Europe at the end of the 20th century. In early June 2005, new tapes showing violent murders in the name of large-group identity shook the Serbian citizenry, as well as the rest of us.

Imagine that a serial killer such as Jack the Ripper is murdering his victims by strangling them with a red scarf. Also imagine that this serial killer is caught, tried and put away. What happens to his murder weapon, the red scarf? It stays in a dusty box in the basement of a court or police building as evidence used during the trial. In short, in the future no one else will use this scarf as a "tool" for murdering people.

Let us go back to Milosevic. At the present time he is on trial because the United Nations considers him responsible for mass murder, among other things. What was Milosevic's "red scarf" and what will happen to it? As I described above, one of Milosevic's prominent "tools" for inciting extreme violence was his reactivation (with the help of some Serbian academicians and people from the Serbian Church) of shared symbols of the Serbian large-group identity: mental representations of loss, humiliation, the Battle of Kosovo, and the Serbian leader Prince Lazar who was killed during this battle.

Now let us imagine that Milosevic is found guilty and is put away, but his "red scarf" is not put away in a basement. Since this "red scarf" belongs to the large group and not to one lone individual, it is possible to use it again in the future. We know this because Milosevic is not the first person to inflame the mental representations of the Battle of Kosovo and Prince Lazar. On June 28, 1914, during an anniversary of the Battle of Kosovo, a Serb named Gavrilo Prencip assassinated Archduke Francis Ferdinand of Austria-Hungary (Austria-Hungary had replaced the Ottoman Empire as the "oppressor" of the Serbs) and his pregnant wife in Sarajevo, thereby beginning World War I.

The political and legal systems have no effective methods to deal with a "tool" that can be used for massive destruction when it belongs to a large group rather than just the man or woman who makes use of it. It can be better understood by the application of psychological insights that illuminate large-group processes in their own right than by logical realpolitik conceptualizations. Who is going to examine "red scarves" that are the property of large groups? I hold that psychoanalysts and others who study human nature are best equipped to do so if they are willing to venture beyond their offices, conduct field work, and collaborate with scholars and practitioners from other disciplines in an effort to understand collective human issues such as politics, diplomacy, wars, terrorism, and the reflection of these things in the realm of public health.

Large Group Regression

When a large-group identity is threatened (and this can be by any variety of things such as the group's enemies) the ethnic, national, religious or ideological large group regresses. (Although I have found 20 signs and symptoms of this kind of regression,[17] I must borrow the term "regression" from individual psychology because we do not have a word that stands only for large-group regression.) When a large group regresses it becomes involved in certain societal processes that serve to maintain, protect and repair the large-group identity. Since large groups as I described them here have their own specific characteristics that are built upon their own centuries-old continua and shared mental representations of history and myth, the examination of signs and symptoms of their regression should also include shared psychodynamics that are specific to each group. We need therefore to go beyond a general description of the emergence of aggression in large groups, when they regress, and their shared paranoid or narcissistic sentiments, and refer to actual manifestations of regression within each specific large group.

Some major signs of large-group regression, such as rallying around the leader—as occurred in the United States immediately following the September 11, 2001 terrorist attacks—have been known since Freud. When Freud[11] wrote about this phenomenon he did not say he was referring to regressed groups, and it was Robert Waelder[30] who brought to our attention that it was in fact regressed groups that Freud was describing. Sometimes the members of a large group continue to rally around a leader for decades and they remain "regressed' in order to modify existing characteristics of their large-group identity. In this situation what we observe is similar to an individual's regressing in the service of progression and creativity. After the collapse of the Ottoman Empire and the establishment of

modern Turkey in 1923 under the leadership of Kemal Atatürk, the Turkish people (in general) continued to rally around Atatürk until his death in 1938. This
was the main factor that supported modern Turkey's cultural revolution and the
modification of characteristics of the Turks' large-group identity.

Often however, a large group regression does not serve a positive outcome.
For example, in certain totalitarian regimes, people rally around the leader in order
to feel personally secure rather than to be punished by the authorities for disobey-
ing the "rules" of the regime. Without being aware of it, they internalize what
Michael Sebek[31] called "totalitarian objects," and blindly follow their leader by
giving up many aspects of their individuality.

When a large group is in a regressed state, the personality and the internal
world of the political leader assumes great importance concerning the manipulation (the "good" or the "bad") of what already exists within the large-group psychology. Therefore, the personality organization of Milosevic, which I describe
elsewhere, was a crucial factor in what happened in the former Yugoslavia, and
demonstrates how political leaders such as Milosevic will bring the large group's
"red scarves" out in the open and use them as tools of mass aggression.

Two types of splitting are also signs of large-group regression. First, a splitting
between "us" and "them" (the enemy outside the regressed large group) becomes
pronounced and the "other" becomes a target for dehumanization. Second, following the initial rallying around the leader, a severe split may occur within the society
itself. This happens especially when the leader cannot differentiate between where
real danger ends and fantasized danger begins, but instead leads the group to
resemble the enemy group in certain areas, such as the curtailing of individual
rights. Without this differentiation the group cannot maintain hope and cannot
tame shared aggression. Just a few years after September 11, 2001 we notice such
a split in the United States. There are various reasons for this, but I believe that
this also reflects the regressed state of America after the massive tragedy, as well as
the American leadership's failure to separate "realistic" dangers from "fantasized"
dangers and its inability to help tame the population's shared anxiety.

A regression within the large group stimulates the population to share primitive mental mechanisms when dealing with the external world. I am referring to
massive introjections (such as the population's "eating up" political propaganda
without making much of an effort to evaluate its validity) and projections, such as
happened under the totalitarian regime of Enver Hoxha when Albanians built
7,500 bunkers throughout Albania in anticipation of an enemy attack that never
occurred. Building these bunkers, which would not stand against modern weapons, was also a reflection of magical thinking, another characteristic of regressed
societies. We see various types of magical thinking, such as the expansion of religious fundamentalism and the increased belief in millennialism in the United
States, which, at the present time, strongly influence political/societal movements
there.

In a regressed society political, legal or traditional borders begin to symbolize
the canvas of the large-group tent. In other words, borders become highly psychol-
ogized and people, leaders, and official organizations become preoccupied with

their protection. Since there is in fact a realistic danger "out there," borders obviously need to be protected and because of this, it is difficult to study the psychological aspects of this preoccupation. In the United States, people are now subjected to the influence of a border psychology almost daily, but because of the real (and fantasized) danger magnified by political propaganda, people may not be aware of the influence of this border psychology during their routine lives. At airports, for example, they deny the assault on individual autonomy at the security check points because of the possibility of real danger. In doing this, they subject themselves to large-group psychology, and their individual psychology that normally would cause them to rebel against the intrusion from outside is put in the background.

When a large group's tent's canvas is attacked and torn apart, "minor differences" between the enemy groups become very major issues, since minor differences are experienced as unchangeable "borders" separating one large group's identity from their enemy's identity. People therefore become preoccupied, not only with major differences between their group and the enemy group, but with minor differences between them as well.

When a large group regresses, traditional family values can be replaced by ideologies, such as happened in Nazi Germany. In some regressed large groups the role of women is reduced to giving pleasure to men (sex), providing food (symbolic milk for the society under stress), and producing children for the survival of the large-group's identity. Certain societal processes begin to remind everyone of the continuing existence of the canvas (large-group identity). Cultural customs are like designs on the canvas illustrating the uniqueness of that particular large-group identity. The group wants to "repaint" such designs on the canvas to ease shared anxiety and to show that the large-group identity still survives. But in reality, the group is helpless, angry, humiliated, and suffering from complicated mourning. Thus, when such designs are "repainted," they do not exactly look like the original designs; they are now sloppy and some aspects of them are exaggerated. This may very easily lead to public health problems. One example of this can be found in what is now the Republic of Georgia. After the collapse of the Soviet Union, bloody fights took place between ethnic Georgians and ethnic South Ossetians living within the same legal/political boundaries, and in fact, South Ossetians declared their own "independent state." Aspects of large-group regression still linger in South Ossetia as well as in Georgia: There had been a playful cultural ritual concerning brides, in which a girl would be symbolically kidnapped and married. The cultural kidnapping customs in South Ossetia have now turned into horrible societal problems in the form of some actual kidnappings and rapes of young women.

We need to study the situation of each large group from many angles in order to find specific elements in large-group processes, to understand their underlying meanings and then begin to plan psychologically informed political strategies for inducing progression within the large group or two or more groups in conflict. The next section provides a summary of a method called the Tree Model that provides such strategies and their application.

The Tree Model and Large Group Progression

The "tree model," which I helped to develop during the course of my 30 years or so of actual involvement with an interdisciplinary team in international relations, uses an image of the slow growth and branching of a tree to illustrate its methods. This methodology has three basic components or phases: 1) psychopolitical diagnosis of the situation, 2) psychopolitical dialogues between members of opposing groups, and 3) collaborative actions and institutions that grow out of the dialogue process. The first phase includes in-depth psychoanalytically informed interviews with a wide range of people who represent the groups involved, through which an understanding begins to emerge concerning the main aspects, including unconscious ones, that surround the situation that needs to be addressed. The psychopolitical dialogues between influential representatives of opposing large groups are conducted under the guidance of a facilitating team and take place in a series of multi-day meetings over several years. As these dialogues progress, resistances against changing the large group's "pathological" ways of protecting its identity are brought to the surface and articulated, so that fantasized threats to large-group identity can be interpreted and realistic communication can take place. In order for the newly-gained insights to have an impact on social and political policy, as well as on the populace at large, the final phase requires the collaborative development of concrete actions, programs, and institutions. This methodology allows several disciplines including psychoanalysis, history and diplomacy, to collaborate to articulate and work through underlying psychological and historical aspects of existing tensions. What is learned is then operationalized so that more peaceful coexistence between the large groups can be achieved, and threats (especially the fantasized ones) to large-group identity coming from the "other" can be tamed. This leads to a progression within the large group. (For details of the evolution and the application of the Tree Model see Volkan[19]).

The signs of a large-group progression include preserving individuality while stabilizing family, clan and professional subgroups, and having a society where individuals and professional organizations establish a capacity for compromise without damaging integrity[22] and an ability to question what is "moral." When a large group is not regressed, there is an increased emphasis on freedom of speech, an end to the devaluation of women and children, and just and functioning civil institutions, especially a fair legal system and mental hospitals with humane care[43]. When a large group is not in a regressed state, its members (in general) can wonder about the enemy's "psychic reality." To understand why the "other" behaved in malignant ways does not mean forgiving and forgetting past wrongs. It means performing the difficult task of "humanizing" even the most destructive perpetrators. Horrible large-scale acts are not performed by "devils," but by humans under the specific influence of large-group psychology. I hope it is clear that here I am not focusing on individuals who, due to their own individual psychology, create chaos and tragedy such as Timothy McVeigh did when he blew up the Alfred Murrah Federal Building in Oklahoma City on April, 1995. I am instead focusing on large-group psychology that leads to hurting and killing people in the name of large-group identity. By studying the "psychic reality" of the enemy as a large group, the attacked group can explore new ways of dealing with the enemy and its threat instead of responding to the enemy and the threat by acting on signs of its own regression.

Becoming Like the Enemy

Al Qaeda divided the world into two categories. After September 11 America did the same (again I am not speaking of individuals here, but referring to a general large-group process) and ideas such as the "clash of civilizations" or religions directly or indirectly was supported within the society. Dividing the world into a clear-cut "us" and "them" is a sign of large-group regression. Responding to an enemy in a non-regressed fashion is a very difficult task. Realistic and logical actions are easily contaminated with emotions that support the human wish to do to the enemy what it did to us. I do not think that humans (as large groups) have ever entertained the idea or developed the ability to refrain from acting like their enemies once they feel threatened or hurt.

I need to be careful not to be misunderstood here. I am not referring, for example, to what the Nazis did and what the Allies did in World War II, and I am not saying that the Allies were like the Nazis. Many factors such as historical circumstances, reactivation of past victimizations, the leader's personality organization, existing military power and, most importantly, the degree of large-group regression can make a large-group dehumanize the "other" and be terribly cruel. In dealing with such an extremely regressed large group, the opposing group need not be identically as regressed as the perpetrating group.

When I speak of a similarity between enemies I am referring to certain large-group processes without considering the degree of their regression or its consequences. First, I am simply saying that when a large group's identity is threatened, the threatened large group automatically begins to hurt the aggressors' large-group identity, thus the attacked group begins to take on similarities to the perpetrator. Second, both groups utilize shared mental mechanisms such as introjection, projection, denial, dissociation, isolation, rationalization, and intellectualization in their consciously or unconsciously motivated political propaganda. This comes from their leadership and/or is wished for and supported by the society. Third, humiliating, hurting, and killing people in the name of large-group identity become acceptable by both sides.

If the leadership does not provide a kind of reality testing that includes an understanding of the enemy's (as large group) "psychic reality" and does not show some attempts to respond to it in humane ways, dangers become magnified and regression sets in or is maintained. Therefore, the idea of a large group becoming like its enemy is an area that needs to be studied openly again and again until new opportunities for different responses (above and beyond military ones) can be conceptualized. In fact, new strategies in international relations that don't include succumbing into large-group regression can be considered, and the so-called diplomatic channels need not be closed until a psychopolitical evaluation of the situation is completed.

A "Microscopic" Examination of Large-Group Psychology's Negative Influence: A Story from Klooga

There are many other concepts related to large-group psychology that are not addressed in this chapter, but with the references to mourning and regression in large groups mentioned above, I tried to illustrate how large-group psychology in its own right needs to be studied. Now, by telling a story from the Estonian village of Klooga, I will illustrate, at a microscopic level, how shared group emotions and perceptions interfere with political/military/legal/ health issues, how we become similar to our enemy, and how we need to pay attention to large-group psychological problems, especially large-group identity issues, in order to find constructive solutions to our conflicts.

After Estonia gained its independence from the Soviet Union in 1991, there were major problems facing the newly independent country, one of them being the fact that one third of Estonia's one-and-a half million population is not ethnic Estonian, but Russian (or Russian speakers who were not ethnic Russians, but who were former Soviet citizens). In other words, when Estonia became independent, every third person was perceived as the "other," the "enemy." When Estonia was separated from the Soviet Union its people asked themselves, "Who are we now and what is our large-group identity now?" This concern with large-group identity necessarily brought about a societal regression that was exaggerated by the existence of huge numbers of "enemy" persons in Estonia who would, it was perceived, contaminate its large-group identity.

I went with an interdisciplinary team to Estonia in 1994 to carry out a diagnostic process and bring together selected individuals to participate in psychopolitical dialogues: high-level Estonians (such as parliamentarians, including the present-day president of Estonia, Arnold Rüütel), high-level representatives from Moscow (such as members of the Russian Duma) and leaders of the Russians (or Russian speakers) living in Estonia. We met over a period of several years, and afterwards we began to apply what we learned from these dialogue series to the population at large (for details see Volkan[16,19]). One place where we wanted to show that coexistence between ethnic Estonians and Russians living in Estonia was possible was a place called Klooga.

When I first went to Klooga in early 1996 it was virtually in ruins and had major public health hazards; it looked to me like a three-mile long and one-mile wide garbage dump. The town is only seven miles from Paldiski, the site of the former Soviet nuclear navy. Like Paldiski, Klooga had housed a Soviet military installation and had been off-limits to Estonians during the Soviet times, but after the withdrawal of the Soviet military some Estonians relocated in Klooga. At the time of my visit its population was about 2000 people, half Estonians and half Russians (including a few Russian-speakers).

The facilitating team's aim in Klooga was to develop some level of community cohesion without inter-ethnic conflict. With the help of our psychopolitical work, the Klooga residents developed a community center which became a place where everyone could come for learning (i.e., classes in computers, English, and Estonian) and for play. Children had a safe place to go after school. Teenagers gathered there too, and the center hosted holiday celebrations for the whole community. Along with the growing sense of community the center engendered, public health and other aspects of life in Klooga improved as well.

There were, of course, inevitable obstacles to our work in Klooga. The following example from our experience there, I believe, illustrates at a microscopic level how shared emotions and perceptions within a group may instigate unrealistic actions, and how members of the group may become "blind," unable to see the consequences of such actions.

The newly established, fledgling Estonian military, with its few colonels in charge, was using a field adjacent to Klooga for live target practice, a situation which greatly concerned Klooga's inhabitants, both Estonian and Russian, because it posed a very real danger to the entire population, especially their children. A hidden script went something like this: We Estonians can now identify with our aggressors. Intellectually, we know that today Klooga is home to Estonian citizens and Estonian children too, but in our minds we continue to see this place as a Soviet military base. Thus, we bomb it repeatedly. The fledging Estonian military could have chosen any other place in Estonia for their target practice, but they insisted on "bombing" Klooga, the "Russian village," even though it was in reality no longer Russian.

The field where live ammunition fell was separated from the village by a 15- to 20-foot wide dirt road. The almost daily heavy artillery fire on the field neighboring Klooga was truly dangerous, and we were afraid that children playing nearby could be injured or killed. There was one incident when an Estonian villager tried to take a shortcut through the field with his old tractor and it was hit by artillery. Incredibly, the man survived. Initially the colonels would inform the village people when the "bombs" were to be dropped, but eventually they began to carry out their target practices without giving notice, which of course made the situation worse.

So, we had to devise a plan that would directly illustrate to Estonian authorities the danger that existed. On July 4, 1997 my team threw a big community-wide party in Klooga. We made no fuss about America and its independence, but everyone was told what the Fourth of July was all about (American Independence Day). We also invited several of the Estonian- and Russian-speaking participants from the original psychopolitical dialogue series, including some parliamentarians, to come with their families. Most of them lived in Tallinn, the capital city, and we were aware that they had never been to Klooga before. The Russian Embassy sent their second-ranking diplomat. The stage was set.

After the party, I invited our guests on a walk around the village, directing them to take the dirt road that separated the village from the field where the live artillery fell. I prayed that the "bombing" practice would resume so that our guests could experience what it was like to live in Klooga. Sure enough, the deafening explosions, "boom, boom," began. The target practice was impossible to ignore and provided unmistakable proof of what Klooga's inhabitants lived with every day. However, in spite of seeing the dangers of this practice for themselves and actually witnessing some Estonian kids playing nearby, our guests from the Parliament still could not bring themselves to do anything about the situation.

The next year I made more direct efforts to stop the "bombing" of Klooga, but there was still great resistance to our requests. Slowly we found ways to "educate" Klooga residents about the psychology of humiliation, the wish to reverse it, and the sometimes strange and dangerous efforts people employ to do so. We also discussed the concept of identification with the aggressor. Without our telling them to do so, Klooga residents (100 of them) wrote a letter to then-Estonian President Lennart Meri and asked that the shooting stop. Living in long-established democratic states we may think that this was a natural, in fact easy, thing to do. But living under communism and assimilating the rules and regulations of that political system made this effort by the villagers a drastic one. It paid off when Klooga began to receive national attention. A television station sent its reporters and cameras to the village and there was a big fuss about the "bombing" of Klooga. The residents of Klooga had learned how to be assertive and use political and media pressure, and although the process took three years, the villagers succeeded in stopping the "bombing."

Last Remarks

This chapter describes large-group identity and how a large group regresses when there is a threat to its identity. Large-group regression may result in destructive acts that kill many people and create serious public health problems. Psychoanalysts and other mental health workers who are willing to study large-group psychology in its own right and take part in interdisciplinary efforts have much to offer toward the understanding and management of deadly large-group conflicts.

Notes

    1. Freud S. "Why War?" Standard Edition, 22; 1932–1964. 197–215.
    2. Arlow J. "Motivations for Peace" in Winnik, R. Moses, M. Ostow. *Psychological Basis of War.* Jerusalem: HZ/Jerusalem Academic Press, 1973. 193–204
    3. Volkan V. D. The Intertwining of the Internal and External Wars. Paper Presented at "Lost in Transmission" conference. Stockbridge, MA: The Erikson Institute, The Austen Riggs Center; October 16, 2004.
    4. Blum H. "Superego Formation, Adolescent Transformation and the Adult Neurosis. *Journal of the American Psychoanalytic Association*, 4; 1985. 887–909.

5. Jokl A. M. Zwei Fällezum Thema "Bewältigung der Vergangenheit" (Two Cases Referring to the Theme of "Mastering the Past"). Frankfurt, AM: Jüdischer Verlag. 1997.

6. Grubrich-Simitis I. Extremtraumatisierung als kumulatives Trauma: Psychoanalytische Studien über seelische Nachwirkungen der Konzentrationslagerhaft bei Überlebenden und ihren Kindern (Extreme traumatization as a cumulative trauma: Psychoanalytic studies on the mental effects of imprisonment in concentration camps on survivors and their children). Psyche, 33; 1979. 991–1023.

7. Ecstaedt I. Nationalismus in der "zweiten Generation:" Psychoanalyse von Hörigkeitsverhältnissen (National Socialism in the Second Generation: Psychoanalysis of Master-Slave Relationships). Frankfurt, AM: Suhrkamp Verlag. 1989.

8. Streeck-Fischer A. "Naziskins in Germany: How Traumatization Deals with the Past." *Mind and Human Interaction*, 10; 1999. 84–97.

9. Volkan V. D., G. Ast, W. Greer. *The Third Reich in the Unconscious: Transgenerational Transmission and its Consequences.* New York: Brunner-Routledge, 2002.

10. Freud S. "Totem and Taboo." Standard Edition, 13; 1913–1955. 1–165

11. Freud S. "Group Psychology and the Analysis of the Ego." Standard Edition, 18; 1921–1955. 65–143.

12. Freud S. "The Future of an Illusion." Standard Edition, 21; 1921–1959. 5–56.

13. Freud S. "Civilization and Its Discontents." Standard Edition, 21; 1930–1959. 59–145.

14. Hendrick I. *Facts and Theories of Psychoanalysis.* New York: Knopf. 1958.

15. Volkan V. D. *The Need to Have Enemies and Allies: From Clinical Practice to International Relationships.* Northvale, NJ: Jason Aronson. 1988.

16. Volkan V. D. *Bloodlines: From Ethnic Pride to Ethnic Terrorism.* New York: Farrar Straus and Giroux. 1997.

17. Volkan V. D. *Blind Trust: Large Groups and Their Leaders in Times of Crises and Terror.* Charlottesville, VA: Pitchstone Publishing. 2004.

18. Volkan V. D. "Politics and International Relations" in E. S. Person, A. M. Cooper, G. O. Gabbard. *Textbook of Psychoanalysis.* Washington, DC: American Psychiatric Press, 2005. 523–33.

19. Volkan V. D. *Killing in the Name of Identity: A Study of Blood Conflicts.* Charlottesville, VA: Pitchstone Publishing. 2006.

20. Bion W. *Experiences in Groups and Other Papers.* New York: Basic Books, 1961.

21. Rice A. K. *Learning for Leadership: Interpersonal and Intergroup Relations.* London: Tavistock Publications. 1965.

22. Turquet P. "Threats to Identity in the Large Group." In L. Kreeger. *The Large Group: Dynamics and Therapy.* London: Constable. 1975. 87–144.

23. Kernberg O. F. "Sanctioned Political Violence: A Psychoanalytic View—Part 1." *The International Journal of Psycho-Analysis*, 84; 2003. 683–98.

24. Kernberg O. F. "Sanctioned Political Violence: A Psychoanalytic View—Part 2." *The International Journal of Psycho-Analysis*, 84; 2003. 683–98.

25. Volkan V. D. *Linking Objects and Linking Phenomena: A Study of the Forms, Symptoms, Metapsychology, and Therapy of Complicated Mourning.* New York: International Universities Press. 1981.

26. Pollock G. H. *The Mourning-Liberation Process*, Vols 1 and 2. Madison, CT: International Universities Press. 1989.

27. Tähkä V. "Dealing with Object Loss." *Scandinavian Psychoanalytic Review*, 7; 1984. 13–33.

28. Frued S. "Mourning and Melancholia." Standard Edition, 14; 1917–1957. 258–77.

29. Volkan V. D., N. Itzkowitz. *Turks and Greeks: Neighbors in Conflict*. Cambridgeshire, England: Eothen Press. 1994.

30. Waelder R. "The Principle of Multiple Function: Observations on Over-Determination." *The Psychoanalytic Quarterly*, 5; 1930–1936. 45–62.

31. Sebek M. "The Fate of the Totalitarian Object." *International Forum of Psychoanalysis*, 5; 1996. 289–94.

32. Rangell L. *The Mind of Watergate*. New York: Norton. 1980.

33. Stern J. "Deviance in the Nazi society." *Mind and Human Interaction* 2001; 12:218–37.

Emotions

Daniel Shapiro and Roger Fisher

Daniel Shapiro founded and directed the Harvard International Negotiation Program, in which he also serves as an associate professor of psychology at Harvard's medical school hospital. His work on emotional and identity-based dimensions of negotiation and conflict resolution shifted our field. Shapiro likes to build theory at home and then test them in the field. His successful conflict resolution initiatives throughout the world speak to the efficacy of his approach. Bouncing between the negotiation program and the medical, he also finds time to contribute to widely read publications, such as the *New York Times*, *O: The Oprah Magazine*, and the *Boston Globe*. The World Economic Forum awarded him the title of Young Global Leader.

Roger Fisher, most well-known for his authorship of *Getting to Yes*, written with William Ury, spent part of his youth in the U.S. Army Air Forces as a first lieutenant during World War II. He helped create the Marshall Plan, which rebuilt Europe after the war. He then went on to Harvard Law School, where he became a professor. The driving question in his early research was, "What advice could I give to both parties in a dispute that would be helpful and lead to better outcomes?" In this piece written with Shapiro, he shows his interest in the role of emotions.

Fisher and Shapiro move us out of Epoch One in their acknowledgment that rational decision-making cannot be used to anticipate or explain behavior. Negotiations, no matter how well-planned or executed, are not simply straight discussions over interests. These authors claim that emotions such as anger and frustration can derail the most straightforward discussions. When expressed, these emotions can injure relationships and end the negotiation. Fisher and Shapiro encourage readers to amplify the "good" emotions that promote collaboration, trust, and curiosity about the other. Emotions are contagious, and creating an atmosphere of positivity creates dividends for everyone.

In this approach, emotions are presented as something to be "dealt with" rather than something to be explored. We learn to manage our own emotions and other's emotions to be more successful in negotiations. A more thorough understanding of the needs and wants of the other seems secondary. The article also suggests that negotiations would be more successful if humans could be the rational beings Epoch One wanted them to be. Sadly, we fail and become emotional. The emphasis becomes the management of ourselves, rather than a deep exploration into what these emotions can tell us about the conflict.

Difficult emotions are presented as problematic rather than emblematic. A group, for example, might be enraged at forced resettlement. This anger could be seen as a healthy response to a devastating policy. To suggest that the anger ought to be "managed" rather than addressed can revictimize certain groups. This allows those in power, likely less enraged, to advocate that the victimized group should control themselves. The division and classification of emotions as good and bad perpetuate binaries of good and evil, victim and perpetrator, which Epoch Three will reconsider.

Questions to consider: Do you think there are good emotions and bad ones? Or do you think all emotions have a role?

Emotions Are Powerful, Always Present, and Hard to Handle

Daniel Shapiro and Roger Fisher

A prospective customer threatens to back out of an agreement just before the final document is signed. The dealer who sold you a brand new car says that engine problems are not covered under warranty. Your eleven-year-old announces there is simply no way she is going to wear a coat to school on this frigid February morning.

At moments like these, when your blood pressure is rising or anxiety is creeping in, rational advice about how to negotiate seems irrelevant. As constructive and reasonable as you might like to be, you may find yourself saying things like:

> "Don't do this to me. If you walk away from this agreement, I'm out of a job."
> "What kind of sleazy operation is this? Fix the engine or we'll see you in court."
> "Young lady, you're wearing a coat whether you like it or not. Put it on!"

Or perhaps you do not express your emotions in the moment, but let them eat away at you for the rest of the day. If your boss asks you to work all weekend to finish something she didn't get to, do you say okay, but spend the weekend fuming while you consider quitting? Whether you speak up or not, your emotions may take over. You may act in ways that jeopardize reaching agreement, that damage a relationship, or that cost you a lot.

Negotiation involves both your head and your gut—both reason and emotion. In this book, we offer advice to deal with emotions. Negotiation is more than rational argument. Human beings are not computers. In addition to your substantive interests, you are a part of the negotiation. Your emotions are there, and they will be involved. So, too, will the emotions of others.

What Is an Emotion?

Psychologists Fehr and Russell note that "everyone knows what an emotion is, until asked to give a definition. Then, it seems, no one knows." As we use the term, an emotion is a felt experience. You feel an emotion; you don't just think it. When someone says or does something that is personally significant to you, your emotions respond, usually along with associated thoughts, physiological changes, and a desire to do something. If a junior colleague tells you to take notes in a meeting, you might feel angry and think, "Who is be to tell me what to do?" Your physiology changes as your blood pressure rises, and you feel a desire to insult him.

Emotions can be positive or negative. A positive emotion feels personally uplifting. Whether pride, hope, or relief, a positive emotion feels good. In a negotiation, a positive emotion toward the other person is likely to build rapport, a relationship marked by goodwill, understanding, and a feeling of being "in sync." In contrast, anger, frustration, and other negative emotions feel personally distressing, and they are less likely to build rapport.[1]

This book focuses on how you can use positive emotions to help reach a wise agreement. In this chapter, we describe major obstacles you might face as you deal with emotions—both yours and those of others. Subsequent chapters give you a practical framework to overcome these obstacles. The framework does not require you to reveal your deepest emotions or to manipulate others. Instead, it provides you with practical ideas to deal with emotions. You can begin to use the framework immediately.

Emotions Can Be Obstacles to Negotiation

None of us is spared the reality of emotions. They can ruin any possibility of a wise agreement. They can turn an amicable relationship into a long-lasting feud where everybody gets hurt. And they can sour hopes for a fair settlement. What makes emotions so troubling?

They can divert attention from substantive matters. If you or the other person gets upset, each of you will have to deal with the hassle of emotions. Should you storm out of the room? Apologize? Sit quietly and fume? Your attention shifts from reaching a satisfying agreement to protecting yourself or attacking the other.

They can damage a relationship. Unbridled emotions may be desirable when falling in love. But in a negotiation, they reduce your ability to act wisely. Strong emotions can overshadow your thinking, leaving you at risk of damaging your relationship. In anger, you may interrupt the long-winded comments of a colleague who was just about to suggest an agreement workable for both of you. And in resentment, he may retaliate by remaining silent the next time you need his support.

They can be used to exploit you.[2] If you flinch at another negotiator's proposal or hesitate before telling them your interests, these observable reactions offer clues about your "true" concerns and vulnerabilities. Careful observers of your emotional reaction may learn how much you value proposals, issues, and your relationship with them. They may use that information to exploit you.

If those are possible results of emotions, it is not surprising that a negotiator is often advised to avoid them altogether.

Emotions Can Be a Great Asset

Although emotions are often thought of as obstacles to a negotiation—and certainly can be—they can also be a great asset. They can help us achieve our negotiating purpose, whether to find creative ways to satisfy interests or to improve a rocky relationship.

President Carter used the power of emotions during the historic peace negotiations between Israel and Egypt. He invited Israel's Prime Minister, Menachim Begin, and Egypt's President, Anwar Sadat, to Camp David. His goal was to help the two leaders negotiate a peace agreement. After thirteen long days, the negotiation process was breaking down. The Israelis saw little prospect for reaching agreement.

By this time, Carter had invested a lot of time and energy in the peace process. He could easily have expressed frustration, perhaps approaching Begin with a warning to accept his latest proposal "or else." But an adversarial approach might have caused Begin to abandon the negotiation process completely. It would also have risked damaging the personal relationship between the two leaders.

Instead, Carter made a gesture that had a significant emotional impact. Begin had asked for autographed pictures of Carter, Sadat, and himself to give to his grandchildren. Carter personalized each picture with the name of a Begin grandchild. During the stalemate in talks, Carter handed Begin the photographs. Begin saw his granddaughter's name on the top photograph and spoke her name aloud. His lips trembled. He shuffled through the photographs and said each grandchild's name. He and Carter talked quietly about grandchildren and about war. This was a turning point in the negotiation. Later that day, Begin, Sadat, and Carter signed the Camp David Accord.

The open discussion between Carter and Begin could not have happened if there were a poor relationship between them. Begin talked to Carter about difficult issues without resisting or walking out. The groundwork of positive emotions allowed nonthreatening conversation about serious differences.

This groundwork did not just "happen." It took work. Honest work. Carter and Begin began to establish rapport at their first meeting more than a year prior to the negotiation. They met at the White House, where Carter invited the Prime Minister for an open, private discussion about the Mideast conflict. Months later, Carter and his wife invited Begin and his wife to a private dinner, where they talked about their personal lives, including the murder of Begin's parents and his only brother in the Holocaust. Later, during the Camp David negotiation, Carter demonstrated that he was looking out for each party's welfare. For example, before Begin met with Sadat for the first time at Camp David, Carter alerted Begin that Sadat would present an aggressive proposal; he cautioned Begin not to overreact.

Carter did not want the negotiation to fail, nor did Begin or Sadat. Everyone had an interest in "winning." And positive emotions between Carter and each leader helped to move the negotiation forward.

In an international or everyday negotiation, positive emotions can be essential. They can benefit you in three important ways.

Positive emotions can make it easier to meet substantive interests. Positive emotions toward the other person reduce fear and suspicion, changing your relationship from adversaries to colleagues. As you work side by side on your problems, you become less guarded. You can try out new ideas without the fear of being taken advantage of.

With positive emotions, you are motivated to do more. Things get done more efficiently as you and others work jointly and with increased emotional commitment. You are more open to listening and more open to learning about the other party's interests, making a mutually satisfying outcome within your reach. As a result, your agreement is more likely to be stable over time.

Positive emotions can enhance a relationship. Positive emotions can provide you with the intrinsic enjoyment that comes from a person-to-person interaction. You can enjoy the experience of negotiating and the personal benefits of camaraderie. You can talk comfortably without the fear of getting sidetracked by a personal attack.

That same camaraderie can act as a safety net. It can allow you to disagree with others, knowing that even if things get tense, each of you will be there tomorrow to deal with things.

Positive emotions need not increase your risk of being exploited. Although positive emotions may help you produce a mutually satisfying agreement, there is a danger that you may feel so comfortable that you make unwise concessions or act with overconfidence. Our advice is not to inhibit positive emotions but rather to check with your head and your gut before making decisions. Before committing to an agreement, check that it satisfies your interests. Draw on standards of fairness. Know each person's alternative to a negotiated agreement, and use that information wisely.

Table 1, which follows, contrasts the effect of positive and negative emotions on a negotiation. This table illustrates the effect of emotions on seven key elements of the negotiation process that are described on page 207.

Dealing with Emotions: Three Approaches that Don't Work

Despite knowing that emotions can harm or help a negotiation, we still have little guidance on how to deal with them. How can we reap their benefits? It is sometimes suggested that negotiators: Stop having emotions; ignore them; or deal directly with them. None of those suggestions helps.

Stop Having Emotions? You Can't.

Table F1.1.   Some Frequent Effects of Emotions

Elements of Negotiation	Negative Emotions Tend to Foster:	Positive Emotions Tend to Foster:
Relationship	A tense relationship filled with distrust	A cooperative working relationship
Communication	Communication that is limited and confrontational	Open, easy, two-way communication
Interests	Ignoring interests; clinging to an extreme demand; conceding stubbornly if at all	Listening and learning about each other's concerns and wants
Options	Two options: our position or theirs	Creating a lot of possible options that might accommodate some interests of each
	Doubts that options for mutual gain are possible	Optimism that with hard work mutually beneficial options can be created
Legitimacy	A battle of wills over why we are right and they are wrong	Use of criteria that should be persuasive to both why one option is fairer than another
	Fear of being "taken"	A sense of fairness
BATNA (*Best* Alternative To a Negotiated Agreement)	Walking away from a possible agreement even if our BATNA is worse	Commitment to the best we can get, as long as it is better than our BATNA
Commitments	No agreement, or commitments that are unclear or unworkable	Well-drafted obligations that are clear, operational, and realistic
	Regret for making (or not making) the agreement	Contentment, support, and advocacy for the agreement

Some Frequent Effects of Emotions

You cannot stop having emotions any more than you can stop having thoughts. At all times you are feeling some degree of happiness or sadness, enthusiasm or frustration, isolation or engagement, pain or pleasure. You cannot turn emotions on and off like a light switch.

Consider the experience of "Michele," a researcher who was just offered a job at a big pharmaceutical company. She was initially excited about her compensation—until she discovered that two other recent hires had been offered higher initial salaries. She was upset and confused. From her point of view, her qualifications far outshone theirs.

Michele decided to negotiate for a higher salary. When asked what her negotiation strategy was, she said, "I plan to negotiate 'rationally.' I'm not going to let emotions enter into our conversation. I just want to 'talk numbers.'" She tried to persuade a company executive that if others of equal caliber received a higher salary, she deserved a similar compensation. Good, principled approach. Unfortunately, the negotiation did not go well. Her emotions failed to stop during the negotiation, even though she presumed she had them under control.

As Michele recalls: "The tone of my voice was more abrasive than usual. I didn't want it to be that way. But it was. I felt upset that the company was trying to hire me for less money than the other two new hires. The company's negotiator interpreted my statements as demands. I was surprised when the negotiator said that he refused to be arm twisted into giving a salary raise to anyone, let alone a new hire. I wasn't trying to coerce him into a salary raise. But my emotions just didn't switch off the way I had hoped."

In most circumstances, negotiators would be foolish to turn off emotions even if they could. Stopping emotions would make your job harder, not easier. Emotions convey information to you about the relative importance of your concerns. They focus you on those things about which you care personally, such as respect or job security. You also learn what is important to the other side. If the other person communicates an interest with great enthusiasm, you might assume that that interest is important. Rather than spend days trying to understand the other side's interests and priorities, you can save time and energy by learning what you can from their emotions.

IGNORE EMOTIONS? IT WON'T WORK.

You ignore emotions at your peril. Emotions are always present and often affect your experience. You may try to ignore them, but they will not ignore you. In a negotiation, you may be only marginally aware of the important ways that emotions influence your body, your thinking, and your behavior.

Emotions affect your body. Emotions can have an immediate impact on your physiology, causing you to perspire, to blush, to laugh, or to feel butterflies in your stomach. After you feel an emotion, you might try to control the expression of that emotion. You might hold back from a smile of excitement or from crying in disappointment. But your body still experiences physiological changes. And suppressing the emotion comes at a cost. A suppressed emotion continues to affect your body. Whether an emotion is negative or positive, internal stress can distract your attention. Trying to suppress that emotion can make it harder to concentrate on substantive issues.

Emotions affect your thinking. When you feel disappointment or anger, your head clogs with negative thoughts. You may criticize yourself or blame others. Negative thinking crowds out space in your brain for learning, thinking, and remembering. In fact, some negotiators become so wrapped up in their own negative emotions and thoughts that they fail to hear their counterpart make an important concession.

When you feel positive emotions, in contrast, your thoughts often center on what is right about you, others, or ideas. With little anxiety that you will be exploited, your thinking becomes more open, creative, and flexible. You become inclined not to reject ideas but to invent workable options.

Emotions affect your behavior. Virtually every emotion you feel motivates you to take action. If you are exuberant, you may feel a physical impulse to hug the other side. If you are angry, you may feel like hitting them.

Usually you can stop yourself before you perform a regrettable action. When you feel a strong emotion, however, careful thinking lags behind, and you may feel powerless to your emotion. In such moments, your ability to censor your thoughts or reflect on possible action is severely limited. You may find yourself saying or doing things that you later regret.

DEAL DIRECTLY WITH EMOTIONS? A COMPLICATED TASK.

Negotiators are often advised to become aware of emotions—both their own and those of others—and to deal directly with those emotions. Some people are naturally talented at dealing directly with emotions, and most can improve their ability. If a negotiator habitually gets angry, for example, he or she can learn helpful skills to recognize and manage that anger.

Yet even for a trained psychologist or psychiatrist, it is a daunting proposition to deal directly with every emotion as it happens in oneself and others. And trying to deal directly with emotions is particularly challenging when negotiating, where you also need to spend time thinking about each person's differing views on substantive issues and the process for working together. It can feel as though you are trying to ride a bicycle while juggling and talking on a cell phone.

Dealing directly with every emotion as it happens would keep you very busy. As you negotiate, you would have to look for evidence of emotions in yourself and in others. Are you sweating? Are their arms crossed? You would have to infer the many specific emotions taking place in you and in them. (Look through the list of emotion words in Table F1.2. on page 369 and think how long it takes simply to read through that list, let alone to correctly identify which emotions you and others are feeling.) You would have to make informed guesses about the apparent causes, which may be multiple and unclear. Is the other person upset because of something you said—or because of a fight with a family member this morning?

You would have to decide how to behave, then behave that way, and then notice the emotional impact of that behavior on yourself and on the other person. If the resulting emotions are negative and strong, there is a great risk that each person's emotions will quickly escalate.

Emotion Words

Emotions are usually contagious. Even if your emotions change from frustration to active interest, the other person is likely to be reacting still to your indignant behavior of a few minutes ago. The impact of a negative emotion lingers long after it has passed. The stronger and more troublesome the emotion, the greater the risk that both of you will lose control.

Table F1.2.   Emotion Words

Positive Emotions	*Negative Emotions*
Excited	Guilty
Glad	Ashamed
Amused	Humiliated
Enthusiastic	Embarrassed
Cheerful	Regretful
Jovial	
Delighted	Envious
Ecstatic	Jealous
	Disgusted
Proud	Resentful
Gratified	Contemptuous
Happy	
Jubilant	Impatient
Thrilled	Irritated
Overjoyed	Angry
Elated	Furious
	Outraged
Relieved	
Comforted	Intimidated
Content	Worried
Relaxed	Surprised
Patient	Fearful
Tranquil	Panicked
Calm	Horrified
Hopeful	Sad
In awe	Hopeless
Wonder	Miserable
	Devastated

Thus comes the question to which this book is directed: How should a negotiator cope with the interacting, important, and ever-changing emotions of each side? Given that we cannot realistically be expected to observe, understand, and deal directly with these emotions as they occur, must we simply react as best we can?

An Alternative: Focus on Core Concerns

This book offers negotiators—and that means everyone—a powerful framework for dealing with emotions. Whether or not you acknowledge emotions, they will have an impact on your negotiation. As the following chapters suggest, you can avoid reacting to scores of constantly changing emotions and turn your attention to five core concerns that are responsible for many, if not most, emotions in a negotiation. These core concerns lie at the heart of many emotional challenges when you negotiate. Rather than feeling powerless in the face of emotions, you will be able to stimulate positive emotions and overcome negative ones.

Notes

1. As a general negotiating strategy, positive emotions are more likely than negative emotions to foster rapport and collaboration. Yet, tactically, even the negative emotion of anger can enable two people to clear the air and get back together. And, to be sure, sometimes negative feelings such as grief can bring people together as they share the grief.

2. In this book, we sometimes use the third person plural—they, them, or their—where strict grammar would suggest using a singular, such as he or she. Other options seem to lead to some sort of stereotyping or distracting language.

Problem-Solving Workshops

Herbert Kelman

Herbert Kelman, professor emeritus at Harvard University, served for ten years as the director of the Program on International Conflict Analysis and Resolution (PICAR) at the Weatherhead Center for International Affairs. Kelman began with a PhD in social psychology from Yale University and, over the years, has won many awards for his contribution to psychology. He spent decades developing his interactive problem-solving workshops described in this article. Many of his efforts sought to bring some hope and resolution to the Arab–Israeli conflict.

Problem-solving workshops bring political elites together to enable them to work collaboratively through the conflicts in their regions. As with mediation, professional outsiders facilitate the meetings. These workshops seek to enhance traditional negotiation or mediation approaches by transforming the conflict parties' relations. Proponents of problem-solving workshops acknowledge that good negotiation skills will have limited effectiveness without receptivity to change on both sides. The workshop approach seeks to transform relations and increase receptivity through a series of pre-meetings and a number of workshops where new ideas are discussed. Issues of confidentially, power, and relationship-building are all also considered to produce high-quality, lasting agreements with sufficient psychological and institutional support.

The belief about conflict here is that distrust and damaged relationships prove as problematic as the lack of a mutually agreeable solution. Relationship-building and exploration are hallmarks of these settings. Because workshops involve predominantly high-level elites who then share this change with their political culture, this is a trickle-down theory of change.

The consideration of context, community influence, and relational dynamics is characteristic in Epoch Two. However, the inclusion solely of elite parties makes this still resonant with Epoch One approaches. In considering limitations to this approach, the question of power remains under-examined in two ways. First, it raises the question as to how parties that come from differing sides of a conflict can erase the power differences while participating in the workshops. Second, it points to the question of reintegration—if attitudes shift during a workshop, what potentially happens when they leave the safety net of the workshops and return back to their homes?

Questions to consider: How might relationship-building enhance traditional negotiations? How might problem-solving workshops move participants away from fixed sum thinking? What are some potential limitations
to this approach? What might happen for individuals who are taken out
of their contexts and shift their ideas and then return back to those same
contexts?

Interactive Problem Solving as a Tool for Second Track Diplomacy

Herbert C. Kelman

For some years, my colleagues and I have been actively engaged in the development and application of an approach to the resolution of international conflicts
for which we use the term "interactive problem solving."[1] The fullest—indeed,
the paradigmatic—application of the approach is represented by problem-solving
workshops (Kelman. 1972. 1979. 1992, 1996b: Kelman and Cohen, 1986).
Although it involves a variety of other activities as well, in fact. I have increasingly
come to see interactive problem solving as an approach to the macroprocesses of
international conflict resolution, in which problem-solving workshops and similar
micro-level activities are integrally related to official diplomacy (Kelman, 1996a).

The approach derives most directly from the work of John Burton (1969,
1979, 1984). While my work follows the general principles laid out by Burton, it
has evolved in its own directions, in keeping with my own disciplinary background, my particular style, and the cases on which I have focused my attention.
My work has concentrated since 1974 on the Arab-Israeli conflict, particularly on
the Israeli-Palestinian component of that conflict. I have also done some work,
however, on the Cyprus conflict and have maintained an active interest in several
other intense, protracted identity conflicts at the international or intercommunal
level, such as the conflicts in Bosnia, Sri Lanka, and Northern Ireland

During the 1970s, as I became more actively involved in work in and on the
Middle East. I collaborated extensively with Ed Azar. He was part of our third-
party team (see Kelman, 1978), which organized and facilitated problem- solving
workshops and other joint activities with Egyptians, Israelis, and Palestinians, and
which also traveled together in the Middle East. In the course of these activities, I
benefited enormously from Ed's insights into Arab politics. culture, and society.
Ed and I shared the view (to be elaborated later in this chapter) that international

conflict is not merely an interstate phenomenon but also an intersocietal phenomenon. This view was reflected in Ed's emphasis on development as an essential context of peace and conflict resolution, a theme that ran through the entire body of his work (sec, e.g., Azar, 1979) and that greatly influenced my thinking about protracted conflict. In my work, the view of conflict as an intersocietal phenomenon is reflected in the emphasis on the role of unofficial interactions as an integral component of the larger diplomatic process. Intrigued by this potential of interactive problem solving, Ed joined our third-party team, later collaborated with Stephen Cohen and with John Burton in other third-party efforts (see, e.g., Cohen and Azar, 1981; Azar and Burton, 1986), and developed his own "problem-solving forum" approach to track-two diplomacy (Azar, 1990, this volume).

Interactive Problem Solving

Interactive problem solving—as manifested particularly in problem-solving workshops—is an academically based, unofficial third-party approach, bringing together representatives of parties in conflict for direct communication. The third party typically consists of a panel of social scientists who between them, possess expertise in group process and international conflict, and at least some familiarity with the conflict region. The role of the third party in our model differs from that of the traditional mediator. Unlike many mediators, we do not propose (and certainly, unlike arbitrators, we do not impose) solutions. Rather, we try to facilitate a process whereby solutions will emerge out of the interaction between the parties themselves. The task of the third party is to provide the setting, create the atmosphere, establish the norms, and offer the occasional interventions that make it possible for such a process to evolve.

Although the distinguishing feature of the approach (in contrast, for example, to traditional mediation) is direct communication between the parties, the objective is not to promote communication or dialogue as an end in itself. Problem-solving workshops are designed to promote a special type of communication—to be described below—with a very specific political purpose. Problem-solving workshops are closely linked to the larger political process. Selection of participants and definition of the agenda, for example, are based on careful analysis of the current political situation within and between the conflicting parties. Moreover, the objective of workshops is to generate inputs into the political process, including the decision-making process itself and the political debate within each of the communities. Most broadly stated, workshops try to contribute to creating a political environment conducive to conflict resolution and to transformation of the relationship between the conflicting parties—both in the short term and in the long term.

Practically speaking, this emphasis usually means that problem-solving workshops are closely linked to negotiation in its various phases, although negotiation does not by any means fully encompass the process of changing international relationships (see Saunders, 1988). In our work on the Israeli-Palestinian conflict in earlier years, problem-solving workshops were designed to contribute to the prenegotiation process: to creating a political atmosphere that would encourage the parties to move to the negotiating table. Thus, in planning and following up on workshops, we focused on the barriers that stood in the way of opening negotiations and on ways of overcoming such barriers—for example, through mutual reassurance. With the beginning of official Israeli-Palestinian negotiations in the fall of 1991, our focus of necessity shifted (Rouhana and Kelman, 1994). During the active negotiation phase, workshops can contribute to overcoming obstacles to staying at the table and negotiating effectively, to exploring options for resolving issues that are not yet on the table, to refraining such issues so as to make them more amenable to negotiation, and to beginning the process of peacebuilding that must accompany and follow the process of peacemaking. Workshops can also be of value in the postnegotiation phase, where they can contribute to implementation of the negotiated agreement and to long-term peacebuilding.

Despite the close link between workshops and negotiations, we have been very clear in emphasizing that workshops are not to be confused with negotiations as such. They are not meant to be negotiations, simulated negotiations, or rehearsals for negotiations, or to serve as substitutes for negotiations. Rather, they are meant to be complementary to negotiations.

Binding agreements can be achieved only through official negotiations. The very binding character of official negotiations, however, makes it very difficult for certain other things to happen in that context—such as the exploration and discovery of the parties' basic concerns, their priorities, their limits. This is where problem-solving workshops—precisely because of their nonbinding character—can make a special contribution to the larger process of negotiation and conflict resolution. This special relationship to the negotiation process underlines one of the central differences between interactive problem solving and traditional mediation: Problem-solving workshops are generally not designed to facilitate or influence the official negotiation process directly, although they do play a significant indirect role. Insofar as we mediate, it is not between the negotiators representing the two parties but between their political communities. What we try to facilitate is not the process of negotiation itself but communication that helps the parties overcome the political, emotional, and at times technical barriers that often prevent them from entering into negotiations, from reaching agreement in the course of negotiations, or from changing their relationship after a political agreement has been negotiated.

Central Features of Problem-Solving Workshops

Until the fall of 1990, the Israeli-Palestinian workshops we organized were all self-contained, one-time events. Some of the participants were involved in more than one workshop, and many were involved in a variety of other efforts at communication across the conflict line. For these and other reasons, there was continuity between these separate events, and they seem to have had a cumulative effect in helping to create a political environment conducive to negotiations. However, because of logistical and financial constraints and a lack of political readiness, we made no attempt before 1990 to reconvene the same group of participants over a series of meetings.

In the fall of 1990, Nadim Rouhana and I convened our first continuing workshop with a group of high-level, politically influential Israelis and Palestinians. The full group met five times between November 1990 and August 1993—a period that included the Persian Gulf crisis and war, the beginning of official negotiations, and the election of a Labor party government in Israel (see Rouhana and Kelman, 1994).[2] After the Oslo agreement (September 1993). Rouhana and I initiated a new project, a Joint Working Group on Israeli-Palestinian Relations (see Kelman, 1996b). This group began meeting in 1994 and held a total of fifteen plenary meetings and a number of sub-committee meetings between the spring of 1994 and the summer of 1999. In contrast to our earlier workshop efforts, the working group was designed to generate and disseminate concrete products in the form of a series of concept papers on final-status issues in the Israeli-Palestinian negotiations and on the long-term relationship between the two societies.[3] The group has published three papers: one on general principles for the final-status negotiations (Joint Working Group. 1999), one on the problem of Palestinian refugees and the right of return (Alpher and Shikaki, et al., 1999), and one on the future Israeli-Palestinian relationship (Joint Working Group, 2000). A fourth paper, on Israeli settlements, is close to completion, but there are no immediate plans to publish it.

To provide a more concrete sense of problem-solving workshops and their underlying logic, I shall describe the format of a typical one-time workshop. It should be stressed, however, that most workshops are in fact "atypical" in one or more respects. Workshops (including continuing workshops) conform to a set of fundamental principles, but they vary in some of their details, depending on the particular occasion, purpose, and set of participants. What I am presenting, then, is a composite picture, which most workshops approximate but do not necessarily correspond to in all details.

Most of our one-time workshops have been held at Harvard University, under the auspices of the Center for International Affairs or in the context of my graduate seminar on international conflict. Workshop sessions usually take place in a seminar room, with participants seated at a round table, although in some cases we have used a living room or a private meeting room at a hotel. The typical workshop is a private, confidential event, without observers. The discussions are not taped, but members of the third party take notes.

Participants in an Israeli-Palestinian workshop usually include three to six members of each party, as well as three to eight third-party members. The numbers have been smaller on some occasions. For example, I have arranged a number of one-on-one meetings, with the participation of one or two third-party members. These meetings have served important purposes and have retained many features of problem-solving workshops, although one major feature—intraparty interaction—is missing. In quite a few of our workshops, the size of the third party has been larger than eight. As an integral feature of my graduate seminar on international conflict, I organized an annual workshop, in which the seminar participants—usually about twenty—served as apprentice members of the third party. Only eight third-party members sat around the table at any one session, however: three "permanent" members (including myself and two colleagues with workshop experience) and five seminar participants, on a rotating basis. When they were not around the table, the seminar participants were able to follow the proceedings (with the full knowledge of the parties, of course) from an adjoining room with a one-way mirror. They were fully integrated into the third party: they took part in all the workshop activities (preworkshop sessions, briefings, breaks, meals, a social gathering) and were always bound by the requirements and discipline of the third-party role. Apart from the large size of the third party, the workshops linked to this graduate seminar were similar to "regular" workshops in their purpose and format, and were widely seen as not just academic exercises but serious political encounters.

The Israeli and Palestinian participants in workshops are all politically active and invoked members of the mainstreams of their respective communities. Many, by virtue of their positions or general standing, can be described as politically influential. Depending on the occasion and the political level of the participants, we may discuss our plans for a workshop with relevant elements of the political leadership on both sides, in order to keep them informed, gain their support, and solicit their advice on participants and agenda. For many potential workshop participants, approval and at times encouragement from the political leadership is a necessary condition for their agreement to take part. Recruitment, however, is generally done on an individual basis, and participants are invited to come as individuals rather than as formal representatives. Invitees, of course, may consult with their leaderships or with each other before agreeing to come. Whenever possible, we start the recruitment process with one key person on each side: we then consult with that person and with each successive invitee in selecting the rest of the team. At times, the composition of a team may be negotiated within the particular community (or subcommunity) that we approach, but the final invitation is always issued by the third party to each individual participant.

As an essential part of the recruitment process, we almost always discuss the purposes, procedures, and ground rules of the workshop personally with each participant before obtaining her or his final commitment. Whenever possible, this is done during a face-to-face meeting, although at times it is necessary to do it over the telephone. In addition to the individual briefings, we generally organize two preworkshop sessions, in which the members of each party meet separately with the third party. In these sessions, which generally last four to five hours, we first review the purposes, procedures, and ground rules of the workshop. We then ask the participants to talk about their sides' perspectives on the conflict, the range of views within their community, the current status of the conflict as they see it and the conditions and possibilities for resolving it, and their conceptions of the needs and positions of the other side. We encourage the participants to discuss these issues among themselves. We make it clear that the role of the third party— even in the preworkshop session—is to facilitate the exchange, in part through occasional questions and comments, but not to enter into the substantive discussion or to debate or evaluate what is being said.

The preworkshop sessions fulfill a number of important functions. They provide an opportunity for the participants to become acquainted with the setting, the third party, and members of their own team whom they had not previously met, without having to confront the other party at the same time; to raise questions about the purposes, procedures, and ground rules of the workshop; to begin to practice the type of discourse that the workshop is trying to encourage; to gain a better understanding of the role of the third party; and to "do their duty" by telling the third party their side of the story and enumerating their grievances, thus reducing the pressure to adhere to the conflict norms in the course of the workshop itself. The preworkshop sessions also give the third party an opportunity to observe some of the internal differences within each team and to compare the ways in which the parties treat the issues when they are alone and when they are together.

The workshops themselves generally last two and a half days, often taking place over an extended weekend. The opening session, typically late Friday afternoon, begins with a round of introductions, in which the participants are encouraged to go beyond their professional credentials and say something about their reasons for coming. We then review, once again, the purposes, procedures, and ground rules of the workshop, stressing the principles of privacy and confidentiality, the nature of the discourse that we are trying to encourage, and the role of the third party. This review, in the presence of all of the participants, serves to emphasize the nature of the contract to which all three parties are committing themselves. After dinner, shared by the entire group, we reconvene for the first substantive session. On the second day, we have two sessions (each lasting one and a half hours) in the morning, with a half-hour coffee break in between. The same pattern is repeated after lunch. That evening, there is a dinner and social gathering for all participants, typically held at the home of the Kelmans. On the third day, there are again two sessions each in the morning and afternoon; the workshop closes late that afternoon. Thus, in addition to ten sessions around the table, workshops provide ample opportunities for informal interaction during meals and breaks. Sometimes participants create additional opportunities for themselves.

In opening the first substantive session, the third party—after describing the political context and the focus of the workshop—proposes a loose agenda. The specific agenda must depend, of course, on the stage of the conflict and the character of the group. The agenda followed in most of our workshops prior to 1992 are appropriate for initial workshops (i.e., workshops whose participants are convening for the first time as a group) in a conflict that is still in a pre-negotiation phase. The main task that we have set for our workshop participants in recent years has been to generate—through their interaction—ideas for bringing the parties to the negotiating table, or for negotiating more productively if they are already at the table. To get the interaction started, we ask the participants to describe their views of the conflict and its current status, to define the spectrum of positions vis-à-vis the conflict in their own societies and to place themselves along that spectrum.

We try to move as rapidly as possible from this more conventional, descriptive discussion into the analytic, problem-solving mode of interaction that is at the heart of the agenda. First, we ask the participants on both sides to talk about their central concerns: the fundamental needs that an agreement would have to satisfy and the fundamental fears that it would have to allay in order to be acceptable to their communities. Only after both sets of concerns are on the table and each side's concerns have been understood by the other are the participants asked to explore the overall shape of a solution that would meet the needs and calm the fears of both sides. Each is expected to think actively about solutions that would be satisfactory to the other, not only to themselves. Next, the participants are asked to discuss the political and psychological constraints that make it difficult to implement such solutions. Finally, the discussion turns to the question of how these constraints can best be overcome and how the two sides can support each other in such an effort. Depending on how much time is left and on the prevailing mood, the participants may try to come up with concrete ideas for unilateral, coordinated, or joint actions—by themselves or their communities—that might help overcome the barriers to negotiating a mutually satisfactory solution.

The agenda described here is not followed rigidly but rather serves as a broad framework for the interaction. The discussions are relatively unstructured and, insofar as possible, are allowed to maintain their natural flow. We are careful not to intervene excessively or prematurely and not to cut off potentially fruitful discussions because they appear to be deviating from the agenda. If the discussion goes too far afield, becomes repetitive, or systematically avoids the issues, the third party—usually with the help of at least some of the participants—will try to bring it back to the broad agenda. In general, the third party is prepared to intervene in order to help keep the discussion moving along productive, constructive channels. At times, particularly at the beginning or at the end of a session, we also make substantive interventions, in order to help interpret, integrate, clarify, or sharpen what is being said or done in the group On the whole, however, the emphasis in our model is on facilitating the emergence of ideas out of the interaction between the participants themselves. Consistent with that emphasis, we try to stay in the background as much as possible once we have set the stage.

Having drawn a general picture of the format and proceedings of a typical workshop, let me now highlight some of the special features of the approach.

ACADEMIC CONTEXT

In my colleagues' and my own third-party efforts, our academic base provides the major venue of our activities and source of our authority and credibility. The academic context has several advantages for our enterprise. It allows the parties to interact with each other in a relatively noncommittal way, since the setting is not only unofficial but also known as one in which people engage in free exchange of views, in playful consideration of new ideas, and in "purely academic" discussions. Thus, an academic setting is a good place to set into motion a process of successive approximations, in which parties that do not trust each other begin to communicate in a noncommittal framework, but gradually move to increasing levels of commitment as their level of working trust increases (Kelman, 1982). Another advantage of the academic context is that it allows us to call upon an alternative set of norms to counteract the norms that typically govern interactions between conflicting parties. Academic norms favor open discussion, attentive listening to opposing views, and an analytical approach, in contrast to the polemical, accusatory, and legalistic approach that conflict norms tend to promote.

NATURE OF INTERACTION

The setting, norms, ground rules, agenda, procedures, and third-party interventions in problem-solving workshops arc all designed to facilitate a kind of interaction that differs from the way parties in conflict usually interact—if they interact at all. Within the workshop setting, participants are encouraged to talk to each other, rather than to their constituencies or to third parties, and to listen to each other—not in order to discover the weaknesses in the other's argument but in order to penetrate the other's perspective. The principles of privacy and confidentiality—apart from protecting the interests of the participants—are designed to protect this process, by reducing the participants concern about how each word they say during the workshop will be perceived on the outside. In order to counteract the tendency to speak to the record, we have avoided creating a record, in the form of audio or videotapes or formal minutes. The absence of an audience and the third party's refusal to take sides, evaluate what is said, adjudicate differences, or become involved in the debate of substantive issues further encourage the parties to focus on each other rather than attempt to influence external parties. These features of the workshop are in no way designed to encourage the participants to forget about their constituencies or relevant third parties; ideas generated in workshops must be acceptable to the two communities, as well as to outside actors, if they are to have the desired impact on the political process. Rather, these features are designed to prevent the intrusion of these actors into the workshop interaction itself, thus inhibiting and distorting the generation of new ideas.

A second central element in the nature of the interaction that workshops try to promote is an analytic focus. Workshop discussions are analytical in the sense that participants try to gain a better understanding of the other's—and indeed of their own—concerns, needs, fears, priorities, and constraints, and of the way in which the divergent perspectives of the parties help to feed and escalate their conflict. It is particularly important for each party to gain an understanding of the other's perspective (without accepting that perspective) and of the domestic dynamics that shape the policy debate in each community. To appreciate the constraints under which the other operates is especially difficult in a conflict relationship, since the parties' thinking tends to be dominated by their own respective constraints. But an analytic understanding of the constraints—along with the fundamental concerns—that inform the other's perspective is a sine qua non for inventing solutions that are feasible and satisfactory for both sides.

Analytical discussions proceed on the basis of a "no fault" principle. While there is no presumption that both sides are equally at fault, the discussions are not oriented toward assigning blame but toward exploring the causes of the conflict and the obstacles to its resolution. This analytical approach is designed to lead to a problem-solving mode of interaction, based on the proposition that the conflict represents a joint problem for the two parties that requires joint efforts at solution.

DUAL PURPOSE

Workshops have a dual purpose, which can be described as educational and political. They are designed to produce both changes in attitudes, perceptions, and ideas for resolving the conflict among the individual participants in the workshop, and transfer of these changes to the political arena—i.e., to the political debate and the decision-making process within each community. The political purpose is an integral part of the workshop approach, whatever the level of the participants involved. Workshops provide opportunities for the parties to interact, to become acquainted with each other, and to humanize their mutual images, not as ends in themselves but as means to producing new learnings that can then be fed into the political process. Some of the specific learnings that participants have acquired in the course of workshops and then communicated to their own political leaderships or publics have included: information about the range of views on the other side, signs of readiness for negotiation, and the availability of potential negotiating partners: insights into the other side's priorities, rock-bottom requirements, and areas of flexibility and ideas for confidence-building measures, mutually acceptable solutions to issues in conflict, and ways of moving to the negotiating table.

Because of their dual purpose, problem-solving workshops are marked by a dialectical character (Kelman, 1979; Kelman and Cohen, 1986). Some of the conditions favorable to change in the workshop setting may be antagonistic to the transfer of changes to the political arena, and vice versa. There is often a need, therefore, to find the proper balance between contradictory requirements if a workshop is to be effective in fulfilling both its educational and its political purpose. For example, it is important for the participants to develop a considerable degree of working trust in order to engage in joint problem solving, to devise direct or tacit collaborative efforts for overcoming constraints against negotiation, and to become convinced that there are potential negotiating partners on the other side. This trust, however, must not be allowed to turn into excessive camaraderie transcending the conflict, lest the participants lose their credibility and their potential political influence once they return to their home communities. Workshops can be seen as part of a process of building coalitions across the conflict line, but the coalitions must remain uneasy ones that do not threaten members' relationships to their own identity groups (Kelman, 1993).

The selection of participants provides another example of a central workshop feature for which the dialectics of the process have important implications. The closer the participants are to the centers of power in their own communities, the greater the likelihood that what they learn in the course of their workshop experience will be fed directly into the decision-making process. By the same token, however, the closer participants are to the centers of power, the more constrained they are likely to feel, and the greater their difficulty in entering into communication that is open, noncommittal, exploratory, and analytical. Thus, on the whole, as participants move closer to the level of top decision makers, they become less likely to show change as a result of their workshop experience, but whatever changes do occur are more likely to be transferred to the policy process. These contradictory effects have to be taken into account in selecting participants for a given occasion or in defining the goals and agenda for a workshop with a given set of participants. In general, the best way to balance the requirements for change and for transfer is to select participants who are politically influential but not directly involved in the execution of foreign policy. The approach can be adapted for use with decision makers themselves, as long as the facilitators are aware of the advantages and drawbacks of participants at that level.

The workshops and related encounters that we have organized over the years have included participants at three different levels of relationship to the decision-making process: political actors, such as parliamentarians, negotiators, part) activists, or advisers to political leaders; political "influentials" such as former officials and diplomats, senior academics (who are leading analysts of the conflict in their own communities and occasional advisers to decision makers), community leaders, writers, or editors: and "pre-influentials," such as younger academics and professionals or advanced graduate students who are slated to move into influential positions in their respective fields. The lines between these three categories are not very precise: moreover, many participants who may have been "pre-influentials" at the time of their workshop have since become influential, and some of our "influentials" have since become political actors. Whatever the level of the participants, a central criterion for selection is that they be politically involved—at least as active participants in the political debate and perhaps in political movements. From our point of view, even this degree of involvement is of direct political relevance, since it contributes to the shaping of the political environment for any peace effort. Another criterion for selection is that participants be part of the mainstreams of their communities and that they enjoy credibility within broad segments of those communities. We look for participants who are as close as possible to the center of the political spectrum, while at the same time interested in negotiations and open to the workshop process. As a result, workshop participants so far have tended to be on the dovish ("moderate" or pro-negotiation) side of the center.

THIRD-PARTY CONTRIBUTIONS

Although workshops proceed on the principle that useful ideas for conflict resolution must emerge out of the interaction between the parties themselves, the third party plays an essential role (at certain stages of a conflict) in making that interaction possible and fruitful. The third party provides the context in which representatives of parties engaged in an intense conflict are able to come together. It selects, briefs, and convenes the participants. It serves as a repository of trust for both parties, enabling them to proceed with assurance that their confidentiality will be respected and their interests protected, even though—by definition—they cannot trust each other. It establishes and enforces the norms and ground rules that facilitate analytic discussion and a problem-solving orientation. It proposes a broad agenda that encourages the parties to move from exploration of each other's concerns and constraints to the generation of ideas for win/win solutions and for implementing such solutions. It tries to keep the discussion moving in constructive directions. Finally, it makes occasional interventions. These may take the form of content observations, which suggest interpretations and implications of what is being said and point to convergences and divergences between the parties, to blind spots, to possible signals, and to issues for clarification; of process observations at the intergroup level which suggest possible ways in which interactions between the parties "here and now" may reflect the dynamics of the conflict between their communities, and of theoretical inputs, which help participants distance themselves from their own conflict, provide them conceptual tools for analysis of their conflict, and offer them relevant illustrations from previous research.

Process observations are among the unique features of problem-solving workshops. They generally focus on incidents in which one party's words or actions clearly have a strong emotional impact on the other—leading to expressions of anger and dismay, of relief and reassurance, of understanding and acceptance, or of reciprocation. The third party can use such incidents, which are part of the participants' shared immediate experience, as a springboard for exploring some of the issues and concerns that define the conflict between their societies. Through such exploration, each side can gain some insight into the preoccupations of the other and into the way these are affected by its own actions. Process observations must be introduced sparingly, and they make special demands on the third party's skill and sense of timing. It is particularly important that such interventions be pitched at the intergroup rather than the interpersonal level. Analysis of "here and now" interactions is not concerned with the personal characteristics of the participants or with their personal relations to each other but only with what these interactions can tell us about the relationship between their national groups.

Social-Psychological Assumptions

The practice of interactive problem solving is informed by a set of assumptions about the nature of international/intercommunal conflict and conflict resolution. These assumptions are meant to be general in nature, although they refer most directly to conflicts between identity groups and may not be equally applicable in other cases. Thus, the problem-solving approach is likely to be most relevant in conflicts in which identity issues play a central role.

In my particular conception of the problem-solving approach, the guiding assumptions derive from a social-psychological analysis, which provides a bridge between individual behavior and social interaction, on the one hand, and the functioning of social systems (organizations, institutions, societies) and collectivities, on the other (Kelman, 1997b). Social-psychological assumptions enter into the formulation of the structure, the process, and the content of problem-solving workshops.

WORKSHOP STRUCTURE

Workshop structure refers primarily to the role of workshops in the larger political context and their place within the social system in which the conflict is carried on. In effect, the focus here is on the relationship between the microprocess of the workshop and the macroprocess of conflict management or resolution. Several assumptions underlie our view of this relationship and hence the way in which workshops are structured.

Conflict as an Intersocietal Process

International conflict is not merely an intergovernmental or interstate phenomenon but also an intersocietal phenomenon. Thus, in addition to the strategic, military, and diplomatic dimensions, it is necessary to give central consideration to the economic, psychological, cultural, and social-structural dimensions in the analysis of the conflict. Interactions along these dimensions, both within and between the conflicting societies, form the essential political environment in which governments function. It is necessary to look at these intrasocietal and intersocietal processes in order to understand the political constraints under which governments operate and the resistance to change that these produce. By the same token, these societal factors, if properly understood and utilized, provide opportunities and levers for change.

This view has a direct implication for the selection of workshop participants. To be politically relevant, workshops do not require the participation of decision makers or their agents. In fact, as proposed in the earlier discussion of the dual purposes and dialectical character of workshops, the ideal participants may be individuals who are politically influential but not directly invoked in the foreign-policy decision-making process. The important consideration is that they be active and credible contributors to the political debate within their own communities and thus be able to play a role in changing the political environment.

Another implication of the view of international conflict as an intersocietal phenomenon is that third-party efforts should ideally be directed not merely to a settlement of the conflict, but to its resolution. A political agreement may be adequate for terminating relatively specific, containable interstate disputes, but it is an inadequate response to conflicts that engage the collective identities and existential concerns of the societies involved.

Conflict Resolution as Transformation of the Relationship

Following from the stress on the intersocietal nature of conflict is the assumption that conflict resolution represents an effort to transform the relationship between the conflicting parties. This assumption has direct implications for the type of solutions that third-party intervention tries to generate. First, solutions must emerge out of the interaction between the parties themselves: the process of interactive problem solving itself contributes to transforming the relationship between the parties. Second, solutions must address the needs of both parties, thus providing the foundation of a new- relationship between them. Finally, the nature of the solutions and the process by which they were achieved must be such that the parties will be committed to them: only thus can they establish a new relationship on a long-term basis.

Diplomacy as a Mix of Official and Unofficial Processes

Another corollary of the stress on the intersocietal nature of conflict is the view of diplomacy as a broad and complex mix of official and unofficial processes. The peaceful termination or management of conflicts requires binding agreements that can only be achieved at the official level. Unofficial interactions, however, can play a constructive complementary role, particularly by contributing to the development of a political environment conducive to negotiations and other diplomatic initiatives (Saunders. 1988). Problem-solving workshops and other informal efforts, as pointed out at the beginning of the chapter, can make such contributions precisely because of their nonbinding character. In such settings—in contrast to official forums—it is much easier for the parties to engage in noncommittal, exploratory interactions, which allow them to test each other's limits, develop empathy, or engage in creative problem solving. Accordingly, many of the features of problem-solving workshops are specifically geared to maximize the noncommittal nature of the interaction: the academic context; the assurance of privacy and confidentiality; the absence (at least in our earlier work) of expectations of specific products; and the emphasis on interactions characterized by exploration, sharing of perspectives, playing with ideas, brainstorming, and creative problem solving—rather than bargaining.

Impact of Intragroup Conflict on Intergroup Conflict

A further assumption relates to the interplay between intragroup and intergroup conflict. In many international and intercommunal conflicts, internal divisions within each party shape the course of the conflict between the parties. This phenomenon represents a special instance of the general observation of continuities between domestic and international politics. Understanding of the internal divisions within each party is essential to the selection of workshop participants, since the political significance of workshops depends on the potential impact these participants can have on the internal debate. The internal divisions in each society are also a major focus of concern within workshops, particularly when the discussion turns to the political and psychological constraints against compromise solutions and ways of overcoming these constraints.

More generally, I have already alluded to my conceptualization (Kelman, 1993) of workshops and related activities as part of a process of forming a coalition across the conflict line—a coalition between those elements on each side that are interested in a negotiated solution. It is very important to keep in mind, however, that such a coalition must of necessity remain an uneasy coalition. If it became overly cohesive, it would undermine the whole purpose of the enterprise: to have an impact on the political decisions within the two communities. Workshop participants who become closely identified with their counterparts on the other side may become alienated from their own conationals, lose credibility, and hence forfeit their political effectiveness and their ability to promote a new consensus within their own communities. One of the challenges for problem-solving workshops, therefore, is to create an atmosphere in which participants can begin to humanize and trust each other and to develop an effective collaborative relationship without losing sight of their separate group identities and the conflict between their communities.

The World System as a Global Society

At the broadest level, my assumptions about international and inter-communal conflict rest on a view of the world system as a global society—a term used here not only normatively but also descriptively. To be sure, the global society is a weak society, lacking many of the customary features of a society. Still, conceiving of the world as a society corrects for the untenable view of nation-states as sole and unitary actors in the global arena. Clearly, nation-states remain the dominant actors within our current global society. The nation-state benefits from the principle of sovereignty and from its claim to represent its population's national identity—perhaps the most powerful variant of group identity in the modern world. (In intercommunal conflicts within established nation-states, the ethnic community is seen as representing the central element of identity and seeks to restructure, take over, or separate from the existing state in order to give political expression to that identity.) Despite the dominance of the nation-state, the world system has many of the characteristics of a society: it is formed by a multiplicity of actors, including—in addition to nation-states—individuals in their diverse roles, as well as a variety of subnational and supranational groups; it is marked by an ever-increasing degree of interdependence between its component parts; it is divided along many complex lines, with the nation-state representing perhaps the most powerful, but certainly not the only, cutting line; and it contains numerous relationships that cut across nation-state lines, including relations based on ethnicity, religion, ideology, occupation, and economic interests. The embeddedness of the nation-state in a global society, in which ethnic and other bonds cut across nation-state lines, accounts in large part for the continuity between the domestic and foreign policies of the modern state.

The view of the world system as a global society provides several angles for understanding the role of interactive problem solving within a larger context of conflict resolution.

First, the concept of a global society with its emphasis on interdependence suggests the need for alternative conceptions of national and international security, which involve arrangements for common security and mechanisms for the nonviolent conduct, management, and resolution of conflicts. Such arrangements and mechanisms, in turn, call for the development of governmental, intergovernmental, and nongovernmental institutions that embody the emerging new conceptions of security. Interactive problem solving can be seen as the germ of an independent (nongovernmental) institutional mechanism, which can contribute to security through the nonviolent resolution of conflicts.

Second, by focusing on multiple actors and cross-cutting relationships, the concept of a global society encourages us to think of unofficial diplomacy in all of its varieties as an integral part of diplomacy and of a larger process of conflict resolution, and not just as a side-show (as it tends to be viewed in a state-centered model).

Finally, the multiple-actor framework central to the concept of a global society provides a place for the individual as a relevant actor in international relations. Interactive problem solving uses the individual as the unit of analysis in the effort to understand resistance to change in a conflict relationship despite changes in realities and interests, and in the search for solutions that would satisfy the human needs of the parties. Moreover, interactive problem solving is a systematic attempt to promote change at the level of individuals (in the form of new insights and ideas), as a vehicle for change at the system level.

WORKSHOP PROCESS

Several social-psychological assumptions underlie our view of the kind of interaction process that workshops are designed to promote.

Direct Bilateral Interaction

One assumption follows directly from the structural analysis that has just been presented on the role of workshops in the larger political context. Somewhere within the larger framework of conflict resolution, there must be a place for direct, bilateral interaction between the parties centrally invoked in a given conflict—such as the Israelis and the Palestinians, or the Greek and the Turkish Cypriots. Such direct, bilateral interactions are not a substitute for the multilateral efforts that are almost invariably required for the resolution of protracted conflicts. Greece and Turkey cannot be excluded from negotiations of the Cyprus conflict, nor can the Arab states and major world powers be bypassed in efforts to resolve the Israeli-Palestinian dispute. Within this larger framework, however, there must be an opportunity for the parties immediately involved—the parties that ultimately have to live with each other—to penetrate each other's perspectives and to engage in joint problem solving designed to produce ideas for a mutually satisfactory agreement between them.

Opportunities for interaction at the micro-level can also contribute some of the needed interactive elements at the macro-level: a binocular orientation, such that each party can view the situation from the other's perspective as well as from its own; a recognition of the need for reciprocity in the process and outcome of negotiations: and a focus on building a new relationship between the parties.

Emergent Character of Interaction

A second assumption underlying the workshop process is that products of social interaction have an emergent character. In the course of direct interaction, the parties are able to observe at first hand their differing reactions to the same events and the different perspectives these reflect: the differences between the way they perceive themselves and the way the other perceives them; and the impact that their statements and actions have on each other. Out of these observations, they can jointly shape new insights and ideas that could not have been predicted from what they brought to the interaction. Certain kinds of solutions to the conflict can emerge only from the confrontation of assumptions, concerns, and identities during face-to-face communication.

The emergence of ideas for solutions to the conflict out of the interaction between the parties (in contrast, for example, to ideas proposed by third parties) has several advantages: such ideas are more likely to be responsive to the fundamental needs and fears of both parties; the parties are more likely to feel committed to the solutions they produce themselves; and the process of producing these ideas in itself contributes to building a new relationship between the parties.

In keeping with our assumption about the emergent character of interaction, we pay attention to the nature of the discourse during workshops (see Pearson, 1990). How does the way parties talk to each other change over the course of the workshop? What are the critical moments in a workshop that have an impact on the continuing interaction? How do new joint ideas come to be formulated in the course of the interaction?

Exploration and Problem Solving

Workshops are designed to promote a special kind of interaction or discourse that can contribute to the desired political outcome. As noted in the earlier discussion of the nature of the interaction, the setting, ground rules, and procedures of problem-solving workshops encourage (and permit) interaction marked by the following elements: an emphasis on addressing each other (rather than one s constituencies, or third parties, or the record) and on listening to each other; analytical discussion; adherence to a "no-fault" principle: and a problem-solving mode of interaction. This kind of interaction allows the parties to explore each other's concerns, penetrate each other's perspectives, and take cognizance of each other's constraints. As a result, they are able to oiler each other the needed reassurances to engage in negotiation and to come up with solutions responsive to both sides' needs and fears.

The nature of the interaction fostered in problem-solving workshops has some continuities with a therapeutic model (Kelman, 1991b). The influence of the therapeutic model can be seen particularly in the facilitative role of the third party, the analytical character of the discourse, and the use of "here and now" experiences as a basis for learning about the dynamics of the conflict (as mentioned in the earlier discussion of process observations). It is also important, however, to keep in mind the limited applicability of a therapeutic model to problem-solving workshops. For example, the focus of workshops is not on individuals and their interpersonal relations but on what can be learned from their interaction about the dynamics of the conflict between their communities. Furthermore, there is no assumption that nations can be viewed as equivalent to individuals or that conflict resolution is a form of therapy for national groups.

Establishment of Alternative Norms

The workshop process is predicated on the assumption that the interaction between conflicting parties is governed by a set of "conflict norms" that contribute significantly to escalation and perpetuation of the conflict (Kelman, 1997b). There is a need, therefore, for interactions based on an alternative set of norms conducive to deescalation. Workshops are designed to provide an opportunity for this kind of interaction. As noted earlier, the academic context provides an alternative set of norms on which the interaction between the parties can proceed. The ground rules for interaction within the workshop make it both possible and necessary for participants to abide by these alternative norms. The safe environment of the workshop and the principle of privacy and confidentiality provide the participants with the protection they need to be able to deviate from the conflict norms.

Individual Change as Vehicle for Policy Change

Finally, workshops operationalize a process that is social-psychological par excellence: a process designed to produce change in individuals, interacting in a small-group context, as a vehicle for change in policies and actions of the political system (Kelman, 1997a). Thus, workshops have a dual purpose— educational and political, or change and transfer—as discussed above. This dual purpose at times creates conflicting requirements that have lo be balanced in order to fulfill both purposes. I have already illustrated how such conflicts may affect selection of workshop participants and the atmosphere of trust that workshops seek to engender. The relationship between change at the individual level and at the system level—which often lends a dialectical character to problem-solving workshops—is at the heart of the workshop process.

WORKSHOP CONTENT

A set of social-psychological assumptions also informs the substantive emphases of workshop discussions. These emphases include human needs, perceptual and cognitive constraints on information processing, and influence processes, as these enter into conflict relationships.

Parties' Needs and Fears

The satisfaction of the needs of both parties—as articulated through their core identity groups—is the ultimate criterion in the search for a mutually satisfactory resolution of their conflict (Burton, 1990; Kelman, 1990). Unfulfilled needs, especially for identity and security, and existential fears about the denial of such needs typically drive the conflict and create barriers to its resolution. By probing behind the parties' incompatible positions and exploring the identity and security needs that underlie them, it often becomes possible to develop mutually satisfactory solutions, since identity, security, and other psychological needs are not inherently zero sum. Workshop interactions around needs and fears enable the parties to find a language and to identify gestures and actions that are conducive to mutual reassurance. Mutual reassurance is a central element of conflict resolution, particularly in existential conflicts where the parties see their group identity, their people's security, and their very existence as a nation to be at stake.

Escalatory Dynamics of Conflict Interaction

The needs and fears of parties involved in a conflict relationship impose perceptual and cognitive constraints on their processing of new information. One of the major effects of these constraints is that the parties systematically underestimate the occurrence and possibility of change and therefore avoid negotiations, even in the face of changing interests that would make negotiations desirable for both. Images of the enemy are particularly resistant to disconfirming information. The combination of demonic enemy images and virtuous self-images on both sides leads to formation of mirror images, which contribute to the escalator dynamic of conflict interaction and to resistance to change in a conflict relationship (Bronfenbrenner, 1961; White, 1965).

By focusing on mutual perceptions, mirror images, and systematic differences in perspective, workshop participants can learn to differentiate the enemy image—a necessary condition for movement toward negotiation (Kelman, 1987). Workshops bring out the symmetries in the parties' images of each other and in their positions and requirements, which arise out of the dynamics of the conflict interaction itself. Such symmetries are often overlooked because of the understandable tendency of protagonists in a conflict relationship to dwell on the asymmetries between them. Without denying these important asymmetries, both empirical and moral, we focus on symmetries because they tend to be a major source of escalation of conflict (as in the operation of conflict spirals) and a major reason that conflicts become intractable. By the same token, they can serve as a major vehicle for de-escalation by helping the parties penetrate each other's perspective and identify mutually reassuring gestures and actions (Kelman, 1978, 1991a).

Mutual Influence in Conflict Relationships

Finally, the content of workshop discussions reflects an assumption about the nature of influence processes in international relations. Workshops are predicated on the view that the range of influence processes employed in conflict relationships must be broadened. It is necessary to move beyond influence strategies based on threats and even to expand and refine strategies based on promises and positive incentives. By searching for solutions that satisfy the needs of both parties, workshops explore the possibility of mutual influence by way of responsiveness to each other's needs. A key element in this process, emphasized throughout this chapter, is mutual reassurance. In existential conflicts, in particular, parties can encourage each other to move to the negotiating table by reducing both sides' fear—not just, as more traditional strategic analysts maintain, by increasing their pain. At the macro-level, the present approach calls for a shift in emphasis in international influence processes from deterrence and compellence to mutual reassurance. The use of this mode of influence has the added advantage of not only affecting specific behaviors by the other party but contributing to a transformation of the relationship between the parties.

The expanded conception of influence processes that can be brought to bear in a conflict relationship is based on a view of international conflict as a dynamic phenomenon, emphasizing the occurrence and possibility of change. Conflict-resolution efforts are geared, therefore, to discovering possibilities for change, identifying conditions for change, and overcoming resistances to change. Such an approach favors "best-case" analyses and an attitude of "strategic optimism" (Kelman, 1978, 1979), not because of an unrealistic denial of malignant trends but as part of a deliberate strategy to promote change by actively searching for and accentuating whatever realistic possibilities for peaceful resolution of the conflict might be on the horizon. Optimism, in this sense, is part of a strategy designed to create self-fulfilling prophecies of a positive nature, balancing the self-fulfilling prophecies of escalation created by the pessimistic expectations and the worst-case scenarios often favored by more traditional analysts. Problem-solving workshops can be particularly useful in exploring ways in which change can be promoted through the parties' own actions and in discovering ways in which each can exert influence on the other (Kelman, 1991a. 1997b).

Relevance of Interactive Problem Solving

The principles of interactive problem solving have some applicability in a wide range of international conflict situations. Indeed. I would argue that problem-solving workshops and related activities—along with other forms of unofficial diplomacy—should be thought of as integral parts of a larger diplomatic process. This type of intervention can make certain unique contributions to the larger process that are not available through official channels—for example, by providing opportunities for noncommittal exploration of possible ways of getting to the table and of shaping mutually acceptable solutions. Moreover, the assumptions and principles of interactive problem solving can contribute to a reconceptualization of international relationships at the macro- level by encouraging shifts in the nature of the discourse and the means of influence that characterize international relations today (Kelman, 1996a). Nevertheless, it must be said that problem-solving workshops, particularly in the format that has evolved in our style of practice, are more directly relevant in some types of conflict than in others and at certain phases of a given conflict than at others.

Since my primary case has been the Israeli-Palestinian conflict, it is not surprising that my approach is most relevant to situations that share some of the characteristics of that conflict. The approach is most directly relevant to long-standing conflicts in which the interests of the parties have gradually converged and although large segments of each community perceive this to be the case, they seem to be unable or unwilling to enter into negotiations or to bring the negotiations to a satisfactory conclusion. The psychological obstacles to negotiation in these cases are not readily overcome despite the changes in realities and in perceived interests.

Interactive problem solving is not feasible if there is no interest among the parties—or significant elements within each party—in changing the status quo. It is not necessary if there are no profound barriers to negotiations; in that event, other forms of mediation—designed to enhance negotiating skills or to propose reasonable options—may be equally or more useful. However, when the recognition of common interests is insufficient to overcome the psychological barriers, interactive problem solving becomes particularly germane. These conditions are likely to prevail in intense, protracted identity conflicts at the international or intercommunal level, particularly conflicts in which the parties see their national existences to be at stake. The Israeli-Palestinian conflict, the Cyprus conflict, and the conflicts in Northern Ireland and Sri Lanka clearly share these characteristics. There are many other conflicts, however, that can benefit from a process designed to promote mutual reassurance and to help develop a new relationship between conflicting parties that must find a way of living together.

Since the goal of workshops is to help the parties translate their interest in changing the status quo into an effective negotiating process by overcoming the barriers that stand in the way of such a process, it is necessary to select workshop participants from those segments of the two communities that are indeed interested in a negotiated agreement. They may be skeptical about the possibility of achieving such an agreement and suspicious about the intentions of the other side, but they must have some interest in finding a mutually acceptable way of ending the conflict. In addition, workshop participants must be prepared to meet and talk with members of the other community at a level of equality within the workshop setting, whatever asymmetries in power between the parties may prevail in the relationship between the two communities. Thus, "participants from the stronger party must be willing to deal with the other on a basis of equality, which generally means that they have come to accept the illegitimacy of past patterns of discrimination and domination; participants from the weaker must be able to deal with the other on a basis of equality, which generally means that they have reached a stage of confrontation in the conflict" (Kelman, 1990: 293–294). In their interactions within the workshop setting, it would be inappropriate for members of the stronger party to take advantage of their superior power, as they might in a negotiating situation. By the same token, it would be inappropriate in this setting for members of the weaker party to take advantage of their superior moral position, as they might in a political rally or an international conference. Workshop interactions are most productive when based on the principle of reciprocity.

As emphasized at the beginning of this chapter, workshops are not intended to substitute for official negotiations, but they may be closely linked to the negotiating process. Thus, our work on the Israeli-Palestinian conflict during the prenegotiation and early negotiation phases helped lay the groundwork for the Oslo agreement by contributing to the development of the cadres, the ideas, and the political atmosphere required for movement to the table and for productive negotiation (Kelman, 1995, 1997c). At a point when active negotiations are in progress, workshops may provide a noncommittal forum to explore options, reframe issues to make them more amenable to negotiation, identify ways of breaking stalemates in the negotiations, and address setbacks in the process. They may also allow the parties to work out solutions to specific technical, political, or emotional issues that require an analytical, problem-solving approach; such solutions can then be fed into the formal negotiating process. In the postnegotiation phase, workshops can help the parties address issues in the implementation of the agreement and explore a new relationship based on patterns of coexistence and cooperation.

The Israeli-Palestinian workshops that we have conducted over the years have suggested some of the ways in which workshops and related activities can contribute to the peace process, helping the parties to overcome the fears and suspicions that keep them from entering into negotiations or from arriving at an agreement. Workshops can help the participants develop more differentiated images of the enemy and discover potential negotiating partners—to learn that there is someone to talk to on the other side and something to talk about. They can contribute to the formation of cadres of individuals who have acquired experience in communicating with the other side and to the conviction that such communication can be fruitful. They enable the parties to penetrate each other's perspectives, gaining insight into the other's concerns, priorities, and constraints. They increase awareness of change and thus contribute to creating and maintaining a sense of possibility—a belief among the relevant parties that a peaceful solution is attainable and that negotiations toward such a solution are feasible.

Workshops also contribute to creating a political environment conducive to fruitful negotiations through the development of a deescalatory language, based on sensitivity to words that frighten and words that reassure the other party. They help in the identification of mutually reassuring actions and symbolic gestures, often in the form of acknowledgments—of the other's humanity, national identity, ties to the land, history of victimization, sense of injustice, genuine fears, and conciliatory moves. They contribute to the development of shared visions of a desirable future, which help reduce the parties' fear of negotiations as a step into an unknown, dangerous realm. They may generate ideas about the shape of a positive-sum solution that meets the basic needs of both parties. They may also generate ideas about how to get from here to there—about a framework and set of principles for moving negotiations forward. Ultimately, problem-solving workshops contribute to a process of transformation of the relationship between enemies.

The continuing workshop that Nadim Rouhana and I convened in 1990-1993 (Rouhana and Kelman. 1994) enhanced the potential relevance of interactive problem solving to the larger political process. A continuing workshop represents a sustained effort to address concrete issues, enabling us to push the process of conflict analysis and interactive problem solving farther and to apply it more systematically than can be done with self-contained, one-time workshops. The

longer time period and the continuing nature of the enterprise make it possible to
go beyond the sharing of perspectives to the joint production of creative ideas.
Moreover, the periodic reconvening of a continuing workshop allows for an iterative and cumulative process, based on feedback and correction. The participants
have an opportunity to take the ideas developed in the course of a workshop back
to their own communities, gather reactions, and return to the next meeting with
proposals for strengthening, expanding, or modifying the original ideas. It is also
possible for participants, within or across parties, to meet or otherwise communicate with each other between workshop sessions in order to work out some of the
ideas more fully and bring the results of their efforts back to the next session.
Finally, a continuing workshop provides better opportunities to address the question of how to disseminate ideas and proposals developed at the workshop most
effectively and appropriately.

The Joint Working Group on Israeli-Palestinian Relations that Nadim Rouhana and I initiated in 1994 has addressed the issue of dissemination more
directly. This project was initiated with the express purpose of producing and
disseminating joint concept papers on the final-status issues in the Israeli- Palestinian negotiations and on the future relationship between the two societies and the
two polities that will emerge from the negotiations. The participants are politically
influential members of their respective communities, some of whom have held
official positions in the past and/or may hold such positions in the future. The
working group has followed the general principles and ground rules that have
governed our previous problem-solving workshops. The principle of confidentiality and nonattribution has prevailed, as in other workshops, until the group has
decided that it was ready to make a particular product public. However, the anticipation that there would ultimately be published papers has focused the discussion
more tightly and reduced the noncommittal character of the interaction. It is a
price worth paying if it yields products that reflect the joint thinking of influential,
mainstream representatives of the two communities and that can be disseminated
under their names to decision makers and the wider public on both sides.

The continuing workshop and the joint working group represent important
new steps in the development of interactive problem solving. The entire field, for
which Ronald Fisher (1993, 1997, this volume) and others use the term "interactive conflict resolution," is still at an early stage of development. A relatively small
number of scholar-practitioners around the world are engaged in this kind of
work, and the experience they have accumulated is still quite limited. However,
the field is maturing. The number of centers devoted to this work is increasing. A
new generation is emerging. My students, among others, are actively engaged in
research and practice in the field and are taking increasing responsibility for organizing their own projects. By establishing their personal identities as scholar-
practitioners in the field, they are giving the field itself an identity of its own. Both
the older and the younger generations are establishing networks, whose members
engage in collaborative work and are beginning to think systematically about the
further development and institutionalization of problem-solving approaches to the
resolution of international conflicts (see Fisher, 1993, 1997). Among the issues
that need to be addressed and that are, indeed, receiving increasing attention are:

the evaluation of this form of practice, the training of new scholar-practitioners, the requirements and pitfalls of professionalization, the formulation of principles and standards of ethical practice, and the development of institutional mechanisms that would strengthen the contribution of interactive problem solving to the resolution of intractable conflicts.

Notes

1. This chapter is adapted from an essay titled "Interactive Problem Solving: Informal Mediation by the Scholar-Practitioner," scheduled to appear in *Studies in International Mediation: Essays in Honor of Jeffrey Z. Rubin*, edited by Jacob Bercovitch and published by Palgrave Publishers Ltd., New York. It appears here by permission of the editor and publisher.

2. The continuing workshop was supported by grants from the Nathan Cummings Foundation, the John D. and Catherine T. MacArthur Foundation, the U.S. Institute of Peace, and Rockefeller Family and Associates. We are greatly indebted to these organizations for making this work possible and to the Harvard Center for International Affairs for providing the institutional base for it. Nadim Rouhana and I were joined on the panel of third-party facilitators by Harold Saunders of the Kettering Foundation and C. R. Mitchell of George Mason University. We are very grateful to them, as well as to the members of the third-party staff, which included Cynthia Chataway, Rose Kelman, Susan Korper, Kate Rouhana, and William Weisberg.

3. The Joint Working Group is a project of PICAR, the Program on International Conflict Analysis and Resolution (Herbert C. Kelman, director; Donna Hicks, deputy director), which was established at the Harvard Center for International Affairs (now the Weatherhead Center) in 1993, with a grant from the William and Flora Hewlett Foundation. The Hewlett Foundation's support of PICAR's infrastructure is deeply appreciated, as is the support of the working group itself by grants from the Nathan Cummings Foundation, the Carnegie Corporation, the Ford Foundation, the Charles R. Bronfman Foundation, and the U.S. Information Agency, as well as the Hewlett Foundation, the Renner Institut in Vienna, and the Weatherhead Center. The third-party team, chaired by Nadim Rouhana and myself, has included Donna Hicks, Kate Rouhana, Rose Kelman, and (in 1994–1995) Eileen Babbitt. Their dedication and skill have been indispensable to the project.

Mediation

Adam Curle

Like Roger Fisher, Adam Curle also served in World War II, but Curle fought as a major with the British Army. Witnessing the trauma experienced by prisoners of war, he was drawn to social psychology at the University of Oxford. Known later as a Quaker peace activist, he co-created the Centre of Peace, Non-Violence and Human Rights in Croatia during the Croatian War in the early 1990s. He is credited with helping establish peace studies as a field.

In the context of warring parties, Curle offers mediation as an approach to address emotions such as anger and fear, which disrupt otherwise mutually beneficial negotiations. Once good relations are re-established—once emotions have softened—the more traditional negotiation strategies can be employed. In effect, mediation helps address destructive emotions, which then allows the rational approaches proposed in Epoch One to work better.

Curle argues mediators can assist because they enter the conflict without the same level of emotion. They can cool anger by building trust, building hope, and demonstrating patience. They do this by helping untangle misunderstandings and helping the conflicting parties identify interests underlying emotions. Curle highlights the importance of understanding the cultural context before entering, noticing, and responding to power imbalances.

Curle's mediators must be approved by involved parties and focus on improving communication. The article, however, focuses more heavily on what Curle believes mediators must not do. They do not accept money, impose ideas, show favoritism, leave early (mediations can last for years), mislead (even white lies), or participate in a mediation whose outcome is fixed.

Questions to consider: What could be some of the long-term benefits in investing in trust building facilitated by a mediator? What might be some of the problems associated with mediation?

Mediation

Adam Curle

Mediators, as the word implies, are in the middle. This is true in two senses. Firstly they are neither on one side nor the other; secondly they are in the center of the conflict, deeply involved in it because they are trying to find a satisfactory way out of it.

Although mediation is considered here in the special context of violent conflict, it is a universal human role. All of us, perhaps even the most intractably aggressive, have practiced it occasionally. We may not have called it that when we tried to persuade members of our family or friends or colleagues to see each other's point of view and stop bickering about some trivial issue. But mediation it was: we were the people in between those who had fallen out, on fairly good terms with both, not taking sides though often pressured to do so; not personally implicated in the dispute, but worried about the situation and hoping to improve it.

What mediators do is to try to establish, or re-establish, sufficiently good communications between conflicting parties so that they can talk sensibly to each other without being blinded by such emotions as anger, fear and suspicion. This does not necessarily resolve the conflict; mediation has to be followed-up by skilled negotiation, usually directly between the protagonists, supported by a measure of mutual tolerance and by determination to reach agreement. But it is a good start.

This would apply whether the conflict were between individuals or nations, and irrespective of culture, political ideology, or religion. Although the circumstances of an international dispute, economic, political and strategic, are very different from the emotional tangle of, for example, a marital one, both ultimately focus on human beings who have to make decisions and to act, and whose passions, fears, hopes, rage and guilt are much the same whoever and wherever they are. This, at least, has been my experience.

Non-Official Mediation

Within the context of violent conflict, the forms of mediation may differ considerably. Some involve short-term missions having a very specific objective, such as those of Terry Waite to secure the release of captives in various parts of the world, or the shuttle diplomacy of a Henry Kissinger hurrying, often without great success, between one capital and another. There is also the longer-term work of United Nations officials such as Dag Hammarsjöld, Brian Urquhart or Sean McBride, struggling year after year to resolve one bitter quarrel after another.

These and many other patterns may be useful and appropriate. What I shall discuss is mediation usually of long duration, carried out by non-official groups or organizations, churches or other religious organizations, charitable bodies, academic bodies, or concerned individuals without institutional backing (although individuals without such support tend to experience difficulty in launching and maintaining their mission, suffer considerable strain and naturally incur considerable costs). I shall not speak of UN mediation, most valuable though it is; the aegis of a great international organization creates conditions, occasionally less favorable where there is unilateral distrust of it, different from those pertaining to both governmental and to private or non-official mediation. What I have to say derives from direct experience of mediation initiated by the Quakers who, of the half dozen or so organizations I know of that have worked in the field, have the longest and most varied experience, as well as from efforts which were personal although carried out with much help from others.

It is perhaps hardly necessary to emphasize that those engaged in private mediation are never, so far as I know, paid, except for their expenses. Nor do they, being constrained by the need for confidentiality, make money or achieve any ego-enhancement by such means as writing articles or giving interviews. Their mediation is perhaps more appreciated because in no sense influenced by the profit motive; there is no reason why they should submit to considerable trouble and inconvenience except to contribute if possible to the reduction of human misery. In the same vein, I sometimes point out to people that I have been retired for several years and would sooner spend my old age at home than gallivanting around the world.

There are, of course, some disadvantages to non-official mediation. There is no automatic entrée, such as an ambassador would have, to recognized authority; there is no established source of intelligence information; there is no help in making appointments and travel arrangements, and with secretarial chores, all of which may be a considerable burden in some conditions; above all, there is no power such as would be enjoyed by the representatives of an important country who could reinforce arguments by a combination of threats and promises. Oran Young (1967, 1972) concluded that private intermediaries without political power and resources, lacked the "saliency" to achieve major diplomatic results.

There is, however, one very considerable advantage. Paradoxically, it derives directly from the major disadvantage. The protagonists with whom mediators work soon discover, if the mediators act correctly, that their sole motivation is concern for the suffering occasioned to both sides by the conflict, and determination to do everything in their power to reduce it. They are not concerned with who wins or loses, they do not take sides, considering the only enemy to be war and the waste and suffering it brings; they are consistent in their honesty, concern and goodwill. Unlike official diplomats, however humane they may be, their aim is not to promote the policy of their own country; by contrast it is recognized that a country's official representative must carry out the instructions of the country he serves, even if they go against the best interests of the one to which he is accredited. Thus in certain respects the non-official or private mediator may be confided in and trusted more than the official. A further advantage of the private position of mediators is that they may be disavowed if for some reason they cause embarrassment, or even expelled from the country without causing a diplomatic furor; they are both useful and expendable.

What then do these people do? First of all if, as may well happen, they are not already well known or have not been specifically invited in, they must get approval for a visit to the country or countries concerned and then gain acceptance from the people with whom they must work, preferably key members of the governments concerned—this process will be considered shortly. Their proper work, when it actually begins, is to open up better communications between the warring parties. This includes such tasks as taking messages from one side to the other, usually enlarging on the implications and the meanings behind the message; they do a considerable amount of explaining the motives and intentions of one side to the other; they interpret the statements or the cryptic "smoke signals" sent up by either combatant; they correct wrong information and mistaken impressions obtained from statements and speeches by leaders of the other side; they attempt to identify the common interests of the protagonists; they make suggestions about how to improve communications between the protagonists and how to avoid obstacles to reaching a settlement; they try to establish friendly relations with as many people as possible, especially decision makers, on both sides; and they try to keep as well informed as possible about the situation so that they can speak about it constructively without making fools of themselves and so discrediting their ability to act in an informed and helpful fashion. In order to carry out these tasks they may often have to make difficult and even dangerous journeys, seek people out in remote camps, and suffer some of the discomforts and privations of wartime conditions. Although, they hope for friendly relations with all concerned, they will probably also make enemies, for there are always some who do not want peace, the hawks who think that it would be possible to get a better deal by continuing to fight. A mediator who favors peace, especially if listened to sympathetically, may be a threat they would wish to dispose of.

We should also consider what mediators do not do and what they are not. They are not negotiators. Negotiators are concerned with the nature and details of any settlement being considered and with the bargaining by which it is achieved. They are usually representatives of the conflicting parties and so by no means impartial. Mediators, on the other hand, have no partisan view on the character of a resolution. By the same token they would consider it improper interference to promote their own solution; their job is to facilitate an acceptable one by helping to clear away obstacles of prejudice and misunderstanding that impede the protagonists in reaching an agreement together. This is not to say, of course, that mediators may not move between the negotiating parties trying to help maintain good communications.

Mediators should also be very cautious of involvement in conflicts in which one side obviously possesses far more power than the other and is genuinely confident of victory. The reason is not that the weaker, and often oppressed, side should not be forsaken, but that mediation simply will not work. The strong are not going to heed any appeal for clemency or compromise. Why should they? They are confident that they can get what they want without giving an inch. If they do not reject the idea of mediation outright, they use the mediators to do their own dirty work by proposing terms to the weak which are tantamount to surrender; terms which, if accepted, would in many cases simply restore the conditions that led to war in the first place. Mediators can only make it clear that they will have no part in such trickery; their purpose is to work for a just and harmonious peace, not the passivity of subjugation. Submission at this stage without any resolution would in any case most probably be followed by a renewal of the conflict, for no situations are permanent.

What else can mediators do in such circumstances? Firstly, before they withdraw, they must ensure that their evaluation of affairs is really correct, that the strong are implacably obdurate, or that the weak have no chance of matching their power and so engaging in fair negotiations. Even if they decide they were in fact right, it could still be wise to try to build up relationships, perhaps with opposition leaders or significant non-official people, which could help initiate mediation when/if the situation eventually changed. For example, friendships made by some mediators with Zimbabwean African leaders several years beforehand greatly facilitated mediation when that became possible.

Mediators may possibly decide that they must temporarily abdicate that role and its impartiality to throw in their lot with the weak; this is purely a matter of personal conscience and judgement. However, if they do decide to serve the victims of violence directly, their best and most appropriate role may be to help empower them through understanding their situation more clearly, and organizing and practicing nonviolent resistance. I might add that in different circumstances, rightly or wrongly, I have responded in all these ways.

LONG-TERM MEDIATION

A major feature of this sort of mediation is its long duration, running often into several years. Admittedly there have often been brief mediations, persuasive arguments brought to bear upon the parties in a quarrel that has suddenly flared up and which, when tempers have died down, is as speedily put right. More often, however, what seems superficially like a short mediation is only an incident, even if a crucial one, in a process that started before and will continue after it; such was the mediation that led to the Camp David agreement; there a process lasting days was preceded by a long preliminary period and is still in some senses going on.

The truth is that peace making of any sort is likely to be a very long process. The greatest virtues for mediators are hope and patience, for during the period they must stick with the intransigent problems of peace making endless obstacles arise, often when the prospects seemed brightest. Sudden changes on the battlefield, the replacement of a "dove" by a "hawk," some external intervention, a rumor, a tactical error, may all demolish months of painstaking preparation for a peace initiative.

But the work of mediation, by its very nature, can seldom be carried out speedily and for the very same reason that conflicts cannot be terminated speedily: they depend more upon human perceptions than on external circumstances, the former being more stubborn and hard to influence than the latter. In the slow move toward negotiation, settlement and the eventual restoration of fully peaceful relations, the significant stages are the changes of vision rather than the signing of agreements that result from them, the gradual erosion of fear, antipathy and suspicion, and the slow shift of public opinion. By contrast, the cessation of actual violence as a result of military victory may lead to a speedy settlement which usually is by no means peace in the sense of harmony and mutual regard. The victors dictate terms which cannot be refused, it is as simple as that.

It is therefore appropriate for mediation to be carried out by non-officials who do not run the risk of being transferred but who can remain with the job, consolidating the relationships on which all peace making depends and following the ramifications of the unfolding situation, the rise and fall of the various actors.

To become associated with such a mediation is to make a commitment to becoming an element in a scene of conflict for a significant period of time. Those I have been involved with have lasted up to four years and never less than two. My colleagues (when I had any) and I were not of course on the spot the whole time; I, for example, would return to my base at home or university and resume my usual activities of teaching and writing and being a husband and father. But the war is never far from the surface of thought, there are letters and telephone calls about it, many meetings in various places; the suitcase remains metaphorically and often literally packed. We keep in touch as closely as possible, debating the meanings of new developments, planning the strategy and timing of the next visit. As soon as we accept this role, we accept responsibility for playing a part in a terrible drama; and the part must go on, unless an understudy can be found, until the tragedy is over.

BEGINNING A MEDIATION

It may be of interest to consider the ways in which mediation begins. Sometimes an organization, or perhaps more likely an individual, is directly approached because of her/his reputation, and asked to mediate, perhaps on a very specific issue. S/he will then no doubt agree and go ahead with whatever support from her/his organization is available. Where there is not a direct approach the entrée is obviously more difficult. In my necessarily limited experience it may happen in a way that is either haphazard or on the contrary well planned. In one case I visited a scene of violent conflict because I was interested in what was happening. It was only after repeated visits that I found I had worked myself into a job, was known to and accepted by a number of people, and that my toing and froing between different groups appeared to be welcomed. So I continued for several years until circumstances made continued work less productive that it had been and I was asked to take part in a more urgent and at the same time more hopeful enterprise. But this kind of more or less solo effort is not often possible, if only for financial reasons.

A more organized effort also tends to begin with the concern of an individual for a particular situation which s/he then brings to, for example, the Quakers.

Then (speaking only for the Quakers with whom I have been through the process several times) the sequence is likely to be something as follows.

The individual discusses the issue with the appropriate group within the Quaker organization and a preliminary decision is reached. This might be to explore further; to say "no" because it is impracticable (there might be no qualified person to undertake it) or it might have lower priority than other projects under consideration; it might be referred to another branch of the Society of Friends, possibly the Australian Quakers if it is a conflict in the Pacific area; or it might seem that the main need is for relief rather than diplomacy.

If, however, it is decided to examine the matter in greater detail, more people will be consulted. Visits will be paid to the local representatives of the parties concerned, to the Foreign and Commonwealth Office in London, the State Department in Washington, to the appropriate branches of the UN in New York and Geneva. The purpose of these visits will be to get further information on the situation; nothing will be said about mediation, because it would be premature to do so.

If these early enquiries appear to favor the possibility of eventual mediation, the next step might well be a reconnaissance. A small group of people will visit the ambassador(s) of the nation(s) involved to express their distress at the suffering caused by the conflict. They will ask if there would be any objection to visiting the country concerned to learn more about the situation, as their organization feels that media reportage is inadequate. The usual response would be to welcome such a visit since it would "enable you to see through the lies of our enemies." It is the first demonstration of the mirror image that the representatives of each protagonist tends to make a similar observation, each implying that they are honest, peace-loving and truthful, while their foes are the opposite.

If all goes well, the reconnaissance team sets off. There will probably be two or three individuals: one is too few as the combined judgement of two or three is desirable; four is too many—they constitute a delegation to whom senior officials speechify rather than converse.

In general the team will find that people are only too willing to talk. It will have to listen, time after time, to almost identical recitals of the wrongs inflicted on them, and of the unrivalled barbarity and ruthlessness of their enemies.

But the transition from fact finding to mediating has yet to be made. The simplest crossing of the gap occurs when the team tell some senior person that they are going to visit the other side and ask "is there anything we can do for you there?" The answer might be, "I would be very interested in your impressions," of "if you see so and so, you might say . . ." and perhaps a message of some slight significance may be given.

I have guessed that such responses are made as much to test the objectivity, impartiality and honesty of the team, as in the hope of learning anything useful. A friend and I met with a good example of this during the Nigerian civil war. At an early stage of our work, before we had met General Gowon, the head of the Nigerian military government, the Quakers had a tentative plan for a secret meeting of senior people on both sides. This, it was thought, could be more effective than previous efforts which had been spoiled by publicity. Such a proposal could be agreed to only by Gowon, but we had great difficulty in making an appointment. Various fairly senior officials tried to arrange one, but we were told that they were always vetoed by someone called Mr. King, whom we imagined to be a white adviser, a sort of eminence blanche (in fact he turned out to be a Nigerian and became a close and valued friend). However, at length the permanent secretary of the Ministry of Foreign Affairs thought our idea was good, and overrode King. We had a meeting with the general, who was slightly interested in the proposal but doubtful over our proposed visit to Colonel Ojukwu, his enemy, the Biafran leader.

"He will simply use your visit for propaganda purposes," he said, "claiming that the Quakers support his cause." We assured him that we would give Ojukwu no cause to say that, and asked if he was actually asking us not to go. "No," he answered, "but please don't say anything that could be taken to mean that you are going at my suggestion. It would be a dangerous mistake for him to think I was taking that sort of initiative. Moreover," he continued, "you will have to fly on one of the rebel pirate arms-carrying planes which my fighter aircraft have orders to shoot down. I am afraid I could not make any arrangements for the safety of your particular flight." We assured him that we would be tactful in our dealings with Ojukwu and that we were prepared to risk the possible dangers of the flight. He then said: "When you see him you might tell him that in the event of a cease fire agreement I shall order my troops to halt their advance and arrange for a neutral buffer force to safe-guard the cease fire." This in fact was an advance on previous conditions. Gowon finally wished us well and said he would be very interested to hear of our experiences and impressions if we returned safely, which he hoped we would. We did, and were given an immediate appointment with the general, who greeted us very warmly. This was the beginning of a very good working relationship which lasted throughout the remaining years of the war.

This is how one mediation began. There had been a round of meetings and discussions at the UN in New York and at Washington, and there had been a reconnaissance lasting several weeks. But the real mediation did not start until we were given a specific message to deliver by General Gowon, returned with a response (not in fact an acceptance, but the idea remained alive) and, as was shown by monitorings of the Biafran radio, our visit had not been used to promote our own publicity or the Biafran cause. The fact that we had been prepared to face a certain amount of danger for no personal gain also counted considerably in our favour on both sides. After this the scope of our activities increased greatly in all the four categories of mediatory work which will be considered in the next section. I should add that in cases where extreme ideological differences are involved coupled with rigid stereotypes derived from them, the process of gaining acceptance may last much longer and be infinitely more complex.

DIFFICULTIES OF MEDIATORS

We have discussed some of the intrinsic difficulties of peace making. To these must be added those peculiar to mediation. The essence of these is that mediators are trying to bridge with friendship the hate-filled gulf between people who may well be killing each other and so generating the paranoid anger and suspicion that justify ghastly excesses. How can the protagonists trust these people who claim also to be on good terms with their sworn enemies? In fact it seems to be a tribute to the genuine desire for peace and essential good sense of most of the leaders I have met, that they were able to tolerate and even develop warm relations with such ambiguous characters.

It is certainly true, however, that mediators have to be constantly alert lest an unguarded word give any suggestion of favoritism of the other side. For example, to refer to Northern Ireland as Ulster to a Republican or as the Six Counties to a Loyalist would immediately put impartiality in question. Even the most tentative suggestion that one accepts the enemy's case, or their explanation of a particular happening, re-arouses suspicions that had been lulled by months of tactful and consistent goodwill. On two occasions in my experience during the Nigerian civil war (the Biafran war) other branches of the Quaker organization concerned, not knowing of the mediation, issued statements implying sympathy with the starving Biafrans. Although the mediators had known nothing about this, a shadow was cast temporarily over their relations with the Nigerian leadership; if these relations had not already been very good, they would no doubt have been broken off. (On the subject of Biafra, to have referred to it as such would have been disastrous; we used instead the euphemism "the other side").

Of course there is no question of concealing from one side one's relations with the other. This is central to mediation. If mediators did not inform X that they were going to visit Y who he hates, they might be spared some embarrassment, but they would be suspected of doing something even worse. If, moreover, they were caught in deception they could be thought of as spies or informers. In any case their usefulness as mediators would be over. No, it is best at all times to be honest and open. It is only by unswerving truthfulness, friendliness and concerned impartiality that mediators earn the conditional right to be on good terms with both sides.

But here let me interpolate another difficulty. Mediators must indeed be truthful if only because even the whitest of lies would, in this highly charged atmosphere, be a proof of mendacity. On the other hand, they must also be true to their principles; they are thought to be motivated by moral values rather than profit and hopes of advancement, but any lapse would throw doubt on their probity. They must, however, not only be truthful but tactful. These three demands upon them may sometimes come into conflict.

Suppose some atrocity is committed, are they to make no protest, in which case the sincerity of their principles will be questioned; or are they to say they are shocked and horrified, thus possibly seeming to imply sympathy with the enemy, and so giving grave offense? Perhaps the best approach is to express sorrow, but in a way that suggests no blame except to the practice of war, which makes such tragedies, committed by either side, inevitable. Faced with this dilemma, I have usually found that taking this line did not violate my conscience. If, however, atrocities are denied or attributed to the enemy with suspicious regularity, mediators must decide whether to risk a blazing row, or to remain pointedly silent.

In the early stages of their work, attempts may be made to use mediators in various ways. In particular the protagonists try to win them over to their side. This appears to be a fairly natural impulse of those engaged in conflict, but if successful, it would obviously subvert any efforts at real mediation. However, if leaders really want the possible fruits of mediation, they soon get the message and exchange the potential propaganda value of "converting" the mediators for collaboration with them. There are also, however, more subtle ways in which mediators may be used. They may be asked to give messages that are intentionally misleading, suggesting, for example, that one side is eager for negotiations when it really hopes to lull the foe into a false sense of security, facilitating the preparation of new positions or the launching of a surprise attack.

It is not always easy to guard against such dishonesty, though at the outset it may help to make a firm but diplomatic statement that any manipulation will mean immediate withdrawal. Fortunately, once their suspicions are aroused, mediators are usually in a position to consult with their own headquarters and/or other concerned and knowledgeable persons on the spot. These might be officials of various embassies, representatives of international agencies, the Commonwealth Secretariat, the OAU and other bodies. In fact, such contacts and consultations are a regular feature of mediation. As a mission proceeds, a network of involved people is developed including such as I have just mentioned as well as members of local churches, human rights organizations, academic institutions and so on. Mediators are seldom completely on their own, though they must always guard scrupulously against revealing what has been told them in confidence—if they did so they would never again be trusted and their mission would be ruined. They must also beware of excessive intimacy with or dependence on friends, for example in their own embassy; such intimacy might be taken to imply bias.

World Café

Juanita Brown and David Isaacs

Juanita Brown and David Isaacs invented the World Café in their living room in the 1990s. Juanita Brown's PhD focused on the role of conversation as a core process for organizational and societal evolution. She has consulted for major brands (IBM, Kraft Foods Group, and others), has also served as a senior affiliate at the MIT Sloan School's Organizational Learning Center, and is the founder of Whole Systems Associates, an international consortium of professionals dedicated to strategic inquiry and the renewal of complex systems. David Isaacs, president of Clearing Communications, designs strategic dialogue forums with senior leaders around the world. He has consulted with Hewlett-Packard, Intel, and others. They both have contributed all of their book royalties to the World Café Community Foundation, which helps the concepts shared in this piece travel worldwide.

This article introduces readers to the thinking behind the World Café: the notion that we are smarter together if we can construct a dynamic and productive conversation. The selection also introduces readers to the structure of a café, should they like to construct one for themselves. The café structure builds on the concept of dynamical systems emphasized in Epoch Two. We think in and we take action within systems. Rather than operating as independent rational actors, as promoted in Epoch One, this approach considers individuals existing in webs of social connection. Therefore, the best way to approach conflict is often by working in and within the web. The webs of conversation utilized in the World Café have been used around the world to address everything from corporate product ideas, fundraising ideas for churches, and political conundrums faced by governments. The uses are endless and embraced by communities and government structures alike.

Consider trying a café in your community and seeing what emerges. You can start with a smaller issue or something tearing a community apart at the seams. For those interested in working with groups, the World Café provides a good dialogue format to practice. Videos on YouTube and the World Café website provide a variety of other resources.

Questions to consider: How might such an approach lead to different solutions than those used in Epoch One? If more people are involved in generating the solutions, might implementation of ideas be easier? What might be the limitations of such an approach?

The World Café
Shaping Our Futures through Conversations That Matter

Juanita Brown and David Isaacs

Beginning the Conversation: An Invitation to the World Café

I am a child of the sixties. During that time of social and political upheaval, many of us were determined to tell it like it is, to see beneath the surface of things to what really mattered. That inner fire that fueled my early years as a social change activist is now tempered by a compassion born of more than thirty years of working intimately with the dilemmas and paradoxes of personal and institutional change in corporate settings. My self-righteousness and certainty have slowly given way to a humility developed out of a growing sense that there are many ways to tell it like it is—that any story worth telling can be experienced from multiple perspectives. It is with this awareness that I share with you the story of the learning journey from which the World Café has emerged and continues to evolve.

When I was growing up in suburban South Miami, Florida, our living room and dinner table were always alive with conversations. These weren't just any kind of conversations. They were passionate discussions about big questions—justice, democracy, and civil rights. From conversations like these in homes and churches, the civil liberties movement in Florida was nurtured and grew into a force for decency and fairness at a time of great turmoil in the South.

I remember, too, the spirited conversations we had at my adopted grandmother's home in southern Mexico when I was a teenager. Trudi Blom had been exiled from Europe during World War II, and there, in the remote state of Chiapas, she founded a global center for dialogue and action on environmental issues—much before it was fashionable to talk about sustainability. At her long dining room table, anthropologists, writers, scientists, and local travelers joined together for delicious meals with Lacandon Maya rain forest people and Chamula highland

Indian guests. The diversity of the group always contributed to learning, discoveries, and connections that never could have been anticipated. Today, half a century later, the Na-Bolom Center still serves as a place where diverse people and perspectives meet in dialogue around the dining room table.

During my early years as a community organizer with Cesar Chavez and the farmworkers' movement, it was in the thousands of informal meetings—conversations among those seated on tattered couches in ramshackle homes and labor camps—that small miracles occurred. Through dialogue and reflection, the underlying assumptions that had kept farmworkers stuck for generations began to shift. As workers shared tortilla and bean suppers, they also shared the if-onlys of their lives and imagined the impossible. With practice, they began to ask the what-if questions. And from the what-ifs came the why-nots!

Over the last quarter-century, my life has taken me to large corporations as a strategist and thinking partner with senior executives as they struggle to embrace the challenges of the knowledge era. In this world, my language and descriptions have changed to those of strategic dialogue and conversation as a core business process. My community-organizing emphasis has evolved to focus on and embrace the informal communities of practice that are the home for social processes of new learning and knowledge creation. But the essential threads of my life remain unbroken. It is still my deepest belief that it is through conversations around questions that matter that powerful capacities for evolving caring community, collaborative learning, and committed action are engaged—at work, in communities, and at home.

Conversations That Matter

Through our conversations the stories and images of our future emerge, and never has this process been more critical. We now have the capacity, through neglect of the planetary commons on which our lives depend, to make this precious earth, our home, uninhabitable. We now have the capacity, through escalating violence and weapons of mass destruction, to make our precious human species, along with many others, extinct. Yet this is also a moment of opportunity. We are connected as never before in webs of communication and information-sharing through the Internet and other media that make our collective predicament visible on a much larger scale than we could have imagined only a few years ago. And for the first time, we now have the capacity for engaging in connected global conversations and action about what is happening and how we choose to respond—conversations that are not under the formal aegis of any one institution, government, or corporation. It is time for us to engage in those conversations more intentionally. Our very survival as a human community, both locally and globally, may rest on our creative responses to the following questions:

- How can we enhance our capacity to talk and think more deeply together about the critical issues facing our communities, our organizations, our nations, and our planet?

- How can we access the mutual intelligence and wisdom we need to create innovative paths forward?

This book is the story of a personal and collective journey shaped by these questions. It is a story in which I have been an active participant, along with my partner, David Isaacs, and a lively global community of inquiry and practice. It is the story of the discovery and evolution of the World Café, a simple yet powerful conversational process for fostering constructive dialogue, accessing collective intelligence, and creating innovative possibilities for action, particularly in groups that are larger than most traditional dialogue approaches are designed to accommodate.

Anyone interested in creating conversations that matter can engage the World Café process, with its seven core design principles to improve people's collective capacity to share knowledge and shape the future together. World Café conversations simultaneously enable us to notice a deeper living pattern of connections at work in our organizations and communities—the often invisible webs of conversation and meaning-making through which we already collectively shape the future, often in unintended ways.

COLLECTIVE INTELLIGENCE
Living Network PATTERN
Café Conversational PROCESS
Integrated Design PRINCIPLES

Engaging the World Café process, principles, and pattern in practical ways empowers leaders and others who work with groups to intentionally host World Café and other types of dialogue as well as to create dynamic networks of conversation and knowledge-sharing around an organization's real work and critical questions.

How Does a World Café Dialogue Work?

Café conversations are designed on the assumption that people already have within them the wisdom and creativity to confront even the most difficult challenges. The process is simple, yet it can yield surprising results. The innovative design of the World Café enables groups—often numbering in the hundreds of people—to participate together in evolving rounds of dialogue with three or four others while at the same time remaining part of a single, larger, connected conversation. Small, intimate conversations link and build on each other as people move between groups, cross-pollinate ideas, and discover new insights into questions or issues that really matter in their life, work, or community. As the network of new connections increases, knowledge-sharing grows. A sense of the whole becomes increasingly strong. The collective wisdom of the group becomes more accessible, and innovative possibilities for action emerge.

In a Café gathering people often move rapidly from ordinary conversations—which keep us stuck in the past, are often divisive, and are generally superficial—toward conversations that matter, in which there is deeper collective understanding or forward movement in relation to a situation that people really care about. The seven World Café design principles, when used in combination, also create a kind of "conversational greenhouse," nurturing the conditions for the rapid propagation of actionable knowledge. These design principles are not limited to a formal Café event. They can also be used to focus and enhance the quality of other key conversations—enabling you to draw on the talent and wisdom of your organization or community to a greater extent than generally occurs with more traditional approaches.

World Café conversations simultaneously create a lived experience of how we naturally self-organize to think together, strengthen community, share knowledge, and ignite innovation. They allow us to see more clearly the importance of conversation as a living force so we can become more intentional about engaging its power. Café conversations demonstrate one innovative way to put living systems theory into practice.

The World Café, both as a designed conversational process and as a deeper living systems pattern, has immediate, practical implications for meeting and conference design, strategy formation, knowledge creation, rapid innovation, stakeholder engagement, and large-scale change. Experiencing a Café conversation in action also helps us make personal and professional choices about more satisfying ways to participate in the ongoing conversations that help shape our lives.

THE WORLD CAFÉ GOES GLOBAL

Since its inception in 1995, tens of thousands of people on six continents have participated in World Café dialogues in settings ranging from crowded hotel ballrooms holding twelve hundred people to cozy living rooms with just a dozen folks present. In a global consumer products company, executives from more than thirty nations used the Café process to integrate a new worldwide marketing strategy. Mexican government and corporate leaders have applied the World Café to scenario planning. Leaders from local communities representing more than sixty countries participated in Café dialogues during the Stockholm Challenge, which offers a Nobel-style prize for those creating technology for the common good.

The World Café can make a special contribution when the goal is the focused use of dialogue to foster productive relationships, collaborative learning, and collective insight.

Faculty members in the United States and Europe are creating virtual, online Knowledge Cafés to conduct distance learning programs. In New Zealand and the United States, the World Café has inspired the creation of local venues for hosting Café conversations on key issues related to business futures, sustainable development, and community collaboration. The World Café has supported Conversation Cafés, Commonway Cafés, and Let's Talk America, key citizen initiatives that invite diverse groups to explore contemporary issues. Local churches and schools have used the World Café process on a smaller scale to build community and access the wisdom of their members.

Whether in business, government, health, education, NGO, or community settings, the World Café can make a special contribution when the goal is the focused use of dialogue to foster productive relationships, collaborative learning, and collective insight around real-life challenges and key strategic questions. This is especially true when working with groups that are larger than most traditional dialogue circles are designed to accommodate.

A COMMUNITY OF INQUIRY AND PRACTICE

The global World Café learning community—as well as this book—have evolved as colleagues from around the world experiment, document their work, share ideas, and learn from each other about the theory and practice embodied in the Café conversation approach.

I will serve as the primary narrator and your host for weaving together the stories, reflections, and conversations among World Café pioneers and others as we share with you our discoveries and the questions at the edge of our "not knowing." In the Perspectives & Observations sections I'll share my own personal aha's and insights, and introduce you to others who are contributing to our learning.

All pioneering ventures are incomplete, reflecting the particular interests and ways of seeing of those who have been part of the journey, and who make the initial maps of the territory. I am but one among many colleagues who are furthering key aspects of this work. Yet I hope your travels with me through these pages will provide glimpses that stimulate new conversations about where to focus special attention and care in your own organizations and communities.

The research for this book and for my own earlier Ph.D. on the World Café (Brown, 2001) was conducted in the spirit of Appreciative Inquiry, an approach to organizational learning and development originated by David Cooperrider and his colleagues at Case Western University (Cooperrider and Srivastva, 1987; Cooperrider and others, 2003; Whitney and Trosten-Bloom, 2003). Appreciative Inquiry deliberately focuses attention on what works, what brings life and vitality to an experience, and what's possible for its evolution. However, keep in mind that the same challenges that come up in any group can arise in a World Café conversation. At the same time, the World Café's focus on intimate exchange, disciplined inquiry, cross-pollination of ideas, and possibility thinking tends to create psychological safety and lessen inappropriate grandstanding and people's attachment to their own points of view. The very design of Café conversations often makes these common challenges easier to deal with than in many group settings.

WHAT YOU'LL FIND INSIDE

Chapter 1 calls on insights from thought leaders across disciplines to reveal the critical but often invisible role of conversation in shaping our lives and our futures.

Chapter 2 invites you to consider a new perspective on conversation as a core process—a fundamental means through which groups and organizations adapt to changing circumstances and co-create the knowledge necessary for success. It also briefly introduces the seven core design principles that are central to understanding the World Café approach to dialogue.

Chapters 3 through 9 share the seven core World Café design principles, with each chapter focusing on one of them. The stories that open these chapters reveal the creativity and imagination with which Café hosts from around the world are using these principles to foster conversations that matter. These real life "learning stories," including the hosts' dilemmas and discoveries, form the heart of the book. More than any abstract treatise, teaching, or training manual, they provide innovative ideas for how to craft a World Café approach adapted to your unique situation. Each chapter then grounds these experiences in a discussion of both the conceptual underpinnings of each design principle and their general application in a wide variety of settings.

Chapter 10 focuses on the practicalities of Café hosting that have not been covered in detail in the earlier exploration of the seven guiding principles. This chapter is designed to stand alone as a World Café hosting guide to help you plan Café dialogues in diverse settings. If you want an initial overview of the specifics of Café hosting, this is the place to start. It provides the information needed for someone with previous group experience to host a successful Café, particularly if you have attended a World Café dialogue yourself.

Chapter 11 begins with several short stories that illustrate ways leaders are using World Café approaches as part of their own conversational leadership—the capacity to engage the collaborative intelligence of their organizations and communities to meet real-life challenges. These form the backdrop for our exploration of both the organizational infrastructures and personal capabilities that conversational leaders can develop in order to nurture greater business and social value using dialogue as a core process.

Chapter 12 highlights the societal implications and the promise inherent in embracing and acting on the insights and practical experiences explored throughout the book. You are encouraged to become a part of the dialogue and deliberation community, sharing your insights and discoveries as you make your own unique contribution to creating a culture of dialogue wherever you may find yourself.

In the epilogue, octogenarian Anne Dosher, Ph.D., the elder of the World Café, shares the questions that have informed her own life's journey and why she has committed her remaining years to nurturing a culture of dialogue. Peter Senge, senior lecturer at the MIT Sloan School of Management and founding chair of the Society for Organizational Learning, then offers an afterword based on our experience together in hosting World Café gatherings with key global leaders.

If you want to learn more about other forms of dialogue, as well as key initiatives that are also making wonderful contributions to the field of dialogue and deliberation, take a look at "Resources and Connections" at the back of the book. And although this book is not an academic treatise, enough reference material has been included in the text to support you in "following the trail" to the conceptual foundations of the World Café and related areas of interest.

HOW TO ENGAGE WITH WHAT'S HERE

Each chapter's learning stories highlight the way the chapter's core ideas are being put into real-world practice.

Having a common architecture as this book unfolded has allowed diverse contributions in a shared framework, enabling you to engage with the material based on your own reading style and preferences. Each chapter begins with a quotation, an illustration, and a question that illuminate the essence of that chapter, so if you look only at the chapter openers you'll gain an overview of the book's main themes. Each chapter's learning stories highlight the way the chapter's core ideas are being put into real-world practice. These stories, although simply "snapshots in time" that continue to unfold, enable you to appreciate the many ways you might introduce and engage Café conversations in your own life and work. In the "Perspectives & Observations" sections that follow, I, as your host, will share multidisciplinary insights from leading edge thinkers as they inform our exploration of dialogue and Café learning. At the end of each chapter, you'll find "Questions for Reflection," a series of questions to consider as you convene and host conversations that matter.

We've purposely included multiple voices and modes of expression as well as graphic illustrations to illuminate key ideas. We've also used the following terms—World Café, Café conversation, and Café dialogue—interchangeably throughout the text to describe the World Café process. In addition, you'll find Café names like Knowledge Café, Leadership Café, Strategy Café, and others that illuminate the many ways people are naming and adapting the basic World Café pattern and process in ways that meet their unique needs and constituencies.

Although this book is not a how-to manual or a detailed recipe for creating a World Café event, you'll find both key ingredients and practical ideas for hosting conversations that matter in many different organizational and community settings. We've discovered that one of the strengths of the World Café approach is its simplicity and versatility. In fact, if you have experience leading or working with groups, a careful reading of the stories that begin each chapter along with a close review of chapter 10 will likely give you enough information to get started. The seven World Café design principles and varied hosting practices you'll find here can be helpful in convening conversations for many different purposes, whether you use the Café format or not. Even if you are not planning to host Cafés personally, the book will provide you with enough perspective to determine if this approach is right for your own organization's meetings, conferences, or retreats.

As I mentioned earlier, "Questions for Reflection," posed at the end of each chapter, encourage you to consider your own experience and process of discovery about conversations that matter. Take a moment to ask yourself these questions now:

- What drew me to this book?
- If I think of this book as a personal conversation with the authors, how will that affect how I approach what they have to share with me?

- What question, if I explore it during my time with this book, could make the most difference in my life and work?

There is ample room for noting your own thoughts and reflections. Imagine yourself in a Café dialogue and think of these pages as Café tablecloths. Notice what connects to your personal experience and your own process of discovery. Jot down your insights about where to focus special attention and care as you engage conversations that matter in your own organization or community. Consider your own questions. Add your voice to the conversation.

In one of his wonderful poems, the Spanish poet Antonio Machado reminds us, "We make the path by walking on it." By joining us on the path that David and I, with the World Café community, are walking, we hope you will find yourself as intrigued as we are by both the power of conversation and the promise of the World Café. We hope you'll find the value generated from Café conversations around the world as an encouraging sign for the future.

Welcome to the World Café!

ADVANCE PREPARATION: CONVENING A WORLD CAFÉ

When you convene and host a Café conversation, you can use your personal imagination and have great fun! Although the traditional setup of Café-like tables and flowers creates a special ambiance, it is by no means the only way to go. We know of exciting World Café designs in which people have moved among conversation clusters in living rooms, rotated between large trees in a forest, or shifted places among several minivans on a learning journey. Whatever specific form you choose, engaging the seven Café principles in combination increases the likelihood of active engagement, authentic dialogue, and constructive possibilities for action. Use whatever space you have available, be creative with the setup and supplies, pay attention to the seven design principles, and use your imagination lo help the World Café achieve your purpose. Be the best host you can, and then trust the process.

Decide If a World Café Gathering Is Appropriate for Your Situation

Designing with the World Café principles in mind allows you to adapt and engage in conversations that matter in almost any circumstance. Cafés have been designed for sessions as short as ninety minutes as well as for conferences lasting several days. A Café can stand alone or serve as part of a larger meeting.

World Café conversations are especially useful for these purposes and in these circumstances:

- For sharing knowledge, stimulating innovative thinking, building community, and exploring possibilities around real-life issues and questions.
- For conducting an in-depth exploration of key challenges and opportunities.

- For engaging people who are meeting for the first time in authentic conversation.
- For deepening relationships and mutual ownership of outcomes in an existing group.
- For creating a meaningful interaction between a speaker and the audience.
- When the group is larger than twelve (we've hosted as many as twelve hundred) and you want each person to have the opportunity to contribute. The World Café is especially suitable for connecting the intimacy of small-group dialogue with the excitement and fun of larger-group participation and learning.
- When you have a minimum of one and a half hours for the Café (two hours is much better). Some Cafés have spanned several days or become part of a regular meeting infrastructure.

The World Café is not an optimal choice under these circumstances:

- You are driving toward an already determined solution or answer.
- You want to convey only one-way information.
- You are making detailed implementation plans and assignments.
- You have less than one and a half hours for the Café.
- You are working with a highly polarized, explosive situation. (Hosting a World Café in this setting requires highly skilled facilitation.)
- You have a group smaller than twelve. In that case, consider a traditional dialogue circle, council, or other approach to fostering authentic conversation.

Set the Context

Once you've determined that a Café conversation is appropriate for your circumstances, you'll need to clarify the context. This means paying attention to the three Ps: purpose, participants, and parameters.

- Determine clearly your purpose for bringing people together, along with the best possibilities or outcomes you can see emerging from your Café. Once you know your Café's purpose, name it in a way that reflects that purpose. For example: Leadership Café, Knowledge Café, Community Café, Discovery Café, Anniversary Café, and so on.
- Identify the participants who need to be included. Diversity of thought yields richer insights and discoveries.
- Take into account the parameters with which you are working (time, money, venue, and so on). See if you need to stretch the parameters in order to achieve your purpose.

Create Hospitable Space

Café hosts around the world emphasize the power and importance of creating a welcoming environment—one that feels comfortable, safe, and inviting for people to be themselves. In particular, consider how your invitation and your physical setup contribute to creating a welcoming atmosphere.

In your invitation, pose an initial question or theme that you believe is important to those you've invited. Choose a question that arouses curiosity and opens the way for more conversation. Craft your invitation to convey that members can expect to have fun, be engaged, and learn new things. When sending a written invitation, find ways to make it stand out from the usual e-mail or written correspondence by making it informal, creative, personal, and visually interesting.

Whether you are convening several dozen or several hundred people, your guests should notice immediately that this is no ordinary meeting. Arrange the room to be as welcoming as possible. Have music playing when people arrive. Natural light and an outdoor view are always inviting. If your room doesn't have windows, bring in plants and greener)' to enliven it. You can quickly transform a dull meeting room into a welcoming space by hanging pictures or posters on the walls. Hospitality and community thrive on food and refreshments; have snacks and beverages available throughout the gathering.

Please don't limit yourself with these suggestions. Look at the room setup and supplies list near the end of this chapter. Then use your own imagination and creativity to create a setting that participants will enjoy.

Explore Questions That Matter

Finding and framing relevant questions that open the way for great conversations is an area where careful thought and attention can produce profound results. Your Café may focus on exploring a single question, or you may develop several lines of inquiry to support an emergent discovery process through successive rounds of dialogue. In many cases, Café conversations are as much about discovering and exploring powerful questions as they are about finding immediate solutions. The question or questions you choose or that participants discover during a Café conversation are critical to its success. As Eric Vogt of the International Corporate Learning Association points out, a powerful question has these characteristics:

- It is simple and clear.
- It is thought-provoking.
- It generates energy.
- It focuses inquiry.
- It surfaces assumptions.
- It opens new possibilities.

Experienced Café hosts recommend posing open-ended questions—the kind that invite exploration. Good questions need not imply immediate action steps or problem solving. They invite inquiry and discovery rather than advocacy and advantage. We've included a list of generative questions near the end of this chapter that can help you craft your own questions for exploration. You'll know you have a good question when it continues to surface new ideas and possibilities. Test questions before using them. Bounce them off trusted friends or colleagues who will be participating in the Café to see if they sustain interest and energy. If you are featuring a speaker, involve that person in helping to create questions that, if explored, could make a difference to the real-life concerns of those attending.

AT THE EVENT: HOSTING A WORLD CAFÉ

A World Café generally consists of three rounds of progressive conversation lasting approximately twenty to thirty minutes each, followed by a dialogue among the whole group. Rounds have gone longer, but people often feel rushed in less than a twenty-minute round. The number and length of rounds prior to the whole-group dialogue will depend on your focus and intent. Feel free to experiment.

The job of the overall Café host (or the hosting team at larger gatherings) begins with welcoming people as they arrive, directing them to the refreshments, inviting them to their seats, and answering any logistical questions before the first round starts. Once everyone is seated, explain the purpose and the logistics of the Café. Let people know that they will be moving from table to table and that the end of a round may come when they are in the middle of an intense conversation, just as happens in life. It is natural to feel some resistance to the interruption, but they can pick up the conversation again at the next table. Explain that when a round ends one person will remain behind as the host of that table, and the other people will travel to new tables to sit with a different mix of people.

The job of the individual table host is to engage in the conversation as a participant and steward, not as a formal facilitator. The added role of this person is to share the essence of the conversation for the guests who arrive for the next round. Everyone at the table is responsible for supporting the host in taking notes, summarizing key ideas, and if so moved, making drawings that reflect interesting thoughts and insights as they unfold. This "table recording" helps the host do the best job possible in conveying to new members the key ideas that have emerged. Be sure to encourage people to write, draw, or doodle on the tablecloths in the midst of their conversations. Often these tablecloth drawings will contain remarkable notes, and they help visual learners link ideas. Members who will be traveling to a new table should bring with them the key ideas, themes, and questions from their last round to seed their upcoming conversation.

Before beginning the first round, it is helpful to introduce the Café assumptions and Café etiquette. You can display our graphics, shown here, on overheads, post them on easel sheets, or distribute them on cards at each table. Or use your own illustration style. Being clear about basic Café assumptions and Café etiquette orients members to underlying beliefs and personal behaviors that are useful in supporting constructive dialogue without being heavy-handed about "shoulds" and "shouldn'ts." Then allow time to answer any final questions prior to commencing the Café dialogue.

You are now ready to pose the question for the first round of conversation. Write the question—even if it's a question that asks people to discover their own question or questions—on flip charts or overheads and if necessary make extra copies to post around the room or distribute on cards to each table. Very often what people think they heard is different from what you thought you said. A visual reference can avoid a lot of confusion. Help clarify the question, if requested, but avoid providing answers or directing the conversation.

Encourage everyone to share their ideas and perspectives freely, and acknowledge that some people's special contribution may be their presence as attentive listeners. Some Café hosts prefer to ask people to identify the table host at the start of the round, while some opt for doing it at the end. Whichever one you choose, make sure that a host is chosen before people change tables.

Upon completing each round of conversation, let people know in a gentle way that it's time to move for the next round. Many hosts use a raised hand that signals others in the room to fall silent and raise theirs as well, marking the end of a round. Encourage the departing travelers from each table to find new tables and different people to sit with. Ask hosts to welcome their new guests. Remind everyone that when they arrive at their new table, they should briefly introduce themselves before the table host shares the essence of the conversation from the previous round. Then the travelers add connections and ideas from the conversations at their previous tables. Ask everyone to listen carefully and build on each other's contributions. Let people know if there is a new question for this round, and make sure it is posted where it can easily be seen.

At times people will participate in the first round, go traveling for the second, and then return to their home table for a final round of synthesis. At other times, members will continue traveling for several rounds while the host stays as the ongoing steward of the evolving conversation and insights at their table. On occasion, people will simply travel for a very brief listening tour to hear what's being explored at other tables prior to returning to their home table to both connect common threads and introduce diverse perspectives. The variations depend on your purpose, as the many stories and examples throughout this book demonstrate.

Encourage Everyone's Contribution

One of the reasons for having only four or five people per table is to enable each voice to be heard. People who are hesitant to speak in a large group often offer rich and exciting insights in a more intimate Café setting. At most Café gatherings, once the question is posed people are encouraged simply to jump into the conversation and begin to explore ideas. Most of the time this works well.

However, we have found it often helpful to have a talking object on the tables to help ensure that no single participant takes over the group's airtime. Originally used by indigenous peoples, a talking object can be a stick, a stone, a marker, a saltshaker—almost any object that can be passed among the people at the table. Ask people to pick tip the talking piece when they are ready to speak, and return it to the center of the table when they are done. The talking piece can also be passed around the circle, or the person who begins can offer it as a gift to whomever he chooses, though people have the opportunity to pass if they wish.

As the host, you can introduce the use of the talking piece as the Café begins or at any appropriate point in the process where you sense that deep listening and "slowing down the action" for more thoughtful engagement may be needed. There are two aspects to the talking object that encourage helpful member participation. Whoever is holding it is encouraged express his or her thoughts as clearly and briefly as possible. Whoever is not holding the talking piece is asked to listen with respect, appreciating the other's perspective as a part of the larger picture.

As host, you can assess what combination of free-flowing exchange and reflective listening to other members using the talking piece will work best. If you anticipate intense emotions or differences of opinion, it's often helpful to begin with a talking piece and then move to a more free-flowing dialogue.

Cross-Pollinate and Connect Diverse Perspectives

Moving among tables, talking with new people, contributing your thinking, and linking the essence of your discoveries to ever-widening circles of thought are hallmarks of the World Café. Patterns emerge, additional perspectives surface, and surprising combinations of insight and creativity reveal themselves in ways people had not previously imagined. The physical movement and cross-pollination of ideas in Café dialogues also reduces the common tendency of participants to "hang onto" their initial positions and opinions.

CONFLICTED CAFÉ? HOW TO DEAL WITH DIFFERENCES AND TENSION

Ken Homer, World Café host and Webmaster
    Cafés often surface differences of opinion and understanding; this is part of their ability to generate new insights. However, differences can foster either energy and excitement or anxiety and dissension. If you anticipate difficulties or discover that a conversation seems to be getting really stuck, then in an upcoming round you might encourage participants to use the following three statements as their dialogue unfolds.

- What I heard you say that I appreciated is . . .
- What I heard that challenged my thinking is . . .
- To better understand your perspective I'd like to ask you . . .

Using this simple discipline appropriately can make the difference between a conversation that is ineffective and divisive and one in which everyone takes advantage of the diversity of thought and opinion for their mutual learning.

Sometimes it is not practical for people to move, but this does not mean people can't cross-pollinate ideas. As the Café host, you can ask all the participants to write one key insight, idea, or theme from their table conversation on a large index card. Each member then turns in a different direction and exchanges the card with a person at a nearby table, thus randomly cross-pollinating insights among table conversations. Members read aloud the "gifts" they've received to provide creative input for a deepening round of conversation.

Listen Together for Patterns, Insights, and Deeper Questions

Noticing patterns and connections lies at the heart of knowledge creation. Dynamic listening plays a key role in realizing such breakthrough discoveries. As the Café host, you can encourage the kinds of listening that will make insight, innovation, and action more likely to occur. At the start of the Café, ask members to enter the conversation with the goal of learning from each person at their table. Encourage people to view different perspectives and assumptions as gifts: even when they make us uncomfortable, they offer fertile ground for discovering new possibilities.

Breakthrough thinking occurs most often when people encourage one another to take their thinking further. Ask participants to give each other their full attention by linking and building on shared ideas rather than going off in random directions or personal tangents. Remind folks to listen together for the insights, patterns, or core questions that underlie the various emerging perspectives that no individual member of the group might access alone. Suggest that they watch for times when it might be helpful to pause between comments, allowing time for new ideas to surface. Finally, encourage each table to take some time to reflect during their inquiry together by asking, What is at the center of our conversation?

Harvest and Share Collective Discoveries

After several Café rounds, it is helpful to engage in a whole-group conversation. These town meeting-style conversations are not formal reports or analytical summaries, but a time for mutual reflection. Give people a few moments of silence to reflect on or jot down what they have learned in their travels, what has heart and meaning, or what is present now as a result of their conversations. Ask anyone in the room to share briefly a key idea, theme, or core question that holds real meaning for them personally. Encourage everyone to notice what discoveries from their own conversations link to this initial sharing.

Solicit additional ideas and insights, making sure to balance new discoveries with moments of silent reflection—for it is often in silence that a deeper intelligence, intuitive flash of new knowledge, or a new action possibility is revealed. Make sure key insights are recorded visually or gathered and posted, if possible. If you want to capture the specifics, ask everyone to contribute by writing a core idea or insight on stickies or index cards, which can then be posted and consolidated for action planning or other purposes.

MAKING COLLECTIVE KNOWLEDGE VISIBLE AND IDENTIFYING ACTION PRIORITIES

In most World Café gatherings, participants write or draw ideas on paper tablecloths, enabling other Café participants literally to "see" what they mean. Here are some additional ways ideas from the Café can be harvested and utilized in practical ways.

- Have a graphic recorder capture the whole-group conversation by drawing the group's ideas on flip charts or a wall mural. These colorful murals act like a big tablecloth for the whole group, enabling people to notice key/insights and action opportunities.
- Take a gallery tour of the tablecloths. They can be hung on a wall so that members can see the group's ideas on a break as a prelude to posting key insights.
- Post your insights. Each participant can write one key insight on a large sticky note and place it on the wall so that everyone can review the ideas during a break. They can be used at the end of a Café for consolidating key themes or action items.
- Create idea clusters. Have volunteers group the insights into affinity clusters so that related ideas are visible. This can help a group plan its next steps.
- Make a story. Some Cafés create a newspaper or storybook to share the results of their work with larger audiences after the event. Or a graphic recorder will create a picture book, often with digital photos, along with text as documentation for future use.

Room Setup and Supplies

The room setup described here is an ideal situation. Your venue may not fit this model exactly. However, by using your imagination, you can improvise and design a World Café dialogue process, with or without Café tables, that reflects your unique situation and embodies the seven basic operating principles. Be creative! For example, if tables aren't available, you can arrange chairs in small U-shaped clusters and ask people to form a circle when the conversation begins. Place index cards or pads of paper on the chairs along with felt-tipped pens for noting key ideas.

Room Setup

- A room with natural light and view of outside foliage. If this isn't possible, place plants or flowers around the room to give the Café a natural feeling.
- Small round or square tables (approximately 36 to 42 inches in diameter) that can seat four or five. Card tables work as well, although round tables tend to create more of a Café ambiance, fewer than four at a table may not provide enough diversity of perspective, while more than five limits the amount of personal interaction.
- A large enough room so that people can move comfortably among tables and Café hosts can mingle without disturbing sealed participants.
- Tables spread in a slightly chaotic fashion, not in rows. Create a random distribution around the room.
- Checkered or other informal-colored tablecloths. If none exist, then white tablecloths will work. Even just putting pieces of easel or flip chart paper on the table alone will work.

Supplies

- Two pieces of white flip chart paper on each table (similar to in cafés, where people often write on the tablecloths). Use more layers it you'll be removing and posting these sheets. Since people record ideas on the tablecloths, flip charts at individual tables are generally not needed.
- Mural or flip chart paper for harvesting and posting collective insights.
- Flat wall space for moral paper or two large rolling whiteboards for the work of a graphic recorder. Wall space is also useful for posting the sheets of paper from tables.
- A mug or wine glass at each table filled with a variety of colored markers (preferably water-based and nontoxic). You can use Crayola watercolor markers, Mr. Sketch, or other pointed felt-tipped pens or markers in darker colors such as red, green, blue, black, and purple.
- One small vase with sprigs of fresh flowers on each table. Flowers should be small so they don't obscure the view. Add a small candle as well, if the venue permits it.
- One additional Café table set up in the front of the room for the host's and presenters' materials.
- A side table for coffee, tea, water, and refreshments for participants.
- Name tags and chairs for all participants and presenters (with capacity to remove extra chairs).

Optional Equipment

- An overhead projector, screen, a table for overheads, and a digital camera.
- A sound system with good speakers that can play both tapes and CDs.
- CDs or tapes of mellow jazz or other upbeat music to play as people enter.
- Microphones with speakers for Café hosts. Two wireless lavalieres, if needed, and two handheld wireless mikes for town meeting-style sessions.
- Two to four flip charts with blank white paper.
- Two or more 4 ft. x 6 ft. or 4 ft. x 8 ft. rolling whiteboards or blackboards.
- A box containing basic supplies: stapler, paper clips, rubber hands, markers, masking tape, extra pens, pushpins, pencils, and sticky note pads.
- Colored 4 in. x 6 in. or 5 in. x 8 in. cards, in colors other than white, if possible—enough cards for each participant to have several for personal note-taking or sharing insights across tables during the gathering.
- Bright-colored 4 in. x 6 in. large sticky notes, divided into small packs of twenty-five sheets, one package for each table. You will need these if you are going to ask people to write ideas and post them.

QUESTIONS FOR ALL SEASONS

Here are generative questions that we and other colleagues have found useful to stimulate new knowledge and creative thinking in a wide variety of situations around the world. Look at these questions to jump start your own creative thinking about the most appropriate ones for your specific situation.

QUESTIONS FOR FOCUSING COLLECTIVE ATTENTION

- What question, if answered, could make the greatest difference to the future of the situation we're exploring here?
- What's important to you about this situation, and why do you care?
- What draws you/us to this inquiry?
- What's our intention here? What's the deeper purpose—the "big why"— that is worthy of our best effort?
- What opportunities can we see in this situation?
- What do we know so far/still need to learn about this situation?
- What are the dilemmas/opportunities in this situation?
- What assumptions do we need to test or challenge in thinking about this situation?
- What would someone who had a very different set of beliefs than we do say about this situation?

QUESTIONS FOR CONNECTING IDEAS AND FINDING DEEPER INSIGHT

- What's taking shape here? What are we hearing underneath the variety of opinions being expressed? What is in the center of our listening?
- What's emerging that is new for you? What new connections are you making?
- What have you heard that had real meaning for you? What surprised you? What puzzled or challenged you? What question would you like to ask now?
- What is missing from the picture so far? What are we not seeing? Where do we need more clarity?
- What has been your major learning or insight so far?
- What's the next level of thinking we need to address?
- If there was one thing that hasn't yet been said but is needed in order to reach a deeper level of understanding/clarity, what would that be?

QUESTIONS THAT CREATE FORWARD MOVEMENT

- What would it take to create change on this issue?
- What could happen that would enable you/us to feel fully engaged and energized in this situation?
- What's possible here and who cares about it?

- What needs our immediate attention going forward?
- If our success was completely guaranteed, what bold steps might we choose?
- How can we support each other in taking the next steps? What unique contribution can we each make?
- What challenges might come our way, and how, might we meet them?
- What conversation, if begun today, could ripple out in a way that created new possibilities for the future of [our situation . . .]?
- What seed might we plant together today that could make the most difference to the future of [our situation . . .]?

Appreciative Inquiry in Mediation

Jeffrey McClellan

Jeffrey McClellan is an associate professor of management at Frostburg State University in Frostburg, Maryland. He is an experienced consultant, teacher, trainer, and speaker. He teaches leadership and management with research interests in servant leadership development, organizational leadership and change, and leadership in Latin America. Jeff earned his PhD from Gonzaga University in Leadership Studies.

McClellan's article opens with a summary of the successes of mediation for interpersonal disputes as well as corporate disputes and those occurring in the criminal context. He cites a study that found that mediation procedures "out performed" courts in a number of areas. The strength of mediation, he says, is its ability to separate the people from the problem, creating the opportunity for people to work through the problem together. The weakness of traditional mediation, he argues, is its propensity to focus on the problem rather than on solutions. He advocates for the inclusion of a positive psychology approach to mediation, which would allow participants and mediators to emphasize what works as much as emphasizing the problematic issues. He backs up his claim with neuroscience, arguing the more we talk about our problems, the more challenging we make them seem. Ultimately, we scare ourselves. Each time we do this, we trigger the amygdala, the part of the brain responsible for emotional responses such as fear, worry, and aggression. Anger builds upon anger. The stress hormones generated hamper creativity and cooperation.

We included this piece under approaches because McClellan's article offers tips for those ready to integrate positive psychology into their work. To do so, he draws on the work of David Cooperrider. Cooperrider's approach, called appreciative inquiry, alters the questions posed by mediators and other conflict resolution practitioners to orient people towards more productive and less descriptive conversations. One question suggested is, "How will your life be different when you solve this problem?"

Whereas Carolyn Nordstrom (ethnography), Robert Irwin Rotberg, and Dennis Thompson (Truth and Reconciliation), and Adam Curle's normative meditation processes promote deep descriptions of conflicts and contexts, McClellan's approach urges the field away from descriptions of problems and towards positive connections and possible alternative futures. Critics of this approach suggest that this type of inquiry leaves differences unaddressed and, therefore, maintains the conditions for further conflict to develop and emerge. Additionally, they claim that appreciative inquiry leaves power unexamined in favor of deeming everyone in the conversation equal no matter their background. This approach has been largely used in organizational development and has been making its way into the field of conflict analysis and resolution.

Questions to consider: What could be some benefits of focusing on the future as much as the problems of the past? How might a future-oriented approach shift policies and contexts?

Marrying Positive Psychology to Mediation

Using Appreciative Inquiry and Solution-Focused Counseling to Improve Progress

Jeffrey McClellan

This article discusses positive psychology and the benefits of combining some of its techniques with traditional mediation. It places specific emphasis on using the "appreciative inquiry" approach and solution-focused counseling. It also suggests how mediators could employ these techniques.

Positive analyses of mediation have been found in numerous studies of divorce mediation, community mediation, school mediation, parent-child mediation and organizational/labor mediation.[1] In a recent survey, even corporate counsel have said that mediation is their favorite process.[2]

Researchers of mediation in the criminal context have found that mediation has performed extremely well on a number of satisfaction scales, some of which are: whether the system was fair, whether the case was handled satisfactorily, whether the parties had an opportunity to tell their story, whether the parties' opinions were adequately considered, whether the judge or mediator was fair, whether the offender was held accountable, whether an apology or offering of forgiveness was given, whether the outcome was fair, and whether the outcome was considered to be satisfactory.

Researchers have found that expressing negative emotions initiates an escalating cycle of emotions in the parties that makes resolution of conflict more difficult.

According to Barton Poulson, who reviewed the available empirical research on victim-offender mediation, victims said mediation "outperformed" courts on every issue except consideration of opinion, while offenders said mediation outperformed courts on all issues except satisfaction with the outcome. In no case did courts perform better than mediation.[3]

The successes of mediation are closely tied to the strength of the traditional mediation process, which invites the parties to "separate the people from the problem," encourages them to work "side by side, attacking the problem, not each other," and focuses not on positional bargaining, but on satisfying "underlying interests."[4]

The Traditional Mediation Model

The traditional mediation process involves a number of steps. How many depends on the model of mediation used by the mediator. However, in all mediations you generally will find these steps. First, the mediator begins with an introductory statement. Typically, this covers the purpose of mediation, the role of the mediator, communication ground rules, confidentiality matters, and the agenda for the session.[5] Importantly, the opening statement emphasizes the voluntary nature of mediation and the parties' consent to continue with the mediation process.

The second step in the mediation process has the parties telling their individual stories in their own words about the dispute.[6] This negative story telling has been considered a vital part of the success of mediation because the parties are able to vent their feelings and explain to each other how they view the facts and circumstances of the dispute. This type of direct, and sometimes emotional, party-to-party communication simple does not occur in court proceedings, which are orchestrated by attorneys in a question-and-answer format.

The third step in mediation has the parties identify the key issues in dispute and the underlying interests of the parties. The mediation then moves into a problem-solving stage that involves an exploration of options.[7]

The last step involves preparing a settlement agreement.

It can be seen from this outline of mediation that early on the process focuses on negative storytelling and then moves into traditional problem solving. I believe that there is great potential to improve this process by taking advantage of certain elements of positive psychology.

The Positive Psychology Movement

The positive psychology movement began as a result of the belief among some psychologists that the field of psychology had "created a deficit bias."[8] They argued that psychology's emphasis on human deficiencies and pathologies merely guided practitioners to bring people to what might be considered a state of normal health. But it did not help people to transcend normalcy.

Positive psychology, by contrast, emphasizes positive experiences and traits. It studies how people flourish, focusing on well-being and the "good life."[9] As a result, it has been said that "positive psychology calls for as much focus on strength as on weakness, as much interest in building the best in life as repairing the worst, and as much attention to fulfilling the lives of healthy people as to healing the wounds of the distressed."[10] This is why positive psychologists and researchers tend to focus on positive subjects such as forgiveness, resilience, virtuousness, gratitude, appreciation, and fostering high quality relationships, strength-based development, leadership and management.[11]

One of the axiomatic principles of the positive psychology movement is expressed in the following statement about the traditional problem-solving approach: "When we talk in earnest about a problem, the problem becomes more increasingly real and increasingly formidable."[12] David Cooperrider, a founder of the "appreciative inquiry," and his co-author, Suresh Srivastva, say that in traditional problem solving, people assume that something is broken and needs fixing. Thus in their words, "the function of problem solving is to integrate, stabilize, and help raise to its fullest potential the workings of the status quo." They see limitations in this process because this goal implies that "one already has knowledge of what 'should be.'" This, they explain, is an "inherently conservative" approach.[13] As a result of this conservatism, Cooperrider asserts that traditional methods of problem solving are "painfully slow," "rarely result in new vision," and "are notorious for generating defensiveness."[14]

Researchers have found that expressing negative emotions initiates an escalating cycle of emotions in the parties that makes resolution of conflict more difficult. One researcher explained this process in neurological terms:

[E]very . . . anger-provoking thought or perception becomes, a minitrigger for amygdala-driven surges of catecholamines, each building on the hormonal momentum of those that went before. A second comes before the first has subsided, and a third on top of those, and so on. . . . [A]nger builds on anger.[15]

As this cycle builds, "edginess" and arousal increase dramatically. Once agitation reaches a high level, the parasympathetic response may take up to 48 hours to restore the body to its original state of calm.

Researchers know that high stress levels tamper creativity and cooperative behaviors. A brain scan of a person who is upset or anxious shows high activity in the amygdala and the right side of the prefrontal area while a brain scan of a person who is in a good mood indicates activity in the amygdala and the left side of the prefrontal area.[16] Activity on the right side of the prefrontal cortex flourishes a negative cycle of emotions, while the right side nourishes positive emotions.

This strongly suggests that allowing participants to share their negative stories early in the mediation process could trigger through emotion to limit the effectiveness of later brainstorming and problem-solving activities.[17]

Thus, it would seem beneficial to find an alternative that has a more positive effect on the participants.

The positive emotions emphasized in positive psychology could have a significant effect on human ability. The transition from negativity to optimism and positive emotions has been found to contribute to motivation, social helpfulness, effective leadership, productive relationships, creativity, resilience, problem solving, improved decision making, learning, and facilitating change.[18] If these positive emotions could be harnessed during mediation, they might facilitate the resolution of the conflict.

According to one researcher, "[E]mbedded within the chaos that fosters conflict is the powerful energy of passion that, if properly harnessed, can lead to progress through actionable agreement."[19] Two practice-oriented outgrowths of the positive psychology movement that could be capable of harnessing this emotional power are the "appreciative inquiry" and solution-focused counseling.

The Appreciative Inquiry

The appreciative inquiry is an organizational development methodology that seeks to foster growth and change by identifying and using the central strengths and resources of an entity or individual.[20] The appreciative inquiry takes organizations and individuals through four stages called the "4-Ds": discovery, dream, design and destiny. First, they discover the factors that "give life to the organization." Second, they dream about what the organization ideally could become. Third, they design their social architecture in a way that would facilitate the desired future. Finally, they seek to make that future happen.[21]

This process seems transferable to alternative dispute resolution mechanisms (ADR) in general and to mediation in particular because ADR is consistent with a founding principle of appreciative inquiry.[22] According to Cooperrider, one of the foundational principles of this methodology is that "[r]elationships thrive where there is an appreciative eye—when people see the best in one another, when they can share their dreams and ultimate concerns in affirming ways, and when they are connected in full voice to create not just new worlds but better worlds." The ability to see the best in others, even in the midst of conflict, requires individuals to reconstruct how they see one another. They need to adopt a different mental attitude, as one of Dostoevsky's characters said, in order to "refashion the world."

It has been said that positive psychology, and in particular appreciative inquiry, helps people discover "positive capacity" in others, which in turn triggers "an increased capacity to "perceive the successes of another, "access from memory the positive rather than negative aspects of the other," and "perceive ambiguous situations for the positive rather than the negative possibilities."[23] Accordingly, the appreciative inquiry can influences people "to respond to the positive images that others have of them."[24] This leads to more social behavior and creates greater alertness, enthusiasm, determination, attentiveness, and energy among the interacting individuals.[25]

Solution-Focused Counseling

Solution-focused counseling is a type of therapy that focuses on peoples' strengths and their potential for accomplishment without regard to any limitations they may have. The basic premise is that people have "a reservoir of wisdom learned and forgotten" that they can use to overcome the problems they face.[26] In solution-focused counseling, counselors help their clients to tap in this reservoir in order to positively deal with, resolve conflicts in their lives.

For example, some questions they might ask a client are: How will your life be different when you have solved the problem? What is different about the times when you do not have this problem? Have you ever solved a similar problem. I overcome a similar challenge in the past? How did you do it?

Because this technique focuses on strength and abilities that an individual already possesses it is innately positive. Therefore, it has the potential to trigger the kind of positive thinking that is needed to diminish conflict.

Improving Mediation

Adding appreciative inquiry and a solution focused discussion to the traditional mediation process could infuse the process with greater positive emotion, unleashing the creativity and collaboration necessary to redirect the parties' focus from past difficulties towards a more positive resolution-oriented future.

The potential for using the positive energy and strength-building that these two methodologies encourage in a mediation setting is exciting to ponder.

Instead of allowing negative storytelling to follow the mediator's opening statement, the mediator could meet privately with each side and focus on fostering appreciation of the other side. For example, the mediator could ask the caucusing party to identify the positive traits and behavior they have witnessed or hope to find in the other side. Possible questions that a mediator might as include:

- What was it about _____ that led you to decide to work with him/her on this project?
- What is it about _____ that leads you to believe that this mediation process will be successful?

The mediator could also ask:

- Tell me about a time when you and _____ were able to successfully work through a conflict in the past. What was it about the other person that made this possible? What did you do to invite the person to respond in this way?
- What has led you to have enough confidence in _____ to be willing to deal with this conflict through mediation?

- What do you believe about _____ that leads you to feel that a win/win agreement might be reached?
- In similar conflicts with others, what have you done that brought the conflict to a positive resolution?
- Tell me about a time when you felt really good about how you solved a conflict with another person that caused the relationship to flourish when you initially did not think it would.

These questions encourage the parties to think more positively about the person they will be negotiating with in mediation. This can only foster positive effect and diminish the tension and defensiveness. Thus, it could be a powerful tool for mediators.

While this initial discussion may prove valuable in a private caucus with each party, additional value is likely to accrue from engaging the parties in an open discussion of these items either after the initial caucus or following storytelling. This open discussion could break down negative perceptual barriers and encourage more positive collaborative interaction throughout the process.

Following the initial invitation to participate in positive discourse, the mediators and the parties would then determine whether to engage in storytelling or to move directly to problem solving. In many cases, telling one's story is essential for the individual to move beyond the experience and achieve both personal and interpersonal resolution. However, storytelling, when preceded by the type of positive conversation described above is likely to result in diminished negativity. In addition, the mediator may establish ground rules that respect the positive context that has been established to ensure that the process proceeds in an affirming way.

As for the solution-focused methodology, the most obvious stage in which the mediator could employ this technique is the problem-solving phase. In doing so, the goal would be to put the parties in a better frame of mind to come up with potential positive solutions to resolve the dispute. As was the case in the process discussed previously, this would largely be achieved through the use of affirming questions. Possible questions the mediator might ask during this phase might include:

- Have you ever solved a similar conflict in the past? If so, how did you do it?
- What was different in your life before you experienced this conflict?
- How do you think your life will be different when you resolve this conflict?

In order to generate possible solutions, the mediator could ask:

- What is the most positive outcome that you can realistically envision happening as a result of this mediation?
- What would it take for this to occur?
- Imagine that five years have passed, this problem is solved and the relationship between you and _____ is positive in nature. What would have happened to bring you to this place?

- What have you done in the past with others whom you care about to solve conflicts you experienced?
- What things, if done by the other person, would you find most affirming and beneficial in resolving this conflict?
- What things do you think you could do that would most positively contribute to the resolution of this conflict and the affirmation of the other person?
- What could you do that would most likely invite the other person to engage in the process in a way that would improve the quality of the mediation process and lead to a positive resolution?

These questions have power to affect the emotions of the parties in a positive manner. They invite the parties to step back from their own positions in the conflict and suggest a more empathetic and positive way of viewing each other and the conflict.[27] This can broaden the parties' perspectives and their understanding of the dispute, increase their commitment to the mediation process, and lead to greater creativity in envisioning possible solutions.

It is worth mentioning, however, that while appreciative and solution-focused questions may prove to be most valuable during the problem-solving or solution-seeking phase of mediation, they can be used throughout the process because they encourage a positive mindset about the process in which they are engaging. This mindset and approach could ultimately transform and reframe the mediation stages.

Conclusion

It is valuable to consider ways to improve an astoundingly effective means of resolving disputes. The appreciative inquiry and solution-focused discourse used in positive psychology have the potential to increase satisfaction with mediation and its outcome, and repair damaged relationships.

Notes

1. *Divorce*: B. J. Bautz, & R. M. Hill, "Divorce Mediation in New Hampshire: A Voluntary Concept," 7(1) *Mediation Quarterly* 33–40 (1989), and C. W. Camplair & A. L. Stolberg, "Benefits of Court-Sponsored Divorce Mediation: A Study of Outcomes and Influences on Success," 7(3) *Mediation Quarterly* 199–213 (1990). *Community mediation*: See generally M. S. Umbreit, Mediating Interpersonal Conflicts: A Pathway to Peace (CPI Pub. 1995), and Z. J. Eigen, "Voluntary Mediation in New York State," 52(3) *Dispute Resol. Journal* 58–66 (1997). *School mediation*: C. T. Araki, "Dispute Mediation in the Schools," 8(1), *Mediation Quarterly* 51–62 (1990), and J. Hart & M. Gunty, "The Impact of a Peer Mediation Program on an Elementary School Environment," 22(1) *Peace & Change* 76–91 (1997). *Organizational/labor mediation*: American Arbitration Association-Sponsored Study, "Dispute-wise Business Management: Improving Economic Outcomes in *Managing Business* (2003), available at www. adr.org/si.asp?id = 4124, and

S. B. Goldberg, "How Interest-Based, Grievance Mediation Performs over the Long Term," 59(4) *Dispute Resol. Journal* 8–15 (1995).

2. Sheri Quakers/ "Survey Says Corporate Counsel Prefer Mediation, Nat'l L.J. Online, April 27, 2007, at www.cpradr.org/pressroom/press2609. pdf; David P. Lipsky & Ronald L. Seeber, "The Use of ADR in U.S. Corporations: Executive Summary" (1997 Joint Initiative of Cornell University, the Foundation for the Prevention and Early Resolution of Conflict (PERC) and Price Waterhouse, LLP).

3. B. Poulson, "A Third Voice: A Review of Empirical Research on the Psychological Outcomes of Restorative Justice," 2003(1) *Utah L. Rev.* 198.

4. R. Fisher et al., *Getting to Yes: Negotiating Agreement without Giving In* 11 (Random House 1981).

5. Umbreit, supra n. 1, at 27; see generally, P. B. Kestner & L. Ray, The Conflict Resolution Training Program Participants Workbook (Jossey-Bass 2002).

6. According to Umbreit, supra, n. 1, at 104, however, "divorce mediation does not usually begin with the parties telling their stories." He explains this exception in the following way: "Opening statements of divorcing couples would usually offer premature solutions or a litany of reasons for the divorce. The parties would then proceed to defend the statements rather than analyze the issues together and consider options." This exception reveals the potential problem of beginning difficult conversations with negative storytelling.

7. Umbreit, supra n. 1, at 27.

8. K. S. Cameron et al., "Foundations of Positive Organizational Scholarship," in *Positive Organizational Scholarship* 7 (Cameron et al., eds., Berrett-Koehler Pub. 2003).

9. K. M. Sutcliffe & T. J. Vogus, "Organizing for Resilience," in *Positive Organizational Scholarship*, supra n. 8, at 98.

10. *Positive Organizational Scholarship*, supra n. 8, at 15.

11. *Forgiveness*: T. Baskin & R. D. Enright, "Intervention Studies on Forgiveness: A Metaanalysis," 82(1) *Journal of Counseling & Dev.* 79–90 (2004). Shan Ferch, "Intentional Forgiving as a Counseling Intervention," 76(13) *Journal of Counseling & Dev.* 261–70 (1998). Resilience: Sutcliffe & Vogus, supra n. 9. Virtuousness: K. S. Cameron, "Organizational Virtuousness and Performance," in *Positive Organizational Scholarship*, supra n. 8, at 48–65. *Gratitude and Appreciation*: D. L. Cooperrider & D. Whitney, "A Positive Revolution in Change: Appreciative Inquiry," in *Appreciative Inquiry*. An Emerging Direction for Organization Development 9–30 (Cooperrider et al., eds., Stipes Pub. 2001). R. Emmons, "Acts of Gratitude in Organizations," in *Positive Organizational Scholarship*, supra n. 8, at 85. *Fostering high quality relationships*: J. D. Dutton & E. D. Heaphy, "The Power of High Quality Connections," in *Positive Organizational Scholarship*, supra n. 8, at 263–78. *Strength-based development, leadership, and management*: D. O. Clifton & J. K. Harter, "Investing in Strengths," in *Positive Organizational Scholarship*, supra n. 8, at 111–21. J. H. Zenger & J. Folkman, *The Extraordinary Leader: Turning God Managers into Great Leaders* (Mc-Graw-Hill 2002).

12. K. J. & M. Gergen, *Social Construction: Entering the Dialogue* 50 (Taos Institute Pub. 2004).

13. D. L. Cooperrider & S. Srivastva, "Appreciative Inquiry in Organizational Life," in *Appreciate Inquiry*, supra n. 11, at 82.

14. D. L. Cooperrider, "Resources for Getting Appreciative Inquiry Started an Example OD Proposal," in *Appreciative Inquiry*, supra n. 11, at 193.

15. D. Goleman, *Emotional Intelligence: Why It Can Matter More than Q.* 61 (Bantam Books 1995).

16. D. Goleman et al., *Primal Leadership: Realizing the Power of Emotional Intelligence* 45 (Harvard Bus. School press 2002).

17. See, generally, E. Jensen, *Teaching with the Brain in Mind* (Association or Supervision & Curriculum Development 1998).

18. *Motivation*: R. P. Bagozzi, "Positive and Negative Emotions in Organizations"; F. Luthans & B. Avolio, "Authentic Leadership Development," in *Positive Organizational Scholarship*, supra n. 8, at 176–93, 241–248; Goleman et al., supra n. 16. *Social helpfulness*: Cooperrider, supra n. 14; Goleman et al., supra n. 6. *Effective leadership*: Goleman et al., supra n. 16; Luthans & Avolio, supra, n. *Productive relationships*: D. L. Cooperrider, "Positive Image, Positive Action: The Affirmative Basis of Organizing," in *Appreciative Inquiry*, supra n. 11. Creativity: Goleman et al., supra n. 16. *Resilience*: Luthans & Avolio, supra n. 18. *Effective problem solving and decision making*: Cooperrider, supra n. 14, Goleman et al., supra n. 16. *Learning*: Cooperrider, supra n. 14, and Jensen supra n. 17. *Facilitating change*: G. Busche, "Five Theories of Change Embedded in Appreciative Inquiry," in *Appreciative Inquiry*, supra n. 11.

19. S. L. Podziba, The Human Side of Complex Public Policy Mediation," 19(4), *Negotiation Journal* 289–90 (2003).

20. Gergen, supra n. 12, at 57.

21. D. Cooperrider et al., *Appreciative Inquiry: The Handbook* 38–41 (1st ed. Crown Custom Pub. 2003.

22. See K. L. Murrell, "International and Intellectual Roots of Appreciative Inquiry," in *Appreciative Inquiry*, supra n. 13, at 109 (shows how using appreciative inquiry in organizations that are experiencing conflict can provide "the energy to correct deficiencies and improve methods").

23. D. L. Cooperrider & D. Whitney, "A Positive Revolution in Change: Appreciative Inquiry," and Cooperrider, "Positive Image, Positive Action: The Affirmative Basis of Organizing, both in *Appreciative Inquiry*, supra n. 11, at 12, 38, 39 & 193. As this occurs, the gratitude that accompanies the appreciative process "serves as a moral motive, stimulating people to behave prosocially after they have been the beneficiaries of other people's prosocial behavior." R. Emmons, "Acts of Gratitude in Organizations," in *Positive Organizational Scholarship*, supra n. 8, at 85.

24. Cooperrider & Whitney, supra n. 23.

25. Emmons, supra n. 23, at 86.

26. W. H. O'Hanlon & M. Weiner-Davis, *In Search of Solutions: A New Direction in Psychotherapy* 1, 13 (W. W. Norton 1989).

27. R. Kegan, & L. L. Lahey, *How the Way We Talk Can Change the Way We Work: Seven Languages for Transformation* 215 (Jossey-Bass 2001).

Rethinking Intractable Conflict

Robin R. Vallacher, Peter T. Coleman, Andrzej Nowak, and Lan Bui-Wrzosinska

Robin Vallacher is a professor of psychology at Florida Atlantic University as well as an affiliate at the Center for Complex Systems at the University of Warsaw in Poland and a research affiliate in the Advanced Consortium on Cooperation, Conflict, and Complexity at Columbia University. His research has been funded by grants from the National Science Foundation and the National Institute of Mental Health. He currently works on developing dynamical models of diverse social psychological phenomena, from self-concept and social judgment to social change and inter-group conflict. Peter Coleman is a professor of psychology and education at Columbia University. In the 1980s, Coleman began his professional career as an actor in New York, working in television, theater, and film. He then worked as a mental health counselor for violent inner-city youth and soon found his way to his true calling. He completed his MA and PhD at Columbia University, where he works today. Coleman is considered a leading expert in intractable conflict. Andrzej Nowak is a professor at the University of Warsaw in Poland, where he is a director of the Center for Complex Systems Research. He is a world expert on the modeling and computer simulations of social processes, such as conflict. Lan Bui-Wrzosinska is an assistant professor of psychology with the Department of Psychology at the Warsaw School of Social Sciences and Humanities and writes about complexity and dynamical systems.

In "What Are Intractable Conflicts?," Heidi Burgess introduces students of conflict to the notion of intractable conflicts—conflicts that, for one reason or another, find themselves resistant to resolution. In this article, the authors study intractable conflicts using principles of complexity and dynamical systems. These authors believe that by looking at these challenging conflicts through this perspective can provide new avenues for resolution. Complexity and dynamical systems approaches can be used to study everything from tornados to a crowded sidewalk. These approaches look beyond root causes or values conflict, and they look instead at the phenomenon as the result of numerous elements coming together to perpetuate the conflict. While this analytical approach comes from mathematics, the authors argue for its relevance to today's conflicts.

One of the most important concepts in this systems' approach to conflict is to understand the concept of attractors. Attractors pull systems back to the same state even after intervention. Without identifying and addressing the attractors, systems will inevitably return to their former pattern—and the conflicts will persist. An example of an attractor could be a deeply held belief of one group by another. Even if conditions change, if that belief persists, the conflict may return at any time. Intractable conflicts often have several attractors.

Questions to consider: Think of a conflict and list at least five interrelated factors in that conflict. How might understanding these factors and understanding their interaction affect how one intervenes in a conflict? What is one attitude circulating that if it does not change will upend any peace efforts?

Rethinking Intractable Conflict

Robin R. Vallacher, Peter T. Coleman, Andrzej Nowak, and Lan Bui-Wrzosinska

Conflict resolution should be easy. Conventional wisdom, enshrined in scholarly analyses (cf. Deutsch, Coleman, & Marcus, 2006), has it that conflict arises when people feel their respective interests or needs are incompatible. Defusing a conflict, then, is tantamount to eliminating the perceived incompatibility and creating conditions that foster common goals and values. A conflict that has become intractable should be especially easy to resolve through such interventions. After all, a conflict with no end in sight serves the interests of very few people, drains both parties' resources, wastes energy, and diminishes human capital in service of a futile endeavor. Even a compromise solution that only partially addresses the salient needs and interests of the parties should be embraced when they realize that such a compromise represents a far better deal than pursuing a self-defeating pattern of behavior that offers them nothing but aversive outcomes with a highly uncertain prospect of goal attainment.

Conflict resolution, of course, is at times anything but easy. To be sure, many antagonistic encounters stemming from incompatible interests are short-lived and run their course without causing irreparable damage to either party. But a small portion of relationships that are mired in conflict become protracted affairs, to the point of seeming intractability. Such conflicts can be extremely detrimental and become self-sustaining, displaying marked resistance to intervention even in the face of rational considerations that would seemingly defuse the animosities at work (cf. Azar, 1990; Bennett, 1996; Bercovitch, 2005; Burton, 1987; Coleman, 2003;

Goertz & Diehl, 1993; Kriesberg, 2005; Marshall & Gurr, 2005; Pearce & Little-john, 1997).

This imperviousness to rationality suggests that the problem of intractability says more about psychology than it does about objective reality. An intractable conflict is one that has become entrenched in cognitive, affective, and social-structural mechanisms, a transformation that effectively distances the conflict from the perceived incompatibilities that launched it. This transformation can occur in conflicts in marriages, in work settings, between political groups in communities, and between warring nations. As a conflict becomes a primary focus of each party's thoughts, feelings, and actions, even factors that are irrelevant to the conflict become framed in a way that intensifies or maintains the conflict. It is as though the conflict acts like a gravity well into which the surrounding mental, behavioral, and social-structural landscape begins to slide. Once parties are trapped in such a well, escape requires tremendous will and energy and thus feels impossible.

The Dynamical Perspective

This simplified scenario of intractable conflict, captured in the gravity well meta-phor, has clear parallels to a wide variety of phenomena not only in the social sciences but also in the physical sciences. Indeed, recent years have witnessed the advent of a perspective in the physical sciences and mathematics that identifies the dynamic and inertial processes that are common to everything from slime molds to galaxy formation. This perspective, which underlies dynamical systems theory and models of complexity, emphasizes the inevitable and spontaneous organiza-tion of discrete elements into global patterns that, once formed, resist disruption and other sources of change (cf. Holland, 1995; Kelso, 1995; Schuster, 1984; Strogatz, 2003). Even a highly volatile phenomenon—whether a tornado, a swarm of locusts, or a crowded sidewalk in Manhattan—can be viewed as the coordina-tion of elements and forces into a higher order entity that becomes self-sustaining and orderly. Our aim in this article is to show the relevance of this perspective for illuminating the nature of intractable conflict and to suggest new strategies for resolving such conflicts that follow from this understanding.

Although developed in mathematics and the physical sciences, the principles of dynamical systems and complexity have potential application to the fundamen-tals of human experience. This potential has become increasingly manifest since the 1990s, and the dynamical perspective has emerged as a primary paradigm for the investigation of psychological processes at different levels of personal and social reality. To date, dynamical models have been advanced to explain and predict a wide range of processes, from self-concept and social judgment to the emergence of public opinion and societal transitions (see reviews by Guastello, Koopmans, & Pincus, 2009, and Vallacher & Nowak, 2007). We feel that the dynamical per-spective is ideally suited to capture the dynamics of intractable conflict, and over the past several years we have begun to reframe this topic in dynamical terms (e.g., Coleman, Bui-Wrzosinska, Vallacher, & Nowak, 2006; Coleman, Val-lacher, Nowak, & Bui-Wrzosinska, 2007; Coleman, Vallacher, Nowak, Bui-Wrzosinska, & Bartoli, in press; Nowak, Vallacher, Bui-Wrzosinska, & Coleman,

2007). Our efforts to date have been largely theoretical, even metaphorical, in an effort to show how conflict intractability can be understood in terms of basic dynamical properties. Having laid this conceptual groundwork, we propose that the next step is to use the propositions and tools of the dynamical perspective to explore well-defined issues in concrete contexts involving real human conflicts.

The Problem of Intractable Conflict

Before we describe the dynamical perspective on intractable conflict, it is important to clarify the scope of the problem with respect to both real-world concerns and theory construction. As the world enters the 21st century, protracted social conflicts represent pressing problems undermining the security and well-being of societies worldwide. Today, there are over 30 wars and violent conflicts being waged around the globe; approximately 40% of intrastate armed conflicts have lasted for 10 years or more, and 25% of wars have lasted for more than 25 years (see http://globalsecurity.org/military/world/war and Marshall & Gurr, 2005). The enduring conflicts in Israel, Palestine, Kashmir, Cyprus, Sudan, and the Democratic Republic of Congo are just a few examples. A study of international conflicts between 1945 and 1995 identified 18 cases of intractable interstate relationships that produced 75 militarized and violent conflicts that resisted hundreds of attempts at resolution and posed serious threats to regional or international security (Bercovitch, 2005). In these settings, entire generations of youths are socialized into conflict, a condition we know to perpetuate destructive conflict. These circumstances often lead to incalculable human suffering, including destruction of vital infrastructure, division of families and communities, and extreme violence, dislocation, and trauma to individuals (Cairns & Darby, 1998; Coleman, 2000). In fact, scholars have linked the events of September 11th, 2001 to the sociopolitical conditions that fester in hot zones of intractable conflict (Crocker, Hampson, & Aall, 2005). Indeed, enduring conflicts have been linked to one half of the interstate wars since 1816, with 10 out of 12 of the most severe international wars emerging from protracted destructive relations (Bennett, 1996). The seeming immunity to resolution has led many scholars to label such conflicts intractable (cf. Coleman, 2003).

Despite the widespread and destructive nature of intractable conflict, this phenomenon has yet to be conceptualized in an agreed-upon and coherent fashion. The failure to achieve consensus regarding the fundamental processes underlying intractable conflict, and the corresponding failure to generate effective strategies for transforming such conflict, is not due to a lack of effort on the part of the scientific and practitioner communities. To the contrary, numerous theories, research initiatives, and intervention strategies have been proposed over the years (cf. http://www.beyondintractability.org; Azar, 1990; Burton 1987; Cairns & Darby, 1998; Coleman, 2003, 2004, 2006 Crocker et al., 2005; Goertz & Diehl, 1993; Kelman, 1999 Kriesberg, 1998, 2005; Kriesberg, Northrup, & Thorson, 1989; Lederach, 1997; Pearce & Littlejohn, 1997; Pruitt & Olczak, 1995). To some extent, the problem in framing a coherent theory reflects the inevitable idiosyncrasies of each conflict. Common factors and processes have been identified, but they represent an embarrassment of riches for theory construction. The task for theory construction is integrating these diverse factors into an account that is coherent yet allows for prediction and a basis for conflict resolution in specific conflict settings.

We propose that adopting the perspective of dynamical systems will promote the emergence of such an account. In particular, we suggest that the proximate causes of intractable conflict (e.g., competition over scarce resources, ideological differences, protection of personal or group identity) belie a more fundamental tendency that can be observed in systems throughout nature—the integration of basic elements into a global state that provides coherence and stability for the system. This tendency, which generates and is maintained by a host of dynamic processes, cannot be reduced to traditional motivational assumptions such as hedonism, self-esteem, or self-interest, whether immediate or long-term. The press for higher order coherence, moreover, is robust with respect to the idiosyncratic features of specific conflict scenarios and thus provides a framework within which the complex nexus of proximate causes of intractable conflict can be understood and investigated. The central issue for conflict resolution in these cases is not how to resolve the issues in dispute but rather how to transform the system from the coordinated ensemble of dynamics perpetuating the conflict to a different coherent state that allows for benign (or positive) relations between the parties.

The Dynamical Perspective on Intractable Conflict: Frequently Asked Questions

Because many readers are unfamiliar with the dynamical systems perspective, it is useful to clarify the key concepts and general hypotheses associated with this approach to intractable conflict. Accordingly, we have developed a set of basic questions[1] concerning intractable conflict for which the dynamical perspective offers fresh insight and testable propositions. Some of these questions represent fundamental features of conflict that have been addressed throughout the years. Others represent seemingly paradoxical features of conflict that are difficult to understand through the lens of canonical models of conflict. All are intended to provide readers with basic concepts and principles of complexity and dynamical systems that are useful for rethinking the nature of intractable conflict and the means by which such conflict can be transformed. We hasten to add that this account does not dismiss classical accounts that trade on notions such as power, justice, competition over resources, identity, entrapment, and in-group–out-group relations. To the contrary, these concepts are incorporated into the heart of the dynamical perspective.

QUESTION 1: HOW DOES DYNAMICAL SYSTEMS THEORY ACCOUNT FOR THE GENESIS AND MAINTENANCE OF INTRACTABLE CONFLICT?

Conflict is not inherently bad. To the contrary, disputes and disagreements are inevitable in human affairs and are essential to the construction of a shared reality, problem solving, participatory governance, and adaptation to changing circumstances. Conflict can escalate beyond a point that has benefits, however, promoting instead protracted malignant relations that are destructive to all parties concerned. How does a basic and largely adaptive feature of social life degenerate into a persistent pattern of behavior that brings out the worst in human nature?

The key to understanding the genesis and maintenance of intractable conflict centers on the notion of attractor. In generic terms, an attractor refers to a subset of potential states or patterns of change to which a system's behavior converges over time. Metaphorically, an attractor "attracts" the system's behavior, so that even very different starting states tend to evolve toward the subset of states defining the attractor. In the absence of an attractor, a system can change and evolve in response to whatever influences and forces it experiences. When a system's dynamics are governed by an attractor, however, the system is resistant to perturbing influences that would otherwise move it to a different state or pattern of changes. An external factor might promote a temporary change in the state of a system, but over time the system will return to its attractor.[2]

An example of an attractor for a simple system is the behavior of a pendulum in the presence of friction. No matter how one swings the pendulum (i.e., regardless of the initial conditions), after some time the pendulum will stabilize pointing downward. Thus, all the trajectories ultimately converge on a single state that represents the attractor for pendulum dynamics, and any disturbance of this state will have only a temporary effect. A system, however, may have more than one attractor. When a coin is tossed, for example, it can land on one of its two sides, each representing an attractor for the coin's dynamics.

In complex systems—systems composed of many interconnected elements—attractors develop as the elements influence each other to achieve a relatively coherent state or pattern of changes that provides coordination for the elements (cf. Haken, 1978; Hopfield, 1982; Strogatz, 2003). The emergence of coherent system-level properties by means of self-organization represents a universal property of nonlinear dynamical systems and provides an important link between areas of science as distinct as biology and economics. The synchronized flashing of fireflies (Strogatz, 2003), for example, seems quite different from the synchronized firing of neurons associated with pattern recognition and consciousness (cf. Hopfield, 1982; Tononi & Edelman, 1998), but both phenomena illustrate the tendency for the elements of a system to become coordinated and to promote the emergence of coherent system-level properties and behavior. Once a system-level property has emerged, it constrains the subsequent behavior of the elements composing the system and resists forces that threaten the system's coherence. An attractor is thus similar to the notion of equilibrium or homeostasis (cf. Cannon,

1932; Miller, 1944[3]). In many systems, the equilibrium is an energy minimum in that it represents a state or pattern that minimizes the incompatibility among the elements.

In psychological and social systems, an attractor can be described as a restricted range of mental states and actions that is commonly experienced by a person or group. At the individual level, the thoughts and feelings that arise in the stream of thought can influence each other to take on a common meaning and promote the emergence of a coherent higher order belief or social judgment (cf. Tesser, 1978; Vallacher, Nowak, & Kaufman, 1994). Once a global mental state develops, it resists subsequent input that threatens to undermine it. In the context of a positive view of someone, for example, information that the person is "critical" may be interpreted as a virtue ("constructive") rather than a vice ("mean-spirited"). Similar dynamics are operative in the emergence and maintenance of norms, attitudes, and fashions in a social system. Individuals, who may differ initially in their personal preferences, influence each other to adopt a shared reality (cf. Kenrick, Li, & Butner, 2003; Nowak, Szamrej, & Latane, 1990). Once a collective state comes to characterize the thought processes of interconnected individuals, there is strong resistance to new information or forces that threaten to undermine it. Thus, discrepant information is discounted or reinterpreted to fit the prevailing view, and individuals holding deviant ideas are subject to intense influence from the local majority or are ostracized.

Attractors do not necessarily represent goals, values, or other desired states. A person with low self-esteem, for example, may initially embrace flattering feedback from an acquaintance, but over time such a person is likely to discount or reinterpret this feedback, displaying a pattern of self-evaluative thought that converges on a negative state (Swann, Hixon, Stein-Seroussi, & Gilbert, 1990; Vallacher, Nowak, Froehlich, & Rockloff, 2002). At an interpersonal level, a person might display a persistent pattern of antagonistic behavior in his or her social relations despite efforts to avoid behaving in this manner. And in an intergroup context, warring factions may display conciliatory gestures when prompted to do so but revert to a pattern of antagonistic thought and behavior when the outside interventions are relaxed (Coleman et al., 2007). In short, when a system's dynamics are governed by an attractor, the system will consistently evolve to a particular state, even if this state is not hedonically pleasant, and will return to this state despite being perturbed by forces that might promote a more pleasant or ideal state.

The attractor concept is illustrated in Figure 1, which reflects the gravity well metaphor noted at the outset. The ball represents the current state of the system and the valleys represent two attractors for the system. The ball will roll down the hill and come to rest at the bottom of the valley, which represents a local energy minimum. Each attractor can be characterized in terms of two basic properties. A basin of attraction specifies the range of states that will evolve toward the attractor. This feature is represented by the width of each valley in the figure. A system with a wide basin "attracts" a broad range of states, including information and events that seem inconsistent with the attractor. A system with a narrow basin "attracts" a smaller range of states and thus is less able to absorb inconsistent ideas and events. In the figure, the basin of attraction for Attractor A is somewhat wider than the basin of attraction for Attractor B. This means that a wider variety of states will evolve toward A than toward B.

An attractor can also be characterized in terms of its strength, or resistance to change. This feature is represented by the depth of each valley in the figure. It is difficult to dislodge a system from a strong attractor even when perturbed by strong external influences, whereas a relatively weak influence can dislodge a system from a weak attractor. In the figure, Attractor B is stronger than Attractor A. This means that once a system is at Attractor B, it is more difficult for it to be dislodged by external influence.

We propose that a protracted malignant conflict reflects a strong attractor with a wide basin of attraction. The strength of the attractor reflects its capacity for maintaining a coherent cognitive, affective, and behavioral orientation among the parties to a conflict. When destructive conflict is associated with a deep attractor (as in Attractor B), an attempt to address the current state of the conflict corresponds to pushing the ball uphill. It not only requires considerable effort but also is likely to be futile, since once the pushing force is relaxed, the ball will roll back to the attractor. This corresponds to some peace agreements, initiated at great expense by the international community, that eventually collapse after the fanfare of the initial breakthroughs subsides. A wide basin of attraction means that a broad range of ideas and action possibilities will eventually evolve toward the dominant mental and behavioral pattern characterizing the parties to the conflict. Even positive information that contradicts the negative view of members of an outgroup is transformed by a variety of cognitive and social mechanisms until it fits the predominant view. Thus, a peaceful overture or a logical appeal emphasizing the nonproductive nature of the conflict might initially be taken at face value but over time will become reframed until it provides evidence in support of, rather than in opposition to, the predominant response tendency of the person or group.

Knowing the attractor landscape of a system is essential when attempting to anticipate the fate of introducing a new element—a communication, an overture, even an unanticipated but significant event—particularly when the element is open to different interpretations or has unclear implications. Assume, for example, that a group has an attractor for negative relations with another group. The width of the basin of attraction determines whether a positive act by the other group will be assimilated to the attractor or instead will represent an inconsistency that holds potential for dislodging the system from the attractor. If the attractor has a wide basin, the positive act (e.g., a conciliatory gesture) might be reframed in negative terms (e.g., as weakness or deception). If the attractor has a narrow basin, the same element cannot be as readily assimilated and might move the system to a different attractor (corresponding to reconciliation).

The strength of the attractor decides whether the inconsistent element (e.g., a positive act) will have any effect in moving the system away from the negative state. If the attractor is relatively weak, the inconsistent element may influence the state of the system, perhaps moving it gradually toward a different pattern of thought and action. Additional inconsistencies might even transform the system, moving it to a different (new or latent) attractor. If the attractor is strong, however,

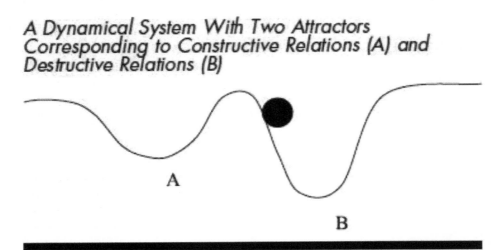

A Dynamical System With Two Attractors Corresponding to Constructive Relations (A) and Destructive Relations (B)

Figure 1.   A Dynamical System With Two Attractors Corresponding to Constructive Relations (A) and Destructive Relations (B)

even very inconsistent information may not affect the state of the system. A highly conciliatory gesture by the other group, for example, is unlikely to change the way the group is perceived. Instead, the gesture will be discounted in importance or suppressed in communication and discussion.

At some point, though, the inconsistent elements may become sufficiently numerous or significant that they succeed in transforming the system. The stronger the attractor, the more numerous or significant the inconsistencies must be to have this effect. When this threshold is reached, the system will show a sudden and qualitative change to a new (or previously latent) attractor. We suggest that these basic processes may underlie the radical shifts observed when communities move rapidly from peace to violence (as occurred in the 1994 Rwandan genocide), or from violence to peace (as seen in the emergence of peace in Mozambique in 1992; see Bartoli, Bui-Wrzosinska & Nowak, in press). After this transformation, the system will display the same resistance to inconsistent (now negative) information and the same nonlinear transformation when a threshold of inconsistency is reached.

This scenario suggests that when a system has two strong attractors (e.g., one maintaining positive relations between two groups and one maintaining negative relations), the same element (an event, a communication, etc.) can be responded to in very different ways depending on which attractor is currently manifest. This tendency, referred to as hysteresis, is a signature phenomenon of nonlinear dynamical systems. With respect to intractable conflict, knowing the respective strength and basins of attraction for the set of attractors defining the relationship between the parties is critical for anticipating the impact of information or events that might have a single unequivocal meaning (e.g., positive or negative) when viewed from outside the conflict.

QUESTION 2: HOW DOES AN ATTRACTOR DIFFER FROM MORE FAMILIAR NOTIONS, SUCH AS "SCHEMA," "GOAL," "ATTITUDE," OR "DISPOSITION"?

The attractor concept has much in common with these and other familiar psychological constructs. Indeed, each of them can be conceptualized as an attractor for a specific type of system. In traditional approaches, however, these phenomena are commonly investigated as fixed structures, with little consideration given to their dynamic properties. By framing them in terms of attractors, we can recapture the dynamics that are often lost in theoretical accounts.

A schema, for example, has attractor properties in that it constrains the dynamics of perception and thinking, causing the stream of thought concerning an object or event to converge on a specific set of values (e.g., interpretations, judgments, beliefs). A goal, in turn, represents an attractor in that it steers actions toward the attainment of a particular state while resisting the temptations of other action possibilities. In similar fashion, the concept of attitude describes the values of thoughts, feelings, and actions that are most often experienced when one is in contact with the attitude object and to which a set of psychological mechanisms promotes convergence after one receives contradictory information. Having a positive attitude toward a person, for example, does not rule out the possibility of experiencing negative feelings toward the person on specific occasions but rather suggests that such feelings are intrinsically unstable and infrequent. A personality disposition, meanwhile, represents a person's tendency to behave in a consistent manner despite interpersonal and situational forces that mitigate against such behavior or promote other types of behavior. It describes not a single value on a dimension of personality but rather the attractor for a system of interacting mechanisms producing and controlling thoughts, feelings, and behaviors in a certain domain.

Reframing these familiar notions in explicitly dynamical terms highlights their common properties and thus provides theoretical unity across otherwise diverse domains and levels of experience. Investigating schemas, goals, and the like from a dynamical perspective thus may illuminate the origin, evolution, and transformation of the collective states that provide stabilization of people's thoughts, feelings, and actions. It is worth emphasizing, too, that a dynamical system may have more than one attractor governing its dynamics. Identifying the structure of attractors in a system thus provides insight into the possible coexistence of different (and potentially conflicting) schemas, goals, attitudes, and dispositions governing a person's functioning under different conditions.

QUESTION 3: WHAT PROMOTES THE DEVELOPMENT OF A STRONG NEGATIVE ATTRACTOR FOR SOCIAL RELATIONS AND CONFLICT?

In benign conflicts (and everyday social relations), the links among different thoughts, feelings, and action tendencies reflect a relative balance between positive (reinforcing) and negative (inhibiting) feedback. Elements linked by positive feedback reinforce and amplify one another's current states. A hostile thought about a person or group, for example, elicits other negative thoughts or transforms neutral thoughts into negative ones, and through repeated iterations of this linkage, the separate thoughts coalesce into a coherent negative judgment. In most social contexts, however, this potential for the spread of negativity and conflict escalation is restrained by inhibitory feedback among elements. A hostile action toward a person, for example, might promote feelings of regret or guilt or perhaps a consideration of the person's benign or positive qualities. Such thoughts effectively restrain the hostile impulses, establishing a tempered stance in the social relationship.

When an attractor begins to develop in a system, the balance between reinforcing and inhibiting feedback is diminished or lost altogether, with elements serving primarily to reinforce or amplify each element's current state through positive feedback loops. By itself, any element is open to change when exposed to other elements with a different meaning or implication for action. Knowing that a person has a political ideology that differs from that of one's ingroup, for example, may set the stage for thinking negatively about him or her, but if other elements of information have not been linked with this element, outside influences could prevent one from forming a negative judgment. Once a global assessment has developed, however, the positive feedback loops among the elements offset the impact of new information that might overwhelm any single element. So if the person's political ideology has become linked to judgments of his or her honesty, intelligence, and patriotism, one's judgment of the person will be more immune to subsequent discrepant information.

In conflict situations, the shift toward reinforcing feedback loops promotes the emergence of strong attractors that are resilient in the face of potentially disconfirmatory events and information. At the individual level, an incongruent piece of information is considered in light of the ensemble of congruent information and is likely to be reframed to fit the prevailing meaning (e.g., Tesser, Martin, & Cornell, 1996). In social systems, communication among group members bolsters the group's attractor for thought and behavior and buffers individuals within the group from outside influence (cf. Nowak et al., 1990). This is particularly evident in isolated, extremist groups of all flavors (see Bartoli & Coleman, 2003). In both cases, a perturbing influence might have an immediate impact on the state of the system, but over time the mutual support among the system's elements restores the system to its attractor.

It remains to be determined what factors are responsible for the breakdown in self-regulatory mechanisms in strong conflict attractors. The balance of power, the degree of interdependence, the level of cooperation versus competition, the salience of ideology and social identity, and the zero-sum nature of resources in some conflicts are plausible candidates. Other likely factors that transcend conflict per se include stress, threat, mortality salience, strong emotions, time pressure, and any condition that undermines controlled (conscious, deliberative) mental processes, which play a central role in self-regulation (Vallacher & Nowak, 1999). Identifying the factors that change the balance between positive and negative feedback in mental and social systems provides an important agenda for empirical research.

QUESTION 4: INTRACTABLE CONFLICTS ARE UNDESIRABLE AND DESTRUCTIVE TO ALL PARTIES, YET THEY ARE MAINTAINED FOR VERY LONG PERIODS OF TIME AND RESIST ATTEMPTS AT RESOLUTION—WHY?

Traditional theories of motivation are hard pressed to explain the persistence of destructive conflict. Apart from being intrinsically unpleasant and defined in terms of negative emotion, protracted conflicts destroy lives, tear apart families and communities, divert attention and energy from more productive pursuits, and rarely produce happiness or even satisfaction. Nor are the goals of conflict often achieved, particularly in cases of intractable conflict that persist through many generations with no end in sight. Hedonism, enlightened self-interest, achievement motivation, and other classic motives fall short in attempting to explain this enduring feature of human existence. Even if such motives could be identified (e.g., ingroup solidarity afforded by outgroup antagonism), there are other means by which these motives could be satisfied without entailing the enormous trade-offs in costs and adverse consequences of intractable conflict.

Despite the self-destructive potential of entrenched conflict, attractors satisfy two basic psychological motives. First, they provide a coherent view of the conflict, including the character of the ingroup, the nature of the relationship with the antagonistic party, the history of the conflict, and the legitimacy of claims made by each party. These views, of course, are often in direct opposition to those of members of the outgroup, as is evident in many accounts of the conflict in the Middle East (cf. Bar-Tal, 2000; Rouhana & Bar-Tal, 1998). Attempts to instill a different view, even one that might allow for peaceful resolution of the conflict, threaten the subjective "accuracy" of the current view and are resisted. Thus, new information might strike an outsider as a basis for rethinking the rationale for a conflict yet be discounted or reinterpreted by the parties themselves in order to make it consistent with the prevailing view of the conflict. This function of attractors is especially critical when the parties encounter information or actions that are open to interpretation. An attractor serves to disambiguate actions and to interpret the relevance and "true" meaning of information.

Second, attractors provide a stable platform for action, enabling each party to a conflict to respond unequivocally and without hesitation to a change in circumstances or to an action initiated by the other party. In the absence of an attractor, the conflicting parties may experience hesitation in deciding what to do or may engage in internal dissent that could prevent each party from engaging in a clear and decisive course of action. At the individual level, such dissent is experienced as ambivalence or uncertainty. At the group or societal level, internal dissent represents disagreement among the individuals comprising the respective ingroups or societies.

A conflict governed by attractor dynamics can appear not only at odds with classic hedonic concerns but also ironic with respect to conventional notions of information processing. Classic theories and lines of research in social psychology suggest that ambiguous and conflicting information makes people vulnerable to new interpretations and attitudes and thus sets the stage for change and transformation at the individual, interpersonal, and collective levels (cf. Deutsch & Gerard, 1955; Festinger, 1954; Sherif, 1936). In mental, interpersonal, or intergroup relationships governed by attractor dynamics, however, we propose that there is an inverse relation between information ambiguity and transformation. When an attractor provides coherence for complex and ambiguous information, it is especially vulnerable to new ideas that provide a different way of integrating such information. Hence, a new perspective regarding an ongoing conflict, although serving the disambiguation function, represents a challenge to the established pattern of thinking and undermines the associated platform for action. Change in response to such information is therefore strongly resisted. We suggest, in fact, that the greatest potential for a sudden eruption of violence exists when there is a challenge to the validity of an attractor providing coherence for information that is difficult to verify. Ironically, when change does occur, it tends to be wholesale rather than incremental in nature, with the party's thoughts, feelings, and action tendencies coalescing into a new attractor or moving to an existing attractor that had previously been latent in the system. This scenario has intriguing but largely untested implications for conflict escalation and resolution (which are developed in the response to Question 10).

The heightened resistance to ideas or interpretations that challenge an attractor based on ambiguous and difficult-to-verify information can be seen at the individual level. When a subjectively important but difficult-to-verify attitude is threatened by an alternative perspective, for example, one or more cognitive mechanisms are engaged to thwart the threat and reaffirm the attitude (e.g., Tesser et al., 1996). Recent theory and research on self-concept, meanwhile, suggest that people who have high self-esteem with an unclear relation to accomplishments and other sources of objective information tend to be the most defensive in response to criticism and unflattering appraisals, often resorting to violence against the source of the threatening feedback (cf. Baumeister, Smart, & Boden, 1996). We suggest that this connection characterizes attractor dynamics at the level of groups and societies as well. If this is indeed the case, it provides insight into certain intractable conflicts that erupt into violence when new information calls into question the legitimacy of one or both parties' stable pattern of thought and behavior. The ironic connection between the complexity and ambiguity of information and a group's resistance to change has yet to be empirically verified and thus provides a promising agenda for research on the dynamics of conflict.

QUESTION 5: AT WHAT LEVEL OF SOCIAL REALITY DO ATTRACTORS OF CONFLICT EXIST?

Attractors represent formal properties of dynamical systems and thus characterize the dynamics of systems at all levels of reality. Cognitive processes and intergroup relations are clearly different phenomena, for example, but each can be described in terms of stable patterns (e.g., interpretation in cognition, social distance in intergroup relations) that provide coherence and unequivocal platforms for action. Accordingly, conflict can be characterized with attractors at different levels of social reality. At the level of the mind, attractors represent stable patterns of thought and affect concerning the parties to the conflict (e.g., oneself and another person in interpersonal conflict, the ingroup and the outgroup in intergroup conflict), as well as the history and nature of the interpersonal or intergroup relationship. At the interpersonal and intergroup levels, attractors represent stable and recurring patterns of relations between the parties to the conflict. The mere mention of the conflicting party—let alone an encounter with the party—may promote well-learned and automatic response tendencies at different levels of action meaning.

Because of the feedback among levels in a dynamical system, an attractor that initially develops at one level of reality is likely to forge attractors at other levels. A conflict may develop over issues of resource allocation, for example, and the negative interactions associated with this conflict could promote psychological attractors (i.e., negative attitudes) that are consistent with, and serve to maintain, the interpersonal conflict. Once a psychological attractor develops, the conditions that generated the conflict (i.e., resource allocation) could be mitigated without resolving the conflict if the attractor is strong and has a wide basin of attraction. The change in objective conditions, for example, could be interpreted in a manner that reinforces rather than undermines the negative feelings toward the other party. In conflict situations, then, an interpersonal or intergroup attractor promotes a social judgment attractor, which then reinforces the interpersonal attractor, and so on, in a reciprocal reinforcing feedback loop.

Because of the feedback linking levels, a conflict initially associated with one level of reality is likely to spread to other levels, creating the potential for overlapping and mutually reinforcing attractors that serve to anchor the conflict. This expansion of attractors can become encoded in cultural beliefs and traditions, adding yet another level to the conflict that can promote long-term intransigence and resistance to attempts at conflict resolution. For example, the annual Orange Walk held in Northern Ireland each July, which celebrates the Protestant victory of Prince William of Orange over King James II in 1690, evokes past grievances and losses associated with the protracted conflict over Ireland that trigger latent psychosocial attractors for more hostile Catholic-Protestant relations.

QUESTION 6: HOW CAN ONE IDENTIFY THE ATTRACTORS IN AN INTRACTABLE CONFLICT?

In one sense, this is a simple issue, almost trivial. If people are embroiled in an ongoing conflict, their respective patterns of thought and behavior are manifest and need only be described. But in another sense, the identification of attractors in a conflict is a very challenging problem. This is true for both descriptive and formal reasons.

Descriptively, the functional equivalence (equifinality) of thought and behavior can make it difficult to determine whether a party to a conflict is displaying a stable pattern, engaging in routine but nonmeaningful action, or acting in accord with very different concerns from one occasion to the next. Consider, for example, a person who attacks someone's line of reasoning, prevents another person from taking a short-cut through his or her territory, and refuses to answer an e-mail message from yet another person. Does this represent a pattern of behavior that could qualify as an attractor, or do these acts each reflect entirely different meanings despite their similarity with respect to an "antagonism" attitude or schema? Perhaps the attack represents "constructive criticism," the territorial defense represents "reinforcing norms of appropriate conduct," and the e-mail neglect represents "setting priorities in one's work." More generally, because actions can be identified and performed with respect to widely different higher level meanings (Vallacher & Wegner, in press), it can prove difficult (and misleading) to judge whether there is a pattern in a person's behavior, and if so, what the pattern is.

Formally, the identification of an attractor is difficult because an attractor is defined mathematically in terms of differential or difference equations and topographically in terms of phase space portraits (cf. Liebovitch, 1998; Nowak & Lewenstein, 1994). In real-world conflict settings, these formal approaches to attractor identification may be unrealistic or impossible (for notable exceptions, see Gottman, Swanson, & Swanson, 2002; Kugler & Coleman, 2009; Losada & Markovitch, 1990).

However, attractor identification is possible because of the two properties described above: the attractor's strength and basin of attraction. The basin of attraction is manifest as the diversity of information or events that are assimilated to the attractor. For an attractor with a wide basin of attraction, even highly discrepant information (e.g., a positive overture by an antagonist) is interpreted or reframed to make it consistent with the attractor. Strength is manifest as the resistance to change in the person or group's pattern of thought and behavior in response to events or information that are outside the basin of attraction. If the attractor is relatively weak, the system might change in response to even a few inconsistencies that are beyond the basin of attraction. If the attractor is strong, however, the system will resist change until a great deal of information or evidence outside of the basin of attraction has accumulated. Such information might be discounted or suppressed until a critical threshold of inconsistency is reached, at which point the system will demonstrate a catastrophic change to a new or previously latent attractor that provides coherence for the perturbing information.

These properties provide basic guidelines for how one might identify the attractors in an intractable conflict. The general strategy is to assess how a person or group responds to conflict-relevant information that varies along a basic dimension (e.g., positive versus negative actions by an outgroup). The range of information on this dimension that is assimilated to the attractor (e.g., by reinterpretation or rationalization) would indicate the width of the basin of attraction. The manner in which a person or group responds to information outside the basin of attraction would indicate the strength of the attractor. A strong attractor would be indicated if a large amount of such information is tolerated before the system undergoes change and if the change is catastrophic (sudden and wholesale), rather than incremental, when it occurs. Before this tipping point is reached, a person or group with a strong attractor is likely to display rapid and highly defensive responses to the inconsistent information. Implementing this general strategy in a systematic fashion to identify the attractors in a conflict situation represents a high priority for research.

QUESTION 7: HOW IS "POWER" INCORPORATED INTO THE DYNAMICAL ACCOUNT OF CONFLICT?

It is probably the exception rather than the rule that two interdependent entities—whether individuals, groups, or nations—have equal power. Personal relations are often characterized by differential dependency, with the less dependent person being in a position to dictate what the dyad does (Rusbult, 1983; Thibaut & Kelley, 1959); social or demographic groups in a society differ in their social capital, wealth, and education, and these assets translate directly into differential influence in shaping public policy (Deutsch, 2006; Sidanius & Pratto, 1999); and nations differ enormously in their respective military prowess, access to resources, and global influence (Zartman & Rubin, 2002). Despite the ubiquity of power asymmetry, intractable conflict is a relatively rare occurrence in social life (Bercovitch, 2005; Fisher, 2006). Such quiescence, of course, could simply reflect recognition of reality and a corresponding resignation concerning its fate on the part of the less powerful entity. Because the more powerful entity is expected to prevail if conflict becomes manifest (e.g., over access to resources), the less powerful entity does not provoke such conflicts and is prepared to settle for less if a conflict cannot be avoided. From this "realism" perspective, if the less powerful entity saw an opportunity to change the power imbalance in its own favor, it would experience little hesitation in doing so.

The dynamical account provides a different way of reconciling power asymmetry with peaceful coexistence among interdependent entities. Over time, the pattern of interaction and influence between such entities is likely to be internalized by both entities as an attractor that serves the key functions of attractors described earlier: coherent understanding and an unequivocal action orientation. Thus, the attractor provides a lens for constructing the past, interpreting the present, and anticipating the future, and it creates a stable platform for the entities' behavior vis à vis one another (e.g., Coleman et al., 2007). And because attractors resist destabilization, perturbations to the relationship will be actively resisted—not only by the more powerful party but by the less powerful party as well. A change in status upsets the equilibrium in the relationship, thereby reducing the coherence of both parties' thoughts and feelings and undermining the relevance of their action scripts. So rather than embracing an opportunity to change the balance of power, the less powerful entity attempts to reinstate the status quo.

Just such counterintuitive effects have been documented in research on system justification theory (cf. Jost, Banaji, & Nosek, 2004) and social dominance theory

(Sidanius & Pratto, 1999). Members of disadvantaged groups (e.g., racial and ethnic minorities), for example, commonly justify the status quo and feel that the social system perpetuating their lot in life is basically fair (see also Lerner, 1980). Even when disadvantaged people publicly express dissatisfaction with the status quo, assessment of their unconscious attitudes often reveals a pattern of ingroup and outgroup evaluation that is consistent with the power asymmetry (Jost, Pelham, Brett, & Carvallo, 2002). As with other instances of attractor dynamics, this tendency illustrates how the functions served by a stable attractor trump the usual panoply of basic motives (e.g., hedonism, enlightened self-interest, achievement, self-esteem).

This state of affairs does not mean that power imbalance is irrelevant to conflict. Asymmetry in influence and access to resources clearly can fuel antagonism between individuals, groups, and nations. Marriages are terminated when dominance and subjugation become unbearable for one of the partners, for example, and social systems undergo civil wars and revolutions in response to real or perceived power asymmetries between groups. In the dynamical account, this effect occurs when one or both parties escape the pull of the existing attractor, which enables information and events to be interpreted in a different way and provides a new platform for action. There are two scenarios by which this can happen (described more fully in the response to Question 10).

First, new information and events can be encountered that are outside the basin of attraction. The more powerful entity, for example, may engage in an especially unwarranted fashion that cannot be rationalized as acceptable (e.g., brutality, humiliation). Or information may come to light about the high-power entity that cannot be reconciled with prevalent beliefs and judgments concerning the entity (e.g., evidence that the high-power entity's flattering history had been falsified). Even if the inconsistent actions and pieces of information are initially discounted or suppressed, they hold potential for sowing the seeds of an alternative attractor for the relationship. Once a threshold of inconsistency is crossed, the relationship can undergo a profound transformation as the attractor loses its power to constrain thoughts, feelings, and actions concerning the relationship. This is the prototypical scenario of many insurgency movements, such as that depicted between the Algerian independence forces and the French in the classic film *The Battle of Algiers*. A new configuration can then emerge to provide coherence and a far different platform for action.

Second, an attractor can lose its pull if the reinforcing feedback loops among elements are weakened or reversed. The disassembly of an attractor is a difficult task, although contemporary research in social psychology provides clues as to how this can be accomplished. Inducing people to focus on the details of an event or a communication, for example, serves to isolate these elements and thus weaken the connections among them (cf. Vallacher, Nowak, & Miller, 2003). This is a tactic often used in mediation when disputants are encouraged to explore the specific needs and interests that underlie their more recalcitrant global positions regarding a conflict or relationship (see Kressel, 2006). The press for coherence associated with attractor dynamics then sets the stage for the emergence of a new pattern of thought and behavior concerning the relationship.

Both scenarios are more likely to alter attractors for power relations under conditions of instability. When marriage partners experience a marked change in their life circumstances (e.g., job loss, winning a lottery), for example, new information and events are experienced that cannot easily be assimilated to their existing attractor for the relationship. And because novel information and events are experienced in detailed (low-level) terms, there is potential for the emergence of an entirely different attractor that links the low-level elements in an alternative configuration. In similar fashion, intergroup relations characterized by power asymmetry can become destabilized during periods of rapid societal transition (Nowak & Vallacher, 2001), setting the stage for the emergence of a new attractor that reflects dissatisfaction with, rather than justification of, the power imbalance. During such periods, those individuals in the low-power group who are better educated or have more social contacts outside the group are typically in the vanguard of change (see reviews by Gurr, 1970, and Tyler & Smith, 1998). Presumably, such individuals have greater access to information that undermines the existing attractor or that suggests alternative perspectives and action possibilities concerning relations with the more powerful group (Gersick, 1991).

In a rapidly changing world, the balance of power between groups and nations may change frequently. Because such changes upset an established equilibrium, they unleash emotions and generate new actions, which can produce a spike in the frequency and intensity of conflict. The group with greater power is likely to feel considerable threat as the attractor connoting dominance is challenged or disassembled. The violence exhibited by lower middle-class males in the southern United States in response to desegregation in the mid-20th century is an example of this scenario. The group with less power, meanwhile, may be especially volatile as negative feelings (e.g., humiliation and anger), unfulfilled wishes, and suppressed actions become manifest. Even if there is progression toward redressing a power imbalance, such feelings may intensify rather than diminish if the rate of change is perceived to be insufficient by the ascendant group. Theory and research on personal satisfaction suggest that the rate of progress in achieving one's goals is more important than the magnitude of the discrepancy between one's current state and the desired state of affairs (Carver & Scheier, 1999; Hsee, Abelson, & Salovey, 1991). This can be seen at the level of intergroup relations as well. Thus, movement toward greater power symmetry may paradoxically lead to increased dissatisfaction in accordance with relative deprivation (cf. Merton, 1957). Such a "rising expectations" scenario characterized the push toward equality on the part of African Americans and women in American society in the 1960s.

From a dynamical perspective, the rate of progress toward a desired state of affairs (such as equality of power) is one of many possible temporal patterns of change in both self-regulatory dynamics (Vallacher & Nowak, 1999) and social change (Nowak & Vallacher, 2001). There may be short bursts of acceleration, for example, that are punctuated by longer periods of stabilization. It remains for future research to identify the dynamic patterns characterizing changes in power relations, both between individuals and between groups, and to map these patterns onto different scenarios of conflict and peaceful transformation.

The dynamical perspective provides a parsimonious integration of conflicting accounts of power asymmetry—one emphasizing stability (e.g., system justification, restoration of the status quo), the other emphasizing the potential for conflict (e.g., dissatisfaction, redress of the power imbalance). Research explicitly addressing these accounts has yet to be conducted, however. Computer simulations, experiments, and archival analyses are needed to identify the critical factors (e.g., social instability) underlying the proposed transformation in attractor dynamics (cf. Nowak, 2004). If an account of power asymmetry is confirmed, an ethical question concerning intervention arises: Is it preferable to promote peaceful relations characterized by power asymmetry or to promote equality if that entails the genesis of conflict and violence? Perhaps the answer to this question lies in developing a better understanding of the necessary yet not destabilizing rate of change between groups in conflict over power.

QUESTION 8: HOW IS "JUSTICE" INCORPORATED INTO THE DYNAMICAL ACCOUNT OF CONFLICT?

Justice is an important foundation for interpersonal and intergroup relations. It tempers self-interest, promotes the emergence of social norms, and can generate cooperative and altruistic behavior. In this sense, a concern with justice serves to stabilize social relations and provides regulatory mechanisms (inhibiting feedback loops) that constrain each party's behavior. But justice is often in "the eye of the beholder," and this subjectivity can serve to intensify rather than mitigate conflict under some circumstances. Particularly when there is an unequal division of resources, the potential for conflict is enhanced when the parties frame the issue in terms of justice. The disadvantaged group may see itself as victimized and view the other group as unfair, greedy, and bad. These perceptions legitimize aggressive action in the service of restoring justice. For its part, the advantaged group may consider its greater access to resources to be a reflection of its superiority and greater deservingness. It may see the other group as inferior and deserving of its lesser access to resources. Both groups, in other words, frame the conflict in terms of justice—but with entirely different notions of what constitutes justice. In effect, justice often amounts to justification (Lerner, 1980) and is therefore prone to the various cognitive mechanisms that are used to protect a coherent worldview against contradictory ideas and actions.

Disagreements about justice are not an inevitable consequence of inequality, however. Once a pattern of thought and behavior concerning an interpersonal or intergroup relationship is established, it functions as an attractor that resists change. If two groups have a long history of inequality, and if this state of affairs is legitimized by cultural values and a shared historical narrative, there may be little impetus for change. Maintenance of the status quo is clearly advantageous for the person or group with greater access to resources. But as noted in the response to Question 7, low-power groups are also inclined to bolster the status quo and thus tend to resist changes that would be to their advantage (Jost et al.,

2004; Sidanius & Pratto, 1999). Attractor dynamics, in other words, may be more important than simple self-interest in dictating how the groups define justice and deal with inequality. As with power asymmetry, basic conditions must be met before injustice in a relationship is recognized and serves to generate actions aimed at restoring justice (see Deutsch, 1985; Gurr, 1970; Merton, 1957). It remains for future research to identify these conditions and document their effects at different levels of social reality (interpersonal, intergroup, international).

QUESTION 9: WHAT IS THE ROLE OF RELIGION IN THE ORIGIN, MAINTENANCE, AND RESOLUTION OF CONFLICT?

Religion can play very different, even inconsistent, roles in conflict. On the one hand, religion provides constraints on actions of a self-serving or hedonistic nature while promoting actions that reflect moral values conducive to peaceful and cooperative relations with other people. Most religions emphasize impulse control, tolerance, and a concern for the welfare of others. These features of religiosity hold potential for the prevention and peaceful resolution of conflict. On the other hand, most religions divide mankind into good versus evil, saints versus sinners. The distinction between good and evil is too often manifest as the distinction between those who share one's religious beliefs and those who do not. Thus, even if someone from a different faith behaves in a morally commendable fashion, he or she may be judged negatively (e.g., as an infidel) by virtue of worshipping a different god or embracing a different creation myth.

When religious faiths fall along ethnic, regional, demographic, or national lines, religiosity tends to intensify the natural tendency to favor one's ingroup (e.g., one's nation) over an outgroup (e.g., another nation). If conditions promote ingroup versus outgroup conflict (e.g., competition over land or resources), the polarization of in-group–outgroup dynamics associated with religion can enhance rather than defuse conflict. Indeed, by perceiving members of the outgroup as evil or damned, the constraints (inhibiting feedback) against aggression and violence are weakened. Ironically, then, religion can promote behavior that is antithetical to the moral values it promulgates.

Framed in dynamical terms, religion captures the defining properties of an attractor. A religious faith provides certainty: a coherent view of the world, both with respect to moral values and cosmological truth, and a stable platform for personal and collective action. Information or events that are inconsistent with the religious worldview represent potential threats to the validity of that view and thus can promote intense defensive reactions (as seen in the current debates between creationism and the theory of evolution). The cognitive biases observed when personal attitudes are contradicted are on full display when information or events challenge a group's religious beliefs. Indeed, because religion by definition reflects faith rather than reason or empirical evidence, discrepant information or events are likely to be experienced as especially threatening and to promote very intense reactions in the service of reinstating the mental and social system at its attractor.

In the modern world, the threats to religions are numerous, from advances in science that challenge the wisdom of sacred texts (e.g., the origin and age of the universe) to increases in contact among people from cultures with different religious convictions and lifestyles. From this perspective, it is not surprising that many intense and prolonged conflicts today are associated with religious differences. Because the central controversies cannot be resolved conclusively (e.g., determining which god is the real one or which prophet is likely to be vindicated), religious-based conflicts are likely to be protracted, with victory and defeat (or genocide, at the extreme) representing the only perceived means of terminating the conflict. This gloomy scenario is especially likely to be manifest under conditions that reinforce a group's conviction that other groups must recognize the zero-sum nature of moral and cosmological truth.

Although religious differences have been associated with intergroup conflicts throughout human history, other factors often must be operative before religion can bring ingroup–outgroup relations to the threshold of serious conflict and warfare. People of different faiths can coexist peacefully, for example, if the available resources do not have a zero-sum quality and the groups are not in a state of confined interdependence (e.g., Hardin, 1968). It is also the case that religion is often used to justify aggression that is actually undertaken for very different reasons. Thus, in-group leaders sometimes exploit religious differences to engage citizens who would otherwise not be inclined to aggress against the outgroup. Finally, most religions converge on moral codes that are beneficial for social relations. Efforts designed to emphasize these rules of interpersonal behavior can offset the intolerance associated with good versus evil categorization. There are numerous instances in history when calls to a higher morality defused conflicts and brought about interpersonal and intergroup harmony.

QUESTION 10: HOW CAN AN INTRACTABLE CONFLICT BE RESOLVED OR AT LEAST TRANSFORMED INTO A BENIGN CONFLICT?

A defining feature of attractor dynamics is the tendency of a conflict to resist external influence and to return to the attractor if influence is temporarily successful. Attempts to challenge directly the validity or practicality of an attractor for intractable conflict are therefore often doomed to fail and in fact are likely to intensify people's beliefs and energize their response tendencies. Imagine, for instance, one's reaction to an acquaintance who takes it upon himself or herself to explain to one in detail why one's pro-choice (or pro-life) position on abortion is erroneous. Odds are, one will likely tune this person out, confront him or her, or move away and avoid him or her in the future. This makes the resolution of intractable conflict a daunting task. There are three basic scenarios, however, by which one might change the dynamics of an intractable conflict.

In one scenario, an understanding of how attractors are created can be used to "reverse engineer" a malignant attractor. Attractors develop as separate elements (e.g., issues, events, pieces of information) become linked by reinforcing feedback to promote a global perspective and action orientation. Reverse engineering thus entails changing some of the feedback loops from reinforcing to inhibitory, thereby lowering the level of coherence in the system. One strategy is to reinstate the salience of individual elements, devoid of their integration with other elements. Psychological research provides clues regarding this "disassembly process" (cf. Vallacher, Nowak, Markus, & Strauss, 1998; Vallacher & Wegner, in press). For example, disruptions to ongoing action tend to make people sensitive to the overlearned details of the action, as do instructions to focus on the details of a narrative rather than on the narrative's larger meaning. Such a situation occurred in Boston in 1994, when a series of violent shootings at family-planning clinics there forced the pro-life and pro-choice communities to carefully reexamine their activities and rhetoric and forge new approaches to the issues. When habitual actions and generalized judgments and beliefs are deconstructed in this way, people become vulnerable to new interpretations that provide an avenue of emergence to a coherent perspective. In effect, the tack is to recapture the complexity of a conflict attractor and reconfigure the elements to promote a more benign form of coherence.

In the second scenario, the key is moving the system out of its manifest attractor into a latent attractor that is defined in terms of benign or even positive thoughts, actions, and relationships. In most interpersonal and intergroup contexts, there are many elements of relevant information and many possible ways of configuring these elements to achieve a coherent perspective and a stable platform for action. Just as perceptual elements can be organized to promote different gestalts, social information can take on a host of different meanings with diverse action possibilities. At any given time, however, only one attractor is likely to be manifest in people's orientation toward other people or groups—just as a single figure-ground relation characterizes perception at a single point in time. The other possible attractors are latent and may be invisible, both to the parties involved and to outside observers. Yet these latent attractors may become manifest in sudden fashion under some circumstances and promote a notable change in the relations among people and groups.

There are reasons for suspecting the existence of latent attractors in relationships whose manifest tendencies are malignant. Many protracted conflicts, for example, involve a long history between the parties, including stretches of time characterized by positive relations. The relations between Ukraine and Poland, for example, go back many decades, and during this time mutually beneficial trade and cultural relations were often manifest. Indeed, the strained relations that developed as a result of World War II can be considered the exception rather than the rule in Ukrainian-Polish relations. Presumably, then, there is a latent attractor for positive relations between the two societies that was supplanted by a negative manifest attractor after the war. With this in mind, it is not surprising that the mutual antagonism gave way in a dramatic fashion to mutual support during the Orange revolution in Ukraine in 2004–2005. In effect, the two countries shifted their respective figure-ground relations and began to interact in a qualitatively different manner that reflected an attractor that had been latent for years.

We propose that latent attractors may be an inevitable consequence of developing a manifest attractor. In emphasizing some elements while ignoring or downplaying others to bolster a particular orientation toward another person or group, people often have to suppress or discount particular ideas, feelings, and action tendencies. These suppressed elements of thought and behavior may become self-organized to promote their own attractor, in the same way that marginalized individuals in a social system form clusters with internal coherence (Nowak et al., 1990). Under certain conditions, the latent attractors formed in this fashion may suddenly become manifest, just as minority groups can suddenly exert significant influence in a social system when various conditions are met (cf. Moscovici, 1985; Nowak & Vallacher, 2001).

This scenario has some surprising, even ironic, consequences. Even a very strong attractor will have a limited basin of attraction and thus will exclude a wide variety of information that is discrepant from the attractor's value. An explicitly peaceful overture by an outgroup, for example, is difficult to reconcile with the ingroup's negative attitude and thus may be discounted as an anomaly. Should enough incidents like this occur, however, they may begin to coalesce into a new attractor reflecting benign or positive attitudes toward the outgroup. At this point, if an event or intervention temporarily defuses the conflict, the newly formed latent attractor could suddenly become manifest and redirect the ingroup's thoughts, feelings, and actions vis à vis the outgroup.

The existence of latent attractors serves as a reminder that change often conforms to a nonlinear scenario. What appears to be sustained antagonism between two groups can suddenly give way to relatively benign or even positive relations if an event—even a seemingly insignificant one—pushes the group out of its current basin of attraction into the basin of a previously latent attractor. Thus, although peacekeeping missions, conflict resolution initiatives, reconciliation processes, and trust-building activities often appear to be largely ineffective in situations with groups locked in a protracted struggle, they may be acting to establish or bolster a sufficiently wide and deep attractor basin for moral, humane forms of intergroup interactions that provide the foundation for a stable, peaceful future. The gradual and long-term construction of a new attractor may be imperceptible, but it prepares the ground for a positive state that would be impossible without these actions. By the same reasoning, of course, peaceful relations between groups may show a sudden change to a negative or even violent pattern of intergroup behavior if conditions have created the foundation for a latent attractor comprised of negative thoughts, feelings, and action tendencies. It remains for future research to assess the viability of this scenario and to identify the conditions that can promote the sudden salience of a previously latent attractor.

The third scenario goes beyond moving the system between its existing attractors to systematically changing the number and types of attractors. In a nonlinear dynamical system, a wide range of variables can produce quantitative effects in the system's behavior, but usually only a small subset of them promote

noteworthy qualitative changes. Small changes in the value of these control parameters can produce bifurcations—qualitative changes in the system's attractor landscape (cf. Nowak & Lewenstein, 1994; Ruelle, 1989). Bifurcations can take many
forms, including a change from a single attractor to two attractors, a change from
a single attractor to a periodic attractor (oscillation between two or more coherent
states), and a sequence of changes from a single attractor through periodic and
multiperiodic attractors to a chaotic attractor (a complex trajectory of behavior
that never repeats and is highly sensitive to initial conditions). In each case, bifurcations occur at specific thresholds in the values of the control parameter.

   To translate this general scenario into a specific strategy for conflict resolution,
it is necessary to identify the relevant control parameters that have the potential
to change the attractor landscape constraining the behavior patterns in an antagonistic relationship. Attention can then be turned to investigating the form that
bifurcations are likely to take in response to changes in the values of these factors.
Does enhancing police security in a community, for example, simply strengthen
the community's attractor for hostile relations with the local government (as was
seen in 2005 when the French government sent SWAT teams into immigrant
neighborhoods to quell unrest), or does it qualify as a control parameter that
transforms the pattern of thinking and behavior of the community regarding the
government? If this factor functions as a control parameter, does it promote the
emergence of a new attractor (e.g., positive relations)? Does it introduce periodic
movement between very different attractors (e.g., oscillation between positive and
negative relations)? Or does it promote a trajectory of chaotic movement over
time between very different patterns (e.g., seemingly random swings in thought
and behavior that are highly sensitive to minor events)?

   The identification of control factors and their effects on the attractor landscape of a system characterized by intractable conflict is a daunting task, but the
potential payoff for success is significant. With this in mind, we have recently
incorporated this approach into a simulation platform for teaching conflict negotiation and peacebuilding (Nowak et al., 2010). Changing the attractor landscape
of a relationship mired in conflict may hold the key to promoting a wholesale
transformation of the relationship and increasing the likelihood of sustainable
peace.

QUESTION 11: WHERE DO WE GO FROM HERE?

The dynamical perspective conceptualizes intractable conflict in terms of generic
processes that underlie diverse phenomena across the social and physical sciences.
This does not mean that intractable conflicts are "nothing but" examples of
generic processes. Human experience is clearly unique in many respects, and one
should never lose sight of the idiosyncratic factors relevant to any particular conflict scenario. The dynamical account provides a scaffolding, though, on which
such factors can be layered and put into perspective.

To build on this scaffold, it is necessary to translate dynamical concepts and principles into hypotheses and develop rigorous and reliable empirical methods to test these hypotheses. Because conflict is a multifaceted phenomenon that is manifest in different ways at multiple levels of social reality, the empirical approach must be correspondingly diverse and flexible, entailing the coordination of laboratory experiments, field research, archival data analyses, and the development of formal models implemented in computer simulations. Accordingly, a cross-disciplinary approach is called for. Our own research team represents the expertise of experimental social psychology, peace psychology, cultural anthropology, nonlinear dynamical systems, and computer science. The following issues, noted in the responses to the basic questions, are currently at the forefront of our research agenda:

- First and foremost, research is essential to verify the connection between conflict intractability and attractor dynamics. Are intractable conflicts, as we propose, associated with attractors that are exceptionally strong and have a wide basin of attraction? Is one property more central to intractability than the other? Are attractor dynamics fundamentally the same for conflicts at different levels of social reality (e.g., interpersonal, intergroup, international)? Although a few studies have provided preliminary support for this proposition (see Gottman, Swanson, & Swanson, 2002; Kugler & Coleman, 2009; Losada & Markovitch, 1990), much work remains to be done.

- What factors promote the imbalance of reinforcing and inhibiting feedback loops that we propose to be responsible for the transformation of a benign conflict into a protracted, malignant conflict? To what extent is the hypothesized breakdown in regulatory dynamics associated with documented antecedents of destructive conflict such as incompatible needs and values, power struggles, perceived injustice, segregated social groups, and ideological differences? Do the factors associated with regulatory failures in everyday life— stress, intense emotion, time pressure, threat, and so forth—also undermine the operation of inhibiting feedback loops in conflict scenarios and thereby promote the evolution of an entrenched attractor for sustained conflict?

- What is the relationship between the complexity and ambiguity of conflict-relevant information and conflict intensity? If, as we propose, a primary motivation of adversaries in a conflict is maintaining the coherence of their respective cognitive, affective, and behavioral orientations, the potential for negative interactions should be enhanced when new information and events threaten one or both parties' attractors. Research directly testing this ironic connection between basic properties of information and conflict remains to be undertaken.

- Can conflicts be transformed by reverse engineering, as we have suggested? Social psychological research has shown that global mental states can be effectively disassembled into their lower level elements, creating the potential for a wholesale change in people's understanding of their own and others' actions (Vallacher & Wegner, in press). Is this approach relevant to the disassembly of strong attractors associated with intractable conflict? If so, what specific strategies would be most effective in breaking the reinforcing feedback loops among elements, in introducing inhibiting feedback loops, or in isolating the elements and thereby increasing the complexity in a coherent system of thought and behavior associated with conflict?

- What is the role of latent attractors in conflict transformation? Do they, as we propose, create the potential for sudden and catastrophic change in the nature of the relationship between adversaries in a protracted conflict? What factors promote the development of latent attractors? Does information that cannot be assimilated to an attractor create the seeds of an alternative pattern of thought and behavior? If so, would attempts to suppress or discount inconsistent information have the ironic effect of undermining a manifest attractor and promoting a transition to a fundamentally different perspective? This possibility resonates with contemporary research in social psychology (e.g., Wegner, 1994) and could be tested in experimental research.

- How and to what extent do concepts known to be relevant to conflict escalation and stalemates configure the dynamic properties of long-term conflicts? Competition over scare resources, power differences, injustice, ideology, and religion, for example, are critical to the genesis, maintenance, and transformation of interpersonal and intergroup relations, but their respective roles have yet to be reframed in explicitly dynamical terms and tested in various conflict scenarios. Identifying the essential control parameters responsible for altering the attractor landscape of intractable conflict (e.g., promoting specific types of bifurcations) is thus a high priority for research.

- Are there asymmetries in the operation of positive and negative attractors? Attractor dynamics are not limited to negative interactions but have been shown to characterize benign and positive social relationships as well (cf. Gottman et al., 2002; Kugler & Coleman, 2009; Losada & Markovitch, 1990; Nowak & Vallacher, 1998). In a close relationship, for example, the psychological and behavioral processes of each party tend to converge on positive states. Negative thoughts and antagonistic actions may be experienced, but these states tend to be short-lived, yielding over time to the positive sentiments and behaviors defining the relationship attractor. Are attractor dynamics symmetric with respect to benign (or positive) and antagonistic relationships? Is the basin of attraction, for example, wider for a relationship characterized by hostility than for one characterized by affection? Assuming one can calibrate the respective intensity of feeling in negative and positive relationships, is there greater attractor strength (resistance to change) in one or the other type of relationship?

Conclusion and Future Iterations

The perspective we have advanced suggests that the most visible causes of intractable conflict—scarce resource competition, ideological differences, and the like—

are not necessarily the critical factors for understanding the genesis, maintenance, and resolution of such conflicts. The proximate causes are not to be trivialized, of course, but they need to be appreciated in the context of basic dynamics that are often opaque—both to observers and to the parties to the conflict. Thus, a conflict progresses toward intractability as specific mental states (thoughts, beliefs, memories) and action tendencies coalesce into a strong attractor that provides coherence and an unequivocal platform for action. Resolving an intractable conflict, then, is tantamount to changing the systems' attractors. To date, we have identified three strategies for doing so: disassembling an attractor for conflict and promoting the emergence of a new (benign) attractor; strengthening a latent attractor for positive relations; and changing the attractor landscape in a system.

Yet other insights into the nature of intractable conflict are destined to emerge as concerted efforts are undertaken to investigate intractable conflict from the perspective of complexity and dynamical systems (see, e.g., Hanson & Sword, 2008). The dynamical perspective has proven to be both integrative and heuristic in many areas of science, establishing invariant principles that link seemingly distinct topics and generating new research agendas in these fields. We anticipate that this approach will serve these functions for the science of conflict as well. But, more important, we hope that the identification of fundamental conflict dynamics will provide new strategies designed to transform conflicts that serve no one's purposes yet seem impervious to resolution. Intractability might turn out to be as much an illusion as the conviction of warring parties that each has a monopoly on truth and value.

References

Azar, E. E. (1990). *The management of protracted social conflict: Theory and cases.* Aldershot, Hampshire, England: Dartmouth.

Bar-Tal, D. (2000). From intractable conflict through conflict resolution to reconciliation: Psychological analysis. *Political Psychology*, 21, 351–365. doi:10.1111/0162-895X.00192

Bartoli, A., Bui-Wrzosinska, L., & Nowak, A. (in press). Peace is in movement: A dynamical-systems perspective on the emergence of peace in Mozambique. Peace and Conflict: *Journal of Peace Psychology*.

Bartoli, A., & Coleman, P. T. (2003). *Knowledge base essay: Dealing with extremists.* Retrieved from University of Colorado, Boulder, Conflict Resolution Consortium website: http://www.beyondintractability.org/m/dealing_extremists/

Baumeister, R. F., Smart, L., & Boden, J. M. (1996). Relation of threatened egotism to violence and aggression: The dark side of high self-esteem. *Psychological Review*, 103, 5–33. doi:10.1037/0033-295X.103.1.5

Bennett, D. S. (1996). Security, bargaining, and the end of interstate rivalry. *International Studies Quarterly*, 40, 157–184.

Bercovitch, J. (2005). Mediation in the most resistant cases. In C. A. Crocker, F. O. Hampson, & P. Aall (Eds.), *Grasping the nettle: Analyzing cases of intractable conflict.* Washington, DC: United States Institute of Peace.

Burton, J. (1987). *Resolving deep-rooted conflict: A handbook.* Lanham, MD: University Press of America.

Cairns, E., & Darby, J. (1998). The conflict in Northern Ireland: Causes, consequences, and controls. *American Psychologist, 53,* 754–760. doi: 10.1037/0003-066X.53.7.754

Cannon, W. B. (1932). *The wisdom of the body.* New York, NY: Norton.

Carver, C. S., & Scheier, M. F. (1999). Themes and issues in the self-regulation of behavior. In R. S. Wyer Jr. (Ed.), *Advances in social cognition* (Vol. 12, pp. 1–105). Mahwah, NJ: Erlbaum.

Coleman, P. T. (2000). Intractable conflict. In M. Deutsch & P. T. Coleman (Eds.), *The handbook of conflict resolution: Theory and practice* (pp. 428–450). San Francisco, CA: Jossey Bass.

Coleman, P. T. (2003). Characteristics of protracted, intractable conflict: Toward the development of a metaframework—I. Peace and Conflict: *Journal of Peace Psychology, 9,* 1–37. doi:10.1207/ S15327949PAC0901_01

Coleman, P. T. (2004). Paradigmatic framing of protracted, intractable conflict: Toward the development of a meta-framework—II. Peace and Conflict: *Journal of Peace Psychology, 10,* 197–235. doi:10.1207/ s15327949pac1003_1

Coleman, P. T. (2006). Conflict, complexity, and change: A meta-frame-work for addressing protracted, intractable conflicts—III. Peace and Conflict: *Journal of Peace Psychology, 12,* 325–348. doi:10.1207/ s15327949pac1204_3

Coleman, P. T., Bui-Wrzosinska, L., Vallacher, R. R., & Nowak, A. (2006). Protracted conflicts as dynamical systems. In A. K. Schneider & C. Honeyman (Eds.), *The negotiator's fieldbook: The desk reference for the experienced negotiator* (pp. 61–74). Chicago, IL: American Bar Association Books.

Coleman, P. T., Vallacher, R. R., Nowak, A., & Bui-Wrzosinska, L. (2007). Intractable conflict as an attractor: Presenting a model of conflict, escalation, and intractability. *American Behavioral Scientist, 50,* 1454–1475. doi:10.1177/0002764207302463

Coleman, P. T., Vallacher, R., Nowak, A., Bui-Wrzosinska, L., & Bartoli, A. (in press). Navigating the landscape of conflict: Applications of dynamical systems theory to protracted social conflict. In N. Ropers (Ed.), *Systemic thinking and conflict transformation.* Berlin, Germany: Berghof Foundation for Peace Support.

Crocker, C. A., Hampson, F. O., & Aall, P. (2005). *Grasping the nettle: Analyzing cases of intractable conflict.* Washington, DC: United States Institute of Peace.

Deutsch, M. (1985). *Distributive justice: A social-psychological perspective.* New Haven, CT: Yale University Press.

Deutsch, M. (2006). A framework for thinking about oppression and its change. *Social Justice Research, 19,* 7–41. doi:10.1007/s11211-066-9998-3

Deutsch, M., Coleman, P. T., & Marcus, E. C. (Eds.). (2006). *Handbook of conflict resolution: Theory and practice* (2nd ed.). San Francisco, CA: Jossey-Bass.

Deutsch, M., & Gerard, H. B. (1955). A study of normative and informational social influence upon individual judgment. *Journal of Abnormal and Social Psychology, 51,* 629–636. doi:10.1037/h0046408

Festinger, L. (1954). A theory of social comparison processes. *Human Relations, 7,* 117–140. doi:10.1177/001872675400700202

Fisher, R. J. (2006). Intergroup conflict. In M. Deutsch, P. T. Coleman, & E. C. Marcus (Eds.), *The handbook of conflict resolution: Theory and practice* (2nd ed., pp. 176–196). San Francisco, CA: Jossey-Bass.

Gersick, C. J. G. (1991). Revolutionary change theories: A multilevel exploration of the punctuated equilibrium paradigm. *Academy of Management Review, 16,* 10–36. doi:10.2307/258605

Goertz, G., & Diehl, P. F. (1993). Enduring rivalries: Theoretical constructs and empirical patterns. *International Studies Quarterly, 37,* 147–171.

Gottman, J., Swanson, C., & Swanson, K. (2002). A general systems theory of marriage: Nonlinear difference equation modeling of marital interaction. *Personality and Social Psychology Review, 6,* 326–340. doi:10.1207/S15327957PSPR0604_07

Guastello, S., Koopmans, M., & Pincus, D. (Eds.). (2009). *Chaos and complexity in psychology: The theory of nonlinear dynamical systems.* New York, NY: Cambridge University Press.

Gurr, T. R. (1970). *Why men rebel.* Princeton, NJ: Princeton University Press.

Haken, H. (1978). *Synergetics.* Berlin, Germany: Springer.

Hanson, B., & Sword, L. D. (Eds.). (2008). Special issue: Chaos, complexity and conflict. *Emergence: Complexity & Organization, 10*(4).

Hardin, G. (1968, December 13). The tragedy of the commons. *Science, 162,* 1243–1248. doi:10.1126/science.162.3859.1243

Holland, J. H. (1995). *Emergence: From chaos to order.* Reading, MA: Addison-Wesley.

Hopfield, J. J. (1982). Neural networks and physical systems with emergent collective computational abilities. Proceedings of the National Academy of Sciences, USA, 79, 2554–2558. doi:10.1073/ pnas.79.8.2554

Hsee, C. K., Abelson, R. P., & Salovey, P. (1991). The relative weighting of position and velocity in satisfaction. *Psychological Science, 2,* 263–266. doi:10.1111/j.1467-9280.1991.tb00146.x

Jost, J. T., Banaji, M. R., & Nosek, B. A. (2004). A decade of system justification theory: Accumulated evidence of conscious and unconscious bolstering of the status quo. *Political Psychology, 25,* 881–919. doi:10.1111/j.1467-9221.2004.00402.x

Jost, J. T., Pelham, B. W., Brett, W., & Carvallo, M. R. (2002). Non-conscious forms of system justification: Implicit and behavioral preferences for higher status groups. *Journal of Experimental Social Psychology, 38,* 586–602. doi:10.1016/S0022-1031(02)00505-X

Kelman, H. (1999). The interdependence of Israeli and Palestinian national identities: The role of the other in existential conflicts. *Journal of Social Issues, 55,* 581–600.

Kelso, J. A. S. (1995). *Dynamic patterns: The self-organization of brain and behavior.* Cambridge, MA: MIT Press.

Kenrick, D. T., Li, N. P., & Butner, J. (2003). Dynamical evolutionary psychology: Individual decision rules and emergent social norms. *Psychological Review, 110,* 3–28. DOI:10.1037/0033–295x.110.1.3

Kressel, K. (2006). Mediation revisited. In M. Deutsch, P. T. Coleman, & E. Marcus (Eds.), *The handbook of conflict resolution: Theory and practice* (pp. 726–756). San Francisco, CA: Jossey-Bass.

Kriesberg, L. (1998). Intractable conflict. In E. Weiner (Ed.), T*he handbook of interethnic coexistence* (pp. 332–342). New York, NY: Continuum.

Kriesberg, L. (2005). Nature, dynamics, and phases of intractability. In C. A. Crocker, F. O. Hampson, & P. Aall (Eds.), *Grasping the nettle: Analyzing cases of intractable conflict* (pp. 65–98). Washington, DC: United States Institute of Peace.

Kriesberg, L., Northrup, T. A., & Thorson, S. J. (1989). *Intractable conflicts and their transformation.* Syracuse, NY: Syracuse University Press.

Kugler, K., & Coleman, P. T. (2009, June). Moral conflict and complexity: The dynamics of constructive versus destructive discussions over polarizing issues. Paper presented at the 22nd Annual Conference of the International Association of Conflict Management. Kyoto, Japan.

Lederach, J. P. (1997). Building peace: Sustainable reconciliation in divided societies. Washington, DC: United States Institute of Peace. Lerner, M. J. (1980). *The belief in a just world: A fundamental delusion.* New York, NY: Plenum Press.

Liebovitch, L. S. (1998). *Chaos and fractals simplified for the life sciences.* New York, NY: Oxford University Press.

Losada, M., & Markovitch, S. (1990). Group analyzer: A system for dynamic analysis of group interaction. In Proceedings of the 23rd Annual Hawaii International Conference on System Sciences (pp. 101–110). Washington, DC: IEEE Computer Science Society.

Marshall, M. G., & Gurr, T. R. (2005). *Peace and conflict.* College Park, MD: Center for International Development and Conflict Management.

Merton, R. K. (1957). *Social theory and social structure.* Glencoe, IL: Free Press.

Miller, N. E. (1944). Experimental studies of conflict. In J. M. Hunt (Ed.), *Personality and the behavior disorders* (pp. 431–465). New York, NY: Ronald Press.

Moscovici, S. (1985). Social influence and conformity. In G. Lindzey & E. Aronson (Eds.), *The handbook of social psychology* (Vol. 2, pp. 347–412). New York, NY: Random House.

Nowak, A. (2004). Dynamical minimalism: Why less is more in psychology. *Personality and Social Psychology Review*, 8, 183–192. doi: 10.1207/s15327957pspr0802_12

Nowak, A., Bui-Wrzosinska, L., Coleman, P. T., Vallacher, R. R., Bartkowski, W., & Jochemczyk, L. (2010). Seeking sustainable solutions: Using an attractor simulation platform for teaching multi-stakeholder negotiation in complex cases. *Negotiation Journal*, 26, 49–68. doi: 10.1111/j.1571-9979.2009.00253.x

Nowak, A., & Lewenstein, M. (1994). Dynamical systems: A tool for social psychology? In R. R. Vallacher & A. Nowak (Eds.), *Dynamical systems in social psychology* (pp. 17–53). San Diego, CA: Academic Press.

Nowak, A., Szamrej, J., & Latané, B. (1990). From private attitude to public opinion: A dynamic theory of social impact. *Psychological Review*, 97, 362–376. doi:10.1037/0033-295X.97.3.362

Nowak, A., & Vallacher, R. R. (1998). *Dynamical social psychology.* New York, NY: Guilford Press.

Nowak, A., & Vallacher, R. R. (2001). Societal transition: Toward a dynamical model of social change. In W. Wosinska, R. B. Cialdini, D. W. Barrett, & J. Reykowski (Eds.), *The practice of social influence in multiple cultures* (pp. 151–171). Mahwah, NJ: Erlbaum.

Nowak, A., & Vallacher, R. R., Bui-Wrzosinska, L., & Coleman, P. T. (2007). Attracted to conflict: A dynamical perspective on malignant social relations. In A. Golec de Zavala & K. Skarzynska (Eds.), *Understanding social change: Political psychology in Poland* (pp. 33–49). Hauppauge, NY: Nova Science.

Pearce, W. B., & Littlejohn, S. W. (1997). *Moral conflict: When social worlds collide.* Thousand Oaks, CA: Sage.

Pruitt, D. & Olczak, P. (1995). Beyond hope: Approaches to resolving seemingly intractable conflict. In B. B. Bunker & J. Z. Rubin & Associates (Eds.), *Conflict, cooperation & justice: Essays inspired by the work of Morton Deutsch* (pp. 59–92). San Francisco, CA: Jossey-Bass.

Rouhana, N., & Bar-Tal, D. (1998). Psychological dynamics of intractable conflicts: The Israeli-Palestinian case. *American Psychologist*, 53, 761–770. doi:10.1037/0003-066X.53.7.761

Ruelle, D. (1989). *Elements of differentiable dynamics and bifurcation theory.* New York, NY: Academic Press.

Rusbult, C. E. (1983). A longitudinal test of the investment model: The development (and deterioration) of satisfaction and commitment in heterosexual involvements. *Journal of Personality and Social Psychology*, 45, 101–117. doi:10.1037/0022-3514.45.1.101

Schuster, H. G. (1984). *Deterministic chaos*. Vienna, Austria: Physik Verlag.

Sherif, M. (1936). *The psychology of social norms*. New York, NY: Harper.

Sidanius, J., & Pratto, F. (1999). *Social dominance: An intergroup theory of social hierarchy and oppression*. New York, NY: Cambridge University Press.

Strogatz, S. (2003). *Sync: The emerging science of spontaneous order*. New York, NY: Hyperion Books.

Swann, W. B. Jr., Hixon, J. G., Stein-Seroussi, A., & Gilbert, D. (1990). The fleeting gleam of praise: Cognitive processes underlying behavioral reactions to self-relevant feedback. *Journal of Personality and Social Psychology*, 59, 17–26. doi:10.1037/0022-3514.59.1.17

Tesser, A. (1978). Self-generated attitude change. In L. Berkowitz (Ed.), *Advances in experimental social psychology* (Vol. 11, pp. 85–117). New York, NY: Academic Press.

Tesser, A., Martin, L. L., & Cornell, D. P. (1996). On the substitutability of self-protective mechanisms. In P. M. Gollwitzer & J. A. Bargh (Eds.), *The psychology of action* (pp. 48–68). New York, NY: Guilford Press.

Thibaut, J. W., & Kelley, H. H. (1959). *The social psychology of groups*. New York, NY: Wiley.

Tononi, G., & Edelman, G. M. (1998, December 4). Consciousness and complexity. *Science*, 282, 1846–1851. doi:10.1126/science.282. 5395.1846

Tyler, T. R., & Smith, H. J. (1998). Social justice and social movements. In D. T. Gilbert, S. T. Fiske, & G. Lindzey (Eds.), *The handbook of social psychology* (Vol. 1, pp. 595–632). New York, NY: McGraw-Hill.

Vallacher, R. R., & Nowak, A. (1999). The dynamics of self-regulation. In R. S. Wyer (Ed.), *Advances in social cognition* (Vol. 12, pp. 241–259). Mahwah, NJ: Erlbaum.

Vallacher, R. R., & Nowak, A. (2007). Dynamical social psychology: Finding order in the flow of human experience. In A. W. Kruglanski & E. T. Higgins (Eds.), *Social psychology: Handbook of basic principles* (2nd ed., pp. 734–758). New York, NY: Guilford Press.

Vallacher, R. R., Nowak, A., Coleman, P. T., Bui-Wrzosinska, L., Bartoli, A., & Liebovitch, L. (2008). The dynamics of conflict: Frequently asked questions. Retrieved from International Center for Complexity and Conflict website: http://www.dynamicsofconflict.iccc.edu.pl/index.php?page = faq

Vallacher, R. R., Nowak, A., Froehlich, M., & Rockloff, M. (2002). The dynamics of self-evaluation. *Personality and Social Psychology Review*, 6, 370–379. doi:10.1207/S15327957PSPR0604_11

Vallacher, R. R., Nowak, A., & Kaufman, J. (1994). Intrinsic dynamics of social judgment. *Journal of Personality and Social Psychology*, 67, 20–34. doi:10.1037/0022-3514.67.1.20

Vallacher, R. R., Nowak, A., Markus, J., & Strauss, J. (1998). Dynamics in the coordination of mind and action. In M. Kofta, G. Weary, & G. Sedlek (Eds.), *Personal control in action: Cognitive and motivational mechanisms* (pp. 27–59). New York, NY: Plenum Press.

Vallacher, R. R., Nowak, A., & Miller, M. E. (2003). Social influence and group dynamics. In I. Weiner (Series Ed.) & T. Millon & M. J. Lerner (Vol. Eds.), *Handbook of psychology*: Vol. 5. Personality and social psychology (pp. 383–417). New York, NY: Wiley.

Vallacher, R. R., & Wegner, D. M. (in press). Action identification theory. In P. Van Lange, A. W. Kruglanski, & E. T. Higgins (Eds.), *Handbook of theories in social psychology*. London, England: Sage.

Wegner, D. M. (1994). Ironic processes of mental control. Psychological Review, 101, 34–52. doi:10.1037/0033-295X.101.1.34

Zartman, I. W., & Rubin, J. Z. (2002). *Power and negotiation*. Ann Arbor, MI: University of Michigan Press.

Notes

1. As background for the set of questions and answers, we encourage readers to visit a website devoted to the dynamics of intractable conflict, http://www.dynamicsofconflict.iccc.edu.pl/, where we present 20 frequently asked questions concerning the relevance and application of dynamical systems theory to social psychological phenomena in general (Vallacher et al., 2008). This question-answer set introduces the basic concepts, principles, and methods we consider to be especially useful in reframing personal, interpersonal, and collective processes. Nonetheless, the present question-answer set on the dynamics of intractable conflict has been written so that it can be understood in its own right by scholars and practitioners in social science, conflict resolution, and peace studies.

2. Three types of attractors have been identified in dynamical systems: fixed point, periodic (including multiperiodic and quasiperiodic), and deterministic chaos. We have found fixed-point attractors to be the most relevant to issues of intractable conflict, and they provide the focus of this article. Periodic and chaotic evolution are expressed in various social processes (Guastello et al., 2009; Vallacher & Nowak, 2007), though, and may prove useful in the investigation of social conflicts as well (see, e.g., Hanson & Sword, 2008).

3. More precisely, a fixed-point attractor corresponds to a stable equilibrium. An unstable equilibrium, referred to as a *repellor,* represents a state that the system tries to avoid.

Contact Theory

Jim A. C. Everett

After finishing his PhD at Oxford University in experimental psychology, Jim A. C. Everett continued on as a post-doctoral research fellow at the Oxford Uehiro Centre for Practical Ethics. Passionate about justice, politics, and dogs, he describes himself as a social psychologist and philosopher, working primarily on human morality and parochial altruism—he wants to know when, why, and how people help their own group members more than members of other groups. He considers these questions primarily in the context of environmental sustainability and poverty relief. His work has great implications for the field of conflict.

This piece considers Gordon Allport's (1954) contact hypothesis that feelings about different groups improve when contact with that group occurs in an environment of equal status, where ingroup cooperation occurs, the group shares common goals, and the group has support from institutional and/or social authorities. Everett's article considers the feasibility of this kind of contact and the possibilities of using this theory to reduce prejudice.

Questions to consider: Do you think that bringing conflicting parties together always promotes peace? Does living alongside someone from a different culture inherently lead to reduced prejudice? What has been your experience?

Intergroup Contact Theory

Jim A. C. Everett

In the midst of racial segregation in the U.S.A and the Jim Crow Laws, Gordon Allport (1954) proposed one of the most important social psychological events of the 20th century, suggesting that contact between members of different groups (under certain conditions) can work to reduce prejudice and intergroup conflict.

Indeed, the idea that contact between members of different groups can help to reduce prejudice and improve social relations is one that is enshrined in policy-making all over the globe. UNESCO, for example, asserts that contact between members of different groups is key to improving social relations. Furthermore, explicit policy-driven moves for greater contact have played an important role in improving social relations between races in the U.S.A, in improving relationships between Protestants and Catholics in Northern Ireland, and encouraging a more inclusive society in post-apartheid South Africa. In the present world, it is this recognition of the benefits of contact that drives modern school exchanges and cross-group buddy schemes. In the years since Allport's initial intergroup contact hypothesis, much research has been devoted to expanding and exploring his contact hypothesis. In this article I will review some of the vast literature on the role of contact in reducing prejudice, looking at its success, mediating factors, recent theoretical extensions of the hypothesis and directions for future research. Contact is of utmost importance in reducing prejudice and promoting a more tolerant and integrated society and as such is a prime example of the real life applications that psychology can offer the world.

The Contact Hypothesis

The intergroup contact hypothesis was first proposed by Allport (1954), who suggested that positive effects of intergroup contact occur in contact situations characterized by four key conditions: equal status, intergroup cooperation, common goals, and support by social and institutional authorities (See Table 1). According to Allport, it is essential that the contact situation exhibits these factors to some degree. Indeed, these factors do appear to be important in reducing prejudice, as exemplified by the unique importance of cross-group friendships in reducing prejudice (Pettigrew, 1998). Most friends have equal status, work together to achieve shared goals, and friendship is usually absent from strict societal and institutional limitation that can particularly limit romantic relationships (e.g. laws against intermarriage) and working relationships (e.g., segregation laws, or differential statuses).

Since Allport first formulated his contact hypothesis, much work has confirmed the importance of contact in reducing prejudice. Crucially, positive contact experiences have been shown to reduce self-reported prejudice (the most common way of assessing intergroup attitudes) toward Black neighbors, the elderly, gay men, and the disabled—to name just a few (Works, 1961; Caspi, 1984; Vonofako, Hewstone, & Voci, 2007; Yuker & Hurley, 1987). Most interestingly, though, in a wide-scale meta-analysis (i.e., a statistical analysis of a number of published studies), it has been found that while contact under Allport's conditions is especially effective at reducing prejudice, even unstructured contact reduces prejudice (Pettigrew & Tropp, 2006). What this means is that Allport's proposed conditions should best be seen as of a facilitating, rather than an essential, nature. This is important as it serves to show the importance of the contact hypothesis: even in

Condition	Meaning	Example	Evidence
Equal Status	Members of the contact situation should not have an unequal, hierarchical relationship.	Members should not have an employer/ employee or instructor/student relationship.	Evidence has documented that equal status is important both *prior* to (Brewer & Kramer, 1985) and *during* (Cohen & Lotan, 1995) the contact situation.
Cooperation	Members should work together in a non-competitive environment.	Students working together in a group project.	Aronson's 'jigsaw technique' structures classrooms so that students strive cooperatively (Aronson & Patnoe, 1967), and this technique has led to positive results in a variety of countries.
Common Goals	Members must rely on each other to achieve their shared desired goal.	Members of a sports team.	hu and Griffey (1985) have shown the importance of common goals in interracial athletic teams who need to work together to achieve their goal.
Support by Social and Institutional Authorities	There should not be social or institutional authorities that explicitly or implicitly sanction contact, and there should be authorities that support positive contact.	There should not be official laws enforcing segregation.	Landis' (1984) work on the importance of institutional support in reducing prejudice in the military.

situations which are not marked by Allport's optimal conditions, levels of contact and prejudice have a negative correlation with an effect size comparable to those of the inverse relationship between condom use and sexually transmitted HIV and the relationship between passive smoking and the incidence of lung cancer at work (Al-Ramiah & Hewstone, 2011). Contact between groups, even in sub-optimal conditions, is strongly associated with reduced prejudice.

Importantly, contact does not just influence explicit self-report measures of prejudice, but also reduces prejudice as measured in a number of different ways. Explicit measures (e.g., How much do you like gay men?) are limited in that there can be a self-report bias: people often answer in a way that shows them in a good light. As such, research has examined the effects of contact on implicit measures: measures that involve investigating core psychological constructs in ways that bypass people's willingness and ability to report their feelings and beliefs. Implicit measures have been shown to be a good complement to traditional explicit measures—particularly when there may be a strong chance of a self-report bias. In computer reaction time tasks, contact has been shown to reduce implicit associations between the participant's own in-group and the concept "good," and between an outgroup (a group the participant is not a member of) and the concept "bad" (Aberson and Haag, 2007). Furthermore, positive contact is associated with reduced physiological threat responses to outgroup members (Blascovich et al., 2001), and reduced differences in the way that faces are processed in the brain, implying that contact helps to increase perceptions of similarity (Walker et al., 2008). Contact, then, has a real and tangible effect on reducing prejudice—both at the explicit and implicit level. Indeed, the role of contact in reducing prejudice is now so well documented that it justifies being referred to as intergroup contact theory (Hewstone & Swart, 2011).

How Does It Work?

Multiple mechanisms have been proposed to explain just how contact reduces prejudice. In particular, "four processes of change" have been proposed: learning about the outgroup, changing behavior, generating affective ties, and ingroup reappraisal (Pettigrew, 1998). Contact can, and does, work through both cognitive (i.e. learning about the outgroup, or reappraising how one thinks about one's own in-group), behavioural (changing one's behavior to open oneself to potential positive contact experiences), and affective (generating affective ties and friendships, and reducing negative emotions) means. A particularly important mediating mechanism (i.e., the mechanisms or processes by which contact achieves its effect) is that of emotions, or affect, with evidence suggesting that contact works to reduce prejudice by diminishing negative affect (anxiety / threat) and inducing positive affect such as empathy (Tausch and Hewstone, 2010). In another meta-analysis, Pettigrew and Tropp (2008) supported this by looking specifically at mediating mechanisms in contact and found that contact situations which promote positive affect and reduce negative affect are most likely to succeed in conflict reduction. Contact situations are likely to be effective at improving intergroup relations insofar as they induce positive affect, and ineffective insofar as they induce negative affect such as anxiety or threat. If we feel comfortable and not anxious, the contact situation will be much more successful.

Generalizing the Effect

An important issue that I have not yet addressed, however, is how these positive experiences after contact can be extended and generalized to other members of the outgroup. While contact may reduce an individual's prejudice toward (for example) their Muslim colleague, its practical use is strongly limited if it doesn't also diminish prejudice toward other Muslims. Contact with each and every member of an outgroup—let alone of all outgroups to which prejudice is directed—is clearly unfeasible and so a crucial question in intergroup contact research is how the positive effect can be generalized.

A number of approaches have been developed to explain how the positive effect of contact, including making group saliency low so that people focus on individual characteristics and not group-level attributes (Brewer & Miller, 1984), making group saliency high so that the effect is best generalized to others (Johnston & Hewstone, 1992), and making an overarching common ingroup identity salient (Gaertner, Dovidio, Anastasio, Bachman, & Rust, 1993). Each of these approaches have both advantages and disadvantages, and in particular each individual approach may be most effective at different stages of an extended contact situation. To deal with this issue Pettigrew (1998) proposed a three stage model to take place over time to optimize successful contact and generalization. First is the decategorization stage (as in Brewer & Miller, 1984), where participants' personal (and not group) identities should be emphasized to reduce anxiety and promote interpersonal liking. Secondly, the individuals' social categories should be made salient to achieve generalization of positive affect to the outgroup as a whole (as in Johnston & Hewstone, 1992). Finally, there is the recategorization stage, where participants' group identities are replaced with a more superordinate group: changing group identities from "Us versus Them" to a more inclusive "We" (as in Gaertner et al., 1993). This stage model could provide an effective method of generalizing the positive effects of intergroup contact.

Theoretical Extensions

Even with such work on generalization, however, it may still be unrealistic to expect that group members will have sufficient opportunities to engage in positive contact with outgroup members: sometimes positive contact between group members is incredibly difficult, if not impossible. For example, at the height of the Northern Ireland conflict, positive contact between Protestants and Catholics was nigh on impossible. As such, recent work on the role of intergroup contact in reducing prejudice has moved away from the idea that contact must necessarily include direct (face-to-face) contact between group members and instead includes the notion that indirect contact (e.g., imagined contact, or knowledge of contact among others) may also have a beneficial effect.

A first example of this approach comes from Wright, Aron, McLaughlin-Volpe, and Ropp's (1997) extended contact hypothesis. Wright et al. propose that mere knowledge that an ingroup member has a close relationship with an outgroup member can improve outgroup attitudes, and indeed this has been supported by a series of experimental and correlational studies. For example, Shiappa, Gregg, & Hewes (2005) have offered evidence suggesting that just watching TV shows that portrayed intergroup contact was associated with lower levels of prejudice. A second example of an indirect approach to contact comes from Crisp and Turner's (2009) imagined contact hypothesis, which suggests that actual experiences may not be necessary to improve intergroup attitudes, and that simply imagining contact with outgroup members could improve outgroup attitudes. Indeed, this has been supported in a number of studies at both an explicit and implicit level: British Muslims (Husnu & Crisp, 2010), the elderly (Abrams, Crisp, & Marques 2008), and gay men (Turner, Crisp, & Lambert, 2007).

These more recent extensions of the contact hypothesis have offered important suggestions on how to most effectively generalize the benefits of the contact situation and make use of findings from work on mediating mechanisms. It seems that direct face-to-face contact is always not necessary, and that positive outcomes can be achieved by positive presentation of intergroup-friendships in the media and even simply by imagining interacting with an outgroup member.

Issues and Directions for Future Research

Contact, then, has important positive effects on improved intergroup relations. It does have its critics, however. Notably, Dixon, Durrheim, and Tredoux (2005) argue that while contact has been important in showing how we can promote a more tolerant society, the existing literature has an unfortunate absence of work on how intergroup contact can affect societal change: changes in outgroup attitudes from contact do not necessarily accompany changes in the ideological beliefs that sustain group inequality. For example, Jackson and Crane (1986) demonstrated that positive contact with Black individuals improved Whites' affective reactions toward Blacks but did not change their attitudes towards policy in combating inequality in housing, jobs and education. Furthermore, contact may also have the unintended effect of weakening minority members' motivations to engage in collective action aimed at reducing the intergroup inequalities. For example, Dixon, Durrheim, and Tredoux (2007) found that the more contact Black South Africans had with White South Africans, the less they supported policies aimed at reducing racial inequalities. Positive contact may have the unintended effect of misleading members of disadvantaged groups into believing inequality will be addressed, thus leaving the status differentials intact. As such, a fruitful direction for future research would be to investigate under what conditions contact could lead to more positive intergroup relations without diminishing legitimate protest aimed at reducing inequality. One promising suggestion is to emphasize commonalities between groups while also addressing unjust group inequalities during the contact situation. Such a contact situation could result in prejudice reduction without losing sight of group inequality (Saguy, Tausch, Dovidio, & Pratto, 2009).

A second concern with contact research is that while contact has shown to be effective for more prejudiced individuals, there can be problems with getting a more prejudiced individual into the contact situation in the first place. Crisp and Turner's imagined contact hypothesis seems to be a good first step in tackling this problem (Crisp & Turner, 2013), though it remains to be seen if, and how, such imagined contact among prejudiced individuals can translate to direct contact. Greater work on individual differences in the efficacy of contact would provide an interesting contribution to existing work.

Conclusions

Contact, then, has been shown to be of utmost importance in reduction of prejudice and promotion of more positive intergroup attitudes. Such research has important implications for policy work. Work on contact highlights the importance of institutional support and advocation of more positive intergroup relations, the importance of equal status between groups, the importance of cooperation between groups and the importance of positive media presentations of intergroup friendships—to name just a few. As Hewstone and Swart (2011) argue, "Theory-driven social psychology does matter, not just in the laboratory, but also in the school, the neighborhood, and the society at large" (Hewstone & Swart, 2011, p. 380).

Nonviolence

Gene Sharp

Gene Sharp, founder of the Albert Einstein Institution, which is dedicated to the study of nonviolent action, taught political science for decades at the University of Massachusetts Dartmouth. His work influenced many anti-government movements around the world. Sharp found himself nominated for the Nobel Peace Prize several times, receiving instead the El-Hibri Peace Education Prize, the Right Livelihood Award, and the Distinguished Lifetime Democracy Award. He began as a masters' student in sociology at Ohio State University, where he also received his BA. Immediately after receiving his masters, Sharp found himself in prison for nine months for protesting the draft called to support the Korean War.

Sharp's article that was chosen for this anthology provides an introduction to nonviolence as an approach of increasing interest in Epoch Two. Even though Mohandas K. Gandhi and Martin Luther King Jr., the most noted leaders of nonviolent movements operated in Epoch One and before, the field saw a renewed interest in these movements as inter-ethnic warfare increased. Nonviolent approaches to conflict, Sharp says, become useful when traditional negotiations fail. Freedom, dignity, justice, and religion cannot be removed for the sake of reaching an agreement. When this happens, there is a stalemate that can lead to nonviolent or violent responses.

Sharp presents the variety of nonviolent approaches by debunking myths about these movements. He challenges that these movements do not only involve disputes with government (they can be between students and universities, workers and employers, etc.). He explains that these are not new approaches only available in industrialized, democratic societies. In fact, nonviolent movements are as diverse geographically (Poland, El Salvador, the United States, the Philippines, China) as they are topically (rights, freedom, independence, etc.).

Sharp also debunks the myth that only those committed to a life of nonviolence can participate in movements supporting these approaches. Many groups choose nonviolent means (boycotts, strikes, leaflets, muting, rallies, marches, etc.) because they may be more powerful tactically than overt violence. These approaches may, in the end, be far more expedient than outright aggression.

Questions to consider: What nonviolent movements have you witnessed or participated in? What has been your impression of these movements and their effectiveness? Have you seen nonviolent movements become violent? If so, when?

Facing Acute Conflict

Gene Sharp

All Conflicts Are Not Equal

We live in a world of many conflicts, and we have a responsibility to face many of them.

Not all conflicts are equal. Some are much more important than others, and in some conflicts the issues at stake are more difficult to resolve in acceptable ways than are those in other conflicts.

Where the issues are of only limited importance, the difficulties in reaching a resolution are often small. Potentially, we can split the difference, agree on a third option, or postpone dealing with some issues until a later time. Even in these lesser conflicts, however, the group with a grievance requires effective means of pressing its claims. Otherwise, there is little reason for one's opponents to consider those claims seriously.

There are, however, many other conflicts in which fundamental issues are, or are believed to be, at stake. These conflicts are not deemed suitable for resolution by any methods that involve compromise. These are "acute conflicts."

Waging Acute Conflicts

In acute conflicts, at least one side regards it as necessary and good to wage the conflict against hostile opponents because of the issues seen to be at stake. It is often believed that the conflict must be waged in order to advance or protect freedom, justice, religion, one's civilization, or one's people. Proposed settlements that involve basic compromises of these fundamental issues are rarely acceptable. Likewise, submission to the opponents, or defeat by them, is regarded as disastrous. Yet, compromise or submission is often believed to be required for peaceful solutions to acute conflicts. Since these are not acceptable options for the parties involved, people therefore believe that it is necessary to wage the conflict by applying the strongest means available to them. These means often involve some type of violence.

There Are Alternatives

Violence, however, is not the only possibility. War and other forms of violence have not been universal in the waging of acute conflicts. In a great variety of situations, across centuries and cultural barriers, another technique of struggle has at times been applied. This other technique has been based on the ability to be stubborn, to refuse to cooperate, to disobey, and to resist powerful opponents powerfully.

Throughout human history, and in a multitude of conflicts, one side has instead fought by psychological, social, economic, or political methods, or a combination of them. Many times this alternative technique of struggle has been applied when fundamental issues have been at stake, and when ruthless opponents have been willing and able to apply extreme repression. This repression has included beatings, arrests, imprisonments, executions, and mass slaughters. Despite such repression, when the resisters have persisted in fighting with only their chosen "nonviolent weapons," they have sometimes triumphed.

This alternative technique is called nonviolent action or nonviolent struggle. This is "the other ultimate sanction." In some acute conflicts it has served as an alternative to violent struggle.

In the minds of many people, nonviolent struggle is closely connected with the persons of Mohandas K. Gandhi and Dr. Martin Luther King Jr. The work and actions of both men and the movements that they led or in which they played crucial roles are highly important. However, those movements are by no means representative of all nonviolent action. In fact, the work of these men is in significant ways atypical of the general practice of nonviolent struggle during recent decades and certainly throughout the centuries. Nonviolent struggles are not new historically. They have occurred for many centuries, although historical accounts frequently give them little recognition.

Widespread Nonviolent Struggle

Nonviolent struggle has occurred in widely differing cultures, periods of history, and political conditions. It has occurred in the West and in the East. Nonviolent action has occurred in industrialized and nonindustrialized countries. It has been practiced under constitutional democracies and against empires, foreign occupations, and dictatorial systems. Nonviolent struggle has been waged on behalf of a myriad of causes and groups, and even for objectives that many people reject. It has also been used to prevent, as well as to promote, change. Its use has sometimes been mixed with limited violence, but many times it has been waged with minimal or no violence.

The issues at stake in these conflicts have been diverse. They have included social, economic, ethnic, religious, national, humanitarian, and political matters, and they have ranged from the trivial to the fundamental.

Although historians have generally neglected this type of struggle, it is clearly a very old phenomenon. Most of the history of this technique has doubtless been lost, and most of what has survived has been largely ignored.

Many cases of the use of nonviolent action have had little or nothing to do with governments. Modern cases include labor-management conflicts and efforts to impose or resist pressures for social conformity. Nonviolent action has also been used in ethnic and religious conflicts and many other situations, such as disputes between students and university administrations. Important conflicts between the civilian population and governments where one side has employed nonviolent action have also occurred very widely. The following examples are often of this type.

Cases of Nonviolent Struggle

From the late eighteenth century through the twentieth century, the technique of nonviolent action was widely used in colonial rebellions, international political and economic conflicts, religious conflicts, and anti-slavery resistance.[1] This technique has been aimed to secure workers' right to organize, women's rights, universal manhood suffrage, and woman suffrage. This type of struggle has been used to gain national independence, to generate economic gains, to resist genocide, to undermine dictatorships, to gain civil rights, to end segregation, and to resist foreign occupations and coups d'état.

In the twentieth century, nonviolent action rose to unprecedented political significance throughout the world. People using this technique amassed major achievements, and, of course, experienced failure at times. Higher wages and improved working conditions were won. Oppressive traditions and practices were abolished. Both men and women won the right to vote in several countries in part by using this technique. Government policies were changed, laws repealed, new legislation enacted, and governmental reforms instituted. Invaders were frustrated and armies defeated. An empire was paralyzed, coups d'état thwarted, and dictatorships disintegrated. Nonviolent struggle was used against extreme dictatorships, including both Nazi and Communist systems.

Cases of the use of this technique early in the twentieth century included major elements of the 1905 Russian Revolution. In various countries growing trade unions widely used the strike and the economic boycott. Chinese boycotts of Japanese products occurred in 1908, 1915, and 1919. Germans used nonviolent resistance against the Kapp Putsch in 1920 and against the French and Belgian occupation of the Ruhr in 1923. In the 1920s and 1930s, Indian nationalists used nonviolent action in their struggles against British rule, under the leadership of Mohandas K. Gandhi. Likewise, Muslim Pashtuns in what was the North-West Frontier Province of British India (now in Pakistan) also used nonviolent struggle against British rule under the leadership of Khan Abdul Ghaffar Khan.

From 1940 to 1945 people in various European countries, especially in Norway, Denmark, and the Netherlands, used nonviolent struggle to resist Nazi occupation and rule. Nonviolent action was used to save Jews from the Holocaust in Berlin, Bulgaria, Denmark, and elsewhere. The military dictators of El Salvador and Guatemala were ousted in brief nonviolent struggles in the spring of 1944. The American civil rights nonviolent struggles against racial segregation, especially in the 1950s and 1960s, changed laws and long-established policies in the U.S. South. In April 1961, noncooperation by French conscript soldiers in the French colony of Algeria, combined with popular demonstrations in France and defiance by the Debré-de Gaulle government, defeated the military coup d'état in Algiers before a related coup in Paris could be launched.

In 1968 and 1969, following the Warsaw Pact invasion, Czechs and Slovaks held off full Soviet control for eight months with improvised nonviolent struggle and refusal of collaboration. From 1953 to 1991, dissidents in Communist-ruled countries in Eastern Europe, especially in East Germany, Poland, Hungary, Estonia, Latvia, and Lithuania, repeatedly used nonviolent struggles for increased freedom. The Solidarity struggle in Poland began in 1980 with strikes to support the demand of a legal free trade union, and concluded in 1989 with the end of the Polish Communist regime. Nonviolent protests and mass resistance were also highly important in undermining the apartheid policies and European domination in South Africa, especially between 1950 and 1990. The Marcos dictatorship in the Philippines was destroyed by a nonviolent uprising in 1986.

In July and August 1988, Burmese democrats protested against the military dictatorship with marches and defiance and brought down three governments, but this struggle finally succumbed to a new military coup d'état and mass slaughter. In 1989, Chinese students and others in over three hundred cities (including Tiananmen Square, Beijing) conducted symbolic protests against government corruption and oppression, but the protests finally ended following massive killings by the military.

Nonviolent struggle brought about the end of Communist dictatorships in Poland and Czechoslovakia in 1989 and in East Germany, Estonia, Latvia, and Lithuania in 1991. Noncooperation and defiance against the attempted "hard line" coup d'état by the KGB, the Communist Party, and the Soviet Army in 1991, blocked the attempted seizure of the Soviet State.

In Kosovo, the Albanian population between 1990 and 1999 conducted a widespread noncooperation campaign against repressive Serbian rule. When the de facto Kosovo government lacked a nonviolent strategy for gaining de jure independence, a guerrilla Kosovo Liberation Army initiated violence. This was followed by extreme Serbian repression and massive slaughters by so-called ethnic cleansing, which led to NATO bombing and intervention.

Starting in November 1996, Serbs conducted daily parades and protests in Belgrade and other cities against the autocratic governance of President Milosevic and secured correction of electoral fraud in mid-January 1997. At that time, however, Serb democrats lacked a strategy to press the struggle further and failed to launch a campaign to bring down the Milosevic dictatorship. In early October 2000, the Otpor (Resistance) movement and other democrats rose up again against Milosevic in a carefully planned nonviolent struggle and the dictatorship collapsed.

In early 2001, President Estrada, who had been accused of corruption, was ousted by Filipinos in a "People Power Two" campaign.

There were many other important examples this past century, and the practice of nonviolent struggle continues.

The Many Methods of Nonviolent Struggle

A multitude of specific methods of nonviolent action, or nonviolent weapons, exist. Nearly two hundred have been identified to date, and without doubt, scores more already exist and others will emerge in future conflicts.

Methods of nonviolent action include protest marches, flying forbidden flags, massive rallies, vigils, leaflets, picketing, social boycotts, economic boycotts, labor strikes, rejection of legitimacy, civil disobedience, boycott of government positions, boycott of rigged elections, strikes by civil servants, noncooperation by police, nonobedience without direct supervision, mutiny, sitins, hunger strikes, sit-downs on the streets, establishment of alternative institutions, occupation of offices, and creation of parallel governments.

These methods may be used to protest symbolically, to put an end to cooperation, or to disrupt the operation of the established system. As such, three broad classes of nonviolent methods exist: nonviolent protest and persuasion, noncooperation, and nonviolent intervention.

Symbolic protests, though in most situations quite mild, can make it clear that some of the population is opposed to the present regime and can help to undermine its legitimacy. Social, economic, and political noncooperation, when practiced strongly and long enough, can weaken the opponents' control, wealth, domination, and power, and potentially produce paralysis. The methods of nonviolent intervention, which disrupt the established order by psychological, social, economic, physical, or political methods, can dramatically threaten the opponents' control.

Individuals and groups may hold differing opinions about the general political usefulness and the ethical acceptability of the methods of nonviolent struggle. Yet everyone can benefit from more knowledge and understanding of their use and careful examination of their potential relevance and effectiveness.

A Pragmatic Choice

Nonviolent struggle is identified by what people do, not by what they believe. In many cases, the people using these nonviolent methods have believed violence to be perfectly justified in moral or religious terms. However, for the specific conflict that they currently faced they chose, for pragmatic reasons, to use methods that did not include violence.

Only in rare historical instances did a group or a leader have a personal belief that rejected violence in principle. Nevertheless, even in these cases, a nonviolent struggle based on pragmatic concerns was often still viewed as morally superior.

However, belief that violence violates a moral or religious principle does not constitute nonviolent action.[2] Nor does the simple absence of physical violence mean that nonviolent action is occurring. It is the type of activity that identifies the technique of nonviolent action, not the belief behind the activity.

The degree to which nonviolent struggle has been consciously chosen in place of violence differs widely among historical examples. In many past cases, nonviolent action appears to have been initiated more or less spontaneously, with little deliberation. In other cases, the choice of a certain nonviolent method—such as a labor strike—was made on grounds specific to the particular situation only, without a comparative evaluation of the merits of nonviolent action over violent action. Many applications of nonviolent action seem to have been imitations of actions elsewhere.

There has been much variation in the degree to which people in these conflicts have been aware of the existence of a general nonviolent technique of action and have had prior knowledge of its operation.

In most of these cases, nonviolent means appear to have been chosen because of considerations of anticipated effectiveness. In some cases, there appear to have been mixed motives, with practical motives predominating but with a relative moral preference for nonviolent means.

What Words to Use?

The type of action in these cases and others has been given various names, some of which are useful and others of which are inappropriate. These names include "nonviolent resistance," "civil resistance," "passive resistance," "nonviolence," "people power," "political defiance," and "positive action." The use of the term "nonviolence" is especially unfortunate, because it confuses these forms of mass action with beliefs in ethical or religious nonviolence ("principled nonviolence"). Those beliefs, which have their merits, are different phenomena that usually are unrelated to mass struggles conducted by people who do not share such beliefs. To identify the technique, we here use and recommend the terms nonviolent action or nonviolent struggle.

Because of the continuing imprecision and confusion about which words to use, it has been necessary over recent decades to refine existing terminology to describe and discuss such action, and even to develop new words and phrases. Therefore, a short glossary has been included for reference at the end of this book.

Exposing Misconceptions

In addition to misconceptions conveyed by unfortunate terminology, there are other areas of confusion in the field of nonviolent struggle as well. Despite new studies in recent decades, inaccuracies and misunderstandings are still widespread. Here are corrections for some of them:

(1) Nonviolent action has nothing to do with passivity, submissiveness, or cowardice. Just as in violent action, these must first be rejected and overcome before the struggle can proceed.

(2) Nonviolent action is a means of conducting conflicts and can be very powerful, but it is an extremely different phenomenon from violence of all types.

(3) Nonviolent action is not to be equated with verbal persuasion or purely psychological influences, although this technique may sometimes include action to apply psychological pressures for attitude change. Nonviolent action is a technique of struggle involving the use of psychological, social, economic, and political power in the matching of forces in conflict.

(4) Nonviolent action does not depend on the assumption that people are inherently "good." The potentialities of people for both "good" and "evil" are recognized, including the extremes of cruelty and inhumanity.

(5) In order to use nonviolent action effectively, people do not have to be pacifists or saints. Nonviolent action has been predominantly and successfully practiced by "ordinary" people.

(6) Success with nonviolent action does not require (though it may be helped by) shared standards and principles, or a high degree of shared interests or feelings of psychological closeness between the contending sides. If the opponents are emotionally unmoved by nonviolent resistance in face of violent repression, and therefore unwilling to agree to the objectives of the nonviolent struggle group, the resisters may apply coercive nonviolent measures. Difficult enforcement problems, economic losses, and political paralysis do not require the opponents' agreement to be felt.

(7) Nonviolent action is at least as much of a Western phenomenon as an Eastern one. Indeed, it is probably more Western, if one takes into account the widespread use of strikes and economic boycotts in the labor movements, the noncooperation struggles of subordinated European nationalities, and the struggles against dictatorships.

(8) In nonviolent action, there is no assumption that the opponents will refrain from using violence against nonviolent resisters. In fact, the technique is capable of operating against violence.

(9) There is nothing in nonviolent action to prevent it from being used for both "good" and "bad" causes. However, the social consequences of its use for a "bad" cause differ considerably from the consequences of violence used for the same "bad" cause.

(10) Nonviolent action is not limited to domestic conflicts within a democratic system. In order to have a chance of success, it is not necessary that the struggle be waged against relatively gentle and restrained opponents. Nonviolent struggle has been widely used against powerful governments, foreign occupiers, despotic regimes, tyrannical governments, empires, ruthless dictatorships, and totalitarian systems. These difficult nonviolent struggles against violent opponents have sometimes been successful.

(11) One of the many widely believed myths about conflict is that violence works quickly, and nonviolent struggle takes a long time to bring results. This is not true. Some wars and other violent struggles have been fought for many years, even decades. Some nonviolent struggles have brought victories very quickly, even within days or weeks. The time taken to achieve victory with this technique depends on diverse factors—including the strength of the nonviolent resisters and the wisdom of their actions.

What About Human Nature?

Despite the widespread occurrence of this type of conflict, many people still assume that nonviolent struggle is contrary to "human nature." It is often claimed that its widespread practice would require either a fundamental change in human beings or the acceptance of a powerful new religious or ideological belief system. Those views are not supported by the reality of past conflicts that have been waged by use of this technique.

In fact, the practice of this type of struggle is not based on belief in "turning the other cheek" or loving one's enemies. Instead, the widespread practice of this technique is more often based on the undeniable capacity of human beings to be stubborn and to do what they want to do or to refuse to do what they are ordered, whatever their beliefs about the use or nonuse of violence. Massive stubbornness can have powerful political consequences.

In any case, the view that nonviolent struggle is impossible except under rare conditions is contrary to the facts. That which has happened in the past is possible in the future.

The extremely widespread practice of nonviolent struggle is possible because the operation of this technique is compatible with the nature of political power and the vulnerabilities of all hierarchical systems. These systems and all governments depend on the subordinated populations, groups, and institutions to supply them with their needed sources of power. Before continuing with the examination of the technique of nonviolent struggle, it is therefore necessary to explore in greater depth the nature of the power of dominant institutions and all governments. This analysis sheds light on how it is that nonviolent struggle can be effective against repressive and ruthless regimes. They are vulnerable.

Notes

1. For bibliographic references to books in English on many of these cases, see Ronald M. McCarthy and Gene Sharp, with the assistance of Brad Bennett, *Nonviolent Action: A Research Guide*, New York and London: Garland Publishing, 1997.

2. It is worth noting that some believers in "principled nonviolence" have even rejected nonviolent struggle because it was a way to wage conflict (in which they did not believe).

Integrated Framework for Peacebuilding

John Paul Lederach

John Paul Lederach remains one of the leading scholars in the field of conflict resolution. Starting with his PhD in sociology from the University of Colorado, he went on to found the Center for Justice and Peacebuilding at Eastern Mennonite University, where he taught for many years. Now a professor of International Peacebuilding at the University of Notre Dame in Indiana, Lederach has received many awards, including the Martin Luther King Order of Peace Medal, has given lectures and commencement addresses the world over, and has been part of peace processes in Somalia, Northern Ireland, Nicaragua, Colombia, and Nepal. While he is most well-known for the elicitive model, his book, *The Moral Imagination*, goes well beyond these earlier models—we recommend all students read his latest works. Lederach is also a member of the Grounded Theory Institute.

Lederach argued for a more integrated approach to peacebuilding. He observed that the solutions emergent in Epoch One often failed to interrupt cycles of violence. After the Cold War ended, the world saw endless cycles of negotiation and confrontation as violence erupted in Somalia, Liberia, Bosnia, and Rwanda. He blames a short-term approach to conflict that favored short-term goals such as cease-fires without taking the necessary steps to plan for long-term peace. Like Robert Irwin Rotberg and Dennis Thompson, who wrote about truth and reconciliation processes, Lederach believes efforts toward reconciliation are as important as the immediate response to humanitarian crises (an end to violence, food, water, shelter, etc.).

This article also advocates for another approach emblematic of Epoch Two—the introduction of systems theory. Systems Theory operates on the premise that no event occurs in a vacuum. All events and people are interconnected; changes in one area will create shifts in another. Therefore, interventions need to be considered holistically. This also shifts the locus of interventions. Before, the power to create change was assumed to only be at the top. With a systems' view of conflict comes a new appreciation of middle-level leaders who may not attend official treaty signings but whose influence and actions nonetheless can be as powerful in maintaining or disrupting peace.

System-level change also requires longer-term efforts. Lederach urges the field to shift from short-term goals to a long-term lens. To do so, he makes a distinction between descriptive and prescriptive approaches. Descriptive approaches focus on describing more accurately the problem and the harms inflicted. We see this descriptive approach promoted in Carolyn Nordstrom's piece on ethnography and in Rotberg and Thompson's piece on truth and reconciliation commissions. The operating notion here is that detailed truth-telling and understanding helps transform the society. A prescriptive approach focuses on solutions and creativity to generate more positive futures. This is similar to the positive psychology approach Jeffrey McClellan urges the field to integrate into mediation. Lederach advocates for both a past- and future-looking approach to peacebuilding and, in doing so, brings under an umbrella the predominant approaches in Epoch Two.

Questions to consider: When peacebuilding, how do you know you have achieved positive peace? How do you help build resilience to help communities handle future issues?

An Integrated Framework for Peacebuilding

John Paul Lederach

Our challenge in this chapter is to outline a framework that brings together the various components of peacebuilding described thus far in a way that is responsive to the realities of contemporary conflict.

In terms of the conflict progression matrix, many contemporary situations seem locked in a vicious cycle of confrontation and negotiation, where sporadic rounds of talks collapse, restart, and collapse again. In the process, high levels of violence continue to produce humanitarian crises of monumental proportions, as we have witnessed in Somalia, Liberia, Angola, and Bosnia in the first half of the 1990s. When these crises are then captured by television cameras, it seems to sear the conscience of the international community, and pressure mounts to do something urgently. As Ernie Regehr points out, the rule of thumb seems to be that "foreign problems not in the headlines should be ignored, but once they have the attention of CNN they should have been addressed yesterday."[1]

The net effect is the loss of the long-term view of the situation, a myopic focus on crisis negotiation, and a failure to appreciate the multiplicity and interdependence of peacebuilding roles and activities. Too little attention is paid to the prevention of conflicts in the latent stages, particularly at the critical transformative period of movement toward armed confrontation. Once the situation has reached the proportions of a humanitarian disaster, the international community tends to shift toward a crisis mentality that is driven by a disaster-management frame of reference. Disaster management focuses on finding a quick political solution, often in the form of intense negotiations and peace accords, but little preparation is made for sustaining the peace process over the medium and long term.

If we want to create a more comprehensive and sustainable process, we must accomplish two things. First, we will need to reconceptualize our time frames for planning and action. Second, we will need to link the various aspects and dimensions of peacebuilding. We start with the perspective on time.

Rethinking Time Frames

As peacebuilders, we have yet to adequately address the nature of our conceptual and operative frameworks in terms of the time frames they represent. For example, in settings of complex emergencies produced by protracted conflict we know that crisis management responses to the humanitarian plight and political reconciliation are linked. What we do not as readily recognize is that they operate within distinctly different time frames. The long view of conflict as progression underscores the importance of recognizing the distinction between the time frame necessary for responding to humanitarian disasters and one that is adequate for the multiple tasks of building peace.[2] It also underscores the relationship between the many forms of crisis-response and peacebuilding activities: Not one is conducted in a vacuum and each has the potential to move the conflict progression forward constructively or to contribute to a stagnating cycle of confrontation. Let us consider this in more detail.

The management of a humanitarian disaster in any situation of war is governed by a crisis framework calling for quick actions that will be evaluated according to their capacity to address the immediate survival needs of the affected population. Yet, while understood in these immediate terms, disaster responses also include planning aimed at making the transition eventually toward rehabilitation and development. The language employed within the NGO relief and development community is reflective of these anticipated shifts.

Thus we talk conceptually about the transition from emergency disaster response to relief operations and to rehabilitation, reconstruction, and development. Central to this framework is the idea that any given immediate intervention is connected to movement toward a longer-term goal, perhaps best articulated as the concept of sustainable development.[3]

This general approach has a clear parallel to the idea of working with the long-term progression of conflict and building toward peace. Both support the idea that the alleviation of immediate suffering must be built upon the concept of transformation, underscoring the goal of moving a given population from a condition of extreme vulnerability and dependency to one of self-sufficiency and well-being. Here, we can put forward two key concepts.

First, transformation at this initial level represents the change from one status to another. In the more specific terms of conflict progression, transformation is the movement from the latent stage to confrontation to negotiation to dynamic, peaceful relationships.

Second, sustainability indicates a concern not only to initiate such movement but also to create a proactive process that is capable of regenerating itself over time—a spiral of peace and development instead of a spiral of violence and destruction.

Combined, the two suggest a critical point of departure that emanates from our discussion of conflict as progression: The process of building peace must rely on and operate within a framework and a time frame defined by sustainable transformation. In practical terms, this necessitates distinguishing between the more immediate needs of crisis-oriented disaster management in a given setting and the longer-term needs of constructively transforming the conflict.

Crisis response tends to involve specific projects with short-term, measurable outcomes. In the interests of transforming the conflict, however, short-term efforts must be measured primarily by their long-term implications. For example, while achieving a cease-fire is an immediate necessity, this goal must not be mistaken for, or replace, the broader framework of peacebuilding activity. Rather, a sustainable transformative approach suggests that the key lies in the relationship of the involved parties, with all that term encompasses at the psychological, spiritual, social, economic, political, and military levels.

The transformation approach suggests another nested paradigm, in this case one that relates time frames and types of peacebuilding activities (see figure 6). In this model, the first circle (on the far left) represents the short-term crisis intervention. For those working in humanitarian aid and development agencies, this type of intervention usually takes the form of emergency relief. For those whose focus is dealing with the conflict, crisis intervention often entails trying to halt the violence and achieve a cease-fire. In an increasing number of situations, both kinds of actions are required—as reflected in the growing use of the term "complex emergencies."

Those people and organizations that undertake crisis intervention think in blocks that rarely go beyond several months: How can we alleviate the excruciating suffering? How can we get the sides to agree to a cease-fire that opens up space for negotiations? The focus is often on the achievement of immediate solutions and goals.

In the second circle, which encompasses the short range, we move to a different modality. To respond more effectively to the proliferation of humanitarian crises induced by conflicts, concerned players in the international arena have increasingly sought to better prepare themselves. The "training" agenda has therefore risen in prominence, particularly in the field of conflict resolution. Training in this context responds to the question: What are the approaches and skills

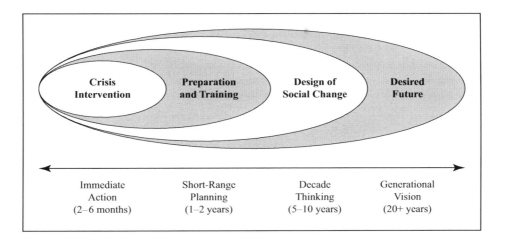

needed to better assess and deal with crises resulting from violent internal conflicts? The nested paradigm suggests that crisis responses should be seen as embedded in the need for better preparation for undertaking crisis management, on the one hand, and for building a capacity to deal more constructively with conflicts before they become full-blown crises, on the other hand. Such preparation envisions a time frame of one to two years, within which a broader array of approaches and skills can be developed and criteria for assessment can be incorporated.

In the fourth circle (on the far right of the model) is the longer-term perspective, which is often adopted by people who seek to prevent conflict and to promote a vision of a more peaceful and socially harmonious future. In this time frame, we think in terms of generations. Elise Boulding talked about this as "imaging" the future.[4] She suggested in reference to peace that we need to have an image, a vision of what we are trying to achieve in order to build toward and reach that vision. In more specific terms, we need to generate within the conflicted settings the space to envision a commonly shared future. Ironically, perhaps, the conflicting groups in settings of protracted conflict often have more in common in terms of their visions of the future than they do in terms of their shared and violent past. Thinking about the future involves articulating distant but nonetheless desirable structural, systemic, and relationship goals: for instance, sustainable development, self-sufficiency, equitable social structures that meet basic human needs, and respectful, interdependent relationships. The point of this time frame is quite simple: If we do not know where we are going it is difficult to get there. This time frame provides us a horizon for our journey.[5]

Between the immediate and long-term approach we find, once again, the middle-range perspective. In terms of time frame, the middle-range thinks in blocks of five to ten years. It is driven by an interest in linking the immediate experience of crisis with a better future in which such crises can be prevented. In other words, the middle-range approach is concerned with the design of social change. This middle-range approach is what a number of conflict resolution practitioners are referring to as "dispute system design."[6] How do we put into place mechanisms that make the transition possible and create a sustainable process that will carry us toward our ultimate goals?

Taken as a whole, the nested paradigm demonstrates that we must respond to immediate crises in a manner that is informed by a longer-term vision. Our capacity to respond to the short-term agenda is more fully developed than is our capacity to take a longer-term view and see distant goals strategically reflected in our short-term action. This is especially important in dealing with protracted conflicts fueled by perceptions dating back generations. As noted in an earlier chapter, one in four current armed conflicts has been under way for more than two decades. I once was nearly thrown out of a conference room in Belfast when I suggested that it will take as long to get out of an armed conflict as it took to get in. While not a literal formula, my suggestion is that we cannot respond with quick fixes to situations of protracted conflict. We must think about the healing of people and the rebuilding of the web of their relationships in terms relative to those that it took to create the hatred and violence that has divided them.

Viewing conflict as a progression provides a set of lenses for rethinking time. It allows us to see not only that humanitarian disasters produced by war require immediate responses that help save lives in the short term, but also that quick fixes in protracted conflict rarely lead to sustainable processes or solutions. More specifically, it suggests that a crisis-driven response to conflict that measures success in terms of arresting disease and starvation and achieving a cease-fire must be embedded within the painstaking tasks of relationship and confidence building, and of the design of and preparation for social change, which ultimately provide a basis for sustaining conflict transformation.

Constructing such a process entails the unfolding of a design "architecture" that moves through stages. The design explicitly envisions short-term crisis responses to protracted internal conflict as embedded in and informed by a long-term point of view. Within the time frame of conflict progression, it is necessary to develop the capacity to think in longer units of time—in decades instead of weeks and months. Such an architecture recognizes and integrates specific roles and functions and their corresponding activities as the dynamic elements that create and sustain the movement along the continuum of constructive transformation over time. What we need are practical mechanisms by which our vision of a desired future can be used to define our response to the crisis; otherwise, the crisis and its dynamics will define the future.

An Integrated Framework

We see here the natural and crucial overlap between the structural and procedural lenses, as elements of a broad peacebuilding paradigm. "Structure" suggests the need to think comprehensively about the affected population and systemically about the issues. "Process" underscores the necessity of thinking creatively about the progression of conflict and the sustainability of its transformation by linking roles, functions, and activities in an integrated manner. Together, the two sets of lenses suggest an integrated approach to peacebuilding, visualized in figure 7 by linking the two nested models into an overall matrix. The vertical axis is taken from the Dugan nested paradigm that allows us to link the foci and levels of intervention in the conflict. The horizontal axis is the time frame model that links short-term crisis with longer-term perspective for change in the society. The two dimensions intersect at five points, each of which represents a distinct—and all too often discrete—community of thought and action in the broader field of peacebuilding. Let us look at each in more detail.

ROOT CAUSES

Those who are concerned with systemic perspectives underlying the crisis tend to pursue a structural analysis of the root causes of the conflict. They often reflect back on the long history of the current crisis to analyze and explain the broader systemic factors that must be taken into account.

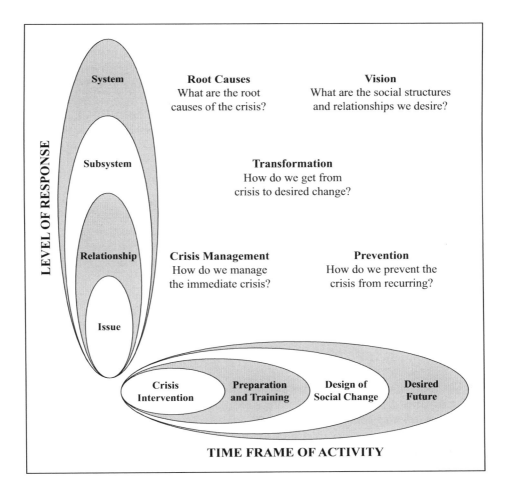

CRISIS MANAGEMENT

People who have the tasks of responding to the immediate issues and ameliorating humanitarian suffering, who seek a respite in the fighting, are most concerned about how to manage the crisis and achieve some agreement between the parties on immediate issues. They rarely have time to review all the information generated by the "root cause" community and are driven by pragmatism and common sense. They want to know what needs to be done and to get it done as soon as possible.

PREVENTION

At the level of the immediate issues but looking toward the future, another set of people concentrate on how to learn the lessons of the crisis in order to anticipate and prevent its recurrence. Their work involves identifying the factors that precipitated the violence, helping the affected society prepare to better handle such situations in the future, and disseminating to other societies the lessons of what went wrong and what went right.

VISION

With a generational perspective on system-level subjects, another group of people focus on desirable social and political structures and future relationships between those groups currently in conflict. The visions they articulate center on the well-being of coming generations.

TRANSFORMATION

Where a focus on the subsystem intersects with a concern to think in terms of decades and to design social change, people pose the strategic question, How to move from this crisis to the desired change? Here, transformation is posited at a middle range, which requires input from the other four communities.

The basic proposal put forward in this book is the need for an integrated approach to peacebuilding. Integration begins with a recognition that the middle range holds special potential for transformation, but that change will be needed at every level of human experience and endeavor. Specifically, the middle-range perspective suggests that we need to achieve integration in at least three strategic ways.

- We must develop the capacity to think about the design of social change in time-units of decades, in order to link crisis management and long-term, future-oriented time frames.
- We must understand crisis issues as connected to systemic roots and develop approaches that explicitly anchor issues within a set of relationships and subsystems.

- We must recognize the integrative potential of middle-range leaders, who by their locus within the affected population may be able to cultivate relationships and pursue the design of social change at a subsystem level, thus helping to make the vertical and horizontal connections necessary to sustain a process of desired change.

Here, we can begin to define an understanding of conflict transformation that goes beyond the resolution of issues. In essence, conflict transformation refers to change that can be understood in two fundamental ways—descriptively and prescriptively—across four dimensions—personal, relational, structural, and cultural.

Descriptively speaking, transformation refers to the empirical impact of conflict—in other words, to the effects that social conflict produces. In this case, we use the word "transformation" to describe the general changes social conflict creates and the patterns it typically follows. At a prescriptive level, transformation implies deliberate intervention to effect change. In this instance, transformation refers to the goals we have as intervenors as we work with conflict.

At both descriptive and prescriptive levels, transformation is operative across four interdependent dimensions. The personal dimension refers to the changes effected in, and desired for, the individual. This involves emotional, perceptual, and spiritual aspects of conflict. From a descriptive perspective, transformation suggests that individuals are affected by conflict both negatively and positively— for example, in terms of their physical well-being, self-esteem, emotional stability, capacity to perceive accurately, and spiritual integrity. Prescriptively, transformation represents deliberate intervention to minimize the destructive effects of social conflict and maximize its potentialities for personal growth at physical, emotional, and spiritual levels.

The relational dimension depicts the changes effected in, and desired for, the relationship. Here we take into consideration the areas of relational affectivity and interdependence, and the expressive, communicative, and interactive aspects of conflict. Descriptively, transformation refers to the effects of conflict on relational patterns of communication and interaction. It looks beyond the tension around visible issues to the underlying changes produced by conflict in the patterns of how people perceive themselves, one another, and the conflict itself, and in their hopes for their future relationship: how close or distant, how interdependent, how reactive or proactive a role to play, what the other party will want. Prescriptively, transformation represents intentional intervention that minimizes poorly functioning communication and maximizes mutual understanding, and that brings to the surface the relational fears, hopes, and goals of the people involved in terms of affectivity and interdependence.

The structural dimension highlights the underlying causes of conflict and the patterns and changes it brings about in social structures. At times understood as the "content" or "substance" of a conflict, the structural dimension may encompass issues such as basic human needs, access to resources, and institutional patterns of decision making. Transformation at the descriptive level refers to the analysis of social conditions that give rise to conflict and the way that conflict affects change in existing decision-making structures and patterns. At a prescriptive level, transformation represents deliberate intervention to provide insight into underlying causes and social conditions that create and foster violent expressions of conflict, and to openly promote nonviolent mechanisms that reduce adversariness, minimize and ultimately eliminate violence, and foster structures that meet basic human needs (substantive justice) and maximize participation of people in decisions that affect them (procedural justice).

The cultural dimension refers to the changes produced by conflict in the cultural patterns of a group, and to the ways that culture affects the development and handling of conflict. At a descriptive level, transformation is interested in how conflict affects and changes the cultural patterns of a group, and how those accumulated and shared patterns affect the way people in that setting understand and respond to conflict. Prescriptively, transformation seeks to understand the cultural patterns that contribute to the rise of violent expressions of conflict, and to identify, promote, and build on the resources and mechanisms within a cultural setting for constructively responding to and handling conflict.

In summary, conflict transformation represents a comprehensive set of lenses for describing how conflict emerges from, evolves within, and brings about changes in the personal, relational, structural, and cultural dimensions, and for developing creative responses that promote peaceful change within those dimensions through nonviolent mechanisms. As such, the integrated framework provides a platform for understanding and responding to conflict and developing peacebuilding initiatives. The overall process of conflict transformation is related to our broader theme of reconciliation inasmuch as it is oriented toward changing the nature of relationships at every level of human interaction and experience.

Conclusion

When we combine the elements in the integrated framework we begin to establish an infrastructure for sustaining the dynamic transformation of conflict and the construction of peace. An infrastructure for peacebuilding should be understood as a process-structure, in the way that quantum theory has proposed. A process-structure is made up of systems that maintain form over time yet have no hard rigidity of structure.[7] Good examples of a process-structure are a glacier or a stream coming down a mountain. These are dynamic processes, flexible and adaptable, yet at the same time they are also structures that have form and move in a particular direction.

In more specific terms, a process-structure for peacebuilding transforms a war-system characterized by deeply divided, hostile, and violent relationships into a peace-system characterized by just and interdependent relationships with the capacity to find nonviolent mechanisms for expressing and handling conflict. The goal is not stasis, but rather the generation of continuous, dynamic, self-regenerating processes that maintain form over time and are able to adapt to environmental changes. Such an infrastructure is made up of a web of people, their relationships and activities, and the social mechanisms necessary to sustain the change sought. This takes place at all levels of the society.

An infrastructure for peacebuilding is oriented toward supporting processes of social change generated by the need to move from stagnant cycles of violence toward a desired and shared vision of increased interdependence. Such an infrastructure must be rooted in the conflict setting. It must emerge creatively from the culture and context, but not be a slave of either. The purpose of the process-structure is reconciliation that centers on the redefinition and restoration of broken relationships. The integrated framework suggests that we are not merely interested in "ending" something that is not desired. We are oriented toward the building of relationships that in their totality form new patterns, processes, and structures. Peacebuilding through the constructive transformation of conflicts is simultaneously a visionary and a context-responsive approach.

Notes

1. Regehr, *War after the Cold War*, 1.
2. See John Paul Lederach, "The Ethics of Military Intervention in Humanitarian Crises," in United Development Programme, *UNDP Training Manual* (New York: United Nations, 1993), 2.
3. Ann Seidman and Anang Frederick, *Towards a New Vision of Self-Sustained Development* (Trenton, NJ: Africa World Press, 1992); Michael Carley and Ian Christie, *Managing Sustainable Development* (Minneapolis: University of Minnesota Press, 1992; and Julie Fisher, *The Road from Rio: Sustainable Development and the Nongovernmental Movement in the Third World* (New York: Praeger, 1993).
4. Elise Boulding, "The Challenges of Imaging Peace in Wartime," *Futures* 23, no. 5 (1991): 528.
5. Lederach, *Journey toward Reconciliation* (see the chapter on time, healing, and reconciliation).
6. Christopher W. Moore, *Dispute Management Systems Design* (Boulder, CO: LDR Associates, 1994).
7. Wheatley, *Leadership and the New Sciences*, 15.

Truth and Reconciliation

Robert Irwin Rotberg and Dennis Thompson

Robert Irwin Rotberg is the founding director of the Intrastate Conflict Program at Harvard University's Kennedy School of Government. He received his PhD from Oxford University. Between 2003 and 2004, he worked under the Secretary of State on an Advisory Panel of Africa. He also received a presidential appointment to serve on the Council of the National Endowment for the Humanities. Dennis Thompson received his PhD in political science from Harvard University in 1968, and after fifteen years teaching at Princeton University, he returned to Harvard as a professor of government at Harvard University's Kennedy School of Government. He has received significant recognition for his contributions to the field of ethics, political theory, and public affairs.

The choices people make in post-atrocity contexts determine whether peace lasts or is upended by simmering hatred and open wounds. Scholars interested in responses in the wake of violence will determine whether peace is lasting and the amount of harm that is addressed if not healed. Transitional justice addresses a variety of issues in the aftermath of atrocity, including compensation, restructuring, transparency, apologies, commemoration, trauma services, and more. This article focuses on truth and reconciliation commissions that occur in some communities after mass violence. These commissions intend to support communities and prevent future outbreaks by bringing those harmed and those who performed the harm into a space in which they can speak openly about what happened during the outbreak.

Truth commission supporters see speech and truth-telling as an important vehicle through which we can return to civilization after barbarism. These commissions often seek a complete accounting of the violent acts, in detail. They seek a "full truth" or a "chain of circumstances." This approach is very resonant with Carolyn Nordstrom's article about ethnography as a research methodology. Both articles promote a granular, deep dive into the details of experience. They aim to bring speech and voice to the silence that violence has created. Through this intimacy with stories and people, the hope is that a cathartic healing and deeper understanding can occur.

Some commissions offer perpetrators amnesty in exchange for their testimony; in doing so, some say commissions privilege truth versus justice. This raises one of the central debates in the field: By trying to bring real culprits forward to confess, are we too quickly replacing criminal justice? Those advocating for amnesty say truth is more important because it creates larger healing and helps form a new nation and new society. Opponents of truth commissions say they simply expunge the culpable parties, worsen relations between parties, and can traumatize victims. Furthermore, they can become national/international dramas rather than vehicles for healing.

Questions to consider: Is truth more important than justice? Is a clear telling of the past necessary to heal and move forward? What might be some of the risks of holding these commissions even for the victims and their families?

Truth Commissions and the Provision of Truth, Justice, and Reconciliation

Robert Irwin Rotberg and Dennis Thompson

"NEVER AGAIN!" is a central rallying cry of truth commissions, and one about which perpetrators and victims can agree. The notion of "never again" captures the response of societies that are recovering their own equilibria, their own dignity, and their own sense of integrity. Truth commissions are intended to be both preventive and restorative.

But if societies are to prevent recurrences of past atrocities and to cleanse themselves of the corrosive enduring effects of massive injuries to individuals and whole groups, societies must understand—at the deepest possible levels—what occurred and why. In order to come fully to terms with their brutal pasts, they must uncover, in precise detail, who did what to whom, and why, and under whose orders. They must seek, at least, thus to uncover the truth—insofar as this aim is humanly and situationally possible after the fact.

Truth commissions generally are created after a totalitarian/authoritarian regime has been succeeded by a democratic one. Sometimes the transition is preceded by civil and economic war bolstered by world public opinion, sometimes by invasion, and sometimes when societal revulsion overwhelms a military junta, a minority dictatorship, or strong arm pseudodemocrats. Massive human rights violations usually accompany such arrogations of power. The mandate of the successor regime is to establish or revive democracy and to prevent any resumption of human rights abuses. It also seeks to reconcile the old and the new, and to move forward in effective harmony.

Truth commissions thus seek, whatever their mandate from a new government, to uncover the past in order to answer questions that remain unanswered: What happened to husbands, sons, wives, and lovers at the hands of the ousted regime? Who gave the orders? Who executed the orders? What was the grand design? Who benefited? Getting the facts provides closure, at least in theory. Making it possible for perpetrators to be confronted by victims and the heirs of victims (as in the South African and Guatemalan cases) can provide further closure. In societies as disparate as Argentina, Bosnia, Cambodia, Cyprus, El Salvador, Guatemala, Haiti, Nigeria, South Africa, and Sri Lanka, and now in Sierra Leone and Kosovo, there is a natural, consuming desire to elicit as complete an accounting as possible of how people disappeared, how they were assassinated, how and why they were flung from airplanes above the Atlantic Ocean, and how and why they were slaughtered in groups and tossed into unmarked graves.

There are the clinical commissions that have tried to discover precisely what happened to persons who vanished during a "dirty war" organized by the defeated regime. They have largely taken testimony behind closed doors and published as accurate a recounting as possible given their constrained circumstances and resources. Sometimes, publication has been delayed or avoided, as in Sri Lanka for some months and in Haiti, for all practical purposes, indefinitely. In several of those cases, especially in the earliest truth commissions, there has been little attempt to go beyond the bare facts—to examine the moral and historical underpinnings of the crimes committed. It has been enough to answer specific questions rather than to affix societal blame. Some, however, have done neither; Haiti's Si M Pa Rele, its National Commission for Truth and Justice, is the prime example.

Those more circumscribed and limited commission efforts reflect both the previous paucity of experience with the truth commission method, and also the bargains struck, as in Guatemala and El Salvador, and in adverse or better than adverse circumstances between an outgoing regime and its successor or between modern governments and human rights watchdogs. Most of the commissions that were formed later had broader mandates and extensive goals. They have sought more than an accounting, and something closer to an approximation of a full truth, about the chain of circumstances that resulted in massive human rights violations, and how each individual atrocity fitted into a carefully constructed mosaic of guilt. These more ambitious commissions have tried to apportion that guilt, both to those who attacked others individually and to those who authorized the dastardly acts by direction or indirection. Ultimately, these commissions wanted to understand the structure of previous abuse, and the extent to which it could be articulated.

The Guatemalan three-man Commission on Historical Clarification (1997–1999) was prohibited from naming names and from apportioning blame directly. Yet the nine-volume report of the United Nations-backed Guatemalan commission found the army responsible for more than 200,000 deaths and disappearances during thirty-six years of civil war. It documented 626 massacres perpetuated by the army and 32 by its opponents, and labeled the military actions genocide. By so doing, the commission nullified a 1996 blanket amnesty that banned prosecution for all other crimes.

South Africa's Truth and Reconciliation Commission (TRC) is the prime example of a commission with a mandate much broader than that of Guatemala's, extensive goals, and a comprehensive vision of how such an effort can prevent future conflict and ensure that "never again!" becomes a societal reality. A book examining the nature of truth commissions inevitably must focus largely (but not exclusively) on the new standard-setting model of the practice.

The TRC, though flawed in many ways, has set a high standard for future commissions.

The importance and rationale of the TRC must be understood in the context of apartheid. The rigid, legalized segregation of South African apartheid began in 1948 when the National Party (led and participated in largely by Afrikaners) won a narrow victory and proceeded to legislate against the vast African majority, against Communism, and against all forms of dissent and disagreement with the political aims of Afrikanerdom. Basic human rights were discarded. Terror gradually became perfected as an instrument of state control. For all Africans, coloreds, and Indians, and even for some white liberals, National Party rule was arbitrary and autocratic, obviously discriminatory, and mean. The police state that was created was supported by atrocities and brutalities equal to if not exceeding those on the other side of the Atlantic Ocean.

After the tyranny of apartheid was removed in 1994, and Nelson Mandela, a long-time prisoner, became the new South Africa's first president, Parliament was established, and he appointed (in 1995) the Truth and Reconciliation Commission to discover the dark facts of apartheid, to report them to South Africa and the world, and to trade amnesty, where necessary, for information. The TRC grew out of an elaborate political compromise that rejected the outgoing regime's demand for blanket amnesty and no retribution in exchange for a mechanism (the TRC) that could grant amnesty for political acts. The origins of the commission are discussed more fully below, in chapters in this volume by Alex Boraine and Dumisa Ntsebeza. They are two among the seventeen original members of the TRC, chaired by Anglican Archbishop Desmond Tutu. The TRC's report, published in 1998, is discussed by nearly all of the contributors, but especially by Wilhelm Verwoerd and Charles Villa-Vicencio, two of its authors.

Whereas the first commissions (Uganda, Bolivia, Argentina, Zimbabwe, Uruguay, the Philippines, Chile, and ten or so more) dared not hear testimony in public for fear that it might be too inflammatory or arouse retaliation from the ousted military officers (who were still around) or their patrons, the South African commission not only insisted on public as well as private testimony, and the public interrogation of accused perpetrators by victims as well as prosecutorial figures from the commission's staff, and by the commissioners themselves, but it also went a step further and permitted press and television reports. Widely disseminated verbatim accounts became the content of an ongoing national drama. Rather than having a distilled version of what had occurred in past times summarized in a commission report, and then released, the South Africans were (with very few exceptions) totally transparent. Their activities educated the new society directly, well before its official findings could be presented to Parliament and the president.

Truth could thus be affirmed by individuals across the land as well as by commissioners. The story of the past could not therefore be just one story, but a million perceptions of what had been revealed before the commission and argued back and forth between those charged with revealing what and why, and the victims, who wanted nothing but the full truth. The South African version of a commission empowered a popular understanding incrementally, rather than comprehensively by polished summary. Moreover, in this way, the new society was able to begin continuously to reconstruct itself—in terms of what it had gone through and how it was going to cope with its travails. As the South African TRC itself learned more and more, it could peel back layer after layer of apartheid atrocity. The report of the TRC, said a commissioner, could "not tell the story of apartheid as a whole, but only the story of its abuses of bodily integrity."[1] The TRC's hearings could slice closer and closer to the bone of terror and inhumanity in a way that the more limited commissions in El Salvador or Haiti never could.

The South African commission has become the model for all future commissions, which is why the chapters in this book examine the experience of the TRC much more fully than they do commissions elsewhere. But this book is about the theory of truth commissioning as well as its practice. It is about the tensions between truth and justice, about the prevention of future conflict through truth commissions, about reconciliation in postconflict situations, about knowledge as opposed to retribution, about victim's as well as perpetrator's rights, and about societal restoration.

There is a strong sense that a society can move forward only after it comes to terms with its collective angst. In the South African case, that meant dealing with outrages committed by whites against Africans, Africans against Africans, Africans against whites, and the African National Congress (ANC) against its own members, as well as with whites coming to terms with the evils of apartheid, perpetrated over more than forty years, with blacks primarily the victims. Tutu asked whites to apologize and take responsibility for their actions during apartheid. Is there no leader of "some stature and some integrity in the white community," he asked in a statement released to the press, who will admit that the whites "had a bad policy that had evil consequences?"[2]

"Moving forward" and "coming to terms with" are figures of speech that provide the rationale for most truth commissions. There is an assumption that a society emerging from an intrastate cataclysm of violence will remain stable, and prosper, only if the facts of the past are made plain. Critics, including several contributors to this book, question that assumption, suggesting that the "truth" that a commission may uncover can only be tentative. Additional truths, they argue, will emerge by encouraging conflict and controversy, not by establishing one truth and declaring consensus. Continuing moral controversy is desirable in a democracy, and fact-finding in the service of reconciliation must take that goal into account.

The rationale for truth commissions, nevertheless, is that the inexplicable should be understood, that actual murders and murderers will be unmasked, that unmarked graves will be located, and, for example, that the bizarre attempt to poison apartheid's opponents will be revealed. As contributors to this book imply, proper remembrances fulfill the collective needs of badly damaged societies. There is too much injury to individuals and nations. Forgetting reinforces losses of self-esteem among victims and even among victims as a group.

Truth commissions exist because of political compromises, in South Africa's recent case as a substitute for the broad amnesty that the outgoing regime wanted, and could not get.[3] But commissions also exist because society is unwilling to forgive and forget, refusing to move on without confronting the repression of its precursor generation. Those who advocate dispensing with truth commissions and simply moving on after a massive regime change argue that the kinds of confrontation engendered by the commission process only make societal tensions more palpable. Opening the old wounds, they argue, harms rather than helps benefi-cially to reconstruct a society in transition. By this logic, the truth commission process retards reconciliation. Indeed, a society cannot forgive what it cannot punish.[4] Thus, the prevailing assumption that postconflict reconciliation is both desirable and possible, as well as necessary, may be incorrect. Similarly, some wonder wisely whether the approach to reconciliation that most of the contribu-tors to this book support may be culturally specific; South Africa may have special qualities that differentiate its potential for reconciliation from a society like Sri Lanka, where a bitter seventeen-year civil war continues.

Most commissions have not tried to reconcile the old, which oppressed, with the new, which enshrines democracy. But the Chilean commission did, and the South African version had as its primary mission the seeking of reconciliation through acquiring and displaying the truth, and, in its chairman's religious design, requesting atonement. Thus, for him and for the other commissioners, uncovering the facts—the truth—of the past was a necessary if not sufficient stage that could prepare the new South Africa to be reconciled, and whites and blacks to be recon-ciled to one another.

Reconciliation may or may not prove possible in the aftermath of an apartheid-riven society. But the TRC operated as if it were, and as if retailing the truth of the deepest machinations of apartheid—the culpability of its highest lead-ers and its mad-doctor schemes of biological and chemical warfare—would some-how set South Africa free to forge a successful multiracial society. To meet those goals—to encourage the kinds of testimony that would reveal apartheid at its moral worst—the TRC had to find a way to compel the real culprits to come forward and confess. Amnesty was the result, as the postamble to the interim constitution prefigured: perpetrators, black and white, would receive perpetual immunity from prosecution if they testified fully and candidly about their terrible deeds and if they could demonstrate (by the loose standards that the TRC used pragmatically) that their crimes were political; that is, that they served political ends or were motivated by political beliefs.

Because the South African TRC is the latest and the grandest example of postconflict truth seeking, it is critical to inquire to what extent truth can be acquired by such means. Can justice in its several forms be served equally well? Would standard forms of prosecution be preferred? Does the amnesty process satisfy various criteria for justice? Does it distort the trial system that societies usually use to punish transgressors and prevent evildoing? Assuming that reconciliation is both desirable and possible, does the truth commission method, with its transparency and attendant publicity, retard or advance the process? How can commissions achieve these goals through the processes of their constituted endeavors and activities, and through the medium of a published report?

Such questions form the core of this book's combined philosophical and pragmatic inquiry. Gutmann and Thompson's chapter raises a central objection to the truth commission endeavor: truth commissions, they write, "sacrifice the pursuit of justice as usually understood for the sake of promoting some other social purpose such as reconciliation." But "trading criminal justice for a general social benefit . . . is, and should be, morally suspect." Indeed, if the moral case for truth commissions in a democratic society is to be made it must satisfy three critical criteria: It must (1) substitute rights and goods "that are moral" and equivalent (or "comparable") to the justice foregone; (2) be broadly inclusive so as to foster social cooperation among all citizens who have legitimate claims on the society being reconstructed; and (3) be "moral in practice," and intimately connected to the democratic ethos of the successor government so that the retribution being sacrificed can be appreciated in terms of the realization of specific, not general, forms of societal benefit.

Gutmann and Thompson assert that the mere stability of a successor government would not satisfy the first criterion, with its emphasis on moral goods. Such social stability only becomes morally relevant when it is part of a new, just dispensation or can be shown to promote justice in the future. Those who defend truth commissions therefore must distinguish moral justifications from the interests of individuals or groups.

The second criterion in their scheme does not mean putting such justifications to a referendum. Rather, there is the test of reason. Gutmann and Thompson want truth commissions to be accessible and inclusive, and they are prepared to take into account the previous history of the country and the conflict, with its critical legacy of injustice. Likewise, the third criterion cannot be satisfied by even a fully moral critique of contemporary violence and injustice for the sake of future peace. The commission is justified best that functions in the democratic spirit of the government which it serves.

Gutmann and Thompson, conscious as they are of the postamble that certified an important political compromise, insist that a political compromise is not necessarily a moral compromise. Providing for amnesty satisfied political needs, not moral ones. What is needed to transform a purely opportunistic, pragmatic political decision into a morally defensible one is the approach that Tutu has articulated so consistently: that criminal justice may be sacrificed for the greater moral justice of enduring societal harmony. This is the restorative justice about which Elizabeth Kiss writes in another chapter of this book.

Tutu also wanted forgiveness and atonement. But those human accomplishments may not be sufficient, morally, to substitute for criminal justice. Forgiveness erases wrongdoing, which has the effect of submitting to evil. According to David Crocker, another chapter's author, "It is morally objectionable as well as impractical for a truth commission . . . to force people to agree about the past, forgive the sins committed against them, or love one another."

Rajeev Bhargava assesses these and other objections to forgiveness. He asks if forgiveness is morally appropriate, and suggests, in any event, that truth commissions cannot bear the burden of bringing about forgiveness by individuals. To forgive is not always appropriate or virtuous. It must, Bhargava concludes, be "consistent with the dignity and self-respect of the victim."

Societal reconciliation is of a different order. Indeed, Gutmann and Thompson claim, "reconciliation is an illiberal aim" if an entire society is expected to embrace one comprehensive moral approach. It is undemocratic, too, for disharmony is desirable and an attribute of a healthy democracy.

A further test of the truth commission method is the extent to which it serves the reciprocal requirements of deliberative democracy. To do so it must practice the democratic principles of the society that a commission is attempting to create. It must share its own views, which the TRC through Tutu has done, with citizens broadly and transparently. Providing a final report that spoke to the entire society also advanced this goal of reciprocity. Unlike a trial, or a series of trials, a truth commission report can express the range of behavior that society needs to judge and condemn, and to which it needs to be reconciled. If it does all that it can do to satisfy such moral criteria, then the goals of societal justice may be satisfied.

The TRC found that the state committed gross violations of human rights, including many of a criminal nature. It condoned the extrajudicial killing of political opponents, and colluded with the Inkatha Freedom Party and others. The highest levels of the apartheid regime were responsible for these crimes. Although the "predominant portion" of the gross violations was perpetrated by the state and its agents, the African National Congress (ANC) also blurred the distinction between military and civilian targets. It tortured and killed alleged defectors and collaborators, and thus committed its own gross violations of civil rights. The TRC report named many names, and pulled few punches.[5] It also uncovered evidence of secret biological, chemical, and weapons experiments; the TRC exposed South Africa's Operation Coast, for instance, which tested biological and chemical weapons on troops from Mozambique and tried to invent infertility drugs to give to blacks only.

Bhargava's essay focuses on restoring a society's norms of basic procedural justice. A truth commission does so by discovering grave past injustices and by encouraging perpetrators to confess to their responsibilities. Only through those means, Bhargava suggests, can a defeated barbaric social formation gradually be transformed into a minimally decent society. That is the overriding objective of a truth commission. Morality flows from the restoration of confidence in procedural justice.

Bhargava's essay distinguishes between barbaric social formations that are asymmetric, where a controlling political group generates evil, and symmetric ones, in which social and political evil is produced collectively by an entire society. The second kind of barbaric social formation is profoundly amoral. The first, where a dominant group violates norms and the rest of society seeks to enforce the rules of procedural justice, is much more promising. It is particularly promising when the dominant group, despite its massive system of evil, still honors the intent of procedural justice, if more in the breach than in practice. When the dominant group is ousted, procedural justice needs primarily to be restored, not introduced (as it would be after a period of societal collapse and amorality).

For Bhargava's analysis, it is essential that the distinction between perpetrators and victims is fully acknowledged by truth commissions. If not, truth commissions will find it almost impossible to help transform a traumatized, postconflict society into a minimally decent society. Nor would they be able to help societies stabilize a system of basic procedural justice, which must be a critical objective.

Kiss's chapter affirms truth commissions as a modern instrument capable of strengthening civil society and providing restorative justice. Because they are simultaneously investigative, judicial, political, educational, and therapeutic bodies, they can pursue morally ambitious ends of profound value to a transitional society. Indeed, their moral ambition makes truth commissions politically innovative. At the heart of this innovation is a concept of justice that is survivor or victim centered, not retributive. It has been praised for being "moral, cultural, psychological, and human rather than . . . solely legal or instrumental"; in short, "the creation of a nation."[6]

Restorative justice emerges from this desire to create a new nation—the desire to reconstruct a just society. Punishment alone for perpetrators, in accord with prosecutions and the requirements of an arms-length criminal system, hinders the achievement of restorative justice. The better path, the believers in restorative justice suggest, is forgiveness and reconciliation preceded by an accounting of violations, a confronting of perpetrators by victims, reparations, and a continuing emphasis on personal motivations and transformations. It is the individual-centered approach of the best truth commissions that contributes meaningfully to restorative justice.

Truth commissions, Kiss asserts, provide a mechanism to do justice to and to acknowledge that there were victims and perpetrators on more than one side. Commissions can be used in promising ways to advance beneficent societal goals despite competing narratives of oppression, and bitter, if opposite, memories of evil. If the goal is to reorient a society that has lost its moral way, truth commissions are more supple and constructive than criminal trials or forms of lustration (the banning of perpetrators from public office). There is positive value in what truth commissions seek, especially those like the Argentinean, the Chilean, and the South African versions—where the explicit goal was to restore a just society.

Crocker's transitional justice, like Kiss's restorative justice, is general and expansive. Rather than confining transitional justice to penal or retributive justice, Crocker employs transitional justice to encompass compensatory and distributive justice. Wisely, he suggests that the challenge for a new democracy is to respond effectively to past evils without "undermining the new democracy or jeopardizing prospects for future development."

Crocker judges the extent to which truth commissions actually serve transitional justice by how well they ferret out the truth, provide salutary platforms for victims and their kin, sanction violators effectively (a weakness of Guatemala's Historical Clarification Commission), uphold and strengthen the rule of law (critical if the new, society wants to distinguish itself from the authoritarianism and institutionalized bias of the outgoing regime), compensate victims through reparations collectively or individually, contribute to institutional reform and long-term national development, reconcile the defeated with the victorious, and foster public debate leading to publicly acceptable compromises.

André du Toit's concept of transitional justice includes truth as acknowledgment and justice as recognition, together providing a coherent alternative to retributive justice. With victims' hearing as a central focus, du Toit suggests that the TRC's form of transitional justice passed moral tests. Differing with Gutmann and Thompson, du Toit avers that moral determination should depend on context; the compromise that was represented by the TRC was justified by postapartheid needs and circumstances.

Chile's special commission compensated the survivors of human rights abuses and the families of victims. The South African TRC' Reparation and Rehabilitation Committee recommended to Parliament who should be compensated, and by how much. But President Thabo Mbeki said that funds were short, and the provision of financial recompense became unlikely. One of the three Sri Lankan commissions of inquiry devoted almost all of its efforts to deciding whom to compensate, and by how much. The principle, which Crocker supports, is that the truth commission process is complete only when victims obtain financial redress as well as knowledge ("truth"), and a moral sense of completion. Reparations and compensation strengthen the rule of law, reconciliation, and the overall process of institutional reform. Martha Minow feels even more strongly: no long-term vision of social transformation is possible if the need for reparations (such as monuments, parks, and renamed buildings as well as cash) is ignored.

Crocker examines the contribution of national and international civil society (transnational nongovernmental organizations for the most part) to the effective accomplishment of transitional justice. The experiences of Honduras and Guatemala, where civic groups succeeded only partially in influencing their nations' postconflict attempts to come to terms with human rights abuses, were very mixed, but Crocker argues that a well-informed international or globalized civil society (including agencies of the United Nations, which Crocker assesses) will increasingly reinforce the work of truth commissions in preventing future intra-state conflicts. Never again! will become a greater reality because of the attention of international civil society.

Boraine, the deputy chairman of the TRC and one of those who originally advocated using an elaborated form of the Chilean commission model to deal with South Africa's "unfinished business" in the aftermath of apartheid, argues for a wide-ranging, powerful, and public investigatory commission capable of extraordinary truth-telling and truth-finding. Creating such a body made it possible to contemplate restoring the nation's moral order, profoundly jeopardized as that order had been by abuses of the rule of law and of fundamental human rights. An attempt by the incoming ANC-led government to hold Nuremberg-like trials would have antagonized any hope of a peaceful transition. (Ntsebeza, another member of the TRC and its chief investigator, also develops this argument in his chapter.) Granting the agents of apartheid a blanket amnesty would have infuriated the long-oppressed majority. Establishing a TRC was an available middle course, and one advocated by important sections of civil society; indeed, only such a forum could provide a collection of individual, but carefully investigated, amnesties. No other method could have legitimized the amnesty or forgiveness process that was essential, Boraine and others argue, if South Africa were to move peacefully from war to peace. Hence the postamble (recognizing the political compromise that overcame apartheid) and the adding of reconciliation to truth as the commission's mandate.

Boraine argues that deeply divided societies cannot rely on punishment to heal and reconcile their several communities. He and Ntsebeza explain what the South African Parliament intended by reconciliation and the development of national unity: understanding not vengeance, reparation but not retaliation, and humanness not victimization. The nature of the TRC's hearings were intended to achieve those goals; its final report (as Villa-Vicencio and Verwoerd make clear) was shaped with that same intent in mind. Boraine believes that acquiring a series of individual truths can contribute to the healing process, albeit partially.

In contrast to most other truth commissions, the manner in which the idea of a South African commission was advanced as an alternative to a potentially costly and inconclusive war crimes tribunal, the nature of its mandate and procedures, and the character and composition of its members were decided upon democratically. Other commissions were presidentially appointed and were composed (as in the Chilean case) by leading figures from the old regime as well as the new.

In South Africa, civil society played a large role in composing the commission and its mandate; Parliament, not a president or prime minister, authorized the TRC. Its striking structure and many goals were mandated by an act of Parliament. Its committees—Human Rights (the one that held hearings and made most of the headlines), Reparation and Rehabilitation, and Amnesty—and their functions were laid down in the act. So was its public nature, its powers of subpoena (which the TRC used sparingly), and the procedures by which amnesty could be granted by the committee that subsequently developed into a specialized commission of its own and was not expected to conclude its work until the end of 2000.

Amnesty was never intended to be easily accessible. It was available in South Africa for individuals only; applicants were required to make full disclosure during open hearings. A long list of qualifications limited the consideration of amnesty only to those whose motives and objects were political and subject to the approval of, or were committed at the behest of, a political body. Boraine and others argue that amnesty was the price South Africa had to pay to achieve a peaceful transition and to achieve a "limited" form of justice—to obtain a series of revelatory truths for victims and kin of victims. Ntsebeza says, indeed, that there was no other way. Likewise, in Brazil, Rwanda, and other countries that were at one time overwhelmed by atrocity, it may be impracticable on multiple grounds to prosecute. For retributive justice to have worked for victims, evidence would have been needed, and only through the amnesty procedures could that evidence have been developed.

"The really big maggots are beginning to come out from beneath the stones," exclaimed the husband and father of two victims of apartheid letter bombs in Angola.[7] Like so many relatives of victims, he preferred retribution, but he also appreciated that persons like himself would have been unlikely to have learned how and why their loved ones were killed by agents of the old South African state without the availability of amnesty. In these late 1998 and 1999 hearings before the Amnesty Committee of the TRC, several of the more mendacious South African operatives sought indemnity from prosecution in South Africa and, if they could achieve it, protection from extradition to Britain, Angola, and Mozambique.

Demanding truth for amnesty, as did the TRC, is suspect because the confessed guilty go unpunished, and in the case of the killers of Amy Biehl, an American Fulbright student, go free retrospectively.[8] When the TRC's amnesty committee granted amnesty to four ANC activists who had killed a black Bophuthatswanan policeman in 1986, the committee said that the applicants had fulfilled the two main conditions for amnesty: "telling the truth and proving a political motive." But in the case of the two whites jailed for killing Chris Hani, an ANC leader, in 1993, the committee ruled that they had failed to tell the whole truth and had acted without the authority of their political party. They did not have the necessary "political mandate." Jeffrey Benzien, a confessed apartheid torturer who demonstrated his "wet bag" methods to the TRC, was pardoned for several murders. Eugene de Kock, involved in 107 cases of murder, torture, and fraud, and serving a 262-year sentence in a high-security prison, was among the last to plead for amnesty, and an escape from incarceration and future punishment. Even he was given an amnesty for some of his crimes, but remains imprisoned for many others.

"It stinks to high heaven," said a prominent black editor of the amnesty process. "To imagine that after confessing, these people who committed the more horrendous crimes will then be patted on the shoulder by the TRC," he complained. Indeed, the editor went on, "The TRC is a denial of justice. Without justice, how can the victims feel healed?" For Boraine, forgiveness was preferable to trials that would not only have been costly but could have caused further division in society. "There was no victor and vanquished," he reminded. "Is it not a better alternative," he asked, "to deal with the past through the means of a commission which has a limited life . . . and move forward into the future?"[9] "We know the decisions are going to upset a lot of people," a spokesman for the amnesty committee said about rulings that indemnified torturers and killers of Africans, "but we really don't have a choice. It is part of the process of reconciliation."[10]

Truth for amnesty is said to achieve justice through reconciliation—an "enriched form of justice." But is this special pleading? According to Christian Tomuschat, coordinator of Guatemala's commission, "no one can today insure that [the] immense challenge of reconciliation through truth can be met with success. In order to do so, the historic facts must be recognized and assimilated into each individual consciousness and the collective consciousness."[11] If amnesty is allowed, the common conception of justice is subordinated to future-oriented societal moral considerations. Gutmann and Thompson remind us that whatever the claims for an enriched form of justice (e.g., strengthening democratic institutions), there is a moral cost that is significant. It is a cost that the families of Steve Biko and Griffiths Mxenge, murdered by the apartheid regime, have paid. The justice that comes with punishment of perpetrators has been denied them (despite their strenuous protests). Gutmann and Thompson also suggest that a genuinely moral compromise implies no blanket amnesties, a condition that the TRC's Amnesty Committee breached in one notorious decision that was subsequently overturned by South Africa's High Court.[12]

Ronald C. Slye supports amnesty as a tool for increasing both the quantity and the quality of information available about the past and its abuses. The South African example is unusually important, he says, because of the innovative nature of the amnesty procedure introduced by the TRC; Slye calls it the most sophisticated ever undertaken for violations of fundamental international human rights. Previously, most amnesties were granted to a cohort, and without demanding testimony. The TRC offered amnesty only in exchange for full individual revelations. (However, the TRC could not later revoke that amnesty if new information were discovered.)

In the search for truth and for individual rehabilitation, the TRC process, unlike that of earlier commissions, provided many of the advantages of a criminal trial. Indeed, Slye's examination of the TRC proceedings found more participation by the accused than in a typical trial. He also discovered that despite the absence of the highly developed rules of evidence, procedure, and proof that govern trials in a Western setting, the quality and quantity of information collected by the TRC was comparable or superior to that which might have been produced in a courtroom.

Another advantage of the process pioneered by the TRC, unlike earlier truth commissions, is that it provided accountability, and thus permitted the possibility of reconciliation. Applicants for amnesty (there were more than 7,000) had to describe their acts, and those seeking amnesty for the most heinous violations of human rights had to participate in public hearings and submit to questions from victims and victims' families. Amnesty applicants were compelled to accept responsibility for their actions. In Sri Lanka, families and parliament refused to accept the amnesty for truth trade-off, and hence received limited answers to questions about disappearances.

In his essay in this book, Kent Greenawalt also asks, "Is the granting of amnesty . . . an injustice?" If it is, can the truth commission process justify such an injustice? Or is it primarily that such an injustice prevents other and larger injustices? One answer is that there are gains in justice from identifying offenders, even if some go free. More will be learned that way. Like Slye, Greenawalt suggests that relying on a truth commission will deliver more justice than criminal prosecutions. But Greenawalt would not want readers to assume that every society would experience "more healing" by avoiding criminal prosecutions; Greenawalt concludes that murderers and torturers do not deserve amnesty; indeed, amnesty for them is not moral.

Greenawalt reviews the American history of granting amnesties and executive grants of immunity (mistakenly called pardons), and provides a detailed checklist of different bases for amnesties. Although political expedience is not justice, amnesties may be highly political and still serve the ultimate ends of justice. Blanket amnesties are not, however, the best ways to proceed. Moreover, he says, amnesty is not a failure to convict. It is something more, with utilitarian results of importance.

Boraine, along the same line, concludes that the truth commission procedure in South Africa at least "broke" the deathly silence surrounding the grotesque consequences of the apartheid system. The new nation and thousands of individuals achieved an important catharsis. Bringing forth truth about what happened helped to create an open society. In addition to knowledge of specific acts, there was an acknowledgment of individual and group collusion with apartheid. Part of "never again!" is the impossibility, thanks to the TRC, of any South African easily ignoring or dismissing the consequences and atrocities of apartheid. Fortunately, too, the generous amnesty process limited renewed victimization and favored forgiveness, thus contributing to the peace of transitional society, or "stable democratization." That is true restorative justice.

Ntsebeza, in his chapter in this book, also focuses on catharsis. The TRC, he says, restored to victims of gross human rights violations their civil and human dignity. The truth did set victims and kin of victims free. It also destroyed a culture of impunity on the part of perpetrators. The public shaming that came through the open nature of the TRC procedures substituted reasonably well for penal justice. Exposure is punishment. It is a powerful component of accountability.

If the goal of healing individuals and society in posttraumatic situations is elevated morally and practically, Minow suggests, the truth commission method might be better than the prosecutorial. Litigation "is not an ideal form of social action." Trials have procedural pitfalls. If resisting the dehumanizing of victims is a societal objective, trials are inadequate. Hence, for public acknowledgement of what happened and who did what to whom, a truth commission provides a safe and effective setting for explicating the truth. In this context, the trade of amnesty for testimony (with amnesty's ability to encourage the lower-ranking perpetrators to implicate higher-ups) is justifiable.

Trials are assumed to proceed by a strict observance of due process. A serious objection to the truth commission endeavor is its inability to operate according to the canons of that process. The chapter of this book that most fully addresses that issue is Sanford Levinson's. He cites Chief Justice Earl Warren's majority opinion in *Hannah v. Larche* (1957), which approved the less than full due process procedures of the U.S. Civil Rights Commission (despite the dissents of Justices William O. Douglas and Hugo Black, two fierce civil libertarians), and supported the flexible quality of due process. This resembles the position advanced by South African Constitutional Court Justices Richard Goldstone and Albie Sachs at a conference in 1998 in South Africa. They both agreed with Levinson that truth commissions need not operate like trial courts since the objectives of the one differ from the other. Trials might deprive individuals of life, liberty, or property; truth commissions seek to piece together the fabric of the past, and thus can operate best—most effectively—with fairness but without the strict requirements of due process. Truth commissions could accept hearsay, even if they evaluated it critically. Courts could not accept it at all.

Levinson also suggests that the granting of amnesties by truth commissions may be considered a special kind of plea bargain. It absolves a perpetrator of legal liability for terrible acts if he or she spells out fully and accurately the extent of the abuse. By waiving their right to a trial, plea bargainers waive their protection against unfounded accusations, which is what the lack of due process does in a truth commission proceeding. They also forfeit their right to counsel, but in that instance as well as one regarding unfounded allegations, the commissioners themselves can attempt effectively to act to protect the accused as well as the victims. (The Chilean and Sri Lankan commissions refused to name names.)

The use of plea bargaining was extended in the twentieth century in part because of numerical burdens on the judicial process. Hence, if the number of persons potentially prosecutable is too high, a commission method of examination is wise. So is a method that gains the most information (the most truth) with the fewest impediments (but still has safeguards). That is the argument that Levinson presents; it was widely discussed by an array of lawyers and jurists at the 1998 meeting.

There is also the question of trauma as a consequence of a truth commission endeavor. After a detailed assessment of how deep and enduring trauma affects individuals in situations like apartheid, and how psychologists of such trauma believe that sufferers can best recover their lives and senses of self, Minow suggests, in chapter XII, that whereas courtrooms carry memories of repression, hearings before the Human Rights Committee of the TRC did not. They created an atmosphere of trust and safety. The absence of adversariality also assisted. So did the TRC's public ability to acknowledge a victim's pain. (Where the TRC failed, many agree, was in its inability to provide sufficient counseling; the need to help victims overwhelmed all the resources available to the TRC.) The TRC proceedings would have failed to provide restorative justice if they had not been seen to be fair, compassionate, and far-ranging.

Minow believes that truth contributes more to reconciliation than does justice. Similarly, she favors final reports that lay out detailed narratives based on the cumulative testimony of perpetrators and victims alike, not a verdict. Commissions can express the complexity of events; tribunals cannot. This process can restore justice through accountability and societal repair, not retribution.

Reports produced by truth commissions follow a process that is less like those of working historians than are criminal trials. Charles Maier, in his chapter, affirms historians' interest in affixing responsibility, which is also the aim of most trials. Truth commissions are less able than either historians or jurists to reach an aggregate judgment about the context of societal responsibility, concentrating as they do on disclosure and contrition. Historians give protagonists their due by exploring their possible choices. Doing justice and doing history, Maier says, are akin because they produce a narrative that is both synthetic and open to conflicting testimony. The narrative is also meant to be coherent, one that interprets, explains, and records. Trials and historians focus on causality, and build a case based on a

chain of verifiable events. Judges and historians, at their best, display jurispruden-
tial wisdom.

Truth commissions can also collect materials for a narrative. They may help
render what Maier calls weak retributive justice. It may be emancipatory, but a
truth commission inevitably produces less than history. Historians, he predicts,
will use truth commission revelations of coercion and abuses of power, but will
integrate such truth commission findings into a wholly different framework Historians evaluate issues of complicity and a chain of events that extends both temporally and morally beyond that usually considered by truth commissions. History
is rendering justice to the nuanced complexities of different assumptions and
divergent views of a chain of events, and all within a single, unified narrative that
is much more than a compromise. In that sense, historians have an obligation to
render judgment, not to reintegrate a society or attempt to heal victims. It might
be harder to satisfy historians than it is victims and kin who want to know what
happened, or who did what to whom. Historians want much more.

The legislative act that created the TRC committed the commissioners, in
their final report, to "establish as complete a picture as possible—including antecedents, circumstances, factors and context of such violations as well as the perspectives of the victims and the motives and perspectives of the persons responsible
for the commission of the violations."[13] But Villa-Vicencio and Verwoerd, who
helped to write the report, explain that the TRC could hardly provide a complete
picture. A lack of resources limited the commission's staffs' ability fully to investigate a number of barbarities. The TRC was unable to do so in the time available
(three years was long enough to open festering sores but too short to have enabled
the TRC to follow up all of the potential leads its witnesses and its own investigations suggested). Its mandate also confined the commission to an investigation of
a narrow range of violations that had occurred within thirty-four years (not the
whole period of apartheid), and to limit it to those who had suffered gross, not
everyday, abuses.

Villa-Vicencio and Verwoerd see the report as a road map rather than a comprehensive history. It is less an expansion of the truth than a reduction in the
number of lies about apartheid that can be circulated unchallenged.[14] The final
report presents decisions in individual cases based on a balance of probability
(rather than beyond all reasonable doubt), given the evidence offered to the commission and an honest attempt on the part of the commissioners and their staff to
examine that evidence and corroborating material in an unbiased manner. Ultimately, the report balances precariously but precisely between the TRC's responsibility to the public interest and to individuals who may be harmed.

Villa-Vicencio and Verwoerd treat as sacrosanct a commission's obligation to
accept what went wrong in the past, without rationalizations, and why. Equally
sacrosanct is an obligation to promote national unity on the basis of the full
acknowledgment of evil. To fail effectively to acknowledge the extent to which an
individual, a state, or a liberation movement violated the rights of others "is to fail
to give a full account of the past." It would be immoral and irresponsible to
sidestep that challenge.

This book seeks to confront that and many other formidable questions. It does so in multiple iterations, for the contributors accept some but not all of the premises of their colleagues. Where they agree with others' premises, they sometimes argue differently. Since they bring the perspectives and training of political philosophers, political scientists, historians, lawyers, theologians, psychologists, and physicians to bear on the myriad issues that affect conclusions about the truth commission process, it is hardly surprising that they speak with more than one voice. Yet, in composite form, that voice is remarkably supportive of the value of truth commissions for developing truth in postconflict societies. There is less agreement, however, about the possibility of achieving societal reconciliation as a result of truth commission activities. In that regard, several of the authors of this book would not be surprised by the results of public opinion polls: an A. C. Nielsen-Market Research Africa survey reported that two-thirds of the South Africans asked believed that the TRC's investigations had led to a deterioration of race relations. An earlier survey by MarkData found that a majority of whites, coloreds, and Indians, and a third of Africans, believed the TRC to be biased and unfair. The leader of the National Party suggested that the people of South Africa were "further apart than when the Truth Commission started."[15] But the contributors to this book, like their South African colleagues in the meeting at Somerset West, feel that such judgments are premature and situational.

The contributors to this book believe the South African TRC remains the most far-reaching, and the most effective of its genre. Indeed, it is obvious that truth commissions as a whole would have been judged more harshly by this volume's authors if the extraordinary work of the TRC had not been before them. Thus, this volume is about both truth commissions as a genre and the practice of truth commissioning as performed specifically in South Africa. Its conclusions apply to both the general and the specific, particularly since the South African commission's mandate and procedures will become the starting point for all future truth commissions. It is the prescription for the next commissions, whether in the Balkans, in Cyprus, or elsewhere in Africa.

Notes

1. Mary Burton, in summary (16) of Somerset West meeting between the authors of this book, the TRC, and invited South African jurists and academics, May 1998.

A much more pointed critique of the TRC appeared in mid-1999. Anthea Jeffery, in an analysis of the Final Report of the commission, called the work of the TRC fatally flawed. It distorted rather than produced "truth." Her Truth about the Truth Commission (Johannesburg, 1999) argues that the TRC relied too heavily on testimony not given under oath and not subject to rigorous cross-examination. Of the more than 22,000 statements by victims, more than 17,000 were based on hearsay. Moreover, when the report was published, only 102 of the 7,000-plus amnesty applications had proceeded through public hearings and thus been subject to cross-examination. In reviewing several instances of massacres and other atrocities, Jeffery also bases her criticisms on the TRC's rejection of official inquest findings, but without convincing explanation.

2. Archbishop Tutu, statement on Truth and Reconciliation, quoted in the *Boston Globe*, 7 August 1998.

3. Albie Sachs and Leon Wessels, speaking at the Truth v. Justice conference in Somerset West, referred specifically to the postamble to the interim South African constitution. It laid out the compromise that resulted in the TRC. See also the chapters in this book by Ntsebeza and Minow.

4. See Martha Minow's chapter in this book for the argument and the context.

5. Excerpts from the Final Report of the TRC, *New York Times*, 29 October 1998.

6. Albie Sachs, quoted in Alex Boraine and Janet Levy (eds.), *The Healing of a Nation?* (Cape Town, 1995), 103; Sachs, quoted in Alex Boraine, Janet Levy, and Ronel Scheffer (eds.), *Dealing with the Past: Truth and Reconciliation in South Africa* (Cape Town, 1994), 146.

7. Marius Schoon, quoted in the *New York Times*, 9 September 1998.

8. On July 28, 1999, the TRC freed the four African killers of Amy Biehl. They had served three years of their eighteen-year sentence for murder. But the TRC decided that they deserved amnesty since their crime was politically motivated. *Boston Globe*, 29 July 1998.

9. *Boston Globe*, 9 September 1998; *New York Times*, 8 April 1999; *Christian Science Monitor*, 9 July 1999.

10. Mdu Lembede, quoted in "S. African Amnesties Reopen Old Wounds," *Boston Globe*, 20 February 1999.

11. Quoted in "The Atrocity Findings: The Historic Facts Must Be Recognized," *New York Times*, 26 February 1999. One critic of the TRC saw its effects as an attempt to execute, shape, and correct memory as needed "to serve as backbone to the new history of the new nation." Breyten Breytenbach, *Dog Heart: A Memoir* (New York, 1999), 21.

12. In late 1997, the Amnesty Committee of the TRC gave blanket immunity to thirty-seven key officials of the ANC. None had appeared before the committee or explained themselves in public. The court overturned the amnesties in May 1998.

13. Promotion of National Unity and Reconciliation Act, no. 34 (1995), Section 3(1)(A). Technically, the Final Report is an interim report, with a final Final Report meant to be produced in 2000 or 2001, when Amnesty processes conclude.

14. See Michael Ignatieff, "Articles of Faith," *Index on Censorship* V (1996): 113. See also Jeffery's critique, in note 1.

15. The Nielsen-Market Research sample was 2,500 persons. The results were reported and summarized in *Southern African Report*, 31 July 1998, 4.

Grounded Theory

Demola Akinyoade

Demola Akinyoade is an associate professor in Peace and Conflict Studies at Afe Babalola University, Ado-Ekiti (ABUAD), Nigeria. He is a scholar-practitioner with over a decade of experience researching, teaching, and practicing conflict resolution. He is the former head of ABUAD Peace and Conflict Studies Unit and currently coordinates its postgraduate programs in Conflict, Peace, and Strategic Studies. He received his MA and PhD degrees in Peace and Conflict Studies from the University of Ibadan, Nigeria, and postgraduate certificates in Peace Studies/Research from the University of Bradford, United Kingdom, and the University of Oslo, Norway. Akinyoade is also a member of the Grounded Theory Institute.

In this article Akinyoade, provides a clear introduction to the research methodology called grounded theory. Grounded theory moves away from hypothesis testing and, in this way, is a shift from the positivist approaches of Epoch One. In Epoch One, researchers would identify a theory and then test its validity in a variety of contexts (see Paul Collier or David Barash and Charles Webel) to test if the theory would hold. In contrast, grounded researchers head into the field and build the theory out of the data gathered on site rather than aiming to test or prove an idea established outside of the context to be studied. Grounded theory approaches operate from the assumption that knowledge comes from socially constructed meaning. Therefore, knowledge is constructed during, as well as a result of, the research process. Instead of well-formed hypotheses, researchers enter the site with open-ended questions, ideally without assumptions about what the findings could be.

As a result, the conclusions are emergent. Researchers produce knowledge through a process of collecting and coding the data. When more data is collected, the previous thematic divisions are reconsidered. Do the groupings still hold? If not, coding is expanded to include room for new findings. In this model, "outlier" data is less likely to be discounted; moreover, outlining or surprising findings can alter the study midstream or give birth to new theories. Grounded theory also reflects back to Epoch Two in its ability to take into account local concerns and to allow different people to have different truths.

Questions to consider: How does this methodology differ from the statistical methods in Epoch One? Whose voices are now included? How might this method produce different kinds of findings? Why might this be important?

Developing Grounded Theory in Peace and Conflict Research

Demola Akinyoade

Introduction

The whole scientific enterprise that scientists engaged in in their quest to build scientific knowledge about the world can be broadly categorized into two—theory testing and theory building. Theory testing scientific research seeks to verify—confirm or confute the claims of existing scientific theory(ies). Theory building empirical research seeks to develop scientific explanations as to the nature and relationships between concepts. Theory is one of the core things that distinguish scientific knowledge-building endeavors from other endeavors (such as journalism, investigation) that attempt to build knowledge through research. Other important aspects of scientific enterprise are data and the relationship between theory and data in scientific knowledge accumulation. So, theory and empirical data play central roles in scientific research. Peace and Conflict students, scholars and researchers must be well grounded in these basics.

Scientific studies verify (test) or generate (build) theory. Theory-testing or theory verification research tests the scientific propositions of a particular theory (ies) (Punch, 1998). Traditionally, positivist (quantitative) research is theory-testing research with clearly defined theory(ies) prespecified before the empirical work of data collection. Theory building or theory generation research, on the other hand, seeks to end with theory, "developed systematically from the data we have collected." (Punch, 1998, p. 16) Qualitative research has typically been involved in theory generation. As Punch points out, while both quantitative and qualitative approaches can be used for both verification and generation, however, theory generation research is more likely to use the unstructured fieldwork techniques of qualitative approach. Theory verification research is useful in areas or fields where there are many unverified theories. Theory generation on the other hand is more suitable in areas or fields with scanty theories.

With relatively fewer theories developed in the field, when compared to older social science disciplines such as Political Science, Sociology, Psychology, International Studies, Economics, etc., one can convincingly argue that theory generation is suitable in peace and conflict studies. However, as a multidisciplinary and trans-disciplinary field, many theories in those other fields are useful in explaining some of the core field definition and distinctive issues of the field. Nevertheless, there have been repeated calls to build more theories to understand and explain contemporary social issues (Punch, 1998), most especially in Peace and Conflict Studies. The need for theory building is pressing in the field of Peace and Conflict Studies, most especially in Africa because of the relatively young status of the field, the complexity and dynamism of its phenomena of interest require new theories to understand, explain, and predict its realities, which are usually contemporary in nature. In *Introduction: Research and Education Fundamental to Peace and Security*, King and Sall contend that the field of peace and conflict studies is " . . . open to a spectrum of conceptualizations, hypotheses, and theories." (King & Sall, 2007, p. 8) They argue further the need for African peace scholars to develop "endogenous and alternative theories, methodologies, and analyses forged in the crucible of the epistemological, social-political, cultural, and economic conditions of African realities." (University for Peace Africa Programme, 2007, p. 75)

This is the main gap this chapter is responding to. It presents grounded theory (GT) approach as a viable research strategy to generate, develop or build the much needed theory in peace and conflict studies. Starting with a brief discourse on the history of grounded theory, it takes the readers through the philosophy or rationale of the approach, its main features, developing grounded theory, the role of literature in GT, the place of GT in peace and conflict research and the grounded theory analysis. Before concluding, it provides useful information on the Grounded Theory Institute as a platform of grounded theory researcher to help interested readers network and build her capacity in GT.

Needless to say, by presenting a method with an explicit orientation for theory building in this medium, the author believes that any interested reader, irrespective of experience, stage in the academic ladder, gender or even intellectual capacity (as long as she can make sense of this write-up) can build relevant and useful theories to explain certain realities germane to peace and conflict through this method. The time is now for African scholars to take upon themselves the responsibilities of putting forward scientifically sound explanations developed systematically from the data they have collected about the epistemological, social-political, cultural, and economic conditions of African realities. Northern scholars, appreciatively, have done more than enough breastfeeding and spoon-feeding us with theories (viable or otherwise) in explaining our realities to themselves and to us. Now is the time for us to provide scientific explanations of our realities ourselves, and the Grounded theory method is a viable method to do just that. There is no better place to begin to champion this cause than in the field of Peace and Conflict Studies.

Grounded Theory

Grounded theory is the systematic generation of a theory from data acquired by a rigorous research method. Grounded theory is not findings, but rather is an integrated set of conceptual hypotheses. It is just probability statements about relationship between concepts (Glaser, 1998, p. 3)

The first thing to know about GT is that it is not a theory. It is a systematic research method, a strategy. That's the simple but fascinating way Punch (1998) put it. "Why then is it called grounded theory," you may want to ask. The answer is because it is a research method that aims at ending with theory that is grounded in the data. That is, its purpose is to generate theory that is rooted or "grounded" in (the analyses of) its data. Hence, its objective is for collecting and analyzing data is to generate theory. Though simply and beautifully described, GT has its peculiar rationale, philosophy, strategy, and techniques to data collection, sampling, literature and analysis of its data. Espousing these is what this chapter is all about. Once people understand it, they soon realize that grounded theory, like most qualitative research methods, is similar to the natural way we gather knowledge and build explanations (that is, theories) about our world on day-to-day basis. So, in a sense we have all been "grounded theorists" or qualitative researchers one way or the other without recognizing it. However, the chapter shows us not only how to recognize it, but how to consciously practice it, especially in our endeavors to build scientific knowledge about the phenomena of interests.

Brief History of Grounded Theory

GT was discovered in the 1960s through a collaborative work in medical sociology by two sociologists—Barney G. Glaser and Anselm L. Strauss. They studied dying in Californian hospitals and developed and used the constant comparative method (later known as grounded theory). They published their first book *Awareness of Dying* (1965), which was a great success. The second book, *The Discovery of Grounded Theory* (1967) was published in response to many methodological questions that followed *Awareness of Dying*. After this publication, Glaser and Strauss seem to disagree on how to conduct GT. Eleven years later, Glaser published *Theoretical Sensitivity* (1978). Nine years after, Strauss published *Qualitative Analysis for Social Scientists* (1987), followed by a joint publication of Strauss and Corbin *Basics of Qualitative Research: Grounded Theory Procedures and Techniques* (1990). In a bid to correct what he saw as misconceptions of GT presented in Strauss and Corbin's book, Glaser published *Grounded Theory Analysis: Emergence vs. Forcing* in 1992. The 1967 to 1992 publications give the basic history of the development of GT and are also the main publications on methodological statements on GT (Punch, 1998). Glaser has published two more publications—*Examples of Grounded: A Reader* and *More Grounded Theory Methodology: A Reader* critiquing Strauss and Corbin's book. Strauss and Corbin wrote a chapter in *Denzin and Lincoln Handbook* (1994) in which they gave and overview of GT methodology and commented on its emerging nature. Strauss died in 1994 and in 1998, Glaser published another book *Doing Grounded Theory: Issues and Discussions* and dedicated it to Strauss "in remembrance of the journey we started in 1967" and to the "the minus-mentorees throughout the world who are doing." In 1999 Glaser founded a non-profit web-based organization—the Grounded Theory Institute (GTI)—dedicated to his own GT methodology. GTI is an online forum for discussion of GT and publishes a journal—*The Grounded Theory Review*.

GT was developed as a method for the study of complex social behavior and was initially presented as a method of analyzing qualitative data. It thus became associated with qualitative research. Although it arose of the quantitative methods in the sense that it was discovered in a bid to bring the statistical analytic methods (e.g., multivariate analysis) into qualitative data analysis. Therefore, Glaser, especially, has argued that it is applicable to quantitative data as well. However, GT is essentially different from positivist theory-testing methodologies in its view of theory. In positivistic research, existing theory are tested for robustness using empirical data. GT, however, does not force data into pre-existing theory or test theory rather it provides researchers with tools to build and generate theory from data. GT has become a general strategy for research found useful in a variety of research contexts including health research, education, and business, which entails studying high impact dependent variables.

Developing Grounded Theory: Key Concepts in Theory and Practice

The crucial idea in developing a grounded theory (from data collected about a phenomenon or phenomena being investigated) is finding a core category, at a high level of abstraction but grounded in the data, which accounts for what is central in the data (Punch, 1998). This is a three-step process, with the first being finding conceptual categories in the data, which is the first level of abstraction. The second is finding relationships between these conceptual categories, which is the second and higher level of abstraction. And the third is conceptualizing and accounting for these relationships at a higher level of abstraction (Punch, 1998). Its goals, therefore, include formulating concepts, developing hypotheses (from these conceptual ideas) and verifying these hypotheses through constantly comparing concepts developed from data. Hence it involves both inductive and deductive thinking processes. Induction and deduction in grounded theory are done through the twin, essentially simultaneous, activities of abstracting and constant comparison. So, abstracting and constant comparing are essential parts of the core activities in GT. Other core activities and tools of GT include theoretical sampling, theoretical sensitivity, theoretical relevance, and theoretical saturation, coding, identifying core variables and saturation. We will now look at how these activities as carried out when conducting a GT research.

There is need to point out at this juncture that the peculiar relationship of data collection and analysis in GT makes it necessary to discuss data collection and data analysis pari passu when presenting this research method. Hence you will find that many of the processes or steps of GT discussed below are executed concurrently with some others in real life GT research activities.

Theoretical Sampling

One of the unique features of GT is the relationship between data collection and data analyses. In most research methods, qualitative and quantitative alike, data collection is a distinctive stage from data analyses. That is, all relevant data are usually collected before analysis commences. But in GT, data collection and analyses are iterative and continues throughout the lifespan of the research. This means there is a back-and-forth movement between data collection and data analyses. This is the concept of theoretical sampling, in which subsequent data collection is guided by theoretical developments that emerge in the data analysis (Punch, 1998). In GT, a researcher, guided by some initial research questions, collects a sample (usually small) of data, codes and analyses them. The next set of data to be collected (what, whom and where) will be guided by the analysis of the previous data collected. This iterative, back-and-forth movement continues until the researcher has sufficient data to describe what is going on in the context or situation under investigation and until the point when theoretical saturation is reached, which is a point when new data collected are no longer adding new information to what is already known. However, there is the argument that one can never be certain that the categories are saturated since induction has its limits. For instance, fresh data may come along that refute the existing theory. This brings in the concept of theoretical completeness as a twin concept to theoretical saturation. In other words, data collection and analysis continues until the researcher has theoretical explanation for what is happening and its key features. That is, when the theory is able to explain the data fully and satisfactorily.

Hence the key issue in sampling here is not representativeness but rather, of allowing the theory to emerge (Cohen, Manion, & Morrison, 2011). Theoretical relevance, that is, "how the data contribute to the emerging theory and its categories" is a critical criterion in the data collection and sampling process. Theoretical relevance requires a skill—theoretical sensitivity. That is, being sensitive to the theoretical possibilities that all data carry. Theoretical sensitivity is a major emphasis in GT. It requires the analyst opening her thinking about the phenomena being studied. Theoretical sampling is getting more popular in other qualitative methods today. And as Punch (1998) pointed out, it resembles the normal way human beings do every day, when we encounter a puzzling situation. Hence it models the way we have always learned. Theoretical sampling may necessitate reviews or total change of the initial research questions. The essential thing is that data drive the direction of the research.

Coding

Having collected sample data as guided by initial research questions, a researcher go about analyzing the data in order for the analysis to inform the next phase of data collection. This brings us to the next activity in GT research—coding. One needs to know what the generic terms "code" and "coding" mean. Codes are names, tags, or labels. Coding is therefore the process of putting names, tags or labels against pieces of data (Punch, 1998). The data may be individual words, phrases, a whole sentence or more, a part of a picture, and so on. Most of us have coded text without knowing. Highlighting part of a text and tagging it with a label to represent what we consider the central idea is a form of coding. Coding serves as index for the data. The first labels also permit a more advanced coding at the latter stage of the analyses. Hence coding is both the first part of the analysis and part of getting the data ready for subsequent analysis. Coding in qualitative research is different from coding as used in quantitative analysis. In the latter data analysts codes data from questionnaire into symbols amenable to statistical operations/manipulations.

Following the three-stage process of developing grounded theory identified above, there are three general types of codes in GT. These are substantive, theoretical and core codes. Substantive codes are the initial conceptual categories generated from the empirical data. However, they are at a higher abstract level than the data. Theoretical codes connect or show the relationship among the categories identified. They bring the substantive codes together and interconnect them using propositions or hypotheses about the data, which will be integrated in the third stage. The core code is the higher-order conceptualization of theoretical codes which account for these relationships and thus form the basis for theory building. (Punch, 1998). From these three codes come the three coding activities in GT. They are open coding which finds the substantive codes; axial coding or theoretical coding, which uses theoretical codes to connect the main substantive codes; and selective coding which isolates and elaborate the higher-order core category (Punch, 1998). Consequently, in coding in GT, the first, second and their objectives are to identify the substantive codes in the data, the theoretical and the core codes respectively. This corresponds with the first, second and third levels of analysis respectively with increasing levels of abstraction. Coding is thus a central issue in GT. However, these coding are likely to overlap and done simultaneously, rather than as separate sequential activities.

Open coding involves "breaking open" or deconstructing the data into manageable chunks. (This is why it is called open coding.) The point is to understand the phenomenon by opening the theoretical possibilities in the data. It aims at generating abstract conceptual categories more abstract than the data they describe. These can then be used later as building blocks for the theory. It involves exploring the data and breaking it into units to code for meanings, feelings, actions, events and so on (Cohen, Manion, & Morrison, 2011). This leads to creation of new codes and categories and subcategories where necessary. It is not about bringing concepts to the data and no a priori coding scheme is used in open coding. Axial coding (or Glaser's theoretical coding) attempts to link together the categories and codes that were created during open coding. In other words, the theoretical possibilities and categories broken apart by open coding are put together again or interrelated by putting axis (that is, link) through the data, howbeit in conceptually different ways. Axial coding involves exploring codes and examining their interrelationships. Selective coding involves deliberately selecting a core code and making explicit its relationship with other codes in those parts of data. Once selected, the core category becomes the centerpiece of the grounded theory. Selective coding includes writing a "story" that builds on the propositions or integrates categories produced by axial coding. The aim of selective coding is integrating and pulling together the developing analysis. The core category being the central focus around which all other concepts, ideas and categories are integrated.

Abstracting

The inductive process of GT is seen in the way its theory emerges from its data through moving from one level of abstraction to the other. Abstracting (as in most other qualitative analysis) essentially means that some concepts are at higher level of abstraction than other. Punch (1998) gives a useful conceptual framework to depict levels of abstraction in data analysis. This is adapted in Figure 1 below. At the lowest level of abstraction are the indicators, which are at the most concrete, descriptive level. As the label goes, indicators indicate, that is, they show the presence of something. For instance, hostile remarks made by someone can be considered indicators of the concept of aggression in a particular research on aggression. A researcher working on such study may include some other indicators of aggression in order to understand aggression in the given context.

Hence indicators are what qualitative researchers collect in the field in form of data. In abstracting, we infer a concept from an indicator in the data. That is we are going upwards from a piece of empirical data to a more abstract concept (Punch, 1998). A concept has many indicators and the indicators are interchangeable with each other for the purpose of inferring the concept. However, rather than have prespecified concepts and indicators, in GT, emerging indicators from the data lead to the development of concept.

Constant Comparison

Comparison is a central intellectual activity in qualitative analysis. It is at the heart of GT analysis as it assists in theory generation. In fact the co-founders of GT described grounded theory analysis as the "constant comparative method." Comparing is essential in abstracting and coding. At the first level of coding, through comparing different indicators in the data, the analyst come up with more abstract

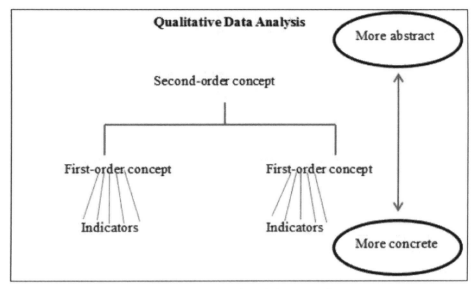

Figure AK.1.   Qualitative Data Analysis. Adapted from Punch, 1988

concepts behind the data. Similarly, at the second stage, it is by comparing categories that we are able to link them. Thus comparison helps in raising the level of abstraction. According to Glaser, constant comparison is the process "by which the properties and categories across the data are compared continuously until no more variation occurs" (1996 cited in Cohen, Manion, & Morrison, 2011, p. 600), that is, until saturation is reached. Theoretical saturation is the aim of constant comparison. It involves using negative, discrepant and disconfirming cases to assist the categories and emergent theory to fit all data by comparing new data with existing data and categories in order for the categories to achieve a perfect fit with the data.

According to Glaser and Strauss (1967, p. 105–13 cit. in Cohen, Manion, & Morrison, 2011, p. 600), constant comparison involves four stages. These are comparing incidents and data that are applicable to each category; integrating these categories and their properties; bounding the theory; and setting out the theory. At the first stage, incidents are coded and compared with former incidents in the same and different groups and with other data in the same category. This involves two processes—unitizing and categorizing. Unitizing involves breaking the narratives into the smallest pieces of information or meaningful text, for example, words, phrases, paragraphs. Categorizing involves bringing together related the unitized text into the same category, devising rules to describe the properties of the categories, and checking for internal consistency within the unitized text within the categories. The second stage is a stage of memoing and further coding, where units being compared change from incidents with incidents to incidents with properties of the category that emerged from previous comparison of incidents. The third stage is a stage of delimitation. The delimitation occurs at the levels of theory and the categories. Major modifications reduce because underlying uniformities and properties are discovered. Theoretical saturation takes place at this stage. The final stage is the stage of writing theory. It occurs when the researcher, having gathered and generated coded data, memos, and a theory, write the theory in full.

To aid reflexivity and accompany constant comparison, the co-founders of GT recommend that memoing should be done simultaneously with constant comparison.

Memoing

"Memos are the theorizing write-up of ideas about substantive codes and their theoretically coded relationships as they emerge during coding, collecting and analyzing data and during memoing" (Glaser, 1998, p. 177). Memoing is the writing down of ideas that occur to the researcher during the process of constant comparison and data analysis. A memo is the write-up of ideas about codes and their relationships as they occur to the analyst while coding (and memoing). It involves writing "ideas, notes, comments, notes on surprising matters, themes or metaphors, reminders, hunches, draft hypotheses, references to literature, diagrams, questions, draft theories, methodological points, personal points, suggestions for further enquiry, etc." (Lempert, 2007, p. 245.; Flick, 2009, p. 434 cited in Cohen, Manion, & Morrison, 2011, p. 600). Memos can be a sentence, a paragraph or a few pages. It expresses the analyst momentary ideas elaborated using certain concepts. Memos could be as varied as the analyst imagination permits. They may be about any part of the data. According to Punch (1998), memos may be "substantive, theoretical, methodological, or even personal." The first two suggest deeper concepts than coding. They Memos are useful throughout the stages of the analysis and even may constitute useful part of the report writing later. Coding and memoing are essential parts of the style of all qualitative data analysis.

Elaborating

As a concept has many indicators, so also, a category has many properties. Elaborating a category is to specify and compare its additional properties by finding additional indicators of the concept until we reach saturation. Elaborating also means developing and examining its variation systematically by specifying, comparing and developing its properties (Punch, 1998).

Grounded Theory Researchers

GT is unique in the sense that it sets aside all preconceived ideas and allows the data themselves to give rise to the theory. This demands certain abilities from the

GT researchers. Glaser (1996) suggests ability to tolerate uncertainty (no preconceived theory), confusion, setbacks (when new data disconfirm emergent theory), to avoid premature formulation of the theory, but through patiently doing constant comparison allow the emergence of the final theory. There is need for openness to the emergent and not forcing data to fit theory by all means. A researcher forces when he lacks the ability to handle confusion and feeling stupid in his study, he argues. GT demands hard work and faithfulness to the rigor of the process. These are summarized as follows:

- Tolerance and openness to data and what is emerging;
- Tolerance of confusion and regression (feeling stupid when the theory does not become immediately obvious);
- Resistance to premature formulation of theory;
- Ability to pay close attention to data;
- Willingness to engage in the process of theory generation rather than theory testing; it is an experiential methodology;
- Ability to work with emergent categories rather than preconceived or received categories (Cohen, Manion, & Morrison, 2011, p. 599).

Evaluating the Grounded Theory

The grounded theory of whatever is being theorized must emerge from the data in an unforced manner and explain the data fully and satisfactorily, that is, account for all the data. There are several criteria against which we can evaluate the adequacy or otherwise of the grounded theory. Those suggested in GT literature include originality, resonance (the data, the phenomenon, the participants" experiences and views), usefulness (for different people and groups, for identifying generic processes, for further research, for advancing the field), workability (practicality and explanatory power), fit with the data, relevance (to the situation, to groups, to researchers, to the field) and modifiability (in light of additional data) (Cohen, Manion, & Morrison, 2011). Glaser and Strauss (1967, p. 237) suggest four key ones. These are:

- The closeness of the fit between the theory and the data;
- How readily understandable the theory is by the laypersons working in the field, that is, that it makes sense to them;
- The ability of the theory to be general to a "multitude of diverse daily situations within the substantive area, not just to a specific types of situation";
- The theory must enable partial control to be exercised over the process and the structures of day-to-day situations that evolve over time, such that the

researcher who is using the theory can have sufficient control of such situations to render it worthwhile to apply the theory to these. (Cohen, Manion, & Morrison, 2011, p. 601)

Criticisms of Grounded Theory Conclusion

With explicit orientation and procedure for theory generation, grounded theory is a viable tool for filling the need for theory-building in Peace and Conflict Research, especially in Africa. It is a complete and rigorous research strategy to develop explanatory theory grounded in the data. It was discovered by Glaser and Strauss in the sixties. Developing grounded theory about phenomena under investigation involves some tools, activities and guiding processes. Central activities in GT are abstracting and constant comparison. Others include theoretical sampling, theoretical sensitivity, theoretical relevance, theoretical saturation, theoretical completeness, coding, memoing, and elaborating. There are criteria for evaluating the adequacy of a grounded theory in theorizing about its phenomena. These are originality, resonance, usefulness, workability, fit with the data, relevance and modifiability. These and similar ones show GT as a rigorous research strategy. GT has been criticized for presuming that it is not informed by other theories whereas data are laden with theories.

Bibliography

Cohen, L., Manion, L., & Morrison, K. (2011). *Research Methods in Education* (7th ed.). Oxon: Routledge.

Glaser, B. G. (1998). *Doing Grounded Theory: Issues and Discussions.* California: Sociology Press.

King, M. E., & Sall, &. E. (2007). *Introduction: Research and Education Fundamental to Peace and Security.* In E. a. McCandless, Peace Research for Africa: critical essays on methodologies (pp. 9–28). Addis Ababa: University for Peace, Africa Programme.

Punch, K. F. (1998). *Introduction to social research: quantitative and qualitative approaches.* London: Sage Publication Ltd.

University for Peace Africa Programme. (2007). Guidelines for Policy and Practice-Relevant Research. In E. McCandless, A. K. Bangura, M. E. King, E. Sall, E. McCandless, A. K. Bangura, M. E. King, & E. Sall (Eds.), *Peace Research for Africa: Critical Essays on Methodology* (pp. 71–82). Addis Ababa, Ethiopia: Author.

Introduction to Ethnography

Brian A. Hoey

Brian Hoey received his PhD in anthropology from the University of Michigan. After a postdoctoral research fellow position with the Alfred P. Sloan Foundation's Center for the Ethnography of Everyday Life, he became an associate professor in the Department of Sociology and Anthropology at Marshall University, where he serves as director for Undergraduate Studies. Using ethnographic and other qualitative methods, he researches personhood and place, migration, narrative identity and life transition, community-building, and environmental health. He conducted a project in Michigan that explored noneconomic, or "lifestyle," migration of downsized corporate workers. He also received a Fulbright to support research in Indonesia studying how people created community in far-flung agrarian settlements within a government relocation program.

As Hoey's piece explains, ethnography is a research methodology that emerged out of the field of anthropology and is now commonly used to describe any kind of qualitative research that is field-based and involves spending significant quantities of time with the people being researched. This time in the field, also sometimes referred to as "participant observation" or "purposeful hanging out," is a core method of ethnography with the aim of describing, interpreting, and developing an understanding of a community, culture, context, or a set of practices. Ethnographers are situated subjectively within the research as opposed to the positivist or quantitative methods in Epoch One, which claimed that researchers were objective. Because of this, researchers using this methodology will locate themselves socially, culturally, politically, racially, and so on within the text to give the reader a clearer understanding of how social and personal identities might inflect interpretations.

Ethnographers might engage in a variety of methods in addition to participant observation (attending cultural events, meetings, family gatherings, etc.), including interviews or informal focus groups, for example. To describe those events and processes in detail, the ethnographer keeps daily field notes. These field notes are critical for creating and understanding or observing the meanings that emerge over time while engaged in the research. In this way, ethnographers spend time reviewing their fields notes and engaging with them to understand not only the events and experiences as described but also to see how one might interpret them differently over time and why. This iterative process keeps ethnographers continuously engaged in the research and challenging their understanding of what they are studying. How a story is told is of important concern for the ethnographer, who is representing the lives of others. Often it is said that it is in the "thick descriptions" offered by ethnographers that we can see ourselves in others. As such, this approach to research is considered to be a bottom-up, emergent process of discovery of patterns that may be theorized. One possible critique of ethnography concerning conflict is that, in this case, the researcher is still representing the voices of the researched or the "Other." In this way, the power structure is not inherently challenged, merely described. The following description of ethnography explains the research process and some of the insights it can offer.

Questions to consider: How might spending time with people in conflict also serve as an intervention? How might people feel about being studied by outsiders? Might there be some challenges if the findings do not lead the researcher to make a favorable analysis of the group they spent so much time studying?

A Simple Introduction to the Practice of Ethnography and Guide to Ethnographic Fieldnotes

Brian A. Hoey

What Is Ethnography?

First, let's review some ideas and set the stage for the primary purpose of this document, which is to set out some useful guidelines for thinking about and doing fieldwork notes from an ethnographic approach.

The term "ethnography" has come to be equated with virtually any qualitative research project where the intent is to provide a detailed, in-depth description of everyday life and practice. This is sometimes referred to as "thick description," which is a term attributed to the anthropologist Clifford Geertz writing on the idea of an interpretive theory of culture in the early 1970s (e.g., see *The Interpretation of Cultures*, first published as a collection in 1973). The use of the term "qualitative" is meant to distinguish this kind of social science research from more "quantitative" or statistically oriented research. The two approaches, i.e., quantitative and qualitative, while often complimentary, ultimately have different aims.

While an ethnographic approach to social research is no longer purely that of the cultural anthropologist, a more precise definition must be rooted in ethnography's disciplinary home of anthropology. Thus, ethnography may be defined as both a qualitative research process and method (one conducts an ethnography) and product (the outcome of this process is an ethnography) whose aim is cultural interpretation. The ethnographer goes beyond reporting events and details of experience. Specifically, he or see attempts to explain how these represent what we might call "webs of meaning" (Geertz again), the cultural constructions, in which we live.

Ethnographers generate understandings of culture through representation of what we call an emic perspective, or what might be described as the 'insider's point of view." The emphasis in this representation is thus on allowing critical categories and meanings to emerge from the ethnographic encounter rather than imposing these from existing models. An etic perspective, by contrast, refers to a more distant, analytical orientation to experience.

An ethnographic understanding is developed through close exploration of several sources of data. Using these data sources as a foundation, the ethnographer relies on a cultural frame of analysis.

Long-term engagement in the field setting or place where the ethnography takes place, is called participant observation. This is perhaps the primary source of ethnographic data. The term represents the dual role of the ethnographer. To develop an understanding of what it is like to live in a setting, the researcher must both become a participant in the life of the setting while also maintaining the stance of an observer, someone who can describe the experience with a measure of what we might call "detachment." Note that this does not mean that ethnographers cannot also become advocates for the people they study. Typically ethnographers spend many months or even years in the places where they conduct their research often forming lasting bonds with people. Due to historical development and disciplinary biases, in the past most ethnographers conducted their research in foreign countries while largely ignoring the potential for work right here at home. This has meant that much of the ethnography done in the United States today is now being done outside of its disciplinary home. Increasing numbers of cultural anthropologists, however, have begun doing fieldwork in the communities where they themselves live and work.

Interviews provide for what might be called "targeted" data collection by asking specific but open-ended questions. There is a great variety of interview styles. Each ethnographer brings his or her own unique approach to the process. Regardless, the emphasis is on allowing the person or persons being interviewed to answer without being limited by pre-defined choices—something which clearly differentiates qualitative from more quantitative or demographic approaches. In most cases, an ethnographic interview looks and feels little different than an everyday conversation and indeed in the course of long-term participant-observation, most conversations are in fact purely spontaneous and without any specific agenda.

Researchers collect other sources of data which depend on the specific nature of the field setting. This may take the form of representative artifacts that embody characteristics of the topic of interest, government reports, and newspaper and magazine articles. Although often not tied to the site of study, secondary academic sources are utilized to "locate" the specific study within an existing body of literature.

Over the past twenty years, interest has grown within anthropology for considering the close relationship between personal history, motivation, and the particulars of ethnographic fieldwork (e.g., see Hoey & Fricke 2007). It is undeniably important to question and understand how these factors have bearing on the construction of theory and conduct of a scholarly life. Personal and professional experiences, together with historical context, lead individual researchers to their own particular methodological and theoretical approaches. This too is an important, even if unacknowledged, source.

Ethnographic fieldwork is shaped by personal and professional identities just as these identities are inevitably shaped by individual experiences while in the field. Unfortunately, the autobiographical dimension of ethnographic research has been downplayed historically if not discounted altogether. This is mostly understandable given a perceived threat to the objectivity expected of legitimate science, to reliability of data, and to integrity of our methodology, if we appear to permit subjectivity to intervene by allowing the ethnographer's encumbered persona to appear instead of adhering to the prescribed role of wholly dispassionate observer.

Most anthropologists today point to Bronislaw Malinowski, author of such landmark ethnographies as *Argonauts of the Western Pacific* (first published in 1922), as a kind of founding father to ethnographic fieldwork, the practice of "participant-observation." Malinowski's early twentieth century ethnographies were written in a voice removed and utterly unrevealing about the nature of the ethnographer and his relationship to people studied. Since Malinowski's time, the personal account of fieldwork has been hidden away in notes and diaries. These "off the record" writings document the tacit impressions and emotional experiences without which we cannot, as ethnographers, fully appreciate and understand the project of our research itself. Malinowski's diaries were published after his death in a revealing autobiographical account of his inner life while in the field (*A Diary in the Strict Sense of the Term*, first published in 1967). We learn in his diaries that, among other details, Malinowski longed to write great novels even as his scientific writing effectively defined the practice of cultural anthropology for much of the twentieth century.

Of many important lessons for anthropologists, Malinowski's diaries hold two especially relevant ones here. First of these is that, at its heart, ethnographic writing is a means of expressing a shared interest among cultural anthropologists for telling stories—stories about what it means to be human. The other is that the explicit professional project of observing, imagining and describing other people need not be incompatible with the implicit personal project of learning about the self. It is the honest truth of fieldwork that these two projects are always implicated in each other. Good ethnography recognizes the transformative nature of fieldwork where as we search for answers to questions about people we may find ourselves in the stories of others. Ethnography should be acknowledged as a mutual product born of the intertwining of the lives of the ethnographer and his or her subjects (e.g., see Hoey 2008).

Fieldnotes

Given that so much of ethnographic fieldwork depends on the researcher's own experience and perspective—i.e., the "I" must be acknowledged—it really does matter where you as that researcher "stand" relative to the process of your own fieldwork and ultimately to the subject of your study. That means not only whether or not you might consider yourself an "insider" or an "outsider" to a group that may be your focus but also the attitudes and/or preconceptions that you bring to that study.

This is true of any science—regardless of whether or not other sciences tend to address the tension between objectivity and subjectivity or ignore it altogether. In any event, it is unavoidably true for ethnographic fieldwork. If you are judgmental in your treatment of your subject, this will affect the product of your work by affecting the process—your capacity to accurately capture the details that become your data, to interpret that data, and to represent the lives of others as well as the account of your fieldwork. That much seems clear.

However, it is more than this. I have found that many students in ethnographic training are reluctant at best and, at times, highly critical of the demands that ethnographic work places on them. Frankly, these students may resent the time and energy it requires. Doing this work can be disruptive to one's everyday life. If you are judgmental of the process itself by being dismissive of the work that you are doing, this can be very harmful as well. It is insidiously distortive and destructive. You need to always be open-minded to allow for possibilities. If you say "nothing happened" then clearly, you've shut off any possibility that there was something there of significance. Do not fall into the trap of not seeing what you have come to take for granted. This is especially hard for those of us who work within our own culture(s) or communities.

Ethnographic fieldwork is, indeed, challenging. It is also immensely rewarding when you allow for that possibility. Keep in mind a few things:

1. While you can and should acknowledge your challenges—e.g., they could become at least some of the "limitations" of your study to be addressed in a report on that research for publication—it isn't a good idea to write in a consistently negative way about the work in which you are engaged.
2. Similarly, it is uncommon to describe either one's field site or the people with whom one works negatively—you may not always enjoy your time, but it is understood that you're expected to do your best to be non-judgmental.

3. It is entirely possible to have a less than stellar ethnographic fieldwork/training experience. This might be measured by how well you are able to collect sufficient data to work with and what conclusions you may be able to draw from that work. It may simply be how well you feel your experience lived up to your own personal or professional expectations or standards. Nevertheless, these experiences may still be analyzed for their potential contribution to a discussion about fieldwork generally—possibility a discourse on methods specifically. Simply stated, we can learn from challenging experience if that experience is examined for insights.

Keep on Writing

Doing ethnography is not at all like doing a research based on books or articles—what is typically referred to as "secondary" research. Although as a student (and even a credentialed scholar) it is possible to neglect writing of the latter sort until the proverbial last minute, such a strategy is a simple recipe for disaster when doing ethnographic fieldwork with the intent to write-up an ethnography—a report or account of that work. Ethnographic fieldwork is primary research and is thus very different what college (and other) students may be used to in secondary research.

Keep something with you at all times in which you can jot down noteworthy observations and impressions. It can be a small (pocket sized) notebook or even just a folded piece of paper. As soon as you can work from these jottings to longer fieldnotes that "flesh out" the bullet points, do so. Some people will nowadays use a small voice recorder to record impressions. If that's your thing, it could work for you. I would still think it necessary to get that information out of the recorder and into some graphical form (e.g., text) so that you can begin to make representations of your experience in the field and to work with that data.

One of the most essential purposes for writing fieldnotes is to—as Geertz would say—turn the events of the moment into an account that can be consulted again (and again) later. That account allows for you to commit what you might not know is important in that moment to memory. It is often the case that you will not know what is important until later. If you don't record things now, they won't be there later. Immediately following from this is the opportunity to recognize patterns. Are there things that people say or do, for example, that appear to suggest consistencies or relationships that are patterned? Does something seem to appear as a "ritual," for example? Remember, "ritual" isn't something far-out and exotic. They happen in voodoo parlors, yes, but they also happen in churches and football stadiums. They're apparent in town meetings and college classrooms. You can find them in the bathroom as well as the bedroom. They're everywhere. Though dated now in some important ways, you may want to take a look at Horace Miner's (1956) article "Body Ritual among the Nacirema" for somewhat timeless insight into how we can make the familiar, unfamiliar.

Normally, ethnographers can spend a good long time (months at least) working in the field so that they can literally discover their purpose through lengthy participant-observation. This is why we refer to ethnographic research as "emergent" or "from the ground up." In most undergraduate courses in ethnographic methods, students should be given a set of training experiences that at least approach what would be typical of the professional ethnographer. In most cases, however, instructors cannot exactly duplicate the full rigors of fieldwork for practical reasons—given that we don't have enough time. Courses should be structured to allow for lots of exploration of the experience of participant-observation and ongoing feedback. This is why it is so important to undergo fieldnote reviews throughout the process of instruction.

So, by now you can see that ethnographers never stop writing. In keeping with the open-mindedness that comes with the approach—in the preliminary stages—ethnographers write about things that interest them generally about their fieldsite. They may even just begin writing about their own lives as a way to raise questions about the world around them.

When a subject is raised—often as a question about a particular group or at least a cultural practice or belief—this begins to give focus and direction to the inquiry and the writing. It is increasingly purposeful. The ethnographer may then spend time discussing in his/her notes how they came to select a given group/community or question/problem/issue. They are writing "thick" descriptions about what is going on with the people in their focused area of inquiry. They are recording what is said, how it is said, where it is said. They are recording their sensory impressions as well as their insights.

Because fieldnotes are where patterns emerge, ethnographers rely extensively on them to provide insight into what qualities may define members in given group: What become essential to understanding group identity, for example? That is to say, ethnographers depend on their fieldnotes to discover, to work toward preliminary understandings, to develop interpretations, and eventually to reach their conclusions. Ethnography, in large part, may be said to take place in and through the fieldnotes. If it isn't in there—as I like to say—you do not have it. As I started this section, rather than waiting until it is time to finish a study and potentially leave a fieldsite, ethnographers are constantly writing-up observations and results, drawing at least tentative conclusions that they will continue to revisit in their fieldwork notes in order that they can continue to refine them. Again, this is an interpretative science in search of meaning. We understand that this meaning is always tentative in some measure so we aim for refinement—as Geertz would say—of debate rather than "the final word" on the subject.

What Sort of Questions Do Ethnographers Ask Themselves?

Basically, our orienting questions are pretty mundane—even journalistic—but they are essential for informing the ongoing process of discovery while in the field. You're just asking yourself: Who; What; Where; When; How; and, Why? Simple stuff, right?

1. Who are key actors in a given context—your defined group, your site, within a putative culture?

2. What happens in a given place and time? What catches your attention? Often we tend to notice what seems "unusual" or "different." That's why working in another culture than our own can be helpful. We tend to notice those things with which we are not familiar. What illustrative occurrences, utterances (what people say), or social interactions would you be able to describe in your fieldnotes that later— when refined in your written account of that fieldwork in a report that will be read—could lead to a keen sense on the part of the reader of the problems or issues that a group faces, to the values that are basic to their behavior, to the quality of the place(s) where they live, work, or play? Are there any keywords that seem to be repeated? What markers of identity are there in this group or at this place? Would the people with whom you are working recognize these markers themselves or does it take an "outsider" to see them as such?

a. While we're on the subject of "what," be sure to ask yourself (as you'll need to answer the question in your final report) what your relationship is to the persons and places in your study. Are you an "insider" or an "outsider?" Explain the relationship and how it changes as you engage in this fieldwork. What drew you to this study?

3. Where do you find the subjects of your study, i.e., the people from whom you are learning? What does this place look like? What does it sound like? Basically, what are your sensory impressions of this place?

4. When do things happen? Do they always happen at this time? Again, we're looking for suggestive patterns. So, do any behaviors, events, or utterances seem to follow a certain order? Are there any non-verbal cues or body language that prompt people to take action in a given situation according to what appears to be some pre-arrangement or understanding?

5. How do things appear to work? That is, are there written rules that people follow? Are there tacit understandings? How do people know how to behave? Is it always the same? Do different "categories" of persons behave differently—young or old, "black" or "white," male or female, newcomer or old-hand?

6. Gradually, as you work through the nuts and bolts, you can begin to think about the larger questions. You start doing this early on because (again) you're trying to develop an understanding. You will need to continue to refine this understanding but start asking things like: Why did this thing happen?

What About after I've Written Notes?

As I have already noted, you should always be conscious of the opportunity to record your fieldwork observations, impressions, and experience. So, you'll be jotting things regularly. After the preliminary notes you take on-the-fly, you should work with them further as soon as you can. Remember, you are processing them. They don't do this by themselves. Fieldnote writing is an interactive, iterative process. You go back and work with and through them. Again, it is leading you toward the interpretations that you must make. Be sure to take time to fill in what may present as "gaps" in your presentation of things in quickly taken notes. At least initially, you are writing for yourself but ultimately you must represent things so that other people can experience—through your account—what you encountered. They need to be able to be there too.

So, that's why you cannot get in the habit of saying "Oh, I remember the details so I don't need to write them down." Imagine that you're describing things to someone in a letter. You're on a trip and writing home to someone you really care about and want to "tell them everything" so that they too can see and understand what's going on. So, you need to have an intimate relationship with your notes. They don't "get done" so that you can forget about them until you look at them later. Ethnography happens through the fieldnotes. You are taking notes on your notes on your notes. You are in a dialog with your notes and with yourself. Think about the following as you go back through, reflect on, and variously process your notes and thus your participant-observations.

1. What are your immediate impressions or responses to the notes that you've previously taken? Do they seem "partial" or "incomplete?" Do you feel like your understanding has changed since you took them? If so, how?
2. Do your notes raise any questions? Are these questions about the subjects of your study? Might they also be about how you're conducting your study? In other words, think not only about who/what you're working with but also about how you're going about your work.
3. Do you need to make any adjustments to your approach? If so, what? How will you go about making those changes and why? What have you learned about the process?
4. What might you need to ask people in order to answer questions raised that you cannot answer on your own based on your observations?
5. Do you find that there are things that you would like to know more about that would require further study? What are these things? What might knowing more about them "do" for you in terms of your emerging project?
6. Much of fieldwork involves serendipity. We unexpectedly find things. We discover. So, there are many "surprises." What surprised you? Why? Listen to your reactions. What was so remarkable about whatever or whoever it was that surprised you?
7. Are there noticeable differences between what you think or believe to be "true" regarding the people and places you are studying and what you are finding that the "locals" or "natives" think or believe about themselves? If so, from where does this difference come? Is it simply the distinction between emic and etic categories, for example? Try to explain the differences—explore them as potential pathways to further insight. Comparison, of many types, if often used to provide the opportunity to learn.
8. How do you think you are perceived/received by the group or in the place where you are working? What is the nature of this relationship? What steps are you taking to assure that you are treating people with respect and that you, yourself, are being treated in this manner? What sort of things do people say and do because of your presence? Sometimes called "reactive effects," these can be very revealing. That is, rather than being "bad" because it suggested that you've caused influence

(or "contaminated" your site), this becomes a form of data. It can be "good," as long as you don't ignore it. Explore it.

Works Cited

Geertz, Clifford. 1973. *The interpretation of cultures: Selected essays*. New York: Basic Books.

Hoey, Brian A. 2008. "American dreaming: Refugees from corporate work seek the good life." Pp. 117–139 in *The changing landscape of work and family in the American middle class: Reports from the field*, edited by E. Rudd and L. Descartes. Lanham, MD: Lexington Books. SEE PDF.

Hoey, Brian A. and Thomas E. Fricke. 2007. "From sweet potatoes to God Almighty: Roy Rappaport on being a hedgehog." *American Ethnologist* 34:581–599. SEE PDF

Malinowski, Bronislaw. 1922. *Argonauts of the western Pacific*. London: Routledge & Sons.

———. 1967. *A Diary in the Strict Sense of the Term*. London: Routledge & K. Paul.

Miner, Horace. 1956. "Body ritual among the Nacirema." *American Anthropologist* 58:503–507.

Shadows of War

Carolyn Nordstrom

Carolyn Nordstrom received her PhD in anthropology from the University of California, Berkeley. Nordstrom moves easily between lecture halls and war zones, studying wars, illegal drug trade, gender relationships, and war profiteering. She has seen battlefields and explored the shadows where diamonds, drugs, and arms are smuggled.

Nordstrom asks, "How do we understand not abstract text-bound definitions of war's violence, but what it lives like, experiences like, tastes, feels, looks, and moves like?" Her article provides some answers to this question. Ethnography offers an approach to research that allows us to move beyond the official discourse of war and perspectives of the leaders. With ethnography, we can explore how war operates in the shadows, those areas not made visible with the methodologies characteristic of Epochs One and Two. By embedding ourselves in the local, we can see how power operates on the ground.

Unlike other methodologies, ethnographic researchers can follow their questions along their natural progression. A full research plan emerges as necessary to answer questions driving the research. With this approach, researchers can understand the pragmatics (i.e., how people trade gems for weapons) as well as "to capture the sight, as well as the smell, feel, taste, and motion of a locale." Researchers observe external behavior as well as explore the dreams, opinions, and doubts of individuals. The materials produced from such studies may be more resonant with what is happening on the ground than more hands-off approaches.

Nordstrom's article does more than explain and advocate for an approach to research; it demonstrates the power of story, intimacy, and narration. Within just a few paragraphs, readers find themselves swept into the riots in Sri Lanka and chatting with a teenage "soldier" in the middle of a bombed-out town in Mozambique. Her rich writing style demonstrates the power of this approach to research.

Questions to consider: What might you better understand after spending months or even years at the site of a conflict rather than conducting a survey? What might be some of the ethical considerations of such research?

Shadows of War

Carolyn Nordstrom

Prologue

> These people say that war is a crocodile which is always hungry. It has
> dishonest eyes and a thrashing tail. It creeps up quietly while you wash
> at the river, while you pound your corn, while you rock your old
> mother in her time of dying.
>
> It is with you always, war, waiting to explode your life and throw
> you down beside a river to die. War wants death, always; war wants to
> quiet your mother's songs. War wants your sorrow.[1]

War is one of those impossible words: it refers to war as a soldier in Sudan
lives it, as a child in Sri Lanka experiences it, as a torture victim in Argentina's
dirty war felt it, as a Greek in Troy died it. A mere three letters covers a sweep of
hundreds of thousands of events across several millennia. How do we understand
so vast a phenomenon while retaining the vibrancy of the lives that constitute it?

There is an image of war that has stuck in my mind for nearly two decades.
It seems to point toward some deep understanding, something that stands just
outside of conscious grasp, or maybe beyond intellectual thought to a more profound conception of . . . what? Not just war, but something that tugs at the heart
of what it means to be human. And in the curious combination that links devastating disasters with the profoundly mundane, this image involves a watermelon
amid some of the worst violence marking recent decades. A Sri Lankan acquaintance and I had traveled to the July 1983 Kataragama religious festival in southeastern Sri Lanka. She is a middle-aged woman from the capital city of Colombo,
a mother with a ready laugh and a maternal charm that holds a bit of impishness.
We had shared a room, and I remember her unpacking her travel bag the first day;
she had a towel, food, and other useful items I had not thought to pack. She
laughingly lectured me: "Carry what you will need."

The 1983 riots in which thousands were killed in seven days broke out the
last night of the festival.[2] No one knew the violence was about to erupt as they
said goodbye to one another and began their journeys home. Almost no one:
curiously, the last two evenings of the festival several of the homeless "mentally
ill" people spoke at length and with great emotion about the impending violence.
One directed his agitated monologue at me, perhaps because I was a foreigner. As
a large crowd gathered around us, he launched into an aggressive explanation of
the cataclysmic violence that was soon to erupt, the blood that would stain the

streets and homes of the country, the screams of pain and anger he could hear, and the ways in which the responsibility for this violence went all the way to my country in cycles of global inequality. The audience around us sought to brush off his belligerent words with a reference to his madness, but a troubling clarity in his speech unsettled all of us.

Just before my traveling companion and I left Kataragama, she found a large watermelon, and bought it to take home to her family. She tried to give me a hug as we parted company to travel to our respective homes and broke out laughing as she juggled her suitcase in one hand and the watermelon in the other.

The bus she took to Colombo arrived at a city overtaken by flames and over-run by mobs. The next time I saw her, she told me of that night:

> We left the Kataragama festival that is meant to put the world together and arrived home to find the world being taken apart. We arrived to a nightmare worse than any the mind could conceive in dream. As we took the bus out of Kataragama, night began to fall, and we were lulled to sleep by the rocking of the bus, the camaraderie of sharing food, and warm memories of the festival. Sometime after midnight as we began to near Colombo, we opened our eyes to a world gone mad. Entire blocks of buildings were in flames, and people broke out of these build-ings aflame themselves. Buses and cars burned in the roads, some with the occupants locked inside. Crowds of people ran in the streets, some shouting and beating people, overturning cars and setting them on fire, attacking homes and businesses . . . others running for safety and for their lives. Nothing made sense. As buses were being stopped, passen-gers being hauled out and killed, and the vehicles firebombed, our bus driver stopped suddenly and turned all of us passengers out onto the street, and drove away. It was nowhere near the bus terminal, and none of us knew where we were.

This fact startles me to this day: I grew up in this city, I know it as home; I know its streets and alleys, its shops and landmarks. I know my way around by a lifetime of knowledge—the pretty wall Mr. Wickramasingham built on this cor-ner, the funny shaped tree in the open field by Mrs. Dharmaratna's shop, the temple my friend took her child to when he fell ill, the movie theatre painted bright blue. But that night, I didn't know where I was, or how to get home. I didn't recognize the city I spent my whole life in. Even that isn't really true: it tore such a cruel wound because I recognized it and I didn't, all at once. Amid the familiar was such horror. Those pretty walls and funny trees, the shops and tem-ples, were in flames or destroyed, the dead and wounded lay there now, and mobs seemed to appear from empty space, overpower all reason, and disappear again, only to be replaced by another just down the road. The police did nothing, or maybe they did too much.

I had all my belongings from my trip with me, my handbag, my wrap, my suitcase, and that large watermelon. I just set my feet moving and tried to find my way home. Every street I turned down seemed as unfamiliar as the last. The horror never stopped. Fires, mobs, beatings, murder. I was exhausted, and my mind could not grasp what it saw. Nothing was clear: not who was killing whom, nor why. Not where it might be safe nor how to get there. Not how to respond nor whom to turn to, and no way of finding out.

I walked for hours. I grew painfully tired, and the things I was carrying seemed to weigh more and more. At some point, I stopped and set my handbag down on the sidewalk and left it there. It just seemed too much to carry. A while later I took my wrap and wiped the sweat and soot off my face, and left the wrap there on someone's fence as I picked up my suitcase and that watermelon and trudged off again in search of my home. Somehow in my mind I thought I'd go back and collect my handbag the next day—I really thought it would just be sitting there where I left it. That's how hard it is to think realistically when everything around you is unrealistic. I left all my identification, my money, everything sitting there on the road while I carried off that heavy unwieldy watermelon with me. Sometime later, it might have been hours or days to my mind, the suitcase became unbearably heavy, and I set that down too and left it. But I never let go of that watermelon. To this day, I can't explain it. But I carried that watermelon all night long through all the chaos and horror, and finally arrived home clutching that darned thing, having left everything else on the road.

You know, my handbag had all my necessities in it: my identification, my money and bank cards, my glasses and licenses. My suitcase had my favorite saris, my daily necessities and medicines, and presents and blessed religious relics for my family. I have always been considered the organized and responsible one of the family. And yet I left all these beside the road and carried home a heavy watermelon through some of the worst rioting imaginable. I will always wonder at that, at the will I had to get home, to keep walking through hell, and to carry a watermelon. How it is we all survive the unbearable.

This is the image that sticks with me: What made my friend drop her bags, with their familial associations and useful documents, in fatigue and terror, but hold on to a watermelon? "Carry what you need," she had said in Kataragama. In the seven days of the rioting, I watched thousands of people act and react to the events at hand, each in his or her own unique way; and hundreds of these people's responses made a strong impression on me. Each story, each behavior I observed during the riots, was a piece of the puzzle, a call to follow the question. But what was the puzzle, what was the question? Perhaps this watermelon is why I study war.

I doubt she would want me to use her real name. I was speaking with her half a world away, and nearly two decades after the Sri Lankan riots. But she would understand the story of the watermelon: she lives in a warzone where one-third of the entire population has been forced to flee their homes, and one-twelfth of the population have lost their lives to war in the last ten years. She had made time in a very busy day to sit and talk with me about the impact of the war on daily life. As the conversation came to an end, I thanked her for her time and asked her if there was anything I could do for her, to reciprocate her kindness.

> Yes, she said, there is. We have tens of thousands of internally displaced
> people in this area who have lost everything to the war. They do any

kind of work to try to make enough to buy food and keep their families alive. This often falls on the women's shoulders: do you know, in most of the camps for the displaced here, the majority of households are headed by a woman? Women and girls scrape together just enough to get some food or goods to sell to make some money to feed their families.

And then you see the police and the military, taking what little these girls and women have. They feel entitled. You see it all the time: a woman will be walking down the street with goods to sell, and the police or the soldiers will just go up and take it.

They have the power, she has nothing now. And she may not make it without that bit to sell—how is she to survive?

What can you do for me? Tell this story. Write about it. Tell the truth of war and what happens to people like these women who stand on the thin line of survival.

For the people standing on that thin line of survival between living and becoming a casualty of war, the impact of these actions is of existential proportions. They may even be cataclysmic. But for most people in the world, these brushes with life, death, and profiteering are largely invisible. They are invisible because militarily, much of war violates human sensibilities; because logistically, the front lines are difficult to document with neutrality; because economically, fortunes are made and lost in less than ethical ways; because politically, power covers its tracks.

The story doesn't end with the women giving up their goods to the police and military. This is just ground zero of the front-line intersections of war and invisible economies that ultimately extend worldwide. Just as these troops demand payment from poor women, so must they pay up the ladder, compensating their commanding officers. And their commanding officers are able to demand far greater goods in their own sphere of work: at the highest levels of power, they may control national concessions over valuable resources, as well as the companies that work the concessions, transport the goods, and oversee the profits. This might be called corruption if it stopped at the national level, but these systems of profit are international. In the shadows, beyond public scrutiny, commanders may partner with international wildcatters who move consumer items, from weapons to cigarettes, into a warzone while moving valuable resources, from diamonds to timber, out to the cosmopolitan centers of the world in less than legal ways.[3] More visibly, they may partner with international state-sponsored vendors to procure expensive weapons and goods—exports that peacetime countries are eager to sell for their own profits, but which rarely match the actual needs of the purchasing country and its war.

Systems of partnership, alliance, coercion, dependency, and outright violation variously mark these transactions, from the poor woman who gives up her only food to the foot soldier all the way to the vast global flows of weapons or resources for hard currency. It is in these intersections that power in its most fundamental sense is forged. In the midst of vast political systems in which riots and wars scar human landscapes and mold global economies, a woman discards her handbags and clutches a watermelon in trying to get home in a city besieged by mobs. This, in total, is the body of war and the hope for peace.

How do we understand, not abstract text-bound definitions of war's violence, but what it lives like, experiences like, tastes, feels, looks, and moves like? Many of the truths of war disappear in unsung deeds and unrecorded acts.[4] "The war tells us: nothing is what it seems. But the war also says: I am the reality, I am the ground under your feet, the certainty that lies beneath all uncertainties."[5] What place do we give to the profound good that beats in the hearts of so many I meet on the front lines that "conventional wisdom" tells us are populated with Hobbesian brutes? At the broadest level these inquiries merge into the question: "What is war?" Or perhaps more accurately, "Why would humans engage in one of the most profoundly unpleasant activities imaginable—one capable of extinguishing humans themselves?"

I soon found that there are no theories of war or—depending on what you are willing to accept as a "theory"—far too many of them. Ask a scholar for an explanation of war, and he or she will most likely snicker at your naiveté in expecting that something so large and poorly defined could even be explained. Ask a non-specialist, however, and you will get any of a dozen explanations, each proffered with utter confidence: it is because of our innate aggressiveness . . . or because of innate male aggressiveness . . . or because of imperialism and greed . . . or overpopulation and a shortage of resources . . . or it is simply a manifestation of unknowable evil. . . . Our understanding of war, it occurred to me, is about as confused and uninformed as theories of disease were roughly 200 years ago.[6]

These questions have led me along a continually unfolding set of inquiries, across several continents, and through two decades of research. After the 1983 Sri Lankan riots I began to study riot phenomena; as the war in Sri Lanka escalated, I went on to research paramilitary, military, and guerrilla warfare. Each inquiry prompted further questions. What happens to women, female guerrillas, children, and healers treating not only war wounds but also entire societies bleeding from assaults on their core institutions and values? How do civilians live their lives on the front lines? Who are the true brokers of war? Of peace? After conducting research in Sri Lanka for a decade, I began comparative work in Southern Africa in 1988, focusing on Mozambique at the height of its war. When Mozambique moved from one of the most destructive wars of the time to a successfully brokered peace, my research explored the "good," as well as the violence, that exists on the front lines and ultimately makes peace possible. In 1996 I began work in Angola, a country in many ways similar to Mozambique, but itself unable to maintain a peace accord until 2002. Violence is defined both by local realities and histories and by internationally forged norms of militarization: a large and well-developed set of networks stretch across the globe and into the most remote battlefield localities to provide everything required by militaries, from weapons to training manuals, food, medicines, tools, and state-of-the-art computers. If war is powerfully shaped by the intersections of individual acts, national histories, and transnational cultures of militarization and economic gain, so too are the more profound questions that attach to studies of war: What is power? Violence? In/humanity? Resolution?

These observations set in motion a new set of research issues: much of this trade passes across boundaries of il/legality. In doing the research for this book, I found these "extra-state" exchange systems—what I here call "shadow" networks—are fundamental to war, and in a profound irony, are central to processes of development, for good or bad. Simultaneously, my research showed that their centrality in world economic and power systems is accompanied by an almost inverse proportion of information on them. As this book will explore, a startlingly large portion of the entire global economy passes through the shadows: 90 percent of Angola's economy; 50 percent of Kenya's, Italy's, and Peru's economies; 40 to 60 percent of Russia's economy; and between 10 and 30 percent of the United States economy enters into extra-state transactions.[7] But a comparable percentage of research and publication does not take place on the non-legal. This of course prompts the question, "Why?"

The repercussions of leaving extra-state realities in the analytical shadows are extensive. Today, trillions of dollars and millions of people circulate around the globe outside of formal legal reckoning. This set of economic and personnel flows ranges from the mundane (the trade in cigarettes and pirated software), through the illicit (gems and timber), to the dangerous (weapons and illegal narcotics).

The trillions generated in these extra-legal financial empires must be laundered to legitimacy, and thus enter global financial markets in uncharted ways. The relative freedom from controls found in warzones and the financial powerhouses found in the cosmopolitan centers of the world combine in ways that tend to merge war and global profiteering.

Complex production, transport, distribution, and consumption systems have emerged to move goods and services through the shadows. Sophisticated banking systems exist to transfer unregulated monies. Highly developed regulatory mechanisms are in place to oversee extra-state trade—from lawyers to conflict resolution specialists. The profits have a substantial impact on the economies of all of the world's countries. And much of this remains invisible to formal state-based accounting systems and theories. We can't, with any accuracy, tell what impact hundreds of billions of dollars worth of illicit weapons gains has on European stock markets; how laundered drug proceeds affect the financial viability of smaller states; how market manipulation of unregulated goods affects interest rates and currency valuations internationally.

Nor, without studying the shadows, can we predict crises such as the Asian market crash in the late 1990s or the September 11, 2001, attack on the United States. The shadows permeate these realms. Extra-state economies are central to the world's power grids.

We have grown used to a world where formal texts on military and economic matters deal only tangentially, if at all, with the extra-state. But this is a dangerous habit: What professional discipline can condone understanding only a part of the scope of its field of inquiry? The consequences of this practice are visible in myriad ways, which the chapters of this book will explore. An example suffices here: The United States intelligence services have taken considerable criticism for not predicting and averting the September 11 attack. But much of what undergirded the assaults took place along shadow channels. The intelligence services, for all their purported interest in the invisible world, function in an epistemological universe that still relies heavily on the classical economic, political, and military texts—texts that take their definitions from the realm of the formal and the state based. If a more developed knowledge of extra-state and extra-legal networks existed, the impending attack—and the activities of those who orchestrated it— would have been more visible. Solutions are predicated on knowing the whole of the problem, not merely the classically visible parts.

. . .

This book follows a very straightforward organizational format: war, extra-state realities, and (the problems of) peace—beginning to end. Each chapter is devoted to a stage along this continuum: the beginnings of political violence; the heights of war and the experiences of violence; the nature of power; the shadowy il/legalities that sustain war; the move toward peace; the impediments to resolution; and the reemergence of shadow powers as a central influence in in/stability, peace, and development on a global scale.

It may be that in the past we could understand a locale solely by focusing our gaze on it. Perhaps not. But today, clearly, locales are not islands surrounded by the vast and churning waters of fluid geographical space. Today humans feel the tug and pull of societal waves generated in regions far afield; they share the currents, even the riptides, that move across vast global stretches. For example, my experiences in Sri Lanka took on greater meaning when I began to do research in Mozambique. When I saw the same cast of characters selling arms, profiteering, and brokering peace in Mozambique as I had in Sri Lanka, I realized that these international players were not necessarily ideologically linked to the causes defining either South Asia or Southern Africa, nor were they necessarily drawn into a national drama for a specific set of reasons unique to this "locale." They were international players. In following the networks brokering war and peace across all distinctions of legal and illegal, I realized that these represent anthropological flows that span the globe both physically and epistemologically—at once dependent on locales and local cultural knowledges but also linking across them.

What, then, is ethnography?

The answer is not the same for everyone. But for me, and for this particular research, ethnography must be able to follow the question. It must be able to capture not only the site, but also the smell, feel, taste, and motion of a locale, of a people that share a common space and intertwined lives. It must be able to grasp at least a fleeting glimpse of the dreams that people carry with them to distant places of world and mind; of the creative imaginary through which people give substance to their thoughts and lives. And quite pragmatically, it must be able to delve into why a soldier pulls the trigger against one human and not another; to illuminate how people suffer the ravages of violence and grieving and still craft humanitarian resistance; to chart the realities of how weapons are traded for diamonds and power, and the lives of those who trade them.

Today, such questions can't be encompassed by studying a single site.[8] The gun that fires the bullet in Mozambique was made in the United States, or Bulgaria, or Brazil, or China. It was traded through a vast network of agents, "advisors," and alliances—all of whom have a say in how the weapon should be used:

who can legitimately be killed (and who cannot, starting with the arms vendors), and how this is all to be justified. Perhaps the weapon was smuggled through the legal world into the shadows, entering another global set of alliances. The soldier who aims the gun aims along years of training, not only on how to kill, but how to draw divisions, hatred, fears, and justifications—a mix of cultural and military lore that has been fed by everything from local grievances through foreign military advisors to global media and music.[9] All of this intersects to shape the lives of everyone involved in war, from the elite decision makers to the youth-soldiers fighting on shifting and hazy front lines.

"We just got a dead Irish Protestant mercenary, you want to see his body?" the fifteen-year-old said as he propped his AK-47 against a tree trunk, sat down next to me, and asked for a cigarette. It was at the height of the war in Mozambique, itself a long way from Europe and the conflicts in Northern Ireland. The boy and I sat in a bombed-out town in the middle of Mozambique, many hundreds of kilometers from the country's capital and cosmopolitan centers. We were, as traditional scholarship would say, in a profoundly "local" setting. "No thanks," I replied, "but how do you know he's a Protestant from Northern Ireland?"

"We looked at his identity papers," the boy said, looking at me as if I were a half-wit. The boy was thin, and dressed only in a pair of tattered shorts and a T-shirt. His gun was strung on an old piece of cloth. He had been press-ganged into joining the military, and had never left his home village region until he walked out as a "soldier" about the time he hit puberty. The boy settled in the sun, and began to talk:

> You know, these white guys are often a whole lot meaner than we are. I mean, we fight and we kill and all, but it's like these white guys think killing is the answer to everything. We have so many white guys, so many foreigners, around; training us, getting mad at us, fighting us, making money from us. Some are OK, I got sent to this training camp faraway, and there were some who were friendly, tried to make sure we got enough to eat, and worked to teach us. People from all over. Got a whole lot of strange ideas, stuff that sometimes' useful, but a lot of times just didn't make a lot of sense, like it was a lot of trouble to do things that way, and dangerous too, I think fighting like that gives them weird ideas about fighting. Bruce Lee, he laughs, now that's who they should send out to train us. That's where it's at. But who knows, it's all beyond trying to guess. Truth is, I don't think a lot of these guys care if we win or lose. We all see them moving on the mines, doing "business." Someone's making a whole lot in this war, and I can tell you, it sure isn't me.

If I were going to understand this war, and this youth's experiences in it, what story would I best follow? I could follow his movements; those of his compatriots and the foreigners he interacted with; the media and movies that shaped his ideas; the war merchants and profiteers from around the world that passed through his life, his country, and its war; the various cultures of militarization that move from warzone to warzone around the world; the vast international systems of economic gain that shape political violence. This "local" youth-soldier was far from "local." The Mozambican war was deeply internationalized. Where does war begin and end?

Ethnography must be able to bring a people and a place to life in the eyes and hearts of those who have not been there. But it must also be able to follow not a place, but "place-less-ness," the flows of a good, an idea, an international military culture, a shadow; of the way these place-less realities intersect and are shaped by associations with other places and other place-less forces. And, as this book will explore in discussing shadow powers, ethnography must be able to illuminate not only a non-place, but also the invisible—that which is rendered non-visible for reasons of power and profit. Power circulates in the corridors of institutions and in the shadows. I will in fact argue that ethnography is an excellent way to study the invisibilities of power—invisibility that is in part constructed by convincing people not to study the shadows, convincing them that the place-less is impossible to situate in study, that it is "out of site." Ethnography gives substance and site to all human endeavor, merely by caring about the day to day of human existence.

In a study such as this, some things must remain in the shadows, unseen. And this in turn requires new considerations of what constitutes ethnography. Anthropology developed as a discipline rooted in fieldwork, and as such it named names and mapped places. In the localized settings in which anthropologists worked, every quote was enmeshed in a web of social relations such that everyone knew who spoke, to whom, and why. It was this "factuality" that lent anthropology an aura of objectivity; and alternatively, the respect of the subject.

But war and the shadows change this equation. Local knowledge is crucial to understanding, yet quoting local informants can mean a death sentence for them. When it comes to massacres, human rights violations, massive corruption, and global profiteering, even situating one's quotes and data in a "locatable" place and person can be dangerous. Academic responsibility here rests in protecting one's sources, not in revealing them.

Traditional scholarship might say that leaving out the names and the places behind the quotes waters down the impact of the research. Having struggled with this question for years now, I have come to disagree. Part of the reason so many aspects of war and extra-state behavior are "invisible" to formal accounting is precisely the problems and dangers of the research: people elect not to publish at all in lieu of endangering their work by asking, and then repeating, the "unspeakable." Perhaps even more important than "naming names and mapping places" at this stage of research into the intersections of war, peace, and shadows is understanding how these systems of human interaction unfold across people's lives and global transactions. The systems of knowledge and action that undergird these realities resonate around the world. Exposing the name of the poor peasant who saw his family murdered will not shed light on the circumstances surrounding that murder—it will merely endanger his life; and exposing the name of the general who is profiteering from war will not illuminate the international networks of extra-legal economies and power—it will merely endanger my ability to return to this field site.

This is not to leave a study hanging in mid-air. The field data presented in my work is all firsthand. In lieu of naming specific names, it sheds light on roles found from one conflict to the next; it maps the flux and flow of violence, shadow powers, and peace-building along connected sites to larger transnational patterns. The quotes throughout this work are from people who populate the immediacy of these realities. In protecting these people and their larger stories, I have given considerable thought as to how to present each story: in some cases I situate it in a locale; in others a region, and in those most sensitive I leave the story sans-locale altogether. When asked to provide more concrete and situated data—the names and places of traditional scholarship—I must respond that endangering those with whom we work endangers the very integrity of our discipline. Weaving together these layers and levels is the best way I know at present to explore, and begin to expose, the visible and invisible realities that attend to war, peace, and shadow powers that are shaping the course of the twenty-first century.

I'll never know why my friend in Sri Lanka left her handbag, wrap, and suitcase in the roadway, yet carried a watermelon as she struggled to get home through the rioting. She says she doubts she will ever figure it out herself. But we speculated about this for months:

> You know, she said, it seems illogical to leave what I might most need in the midst of a'life-threatening night. But, when you think of it, it seems illogical to kill people for an identity: are you Tamil, Sinhalese, Hindu, Muslim, Buddhist? It seems illogical to target people on their jobs and associations, voter registration designations, and location of their homes. My handbag was filled with such "identity": my registrations and designations, licenses and addresses. It just occurred to me: these are like licenses to kill. Leaving my glasses, my keys? Perhaps I just didn't want to see what was going on; and what are keys but an illusion of safety shattered by mobs who just break windows and enter houses? What did I care that night if I broke my window to get into my home? If I had to break in, that would be wonderful, it would mean my house had not been attacked. My suitcase? It was heavy, and when your life is on the line, all those pretty saris and comfortable shoes don't mean a whole lot. But I think it was more: all around me people were looting the goods of the maimed and the murdered, of the burning shops and the deserted houses. What have we humans become, I believe I worried that night, that we will feast on the dead for a television or a trinket? When did we begin to value goods above good? My suitcase, filled with my goods, became heavy in more ways than one. I left those behind. I left behind the presents I bought for my family. Somehow I think they seemed to embody the religious strife that was tearing my country to shreds that night. But that watermelon. It was heavy, and unwieldy, and I can't imagine what I looked like, an old mother struggling down burning streets covered in dirt and ash carrying a large watermelon in her arms. But it was something pure of violence; a present for my family that cost no one their life; something that seemed to

represent sanity and succor in a world gone mad. A watermelon carries its own seeds for the future. Perhaps that is what I was trying to do.

Notes

1. Mattijis van de Port, *Gypsies, Wars, and Other Instances of the Wild: Civilization and Its Discontents in a Serbian Town* (Amsterdam: Amsterdam University Press, 1998), 27.

2. Ibid., 28.

3. Ibid., 103–3.

4. Arthur Redding, *Raids on Human Consciousness: Writing, Anarchism, and Violence* (Columbia: University f South Carolina Press, 1998), 14.

5. Ibid., 34.

6. P. Gaspatini Alves and D. Cipollone, *Curbing Illicit Trafficking in Small Arms and Sensitive Technologies: An Action-Oriented Agenda* (Geneva: United Nations Institute for Disarmament Research, 1998).

7. Karl Maier, *Angola: Promises and Lies* (Rivonio, IL: William Waterman, 1996), 59.

8. For an excellent study of war economies and the politics of the invisible, see Mark Chingono, *The State, Violence, and Development: The Political Economy of War in Mozambique, 1975–1992* (Aldershot, UK: Avebury, 1996), 127.

9. Charles Tilly, "War Making and State Making as Organized Crime," in *Bringing the State Back In*, ed., Peter B. Evans et al. (Cambridge: Cambridge University Press, 1985), 169–91.

Case Study

Sarah Federman

Sarah Federman is an assistant professor of Negotiations and Conflict Management in the College of Public Affairs at the University of Baltimore. Prior to her work in academia, Federman spent more than a decade as a senior global advertising executive, negotiating with companies throughout North America, Europe, the Middle East, Africa, and Asia, including Google, the NFL, Viacom, Expedia, the Discovery Channel, and many of the world's largest advertising agencies. During her professional career, she completed Harvard Business School's Key Executive Program.

Her job transferred her from New York to Paris. One day walking around the city, she saw her own name on a Holocaust memorial wall. She began to explore France's Holocaust history, especially the role of the French National Railways (SNCF). She studied both the war years and the ongoing conflict in the U.S. in France over whether the company has made sufficient amends.

This article describes the SNCF conflict as a case study used to highlight some of the complexities of holding corporate actors accountable for their complicity in mass atrocity. Case studies consider how a particular situation, person, place, or group develops over time. The details of the particular context can be used to demonstrate various theoretical constructs. Case studies can involve qualitative or quantitative data and analysis. The research strategy used by case studies, vis-à-vis methods used in Epoch One, is the focus on particular contexts rather than generating sweeping studies that consider the world over (i.e., the Global Peace Index, or GPI) or make sweeping claims about human nature (Human Needs Theory). Researchers using a case method must define what and who they will study and over what period of time. They must also answer a question: "What is this a case of?" For example, is the SNCF conflict an example of corporations skirting responsibility or of the varied ways people can seek justice over time or of the complex personal and societal needs mass atrocity creates?

Questions to consider: What does a close examination of a particular case make possible? What might be some of the challenges for researchers who use a case study method? How does this research method add to the larger-scale survey methods prevalent in Epoch One approaches?

Genocide Studies and Corporate Social Responsibility

The Contemporary Case of the French National Railways (SNCF)

Sarah Federman

Introduction

The revenues of transnational corporations increasingly exceed the GDPs of some of the countries in which they operate. Wal-Mart's revenue now exceeds the GDP of 170 countries, for example, and the trend is on the rise.[1] The transnational nature of business also means any region with violent outbreaks has large market actors either participating in or suffering from the disruptions of violence—sometimes both. Violent outbreaks in Darfur, for example, cost the Chinese oil industry millions of dollars, as did the violence during the fall of Muammar Gaddafi in Libya. Long-term market actors often have much to lose during violence, but—of course—some profit tremendously in the interim. These relationships are complicated, shifting, and intertwined. This article argues for greater inclusion of market actors in genocide studies both to understand and respond to the complex roles these actors play in both participating in and interrupting mass atrocity.

This article defines market actors as any business, transnational or domestic, of any size and considers questions of both accountability and responsibility. Corporate accountability refers to the amends a market actor attempts in the aftermath of human rights violations. Responsibility refers to the activities and/or the ethos of the company to promote human betterment. The United Nation's Guiding Principles on Business and Human Rights address questions of both responsibility and accountability. The first two guiding principles consider prevention and the third, remedies.[2]

1. States' existing obligations to respect, protect and fulfill human rights and fundamental freedoms;
2. The role of business enterprises as specialized organs of society performing specialized functions, required to comply with all applicable laws and to respect human rights;
3. The need for rights and obligations to be matched to appropriate and effective remedies when breached.[3]

The UN Guiding Principles address States, urging them to oversee business behavior. This article, however, locates the responsibility back in the business enterprise—where many activities and decisions originate.

After making the case for greater development of this intersection between market actors and genocide studies, this article uses the contemporary debates over French National Railways (SNCF-Société Nationale des Chemins de Fer Français)'s role in the transport of deportees towards death camps during World War II as a case study. The purpose of this article is not to condemn or expunge the SNCF, rather to consider how the various iterations of the ongoing conflict highlight many of the contemporary conundrums when we consider corporate complicity in genocide and massive human rights violations. When the Germans occupied France during World War II, they requisitioned the rolling stock of the railroad. The SNCF carried out German requests as well as those required to keep France running. The German demands, which included shipments of soldiers and armaments, also included the order to transport roughly 76,000 mostly foreign-born Jews to the German border where a German driver then took them to Auschwitz. Most deportees suffered during the thirty-six hours that they were packed in merchandise cars with no food, water, light, or sanitation. Current estimates say that only 3,000–5,000 of the original 76,000 Jews transported survived the voyage and the death camps.

After the war, the company went on to become a successful global rail company, bidding for contracts also in the United States where a small, but powerful group of survivors and their lawyers vowed to keep the company out of the country until it paid survivors directly for their losses. Via lawsuits and legislation, the conflict has rolled on for decades. The SNCF's head of Corporate Social Responsibility—Bernard Emsellem—and SNCF America CEO Alain Leray were both tasked with handling the SNCF's response to repeated attacks.

While the question of the company's guilt and innocence is of great interest and the focus of other works, this article considers the SNCF conflict in order to understand how post-conflict treatment of corporations can unfold and the lessons learned from this process.[4] Additionally, deep consideration of the role of market actors requires moving beyond simple binaries of guilt and innocence. Tyranny and mass violence create extreme and complicated contexts in which individuals operate and make moral decisions. At the moment they are made, these decisions may not appear as moral choices or even as decisions. But they can have serious repercussions. To embrace the complexity, this article addresses how victimized individuals sought amends, how the company responded, and how the field currently addresses and/or avoids conundrums relevant to corporate accountability.

The scholarship emerging from the field of corporate social responsibility (CSR) can help genocide studies tackle difficult questions, such as: Where within a business does accountability reside? Are agents, shareholders, or executives responsible? For how long? The field of CSR can also help guide discussions around the ethos of businesses giving rise to policies and behaviors that prohibit or promote life-supporting behavior. In return, genocide studies—and the related field of transitional justice—can help expand CSR beyond labor rights and environmental issues to more fully consider forms of remedies and prevention necessary in the context of mass violence.

Genocide Studies, Transitional Justice, and Market Actors

Traditionally in genocide studies, peace studies, and conflict studies, discussions involving market actors falls into two categories: economic crimes (looking backward) and economic rights (looking forward).[5] Economic crimes range from pillaging, ill-gotten gains, and starvation, to more general accusations of corruption and greed. The second category speaks to the ways in which industry figures into long-standing economic inequality both as a complicit actor and a means of advancing Social, Economic and Cultural (SEC) rights.[6] This article focuses on economic-related crimes.

Historically, genocide studies and related disciplines have sidelined issues of economic crimes. Current discussions remain relatively sparse.[7] Zinaida Miller notes that Ruti Teitel's respected genealogy of transitional justice, for example, only addresses economics as it relates to the widening gap between the rich and poor in the post-Cold War era. Miller says John Elster also treats economics as a separate domain.[8]

In post totalitarian regimes, questions of the ill-gotten gains of individuals—rather than role of corporate entities—dominate economic and business related discussions. In 2005, the UN Convention Against Corruption (UNCAC) declared asset recovery a primary goal, along with establishing corruption as a criminal offense.[9] Within its charter, the International Criminal Court (ICC) has the right to obtain proceeds from ill-gotten gains and use the gains to support victim recovery programs. The new Peruvian government, for example, successfully recovered assets from Peru's former President, Alberto Fujimori and his collaborators, and then used these funds to support reparations and truth seeking programs.[10] Ruben Carranza claims that the field focuses primarily on asset recovery because it is the easiest corruption-related issue to address. However, focus on asset recovery can obscure the powerful role market actors continue to play.

While the post-war SNCF conflict about amends began as fight about the company's complicity in genocide, because of legal lacuna, the most recent lawsuits focus on theft (i.e., ill gotten gains). The April 2015 class action lawsuit filed against the company focuses on items, "illegally, improperly and coercively taken from the ownership or control of an individual during the deportations."[11] This article will consider the treatment of market actors in the field of genocide studies before turning to the SNCF conflict.

The Marginalization of Corporate Accountability

To encourage discussion about market actors, it is helpful to consider what contributes to a general sidelining of these issues. Corporations so powerfully structure culture socially, economically and politically, marginalizing them in conflict work seems dangerous. Proposed scholarly explanations for the marginalization of business in genocide studies include:

1. legal lacunae,
2. development and post-conflict work prefers short-term projects, and
3. power elites and structural forces mask culpability.

A number of scholars note how the structure of international law makes it difficult to discuss the culpability of economic actors in mass atrocity.[12] The ICC has no teeth with which to bite down on corporate giants. The court can only prosecute a natural person not a legal person. Even if the ICC and other criminal courts could try legal persons, the prosecution would have the difficult task of proving the accused entity possessed both a mens rea (guilty mind) and an actus reus (guilty act). The question of whether the corporate consciousness resides solely within the company's agents or exists as something greater than the whole, has vexed scholars for years.[13]

During genocidal periods, enterprises may have only contributed to bodily harm indirectly. This makes ascribing accountability difficult. Enterprises may have transported soldiers, provided fuel, housed monies, or fabricated materials used in combat. What accountability would Hugo Boss' company, for example, have for proudly producing Nazi SS uniforms? In the case of Rwanda, Radio-Television Libre des Mille Collines (RTLMC) was launched by Hutu extremists to foster hate and galvanizing support for the forthcoming genocide. What is the responsibility of this station for its role? These questions remain difficult to answer and as a result the enterprises find themselves largely expunged.

Concerns about Corporate Accountability

Some scholars avoid corporate accountability because they fear it promotes collective guilt, which leads to blame and shame cycles that impede reconciliation and healing.[14] Former U.S. Secretary of State Madeleine Albright, agrees. She believes moving forward requires holding individuals accountable in order to expunge the collective.[15] Lars Waldorf attributes the avoidance of market actors more to the failure of communism and the general decline of the left.[16] This decline led to what Louise Arbour—former UN High Commissioner for Human Rights—calls a "deep ambivalence within justice about social justice."[17] Ruben Carranza believes this ambivalence created resistance within human rights discourse to unite political and civil rights issues with economic ones. Economic issues became taboo. Elie Wiesel observed this taboo. He noted that people often argued that negotiations of ill-held bank accounts distract from the more "noble" work of remembering the dead.[18]

Privileging Easy Success

Short-term "transition" projects with proven models of success take precedence over messy business issues.[19] Transitional justice scholar Lars Waldorf purposefully marginalizes questions of market actors arguing that inclusion could make the field so enormous as to be meaningless.[20] Others express concern that issues of corruption, fraud, and business crime, may be too difficult for the field to disentangle.[21]

Power Elite Obstruct Access

Perhaps the most difficult challenge to accountability for market actors is that powerful elites refuse to allow their financial streams to be interrupted. Structural changes may anger elites upon whom development and peacebuilding depends.[22] After the fall of regimes in Latin America and Eastern Europe, for example, prior leaders and their military supporters retained much power and could reignite violence. It would have been too much, Naomi Roht-Arriaza argues, to prosecute this elite for all their corruption. Trials would have destabilized the state.

Even in peacetime, corporations and their agents create and reinforce power structures that resist accountability. According to Johan Galtung, "when the structure is threatened, those who benefit from structural violence, above all those at the top, will try to preserve the status quo so well geared to protect their interests."[23] France was no exception. For years, French President Mitterrand protected befriended collaborators from legal and political attack. The French Catholic Church and Georges Jean Raymond Pompidou (France's Prime Minister 1962–1968) also sought to preserve the structural elite. Together they pardoned Paul Touvier, a lead French collaborator with the Nazis. Eventually, Touvier became the first convicted in France for crimes against humanity. Prior, Touvier, along with René Bousquet and Maurice Papon (who ran the Vichy police that organized and conducted the round-ups) all had great post-war careers both in government and business.[24]

Most corporate leaders involved in and profiting from Nazi efforts and slave labor largely walked away.[25] Their companies remained intact. The 2nd Military Tribunals conducted by the U.S. military moved to hold a dozen corporate board members held accountable at Nuremberg for their companies' support of the Nazi war effort or various crimes against humanity. While the trials served as a birthplace for corporate liability for crimes against humanity, no corporate mogul served more than eight years in prison. Most went on to build post-war Europe in various capacities.

In spite of this light treatment, these trials served as the beginning of corporate accountability debates. Kevin Jon Heller and other distinguished Nuremberg scholars argue that accountability of legal persons (corporations) first began after the war. Heller and his colleagues pointed to the Allied Control Council, an international body operating in Germany after the war, which held corporations accountable. The work of this council led to the

> dissolution of corporations and the seizure of their assets. Indeed, even before the first Nuremberg trial began, the Allied Control Council had already dissolved a number of German corporations, including most prominently the world's largest chemical corporation Interessengemeinschaft Farbenindustrie Aktiengesellschaft ("I. G. Farben"), and seized their assets.[26]

Heller asserts that the origins of corporate accountability actually reside in Holocaust-implicated companies. The SNCF conflict and other contemporary conflicts offer an opportunity to see how little or much the field has advanced since 1949 when the Council completed its work.

The Resources to Skirt Accountability

Today corporate structures as compared to war-torn World War II companies have even more momentum and means to support the status quo. Many corporations and elites who play large economic roles have political and financial means to prolong and appeal lawsuits, delaying or nullifying payments. Ruben Carranza notes how Pinochet, Marcos, and Suharto all used their stolen assets to stop or limit investigations. More recently, in 2012, a court in Ecuador attempted to hold Chevron accountable for environmental damage since the 1960s. However, the $18 billion settlement has been called unenforceable. The company refuses to pay and the government has no means by which to demand payment.[27] The SNCF used its legal counsel, clout, lobbying, and its relationship to the French government to avoid all direct liability. In 2014, the SNCF spent over $250,000 on U.S. based lobbying efforts related to WWII-related accusations.[28] In contemporary conflicts, lawyers and lobbyists can walk away with significant financial gains.

French National Railways (SNCF) and the Holocaust[29]

The contemporary conflict involving the SNCF provides a rich opportunity to consider corporate accountability in the wake of atrocity. Even though the events occurred over seventy years ago, the case study provides a rich opportunity to see how corporations can skirt legal liability. As noted earlier, this article is not a polemic for or against the legal battles, but rather uses them to demonstrate larger points about corporations' ability to circumvent legal liability, even for participation in the worst crimes.

Created in 1938, the SNCF began as a conglomerate of five major private rail companies operating in France. When they came together, the former private owners retained a 49% share of the company; the state acquired 51%. The company would be considered state-owned but tried under civil law. (This hybrid public-private identity would complicate questions of accountability for decades to come.) At the start of the war, the company boasted 400,000 employees.[30] The 1940 Armistice signed with the Germans placed the railroad's rolling stock under Nazi command. While the SNCF maintained daily operations, the company also transported German soldiers, armaments, livestock, and other goods for a fee. The Germans rarely paid the full amounts billed by the SNCF. Germans also ordered the deportations which SNCF workers, reluctantly or not, carried them out. Almost eighty-thousand Jewish deportees found themselves crammed aboard cattle cars headed towards their death. The SNCF did not plan this annihilation, though—at least in France—the successful deportation of the Jews required the company's participation. Even if the SNCF workers could claim ignorance regarding the destination, the sight of the deportations themselves were a clear massive human rights violation.

A French military policeman who managed the convoy leaving from Gurs— the French internment camp—September 1, 1942 provided the following description:

> In truth, the special train of September 1st was transporting a mixed group of men, of women; of elderly, of sick and wounded were left to their fate once the train had departed. With the exception of those traveling in the two passenger cars, the group was parked on straw, humid with urine. The women were desperate, without hope, to satisfy their natural needs out of the sight of strangers. The site of this train left a powerful and negative impression on the non-Jewish French population who saw it.[31]

Over seventy convoys left France for Auschwitz. Every train reached its destination and no documents yet found indicate direct resistance from the SNCF management.[32] Some post-war accounts by SNCF cheminots (railway workers) indicate concern and sympathy for those crammed into these transports by French police.[33] The transports could not have occurred without the SNCF and the company's ability to resist remains a question. Could more have been done? Are contemporary SNCF executives and shareholders responsible for the inability and/or refusal of its predecessors to successfully resist? What has been the response of other complicit companies?

Though created as a state-owned enterprise in 1938 and then placed under German control during the war, the SNCF liked to think of itself as operating independently.[34] In many ways, the company organized its daily operations. In 1940, Nazis briefly set up a transportation division in Paris and within a month returned all control, except for the costal operations, back to the French. As a result, from 1939 to 1941, the SNCF fulfilled (and billed for) all German requests while retaining majority of control over its operations. The SNCF usually consulted the Vichy government, not the Germans, regarding its activities. During these years, the Germans rarely issued orders but when they did, the SNCF responded unenthusiastically to German involvement in its affairs. December 29, 1942, President Munzer, the Nazi responsible for French rail activity, wrote a letter to the SNCF saying, "The spirit of collaboration within the SNCF leaves something to be desired."[35] The transportation division of over which Munzer presided, issued a number of statements expressing its dismay over the SNCF's lack of willingness to collaborate. The lack of enthusiasm at the executive level became most visible after the German defeat at Stalingrad in February of 1943.[36] The railroad sabotage increased throughout the war, climaxing on D-day and continuing until the liberation of France.

The acts of resistance were vital and required great bravery. There were heroes and many engaged in heroic acts silently. Throughout the war, however, as an organization the disgruntled SNCF cooperated more than it resisted, fulfilling most German orders on time and with relatively little supervision. The Nazis had relatively few Germans to spare to manage the French occupation. A relatively small group of 60,000 German soldiers arrived in France to oversee forty million people. Only 6,000 Nazis monitored 400,000–500,000 SNCF workers. Supervising so many individuals with so few Germans required complicity on many levels. Successful occupation relied on a variety of insiders who become necessary accomplices.[37] Some provided these services fearing the consequences of non-adherence and others, less gloriously, used the occupation to advance their careers or status. Germans demanded complicity with greater intensity as the war went on. The question of whether the SNCF collaborated with or resisted the occupation is a large and complicated subject handled by my dissertation and Ludivine Broch's work.[38] For the scope of this article, the story has been compressed. Ultimately, the SNCF did not like being under the German thumb. There were acts of the resistance among some of the railway workers, but the executives seemed to largely collaborate. Most acts of resistance sought to disrupt the occupying forces rather than to save the deportees. The few attempts on the behalf of those crammed aboard the cattle cars, however, were well remembered and much appreciated.[39] The question of whether the SNCF knew the destination of the cattle cars remains debated. The executives likely knew, though the train drivers who descended at the German border could likely not imagine the death camps at the end of the

line. Deportees themselves could hardly believe the rumors of Jews being inciner-
ated upon arrival. While knowledge of the destination had been limited, clearly
the horrendous conditions were visible to all near the wagons. The screams and
lack of food, air, water, sanitation and space were themselves torture. Even
bystanders, like Edith Thomas, witnessed these conditions. She said,

> I saw a train pass by; at the head of the train, a wagon containing the
> French military police and the German soldiers. Then, came the cattle
> cars, packed. The skinny arms of children clinging to the bars. A hand
> outside flapping like a leaf in a storm. When the train stopped voices
> cried, "Mamma!"[40]

The German occupier ordered the deportations. They mostly determined the
conditions and the SNCF workers carried them out.[41] The company, a complex,
enterprise of almost half a million employees embodied the complexities of France
and the complexities of occupation. On a daily basis, there were moments of
collaboration, resistance, bravery, cowardice, and everything in between. This further complicates the question of accountability. Who is responsible for the
SNCF's role in the deportations? Contemporary executives? The French taxpayer?
And for how long? SNCF executives, engineers, conductors, and others enabled
those trains to depart. As of 2016, all of the involved individuals have passed
away—only questions of accountability remain. The answers are not clear, even
to the survivors. Of the over 80 Holocaust survivors interviewed for this research,
the majority were unsure about whether holding the contemporary company
accountable made any sense.[42] While unsure about what to do with the contemporary company, most agreed that France's moves toward accountability were frus-
tratingly slow.

Post-War France

Immediately after the war, Holocaust victims remained unrecognized as a distinct
group, having suffered persecution as well as war wounds. Of the eighty survivors
interviewed for this research, only a couple boasted more than sixteen-years of age
at the time of the war. Many recalled a postwar home life more brutal than the
war itself. Many had lost families and identities and struggled to find food, money,
education, and any feeling of safety. After surviving Auschwitz, Daniel—age fourteen—recalls approaching the bank to withdraw the little money left by his parents
both murdered in the camp. The bank sent him away explaining the account had
been closed for disuse. "I understood they had their policies," he explained, "but
it was deeply painful to be sent away like that."[43]

The bank held and made use of the assets until the 1990s when the French-
initiated Mattéoli Commission and a U.S. class action lawsuit would return those
assets. Immediately after the war, many found not just their assets frozen, but their
voices too. They were unable to speak freely. At home, they could ask nothing of
their parents and express little of their own suffering. They said people wanted to

move on and with scarce food and jobs; few had time or energy to pursue justice or lick wounds. Survival came first, concerns about justice came later.

In France, however, little by little people started to speak up by recording their memories, requesting archival material, or making claims for lost possessions. Some worked to reveal collaborators or in other ways make sure their experience was included in the collective memory. Time, global events, as well as historical works also helped upend the silence. After forty years, some public archives opened, enabling people to access information about accounts and government activities. Raul Hilburg's *The Destruction of European Jews* (1961), based on German documents, detailed in six volumes the bureaucracy of annihilation. The fall of the Berlin Wall, leading to the end of the Cold War, meant the United States no longer needed Germany and Switzerland to help protect it from the U.S.S.R. Tens of thousands of survivors, many of who lived in the United States, could launch transnational holocaust litigation for stolen assets. French documentarian, Claude Lanzmann, prompted conversation through his nine-hour documentary, Shoah, in which he interviewed the individuals who perpetrated the crimes. France was also shaken by archival work of Robert Paxton and Michael Marrus's archival work, which proved the anti-Semitic policies initiated by France without German interference. With increased voices came additional political trials, compensation programs, and the unleashing of transnational holocaust litigation. During this time, the SNCF found itself in court. (See Table A for related lawsuits)

SNCF Accountability Debate

While the events of the Holocaust date back seventy years, genocide scholars and justice seekers continue to live in the questions the atrocity provoked. Some of those touched by the persecution demand financial compensation. A powerful group of lawyers, legislators, and survivors linking Holocaust injustice to United States regional and high-speed train bids continue to make headlines with their calls for justice. The group fighting the company wants the SNCF to be more transparent regarding its wartime role and to compensate victims before advancing business interests in the United States where it and its subsidiary Keolis bid for contracts.

Since the war, the SNCF's power and reach had increased nationally and internationally. The shift away from coal reduced the need for employees by 50% (now down to 250,000). The SNCF had become and continues to be a world class railway and transport company. The SNCF is a strong competitor against Japanese, German, and other leaders in rail travel. The SNCF's earnings reflect its global strength. In 2013, the company reported its worldwide revenue as 32.2 billion Euros (roughly $44 billion dollars).[44] The company remains a public-private hybrid as it has since its inception. According to Bernard Emsellem, SNCF's head of Corporate Social Responsibility, today France classifies the SNCF as an Etablissement Public Industriel et Commercial (EPIC)—a public establish-ment of industrial and commercial nature. This means the company is still state-owned but can participate in commercial activities normally prohibited by state entities.[45] Holding this global, partially state-owned enterprise legally accountable for Holocaust crimes has proved impossible.

The company's social notoriety also makes it a difficult target. Julius, who lost his parents and siblings in the deportations points out one of the primary reasons, "You are well aware, I am sure, that the subject is very 'delicate.' La SNCF, C'est la France!"[46] The SNCF is France! The company logo closely resembles the French flag and is almost as ubiquitous as the McDonald's sign in the United States. The trains serve as the veins through which nearly every person and product eventually flows. Do these trains bear the responsibility?

The father of Holocaust research Raul Hilberg was not so quick to dismiss the accountability of the individual railway man. He argued in 1976 that these railway workers were "not mindless robots. As intelligent men they were capable of understanding the tenor of their time."[47] Among scholars, his view is not the most common one today. Many site the complexity of the times and the complex-ity of collective accountability. Ralph Steinhardt argues, for example, that corpora-tions cannot be held accountable for the government's poor decisions,

> No one can be held responsible for acts beyond his or her control . . .
> a corporation cannot be held liable for a host government's systemic
> violations of civil, political, and cultural rights, unless the corporation
> contributes to the violation.[48]

Steinhardt, therefore, would likely expunge the SNCF past and present arguing that the SNCF found itself caught up in the government's political com-mitments. In addition to governmental control, the SNCF had its own set of norms and structures that might have made widespread resistance difficult. Vichy historian, Ludivine Broch observed the powerful forces of "hierarchy, obedience, and personal advancement" that existed within the SNCF.[49] Her scholarship sug-gests that cheminot fidelity to the trains and each other superseded any notions of human rights or any larger moral imperative.

Questions of group accountability within the moral framework of an agency remain a much-debated subject. Vichy historian Michael Marrus challenges the accountability Hilberg promoted, saying that it creates a slippery slope, "After the trains, people went on buses," Marrus says,

> So are you going to sue the bus company? What about the postal service
> for notices sent to Jews during the War? . . . Anyone who showed
> any signs of independent activity, anyone who would not discharge the
> requirements of the Reich, was purged.[11]

Marrus claims the consequence of any deviance was death; the price proved too high to expect anyone to rebel. Others argue that the SNCF's affiliation with the Nazis was too loose to ascribe accountability. In 2011, French radio journalist Hervé Gattegno made this bold comparison,

I don't think we can say that SNCF as a company was any more associated with this atrocity than the American airline companies were with the 9/11 attack. And I don't see why SNCF agents today should have to bare [sic] the burden of this terrible past.[51]

Public pressure and lobbying have continued for over ten years, providing ongoing opportunities to discuss these issues. The efforts of the plaintiffs catalyzed a large French settlement—discussed later in the article—and helped the SNCF become a large supporter of Holocaust commemoration in France. The courts, however, remain inaccessible to those trying to ascertain legal liability.

French Lawsuits

This article addresses the challenges of holding market actors legally accountable for participation in atrocity, beginning with the SNCF. For years, in France no one was allowed to even sue the State for Vichy policies. In 1952, the Conseil d'Etat, France's highest administrative court, considered the Epoux Giraud case. The court rejected demands for compensation for victims suffering under the anti-Semitic legislation and deportations policies on the basis that the policies never existed. The court based this ruling on the August 9, 1944, ordinance which declared the Vichy Regime a de facto government and thereby considered all its policies null and void.[52] The state declared this policy while deporting individuals to Auschwitz. Convoy 78, left Lyon two days after the declaration on August 11, 1944, crammed with 650 people (438 men, 12 children, and 200 women). Only in 2002, did the Conseil d'Etat open the possibility of state responsibility. Despite this eventual transformation, no one ever succeeded against the French railway company.

The French cases and the rulings demonstrate some of the difficulties in holding market actors accountable even in countries with established court systems. The high courts had closed its doors to victims for roughly sixty years. When the gates opened, they did so only partially. Claimants had much work ahead of them. Class action lawsuits allow large numbers of people to sue without baring legal fees individually. Class action lawyers often work on contingency fees, meaning they receive payment only if they win the case. Without this system, survivors wanting to sue in France would have to pay their own legal fees without guarantee of regaining lost assets. This also means the court must hear each individual case. For tens of thousands of victims, this could occupy the court for decades. Furthermore, any winnings would only belong to the individual claimant and would not help survivors with similar losses.

In spite of these barriers, several individuals in France, with the means to do so, battled the SNCF for personal and financial reasons. The first lawsuit, *Kurt Werner Schaechter v SNCF* was issued by a survivor who found invoices in the Toulouse archives demonstrating that the SNCF received payment for transports within France. In *Jean-Jacques Fraenkel v SNCF* the *Tribunal de Grande Instance Paris* rejects the case arguing insufficient evidence.

The most infamous French case, that of the Lipietz family, never led to financial compensation, but the legal reasoning used provides insight into how corporate accountability cases may be considered. On November 14, 2001, Alain and Georges Lipietz (son and father, respectively) filed against the French state for their losses related to the deportations. Their lawyer, Rémi Rouquette, advised the plaintiffs to add the SNCF to their claim. Alain Lipietz claims that his father, for whom he launched the suit, had no grudge against the SNCF, but added the company because Rouquette argued the SNCF was a distinct juridical entity, separate from the State and therefore suable.[53] They filed the case in the Administrative Court in Toulouse, citing injuries suffered by Alain's mother, father, and step-father by their arrest by the Gestapo on May 8, 1944, the SNCF trip May 10 and 11 from Toulouse to Paris-Austerlite, and their internment at Drancy from May 11 through August 17, 1944.

Arno Klarsfeld representing the SNCF, also son of renowned French Nazi hunter Serge Klarsfeld, emphasized that the Gestapo organized transport to the Drancy internment camp (not the SNCF) and that Georges Lipietz never took the trip from France to Auschwitz.[54] Arno Klarsfeld's claim suggests that the SNCF had no control over the management of the voyage. Furthermore, if Georges only traveled to Drancy, he did not endure the same transport conditions as the deportees travelling over thirty-six hours to Poland to a death camp. While George was not a willing passenger, his experience was not the grave crime against humanity suffered by over 75,000. Without class action, the SNCF only had to prove that the Lipietz family did not experience immense tragedy. The tragedy of others is irrelevant in the judge's decision.

Post-war lawsuits faced ongoing critiques. One critique is that post-war trials can be so lengthy they limit their impact.[55] Cases can outlive their litigants. The Administrative Court of Toulouse read its decision to a large room of jurists, students, and journalists among others on June 6, 2006, five years after the case was filed and three years after the death of Georges Lipietz. Prosecuting lawyer, Rémi Rouquette made the following statement,

> The Lipietz family did not want to go to Drancy. . . . [T]hey did not buy a ticket to Paris and were not, in effect, customers of the SNCF. So the railway had no business having them on the train. . . . It never did anything, or tried to do anything, to slow down the rhythm of the convoys, even after the Allied landings.[56]

In response, the SNCF's attorney reiterated the argument that the company had no autonomy during the war. He then argued a legal technicality—at the time of these events the company operated under private law. Therefore, any cases against the SNCF for these offenses would need to take place in a civil or criminal court, not an administrative one. This highlights a legal lacuna that makes it hard to convict the company—while a public company, it operates under private law. Private law largely handles individuals, rather than collective entities; in other words, an individual criminal. In this case, the court was faced with a company who no longer employed anyone who perpetrated the crimes. They were all dead.

A Partial Win

Christophe Truilhé, the French government's commissariat, responded with the court's ruling.[57] While France has no statute of limitations on crimes against humanity, this only applies to charges in criminal courts, not administrative courts like this one. The court ruled that the SNCF went beyond the demands of both the Vichy government and the Nazis. The SNCF's autonomy to pursue its financial interests during the war prevented it from being able to argue that the company could not choose the transport conditions. As a result, the State and the SNCF found themselves condemned by the Tribunal of Toulouse for their role in the deportations. The SNCF appealed while the French State paid the beneficiaries €62,000. This was a symbolic win for many and a financial gain for just a few. As mentioned earlier, without class action lawsuits, only those who launch and pay for the lawsuit receive any winnings. The decision did not create a compensation program for others.

SNCF Wins and French Courts Close

In March 2007, the Administrative Court of Bordeaux granted the SNCF the appeal, claiming the SNCF operated according to private law at the time and could not be viewed as executing a public service. Now, the Lipietz family appealed, this time before the Conseil d'Etat (the Supreme Court for administrative cases). The Conseil d'Etat found the SNCF not liable, arguing the company did not have the initiative to deport people. They claimed, however, if the SNCF had to conduct these transports, they surely did not for a minute reflect upon the consequences. In other words, the SNCF was neither a lead resistant nor lead perpetrator. This case, while not resulting in financial compensation, was a major blow to the prevailing narrative that the SNCF played a solely heroic role in the war.[58] This symbolic success unleashed a chorus of demand. Victims felt encouraged by the Lipietz near win they and their descendants filed an estimated 1800 complaints against the SNCF.[59]

By 2009, however, the French courts closed all Holocaust-related cases, corporate and otherwise. The court ruled on *Hoffmann-Glemane v France and SNCF* that while the crimes themselves were incommensurable, pragmatically speaking, there would have to be a financial cap. No more individual cases would be heard. Michael Marrus calls the February 16, 2009, decision the decisive ending to French Holocaust litigation.[60]

Most Vichy historians found this ending acceptable; they believed the SNCF had done what it needed to do. French historian Henry Rousso and Arthur Goldhammer's seminal *The Vichy Syndrome* (first released in 1987) addresses how the French handled Nazi occupation. In his book he coins the famous phrase, "The past that does not pass." Today, over twenty years later, Rousso believes some kind of transition has occurred. He now says, "The past is past. It's not forgotten, but it has finally found its place."[61] His colleagues seem to agree. According to *The New York Times*,

> some French historians and Holocaust experts have called the legal pressure and campaign against the SNCF in the United States uninformed and unfair. They contend that the SNCF has taken on more than its fair share of guilt, given the Nazi occupation of France and the Germans' use of French national institutions as their own.[62]

Michael Marrus, professor emeritus of Holocaust studies at the University of Toronto and leading expert on Vichy France, thinks the SNCF has paid its dues. Marrus finds today's efforts against France misguided. After doing archival work for the SNCF, Marrus said he is "a bit exasperated" by efforts to ban the railway from U.S. government contracts and thinks "these matters should be put to bed." He goes on to say,

> I don't diminish the tragedy or the pain and suffering, but I think at the end of the day, there will never be justice in the sense that most of the perpetrators have died by now and most of the people who suffered directly have died by now, I just don't see any merit in continuing this, especially when [there has been] open acknowledgment and contrition.[63]

Noted French historian Annette Weiviorka agrees with Marrus that the SNCF ought to be absolved,

> The SNCF has largely taken responsibility for its role in the Holocaust. Since the 1990s, the company opened its archives. In all of the train stations, it had an exposition on the deportation. Saying that the company did nothing for commemoration, like certain members of this case are saying, is unlikely. This approach is scandalous.[64]

French historian Georges Ribeill also discredits this conflict against the SNCF. In 2008, Ribeill wrote a fifty-six-page article on the SNCF's role in the deportations for the publication *Historail*. In the article, he considers the invoices produced by Kurt Schaechter in 1992 and the Lipietz family lawsuit "harassment" of the company. After completing his extensive search in the SNCF archives, Ribeill believed that French lawyers were fighting the company with judicial arguments based on little historical founding.[65] The French Jewish leadership shares the sentiment of the courts and Vichy historians that France has appropriately addressed the Holocaust.

The SNCF's successful appeal and the overall closure of the French courts to Holocaust-related litigation thwarted all French legal efforts to hold the company accountable. Litigants turned to the United States where class action lawsuits flourished. One reached out to New York-based lawyer Harriet Tamen known for her work in the mid-1990s challenging the French banks for freezing victim bank accounts.

U.S. Legal Battle

In 2000, Tamen launched the class action lawsuit *SNCF v Abrams et al.* in the District Court for the Eastern District of New York. The court dismisses the complaint by pointing to the SNCF's immunity due to the Foreign Sovereign Immunities Act.[66] The Court of Appeals reinstated the case only to have it dismissed by the Supreme Court in 2005.

The SNCF lawsuits demonstrate the kinds of legal lacuna that allow market actors to skirt around the legal system. The SNCF escaped liability because of its hybrid public-private identity. In the United States, the company positioned itself as part of the French government. In France, the company used its private identity which placed it under private law. In addition to legal loopholes, market actors have greater funds to throw at cases. Tamen took on the case pro bono.

When Courts Fail: Lobbying and Legislation

When courts fail in the United States, lobbying and legislation can be used to mount pressure. Plaintiffs against the company succeeded at this. The SNCF and its subsidiary Keolis bid for a variety of commuter, regional, and high-speed rail contracts. Many of these states have sizable Jewish populations. This helped Tamen and her supporters succeeded in their lobbying efforts. Five states— Virginia, Maryland, New York, California, Florida—drafted legislation to create barriers for the SNCF. The legislation brought the debate national and international attention. As of January 2016, only Maryland has passed a bill. Then-Governor Martin O'Malley signed Maryland House Bill 520, which required the SNCF to digitize its archives before bidding for the MARC (Maryland Area Regional Commuter) contract. The SNCF, the favored company, complied, but ultimately lost the bid—allegedly because the competitor offered a lower bid.

The issue resurfaced in Maryland when the SNCF bid for the Purple Line contract. Joan Carter Conway (D-MD) proposed Maryland House Bill 1326 requiring the SNCF to pay restitution before bidding for the contract the federal government interceded. The U.S. State Department considers the SNCF an extension of the French state. Therefore, any complaints must be handled diplomatically. To make themselves heard, the federal government threatened to withdraw $900 million from the project if Maryland passed the legislation. The bill died.

These state-level scuffles led to bad press and cost the SNCF considerable time and money. The U.S. public is very sympathetic to Holocaust survivors, generally even more so than the French public. These remaining survivors, all children during the war, are now quite elderly and frail. This makes the U.S. public even more sympathetic. A foreign, faceless multi-national train company becomes all too easy to hate. Being a train company in particular makes the SNCF's position doubly challenging. Trains remain arguably the symbol of the Holocaust. Holocaust scholar Raul Hilberg argues that while many organizations

(S.S., industrial enterprises, banks, etc.) contributed the destruction of Jews in Europe, the railroads were "indispensable at its core."[67] He cites Auschwitz's forty-two parallel tracks as an example. While the 50,000 death and work camps differed in their conditions and survival rates, almost all arrived by rail. It remains the one shared experience. While Nazis succeeded in killing hundreds of thousands with bullets, the annihilation of over six million Jews could not have occurred without the railroads transporting them to death camps. Firstly, without railroads, so many Jews and other deportees could not have been taken to the camps. Trucks crammed with victims would not have been able to bring so many people such great distances. Mass atrocity requires massive efficiency—trains provided this.

The Conflict Climax

The pressure exerted by state legislation and national visibility pushed this conflict towards what seems to be the climax, if not the end. On February 6, 2014, the U.S. State Department officially began negotiating with the French government over the issue of the deportees transported on French trains.[68] After months of negotiation, the two countries signed a $60 million settlement at the U.S. State Department in December 2014 to compensate an estimated 2,000 victims and descendants around the world not covered by other French programs.[69] Negotiations had been slowed by debates over how to determine nationality (many lost French nationality due to anti-Semitic legislation), retroactivity, and wording created significant challenges. While the resulting agreement was not about the SNCF, the treaty required the SNCF to donate an additional $5 million for Holocaust related research, commemoration, and programming. As of January 2015, the U.S. State Department is working ardently to distribute funds to survivors before they pass away. Monies issued today are not trivial in sum—$100,000—awarded to deportees not covered by other programs. As many said in interviews, they most needed the money right after the war when they had no parents, homes, or money. For those living today in impoverished conditions, however, this money would greatly impact their comfort in their remaining years. For others it will be largely symbolic and mostly passed on to their children.

The French and U.S. governments, along with the SNCF said they hoped the December 8, 2014, settlement would stop the lawsuits and legislation. Within four months, however, on April 16, 2015—Holocaust Remembrance Day—descendants of deportees filed a class action lawsuit in Chicago attempting to hold the company accountable for theft. The conflict continues, though with far less force than before.

SNCF Amends Making

By the close of 2014, the SNCF had made roughly $10 million in contributions toward commemoration, research, and education.[70] To demonstrate a commitment to transparency, the company opened its archives and commissioned independent research on its history. The company has also issued several formal apologies. As a result of these efforts, the French Jewish leadership now considers the SNCF a partner in Holocaust commemoration and memory. National Jewish groups in the United States—the Anti-Defamation League and the American Jewish Congress—also consider the SNCF as having paid its dues. Some smaller Jewish organizations throughout the United States, a small group of survivors, their lawyers and legislators claim that without direct restitution such efforts remain insufficient. With the courts closed, they used state power to exert pressure on the company.

The SNCF Conflict: Lessons Learned

For scholars, the SNCF conflict illuminates many of the issues common across market actors. The conflict raises the question of who is accountable and for how long. The conflict also demonstrates the kind of legal lacunae making legal liability difficult to establish, even if culpability is clear. The economic power of corporations to handle the legal attacks also creates an unfair fight, especially in France where litigants had to pay their own legal fees. (Europe has begun to allow class action lawsuits, which may make corporate accountability cases largely more likely and more effective.) Without legal means to fight the company, victims used social pressure to advocate for transparency, compensation, and an apology.

For executives struggling with violations of their predecessors, the SNCF conflict also provides some learning opportunities. In *Moral Repair*, Walker claims accountable entities must accept a certain amount this hostility and indignation, but stop short of letting themselves become a scapegoat.[71] Corporations more often could serve as an important vehicle through which injured parties can work out their justified rage. Keeping corporations out of the discussion might remove important contexts through which justice can be deliberated and agreed upon. Corporations may struggle, however, to prevent themselves from becoming a scapegoat or caught in double-binds. When the SNCF apologized, for example, some rejected the apology, believing it to be motivated by business interests. If the company did not apologize, however, its management would be considered cold and heartless. This double-bind is known as "damned if you do damned if you don't."[72] Other formerly complicit actors will also face this conundrum. Still, knowing this may occur can help them think through how they might address victims' concerns about sincerity.

The SNCF's public-private identity also makes this a useful case. In many post-conflict contexts, the largest industries are tied into governments (legally or through corruption). Even if not literally connected, many governments want and need large corporate entities to generate wealth and provide jobs. Governments can be protective of national industries. The United National Guiding Principles offers guidance on how governments can respond to market actors complicit in human rights violations. The SNCF conflict fought the conflict largely on its own for several decades until the State stepped in and led negotiations. Those fighting the company wanted the SNCF to pay, not the State. This had symbolic importance for them. Even if legally considered state-owned, some businesses may need to make contributions from their own coffers to provide victims the acknowledgement they require. Direct payment to survivors provides public admission of the harm and suggests it will not be repeated. If the State simply pays, it seems as if the complicit entity has made weaker promises about changing future behavior.

Finally, practitioners working in the aftermath of conflict will benefit by noting the public strength of victims' voices. U.S. based Holocaust survivors have political and economic power. U.S. public sympathy for the survivors enabled those challenging the company to win support in many states. This is often not the case. In most post-conflict contexts, survivors lack the power and voice to challenge large corporate entities, especially ones protected by the State. Victims of the 1965 genocide in Indonesia, for example, still have far less power and support for any claims. Some of those complicit in the genocide are still in power. The government has not formally recognized the genocide and innocent individuals are still barred from various government positions because of unsubstantiated claims that they were enemies of the state in the 1960s. Without public recognition of the victims, public sympathy cannot be easily expressed and pressure cannot be exerted. In contexts where victims lack strong public legitimacy and recognition, additional outside support and sponsorship might be required.

The Genealogy of CSR: Primed for Human Rights Dialogues

While the SNCF conflict became vitriolic, the relationship between business and development, peacebuilding and/or genocide prevention does not always have to be contentious. Corporate social responsibility (CSR) literature could help scholars find productive ways to engage these paradoxically ubiquitous yet hard to access entities. CSR, like transitional justice, emerged in the wake of World War II and now offers increasingly sophisticated frameworks that might be of interest to the field. After World War II, Howard Bowen and F. Earnest Johnson's "Social Responsibility of the Businessman" introduced the notion that business should improve American social and economic life basing his argument on Christian ethics.[73] Until the late 1970s, however, the business community mocked corporate social responsibility.[74] Milton Friedman sharply dismissed the field as anti-free market, claiming the concept placed an unfair burden on shareholders and executives.[75] Moreover, Friedman and others have expressed the concern that this turn toward corporate social responsibility is at odds with the shareholder primacy principle.[76] This principle states, that companies must first and foremost operate on behalf of the shareholders. Friedman argued to place social good before the needs of the shareholder who invests in the company upends the whole free market mechanism. Many agreed with Friedman that CSR and most business ethics programs undercut the underpinnings of business.[77]

In spite of these concerns, by the late-1990s, the term became ubiquitous. Business scholars succeeded in developing models that more convincingly coupled profits with CSR. This peaked the interest of the business community, which faced an increasingly savvy and vocal consumer base that commented on everything from labor practices to the environmental impact of production. The development field also began engaging more deeply with corporations. The World Bank and United Nations authored CSR guidelines and dedicated departments to CSR. John Ruggie's work contributed to the formulation of UN Global Compact, inviting businesses into human rights dialogues with the United Nations.[78]

Leveraging Corporate Interests

CSR literature has proliferated beyond what this narrow introduction can fully present; however, the following section addresses several areas of special interest to the field genocide studies. The increased coupling of CSR with corporate financial performance (CFP) can assist those looking to gain leverage over companies operating in fragile post-conflict states. Threats to profit provide leverage in many Holocaust-related settlements. Stuart Eizenstat, for example, claims the French, German, Swiss, and Austrian banks settled World War II cases because shareholders found the case too costly, not because of conscience.[79] Playing hardball with corporations threatens their bottom line.

Reputation can also be used as leverage when working with corporations. Better understandings of reputation as a motivating factor could help practitioners skillfully include business in post-conflict processes. The SNCF has used lobbying and other means to improve its poor image in the United States. Their opponents have done the same. The national and international press reports on its Holocaust history have severely challenged its reputation in the United States. This branding problem continues to vex and exhaust current executives who are wrapped up in the challenges of competing in an international market. For public companies, poor reputations can impact stock prices. Deborah Sparr argues that the proliferation of the Internet has amplified the spotlight effect. People watch what companies do and hold them accountable for their actions impacting the behavior of companies.[80] Reputation is powerful. It is far easier to improve a neutral reputation than to turnaround a tarnished one. Just ask the SNCF.

CSR and Genocide Studies: The Time is Right

New CSR models offer some tantalizing places to start. Thomas Jones and Michael Porter advanced theories linking CSR and CFP through the now popularized stakeholder theory and the strategic philanthropy model.[81] Michael Porter believes that corporate aims do not inherently work against human rights. He argues that business has the moral obligation and commitment to develop healthy long-term business/society relationships that promote sustainability, transparency, and increase dialogues with citizens and activists. Other CSR theories could also provide a better bridge between market actors and genocide scholars and related disciplines. In 2002, Christine Parker advanced the idea of a democratically self-regulating "open corporation" as a means of advancing corporate accountability. This model promotes corporate independence while challenging the corporation to alter its internal norms and practices to avoid human rights violations. Corporations can do this, she believes, through "the marriage of management, democracy and law."[82] This scholarship supports, in the words of Harvard University's Kennedy School CSR Initiative, the "public contribution of private enterprise."[83]

Without this overlay with CSR, practitioners and scholars may feel as if they are trying to hold back giants with rubber bands or unravel hopelessly enormous knots of corruption. Natural synergies are possible by aligning CSR business interest models with the interests of peace, justice, truth, and freedom. At the same time, CSR would benefit from the overlay of genocide studies. The majority of this scholarship currently concerns itself with environmental issues and labor rights issues.

The SNCF's involvement in restitution, commemoration, apologies, education, research, and dialogues point to many ways corporations can be involved. My dealings with the company, specifically, their openness to my research makes me think they might be willing to work on other related projects. Perhaps the company's efforts could turn toward addressing rising anti-Semitism and barbarism in France and throughout Europe.

Conclusion

Those who become most visible in the aftermath of atrocity are not necessarily the most culpable. This article emphasizes the cost of permitting market actors to escape accountability simply because their wealth and size may enable them to hide their activities. Legal lacunae also make accountability challenging. Beyond accountability, market actors can become significant allies in failing societies, offering jobs, stability, and growth. By uniting CSR and genocide studies positions corporations can be seen as both part of the problem and part of the solution. Market actors are participants in a society and like everyone else play complicated roles as both perpetrator and even victim, often losing out when violence strikes. This is as much during the atrocity as after. Some harbor stolen funds or benefit from enrichment due to enslaved labor. Market actors can also fund post-conflict restitution and commemorative programs as well as provide needed jobs. To consider them solely perpetrator or victim betrays the truth of what happened and cuts of important areas of discourse.

The SNCF conflict demonstrates the ways in which some try to hold corporate actors accountable even seventy years into the aftermath. The legal lacuna that provides SNCF impunity provides insight into the kinds of mechanisms protecting others. Lobbying and legislation demonstrate the power of local voice in the United States. Yet, this can only occur in a government with legislators who are not protecting business interests and in a society where victims have voice. This is usually not the case. Most victims still struggle for public legitimacy or what the French call reconnaissance. This is true for Armenians, Indonesians, and many others. The market actors complicit in genocides will likely continue to march along unimpeded. The sidelining of market actors also blinds the field to allies. In South Sudan, for example, China's oil interests make them a partner for peace. They have sent troops to the UN Peacekeeping force and make public statements to demand a cessation of violent outbreaks.

Corporations are here to stay. Market actors become increasingly important. To neglect their role is to neglect the reality in which these atrocities take place.

Notes

1. Steven Coll, interview by Amy Goodman, *Democracy Now*, May 4, 2012.

2. The UN term "remedy" suggests that the problem can be fixed. In the cases discussed in this article, the harm is irreparable and cannot be remedied as a case of poison ivy might be. Instead, this article refers to responding to human rights violations rather than providing remedies.

3. John Ruggie, Guiding Principles on Business and Human Rights: Implementing the United Nations "Protect, Respect, and Remedy" Framework (New York and Geneva: United Nations Human Rights, 2011), 1. Sarah Federman, "Genocide Studies and Corporate Social Responsibility: The Contemporary Case of the French National Railways (SNCF)" *Genocide Studies and Prevention* 11, 2 (2017): 13–35. ©2017 Genocide Studies and Prevention. http://doi.orq/10.5038/1911-9933.11.2.1390

4. For more information on the SNCF's complicity during WWII please see: Sarah Federman, Aller Simple (One-Way Ticket) Corporate Accountability for Mass Atrocity: A Study of the French National Railroads. Dissertation. George Mason University, 2015; and Ludivine Broch, *Ordinary Workers, Vichy and the Holocaust: French Railwaymen and the Second World War* (Cambridge, UK: Cambridge University Press, 2016).

5. Zinaida Miller, "Effects of Invisibility: In Search of the 'Economic' in Transitional Justice," *International Journal of Transitional Justice* 2, no. 3 (2008), 266–291. See also Wendy Lambourne, "Transitional Justice and Peacebuilding after Mass Violence," *International Journal of Transitional Justice* 3, no. 1 (2009), 28–48.

6. SEC rights include the right to education, housing, and health. The International Covenant on Economic, Social and Cultural Rights (ICESCR) serves as the international legal guideline for these rights. These rights address questions of access, but not necessarily structural factors.

7. Ruben Carranza, "Plunder and Pain: Should Transitional Justice Engage with Corruption and Economic Crimes?" *International Journal of Transitional Justice* 2, no. 3 (2008), 310–330. See also Miller, *Effects of Invisibility*. Louise Arbour, "Economic and Social Justice for Societies in Transition," *New York University Journal of International Law and Politics*, 40, 1 (2007), 4; Ismael Muvingi, "Sitting on Powder Kegs: Socioeconomic Rights in Transitional Societies," *International Journal of Transitional Justice* 3, no. 2 (2009), 163–182; Hugo Van der Merwe and Audrey R. Chapman, Assessing the Impact of

Transitional Justice: Challenges for Empirical Research (Washington, DC: United States Institute of Peace, 2008); R. L. Nagy, "The Scope and Bounds of Transitional Justice and the Canadian Truth and Reconciliation Commission," *International Journal of Transitional Justice* 7, no. 1 (2012), 52–73; E. F. Drexler "Fatal Knowledge: The Social and Political Legacies of Collaboration and Betrayal in Timor-Leste," *International Journal of Transitional Justice* 7, no. 1 (2013), 74–94; Lauren Marie Balasco, "The Transitions of Transitional Justice: Mapping the Waves from Promise to Practice," *Journal of Human Rights* 12, no. 2 (2013), 19–-216; Kora Andrieu, "Dealing With a 'New' Grievance: Should Anticorruption Be Part of the Transitional Justice Agenda?" *Journal of Human Rights* 11, no. 4 (2012), 537–557; Tricia D. Olsen, Andrew G. Reiter, and Eric Wiebelhaus-Brahm, "Taking Stock: Transitional Justice and Market Effects in Latin America," *Journal of Human Rights* 10, no. 4 (2011), 521–543.

8. Miller, Effects of Invisibility, 266–291.

9. United Convention Against Corruption, UN General Assembly Resolution A/RES/58/4. Implemented 14 December 2005. Examples of ill-gotten gains include Augusto José Ramón Pinochet who had multiple offshore accounts, Sani Abacha from Nigeria amassed four billion dollars in assets, the DRC's Mubuto Sese Seko collected an estimated twelve billion dollars, and Indonesia's Suharto hoarded nine billion dollars in assets. See Carranza, *Plunder and Pain*. The U.S. Alien Tort Statute (ATS) from 1789 was enacted in the in 2004 trial against the Marcos family in the Philippines (*Hilao v. Estate of Ferdinand Marcos*) regarding their billion-dollar estate. Most of embezzlement remains at large.

10. Carranza, Plunder and Pain.

11. AFP, "US families of Holocaust victims sue SNCF," The Local, April 17, 2015, accessed January 2, 2017, http://www.thelocal.fr/20150417/holocaust-victim-descen dants-sue-frances-sncf-in-us.

12. Arbour, *Economic and Social Justice*, 1. See also Kieran McEvoy, "Beyond Legalism: Towards a Thicker Understanding of Transitional Justice," *Journal of Law and Society* 34, no. 4 (2007), 411–440. Miller, *Effects of Invisibility*. Rosalind Shaw, Lars Waldorf, and Pierre Hazan, *Localizing Transitional Justice: Interventions and Priorities after Mass Violence* (Stanford, CA: Stanford University Press, 2010).

13. John Dewey, "The Historic Background of Corporate Legal Personality," *Yale Law Journal* 35 (1925), 655. Sir John William Salmond and Patrick John Fitcegerald, *Salmond on Jurisprudence* (London: Sweet & Maxwell, 1966). William S. Laufer, "Corporate Bodies and Guilty Minds," Emory Law Journal 43 (1994), 647.

14. Martha Minow, *Between Vengeance and Forgiveness: Facing History after Genocide and Mass Violence* (Boston: Beacon Press, 1999). John Braithwaite, "Restorative Justice: Theories and Worries," Visiting Experts' Papers: 123rd International Senior Seminar, Resource Material Series 63 (2004).

15. Madeleine Albright, From Words to Action, the Responsibility to Protect, The United States Holocaust Memorial Museum, 23 July 2013.

16. Lars Waldorf, "Anticipating the Past: Transitional Justice and Socio-Economic Wrongs," *Social & Legal Studies* 21, no. 2 (2012), 171–186.

17. Arbour, *Economic and Social Justice*, 1.

18. Stuart Eizenstat, *Imperfect Justice: Looted Assets, Slave Labor, and the Unfinished Business of World War II* (New York: Public Affairs, 2009), x.

19. Miller, Effects of Invisibility. Paige Arthur, "How 'Transitions" Reshaped Human Rights: A Conceptual History of Transitional Justice," *Human Rights Quarterly* 31, no. 2 (2009), 266–291.

20. Waldorf, "Anticipating the Past," 171–186. Paul Gready, *The Era of Transitional Justice: The Aftermath of the Truth and Reconciliation Commission in South Africa and Beyond* (London: Routledge, 2010).

21. Alan Doig and Stephanie Mclvor, "Feature Review Corruption and its Control in the Developmental Context: An Analysis and Selective Review of the Literature," *Third World Quarterly* 20, no. 3, (1999), 657–676.

22. Graham Brown, Corinne Caumartin, Arnim Langer, and Frances Stewart, "Addressing Horizontal Inequalities in Post-Conflict Reconstruction," in *Rethinking Transitions: Equality and Social Justice in Societies Emerging from Conflict*, ed. Gaby Ore Aguilar and Felipe Gomez Isa (Portland, OR: Intersentia, 2011).

23. Johan Galtung, "Violence, Peace, and Peace Research," *Journal of Peace Research*, 6, no. 3 (1969), 179.

24. Richard J Golsan, "Crimes-against-Humanity Trials in France and Their Historical and Legal Contexts: A Retrospective Look," in *Atrocities on Trial: Historical Perspectives on the Politics of Prosecuting War Crimes*, ed. Patricia Heberer and Jürgen Matthäus (Lincoln: University of Nebraska Press, 2008).

25. See Benjamin B. Ferencz, *Less Than Slaves: Jewish Forced Labor and the Quest for Compensation* (Cambridge, MA: Harvard University Press, 1979).

26. Kevin Jon Heller, "Nuremberg Scholars Amicus Brief in Kiobel," *Opinio Juris*, December 23, 2011, accessed February 17, 2017, http://opiniojuris.org/2011/12/23/nuremberg-scholars-amicus-brief-in-kiobel/. I. G. Farben was disbanded for its role in the German war effort, not for its production of the Zyklon B gas used to kill Jews and other deportees. Note, the brief was signed by a variety of Nuremberg scholars including, Omer Bartov, Michael Bazyler, Donald Bloxham, Lawrence Douglas, Hilary Earl, Hon. Bruce Einhorn, David Fraser, Sam Garkawe, Stanley A. Goldman, Gregory S. Gordon, Michael J. Kelly, Matthew Lippman, Michael Marrus, Fionnuala D. Ni Aolain, Kim Priemel, Cristoph Safferling, and Frederick Taylor.

27. Manuel A. Gomez, "The Global Chase: Seeking the Recognition and Enforcement of the Lago Agrio Judgment Outside of Ecuador," *Stanford Journal of Complex Litigation* 1, no. 199 (2013), 13–14.

28. Open Secrets.org, Center for Responsive Politics. *SNCF America Issues*, 2014, accessed January 2, 2017, http://www.opensecrets.org/lobby/clientissues.php?id = D000065089fcyear = 2014.

29. These findings are based on archival work and over 120 interviews with involved parties in France and the United States. Research also included participant observation at commemorative sites, legislative debates, the State Department Treaty signing, and pro bono work at the House of Representatives and the U.S. State Department.

30. As a result of the transition away from coal, today the company employs closer to 250,000 individuals.

31. Marie-Noëlle Polino, Association pour l'histoire des chemins de fer en France (AHICF), Une entreprise publique dans la guerre la SNCF 1939–1945. Paris, Assemblée Nationale: 21–22 Juin 2000 (Paris: Presse Universitaires de France (PUF), 2001), 200.

32. Note: While this thesis focuses specifically on the Jewish deportations, political prisoners and others also found themselves on these trains to Auschwitz. My dissertation outlines the information available and the debates that remain over the SNCF's ability to resist and any say it had over the conditions of the transports. Federman, Aller Simple (One-Way Ticket).

33. Paul Durand, *La SNCF pendant la guerre* (Paris, France: Presses Universitaires de France, 1968).

34. Vichy historians differ over the amount of independence the clause afforded. Historian Georges Ribeill interpreted the Armistice as forcing the SNCF to operate exclusively under German authority. Historian and economist Michel Margairaz agreed, arguing that the SNCF operated under the thumb of both the complicit French government and the German occupier. Georges Ribeill, "Dossier SNCF et Déportations," *Historail* 4 (2008); 46. Annette Wieviorka, however, interpreted the clause differently, arguing the SNCF retained ownership of its materials (trains, wagons, etc.) while the German head of transport managed all of the operations of the trains (schedules, etc.) Wieviorka claims this perceived additional independence afforded the railway company created a bit of 'jealousy' within the Vichy regime wished greater independence from the Germans.

35. Monsieur de Directeur Général with M. le Président Münzer à la HVD, le 29–12–42. 3 January 1943, Box 72 AJ 474. National Archives of Paris, France.

36. Christian Bachelier and Centre National de la recherche scientifique (CNRS), *La SNCF Sous L'Occupation Allemand 1940–1944* (France: AHICF, 1996). Note: the battle of Stalingrad, August 23, 1942 through February 2, 1943, is seen as the turning point of the war. The Germans never regained their positions after this defeat to the Soviets.

37. Michael R. Marrus and Robert O. Paxton, *Vichy France and the Jews* (New York: Basic Books, 1981), xvi.

38. Federman, Aller Simple (One-Way Ticket). Ludivine Broch, *Ordinary Workers, Vichy and the Holocaust: French Railwaymen and the Second World War* (Cambridge, UK: Cambridge University Press, 2016).

39. These attempts are addressed in Federman, Aller Simple (One-Way Ticket), Paul Durand, *La SNCF pendant la guerre* (Paris: Presses Universitaires de France, 1968). Broch, Ordinary Workers.

40. Robert Paxton, Stanley Hoffman, and Claude Bertrand, *Vichy France: Old Guard and New Order, 1940–1944* (New York: Knopf, 1972), 180.

41. Surviving invoices suggest the SNCF received payment for transporting deportees to various internment camps within France. No remaining invoices prove the SNCF received payment to transport deportees to the German border crammed in cattle cars.

42. These interviews were conducted in France and the United States with individuals who fled the persecution of the Jews in France during the war.

43. Interview, April 30, 2016.

44. SNCF, *Profile and Key Figures* (Booklet), 2013.

45. Email correspondence. March 9, 2015.

46. Phone Interview July 7, 2014. Note: names of survivors have been changed.

47. Raul Hilberg, German Railroads/Jewish Souls, *Society* 14, no. 1 (1976), 7.

48. Ralph G. Steinhardt, "Corporate Responsibility and the International Law of Human Rights: The New Lex Mercatori," in *Non-State Actors and Human Rights*, ed. Philip Alston (Oxford and New York: Oxford University Press, 2005), 217.

49. Ludivine Broch, "Professionalism in the Final Solution: French Railway Workers and the Jewish Deportations, 1942–4," *Contemporary European History* 23, no. 3 (2014), 359–801.

50. Amar Toor, "The Holocaust's Legacy Threatens One Company's US Rail Projects," *The Verge*, March 7, 2014, accessed February 17, 2017, http://www.theverge.com/2014/377/5480714/the-holocausts-legacy-threatens-sncf-france-us-rail-projects.

51. SNCF, "History and Memory: SNCF & World War II" (Paris: SNCF, 2012).

52. "16 Février 2009—Hoffman-Glemane," Le Conseil d'Etat et La Jurisdiction Administrative, September 28, 2015, accessed February 17, 2017, http://www.conseil-etat.fr/Decisions-Avis-Publications/Decisions/Les-decisions-les-plus-importantes-du-Conseil-d-Etat/16-fevrier-2009-Hoffman-Glemane.

53. Alain Lipietz, *La SNCF et la Shoah: le procès G. Lipietz contre État et SNCF: Essai.* (Paris: Les Petits Matins, 2011).

54. Arno Klarsfeld, "La SNCF et les trains de la mort," *Le Monde*, June 3, 2006.

55. Naomi Roht-Arriaza and Javier Mariezcurrena, *Transitional Justice in the Twenty-first Century: Beyond Truth Versus Justice* (Cambridge, UK and New York: Cambridge University Press, 2006).

56. Lipietz, *La SNCF et la Shoah.*

57. A commissariat is an independent magistrate, specializing in administrative law. A commissariat is not a judge, but confers with the judge throughout the case. Their comments are influential and often reflect that of the judge at the time they are read.

58. René Clément, *La bataille du rail*, directed by René Clément (1946; Paris: Coopérative Générale du Cinéma Français), Film. This film proliferated the heroic narrative of the SNCF. As did Paul Durand's government supported, La SNCF Pendant la Guerre.

59. Michael R. Marrus and Robert O. Paxton, *Vichy France and the Jews* (New York: Basic Books, 1981).

60. The court ruled specifically on claims sought by Madeline Hoffman-Glemane from the French State and the SNCF totaling 280,000, for the deportation and murder of her father and for her own suffering. The administrative court in Paris passed the question to the Conseil d'Etat. The state dismissed the claims against the SNCF referring to the decision issued on the Lipietz case.

61. Johannes Weteel, "'The Past Doesn't Pass'—A German Look at France's Nazi Collaboration," *World Crunch*, October 15, 2012.

62. Maia de la Baume, "French Railway Formally Apologizes to Holocaust Victims," *The New York Times*, January 25, 2011.

63. Katherine Shaver, "Maryland Lawmaker Says He Won't Jeopardize Purple Line Funding with Holocaust Bill," *Washington Post*, March 11, 2014. Note, Aaron Greenfield, lobbyist working against the SNCF in Maryland, discredits Marrus arguing that he is on the SNCF payroll and attends many SNCF-sponsored events. Other world-renowned Vichy experts and Holocaust activists have spoken in defense of the SNCF and have been discredited for doing so.

64. Annette Wieviorka, "La SNCF, la Shoah et le Juge," *L'Histoire* 316 (January 2007).

65. Georges Ribeill, "Dossier SNCF et Déportations," *Historail* 4 (January 2008).

66. FSIA (the Foreign Sovereign Immunities Act of 1976) prevents lawsuits against sovereign nations.

67. Hilberg, "German Railroads/Jewish Souls," 70.

68. U.S. State Department office of Holocaust Issues confirms this date.

69. There have been French restitution programs for years. This agreement covers survivors living in countries that did not sign agreements with France to cover resident survivors. Only the United Kingdom, Poland, the Czech Republic, and Belgium signed such agreements. Why the United States did not sign an agreement remains unclear. Even former Ambassador Douglas Davidson who managed the office of Holocaust Issues at the U.S. State Department could not recall why the United States never wrote such an agreement. For a detailed description of French restitution programs, see Federman, *Aller Simple* (One-Way Ticket), 275.

70. SNCF America CEO Alain Leray, e-mail exchange to author, March 15, 2016.

71. Margaret Urban Walker, *Moral Repair: Reconstructing Moral Relations after Wrongdoing*, 1st ed. (Cambridge, UK: Cambridge University Press, 2006).

72. Carlos E. Sluzki, Donald C. Ransom, and Gregory Bateson, *Double Bind: The Foundation of Communicational Approach to the Family* (New York: Psychological Corp., 1976).

73. Howard R. Bowen and F. Ernest Johnson, *Social Responsibility of the Businessman* (New York: Harper, 1953); Min-Dong Paul Lee, "A Review of the Theories of Corporate Social Responsibility: Its Evolutionary Path and the Road Ahead," *International Journal of Management Reviews* 10, no. 1 (2008), 53–73.

74. Steven D. Lydenberg, *Corporations and the Public Interest: Guiding the Invisible Hand* (San Francisco: Berrett-Koehler Publishers, 2005).

75. Milton Friedman, *Capitalism and Freedom* (Chicago: University of Chicago Press, 1962).

76. H. Jeff Smith. "The Shareholder v. Stakeholder Debate." *MIT Sloan Management Review.* Summer 2003.

77. Scott Pegg, "An Emerging Market for the New Millennium: Transnational Corporations and Human Rights," *Transnational Corporations and Human Rights* 1, no. 17 (2003), 1–33. David Henderson, *Misguided Virtue: False Notions of Corporate Social Responsibility* (London: IEA, The Institute of Economic Affairs, 2001).

78. The Global Compact invites businesses to join the United Nations in its promotion of human rights. Companies agree to adhere to certain principles and then the UN lists the companies as part of the compact.

79. Stuart Eizenstat, *Imperfect Justice: Looted Assets, Slave Labor, and the Unfinished Business of World War II* (New York: Public Affairs, 2009).

80. Debora L. Sparr, "The Spotlight and the Bottom Line: How Multinationals Export Human Rights," *Foreign Affairs* 77, no. 2 (1998), 7–12.

81. Thomas M. Jones, "Instrumental Stakeholder Theory: A Synthesis of Ethics and Economics," *Academy of Management Review* 20, no. 2 (1995), 404–437; Michael E. Porter and Mark R. Kramer, "Strategy and Society," *Harvard Business Review* 84, no. 12 (2006), 78–92.

82. Christine Parker, *The Open Corporation: Effective Self-Regulation and Democracy* (Cambridge, UK: Cambridge University Press, 2002), ix.

83. Harvard Kennedy School Corporate Social Responsibility Initiative, 2013, Harvard University, accessed February 17, 2017, http://www.hks.harvard.edu/centers/mrcbg/programs/csri.

Bibliography

Aguilar, Gaby Oré and Felipe Gómez Isa. *Rethinking Transitions: Equality and Social Justice in Societies Emerging from Conflict.* Cambridge, UK and Portland, OR: Intersentia, 2011.

Andrieu, Kora. "Dealing With a 'New' Grievance: Should Anticorruption Be Part of the Transitional Justice Agenda?" *Journal of Human Rights* 11, no. 4 (2012): 537–557. https://doi.org/10.1080/ 14754835.2012.702471

Arbour, Louise. "Economic and Social Justice for Societies in Transition." *New York University Journal of Law and Politics* 40 (2007): 1–27.

Arthur, Paige. "How 'transitions' reshaped human rights: A conceptual history of transitional justice." *Human Rights Quarterly* 31, no. 2 (2009): 321–367. https://doi.org/ 10.1353/hrq.0.0069

Aukerman, Miriam J. "Extraordinary Evil, Ordinary Crime: A Framework for Understanding Transitional Justice." *Harvard Human Rights Journal* 15, (2002): 39–97.

Balasco, Lauren Marie. "The Transitions of Transitional Justice: Mapping the Waves From Promise to Practice." *Journal of Human Rights* 12, no. 2 (2013): 198–216. https:// doi.org/10.1080/1475 4835.2013.784858

Baume, Maia de la. "French Railway Formally Apologizes to Holocaust Victims." *The New York Times*, January 25, 2011. Accessed February 17, 2017. http://www.nytimes.com/2011/01/26/world/europe/26france.html?r=0.

Bowen, Howard R. and F. Ernest Johnson. *Social Responsibility of the Businessman*. New York: Harper, 1953.

Braithwaite, John. "Restorative Justice: Theories and Worries." Visiting Experts' Papers: 123rd International Senior Seminar, Resource Material Series vol. 63 (2004): 77–56.

Broch, Ludivine. Ordinary Workers, *Vichy and the Holocaust: French Railwaymen and the Second World War*. Cambridge, UK: Cambridge University Press, 2016. https://doi.org/10.1017/ CB09781139600453

Broch, Ludivine,"Professionalism in the Final Solution: French Railway Workers and the Jewish Deportations, 1942–4." *Contemporary European History* 23, no. 3 (2014): 359–801. https://doi. org/10.1017/S0960777314000186

Brown, Graham, Corinne Caumartin, Arnim Langer, and Frances Stewart, "Addressing Horizontal Inequalities in Post-Conflict Reconstruction," in *Rethinking Transitions: Equality and Social Justice in Societies Emerging from Conflict*, edited by Gaby Oré Aguilar and Felipe Gomez Isa. Cambridge, UK and Portland, OR: Intersentia, 2011, 11–46.

Carranza, Ruben. "Plunder and Pain: Should Transitional Justice Engage with Corruption and Economic Crimes?" *International Journal of Transitional Justice* 2, no. 3 (2008): 310–330. https://doi.org/10.1093/ijti/iin023

Chatterjee, Pratap. "Chiquita Banana to Face Colombia Torture Claim." *CorpWatch*, March SD, 2D12. Accessed February 17, 2017. http://www.corpwatch.org/article.php?id=15697.

Clément, René. *La bataille du rail*. Directed by René Clément. 1946. Paris: Coopérative Générale du Cinéma Français. Film.

Collier, Paul and the World Bank. "Breaking the Conflict Trap: Civil War and Development Policy." World Bank Publications, 2003.

"16 Février 2009—Hoffman-Glemane." Le Conseil d'Etat et La Jurisdiction Administrative, September 28, 2015. Accessed February 17, 2017. http://www.conseil-etat.fr/Decisions-Avis-Publications/Decisions/Les-decisions-les-plus-importantes-du-Conseil-d-Etat/16-fevrier-2009-Hoffman-Glemane.

Dewey, John. "The Historic Background of Corporate Legal Personality." *Yale Law Journal* 35, (1925): 655–673. https://doi.org/10.2307/788782

DeWinter, Rebecca. "The Anti-Sweatshop Movement: Constructing Corporate Moral Agency in the Global Apparel Industry." *Ethics & International Affairs* 15, no. 2 (2001): 99–115. https://doi.org/10.1111/j.1747–7093.2001.tb00361.x

Doig, Alan and Stephanie McIvor. "Feature Review Corruption and its Control in the Developmental Context: An Analysis and Selective Review of the Literature." *Third World Quarterly* 2D, no. 3 (1999): 657–676. https://doi.org/10.1080/01436599913749

Drexler, E.F. "Fatal Knowledge: The Social and Political Legacies of Collaboration and Betrayal in Timor-Leste." *International Journal of Transitional Justice* 7, no. 1 (2013): 74–94. https://doi.org/10.1093/ijtj/ijs037

Drumbl, Mark. "Collective Violence and Individual Punishment: The Criminality of Mass Atrocity." *Northwestern University Law Review* Winter (2005): 538–610.

Durand, Paul. *La SNCF pendant la guerre*. Paris: Presses Universitaires de France, 1968.

Echlin, John. "Undercutting the Political Economy of Conflict Is Bosnia and Herzegovina: A Transitional Justice Approach to Prosecuting Systemic Economic Crimes." *Columbia Journal of Transnational Law* 48 (2009): 353–398.

Eizenstat, Stuart. *Imperfect Justice: Looted Assets, Slave Labor, and the Unfinished Business of World War II*. New York: Public Affairs, 2009.

Farmer, Paul. *Pathologies of Power: Health, Human Rights, and the New War on the Poor.* Berkeley: University of California Press, 2003.

Federman, Sarah. Aller Simple (One-Way Ticket) Corporate Accountability for Mass Atrocity: A Study of the French National Railroads. Diss. George Mason University, 2015.

Ferencz, Benjamin B. *Less Than Slaves: Jewish Forced Labor and the Quest for Compensation.* Cambridge: Harvard University Press, 1979.

Friedman, Milton. *Capitalism and Freedom.* Chicago: University of Chicago Press, 1962. From Words to Action, the Responsibility to Protect. The United States Holocaust Memorial Museum, 23 July 2013.

Galtung, Johan. "Violence, Peace, and Peace Research," *Journal of Peace Research* 6, no. 3 (1969): 167–191. https://doi.org/10.1177/002234336900600301

Golsan, Richard J. "Crimes-against-Humanity Trials in France and Their Historical and Legal Contexts: A Retrospective Look." In *Atrocities on Trial: Historical Perspectives on the Politics of Prosecuting War Crimes*, edited by Patricia Heberer and Jürgen Matthäus, 247–261. Lincoln and Washington, DC: University of Nebraska Press; Published in association with the United States Holocaust Memorial Museum, 2008.

Gomez, Manuel A. "The Global Chase: Seeking the Recognition and Enforcement of the Lago Agrio Judgment Outside of Ecuador." *Stanford Journal of Complex Litigation* 1, no. 199 (2013): 13–14.

Gready, Paul. *The Era of Transitional Justice: The Aftermath of the Truth and Reconciliation Commission in South Africa and Beyond.* London: Routledge, 2010.

Harvard Kennedy School Corporate Social Responsibility Initiative. Harvard University, 2013. Accessed February 17, 2017. http://www.hks.harvard.edu/centers/mrcbg/programs/csri.

Hayner, Priscilla B. *Unspeakable Truths: Transitional Justice and the Challenge of Truth Commissions.* New York: Routledge, 2010.

Heller, Kevin Jon. "Nuremberg Scholars Amicus Brief in Kiobel." *Opinio Juris*, December 23, 2011. Accessed February 17, 2017. http://opiniojuris.org/2011/12/23/nuremberg-scholars-amicus-brief-in-kiobel/.

Henderson, David. *Misguided Virtue: False Notions of Corporate Social Responsibility.* London: IEA, The Institute of Economic Affairs, 2001.

Hilberg, Raul. "German Railroads/Jewish Souls." *Society* 14, no. 1 (1976): 60–74. https://doi.org/10.1007/BF02694653

Jones, Thomas M. "Instrumental Stakeholder Theory: A Synthesis of Ethics and Economics." *Academy of Management Review* 20, no. 2 (1995): 404–437.

Klarsfeld, Arno. "La SNCF et les trains de la mort." *Le Monde*, June 3, 2006.

Lambourne, Wendy. "Transitional Justice and Peacebuilding after Mass Violence." *International Journal of Transitional Justice* 3, no. 1 (2009): 28–48. https://doi.org/10.1093/ijtj/ijn037

LaPlante, Lisa J. "On the Indivisibility of Rights: Truth Commissions, Reparations, and the Right to Develop." *Yale Human Rights & Development Law Journal* 10 (2007): 141–177.

Laufer, William S. "Corporate Bodies and Guilty Minds." *Emory Law Journal* 43 (1994): 648–730.

Lee, Min-Dong Paul. "A Review of the Theories of Corporate Social Responsibility: Its Evolutionary Path and the Road Ahead." *International Journal of Management Reviews* 10, no. 1 (2008): 53–73. https://doi.org/10.1111/j.1468-2370.2007.00226.x

Lipietz, Alain. *La SNCF et la Shoah: le procès G. Lipiek. contre Etat et SNCF: Essai.* Paris: Les Petits Matins, 2011.

Lydenberg, Steven D. *Corporations and the Public Interest: Guiding the Invisible Hand.* San Francisco: Berrett-Koehler Publishers, 2005.

Marrus, Michael R. and Robert O. Paxton. *Vichy France and the Jews.* New York: Basic Books, 1981.

McEvoy, Kieran. "Beyond Legalism: Towards a Thicker Understanding of Transitional Justice." *Journal of Law and Society* 34, no. 4 (2007): 411–440. https://doi.org/10.1111/j.1467-6478.2007.00399.x

Miller, Zinaida. "Effects of Invisibility: In Search of the 'Economic' in Transitional Justice." *International Journal of Transitional Justice* 2, no. 3 (2008): 266–291. https://doi.org/10.1093/ ijtj/ijn022

Minow, Martha. Between *Vengeance and Forgiveness: Facing History after Genocide and Mass Violence.* Boston: Beacon Press, 1999.

Muvingi, I. "Sitting on Powder Kegs: Socioeconomic Rights in Transitional Societies." International *Journal of Transitional Justice* 3, no. 2 (2009): 163–182. https://doi.org/10.1093/ijtj/ijp010

Nagy, Rosemary L. "The Scope and Bounds of Transitional Justice and the Canadian Truth and Reconciliation Commission." *International Journal of Transitional Justice* 7, no. 1 (2012): 5273. https://doi.org/10.1093/ijtj/ijs034

Olsen, Tricia D., Andrew G. Reiter, and Eric Wiebelhaus-Brahm. "Taking Stock: Transitional Justice and Market Effects in Latin America." *Journal of Human Rights* 10, no. 4 (2011): 521–543. https://doi.org/10.1080/14754835.2011.619411

Ortega, Olga Martín. "Deadly Ventures? Multinational Corporations and Paramilitaries in Colombia." *Revista Electrónica de Estudios Internacionales* no. 16 (2008): 1–13.

Parker, Christine. *The Open Corporation: Effective Self-Regulation and Democracy.* Cambridge, UK: Cambridge University Press, 2002. https://doi.org/10.1017/CBO 9780511550034

Paxton, Robert, Stanley Hoffman, and Claude Bertrand. *Vichy France: Old Guard and New Order, 1940–1944.* New York: Knopf, distributed by Random House, 1972.

Pegg, Scott. "An Emerging Market for the New Millennium: Transnational Corporations and Human Rights." In *Transnational Corporations and Human Right,* edited by Jedrzej George Frynas and Pegg Scott, 1–33. Houndmills, Basingstoke, Hampshire: Palgrave, 2003. https://doi.org/10.1057/9781403937520_1

Polino, Marie-Noëlle. Association pour l'histoire des chemins de fer en France (AHICF). *Une entreprise publique dans la guerre la SNCF 1939–1945.* Paris, Assemblée Nationale: 21–22 Juin 2000. Paris: Presse Universitaires de France (PUF), 2001.

Porter, Michael E. Porter and Mark R. Kramer. "Strategy and Society." *Harvard Business Review* 84, no. 12 (2006): 78–92.

Ribeill, Georges. "Dossier SNCF et Déportations." *Historail* 4 (2008): 34–87.

Roht-Arriaza, Naomi and Javier Mariezcurrena. *Transitional Justice in the Twenty-first Century: Beyond Truth Versus Justice.* Cambridge, UK and New York: Cambridge University Press, 2006. https://doi.org/10.1017/CBO9780511617911

Rousso, Henry and Arthur Goldhammer. *The Vichy Syndrome: History and Memory in France since 1944.* Harvard University Press, 1994.

Ruggie, John. "Guiding Principles on Business and Human Rights: Implementing the United Nations 'Protect, Respect, and Remedy' Framework." New York: United Nations Human Rights, 2011.

Salmond, Sir John William and Patrick John Fitzgerald. *Salmond on Jurisprudence.* London: Sweet & Maxwell, 1966.

Shaver, Katherine. "Maryland Lawmaker Says He Won't Jeopardize Purple Line Funding with Holocaust Bill." *Washington Post*, March 11, 2014.

Shaw, Rosalind, Lars Waldorf, and Pierre Hazan. *Localizing Transitional Justice: Interventions and Priorities after Mass Violence*. Stanford, CA: Stanford University Press, 2010.

Smith, H. Jeff. "The Shareholder v. Stakeholder Debate." *MIT Sloan Management Review*, July 15, 2003.

SNCF. "History and Memory: SNCF & World War II." Paris: SNCF, 2012.

SNCF. *Profile and Key Figures*, 2013.

Sparr, Debora L. "The Spotlight and the Bottom Line: How Multinationals Export Human Rights," *Foreign Affairs* 77, no. 2, (1998): 7–12. https://doi.org/10.2307/20048784

Steinhardt, Ralph G. "Corporate Responsibility and the International Law of Human Rights: The New Lex Mercatoria." In *Non-State Actors and Human Rights*, ed. Philip Alston. Oxford: Oxford University Press, 2005.

Toor, Amar. "The Holocaust's Legacy Threatens One Company's US Rail Projects." *The Verge*, March 7, 2014.

United Convention Against Corruption, UN General Assembly Resolution A/RES/58/4. Implemented 14 December 2005.

Van der Merwe, Hugo and Audrey R Chapman. *Assessing the Impact of Transitional Justice: Challenges for Empirical Research*. Washington, DC: United States Institute of Peace, 2008.

Waldorf, Lars. "Anticipating the Past: Transitional Justice and Socio-Economic Wrongs." *Social & Legal Studies* 21, no. 2 (2012): 171–186. https://doi.org/10.1177/0964663911435827

Walker, Margaret Urban. *Moral Repair: Reconstructing Moral Relations after Wrongdoing*. 1st edition. Cambridge, UK: Cambridge University Press, 2006. https://doi.org/10.1017/CBO9780511618024

War, Glenn T. and Gregory P. Noone, "The Culture of Corruption in the Postconflict and Developing World." In *Imagine Coexistence: Restoring Humanity after Violent Ethnic Conflict*, edited by Antonia Handler Chayes, Martha Minow, and Program on Negotiation at Harvard Law School, 191–209. San Francisco, CA: Jossey-Bass, 2003.

Weteel, Johannes. " 'The Past Doesn't Pass' – A German Look At France's Nazi Collaboration." *World Crunch*, October 15, 2012.

Wieviorka, Annette. "La SNCF, la Shoah et le Juge" *L'Histoire*. 316 (January 2007): 89–99.

End of Epoch Questions

Questions for Discussion

- What events shifted the field in Epoch Two?
- What distinguishes Epoch Two from Epoch One? What does this now make possible?
- What disciplines are now included in the field?
- Name (or find) some kinds of events that might use Epoch Two discourses.
- What might a university department operating in an Epoch Two discourse be called?
- What might be some frictions between those operating in Epoch Two and Epoch One discourses? Where might they disagree?

Activities

Visit the World Café website at www.theworldcafe.com. In class, at work, or in your organization, try hosting a World Café. These cafés are dialogue circles that draw on the collective intelligence of the group by shifting the groups in conversation.

PART III

EPOCH THREE: TRANSBOUNDARY CONFLICTS, 2001–PRESENT

Epoch Three (2001–Present)
September 11th Through the Present

Transboundary Conflicts

Discourses of conflict resolution shifted dramatically again after the terrorist attack in the United States on September 11, 2001. In this now infamous attack, terrorists used passenger-filled planes to hit important symbolic targets in the United States, bringing New York's World Trade Center to the ground and severely damaging the Pentagon in Washington, DC. Thousands of people died that day, and the country went into mourning for the dead.

The destruction of the World Trade Center and the loss of life (more than 3,000) came as a shock to the world and raised new important questions about how to think about and approach such atrocities. Neither the predictive models of conflict, developed in Epoch One, nor the identity-based approaches to conflict developed in Epoch Two, helped us understand or respond to these acts of terrorism. Indeed, cooperating in this new world of terrorism required a redefinition of "war" and "enemy." Terrorism—the use of violence for ideological aims—became the primary tool of war, and this new nameless, faceless enemy was not easily characterized by geographical boundaries; this entity operated in the shadows and could emerge anywhere at any time. Fear escalated, for it was/is the general public that became the target, not members of professional armies. Additionally, there was little understanding about why the attacks occurred. Epoch One strategies sought to make sense of the events in game theory terms, yet the actions seemed irrational. Epoch Two identity-focused approaches could not explain cultures that used suicidal members as weapons targeting civilians. This was a "faceless, nameless" kind of killing, and general terror and insecurity was the goal, not an increase in territory or righting historical injustices.

After 9/11, conversations about "security" dominated the sociopolitical landscape, and the general public in the United States began to see the effects of this discourse on their daily lives. Air travel security increased, surveillance further increased (the Patriot Act), and news outlets announced daily "terror alerts" (red, orange, yellow). Electronic signs over highways encouraged the public to contact the police if they had "suspicions." The Department of Homeland Security was born, charged with protecting the "Homeland," and today, they have developed the "See Something, Say Something" campaign,[1] where people are asked to be alert to potential threats and to notify police. The field of conflict resolution began to reflect on the impact of trauma as a consequence of violence and the kinds of needs this trauma creates over time (Fassin and Rechtman 2009). The fear that was generated by these acts of terrorism had multiple important secondary effects.

In the United States, nationalism became the rallying cry in response to terrorism. American flags proliferated, appearing on lawns, clothing, cars, and more, in numbers never before seen. This was, of course, an "in-group" response to a threat from an "out-group." There was, for example, tremendous opposition to the building of a mosque (the so-called Ground Zero Mosque) close to the 9/11 Memorial and Museum[2]; there was a growing national conversation about the nature of Islam—whether it was a peaceful or violent religion—and this conversation has been divisive.[3] These trends have continued in the years following 9/11, most recently materializing in President Donald Trump's proposed travel ban (Executive Order 13769 and 13780). In June 2018, the U.S. Supreme Court upheld the order in a 5–4 decision. Proponents of the travel ban argue that keeping out travelers from six Muslim-majority countries increases the security of the United States, while those disagreeing with the travel ban argue that doing so is an act of discrimination against people of the Islamic faith. Here our point is that these divisions were the downstream consequence of 9/11 and the wars in Afghanistan, Iraq, Lebanon, and Syria. Out of the ashes of the Twin Towers emerged a new nationalism in the United States, one that was predominantly anti-Muslim. However, this event also has had a tremendous impact on the field of conflict resolution.

Despite these divisions and the development of "patriotic" nationalism in the United States, there was also new self-examination occurring in the United States—a recognition that we just did not understand why these terrorists had committed their heinous acts. "Why Do They Hate Us?" was a refrain in speeches by public leaders and in new media. This was at the beginning of an effort to understand our relationship with the Islamic world. While the less-reflective answer was "They hate our freedoms,"[4] this was easy because it did not require us to trace the consequences of our foreign policy on the emergence of extremism within the Islamic world. Following 9/11, there was considerable effort made to understand the history of Islamic extremism and examination of the U.S.'s relation to the Islamic world, more generally. This was a reflexive effort to consider the nature of the relationship between the "West and the rest," the partial title of Niall Ferguson's (2011) seminal book exploring the rise of the West (*Civilization: The West and the Rest*), which argues that the biggest threat to the West is not from the outside, such as from a rising power or insurgent groups, but from within, as a consequence of our own policies. In the field of conflict resolution, reflexive inquiry (how do "we" contribute to conflict with "them") is characteristic of Epoch Three approaches to conflict analysis and resolution. Rather than externalize responsibility for conflicts, Epoch Three discourse fosters an examination of how the conflict system works and what "our" role is in the production of the conflict.

However, since 9/11, there has been significant deployment of Epoch One and Epoch Two discourses to try to understand terrorism. Epoch One analysis has focused on how to predict terrorism—who would become a terrorist and which messages resonate with youth, for example. Profiling emerged at airports as violence became associated, statistically, with people of a certain ethnic and religious background. This has failed to prevent acts of terrorism, especially the "home-grown" version, where citizens within a country commit acts of terrorism. Largely because Epoch One discourse presumes that people are rational, it has had little to contribute to the study of terrorism, except for promulgating the presumption that terrorists are irrational and, therefore, inhuman. Imagine how different the global response to terrorism would have been if governments had presumed that terrorists were rational and were making reason-based, cost-benefit calculations about how to achieve their goals. From this perspective, the Epoch One discourse blinded the world to the logic of terrorists and disabled, de facto, the world from building forums for hearing complaints from extremist groups and negotiating for joint outcomes.

Since 9/11 there have also been Epoch Two efforts to assess and intervene in terrorism. When we examine the cost of the wars since 9/11 in terms of lives lost and money spent, we can begin to see the ineffectiveness of Epoch Two solutions to terrorism. For example, Samuel Huntington's *Clash of Civilizations* (2007) framed these conflicts as the inevitable result of *different* civilizations coming head-to-head; this is an explanation anchored by the discourse of cultural (identity-based) differences. While these civilizations seemed to share a desire for advancement, in this Epoch Two discourse, different civilizations populated the planet and these civilizations changed at different rates, in different directions, and with different notions of human rights. Taking to heart Huntington's work, Kofi Annan, Secretary-General of the United Nations between 1997 and 2006, sought to respond to terrorism by trying to unify these seemingly disparate civilizations via the United Nations Alliance of Civilizations (UNAOC). Established in 2005, just a few years after the September 11 attacks, Annan tasked experts with sorting through the nature of this polarization between societies. The resulting report encouraged a focus on education, youth, migration, and media (United Nations Alliance of Civilizations 2018). Annan's initiative resembled an Epoch Two response to the attacks because it called for coexistence through greater unity, brought about through strategies to increase cultural understanding and reduce identity-based differenced. This approach to terrorism is very different from that which could, in a self-reflexive examination, explore collective, as well as personal, responsibility for conflict production, as well as conflict transformation.

Because such reflexive self-examination has forced those in the West to consider their own place in the world, this has opened up a space for critical self-reflection previously absent in conflict analysis. The "war against terror" continued on for over a decade and civilian deaths from acts of terrorism increased. Involved in wars in Afghanistan, Lebanon, Syria, and Iraq, the United States, especially the military, began to openly question its own strategy. These were not wars that could be won militarily. These were wars where the mere presence of U.S. forces, on the ground, contributed to increased antipathy toward the United States, and the West more broadly. The U.S. military raised these questions, discussing its failures in the "decade of war" in a rather astounding publication that reflected on errors at the strategic level, as well as at the operational level.[5] This is an excellent example of the practice of reflection that has helped us understand conflict as a system, where "we" interact with "them" in a manner that can either promote violence or engender peace.

September 11 had other ripple effects. During this time, in the name of increased security, the countries promoting global human rights often failed to protect them. The policies and practices of the West used in the war on terror included unlawful detaining procedures, such as the suspension of habeas corpus[6] and the presence of state-sanctioned torture on terrorist suspects in prisons at Abu Ghraib and Guantanamo Bay. These abrogations of rights shocked the world, as the United States had clearly put security concerns before the rule of law. The United States, in the name of security, also began sending drones to do extra-judicial killings of both U.S. citizens living abroad, as well as citizens of other nations.[7] "Security" has also driven an increase in surveillance of U.S. citizens within the United States.[8] Now the *tools* of war became as nameless and faceless as the enemy; the West began breaking its own moral code, blurring the lines of victim and perpetrator, villain and hero.

The United States, which had maintained a position of heroism since its engagement in World War II, began Epoch Three as a victim of the September 11 terror attacks. However, as the United States responded to the attack, launching wars in Afghanistan and Iraq and developing "enhanced" interrogations and suspending habeas corpus at Guantanamo, it began to look like a perpetrator as well. Civilian deaths in Afghanistan and Iraq far surpassed the deaths of U.S. forces.[9] Other Western countries such as France also began bending the legal rules protecting civil rights when terrorism exploded on their streets. France declared an *etat d'urgence* (state of emergency) on November 14, 2015, after terrorist attacks killed 130 people. The state of emergency permits the government to search without warrants, conduct raids, and engage in other activities not normally permitted. French journalists and others expressed concern about potential abuse during this period. During this period, in response to such concerns, the United Nations formed the Universal Periodic Review process, which now reviews the human rights records of all UN Member States as a check on the suspension of rights.

In the aftermath of 9/11, not only the treatment of foreigners came under review, but also the treatment of a state's own people also became a core concern. The murder of Trayvon Martin by a community watch member and later the deaths of Eric Garner, Michael Brown, Walter Scott, Sandra Bland, Korryn Garnes, and Freddie Gray, all at the hands of police sparked protests across the United States. All of the victims were Black—igniting the Black Lives Matter movement, a contemporary iteration of the civil rights movement that emerged in Epoch One. People of color living in economically disadvantaged communities could make valid claims of ongoing human rights violations. With widespread gun possession, altercations continue today, and many police remain terrified to enter some gang-filled communities. While one could argue that there is little to no relation between the death of Blacks at the hands of the police and the attacks of 9/11, these violent events indeed resonate as both calls for the examination of marginalized voices and the interrogation of the militarized violence of the state toward civilians in the United States and abroad, as well as the application of the rule of law, national and international, to all peoples, all the time. This kind of interrogation, examination, and critique function as a form of moral inquiry into who "we" are and how we treat the various kinds of "them."

We can see that the "enemy" is not just disguised members of Al Qaeda, the Taliban, or ISIL, but for the Black people in the United States, it is the police, and for the police, it is, all too often, Black men. This moral inquiry has also moved into the national conversation about gun violence—in the United States alone there have been more than a hundred school shootings since 2000. The 2018 shooting (which resulted in the murder of seventeen people) at Stoneman Douglas High School in Parkland, Florida, ignited a social movement for gun control, focusing again on the morality of access to assault weapons.[10] Unlike the Cold War, terrorism, racial violence, and school shootings all involve non-state actors, often individuals acting on the basis of their own stories and their own belief systems. This violence is neither predictable nor rational. The impact of the violence, given the prevalence of social media, is felt across the country and beyond. Racial violence has the Black community outraged and afraid, while the White community ponders questions of privilege and allyship. The school shootings deepen the cultural polarization in the United States, as many liberals seek to change policy and many conservatives line up behind the NRA. The acts of terrorism within the homeland increase fear of the Other and make uncertainty a part of daily life. Conflict marauds outside the boundaries of law and of justice. Polarization within our communities, even our families, has grown.[11]

This new world of conflict requires a rethinking of conflict dynamics and our binary characterizations of "good" and "evil" as we question our own assumptions about morality. Moreover, we would argue that this is a welcomed feature of our world today, precisely because of "interdependence"—we live in a world where terrorism in France calls for the reflection on marginalized Muslim populations in that country, and elsewhere; the school shootings in the United States call for reflection on the safety of children everywhere, and the racial violence in the United States reverberates in our conversations about the Other more broadly as we consider immigration policy, as well as strategies for addressing (or not) the social and economic needs of those Others. As these forms of violence contribute to polarization across national boundaries, especially in social media, the fragile nature of our relationships comes into sharp focus—they are easily damaged by accusations and counteraccusations, and there are rarely opportunities to listen to and learn about the Other's perspective. And yet, this is precisely what we argue is the focus for Epoch Three approaches to conflict analysis and resolution. In the sections that follow, we describe the conflict theories pertinent to and required to understand transboundary conflicts, the research methods used in the analysis of transboundary conflicts, and the practices that support the resolution, or perhaps evolution, of transboundary conflicts.

Conflict Resolution Theories in Epoch Three

The critical self-reflection in Epoch Three, calls for a set of reflexive questions that require "us" to examine our own role in the production of the conflict, as well as possible contributions to its evolution, if not resolutions:

- What role do we see ourselves playing in the creation/maintenance of the conflict?
- What kinds of assumptions underlie the actions of the Others? Where did those assumptions come from or how were they developed?
- What are the assumptions we are making about the Others that would be at odds with their descriptions of themselves?
- What do the Others not seem to know about "us" and what have we done that has enabled that ignorance to flourish?
- How have the Others tried to solve or address the conflict? What did we miss regarding their overtures for peace or reconciliation or collaboration?

All of these questions call for a critical examination of the meanings that are important to both "them" and "us"—the core stories that lie at the heart of violent actions, as well as reactions to violence. This builds on Epoch Two, which encouraged a deeper understanding of what shaped people's worldviews and how differences led to conflict. However, in Epoch Three, the effort is reflexive and meant to evaluate ourselves concerning the role we play in producing the conditions that support violence, including the stories and events that shape our interpretations of the world and our perspectives on conflict. In doing this reflexive exercise, we can see the limited nature of understanding and the need for a more robust inquiry into both Self and Other.

Our interpretations of the world can be understood as discourses circulating in the interpersonal realm, anchored by broader cultural and societal norms, rendering certain meanings more legitimized than others, shaping what is considered "normal." For example, the shifts in gay rights in the 2000s, including allowing marriage between gay people, have been widely accepted in the general population. The recent Me Too Movement[12] has opened up a new discourse that enables women, across different domains and geographies, to discuss their experience of sexual violence. While sexual violence has long existed, there is suddenly a new set of norms, and men, across multiple industries, are being fired or are resigning as a result of credible allegations of sexual predation. Over time, certain discourses are normalized and become dominant while others remain marginalized. For this reason, in Epoch Three we explore the role of discourses in producing and reproducing inequalities. Accordingly, Epoch Three's approaches to conflict focus on the analysis of power in discourses and narratives as the architecture for both meaning and action.

Epoch Three conflict scholars consider how dominant narratives marginalize particular ways of knowing and forms of action, providing the conditions for conflict. For example, say a college student attends a liberal university but has some conservative perspectives; these perspectives can be difficult to articulate in the classroom where they feel that the dominant perspective is liberal. Unable to voice their perspectives on abortion, gun control, religion, and so on, the student withdraws, feels isolated, and joins an anarcho-capitalist student group that promotes vandalism as a means of overthrowing the system. If the student could have expressed her views in the classroom and been treated with dignity when doing so, she could have debated with her peers rather than fought them. A similar example could be a liberal gay student attending college in a more conservative environment; this student might feel compelled to deny his sexuality to avoid conflict and, in response to the isolation, commits violence against himself through suicide. In both of these cases, we see not the rational game (Epoch One), or just cultural differences (Epoch Two), but the power of the discourses and the narratives involved to silence, marginalize, and eliminate Others.

From this perspective, conflict becomes a product of voices that cannot be heard and stories that cannot be shared. Cynthia Enloe (2014) addresses these dynamics using a gender lens, encouraging scholars and practitioners to explore the domestic realm, often left out of policy-making and politics. Coinciding with Enloe's work, Leslie Dwyer (2009) encourages the field of conflict resolution to consider the complex role of silence in these marginalized spaces. Silence does not always mean acceptance or repression. Dwyer demonstrates how silences have their own history and are often held in place by social, economic, and/or political forces. One way to identify these sociopolitical forces is through narrative analysis (Cobb 2013).

Sara Cobb directs the field to explore the narratives (or stories) we have about ourselves, what work these stories do, and how these stories exist relationally with "Others." Narrative approaches critically examine how we characterize Others. For example, once society labels someone a "terrorist" or a group as a "terrorist organization," this framing invites certain responses. When parts of the West excused itself from having to honor the human rights of certain individuals, this understanding of the labeling process became paramount. The exclusion of certain groups, first discursively, often leads to the justification for the use of violence against the excluded group (Jabri 1996). For example, Suharto took power in Indonesia in 1965 by first excluding anyone his regime considered a "communist." Once he created an enemy responsible for all the country's problems, he could more easily justify their murder and take power. The Nazi regime used a similar approach when it held the Jews responsible for the world's economic and social problems. First exclusion and then hatred can be a way to justify grabs for power and can lead to mass violence. Epoch Three approaches caution us to tread carefully when constructing insiders and outsiders, by considering these labels critically, as delegitimizing labels that clearly foment conflict.

There are many ways in which narrative, as a framework for understanding, contributes to our theories of conflict. Thus, across the work of Sara Cobb, Sarah Federman, and Alison Castel, we see that narrative informs how we understand conflict dynamics using narrative as a characterization of stories about Self and Other (Cobb 2013), dynamics of master narratives (Castel 2016), and narrative constructions of victims and perpetrators (Federman 2018).

Federman's work on perpetrators considers how—in the case of mass violence—certain perpetrators come to stand for the many, expunging multitudes of collaborators. How are these few selected? She has developed a framework to help us understand what attributes these "ideal perpetrators" share and why they stay in the spotlight when many other culpable actors hide in the shadow (Federman 2018). We focus on these few to help prevent revenge cycles, but can sidestep the important work of reflexivity. How do we, even when perpetrators are not the guiltiest? Therefore, across the work of Cobb, Federman, and Castel, we see that narrative informs how we understand conflict dynamics.

Castel's ethnographic work in rural Colombia explores the dynamics of dominant narratives and counternarratives in interaction between the state and historically marginalized communities during the processes related to reparations and healing. This work explores how globalized discourses are constituted and mediated by institutions and how they are translated, resisted, appropriated, and reconstituted in local practices and relationships. It considers what stories can and cannot be told in these contexts and which stories are privileged over others. These dynamics uncover ways that current neoliberal peacebuilding approaches continue to marginalize the voices of those most impacted by violence and the ways in which grassroots organizing with the support of community-based organizations facilitate the emergence of new kinds of narratives to make communities legible to the state (Castel 2016).

We see how the stories we tell about ourselves and others have very real effects on our responses to conflict. In any conflict, if we consider ourselves solely as victims, we cannot discover our contribution to the conflict or our power to make a positive contribution. Understanding our contribution to any conflict is necessary for conflict transformation and conflict prevention. Self-reflection and discourse analysis does not excuse the actions of others; it simply places these actions in a larger context, helping us access the deeper dynamics perpetuating conflict. This reflexive inquiry challenges the idea of neutrality in Epoch One and the unbiased listening promulgated in Epoch Two. Our perceptions are always informed by our experiences, which means that our understanding is always limited and partial. Unlike Epoch One where there was an assumption that it was possible to understand conflict "objectively," Epoch Three theories presume that knowledge is not always dependent on the experiences of a person but also the dynamics of the macro-level cultural narratives in which they are embedded. For this reason, in Epoch Three, neutrality, central to the rule of law and the promotion of justice, also came into question. The challenge to law's neutrality became central when the International Criminal Court (ICC) was challenged because all of the initial cases were from Africa. Some African nations withdrew from the Rome Charter, including South Africa, Burundi, and Gambia. In March 2019, the Philippines left. This effectively blocks the capacity of the ICC to prosecute crimes against humanity within their countries. A reminder that the United States and Russia signed, but never ratified the Rome Statute. China, India, Turkey, Saudi Arabia, Libya and others never even signed. The power of the court is in question. We see here that the discourses that anchor Epoch Three prompted moral questions including questions regarding the viability and integrity of international, national, and social institutions.

Indeed, this is an uncomfortable period for many; we know that people prefer feelings of certainty to feelings of uncertainty, and yet this new approach to conflict challenges the accepted wisdom of everyday constructions of ourselves and others. Cognitive dissonance,[13] a term from psychology, describes the uncomfortable feeling when we discover information that conflicts with our beliefs. Cognitive dissonance can occur in domestic situations; say your father harmed you as a child and then as a young adult supports you in ways you could never have imagined after getting help for his alcoholism. These conflicting behaviors can be difficult to hold simultaneously. Is your father a victim or perpetrator? Or is he simply a flawed human? Long-held beliefs resist new information and, for this reason, can anchor large-scale and long-term conflict. Epoch Three demands of us all a higher tolerance for cognitive dissonance and a willingness to blur the lines between victims and perpetrators.

Cognitive dissonance occurs in other contexts too. It can be seen when, for example, Palestinians and Jews participate in peace programs and find that the "enemy" is just like them. However, they then struggle when each returns home to explain to their friends and family their new understanding; for indeed, the new "understanding" is essentially a new narrative, one that challenges the dominant narrative in their social network. From this perspective, social networks "police" what stories can be told, maintaining the conflict narratives, and by extension relationships, that can anchor polarization and violence.

When new events or conflicting information cause people to question themselves, many step back or sometimes even delete (often unconsciously) the information that does not support their worldview (this is also known as confirmation bias). This can help explain the Facts Matter movement that has sprung up in the United States during the Trump presidency; people discover facts that are ignored or even twisted to serve various political agendas. People will more often bend the facts to fit their worldview rather than construct their worldview based on facts revealed. At a broader level, the entire conversation about "fake news" or "fake science" reveals that "truth" itself seems to have been a casualty of Epoch Three discourses—once we presume that social reality is constructed, not revealed, then we are living in a "reality" where no one group, or one perspective, has any legitimate foundation for being "right." Moreover, we no longer have the luxury of "facts" to provide frameworks for decisions or policies.

Epoch Three theories and approaches embrace messiness, complex stories about conflict, conflicting facts (stories), and overlapping identities. Therefore, narrative approaches emphasize *how* stories operate rather than evaluate them for their truthfulness. If a story has influence, it has power, even if it is untrue. This era proves a struggle for those comfortable with the juxtaposition of seemingly simpler good and evil constructions promoted in prior wars, including the Cold War. However, this is not to say that the Epoch One's discourse has not been applied to conflicts since 9/11; indeed terrorism, as a label, frames the terrorist as "evil," as inhuman. Moreover, this discourse made it possible to use drones for extra-judicial killings, of both U.S. citizens as well as foreigners, along with the use of "enhanced" interrogation. In fact, much of the response to 9/11 has been in Epoch One discourses, where "winning" the war on terror has been a military objective, or Epoch Two, where terrorism is framed as a "clash" of cultures. Identifying terrorists remains the focus as does understanding and blocking terrorist recruitment efforts on social media. However, despite the fact that 9/11 ushered in a new era in conflict resolution, one that focused on reflexivity, Epoch Three discourse is only now, many years after 9/11, beginning to be used to understand the Arab world. Indeed, the Arab Spring in 2011 opened the West's eyes to the historical, cultural, and economic factors contributing to these uprisings. The West began to see how the United States' support of Arab dictators and corrupt governments since the colonial era began to be challenged by local peoples suffering under these regimes.[14]

Epoch Three's reflexive stance accompanies a systems perspective on conflict dynamics, which is an approach to conflict analysis and resolution that is anchored on a set of assumptions arising from systems theory:[15]

- *The whole is greater than the sum of the parts*: Applied to conflict analysis and resolution, this assumption locates the conflict as a system of inter-related parts. We can only understand the conflict by looking at how all the parts interact as a whole. We cannot understand the conflict as a list of factors, for this will not tell us about the dynamics of the conflict. For example, to understand the terrorism promoted by violent jihadists, we need to look at the participation of the role of the West, in the Arab world, positive and negative, and see how the Arab world has reacted. When we look at the conflict this way, we see that "they" do not attack "us" for no reason, akin to zombies, but rather they have chosen to commit heinous acts of violence to make their grievances "heard" in a context where they feel their requests/proposals (to the West) have been ignored. From a systems perspective, we can see that terrorists are in a "conversation" with the West, where the West is (relatively) impervious. A systems perspective does not excuse or justify the violence of terrorism; rather, it calls conflict analysts to consider the actions of the parties involved as contributors to the dynamics of violence.
- Reality is socially constructed; that is, people make sense of the world through interaction with other people. This "sense-making" involves the use of frames and stories. In turn, these frames are derived from the broad cultural myths and stories that circulate in society, as well as from the experiences that shape an individual's perspective. Conflict analysis requires attention to the nature of the meanings that are being produced and reproduced; conflict resolution requires intervention into the interaction to generate changes in the frames and stories that are in circulation in the conflict. When we look at conflict this way, we see how important stories are, as indeed people make sense of themselves, and Others, using stories.
- Change is a dynamic process and cannot, therefore, be understood as a function of linear causal factors but rather must be understood in light of the complexity in the context of any given conflict, which shapes and structures the interactions between people. Rather than set out to determine the causes of conflict, the systems approach characteristic of Epoch Three frameworks focuses instead on the feedback loops that contribute to conflict escalation, or support its de-escalation. Conflict resolution involves interrupting the feedback loops that breed distrust and increase polarization between groups, fostering the feedback loops associated with the development of new relational connections and collaborative processes.

This set of assumptions is accompanied by the reflexive effort to understand our own stories, our own frames of reference, not as the truth but as one approach to the world that arises from our histories and core values. In Epoch Three, we discover that conflict narratives (stories that perpetuate conflict) occur as closed in their constructions. People speak of "us versus them," "good versus evil," "right versus wrong," "victims versus perpetrators," and so on. These binary constructions, reminiscent of Epoch One characterizations of conflict, promote "win-lose" approaches to conflict. Within these categorizations, morality is constructed as black-and-white with no possibility for gray; and those who are with "Us" are considered to be infallible—"right," "good," and otherwise "victims" in the circumstance—consequently leaving the "Them" to be "evil," "wrong," and "perpetrators." Narrow characterizations do not allow for alternative constructions of "Us" and "Them" and, therefore, provide the conditions for war and preclude any path to peace. Vivienne Jabri (1996) argues that these characterizations of good and evil are, in fact, violence. Once we exclude a group, the process of separation begins, and violence of various kinds can be legitimized against them.

This approach to conflict also works with tensions within smaller groups (family, friends, organizations, etc.). Think about someone with whom you find yourself in conflict. How do you describe them? Do you describe them as having multiple attributes or can you only focus on them as a wrong-doer? Can you talk about the good times as easily as you talk about the difficult times? When we are in conflict, it can be difficult to hold multiple or competing views toward the same person or group.

Here is an example of how we can move from simplistic narratives to more complex ones. A couple living in a wealthy suburban community in Maryland complained to their friends about the neglected yard of their neighbor, expressing disappointment that this neighbor felt no need to keep the street looking good. They considered this neighbor "slovenly" and "irresponsible" and, therefore, different from the other well-behaved families on the street. One day, rather than just continuing to complain, the couple decided just to mow this neighbor's lawn after mowing their own. In reaching out, they discovered that the "neglectful" family was an elderly couple; the man had been a political prisoner in Burma. After years of torture, he could not maintain the yard or even work, and the wife had undertaken two jobs to support them. With this new information, the community could then talk about this couple not as "troublemakers" but instead as victims of a repressive regime and in need of help and support. This new construction of their identity created new pathways of communication and resolution.

The couple had to reach out to make these discoveries. In certain contexts, reaching out is not so easy. The United States forbids citizens from talking with Hamas or other terrorist organizations, for example. Furthermore, many of these organizations would not come to a negotiation table, even if one existed. While Epoch Two approaches rely on our ability to dialogue, conflict experts from an Epoch Three perspective note how many dialogues are cut off by law and simple divisiveness. The polarization in the United States between Democrats and Republicans reflects this inability and unwillingness to speak across conflict divides. Moreover, these differences, even if discussed, would likely not go away or be resolved if there were not changes made to the frames and stories people were using to make sense of themselves. Dialogue may, at times, contribute to make this happen, but at other times, if it functions as an opportunity to share views, without leading to any changes in the meaning systems or in the discourse. How can groups come together for the kinds of interaction and engagement that might contribute to shifts in the meaning, in the way reality is socially constructed? Epoch Three praxis provides new approaches that support the kinds of systems change the frames and stories, generating not just agreements or consensus, but a new foundation for collaboration, if not peace.

Conflict Resolution in Epoch Three-Praxis

In Epoch One, we talked about responses to conflict as *tactics* and *strategies* because the goal was to outwit the other side, often in a win-lose and sometimes in a win-win model. In Epoch Two, we called responses *approaches* because we want to understand the "Other" and not just beat them to meet our needs. We actually *approach* the other party to dialogue, attempting to understand and even befriend. In Epoch Three, we call intervention *praxis*. We draw on the definition of praxis articulated by Pablo Freire in his work *Pedagogy of the Oppressed* (2018) as well as the work of Toran Hansen (2008) included in this anthology. Freire considered praxis as critical self-reflections, as well as the actions taken to transform oppressive structures in society. In other words, words matter, and for this reason Freire argued that critical self-reflection was foundational to social change and the movement toward social justice. Epoch Three praxis looks to transform structures of inequality and marginalization through narrative intervention, radical care, and identification of power dynamics.

Indeed, the critical analysis of power is at the heart of Epoch Three praxis, by seeking the transformation of social relationships by shifting power dynamics. Critical self-reflection calls on us to explore how we may uphold systems of inequality in our daily behavior. When we can see how we contribute to inequality and oppression, we can more effectively help improve conditions. This form of praxis blocks the kind of externalizing blame that is so characteristic of conflict dynamics, and it helps us as practitioners, and as human beings, to include ourselves in the problem-system, perhaps contributing to privilege some voices (and ways of speaking) while silencing/marginalizing others. Being silent or neutral in the face of inequality within systems upholds the status quo, privileging those in power. Scholars now critique the neutrality and balanced perspectives approaches promoted in Epoch Two because such passivity perpetuates unfair systems.

We noted in Epoch One how, in 1963, Martin Luther King Jr. pointed to the dangers of the white moderate who can, through their neutrality, inadvertently support systems of injustice. Epoch Three praxis begins with the critical analysis of the role of Self and our role in the production of conflict; from this perspective, Epoch Three practitioners are constantly working to understand themselves, in context and the conflicts where they "work" are connected to the conflicts in their own lives, in their own social setting.

Some earlier approaches from Epoch Two have proved adaptable enough to serve the new context of Epoch Three. For example, the World Cafés and scenario building can address contemporary challenges precisely because they engage people in deep reflections about their own position as well as how to legitimize the positions of others. Additionally, both of these approaches attend to the meanings people are making. The World Café is designed to generate layers about prior conversations—as people move from table to table, changing conversational partners over the course of the process, each round of conversation is reported out as a foundation for subsequent conversations. In this way, people pay attention to how they, and others, are constructing the meanings that are circulating. Likewise, with scenario building all participants together deconstruct the ways that problems or issues are being formulated and, again, the meaning itself is a focus of attention as people reflect on their preferred futures together.

Epoch Three praxis is not equivalent to "sharing your story" in a dialogue process, for such sharing does not necessarily lead to changes arising from critical reflection, nor does it necessarily lead to changes in interactions between people. For this reason, we can note that in Epoch Three "sharing stories" as a response to conflict does not go far enough. Transforming spaces, institutions, and communities requires working with and altering the stories about self and other that anchor and support the maintenance of the conflict.

To transform meaning and shift narratives, Epoch Three practitioners recognize that *intra*-party processes for critical reflection must first be done prior to designing processes for *inter*-party dialogue or problem-solving. Intra-group reflection is a precursor for working across divides, precisely because it enables people to consider their role in the conflict without fostering defensiveness. For example, Showing Up for Racial Justice (SURJ) is an organization in which White people examine and deconstruct their privilege and then work in concert with Black organizations to support change. Said another way, in Epoch Three, *intra-group* work occurs before *inter-group* work. Moreover, there are cases where practitioners only work with one party precisely because Epoch Three praxis presumes that shifts in the narratives one group has about Self and Other will automatically engender changes in the interaction between groups.

Articles selected for Epoch Three praxis discuss *how* one person in a conflict can conduct self-reflection and intervene at a discourse level by shifting the dynamic of the relationship with the Other via changes in their discourse and narratives. Gerald Monk and John Winslade (2012) promote in their book, *When Stories Clash*, analysis of the features of narratives that anchor a conflict. They note that there are often "totalizing" narratives about Self and Other that operate as generalizations, erasing nuance, exceptions, and variation. These totalizing narratives perpetuate the conflict. Intervening in the narrative constructions helps parties transform their relationships and create new descriptions, which shift the nature of the interaction in a more positive direction. These changes to the narrative themselves have the potential to develop sustainable solutions to problems because parties have new ways of making sense of their history, as well as the issues they face. In turn, this benefits not just the conflict parties but their communities and the organizations with which they engage—the system of which they are a part.

When we locate our own contribution to conflict and recognize that we are not blameless, we have power. We are not reliant on others to change for us to have a better life. Ironically, self-reflection that challenges us at an ego level makes us stronger in the long term. We can find our agency—our area of influence, voice, and choice—when we see where we contribute to conflict or its resolution at the individual and/or community level.

Hilde Lindemann Nelson, in her book *Damaged Identity, Narrative Repair* (2001), highlights the connection between voice, agency, and narrative. She tells the story of a group of nurses in a hospital that come together to organize a yearly "Nurse Recognition Day." As they discuss their experiences in the hospital, they begin to understand how their knowledge and practices are trivialized and under-valued by the expertise of the doctors and hospital administration (an irony, indeed, as they planned their "Recognition Day"). As they examined the harmful dominant narratives that demeaned or erased their contributions to patients and their families, they begin to re-story themselves in ways that valued the knowledge and approaches that they brought to medical care at the hospital, reclaiming what Nelson calls their "moral agency." She argues that we can only really have agency if and when others see us as able to make moral decisions, able to be a moral actor. It is not enough for the nurses to have a high opinion of their own capacities for moral decision-making—they must be framed by Others as moral agents. However, as the nurses created more complex descriptions of their contributions to patient care, they began interacting with the doctors and administrators differently, demonstrating their moral agency. As a result, the doctors began to treat them differently. The system changed.

Shawn Ginwright (2010) reinforces Nelson's narrative approach in his work with Black youth in Oakland. By engaging in what he calls "radical care," Ginwright describes the everyday trauma and violence experienced by Black youth within urban communities in the United States. Through programming and advocacy, he helps youth experience themselves outside of the narratives that frame them as "lazy," "inherently violent," and "uneducated." In conversations with the youth, he re-stories them as part of a larger system of disenfranchisement, stemming back to slavery and continued into the present day. Caring can be understood as political; providing a space for youth to discover themselves enables them to more easily cast off and challenge inherited structures of inequality. Through this transformation of social relationships, Ginwright helps participants increase their social capital, the resources they have that can help them navigate their social worlds, to become greater agents in their own lives. Constructing a richer identity of oneself happens *with* others, not alone, and requires a critical understanding of society, the narratives that predominate in it, and how these narratives operate. This perspective is predicated on social constructionist views which posit that social categories and their meanings are created in and through social interactions that are anchored on historical understandings and embedded in institutions (Gergen 1999). Recognizing that it is through the process of social construction that normative assumptions about what is inherently "good" or "right" are developed, it opens up possibilities for new understandings to emerge—at least once we can interrogate those assumptions. Likewise, identities are not preexisting and fixed; rather, they are continually produced and conferred in social interactions through communication, performance, and other social processes (Gergen 1999). A narrative approach helps us enrich our understanding of ourselves and others. While social constructionism preceded the events that precipitated Epoch Three, September 11 and its aftermath pushed conflict scholars to consider what social constructionism could contribute to the field.

Whereas the earlier Epochs advocated short-term interventions (negotiations, truth and reconciliation commissions, problem-solving workshops, mediations, etc.), Ginwright demonstrates the power of practitioners entering into and remaining in the communities they wish to serve. Relationships inspire transformation, Ginwright found, when interveners become part of the social fabric to work with those carrying and perpetuating the stories (about themselves and others) that keep them imprisoned in stories they did not choose and cannot change.

We all operate within storylines that provide us with advantages and disadvantages and have material effects on us as well as others. When we locate the problem in the person, or a group, then we must remove the people to remove the problem. Externalizing responsibility for the conflict is a typical narrative construction—it confers legitimacy on Self while denigrating the Other. This is a problematic narrative construction since it generates the struggle for legitimacy and makes it more likely that "we," once we get into power, replicate the same kinds of oppression and marginalization on Others, as was done to our group. So how do we radically upend systems of injustice without simply reenacting the same violence on others?

We can see so clearly the presence of reciprocal blaming on the Internet; while social media provides a new domain for the analysis of narratives, it can also be a domain that fosters polarization, as well as the potential for large-scale social movements, such as the Arab Spring in 2011. Social media is a critical domain for understanding how the politics of "voice" have been transformed, allowing for otherwise repressed narratives to emerge, such as in the case of the Arab Spring (Castells 2015). In summary, Epoch Three praxis is one that is founded on the analysis of and engagement with meaning structured as frames, stories, discourses, and narratives. This focus on meaning highlights the role of critical self-reflection and intra-party work, enabling narratives to shift interactions and conflict dynamics at a larger scale. From this perspective, Epoch Three praxis is a social change praxis, one that seeks to redress oppression and reduce marginalization, moving beyond the aims of Epoch Two (consensus or even mutual understanding) and surpassing the goals of Epoch One (settlements via integrated bargaining). However, the praxis does not arise from an intuition but instead from research on how narrative systems function.

Research in Epoch Three

Research in Epoch Three responds to these changing narrative landscapes and conflict dynamics, moving away from the top-down approaches in Epoch One, where the researcher sought to be objective and omniscient. In Epoch One, the perspective of the researched was absent altogether. In Epoch Two, the researcher is more visible, as ethnographers grapple with their biases, limitations and ethical questions. They provide "think descriptions" (Geertz, et al 2000) that often includes their own presence. Grounded Theory, which codes data, often leads to a more invisible researcher. However, in Epoch Three, methods researchers work to account for the power dynamics of research itself. Who carries out the research, analyzes it, and eventually writes the finished product? Research approaches in Epoch Three address these challenges by embedding the researcher in the contexts as well including the people most affected by conflict or an issue as participants in the research process. For example, Participatory Action Research (PAR) makes the participants a part of the study construction, collection, and evaluation. In this research tradition, participants are empowered to lead the research as stakeholders in the process. This proves quite a departure from Epoch One approaches that consider the researcher's job to study conflict as an "object" separate from themselves. In Epoch Three, researchers frame themselves as "learner" rather than expert, acknowledging that knowledge production has historically been the domain of the dominant and the privileged, but also recognizing that the scientific enterprise has itself functioned to preserve that privilege. From this perspective, the research on conflict has contributed to erase or sideline the frames that local indigenous people would make about problems/conflicts, deepening their marginalization. For Epoch Three researchers, people are not research "subjects" but rather partners in the inquiry process; they are stakeholders in the research process, as they are the ones that are impacted by the framing of the problem/research focus, as well as the findings/solutions that could emerge from the research. In this way, Epoch Three research is more likely to be applied collaboratively—focused on how to address problems *with* people rather than trying to understand conflicts as abstract puzzles, distinct from the people who are living the conflict.

Ultimately, Epoch Three approaches also call upon the greater reflexivity in the researcher, asking her to consider how her own identity and perspective impacts the methodology and knowledge that the study produces. Through this reflexivity, the researcher can begin to see and release any embedded colonial tendencies.

Epoch Three seems like a long-awaited response to Albert Einstein's insight that "no problem can be solved from the same level of consciousness that created it." Together, in Epoch Three, we search for the level of consciousness where the problem is solved and then advocate that others join us in this shift. This means giving up the problem and looking critically at ourselves while using our imaginations to construct better futures.

Keywords for Epoch Three: reflexivity, voice, silence, power, marginalization, radical care, narrative mediation, conflict transformation, praxis, participatory action research, mutual liberation.

References

Castel, Alison. *The Politics of Legibility: Narrative Dynamics of Transitional Justice in Rural Colombia.* George Mason University, 2016 Ann Arbor ProQuest.

Clifford, James, George E. Marcus, Mike Fortun, and Kim Fortun. *Writing Culture: The Poetics and Politics of Ethnography, 25th Anniversary Edition.* 2nd ed. Berkeley, CA: University of California Press, 2010.

Fassin, Didier, and Richard Rechtman. *The Empire of Trauma: An Inquiry into the Condition of Victimhood.* Princeton, NJ: Princeton University Press, 2009.

Federman, Sarah. "The Ideal Perpetrator. Considering the Social-construction of Accountability: A Study of the French National Railways (SNCF)." *Security Dialogue*, Volume 49, Issue 5: 327–44 (2018).

Ferguson, Niall. *Civilization: The West and the Rest.* New York: Penguin, 2011.

Freire, Paulo. *Pedagogy of the Oppressed: 50th Anniversary Edition.* New York: Bloomsbury Publishing, 2018.

Gergen, Kenneth J. *An Invitation to Social Construction.* Thousand Oaks, CA: SAGE, 1999.

Huntington, Samuel P. *The Clash of Civilizations and the Remaking of World Order.* New York: Simon & Schuster, 2007.

Monk, Gerald and John Winslade. *When Stories Clash: Addressing Conflict with Narrative Mediation.* Chagrin Falls, OH: Taos Institute Publications, 2012.

United Nations Alliance of Civilizations. "Who We Are," 2018. Web. Accessed January 11, 2018. https://www.unaoc.org/who-we-are/.

Notes

1. See a description of the campaign at https://www.dhs.gov/see-something-say-something.

2. See the 9/11 Memorial and Museum website at https://www.911memorial.org/museum.

3. See Karen Armstrong's interview that addresses questions on the nature of religious violence at https://www.nieuwwij.nl/english/karen-armstrong-nothing-islam-violent-christianity/; in this link, her books on the topic of religion and violence are mentioned. See also Graeme Wood's article, "What ISIS Really Wants," where he discusses the violent nature of Islam: https://www.theatlantic.com/magazine/archive/2015/03/what-isis-really-wants/384980/.

4. See the text of President George W. Bush's speech where he answers this question at http://www.washingtonpost.com/wp-srv/nation/specials/attacked/transcripts/bush address_092001.html.

5. See "Decade of War: Volume I, Enduring Lessons from the Past Decade of Operations," which is the U.S. military document that reflects on the failures of the prior decade of war, at https://searchworks.stanford.edu/view/10402947.

6. See https://en.wikipedia.org/wiki/Habeas_corpus for a definition of "habeas corpus" and its history.

7. See the argument against "extra-judicial" killings at https://www.theguardian.com/commentisfree/2012/jun/11/obama-drone-wars-normalisation-extrajudicial-killing; see an article in favor of the use of drones at https://www.brookings.edu/articles/why-drones-work-the-case-for-washingtons-weapon-of-choice/.

8. For a description of the history of mass surveillance in the United States, see https://en.wikipedia.org/wiki/Mass_surveillance_in_the_United_States.

9. See this link to Brown University's Watson Institute "Costs of War" project that provides data on civilian deaths for the wars in Afghanistan and Iraq: http://watson.brown.edu/costsofwar/costs/human/civilians.

10. See the article that describes the conflict between students-as-victims and the NRA at http://www.baltimoresun.com/entertainment/tv/z-on-tv-blog/bs-fe-zontv-nra-stoneman-douglas-pr-battle-20180226-story.html.

11. See the reports documenting increases in polarization at the Pew Research Center: http://www.pewresearch.org/topics/political-polarization/2018/.

12. See the Me Too Movement at https://metoomvmt.org/.

13. See the Wikipedia entry on "cognitive dissonance," which provides a short description, as well as a list of key theorists: https://en.wikipedia.org/wiki/Cognitive_dissonance.

14. See Goldstone, J. (2011). "Understanding the Revolutions of 2011." *Foreign Affairs* 3: 8–16.

15. For the list of assumptions associated to systems theory, see Dent, E. and Umpleby, S. (1998). "Underlying Assumptions of Several Traditions in Systems Theory and Cybernetics." In Robert Trappl (ed.) *Cybernetics and Systems '98; Vienna: Austrian Society for Cybernetic Studies*, 1998, 513–18.

Power

Vivienne Jabri

Vivienne Jabri, professor of international politics in the Department of War Studies at King's College London has a special interest in the politics of conflict, violence, and security practices. In addition to academic scholarship, she has also worked in the arts on exhibitions about war. She recently won the Leverhulme Artist in Residence Award to work on a project titled "The Fabric of War," which looks at war in the everyday. She also won the International Studies Association's Distinguished Scholar Award in 2015.

Jabri's piece opens with a genealogy of the field of conflict resolution; her descriptions align with the genealogy outlined in this book. She discusses the Cold War (Epoch One) and the post-Cold War period (Epoch Two) and then critiques the approaches the field of conflict resolution has used to understand and respond to mass violence. Even though she wrote this piece during the heart of the interethnic warfare that defined Epoch Two, Jabri's theories reflect Epoch Three because she studies the discursive dynamics that produce and perpetuate violence.

Jabri explores "the social continuities in life which enable war and give it legitimacy, backed by discursive and institutional structures" (1996, 6). In Epoch One, Johan Galtung and John Burton pointed to institutions as sites of structural or latent violence; Jabri goes further, arguing these institutions also provide the cultural norms and structural support for active violence. When individuals interact with the continuities produced by these institutions, they are led to war as a viable option. She challenges the theory that war spawns from the innate "makeup" of human beings, the result of leadership, or a natural response to external environmental or economic factors. She locates the origins of war at the intersection of self and society. If social practices legitimize war as a means to address conflict, upending war requires intervening at the discursive sites in societies that offer war as a viable solution to problems.

Once a society legitimizes violence against a group, mass expulsions, ethnic cleansing, torture, rape, and so on can occur and are interpreted by the society as a necessary, if unfortunate, fact of war. In Machiavellian terms, during war, the ends (winning) justify the means. For harm to be acceptable, the society must first construct a mythology around inclusion and exclusion, those worthy of life and those whose lives must come at the expense of the greater project. This framing of insiders and outsiders produce moral certainties that, paradoxically, can evoke the uncertainties of war.

Questions to consider: Where in your community do you hear justifications for excluding certain individuals or groups? Against whom has your society legitimized violence (terrorists, illegal immigrants, felons, etc.)? What words are used to justify physical force against these individuals?

Discourses on Violence

Vivienne Jabri

> *War is not only a state of affairs, but a process of gradual realisation. First, one has to get used to the idea of it. The idea then has to become part of everyday life. Then rules can change, rules of behaviour, of language, of expectations.*
>
> —Slavenca Draculic, *Balkan Express* (1993)

War is a widespread human phenomenon. It is an option that is available to states and communities as conflicts emerge and relations break down. With the exception of pacifism, the belief that war is unacceptable under any circumstances, the predominant view is that violence may be resorted to in conditions of high salience, for causes that are deemed worthy of the human and material destruction which is war. The constitutive element of war as violent conflict is that it is aimed at social/political objectives requiring human sacrifice in an environment of threat. As a form of behavior, violent conflict is not confined to inter-state relations, but involves communities within and across state boundaries involved either directly in combat or indirectly through economic and symbolic support. Our understanding of war cannot, therefore, be limited to inter-state conduct or to the definition of world politics as the external relations of states as behavioral entities. War as a social phenomenon involves individuals, communities and states and any attempt to uncover its genesis must incorporate the discursive and institutional continuities which render violent conflict a legitimate and widely accepted mode of human conduct.

The advent of nuclear weapons and the Cold War stand-off in the European arena invited suggestions that war had come to be an obsolete phenomenon, its ramifications too costly for its continuance as a technique of statecraft. Increasing economic interdependence and the spread of international organizations instituted linkages which enabled the resolution of conflicts and competition over resources within cooperative interactions. The "war generation" was a label applied to those who had directly experienced the First and Second World Wars. Future generations would not again be allowed to experience such devastation. Nuclear weaponry and a policy of deterrence would be their insurance policy against the onset of further wars. Any conflicts and competitions for global influence would be fought out by proxy, in arenas outside the European "theatre," involving combatants from elsewhere, "clients" engaged in "hot" wars to sustain the North's "cold" conflict.

The end of the Cold War was deemed to have brought forth a "new world order," free of threat, concerned with progress, international trade, and individual material contentment. Protracted conflicts such as the Arab-Israeli conflict and conflict in southern Africa witnessed transformations towards resolution, possibilities unforeseen and unpredicted in the previous era. The breakdown of the Soviet Union, the democratisation of formerly authoritarian states, and increasing calls for popular democracy elsewhere focused attention on a world politics based on representation and human rights. Security could no longer be defined in military terms but in terms of shared threats and concerns the resolution of which demanded cooperation rather than confrontation.

However, just as the Cold War era was based on violence and high military expenditure, so too the post-Cold War situation has produced new uncertainties, new demands for sovereignty, intercommunal violence, and military intervention. The war in the former Yugoslavia and the 1991 conflict in the Gulf brought into sharp focus the readiness with which leaders and their populations resort to violence as a form of behavior in emergent conflicts. These and other conflicts throughout Europe, Africa, the Middle East, Asia, and the American continent show that violence for political ends continues to constitute an aspect of the human condition. The inter-state conflict in the Gulf and inter-communal conflicts in Rwanda, Yugoslavia, Algeria, and elsewhere illustrate with vivid clarity the ability of leaderships to mobilize support for violence and, in certain civil wars, the involvement of mass populations in direct combat against former neighbors and fellow citizens. The phenomenon of violent conflict cannot, therefore, be understood simply through analyses of leadership decision-making, but calls for uncovering the continuities in social life which enable war and give it legitimacy, backed by discursive and institutional structures.

The study of war has produced a number of often conflicting answers to Quincy Wright's question, "Why is war thought? Why is war fought?"[1] The history of human political violence has shown that we cannot produce monocausal explanations of war. Studies which concentrate on assumed innate human characteristics fail to account for the societal factors which are implicated in what is essentially an interactive and dynamic process. Similarly, investigations which link attributes of the international system, such as balances of power, not only produce contradictory findings, but seem to negate human decision-making and psychological processes in the onset of war in specific conditions. Studies of violent conflict aspire to uncover, through empirical investigation, patterns of behavior which lead to war. As indicated by Holsti, studies of war may be divided into those which emphasize structural or "ecological" variables, such as the distribution of power capabilities within the system, and those which emphasize "decision-making, values, and perceptions of policy-makers" in attempts to isolate common features leading up to the decision for war.[2]

This book does not aim to review the empirical findings of the above investigations. Rather, it seeks to use social and political theory in an attempt to locate violence in the relationship between self and society. It is primarily an ontological investigation of the constitution of self and society, or action and social structure, and the place of war therein. The primary assumption made in the study is that war or violent conflict are social phenomena emerging through, and constitutive of, social practices which have, through time and across space, rendered war an institutional form that is largely seen as an inevitable and at times acceptable form of human conduct. The study specifically utilizes Giddens's structuration theory,[3] a statement on the ontological relationship between action and structure, in seeking to understand the institutionalization of war as human practice. The assumption is that our understanding of violent human conflict cannot simply be based on instrumental rationality but must situate the agent, or acting subject, in relation to the structural properties which render war a continuity in social systems. The relationship between human action and social structure is at the heart of social theory and is central to developing an understanding of violent conflict if we assume that this mode of conduct is a continuity in patterned social systems. As stated by Giddens, structuration theory is concerned with the "conditions governing the continuity or transformation of structures, and therefore the reproduction of systems," which in turn are "reproduced relations between actors or collectivities, organized as regular social practices."[4] The relevance of structuration theory for developing an understanding of war is located in this theory's concern with the reproduction of social systems, or aspects of social life, through the activities of situated actors drawing upon and reproducing the structural features of social systems. The starting assumption is that violent conflict is not a product of characteristics innate within the "make-up" of human beings or of instrumental reason, nor is it a product of the structure of the international system, but derives from the ontological relationship between agency and structure, where war as human action is a product of human decisions made within the context of structured social relations. The argument is that violent conflict is itself structurated through the actions of agents situated in relation to discursive and institutional continuities which both enable war's occurrence and legitimate it as a form of human behavior.

Structuration theory and its relevance to the understanding of violent conflict will be returned to in chapter three. The remaining sections of this chapter begin with a discussion of the implication of violent conflict as a human condition. The second section locates the parameters of conflict analysis as currently defined by the field of conflict studies. The third and final section of the chapter identifies the premises made in a specifically critical approach to the study of conflict.

The Social Meaning of War

Slavenca Draculic's description quoted at the outset of this chapter is based on her experience of the ethnic nationalist wars which led to the breakdown of Yugoslavia. It illustrates with vivid clarity the two prominent aspects of that peculiarly human condition which is war, namely its cruel reality and its immediate impact on the everyday and the mundane. Its physical manifestation has an equivalent impact upon discourse which, in a self-fulfilling prophecy, renders the destructive element of human violence acceptable or legitimate to those who perceive war in strategic terms.

War has no exclusionary clauses. As shown by the civil wars in the former Yugoslavia, Somalia, Angola, Rwanda, and the 1991 war in the Gulf, while the decision to go to war is confined to the few making up the "war cabinet," its consequences go far beyond and affect the armed as well as the unarmed. Telecommunications advances also render proximate events which could, in the past, be perceived as sufficiently distant to warrant inaction or indifference. Combatants vie for the onlookers' support and their actions, even in combat, may be directed more at these external others than at the enemy. Official and non-official responses to a conflict are greatly influenced by the proximity of the media to a particular conflict. Protracted and ongoing conflicts perceived as unnews-worthy in the editorial rooms remain hidden from view and therefore beyond any ethical or moral consideration by policy-makers and/or audiences.

War brings with it other socially constitutive manifestations. Affiliation and identity come to be defined in terms of exclusionist social boundaries. To be a dissenting voice is to be an outsider, who is often branded as traitor to the cause and, therefore, deserving of sacrifice at the mythical altar of solidarity. What would previously have been blurred social boundaries become sharpened primarily through a discursive focus upon features, both symbolic and material, which divide communities to the extent that the desire for destruction of the enemy is perceived to be the only legitimate or honorable course to follow. Again, Slavenca Draculic expresses this experience of war:

> After a year of violence, with the dead numbering approximately 200,000, with many more wounded and over two million refugees flooding Europe, there came the story of concentration camps. And all of a sudden in a thin desperate man behind barbed wire the world recognized not a Moslem, but a human being. That picture, the words "concentration camp" and "holocaust" finally translated the true meaning of "ethnic cleansing". At last people in the West began to grasp what was going on. It was suddenly clear that Europe had not learned its lesson, that history always repeats itself and that someone is always a Jew. Once the concept of "otherness" takes root, the unimaginable becomes possible. Not in some mythological country but to ordinary urban citizens, as I discovered all too painfully.[5]

As a conflict escalates towards violence and as the "war mood"[6] takes hold of entire populations, the dissident from either camp or the peacemaker from the onlooking external world can become subject to social contempt and censure rather than admiration.

Once violent destruction of the enemy and its valued resources comes to define a relationship, the rules of the game or the rules of "everyday life" change. Behavior that is unacceptable in peacetime becomes legitimate in time of war. Specifically killing, torture, rape, mass expulsions, ethnic cleansing and the creation of concentration camps are explained by such terms which essentially state that while war goes on we must expect such occurrences, or simply not be surprised by them. They form part of the strategic calculations perceived as necessary when the prime motivation is winning in war.[7] The existence of conventions on the conduct of war, on such matters as the treatment of prisoners of war, or of populations under occupation, may suggest a basis of ethical norms which interconnect international society. The very existence of these laws may, on the other hand, be interpreted as humanity's acknowledgement of war as an unavoidable aspect of social interaction.

War has a certain dialectic which incorporates both normality and abnormality. Its normality derives from the assumption, held predominantly by the "realist" school of thought in international relations,[8] that war has always been a tool, or a mode of behaviour, to which individuals and groups may have recourse in times of conflict with other individuals and groups. The Hobbesian emphasis on the state of nature as being inherently conflictual and violent suggests that nonviolent interaction is an artificial condition achieved only through an imposed contractual order. The breakdown of social order, according to Hobbes is a mere reversion back to what is naturally human: "Hereby it is manifest, that during the time men live without a common Power to keep them all in awe, they are in that condition which is called Warre; and such a warre, as is of every man, against every man."[9] As pointed out by Chanteur, the Hobbesian analysis is based on an ahistorical and apolitical state of nature where the universal driving forces are centered at one and the same time around fear and desire. Human beings fear not so much the natural world around them but other human beings where the desire to dominate is the basic need defining what it is to be human.[10]

War is also an abnormal condition. War implies the breakdown of an existing order defining either domestic or international situations. War constitutes behavior which is unacceptable in times of peace, or non-war. War breaks down taboos against killing and the deliberate and direct infliction of suffering against fellow human beings. The mechanism by which war specifically breaks down taboos is distinguished by the relatively short timespan between the existence of a taboo, its breakdown and its re-establishment. The moral boundary between war and non-war is defined by the acceptance or legitimacy conferred on violence as a form of human behavior.

The discourse of war aims at the construction of a mythology based on inclusion and exclusion. This categorization sharply contrasts the insiders from the outsiders who are the "others," or the deserving enemy. This process cannot be confined to the definition of the enemy but incorporates the inclusion of texts which valorize the history and cause of one party to a conflict while depicting the claims of the enemy as unfounded, unjust or even diabolical. The discoursed inclusion and exclusion cannot allow uncertainty or doubt, so if such are expressed, they must be represented as irrational or even treacherous. Any representation which blurs the inclusion/exclusion boundary breaks down certainties constructed in the name of war and forms a counter-discourse which deconstructs and delegitimates war and thereby fragments myths of unity, duty and conformity.

Conflict, and specifically violent conflict, is constitutively defined in terms of inclusion and exclusion and any understanding of war must incorporate the means through which such systems are perpetuated and implicated in violent action. Linklater rightly points out that "questions of inclusion and exclusion are central to international relations, since states and the state system are, in themselves, systems of inclusion and exclusion."[11] Systems of inclusion and exclusion generate a "normative" discourse concerned with the justifications of such formations, a "sociological" discourse centered around the workings and maintenance of systems of inclusion and exclusion, and "praxeological" questions related to the practical implications of such systems.[12] While the normative implications of such systems defined in the cosmopolitan/ communitarian debate will not be dealt with,[13] the sociological and praxeological components form a central focus for the framework of understanding developed in this study. As will be argued later, systems of inclusion and exclusion are structured through identiational discursive and institutional practices implicated in the legitimation of and support for violent conflict.

War is a social condition and takes place within the realm of society. Analyses of war based on notions of innate drives or basic needs fail to recognize the social and political origins of what Diderot referred to as "the convulsive and violent disease of the body politic."[14] To conceive of the individual as somehow separate from society is to negate the constitutive implications of normative and discursive processes which define the institutional continuities of social life. War is a product of social interaction. It emerges or is made possible through processes of group formation; for example, the institutionalization of difference as reflected in the division of humanity into a world of separate states, and the establishment of machineries aimed specifically at the war-making process. The interplay between self and society comes into sharp focus especially in time of war when identity, affiliation and the will to sacrifice are tested against criteria defining loyal citizenship.

Although war is a product of social life, it reflects a drastic change in the rules of conduct where actions take forms which are qualitatively different from interaction in times of non-war. Quincy Wright's seminal work on the study of war concentrates on interstate war in pointing to the "legal condition which equally permits two or more hostile groups to carry on a conflict by armed force." The term conflict, according to Wright, suggests that "war is a definite and mutually understood pattern of behavior, distinguishable not only from other patterns of behavior in general but from other forms of conflict."[15] War reflects a breakdown in the rules of everyday life, possesses its own socialized customs, but is, even so, a product of social and inter-social formations.

In answer to the question "where are the major causes of war to be found?", Kenneth Waltz suggests three "images" encompassing individual traits, internal structures of states, and the interstate system as having prevalence in Western political thought.[16] He provides a devastating critique of the first two and concludes that any explanation of war must recognize that it is a product of social formations and more specifically the anarchical inter-state system. In relation to perspectives which assume innate human characteristics, his conclusion is that "To attempt to explain social forms on the basis of psychological data is to commit the error of psychologism: the analysis of individual behavior used uncritically to explain group phenomena."[17] This view has its supporters in the field of social anthropology where researchers argue both against essentialism and in support of the view that war is a distinctly social phenomenon.[18] In rejecting universalist premises on human characteristics, Howell and Willis point to the implications of essentialist criteria for social research:

> An accepted notion that aggression is a given characteristic in humans everywhere leads to a search for it in various social settings. This, however, begs the question and determines the formulation of research, phrasing the questions in terms of how aggressive drives are handled. The vocabulary of the debates reflects this, for the contrast is drawn between aggression and non-aggression, violence and non-violence; it is the absence of conflict not the presence of something else that is noted.[19]

Just as inter-personal and inter-societal behavior must be located within the ideological and cultural settings of societies, so too the linguistic constructs within research derive from and construct the settings which they seek to understand.

Waltz argues that explanations of war based on the internal structures of states are similarly reductionist in orientation and remain inadequate as bases for explaining inter-state violent conflict. He specifically directs his attack against the liberal assumption that "democracy is preeminently the peaceful form of the state" arguing that "faith in public opinion or, more generally, faith in the uniformly peaceful proclivities of democracies has proved utopian."[20] Instead of providing an alternative theory of the state, Waltz suggests that inter-state war must be situated in the anarchical structure of the inter-state system which contains specific characteristics peculiar to the game of international politics where "(1) the stakes of the game are considered to be of unusual importance and (2) . . . in international politics the use of force is not excluded as a means of influencing the outcome."[21] This forms the basis of Kenneth Waltz's neo-realist perspective on international relations generally and on war in particular. It is a perspective which Waltz later develops as a specifically structural approach to the study of international relations and which Gilpin adopts in his analysis of the impact of war on change in world politics.[22] Structure is here recognized as both determining and constraining the behavior of states within the anarchic condition of the inter-state system, and the distribution of capabilities is a central feature in the analysis of state behavior.

Does this structuralist orientation to the explanation of violent human conflict provide an improvement on explanations based on individual traits or instrumental reason? The first argument against the approach is that it suffers from the same linguistic determinism as that which Howell and Willis direct against the essential-ist premises which underpin explanations based on individual innate char-acteristics.[23] The second argument is that, as Wendt has pointed out, Waltz's understanding of system structure is "ontologically reductionist"[24] in that it con-ceives structure as constraining the agency of pre-existing states rather than as "generating" state agents themselves. Given this, the theory fails to provide a social conception of the state or of agency. The third argument against the approach that is relevant to our present objectives is that it fails to provide an adequate framework for understanding the social formations which generate violent human conflict across the boundaries of the state. Conflict is not confined to inter-state relations but, as argued above, involves both state and non-state actors. The state itself is a container of individuals and communities existing within shared worlds of meaning, symbolic orders, and institutional frameworks which are, as will be argued in this study, implicated in the generation of violent human conflict. The agent-structure problem will be returned to in an elaboration of structuration theory later in this study. The following section provides a brief overview of the field which is specifically devoted to developing explanations of conflict and con-flict resolution.

Conflict Analysis and the Understanding of War

The study of conflict seeks to broaden the analysis of political violence beyond the inter-state level of analysis and adopts a more specifically decision-making framework. The boundaries of conflict and peace studies relate to two fundamen-tal assumptions: firstly, conflict is a generic phenomenon, and as such requires a multidisciplinary approach; and secondly, the field has a normative orientation based on a concern to alleviate the dysfunctional aspects of violent conflict. These central assumptions, while providing a basis of identity for the conflict researcher, do not immediately suggest the existence of a hard core of theory around which what Lakatos terms a "scientific research programme" is conducted.[25] Groom sug-gests a division of the field between conflict research and peace research, where the former considers conflict as a subjective phenomenon resulting from individ-ual and group decision-making, while the latter concerns structural inequalities and exploitation as bases of conflict.[26] Nicholson suggests that the former consti-tutes a "social science" as it concerns "a description of how social groups actually behave" while the latter constitutes "social engineering" as it is a "prescription for achieving specified goals in the light of the propositions discovered by the social scientists."[27] The two approaches have been presented as a dichotomy whereby the hard core of conflict research is rational actor decision-making while the hard core of peace research looks to structures which perpetuate domination and depen-dency, defined by Galtung as "structural violence."[28]

The debate has its origins in the 1960s when neo-Marxist West European peace researchers, such as Herman Schmid, criticized the empiricist and uncritical orientation of the field, calling for an explicit statement on the concept of peace as a clearly-defined value orientation.[29] The call was for a critical mode of inquiry that would transcend the behavioralist consensus which became prevalent in the late 1960s and early 1970s, as evidenced by the nature of articles published in the United States-based *Journal of Conflict Resolution*. Krippendorff, for example, suggested that while this methodological consensus brought peace research a certain legitimacy, the cost was that it "lost its significance for a reorientation of the social sciences,"[30] which could only be restored by a return to fundamental questions of ontology and epistemology. Despite such calls for reorientation and theoretical and methodological clarity, the conflict research/peace research dichotomy has largely remained static. The field has not experienced the level of theoretical debate prevalent in other social sciences, including international relations. As pointed out by Reid and Yanarella.

> The controversy has simply run aground as the concern for communication and dialogue across schools of peace research has dwindled. Radical peace researchers have an important stake in renewing this controversy, going beyond the limits of the earlier phase of conflict.[31]

The field has been so dominated by a positivist orientation that questions of ontology and epistemology have been largely ignored, since the methods of the natural sciences have been assumed to be applicable to the study of social phenomena such as conflict.

As succinctly pointed out by Burton, conflict studies is "not merely concerned with conflict as a specific and overt happening, but with the underlying human and institutional problems that create it."[32] The primary aim of conflict research may be explanation, but the field also has a self-consciously practical aim. It is assumed that greater understanding of conflict processes leads to the amelioration of their most destructive implications. As pointed out by Nardin, "Conflict research reflects a commitment to what is regarded as theoretical illumination, but it is also practically motivated. Like many other branches of inquiry, it is the offspring of a wish to ameliorate the human condition."[33]

The parameters of conflict research start from explanations of the causes of conflict, and develop into analyses of its dynamics and development, namely escalation and de-escalation processes, to conflict resolution. Developments in the latter theme have focused on mediation and negotiation processes and, as a result of Burton's unparalled contributions to the field, on innovative modes of conflict resolution.[34]

Conflict research is based on the assumption that conflict is a generic phenomenon and that any separation of types of conflict based on levels of societal interaction is an artificial one built on the exigencies of the division of the social sciences into separate academic disciplines. Inter-personal conflict becomes as much a valid point of departure as conflict between states. The focus of investigation is, therefore, on what Kriesberg terms "social conflict," where it is assumed that theories on the origins, dynamics and termination of conflict have explanatory potential in investigations of such seemingly diverse conflicts as college-based disputes, gender-related, inter-racial and international conflicts.[35] The basic mode of inquiry is to isolate the conflict system, which becomes the unit of analysis. Propositions linking sets of variables are tested against empirical observations. Sets of interrelated hypotheses deemed successful after empirical testing are then formulated into an empirical theory.[36] The most important feature of this approach is that it is dependent on a *decision-making framework* which seeks to explain the interaction process between parties in conflict and the social environmental influences on this interaction.

One major focus of inquiry has been what Kriesberg terms "conflict mitigation" which suggests that "one seeks to control the adverse consequences of the way a conflict is waged."[37] This approach takes as its baseline the specific conflict under investigation and focuses on the modes by which it may be resolved, from negotiation, to mediation, to problem-solving.[38] This form of research has produced ideas on the suitability of different modes of peacemaking in international conflict and has been successful in highlighting the dynamics of the conflict resolution process. If empirical theory is the primary aim of this research, then the combined efforts of empirical researchers have pointed to the nature of the conflict resolution process; the spectrum of activity which defines it; and the suitability of different modes of peacemaking in different conflict situations.[39] The practical aim is to develop frameworks which may be applied in the international arena both through the incorporation of mediation within institutional settings,[40] and through the direct participation of conflict researchers as conflict resolvers.

The analysis of conflict, investigations of the dynamic processes involved in the generation and escalation of conflict, have the purpose of informing conflict mitigation. The question of "why war?" is approached by defining factors, or independent variables, which explain the escalation of conflict situations towards the use of violence. War is defined as a contest or conflict over valued resources and belief systems carried out through the use of violence by one group against another. The aim is to uncover a causal sequence specifying factors which may lead to war in a specific situation. As Vasquez points out, "war is fundamentally a political institution that serves crucial political functions."[41] This instrumentalist view sees war as a tool of policy that is available to the decision-maker where conflicts of interest escalate to such a degree of intensity that violence is deemed an appropriate method of achieving desired outcomes. Whether a contention over issues and desired outcomes is carried out violently or through nonviolent modes of interaction is dependent on a number of factors related to the issues at stake, the relationship between the parties, resources available to the parties, the ideological disposition of the parties, and the impact of the social environment.[42] This last factor also incorporates the "institutional context" in which issues arise, agendas are formed and interaction between contending parties regulated.[43] Violence, whether used by state or non-state actors, is one form of conflict behavior and a component part of the life cycle of a conflict. War is understood as part of a wider interaction process. The emergence of goal incompatibilities between contending parties leads to the adoption of behaviors aimed at achieving desired outcomes.

The framework of analysis which underpins empirical investigations in the study of conflict is one of *interactive decision-making* and the model is a "modified rational actor model."[44] It is "modified" since it incorporates subjective expected utilities, recognizing the potential diversity of conflict goals which may range from the economic to the ideological, and of subjective probabilities influenced by misperceptions, informational distortion and ideological biases. The approach centers around conflict processes within the life cycle of a conflict which can be considered as having "causal importance"[45] in escalation to the use of force. Such factors as misunderstood signals, perceived changes in the balance of advantage between the protagonists, prior relationships, and the input of allies and interested others could, either singly or in combination, influence the course of a conflict and behaviors therein.

The notion of "intent" or purposeful behavior is central to the perspective outlined above. Mitchell defines conflict behavior as aimed specifically at gaining desired outcomes by influencing the adversary's evaluations of the issues in conflict and altering their perceptions of the merits of their actions.[46] Himes defines social conflicts as "purposeful struggles between collective actors who use social power to defeat or remove opponents and to gain status, power, resources, and other scarce values."[47] The idea of purposeful behavior suggests the existence of an element of choice between alternative courses of action. Kriesberg suggests that the "use of the word choice should not be interpreted to mean that all alternatives are consciously weighed by each party and that, after due calculation, a course of action is selected." Interest is, rather, focused on the "factors that influence and constrain the course. Followed."[48] Such influences and constraints derive from the dynamics of the conflict and its social environment. The purposefulness of conflict behavior is stressed by Kriesberg when he states that "there must be an intention to induce the other side to yield what the coercer wishes to obtain."[49]

Two questions emerge from the above. The first relates to the influences and constraints which determine the course of action adopted. An instrumentalist perspective suggests that primary constraining or enabling factors would include the balance of advantage between the protagonists, prior relationships linking the parties, as well as constituency and third party input. Enabling and constraining factors could also be conceptualized in terms of structural continuities within which decision-making takes place. The constraining and enabling inputs which determine the mode of behavior within situations of conflict cannot merely be analyzed in terms of immediate cost/benefit evaluations, but must also incorporate the institutional and discursive continuities which form the backdrop to conflict behavior. This second concern is central to a "critical" approach adopted in this study and will be returned to later.

The concern of the remainder of this chapter is to highlight the questions and the research problems which have emerged from the "modified rationality" model or the interactive decision-making approach. The focus of the review is drawn to two interrelated analytical problems, namely the parties to a conflict and the issues which lead to the emergence of violent conflict.

The first question relates to the "parties" in conflict and the ways in which these are defined in the conflict research literature. One method is to adopt Bueno de Mesquita's assumption that decisions about the onset of war are controlled by either a single leader or a centralized and well-defined leadership such as a "war cabinet," both of which are taken to act as "rational expected utility maximisers." According to Bueno de Mesquita, a necessary condition for a nation or a party to go to war is that its leader must calculate it to be in his or her interest which is itself equated with the "national" or group interest.[50] While Bueno de Mesquita "recognizes that decision making about the use of force is a process of social choice, he adopts a simplifying assumption that collapses the process into the hands of a single dominant leader."[51] As Haney et al. rightly point out, this is consistent with the assumptions of the realist approach in international relations which views states as single, unitary, rational actors.

The central problem with Bueno de Mesquita's treatment of the problem is that it precludes analysis of the involvement of non-leadership levels of society which are involved in the process of war. How do we, therefore, delimit the boundaries of the "parties" in conflict? The answer has a number of implications for both conflict analysis and practical concerns with conflict resolution. Leaderships may choose war, but it is the entire social framework which becomes involved in war, defining itself in terms of the contending sides to the conflict. How we define the parties to a conflict may also be a reflection of dominant discourses around a particular conflict situation which legitimize or render visible the claims of one while delegitimizing those of the other. Scholarly analyses or journalistic accounts of particular conflicts may also directly or indirectly influence practical approaches adopted by potential mediators in the resolution of conflict such that mediation becomes a legitimating exercise for those chosen as "representatives" of the protagonists.

That party boundaries are, in some types of conflict, difficult to define is especially reflected in conflicts involving diffuse categories such as classes, genders or ethnic groups. As indicated by Blalock, "In such instances there may be highly active members of both parties but also many others whose behaviours and loyalties are difficult to classify as being clearly on the one side or the other."[52]

Difficulties in unambiguously classifying parties emerge especially in inter-communal civil war where the boundaries between the armed and the "unarmed" become seriously blurred. The diffuse nature of the conflict in the former Yugoslavia and that in Rwanda demonstrates that in certain conflicts the combatant/civilian divide is problematic. Within the former Yugoslavia, an already armed and militarized civilian population rapidly became involved in inter-communal hostilities involving households, neighborhoods and ultimately entire regions. Inter-communal violence on a massive scale in Rwanda similarly shows the ease with which a civilian population is recruited directly into active combat. The dividing line between decision-makers and combatants on the one hand and the non-combatant population on the other in situations of inter-communal conflict is not as unambiguous as in inter-state conflict. Even in such seemingly well-defined conflicts, however, it is important to analyze the relationship between the war-making machinery of the state (which includes the war cabinet as well as the armed forces) and the civilian population, whose support is mobilized towards the war effort. The gathering of information and its dissemination may in such instances be used to ensure popular support for a military solution to an emergent dispute. Tilly's emphasis on "resource mobilization" as a central aspect of the escalation of conflict towards violence becomes highly relevant in investigations of the legitimation of violence as a mode of conflict behavior. It also provides a behavioral link between decisions made by policymakers and the support conferred on these decisions by the wider constituency.[53] To confine analysis to the role of leadership decision-making and instrumentalist calculation is, therefore, to negate the crucial role played through societal processes in the legitimation of war.

Empirical investigations of conflict have also sought to analyze the relationship between issue type and the emergence of violent conflict. The consensus in the literature is that, rather than developing typologies of issues around which conflicts evolve, it is more fruitful to uncover processes through which some issues become so salient as to enable leaders to mobilize support for a course of war as opposed to peaceful resolutions of emerging disputes.

A number of typologies have been suggested as a means to understanding the role that issues play in the emergence of violent conflict. Aubert defines issues in terms of those which are "consensual" as opposed to those which are "dissensual."[54] Consensual conflicts are where parties agree about the value of what they seek, but a conflict arises where one obtains more of what it wants and the other achieves less. These are conflicts of interest where there is agreement on the value of the resources sought and disagreement over the distribution of scarce resources such as territory, leadership positions, access rights and competitions over markets. Dissensual conflicts, on the other hand, exist where parties differ in belief systems and where one seeks the conversion, persecution, or even the destruction of the other.

The sources of differences or incompatibilities between individuals, groups and states are variously labelled the "conflict situation," the "bases of conflict," or the "structure of conflict."[55] Empirical observations suggest that contentions over territorial boundaries and ethnic separation seem to be the dominant sources of violent disputes in present-day world society. The rise of ethnic nationalism in the former territories of the Soviet Union, the breakdown of Yugoslavia, the Israeli-Palestinian conflict, and the Hutu-Tutsi warfare in Rwanda and Burundi seem to confirm the relationship between ethnic territoriality and the escalation of conflict towards violence. Conflicts of belief systems relating to the organization and governance of society can also be a source of violent conflict and tend to be a more intractable form of conflict. Mere difference in belief is not in itself a basis for conflict but becomes so when one party seeks to convert, undermine, or, in extreme situations, eliminate members of groups holding differing belief systems. The rise of Islamist groups in certain Middle Eastern states has led to conflicts between these and adherents of secular modes of governance. Conflicts of interest over tangible resources are rendered graver in intensity where they overlap an ideological or religious conflict. As pointed out by Druckman, "conflicts of interest linked to differences in ideology are more difficult to resolve than conflicts that do not derive from contrasting ideological orientations and . . . the more polarized the parties in ideological orientation, the more difficult it is to resolve a related conflict of interest."[56]

One difficulty associated with the identification of issues as bases of conflict is that specific disputes could reflect both consensual and dissensual differences. As pointed out by Kriesberg, "The relative importance of each varies in different conflicts, it also varies among the different segments of each party and probably changes in the course of a struggle."[57] Thus, even in cases where there is a clear case of dissensual conflict, such as exists between those striving for theocratic governance as opposed to secularist leaders, both antagonists value the same leadership positions which are seen as the vehicles for social control. The dynamic nature of the conflict process also means that the issues which lead to the emergence of conflict are not necessarily those which cause its intractability or longevity.

Another difficulty in attempting to build an empirical relationship between issues and violence relates to the salience of grievances which underpin a conflict as indicated by Paul Diehl.

It is even more problematic to develop an empirical measure of the salience of those issues involved in the conflict. In some conflicts, the stakes in the conflict are not as tangible as might be the case with conflicts over territory or markets. Scholars also cannot easily point to characteristics of the issues to identify which, if any, are most salient. Furthermore, one runs into the problem of perception; it is difficult to determine if what appears objectively to be very salient is perceived as such by decision-makers (or vice versa).[58]

It would seem, therefore, that identification of the issues is not as clear-cut as would be suggested by Clausewitz when he suggests that "The political object— the original motive/issue for the war—will thus determine both the military objective to be reached and the amount of effort it requires."[59] A conflict is not merely constituted by a set of incompatibilities, but incorporates salience of desires and beliefs which could determine the choice of violence as a mode of conflict behavior. Salience as identified by the investigator may not reflect the "operating frames of reference"[60] influencing policy-makers' choices of action.

Empirical investigations of the role of issues in the generation of violent conflict assume that policy-makers are purposive actors seeking particular ends through action deemed as the most effective in achieving desirable outcomes. One purpose which seems to have led overwhelmingly to the emergence of war is the creation of states. As indicated by Holsti:

> When we aggregate three issues—national liberation/state creation, national unification/consolidation, and secession—we deal with similar values and stakes if not behaviours. They all identify efforts to create states and symbolize that long historical process that began in Europe in the fifteenth and sixteenth centuries and that has extended into the non-European parts of the world in the twentieth century.[61]

In his inductive study of the role of issues in generating war, Holsti finds that state creation ranks highest as the cause of war, standing at 52 per cent of the wars of the post-1945 period. He also finds that ideological conflicts, those concerned with the political principles which underpin governance, have also been a frequent cause of international conflict, standing at 42 per cent of post-1945 conflicts, constituting "the second highest issue cluster after state creation."[62] Another major cause of war is found to be what Holsti refers to as "human sympathy" with those considered ethnic, religious or ideological kin, vindicating the importance or salience of identity as the basis of conflict while conflicts over tangible resources, such as territory and wealth have declined in relative importance. It also shows that while conflicts over tangible resources may be amenable to compromise or the creation of regimes aimed at the management of such disputes, conflicts centered around national self-determination and belief systems seem to be less amenable to compromise and accommodation.

The dichotomous distinction between conflicts over belief systems and those over tangible resources and the related assumption that the former are less amenable to resolution than the latter becomes questionable when we distinguish between *values* underlying a conflict, the specific *issues* which define a conflict situation, and the *stakes* involved (cf. Holsti, 1991). An example which could be used to illustrate this distinction may be drawn from the Israeli-Palestinian conflict. This particular conflict may be broken down into a number of issues which are salient to the parties involved and around which negotiation has taken place. These include territorial boundaries, the nature of Palestinian autonomy in the disputed territories, the numbers and location of Jewish settlements in these territories, economic rights, the future of diaspora Palestinians, the treatment of political prisoners, and the maintenance of law and order. The values which underlie these issues center around national identity, political self-determination, and the right to security. The stakes for the leaderships of either side include the maintenance of unity, legitimacy and support from their respective constituencies and allies in the external world. The success or failure of a process of conflict resolution may be determined by whether it begins with addressing the underlying values, the specific issues or the stakes involved.

Apart from the practical conflict resolution implications of the distinction between values, issues and stakes, the theoretical concerns which emerge from this trilateral conception relate more immediately to the concerns of this study. One central question revolves around processes which constitute underlying values, including the construction of social identity, and how these come to dominate discourse around a particular conflict. A related concern is how one form of identity, namely national identity, acquires primacy over other formations which could identify cross-cutting interests across the conflict divide. Understanding social conflict must begin with these continuities of social life, namely the processes through which a value system or a mode of discourse come to define the relationship between the individual and society. It is only then that we may begin to analyze how dominant values and discourses translate into specific issues and stakes around which parties come to be willing participants in violent conflict.

Vasquez distinguishes between "underlying" and "proximate" causes of conflict where "Underlying causes are fundamental causes that set off a train of events (the proximate causes) that end in war."[63] War is the outcome of sequences of actions and decisions carried out by defined decision-makers: "Those who made war decisions implicitly or explicitly calculated that the potential costs of men, *matériel,* property, and the possibility of humiliating defeats and terms of surrender did not outweigh the values and purposes that they sought or that were being challenged or threatened by opponents."[64] This approach to the study of conflict assumes that the emergence of violent conflict is an extraordinary activity undertaken in response to extraordinary circumstances. In confining analysis to the decision-making process in specific conflicts, taken as discrete events, this form of investigation precludes an understanding of the relationship between everyday forms of interaction and the emergence of support for war as a form of conflict behavior. Furthermore, it fails to develop an understanding of the relationship between the discursive and institutional continuities of social life and their role in the relationship between the individual and society and the place of war therein.

A Critical Investigation

The aim of conflict studies from its inception has been to explain war, or human violence in time of conflict, in terms of its origins, its dynamics in escalation and de-escalation, its consequences, and the means by which it comes to an end. While we may explain the peculiar and the specific, the central aim of the field must lie in explaining the basis of support for war and its legitimation through time and geographic space.

Historical accounts of major wars, inter-state or civil, concentrate on those who make decisions, the leaders as opposed to the led, ignoring thereby the internalization of war which inevitably leads to its normalization. Until an explanation is elaborated of the non-combatants' willingness to support war, violence as a mode of conflict behavior will remain a central element of the human condition.

Any investigation of war as a form of human action must begin with a conceptualization of action itself. War is a consequence of human actions and human decisions. The central focus of this study is violence used in time of social conflict. Such conflict may be at the inter-communal level within domestic society, as for example in times of civil war or civil insurrection, or it may be located at the transnational level, where both state and non-state actors are involved in conflict, or at the inter-state level, where two or more states become involved in conflict.

The methodology conventionally adopted in the field of conflict research is the search for explanation, defined in terms of scientific statements of the cause-effect variety. The object for explanation, or the dependent variable, requires the identification of independent variables which "explain" the phenomenon under observation. The methods of the natural sciences are assumed to apply to the social sciences in general and to the study of war in particular. The aim is to discover objective laws which would be devoid of normative considerations and as such would lend legitimacy to a field which could easily be accused of activist-led emotionalism. To discover a statement of the "if X then Y" variety would be to emulate the methods of the natural sciences, perceived as the harder, more legitimate sciences. Under the behavioralist revolution, a correlation between events

was seen as a means of discovering explanation. Under this epistemological framework, theories are based on regularities which, if they withstand empirical testing,
stand as explanations. If anomalies arise, the theories are either modified or
rejected altogether. This is essentially the positivist idea that hypotheses can be
tested by comparing their implications with objective, neutral facts of experience.[65]

The objective of this book is to develop a critical understanding of war as a
social continuity. While it appreciates the empirical studies of conflict reviewed
above, it seeks a critical understanding by situating war and violent conflict in the
constitution of the human self and human society. It assumes that specific
instances of war are a manifestation of the longer-term processes which have established war as a form of institution linked to discursive and institutional practices
which define societal continuities. Furthermore, the study assumes that a critical
interpretation must incorporate both understanding and the practical intent of
promoting emancipatory social transformation. It seeks to uncover the ideological
basis of discourses on any social phenomenon and their relations to the constitution of human practices. It assumes that knowledge of human phenomena such as
war is, in itself, a constitutive part of the world of meaning and practice. Any
critical interpretation situates knowledge within specific historical contexts and in
doing so sees knowledge and history as the products of the constituting labor of
the human species. Knowledge as such is both historically bound and interest
bound. As pointed out by Held, "The plausibility of critical social theory depends
on an acceptable explication of the relation between language, action and history."[66] Tradition, or the historical context, must be an integral part of understanding, and knowledge itself is generated and made possible within the framework of
traditions. Chapter two, therefore, starts this project by locating understandings
of war within political theory and moral philosophy as discourses which have
influenced our assumptions about human political violence. While the symbolic
mediation of social action is central to understanding action, the world of meaning
is in itself part of a wider complex shaped by material conditions.[67] Such material
conditions situate the worlds of meaning and practice within the wider institutional continuities which define particular social formations. Chapter three provides an analysis of human action which takes human conduct and social
discursive and institutional continuities as mutually constitutive processes and, for
this purpose, makes use of the writings of Anthony Giddens and his theory of
structuration. The aim of this chapter is to argue that (i) war can only be understood within a wider understanding of human action, and (ii) war is both a product and a constitutive part of the relationship between the self (agency) and
societal structures.

Any critical interpretation of a social phenomenon must incorporate within
its conceptual scheme the two themes mentioned above, namely the place of discursive practices as well as structural systems of domination which have homoge-
nizing and conforming tendencies. As pointed out by Best and Kellner, "Using
the dialectical category of mediation, critical theory attempts to describe how
concrete particulars are constituted by more general and abstract social forces,
undertaking an analysis of particulars to illuminate these broader social forces."[68]
A critical interpretation thus seeks to analyze the connection or mediation between

particularities and totalities, parts and wholes, individual artifacts and events and social processes and structures. The central focus is therefore on the constitution of phenomena and the interconnections between them. Thought and knowledge are a product of discourse, social experiences, and institutions while society is a product of language, social determination and human practices. Chapter jour seeks to analyze the discursive orders and ideological frameworks which have legitimated war across time and space. It specifically concentrates on a *"language of war"* based on militarism and notions of justice which have structured war as a continuity in social systems. The relationship between specific decisions for war, support for war, and the institutional frameworks of society are located in the construction of identity which, it is argued in chapter . . . five, must remain the central focus in our attempts at understanding war as a social continuity. Emancipatory knowledge incorporates the basis of social transformation and, with this in mind, chapter six seeks to define discourses on peace. This chapter argues that the condition of peace and the elimination of war must rest upon transformed discursive and institutional practices which have legitimated violence in human history. Language and forms of communication are seen as central to the development of new forms of social solidarity which reject discourses based on the dichotomy of inclusion and exclusion, self and other, and processes which legitimate violent fragmentation. The concluding chapter seven provides a critical reflection on the approach adopted in this study.

Notes

1. Q. Wright, *A Study of War* (University of Chicago Press, Chicago and London, 1966), p. 20.

2. K. J. Holsti, *Peace and War: Armed Conflicts and International Order 1648–1989* (Cambridge University Press, Cambridge, 1991), p. 5.

3. Anthony Giddens defines his theory of structuration in *Central Problems in Social Theory* (Macmillan, London, 1979) and *The Constitution of Society* (Polity Press, Cambridge, 1984).

4. A. Giddens, *op.* cit., p. 66.

5. S. Draculic, *Balkan Express* (Hutchinson, London, 1993), p. 3.

6. L. F. Richardson, "War Moods," *Psychometrica,* Vol. 13, Part 1 (1948), pp. 147–174.

7. Vanessa Vasic Janekovic illustrates this point in relation to ethnic cleansing in the Bosnian conflict where, in geographic areas containing Muslim populations which complicated Serb aspirations of a Greater Serbia, "the Serbs came to a simple solution: displacement. The improvised mass murder that evolved was only a logical extension of the game." See Vanessa Vasic Janekovic, "Beyond the Detention Camps," War Report, *Bulletin of the Institute for War and Peace Reporting* (October 1992), p. 12, quoted in L. Freedman (ed.), *War* (Oxford University Press, Oxford, 1994), p. 63.

8. Representatives of this school include K. Waltz, *Man, the State and War* (Columbia University Press, New York, 1954) and H. J. Morgenthau, *Politics Among Nations* (Alfred Knopf, New York, 1985).

9. T. Hobbes, *Leviathan* (Penguin Classics, Harmondsworth, 1985), p. 185.

10. J. Chanteur, *From War to Peace* (Westview Press, Boulder, CO, 1992), pp. 42–50.

11. A. Linklater, "The Question of the Next Stage in International Relations Theory: A Critical-Theoretical Point of View," *Millennium,* Vol. 21, No. 1 (1992), p. 78.

12. *Ibid.,* p. 78.

13. For the normative divide between cosmopolitanism and communitarianism in international relations, see C. Brown, *International Relations Theory: New Normative Approaches* (Harvester Wheatsheaf, Hemel Hempstead, 1993); A. Linklater, *Men and Citizens in the Theory of International Relations* (Macmillan, London, 1990). For a philosophical discourse on the liberal/communitarian debate, see S. Mulhall and A. Swift, *Liberals and Communitarians* (Blackwell Publishers, Oxford, 1992).

14. Quoted in Wright, *op. cit.,* p. 10.

15. Wright, *op. cit.,* pp. 8–9.

16. Waltz, *op. cit.,* p. 12.

17. *Ibid.,* p. 28.

18. See R. B. Ferguson (ed.), *Warfare, Culture and Environment* (Academic Press, Orlando, FL, 1984); P. Marsh and A. Campbell (eds), *Aggression and Violence* (Blackwell, Oxford, 1982); D. Riches, *The Anthropology of Violence* (Blackwell, Oxford, 1986); and G. Siann, *Accounting for Aggression: Perspectives on Aggression and Violence* (Allen and Unwin, Boston, 1985).

19. S. Howell and R. Willis (eds), *Societies at Peace: Anthropological Perspectives* (Routledge, London and New York, 1989), p. 8.

20. Waltz, *op. cit.,* pp. 101–102.

21. *Ibid.,* p. 205.

22. K. N. Waltz, *Theory of International Politics* (Addison-Wesley, Reading, MA, and London, 1979); R. Gilpin, *War and Change in World Politics* (Cambridge University Press, Cambridge, 1981).

23. See note 19 above.

24. A. E. Wendt, "The Agent-Structure Problem in International Relations Theory," *International Organisation,* Vol. 41, No. 3 (1987), p. 342.

25. I. Lakatos, "Falsification and the Methodology of Scientific Research Programmes," in I. Lakatos and A. Musgrove (eds.). *Criticism and the Growth of Knowledge* (Cambridge University Press, Cambridge, 1970).

26. A. J. R. Groom, "Paradigms in Conflict: The Strategist, the Conflict Researcher and the Peace Researcher," in J. W. Burton and F. Dukes (eds.), *Conflict: Readings in Management and* Resolution (Macmillan, London, 1990).

27. M. Nicholson, *Rationality and the Analysis of International Conflict* (Cambridge University Press, Cambridge, 1992), p. 22.

28. J. Galtung, "Violence, Peace, and Peace Research," *Journal of Peace Research,* Vol. 6, No. 3 (1969), pp. 167–191.

29. H. Schmid, "Peace Research and Politics," *Journal of Peace Research,* 5 (1968), pp. 217–232. For a discussion of this early debate, see A. Eide, "Dialogue and Confrontation in Europe," *Journal of Conflict Resolution,* Vol. 16 (1972), pp. 511–522.

30. E. Krippendorff, "Peace Research and the Industrial Revolution," *Journal of Peace Research,* Vol. 10 (1973), p. 184.

31. H. G. Reid and E. J. Yanarella, "Toward a Critical Theory of Peace Research in the United States; The Search for an 'Intelligible Core,'" *Journal of Peace Research,* Vol. 13 (1976), p. 318.

32. J. W. Burton, "Introduction," in J. W. Burton and F. Dukes (eds.), *Conflict: Readings in Management and Resolution* (Macmillan, London, 1990), p. 2.

33. T. Nardin, "Theory and Practice in Conflict Research," in T. R. Gurr (ed.), *Handbook of Political Conflict* (Free Press, New York, 1980), p. 463.

34. For the major themes of inquiry in the field, see C. R. Mitchell, "Conflict Research," in M. Light, and A. J. R. Groom (eds.), *Contemporary International Relations: A Guide to Theory* (Pinter, London, 1994). For Burton's work on conflict resolution, see his *Resolving Deep-Rooted Conflict* (University Press of America, Lanham, MD, 1987) and *Conflict Resolution and Provention* (Macmillan, London, 1990).

35. L. Kriesberg, *Social Conflicts* (Prentice Hall, Englewood Cliffs, NJ, 1982).

36. This is the approach adopted by H. Blalock in *Power and Conflict: Toward a General Theory* (Sage, London, 1989), and by M. Nicholson, *Rationality and the Analysis of International Conflict* (Cambridge University Press, Cambridge, 1992).

37. L. Kriesberg, "Conflict Resolution Applications to Peace Studies," *Peace and Change,* Vol. 16, No. 4 (1991), p. 404.

38. Conflict resolution is one of the fastest growing research areas in the field of conflict studies. See C. R. Mitchell and K. Webb (eds.), *New Approaches to International Mediation* (Greenwood Press, Westport, CT, 1989).

39. V. Jabri, *Mediating Conflict* (Manchester University Press, Manchester, 1990); K. Kressel and D. Pruitt (eds.), *Mediation Research* (Jossey-Bass, San Francisco, 1989); S. Touval and I. W. Zartman (eds.). *International Mediation in Theory and Practice* (Westview Press, Boulder, CO, 1985).

40. The development of a mediation framework within the CSCE to prevent the escalation of ethnic conflict in Eastern Europe is an area which may potentially benefit from the conflict resolution literature.

41. J. A. Vasquez, *The War Puzzle* (Cambridge University Press, Cambridge, 1993), p. 44.

42. For general reviews of the relationship between these factors and the onset of violent conflict, see Kriesberg (1982), *op. cit.,* pp. 66–106; Vasquez, *op. cit.,* chapters 4 and 5; and Blalock, *op cit.,* chapters 2, 3 and 6.

43. Vasquez, *op. cit.,* p. 46.

44. Blalock, *op. cit.,* p. 5.

45. *Ibid.,* p. 6.

46. C. R. Mitchell, *Structure of International Conflict* (Macmillan, London, 1981), pp. 120–121.

47. J. S. Himes, *Conflict and Conflict Management* (Georgia University Press, Athens, GA, 1980), p. 14.

48. Kriesberg (1982), *op. cit.,* p. 114.

49. *Ibid.,* p. 115.

50. B. Bueno de Mesquita, *The War Trap* (Yale University Press, New Haven, CT, 1981), p. 20.

51. P. J. Haney *et al.,* "Unitary Actors, Advisory Models, and Experimental Tests," *Journal of Conflict Resolution.* Vol. 36, No. 4 (1992), p. 605.

52. Blalock, *op. cit.,* p. 11.

53. On the concept of resource mobilisation, see C. Tilly, "Do Communities Act?" *Sociological Inquiry,* Vol. 43 (1974), pp. 209–240, and C. Tilly, *From Mobilization to Revolution* (Addison-Wesley, Reading, MA, 1978).

54. V. Aubert, "Competition and Dissensus: Two Types of Conflict and Conflict Resolution," *Journal of Conflict Resolution,* Vol. 7 (1963), pp. 26–42.

55. See D. Druckman, "An Analytical Research Agenda for Conflict and Conflict Resolution," in D. J. D. Sandole and H. van der Merwe (eds.), *Conflict Resolution Theory and Practice* (Manchester University Press, Manchester, 1993).

56. *Ibid.,* p. 28.

57. Kriesberg (1982), *op. cit.,* p. 42.

58. R. F. Diehl, "What Are They Fighting For? The Importance of Issues in International Conflict Research," *Journal of Peace Research,* Vol. 29, No. 3 (1992), p. 335.

59. C. von Clausewitz, *On War,* translated by J. J. Graham (Routledge and Kegan Paul, London, 1966), p. 81.

60. Holsti, *op. cit.,* p. 18.

61. *Ibid.,* p. 311.

62. *Ibid.,* p. 313.

63. Vasquez, *op. cit.,* p. 7.

64. Holsti, *op. cit.,* p. 306.

65. M. Hollis and S. Smith, *Explaining and Understanding International Relations* (Clarendon, Oxford, 1991), p. 54.

66. D. Held, *Introduction to Critical Theory* (Polity Press, Cambridge, 1980), p. 311.

67. See J. Habermas, "A Review of Gadamer's *Truth and Method*," in F. Dallmayr and T. McCarthy (eds), *Understanding Social Inquiry* (Notre Dame Press, Notre Dame, IN, 1977), quoted in Held, *op. cit.,* p. 316. Also see J. Habermas, *Knowledge and Human Interests,* trans. J. J. Shapiro (Heinemann, London, 1972). For an international relations perspective, see M. Hoffman, "Critical Theory and the Inter-Paradigm Debate," *Millennium,* Vol. 16, No. 2 (1987), pp. 231–250.

68. S. Best and D. Kellner, *Postmodern Theory: Critical Interrogations* (Macmillan, London, 1991), p. 223.

Politics of Voice

Sara Cobb

Dr. Sara Cobb is the Drucie French Cumbie Professor at the School for Conflict Analysis and Resolution (S-CAR) at George Mason University, where she was also the director for eight years. In this context, she teaches and conducts research on the relationship between narrative and violent conflict; she is also the director of the Center for the Study of Narrative and Conflict Resolution at S-CAR, which provides a hub for scholarship on narrative approaches to conflict analysis and resolution. Formerly, she was the director of the Program on Negotiation at Harvard Law School and has held positions at a variety of tier-one research institutions, such as the University of California, Santa Barbara, the University of Connecticut, and, more recently, at the University of Amsterdam. She has also consulted to and/or conducted training for a host of public and private organizations, including UN High Commission on Refugees, UNDP, La Caxia Bank, Exxon, the American Bar Association, and Fox Learning Academy, as well as a number of universities in Europe and Latin America. Cobb is widely published. Her book *Speaking of Violence: The Politics and Poetics of Narrative in Conflict Resolution,* from which this selection comes, offers a narrative perspective on both conflict analysis and conflict resolution. She has been a leader in the fields of negotiation and conflict resolution studies, conducting research on the practice of neutrality.

In this piece, Cobb argues words do more than represent the world; they create it. Words through narratives create policies and institutions, negotiate relationships and identities, and are used by governments to legitimize violence (structural or active). Because stories about Self and Other both produce and perpetuate conflicts, analyses of conflicts must include a narrative analysis. Without also including intervention at the narrative level, any ceasefire or treaty will likely be upended by the rhetorical positions that produced the violence.

Because local language is the site of global meaning-making, narrative work—in alignment with Epoch Three approaches—collapse the divide between the global and the local. They simply operate at the level of voice, the transitional moment when belief moves from an internal environment (self) to an external one (society). Here we see a resonance between Cobb and Vivienne Jabri, who also located violence in this intersection between self and society.

> Beyond violence, narratives of violence debilitate individuals from serving as agents in their own lives. A defining characteristic of Epoch Three approaches is to consider individuals not as simply acted upon (by leaders, biological aggression, human needs, inter-ethnic war, etc.) but sites and sources of violence produced and reproducing the violent social structures that encase them.
>
> Narrative approaches to conflict seek to interrupt the thin or problematic narratives, replacing them with richer and more complex narratives. Complexity (rather than simply good-evil binaries) offers more opportunities to build relations between and across groups. Cobb urges the field of conflict resolution to move beyond "interest-based analysis toward understanding the dynamics of meaning-making" (2013, 11).
>
> Questions to consider: What are examples of characterizations of "Self" and "Other" that lead to conflict? What are some of the narratives circulating in a conflict of interest to you? Do they suggest reconciliation or ongoing conflict?

Speaking of Violence

Sara Cobb

Introduction

Stories matter. They have gravitas; they are grave. They have weight. They are concrete. They materialize policies, institutions, relationships, and identities that circulate locally and globally, anywhere and everywhere. The story told by Israel about Hamas is not just a set of words, it is an account of the history, in the present, toward a selected or preferred scenario that rationalizes walls, continued settlements, ongoing humiliations via the patchwork of checkpoints, and authorizes violence. Likewise, the Palestinian story about "Nakba," the catastrophic event that established the state of Israel and disenfranchised the Palestinians, is a story, not in the sense of a representation of the events themselves but in the sense that it creates underground tunnels, it authorizes networks of insurgency while legitimizing Hamas for its role in reducing suffering within the Palestinian community, defining the contours of Palestinian identity itself. The Middle East conflict, as a story, is foundational and mythic, primordial, within both the Middle East and the Western worlds. It helps anchor the divisions across the world, between religions, nations, and cultures, and is toxic to peace everywhere for this reason.

This conflict, like all conflicts, is a function of the stories that are told, retold, and foretold about the conflict (Harré and van Langenhove, 1991, 1999; Pearce, 2008; Tan and Moghaddam, 1999; Winslade and Monk, 2000). And, indeed, one can argue that the persistence of this conflict is our collective failure to treat it as the mythic struggle for life and legitimacy that the stories about it reveal. It is not just a conflict over specific issues—and there are many. Even if there could be consensus regarding the "right of return" or the settlements, the conflict narratives, breeding "brittle" relationships, remain. Indeed, the specific issues associated with the conflict, such as borders, settlements, and the fate of Jerusalem, arise from the conflict narratives, the overlapping and layered stories that provide a plot sequence, a set of characters, and moral frameworks that authorize and legitimize a particular history, a given identity. And these stories are not simply representations of history, even though they operate as if that is all they do. Rather, these stories provide the architecture for hate and distrust at all levels of social relations, from international to interpersonal conflicts (Entman, 1991; Halverson, 2004; Porat, 2004; Tilly, 1998).

On the global stage, the war between Al-Qaeda and the West rests on the (rather incomplete) story on either side about the Other. Immediately after 9/11, the U.S. administration began to tell a story about "why they hate us"—the cause of the hatred was their fear of our freedom and envy for our wealth. In what Jackson calls the "myth of exceptional suffering," the U.S. administration and the press advanced a story in which the United States was an exceptional victim (Jackson, 2005). This story has not only provided a rationale for war in Afghanistan, but has also been used, retrospectively, post-invasion, to justify the war and continued U.S. occupation in Iraq. In symmetry with the destructive force of what this narrative affords or makes possible in terms of violence, it is equivalently violent in terms of what it constrains—we, in the West, are disabled from exploring the Other(s) in all their complexity, doomed, in a very tragic sense, to create the enemy we then seek to destroy. And, of course, on the Other side, the Muslim "terrorists," a largely undefined category of Others made up of anyone (presumably Muslim) intent on violence against the West (the United States), continue to resist and confront the West, in Gaza, in Iraq, in Pakistan, in Afghanistan, and in Southeast Asia, for example. In a terrible cycle of irony, the narratives create the evidence for their own presence and persistence (Jackson, 2005).

However, the interventions intended to eliminate or control terrorists, ranging from wars to prisons such as Guantanamo, to aerial bombing, to counterinsurgency strategies, have clearly increased the antipathy within the Muslim world toward the United States, and, in fact, there is some empirical evidence that the Global War on Terror (GWOT) is responsible for actually increasing terrorists attacks (Sheehan, 2007). Lake (2002, cited in Sheehan) has also argued that the policy of "preemption" has mobilized extremists and contributed to their consolidation, enabling them to increase their resources and their organizational strength.

Efforts have been made, on the part of the West, at building "understanding" within the Muslim world. These have appeared under the banner of "public diplomacy" and have been efforts to market the United States in particular and democracy more broadly; these efforts to gain "soft power" (Nye, 2004) are not focused on increasing the understanding of the "terrorists" by the United States, but rather they are intended to influence "hearts and minds," reducing insurgencies and/or cooperation with the enemies of the West. Public diplomacy has not, however, yet focused attention on the *dynamics* of the broad cultural narratives that shape the conflict between these two cultures. And yet, without an understanding of not only the narratives of extremists and those who advocate terrorism and without reflective awareness of how those narratives are, in turn, fueled by the narratives told by the United States (the West), strategies for reducing terrorism will continue to focus on control and containment while public diplomacy is deployed as an effort to increase soft power. Clearly, these global narratives that criss-cross the world play a critical role in the production of violence, as well as in the international policies and practices that seek to contain or reduce it.

Local conflicts can also be understood in terms of the narratives told and retold by parties to the conflict. In the Niger Delta region, parties themselves explain the violence in the region via what can be called the "criminal narrative," referring to the theft of oil by militias creating a black market where illegal trading of weapons and oil cause the conflict between the government, backed by the multinational oil companies and the armed groups. In this story, the militias are a criminal force, motivated by greed and a lust for power. Conversely, the "social justice" narrative, told by locals in the community and militia leaders authorizes the use of force to right the wrongs done to the communities in the south over the past sixty years. During that time, the story goes, the government and the multinational oil companies robbed the south of its natural resource, polluted its communities, and failed to compensate the people for that resource. In this narrative, the people of the Delta region have been forced to take matters into their own hands in an effort to gain a greater share of the wealth that has been stolen from them. The "environmental justice" narrative, a permutation of the "social justice" narrative, adds to the complexity of the conflict as international environmental groups echo the narrative of the local people, who live with the open flames from nearby refineries. And, finally, there are many within Nigeria, as well as in the international community, who account for the conflict using ethnicity as a frame; this account tells the story of the historical struggle between tribes and attributes current violence to those divisions. Of course this "ethnic" narrative disqualifies the logic and legitimacy of the social and environmental justice narratives and sidelines the role of the multinational oil companies altogether. The narrative politics of this conflict are extremely complex because, not only are there multiple narratives at play, each struggling for elaboration and legitimacy, but there are also local, national, and international actors, and the narratives at play are variously, even if predictably, advanced and defended by speakers and their affiliated groups.

But it is not just that there are different and competing narratives in the Niger Delta; narrative politics takes place in a context that Watts (2005) calls the "oil complex," as a set of institutional practices, struggles to marginalize, co-opt, and otherwise delegitimate the narratives from those that would oppose it. The narrative playing field is not "level"; institutional authority (note the root word "author") regulates the public sphere in which narratives of dissent, alternative to the state narrative, can appear. Banished narratives or "hidden transcripts" are the foundation for resistance (Scott, 1990) if not violence. As Scarry (1987) has noted, violence fills up the spaces where words are not allowed.

Within the United States, a "local" conflict erupted in Manassas, Virginia, over the "Rule of Law Resolution" that was passed in 2007, which allowed police to stop anyone and conduct a background check of immigration status using a "probable cause" standard; Help Save Manassas, a local citizen group, mobilized the community in favor of this legislation, with an overarching narrative that illegal immigrants were taking jobs from citizens, committing crimes, infesting the community with gangs, and getting access to services supported by tax dollars. The human rights community, along with Latino advocates, told a different story: This country was founded and built by immigrants, and these immigrants, regardless of their legal status, pay taxes and contribute to the diversity of the community. Further, the Resolution dramatically reduced the civil liberties of all citizens and promoted racial/ethnic profiling, thus fostering discrimination.

Even though the legislation was amended in 2008 for practical reasons having to do with the complexity of implementation, the narrative struggle persists; the community continues to be polarized. Further, the narrative about illegal immigrants began to resonate with communities all over the country, giving it momentum and anchoring the emergence of other groups, permutations of Help Save Manassas. And, in turn, this narrative has resonance across many parts of the world. Like the narratives that characterize the conflict between extremists and the West, these narratives regarding immigration are both local and global. Indeed, the narratives of inclusion/exclusion demarcate the boundaries of belonging, citizenship, and community itself (Wodak, 2006).

They are always local in the sense that narrative conflict is performed in a particular setting, with particular people. However, these are also always global in that they operate as narrative resources that are "downloaded" into particular settings as sense-making devices, structuring what Taylor refers to as "the intersubjective web of meaning" on which both consensus and dissensus are constructed (Taylor, 1985). Consider the stories that defined the murder of Theo van Gogh in the Netherlands in 2004; this event unleashed violence against local mosques, as well as some churches, and polarized the region—*autochtonen* (those of Dutch descent) expressed alarm over the militancy of a portion of the large immigrant Muslim population, while the Muslim community reacted not only with fear but with a narrative about their own exclusion within Dutch society. The post-9/11 narratives colonized the meaning of the murder of van Gogh and today the Netherlands still struggles to reconcile the narratives of the *autochtonen* with those of the Muslim community; the government is working to design policies and processes that address the needs of what has been named "problem neighborhoods" (Smetsand Uyl, 2008).

To complete the tracing of narrative across levels of conflict, interpersonal conflicts are also a function of the narratives that are enacted. As many scholars have noted (Killian, 2002; Labov and Waletzky, 1967; Sarbin, 1986; Walzer and Oles, 2003; White and Epston, 1990; White and Taket, 2000), the stories that individuals tell about Self and Other, in everyday conversations, structure the nature of interpersonal interactions (Shotter, 2008), as well as intrapsychic dynamics (Spence, 1986). The divorcing couple, family business conflicts, organizational conflicts, and sibling conflicts, as well as family conflicts of all kinds, all are enacted in conversations, within a network divided into "us" and "them," known as the "enmity system" (Coleman et al., 2007). The division between people within this system is a boundary constructed by the story about the conflict and its associated issues.

For example, a conflict in a family business can be analyzed in terms of the stories that are told, to whom, about what, as stories of suffering, loss, and pain. In one such case in Latin America, there was a set of siblings whose uncle controlled their (considerable) assets, after their own father died early. Over time, the uncle clearly began to favor his own children, doling out cash, professional opportunities, and special privileges to them. As the siblings grew, so did their story of displacement and exclusion. As these narratives developed and hardened, one of the siblings began to wear reflective sunglasses and T-shirts and march in antigovernment protests. The uncle admonished his nephew, who then openly and repeatedly defied his uncle. At one point, homemade bombs were thrown over the wall of the uncle's family compound, in broad daylight. All of this had dire consequences for the financial opportunities of the siblings. They were effectively banished from the family business, and there were no formal laws in place that could adequately restore these siblings to their prior standing, with access to collective assets. The uncle clearly had a negative story about the siblings anchored by the central character, the errant brother, whereas the siblings felt themselves "imprisoned" in their uncle's illegal regime. These stories were not only toxic to the relationships across the entire family, but they also had serious material consequences for both the group of siblings, who kept trying to control their "radical" brother, but also for the uncle, who was repeatedly called out in public by *"el mal educado."* Although some in the field of conflict analysis and resolution would not consider a "family feud" a real conflict, for those involved, it has the markers of violence, exclusion, and displacement in which relationships, assets, and the future are at stake.

Furthermore, narratives of violence maraud across the relational field, infecting even the intrapsychic space, debilitating a person's capacity to be an agent in his own life, rupturing his relation to his own narrative processes. Not only do individuals "smooth" narratives, as Spence (1986) has noted, editing out portions that might destabilize their own legitimacy, but their development depends on their ability to story their Other as legitimate, which in turn reflects on their capacity to manage and resolve conflicts (Goboda-Madikizeal, 2008). As Bauer, McAdams, and Pals (2008) have noted, "happiness" itself is a function of the nature of the narratives we tell about Self and Other.

In addition to the narrative complexity at the intrapersonal level, interpersonal narrative dynamics, enacted in conversations, reflect the tremendous complexity of conversations at the intersection of global, local, interpersonal, and intrapersonal narratives. These "conversations" can be thought of as interactions between speakers, exchanges that may not be face-to-face or exchanges in which only one interlocutor participates, imagining their Other, "conversing" via the media, in blogs, or in art, as well as in all manner of public forums. I am here using the notion of "conversation" not as the discrete turn-taking between parties, consistent with conversational analysis, but rather referring to the struggle over meaning, in which parties to that process offer interpretations in response to Others, and these interpretations become the context for the next round of what Bateson called "proposals" of how I see you seeing me, seeing you (Bateson, 1979; Laing, 1998).

Because conversations-as-proposals are the domain for the enactment of narrative, the distinction between "micro," "mezzo," and "macro" is not only unnecessary, because these conversations populate all these levels, but it is problematic, as it implies that macro is more critical, providing context for "lower levels." Although it is certainly the case that large-scale narratives do provide context for interaction at mezzo and micro levels, it is also the case that the micro-level conversations where narratives are adopted, elaborated, and promulgated are extremely critical to the macro level. Local actors develop what Hajer (1995) refers to as "storylines" in the course of addressing conflict or problems, drawing on the discursive resources that are present and available, explaining the past and forecasting a future. In turn, these discursive resources are comprised of event sequences, characters, and themes that circulate in their culture; the "origin" of these resources, although archeologically traceable, is less important to this project than their deployment. For this reason, I resist, in this book, following the "levels of analysis" approach and prefer to develop case studies that exemplify the circulation of narratives as conversations across global, local, organizational, and interpersonal contexts, accenting, where data permit, the circulation of stories across these contexts as well. In this mediated age, conversations between people careen around the globe, contributing to break down the distinction between discrete levels of analysis. The "Global War on Terror" narrative populates the stories in the Niger Delta conflict, and those narratives ricochet off discussions of security and economic development in Africa, which reverberate in conversations at affected oil companies and a host of national and international nongovernmental organizations (NGOs) that deal with human rights, environmental justice, aid, peacemaking, and more. The effort to understand the level of analysis is an effort to try to isolate the origin of meaning itself or to try to understand meaning as though it could be contained by the "level" itself.

The conversations to which I refer are not conversations over the color of tablecloths. They are not ordinary conversations, but are instead extraordinary precisely because of what is at stake—literally life, well-being, and the access to resources and rights. These are conversations in which violent narratives are in motion, unleashed onto a social context and, all too often, uncontained, if not uncontainable. These are conversations about "differends" (Lyotard, 1989), narratives that "uncover and find idioms for wrongs, to remember and reconstitute publically the traces and remainders of horrific events" (Smith, 2008).

As Smith (2008, p. 167) has noted, any discussion of the "differends" (wrongs suffered and silenced) is not only a conversation in which there is a struggle over meaning—meaning that does not originate in that particular conversation—but also it is a conversation in which meaning itself is uncontrollable, multifaceted, and often opaque. These are conversations in which power is visible, where irony abounds, and the materiality of discourse, of narrative, as a doing, as a practice, is a "fact," as in "factum," or "something done."[1]

Communication theorists have studied these practices. They have noted that anything that is said is structured by the frame provided by the context (Austin, 1975; Pearce, 2008); they have noted that anything that is said is regulated by the constitutive and regulative rules that govern interaction in that context (Huspek, 1994; Pearce, 2008); they have explored the ethnomethods associated with specific cultures, in terms of language pragmatics (Carbaugh, 2005; Wodak, 2006). These lines of research, and the pragmatic tradition from which they arise, presume that speech is enacted by agents who are "getting on" in the Wittgensteinian (1953) sense, mobilizing language and stories toward preferred outcomes and relationships (Searle, 1997).

But what the pragmatic approach to discourse does not accent is that agency itself is all too often a casualty of conflict. In order to "get on," people must be able to tell a story in which they are positioned as agents, able to describe and account for their own victimization, able to respond humanely to the stories of others. However, conflicts are precisely the context in which the capacity for action, for narrative action, is carefully circumscribed by institutional practices (Smith, 2008), by master narratives (Johnson, 2008), by structural and physical violence (Burton, 1996; Galtung, 1990). Narrative and discourse are not only practices in which the social is constituted and relationships negotiated, as the pragmatists would have it; they are highly political processes by which some forms of life thrive and others are banished.

But the political process of narrative erasure, marginalization, or colonization is not simply a process in which the powerful work strategically, in line with their own interests, to reduce the agentic narrative capacity of their Others. If this were the case, narrative would be the instrumental manifestation of the intentions of the powerful, and the politics of narrative in conflict processes would collapse back into game theory and behavioral economics—narratives would be the surface manifestation of the deep structure, the intentions of actors. Although narratives can certainly be the instruments of the powerful, manifestations of intentions to dominate, narratives are, in and of themselves, discursive "matter" that, obedient to social structure and cultural capital, provide the habitus that affords and constrains what is possible (Bourdieu, 1977). And this habitus appears in conversations, in talk, in interaction.

This book explores the politics of narrative processes in the context of conflicts across global, local, organizational, and interpersonal contexts. First, I offer a theoretical framework for understanding conflict as a narrative process, describing both the structural and dynamical features of conflict narratives. Drawing on narrative theory and language pragmatics, episodic structures, character roles, and the moral themes of conflict narratives will be explored in a set of case studies. Dynamical features of conflict narratives, including critical moments and turning points, as well as the production of liminal phases, will be described. Part I will end with a critique of narrative pragmatics and positioning theory; drawing on Arendt, I will explore "radicalized" narratives that form the basis for cultural archetypes that contain and manage discourse, debate, and dialogue, severely delimiting our collective capacity for the deliberative processes that Carlos Nino (1998), John Dewey (1929), and others (Hirst, 1994) had hoped would be the foundation for democracy itself.

Against the backdrop of "radicalized narratives," Part II offers a theory of narrative violence that accounts for and describes the marginalization of narratives through a series of discursive practices. Following a critique of Habermas's (1996) approach to emancipation, I will offer a normative view of narrative, one that will build on the work of Nelson (2001), Scarry (1987), Jabri (1996), Arendt (1998), Oliver (2001), Lara (2007), and others; this normative view will be the foundation for evaluating and interrogating conflict narratives and will provide the framework for a narrative perspective on power, a critical theory of narrative. Again, I will be drawing on cases to illustrate the model.

Finally, in Part III, I will explore the implications of this narrative lens on conflict dynamics for conflict resolution practice, advancing a theory of narrative transformation that is founded on a normative approach to narrative. This normative narrative model provides a framework for assessing narratives as regards their ethical and aesthetic characteristics and features, in the context of conflict processes and in light of the critical narrative theory discussed in Part II. The implications of normative narrative theory, as a revolution of conflict resolution practice, will be discussed. My goal in Part III is to provide a framework for narrative practice that provides the foundation for a critical analysis, as well as a framework for ethical intervention.

Advancing a Theory of Practice: Narrative Contribution to Conflict Resolution

My motivation for this book, more broadly, is to build on the excellent work that is being done in narrative theory and practice, across many disciplines, in order to connect this work to conflict analysis and resolution. Not only is there an increasing body of research on narrative processes, but there is an increasing gap between the approaches to conflict analysis and resolution, founded on game theory and augmented by social psychology, and the effective practice of conflict resolution as a practice in which the meanings that anchor conflict and constitute relational divisions evolve.

But, more specifically, I hope this book, which outlines the contours of critical narrative theory, will provide the theoretical framework to assess and advance existing conflict resolution practices. At present, there are significant challenges to the resolution methods that presume that conflicts can be resolved via changes in attitudes or via meeting needs/interests as a function of negotiated settlements. We know that a large percentage of peace agreements collapse post-agreement (Stedman, Rothchild, and Cousens, 2002); we know that even when agreements are in place, the conflict between peoples can become "frozen," as is the case in Bosnia (Borgen, 2007; Kemp, 2004); positive peace cannot be legislated. Although negotiation is certainly an advance over deterrence as a peace strategy, it is not a process that can easily adapt to the complexities of, for example, the U.S./Iran relationship, in which there is a history of violence, asymmetric power relations, and a vast difference in culture. "Negotiation" that presumes "rationality" is just as likely to contribute to escalations, as parties struggle to outline the conditions for any talks. All too often, failures in peace negotiations are attributed to the absence of "ripeness" or to the presence of "spoilers" who seek to continue the conflict for personal gain; although these explanations are certainly viable, they lay blame on the context and the parties for the failures of conflict resolution practice. And when there is "success," it is also attributed to "hurting stalemates" (Zartman, 1995) that generate the conditions for ripeness/readiness. The issue for the field of conflict resolution is not the viability of ripeness theory as an explanatory tool, but rather the underlying assumption that parties know and will rationally discern and address their interests/needs.

The violence associated with terrorism is riddled with interest-based discourse. Either, as in the case of suicide bombers, experts continue to apply an "interest-based" discourse, framing "terrorists" as irrational (as a function of the misalignment of actions with interests) (Caplan, 2006) or they construe the interests of terrorists as seeking media attention and instilling fear/terror. However, in neither case have experts actually interviewed extremists in order to understand (stand under) the stories that the extremists themselves would tell, the stories that require violence and the generation of fear. In this context, the application of a negotiation paradigm and interest-based discourse by the West has not only been costly in terms of lives and money, but it has also very likely fueled the very narratives that undergird the violence itself. Increasing the effectiveness of conflict resolution will require the field to move beyond interest-based analysis toward understanding the dynamics of meaning making itself.

But a focus on narrative would do more than make conflict resolution practices more effective; it would also encourage the development of an ethics of practice equipped to favor the development of stories that redress marginalization and anchor people's capacity for moral agency. Existing conflict resolution practices, such as mediation and facilitation, may be effective at generating agreements, but may themselves lack criteria for assessing either the ethics of the agreements (as parties to the conflict make those assessments themselves, often from within asymmetric power relations) or the evolution of the problematic relationship, if there was an evolution. Deliberative processes can indeed generate community as well as consensus, but they can just as easily cover over injustice and perpetuate marginalization, as Hajer and Wagenaar (2003) and others have shown.

Other approaches to conflict resolution, such as problem-solving workshops, do indeed attend to the meanings that parties assign to problems and the associated construction of relationships. Problem-solving workshops have certainly been advanced by the field as a strategy for promoting understanding across divisions fueled by violence and hatred (Fisher, 1997; Kelman and Cohen, 1976). However, they all too often "symmetrize" the conflict and contribute to justify the relationships that are formed, even in the context of oppression and continued violence (Rouhana, 2004), even in the face of the complexities of "re entry"—participation in a problem-solving workshop can be read as "defection" from within a group, endangering the lives of those who participate (Pearson d'Estrée, Fast, Weiss, and Jakobsen, 2001). Even in the case in which the knowledge "transfer," via re entry, is strategically orchestrated, there is still little work that evaluates the effectiveness or the ethics of the movement of meaning/stories through networks. A more developed approach to narrative and conflict resolution would shift the grounds for problem-solving workshops and help link networks to narratives in practice.

Dialogue is another important conflict resolution practice anchored in the exploration of meaning, but, like other practices, it cannot only cover over asymmetries—as dialogue itself is often advocated as a practice that foster "authentic" relations—it can also set up parties for a connection between "revelation/reflection" (as if sharing alone breeds understanding) and relational healing. Also, dialogue is often promoted as a means for obtaining consensus, as if communion would generate the grounds for addressing injustice, suffering, and oppression. Perhaps the most pernicious aspect of dialogue as a conflict resolution practice is the concept of "recognition" that lies at its heart, a concept I will review later in this book. Oliver (2001) has offered a powerful critique of the way parties "exchange" granting the Other status as a human being on the basis of similarities they see they have with the Other. Clearly "recognition" should not be a commodity to be traded in a dialogue process, but if we are to avoid the ethical dilemmas that Oliver has underlined, we need to advance the theory that undergirds the practice of dialogue. Attending to the nature of the stories that are constructed in a dialogue process would provide a method for tracking the commodification of recognition and establish a narrative framework that fosters reflection and learning along with relational development.

Deliberation, as a practice often twinned to dialogue, has a rich theoretical foundation linked to the pragmatics of meaning making. Habermas (2001) has provided a framework for deliberation as a practice core to democratic practice, enacted via the construction of ideal speech acts. Although a more thorough review of this contribution is included in this book, I am here making the point that this work has been, to date, one of the only efforts to provide a critical theoretical base for designing and evaluating deliberative processes, attending to meaning making. However, as McAfee's (2009) analysis of deliberative practice reveals, the discourse of interest-based processes is retained even though there is also an abiding concern for the production of meaning in communities. There is new and important work being done on the production of meaning in deliberation in which scholar-practitioners are developing theories to account for reframing practices and the "negotiation" of meaning as communities come together to work through identity conflicts. Reviewed later in more detail, this line of research is drawing on narrative theory and developing a narrative lens on public policy practice. It is an excellent example of innovative research in deliberative process.

Peacemaking is yet another conflict resolution practice aimed at relational development, outside the parameters of interest-based discourse. Described by Lederach (1998, 2005) and anchored in the nonviolent tradition of Gandhi and Martin Luther King, Jr., peacemaking and peacebuilding are certainly critical to the resolution of protracted conflict and to the emergence of a sustainable positive peace. Peacemaking itself is grounded in an ethics of participation that seeks to ensure that the peace that emerges promotes equality among and across the parties, often twinned to processes promoting justice (Abu-Nimer, 2001a, b; MacGinty, 2008).

Although there have been excellent examples of the successes of peacemaking (Dayton and Kriesberg, 2009), peacemaking itself is increasing co-opted by counterinsurgency processes, such as those practiced in Iraq or those under development in Afghanistan; peacebuilding has become "nation-building" and is all too often aligned with the objectives (narratives) of the occupying force, as has been the case in wars in Iraq and Afghanistan. Although Lederach (2005) and others (Cousens, Kumar, and Wermester, 2001; Jeong, 2005; Reychler and Paffenholz, 2001) have outlined the parameters of effective peacebuilding practices, the issues surrounding power and justice remain, the issues surrounding marginalization can persist, even as peace agreements are reached. Peacebuilding and peacemaking would both benefit practically and ethically from a redefinition anchored in narrative theory, tuned to the features of the stories that populate a given conflict and effective at fostering their evolution.

Somalia provides a case in point: The power-sharing agreements that were negotiated in Somalia have not resolved the "meaningful" issues—relationships continue to the damaged, and power-sharing has not led to reconciliation. As Nadler, Malloy, and Fisher (2008, p. 41) point out, power-sharing agreements fall into the category of "instrumental reconciliation," which seeks to promote trust through collaboration or cooperation. This is very different from a focus on what they term "socioemotional reconciliation," which is designed to build trust by altering the way parties construct their sense of Self and their sense of the Other; these changes in identity, in turn, provide a foundation for a new relationship. It is clear that in instrumental reconciliation there is little evolution in the nature of the conflict narratives—collaboration is expected to be the force that creates those changes. In the case of Somalia, instrumental reconciliation has not worked— fourteen different reconciliation agreements did not heal the past or increase the presence of positive peace.

But even in the case of socioemotional reconciliation, the theory about how identity is transformed through interaction/engagement is limited in terms of our understanding of *how* the meaning that undergirds the construction of identity evolves over time and, in a positive manner, in the context of a relationship that is historically violent. Although research has expanded our understanding of the process of reconciliation, it has yet to document the evolution of the stories parties tell, on the ground, about the conflict, about themselves, and their relation to others. Without this level of detail, we may presume reconciliation has taken root in a post-conflict environment on the basis of evidence that there are acts of "forgiveness" (widely circulated in the media, as they were in the national reconciliation project in South Africa, set in motion by the Truth and Reconciliation Commission [TRC]) or collaborations in progress. These acts of reconciliation not only may be limited in nature, but they may also cover over ongoing resentment associated with marginalization. A narrative lens would enable analysts and interveners, who are working to promote reconciliation, to attend to the evolution (or lack thereof) of the stories told in a post-conflict region.

Additionally, reconciliation processes are often critiqued for bypassing justice—transitional justice itself often relies on amnesty, and even when truth and reconciliation processes, such as the one in South Africa, foster forgiveness, social inequality and marginalization persist (Mendeloff, 2004; Nagy, 2004). Some have argued that "truth-telling" without accountability neither fosters reconciliation nor supports the emergence of justice (Gibson, 2004; Nattrass, 1999; Quezada, Rangel, and Pallais, 2006). And there have been many critiques of transitional justice processes for either failing to promote reconciliation, as in the case of Chile (Cobb and Wasunna, 2000), or failing to promote justice, as has been the critique of South Africa's TRC, as well as many other cases in which "truth-telling" was either accompanied by amnesty or no effort was made to assign blame, as has been the case in many TRCs to date. Attention to the narrative structure and reconciliation processes would not only provide an additional assessment for evaluation of the process, it would also provide the foundation for more effective, targeted policies that address and reduce marginalization and promote integration across identity divisions.

In summary, the practices of conflict resolution available to practitioners today, although certainly effective in many cases, are inevitably limited, either because they are not able to effect agreements or alter the nature of the conflict, or because the peace that is created is partial, unstable under the weight of historical injustice and the threat of renewed violence. Although the interest-based discourse has certainly contributed to conflict resolution, it has fit, hand-in-glove, to the discourse of rational choice theory, which disattends to the presence and creation of meaning systems and their relation to violence. After all, it is not as though people can "create new meaning for mutual gain" when it is the existing frameworks for meaning that reproduce the conflict. One can argue that the glass is half empty and return to advocate "Realpolitik," using the logic that conflict resolution practices are "soft" and flawed.

However, I want to argue the opposite—the glass is more than half full. We have sets of conflict resolution practices, emerging around the world, in conflict and post-conflict zones, in business settings, in law, in formal diplomatic processes and grass-roots social movements. But what we need is a lens, a way of tracking the conversations in these practices that attends to the nature of the stories in play, as well as to their transformation. Narrative provides a "plumb line" for understanding, tracking, and altering the meanings that anchor conflict and support its resolution. It provides a lens for both planning and assessing the nature of the change that is effected; and critical narrative practice goes further—it will provide us means to differentiate the "better" from the "worse" stories, and, in the process, it holds out the promise of an ethics for narrative approaches to conflict resolution that can address, if not redress, marginalization.

What all the conflict resolution processes have in common is that they all are enacted in conversations in which stories are launched, elaborated, destabilized, and otherwise unfolded. Elaborating a theory of conflict and its resolution from a narrative lens will provide not only a foundational theory for the analysis of conflicts, but will also enable practitioners to assess the evolution of narratives on the basis of a narrative ethics that denounces narrative violence and calls for the reduction of marginalization, story by story, conversation by conversation. Conflict resolution does indeed aspire to more than simply settlement or agreement. In keeping with Burton's aspirations (1996), it should seek to redress marginalization, which is the handmaiden of structural violence (Galtung, 1990; Laclau and Mouffe, 1987). In the end, it is my hope that this book will not only advance the theory of conflict resolution, but will also support the evolution of conflict resolution practice in line with an ethics for narrative engagement that addresses the critical workings of power and ideology. Moving beyond the very important observation that we live in narrative, this book provides a pragmatic and ethical framework for understanding conflicts and their evolution, as narrative processes, as well as a framework for practice that recognizes and contains, as it reduces, narrative violence.

Bibliography

Abu-Nimer, M. 2001a. "Conflict Resolution, Culture, and Religion: Toward a Training Model of Interreligious Peacebuilding." *Journal of Peace Research* 38 (6): 685.

———. 2001b. *Reconciliation, Justice, and Coexistence: Theory and Practice.* Lanham, MD: Lexington Books.

Arendt, H. 1998. *The Human Condition.* 1st ed. Chicago, IL: University of Chicago Press.

Aristotle. 1987. *The Poetics of Aristotle: Translation and Commentary.* Trans. Stephen Halliwell. Chapel Hill: University of North Carolina Press.

Austin, J. L. 1975. *How to Do Things with Words: Second Edition.* 2nd ed. Boston, MA: Harvard University Press.

Borgen, C. J. 2007. "Imagining Sovereignty, Managing Secession: The Legal Geography of Eurasia's Frozen Conflicts." *Oregon Review of International Law* 9: 477.

Bosco, L. 2011. "Competition for Power and Altruism." Forum for Social Economics (April 10). http://www.econ-pol.unisi.it/quaderni/562.pdf.

Bruner, J. 1991. "The Narrative Construction of Reality." *Critical Inquiry* 18 (1): 1–21.

Burton, J. W. 1996. *Conflict Resolution.* 1st ed. London: The Scarecrow Press, Inc.

Caplan, Bryan. 2006. "Terrorism: The Relevance of the Rational Choice Model." *Public Choice* 128 (1) (July 1): 91–107. doi:10.1007/slll27-006-9046-8.

Carbaugh, Donal A. 2005. *Cultures in Conversation.* Mahwah, NJ: Lawrence Erlbaum Associates.

Cobb, S., and A. Wassuna. 2000. Humanizing Human Rights: Transitional Justice as Moral Discussion. Presented at Law 8t Society Annual Association Meeting. Miami, Florida.

Coleman, P. T., R. Vallacher, A. Nowak, and L. Bui-Wrzosinska. 2007. "Intractable Conflict as an Attractor: Presenting a Dynamical Model of Conflict, Escalation, and Intractability." *American Behavioral Scientist* 50 (11): 1454–1475.

Cousens, E. M., C. Kumar, and K. Wermester, eds. 2001. *Peacebuilding as Politics: Cultivating Peace in Fragile Societies.* Boulder, CO: Lynne Rienner Publishers.

Dayton, B. W., and L. Kriesberg. 2009. *Conflict Transformation and Peacebuilding: Moving from Violence to Sustainable Peace.* Oxford: Routledge.

Deitelhoff, N., and H. Müller. 2005. "Theoretical Paradise—Empirically Lost? Arguing with Habermas." *Review of International Studies* 31 (1): 167–179.

Deleuze, G. 1995. *Negotiations.* Trans. M. Joughin. New York: Columbia University Press.

Dewey, John. 1929. *The Quest for Certainty.* New York: Putnam.

Entman, R. M. 1991. "Framing U.S. Coverage of International News: Contrasts in Narratives of the KAL and Iran Air Incidents." *Journal of Communication* 41 (4): 6–27.

Feldman, A. 1991. *Formations of Violence: The Narrative of the Body and Political Terror in Northern Ireland.* Chicago: University of Chicago Press.

Fernea, E. W., and M. E. Hocking. 1992. *The Struggle for Peace: Israelis and Palestinians.* 1st ed. Austin: University of Texas Press.

Fisher, R. 1997. *Interactive Conflict Resolution.* 1st ed. Syracuse, NY: Syracuse University Press.

Galtung, J. 1990. "Cultural Violence." *Journal of Peace Research* 27 (3): 291–305.

Genette, G., and A. Levonas. 1976. "Boundaries of Narrative." *New Literary History* 8 (1): 1–13.

Gibson, L. J. 2004. *Overcoming Apartheid: Can Truth Reconcile A Divided Nation?* New York: Russell Sage Foundation.

Goboda-Madikizeal, P. 2008. Transforming Trauma in the Aftermath of Gross Human Rights Abuses: Making Public Space Intimate Through the South African Truth and Reconciliation Commission. In *The Social Psychology of Intergroup Reconciliation,* ed. A. Nadler, T. Malloy, and J. Fisher, 57–76. New York: Oxford University Press.

Habermas, J. 1996. *Between Facts and Norms: Contributions to a Discourse Theory of Law and Democracy.* Cambridge: MIT Press.

Habermas, J. 2001. *The Postnational Constellation: Political Essays.* Cambridge: MIT Press.

Hajer, M. A. 1995. *The Politics of Environmental Discourse: Ecological Modernization and the Policy Process.* New York: Oxford University Press.

Hajer, M. A., and D. W. Laws. 2006. Ordering Through Discourse. In *The Oxford Handbook of Public Policy,* ed. M. Moran, M. Rein, and R. E. Goodin. New York: Oxford University Press, pp. 251–268.

Hajer, M. A., and H. Wagenaar. 2003. *Deliberative Policy Analysis: Understanding Governance in the Network Society.* Cambridge: Cambridge University Press.

Halverson, E. R. 2004. Narrative and Identity: Constructing Oppositional Identities in Performance Communities. In *ICLS '04 Proceedings of the 6th International Conference on Learning Sciences,* 246–253. Santa Monica: International Society of the Learning Sciences.

Harré, R., and L. van Langenhove. 1991. "Varieties of Positioning." *Journal for the Theory of Social Behaviour* 21 (4): 393–407.

Harré, R., and L. van Langenhove, eds. 1999. *Positioning Theory: Moral Contexts of Intentional Action.* Oxford: Blackwell.

Hewstone, M., J. B. Kenworthy, E. Cairns, N. Tausch, J. Hughes, T. Tam, A. Voci, U. von Hecker, and C. Pinder. 2008. Stepping Stones to Reconciliation in Northern Ireland: Intergroup Contact, Forgiveness, and Trust. In *The Social Psychology of Intergroup Reconciliation,* ed. A. Nadler, T. E. Malloy, and J. D. Fisher, 199–226. Oxford: Oxford University Press.

Hirst, P. Q. 1994. *Associative Democracy: New Forms of Economic and Social Governance.* Amherst: University of Massachusetts Press.

Huspek, M. 1994. "Oppositional Codes and Social Class Relations." *British Journal of Sociology* 45 (1): 79–102.

Jabri, V. 1996. "Textualising the Self: Moral Agency in Inter-Cultural Discourse." *Global Society* 10 (1): 57–68.

Jackson, R. 2005. *Writing the War on Terrorism: Language, Politics and Counter-terrorism.* Manchester: Manchester University Press.

Jakobson, R. 1960. Linguistics and Poetics. In *Style in Language,* ed. T. A. Sebeok, 351–377. Cambridge, MA: MIT Press.

Jeong, Ho-Won. 2005. *Peacebuilding in Postconflict Societies: Strategy and Process.* Boulder, CO: Lynne Rienner Publishers.

Johnson, A. 2008. " 'From Where We're Sat . . .': Negotiating Narrative Transformation Through Interaction in Police Interviews with Suspects." *Text & Talk—An Interdisciplinary Journal of Language, Discourse Communication Studies* 28 (3): 327–349.

Johnson, M. 2007. *The Meaning of the Body: Aesthetics of Human Understanding.* Chicago: University of Chicago Press.

Kelman, H. C,, and S. P. Cohen. 1976. "The Problem-Solving Workshop: A Social-Psychological Contribution to the Resolution of International Conflicts." *Journal of Peace Research* 13 (2): 79–90.

Kemp, W. A. 2004. "The Business of Ethnic Conflict." *Security Dialogue* 35 (1): 43–59.

Killian, K. D. 2002. "Dominant and Marginalized Discourses in Interracial Couples' Narratives: Implications for Family Therapists." *Family Process* 41 (4): 603–618.

Labov, W., and J. Waletzky. 1967. *Narrative Analysis: Oral Versions of Personal Experience.* Seattle: University of Washington Press.

Ladau, E., and C. Mouffe. 1987. "Post-Marxism Without Apologies." *New Left Review* 166: 79–106.

Laing, R. D. 1998. *Knots: Selected Works of R. D. Laing.* Reprint. New York: Routledge.

Lakoff, G., and M. Johnson. 1999. *Philosophy in the Flesh: The Embodied Mind and Its Challenge to Western Thought.* New York: Basic Books.

Lara, M. P. 2007. *Narrating Evil: A Postmetaphysical Theory of Reflective Judgment.* New York: Columbia University Press.

Laws, D. 1996. "The Practice of Fairness." *Environmental Impact Assessment Review* 16 (2): 65–70.

———. 2001. Enacting Deliberation: Speech and the Micro-Foundations of Deliberative Democracy. Paper presented at the EPCR Joint Sessions, Workshop 9. Grenoble.

Laws, D., and M. Rein. 2003. Reframing Practice. In *Deliberative Policy Analysis: Understanding Governance in the Network Society,* ed. M. A. Hajer and H. Wagenaar. Cambridge: Cambridge University Press, pp.172–206.

Lederach, J. P. 1998. *Building Peace: Sustainable Reconciliation in Divided Societies.* Washington, DC: United States Institute of Peace.

———. 2005. *The Moral Imagination: The Art and Soul of Building Peace.* New York: Oxford University Press.

Lerche, C. O. "Truth Commissions and National Reconciliation: Some Reflections on Theory and Practice." *Peace and Conflict Studies* 7 (1): 2–23.

Lyotard, J. F. 1989. *Differend: Phrases in Dispute.* 1st ed. Minneapolis: University of Minnesota Press.

MacGinty, R. 2008. "Indigenous Peace-Making Versus the Liberal Peace." *Cooperation and Conflict* 43 (2): 139–163.

McAfee, N. 2009. "Democracy's Normativity." *Journal of Speculative Philosophy* 22 (4): 257–265.

Mendeloff, D. 2004. "Truth-Seeking, Truth-Telling, and Postconflict Peacebuilding: Curb the Enthusiasm?" *International Studies Review* 6 (3): 355–380.

Nadler, A., T. Malloy, and J. D. Fisher. 2008. *Social Psychology of Intergroup Reconciliation: From Violent Conflict to Peaceful Co-Existence.* 1st ed. New York: Oxford University Press.

Nagy, R. 2004. "The Ambiguities of Reconciliation and Responsibility in South Africa." *Political Studies* 52 (4): 709–727.

Nattrass, N. 1999. "The Truth and Reconciliation Commission on Business and Apartheid: a critical evaluation." *African Affairs* 98 (392): 373–391.

Nelson, H. Lindemann. 2001. *Damaged Identities, Narrative Repair.* Ithaca, NY: Cornell University Press.

Nino, C. S. 1998. *Radical Evil on Trial.* New Haven, CT: Yale University Press.

Nye, J. S. 2004. *Soft Power.* New York: PublicAffairs Press.

Oliver, Kelly. 2001. *Witnessing: Beyond Recognition.* Minneapolis: University of Minnesota Press.

Pearce, W. Barnett. 2008. *Making Social Worlds: A Communication Perspective.* Chichester, UK: Wiley-Blackwell.

Pearson d'Estree, T., L. Fast, J. Weiss, and M. Jakobsen. 2001. "Changing the Debate About 'Success' in Conflict Resolution Efforts." *Negotiation Journal* 17 (2): 101–113.

Porat, D. A. 2004. "It's Not Written Here, But This Is What Happened: Students' Cultural Comprehension of Textbook Narratives on the Israeli-Arab Conflict." *American Educational Research Journal* 41 (4): 963–996.

Prince, G. 2003. *A Dictionary of Narratology.* Lincoln: University of Nebraska Press.

Pruitt, D. G. 2007. "Readiness Theory and the Northern Ireland Conflict." *American Behavioral Scientist* 50 (11): 1520–1541.

Quezada, S. A., and J. Trevino Rangel. 2006. "Neither Truth nor Justice." *Latin American Perspectives* 33 (2): 56–68.

Reychler, L., and T. Paffenholz, eds. 2001. *Peacebuilding: A Field Guide.* Boulder, CO: Lynne Rienner Publishers.

Rouhana, N. N. 2004. "Group Identity and Power Asymmetry in Reconciliation Processes: The Israeli-Palestinian Case." *Peace and Conflict: Journal of Peace Psychology* 10 (1): 33–52.

Sarbin, T. R., ed. 1986. *Narrative Psychology: The Storied Nature of Human Conduct.* New York: Praeger.

Scarry, E. 1987. *The Body in Pain: The Making and Unmaking of the World.* 1st ed. New York: Oxford University Press.

Schopenhauer, A. 1966. *The World as Will and Representation.* New York: Dover.

Scott, J. C. 1990. *Domination and the Arts of Resistance: Hidden Transcripts.* New Haven, CT: Yale University Press.

Searle, J. R. 1997. *The Construction of Social Reality.* New York: Free Press.

Sheehan, I. S. 2007. *When Terrorism and Counterterrorism Clash: Vie War on Terror and the Transformation of Terrorist Activity.* Amherst, NY: Cambria Press.

Shotter, John. 2008. *Conversational Realities Revisited: Life, Language, Body and World.* 2nd ed. The Taos Institute Publications.

Siegel, M. 1995. "More than Words: The Generative Power of Transmediation for Learning." *Canadian Journal of Education/Revue canadienne de l'éducation* 20 (4): 455–475.

Smets, P., and M. den Uyl. 2008. "The Complex Role of Ethnicity in Urban Mixing: A Study of Two Deprived Neighbourhoods in Amsterdam." *Urban Studies* 45 (7): 1439–1460.

Smith, A. R. 2008. "Dialogue in Agony: The Problem of Communication in Authoritarian Regimes." *Communication Theory* ("10503293; 18 (1) (February): 160–185. doi:10.1111/j.l468-2885.2007.00318.x.

Spence, D. P. 1986. "Narrative Smoothing and Clinical Wisdom." In *Narrative Psychology: The Storied Nature of Human Conduct,* ed. T. Sarbin, 211–232. New York: Praeger.

Stedman, S. J., D. Rothchild, and E. M. Cousens. 2002. *Ending Civil Wars: The Implementation of Peace Agreements.* Reprint. Boulder, CO: Lynne Rienner Publishers.

Stewart, G. 1999. *Between Film and Screen: Modernism's Photo Synthesis.* Chicago: University of Chicago Press.

Tan, Sui-Lan, and F. M. Moghaddam. 1999. "Positioning in Intergroup Relations." In *Positioning Theory: Moral Contexts of Intentional Action,* ed. R. Harré and L. van Langenhove, 178–194. Oxford: Blackwell.

Taylor, C. 1985. *Human Agency and Language.* Cambridge: Cambridge University Press.

Tilly, C. 1998. "Contentious Conversation." *Social Research* 65 (3): 491–510.

Walzer, S., and T. P. Oies. 2003. "Managing Conflict After Marriages End: A Qualitative Study of Narratives of Ex-Spouses." *Families in Society* 84 (2): 192–200.

Watts, M. 2006. "The Sinister Political Life of Community: Economies of Violence and Governable Spaces in the Niger Delta, Nigeria." In *The Romance of Community,* ed. G. Creed, 101–142. Santa Fe, NM: SAR Press.

Watts, M. J. 2005. "Righteous Oil? Human Rights, the Oil Complex, and Corporate Social Responsibility." *Annual Review of Environment and Resources* 30 (1): 373–407.

Watzlawick, P., J. Beavin Bavelas, and D. D. Jackson. 2011. *Pragmatics of Human Communication: A Study of Interactional Patterns, Pathologies, and Paradoxes.* New York: W. W. Norton.

White, L., and A. Taket. 2000. "Exploring the Use of Narrative Analysis as an Operational Research Method: A Case Study in Voluntary Sector Evaluation." *Journal of the Operational Research Society* 51 (6): 700–711.

White, M., and D. Epston. 1990. *Narrative Means to Therapeutic Ends.* 1st ed. New York: W. W. Norton.

Winslade, J. 2009. "Tracing Lines of Flight: Implications of the Work of Gilles Deleuze for Narrative Practice." *Family Process* 48 (3): 332–346.

Winslade, J., and G. D. Monk. 2000. *Narrative Mediation: A New Approach to Conflict Resolution.* 1st ed. San Francisco: Jossey-Bass.

Wittgenstein, L. 1953. *Philosophical Investigations.* Oxford: Blackwell Publishing.

Wodak, R. 2006. "'Doing Politics': The Discursive Construction of Politics." *Journal of Language & Politics* 5 (3): 299–303.

Zakaria, F. 2001. "The Politics of Rage: Why Do They Hate Us?" *Newsweek,* October 14. http://www.thedailybeast.com/newsweek/2001/10/14/the-politics-of-rage-why-do-they-hate-us.html.

Zartman, 1.1995. *Cooperative Security: Reducing Third World Wars.* 1st ed. Syracuse, NY: Syracuse University Press.

Note

1. See the dictionary definition of "factum" at http://oxforddictionaries.com/definition/english/factum.

Beyond Coexistence

Leigh Payne

Leigh Payne is a professor of sociology at Oxford University. She received her PhD in political science from Yale University, where she then taught until accepting a position at the University of Wisconsin-Madison. Within Oxford's Latin American Centre, she focuses on human rights violations in Latin America, exploring how to develop human rights cultures that prevent violence as well as overcome impunity for past abuses. She does this through the lens of transitional justice, which is the set of mechanisms used to address past human rights violations in dictatorships and armed conflict. Her work has attracted not only the interest of scholars but also that of victim groups and international and domestic governmental and non-governmental organizations interested in her findings. Her book, *Unsettling Accounts*, from which we selected this excerpt, analyzes the confessions of perpetrators of state violence in Argentina, Brazil, Chile, and South Africa.

Instead of aiming for consensus or peace, focuses of Epoch Two scholarship, Payne advocates for what she calls "contentious coexistence." She claims active sites of contentious dialogue can be a sign of a healthy, rather than a failing, democracy. Healthy contentious spaces invite multiple truths not because "truth can set one free" or because certain truths are dangerous if exposed too directly, but rather because adding voices to the public discursive space provides the greatest chance for a positive peace, including greater equality and decreased outbreaks of violence. This approach is far less teleological. This is unlike Epoch Two, which employs mechanisms like truth and reconciliation councils that sometimes seek unifying truths or to produce a kind of reconciliation. Payne's approach focuses more on the process and less on the results.

Community members can offer "unsettling accounts" of violence (active or structural) or other issues without having an agenda. In this context, conflict resolution professionals do not need to push these accounts into shape or find links between one account and another. Epoch Two dealt with diversity by looking for commonality. Epoch Three creates spaces for difference.

Payne's approach also speaks to some early critiques of conflict resolution, which argued that the pressure to find a solution could bury structural inequalities. Contentious coexistence creates space for reform, revolution, or other means of change to address various forms of injustice. Democracies will be made stronger by contention than by forced consensus, Payne argues. In this approach, stifling debates can be seen as the most dangerous threat to democracies. She provides a caveat about what she calls injurious speech or direct threats of violence, which she concedes could provide a threat to the well-being of a community.

For practitioners of conflict resolution, Payne's approach requires a shift in orientation. New skills need to be developed to lead contentious dialogues. Articles by Shawn Ginwright, John Winslade, and Michael Gardner provide some guidance on the kinds of skills and techniques that create space for unsettling accounts.

Questions to consider: Do you think, as communities, rather than developing "safe spaces," we would benefit from becoming more comfortable with difference and disagreement? What might conflict resolution look like if we allowed for, rather than tried to assuage, tensions?

Contentious Coexistence

Leigh Payne

People can die of an excessive dose of the truth, you know.

—Ariel Dorfman, *Death and the Maiden*

Democratic theorists and governments alike endorse the above-stated claim by Gerardo in Ariel Dorfman's play *Death and the Maiden*. The scholar Stephen Holmes quips, "Repression can be perfectly healthy for democracy" and "Tongue-tying . . . may be one of constitutionalism's main gifts to democracy."[1] With the exception of South Africa, the democracies analyzed in this book generally concurred with Gerardo and Holmes. Argentina, Brazil, and Chile have tried, mainly unsuccessfully, to keep contentious issues off the public agenda in order to protect fragile political systems from polarizing debate and to avoid provoking authoritarian reversals. Despite their failure to silence the past, these democracies have survived and flourished.

In *Unsettling Accounts* I have thus challenged the "fatal overdose of truth" notion prevalent in democratic theory and practice. But I have also disputed the opposite claim, espoused by Paulina in *Death and the Maiden* and some theorists and practitioners of transitional justice, that the truth sets one free and settles accounts with the past. "Healing truths" have proved equally elusive. Most countries emerging from authoritarian rule have not adopted South Africa's model of reconciliation through truth, because they recognize the unlikelihood of establishing one truth about the past that will resolve the deep and enduring political divisions they confront.

Between the cautionary and Utopian extremes of conflict resolution lies a more practical model: contentious coexistence. Contentious coexistence rejects ineffective gag orders and embraces democratic dialogue, even over highly factious issues, as healthy for democracies. It rejects infeasible official and healing truth in favor of multiple and contending truths that reflect different political viewpoints in society. Contentious coexistence does not require elaborate institutional mechanisms, but rather is stimulated by dramatic stories, acts, or images that provoke widespread participation, contestation over prevailing political viewpoints, and competition over ideas. Contentious coexistence, in other words, is democracy in practice.[2]

This book has explored unsettling accounts and the contentious coexistence they have spawned through perpetrators' confessions. Similar processes have unfolded in other countries at different stages of democratic development, suggesting the absence of inoculation from the assumed fatal dose of truth. Consider, for example, the dramatic accounts of honor killings and stoning of allegedly adulterous women in Iran, Jordan, Nigeria, Pakistan, and elsewhere. These stories did not initiate friction over the interpretation and application of Sharia laws, which regulate public and aspects of private life, in contemporary Muslim societies. But nongovernmental organizations within and outside these countries used these stories to mobilize broad participation and debate and to demand political change. Similarly, while the banning of Muslim girls from French public schools did not instigate conflict over the secular state and religious freedom, it did heighten the political drama surrounding the debate and drew in a surprising range of perspectives. These examples of deep and seemingly unresolvable conflicts occurred without undermining democracy, but also without establishing a reconciling truth. Unsettling accounts unleash a society-wide probing into how to interpret the stories and what they mean for contemporary political life. Response to the photographs that exposed U.S. abuses in the Abu Ghraib prison in Iraq extends the arguments in this book to established democracies. These photographs and perpetrators' confessions sparked contentious coexistence in different political contexts and affected democratic practice and outcomes.

"The Photographs Did Not Lie"

After the September 11, 2001 bombing of the World Trade Center, preventing another terrorist attack obsessed the U.S. government and public. The scholar Alfred McCoy noted that "a growing public consensus . . . in favor of torture" prevailed at the time.[3] That consensus hinged on a "ticking bomb" theory: torture provided an effective and necessary means of extracting information from terrorists to prevent planned attacks on civilian populations.[4] The photographs from Abu Ghraib prison, however, changed that perception. They revealed depraved behavior by U.S. prison guards:

> The photographs did not lie.
> American soldiers, male and female, grinning and pointing at the genitals of naked, frightened Iraqi prisoners; an Iraqi man, unclothed and leashed like a dog, groveling on the floor in front of his female guard; a prisoner standing on a box with a sandbag over his head and wires attached to his body beneath a poncho. These were not enemy propaganda pictures; these showed real atrocities actually inflicted by Americans.[5]

Eroding the previous consensus, the images catalyzed a "serious nationwide political debate" and an "epic political struggle" that involved "ordinary Americans" among "a surprisingly diverse range of voices . . . breaking the public climate of timid compliance."[6] The journalist Mark Danner attributed outrage not only to the photographs but also to the context in which they emerged: "Details of the methods of interrogation applied in Guantánamo and at Bagram Air Base, began to emerge more than a year ago. It took the Abu Ghraib photographs, however, set against the violence and chaos of an increasingly unpopular war in Iraq, to bring Americans' torture of prisoners up for public discussion."[7] The public reaction to the photographs eroded consensus and challenged the Bush administration's strategies. As the essayist Susan Sontag wrote, "Apparently it took the photographs to get their attention, when it became clear they could not be suppressed; it was the photographs that made all this 'real' to Bush and his associates."[8]

The photographs from Abu Ghraib fit the definition of unsettling accounts: dramatic performances, speech, or events that rupture political silence or prevailing political consensus and engage a broad sector of society in the democratic practices of participation, contestation, and competition. These dramatic political spectacles prompt even cautious or complicit media outlets to cover them. By widely disseminating emotionally charged images and narratives, media portrayals draw out a diverse range of perspectives. Unsettling accounts obliterate passivity even among audiences otherwise reluctant to discuss politics. They spark debate in public and private sites: families, schools, barbershops, coffee shops, churches, neighborhoods, communities, blogs, on television, on the radio, and in the newspapers. Controversies, normally limited to a small, specialized sector of society, now reach individuals without any personal or direct connection to the underlying events. Moral outrage and political challenges to prevailing political views are aired publicly, sometimes for the first time. The unsettling photographs from Abu Ghraib have even prompted former prisoners of U.S. detention centers to speak out—voices not previously heard.[9]

Unsettling accounts do not merely amplify existing political views in society; they provoke new ways of thinking about politics among newly engaged sectors. Perpetrators' confessions, for example, did not only magnify the existing political demands of victims and survivors; they also presented new views from within the security apparatus and among former regime supporters. They challenged a prevailing view. Whether perpetrators confessed their remorse for past atrocities, bragged about their heroic accomplishments, or expressed salacious pleasure at having inflicted pain, they broke the regime's silence and denial of violence. Regime supporters who had previously believed, or wanted to believe, that victims and survivors had invented stories of atrocity for political gain could not easily ignore evidence to the contrary presented by the perpetrators of that violence.

Similarly, the Abu Ghraib photographs graphically revealed what the formerly abstract consensus around torture really meant. The Bush administration refused to label the acts portrayed in the photographs as "torture," using the language of "humiliation" instead. But even the administration's defenders ignored the euphemism. Senator Bill Frist (Republican, Tennessee) remarked, "What we saw is appalling."[10] Rejecting President Bush's notion that only a "few rotten apples" had committed the abuses, Senator Lindsey Graham (Republican, South Carolina) asserted, "Some of it has an elaborate nature to it that makes me very suspicious of whether or not others were directors or encouraging [the acts]."[11] Senator John McCain (Republican, Arizona) blamed the photographs, and presumably what they depicted, for weakening national security: "I would argue the pictures, terrible pictures from Abu Ghraib, harmed us not only in the Arab World, . . . but . . . also harmed us dramatically amongst friendly nations, the Europeans, many of our allies."[12] As a result of the photographs, McCain sponsored a "torture amendment" that would firmly ally the United States with the international ban on torture. President Bush, responding to pressure from within and outside his party, backed down from his initial decision to veto the amendment. As one journalist noted, "The American people spoke. Both chambers overwhelmingly passed this law [the torture amendment] by veto-proof majorities. It's shameful Bush had to be bullied into supporting it."[13]

Perpetrators' confessions and the Abu Ghraib photographs demonstrate that deeply contentious issues provoke debate without destroying or even threatening democracies. Unsettling accounts, while they do contest prevailing political views, do not replace them with an alternative, "healing" truth, however. Instead, political groups clash over how to interpret unsettling accounts and their meanings for contemporary political life.

"Withholding Pancakes"

Unsettling accounts break down consensus because individuals dissociate themselves from the viewpoints represented in them. Not all audiences, however, reject the viewpoints represented in the unsettling accounts. Indeed, debate erupts because some individuals and groups maintain the prevailing view. These individuals and groups reinterpret unsettling accounts, trying to give them new political meaning in the hope of rebuilding political consensus. Political groups, in other words, compete over the interpretation of unsettling accounts. Reflecting on the Abu Ghraib photographs, a journalist remarked that their "ubiquity . . . suggests not only their potency but their usefulness and their adaptability."[14] Unsettling accounts do not replace one consensus with another, but rather intensify public debate over political events and their meaning for contemporary life.

Regime supporters, therefore, neither defend nor endorse atrocities or sadism; they reframe the confessions that depicted such acts using a variety of narrative techniques. They denigrate some perpetrators—particularly those who issue betrayal, remorseful, and sadistic confessions—as opportunists, liars, and psychopaths. If the confessed acts did occur, so they argue, they were carried out by a few rotten apples and did not represent either the noble security forces who defended the country or the regime's war strategy. Regime supporters publicly defend human rights, arguing that the regime had to protect the country from "terrorists." They use the language of "never again" to call on the country to remain vigilant against subsequent national threats. They also accuse the media and the left wing of misrepresenting, misinterpreting, or staging obscene confessions to slander the previous regime and its heroic accomplishments.

These narrative techniques rarely persuade objective observers. They do provide rhetorical cover, however, for individuals seeking an excuse to defend prevailing political views against the damaging evidence provided by unsettling accounts. President Bush's approach to the Abu Ghraib photographs, Sontag argued, aimed to "limit a public-relations disaster . . . rather than deal with the complex crimes of leadership and of policy revealed by the pictures."[15] Bush-administration supporters tried to reframe the images as "pranks," rather than as abuses, as did the talk-radio host Rush Limbaugh: "This is no different than what happens at the Skull and Bones initiation, and we're going to ruin people's lives over it, and we're going to hamper our military effort, and then we are going to really hammer them because they had a good time."[16] Another reframing device used by Bush-administration supporters involved emphasizing the threat of a terrorist attack and the importance in protecting U.S. citizens with "coercive interrogations," "tough measures," or other euphemisms for what the photographs depicted. Senator Trent Lott (Republican, Mississippi), for example, quipped, "Interrogation is not a Sunday-school class. . . . You don't get information that will save American lives by withholding pancakes."[17]

Unsettling accounts do not replace one prevailing political view with another. Instead, they generate political competition over how to interpret dramatic political events, how to use them, and what they mean for contemporary political life. Such a rhetorical war does not end by killing off democracy or saving it. Instead, it puts into practice the art of competition over ideas and the possibility of building consensus around democratic values.

"Nuance, Passion, and . . . Erudition"

Political groups feel compelled to publicly associate or, more likely, disassociate, themselves from the repulsive acts represented in unsettling accounts. For those groups that had failed to successfully oppose prevailing opinion, unsettling accounts provide an opportunity to do so and thereby strengthen their political claims. Perpetrators' confessions, therefore, help victim and survivor groups raise public awareness of a regime's atrocities and the need for building rule of law to end impunity. Similarly, human-rights groups who condemned the use of torture by the United States employed the Abu Ghraib photographs to show the American public what torture looked like and why it should be outlawed. Such groups use unsettling accounts to persuade audiences to accept their political perspectives; they may even win over former opponents.

This is not, however, a one-sided battle: groups must compete with others' efforts to reframe unsettling accounts. The ensuing debate forces both sides to make more persuasive arguments in vying for political power. The result is often what McCoy described in the aftermath of the Abu Ghraib photographs: "a substantive public discussion . . . marked by nuance, passion, and even, at times, erudition."[18] Unsettling accounts thus render old shibboleths obsolete and demand new arguments to address a new reality.

Sometimes this process involves simply repackaging old ideas in new ways. That effort, however, requires understanding how various perspectives on politics will resonate with a society stunned by unsettling accounts. Groups thus weed out language that legitimates the atrocities depicted, even when those groups concur with the political perspective behind the unsettling accounts. To maintain their base of support, they must show that what they defend differs from atrocity. That process involves a capacity for nuance and rhetorical sophistication.

Simply coding language to hide support for atrocity will maintain support for the group among its most ideologically committed members. Others will see the coded language for what it is and withdraw their support. The latter implicitly endorse the perspectives held by their political enemies, building a broader public consensus around those viewpoints.

Perpetrators' confessions illustrate this process, with former regime supporters, scandalized by tales of atrocity, aligning themselves in support of the protection of human rights. However, these groups do not always, or necessarily, condemn the authoritarian regime as a whole. In Chile, for example, some of Pinochet's former supporters condemned the human-rights violations committed by the regime, but endorsed the regime's economic strategies. In Argentina, the head of the navy decried officers who made, and soldiers who followed, illegal orders, but he did not condemn the "war against subversion."

Similarly, two years after the fact, President Bush declared Abu Ghraib the "biggest mistake" in the war on global terror, stating. "We've been paying for that for a long period of time."[19] The fog of war—a strategy Vice President Dick Cheney advocated five days after 9/11, when he said, "A lot of what needs to be done here will have to be done quietly, without any discussion"—failed to shield the administration's policies from public scrutiny.[20] The Pentagon and the Defense Department rejected Cheney's strategy of creating secret manuals on interrogation techniques, a move that implicitly allied them with the position on torture held by human-rights groups. As Elisa Massimino, the Washington director of Human Rights First, stated, "If the Pentagon is stepping back from that, it's a welcome sign that they now understand the need for transparency and clarity."[21] The unsettling photographs from Abu Ghraib and resulting widespread outrage no doubt contributed to this policy shift.

The understanding generated by unsettling accounts and contentious coexistence, in turn, leads to fragmentation within formerly entrenched political poles. Thus, rather than there being only two contending perspectives in society, a range of views and cross-cutting alliances develop. Some authoritarian-regime supporters in South Africa and Latin America, for example, unambiguously condemn the atrocities those regimes committed, thereby allying themselves with victims and survivors. On the other hand, some victims and survivors share with authoritarian security forces the desire to censor perpetrators' confessions. Still others persist in their original condemnation of or support for those regimes. But all of these political perspectives reflect growing consensus around the importance of protecting human rights, even as they diverge on how to define those rights and who has historically abused them.

"The Pictures Will Not Go Away"

Unsettling accounts and contentious coexistence lead to political transformations. Perpetrators' confessions contributed to the reversal of amnesty laws in Argentina and Chile, thus eroding the culture of impunity by making those criminal abuses undeniable. Perpetrators' confessions in South Africa's TRC also erased previous denials of apartheid state violence. The Abu Ghraib photographs compelled the White House to retract its earlier definition of torture as only "serious physical injury, such as organ failure, impairment of bodily function, or even death."[22] It also investigated, tried, and found guilty those who had committed the Abu Ghraib abuses. It signed the torture amendment. The uproar over the photographs no doubt contributed significantly to these developments.

Some contend, however, that these political changes mark only superficial, and not fundamental transformations of policies. Unsettling accounts in Brazil, for example, have not contributed to any changes in its amnesty laws. Perpetrators denied amnesty by the TRC have not faced prosecution in South Africa. Changes in amnesty laws have brought few perpetrators to prison for their violations in Argentina and Chile. And the Bush administration has found ways to circumvent the constraints on its policies imposed in the aftermath of the debate over the Abu Ghraib photographs. Specifically, none of those responsible for preparing the legal memos bypassing international bans on torture have lost their positions in the Bush administration, and some have even received promotions.[23] The commanders of those who committed the atrocities have avoided investigation, trial, or even criticism. President Bush tried to sneak past the U.S. public a measure granting him the power to interpret the torture amendment as needed.[24] The new consensus that emerged from the Abu Ghraib photographs, some cynics contend, was to hide torture better, not ban its use. Even without such cynicism, evidence suggests that the uproar over the Abu Ghraib photographs failed to end the use of torture in prisons in Guantanamo Bay, Afghanistan, and third-party accomplice states as part of the war on terror.[25] Danner asks, "Is what has changed only what we know, or what we are willing to accept?"[26]

Unsettling accounts and contentious coexistence do not heal democracies. Indeed, they cannot even guarantee particular policy changes. What they do is change the political context and put into practice the democratic art of participation, contestation, and competition. The political scientist David Art concisely summarizes the ambiguous results of the democratic processes they engender: "Public debates create new frames for interpreting political issues, change the ideas and interests of political actors, restructure the relationships between them, and redefine the limits of legitimate political space. These changes do not occur because the better argument carries the day, but rather because public debates set in motion a series of processes that reshape the political environment in which they occur."[27]

In other words, some unsettling accounts and forms of contentious coexistence may prove more successful than others in transforming the political landscape. The performative analysis I have adopted in this book identifies the factors that constrain and enhance the role of unsettling accounts and contentious coexistence in democracies. Some performances fare better than others in catalyzing responses from individuals. Thus, any response to the fictional text written by an unknown pilot who witnessed, but did not commit, violence and who could not remember key details in Brazil cannot compare with the outrage when someone confesses to having killed thirty people by dropping them from a plane in Argentina, or expresses pleasure at sexually torturing women in Chile, or demonstrates the wet-bag torture technique in a media circus in South Africa. The power of unsettling accounts varies with the power of the performance: who makes it (actor), what they recount (script), and how they recount it (acting).

Factors external to the perpetrators' confessional speech—institutional mechanisms (staging), political context (timing), and public response (audience)—also shape the power of unsettling accounts to stimulate debate and engender political change. Governments that control the staging of unsettling accounts may also limit the participation and contestation they create. These controls take the form of censorship, speech laws, and limiting access to information. In addition, media that share political perspective with the government or political actors challenged by unsettling accounts tend to provide thin and highly edited coverage of those accounts, thus dampening their political impact. The Chilean media fits this description, with its limited coverage of perpetrators' confessions and its decision to present an edited version of Romo's only after it had provoked an uproar outside the country. The success of the Bush administration in keeping the unedited file of photographs from Abu Ghraib out of the mainstream media helped its efforts in minimizing the acts portrayed as "humiliations," rather than torture.

Others blame the public's preoccupation with another terrorist attack on U.S. soil for its acceptance of the Bush administration's strategy in the "war on terror." The journalist Joseph Lelyveld, for example, argues that "when it comes to imminent threats of terrorism, the democratic process doesn't demand open debate."[28] Danner, however, remains baffled by the muted response from U.S. audiences to the Abu Ghraib photographs: "It is not about revelation or disclosure but about the failure, once wrongdoing is disclosed, of politicians, officials, the press, and, ultimately, citizens to act. The scandal is not about uncovering what is hidden, it is about seeing what is already there—and acting on it. It is not about information; it is about politics."[29] Abu Ghraib suggests that political timing, particularly when more pressing political issues prevail, limits the power of unsettling accounts to catalyze political participation and contestation. Similarly, perpetrators' confessions that occur long after the end of the abuses, as in Brazil, may shock audiences without mobilizing them behind political change.

This is particularly true if there are few politically mobilized sectors in society capable of keeping unsettling accounts on the democratic agenda. The further back in time the political events occurred, and the fewer the sectors of the population they affected, the harder it will be to keep political actors mobilized to fight for political change. Sontag wrote, "The pictures will not go away," referring to the enduring images from Abu Ghraib.[30] But for those pictures to be used effectively to promote specific political ends, an organized group or set of individuals must use them. Mobilized groups, as perpetrators' confessions have illustrated, can transform even inauspicious unsettling accounts into catalysts for political action. In Argentina human-rights activists turned heroic confessions into evidence of atrocities committed and thus were able to demand justice. In Chile and in South Africa they filled in details missing from denials and amnesia confessions to challenge impunity. They even overcame silence in Brazil, using a mere whisper of a confession to reveal hidden atrocities.

The success of these groups also depends on their ability to overcome other organized sectors of society poised to combat the political change they advocate. In this battle, the best, most ethical, democratic, or even legal argument will not necessarily win. Unsettling accounts may bring forth previously silenced views, but they do not guarantee that those views will prevail in a power struggle with the opposition.

"Good Counterspeech Is One Remedy for Bad Speech"

In *Unsettling Accounts* I advocate political participation to contest prevailing views that have impeded the promotion of democratic values, like human rights and rule of law. I recognize that political competition means that groups advocating those values will not always succeed in achieving the specific policy outcomes they desire. But by provoking participation, contestation, and competition, unsettling accounts contribute to building stronger democratic practices, if not policies.

The contentious-coexistence model, moreover, proves more realistic and effective than its alternatives. Both the "fatal overdose of truth" and "healing truth" theories suffer from the same Utopian assumption that democracies can successfully gag contentious issues. Little evidence supports this assumption. Efforts by the Bush administration to run the global war on terror in secret failed to stifle the photographs from Abu Ghraib or other abhorrent tales of U.S. abuses. Strategies to impose one official truth to reconcile conflict over the apartheid state in South Africa or military regimes in Latin America also failed. Perpetrators' confessions broke the pact of silence among the military in Latin America. They even defied speech laws aimed at protecting society from harmful justifications by perpetrators for their past crimes. South African government officials, most famously the former president P. W. Botha, publicly denounced the TRC and the healing truth it imposed. A reluctant media in the United States and in Chile, wary of exposing an unfavorable view of past and present governments and their policies, still presented enough of the unsettling accounts to unleash outrage. Powerful political groups defending the status quo—like the militaries in Latin America—could not even keep their own members from defying gag rules.

Not only are such efforts at stifling debate infeasible, but they also prove dangerous. They drive strongly held, but silenced, views underground and beyond the scrutiny and judgment of public debate. Certainly some forms of speech require prohibition, specifically direct and credible threats of violence aimed at specific individuals, or injurious speech that violates individuals' right not to listen.[31] For other kinds of speech, however, democracies benefit most from unfettering them, compelling them to compete with better—more democratic-ideas. As the adage goes, "Good counterspeech is one remedy for bad speech."[32]

What I have described is a messy process. It involves coping with heightened tensions, sometimes at very early stages of democratic development. It exposes citizens to uncomfortable facts and perspectives that they would rather avoid, and indeed have sometimes managed to avoid for some time. And the outcomes, at least in terms of specific policies, are uncertain. But this messy process is unavoidable and healthy in new and established democracies.

Notes

All translations of material in other languages are my own, unless otherwise specified.

Epigraph from Dorfman, *Death and the Maiden*, 55.

1. Holmes, "Gag Rules or the Politics of Omission," 203, 204.

2. Dahl, *Polyarchy*.

3. McCoy, *A Question of Torture*, 110.

4. McCoy includes examples from the *Washington Post, Los Angeles Times, Wall Street Journal, Newsweek*, and PBS's *McLaughlin Group* as part of the "media swagger" in favor of torture. McCoy, *A Question of Torture*, 110–11. Memos discussing the use of torture in the war on terror, which were prepared for the George W. Bush administration, have been reproduced in Danner, *Torture and Truth*, 78–214. The ticking-bomb defense from self-identified liberals includes Alan M. Dershowitz's *Why Terrorism Works* and Michael Levin's "The Case for Torture," which refers to the use of torture in some situations as "morally mandatory." Michael Ignatieff makes a similar, but more nuanced argument, in "Lesser Evils."

5. Whitney, Introduction, vii.

6. McCoy, *A Question of Torture*, 150, 179, 180.

7. Danner, *Torture and Truth*, 22–23.

8. Sontag, "Regarding the Torture of Others."

9. See, for example, Mourad Benchellali's testimony about his experiences in the Guantanamo Bay prison, in a book written with Antoine Audouard and excerpted as "Detainees in Despair," *New York Times*, 14 June 2006, A23.

10. Charles Babington, "Lawmakers Are Stunned," *Washington Post*, 13 May 2004, A1.

11. Sontag, "Regarding the Torture of Others."

12. McCoy, *A Question of Torture*, 186.

13. "McCain's Effort Saves Nation's Soul: Anti-torture Measure Wins Because It Keeps America on Right Side Legally," *Buffalo News*, 21 December 2005, A8.

14. Danner, *Torture and Truth*, 27.

15. Sontag, "Regarding the Torture of Others."

16. Quoted in ibid.

17. Deborah Solomon, "Questions for Trent Lott," *New York Times Magazine*, 20 June 2004, 15, quoted in McCoy, *A Question of Torture*, 153.

18. McCoy, *A Question of Torture*, 150.

19. David E. Sanger and Jim Rutenberg, "Bush and Blair Concede Errors, but Defend War," *New York Times*, 26 May 2006, a12.

20. Jane Mayer, "Outsourcing Torture: The Secret History of America's 'Extraordinary Rendition' Program," *New Yorker*, 14 February 2005, 106.

21. Eric Schmitt, "Pentagon Rethinking Manual with Interrogation Methods," *New York Times*, 14 June 2006, A19.

22. Memorandum Opinion for the Deputy Attorney General, 30 December 2004, www.usdoj.gov/.

23. Alfred McCoy reviews the career trajectory of these individuals, including those of Alberto Gonzales, president's counsel, who famously referred to the Geneva Convention's limitations on interrogations as "obsolete" and "quaint"; Jay Bybee, assistant attorney general, who prepared the memos for Gonzales, thus creating the legal cover for torture in Iraq and elsewhere; and John Yoo, the justice-department lawyer who drafted the notion of the "unitary executive," which argued for a secret emergency constitution that would give the president unlimited powers in the "war on terror." McCoy, *A Question of Torture*, 160–61.

24. "Veto? Who Needs a Veto?" *New York Times*, 5 May 2006, a22.

25. McCoy, *A Question of Torture*, 188–209.

26. Danner, *Torture and Truth*, 9.

27. Art, *The Politics of the Nazi Past in Germany and Austria*, 14.

28. Lelyveld, "Interrogating Ourselves," 39.

29. Danner, *Torture and Truth*, xiv.

30. Sontag, "Regarding the Torture of Others."

31. Downs, "Racial Incitement Law and Policy in the United States," 117–18.

32. Ibid., 128.

Politics of Victimhood

Diane Enns

Diane Enns describes herself as a writer first, then a professor of philosophy. She teaches at McMaster University in Hamilton, Ontario, Canada. She says one of her inspirations is Hélène Cixous, poet-philosopher extraordinaire, who wrote that "what is most true is naked life," and Virginia Woolf, who insists not only that we need money and a room of our own in order to write but also "the courage to write exactly what we think." In her own room, Enns has the courage to write not only about war and victimhood, but she also writes about the philosophy of love. Her approach to philosophy is informed by Hannah Arendt as well as the French post-structuralist traditions (Étienne Balibar, Jacques Derrida, and Maurice Merleau-Ponty). The book from which this selection is taken, *The Violence of Victimhood,* investigates the status and condition of the victim of political violence, raising questions regarding the responsibility of victims and the concepts of judgment, forgiveness, and mercy as responses to collective injury.

In taking on these subjects, Enns tackles a theme characteristic to Epoch Three scholars; the upending of simple binaries such as good versus evil and victim versus perpetrator. The neat lines of good and evil are perfectly suited for the legal pursuits of retributive justice and the efforts to promote security by identifying and removing dangerous parties. Enns highlights another binary operating as the subtext to many acts of genocide: native versus settler. These binary pairs dangerously and endlessly keep parties at war. In the contexts of Israel–Palestine as well as colonialism, she examines how when victims become perpetrators, they often maintain rather than upend conflict. The cycle repeats with different characters playing each role.

The work here is for those within and those studying conflicts to allow multiple victims and perpetrators as well as overlapping roles. Epoch Three invites complexity, first of all at the level of defining parties. Media and people in positions of power articulate conflicting parties in ways that often perpetuate conflict, either by communicating a particular storyline or justifying the use of violence. Epoch Three scholars can observe violence through the language used to describe the parties. Enns' article makes room for narrative praxis of Epoch Three, which seeks to intervene at the level of language and to enrich understanding of complex positions.

Questions to consider: Are there times when oppressed people need or ought to use violence? How can we teach appreciation of various perspectives without justifying the use of violence? Does violence always provoke more violence, or can it make room for a positive peace between peoples?

When Victims Become Killers

Diane Enns

I have related my experience of being accused of racism in order to set up the problem that drives this book. The moral authority of the victim and the moral failure of the privileged are in dispute here, not the facts of privilege and oppression. In the months that followed the accusation, I struggled to understand this event and the responses to it from a faculty and student community informed by feminist ideals. I spent the next six months wondering if I would have to face a university hearing, unable to trust that any of my new colleagues would support me—for who would dare to question the experience of a black student in such a matter? Those whom I did trust with my story spoke to me gently about the challenges of teaching in a multicultural environment, referring me to campus services that could train me to be more sensitive to issues of race in the classroom. Even several years later, long after one of the students dropped her accusation and expressed regret over the incident to one of my colleagues, I remained surprised that no one in this apparently close-knit feminist community ever commented on the injustice of the charge against me. Indignation and empathy were reserved for the female faculty member who was subjected to sexual harassment by a student via e-mail—a safer ground for solidarity.

What I felt, immediately and for many months afterward, was a profound sense of injustice but at the same time persistent self-doubt. This led to a certain defensiveness when explaining the incident to others who were not immediately sympathetic. The less understanding I perceived in my listener, the more defensive I would become. At the same time, attempting to look at myself from my accuser's perspective, I asked myself whether she could have been right, whether I had indeed committed an act of racism. I wanted to say that I was unjustly accused of racism, but what I had learned from decades of scholarly emphases on difference and marginality made these words difficult to say. Feminism had taught me that the experience of victimhood is sacrosanct, beyond critique or judgment. Vindicating myself entailed making a judgment against a black woman who experienced racism in my classroom, something we are not prepared to do.

This confusion brought home to me how far we have come in bestowing on the "other" the status of innocent victim, a status that in this case was superficially equated with skin color. The question whether this young, assertive black woman bore any responsibility for the events that transpired was never raised. Her motivation, perception, and interpretation were considered guileless, and only because of the facts of her skin and mine, mere accidents of birth. Hers rendered this student an innocent victim; mine, a perpetrator of racism.

When Victims become Killers

> *So, if we want to remain alive, we will have to kill and kill and kill. All*
> *day, every day. If we don't kill, we will cease to exist.*
> *Victory for us is to see you suffer.*

Humans are capable of carrying out extraordinarily evil deeds while feeling righteous.[1] Perpetrators of violent actions may fervently believe that they are committing an act of self-defense. Killers may see themselves as victims balancing the scales of justice. Constructing a narrative that justifies one's actions seems a requirement in order to injure or kill another without compunction; otherwise, many perpetrators could not live with themselves.

The title of this chapter is borrowed from Mahmood Mamdani's remarkable analysis of the 1994 genocide in Rwanda, *When Victims become Killers: Colonialism, Nativism, and the Genocide in Rwanda*. Mamdani describes the genocide as the natives violent response to the settler—to use Frantz Fanon's terms—the violent impulse of those who considered themselves sons and daughters of the soil, their mission one of "clearing the soil of a threatening *alien* presence."[2] Mamdani makes an analogy that is useful for my purposes here. He warns of the dangers of becoming locked into the world of the rat and the cat, that is, the political world of the Hutu and the Tutsi, or the native and the settler. It is a world in which identities are generated endlessly in binary pairs. The rat believes his worst enemy is the cat—not the lion, the tiger, or the elephant—while the cat thinks there is nothing more delicious than the rat. In a world where cats are few and rats are many, the cats come up with a clever way of stabilizing their rule: they make distinctions based on ethnic and racial origins that become normalized into a political order. Ruts are tagged through "a discourse on origins, indigenous and nonindigenous, ethnic and racial." It is quite possible that in a world in which rats have managed to triumph over cats, rats may continue living in a world defined by cats, that is, by identities generated in the era when cats ruled.[3]

My objective in this chapter is to look carefully at the logic of Mamdani 8 analogy in the context of the ongoing crisis in Israel and Palestine. When victims of a political regime bent on eliminating a people become killers themselves, he argues—crying out to their oppressor, "never again!"—they confirm rather than transform the binary worldview that rendered them less than human, able to kill with impunity. They remain locked in the worldview of the victim, no less dangerous than that of the perpetrator, for it is a worldview bound by the same terms. Without acknowledging the limits of this binary perspective, without questioning the historical context of its instigation and reification, a victim's identity "is likely to generate no more than an aspiration for trading places," and "every pursuit of justice will tend toward revenge, and every reconciliation toward an embrace of institutional evil."[4] While the historical and political circumstances that led to the genocide in Rwanda are very different from those that gave rise to the current situation in Israel and Palestine, Mamdani's analysis of the logic of victimhood helps us to understand a largely misunderstood dynamic of the conflict, one that contributes considerably to its impasse.

I began writing this chapter at the start of Israel's massive military assault on Gaza in December 2008. Three weeks later, Israel and Hamas declared a ceasefire. The details are by now familiar and the severity of the violence frozen into statistics: the operation included air strikes and a ground offensive, killed between I,387 and I,417 Palestinians—roughly a third of them children—injured more than five thousand, and uprooted thousands of Gazan civilians from their homes, many of which were reduced to rubble. Hamas rockets and mortars killed four Israelis, three of them civilians; five Israeli soldiers died during the fighting in Gaza, and four more were killed by friendly fire. Gaza's infrastructure—such as it was for this virtual open-air prison of 1.3 million people, 80 percent of whom subsist on less than $2 a day—was destroyed, to the tune of $3 billion in damages.[5]

It is difficult to fathom the stunningly disproportionate terms on which the war was fought. The crushing force of military muscle against an imprisoned population without means of escape except through death, the dismembered and dying children deprived of medical care, the venom and lack of compunction expressed in daily blogs responding to the assault in such media outlets as *Ha'aretz*—these facts would appear to demand immediate moral condemnation of state brutality. And yet the Canadian government felt confident enough to be the only nation (of forty-seven member nations) to oppose a UN Human Rights Council motion calling for an investigation into Israel's "grave" human rights violations and the ensuing humanitarian crisis.[6] Canada's representative explained that the language of the motion was "unnecessary, unhelpful and inflammatory" and did not make clear that Hamas rockets "triggered the crisis."[7] Thirteen other nations, mostly European, abstained. Intelligent, politically astute scholars on campuses across North America stayed mute and believed they had good reasons for their silence. Campus events attempting to respond to the conflict struggled to stave off the seemingly inevitable eruptions of blame and exoneration, accompanied by sporting event-style cheers. In this, they mostly failed.

In Israel and Palestine we are witnessing the pernicious effects of the worldview of the victim, mirrored on both sides of the conflict. What is played out on the land to which Jews and Arabs lay claim is the victim's struggle to exercise all the vengeance it can, in the name of morally legitimate self-defense—*"victory for us is to see you suffer."* We witness here the same dynamic and effects described in the previous chapter, only in this case the stakes are drastically higher. The moral power of the victim results in death, destruction, and the silencing of dissent. There is no parity in this case, however, in anything but the logic of blame and revenge and the unwavering belief in the virtue of one's own position. Power over life and death are not on par. How do we take this incontrovertible fact into account when considering matters of judgment and responsibility? I would submit that the demand for "balance" amounts to a refusal to accept responsibility, to judge, and to act. As observers of conflict, we can and must make moral judgments of individual acts on both (or all) sides of a political conflict, even while declaring that one side is more responsible for the crisis than another. How we achieve this without dissolving all discussion into a game of blame and vindication requires a vigilant focus on one's own responsibility, acting as if the other will do the same.

These issues have plagued me in recent years, as discussions of the Israeli-Palestinian conflict have degenerated into a terrible deadlock, causing many to disengage from any discussion of the crisis altogether. To those who have asked why I would want to write on this issue, when so many others have done so (seemingly in vain), and when we write from a safe distance, untouched by bombs, bulldozers, or stones, I respond that the deadlock speaks precisely to the global significance of the crisis, and hence to our responsibility to engage with the questions it raises.

As Étienne Balibar suggests, Palestine is "a universal cause," a "concentrated and reduced but also intensified image of the kind of problem that has to be solved in a post-colonial era, if we are not to have prominent wars and latent or rampant processes of extermination everywhere in the world. In a sense, they are testing for us the possibility of inventing post-national politics, and in the most difficult of conditions since it is not a dialogue among equals." "Something has to be invented," Balibar argues, which is why Palestine is so important: a postnational politics or, I would venture awkwardly, a *post-identity-politics* politics that will interrupt the "irreversible process" of colonization on which Israel embarked in 1948 and from which it cannot or will not now extricate itself.[8] Such a politics must succeed in overcoming the deadlock caused by death-defying claims to victimhood.

At this excruciating time, when a solution appears unattainable, when the Israeli government and many of its citizens are fed up with years of intermittent rocket fire and feel justified in the states terrible demonstration of military might,[9] and when Palestinians are suffering from the occupation, their own violent internal politics, the world's indifference, and the brutal reprisals for their own retributive acts of terror, it is necessary for us to think further about the conceptual framing of the conflict. The deadlock has much to do with the moral power of the victim granted in the wake of our unwillingness, as bystanders, to judge wrongdoing.

Critique of Counterviolence

Several years ago, in an undergraduate philosophy course I taught on violence and self-determination, I introduced the students to readings that I hoped would help them understand the phenomenon of suicide bombing as it is practiced by Palestinians. I shared the worries of Ghassan Hage, who warned, after Israel's reinvasion of the West Bank in March 2002, of a clear political risk in trying to explain suicide bombings. Hage claims that there is a "condemnation imperative" in the Western public sphere that censors any attempt to explain why suicide bombers act as they do, rendering it a challenge to "leav[e] condemnation aside in order to concentrate on explanation, without this being seen as a form of 'justification.' "[10]

What surprised me was that there was in fact little resistance in the class to understanding the motivation of suicide bombers. I had hoped that they would suspend their moral condemnation long enough to understand why a young man or woman would decide to take up arms in this horrific act of murder and self-destruction. But most of the students who spoke in class appeared not to be disturbed at all by the justification of violence as a political response to violence, accepting that violent retribution could set the scales of justice right again. As the chorus of "what else can they do?" reached the front of the classroom, I found myself backpedaling, worried that the texts they read had justified for them this egregious form of violence simply and neatly, before any hard questions could be asked. For these students, condemning the violence of the victimized group—in this case, the suicide bombers—seemed immediately to affirm the legitimacy of Israeli state violence. I thus discovered a profound investment in upholding the victim groups immunity to moral judgment—an investment difficult to criticize without appearing to contribute to the group's victimization. Furthermore, I discovered that this dynamic in my classroom betrayed my own ambivalence regarding the violence of the victimized. In my desire to understand suicide bombing, and in my compassion for the plight of the Palestinians, who continue to appear superfluous in the eyes of the world, I also resisted expressing an explicit moral condemnation of suicide bombing. It seems that we can only accept one perpetrator and one victim in any account of conflict. The violent response of the victim to victimization is particularly difficult to condemn.

What moral distinction is thus accepted in the very term "counterviolence," and what are its effects? To answer these questions, we could return to one of the most extensive descriptions of the condition of the colonized, a condition that fosters the desire for vengeance. Frantz Fanon's *The Wretched of the Earth* is a pivotal text on colonialism and decolonization, responsible for influencing a number of twentieth-century social movements and transforming our perceptions of the victims of oppression. Fanon poignantly and forcefully describes the relation between the native Algerian and the French settler, and the violence that produces and sustains it. While he argues that the native is brought into being by the settler and acknowledges the ambiguity of such an identity, Fanon insists that the native's self-determination requires that he reclaim this very identity and, through violence, replace one species of men with another. The native thus embarks on the path from victim to perpetrator, from the colonized, native Algerian who freezes under the dehumanizing gaze of the French settler, to the decolonized man who grasps history through a murderous desire to annihilate the settler, albeit with a violence implanted by the colonizer. Here we see already that the victim is considered innocent to begin with, the potential for violence not simply a human attribute that can be provoked but a seed sown by the colonizer.

Fanon's claim that decolonization is "always a violent event" has been read variously as a justification of violence in the name of liberation or as descriptive rather than prescriptive, contingent rather than universal.[11] While he may have been the first critic of decolonizing violence, Fanon's visceral and moving descrip-tion of the natives experience of oppression and desire for freedom has often foreclosed any critique of the violence of the victim. What is both remarkable and disturbing about Fanon's account is that we are permitted a glimpse into the violent dreams of the victims of colonization. Without mincing words, he exposes his reader to an unabashed desire for the death of one's oppressor, yet he solicits our compassion toward the fundamental humanity of the suffering native. We come to *understand* the impulse to violence; it appears a natural and necessary means to dignity and self-determination for a disenfranchised, dehumanized population.

The violence of the colonized therefore presents us with a kind of moral ambiguity that the settler's violence does not. For Fanon, the settler is responsible for the Manichean world the native must burst apart; the native's very humanity is at stake. From this perspective, that the native Algerians risked their lives was the proof of their humanity, their killing of French settlers a terrible outcome, but the lesser of two evils. Here we find a compelling presentation of the logic repeated in every violent struggle for liberation: "counterviolence" is the violence of self-defense—the violence of victimhood—and must therefore be considered in a dif-ferent moral light. It is justifiable because necessary. It is the final recourse of a desperate people who have exhausted all avenues in the attempt to reclaim the humanity that was stripped from them.

Unfortunately, in addition to Fanon's tremendous insight into the plight of the colonized, his legacy includes a notion of justice as vengeance, and the dis-placement of politics by violence. *The Wretched of the Earth* has been read as a revolutionary manifesto, and cautionary criticism of nationalist fervor in Fanon's work has been sadly neglected. The polemical tone of Jean-Paul Sartre's preface to the book clearly demonstrates a Manichean logic that works on the guilt of the European reader. Sartre warns his French audience that the violence of the native will return to them: "we [Europeans] will only be fueling in their bodies a volcanic fury whose power matches the pressure applied to them. They only understand the language of violence, you were saying? Of course; at first the only violence they understand is the colonist's, and then their own, reflecting back at us like our reflection bouncing back at us from a mirror."[12] Sartre asks why the European cannot recognize his own cruelty, now turned against him, and remains vehe-mently unapologetic about the reciprocation of this cruelty. If anything, we detect here a smug moralism— the guilt-ridden liberal European advocating on behalf of the oppressed. The innocence of the native seems unquestionable, as though the very potential for violence arrived only with the settler, rendering actual vio-lence, the native's counterviolence, unavoidable. Evidently, the agency and responsibility that Sartre demands of the European isn't required of the Algerian.

In the scholarly response to Fanon's commentary on counterviolence, Hannah Arendt's critique stands out for its decided rejection of the use of violence to advance the cause of freedom and social justice. Writing in the midst of the Ameri-can civil rights movement and student protests around the world, Arendt com-plains of the "glorification" of violence in Fanon and Sartre, which she holds partly responsible for the turn to violence in some of the protests of the 1960s. If it were true, as Sartre claims, that "violence, like Achilles' spear, can heal the wounds it has inflicted,"[13] then revenge would cure most of our ills, Arendt comments wryly. Sartre's declaration is an abstract myth, she notes, as mythical as Fanon's worst rhetorical excesses. Who has ever doubted that the violated dream of violence, Arendt asks, or that the oppressed dream of taking the oppressor's place? As Marx ventured, dreams never come true. The "mad fury" that Sartre warned his European audience about could turn everyone's dreams into nightmares.[14]

Unfortunately, the romanticization of revolutionary violence by those on the political left has carried on unabated, encouraged by a philosophical preoccupation with a violence ever more abstractly and nebulously defined. The poststructuralist tradition carries out a deconstructive operation that demonstrates beautifully the contradictions inherent in violence but leaves us with no mandate or method for judging violent acts. Thus we learn that violence occurs in the very operation of language as a kind of colonizing force, that law itself is violent when it declares that those who do not uphold it are violent, that since every state is founded in violence, the distinction between legitimate and illegitimate violence crumbles, and that violence may be found even at the heart of a blind political preference for peace.[15] We end up mired in the bog of Slavoj Žižek's bizarre logic when he argues that "the same act can count as violent or nonviolent, depending on its context; sometimes a polite smile can be more violent than a brutal outburst." Violence, according to Žižek, means a "radical upheaval" of basic social relations. "Crazy and tasteless as it may sound," he concludes, "the problem with historical monsters who slaughtered millions was that they were not violent enough. Sometimes doing nothing is the most violent thing to do."[16] Perhaps this is why Che Guevara T-shirts are everywhere worn in good conscience.

If violence is inescapable, as many would have it, then the only recourse is to choose the lesser violence.[17] Balibar is right to suggest that if this is the case, then the field of politics has progressively permeated the field of violence, to the extent that extreme violence has become built into the very heart of emancipatory politics.[18] Choosing the lesser violence, as Arendt reminds us, is still choosing violence.[19]

Last Recourse

The acceptance of counterviolence as morally distinct from "originary" violence and therefore as defensible is embedded in narratives that describe Palestinian suicide bombing as the political resistance of a people struggling to be free. Significantly, resistance is always depicted as a last resort—*we had no choice*. It is a romanticized view of victims' violence that betrays a binary logic of innocent victim versus guilty perpetrator, defending the victim as bereft of historical responsibility and *entitled* to carry out acts of brutality. Substitute Israeli state violence for Palestinian violence in this equation and the resulting logic is the same. If our moral judgments depend on whether violence is originary or retributive, the distinction becomes paramount, which explains the current impasse in discussions of the conflict in Israel/Palestine; each side must vie for the position of innocent victim. "Beware a people that boasts its own virtue."[20]

As we will see, in this particular context, self-defense as a justification for violent retribution will never open avenues to a resolution. Every perpetrator could have been a victim at one time, and before that a perpetrator, and so forth. How far back do we search in history for the "original" act of violence? We could return to 1967, when Israel fought and won the Six-Day War. We could go further back, to 1948, when the state of Israel was declared and some eight hundred thousand Palestinians were displaced. We could return to the period of Irgun terrorism in the 1930s, to the Palestinian massacre of Jews at Hebron in 1929, to a time when the land belonged to Jews, or earlier, when it belonged to the peoples of Canaan, ad infinitum. A critical analysis of this desperate search for vindication is necessary if we are at all concerned about the human rights violations of a global politics premised on the priority of security at all costs. If any act of violence can be excused by the perpetrator as a response to an earlier violation, then violence ceases to be a moral issue at all.

Since the beginning of the second intifada, a discussion of Palestinian suicide bombing has developed among leftist scholars and commentators that resonates with Fanon's analysis of revolutionary violence. The occupied Palestinian stands in for the Algerian native, his or her existence constituted by the Israeli occupier as less than human, rendering violent resistance inevitable in the attempt to regain dignity and human worth. From this perspective, the suffering Palestinian has no other recourse. Destroying one's body and murdering innocent bystanders in order to exact revenge on the occupiers is thus considered a legitimate response to despair. It is an act of self-defense, of political resistance in the name of self-determination and the struggle for human rights. Such an act of violence can be interpreted as the recuperation of meaning for a people who found it increasingly impossible to create such meaning—a redemptive act, in other words, one that restores to life the significance it lacks.

It is a seductive argument, particularly in a Western world that has become more attuned to the suffering of victims. We read about the appalling conditions of life in Palestinian refugee camps, breeding grounds for young men and women willing to sacrifice their lives for a better future. The refugee camp has come to symbolize the expulsion of the Palestinians, the place where, according to Faisal Darraj, conditions are "so wretched that rebelling, and taking up arms, eventually becomes *the only understandable response*" (emphasis added).[21] The "social unavailability" of the opportunity to make something of one's life in the camps means that throwing stones, facing the tanks, risking death, and wishing for martyrdom all become meaningful events that create the strong sense of individual or collective identity that Palestinians are normally denied. After fifteen-year-old Mohammed Dauoud was killed while throwing stones at a main clash point in Al-Bireh during the early days of the second intifada, his sister Soha said in an interview with Wendy Pearlman, "How can you express yourself other than going to the checkpoint and throwing a stone? . . . You feel like you have to do something, even if you know that the stone won't even reach them—even if you know that, in the end, it's useless."[22]

The violent response of the Palestinians is considered a direct consequence of the inhumanity of their occupiers. Eyad El-Sarraj, a frequently quoted psychiatrist and human rights activist from the Gaza Strip, draws attention to the fact that suicide bombers are the children of the first intifada, more than half of whom witnessed the killing or humiliation of their fathers at the hands of Israeli soldiers. El-Sarraj concludes that witnessing this helplessness, and the inability of fathers to protect their children, has a devastating psychological impact: "Children who have seen so much inhumanity . . . inevitably come out with inhuman responses. That's really how to understand the suicide bombings."[23]

I do not want to make light of the despair and trauma that the Israeli occupation has caused, or of its debilitating and enduring effects, but we should be asking why so many have come to accept that such despair *necessarily* leads to violence, justifies retaliatory killing, and grants moral immunity to the victim-turned-perpetrator. How far are we willing to go in our sympathetic understanding of "emancipatory" violence? For the British philosopher Ted Honderich, Palestinian suicide bombing is both a sign of desperation *and* an act of terror—but a legitimate one. If the highest moral principle is, as he believes, to take "rational steps to get people out of lives of wretchedness and deprivation," then Palestinians have "a moral right to their terrorism." The critical question for Honderich is whether a particular practice of terrorism can be proved to be an act of violence *for* humanity. He calls this kind of violence "terrorism for humanity," defining it as "terrorism with the aim of the principle of humanity, "which means getting people out of "lives of wretchedness and other deprivation."[24]

Honderich concludes that since Palestinians have been denied freedom, power, and respect in their homeland since the start of a new Zionism in 1967, and given that terrorism is an "established necessity" due to the absence of any alternatives, Palestinian terrorism is a paradigmatic case of "terrorism for humanity." In fact, he writes, terrorism "is their only effective and economical means of self-defense, of liberating themselves, of resisting degradation."[25] The suicide bomber who kills an Israeli child, therefore, in Honderich's words, "was morally permitted if not obliged to do what she did."[26]

Honderich's claims reveal the morally repugnant ends to which an emphasis on the pure innocence of victimhood—and the moral immunity this status implies—leads. In its insistence that there is no alternative to violent retribution, the argument lacks political vision; it fails to imagine a future beyond a global human community in which the only certainty is that violence in an inevitable and necessary response to violence. It exchanges politics for violence, as Ghassan Hage implies when he argues that such a perspective "risks normalizing the situation rather than perceiving it as the product of an inviable political framework . . . It is only because of the failure m the political that such a state of nature becomes the cultural norm and violence emerges as a matter-of-fact possibility."[27] This failure is spectacularly evident in the consequences of suicide bombing for Palestinians, although thin point is often ignored by the Left. As Balibar reminds us, the violent retribution of suicide bombing not only creates Israeli victims; it is "deeply self-destructive" and "catastrophic for the struggle of Palestinian people."[28] An act of violence—even if it meets Honderich's criteria for "terrorism for humanity"—will simply create more victims, who will in turn be "obliged" to kill in the name of humanity. It is a self-defeating argument.

Thus we have an argument from the political Left that, in defining Palestinian suicide bombing as a political act of resistance for a people that has no other recourse, ultimately imprisons Palestinians in their own agent-less victimhood. We set the bar very low in terms of intelligent political solutions when we argue that there is nothing Palestinians can do but blow themselves up in order to kill innocent civilians. Furthermore, it absolves the bystander of responsibility.[29] This perspective confirms rather than transforms the Manichean world of the victim and perpetrator, merely turning the tables. To argue that desperate people have no other choice but to commit acts of terror would be to claim that there has never been as desperate a people as the Palestinians. How can we know when we have reached the "last recourse?" If human history has not given us many examples of liberation struggles that succeeded without violence, it has certainly given us numerous examples of violent struggles that failed miserably.

Apology for Terror

The "last recourse" argument inevitably leads to an apology for terror. It is, sadly, characteristic of the Left's response to violent acts carried out in the name of emancipation, and is the logical consequence of justifying violence on the basis of the moral status of victimhood. For example, Simon Cottee points to the leftist logic underlying commentaries on the terrorist attacks in the United States on September 11, 2001: "Yes, what happened was awful, but it was hardly very surprising." From the perspective of the far Left, according to Cottee, the root cause of terrorism lies in "the humiliations and injustices visited upon the Arab and Muslim world by the West, particularly the United States." Terror is a response—the wrong response, of course—but a response nonetheless, and the only way to circumvent terror is to put an end to the evils that nurture it. This would mean, for example, that withdrawing financial and military aid from Israel would appease the jihadist terrorists. Cottee cites a number of examples: Gore Vidal writes of the provocations that "drove" the 9/11 terrorists to such terrible acts. Tariq Ali warns that the war against terror will only "push" young Muslims into violence. Douglas Kellner points to the failures of the U.S. government's foreign policy and intelligence systems but does not, Cottee observes, even mention the actual perpetrators of the 9/11 attacks.[30]

The result of this apologetic discourse, according to Cottee, is a refusal on the part of the Left to assign moral blame to those who seek revenge against the criminality of the West. The more appropriate object of moral condemnation is the West—here we find the real culprits, while those who take revenge are merely caught in a set of historical circumstances over which they have no control. Cottee concludes that two denials occur simultaneously here: responsibility is denied, and the "real victim" is denied. The perpetrator (in this case the terrorist) assumes the position of an avenger, and the victim (the United States) is transformed into a wrongdoer. "At no point in this discourse," he remarks, "is it entertained that young Muslim fanatics are morally autonomous human agents, responsible for the consequences that follow from their independently chosen actions. Nor is it made explicit— still less demonstrated—how the West, particularly in the form of George W. Bush and Tony Blair, is morally responsible for the murderous actions of the fanatics themselves."[31]

Of interest in Cottee's analysis is the fact that horrible deeds can be justified on the basis of tolerance or political interests when they are carried out by individuals or groups perceived to be victims with a claim to absolute innocence. But Cottee himself slips into the binary logic of the victim/perpetrator. In defending the United States against its leftist critics, he appears to maintain its complete innocence, using the logic of Norman Geras: that someone else contributes causally to a crime does not mean that he is as morally responsible as the direct agents are, if what he has contributed causally is not wrong in itself. This argument would require believing that the U.S. foreign policies that preceded the war on terror were not wrong.

This is the road that Arendt warned against during the violent turbulence of the anticolonial and civil rights struggles of the 1960s and 1970s. We have reified the categories of victim and perpetrator to such an extent that innocence and culpability are viewed as clean, discrete, and incommensurable categories, and responsibility is reduced to a question of blame. We demand that the victim be absolutely innocent and the perpetrator absolutely guilty in order to justify violence in the name of victimhood and to claim the moral power of the victim. This is by no means an innocent or innocuous power. If we remain caught in this dynamic, the conflict between Jewish Israelis and Palestinian Arabs will never end. Alternatively, we could acknowledge that there are different degrees of responsibility and accountability. Rather than look to the past to justify actions in the present, we need to assess the current situation. Who is responsible for what? Who has the resources and capacity to change the circumstances? Who has the fortitude and foresight to be the first to lay down their arms?

While Cottee provides an important critique, he continues to play according to the rules of the blame game. He exposes the same kind of apology proffered by the feminists and multiculturalists discussed in chapter 1: we are bad imperialists, responsible for oppressive colonization, and we understand why the subjects of our imperialist gestures would dislike us. Consequently, we must accommodate them, not judge them. But even if this argument were sound, it is completely powerless to transform the circumstances of conflict. The rather masochistic attitude arising from Western academic discourses—we started it; go ahead and hit us back—has no politically transformative effects. It is another manifestation of the belief that the other—even the terrorist other—is a good other. We must ask how this acceptance of violent counterinsurgency, and the essentialized categories of us and them on which it relies, makes "us"—the bystanders—complicit in the worst forms of terror.

Palestinians must bear the responsibility for their actions, as we have witnessed the terrible consequences of Hamas's tactics for its own people, and for innocent Israeli citizens. But their capacity to alter their situation is severely restricted. Prisoners of an occupation that is suffocating the possibility of collective political action, and captives of extremist factions among their own population, their options are limited. This is not an apology for terror. On the contrary, if we are to have productive discussions concerning the conflict in Israel and Palestine, those who are working toward equality and freedom for Palestinians (and therefore for all Israelis as well) must resist the temptation to excuse the death and destruction caused by suicide bombings and rockets.

The defensive position leads nowhere. Beyond the reasons already provided, it is a position that the Israeli government and those who agree with its policies have mastered to far better effect.

The reader at this point may either cheer at my criticism of Palestinian terrorism or condemn me for supporting the Israeli occupation and destruction of Palestinian lives. If the intent is to criticize state as well as insurgent violence, then the critic has no "side" with which to claim solidarity; one is anti-Israeli (or anti-Semitic) according to one camp and anti-Palestinian (or anti-Arab) according to the other. There is no exit from this seamless operation except to resist the defensive impulse and carry on in uncharted territory. But judgment must be a part of this discussion. It is essential that we criticize all excuses for violence yet acknowledge that the burden of responsibility for change must be disproportionately borne by the Israeli government and its people, for the simple reason that they disproportionately hold the power to dictate the terms of Palestinian-Israeli relations. This does not mean, however, that the Palestinians are absolved of the burden of finding political solutions. With the right leadership and global support, they could be the first to lay down their arms.

Never Again

When we examine the discourse of victimhood in Israeli society, we find evidence of the same moral power and reprieve from responsibility granted to the Palestinian as victim. While we often hear of the culture of martyrdom growing in Palestinian society, backed by images of grieving but proud families holding up the photos of their martyred loved ones, we hear less of the culture of victimhood in Israeli society. "Never again" is the sentiment that symbolizes the response to Jewish victimhood—the standard by which all victimhood is measured, at least in the West. It is the Holocaust victim of Nazi Germany, particularly the camp survivor, who symbolizes absolute victimhood—pure innocence—for us today.

It is not my intent to trace the history of the status of victimhood in Israeli society. I can only gesture to a development we rarely hear about, despite the number of Israeli writers and academics who seek to analyze it, particularly since the current demand for security against terror has become a dominant discourse. Avraham Burg, a prominent Israeli politician, describes the constant presence of the Shoah in his life as a "buzz" in his ear. "The list of Shoah manifestations in daily life is long," he explains. "Listen to every word spoken and you find countless Shoah references. The Shoah pervades the media and the public life, literature, music, art, education. These overt manifestations hide the Shoah's deepest influence. Israel's security policy, the fears and paranoia, feelings of guilt and belonging are products of the Shoah. Jewish-Arab, religious-secular, Sephardi-Ashkenazi relations are also within the realm of the Shoah. Sixty years after his suicide in Berlin, Hitler's hand still touches us." Burg goes so far as to suggest that the Shoah has caused Israel to become "the voice of the dead, speaking in the name of those who are no longer, more than in the name of those who are still alive."[32] It is a powerful comment about victims living in the grip of history, unable to escape the prison of a victim's worldview.

Burg and others make clear the relationship between this ever-present history of victimhood and Israel's military response to its neighbors and to the people of its occupied territories. According to Yael Zerubavel, it was the 1973 Yom Kippur War that transformed an earlier perception of Holocaust victims in Israel, altering the meaning of victimhood for Israeli Jews. The shocking discovery of the state's own vulnerability during this war "weakened earlier condemnation of the [Holocaust] victims for going like sheep to the slaughter." A new identification with Holocaust survivors grew out of the embrace of survival as a form of resistance to the Nazis, and of "evidence of inner, if not physical, strength."[33] The victim became the new model of moral and spiritual strength to inspire Israeli soldiers. This transformation is reflected, Zerubavel believes, in changes over the final several decades of the twentieth century in the Israeli commemoration of one of their most important historical events. Masada is the name of the site where approximately nine hundred Jews allegedly committed suicide to avoid being captured by the invading Roman army in the first century CE.[34] In the early years of Israel's existence as a Jewish state, Zerubavel explains, narratives based on the ghetto uprisings and other forms of Jewish resistance were promoted, while the traumatic aspects of the Holocaust or of Masada were downplayed. In recent decades, however, these narratives have been transformed into tragic histories. They have turned vulnerability into strength. The determination never to allow such deadly events to recur—captured in the expression "Never again!"—turns victimhood into victory and accepts, even glorifies, the violent retribution of the victim.[35]

This evolution of Israeli identity is corroborated by others. Idith Zertal, an Israeli historian, claimed at the start of the second intifada in 2000 that "there has not been a war in Israel, from 1948 till the present ongoing outburst of violence . . . that has not been perceived, defined, and conceptualized in terms of the Holocaust." Auschwitz, she maintains, has become "Israel's main reference in its relations with a world defined repeatedly as anti-Semitic and forever hostile." The result is that Israel "has rendered itself immune to criticism, and impervious to a rational dialogue with the world around her."[36] We have only to consider our own responses to the conflict in Israel and Palestine to find evidence of the power of this immunity and imperviousness. The fear of offending Jews and appearing anti-Semitic stifles moral judgment and promotes a complicit silence. There appears to be no such corresponding fear of offending Palestinians and attendant worries about anti-Arab sentiment.

We would do well to heed Mamdani's warning that victor's justice comes with a price: an increased need to secure one's position as victor. The jailor becomes as tied to the jail as the prisoner, and so the victor must live in fear of the next round of battle. A permanent civil war ensues.[37] Burg concurs. The devastating consequences of such a defensive position are clear: "A state that lives by the sword and worships its dead is bound to live in a constant state of emergency, because everyone is a Nazi, everyone is an Arab, everyone hates us, the entire world is against us."[38] It leads to the worst excesses of the self-defense alibi, starkly evident in Arnon Sofer's proclamation in the epigraph to this chapter: "So, if we want to remain alive, we will have to kill and kill and kill. All day, every day. If we don't kill, we will cease to exist." As Giorgio Agamben puts it, the state that promotes a politics of security exercised by violence against terrorism turns itself terroristic, ironically transforming itself into a fragile organism. Security and terrorism then form a single deadly system, mutually justifying and legitimizing each other's actions.[39]

The victim thus occupies a very powerful place—a contentious claim, given that it flies in the face of decades of efforts to bring the plight of victims to our attention and recognize their rights. But the implications and effects of these efforts, particularly concerning questions of moral judgment and responsibility in the political realm, have not been fully explored. We might consider, for example, Israeli accounts of the January 2009 attacks on Gaza, in which we find no reference to the occupation, no acknowledgment of the displacement of Palestinians or of the fact that the living conditions in Gaza—the lack of freedoms, rights, and basic necessities—have anything to do with this occupation. Many responses to those attacks in fact demonstrate a frightening logic: "You forced us to kill you."[40] Thus, while the disproportionate brutality is undisputed, this does not matter in countless discussions of this military offensive. Any mention of factors that tarnish the image of Israel as anything but a victim state is silenced. Israelis must believe that *they* are the victims—displaying willful blindness, as many have argued—in order to carry on the occupation. "In this myopic fantasy land," wrote Seamus Milne in the *Guardian*, as the attacks on Gaza raged, "there is no 6-year national dispossession, no refugee camps, no occupations, no siege, no multiple Israeli violations of UN security council resolutions and the Geneva conventions, no illegal wall, no routine assassinations, no prisoners and no West Bank."[41]

"Never forget" has been the mantra of Jewish and Israeli politics for three decades, according to Baruch Kimmerling, who argues that the obsessive commemoration of Jewish victimhood has blinded much of the Jewish community to Israel's real position in the world. The result has been this willful blindness toward the humanity of Palestinians, and to a reasonable political solution to the conflict. Kimmerling asks whether "the cult of death" in Israel has come to an end, or whether the prevailing ideology will last another hundred years. "To choose the former option is to grant priority to the lives of Israel's citizens, Jewish and Arab. To choose the latter is to remain a community of victims," which can only lead to disaster.[42] Kimmerling wrote these words in late 2004. Seven years later, we are no closer to the better option.

"Something Has to Be Invented"

At the end of Gwynne Dyer's comprehensive account of the history of war, he relates a story about a group of olive baboons in Kenya called the "Forest Troop," a group that Robert Sapolsky and Lisa Share have studied since 1978. Over several years in the 1980s, the most brutal and despotic alpha males of the troop, who ate frequently from the dumpsters of a nearby tourist lodge, became infected with bovine tuberculosis and died. This meant that the less aggressive males—those who steered clear of the dumpster so as to avoid fights with the alpha males—survived. After the death of the alpha males, the normally vicious baboon society changed completely. As Dyer puts it, "the surviving members relaxed and began treating one another more decently."[43] The males still fought, but aggression was more likely to occur between males of equal rank rather than between the strong and the weak. At the same time, an increase in grooming was observed, and hormone samples revealed far lower stress levels in even the lowest-ranking males than in other, more aggressive troops.[44] Females stopped being attacked at all. Years later, when the range of male personalities in the Forest Troop had returned to the normal distribution of dominant alphas and submissive, timid types, the behavior of the troop still had not returned to normal: the new behaviors had become entrenched in the troop's culture. As one biologist put it, the aggressive new males were obviously learning that "we don't do things like that around here."[45]

   This marvelous anecdote, about animals typically seen as "shackled by their genes to viciously aggressive norms,"[46] unsettles our assumption that violence is necessary or inevitable, particularly as a response to violence. It is easy to forget that there are alternatives to violence when violence is normalized. During the trial of Adolf Eichmann, which Hannah Arendt covered for the *New Yorker*, stories were shared of Germans who assisted Jews during the Nazi years. Arendt recalls the story of a German sergeant, Anton Schmidt, who helped members of the Jewish underground for five months before his arrest and execution. While other German soldiers testified that their own disobedience would have led to a useless sacrifice, since they would have died in anonymity, Arendt argues that such dissent would not have been practically useless, at least not in the long run. Someone always lives to tell the story. The lesson is simple: "Politically speaking, it is that under conditions of terror most people will comply but *some people will not,* just as the lesson of the countries to which the Final Solution was proposed is that 'it could happen in most places but *it did not happen everywhere.* Humanly speaking, no more is required, and no more can reasonably be asked, for this planet to remain a place fit for human habitation."[47] We spend an inordinate amount of time considering the cases of those who do comply rather than looking for the cases of those who resist. For Ted Honderich to be right that terrorism is the

Palestinians' only recourse would mean that every nation or people *without exception* must turn to violence in the struggle for freedom. If even one person or group chooses another path, then nonviolent action remains a permanent possibility. Arendt is making a forceful claim: all that is required for this planet to remain fit for human habitation is the knowledge that some people will dissent under conditions of terror. There is always a choice, always agency, even if severely restricted. And as the anomaly of the Forest Troop baboons tells us, alternatives can establish new patterns and unsettle long accepted norms. If the baboons can do it, why can't we?

A direction out of the quagmire of the Israeli-Palestinian conflict, then, is to start with those dissenting voices and actions that *do not comply*. Like Arendt's anecdote about the German soldier, we have numerous examples, rarely drawn to our attention, that prove that this planet is fit for human habitation. Rami Elhanan, in a documentary called *ScaredSacred*, relates the terrible story of the day his daughter was killed by a suicide bomber in Jerusalem. There is no blame in his response, but a conscious and concerted effort to accept mutual responsibility for a different kind of future. After hearing about a bombing in the center of Jerusalem, Elhanan finds himself running through the streets in search of his daughter. Later that evening he is at the morgue, witnessing a sight that he "will never, ever be able to forget for the rest of [his] life." From that moment on, he explains, he became a different person:

> You change completely—set of values, perspectives, everything, your genes change. You come back home and you are alone and you have to look yourself in the mirror. Where are you going to take this new and unbearable pain? What are you going to do with the rest of your life, now that you are a different person? And there are only two alternatives. The one is the obvious and the natural and the way most people choose, which is the way of retaliation and revenge because when someone kills your fourteen-year-old little girl and you are very, very angry and you want to get even. This is natural, this is only natural.
>
> You start to think, will killing someone else bring back my baby? Will causing pain to someone else ease my pain in any way? Of course not. And it takes time, a long time, to choose the other way. The other way is the way of understanding. Why did it happen? How could such a thing happen? And the most important thing: what can you do, now that you have the burden on your shoulders to prevent it from happening to others?[48]

This is an extraordinary and powerful passage. Elhanan acknowledges that the loss of his daughter, Smadar, who was killed by two Palestinian suicide bombers while shopping for schoolbooks with friends on September 4, 1997, provoked in him "an urge for revenge that is stronger than death."[49] It was a meeting with others who had lost beloved family members that changed his perspective. Elhanan became one of several hundred members of an organization called the Parents Circle-Families Forum (PCFF) that has brought together bereaved Palestinian and Israeli families since 1995 in order to promote peace and reconciliation, provide mutual support, influence the public and policymakers, and "prevent the usage of bereavement as a means of expanding enmity between our peoples."[50] The organizing principle is that the unbearable pain of losing a family member is an experience common to all human beings. Such suffering establishes common ground by rendering everyone who loses a loved one a victim of the conflict.

There is no dearth of similar stories in Israel and Palestine of individuals who attempt to reach out across the multiple barriers—both material and psychological—thrown up by the occupation, to establish contact with those on the other side, or of groups who work tirelessly to bridge the gaps of understanding between two peoples.[51] They provide us with examples of those who do not comply, often at great risk to their own lives. Like Elhanan, they decide that hostility and revenge are not the destiny of the Israeli and Palestinian people. "Nowhere is it written that we must continue dying and sacrificing our children forever," Elhanan declares in *ScaredSacred*, in what has become a vicious circle of violence and retribution. The intolerable pain of losing a family member can lead to cooperation and strength. "Our blood is the same color, our pain is the same pain, the taste of our tears are as bitter," Elhanan insists. "If we can talk to one another, then anyone can. And this really gives you a reason for existence." It is a dramatic rewriting of the script: from "victory for us is to see you suffer" to "victory for us is to feel your suffering." This is a critical starting point.

It is important to note that the effectiveness of groups like the PCFF depends on the destabilization of the victim/perpetrator opposition, mapped onto the identity of one group in conflict with another. Members of the PCFF exemplify the kind of inventiveness Balibar alludes to when he calls for a postnational politics. Suffering is the unifying factor; it no longer matters whether the parent who grieves the loss of her child is an Israeli Jew in Jerusalem or a Palestinian Arab in the Gaza Strip. Their pain is the same.

The "way of understanding," however, must extend into the realm of politics. Groups that seek to educate for peace by bringing hostile individuals and communities into dialogue provide us with essential examples of noncompliance, examples that make it impossible to ignore the agency of victims and perpetrators alike and allow us to see the dehumanized other as human. It introduces empathy into the equation. But we must be wary of projects and analyses that do not challenge the imbalance of power. Unfortunately, individual change and empathy are not enough if there is no corresponding change at the political and institutional level. What is required is the opportunity for a people to organize and act as a political entity. There must be allowances for dissent, and the acknowledgment of grief before it turns to grievance, and this must occur at all levels of political decision making. Groups like PCFF and individuals like Rami Elhanan demonstrate that identities can be transcended, but without a corresponding change in the structures of power that keep these identities in place, the way of understanding won't help much. The Palestinian and the Israeli, sharing tea in friendship, return to drastically different political and economic realities when they go home.

Could we not make the quest for political solutions, rather than violent ones—taking for granted Arendt's distinction between these terms—the common denominator when working toward a resolution of conflict? Mamdani elaborates an idea he calls "survivor's justice," which does not mean justice only for the surviving victims but for all those who have survived a civil war or genocide. It is a notion he uses to transcend the bipolar terms of victim and perpetrator. He asks, in the context of Rwanda today, whether we couldn't invite into the community of those concerned with political transformation and the creation of a future *only* those willing to forgo violence. It is the victor who must reach out to the vanquished, as only the victor can transcend the opposition between the two by defining both as survivors. The crucial point here is to destabilize the binary opposition between victim and perpetrator, give up the right to hate, as Fanon urged, relinquish claims to being the first and most aggrieved victim, and come to terms with the fact that power is not the precondition for survival. As Mamdani puts it, we must consider the opposite possibility "that the prerequisite to cohabitation, to reconciliation, and a common political future may indeed be to give up the monopoly of power."[52]

Those who exist under the conditions imposed on Palestinians in the occupied territories, who survive a suicide bomb attack and live with the perpetual fear of terror, or who live through genocide, may scoff at this suggestion. Mamdani is aware of this when he writes that we cannot ignore the fact that "must weigh like a nightmare on the minds of the Tutsi survivors": that they are an imperiled minority living under a dark cloud of fear that they will once again have to submit to the very majority that attempted to eliminate them.[53] How dare we ask a victimized population to make themselves vulnerable again, to give up the balance of power that leads to the perception of greater security?

The enormity of this request hit home when I participated in what turned out to be a politically contentious conference (contentious for all the wrong reasons) in 2009 at York University in Toronto called "Israel/Palestine: Mapping Models of Statehood and Paths to Peace." An Israeli academic spoke eloquently and sincerely about the terrible fear that governed the everyday lives of his fellow Israelis. There was a loud chorus of both sympathy and protest from the audience, activists and academics alike. We who are personally untouched by the conflict could perhaps understand this man's plea, could try to put ourselves in the shoes of those who live with political insecurity and instability but the Palestinians were enraged and hurt. How could you be so audacious, they cried, as to ask for understanding for your security needs when we (or our families) live under the occupation of your government? They found it outrageous that the Israeli occupiers could portray themselves as a victim nation bobbing precariously in a sea of Arab hostility. But Israeli fear is nurtured on a daily basis—its only antidote, political and military power.

In effect, Jeff Halper is asking Israelis to work toward survivor's justice. An Israeli anthropologist and the coordinator of the Israeli Committee Against House Demolitions (ICAHD), Halper advocates a "reframing" of the conflict that stresses three points: first, that an occupation exists and is the center of the conflict; second, that Israel is the strong party in the conflict and thus the only one that can actually end the occupation and be held accountable for its policies and actions; and third, that the occupation is "not defensive or reactive" but a vehicle for establishing Israel's permanent control over the entire country. Central to

ICAHD's reframing is the rejection of Israel's security reasoning and its result: the casting of itself as a victim in what Israeli prime minister Benjamin Netanyahu calls "a tough neighborhood of bullies." "This is a crucial part of the security framing," Halper writes, "since it relieves Israel of all responsibility. A victim, after all, is a victim and cannot be held accountable, since his or her actions come merely out of self-defense. Being a victim, however, is a very powerful place to be. Israel can be a regional superpower and an occupying power, yet have responsibility. Indeed, it is the flight from responsibility that impels the security framing." Halper explains the distortion that must occur for Israel to cast itself as a victim, given that Zionists have held disproportionate power since the turn of the twentieth century, when the Zionist movement gained international support denied to Palestinians and other Arabs. It also gained economic and military superiority. Israel is now a regional superpower, with an economy three times larger than those of Egypt, Palestine, Jordan, Syria, and Lebanon put together (it is more than forty times the size of the Palestinian economy), and receives more than $3 billion annually in military aid from the United States. In addition, it is the world's fourth-largest nuclear power and an occupying power. This asymmetry of power, Halper insists, demands an asymmetry of responsibility from Israel.[54]

ICAHD defines itself us "a nonviolent Israeli direct-action organization" established in 1997 to end the occupation. The focus of its resistance is the demolition of Palestinian homes in the occupied territories by the Israeli military. Since 1967 more than twenty-four thousand Palestinian homes have been destroyed, more than 95 percent of them for political reasons having nothing to do with security. The intent is "to either drive the Palestinians out of the country altogether, or to confine the four million residents of the West Bank, East Jerusalem and Gaza to small, crowded, impoverished and disconnected enclaves, thus effectively foreclosing any viable Palestinian entity and ensuring Israeli control." Members of ICAHD operate on several levels. They physically block bulldozers about to demolish homes and raise funds abroad to facilitate the rebuilding of new homes; advocate within Israel and internationally for a just peace by disseminating information and networking; and collaborate with Palestinian organizations and communities, providing strategic practical support, including legal assistance to families facing demolition.[55]

Once again we encounter an organization whose focal point is shared human need and a concerted effort to work together on a common project. In this case it is not the emotional work of grief that is shared but the construction of homes. But "reframing" the conflict is a challenge, given that in any debate, the party that succeeds in framing the issue and determining the terms of the discussion inevitably wins. Israel has a great advantage, Halper points out, since it determines the logic of the debate, leading to its desired conclusions. The Israeli peace camp and the Palestinians themselves lack the support of the state agencies, public relations agencies, professional spokespersons, and access to the media that Israel enjoys. "We are thus thrust into the weak position of refuter," Halper concludes, "left only to respond to Israel's charges yet without the space to present a coherent, credible and persuasive alternative framing of our own. Confined to countering the arguments of the 'framer,' respondents (called the negative side in debates) invariably come across as defensive, inarticulate and unconvincing."[56] The problem is not how to make peace—Halper sees viable solutions and an overwhelming will for peace among Israelis and Palestinians—"but how to overcome the fear and obfuscation by which Israel's gatekeepers deflect all attempts to arrive at a just peace, manipulating the thought and feelings of peoples and governments that don't, or won't, get it." It isn't about taking "sides," then, but about generating critical political discussion and effective action that will help Israelis, Palestinians, peoples of the wider Arab and Muslim worlds, and all others affected by this conflict to get out of "this mess we share and suffer from."[57]

Dreams

We can conclude from this brief discussion that in the case of Israel/ Palestine, *which* victim's worldview we defend depends on a number of factors, including which side of the political spectrum we find ourselves on and whose interests are being promoted. There is compassion for Israel as a nation of victims—both historically, as the victims of genocide in Nazi Germany, and currently, as the victims of terrorism—and a corresponding apology or acceptance of the need for violent security measures. There is compassion for Palestinians as an occupied people, displaced by the creation of the state of Israel and collectively punished for existing at all, and accompanying excuses for the acts of revenge on the part of Hamas. What they have in common is that they respectively stake their claims to ultimate victimhood and justify their actions with the moral power these claims confer. What the Palestinians do not share with Israel is military strength; the economic, military, and political support of the United States, Canada, and other Western nations; wealth; readily available water and electricity; freedom of movement; basic human rights; and a thriving civil society.

Our responses to the conflict are already conditioned by a conceptual framework that is not easy to question. While victim discourses on both sides have very different origins, they share an oppositional understanding of victim versus perpetrator that sabotages every attempt to refuse to take sides and demand responsibility—albeit to different degrees—of all actors. This is why, at teach-ins or academic panel discussions, the audience is immediately sucked into choosing sides by an almost irresistible competition for ultimate victim status. I am always shocked by what happens at these events—how reasonably intelligent, otherwise considerate and level-headed faculty and students can be seen hurling insults at one another, or crying while others hiss and boo. The impulse to defend and justify oneself or one's political cause is powerful.

Rather than continue this failed dialogue between two sides, unequal in power yet equally entrenched in a victim's binary worldview, we need to reframe the conflict in a way that will lead to alternative political solutions. No one is suggesting that such alternatives are easy to carry out, but we who merely write about them are the first to complain about our own armchair thinking and throw up our hands in despair that there are no solutions. Alternative examples of a different political path are not hard to find if we only look. This is the challenge we need to meet: to sift through the misinformation and the dogma, resist the invitation to believe only in dualistic identities, and listen to those voices of sanity that are no less in the midst of the crisis than many of those who mislead us. We must not forget that there are world leaders and people in positions of power who want us to believe that there are only military solutions. Some of the best critical analyses of the Israeli Occupation of the Palestinians, and of this seemingly irresolvable conflict, are coming from extraordinarily courageous Israeli Jewish and Palestinian scholars and activists. We need to keep in mind that Israelis and Palestinians are not necessarily who we think they are, and may not hold the views we think they do, especially since most of what we know of them comes from media and government sources, all promoting a particular agenda. We are led to believe that Israelis present a united front in support of their government policies, and that Palestinians are united in their support of terrorism and their desire to eliminate the state of Israel. While it does not look good for Israeli activism against the occupation at the moment, thousands of Israeli citizens protested the war on Gaza in early 2009—voices we did not hear in the mainstream media.

I return to my opening point that humans are capable of carrying out extraordinarily evil deeds while feeling righteous. Each time I hear the demand that the perspectives of "both sides" be presented in any discussion of the Israeli-Palestinian crisis—from intelligent, compassionate individuals who are normally severely critical of the use of violent means to end conflicts—I am struck anew by the terrible power of this righteousness. This power is the result of the moral status we give to victims. But it is not only as victims of one of the worst genocides of the twentieth century that Israeli Jews benefit from the support of the United States, Canada, and other complicit or indifferent states the world over. It is as victims of terrorism.

The "globalization of terror" gives Balibar reason to believe that the Palestinian struggle is "a universal cause." Israel, he notes, long ago began to identify Palestinian armed resistance with "international terrorism," and the globalization of terror has become the common goal of both Islamic fundamentalists and the U.S. administration since 2001. Halper draws our attention to the global implications of what he calls a new "global system of pacification" that includes extensive surveillance and control measures. It is a system promoted and perfected by the Israeli government in collusion with governments like our own, a system in which the brutal quelling of insurgency, in the name of security for a people under attack, is not only tolerated by the world but confidently justified.[58] The conflict is not the "Palestinian problem," as it is often called by the world's leaders and media, but has an impact far beyond the Middle East. Halper cites Martin Luther King's famous dictum that "injustice anywhere is a threat to justice everywhere." Like all conflicts, Halper concludes, the Israel-Palestine conflict ultimately affects all of us, especially in that the occupation could not be maintained without the active complicity of our own governments, wherever we are.[59]

A world in which the paradigm of terror and security structures all our global relationships will ultimately become unlivable. What we need instead is to focus on forming a new community of political subjects that is not founded on victimized identities that righteously secure themselves from vulnerability and accountability. We really have no choice but to find a way to live together. Neither the Palestinians nor the Israelis are going anywhere. The dream of an end to the Jewish state is as unviable and catastrophic as the desire to eliminate all Palestinians.

> *Twenty-two years later I am still dangling over the ground by dislocated arms, panting, and accusing myself.*
> *I am not the same person who set off, singing, on that sunny Fourth of July in the French countryside. I left her in a rocky creek bed at the bottom of a ravine. I had to in order to survive.*

These are the words of victims who have survived brutal acts of violence.[60] They provide heartrending glimpses into what it means to be reduced to a suffering body, and to survive the betrayal, exposure, and humiliation of another's dehumanizing act. Listening to a victim recounting an experience of violation invites a profound identification with the suffering of another, the vulnerability we share exposed on the face of the speaker or the white of the page. Those of us who have never been victims of violence are unsettled or perhaps frightened by the knowledge that we too could be tortured, murdered, or raped. We may imagine the sensations of pain in our own bodies, or entertain for a brief, terrible moment what it would feel like to witness the victimization of someone we love. While we may never be able fully to comprehend suffering we have not ourselves experienced, we can identify with another's pain at some level; we can attempt through imagination to feel as others feel. This is empathy—imaginatively inhabiting the other's body and emotive being. Without it, we appear less than human, able to witness or perhaps even commit acts of cruelty without compunction.

Notes

1. The epigraph for this chapter is a statement by Arnon Sofer, a professor of geology at Haifa University, made during an interview published in the *Jerusalem Post*, May 21, 2004, quoted in Jeff Halper, *Obstacles to Peace: A Re-framing of the Palestinian-Israeli Conflict* (Jerusalem: ICAHD, 2009), 47.

2. Mahmood Mamdani, *When Victims Become Killers: Colonialism, Nativism, and the Genocide in Rwanda* (Princeton: Princeton University Press, 2001), 14.

3. Mahmood Mamdadni, "Making Sense of Political Violence in Postcolonial Africa," in *Experiments with Truth: Transitional Justice and the Processes of Truth and Reconciliation, Documenta11_Platform2*, ed. Okwui Enwezor et al. (Ostfildern-Ruit, Germany: Hatje Cantz, 2002), 37.

4. Ibid., 36–37.

5. NGOs estimated Palestinian deaths between 1,387 and 1,417; Gaza authorities put the number at 1,444 and the Israeli government at 1,166. See the UN report on Gaza, "Human Rights in Palestine and Other Occupied Arab Territories: Report of the United Nations Fact Finding Mission on the Gaza Conflict," September 12, 2009, 10, http://www1.ohchr.org/english/bodies/hrcouncil/specialsession/9/factfindingmission.htm (accessed February 11, 2011).

6. Canada was a member of the UN Human Rights Council from 2006 to 2009. The United States was not a member at the time of this motion. For current and past lists of the forty-seven member nations, see http://www2.ohchr.org/english/bodies/hrcouncil/membership.htm.

7. Bruce Camion-Smith and Les Whittington, "Canada Votes Alone for Israel," *Toronto Star*, January 13, 2009, http://www.thestar.com/article/569872 (accessed February 1, 2009).

8. Quoted in Diane Enns, "A Conversation with Étienne Balibar," *Symposium* 9, no. 2 (2005): 390.

9. "Israel Hits Hamas Targets in Gaza," BBC News, February 1, 2009, http://news.bbc.co.uk/2/hi/middle_east/783500.stm (accessed February 10, 2009). Speaking at the weekly Israeli cabinet meeting, Mr. Olmert warned that Israel would respond forcefully to renewed rocket fire. "We've said that if there is rocket fire against the south of the country, there will be a disproportionate Israeli response to the fire on the citizens of Israel and its security forces," he said. "The response will come at the time, the place and the manner that we choose."

10. Ghassan Hage, "'Comes a time we are all enthusiasm': Understanding Palestinian Suicide Bombers in Times of Exighophobia," *Public Culture* 15, no. 1 (2003): 68.

11. Frantz Fanon, *The Wretched of the Earth*, trans. Richard Philcox (New York: Grove Press, 2004), 1.

12. Jean-Paul Sartre, preface to ibid., li.

13. Ibid., lxii.

14. Hannah Arendt, *On Violence* (New York: Harcourt Brace, 1969), 21–22.

15. See Étienne Balibar, "Outline of a Topography of Cruelty: Citizenship and Civility in the Era of Global Violence," in *We, the People of Europe? Reflections on Transnational Citizenship*, trans. James Swenson (Princeton: Princeton University Press, 2004), 115–32; Walter Benjamin, "Critique of Violence," trans. Edmund Jephcott, in Benjamin, *Selected Writings*, vol. 1, *1913–1926* (Cambridge: Belknap Press of Harvard University Press, 1996), 236–52; Jacques Derrida, "Violence and Metaphysics: An Essay on the Thought of Emmanuel Levinas," in Derrida, *Writing and Difference*, trans. Alan Bass (Chicago: University of Chicago Press, 1978), 79–153; Emmanuel Levinas, *Totality and Infinity: An Essay on Exteriority*, trans. Alphonso Lingis (Pittsburgh: Duquesne University Press, 1969).

16. Slavoj Žižek, *Violence* (London: Picador, 2008), 213, 217.

17. See Michael Ignatieff, *The Lesser Evil: Political Ethics in an Age of Terror* (Princeton: Princeton University Press, 2004).

18. Balibar, *We, the People of Europe*, 131.

19. Hannah Arendt, ersonal Responsibility Under Dictatorship," in Arendt, *Responsibility and Judgement*, ed. Jerome Kohn (New York: Schocken Books, 2003), 36.

20. Jacqueline Rose, *The Last Resistance* (London: Verso, 2007), 113.

21. Faisal Darraj, "Ethics of Resistance," an open letter to Étienne Balibar, *Al-Ahram Weekly*, May 2–8, 2002, http://weekly.ahram.org.eg/2002/584/op2.htm (accessed February 10, 2011).

22. Quoted in Wendy Pearlman, *Occupied Voices: Stories of Everyday Life from the Second Intifada* (New York: Thunder's Mouth Press/Nation Books, 2003), 88.

23. Eyad El-Sarraj, "Suicide Bombers: Dignity, Despair, and the Need for Hope," *Journal of Palestine Studies* 31, no. 4 (2002): 72.

24. Ted Honderich, "Terrorism for Humanity" (lecture given at the International Social Philosophy Conference at Northeastern University, Boston, revised March 4, 2004), 5, 6, http://www.ucl.ac.uk/~uctytho/terrforhum.html (accessed February 9, 2010).

25. Ibid., 7.

26. Ted Honderich, "Obligations to the Future: Palestinian Terrorism, Morality, and Germany," *Counterpunch*, October 25–26, 2003, http://www.counterpunch.com/honderich10252003.html (accessed January 6, 2009).

27. Hage, "'Comes a time we are all enthusiasm,'" 75.

28. "Il est de toute façon catasrophique pour la lute du people palestinien. . . . Il est donc profondément autodestructeur." Étienne Balibar, "Universalité de la cause palestinienne," *Le Monde Diplomatique*, May 2004, 26–27.

29. For an excellent discussion of the bystander's responsibility, see Erwin Staub, *The Psychology of Good and Evil: Why Children, Adults, and Groups Help and Harm others* (Cambridge: Cambridge University Press, 2003).

30. Simon R. Cottee, "Excusing Terror," *Journal of Human Rights* 5 (2006): 152, 153, 158.

31. Ibid., 158.

32. Avraham Burg, *The Holocaust is Over; We Must Rise from Its Ashes* (New York: Palgrave Macmillan, 2008), 13, 23, 24.

33. Yael Zerubavel, *Recovered Roots: Collective Memory and the Making of Israeli National Tradition* (Chicago: University of Chicago Press, 1995), 193.

34. Apparently, Israeli soldiers take an oath there: "Masada Shall Not Fall Again." It is one of the most important symbols for Jews, epitomized in the idea that it is better to die than be a slave. One can even buy a T-shirt with the oath. See http://www.zahal.org/products/massada-shall-not-fall-again-shirt (accessed September 16, 2010).

35. Zerubavel, *Recovered Roots*, 194.

36. Idith Zertal, *Israel's Holocaust and the Politics of Nationhood*, trans. Chaya Galai (New York: Cambridge University Press, 2005), 4.

37. Mamdani, *When Victims Become Killers*, 270–72.

38. Burg, *Holocaust Is Over*, 24.

39. Giorgio Agamben, "Security and Terror," trans. Carolin Emcke, *Theory and Event* 5, no. 4 (2001), http://muse.jhu.edu/login?uri = /journals/thoery_and_event/v0 05/ 5.4agamben.html (accessed February 12, 2011).

40. See the daily blogs on *Ha'aretz* at http://www.haaretz.com/.

41. Seamus Milne, "Israel and the West Will Pay a Price for Gaza's Bloodbath," *Guardian*, January 8, 2009, http://www.guardian.co.uk/commentisfree/2009/jan/08/gaza-israel-h amas-us (accessed January 22, 2009).

42. Baruch Kimmerling, "Israel's Culture of Martyrdom," *Nation*, December 22, 2004, 7, http://www.thenation.com/doc/20050110/kimmerling/print (accessed February 26, 2009).

43. Gwynne Dyer, *War* (Toronto: Vintage Canada, 2005), 419. See also Natalie Angier, "No Time for Bullies: Baboons Retool their Culture," *New York Times*, April 13, 2004, http://www.primates.com/baboons/culture.html; and "Emergence of a Peaceful Culture in Wild Baboons," http://www.ncbi.nlm.nih.gov/pmc/articles/PMC387823.

44. See Angier, "No Time for Bullies."

45. Ibid., quoted in Dyer, *War*, 420.

46. Ibid.

47. Hannah Arendt, *Eichmann in Jerusalem: A Report on the Banality of Evil*, rev. and enl. ed. (New York: Penguin Books, 1977), 233.

48. From the documentary *ScaredSacred*, directed by Velcrow Ripper (Toronto: ScaredSacred Films, Inc./Mongrel Media, 2006).

49. See Elhanan's personal story at http://www.theparentscircle.com/stories.asp.

50. See http://www.theparentscircle.com/ (accessed February 17, 2010).

51. For an extensive list of such organizations, see the Palestinian-Israeli Peace NGO Forum at http://www.peacengo.org/.

52. Mamdani, *When Victims Become Killers*, 279. For a provocative discussion of survivor's justice, see 272–82.

53. Ibid., 279.

54. Halper, *Obstacles to Peace*, 35, 40, 41.

55. Jeff Halper, *An Israeli in Palestine: Resisting Dispossession, Redeeming Israel* (London: Pluto Press, 2008), 5–6 (quotation on p. 5).

56. Halper, *Obstacles to Peace*, 42.

57. Ibid., 5.

58. Jeff Halper, "Reframing the Israel/Palestine Conflict" (lecture, McMaster University, Hamilton, Ontario, January 21, 2009).

59. Halper, *Israeli in Palestine*, 11.

Feminist Theory

Cynthia Enloe

Cynthia Enloe taught for many years at Clark University, serving both as the chair of the Political Science Department and the director of Women's Studies. She received her PhD in political science at the University of California, Berkeley. In addition to receiving widespread recognition for her scholarship, Enloe received the Clark University's Outstanding Teacher Award three times. Academically, she is well-known for her work on feminist and gendered politics. She considers how understandings of gender shape politics, paying specific attention to how women are exploited for their labor. While now a professor emeritus of Clark University, Enloe still lectures, publishes, and works on editorial boards of scholarly journals.

Enloe invites curiosity about gender, not simply to consider how men and women process the world differently, but to consider how power dynamics determine who creates the world and what is created. First, she encourages the conflict professional to seek out the predominantly invisible woman (domestic workers, secretaries, women diplomats/women married to diplomats, mistresses to the elite, women soldiers, etc.). She advocates digging into their complex experiences and ideas. Traditionally, the field of international politics considers the spaces these women inhabit as trivial. However, these women and the spaces they inhabit can "pull back the curtain on the political workings in lofty state affairs." Conducting such an investigation will require new skills, including genuine humility and curiosity as well as an appreciation of what an understanding of these spaces can bring to international politics. Enloe considers this work as an investigation into power. In this article, we see Enloe's discussion of gender push far beyond her Epoch Two counterparts, who often discussed gender roles as the result of tradition, norms, or natural or cultural differences but rarely to power differentials. Her article also uncouples the often-unchallenged concept of "women and children," a term ubiquitous in international politics. This coupling positions women as children, as victims of, but not creators of, agents in an adult world.

The security narrative dominating the international landscape in response to crises in the Middle East, terrorist threats, and local gun violence further the position of women as needing protection. Enloe also challenges the seemingly women-promoting encouragement to stay up-to-date with foreign affairs. The encouragement tends to suggest that women are acted upon by these affairs but that they are not agents in its production nor encouraged to define the problem or its causes. A response to this is a redefinition and remapping of the boundaries of the political and international understanding of how personal choices shape the world. In this way, Enloe goes beyond adding women's voices to the current discussion, but she broadens the topography of the political space in a way that more naturally includes and, therefore, values the diverse experiences of women.

Questions to consider: In what ways does Enloe see the perspectives of secretaries and housewives as critical and able to create holistic security strategies? How is this perspective different from your understanding of what is usually privileged in policy creation?

Bananas, Beaches, and Bases
Making Feminist Sense of International Politics

Cynthia Enloe

Where Are the Women?

Perhaps you have never imagined what it would feel like if you were a woman fleeing your home with your young children, escaping a violent conflict between government troops and rebel soldiers, crossing a national border, pitching a tent in a muddy refugee camp, and then being treated by aid staff workers as though you and the children you are supporting were indistinguishable, "women and children."

Maybe, if any of your aunts or grandmothers have told you stories about having worked as domestic servants, you can more easily picture what your daily life would be like if you had left your home country to take a live-in job caring for someone else's little children or their aging parents. You can almost imagine the emotions you would feel if you were to Skype across time zones to your own children every week, but you cannot be sure how you would react when your employer insisted upon taking possession of your passport.

It probably feels like a stretch to see yourself working in a disco outside a foreign military base. It is hard to think about how you would try to preserve some modicum of dignity for yourself in the narrow space left between the sexualized expectations of your foreign male soldier-clients and the demands of the local disco owner who takes most of your earnings.

While you might daydream about becoming a senior foreign policy expert in your country's diplomatic corps, you may deliberately shy away from thinking about whether you will be able to sustain a relationship with a partner while you pursue this ambition. You try not to think about whether your partner will be willing to cope with both diplomacy's social demands and the pressures you together will endure living in a proverbial media fishbowl.

If you keep up with the world news, you may be able to put yourself in the shoes of a women's rights activist in Cairo, but how would you decide whether to paint your protest sign only in Arabic or to add an English translation of your political message just so that CNN and Reuters viewers around the world can see that your revolutionary agenda includes not only toppling the current oppressive regime but also pursuing specifically feminist goals?

As hard as this will be, it will take all of this imagining—and more—if you are going to make reliable sense of international politics. Stretching your imagination, though, will not be enough. Making feminist sense of international politics requires that you exercise genuine curiosity about each of these women's lives—and the lives of women you have yet to think about. And that curiosity will have to fuel energetic detective work, careful digging into the complex experiences and

Figure EN.1.   Egyptian women protesting sexual harassment hold up signs in Arabic and English, Cairo, 2013. Photo: OPantiSH

ideas of domestic workers, hotel chambermaids, women's rights activists, women diplomats, women married to diplomats, women who are the mistresses of male elites, women sewing-machine operators, women who have become sex workers, women soldiers, women forced to become refugees, and women working on agribusiness plantations.

That is, making useful sense—feminist sense—of international politics requires us to follow diverse women to places that are usually dismissed by conventional foreign affairs experts as merely "private," "domestic," "local," or "trivial." As we will discover, however, a disco can become an arena for international politics. So can someone else's kitchen or your own closet.

And so can a secretary's desk. Consider, for instance, women who work as secretaries in foreign affairs ministries. They are treated by most political commentators as if they were no more interesting than the standard-issue furniture. But women as secretaries have played interesting roles in international events as significant as the controversial Iran-Contra Affair, which exposed the clandestine American military intervention in Nicaragua in the 1980s, and as the secret Israel-Palestine peace negotiations in Oslo in the 1990s. Who pays attention to women as clerical workers when, allegedly, it is elite men (and a handful of elite women) who determine the fates of nations? Feminist researchers do. They challenge the conventional presumption that paying attention to women as secretaries tells us nothing about the dynamics of high-level politics. Feminist-informed investigators pay attention to low-status secretarial women because they have learned that paying attention to (listening to, taking seriously the observations of) women in these scarcely noticed jobs can pull back the curtain on the political workings in lofty state affairs. Devoting attention to women who are government secretaries, for instance, exposes the far-reaching political consequences of feminized loyalty, feminized secrecy, feminized record-keeping, feminized routine, masculinized status, and masculinized control.[1]

Thanks to innovative research by feminist-informed scholars, we know to look for secretaries throughout international politics. For instance, we recently have learned that in the 1920s and 1930s, some enterprising women—German, British, Dutch—pursued jobs in the newly launched League of Nations, the international organization founded in the wake of horrific World War I to remake interstate relations. These women were breaking new ground not only by becoming the first international civil servants but also by, as women, pursuing their own careers far from home. Working as secretaries and also as librarians, these women were the ones who ensured that the League of Nations documents would be produced and archived professionally. Because of these staff women's efforts, we now can launch our provocative reassessments of the League as a site not only for preventing war but also for promoting international social justice. These women did not think of themselves as furniture.[2]

Some women, of course, have not been treated as furniture. Among those women who have become visible in the recent era's international political arena are Hillary Clinton, Mary Robinson, Angela Merkel, Christine Lagarde, Michelle Bachelet, Ellen Johnson Sirleaf, and Shirin Ebadi.[3] Each of these prominent women has her own gendered stories to tell (or, perhaps, to deliberately not tell).

But a feminist-informed investigation makes it clear that there are far more women engaged in international politics than the conventional headlines imply. Millions of women are international actors, and most of them are not Shirin Ebadi or Hillary Clinton.

To make reliable sense of today's (and yesterday's) dynamic international politics calls both for acquiring new skills and for redirecting skills one already possesses. That is, making feminist sense of international politics necessitates gaining skills that feel quite new and redirecting skills that one has exercised before, but which one assumed could shed no light on wars, economic crises, global injustices, and elite negotiations. Investigating the workings of masculinities and femininities as they each shape complex international political life—that is, conducting a gender-curious investigation—will require a lively curiosity, genuine humility, a full tool kit, and candid reflection on potential misuses of those old and new research tools.[4]

Most of all, one has to become interested in the actual lives—and thoughts —of complicatedly diverse women. One need not necessarily admire every woman whose life one finds interesting. Feminist attentiveness to all sorts of women is not derived from hero worship. Some women, of course, will turn out to be insightful, innovative, and even courageous. Upon closer examination, other women will prove to be complicit, intolerant, or self-serving. The motivation to take all women's lives seriously lies deeper than admiration. Asking "Where are the women?" is motivated by a determination to discover exactly how this world works. One's feminist-informed digging is fueled by a desire to reveal the ideas, relationships, and policies those (usually unequal) gendered workings rely upon.

For example, a British woman decides to cancel her plans for a winter holiday in Egypt. She thinks Egypt is "exotic," the warm weather would be welcome, and cruising down the Nile sounds exciting; but she is nervous about political upheaval in the wake of the overthrow of Egypt's previous regime. So instead she books her winter vacation in Jamaica. In making her tourism plans, she is playing her part in creating the current international political system. She is further deepening Egypt's financial debt while helping a Caribbean government earn badly needed foreign currency. And no matter which country she chooses for her personal pleasure, she is transforming "chambermaid" into a major globalized job category.

Or consider an American elementary school teacher who designs a lesson plan to feature the Native American "princess" Pocahontas. Many of the children will have watched the Disney animated movie. Now, the teacher hopes, she can show children how this seventeenth-century Native American woman saved the Englishman John Smith from execution at Jamestown, Virginia, later converted to Christianity, married an English planter, and helped clear the way for the English colonization of America. (The teacher might also include in her lesson plan the fact that Pocahontas's 1614 marriage to John Rolfe was the first recorded interracial marriage in what was to become the United Sates.) Her young students might come away from their teacher's well-intentioned lesson having absorbed the myth that local women are easily charmed by their own people's foreign occupiers.

The lives of Hollywood actresses can take on new international import when viewed through a feminist analytical lens. For example, in the 1930s, Hollywood moguls turned the innovative Brazilian singer Carmen Miranda into an American movie star. Then they put Miranda to work bolstering President Franklin Roosevelt's efforts to promote friendlier relations between the United States and Latin America. Soon after, an international banana company made her image into their logo, creating a new, intimate relationship between American housewives and a multinational plantation company. Today, however, Carmen Miranda has become an archetype of a certain over-the-top Latinized femininity. Men and women dress up with fantastic fruit-adorned hats and put their Carmen Miranda look-alike images up on YouTube and their Facebook pages.

Or consider the implications of a gendered encounter between a foreign male soldier and an impoverished, local woman today: an American—or Australian or Canadian or Ugandan—male soldier on an international peacekeeping or humanitarian mission responds to his comrades' homophobic innuendos by finally going along with them to a local brothel in order to prove that he is "one of the boys." Though he may think of himself as simply bolstering his own manly credentials, his attempts to compensate for his insecure masculine identity help shape power relations between his country's military and the society it is supposed to be protecting. He is also reinforcing one of the crucial bulwarks of today's militarized international political relations: heterosexualized masculinity.

The woman tourist and the chambermaid; the schoolteacher and her students; the film star, her studio owners, the banana company executives, the American housewife, and contemporary YouTube enthusiasts; the male soldier, the brothel owner, and the woman working as a prostitute—all are dancing an intricate international minuet. Those who look closely at the gendered causes and the gendered consequences of that minuet are conducting a feminist investigation of today's international political system.

These "dancers," however, are not in a position to call the tune. Yet even a woman who is victimized is not mindless. It is crucial to this feminist-informed investigation into unequal international relations that we not create a false (and lazy) dichotomy between the allegedly "mindless victim" and the allegedly "empowered actor." Women who are pushed to the far margin of any power system continue to assess and strategize even with the minimal resources they have available; sometimes they move beyond private strategizing to collective organizing. Nonetheless, acknowledging the severely restricted agency exercised by women pushed to the margins is not to deny that some international actors wield a lot more influence and garner far more rewards than do others. Thus, to investigate the gendered workings of international politics we will have to make power visible—power in all its myriad forms. This exploration can be uncomfortable.

Where Does Power Operate?

To do a gender investigation fueled by a *feminist* curiosity requires asking not only about the meanings of masculinity and femininity but also about how those meanings determine where women are and what they think about being there.

Conducting a feminist gender analysis requires investigating *power:* What forms does power take? Who wields it? How are some gendered wieldings of power camouflaged so they do not even look like power?

A feminist gender analysis calls for continuing to ask even more questions about the genderings of power: Who gains what from wielding a particular form of gender-infused power? What do challenges to those wieldings of that form of power look like? When do those challenges succeed? When are they stymied?

Most of us, understandably, would prefer to think that the appeal of a company's marketing logo is cultural, not political. We would like to imagine that going on holiday to Jamaica rather than Egypt is merely a social, even aesthetic, matter, not a political choice. Many women and men would also prefer to think of sexual relationships as existing in the intimate realm of personal desire and attraction, immune to political manipulation. Yet corporate executives choose certain logos over others to appeal to consumers' stereotypes of racialized femininities. Government officials market their women's alleged beauty or their deferential service in order to earn needed tourism revenues. To foster certain bases of "social order," elected legislators craft particular laws to punish certain sexual attractions while rewarding others. Power, taste, attraction, and desire are not mutually exclusive.

If one fails to pay close attention to women—all sorts of women—one will miss who wields power and for what ends. That is one of the core lessons of feminist international investigation.

Power operates across borders. Think about the power dynamics of marriage. Whose marriage to whom is recognized by which governments for which purposes? To answer this multifaceted question, one has to pay attention to power. One has to investigate who has the power to rule that a male citizen can marry a woman or a man of another country and thereby confer his own citizenship status on his new spouse, whereas a woman who marries a person from another country cannot. Those with access to political power use that power to control marriage because marital relationships between people of the same or opposite sex affect transnational immigrations and access to the privileges of state-bestowed citizenship. Marriage is political. Marriage is international.

The politics of marriage can become even more intensely international as a result of gendered pressures from outside: colonial rule, new international norms of human rights, transnational religious evangelizing, and membership in new interstate unions whose standards have to be met. A family's wedding album rarely shows what power was wielded nationally or internationally and by whom in that ceremony. One has to dig deeper, even when the digging makes one uneasy.

One of the most important intellectual benefits that comes from paying serious attention to where women are in today's international politics—and investigating how they got *there* and what they *think* about being there—is that it exposes *how much more political power is operating than most non-gender-curious commentators would have us believe.*

This assertion—that many commentators underestimate power—may seem odd, since so many gender-*in*curious commentators appear to project an aura of power themselves, as if their having insights into the alleged realities of power bestows on them a mantle of power. Yet it is these same expert commentators who gravely underestimate both the amount and the kinds of power it has taken to create and to perpetuate the international political system we all are living in today. It is not incidental that the majority of the people invited to serve as expert foreign affairs commentators are male. For instance, one study revealed that, although white men constitute only 31 percent of today's total U.S. population, they made up 62 percent of all the expert guests on the three most influential American evening cable news channels.[5]

The flaw at the core of these mainstream, seemingly "sophisticated" commentaries is how much they take for granted, how much they treat as inevitable, and thus how much about the workings of power they fail to question—that is, how many types of power, and how many wieldings and wielders of power, they miss.

Too often gender incurious commentators attribute women's roles in international affairs to tradition, cultural preferences, and timeless norms, as if each of these existed outside the realms where power is wielded, as if they were beyond the reach of decisions and efforts to enforce those decisions. What sacrifices a woman as a mother should make, what priorities a woman as a wife should embrace, what sexualized approaches in public a woman should consider innocent or flattering, what victim identity a refugee woman should adopt, what boundaries in friendships with other women a woman should police, what dutiful-daughter model a girl should admire—in reality, all of these are shaped by the exercise of power by people who believe that their own local and international interests depend on women and girls internalizing these particular feminized expectations. If women internalize these expectations, they will not see the politics behind them. Political commentators who do not question these internalizations will accept the camouflaged operations of power as if there were no power at work at all. That is dangerous.

Women's collective resistance to any one of these feminized expectations can realign both local and international systems of power. As we will see, even stymied or only partially successful resistance by women can expose both who wields power to sustain the gendered status quo and what those power-wielders fear they will lose if women's resistance succeeds. This is why every suffrage movement in every country—the United States, Britain, Brazil, Mexico, China, Egypt, Kuwait—has raised such intense political alarm. Today, likewise, every effort by immigrant domestic workers to unionize—and every attempt by women garment and electronics workers to go out on strike, every move by women banana workers to be heard inside a male-led labor union, every campaign by an "out" lesbian to gain elective office, every demand by women married to soldiers and diplomats to pursue their own careers—not only has the potential to upset the gendered norms and roles on which the current global system has come to rely but also exposes where power operates to sustain the gendered status quo, as well as who benefits from that current gendered status quo.

Thus, if one is interested in gaining a reliable sense of national and international politics, one should be curious about all sorts of women's resistance, whether or not that resistance succeeds.

As one learns to look at the world through gender-curious feminist eyes, one learns to ask whether anything that passes for natural, inevitable, inherent, traditional, or biological has been *made.* One asks how all sorts of things have been made—the receding glacier, the low-cost sweatshirt, the heavily weaponized police force, the masculinized peace negotiation, the romantic marriage, the all-male Joint Chiefs of Staff. Asking how something has been made implies that it has been made by someone with a certain kind of power. Suddenly there are clues to trace; there is blame, credit, and responsibility to apportion, not just at the start but at each point along the way.

That is, a feminist, gender-curious approach to international politics offers a lot more topics to investigate because it makes visible the full workings of myriad forms of power.

Who Takes Seriously the Ideas of Transnational Feminists?

Despite the remarkable activist engagement that has generated today's multistranded transnational women's movement, many journalists (and the editors who assign their stories), foreign policy experts, and policy decision makers remain oddly confident in their dismissal of feminist ideas.

Among the most loosely organized, social-media-energized, recent transnational women's movements have been Girl Rising, Slut Walks, Femen, and Vagina Monologues, with its accompanying V Day. Each tends to be fluid and not to depend on paid staffs or brick-and-mortar headquarters. The activists in each adapt their actions and messages to suit local needs and conditions. The organizations' distinguishing features are Internet savvy, feminist creativity, and convention-defying public performance.[6]

Simultaneously, a host of more explicitly organized transnational feminist groups and networks challenge the conventional workings of international politics today. Here is an admittedly incomplete list:

- Women Living Under Muslim Laws
- International Network of Women in Black
- Women's Global Network for Reproductive Rights
- International Women's Health Coalition
- Our Bodies Ourselves Global Network
- Equality Now
- International Action Network on Small Arms Women's Network
- Women's Initiatives for Gender Justice
- International Domestic Workers Network
- International Gay and Lesbian Human Rights Commission
- Women's International League for Peace and Freedom
- NGO Working Group on Women, Peace and Security
- Women in Conflict Zones Network

Figure EN.2.   Anna Hutsol, cofounder of the topless direct-action feminist group Femen, and her mother in their Ukrainian home village, 2013, prior to physical attacks aimed at Hutsol and other Femen activists. Photo: Dmitry Kostyukov/*The New York Times*/Redux

The Women's International League for Peace and Freedom was founded a century ago by transnational feminist peace activists in the midst of World War I.[7] Many groups on this partial list, by contrast, have been created in the years since the 1990s. New transnational networks and coalitions are on the brink of being launched today. Each network has its own gendered international political history.

Their feminist activists do not always agree. Their members debate each other over what is causing what, which goal should be prioritized, which international power-holder should be the focus of protests or lobbying. They debate with each other over which compromises can be swallowed and which cannot. But the activists working in these organized groups also have come to share much in common: each is headed by women leaders; each, simultaneously, fosters autonomy among its grassroots activists; each urges women to take part in not only local but also international politics; each builds alliances with other all-women groups and with mixed men's and women's networks; each depends on donors, interns, and volunteers; each monitors trends and decisions in a particular arena of international politics; each posts data and analyses on its own website, usually in several languages; each uses its own gender-conscious investigations and analyses as a basis for crafting strategic campaigns to challenge both the oppression women experience and the practices that privilege certain men and certain masculinities; each aims its political campaigns not only at governments but also at the media, international agencies, and corporations.[8]

Why do most of us not hear the names of these organizations regularly on the nightly news or on the main Internet news sites? Editors, mainstream experts, and some academic scholars employ several strategies to dismiss the analytical (that is, explanatory) value of these groups' insights and impacts. One common rationale for ignoring the work of these transnational feminist networks is to dismiss them as representing only a "special interest." By contrast, the international expert is, so he (occasionally she) claims, interested in "the Big Picture." That is, the common assumption is that one-half of the world's population is equivalent to, say, logging companies or soccer clubs; thus, the thinking goes, their actions do not shed light on the world but simply are intended to advance their own limited self-interests.

A second rationale for not taking seriously the ideas and actions of these contemporary globalized women's advocacy groups—ideas and actions that should be thoughtfully weighed, not automatically accepted—is that the arenas of politics that these feminist activists do expose are presumably merely domestic or private, as opposed to, for instance, the allegedly "significant" public arenas of military security or government debt. In other words, the conventional failure to take seriously the thinking behind transnational women's advocacy is itself rooted in unrealistically narrow understandings of "security," "stability," "crisis," and "development." All four concepts are of utmost concern to those worried about the international Big Picture. Each of these four concerns—security, stability, crisis, and development—is routinely imagined to be divorced from (unaffected by) women's unpaid and underpaid labor, women's rights within marriage, the denial of girls' education, women's reproductive health, and sexualized and other forms of male violence against women, as well as the masculinization of militaries, police forces, and political parties. The conventional Big Picture, it would appear, is being painted on a shrunken canvas.

Third, these feminist transnational groups' analyses and actions can be ignored—their reports never cited, their staff members never invited to speak as experts, their leaders or activists never turned to for interviews—on the questionable grounds that their campaigns are lost causes. Behind this justification is the notion that challenging entrenched masculinized privileges and practices in today's international affairs is hopeless, therefore naive, therefore not worthy of serious attention. Further underpinning this final argument are the stunningly ahistorical assertions that (a) any advancements that women have gained have come not as a result of women's political theorizing and organizing but because women have been given these advancements by enlightened men in power, and (b) we collectively have "always" understood such useful political concepts as "reproductive rights," "sexual harassment," "systematic wartime rape," and "the glass ceiling." This latter assertion overlooks the fact that each of these revelatory concepts was hammered out and offered to the rest of us by particular activists at particular moments in recent political history.

All three of these spoken or unspoken rationales, and the assumptions they rely upon, are themselves integral to how international politics operates today. All three assertions that deny the significance and analytical value of transnational feminist organizing *are* the very stuff of international politics.

The very rarity of professional international political commentators taking seriously either women's experiences of international politics or women's gender analyses of international politics is, therefore, itself a political phenomenon that needs to be taken seriously. What so many non-feminist-informed international commentators *ignore* has been explored by the burgeoning academic field of gender and international relations. That is, paying close attention to—and explaining the causes and consequences of—what is so frequently ignored can be fruitful indeed.[9]

At the same time, we can be more curious about who does not pay attention to women's experiences—of war, marriage, trade, travel, revolution, and plantation and factory work. Who reaps rewards when women's experiences of these international affairs are treated as if they were inconsequential, mere "human interest" stories? That is, one becomes an international political investigator when one seeks to figure out who is rewarded if they treat women's experiences and women's gender analyses as if either were mere embellishments, almost entertainment, as if neither sheds meaningful light on the causes of the unfolding global events. Rewards are political.

Consider one common journalistic trivializing device: using a photograph or a bit of video footage of women to illustrate a news story—women shown grieving seems especially alluring to editors—but then interviewing only men for the main content of the journalistic account. Most coverage of international affairs is crafted with the presumption that only men—diverse men, rival men—have anything useful to say about what we all are trying to make sense of. Feminists routinely count how many men and how many women are interviewed in any political news story. A ratio of six to one or seven to zero is common.[10]

Since 2000, new social media have been used by many women, especially young women, to break through the masculinity-privileging walls of mainstream, established media. Women have become skilled bloggers, users of Twitter, Tumblr, YouTube, and Facebook. In addition, some feminist journalists have created alternative, independent international outlets, most prominent being the online international news service Women's eNews, which commissions local women journalists to cover stories about women's politics that the bigger media companies ignore.[11]

These recent media innovations are not the first time that women have tried to fashion alternative media in order to make visible women's political issues, women's critical analyses, and women's political activism. Suffragists in the early 1900s set up their own printing presses and publishing houses to put out independent broadsides, pamphlets, and newspapers to let their fellow citizens know why women campaigners were demanding voting rights for women on the same terms as for men.

Then, in the 1980s and 1990s, scores of new magazines, publishing houses, archives, and bookstores were established by feminists in India, Mexico, Britain, the United States, Canada, Italy, Germany, Netherlands, Switzerland, Spain, Australia, South Africa, Japan, South Korea, Sweden, Pakistan, and Turkey in order to provide media outlets for literally thousands of women who were writing feminist-informed histories, novels, poetry, memoirs, political theory, health guides, investigatory journalism, and cinema reviews. Other women started women's radio

Figure EN.3.   Mary Phillips, a Scottish suffragette, selling the British suffragist news-paper *The Vote*, 1907. Photo: Museum of London

programs and documentary film distribution companies. Many of the women involved in these media politics were aware of women in other countries doing the same; they read and distributed each other's publications, visited each other's bookstores, and traded encouragement and practical advice across national boundaries.[12]

As influential as these past and present local and international feminist media innovations were—and still are—in offering alternative information and perspectives, they did not and still do not have sufficient resources (for instance, for news bureaus in Beijing, Cairo, Nairobi, London, Tokyo, and Rio de Janeiro). Nor can they match the cultural and political influence wielded by large well-capitalized or state-sponsored media companies—textbook publishers, network and cable television companies, national radio stations and newspapers, Internet companies, and major film studios. These large media companies have become deliberately international in their aspirations. They are not monolithic, but together they can determine what is considered "international," what is defined as "political," what is deemed "significant," and who is anointed an "expert."[13]

Thus it is important to investigate, despite their differences, these influential media companies' common dismissal of unorganized and organized women as insignificant and to weigh carefully the risks that such dismissals carry. Each dismissal hobbles us when we try to explain why international politics takes the path it does.

What We Miss: Two Brief Case Studies

First case: the transatlantic antislavery movement. Despite the emergence of feminist historians, it is easy to portray the transatlantic antislavery movement of the early and mid-1800s as an all-male movement. The slave trade—and the profitable exports of cotton, tobacco, and sugar that the slave trade enabled—was a globalized business. Challenging that trade would drastically alter the international politics of the time. That is accepted. But it is the American male antislavery activists Frederick Douglass, John Brown, and William Lloyd Garrison, and their British ally the abolitionist William Wilberforce, who continue to be publicly celebrated. Thanks only to the work of African American feminist historians have the political contributions of abolitionist Sojourner Truth been recognized.[14] Overlooked by all but feminist historians have been the lesser-known British and American women antislavery activists, women who created mass movements in the early and mid-1800s. Not only did they strategize and campaign (e.g., British antislavery women provided the backbone for the sugar boycott and introduced mass petitioning), but these women activists, black and white, also overcame their lack of voting rights, their exclusion from the halls of governments, and the obstacles to travel and communication (letters from London took more than two weeks to reach Boston's antislavery hub) to create an effective transatlantic alliance, one of the world's first transnational women's movements.[15]

What do we miss if today we persist in portraying this important early international political movement as an all-male affair? First, we grossly underestimate how much racialized gendered power it took for proslavery advocates to sustain the slave trade and systems of slave labor for as long as they did. If those with vested interests in maintaining slavery had faced only male opponents, without the energy, political innovations, and knowledge of domestic consumption that women abolitionists contributed, they might have been able to sustain the exploitive racist system longer or at lower political cost.

Second, if we continue to ignore the distinct ideas and actions of the British and American women abolitionists, we will underestimate the internal tensions that marked the transatlantic antislavery movement itself: to sustain their movement over decades and in the face of formidable opposition, male and female antislavery activists not only had to reconcile their differing ideas about race, property, freedom, and the meaning of humanity, but they also had to work out among themselves their contentious differences over femininity, masculinity, respectability, and marriage (e.g., was marriage itself, in its then-current form, as some women abolitionists came to believe, just a more polite form of slavery?).[16]

Finally, if we persist in taking seriously only the male anti-slavery campaigners in the international movement to abolish the slave trade and slave labor, then we are bound to miss one of the most significant consequences of that political movement: the mobilization in the late 1800s and early 1900s of campaigns to end the political systems of male-only suffrage. The suffrage movement, despite its contradictions and shortcomings, became one of the world's most radically democratizing movements. And it was globalized.[17]

Yet investigations of the international gender politics of both abolitionism and women's suffrage campaigning are virtually absent from most university courses purporting to train students in the skills they will need to make reliable sense of democratization, political mobilization, and international politics.

Second case: the international Arms Trade Treaty. It took eight years. Money had to be raised. Gender-disaggregated data had to be collected. Women had to be interviewed. Interviews had to be translated. Consciousnesses had to be raised. Meetings had to be organized. Visas and plane tickets to New York had to be obtained. Different priorities and understandings had to be aired and reconciled. Alliances had to be forged, then tended and reforged.[18] But on April 2, 2013, by a majority vote (154 in favor, 3 against, 23 abstaining), member states of the United Nations General Assembly adopted the world's first-ever international Arms Trade Treaty. For the first time, governments and companies exporting small arms—rifles, pistols, grenade launchers, and the parts and ammunition for these weapons—would be bound by international law to explicitly assess whether those arms would be used in the importing country for purposes that violated international human rights. This was new.

Buried in its thirteen pages of formal diplomatic language was a transnational feminist success: article 7, paragraph 4. It reads, "The exporting State Party, in making this assessment [of the potential 'negative consequences' of permitting the export of small arms], shall take into account the risk of the conventional arms covered under Article 2 (1) of the items covered under Article 3 or Article 4 being used to commit or facilitate serious acts of gender-based violence or serious acts of violence against women and children."[19]

Eight years and multinational attentiveness and transnational lobbying by scores of women produced this crucial phrase: *gender-based violence.* And not only that. The hotly contested phrase—*gender-based violence*—was placed here, in this section of the Arms Trade Treaty that made it binding (not simply advisory) on the ATT's government signatories.

Including "gender-based violence" as a criterion for government officials when they assessed the legality of exporting any small arms from their own countries' gun manufacturers was a criterion strenuously resisted by certain influential organizations and by officials from powerful governments.

The alliance that developed the reasoning for "gender-based violence" as an assessment criterion was feminist-led and transnational. At its core were three organizations: the Women's International League for Peace and Freedom (WILPF), especially its international staffs in Geneva and in New York, across the street from the UN; the International Action Network on Small Arms (IANSA), Women's Network; and Global Action to Prevent War and Armed Conflict.

Together, these three organizations had activist affiliates around the world. While their combined lobbying to persuade governments' UN delegates to support the inclusion of the words *gender-based violence* in the ATT and to "make it binding" is a story yet to be fully told in all its twists and turns, a crucial part of that story was these activists listening to women, asking where women are in today's international politics of guns.

Most of the non-feminist-informed activists who pushed for the Arms Trade Treaty focused their attention on export figures, import figures, patterns of armed conflict, and gun-exporting governments' and their weapons manufacturers' complicity in enabling those damaging armed conflicts. It was their analyses, too, that informed most mainstream news coverage. What the women of IANSA, WILPF, and Global Action did was distinct: they looked deeper into armed conflicts to chart the gendered dynamics of guns, both gun violence's causes and its consequences. IANSA's women activists in Mali, Congo, Brazil, the Philippines, and other countries that had experienced years of violence played a crucial role. They asked, "Where are the women?" And "Where are the guns?" They interviewed women about where guns were in their own daily lives. They revealed how politicized conflict became gendered conflict. They exposed the causal connections between group armed violence and violence perpetrated inside homes and families. And they demonstrated how those guns when not even fired could infuse relationships between women and men with fear and intimidation. Listening to women's diverse experiences of living with guns in their communities and their homes, they painted a Big Picture: the massive international exports of guns sustained gender-based violence as a pillar of international and national patriarchy.

The Vatican was a crucial player in the UN Arms Trade Treaty negotiations. The Vatican has "observer status" at the UN (as does the Palestinian delegation). This status gives the Vatican's delegates access to crucial discussions among voting state delegations, where its opinions and interpretations often carry significant weight. In each UN treaty negotiation process, the state participants decide whether or not observers will be allowed to cast votes on the final proposed document. In the Arms Trade Treaty process, observers were not allowed to vote. But throughout the multistage negotiations, the Vatican's delegates were omnipresent and influential. Its delegates helped to create what feminists called the "unholy alliance" between the UN delegates of the Vatican, Russia, Syria, and Iran. The Vatican led the resistance to including the phrase *gender-based violence* in the Arms Trade Treaty. Over the years, the Vatican's delegates have treated social constructions of male and female as anathema. Thus no "gender." They pressed, instead, for the more patriarchal phrase *violence against women and children*. Furthermore, the Vatican pushed to have *violence against women and children* inserted only in the treaty's opening preamble. That is, they were comfortable with including *violence against women and children* in the final treaty as a motivating reason for creating this new interstate agreement, but were opposed to it being made a binding criterion that governments would be obligated to use when they assessed their own gun exports.

The Vatican was not alone. By itself, its role is never decisive. Numbers of governments and lobbying groups were willing to allow the conventional phrase *violence against women and children* to be inserted and to have it listed merely as one reason among many for limiting the international trade in small arms. What they did not accept was the insertion of the more politically salient analytical phrase *gender-based violence,* or for that to become a formal criterion imposed on governments when they assessed the legality of exporting weaponry.

Ideas matter. Words matter. Placement matters. The strategists of WILPF and IANSA's Women's Network and Global Action, women such as Ray Acheson and Maria Butler, went from state delegation to state delegation to explain why neither the phrase *violence against women and children* nor its placement solely in the nonbinding preamble were sufficient—that is, why neither matched the realities of women's lives. Eventually, more than one hundred state delegations publicly backed the inclusion of the term *gender-based violence* and its placement in the section that would make it a binding criterion in each exporting government's assessment process. The UN delegates of Iceland and Lichtenstein, though representing small countries, were especially helpful in supporting WILPF's and IANSA's feminist campaigners.

The wide governmental support that the feminists ultimately gained was the outcome of scores of women activists spending hours explaining, first, that "women and children" should not be lumped together and treated as mere victims. Second, feminist activists working the corridors of the UN explained to delegates that when violence is described as "gendered" it makes the workings of masculinities and the politics of misogyny visible in the international politics of gun exporting. Third, they explained to scores of delegates that, to be meaningful, the treaty had to legally obligate exporting governments to explicitly determine whether any small arms were likely to be used in the importing country to perpetrate widespread gender-based violence.

The intricately crafted final version of the Arms Trade Treaty was passed by the General Assembly on April 2, 2013 (with the delegates of Syria, Iran, and North Korea casting the three "no" votes). Its passage was the result of many actors, many efforts, many forms of analysis. But if one does not ask, "Where were the women?" one will miss who tried to dilute the ATT and why. If one ignores the thinking and the activism of the WILPF and IANSA women, one also will miss the innovative feminist thinking that causally linked international gun political economies to the political economies of sexualized wartime violence, domestic violence, and the processes of intimidation that severely limit women's economic and political participation. Moreover, one will miss the feminist-informed listening, data collection, analysis, and strategizing that transformed a groundbreaking international agreement between governments into an instrument for furthering women's rights.

The Arms Trade Treaty's gendered politics had taken years to create, but in April 2013 those gendered politics had just begun. To become operational, the ATT would have to be ratified by individual governments. In each country there would be multiple bases for support and for rejection of the treaty. Who in each country would balk at making "gender-based violence" a binding criterion? Who would argue that its inclusion was one of the positive strengths of the ATT? Charting each of these ratifying debates, country by country, will shine a light on the genderings of the international political economies of rifles, pistols, and grenade launchers. Then there will be still further chapters in the gendered ATT story: in those countries that ratify the ATT (that is, which sign on to its binding obligations), who will officials turn to for expert advice when they have to assess whether the guns they are about to export will be used to inflict widespread gender-based violence? The women of IANSA?[20]

Where Are the Men?

Most of the time we scarcely notice that many governments still look like men's clubs, with the occasional woman allowed in the door. We see a photo of members of Russia's cabinet, Wall Street's inner circle, the Chinese Politboro, or Europe's central bankers, and it is easy to miss the fact that all the people in these photographs are men. One of the most useful functions that the British prime minister Margaret Thatcher served during the 1980s was to break through our gender numbness. Thatcher herself was not an advocate for women, but when she stood at a 1987 meeting in Venice alongside France's Mitterand, Japan's Nakasone, the United States' Reagan, and the other heads of government, we suddenly noticed that everyone else was male. Twenty-five years later, Angela Merkel, the German chancellor, provided a similar gender-consciousness-raising function when she stood for a photograph with the other heads of government in the Group of Eight, the world's economic powers. One woman in a photo makes it harder for us to ignore that the men are *men*.

Once we start looking at men as men, we are more likely to become curious about masculinities—what it means to be manly—and about the contests over diverse, unequally ranked sorts of masculinity.

It is widely asserted today that we live in a "dangerous world." It was commonly stated during the four decades of the Cold War, when the threats posed by nuclear weapons were used by both the United States and the Soviet Union to raise the stakes of international rivalries. The notion that we live in a dangerous world gained new saliency after the attacks on New York's towering World Trade Center in September 2001. Since 2001, countless American politicians have based their calls for rolling back citizens' privacy rights, curtailing due process legal protections, giving surveillance agencies free rein, equipping local police forces with heavier weaponry, casting new immigrants as potential threats, launching weaponized drones, and turning a blind eye toward the antidemocratic actions of U.S. international allies by justifying each move as a contributor to the "war on terror."

Among its many questionable consequences, the absorption of the idea that we live in a dangerous world serves to reinforce the primacy of particular forms of masculinity while subordinating most women and femininity itself. Men living in a dangerous world are commonly imagined to be the natural protectors. Women living in a dangerous world allegedly are those who need protection. Those relegated to the category of the protected are commonly thought to be safe "at home" and, thus, incapable of realistically assessing the dangers "out there."

Figure EN.4.   Group of Seven summit meeting, including Margaret Thatcher, Venice, 1987. Photo: Daniel Simon/Frank Spooner Pictures, London

Figure EN.5.   Leaders of the Group of Eight industrialized nations, including Angela Merkel, joined by European Commission and European conflict officials, summit meeting, Northern Ireland, 2013. Photo: Matt Cardy/Getty Images News

Notions of masculinity are not identical across generations or across cultural boundaries. That is why one needs to explore the workings and rankings of masculinities in particular places at particular times—and then track them over generations.[21] Comparison may reveal striking similarities but also expose significant differences. A masculinized rivalry is one in which diverse masculinities are unequally ranked and contested: there is a contest over which expression of manliness is deemed most "modern," which most "rational," which the "toughest," which the "softest," which the "weaker." In such rivalries, women are marginalized unless (withstanding ridicule as "unfeminine") they can convincingly cloak themselves in a particular masculinized style of speech and action. Thus a common British assessment of Britain's first and only woman prime minister: "Margaret Thatcher was the toughest man in the room."

While political contests over masculinity marginalize all but a very few women, such contests always put femininity into play. In a patriarchal society—a society whose relationships and inequalities are shaped by the privileging of particular masculinities and by women's subordination to and dependence on men—anything that is feminized can be disparaged. Consequently, rival men are prone to try to tar each other with the allegedly damning brush of femininity. The intent is to rob the opposing man of his purchase on such allegedly manly attributes as strength, courage, and rationality.[22] This masculinized wielding of femininity happens not only on the playground and in local elections but also in international nuclear politics.[23]

Furthermore, this femininity-wielding masculinized contest between men shapes not only the international politics of war and national security but also the international politics of domestic servants, sex workers, wives, women factory workers, and women plantation workers. This contest determines what is considered mere "women's work" and thus unfit for any manly man. What presumptions about a manly man's access to any woman's sexuality fuels sexual harassment of women on and off the job?

In conventional commentaries, men who wield influence in international politics are analyzed in terms of their national, ethnic, and racial identities; their positions in organizations; their class origins; their paid work; and sometimes their sexual preferences. Rarely, though, are men analyzed as *men,* people who have been taught, since childhood, how to be manly, how not to be a "girl," how to size up the trustworthiness or competence of other men by assessing their manliness. If international commentators do find masculinity interesting, it is typically when they try to make sense of "great men"—Napoleon Bonaparte, Abraham Lincoln, Mao Zedong, Nelson Mandela—not when they seek to understand the actions of male factory owners, male midlevel officials, male banana workers, or male tourists. It is a lack of feminist curiosity that makes comfortably invisible such men's efforts to be seen by other men as masculine in doing their jobs, exercising influence, nurturing alliances, or seeking relief from stress. In so doing, such a lack of feminist curiosity also makes dangerously invisible these men's attempts (sometimes thwarted) to use diverse women in their daily pursuits of precarious masculine status.

Beyond the Global Victim

Some men and women active in campaigns to influence their country's foreign policy—on the right, as well as the left—have called on women to become more educated about international issues, to learn more about "what's going on in the world." Women are told, "You have to take more interest in international affairs because it affects how you live." The gist of the argument is that women need to devote precious time and energy to learning about events outside their own country because, as women, they are the *objects* of those events. For instance, a woman working for a software company in Ireland is told she should learn more about the European Union because what the EU commissioners decide in Brussels is going to help determine her wages and maybe even the hazards she faces on the job. An American woman similarly will be encouraged to learn about the ongoing fighting in Syria because political contests in the Middle East will affect her children's chances of a safe future.

There are two things striking about this conventional line of argument. First, those who are trying to persuade women to "become informed" are not inviting women to reinterpret international politics by drawing on their own experiences as women. If the explanations of how the EU and Middle East politics work do not already include any concepts of femininity, masculinity, or patriarchy, they are unlikely to do so after more women start listening to the recognized gender-incurious international experts. Because these persuaders are not curious about what paying close attention to women's complex experiences could contribute to an understanding of international politics, many women, especially those whose energies are already stretched to the limit, may be understandably wary of spending precious time reading about fighting in Syria or decisions made in Brussels.

When the common women-need-to-learn-more-about-foreign-affairs approach is articulated by gender-incurious activists (women or men), women are usually portrayed as the objects, even victims, of the international political system. Women should learn about capitalist globalization, or the Middle East's Arab Spring, or the workings of the United Nations, or climate change because each has an impact on them. In this worldview, women are forever being acted *upon*. They are the victims of garment factory disasters; they are the targets of sexual assaults in wartime; they are the trafficked, the low paid, the objectified. Rarely are women seen as the explainers or the reshapers of the world. Rarely are they made visible as *thinkers* and *actors*.

If women are asked to join an international campaign—for peace, for refugees, against war, for religious evangelism, against hunger—but are not allowed to define the problem and its causes, it looks to many locally engaged women like abstract do-gooding with minimal connection to the battles they are waging for a decent life in their households and in their own communities.

A lot of books about international politics leave their readers with a sense that "it's all so complex, decided by people who don't know or care that I exist." The spread of capitalist economics, even in countries whose officials call themselves socialists, can feel as inevitable as the tides (which, we are learning, are actually not inevitable). Governments' capacities to wound people, to destroy environments and dreams, are constantly expanding through their uses of science and bureaucracy. International relationships fostered by these governments and their allies use our labor and our imaginations, but it seems beyond our reach to alter them. These relationships seem to have created a world that can turn tacos and sushi into bland fast foods, destroy rain forests, melt arctic ice, globalize pornography, and socialize men from dozens of cultures into a common new culture of high-risk banking. One closes most books on "international security" or "international political economy" with a sigh.

They purport to explain how it works, but they offer knowledge that makes one feel as though it is more rewarding to concentrate on problems closer to home.

Most important, many of these analyses of international affairs leave one with the impression that "home" has little to do with international politics. When home is imagined to be a feminized place—a place where womanly women and feminine girls should feel most comfortable, and where manly men and real boys should stop in now and then for refueling—then this consequence of many mainstream explanations can send the roots of masculinized international politics down even more deeply.

There is an alternative incentive for delving into international politics. That is, seeing oneself in it, not just being acted upon by it. To do this, however, requires remapping the boundaries of the "international" and the "political": it requires seeing how one's own family dynamics, consumer behaviors, travel choices, relationships with others, and ways of thinking about the world actually help shape that world. We are not just acted upon; we are actors. Though, even recognizing that one is not part of any elite, acknowledging oneself as an international actor can be unnerving. One discovers that one is often complicit in creating the very world that one finds so dismaying.

The world is something that has been—and is being—made every day. And ideas about and practices of both femininity and masculinity, combined with attempts to control women, are central to that world-making. So are challenges to those conventions and resistance to those attempts. It is not always easy to see those attempts and, thus, to resist them. Policy makers may find it more "manly" (even if some of the policy makers themselves now are women) to think of themselves as dealing in guns and money, rather than in notions of femininity, marriage, and sexuality. So they—and most of their critics as well—try to hide and deny their reliance on women as feminized workers, as respectable and loyal wives, as "civilizing influences," as sex objects, as obedient daughters, as unpaid farmers, as coffee-serving campaigners, and as spending consumers and tourists. If we can expose their dependence on feminizing women, we can show that this world is also dependent on artificial notions of masculinity.

As a result, this seemingly overwhelming world system may begin to look more fragile and open to radical change than we have been led to imagine.

Thus this book is only a beginning. It draws on the theoretical and organizational work of women in Britain in the 1890s, Algeria in the 1950s, the Philippines in the 1980s, Chile in the 1990s, and Egypt in the beginning of the twenty-first century. Most of the conclusions here are tentative. What readers themselves write in the margins of these pages as they test the descriptions and explanations against their own experiences of the internationalized politics of femininity and masculinity will be at least as valuable in creating a different world as what appears here in deceptively solid print.

Notes

1. For suggestive clues on what taking seriously women as secretaries would reveal about the Iran-Contra affair, see Barbara Gamarekian, "Consequences of Fawn Hall," *New York Times,* February 28, 1987; Mary Sit, "Hall Tells Secretaries: 'Stand by Your Boss,'" *Boston Globe*, September 30, 1988. For a feminist political analysis of the surprising roles that women as secretaries played in the otherwise masculinized Israeli-Palestinian peace negotiations, see Sarai Aharoni, "Gender and Peace Work: An Unofficial History of Israeli-Palestinian Peace Negotiations," *Politics and Gender* 7, no. 3 (2011): 391–416. For a feminist study of women as secretaries, based on interviews with five hundred Australian secretaries, see Rosemary Pringle, *Secretaries Talk: Sexuality, Power and Work* (London: Verso Books, 1988). An eye opening study revealing how differently working-class and middle-class Israeli women have interpreted their work as conscript secretaries in the Israeli Defense Force is: Edna Lomsky-Feder and Orna Sasson-Levy, "Serving the Army as Secretaries," *British Journal of Sociology* (2014)).

2. I am deeply indebted to feminist scholar Gyoung Sun Jang for opening my eyes to the still barely acknowledged history of diverse women's work inside the League of Nations. Her fascinating dissertation is: Gyoung Sun Jang, "The Sexual Politics of the Interwar Era Global Governance: Historicizing the Women's Transnational Movements with(in) the League of Nations, 1919–1940" (PhD diss., Women's Studies, Clark University, Worcester, MA, 2009).

3. Hillary Clinton is the U.S. lawyer who has served as First Lady (that is, the wife of the male president), been elected U.S. senator from New York, and been appointed U.S. secretary of state; Mary Robinson is the Irish lawyer who has been elected president of Ireland, served as the United Nations high commissioner for human rights, and served as the U.N. secretary general's special envoy for the Great Lakes Region of Africa; Ellen Johnson Sirleaf is the Liberian economist who has been a World Bank economist, elected president of Liberia, and awarded a Nobel Peace Prize; Shirin Ebadi is the Iranian lawyer who, for her work defending Iranians' human rights, was awarded the Nobel Peace Prize; Angela Merkel is leader of Germany's Christian Democratic Party and the German chancellor (head of government); Christine Lagarde has been France's minister of finance and is the first woman ever appointed managing director of the International Monetary Fund.

4. Two books that bring together thoughtful reflections on how to conduct investigations of women's experiences of international politics and the workings of masculinities and femininities in their often tension-filled lives are: Dyan Mazurana, Karen Jacobson, and Lacey A. Gale, eds., *Research Methods in Conflict Settings: A View from Below* (New York: Cambridge University Press, 2013); Brooke Ackerly, Maria Stern, and Jacqui True, eds., *Feminist Methodologies in International Relations* (New York: Cambridge University Press, 2006).

5. These figures come from a study by the independent monitoring group Media Matters for America, which examined evening programs during the month of April 2013 broadcast on CNN, Fox News, and MSNBC. Rob Savillo and Oliver Willis, "Report: Diversity on Evening Cable News in 13 Charts," *Media Matters for America*, May 13,

2013, http://mediamatters.org/research/2013/05/13/report-diversity-on-evening-cable
-news-in-13-ch/194012. The British group Women in Journalism revealed a similarly masculinized pattern when, in 2012, they surveyed the front-page stories in nine of Britain's
national newspapers. Enloe, Cynthia. *Bananas, Beaches and Bases: Making Feminist Sense
of International Politics*, University of California Press, 2014. ProQuest Ebook Central,
http://ebookcentral.proquest.com/lib/mcgill/detail.action?docID=1687669. Created
from mcgill on 2019–05–04 06:38:25. They found that, of the nine papers, only one
(*Daily Express*, a tabloid) gave 50 percent of its front-page stories to women journalists.
On the front pages of the well-known and influential *Times*—sometimes referred to as
"the Times of London"—male journalists had 82 percent of the bylines, while women
journalists had a mere 18 percent. This same study found that of all those quoted or
mentioned by name in the lead stories of Britain's nine national papers, 84 percent were
men. Jane Martinson, Kira Cochrane, Sue Ryan, Tracy Corrigan, Fiona Bawdon, "Seen
but Not Heard: How Women Make Front Page News," Women in Journalism, October
15, 2012, www.womeninjournalism.co.uk/wp-content/uploads/2012/10/Seen_but_
not_heard.pdf. For more data on the likelihood of men rather than women being chosen
by television news producers to appear as experts on their shows, see Cynthia Enloe and
Joni Seager, "Media," *The Real State of America Atlas: Mapping the Myths and Truths of the
United States* (New York: Penguin Books, 2011), 40–41.

6. For a description of the three Ukrainian young women who launched Femen,
noted for its bold feminist protest uses of feminine nudity, see David M. Herszenhorn,
"Ukraine's Feminist Shock Troops," *International Herald Tribune*, June 1–2, 2013. For a
report on physical assaults on Femen activists, see David M. Herszenhorn, "Feminists Ask
Protection after Attack in Ukraine," *New York Times*, August 19, 2013.

7. See Catia Cecilia Confortini, *Intelligent Compassion: Feminist Critical Methodology
in the Women's International League for Peace and Freedom* (Oxford: Oxford University
Press, 2012).

8. Learn more about each of these transnational feminist groups by going to their
respective websites: Women Living Under Muslim Laws, www.wluml.org; International
Network of Women in Black, www.womeninblack.org; Women's Global Network for
Reproductive Rights, www.wgnrr.org; International Women's Health Coalition, http://
iwhc.org; Our Bodies Ourselves Global Network, www.ourbodiesourselves.org; Equality
Now, www.equalitynow.org; International Action Network on Small Arms Women's Network, www.iansa-women.org; Women's Initiatives for Gender Justice, www.iccwomen
.org; International Domestic Workers Network, www.idwn.org; International Gay and
Lesbian Human Rights Commission, www.iglhrc.org; Women's International League for
Peace and Freedom, www.peacewomen.org; NGO Working Group on Women, Peace
and Security, www.womenpeacesecurity.org; and Women in Conflict Zones Network,
www.yorku.ca/wicznet. For an exploration of how feminist groups become globalized and
with what consequences, see Mary Hawksworth, *Globalization and Feminist Activism* (Lanham, MD: Rowman and Littlefield, 2006).

9. Among the outpouring of feminist-informed academic explorations that has
helped create and enliven the academic field of gender and international relations are: J.
Ann Tickner, *Gendering World Politics* (New York: Columbia University Press, 2001);
J. Ann Tickner and Laura Sjoberg, eds., *Feminism and International Relations* (London:
Routledge, 2011); Christine Sylvester, *Feminist International Relations: An Unfinished Jour-
ney* (Cambridge: Cambridge University Press, 2001); V. Spike Peterson and Anne Sisson
Runyan, *Global Gender Issues in the New Millennium* (Boulder, CO: Westview Press,
2010); Jan Jindy Pettman, *Worlding Women: Feminist International Politics* (London:
Routledge, 1996); Laura Shepherd, *Gender, Violence and Security* (London: Zed Books,

2008); Shirin Rai, *The Gender Politics of Development* (London: Zed Books, 2008); Elisabeth Prugl and Mary Meyer, eds., *Gender and Global Governance* (Boston: Rowman and Littlefield, 1999); Laura Sjoberg, ed., *Gender and International Security: Feminist Perspectives* (London: Routledge, 2010); Annick T. R. Wibben, *Feminist Security Studies* (London: Routledge, 2011); Marianne Marchand and Anne Sisson Enloe, Cynthia. *Bananas, Beaches and Bases: Making Feminist Sense of International Politics*, University of California Press, 2014. ProQuest Ebook Central, http://ebookcentral.proquest.com/lib/mcgill/detail .action?docID = 1687669. Created from mcgill on 2019–05–04 06:38:25. Copyright © 2014. University of California Press. All rights reserved. Runyan, eds., *Gender and Global Restructuring* (London: Routledge, 2000); Carol Cohn, ed., *Women and Wars* (Cambridge: Polity Press, 2013); Marysia Zalewski, *Feminist International Relations* (London: Routledge, 2013); Joyce Kauffman and Kristen Williams, *Women, the State and War: A Comparative Perspective on Citizenship and Nationalism* (Lanham, MD: Lexington Books, 2007); Cynthia Weber, *International Relations Theory* (London: Routledge, 2014); Laura Sjoberg, *Gender and International Relations* (New York: Routledge, 2009); Laura Shepherd, ed., *Gender Matters in Global Politics* (New York: Routledge, 2014); Cynthia Weber, *Queer International Relations* (Oxford: Oxford University Press, 2014). The academic journal that has been created to provide an interdisciplinary space for feminist-informed studies of international politics is the *International Feminist Journal of Politics.* Among *IFJP*'s contributors and editors are many of these same authors, but also many scholars from dozens of countries who more recently have entered and shaped the field of gender and international relations.

10. For comparative data on women and men in U.S. print, television, radio, and Internet news outlets, see Diana Mitsu Klos, *The Women's Media Center: The Status of Women in the U.S. Media 2013*, Women's Media Center, 2013, www.womensmedia center.com/pages/statistics. The Women's Media Center conducts regular research on the treatment of women in the media, as well as on the conditions of women as professional media producers, editors, and reporters. The Center was founded by Gloria Steinem, Robin Morgan, and Jane Fonda. For British gender monitoring of news media, see Women in Journalism, http://womeninjournalism.co.uk.

11. Women's eNews, http://womensenews.org/.

12. Copies of these lively publications from the late 1800s to the present, as well as the records of the influential feminist bookstores, such as New Words of Cambridge, Massachusetts, are collected and available to the public at several women's history libraries and via their online sites: the Schlesinger Library on the History of Women in America, Radcliffe Institute, Harvard University; the Sophia Smith Collection, Smith College, Northampton, MA; the Women's Library (formerly the Fawcett Library), London School of Economics; the Lesbian Herstory Archives, Brooklyn; the Lesbian Archives, Amsterdam.

13. When the Center for Women's Global Leadership brought together activists and scholars to create a strategy for pressing the UN to take explicit account of women in its post-2015 development goals, one of the topics they put on their agenda was making media aware of the expertise of feminist economists: *Towards the Realization of Women's Rights and Gender Equality: Post 2015 Sustainable Development* (New Brunswick, NJ: Center for Women's Global Leadership, Rutgers University, 2013), www.cwgl.rutgers.edu.

14. See Nell Irvin Painter, *Sojourner Truth: A Life, a Symbol* (New York: W. W. Norton, 1996); Margaret Washington, *Sojourner Truth's America* (Urbana: University of Illinois Press, 2009).

15. Claire Midgley, *Women against Slavery: The British Campaigns, 1780–1870* (London: Routledge, 1992).

16. A exciting new biography of the mid-nineteenth-century American writer, editor, and women's rights advocate Margaret Fuller reveals how she came to make the connection between the enslavement of Africans in the United States and the slavery-like conditions experienced by white married women. Megan Marshall, *Margaret Fuller: A New American Life* (Boston: Houghton Mifflin Harcourt, 2013).

17. See, for example, Margot Badran, *Feminists, Islam and Nation: Gender and the Making* Enloe, Cynthia. *Bananas, Beaches and Bases: Making Feminist Sense of International Politics*, University of California Press, 2014. ProQuest Ebook Central, http://ebookcentral.proquest.com/lib/mcgill/detail.action?docID=1687669. Created from mcgill on 2019–05–04 06:38:25. Copyright © 2014. University of California Press. All rights reserved. *of Modern Egypt* (Princeton: Princeton University Press, 1995); Bonnie S. Anderson, *Joyous Greetings: The First International Women's Movement, 1830–1860* (Oxford: Oxford University Press, 2000); Caroline Daley and Melanie Nolan, eds., *Suffrage and Beyond: International Feminist Perspectives* (New York: New York University Press, 1994). For a huge online database (already 150,000 pages and still growing) of documents and reports on women's international organizing from the mid-nineteenth century to the present, see Kathryn Sklar and Thomas Dublin, eds., *Women and Social Movements, International, 1840 to Present* (Alexandria, VA: Alexander Street Press, n.d.), http://alexanderstreet.com/products/women-and-socialmovements-international.

18. This account is based on conversations and email exchanges by the author between March and July 2013 with Ray Acheson, Maria Butler, Madeleine Rees, and Abigail Ruane, all of the Women's International League for Peace and Freedom (New York and Geneva offices), and Sarah Taylor of the NGO Working Group on Women, Peace and Security, based in New York. Each played a key role in the multiyear, transnational feminist activist campaign to insure that gender-based violence was specifically and effectively addressed in the historic 2013 Arms Trade Treaty. Written sources for this narrative include: WILPF, IANSA Women's Network, Amnesty International, and Religions for Peace, "A United Call to Explicitly Include Gender-Based Violence in the Criteria," June 2012, www.wilpfinternational.org; International Action Network on Small Arms Women's Network, "About the IANSA Women's Network": www.iansa-women.org/about.html, accessed May 10, 2013; IANSA Women's Network, "IANSA Women Continue to Push for a Strong ATT That Will Prevent Gender-Based Violence": www.iansa-women.org/node/819, accessed May 10, 2013; Women's International League for Peace and Freedom, "Make It Binding: Include Gender-Based Violence in the ATT," PeaceWomen, April 2013; www.peacewomen.org/pages/att; Ray Acheson, "A Tale of Two Treaties," *Arms Trade Monitor*, no. 6.9 (March 27, 2013), http://reachingcriticalwill.org/images/documents/Disarmament-fora/att/monitor/ATTMonitor6.9.pdf; Rebecca Gerome (IANSA Women's Network) and Maria Butler (WILPF's PeaceWomen), "A Step Back? 'Gender-Based Violence' vs. 'Violence against Women and Children,'" *ATT Monitor*, no. 5.11 (March 2013), www.peacewomen.org/assets/file/ATT/att_and_gbv.pdf; Ray Acheson, Maria Butler, and Sofia Tuvestad, "Preventing Armed Gender-Based Violence: A Binding Requirement in the New Draft ATT Text," WILPF, March 28, 2013, http://peacewomen.org/assets/file/article_gvb_march28_final.pdf; Ray Acheson and Beatrice Fihn, "The Failure of Consensus," *Arms Trade Treaty Monitor: The Blog*, April 1, 2013, http://attmonitor.blogspot.com/2013/04/the_failure_of_consensus_html; Robert Zuber, "Distance Runner," *Arms Trade Treaty Monitor: The Blog*, April 1, 2013, http://attmonitor.blogspot.com/2013/04/distance-runner.html; Katherine Prizeman, "Looking to the Future of the ATT: Shifting Attention to Implementation," *Arms Trade Treaty Monitor: The Blog*, April 2, 2013, http://attmonitor.blogspot.com/2013/04/looking-to-future-of-attshifting.html; Ray Acheson, "The ATT: A Start to Challenging the Status Quo," April

2, 2013, http://attmonitor.blogspot.com/2013/04/the-att-start-to-challenging-status
-quo.html; Maria Butler, editorial, *PeaceWomen Enews*, April 2013, www.peacewomen.org.

19. United Nations General Assembly, *Final United Nations Conference on the Arms Trade Treaty, Draft Decision, Submitted by the President of the Final Conference: The Arms Trade Treaty* (New York: United Nations, March 27, 2013), 6. To take effect internationally, the Arms Enloe, Cynthia. *Bananas, Beaches and Bases: Making Feminist Sense of International Politics*, University of California Press, 2014. ProQuest Ebook Central, http://ebookcentral.proquest.com/lib/mcgill/detail.action?docID=1687669. Created from mcgill on 2019–05–04 06:38:25. Copyright © 2014. University of California Press. All rights reserved. Trade Treaty will have to be both signed and ratified by at least fifty governments. The U.S. government, as of the end of 2013, had only signed the ATT, without even a date scheduled for its ratification to be debated and voted upon by the U.S. Senate. Prospects for the ATT's adoption by the U.S. government are deemed slim, owing to the political influence wielded in American politics by the pro-gun lobby, led by the National Rifle Association. "Editorial: Containing the Conventional Arms Trade," *New York Times,* October 1, 2013. On the other hand, several recent international treaties (e.g., the treaty banning land mines and the treaty establishing the International Crimes Court) have garnered sufficient numbers of government ratifications to go into effect without ratification by the United States.

20. A rare effort to chart and compare murders of women (as distinct from women's wartime deaths) around the world is: Joni Seager, "Murder," *Penguin Atlas of Women in the World* (New York: Penguin Books, 2009), 30–31.

21. There is a growing body of provocative studies that track the evolutions of, and contests between, masculinities within particular countries, many of them conducted by gender-curious ethnographers. See, for instance, John Osburg, *Anxious Wealth: Money and Morality among China's New Rich* (Stanford, CA: Stanford University Press, 2013); Robin Le Blanc, *The Art of the Gut: Manhood, Power, and Ethics in Japanese Politics* (Berkeley: University of California Press, 2010); Daniel Conway, *Masculinities, Militarisation and the End Conscription Campaign: War Resistance in Apartheid South Africa* (Manchester: Manchester University Press, 2012). Among the innovative cross-national studies of diverse masculinities, their interactions, and their political implications are: Marysia Zalewski and Jane Parpart, eds., *The "Man" Question in International Relations* (Boulder, CO: Westview Press, 1998); Jane Parpart and Marysia Zalewski, eds., *Rethinking the Man Question: Sex, Gender and Violence in International Relations* (London: Zed Books, 2008); Paul Kirby and Marsh Henry, eds., "Rethinking Masculinity and Practices of Violence in Conflict Settings," special issue, *International Feminist Journal of Politics* 14, no. 4 (2012); Paul Higate, ed., *Military Masculinities: Identity and the Sate* (Westport, CT: Praeger, 2003); Paul Amar, "Middle East Masculinity Studies," *Journal of Middle East Women's Studies* 7, no. 3 (Fall 2011): 36–71; Terrell Carver, "Being a Man," *Government and Opposition* 41, no. 3 (2006): 477–95.

22. Sandra Harding, a pioneering theorist in the feminist studies of science, has written extensively on how rational thinking has been presumed to be a hallmark of masculinity. See, for instance, Sandra Harding, *The Science Question in Feminism* (Ithaca, NY: Cornell University Press, 1986); Sandra Harding, *Sciences from Below: Feminisms, Postcolonialities and Modernities* (Durham, NC: Duke University Press, 2008).

23. Carol Cohn, "Sex and Death in the Rational World of Defense Intellectuals," *Signs* 12, no. 4 (1987): 687–718; Carol Cohn with Felicity Hill and Sara Ruddick, *The Relevance of Gender in Eliminating Weapons of Mass Destruction* (Stockholm: Weapons of Mass Destruction Commission, 2005).

Silences

Leslie Dwyer

Leslie Dwyer is an associate professor and director of the Center for the Study of Gender and Conflict at S-CAR at George Mason University. She joined the faculty of S-CAR in 2009. She is a cultural anthropologist (BA, University of Pennsylvania; MA/PhD, Princeton University) whose academic research focuses on issues of violence, gender, post-conflict social life, transitional justice, and the politics of memory and identity. Her most recent project, supported by grants from the MacArthur Foundation, the Harry Frank Guggenheim Foundation, and the United States Institute of Peace, is an ethnographic study of the aftermath of political violence in Indonesia, where she has worked for more than twenty years. Her book on this research, titled *'A World in Fragments': Aftermaths of Violence in Bali, Indonesia*, will be published as part of the University of Pennsylvania Press "Pennsylvania Studies in Human Rights" series. She is a documentary filmmaker whose most recent film, *The Black Highway*, engages critically with post-conflict peacebuilding practices in Aceh, Indonesia. Today, she finds herself actively involved in Indonesian efforts to transition the palm oil industry to a more sustainable model that does not require the destruction of ancient forests and the voluminous release of toxins used in the process.

Dwyer's article considers silence in the wake of atrocity as not necessarily indicative of forgiving, forgetting, or moving on. Nor is it necessarily a natural response to terror. Dwyer demonstrates that silences have genealogies, often held in place by social, economic, and/or political forces. She demonstrates the power imposed upon speech in the context of post-genocide Bali. In step with Epoch Three thinking, Dwyer challenges binary models. In this case, binary models of silence that consider silence as simply the absence of speech and/or memory.

Dwyer also resists the easy binary framing that could propose speaking as the obvious response to long-held silences. Truth-telling, confession, and productions of linear histories cannot fully access the local experiences of those living in the wake of genocide, nor would they be produced totally outside the political repression that prompted the violence. She also offers the possibility that silence too may be an expression of some form of power by the individual. The notion that speaking is healing, a prevalent idea in Western psychology, as well as within transitional justice, has a genealogy as well, descending from the Christian confessional tradition.

   While included as a Topic article in Epoch Three, this article can also be of use to researchers. Initially, Dwyer challenges an approach to silence as treating speech and memory as artifacts to be excavated. She also suggests that if someone is unwilling or unable to speak during an interview, it may not be because of an inability to remember or because of lack of a rapport with the researcher. The silence can be the footprint of a political and/or social repression or a form of resistance.

   Questions to consider: How do you interpret silence? How might you better access what silences mean in the conflicts you study?

A Politics of Silences

Violence, Memory, and Treacherous Speech in Post-1965 Bali

Leslie Dwyer

One of the first questions motivating my research on the violence of 1965–1966 in Bali, Indonesia, was that of silence. It was 1998, almost 35 years after the state-sponsored massacres of alleged communists had left some one million Indonesians dead and hundreds of thousands of others deprived of basic civil rights. Yet these events, and their deep repercussions, remained relatively unreferenced outside the communities they had devastated.[1] In Bali, where some 80,000 to 100,000 people (or 5 to 8 percent of the population)[2] had lost their lives over a span of less than six months, stories of the violence were rarely found in the guidebooks carried by the two million-plus tourists who by the turn of the twenty-first century were visiting the "Island of the Gods" each year. Neither did the substantial scholarly literature on Bali offer much insight into what had happened or what the continuing implications might be.[3] Despite its domination by anthropologists, whose in-depth engagements with Balinese lives would seem likely to have turned up traces of violence, Balinese studies tended to echo official Indonesian histories by circumscribing and distancing the massacres as an extraordinary "incident" located safely in the past. Those few scholars who did mention 1965–1966 tended to conclude that Balinese no longer wished to speak about this troubled time, having either forgotten, forgiven, worked through, or moved on from the past.[4] Even among Balinese themselves there seemed to be little public acknowledgment of the massacres. Reference to them was missing from the national history textbooks,[5] the

Balinese media, and the pronouncements of public officials. Granted, when I began my research Indonesia was just emerging from over three decades of repressive rule, during which utterances perceived to be political risked harsh responses from the state. Yet by December 2002, four years after the fall of Suharto's dictatorship and two months after terrorist bombs exploded in a crowded nightclub in one of Bali's tourist districts, the 202 fatalities, mostly tourists, could be termed by the governor of Bali "the worst tragedy the island has experienced," with few voices in the domestic or international media to contradict him.[6] Similar settings of mass violence around the world had—if not immediately, then in the years and decades that followed—come to serve the public imagination as shorthand for human brutality: Armenia, Nazi Europe, Cambodia, Argentina, Guatemala, Bosnia, Rwanda, Sudan. Why, then, did 1965–1966 seem to have disappeared not only from so-called expert attention but also from the lives of the Balinese themselves?[7] Were these silences indicative of an absence of interest or meaning? Or were they spaces of cultural and political signification with their own complex and contested genealogies? Starting from these questions, this essay—part of a larger collaborative research project on the aftermath of 1965–1966 in Bali—explores some of the troubled terrain of postmassacre Bali, focusing on the processes of remembering and forgetting, and of speech and silence, that have marked it.[8]

One of my earliest encounters with the violence in fact took the form of questioning an absence. It was July of 1998, two months after Suharto's resignation from the helm of the country he had ruled for 32 years, and I was in Bali conducting research on women's participation in the political activism that had ushered in the end of his New Order (Orde Baru) regime. A Balinese colleague, Degung Santikarma—who would soon become my research partner and husband—invited me to his family compound, a warren of alleyways, pavilions, sleeping quarters, and shrines where some 150 people lived in tight proximity. It was close to dusk, and the compound was busy with a familiar Balinese bustle of children being bathed, food being shared, and ritual offerings being prepared to the soundtrack of the evening soap operas. But something struck me, my attention so recently trained on gender, as unusual about the scene. While there were women of all ages visible, there were no men older than around 50 to be seen. I commented on this to my colleague, who gave me a look of surprise, saying that no one had ever pointed this out to him before. Later, away from those who could overhear us, he told me how his father, several uncles, and other relatives had been killed in late 1965 and early 1966, and how the few men who had survived had chosen to leave the family compound to escape the memories it held and the scrutiny of the state it enabled. "Many people are now talking about the end of the New Order," he warned me. "But it's still hard to talk about how it began."[9]

At the time it was difficult for me to imagine that I was indeed the first person to comment on what appeared to me as a striking absence. My colleague had a large international network of fellow scholars and friends, some of whom must surely have known about the massacres. Yet as I learned more about what had happened in Bali during and after the violence, I began to see how the production, maintenance, and negotiation of silences had become a crucial feature of the everyday lives of Balinese and of their self-presentations on a global stage. Popular belief often holds that exposing genocidal violence to international scrutiny is among the most effective ways of halting it. Violence, in such framings, is something done in the dark, on the isolated edges of a civilized international community whose attention promises to spotlight and thus banish injustice. In Bali, however, an increasing incorporation into transnational flows of power, profit, and knowledge in the form of tourism, scholarship, and various modes of state-mediated modernity has served overwhelmingly to strengthen rather than slacken the force of silence. While I was undoubtedly far from being the first person to have noticed one of the many traces of violence marking my colleague's family—indeed, as I came to know them better, I began to see just how visible this history was to those in their community—I was, however, among those naive enough to think that verbalizing my notice, both as an American scholar and as someone being pulled closer into the dense social politics of survivors' worlds, was a simple matter.[10]

As I began to work collaboratively with my colleague to try to understand the political and cultural aftermath of 1965–1966 in Bali, I realized that such silences are not simply blank spots on a communicative landscape; rather, they constitute social products with particular genealogies. In large part the silences surrounding 1965–1966, and the enduring resonance of violence that they often signal, can be traced to the cultural work of the state. Suharto's New Order regime (1966–1998) engaged in persistent attempts been seen as atypical of or external to Bali, even contemporary scholars have been able to presume the existence of orderly, stable, and consensual symbolic systems in both pre-1965 and post-1965 Bali, bracketing the violence as optional to either historical scholarship or cultural analysis.[11] To take but one recent example, the anthropologist Michele Stephen (2006), in an essay for an edited volume titled *Terror and Violence: Imagination and the Unimaginable*, offers a brilliant analysis, drawing on the work of the psychoanalyst Melanie Klein, of "imaginary violence," sorcery, and the figure of the "terrible mother" in Bali—without once acknowledging that in 1965–1966 tens of thousands of Balinese in fact experienced horrific violence that continues to haunt personal and social imaginations.[12]

By highlighting how scholarship on Bali has persistently failed to give sustained attention to the massacres, I am not just suggesting that anthropologists have lost opportunities for a more complete or complex understanding of Bali, or that they have refused a politically responsible engagement with their interlocutors' suffering—that they have been "missing the revolution," as Orin Starn (1991) described anthropologists' similar failure to see social tensions in 1980s Peru. Although these scholarly representations of Bali are rarely consumed as original texts by those other than upper-class, educated Balinese, they do not exist in some ivory tower far removed from everyday life, but have filtered into popular Balinese culture via the mass media and, especially, via the tourism industry. Tourist ignorance is, of course, often glibly dismissed as irrelevant to the real matters of scholarly pursuit. Jokes abound in Bali (often told by other tourists) about the holidaymaker who arrives at the airport immigration counter only to exclaim furiously that the plane was not supposed to have been going to Indonesia. But it becomes harder to ignore the place of tourism in the aftermath of massacre if one recognizes that an estimated 80 percent of Balinese depend, directly or indirectly, on the industry for their livelihoods. Tourism has simplified and commodified scholarly representations of a harmonious Bali, turning them into spectacular commercial displays used to advertise the island as an outpost of peaceful, premodern culture where life revolves around ancient, apolitical Hindu-Balinese ritual and where social relations are based on consensus.[13] In their roles as tour guides, drivers, wait staff, vendors, and performing artists, Balinese are expected to reproduce such images for tourist consumption, with the articulation of alternative views seen as not only politically dangerous but economically irrational. Balinese themselves have also become subjects of a representational regime that defines appropriate touristic subjectivity through campaigns such as the New Order-era Sapta Pesona, "The Seven Charms/Seductions," which exhorted Balinese to be clean (bersih), friendly (ramah), orderly (tertib), beautiful (indah), safe (aman), preservationist (lestari), and memorable (kenangan) to maintain their ability to attract tourists.[14] Through such discourses tourism became an instrument of state control, with Balinese admonished not to protest against injustices nor to call public attention to histories of violence because a fickle tourist audience might be watching, ready to depart for a more peaceful paradise island. Tourism has attempted to cover up violence with layers of alluring images, at the same time as it often literally covers up traumatic history, as in the case of one five-star, 500-dollar-a-night beachfront resort in Seminyak, South Bali, whose lushly landscaped grounds are known by the local community (but not, of course, by the vast majority of its guests) to cover a mass grave containing victims of 1965–1966.[15] Indeed, one of the many ironies of 1965–1966 is that survivors of the violence who were marked as linked to communism and thus were barred from obtaining the official "letter of good behavior" (surat kelakuan baik) and "letter of noninvolvement in the PKI's September 30th Movement" (surat keterangan bebas G-30-S-PKI) required for most salaried employment were often forced into the informal economic sector. Many survivors who began by selling trinkets to tourists or by offering them massages on the beach in the early 1970s when mass tourism began have ended up deeply invested in the industry and thus have a serious economic incentive to censor their own memories. While anthropologists often position themselves as external to or critical of this tourist economy of images, ethnographic representations of Bali that disregard its legacies of violence often fit all too comfortably with tourist and state visions of peaceful, apolitical, "well-behaved" Balinese. Ethnographic representations taken up and used to authorize the economic and political projects of tourism help to shape the limits and possibilities of what can be said in and about Bali.

The failure of the majority of the extensive area studies literature on Bali to address the violence and its aftermath has not, however, simply resulted from a willful uncaring about Balinese suffering or a theoretical and ethnographic gaze that rests more comfortably elsewhere. Indeed, if it did, it might be far more straightforward to challenge. Scholarly inattention has no doubt worked to strengthen the Indonesian state's long-standing resolve to remain silent on its own implication in the violence and on the continuing pain it has engendered, but it has been motivated by a complex set of causes. Foreign scholars' concerns have ranged from the pragmatic fear of losing hard-won government permission to

conduct important research to encompassment by the habitual ways of understanding Bali that have built up over a century of academic production. Silences
have been rendered easier—even "locally sensitive"—by the fact that under the
New Order regime, a "clean environment" letter certifying one's lack of leftist
family ties was required of Indonesian university scholars, who often served as
research sponsors and assistants for foreign anthropologists and steered them away
from matters considered dangerously political. A reluctance to engage with matters
of violence has also, ironically, been supported by narratives of concern for the
tenuous and troubling situation of victims of violence in the years following 1965–
1966, in which scholarly silence is presumed the most appropriate way of protecting the communities with which one works. Commonplace anthropological
practices of offering pseudonyms to one's informants or of disguising place names
and identifiable incidents here shade into a more general hesitancy to speak of
dangerous matters or to see the powers that may take strength from such silences.
Even those willing to acknowledge the place of violence face a more general challenge in that anthropology, as a rule, has found it difficult to engage with what
seem to be absences, rather than easily accessible and narratable presences. In part,
this is a methodological issue: it is much easier, and seems to make much more
common sense, to ask people about what they remember of the past than about
what they have come—or decided, or been forced—to forget. Yet this approach
has implications both theoretical and ethical: a failure to think through the politics
of silence has meant that the anthropological literature offers far more sophisticated understandings of how people enact practices of history making, memory,
or commemoration than of how they engage in forgetting and silence. In the case
of 1965–1966, it means that scholarship has often elided its own reluctance to
speak about violence or its own privileging of familiar narrative forms of history
telling, with the conclusion that Balinese also do not concern themselves with
such things.

   While acknowledging that many Balinese have spoken—generally in contexts
they deem nonpublic and "safe"—about the violence, my primary focus in this
essay is on how terror has been articulated less through direct speech than through
non-narrative practices including ritual, magic, community politics, and gender
relations. I argue that far from being definitively past, the events of 1965–1966
continue to channel and block possibilities for speech, social action, and political
agency in Bali. Yet at the same time as I highlight how 1965–1966 still saturates
the islands social, cultural, and political landscape, I also explore the theoretical,
methodological, and political challenges of including ethnographies of silence and
forgetting in our approaches to the aftermath of violence. Posing anthropology's
desire to locate and excavate sites of memory—often assumed to be staging
grounds for liberatory challenges to official histories and repressive silences—
against Balinese practices of concealment, suppression, and redirection, I show
how a dialectic of social remembering and forgetting reworks relations of power
and provides a means of ensuring a continuing coexistence in communities in
which the lines dividing "perpetrators" from "victims" have been highly blurred
and in which particular versions of the past have become commodities of touristic
value. I conclude with a brief consideration of concepts of reconciliation, arguing

that a reliance on models that privilege truth telling, confession, and linear historical narrative may fail to account for local experiences of living in the wake of mass
violence and genocide.

Powers of Speech and Silence

To express something of the ways in which 1965–1966 shifted the discursive
topography of Bali, I first tell a story. Although I present it in the form of a
narrative, it is a story marked with silences, one that refers to the powers of the
unsaid and to memory's ambivalent relationship to discourse. As the story of one
of the women I noticed the first time I entered my colleague's family compound,
it speaks to both the visibility and the concealment of violent history in everyday
Balinese relations. Parts of this story were told to me by its subject, Ibu Ari, and
parts I pieced together from other people's tales and from what I have seen and
heard of how people speak and stay silent. Although it shows how people are not
simply silenced by the state or by the pain of the past, this story does not exist
spoken in the form I write it here, as a concise oral history, a point that is crucial
to understanding both its power and its limits. By focusing here on one woman's
experiences during and after 1965–1966, I do not claim to portray a representative
victim of the violence. Indeed, one of the key insights I gleaned from this and
other Balinese stories is that violence does not necessarily lead to solidarity, a
collective memory, or a shared subjectivity or political position among those it
affects (Das 2000). Instead, violence often fragments communities and casts social
interactions into tense configurations. What Ibu Ari's story offers, however, is a
detailed account of the complexities and ambiguities that constitute much of what
it means in Bali to live after attempts to annihilate life.

Ibu Ari was a new bride in December 1965 when a group of nationalist
paramilitaries entered her family home and took her husband and her younger
brother away, never to return. Soon after these two men disappeared, another one
came to see her: Bli Made, a neighbor and village leader of the anticommunist
Indonesian Nationalist Party (Partai Nasionalis Indonesia, or PNI), who was
rumored to have had his eye on Ibu Ari for years. No one in the family compound
dared deny Bli Made entrance that afternoon when he marched in wearing the
heavy boots of a soldier, accompanied by half a dozen of his thugs and saying he
was there to carry out an "inspection" (periksa), searching for proof of the family's
communist allegiances. That afternoon, the "proof" they were searching for was a
hammer and sickle tattoo, said to have been drawn by women sympathetic to the
communist cause on their vaginas, thighs, or lower abdomens. When he ordered
Ibu Ari to climb up the ladder to her family's rice barn, followed her up, and
closed the door behind them, no one, they now say, could move or speak or see
anything but their feet for the hour until the door opened again. And when Ibu
Ari came down from the rice barn clutching her batik cloth across her breasts, she
said nothing, and her family never asked. "We knew that she couldn't tell us what
happened," says one of her cousins, a woman a few years younger than Ibu Ari.

"How could we speak of it? Death we could speak of; death was different. Even if we were afraid, death was something ordinary. But 'inspecting' women, who could speak of it? We were afraid of the words themselves."

Ibu Ari still says nothing about that afternoon, only shakes like a tree in a storm if someone mentions Bli Made, who now appears regularly on television after having become a member of Bali's provincial legislature in 1999. Ibu Ari does not speak about it, but many in the family remember what no one knows happened or not, so they say nothing when suddenly, in the midst of the daily women's work of weaving ritual offerings, Ibu Ari will sometimes start speaking to no one they can see or hear, gripping her hands together in front of her chest, closing her eyes and rocking back and forth with the motions often used by women in trance to welcome deities into their bodies. Behind her back, though, they say that Ibu Ari Is crazy, the kind of crazy, maybe, that happens when an unquiet history returns to inhabit the present.

"But what else could have been done?" Ibu Ari asks. Two years after her brother and husband disappeared she went with a group of women relatives to consult a balian peluasan, or spirit medium, who she hoped could tell her where the bodies had been buried. She could not, she felt, tell the medium that the men had certainly been killed—that would have immediately and openly identified her as coming from a family of alleged communists—so she said that their deaths had been salahpati, "wrongful deaths" that arise from suicide or accident, the kinds of deaths that might result in a missing body. She knew it was wrong to say this: It is no suicide when you have no power to resist, is it? And is it an accident, she asks, when someone—someone who has had their eye on you for a long time—comes one day and takes you away from your family, showing less mercy than one might show a dog? The medium told Ibu Ari where to look for the bodies, but she never found them; she speculates that maybe the medium guessed the truth behind her he and lied to her "for politics," or maybe that her own diverted speech detoured the medium on her path to the truth. Whatever the case, she recounts how with no bodies to cremate, she and the other widows in the family went to their village graveyard one quiet night in 1968 and took some earth home to shape into effigies of bodies (adegan), which they then wrapped in white cloth. Standing in front of the gates to the family compound, they called out softly to the spirits of their family members to come home and inhabit the effigies, which they then cremated secretly, without the usual acknowledgment and assistance of the hamlet (banjar) association. These were proper cremation ceremonies, she insists, with seven kinds of holy water and a complete set of offerings, but she admits that after they were over, she still did not feel "satisfied" (puas) in her heart. She had done everything she could, but were the pedanda (Brahmana priests) from the Parisadha Hindu Dharma Indonesia, the official Hindu body of the state Department of Religious Affairs, right about what they were saying in the years following the violence, that it was the purification of the soul that made a cremation real, not the material body? Now, she says, she believes that the priests' pronouncements were political, part of the state's attempt to hide what really happened by denying the importance of the bodies of the missing. But back then, when the world was so confused, how could she know? After all, she was no Brahmana who might know such things. And who could she trust to answer her doubts about a ritual that had been carried out in secret, for men who were now said by the government, in its official comments on 1965, to have been atheists out to destroy religion and raise up the gods of Marx and Lenin?

There was so much in those days that was not spoken, she says. People used to talk about 1965 as the time when *ulian raos abuku matemahing pati* (you could die just because of a word). Spoken words are said in Bali to evoke actions, like the holy mantras of priests or the stories of shadow puppeteers that resonate across the visible (sekala) and the invisible (niskala) worlds, temporarily binding and directing energies, channeling the impersonal potency known as sakti that imbues the organic and inorganic universe. The word of a curse, spoken by the powerful, can bring illness or even death, and words can invest the inanimate—a mask, a jar of holy water—with taksu, or charisma. But in 1965 words became new kinds of triggers. Improperly articulated words—an insult never quite forgotten, coarse low Balinese language spoken to someone who thought they should have been addressed in refined high Balinese, flirting exchanges with someone else's wife— could return from the past to provoke horrifically exaggerated responses. A 15-year-old neighbor of Ibu Ari's who "talked too much" for some people's liking was corralled in a wicker cage used to transport pigs and then thrown into the river to drown. A man who witnessed his neighbor helping burn down someone's house called out in protest and the next day was dead. A woman food stall vendor whose welcoming small talk was heard as a promise saw her husband killed by her would-be suitor. And one word above all, communist, held the power to determine who lived and who died, a power no one word had ever been known to have before. Uttering the word communist, speakers shifted social assumptions: no longer did the powerful alone speak words of power, but the word itself, for those who dared to speak it in accusation, was imagined capable of saving one's own life and determining others' destinies. Heady, extraordinary, horrific; language became an unstable weapon in terrors fantastic arsenal, like a mythical keris-dagger blade loose in the hilt, which could slip and wound its bearer should the flow of battle turn backward. For as the word communist was wielded, it came to mean far more than one who had pledged to party membership or felt sympathy for the PKI's aims. As the ambitions of those who spoke it extended beyond the military mandate of "uprooting the PKI" to staking social claims, exacting revenge, or protecting themselves and their families in a treacherously shifting landscape, communist transmuted from a symbol of political affiliation in the narrow sense to an indexical sign marking the instability of knowledge and language themselves, and the impossibility of accurately reading another's signs in an opaque field of highly charged power relations. As another of Ibu Ari's cousins expressed it: "Today you call me a communist, tomorrow someone calls you a communist. Anyone could be a communist as long as someone was willing to name them as one."

Not only were words imbued with dangerous new potential but they also became disarticulated from the things they had been thought to represent: sentimen, an Indonesianized English word, was popularized in 1965 by army propagandists to refer to local affective ties, with people urged to sever their emotional bonds to root out communist evil in their families and villages. Jatah, an Indone-sian word meaning an allotment or quota, was used prior to 1965 to refer to the rations of kerosene, rice, and sugar given by the government to supplement civil servants' wages, or to the share of the rice earned by a hamlet harvesting society (*sekehe manyi*) that was distributed to each member. But as the killings got under-way a. jatah became the number of men a paramilitary group aimed to execute in a particular night—a gift from the state to those who served it, the fruit of one's cooperative labors, became one's gift to the state's vision of a new order through the violent dismemberment of the social body. And a periksa, or "inspection,"[16] an Indonesian word reeking of state authority and of efficient, top-down bureau-cracy, could enter the intimate space of one's family home or enact its control on a woman's body, bringing the state and its subjects into a terrifying new embrace as men like Bli Made claimed to be guarding the nation against what might be written—literally—on a woman's vagina. Even words like sibling or neighbor or friend turned slippery and treacherous, transformed into new hazards like inform-ers, collaborators, and provocateurs. And the emotions this speech engendered—the fear Ibu Ari's cousin speaks of as being "afraid of the words themselves"—grew so strong as to choke off streams of language and to channel meaning into silent forms.

This sense of the dangerous ambiguity inherent in everyday social interaction, and of the ability of words to conceal as well as to reveal intentions, was not new to Balinese. I interpret it as having drawn on and strengthened Balinese notions of fundamental social uncertainty that coalesce around the figure of the leak, a shape-changing sorcerer capable of causing illness or death. Although people may whisper their suspicion that a certain person is a leak—whispering so as not to anger the sorcerer—leak are not always identifiable, even to their most intimate relations. Among Ibu Ari's family it is often said that the most effective sorcerers are in fact those who prey on the people who worship at the same merajan temple as they do,[17] a merajan's congregation comprising those who share patrilineal descent from a common ancestor. The closeness of social relationships, which promises comfort and communication, thus also enables the possibility of treach-ery and harm. This understanding that relationships between neighbors like Bli Made and Ibu Ari, or even among members of the same family, could be shot through with suspicion and unknown intentions, was heightened by the military's propaganda in 1965, which called on people to uncover the hidden "enemy within the blanket" (musuh dalam selimut) in the service of destroying communism "down to its roots" (sampai ke akar-akarnya).

This newly forceful semiotics of terror perhaps explains why when Bli Made came back every few months after his "inspection" to ask Ibu Ari for money, she did not say anything, just sold what jewelry she had to keep up the payments. As a widow marked as "politically unclean" (tidak bersih lingkungart),[18] with no brother or husband to protect her, she was acutely vulnerable, painfully conscious of what actions a word of hers could evoke from him or what unwanted words from him any action of hers could set loose. But Ibu Ari's payments to Bli Made were part of an exchange that never quite managed to substitute money for memory—the memories of either party to the transaction or the memories of those who witnessed something, no one quite sure what, change hands. In the months and years that followed the inspection, Bli Made would sometimes see Ibu Ari at village temple ceremonies or in the nearby market, making her way through the crowd. Once she was within shouting distance, he would yell out to her, "Oh, you want that money I borrowed from you, don't you?" As the years passed, however, and new young toughs and political party configurations emerged to eclipse Bli Made's standing in the neighborhood,[19] and as the rumors multiplied about the number of women—and not only PKI-linked women—he had sexually harassed, abused, and threatened, his public calls to Ibu Ari began to sound, people said, more and more like the desperate pleas of a debtor and less like the boasts of an invulnerable assailant. Uttering words that reduced what had transpired between them to a loan of money, Bli Made was met by silence. Ibu Ari never responded with the language of a true woman trader, with marketplace banter, or with aggressive coaxing, and with that absence of language sent out signs that grew all too easy for others to interpret. Ibu Ari took on silence as a barricade, protecting herself from the pain of memory and from the possibility of inciting more violence on her. But even as she erected this wall she opened another door to memory, her own memory of just what karmic debt had been incurred in the rice barn, and the memories of her family and neighbors, which were elaborated from an image of a closed door into an imagination of what lay beyond it during that hour when no one dared to see. Her silence did not preclude semeiosis, involving as it did an awareness of relations of signification on the part of she who does not speak and an interpretation on the part of those who do not hear (see Daniel 1996:122). She was "muted," yet her muteness spoke memory.

Nor did Ibu Ari forget other things. She thought sometimes about her husband, whom she had never had a chance to grow close to after their arranged marriage, but she thought more often about her younger brother. "He was the one person in the world I could really talk with," she remembers. "We could tell each other everything, even if we didn't always agree" Ibu Ari had not, for instance, agreed with her brother's insistence that Balinese ritual should be simplified to take account of one's economic condition. This "Hindu rationalist" movement had grown popular in the early 1960s among the young leftist men of her family, who were high caste but poor in land and the hard currency that came with it. Their thinking had led to conflict among the family, especially after 1964, when Ibu Ari's uncle died and his PKI-member son and some other young leftist men, including Ibu Ari's brother, insisted that the family hold a simple cremation ceremony for him, arguing that the essence of the ritual, its practical effects of purifying the dead so that they may take their place among the divine ancestors and later reincarnate into the family, did not require the trappings of social hierarchy represented by a vast and expensive variety of ritual offerings. Most of the women of the family, including Ibu Ari, who were used to devoting their days to making offerings and organizing their use for family rituals, were uncomfortable, feeling that such a cremation would not only undermine the value of women's ritual expertise but would also surely evoke curses from their ancestors and shame the family socially. It was a measure of Ibu Ari's closeness with her brother that they could openly debate such matters of great importance to the family, with no need to gloss their disagreement with the careful language and etiquette indicative of a woman's deference to her male relatives. Indeed, it was the language they used—the coarse Balinese ci/ciang for "you/me"—that Ibu Ari references to remember their intimacy.

This relationship with her beloved brother was cut short by his disappearance, but even then, the tie was not completely severed:

> We were so close, so very close. So close that when he died that after-noon, when he was killed, who knows where, nobody knew the place, that same night he came looking for me. He called out to me three times. I had already fallen asleep over there, next to that small coconut tree. Already he was looking for me. We were so close. He would tell me everything. If he spoke to our older brother once a day, he would speak to me ten times. He had left his watch behind. The day he died, his first son was just 42 days old, it was the day of his dedinan [infancy] ceremony. He said to me [about the child], "Later, when he's grown, don't forget about him. It doesn't matter if you have nothing to eat, you must give him the food from your own mouth, for this child who still lives." He told me to sell the watch to pay for the dedinan cere-mony. Three times he came to me, coming back and forth, telling me, "Remember, remember, remember." I was so shocked. I didn't know that he was dead until the next day, when someone came to tell us he had been killed. They never told us where the place was where he had died, just that he was dead. He told me to remember.

As the years passed and Suharto's New Order continued its project of history making, characterizing the men who died in 1965 as communists willing to under-mine family, religion, and state in pursuit of evil aims and erasing from national discourse the sexual assaults on women said to be wanton destroyers of society itself, Ibu Ari continued to receive visits from her brother. Often he would just greet her and then depart, but sometimes he would give her instructions about family ritual matters. These instructions had little to do with his former stance in favor of simplifying and rationalizing religious ritual—a stance later glossed by the state as communist atheism—but instead directed Ibu Ari to make additions to the offerings she was preparing to make them more complete. That her brother, who had exhibited little interest while alive in the women's work of offering mak-ing, was now instructing her in ritual procedure did not appear odd to Ibu Ari; she was aware that once a spirit entered the realms of the dead he or she could change in character. Indeed, in the early 1970s, when Ibu Ari was among a group of women visiting a spirit medium to inquire as to who had reincarnated in a child of the family, it was she who was addressed by name through the medium with the voice of her PKI cousin, who before his death in 1965 had caused so much controversy in the family by arguing that his own father should be cremated simply. This cousin, Ibu Ari said, told her that he had changed, that he was now a woman, and exhorted her, as her brother had, to "remember."

Perhaps it was the strength of Ibu Ari's nostalgia for an imagined time before the violence when she believed language could serve as a means of intimacy, rather than as an implement of social fragmentation, that kept the door open between her and her brother. Perhaps it was Ibu Ari's desire to be free of the stain of communism with which the state had smeared her family that led her to hear her brother as having been religiously rehabilitated, worthy of a return to history. Perhaps it was her vulnerability as a widow that left her prey to people like Bli Made that evoked in her a desire for protection from her own patriline in the spirit of her brother or, conversely, her struggle to maintain women's centrality to ritual practice that caused her to voice her brother's instructions as authoritative. But these are all anthropological attempts to come to terms with the uncanny, to strip it of its mystery. Ibu Ari herself is not interested in such explanations. Whatever the reason—and how, she asks, could the living ever really know what goes on in the realms of the dead?—even after the secret ceremony that should have freed Ibu Ari's brother from his worldly ties and allowed him to move toward reincarnation, he still visited Ibu Ari. The last visit she described took place in 2003, when she went with her family to a major ceremony at the Pura Dalem Puri, a temple associated with death rituals near the Besakih temple complex. In the midst of a crowd of hundreds, Ibu Ari felt a pair of hands descend on her shoulders. Not knowing who had touched her, she called out questioningly, "Bapak?"—the formal Indonesian term of address for a man, the word one might use to speak to a government bureaucrat, a soldier, or a stranger. She heard a voice chide her in low Balinese: "Who are you calling 'Bapak'? Don't you [ci] know me [ciang]? Have you forgotten already?" No, Ibu Ari replied, she still remembered.

Madness and Unconscripted Memory

Listening closely to the story of Ibu Ari—and to the silences that are so much a part of it—we can, if we are so inclined, identify elements of the heroic. By refusing to speak with Bli Made, Ibu Ari refused to occupy the space that his talk of borrowing and paying back allotted her: the space of one owed a debt that could be satisfied, a space from which closure on past losses is possible. In her silences and their significations Ibu Ari expresses the persistence of memory, its ability, despite the pain and terror it evokes, to circumvent the treacherous realm of language and to find a social existence, no matter how tenuous and fragmentary. Speaking with her dead brother, and in the maintenance of memory she pledges to him, Ibu Ari recasts official state narratives of 1965 that would silence the dead and their families and preclude mourning for those disappeared and exiled from national belonging. By articulating her positions through ritual practice, rather than by attempting to express her suffering through a more straightforwardly referential speech, she bypasses some of the potential dangers of language in the aftermath of terror, rooting herself in a realm of religion that can also protect her from accusations of "atheist communism." But these moments of potential defiance, when she will not accept dominant narratives of truth ("what really happened") or of memory (as subordinate to state history or the erasures attempted by the

perpetrators of violence), are precisely when Ibu Ari finds herself most marginalized. Even as her silences and her speech position themselves against power, they
deprive her of a stable place within a community of victims—showing up the
fragile fictions on which such a notion of social coherence rests in post-1965 Bali.
Her own family cannot break down the door of her silence to incorporate her
pain into a collective narrative of suffering, and in her speech they find signs of
madness.

Ibu Ari knows that there are those who think she is crazy, but she shrugs it
off with a dismissive laugh. "Let them think I'm crazy. They don't hear my brother
speak; I do," she explains. But if Ibu Ari holds on to her experience as its own
truth, incommensurable in its phenomenological and historical uniqueness, it is
this specificity that others critically engage as they characterize her as mad. Her
family insists that her madness could not be located in any particulars of her
history, in any painful experiences that she alone underwent, which might have
transformed her into someone who could speak with one who died violently. We
were all victims, they say, each with our own impossible tale, each with our own
unspeakable losses. All victims, but no one else they know speaks with the dead of
1965 in their waking hours, even if many hear the whisperings (pawisik) of deified
ancestors, or even unnamed gods, in their dreams, and many more are possessed
in trance by gods, who may themselves be long-ago ancestors, at temple ceremonies when the gods and the ancestors are called down to earth. All victims, but only
Ibu Ari gives voice to a victim whose death has not yet congealed into history,
who is neither a vilified enemy of the state nor a divine ancestor but someone far
more complexly present in everyday life. All victims, but only one woman whose
weighted silences and uncanny speech carve cracks into the family consciousness.
All victims, but Ibu Ari is the one who is crazy.

But if her family doubts Ibu Ari's sanity, they do not doubt that what she
experiences is real. In their eyes, hers is not a madness of delusion, a madness of
failing to grasp the reality of the world around her. Ibu Ari is mad, they say, but
it is not a madness that fills into any established categories. Indeed, one of the
most striking aspects of the talk concerning Ibu Ari's supposed madness is its
resistance to conscription. There seems to be no term in Balinese—a language not
lacking in descriptions of mental illnesses or in speculations as to their various
causes—that can comfortably encompass it. Asked to describe her madness, her
family members sift through and reject a series of typical Balinese diagnoses: it is
not the madness that afflicts victims of black magic or sorcery; it is not the madness that may occur when some ritual responsibility is overlooked and one is
cursed by one's ancestors; it is not the madness that is risked when someone
unwittingly disturbs one of the spirits inhabiting one's environment. Nor do they
describe Ibu Ari using the lexicon of modern psychology that has filtered into
popular Balinese culture through the Indonesian-language media: skizofrenia,
depresi, stres, trauma. Most often they describe her simply as gila, an Indonesian
word meaning "crazy" that is equally applicable to persons, mad dogs, or bizarre
situations, or as sinting, an Indonesian word that might best be translated as "not
quite all there." By using their second language, the formal national language of
Indonesian, the members of Ibu Ari's family distance not only Ibu Ari but also

her madness itself, placing it in a register that, if not exactly alien, remains far from intimate family speech. Yet even as they call her mad, they do not treat her as if she were suffering from a pathological illness. No one has ever suggested she seek a cure from a psychic healer or from a modern psychiatrist, as they have with a number of other family members afflicted with more easily classifiable mental illnesses. In fact, the reverse holds true: When Ibu Ari says that her brother has told her that the family must add specific offerings to the preparations for the family temple anniversary, or that they must seek out holy water from a particular temple to make a ceremony complete, her word is followed without question. For who knows what happens to those who have passed on through death, disappeared from a time when fundamental social certainties wavered and splintered? Even as it is excluded, Ibu Ari's madness returns to family practice—not quite all there, but not all elsewhere either.

Some members of the family who have witnessed Ibu Ari speaking to her brother in what appears to them as a state of trance have attempted to push her into a more familiar cultural framework, suggesting that she could perhaps herself become a spirit medium, claiming social significance as a conduit through which the living can speak to the dead. They warn that someone who has received the gift of the medium and refuses to accept it as a social role risks being cursed by the gods with madness, as can a psychic who shows arrogance in his or her personal power at the expense of acknowledging that this gift comes from the divine. Yet Ibu Ari insists that her experience is not the trance of a medium, but rather normal waking consciousness. She denies any agency in initiating this communication: her brother enters her everyday world; she does not purposely try to open a door to the unseen realm where he dwells. She rejects the idea of playing the public role of a medium, saying she has no desire for such power. She speaks with her brother, the only person she could ever really speak with, and she has no interest in speaking with others or their dead. Ibu Ari knows that many psychics repeatedly refuse to take up a social role before finally acquiescing to the unceasing demands of the divine, but she claims that there is no possibility of changing her mind. After all, she adds, who would consult a psychic who was known to have communist ties? And were her ability to speak with the dead made public, would people start talking again about what she wished them to forget: That she was the widow and the sister of men who had been marked as communist? And would they try to force open the closed door of the rice barn, to put into language what had become for her and her family a silence weighted with ambiguous memory and ambivalent forgetting? The politics of speaking, even with the dead, are, Ibu Ari knows, treacherous indeed.

It is here, at the nexus of one woman's experience and the traumatic history her family members imagine themselves to share—to share, especially, after the fact, as they all, young and old, men and women, sympathetic or disinterested in the aims of the PKI, were marked by the state as sharing an "unclean environment"—that madness is identified. Ibu Ari is considered mad not because her behavior or the state of mind that people attribute to her can be fit into what they know of madness, but precisely because it cannot be clearly diagnosed. Although Ibu Ari is considered by her family to be one of a community of victims who have experienced similar suffering, her madness refuses a place in shared knowledge or practice, as it unsettles awareness about what can be shared. Private speech challenges collective memory, violent disappearance evokes an uncanny presence, and language grows alien and inexact as it flows through the figure of the woman searched for signs of communism. Ibu Ari's speech engages an absence familiar to all members of her family, each of whom acknowledges the deaths of loved ones during 1965, but it does not become an allegory of communal loss, a public lament of mourning, memory, and recovery.

Thinking with Silences

Models that hold silence to be simply the absence of speech, or forgetting the absence of memory, promise a relatively straightforward engagement with the aftereffects of mass violence. Operating within such frameworks, the scholar has only to wield questions about the past as tools in an excavatory process in which speech is recovered from silence and memory is released from forgetting, these absences left to the side like earth that has given up its buried artifacts. The work may be slow and painful, touching as it does on the fragments of terror still embedded in selves and society, but the main challenges are technical ones: reaching truths, recognizing references, and placing responses within a cultural and political context that can render the unthinkable subject to sense. Yet in reflecting on the silences that obtain in the wake of 1965–1966, such models seem insufficient. Keeping the experiences of Ibu Ari and other survivors of 1965–1966 in mind, I offer a brief consideration of some of the complexities of the engagement with silences, touching on several key concerns that may resonate across other contexts of genocide and mass violence.

One of the most pressing questions many scholars of violence face is that of the ineffability of terror, its presumed inability to be fully expressed and understood through the limited medium of language. While a number of artists, theorists, and memoirists have noted their own inability to capture extreme violence in words, Scarry has perhaps gone furthest in asserting the generic nature of pain's resistance to language, arguing that the experience of torture, rather than provoking a confessional flood of truth, in fact blocks its narration, reverting the tortured to a primordial, prelinguistic state of inarticulate embodiment (1985). In a similar vein—albeit one far more attuned to the specificities of sociopolitical location—E. Valentine Daniel describes how Sri Lankan torture victims may find it impossible not only to voice their own suffering but to hear the truth of pain in the words of others (1996). Such phenomena, Michael Taussig suggests, demand that the engaged scholar "write against terror" in a way that combats the oppressive power of silence without reproducing the reductive rationality of didactic speech that claims to have encompassed the causes and effects of extreme violence; or, as he phrases it, in a way that can "penetrate the veil while retaining its hallucinatory quality" (1987:10).

Writing in the aftermath of terror in Bali, such concerns about the relations of silence and speech to violence are highly relevant. The violence of 1965–1966 has produced silences both among Balinese and among those who author representations of them, and the events spoken of often seem to exceed language's ability to capture their chilling experiential reality. Neither Ibu Ari nor her cousin—"afraid of the words themselves"—could turn Bli Made's act of terror into narrative. Yet I argue that silence is neither a natural response to physical or psychic pain nor a blunt barrier blocking the analyst—or those people who share a social space in the wake of terror—from full description and comprehension. Silence, like speech, is a cultural and political creation that takes place in particularly contoured settings, with certain interlocutors—or eavesdroppers, or informants—in earshot or mind. As Rosalind Shaw reminds us, "there are different kinds of silence" (2006:89), and each may perform particular cultural and political tasks. The interplay of silence and speech may sketch spaces of fear, secrecy, and suspicion, with the urgency of such mapping intensified in settings of violence. Speech, like silence, can conceal, accuse, and redirect, while silence, like speech, can have semiotic effects, making silences never purely monochrome, any more than speech can be strictly monologic. Ibu Ari could not tell me (likely because she could not be certain how her words would then be transmitted), but I heard it whispered by others in the family that perhaps the reason 1965 sparked a strange kind of madness in her was that it was one of her own cousins who informed on her brother as part of a plan to claim his rice land. Her own silence about this matter—and her relatives' ability to send tendrils of gossip about it through their local networks in a way they could not about her experience in the rice barn—marked a different kind of political claim than that staked by her silence at Bli Made's offer of "compensation."

Fieldwork, of course, participates in such contexts, often without realizing it. This makes it crucial not to mistake a reluctance to speak to the anthropologist for a more general absence of memory or voice, an issue that cannot be resolved by reference to such notions as rapport. Given this, I suspect that "penetration" is not the most apt of metaphors for engaging with the silences that have emerged in the wake of violence in Bali. Even if we ignore its masculinist and militarist presumptions, silence is not an even fog barricading events and emotions from view, but a variegated landscape that Balinese navigate with what knowledge and caution they can muster, sometimes drawing on local notions of how speech is channeled and dammed and sometimes moving blindly, the certainty that one can find direction on a shifting social topography undermined in the experience of terror. By describing some of the shapes, textures, and motions of Balinese silences, and the cultural and political relations in which they are enmeshed, I hope to question analytic binaries that hold speech and silence, memory and forgetting, expression and its repression, in rigid opposition, pointing toward the more complex and politically fraught processes of semiosis that have emerged in the aftermath of 1965.

Another question raised by placing forgetting and silence within one's analytic purview is that of the relationships between what took place during 1965–66 and contemporary Balinese lives. How does one know, in the frequent absence of explicit statements to that effect, that phenomena are connected, that what emerges in the present can be traced back to violence in the past? To take but one example of what I mean, I remember being struck by the intensity of a debate over another elderly woman, a cousin of Ibu Ari's. The discussion flared up around whether her foot, which was to be amputated due to an infection exacerbated by uncontrolled diabetes, should be saved to later be cremated with the rest of her body on her death. Family members educated in a modernist Balinese Hindu theology that sees the coarse material body (awak) as separate from and subordinate to the soul (atma) argued that this was not only unnecessary but disgustingly unhygienic and backward. She and others less influenced by contemporary theological claims insisted that a body lacking wholeness would follow her into her next incarnation. This debate was, I thought, "about" a number of things: Competition among divergent religious interpretations and resistance by an older generation to a state-sponsored, rationalist Hinduism; the pain and stress felt by a woman whose poverty and thus lack of access to decent medical care in part derived from her family's supposed association with the Communist Party; and an attempt by a woman known as a respected ritual expert to claim authority both over religious practice and over what little—her body, her death, her movement through cycles of reincarnation—she could, at least partially, call her own. Yet the anxiety surrounding this topic also seemed to me to parallel the feeling with which that same woman had told me stories of nationalist paramilitaries dismembering alleged communists and placing their body parts about her village; entrails on the victim's doorstep and limbs marking the village's boundaries. Such stories in turn seemed to evoke, in grotesque parody, the manipulation of a Balinese ritual animal sacrifice (caru), in which the parts of a chicken or of another animal are ordered in space according to the Balinese compass points. And all this seemed to fit with tales I heard spoken in the intimate whispers of family gossip about the karmic consequences of violence said to work through the body, including that of the former paramilitary member known for hacking his victims apart whose child was later born with stumps as arms and legs.

To me such connections seemed reasonable, and I took them both as indications of the hold the events of 1965–1966 continued to have on Balinese lives and as a reminder to look for violence not simply in purposeful physical harm or in straightforward recollections of it. Yet I also wanted to understand how the connections I was drawing differed from those this woman and her family articulated, and how all our historical diagnoses took place within a power-charged field in which making links to the violence is often perceived as a dangerous endeavor. In such settings, the challenge for the analyst becomes placing people's utterances about a violent past within frameworks both of sense making and of silence, neither reducing the present to mere reproductions of the past nor engaging in a shallow neofunctionalism that locates the pasts meaning, power, and relevance solely in present concerns (Shaw 2002; Trouillot 1995). Such analyses run interpretive risk, but it is only by attempting to trace links between the past and the present, by attending to how silence blocks the emergence of certain conclusions and enables the articulation of others, that we can avoid the ahistoric and apolitical stance taken by many observers of Bali, who see "Balinese culture" as an unproblematic category, with the violence standing as an aberrant occurrence, reassuringly enclosed by historical remove.

Yet perhaps the most important question surrounding silence in Bali is that of its ethics and politics. The questions of why not only outside observers of Bali but Balinese themselves have frequently remained silent on the matter of 1965–1966, and what is the continuing relevance of the violence for Balinese life, are closely entangled with the question of what it means for me—or anyone else concerned with these issues—to probe into the shapes and textures that silences take. Clearly, an analysis of, say, a Balinese temple ritual that sought to debunk its assumptions and expose it as mere mystification or trickery would be received in most quarters as highly problematic. Yet anthropology's long tradition of relativistic neutrality on matters of belief, which has often complicated activist positions, has rarely extended to silences, which are often assumed, following the convergent models of psychoanalysis, juridical witnessing, and Christian confessionalism, to result from powerful structures of repression whose dismantling promises empowerment: "But only say the word and you shall be healed." That silence itself may offer certain forms of agency that are not simply the absence of speech, that it may be striated with a more complex politics than merely a cowed acquiescence to power, has remained an underexplored possibility. If, however, we understand something of the specific social and political relations that give rise to silences—which in Bali include not only engagements with a repressive state, an overwhelmingly ignorant or indifferent international community, and a tourism industry that commodities the erasure of violence from images of Bali but also everyday practices of living within families and communities fractured by betrayals, complicities, or suspicions—it is not at all clear that breaking the silence constitutes a sure route to liberation. Certainly Ibu Ari does not see it as such. Here I caution not simply that asking people to speak risks exposing them to the psychic pain of memory—although that is an issue for which anthropologists have often been unprepared. Indeed, such concerns must be weighed against the patronism they often imply and against the way in which they tend to paint survivors of violence as uniformly delicate victims to be approached with clinical care.[20] Ibu Ari is willing to speak of pieces of her past, and to let that speech evoke accusations of madness, to keep her commitments to memory and truth. I do, however, wish to stress that to the extent that silence arises as a response to political risk, as a tactic to ensure that new violence does not erupt within families and communities among whom memory remains poignantly present, or simply as a way to attract desired tourist dollars, attempts to excavate the remains of violence in the service of social healing or activist truth telling cannot constitute a straightforward endeavor. If I began this essay with an anecdote of questioning absence that risks being read as a classically heroic ethnographic tale of discovery, insight, and exposure, I hope to end it by urging a more complex consideration of the ethics of speech and silence and of the ramifications of how we write about them.

Rethinking our approaches to silence, and questioning analytic binaries that pose it in sharp opposition to speech, has much more than academic significance. Since the fall of Suhartos dictatorship Indonesians have wrestled with concepts of reconciliation and have begun a process—slowly, and hampered by a reluctant state—to put a National Truth and Reconciliation Commission in place (see Agung Putri 2003; Zurbuchen 2001). Most calls for reconciliation at the national level have advocated models laid out in South Africa, whose Truth and Reconciliation Commission encouraged victims of human rights abuses to speak publicly of their experiences in the service of national "healing." Yet stories like Ibu Ari's offer caution that such processes may be less than straightforward in Bali. Speaking memories of violence does not simply place one in relation to a distant past but also engages with a complex politics of the present and its articulation and concealment in social practice. A truth commission's work in Bali could not be expected to bring closure to the past—to the extent that such a possibility ever exists—but rather will open new challenges as Balinese rethink what it means to speak of and to power.

Notes

My research in Bali has been carried out in collaboration with the Balinese anthropologist Degung Santikarma. I gratefully acknowledge the support I have received from a John D. and Catherine T. MacArthur Foundation Research and Writing grant (2000, 2001), an H. F. Guggenheim Foundation grant (2003–2004), a grant from the Haverford College Faculty Research Fund (2005), and a grant from the United States Institute of Peace (2005–2007). For intellectual inspiration and support as I worked through the ideas in this essay, I thank Degung Santikarma, Alex Hinton, John Roosa, Gung Ayu Ratih, Hildred Geertz, Anita Isaacs, Rob Lemelson, Diyah Larasati, and Dag Yngvesson. I also thank the anonymous reviewers for Duke University Press for their comments.

1. The exact number of Indonesians killed is unknown and will likely remain so, despite recent efforts at fact-finding by victims' advocacy groups such as the Yayasan Penelitian Korban Pembantaian (Foundation for Research on the Victims of Massacre). Estimates have ranged from around three hundred thousand deaths to as many as three million, with a figure of one million frequently cited in academic and journalistic accounts of the violence. The politics of numbering the dead is, of course, far from straightforward, speaking both to the state's desire to block access to nonofficial historical research and to activists' desires to ground calls for attention to the violence in statistical claims of its significance. It is important to note, however, that while the extent of the suffering wrought by the violence of 1965–1966 should be undeniable, survivors often locate its import not in its scope but in its intimacy, not in its manageable facticity but in its destabilizing incomprehensibility, not in its right to a place in the annals of the twentieth century's greatest tragedies but in its continuing power to inflect possibilities for living in the present. Gyanendra Pandey discusses a comparable politics of enumerating the deaths that occurred during the partition of British India in 1947, suggesting that such "extravagant, expandable, unverifiable but credible" (2001:91) statistics function to obscure the social production of history and its qualities of rumor. For more on the challenges of estimating the death toll in 1965–1966, see Cribb 1001.

2. Robinson 1995, based on research carried out while Suharto was still in power, gives an estimate of 80,000 deaths in Bali. Activists conducting fact-finding projects after Suharto's resignation have estimated the figure to be closer to 100,000.

3. The major—and until recently, only—exception is Geoffrey Robinson's (1995) important work on twentieth-century Balinese politics, which includes a substantial discussion of the events leading up to the violence of 1965–1966 and an analysis of the patterns it took. Since then a handful of works discussing 1965–1966 in Bali have been published, including Darma Putra 2003 on the politics of Balinese literature in the years prior to the violence; Parker 2003, chapter 4, on memories of 1965–1966; Dwyer 2004 on the gender politics of the violence and its aftermath: and Dwyer and Santikarma 2003, 2007 on the cultural and political landscape of post-1965 Bali. For an overview of recent work on 1965–1966 elsewhere in Indonesia, see Zurbuchen 2002.

4. In his popular history of Bali, Adrian Vickers writes: "Understandably, few Balinese want to relive this time in conversation and most, like survivors of other conflicts, prefer to block it out of their memories" (1989:172). Graeme MacRae echoes this characterization: "Most people in Ubud [Bali] who remember this era prefer not to think or, at least, not to talk about it" (2003:44).

5. The national high school and junior high school textbooks were revised in 1999 after the fall of Suharto's dictatorship to include a brief statement that the history of 1965 is debated by historians. The high school textbooks also include a new section presenting differing theories about the alleged coup and about whether it really was carried out by the PKI. The textbooks still do not make mention of the violence against alleged communists.

6. From Berata 2002. On the contrast between the Indonesian state and international media's responses to the Bali bombings and to the violence of 1965–66, see Santikarma 2004.

7. For more on the events of September 30, 1965, see Anderson and McVey 1971; Cribb 1990; Crouch 1978. For an overview of the events in Bali, see Robinson 1995. For an examination of the cultural and political repercussions of the violence in Bali, see Dwyer 2004; and Dwyer and Santikarma 2003, 2007. For discussions of the important place that 1965 as history, imaginary, and threat has held in state discourse and in public culture, see Anderson 1994; Pemberton 1994; Siegel 1998; Steedly 1993; Shiraishi 1997; Heryanto 1999.

8. While the international media at the time tended to describe the killings as an irrational outburst of primitive emotion, describing "orgies" of bloodshed and a "frenzy" of anticommunist fervor (the Pulitzer Prize winner John Hughes's book on 1965, *Indonesian Upheaval*, recently reissued as *The End of Sukarno: A Coup That Misfired; A Purge That Ran Wild* (2003 [1967]), offers perhaps the best example of this sensationalist genre), state accounts instead stressed the savage excess of the left, framing military and civilian violence against alleged communists as the careful, calculated, and justified enactment of bureaucratic rationality on those who had forfeited claims to citizenship.

9. Honna 2001 details how Indonesian military ideology framed and refrained the notion of communism from 1966 to 1998 to address changing "threats" to its power, ranging from pro-democracy activism to globalization. Heryanto 1999 discusses the deployment of and resistances to the term communist under the New Order. Despite the fall of Suharto's dictatorship, anticommunist rhetoric continues to be used in Indonesia in attempts to effect various political ends. To take only a few examples: In Java, some Islamist groups have gained support for their agendas by evoking an "atheist" communist genealogy to contemporary secularist movements; in Bali, a labor strike against a tourist facility was followed by the "mysterious" appearance of posters tacked to walls and trees warning against a potential resurgence of communism; in Jakarta, in preparation for an interview for a permanent resident visa at the U.S. embassy, my husband was required to be interviewed by the local police, who interrogated him from a standard set of questions

that referred, among other matters, to his family's political affiliations in 1965—a new level of surveillance made possible by U.S. funds for the Indonesian police to enlist in the so-called war on terror.

10. For a discussion of romantic conceptions of the Balinese desa adat, or customary law village, see Warren 1993.

11. One notable exception to the tendency of this earlier generation of anthropologists to bracket violence is H. Geertz 1991, in which the author discusses a "ritual drama" performed in 1947 that involved the communal beating and torture of a group of men arrested for their participation in the anticolonial movement and for their rejection of the political authority of the traditional Kingdom of Gianyar, which had allied itself with the Dutch. Geertz argues that rather than reproducing or enacting harmony among Balinese and between humans and the unseen world, as so many other observers of Balinese ritual have argued, Balinese ritual drama has "agonistic violence at its core" (1991:180).

12. Robinson 1995 makes a similar critique of classical scholarship in Bali.

13. For a discussion of how related concepts of tourism and politics operate in Ubud, the Balinese village that reinvented itself in the 1950s as Bali's "center of art and culture," see MacRae 2003.

14. For a discussion of how tourism and state developmentalism have shaped discourses of Balinese culture in the service of state control, see Santikarma 2001.

15. Much of the work of the small group of advocates for the rights of victims of 1965–1966 in Bali has consisted of trying to identify mass graves from 1965–1966. Hopes for exhuming the bodies they contain are slim, however. Such land is considered by Balinese to be tenget—spiritually "hot" or "contaminated"—and thus unfit for Balinese to inhabit or cultivate. Much of this land was therefore sold to non-Balinese or, in South Bali, used to build tourism facilities, meaning that any attempt to find what lies beneath the ground would most likely face serious opposition from the owners of what now lies above the ground. As one activist reminded us: "Tourism is big business, big money. If you take on tourism, the next thing you know you're a communist, and the corrupt aparat ('security apparatus,' military and police] make sure that you're buried as well."

16. Scholars of Indonesia reading my work have pointed out that the Indonesian noun for inspection should be pemeriksaan, not periksa. This is true; however, Balinese do not always speak Indonesian as they "should." Grammatically proper or not, Balinese identify periksa—both the word and the events—as emanating from the central Indonesian state.

17. Merajan is the term used by Bali's triwangsa ("three peoples") or upper-caste nobles. A non-triwangsa family would use the term sanggah.

18. The New Order's infamous "clean environment" (bersih lingkungatt) policy claimed that spouses, parents, siblings, children, and even grandchildren of those marked as communists were contaminated by "political uncleanliness" and thus to be barred from participation in government or civil society. Officially the policy applied only to those who were over 12 years old at the time of the violence, with the exception of younger children of those considered to be leaders of the PKI. In practice, however, entire families, especially if they lived together in family compounds, were often considered unclean for local political purposes. Relatives of alleged communists who themselves had never been charged with crimes were barred from obtaining the surat keterangan bebas G-30-S-PKI, or letter of noninvolvement in the PKI's September 30th Movement, a document necessary to obtain permission to join the vast government bureaucracy, to work in the media or in social welfare, or to obtain a university teaching position or scholarship.

19. By 1972 the New Order state had grown uneasy with the power that the PNI had gained as a result of its participation in the massacres of the PKI, and it began a

process of reconfiguring the political party landscape in which the PNI was banned and the government "functional group" Golkar was ensured dominance through the mandatory membership of the military, government officials, and vast national civil service.

20. I thank Gung Ayu Ratih for stressing this point in conversation, as well as in an unpublished paper authored with John Roosa on how we might rethink methodologies of oral history on 1965–1966 in Indonesia.

References

Agung Putri
2003   *Evading the Truth: Will a Truth and Reconciliation Commission Ever Be Formed?* Inside Indonesia 73. http://insideindonesia.org.

Anderson, Benedict
1994   *Language and Power: Exploring Political Cultures in Indonesia*. Ithaca, NY: Cornell University Press.

Anderson, Benedict R., and Ruth T. McVey, with Frederick P. Bunnell
1971   A Preliminary Analysis of the October 1, 1965, Coup in Indonesia. Ithaca, NY: Modern Indonesia Project, Cornell University.

Bateson, Gregory
1970   Bali: The Value System of a Steady State. In *Traditional Balinese Culture*. Jane Belo, ed. Pp. 384–401. New York: Columbia University Press.

Bateson, Gregory, and Margaret Mead
1942   *Balinese Character: A Photographic Analysis*. New York: New York Academy of Sciences.

Berata, Dewa
2002   The Kuta Tragedy and the Present-Day Bali (A Report by the Governor of Bali). Paper presented at the ASEAN +3 NTO meeting, Denpasar, Bali, December 11–12.

Cribb, Robert
2001   How Many Deaths? Problems in the Statistics of Massacre in Indonesia (1965–1966) and East Timor (1975–1980). In *Violence in Indonesia*. Ingrid Wessel and Georgia Wimhöfer, eds. Pp. 82–98. Hamburg: Abera.

Cribb, Robert, ed.
1990   *The Indonesian Killings of 1965–66: Studies from Java and Bali*. Clayton, Victoria: Centre of Southeast Asian Studies, Monash University.

Crouch, Harold
1978   *The Army and Politics in Indonesia*. Ithaca, NY: Cornell University Press.

Daniel, E. Valentine
1996   *Charred Lullabies: Chapters in an Anthropography of Violence*. Princeton, NJ: Princeton University Press.

Darma Putra, I Nyoman
2003   Reflections on Literature and Politics in Bali: The Development of Lekra, 1950–
1966. In *Inequality, Crisis, and Social Change in Indonesia: The Muted Worlds of Bali.*
Thomas Reuter, ed. Pp. 54–85. New York: Routledge Curzon.

Das, Veena
2000   The Act of Witnessing: Violence, Poisonous Knowledge, and Subjectivity. In *Violence and Subjectivity.* Veena Das, Arthur Kleinman, Mamphela Ramphele, and Pamela
Reynolds, eds. Pp. 205–225. Berkeley: University of California Press.

Dwyer, Leslie
2004   The Intimacy of Terror: Gender and the Violence of 1965–66 in Bali. Intersections: Gender, History, and Culture in the Asian Context (10)2. hltp://inter
sections.anu.edu.au.

Dwyer, Leslie, and Degung Santikarma
2003   "When the World Turned to Chaos": 1965 and Its Aftermath in Bali, Indonesia.
In *The Specter of Genocide: Mass Murder in Historical Perspective.* Ben Kiernan and Robert
Gellately, eds. Pp. 289–306. New York: Cambridge University Press.
2007   Speaking from the Shadows: Memories of Massacre in Bali. In *Mass Crime and
Post-Conflict Peacebuilding.* Beatrice Pouligny, Simon Chesterman, and Albrecht Schnabel,
eds. Pp. 190–215. Tokyo: United Nations University Press.

Geertz, Clifford
1973   *The Interpretation of Cultures: Selected Essays.* New York: Basic Books.

Geertz, Hildred
1991   A Theatre of Cruelty: The Contexts of a Topeng Performance. In *State and Society
in Bali: Historical, Textual, and Anthropological Approaches.* Hildred Geertz, ed. Pp. 165–
197. Leiden: KITLV Press.

Heryanto, Ariel
1999   Where Communism Never Dies; Violence, Trauma, and Narration in the Last
Cold War Capitalist Authoritarian State. *International Journal of Cultural Studies* 2(2):
147–177.

Hinton, Alexander Laban
2005   *Why Did They Kill? Cambodia in the Shadow of Genocide.* Berkeley: University of
California Press.

Honna, Jun
2001   Military Ideology in Response to Democratic Pressures during the Late Soeharto
Era: Political and Institutional Contexts. In *Violence and the State in Suharto's Indonesia.*
Benedict R. O'G. Anderson, ed. Ithaca, NY: Cornell Southeast Asia Program Publications.

Hughes, John
2003[1967]   *The End of Sukarno: A Coup That Misfired; A Purge That Ran Wild.* Singapore: Archipelago. [Originally published as *Indonesian Upheaval.*]

MacRae, Graeme
2003   Art and Peace in the Safest Place in the World: A Culture of Apoliticism in Bali. In *Inequality, Crisis, and Social Change in Indonesia: The Muted Worlds of Bali*. T. Reuter, ed. Pp. 30–53. New York: Routledge Curzon.

Pandey, Gyanendra
2001   *Remembering Partition: Violence, Nationalism, and History in India*. Cambridge: Cambridge University Press.

Parker, Lyn
2003   *From Subjects to Citizens: Balinese Villagers in the Indonesian Nation-State*. Copenhagen: Nordic Institute of Asian Studies.

Pemberton, John
1994   *On the Subject of "Java."* Ithaca, NY: Cornell University Press.

Robinson, Geoffrey
1995   *The Dark Side of Paradise: Political Violence in Bali*. Ithaca, NY: Cornell University Press.

Roosa, John
2006   *Pretext for Mass Murder: The September 30th Movement* and *Suharto's Coup D'état in Indonesia*. Madison: University of Wisconsin Press.

Santikarma, Degung
2001   The Power of "Balinese Culture." In *Bali: Living in Two Worlds*. Urs Ramsayer, ed. Pp. 23–36. Basel: Museum der Kulturen and Verlag Schwabe.
2004   Monument, Document, and Mass Grave. In *Beginning to Remember: The Past in the Indonesian Present*. M. Zurbuchen, ed. Pp. 312–323. Seattle: University of Washington Press.

Scarry, Elaine
1987   *The Body in Pain: The Making and Unmaking of the World*. Oxford: Oxford University Press.

Shaw, Rosalind
2002   *Memories of the Slave Trade: Ritual and the Historical Imagination in Sierra Leone*. Chicago, IL: University of Chicago Press.
2006   *Displacing Violence: Making Pentecostal Memory in Postwar Sierra Leone*. Cultural Anthropology 22(1):66–93.

Shiraishi, Saya S.
1997   *Young Heroes: The Indonesian Family in Politics*. Ithaca, NY: Cornell University Southeast Asia Program.

Siegel, James T.
1998   *A New Criminal Type in Jakarta: Counter-Revolution Today*. Durham, NC: Duke University Press.

Starn, Orin
1991   *Missing the Revolution: Anthropologists and the War in Peru*. Cultural Anthropology 6(1):63–91.

Steedly, Mary Margaret
1993   *Hanging without a Rope: Narrative Experience in Colonial and Postcolonial Karoland.*
Princeton, NJ: Princeton University Press.

Stephen, Michele
2006   Imaginary Violence and the Terrible Mother: The Imagery of Balinese Witchcraft.
In *Terror and Violence: Imagination and the Unimaginable.* Andrew Strathern, Pamela J.
Stewart, and Neil L Whitehead, eds. Pp. 192–230. London: Pluto.

Taussig, Michael
1987   *Shamanism, Colonialism, and the Wild Man: A Study in Terror and Healing.* Chicago: University of Chicago Press.

Trouillot, Michel-Rolph
1995   *Silencing the Past: Power and the Production of History.* Boston, MA: Beacon.

Vickers, Adrian
1989   *Bali: A Paradise Created.* Hong Kong: Periplus.

Warren, Carol
1993   *Adat and Dinas: Balinese Communities in the Indonesian State.* Kuala Lumpur:
Oxford University Press.

Zurbuchen, Mary
2001   Looking Back to Move Forward: A Truth Commission Could Bring Healing for a
Tragic Past. Inside Indonesia 65. http://insideindonesia.org.
2001   History, Memory, and the "1965 Incident" in Indonesia. *Asian Survey* 42(4):
564–581.

Narrative Repair

Hilde Lindemann Nelson

Hilde Lindemann (formerly Nelson) is a professor of philosophy at Michigan State University. She received her BA from the University of Georgia studying German language and literature. She received a Fulbright grant during this time and then went on to pursue a masters' in theater studies. Two decades later, she returned to academia to pursue her PhD in philosophy from Fordham University in New York. In 2003, she received the American Society of Bioethics and Humanities Distinguished Service Award; from 2007–2008, she served as their president-elect. She has written numerous books and dozens of articles. Her interests include feminist bioethics, feminist ethics, the ethics of families, and the social construction of persons and their identities. Her work highlights a number of central themes in Epoch Three.

Epoch Two scholars highlight the importance of *identity* when addressing conflict; Epoch Three scholars explore how to transform damaging stories about people or groups. Through a story about the nurses of Cranford Community Hospital, a small hospital in the Midwest, Nelson offers an example of how an intervention at the level of identity can occur.

Virginia Martin joined the "Nurse Recognition Day" planning committee. The diverse nursing team found they had something in common beyond the title of "nurse": the majority felt the doctors treated them as not-very-bright children, capable of handling touchy-feely stuff but not real medicine. Through shared stories about this demeaning treatment, the committee transformed from a party-planning group to a group that actively strategized how to upend this perception about nurses.

Nelson's essay details how the nurses shifted the perception of identity through small and continuous actions. The group, instead of taking on the doctors directly, first engaged in significant *intra-group* work, meaning they first struggled with their own sense of differences, similarities, and desires amongst themselves. The method of engaging in intra-group work before confronting the offending party is distinctive of Epoch Three. Mediation, problem-solving groups, and Truth Commissions fostered in Epoch Two promoted inter-group work, often overlooking the important role of starting with one's own community before interacting with outsiders.

Also, typical of Epoch Three, Nelson's piece demonstrates the space for storytelling and shared support that created the context through which transformation could occur. Martin's exposure to the stories of others helped her recognize her own indignation. Prior to the meetings, she had largely accepted and internalized the treatment of nurses as disappointing but not worth ruffling feathers over.

To explain how the nurses challenged the stories about them, Nelson introduces the concepts of *master narratives* and *counterstories*. Master narratives are the archetypical, recognizable storylines in any culture that seek to define roles and reinforce cultural norms. Counterstories work to challenge these dominant narratives by providing alternative storylines, enriching old ones, or by directly challenging them. To be effective, those developing counterstories must first identify the problematic threads in the master narrative and then articulate the marginalized group as morally trustworthy persons. In this story, the nurses challenged the dominant narratives by re-storying themselves as legitimate and vital agents in the care of patients. This article reflects Epoch Three because the case study demonstrates how narrative dynamics can produce marginalization and challenge it.

Questions to consider: What are some of the stories or the beliefs about people circulating in the conflicts you study or have experienced? How might you work to challenge those narratives that constitute potentially damaging identities?

Reclaiming Moral Agency

Hilde Lindemann Nelson

Multiplication is vexation,
Division is as bad;
The rule of three doth puzzle me,
And practice drives me mad.

—Elizabethan manuscript, 1570

In the small city of Cranford somewhere in the Midwest there was a 225-bed hospital. Virginia Martin did her floor training there when she was a nursing student at Eton College, and when she graduated in 1989 she found full-time work on the orthopedic service almost immediately. She was thirty then, kindly and plump, married since nineteen. She'd have liked to go to medical school and was certainly bright enough to get the degree, but since her husband's law school loans still had to be repaid and their two children needed her, nursing seemed the next best thing. She was good at it. She liked it.

Virginia Martin's hospital had four different kinds of nurses. Many of them were young or middle-aged baccalaureate nurses like herself, trained in the work of a particular unit and qualified to rise to the rank of head nurse. The older nurses tended to be diploma nurses with years of practical experience. Then there were RNs with associate degrees, many of whom were part-timers. And finally there were RNs with master's degrees, who served as the hospital's nurse-educators and directed the chemotherapy and nuclear medicine units. Since only 6 percent of nurses in the United States are men, perhaps it's not surprising that, at the time when these events unfolded, all the nurses at Cranford Community Hospital were women.

Like all hospitals, Cranford Community had its frictions. The diploma nurses were galled when they trained a baccalaureate nurse to the work of the unit, only to see her promoted to be their head nurse. As a cost-cutting move, the hospital administrators had hired more unlicensed personnel to do bedside tasks that none of the nurses considered them qualified to do. And physicians at Cranford continued to see their job as "managing the numbers"—getting white cell counts down to normal levels, measuring blood gases, monitoring electrolyte imbalances-while leaving the nurses to do what the chief of medicine was once overheard to call the "touchy-feely stuff" of providing patients and their families with human sympathy.

Every year in the first week of May the nurses at Cranford Community Hospital and Eton College sponsored a Nurse Recognition Day, involving speakers, student events, media attention, and a sit-down dinner for four hundred of the city's RNs to honor the recipient of that year's Distinguished Service Award. Virginia Martin volunteered to serve on the steering committee, which met twice a month throughout the year. She wasn't sure why she'd taken it on. If you needed a Recognition Day, it must be because you knew you weren't recognized, and why would you want to draw attention to that? Doctors don't bother with recognition days, she thought. She found, however, that she really enjoyed getting to know the fourteen other members of the committee. They quickly coalesced into their own little community.

And a diverse community it was. Nursing was about the only thing the committee members had in common. One of them was a fundamentalist Christian, some were atheists, two were observant Jews. Political stances ranged from left-leaning (like herself), to apathetic, to those who favored big business. Three sexual orientations were represented: lesbian, bi, and straight. Most committee members had full- time careers; three were "refrigerator nurses" who saw their jobs mainly in terms of supplemental income. Some, like herself, were comfortably maternal, some feisty and funny, still others quietly elegant, or timid, or driven.

As the committee sifted through the nominations and planned the events, the conversation moved naturally to the qualities that make someone an admirable nurse and to the future of the profession. But the talk also drifted to the ethical problems the nurses encountered in the course of their work. Linda Adams, a public health nurse, had visited a new mother and baby in a tumble-down farm-house and suspected the baby's failure to thrive was caused by the mother's inabil-ity to cope—it was just a feeling she'd had when she was there. Sally Martinson, the emergency room nurse, had started an intravenous drip on a patient without orders because the physician seemed slow and unsure of herself. Chris Johnson, the director of the chemotherapy unit, remarked that she never knew how much she should tell her patients about side effects, since she believed in honesty but not in "truth-dumping." And so on.

At the fourth meeting of the Nurse Recognition Day Committee, Pilar San-chez arrived with a tale of a sixteen-year-old patient who had been in and out of the hospital many times over the last few years with a form of leukemia that's usually curable in kids of his age. Jake was unlucky, though. His oncologist thought he had defeated the cancer but it came back, and now even a last-ditch bone marrow transplant had failed. Jake's mother insisted that he not be told that he's dying, and the physicians, saying they had to respect her wishes, forbade the staff to discuss Jake's prognosis with him. Pilar Sanchez, who had been taking care of Jake every time he was hospitalized, was very troubled by this. She was con-vinced that he could handle the truth, and she felt as if she'd lied to him every time she smiled encouragingly when he told her about his plans for the future. She tactfully tried to broach the subject with Jake's oncologist, but he was abrupt, telling her that she was emotionally overinvolved and professionally out of line.

Everybody on the committee was interested and indignant, and everybody had something to say. In Sally Martinson's opinion, this was yet another case of physicians' treating nurses like not-very-bright children. Chris Johnson declared that the reason doctors didn't listen to you is that they didn't take you seriously, and the reason they didn't take you seriously is that you were only doing women's work. Linda Adams bitterly agreed. They do the science. We just do the touchy-feely stuff. Pilar Sanchez added that the oncologist might just as well have said right out that she was an excitable Hispanic. Virginia Martin didn't think they needed to drag gender or ethnicity into this—it was just a doctor-nurse thing. It happened all the time. Only last week, one of the orthopedic surgeons on her unit had put her off when she asked him for a medical consult for a patient with high blood pressure. She hated that. She was the one who would have to cope if the patient stroked out.

And so the committee settled down to a full-bodied grouse.

Then the eldest member, Patricia Kent, a crisply tailored professor of nursing at Eton College, suggested that instead of merely complaining about the friction at the hospital, the committee might take some time at each meeting to figure out how to challenge the "technical" versus "touchy-feely" division of labor between doctors and nurses. A picture of nursing seemed to be holding the physicians captive—the nurse as Earth Mother with the Bedpan, you might call it. The Earth Mother, of course, was a character in an old story that badly needed to be updated. What better story could be told about the nurses' professional identity that would allow the physicians to see them more clearly? If the nurses could challenge the story about Mothers that the physicians seemed to be telling themselves and sub-stitute one that invited more respectful treatment, maybe it would be easier for them to do their jobs properly.

Nancy Schmidt, one of the older diploma nurses, thought all this business of nursing as a profession had been taken too far, and that if nurses wanted to be professionals, they should become doctors. Virginia Martin secretly agreed with her, but aloud she merely pointed out that there didn't seem to be any one story they could all tell about their professional identity. There were too many differences among them.

Perhaps, Patricia Kent suggested, they could at least agree that the "touchy-feely" story was a damaging one, because it got in the way of their work. And she traced the history of that story, reminding the others of its connections to nineteenth-century military models of nursing, where male officers gave the orders and female nurses served and obeyed them. If the committee members were to resist the "touchy-feely" identity, she argued, they would have to challenge the stories that fed it, including those that identified women as subservient to men, as emotional rather than rational, as mothers rather than scientists. Those were the stories the physicians seemed to endorse. To get them to stop, the nurses would have to counter the destructive stories with better ones of their own.

Virginia Martin drove home feeling a little flat, like a tire without quite enough air. She'd managed to stay clear of the frictions at the hospital by being nice to everybody and keeping her mouth shut, but she'd hoped that this strategy wouldn't be necessary in her newly acquired circle of friends. While she was all for equality with men, she was no feminist. The thought of quoting Gloria Steinem to the orthopods on her unit made her blink. *There* was an image for you. Why were the committee members making such a fuss over what was, after all, just a case of docs being docs? A savvy nurse soon learned how to work around these petty obstructions.

Still, as the weeks went by and many committee members continued to want to use some of the meeting time to think about who they were and whether the physicians would let them be it, Virginia Martin and Nancy Schmidt reluctantly went along. The anecdotes about encounters with physicians displayed a disturbing pattern. For example, there was the story of a dehydrated and disoriented elderly patient with no previous history of dementia who, after being restrained in the emergency room, managed to free her right arm, pull out her IV tubes and Foley catheter, and tangle herself in the bedding, all the while wailing loudly. Sally Martinson helped her to sit in a chair while she remade the bed, gave her juice and water to drink, calmed her by stroking her forehead, roused her hourly all night for fluids, toileting, and neurological checks, and by morning found her oriented and talking of going home. The patient was discharged that afternoon. A week later, the night-shift supervisor formally reprimanded Sally for not following the physician's orders concerning restraints, IVs, and Haldol. Apparently the physician had gone straight to the supervisor to complain. Virginia Martin could identify with this story. She too had been the target of complaints from physicians who didn't bother to talk to her first. And somehow that brought to mind her husband's law firm, where the senior partner had recently made it clear—to her husband, not to her—that he expected her to give a dinner party for an important client.

Over time, Virginia Martin's perception of the hospital underwent a significant shift. In the beginning this was largely due to her respect for Patricia Kent. She had a great deal of affection for her witty and magisterial former professor, and an equally high opinion of her intelligence. And Sally Martinson, who was no fool either, took almost as radical a view as Patricia Kent. Virginia Martin's trust in these women allowed her to try on their perspective.

The stories ultimately contributed just as much to her change of heart as the people who told them, however. They spoke to her own experiences, but because they were the other people's stories, the stories of people she was fond of, they aroused feelings of indignation that her own experiences had never seemed to merit. And since they were *her* stories as well, the patterns they displayed of contempt for women had to be acknowledged as a pattern in her own life. That acknowledgment made it possible for her to agree that the doctors' story about nurses, as the others were piecing it together, needed to be resisted. She saw that, despite their differences, she and the others could construct a better story—one that identified nurses more accurately and respectfully as skilled professionals with serious responsibilities.

Bit by bit, the nurses connected one fragment of their story to another, offering ethical interpretations of the various anecdotes and telling fresh ones that, in the light of these interpretations, now seemed relevant. Some were stories of admirable nursing practice. Patricia Kent, for instance, told the others of the time when Virginia Martin, while a nursing student, had arranged for a dying patient to take a little walk outside the hospital in the spring rain and gotten thoroughly soaked while keeping him company. Others were stories of why the nurses had been attracted to nursing in the first place. As the narrative work went on, the committee members came to a clearer, shared understanding of who they were on the job.

They realized that this shared understanding was only a first step. They knew they'd have to start telling their improved story *within* the hospital if their work conditions were ever to change. Moreover, the physicians would not only have to hear that story but accept it and alter their behavior accordingly. And that would take a lot of doing. The day they succeeded would indeed be a Nurse Recognition Day.[1]

Counterstories

The cluster of histories, anecdotes, and other narrative fragments the nurses began weaving together is a *counterstory*—a story that resists an oppressive identity and attempts to replace it with one that commands respect (Nelson 1995). By "identity" I mean the interaction of a person's self-conception with how others conceive her: identities are the understandings we have of ourselves and others. In piecing together the fragments of various narratives that have constructed their oppressive identity and challenging the unjust assumptions that lie hidden in those narrative fragments, the nurses have begun to develop a counterstory that identifies them more accurately and fairly.

The counterstory positions itself against a number of *master narratives:* the stories found lying about in our culture that serve as summaries of socially shared understandings. Master narratives are often archetypal, consisting of stock plots and readily recognizable character types, and we use them not only to make sense of our experience (Nisbett and Ross 1980) but also to justify what we do (MacIntyre 1984). As the repositories of common norms, master narratives exercise a certain authority over our moral imaginations and play a role in informing our moral intuitions. Our culture's foundation myths—the Passion of Christ, for example, or Washington Crossing the Delaware—are master narratives. So are the best-known fairy tales, landmark court cases, canonical works of great literature, movie classics. Although master narratives need not be oppressive, those that figure into the physicians' understanding of who nurses are supposed to be seem to be sexist, classist, and possibly ethnocentric. It is master narratives of this kind that counterstories resist.

Many counterstories are told in two steps. The first is to identify the fragments of master narratives that have gone into the construction of an oppressive identity, noting how these fragments misrepresent persons—here, nurses—and situations. The second is to retell the story about the person or the group to which the person belongs in such a way as to make visible the morally relevant details that the master narratives suppressed. If the retelling is successful, the group members will stand revealed as respect worthy moral agents. Since a powerful group's misperception of an oppressed group results in disrespectful treatment that can impede group members in carrying out their responsibilities, the counterstory also opens up the possibility that group members can enjoy greater freedom to do what they ought—Virginia Martin and her colleagues may now be able to care for their patients properly.

In what follows, I argue that through their capacity for narrative repair of identities damaged by oppression, counterstories can provide a significant form of resistance to the evil of diminished moral agency. First, by interacting in a number of different ways with master narratives that identify the members of a particular social group as candidates for oppression, counterstories aim to alter the *oppressors'* perception of the group. If the dominant group, moved by the counterstory, sees subordinates as developed moral agents, it may be less inclined to deprive them of the opportunity to enjoy valuable roles, relationships, and goods. This allows members of the oppressed group to exercise their agency more freely.

Second, counterstories aim to alter, when necessary, an oppressed person's perception of *herself.* Oppression often infiltrates a person's consciousness, so that she comes to operate, from her own point of view, as her oppressors want her to, rating herself as they rate her. By helping a person with an infiltrated consciousness to change her self-understanding, counterstories permit her to put greater trust in her own moral worth. If the counterstory moves her to see herself as a competent moral agent, she may be less willing to accept others' oppressive valuations of her, and this too allows her to exercise her agency more freely.

This book is a work of philosophy, but not a philosophy restricted to conceptual analysis in the classical sense. My claims about counterstories are motivated by a combination of purely conceptual points and an attention to broad, general features of human life—features that in themselves are not recondite, although their implications for resisting some of the effects of oppression have not been well understood. Although I won't attempt to identify all the social and material conditions under which counterstories can actually repair a damaged identity, focusing instead on the features that make a counterstory morally desirable, I will rough out the epistemic context that is required for counterstories to be effective. The project I have undertaken, then, is to develop the concept of the counterstory and to offer criteria for assessing stories of this kind.

Counterstories are created much like any story whose aim is to make moral sense of something: their creators choose particulars from the array of experience and look at them in the light of important moral concepts, which in turn show up the relevance of other particulars, which suggest the relevance of other moral concepts, and so on, until the particulars and their moral interpretations have been set into an equilibrium that points to a specific understanding of the state of affairs.[2] Counterstories are the subset of stories developed in this manner that constitute a revised understanding of a person or social group. They are stories that define people morally, and are developed for the express purpose of resisting and undermining an oppressive master narrative. They ordinarily proceed by filling in details that the master narrative has ignored or underplayed. Through augmentation and correction, the master narrative is morally reoriented, thus allowing the counterstory teller to dissent from the interpretation and conclusion it invites. Counterstories take up an oppressive but shared moral understanding and attempt to shift it, rejecting its assumption that people with a particular group identity are to be subordinated to others or denied access to personal and social goods. They are, then, narrative acts of insubordination.

The task of this chapter is to introduce the concept of the counterstory, to explain the kind of moral work that this philosophical tool can do, and to show how a counterstory, by reidentifying a person, can loosen the constraints on her moral agency. Along the way, I begin to collect some of the working parts needed to develop the concept. Counterstories, typically told within the moral space of a *community of choice,* are *stories* of *self-definition,* developed in response to the twin harms of *deprivation of opportunity* and *infiltrated consciousness.* Through their function of *narrative repair* they resist the evil of diminished moral agency. After discussing each of these ideas at some length, I'll begin the central argument by securing the connection between identity and agency that is crucially presupposed by a counterstory.

Found Communities and Communities of Choice

Marilyn Friedman (1992) has drawn a useful distinction between two sorts of communities. The communities into which we are born and reared—families, neighborhoods, nations—have been accorded special significance by communitarians such as Alasdair MacIntyre and Michael Sandel, who see them as constitutive of self-identity and the source of binding moral norms. But as Friedman points out, these "found" communities have tended to exclude and suppress nongroup members while exploiting and oppressing certain members within the group; women, she observes, have often been on the receiving end of both sorts of treatment. While Friedman grants that found communities play a role in constituting "the unreflective, 'given' identity that the self discovers when *first* beginning to reflect on itself" (Friedman 1992, 92), she notes that on reaching adulthood, women can form radically different communities, those based on voluntary association. She invokes both friendship and urban relationships (her examples are trade unions, political action groups, and support groups) as communities of choice. These, she argues, "foster not so much the *constitution* of subjects but their reconstitution. We seek out communities of choice as contexts in which to *relocate* and *renegotiate* the various constituents of our identities" (95). This relocation and renegotiation is not always benign, of course. As the Ku Klux Klan reminds us, communities of choice can endorse all kinds of evil that aren't countenanced by a found community.

The distinction between found and chosen communities isn't a hard and fast one, as the associations we elect voluntarily are typically nestled within the larger communities we inherit at birth or through forcible displacement. Some found communities can be exited at will while others can't, or can't easily. A neighborhood into which one chooses to move isn't as "found" as the neighborhood in which one has lived all one's life; the long-term, intimate relationships one enters into aren't as "found" as are one's affinities to parents, siblings, and other blood kin. The boundaries may be blurred, but there is nevertheless a difference between the two sorts of communities that has important implications for the viability of a counterstory: a found community operates on a given set of shared moral understandings, while a chosen community can operate on quite another. I'll argue, in Chapter 5, that the alternative evaluative standards of a chosen community are what make it possible to legitimate the person who develops a counterstory.

Both kinds of communities are present in the story about Virginia Martin. Cranford Community Hospital is arguably a found community. While it's true that the nurses chose their profession, most did not choose the setting in which they practice it. Virginia Martin, for example, is restricted because of her husband's job to the city of Cranford, which has only the one hospital. If she wants to be a floor nurse—and she does—then the hospital is her community. Like some other found communities, this one is "exploitative and oppressive toward many of [its] own members, particularly women." Like some other found communities, this one *"complicate[s]* as well as *constitute[s]* identity" (Friedman 1992, 91, 93).

The steering committee, by contrast, is clearly a community of choice. Its members are all volunteers. Virginia Martin, like the other committee members, gravitated toward the committee out of her "own needs, desires, interests, values, and attractions, *rather than* ... from what is socially assigned, ascribed, expected, or demanded" (Friedman 1992, 94). Virginia Martin thinks of the committee members as friends, not just colleagues. And as we have seen, it is in this community, rather than in the hospital where many of the members happen to work, that the nurses have found a context in which to "relocate and renegotiate" the various constituents of its members' identities.

Either kind of community could function as a moral space (Walker 1993) in which people subject what they do to ethical examination and reflection, but in our story, Virginia Martin and her friends used the community of choice for this purpose. We saw them undertaking such an examination as they worried about the baby in the farmhouse, the emergency room physician who seemed unsure, the chemotherapy patients who wanted to know the truth. And because nursing practice says something significant about the nurses' identities, the moral space created by the chosen community was also a space for reflecting on who the nurses are and want to be.

When a person engages in ethical reflection within the moral space of a chosen community, the others who inhabit that space perform a number of useful functions that fit roughly under the heading of what Cheshire Calhoun has called "emotional work"—the work of managing another's feelings. Calhoun argues that the work of "soothing tempers, boosting confidence, fueling pride, preventing frictions, and mending ego wounds" (Calhoun 1992, 118) is critical to the transformation of moral belief systems. "Because what we feel is tied to how we interpret situations," she writes, "helping others get the right moral perspective cannot be detached from working to correct their emotional attitudes" (120). The members of the chosen community thus help the deliberator to manage her emotions about what she has done or what has been done to her, and they tell stories that help her to correct inappropriate feelings arising from misinterpretation of other people's intentions. They supply further information that is relevant to the deliberations, or fresh perspectives on the morally troubling situation. They serve as a check on the deliberator's self-understanding by providing new interpretations of her interactions with others—"was the ER physician really slow, or were you feeling especially impatient that day?"—and offering their own intuitions as sounding boards against which to test her conclusions. And because the knowledge of what she ought to do now or how she should feel about what has already happened is not already there, fully formed, inside the deliberator's consciousness, the others within her moral space lend a hand in shaping her deliberations. They help her to know her own thoughts.

Stories

What makes a counterstory a *story*? Does just any depiction of a logically related, chronological sequence of events count? How are the elements of a story connected to one another? Where do a story's meanings come from? I want here to draw attention to the features of stories that are important for my purposes: they are *depictive*, being representations of human experience; they are *selective* in what they depict; they are *interpretive,* offering a particular way of construing the acts, events, and personae that are represented; and they are *connective,* creating relationships among their own elements and to other stories.[3] Once we have rehearsed a story's characteristics, it will be easier to see how stories figure into the construction of an identity. Throughout this work, I'll use the terms "story" and "narrative" interchangeably.

First, a story is *depictive.* It is a representation of some actual or imaginary set of events, brought about or suffered by actors, that takes place over time. The raw material for any story is the stuff of actual people's lives—the things they do and experience, what they believe, their interactions with other people and the rest of the world.[4] Stories depict these events and experiences by describing them in words or other symbolic systems that are capable of representing a temporal sequence. Not all symbolic systems can depict successive moments in time; photographs, for example, usually represent only one such moment. Narrative representations, by contrast, must depict time passing.

Depictions of logically related events, actors, and places can be arranged into a simple chronological succession, but this is not yet a story. It is simply a *chronicle.* A chronicle represents events as occurring in a strict temporal sequence, but the events of a story can deviate from this sequence. Stories can contain flashbacks or flash-forwards, or rapid switches between the two. An event can be separated by an interval from the narrative present ("Last year I went to India") or it can be presented as occurring at some unspecified time. A story can linger over an event so that its representation takes up more time than did the event itself, or time can be compressed or skipped. An event that occurs only once can be presented a number of times, or a whole series of similar events can be presented simultaneously (Bal 1985, 49–79). In a story, then, time's arrow can fly in a number of directions.

Second, stories are *selective* in what they depict. Chronicles too are somewhat selective—a chronicle of the kings of England doesn't contain depictions of, say, domestic life in a contemporary Inuit village—but they are indiscriminate about which events in the lives of the kings they might include. Unlike a chronicle, which simply tells you that this happened, and then this, and then this, the elements of a story must be chosen in such a way as to represent a "process of happening, which is thought to possess a discernible beginning, middle, and end" (White 1973, 5). The chronicle becomes a story when its elements are restricted to inaugural, transitional, or terminating motifs. "Chronicles are, strictly speaking, open-ended. In principle they have no *inaugurations;* they simply 'begin' when the chronicler starts recording events. And they have no culminations or resolutions; they can go on indefinitely. Stories, however, have a discernible form (even when that form is an image of a state of chaos) which marks off the events contained in them from the other events that might appear in a comprehensive chronicle of the years covered in their unfoldings" (6).

Third, stories are *interpretive.* They don't just select the actors, events, and places that go into their creation—they characterize these elements. One means of characterizing the actors in a story is by showing what they do, and when characters are depicted as doing certain things repeatedly, we conclude that they have particular preoccupations or habits. *Round* characters are complex and undergo change; *flat* characters are stable stereotypes (Bal 1985, 79–80). The protagonist may, depending on how the story is plotted, be an active and successful hero, an unsuccessful victim (tragic hero), or a patient who suffers events rather than bringing them about (think of the character Dude, the protagonist of the Cohen brothers' film *The Big Liebowski*). Places are characterized in terms of the events that occur in them, or through descriptions that create an atmosphere inviting a particular emotional response.

The elements of a story can also be interpreted through a character who perceives and reacts to them—through what the character sees, hears, or touches. In a story (but not a chronicle), the depictions of time, events, actors, and places are always presented from within a point of perception—from a particular angle or way of seeing that offers a specific interpretation of what's going on. Mieke Bal's term for the relation between the elements that are presented and the perspective through which they are presented is *focalization* (Bal 1985, 100), and the person from whose point of view the story is told is the focalizer. Sometimes the story in its entirety is seen from a particular focalizer's point of view, but different people can also play the role of focalizer at different points in the story. In one scene we might see a setting or character from one character's angle of vision, while in the next the focalizer might be someone outside the action, such as the narrator.

A story offers an interpretation of its characters and events not only through its focalizers and what it shows people doing, but through its plot and the genre to which that plot belongs. A story's plot invites the receiver of the story (the reader, spectator, listener) to draw a conclusion about what happened: he really loved her but didn't know how to show it; the wrath of Achilles was the cause of the trouble; it was sad when the great ship went down. The *mode* of emplotment, or genre, invites the receiver of the story to interpret the depiction of events as farcical, as tragic, as an instance of chaos in a meaningless universe, and so on. The mode of emplotment thus relates a given story to other stories that offer the same kind of explanation of people's place in the cosmic (or local) order of things, of whether reconciliation among people is possible, of whether what happened was inevitable or just a matter of bad luck.

In the mode of emplotment's ability to relate one story to another we can see a fourth feature of stories: they are *connective*. They draw connections not only among themselves but also within themselves. As we just saw, setting can be related to event or character, and action is often related to character as well: the courtier's kiss shows him to be a traitor; the stifled laugh displays the worker's contempt for a colleague. By depicting events as causally (and not just temporally) linked; by the use of symbolism, which allows the depiction of a person or thing to stand for something greater than itself; by patterns and motifs that connect one set of events to another; and by connections between setting and event (such as a declaration of love on a moonlit balcony), the story's capacity for connection allows us to make sense of what has been represented.

Stories create meanings through the relationships of their internal elements, but also through their relationships to one another. While a story's mode of emplotment connects it to other stories generically, stories also draw explicit connections to particular stories (Bal 1985, 7). A contemporary story, for example, can contain a reference to a "Judas" or a "Scrooge" and so establish a narrative connection to the Passion of Christ or Dickens's *Christmas Carol*. This narrative connection, established through allusive nods to other stories, also sets up inter-connections among various elements *within* the story. Character types and the stock plots that are associated with these characters can be lifted from stories that are familiar cultural staples and be reworked as variations on old themes. Or fragments of one story might be spliced to those from another story and so shed light on both. As we'll see later on, the connective feature of stories is absolutely central to the narrative construction of identities.

The depictive, selective, interpretive, and connective features of a story all work together to give the story its overall meaning. Indeed, it's in a story's ability to mean and to convey meaning that it differs most notably from a chronicle. A chronicle is just one damned thing after another, whereas a story embodies an understanding. Through its selective, interpretive, and connective representation of human experience over time, it makes a certain sort of sense of some part of what it is to be human. A personal identity likewise embodies an understanding. Through one's own and others' selective, interpretive, and connective representations of the characteristics, acts, experiences, roles, relationships, and commitments that contribute importantly to one's life over time, an identity makes a certain sort of sense of who one is. It does so because it is essentially narrative in nature.

Self-Definition

Counterstories are stories of self-definition. In general, stories of self-definition can be grouped roughly into three categories: nonmoral self-definition, weak moral self-definition, and strong moral self-definition. They might be stories that define (or redefine) a group to which an individual belongs and from which the individual takes some significant part of her identity, or they might be stories that define (or redefine) the individual directly.

A story of group nonmoral self-definition merely identifies the group as one thing rather than another—the board of directors of a theater company, for example, might recount the history of past performances as a way of identifying the theater primarily with comic revivals instead of contemporary drama. Similarly, a story of individual nonmoral self-definition might identify the person as a good cook. A story of weak moral self-definition constructs a group or an individual as morally competent. A corporation tells such a story when it advertises itself as socially and environmentally responsible, and a teenager does the same when she recounts instances of good judgment to persuade her parents that she can be trusted with the car keys.

The concept of strong moral self-definition requires a more extensive explanation. In Margaret Urban Walker's terms, strong moral self-definition is a kind of moral competence. It is "the ability of morally developed persons to install and observe precedents for themselves which are both distinctive of them and binding upon them morally" (Walker 1987; 173). Walker has argued that, contrary to universalist moral theories, which assume that all relevant considerations regarding what any moral agent is required, permitted, or forbidden to do in a situation are exactly the same for any other agent similarly placed, there are identity-constitutive features of a moral agent's life that can give content to the particular ways in which this particular agent may or must act. On Walker's view, *this* agent might have commitments or priorities that differ from those of another agent in a similar situation. She might not need to do what the similarly situated agent does; she might aim to be a different kind of person from the one the similarly situated agent tries to be.

In deliberating about what she ought to do, the agent reviews her personal history, weighs the particulars of her past in terms of more general moral values, and discerns or constructs a course of action that expresses a commitment to those particulars. The person either ratifies her history—"I've always believed in telling the truth, but not in truth-dumping"—and remains on her present course, or repudiates it and charts a new course: "I've always been too quick to blame the mother when a baby doesn't thrive. I'll try not to do that this time." Either way, she creates a moral track record that commits her to certain values for the future. The review of her history is a backward-looking story that explains to her who she has been. The commitment to a future course of action is a forward-looking story that shows her where she wants to go. Strong moral self-definition thus allows certain individuating features of the person's life to matter in ways that aren't universally generalizable but remain specific to the person and so contribute to her identity.

We may contrast purposeful strong moral self-definition, whereby the agent deliberately sets out to define herself in terms of the values, experiences, and commitments she takes to be identity-constituting, with inadvertent strong moral self-definition, whereby the agent non-purposefully and perhaps even unconsciously makes of herself a particular sort of person. Consider Virginia Martin's young friend Megan O'Brien, a nurse-practitioner at a not-for-profit family planning clinic. A year or so ago, shortly after she began her practice, a sixteen-year-old high school dropout asked Megan O'Brien for birth control. On being presented with a number of options, the girl thought a long-acting contraceptive would be best, so Megan O'Brien gave her Norplant, inserting six flexible strips under the skin on the girl's upper arm. The implants, designed to release the hormone progestin slowly, protect the recipient against pregnancy for five years. Nine months later, however, the girl returned to ask that the Norplant be removed, because she was experiencing breakthrough bleeding and her boyfriend didn't like the feel of the strips under the skin. Megan O'Brien hesitated. As she started to think about it, she concluded that her patient was too young to appreciate fully what a disaster for her a pregnancy at this point would be. Moreover, she didn't trust the girl to remember to take a daily birth control pill. So she refused to remove the implants.[5]

This is a moment of strong moral self-definition, but it's inadvertent. Megan O'Brien might purposefully have mined her past for the commitments and experiences that have made her who she now is, and used these particulars not only to guide her care of the young patient but to set a precedent for the care of future patients. That she didn't do this, however, doesn't mean that she is not now defining herself morally. In acting as she does, she has begun to fashion herself into a nurse who controls and manipulates underage patients. If she controls and manipulates often enough, she becomes a controlling person.

When she originally inserted the contraceptive, something important about her action was indeterminate. Was she acting as her young client's agent? Was she implementing her own views about adolescent sexuality, or attempting to stand in for the girl's parents? None of this was clear, either to herself or to anyone else. The girl thought it was clear, however. She had agreed to accept Norplant on the understanding that she was in charge of her own body. But now, by refusing to remove the implants, Megan O'Brien retroactively changes what it was that her patient originally consented to. Her present refusal makes visible what could not be seen earlier—that not only for the immediate moment but for the past nine months the contraception has been coercive. Christine Korsgaard echoes this idea of strong but retrospective moral self-definition when she writes,

> You cannot, just by making a resolution, acquire a virtue or recover from a vice. Or better still, we will say that you can, because you are free, but then we must say that only what happens in the future establishes whether you have really made the resolution or not. I do not mean that only the future will produce the evidence: I mean that only what you do in the future will enable us to correctly attribute a resolution to you. There is a kind of backwards determination in the construction of one's character. (Korsgaard 1989, 45)

The backward determination of a morally opaque action that is nevertheless identity-constituting is more complicated in a case of purposeful strong moral self-definition, because there the agent, *intending* that the action should say something about who she is, issues herself a promissory note which she must later make good. How well she succeeds in this depends in part on her later choices, but these may be constrained by events over which she has little control. She cannot know until her life-story plays itself out whether the commitment she made could actually be adhered to in the way she anticipated. Something might turn up or have been overlooked that sends her story off in an unexpected direction, so that, in the event, there is cause for regret.

A story of strong moral self-definition is always told *from here,* but like any sort of moral choice, its assessment is necessarily *from there* (Williams 1981a, 35). Whether a person has succeeded in defining herself by charting a present course of action depends on how well she stays on course, and that depends not only on her own resolve but on whether subsequent events knock or nudge her in a different direction. Living up to one's resolutions requires luck as well as persistence. Because one can't foresee how one's life will go, from here it is somewhat indeterminate; from there, it might mean something morally that can't now be seen.

Two Kinds of Counterstories

Unlike an act of backward determination, which defines a past that has been, until now, morally opaque, counterstories redefine a past that has been, until now, characterized incorrectly. They take a story that has (for the moment at least) been determined, undo it, and reconfigure it with a new significance. If individuals or groups can *identify* themselves through stories of nonmoral self-definition, weak moral self-definition, or strong moral self-definition, though, they can *repair* their identities only through the last two kinds. Counterstories such as the ones the nurses told in the moral space of the steering committee are stories of strong moral self-definition, told both for the individuals and the group. Each person uses the story to repudiate an incorrect understanding of who she is, and replaces this with a more accurate self-understanding. Reidentifying herself in this way commits her to a future course of action that expresses who, morally, she takes herself to be.

Other counterstories do their repair work more minimally, resisting master narratives' morally degrading depictions of an oppressed group by representing the group members as morally upright human beings. These are stories of weak moral self-definition. Harper Lee's *To Kill a Mockingbird* is such a counterstory, bidding readers to resist the master narratives that identify black men as sexual predators of Southern white women. While the counterstory concerns a particular black male character, there is no one existing person who is reidentified by it. Instead, the story can be set to the moral task of shifting racist understandings of black men in general. If it succeeds, then individual black men whose identities have been damaged by those same master narratives can also be seen as morally trustworthy.

Individual and group counterstories can shade off into one another. Just as a counterstory could be developed by an individual to define herself morally, so a counterstory that reidentifies an individual can be generalized to revise a moral understanding about the group to which the individual belongs. Counterstories move in this way between individuals and groups because oppressive identities are imposed on individuals precisely because of their membership in a despised group.

No counterstory can be nonmorally self-defining, though it may identify the individual or group in nonmoral terms. For example, I might tell a story to establish that, despite what others may think, I am bad at managing money and have no head for business. If I am a Jew and am purposefully resisting the stereotypes that depict Jews as avaricious usurers, my story is a counterstory even though it doesn't employ moral terms, because it repudiates a pernicious master narrative. Groups too can tell self-defining counterstories that, on their face, say nothing about their moral character but instead identify them in non-moral terms. The nonmoral terms take on a moral valence when the stories are used to repair the group identity.

Counterstories can be created *by* or *for* the person whose identity needs repair. In the moral space within a corporation (perhaps by the water cooler) I can construct a story with my coworkers that lets me reidentify a gay colleague, who has been isolated and passed over for promotion on account of his sexual orientation, as a talented and trustworthy person. If my gay colleague takes up my counterstory, it has corrective powers not only for me and my coworkers but also for him. We now see him as someone to be respected and treat him accordingly, and he too, perhaps, sees himself in a new light. The reason that counterstories can be told to reidentify someone other than the teller, as I'll explain in Chapter 3, is that identity is a function not only of how a person perceives himself but also of how others perceive him. Counterstories told to repair someone else's identity obviously aren't self-defining, but they can identify the other person in terms that acknowledge the person's moral competence. They are, in other words, stories of weak moral definition. In certain instances of prolonged and deep intimacy it may also be possible for one person to define another in strong moral terms (J. Nelson 1999), but I shall not explore that possibility here.

Narrative Repair

The immediate purpose of a counterstory is to repair identities that have been damaged by oppression. Identities are complex narrative constructions consisting of a fluid interaction of the many stories and fragments of stories surrounding the things that seem most important, from one's own point of view and the point of view of others, about a person over time. Because identities are constructed from both points of view, there are, broadly speaking, two ways in which they can be damaged. First, a person's identity is damaged when powerful institutions or individuals, seeing people like her as morally sub- or abnormal, unjustly prevent her and her kind from occupying roles or entering into relationships that are identity-constituting. If a woman is denied custody of her child solely on the grounds that she is lesbian, her relationship with her child is attenuated; this impairs her ability to hold on to her identity as a mother. If a company's offices are accessible only by means of stairs and this prevents a person in a wheelchair from taking a lucrative job there, the person's potential relationship with the company never gets off the ground; this slightly erodes his identity as an economically self-sufficient person. Japanese Americans interned during World War II were forcibly confined because of their supposed threat to the country; their identities as U.S. citizens were taken away from them. And in the story of the Nurse Recognition Day committee, the physicians' "touchy-feely" characterization of nurses makes it difficult for them to fulfill their nursing roles; this is an injury to their professional identities. Harm to an oppressed person's identity that takes this form may be called *deprivation of opportunity*. The kind of counterstory that is required to repair deprivation of opportunity is one that will change others' perception of the person. The judge, the employer, the government,[6] the physicians must either *endorse* counterstories told by those suffering the deprivation or *develop* counterstories on the sufferers' behalf.

Although oppression always damages people's identities by depriving them of opportunity, it frequently also has a second kind of destructive impact. A person's identity is twice damaged by oppression when she internalizes as a self-understanding the hateful or dismissive views that other people have of her. The lesbian mother, the wheelchair-bound worker, the Japanese American might all come to see themselves in the terms reserved by the oppressive institutions of their society for people like them. They then lose, or fail to acquire, self-respect. If John Rawls is right in identifying self-respect as a primary good (Rawls 1971, 178), then its absence is perhaps even more significant a harm than the deprivation of an identity-constituting role or relationship. This second sort of damage to an oppressed person's identity can be called *infiltrated consciousness*.

Notice that, like deprivation of opportunity, infiltrated consciousness admits of degrees. In the story of the Nurse Recognition Day committee, Virginia Martin had partially internalized the physicians' opinion of nurses. She had unreflectively believed that physicians did the real work in the hospital and that the nurses' work was not merely different but somehow second best. She would have gone to medical school rather than nursing school if she could; she dismissed the physicians' lack of respect toward nurses as simply a matter of docs being docs. But she also took pride in her work and enjoyed doing it. To the extent that the physicians' characterization of who nurses are had invaded her own sense of herself, her identity has been damaged. The kind of counterstory that is required to repair an infiltrated consciousness is one that will change the person's self-perception. The person must either tell a counterstory for herself or endorse one that is told on her behalf.

Identity and Agency

So far, I have been collecting some of the working parts that contribute to the concept of the counterstory: community of choice, story, self-definition, deprivation of opportunity, infiltrated consciousness, narrative repair. Now I want to secure the connection between identity and agency. My claim, if you recall, is that counterstories allow oppressed people to refuse the identities imposed on them by their oppressors and to reidentify themselves in more respect worthy terms. I further claim that this reidentification permits oppressed people to exercise their moral agency more freely. These claims are plausible only if identity and agency are closely connected. With the help of two important papers by Paul Benson (1990, 1994), I argue that the connection between the two is an internal one, since not only do my actions disclose who I am, but who I am taken—or take myself—to be directly affects how freely I may act.

Identity is a question of how *others* understand what I am doing, as well as how *I* understand what I am doing. If other people perceive my actions to be those of a morally trustworthy person, then they will permit me to act freely. In addition, though, I must see *myself* as a morally trustworthy person if I am to act freely. Both others' recognition that I am a morally responsible person and my own sense of myself as a morally responsible person, then, are required for the free exercise of moral agency.

Following Benson, I argue that agency is freer or less free to the extent that two conditions obtain. The first, control over one's actions, ranges over both one's ability to act willfully and the ability to regulate one's will reflectively. The second, normative competence, involves three capacities: (1) the ability to understand moral norms, act in accordance with them, and reveal who one is, morally speaking, through what one does; (2) the ability of others to recognize by one's actions that one is a morally responsible person; and (3) the ability of the agent to see herself as a morally responsible person. If others' conception of who I am keeps them from seeing my actions as those of a morally responsible person, they will treat me as a moral incompetent. This is the problem of deprivation of opportunity. If my own conception of who I am keeps me from trusting my own moral judgments, I will treat *myself* as a moral incompetent. This is the problem of infiltrated consciousness.

I'll make my argument in two steps. First, I'll make the case that how others identify me has a direct bearing on how freely I can exercise my agency. Second, I'll demonstrate that how I see myself also determines how freely I can act.

How Others Identify Me: Deprivation of Opportunity

Modern and contemporary philosophers often talk of moral agency as if it were merely a capacity one has, involving competencies that we possess in our own right. Many prominent contemporary theories, including Gerald Dworkin's (1970, 1988), Harry Frankfurt's (1971), Wright Neely's (1974), Gary Watson's (1975), and Daniel Dennett's (1984), have characterized free agency as consisting in the competency to govern one's conduct willfully and the capacity to regulate one's will reflectively—neither of which is represented as having anything at all to do with one's relationships to other people. In his classic "Freedom of the Will and the Concept of a Person," for example, Harry Frankfurt writes,

> The unwilling addict identifies himself . . . through the formation of a second-order volition, with one rather than with the other of his conflicting first-order desires. He makes one of them more truly his own and, in so doing, he withdraws himself from the other. It is in virtue of this identification and withdrawal . . . that the unwilling addict may meaningfully make the analytically puzzling statements that the force moving him to take the drug is a force other than his own, and that it is not of his own free will but rather against his will that this force moves him to take it. (Frankfurt 1971, 13)

Similarly, Wright Neely contends:

> A man is freer not only to the extent that he does as he pleases and to the extent that his pleasing as he does follows from a coherent life plan, but also to the extent that this life plan and the character which goes with it have been forged by him through time with due attention to the satisfactions which he may be missing as a result of lacking certain desires, with due consideration of those of his character traits which lead to painful consequences, and with due sensitivity to other types of lives which may serve as ideals for him to follow. (Neely 1974, 54)

Although Susan Wolf does not restrict her account to the content-neutral capacities of governing one's conduct and regulating one's first-order desires, her theory of agency is just as individualistic as the others. She argues that free agents must have a metaethical commitment to some degree of objectivism, as this grounds "the ability to do the right thing for the right reasons" and "the ability to act in accordance with, and on the basis of, the True and the Good" that are, on her view, necessary for moral agency (Wolf 1990, 71). Here again, though, there is no acknowledgment that the agent acts in conjunction with other agents, much less that this fact might have a bearing on the conditions for free agency.

It's my contention, however, that freedom of agency requires not only certain capacities, competencies, and intentions that lie within the individual, but also recognition on the part of others of *who one is,* morally speaking. To see how this works, let's return to the story of the young leukemia patient who was not told that he was dying. Because the physician identified Pilar Sanchez as a fond (in the sense of foolish) care giver, her considered moral judgment that Jake be told of his prognosis didn't get registered as a *moral* judgment at all. It got registered as emotional overinvolvement—assisted, perhaps, by ethnic stereotypes about excitable Hispanics. The physician's inability to identify Pilar Sanchez as a morally developed agent forecloses the possibility of any discussion with him, let alone a case consult, and this deprives her of the opportunity to care for Jake as well as she thinks she should.

In "Feminist Second Thoughts about Free Agency," a paper that develops the point about recognition, Paul Benson contends that most theories of free agency have misdescribed cases of diminished freedom in which the agent is, say, a young child or someone who has been diagnosed with a serious mental illness. In cases of this kind, the theories hold, the agents have no "power to control their conduct through deliberate choices which express what they 'really' want to do" (Benson 1990, 52). So, for example, Frankfurt classifies young children as "wantons," incapable of adopting second-order desires that control which first-order desires they are willing to act on (Frankfurt 1971). The insistence on a control condition as sufficient for free agency, Benson suggests, is a mistake that could only be made by a philosopher who has never been the primary care giver of a young child. Who else would think that a five-year-old boy who has been warned not to tease his baby sister but does it anyway must be out of control, incapable of stopping what he is doing? That the control condition is inadequate is, to harken back to the title of the essay, Benson's "first feminist thought" about free agency.

The five-year-old may be perfectly capable of leaving his sister alone, says Benson. What he has not yet developed, however, is the capacity for "normative self-disclosure"—the ability to reveal through his actions who he is as a person (Benson 1990, 53). To revert to the language I was using earlier, the little boy's teasing does not count as an instance of inadvertent strong moral self-definition. Unlike Megan O'Brien's refusal to remove her patient's contraceptive device, which disclosed a controlling and manipulative streak in her character, the boy's behavior doesn't tell us anything much about who he is. Since the capacity for normative self-disclosure is, for Benson, a crucial component of normative competence, and the boy hasn't fully attained normative competence, his agency isn't free even though he *can* control his behavior.

On Benson's view, then, agency is free to the extent that two conditions are present. One is the control condition, and the other is normative competence, which involves the ability to express one's identity through what one does. As Benson puts it,

> Powers of control are only one part of a much broader, and hopefully more adequate, conception of free agency. On this new conception, free agency requires *normative competence,* an array of abilities to be aware of applicable normative standards, to appreciate those standards, and to bring them competently to bear in one's evaluations of open courses of action. . . . At the heart of free agency is the power of our actions to reveal who we are, both to ourselves and to others, in the context of potential normative assessments of what we do. Our level of awareness and understanding of the standards expressed in those assessments is as crucial to our freedom as our ability to control what we do. (Benson 1990, 55)

In keying free agency to the power of our actions to reveal who we are, Benson points to something that P. F. Strawson has famously described in "Freedom and Resentment." In that essay, Strawson contrasts our ordinary attitudes of interpersonal engagement, such as "gratitude, resentment, forgiveness, love, and hurt feelings" (Strawson 1962, 62), which we display toward people whose actions reveal them to be participants in the moral community, with attitudes that preclude such engagement, because the persons' deeds show them to be morally sub- or abnormal. "Participant reactive attitudes," says Strawson, "are essentially natural human reactions to the good or ill will or indifference of others towards us, as displayed in *their* attitudes and actions." They are attitudes we take toward people who by their attitudes and actions have shown themselves to be among "the normal and the mature" (Strawson 1962, 67).

Objective attitudes, by contrast, are those we exhibit toward people whose actions disclose them to be psychologically abnormal or morally undeveloped (note that these are Benson's two cases of unfree agency). "To adopt the objective attitude to another human being," as Strawson memorably puts it, "is to see him, perhaps, as an object of social policy; as a subject for what, in a wide range of sense, might be called treatment; as something certainly to be taken account, perhaps precautionary account, of; to be managed or handled or cured or trained" (Strawson 1962, 66). Which attitude we take toward someone depends on whether we think they are morally responsible or morally defective, and we decide this by interpreting, in accordance with some set of evaluative standards, what their actions say about who they are. How we register what someone is doing thus determines whether we will allow them to exercise their agency freely, on the one hand, or constrain them by disciplining them, refusing them a driver's license, denying them custody of their children, or confining them to a locked psychiatric ward, on the other.

But, as Benson goes on to point out (this is his "second thought"), whether we will be seen as the sorts of people who can be held morally responsible for what we are doing has as much to do with the norms of those who assess us as with our ability to understand those norms (58). Not all of us who fail to qualify as fully free agents do so because we don't appreciate the evaluative standards that others use to take our measure. We may know those standards very well but reject them, and so court persistent misreading. Here Benson is thinking, for instance, of a woman in a sexist society. She may be perfectly aware of how others will perceive her "unladylike" behavior, but not accept mainstream standards of how a lady should behave. It's possible that those in the mainstream will then judge from her actions that she is not morally trustworthy—she obviously doesn't know the rules. As Benson points out, agents who are at the margins of society are particularly open to having their actions evaluated as evidence of sub- or abnormality, precisely because they don't conform to the standards adopted by those in the mainstream.

If Benson is right—and I think he is—then normative competence isn't just a matter of capacities and capabilities that reside within the agent. As capacities and capabilities are always relative to an environment, the ability to exercise them successfully depends in part on the others who inhabit that environment. Normative competence is therefore genuinely interpersonal: the capacity for normative self-disclosure embraces not only the agent's ability to appreciate the moral construction that others will place on her actions but also the recognition by those others that her actions are those of a morally developed person. The role that other people's recognition of one's identity plays in Benson's account of free agency explains, in a way that most contemporary theories can't, what went wrong between Pilar Sanchez and the dismissive oncologist. According to the standard theories, Pilar Sanchez is a free agent. She is able to govern her behavior by means of her will and is also capable of regulating the content of her will. So the control condition is met. Yet there are good reasons to think that her moral agency is less than fully free, and that is because one component of the normative competence condition is not met. She is aware of and appreciates applicable normative standards and can bring them to bear in her assessments of her options, but she can't make her actions reveal who she is, because others have imposed an oppressive identity on her.

The oncologist has perceived Pilar Sanchez's involvement with her young dying patient as saying something morally discreditable about her. He sees her as a defective agent, and therefore in no position to hold him accountable. By his standards, which are the mainstream standards in the hospital, she is someone to be managed or handled (if not cured or trained). The problem is not, however, that Pilar Sanchez is morally underdeveloped. Rather, it's that there is something wrong with the norms in the mainstream. These norms produce the oncologist's objective attitude toward her, and it's that which keeps her from being fully free.

If the constrictions on her agency are to be loosened, the oncologist must be persuaded to identify Pilar Sanchez differently. If he comes to perceive her as a colleague rather than an emotional Latina, he is more likely to include her in the moral deliberations regarding Jake's care. The damage the oncologist has inflicted on her identity is that of deprivation of opportunity. The counterstory that's required to reidentify her, then, is a story about her moral trustworthiness that *he* is willing to endorse. The difficulty, of course, lies in getting the oncologist to listen to such a story.

So far, it looks as if the degree to which agency is free depends on how well two conditions are met. One is the control condition, which ranges over both one's ability to act willfully and the ability to regulate one's will reflectively, and the other is normative competence, conceived as (1) the ability to understand moral norms, act in accordance with them, and reveal who one is, morally speaking, through what one does; (2) the ability of others to recognize by one's actions that one is a morally responsible person. Alternatively, the normative competence condition may be thought of as a refinement of the control condition: control over one's actions requires that others not put obstacles in one's path. Seeing that self-disclosure is a matter of what others perceive, as well as what a person expresses, helps us to explain why repairing the damage to a person's identity allows her to exercise her agency more freely, at least when the damage in question is that of deprivation of opportunity.

How I Identify Me: Infiltrated Consciousness

When we consider the *other* sort of damage that oppression inflicts on people's identities, however, it quickly becomes apparent that our understanding of the normative competence condition needs to be expanded. In a second paper, "Free Agency and Self-Worth," Benson considers the problem of what I have been calling infiltrated consciousness, arguing that in addition to whatever other capacities are necessary, "free agents must have a certain sense of their own worthiness to act" (Benson 1994, 650). In other words, not only do others have to identify the agent as morally trustworthy—she has to identify herself as trustworthy as well.

Benson begins by looking at an instance, not of oppression, but of personal domination.[7] In the 1944 film *Gaslight*, the character played by Ingrid Bergman is the wife of an evil man, played by Charles Boyer. The Boyer character, who has murdered the Bergman character's aunt, marries the Bergman character so that he can steal the valuable jewels the aunt hid before she died. Bergman, of course, is unaware of his nefarious intent and believes he truly loves her. To keep her from finding out what he is doing, Boyer tries to confuse and disorient her, making her believe that she can't remember things she has recently done, that she loses things, that she has hallucinations. Through plausible suggestions he isolates her from people, reducing her to bewildered helplessness. By these means he dramatically diminishes her freedom as an agent.

She can act intentionally even though she believes she is going mad, and her will doesn't seem to be plagued by unregulated motives. As most free agency theorists understand it, then, the control condition is met. Likewise, her normative competence, as we understand it so far, seems to have survived intact. She can wield moral norms and reveal herself through her actions, and others identify her as the sort of person toward whom one appropriately takes the reactive attitude. But she is still not free. Why? Benson's answer is that "she has lost her former sense of her own status as a worthy agent. She has ceased to trust herself to govern her conduct competently" (Benson 1994, 657). If he's right, then we have to refine the normative competence condition. We must now conceive of normative competence as: (1) the ability to understand moral norms, act in accordance with them, and reveal who one is, morally speaking, through what one does; (2) the ability of others to recognize by one's actions that one is a morally responsible person; and (3) the ability of the agent to see herself as a morally responsible person.

Benson thinks that a historical theory of free agency, such as John Christman's (1991), could explain Bergman's lack of freedom by showing that the process by which she came to her present beliefs couldn't bear her scrutiny. If she knew what Boyer had done to manipulate her, "she would surely resist the beliefs and desires that resulted from it" (Benson 1994, 656). So Benson moves to a case of oppression, which he views as blocking this response. He imagines a feminist remake of *Gaslight*, also set in the 1880s, in which the husband is a kindly soul who takes his wife's interests to heart, but, because he is a physician and the medical science of his day pathologizes women, he regards the wife's active imagination and strong passions as symptomatic of a serious psychological illness. The wife trusts her husband's diagnosis and comes to believe that she is mentally ill. In this case, Benson argues, "the woman would not be likely to resist the process by which her beliefs and desires were altered in the wake of her diagnosis, if she were to attend reflectively to that process. For she arrives at her sense of incompetence and estrangement from her conduct on the basis of reasons that are accepted by a scientific establishment which is socially validated and which she trusts" (657).

Here the loss of free agency extends beyond the institutional impediments that others place in the agent's way. Whereas the social mechanisms that sustain oppression thwarted Pilar Sanchez's ability to register a moral judgment regarding her young patient, the mechanisms reach even further in Benson's case of medical gaslighting, infiltrating the agent's consciousness and destroying her sense of who she is. Oppression takes the place of Boyer's machinations to bring it about that the medically gaslighted wife should lose, to a significant degree, confidence in her worthiness to be the author of her own conduct. Like Bergman in the original film, her view of herself has been altered so that she no longer regards herself as competent to answer for her actions in light of normative demands that she herself thinks other people might reasonably apply to her (Benson 1994, 660).

While Benson's explanation of why someone with an infiltrated consciousness is not a free agent strikes me as largely correct, I believe that he has misdescribed what happens when one is gaslighted by deceit, as opposed to being gaslighted by oppression. Benson accepts Christman's view that an agent's regulative power over her will is free just in case "the agent's will was acquired through a process that could be sustained under reflection" (Benson 1994, 654). Under reflection, the agent concludes that her beliefs about her will have been formed in the right way: they have been properly connected to reality and are therefore warranted. Because Bergman's belief that she ought not to trust her judgment was formed by Boyer's systematic deception, rather than by any actual psychological impairment, it is not warranted, and so, Christman would say, she is not free.

Benson endorses this account of how deception takes away an agent's freedom and follows it up by a psychological claim: when an agent whose beliefs about her unworthiness to act aren't warranted, she can repair the damage and free her will simply by reflecting on the process by which her beliefs were formed. That's why Benson thinks that if Bergman were aware of Boyer's manipulation, she would "surely resist the beliefs and desires that resulted from it." This is an argument about transparency. Benson claims that if Boyer's chicanery could be made transparent, Bergman would drop her beliefs that her judgments are worthless: what was done by deceit can be undone by unmasking the deceiver. The unstated inference is that because the medically gaslighted wife has no way to see through the medical ideology of her day, she cannot, like Bergman, free herself.

But Benson ought not to suppose that the Bergman character would "surely" resist the belief in her own unworthiness if only she knew the belief wasn't warranted. He attaches too much importance to the consequence of being shown the hidden mechanism. Knowing that there is no rational warrant for the belief that she is morally untrustworthy doesn't guarantee that the agent can rid herself of the belief. Her ability to resist depends on *her ability to trust her own judgments,* and in both of the gaslighting cases, that is precisely what has been so badly broken down.

In the original case, Bergman might discard the belief in her own untrustworthiness if she knew of Boyer's deception and if he had only been playing with her mind for a few days or weeks, because that is too short a time to do a thoroughgoing job of corrupting someone's sense of self-worth. Self-worth is resilient and survives repeated blows. As long as Bergman retains enough of it to believe that her mental processes are reliable, she may be able to assess the evidence pointing to her husband's machinations and draw her own conclusions, and that will be enough to restore her to her premarital level of confidence in her agency.

If, however, Boyer is given sufficient time to destroy Bergman's sense of self-worth altogether, and if her loving trust in him causes her to accept his verdict regarding her mental state as definitive, then Bergman will not be able to rely on her judgments, no matter how much evidence presents itself regarding her husband's deception. Her beliefs will be evidence-resistant, precisely because she no longer trusts herself to exercise her moral agency competently. She is then in no better an epistemic position than the medically gaslighted wife who, having lived all her life in a society that discounts women's judgments, and having now been authoritatively diagnosed as seriously ill, no longer regards herself as mentally competent. For the doctor's wife too, the ability to resist the belief that she is crazy depends less on *whether* she is shown the hidden mechanism that drives the diagnosis than on *when.* If the evidence that the science is wrong comes too late and she no longer has any faith in her ability to judge it for herself, the evidence will not free her.

The relevant difference between the two gaslighting cases, then, is not (as Benson supposes) that there is something the wife could find out that would free her agency in the first case but not in the second. Rather, the difference is that, in the first case, the wife's sense of self-worth hasn't yet been completely corrupted. If it were, what she knew or didn't know about the warrant for her beliefs could make no positive difference to her, because her ability to know anything would be precisely what she no longer trusted. Indeed, the knowledge that her beliefs are without rational warrant could well serve to make her feel even more crazy.

There are other relevant differences, too, and these have to do with both the extent to which the women's beliefs have been manipulated and the means used to manipulate them. The woman who has been medically gaslighted has been extensively manipulated. Because hers is a case of oppression, she has perhaps never seen herself as a fully competent moral agent. Those in authority are likely always to have treated her as if she were morally deficient, and this means the normative competence condition was never fully met. The social constriction on her agency would then have been compounded by the medical judgment that she is hysterical, which corrupts what little sense of self-worth she might once have had. She, having internalized both the prevailing judgment about women and the judgment of medical science, is thereby thrice bound: once by patriarchy, again by doctors, and finally by herself. As she has never exercised her agency very freely, talk of narrative *repair* seems inappropriate. What the medically gaslighted woman needs are stories that let her *acquire* ordinary levels of free agency for the first time. She needs counterstories that her husband and his colleagues will endorse and counterstories that she can endorse. Only when her identity is more fully formed—in terms of how others see her and how she sees herself—can the normative competence condition be satisfied. The resources available to her for telling either kind of story lie in her communities, especially her communities of choice.

The Bergman character's problem lies more in the *means* by which her beliefs are manipulated. Once, it appears, she enjoyed normal levels of free agency: before she was married, both conditions for freedom were met reasonably well. That being the case, we can say that her beliefs have not been extensively manipulated. Nevertheless, if Boyer had been given a long enough time, he might have been able to corrupt her will even more thoroughly than did the husband of the medically gaslighted woman because the means Boyer employed were Bergman's own love and trust in him. He used the special vulnerability that is attendant on intimacy to bend her to his will, taking advantage of the confidence she placed in him, not only to implant the suggestion that she was going mad, but also to isolate her from anyone who might reassure her as to her sanity.

Had he been completely successful in this program of personal deception, he might well have stripped her of all the resources that would allow her to take back her normal epistemic position. Bereft of everything except her intimacy with him and no longer able to trust herself, she would have had to rely entirely on his judgments rather than her own. There would be no communities to which she could turn for help, for her world would now contain only herself and her husband. In that world there would be no one to free her, for she could no longer convincingly tell a counterstory on her own behalf and her husband would be the last person to tell it for her.[8]

Sustained and systematic deception by an intimate, then, is potentially even more destructive to a person's sense of her own worthiness to act than is oppression. In either case, however, the difficulty for someone who identifies *herself* as unworthy of answering for her own conduct is that she can't reidentify herself as morally accountable simply by coming to the rational conclusion that her feelings of worthlessness aren't warranted, or by having others point this out to her. Because she doesn't trust her own judgment, it will be hard for her to hear, much less create, a counterstory that reidentifies her as a worthy person. She can always come up with another story that explains why she *ought* to be treated badly. She can always remind herself, as Virginia Martin did, that docs will be docs.

How, then, can a counterstory serve to repair an infiltrated consciousness? The short answer is that sometimes it can't. As in the case of deprivation of opportunity, where there can be a great deal of difficulty in getting the persons who are misperceiving someone to endorse a counterstory that identifies the person as morally competent, so, in the case of infiltrated consciousness, the necessary story of weak or strong moral self-definition may be impossible for the oppressed person to develop. Since, however, consciousnesses can be infiltrated to greater or lesser degrees, the agent whose trust in herself is not yet completely corrupted might be able, under the right conditions, to tell the story she needs in order to free herself.

Virginia Martin, for example, has a comparatively mild case of infiltrated consciousness. When the Nurse Recognition Day committee meetings first began, she shared the mainstream view in the hospital that a nurse is a kind of second-rate doctor who doesn't deserve a great deal of professional courtesy. When she encountered evidence that this view was unwarranted, she was generally able to resolve the cognitive dissonance this set up in her by dismissing the evidence as unimportant or telling a story about it that made it fit better with her other beliefs.

She resisted the idea that she and her colleagues needed to reidentify themselves and was equally suspicious of the move to link this reidentification to any kind of feminist framework.

Because the committee meetings provided a moral space in which to reflect—in the company of other nurses whose opinions she respected—on who she was, and because these others had a very different view of nurses from the one that infiltrated her consciousness, a cognitive dissonance arose that she couldn't simply dismiss. She tried to laugh it off, caricaturing the project of strong moral self-definition as a Gloria-Steinem-meets-orthopedic-surgeon absurdity. Ultimately, however, her affection for, and trust in, her former professor and the new friends of her chosen community made it possible for her to take for her own the counterstory the others were telling about themselves.

As Benson's two papers suggest, identity and agency are both interpersonal notions. Who I am, morally speaking, is in some measure a matter of who others say I am, and this has a direct bearing on how freely I am able to exercise my moral agency. Moreover, how others perceive me also influences how I perceive myself, and that too has a direct bearing on my freedom to act.

Questions Raised by Counterstories

Counterstories, I have argued, permit people whose identities have been damaged by oppression to see themselves, and to be recognized by others, as morally trustworthy persons. But it is important to note precisely what role recognition plays here. By itself, recognition does not stop persons from being oppressed, as oppression is the product of a dialectic between people's understanding of themselves and of one another, on the one hand, and the material conditions of an oppressive community of place, on the other. The nurses' counterstory cannot—is not designed to—end oppression. It is instead a tool for reidentifying the nurses as respect worthy professionals, and so freeing their agency.

The story of the nurses raises a number of philosophical and ethical questions. First, what is it about the story that allows the nurses to refigure their own role? This is a question about *identity*. Second, what is the connection between the stories they have been hearing in their community of place and what is morally owed them? This is a question about *oppression*. Third, how should the nurses respond? This is a question about *resistance*. In the chapters to come, I take up each of these questions, using the concept of the counterstory to trace the connections among them.

Before doing so, however, I wish to situate my project with respect to other recent philosophical work. The growing body of literature within moral philosophy that has argued for the importance of narratives to the moral life has not paid much attention to oppressive identities and the possibility of narrative resistance. In the next chapter, then, I survey the work that has been done and examine some of the difficulties that arise as a consequence of this neglect.

Notes

1. Jeannine Ross Boyer, RN, supplied the texture for this story. The anecdote told by Pilar Sanchez is adapted from a case study presented by Wayne Vaught at the annual meeting of the Society for Health and Human Values, Baltimore, Md., November 1997. Sally Martinson's story is taken from the *American Journal of Nursing* 89, no. II (1989): 1466–67.

2. The method is similar to one that has been famously described by John Rawls (1971). Rawlsian reflective equilibrium, however, balances intuitive moral judgments about particular cases against a moral theory, not nonmoral descriptions against moral concepts.

3. My thanks to Elise Robinson for these four rubrics.

5. Even a fantasy begins with the stuff of actual people's lives: the depiction of a planet that is lit by two green suns draws on the actual experiences of "green" and "sun."

5. For ethical analyses of health care providers' refusal to remove Norplant, see Macklin 1996.

6. I take it that collectives and not just individuals are capable of moral agency. For arguments in defense of the idea that collectives can be persons, see Rovane 1998.

7. Oppression consists in systematic institutional processes that prevent certain groups of people from developing and exercising their capacities or gaining access to material goods (Young 1990, 38, 40). Personal domination consists in one person's preventing another from determining her own actions.

8. In the film, Boyer makes the mistake of permitting his wife to go out with him on a sightseeing expedition. Her beauty and mystery attract the attention of a handsome police investigator, played by Joseph Cotten, who ultimately comes to Bergman's rescue. So her world never does consist of just herself and her husband.

Critical Theory

Toran Hansen

Toran Hansen is an associate professor and graduate director of Conflict Analysis and Dispute Resolution at Salisbury University in Maryland. He previously worked as an assistant professor at Nova Southeastern University's Department of Conflict Analysis and Resolution in Florida. He received his PhD in social work from the University of Minnesota. He has worked as a mediator and a facilitator for the Minnesota Department of Corrections, the Palm Beach County Courthouse, and Nova Southeastern University. He was a Peace Corps volunteer in Guinea, West Africa. Hansen's research interests are in conflict transformation, as well as social, restorative, and transitional justice.

In this article, Hansen makes a case for bringing the work of critical theory into conflict resolution. His genealogy of critical theory traces the field from its origins in Marx and Engels through Foucault and Freire. While the critical approach has developed over time, many theorists share this goal of upending systems and structures that oppress various groups either socially, economically, and/or politically. Positioning social structures and culture as creations, rather than reflections of absolute truth, means conflict resolution practitioners must locate the groups and norms creating culture. This is the standpoint from which Epoch Three theorists explain their focus on power. If culture is created, one must consider who or what is creating it and how these lines of power produce and reproduce systems of oppression. By challenging notions of neutrality, conflict resolution acknowledges an understanding of how power operates and the oppression it can produce. If neutrality cannot exist, then practitioners must acknowledge, and then account for, power imbalances in conflict contexts; otherwise, the field risks replicating systems of oppression.

Hansen's call for praxis—rather than practice—challenges conflict resolution professionals to seek answers to real-world problems rather than abstract theory. Praxis is future-focused and is reflexive in nature, requiring constant reflection on the theory-action relationship and constant revision in response to these reflections.

Questions to consider: How might a study of power provide a new vantage point from which to study conflict? What might we better understand that was maybe overlooked before? Do we risk eliminating agency (people's ability to take action in their own lives) or accountability (holding people responsible for injustices) when we ascribe too much fault onto society?

Critical Conflict Resolution Theory and Practice

Toran Hansen

This article brings together a variety of ideas from critical theorists and practitioners in order to present a coherent critical approach for the field of conflict resolution. The historical roots of critical theory are briefly presented, along with critical practices that conflict resolution practitioners and theorists have developed. This leads to a discussion of critical strategies that are employed by conflict resolution practitioners who have aligned their practice and values with critical ideology. The potential place of critical theory and practice in the field of conflict resolution is stressed, highlighting new forms of practice and new roles for practitioners. As Alinsky wrote, "Conflict is the essential core of a free and open society" (1971, p. 12).

Critical theory has a long tradition in the social sciences and has contributed insights to many professional fields. The legal profession has used it to confront social justice concerns both in and out of the courts (Cornell University, n.d.; Ward, 1998). Teaching, in particular in higher education, has emphasized critical pedagogy in an effort to develop analytical thinking skills and promote critical ideas among students in critiquing the treatment of marginalized and oppressed populations (Knupfer, 1995). Social work has used critical theory to confront the social justice concerns faced by the clientele they serve daily (Payne, 2005). In fact, critical social workers such as David Gil (1998) have gone so far as to develop practice principles that guide a would-be critical social worker in community practice (see Exhibit 1). The field of conflict resolution and practitioners interested in addressing social justice concerns can benefit greatly by learning from this body of critical theory and practice wisdom. It is precisely this important societal concern for social justice and improving the lives of oppressed people that makes this endeavor worthwhile, for those entreated with assisting people in managing their social conflicts.

Exhibit 1. Critical Social Work Practice Principles

1. Rejecting the idea of political neutrality and believing in social justice and liberation
2. Choosing values consciously: equality, liberty, cooperation, and community
3. Transcending technical and professional approaches
4. Facilitating critical consciousness through dialogue
5. Advocating human rights
6. Confronting obstacles to needs fulfillment
7. Analyzing oppression in one's personal life
8. Analyzing future possibilities
9. Spreading critical consciousness and building social movements *Source:* Gil (1998), pp. 104–108.

Historical Roots

The origins of critical theory come from the work of Karl Marx and Friedrich Engels in the mid-1800s. At that time, Marx and Engels developed a critique of the capitalist system by analyzing the social structure from which it emerged (Collins, 1985). This analysis was based on considering how capitalism perpetuated the social classes. Marx and Engels argued that the lower class (the proletariat) was dominated by the upper class (the bourgeoisie) which controlled the societal resources and the means to produce them, concentrating societal wealth through political, ideological, and economic hegemony (see, for example, Collins, 1985). A particularly important means of control used by the bourgeoisie was ideological, with the lower classes accepting the social structure and the rules supporting it and adopting the interests of the elites as their own, though the social structure did not support their interests (Marx and Engels, 1985). This process was later termed "false consciousness." Overcoming this domination required the lower classes to revolt against their oppressors (Marx and Engels, 1969). Initially termed Marxist, this theoretical framework was later called "radical."

A recent period of great activity for radical activists and theorists was the 1960s and 1970s (Galper, 1976). In this era, the civil rights movement drew heavily on radical theory and practice in attempting to overturn unjust societal institutions and structures (Piven and Cloward, 1979). Constructivists such as Michel Foucault (who did not consider himself a Marxist or radical theorist) and Paulo Freire had a great impact on radical theory. Foucault reconsidered common understandings of social phenomena such as power and grounded them in the details of language, challenging the notions of neutrality and objectivity (Chambon, Irving, and Epstein, 1999). To Foucault, social understandings were created by those responsible for naming the social phenomena and norms in a society. In this sense, things were "true" only insofar as they were legitimized through language, which gave societal power to those who created the societal discourse, the societal elites (Chambon, Irving, and Epstein, 1999; Foucault, 1994a).

Freire's thought (1997) emerged directly from his work with the poor in Brazil who were facing the day-to-day reality of their oppression. Freire determined that societal change would emerge from a kind of education, one based on dialogue and self-discovery that would assist oppressed groups in understanding the structural obstacles to their hopes for social justice and equality. He called this awareness based on these new understandings "critical consciousness" (Freire, 1997). Educating for critical consciousness gave critical theorists a means for supporting marginalized groups in attaining their societal goals. These constructivist ideas had a profound impact on radical thought, and "critical theory" emerged from this union.

Critical theory has thus evolved over time. Different iterations were responses to social conditions and circumstances in various eras, when the public mood vacillated between more conservative and more liberal ideologies (Galper, 1976). In general, critical thought submerged in conservative eras when it was not favored and emerged again in favorable social and academic climates that were typically more liberal and less affluent (Galper, 1976). Theorists and practitioners working on behalf of diverse social movements have over time drawn on critical theory to explain and confront the oppression of various marginalized populations such as African Americans; Native Americans; women; gay, lesbian, bisexual, and transgender (GLBT) groups; and the physically and mentally challenged (Galper, 1976; Gil, 1998). The current conservative era (from the 1980s to the present), with increasingly consolidated wealth, a greater emphasis on military security, mainstream media that do not tend to question the status quo, and the relative absence of critical social analysis, supports the hypothesis that critical thought tends to submerge in affluent, conservative eras such as the one we are presently living through (Kincheloe and McLaren, 2000; Longres, 1982).

Important Concepts

Critical theory is relevant for the field of conflict resolution because it offers conflict resolution practitioners and scholars a framework that can guide them in assisting parties to overcome societal and interpersonal oppression and injustice:

> Oppression refers to a mode of human relations involving domination and exploitation—economic, social, and psychologic—between individuals; between social groups and classes within and beyond societies; and globally, between entire societies. . . .
>
> Injustice refers to coercively established and maintained inequalities, discrimination, and dehumanizing, development-inhibiting conditions of living (e.g., slavery serfdom, and exploitative wage labor; unemployment, poverty, starvation, and homelessness; inadequate healthcare and education), imposed by dominant social groups, classes, and peoples upon dominated and exploited groups, classes, and people [Gil, 1998, p. 10].

Societal oppression therefore adversely affects the entire society, oppressors and the oppressed alike, by dehumanizing them and giving certain groups advantages at the expense of others. The oppressed are dehumanized when they are denied opportunities that oppressors take for granted in pursuing their rights and in getting their needs met (Freire, 1997). Oppressors are dehumanized by controlling and violating the rights of the oppressed and becoming dominators, polarizing their communities, and denying their compassion for their fellow human beings (Freire, 1997).

Oppressive societies reinforce the exploitation of certain societal members for the benefit and privilege of others, resulting in unequal rights, conditions of living, and distribution of resources (Gil, 1998). These systemic social imbalances call for systemic alterations to the social structure and the taken-for-granted social order to address them, creating greater parity between groups (Galper, 1975). This is the essence of social justice, the principal goal of critical work. The National Association of Social Workers (1999) defines social justice as "pursu[ing] social change, particularly with and on behalf of vulnerable and oppressed individuals and groups of people. . . . Social change efforts are focused primarily on issues of poverty, unemployment, discrimination, and other forms of social injustice. These activities seek to promote sensitivity to and knowledge about oppression and cultural and ethnic diversity [and] strive to ensure access to needed information, services, and resources; equality of opportunity; and meaningful participation in decision making for all people."

The ultimate goal of critical theory is thus to transform societal relationships and institutions that are exploitative, creating a more equitable society.

Power in social relationships is the central organizing concept around which critical theory is organized. Marx and Engels (1985) originally conceived social power as arising out of historical relationships based on domination. Power is located in the hands of the oppressors and controlled by them in shaping societal ideologies. In the process, their interests become hidden, appearing as though they represent the interests of the entire society including oppressed groups (Marx and Engels, 1969, 1985). This "false consciousness" gives the upper class in a society ideological domination, thereby contributing to the control of the lower classes. The upper class also dominates a society through economic means, systematically concentrating societal wealth (Collins, 1985; Marx and Engels, 1969).

In overcoming oppression, the oppressed must awaken their awareness of the repressive dimensions of this oppressive societal ideology and rise up in a revolution to wrest ideological, economic, and political power from the hands of their oppressors (Marx and Engels, 1969, 1985). Overthrowing the oppressors in a social revolution is therefore paramount in Marxist thought and is transformative, altering society and its ideology wholesale rather than incrementally by nibbling away at the dominant societal ideology (Marx and Engels, 1969, 1985). Later iterations of critical theory have since challenged this notion of complete societal revolution as the only means to accomplish critical ends, in favor of incrementalism.

Foucault suggested that power as originally conceived by Marx and Engels was too simplistic. Instead of existing within the oppressors, like a thing that was

inevitably repressive, Foucault felt that power existed throughout the social network of relationships and had to be exercised in specific social contexts (Foucault,
1994a). To Foucault, power could be used for either productive or repressive ends
(Foucault, 1994b). However, the societal members who controlled the creation
and maintenance of language controlled the power in relationships by determining
how social phenomena were named and discussed (Foucault, 1994b). This process
creates what is perceived as the truth in any society. For this reason, Foucault
looked at the transformative potential of societal discourses as a means to change
society, rather than revolution as advocated by Marxist thought (Chambon,
Irving, and Epstein, 1999). Such transformation could be attained by disturbing
common understandings of social phenomena and relationships, destabilizing
societal discourse through analysis and language use rather than by force as envi-
sioned by Marx and Engels (Chambon, Irving, and Epstein, 1999; Foucault,
1994b). These constructivist ideas allowed analysts to see more complexity when
conceptualizing power, making societal transformation incremental (and less
objectionable) while retaining an analysis of ideological societal domination and
false consciousness.

Critical theory therefore calls for an analysis of power in overcoming societal
injustice and oppression. Expressions of power can be either covert or overt, and
a practitioner must consider both of these modalities of expression if they wish to
overturn its unjust application (Gil, 1998; Piven and Cloward, 1979). However,
societal discourse is frequently controlled by elites who can inhibit an official
power analysis on a societal level, in order to protect the prevailing social order
(Freire, 1997). Freire has suggested that overcoming these obstacles can be
achieved through a new kind of education, called "problem-posing education."
Students learn to deconstruct the societal ideology affecting them in their everyday
lives, see how it inhibits attainment of their interests, and visualize possible societal
changes that could better serve their interests. Problem-posing education ultimately results in "critical consciousness," which can be emancipatory for oppressed
individuals who can then seek to alter their world and the prevailing oppressive
societal ideology in accordance with their new understandings.

Traditionally, education and societal institutions have objectified people,
denying them opportunities for probing into important societal discourse in order
to deconstruct it for their benefit as "subjects" capable of questioning and transforming their world (Foucault, 1994a; Freire, 1997). To allow oppressed individuals and populations to become subjects, their voices must come to the fore and be
counted. In meeting the needs of the oppressed, more equitable societal alternatives should be conceived by them, as a grassroots approach, rather than being
imposed on them from more powerful social groups (Galper, 1975). The common
interests of various oppressed groups can be used as a means to galvanize their
solidarity of voice, which could then create the leverage needed to generate social
change (Freire, 1997). Preventing their voices from entering the societal discourse
is a form of violence perpetrated against the oppressed and must be overcome in
order to create and maintain a just society (Freire, 1997).

When individuals reach critical consciousness, it allows them to become subjects in their world, actively and consciously co-creating it, rather than passive

"objects" who accept their social reality (Chambon, Irving, and Epstein, 1999; Foucault, 1994a; Freire, 1997). In this way, critical theory calls for *praxis*, addressing real-world problems and constraints, rather than armchair theorizing. *Praxis* is the reciprocal, dynamic, and reflexive relationship that practitioners engage in when their theorizing about societal oppression informs their actions taken to challenge that oppression, and vice versa (Marx and Engels, 1985). *Praxis* also puts the scholar or practitioner in a position of continuous reflection, questioning the theory-action relationship in order to continuously revise his or her approach. A *praxis* orientation is inherently future-oriented and hopeful, with scholar-practitioners creating new visions for societal relationships in overcoming societal domination, which in turn are an impetus for further societal analysis and action (Freire, 1997; Scanlon and Longres, 2001).

There have been many important and valid criticisms of critical theory since the time that Marx and Engels originally conceived it. As was already stated, concepts of power employed by critical theorists have been criticized for being too narrow, focusing on collective rather than individual justice and exclusively considering domination by elites when "powerless" groups can use both violence and social power to further their own ends as well (Payne, 2005; Spencer, 1991). In conflict resolution, this can create a problem when the subjective experiences of clients and their understanding are minimized (ideological concerns) in favor of paternalist practitioner understandings based on society as a whole (materialist concerns; Eide, 1972; Heyworth, 1991; Spencer, 1991). At its worst, critical theory can be used to blame an individual's social environment and his or her assumed place in it for all of the problems and conflicts, eliminating personal agency and responsibility for ameliorating those concerns (Payne, 2005). Likewise, "the establishment" (societal elites) are thought of by critical theorists in very stereotypical, one-dimensional terms (Kent, 1971; Spencer, 1991), which can create further polarization between parties in conflict. Paying attention to such criticisms can help critical theorists and practitioners recognize the limitations of their analysis. In the field of conflict resolution, these limitations can help guide decisions as to when it would be appropriate to employ a critical analytic framework and when it would not.

The Place of Critical Theory in Conflict Resolution Theory

Critical theory is not altogether new to the field of conflict resolution. In the early 1970s, Rapoport initiated a debate considering the proper place of critical theory and practice in international conflict resolution and peace studies. Kent (1971), Eide (1972), and Stohl and Chamberlain (1972) were among those to respond to this discussion. Rapoport (1970) suggested that conflict resolution could potentially be seen as a tool of "the establishment" in attempting to pacify conflicting parties, potentially undermining the attempts of marginalized populations in attaining social justice. In this vain, Stohl and Chamberlain juxtapose the goal of social justice with that of social stability, questioning whether it is possible for conflict resolution practitioners to pursue both goals simultaneously. Eide went further to say that the quest for neutrality in the profession may in fact mask underlying inequitable power governing the relationships of conflicting parties. This stance suggests that true neutrality is not possible in conflict resolution as the societal elites benefit from such a position, holding power and privilege outside the conflict resolution process itself. Hence conflict resolution processes would be biased toward societal elites rather than "underdogs," reinforcing the status quo.

These arguments embed individual conflicts firmly in the social structures where they have arisen, thus broadening the field of conflict resolution to consider the impact of significant external societal factors (such as power) on any particular conflict, and their potential implications for its management or resolution. In a rebuttal to the premise that conflict resolution was being used as a tool by the establishment, Kent (1971) suggested quite the opposite: that conflict resolution was not a tool of the establishment and conflict scholars have had sufficient autonomy to critically examine conflicts and conflict resolution processes. In fact, their independence is what enabled them to aid parties in discovering the causes of their conflicts and help craft just resolutions. He believed that researchers and practitioners were not so much a part of the establishment but rather were not being thorough and contemporary enough to ensure that their work went outside the bounds of the expectations of the establishment.

Today, this debate is still very much alive in considering the potential utility of critical theory and practice in international conflict resolution. Quille (2000), for instance, suggested that critical theory might have an important role to play in informing peacekeeping operations. Quille indicates that creating a sustainable peace involves more than placating or pacifying conflicting parties; any resolution should also ensure the human and economic rights of parties in conflict. This type of peace building differs from traditional peacekeeping operations by empowering and developing local communities. Martin (2005) states that such support for the underdogs ensures that peace building protects minorities and human rights, rather than supporting a conservative, elite-legitimated social order. Traditional notions of peacekeeping may tend to quell hot conflict by military or political means in advance of any thorough consideration of the implications of halting the conflict before the underlying social issues are addressed.

Critical theory and practice can also be applied to domestic conflict resolution settings. Certain conflicts, where social justice considerations are present (such as those involving racial, gender-based, and other social justice-related concerns), may call for an approach supporting the party in conflict who is the underdog. Such contexts necessitate attention to the structural causes of and remedies for conflicts, which are considered embedded in the social structure and societal discourse. Conflict resolution is a pluralistic field with a variety of theoretical orientations possible, owing to their specific practice contexts and goals. Critical practice can fill a specific niche in the field of conflict resolution outside of traditional settings where a neutral third-party stance is desirable or essential (as with mediation in the courts, for instance).

Bush and Folger (1994) show us that mediation as a form of conflict resolution, for example, is a diverse enterprise in outlining four mediation conceptions: "the satisfaction story," "the social justice story," "the transformation story," and "the oppression story." The satisfaction story's primary goal is satisfying the needs of parties in conflict by settling their dispute through problem solving. In the transformation story the primary goals are promoting empathy between the parties (recognition) and empowering them in their decision making (empowerment). The social justice story considers mediation a tool for overcoming societal oppression, while the oppression story suggests that it may actually be used as a tool to promote and perpetuate the status quo of societal domination. Although critical theory aligns with the social justice story, Bush and Folger suggest that the satisfaction story has dominated the field of mediation to the detriment of both the social justice story and the transformation story. Mediation scholarship and practice may therefore be artificially narrowed in the field of conflict resolution, stifling potential opportunities for tension and debate that could broaden and improve it.

The satisfaction story relies heavily on the mediator taking a neutral stance as a conflict intermediary (Bush and Folger, 1994). Such a neutral, disinterested stance suggests that a mediator can stand apart from his or her social, economic, political, and cultural context (Cotter, Monk, and Winslade, 1998). For the conflict resolution practitioner, however, true neutrality may be more of a myth or "folklore" than an actual attainable goal (Rifken, Millen, and Cobb, 1991). The world in which conflict resolution practitioners live is situated in a specific historical, social, and political context, and they are subject to that context, including many established social patterns and norms that are invisible to them (Chambon, Irving, and Epstein, 1999; Foucault, 1994a, 1994b; Freire, 1997; Gil, 1998). A neutral stance, without an analysis of power between the parties in conflict, can obfuscate the power differential that exists between parties in conflict and actually undermine the efforts of oppressed people by tacitly or explicitly supporting the prevailing ideology and social order oppressing them (Eide, 1972; Townley, 1994). Because social actions are not politically neutral, conflict resolution practitioners may erroneously believe that they have conducted themselves in a neutral and impartial manner as mediators. In actuality, they may have unwittingly supported societal norms that oppress the very people they are serving, upholding an oppressive social order. Critical theory does not rely on this neutral position but rather calls for conflict resolution practitioners to explicitly state power imbalances, take a partial position with the underdog, and seek to go beyond conflict settlement, helping parties change oppressive social relationships.

Critical theory fits well with various core ideas in conflict resolution theory. Conflict theorists from a variety of disciplines and practicing in different settings have sought to uncover and remedy the underlying causes of conflicts, including oppression. Johan Galtung's vision of conflict resolution, for instance, corresponds very well to many central ideas in critical theory. Galtung's notion (1969, 2000) of positive peace entrenches individual conflicts in the societal structure where they have arisen. For a negative peace to exist in a society, that society must be free of physical violence, but for positive peace to exist it must be free of both direct physical violence and structural violence. Structural violence occurs when stable social patterns perpetuating imbalances are embedded in a society, thus harming individuals or social groups and preventing those people from realizing their potentialities. Even though the conflictual behaviors of the parties in conflict represent the parties themselves, their underlying relationship emerges from their social structure (Eide, 1972). In this way, the achievement of peace involves more than the absence of societal violence, instead requiring the presence of social justice. A practitioner should not simply assist parties in conflict to reach a decision, placating them and potentially fostering negative peace, but should instead help them reach a decision that is just, fostering positive peace.

Feminist conflict resolution theorists have also drawn heavily from critical theory in their work. Betty Reardon (1990), for instance, recognizes that the concepts of peace and justice are inherently tied to one another; her feminist conflict analysis is not intended to be neutral but rather to challenge deep-rooted gender oppression, bringing about positive peace. Furthermore, she ties militarism to masculine societal domination and contrasts this against traditionally feminine, nurturing practices and social mores. Reardon links the fulfillment of needs with peace, which would ultimately serve to challenge masculine societal domination and notions of security that emphasize military and police protection. Brock-Utne (1990) also seeks to challenge sexist social practices that lead to violence and negative peace. Her analysis challenges societal sexism and the institutions that support it, ultimately leading her to consider ways of redistributing societal resources to women and assisting women in attaining institutional positions of power in society. Both of these feminist scholars seek to challenge the oppressive status quo and bring about societal reform through conflict resolution.

There are a variety of other conflict resolution theorists whose ideological orientation and practice align to varying degrees with critical theory and practice. John Burton's problem-solving workshops (1996) call for participants representing conflicting parties to recognize each other's basic human needs and creatively discover ways of meeting those needs together. Burton saw his approach as essentially preventative, calling the process "provention," attempting to address causative factors that gave rise to the conflict to begin with. When these factors are understood, workshop participants can then be given the skills to dialogue with one another, problem-solving means of overcoming these obstacles. Hence conflict settlement is intimately connected to conflicting parties' understanding of the societal structures shaping their behaviors (such as a lack of human and economic rights), while fostering individual and community empowerment by giving them the skills to discuss these imbalances.

Critical theory also aligns well with John Paul Lederach's elicitive training model for peace building. Lederach (1995) suggests that conflict resolution practitioners training individuals and communities to address and overcome conflict must necessarily prioritize the voice of the trainees. Lederach illustrates how this approach to training can help to overcome cultural biases in cross-cultural settings. Equally important, like Freire, Lederach recognizes that emphasizing the voices of the populations one is working with helps the practitioner gain credibility and meet the needs of the people in conflict, while acknowledging that potential resolutions should be grounded in local knowledge and language. The elicitive approach illustrates how ground-up decision making can simultaneously help conflicting parties better meet their immediate needs and realize their long-term structural goals. When oppressed people achieve critical consciousness, they identify their own needs, obstacles, and potential solutions to their problems in light of their new understanding of societal power. When calling for the voices of the oppressed to identify their own concerns and their potential resolutions, grassroots participatory democracy is promoted (O'Brien, 2005).

Implications for Conflict Resolution Practice

Applying critical theory to the field of conflict resolution points conflict resolution practitioners in a new and important direction. This does not mean that other forms of conflict resolution practice should not be valued or practiced in our society; conflict resolution is a pluralistic discipline requiring a number of conceptions and methods to address different kinds of conflict. Critical conflict resolution puts practitioners in a new role in order to address and ameliorate societal oppression. Oppression and social injustice are considered multitiered, nested conflicts, simultaneously existing at the individual, community, and societal levels. Critical conflict resolution becomes a means to challenge social injustice and oppression. Social welfare, for instance (nonprofit and government services for poor and marginalized communities), could be considered a means to mediate class, gender, and ethnic conflicts, either masking or managing these conflicts depending on its implementation (Chatterjee, 1996). Conflict resolution practitioners working with social welfare agencies could use a critical lens to manage individual, group, and organizational conflicts within that system, as dialogue facilitators who foster productive communications between individuals or groups with differing levels of power.

Critical conflict resolution practice calls for both short-term and long-term strategies to challenge societal oppression. Gil (1998) suggests that even though critical practices emphasize long-term, structural social change in assisting oppressed populations, short-term strategies are called for as well. Short-range strategies are necessary to ameliorate the "symptoms" of oppression and reduce or eliminate oppressive practices targeting specific oppressed individuals or groups in given situations. Long-range strategies, on the other hand, seek to eliminate the root causes of oppression, hoping to create a just society free from oppression. Both short-term and long-term strategies would be enhanced with conflict resolution practitioners who promote and enhance communications between the oppressed and their oppressors as well as facilitate discussions among oppressed individuals to help them determine their needs and their preferred means to meet them.

Regardless of whether strategies are short-term or long-term, however, they imply a very different ethical code than is presently emphasized in many conflict resolution circles. The American Arbitration Association, the American Bar Association, and the Association for Conflict Resolution highlight self-determination, impartiality, avoiding conflicts of interest, competence, confidentiality, quality of the mediation process, responsible solicitation of services, reasonable fees, and advancing mediation practice as their ethical standards in their Model Standards of Conduct for Mediators (2005), but critical practice suggests a very different set of ethical principles. Critical ethical principles tend to focus less on the professional role of the practitioner and more on their commitment to social justice, including a concern with the common welfare of humanity, meeting the needs of all in society, consistent critical values in one's personal and professional lives, advancing critical theory and practice, supporting fellow critical practitioners and holding them to critical ethical standards, valuing the freedom of all people, seeking to uphold democratic and humanistic ideals, and working to change society to match these ethical principles (Galper, 1975). Ethical frameworks for advocates may be more suitable for such an approach and already exist within the fields of social work and the law. Consequently, these other professions furnish ethical frameworks that might offer ethical insights for critical conflict resolution practitioners.

Critical practitioners should abide by certain practice guidelines in conducting their work: developing oneself to reflect critical ideals; linking one's work to broader social movements and political solutions to social problems; and focusing on conflict prevention with long-term, durable, just resolutions. To assist others in overcoming oppression, practitioners need to first reflexively question their own values and experiences with oppression as their practice will undoubtedly reflect their personal theoretical orientation and values (Galper, 1975, 1976). Critical theory also emphasizes egalitarian relationships with one's clients and colleagues (Galper, 1975, 1980). This means shedding the "expert" role in favor of reciprocal learning and client-driven practice. Once oppressed individuals have reached critical consciousness by being educated about structural power imbalances, they become empowered to identify manifestations of oppression and determine means for addressing them. Critical practitioners are charged with facilitating critical discussions of societal discourse that draw out personal perspectives of oppression, obstacles to transforming oppressive relationships, and the potential means for overcoming those obstacles from the oppressed themselves (Freire, 1997; Galper, 1980; Galtung, 2000). Hence critical dialogue includes reflection by the oppressed on societal norms, institutions, language, and values, as well as discussions of actions to be taken to alter these phenomena in order to promote social justice (Chambon, Irving, and Epstein, 1999; Freire, 1997; Galtung, 2000).

Critical practice also calls for efforts to build local collectivities and organizations that link to larger movements: "Change comes from power and power comes from organization" (Alinsky, 1971, p. 113). The process of community organizing means acquiring and expanding a network of allies (Alinsky, 1971; Galper, 1975, 1980; Gil, 1998). When linked to broader social movements, communities of the oppressed can maximize their "disruptive power" in challenging oppressive societal practices and the social order (Galper, 1975; Piven, 2006, Piven and Cloward, 1979). In changing societal discourse, inevitably critical practice must bring the voice of the oppressed to the political stage. Policies involving health care, unemployment, and other such concerns inevitably affect the oppressed, and their voices must be shared with policymakers in an effort to influence them (Eide, 1972; Gil, 1998). Conflict resolution practitioners can use mediation, negotiation, and facilitation skills to bring oppressed allies together, communicate with potential supporters from larger social movements, and struggle for political changes that could ameliorate their circumstances.

Critical practice demands that practitioners go beyond a reactive stance that tends to modify the status quo, seeking instead to address the underlying causes of oppression. As conflict resolution practitioners, Burton (1996) and Galtung (2000) emphasize preventative conflict resolution approaches. The underlying assumption suggested in their work is that meeting people's basic human needs may prevent a harmful conflict from arising or escalating. Preventative critical conflict resolution entails facilitating productive dialogue to assist oppressed people in receiving the services, skills, and resources they need by advocating with them to ensure that their needs are met so that resolutions are consequently durable (O'Brien, 2005).

The question remains, however, as to what the incentive would be for an oppressor to come to the bargaining table with the oppressed and a conflict resolution practitioner who is partial to their plight. There are three potential reasons an oppressor would participate in such a venue. First, the oppressor may be educated as to the injustice experienced by the oppressed party and want to ameliorate it. Freire (1997) terms these oppressors "converts," who desire to overturn an unjust social order. Second, the oppressor may be compelled to come to the table in being regulated to do so either by a higher authority or by the oppressed themselves, who can use shaming, nonparticipation in the social structure, or other direct action to force the oppressor to act. Martin Luther King Jr. used such nonviolent tactics to dramatize racial injustice in order to "create such a crisis and foster such a tension that a community which has constantly refused to negotiate is forced to do so" (King, 1992, p. 116). In contrast to Dr. King's approach, the use of legal authority, such as that coming from *Brown v. Board of Education* in 1954, compelled schools to face the issue of racially integrating school systems across the United States (King, 1992). The third reason an oppressor may come to the bargaining table with a critical conflict resolution practitioner is that just solutions tend to be more durable, long-term solutions. Resolutions that give the oppressed more power to control their own lives and problems by reducing societal inequities, eliminating structural forms of oppression, and ensuring that the needs of the oppressed party are met are likely to be more sustainable (Galtung, 2000; Martin, 2005; O'Brien, 2005; Quille, 2000).

Critical Conflict Resolution Practice

As has been suggested, critical conflict resolution places conflict resolution practitioners in roles and settings that are different from those of traditional conflict resolution practitioners. Rather than third-party neutrals, conflict resolution practitioners might more suitably take on the roles of catalyst, educator, advocate, advisor, systems navigator, or another that would assist oppressed people in challenging oppression by fostering productive dialogue (Kent, 1971; Knupfer, 1995; Stohl and Chamberlain, 1972). There are already many conflict resolution practitioners and scholars who have adopted such atypical roles, as with conflict resolution education for instance, where practitioners educate and advocate rather than mediate. These emerging, diverse roles within the conflict resolution profession may also call for new and innovative settings for novel forms of conflict resolution practice to be nurtured, as in nonprofit organizations such as peace and justice centers that educate community members for critical consciousness, train them in communication skills, and cultivate social justice discourse.

Traditional conflict resolution practitioners do not use a critical framework for conflict analysis or practice. However, practitioners in the field of conflict resolution are positioned well professionally to do critical work because they are the only professionals to holistically examine social conflicts and are skilled at various core processes for intervening in conflict: negotiation, mediation, arbitration, early neutral evaluation, community conferencing, negotiated rulemaking, communication and problem-solving training, and efforts to reduce violence in schools (Association for Conflict Resolution, n.d.). These skill areas make conflict resolution practitioners uniquely suited for certain forms of critical practice, intervening in social justice—related conflict. Here we offer several examples of how the core conflict resolution processes of mediation, negotiation, facilitation and training, and conflict resolution education can be conducted in using a critical practice framework.

Prior to conducting critical conflict resolution, practitioners must undertake a power analysis of the parties in conflict. In a power analysis, a practitioner "examine[s] how power is distributed in a given situation in terms of, for example, race, gender, education, economics, sexual orientation, or socio-political history. Through power analysis the [practitioner] and client[s] come to a more informed and context-sensitive understanding of beliefs, choices, perceptions, and behaviors. An important component of power analysis is understanding the meaning and effects of privilege" (McWhirter and McWhirter, 2007, p. 423).

In such an analysis, the practitioner should conduct a self-analysis to understand the role power might play in interactions with parties in conflict, as well as an analysis of the parties themselves (McWhirter and McWhirter, 2007). In conducting a power analysis, a practitioner considers both societal power imbalances and those stemming from practitioner and party cultures, institutions, organizations, languages, and idiosyncratic belief systems (Roy, 2007). The relevant forms of power to be mapped out are context-dependent and may include other forms of power and privilege such as those that come with age or physical ability, for instance (McWhirter and McWhirter, 2007). The conflict resolution practitioner uses this power analysis over the course of working with the parties to educate them as to how societal power could be affecting their thoughts, feelings, and behaviors, enabling them to overcome social justice—related obstacles to dialogue and conflict resolution.

CRITICAL CONFLICT RESOLUTION
MEDIATION

Critical mediation, particularly with therapeutic mediation models, involves drawing attention to power differentials as a result of gender, class, racial, ethnic, or other group membership. In fact, Roy (2007) suggests that all mediations involve "rearranging power" to some extent between parties in conflict. In this sense, it is not possible for a mediator to be neutral; rather, the practitioner should advocate for those who have less power in the mediation according to the social structure: "The job of the mediator is to persuade those with more power to see where their own interests join with their subordinates' in recasting roles and relationships, as well as teaching leaders the difference between the cooperative use of power and its hierarchical abuse" (Roy, 2007, p. 84). In this mediation model, there is a clear mandate to help facilitate more egalitarian relationships between conflicting parties and support the rights of weaker parties.

Narrative mediation also calls attention to societal power differentials between parties in conflict. Winslade and Monk (2001) illustrate examples of mediating disputes between spouses and ex-spouses in which the men in conflict have a sense of patriarchal entitlement. They show how the use of "externalizing language" (separating the people from the problem) can be used to draw attention to such power differences without creating defensiveness or loss of face on the part of the male power abuser. This mediation model places the specific conflict being mediated in the overarching societal discourse around patriarchy and male entitlement. The mediation venue is used to show the parties in conflict how their conflict fits into that discourse and the negative effects the discourse has on their lives and the conflict. That being clarified, they are in a position to change their relationship with the overall discourse and resolve their conflict accordingly.

CRITICAL CONFLICT RESOLUTION
NEGOTIATION

Critical negotiation plies many of the same skills of traditional negotiation toward critical ends, while involving a degree of uniqueness. For instance, Kritek (2002) presents several examples of negotiations that she was a part of in health care as a nurse and administrator, which she used as opportunities to challenging existing systems of power for the benefit of marginalized groups. She engaged in negotiations with a state funding agency, social service agencies, university groups, and neighborhood residents to get more community control in a clinic serving the needs of racially diverse community residents. She also engaged in negotiations with her university's administration to establish mechanisms for women to participate more fully in university governance and to recruit more students of color. Kritek believes that negotiating at "uneven tables" in order to struggle against existing power structures involves unique "ways of being" in order to be successful. Though all negotiators should be authentic, honest, innovative, open to learning, and take responsibility for change, less powerful groups must be particularly innovative, be even clearer on what their limits are, expand discussions to wider and deeper outcome and process visions, and know how and when to leave the bargaining table.

Critical negotiators thus work as advocates, laboring for the cause of social justice and against oppressive institutions. This fits within the purview of social workers as well, who have defined social advocacy as "the exclusive and mutual representation of a client(s) or a cause in a forum, attempting to systematically influence decision making in an unjust or unresponsive system(s)" (Schneider and Lester, 2001, p. 65). In fact, as alluded to earlier advocacy is entrenched in the National Association of Social Workers *Code of Ethics* (1999), linking social work's commitment to advocacy with the value base of the profession, which includes striving for social justice, placing clients' needs in their environmental context, and considering the general welfare of society (Schneider and Lester, 2001). Advocacy can be done case-by-case (advocating for client needs), for a cause (advocating for systemic change to benefit entire social groups), on the legislative level (advocating for political and regulatory change), or as a social service administrator by changing one's agency to reflect social justice goals (Schneider and Lester, 2001). Conflict resolution practitioner skills in conflict analysis and negotiation are well suited to engaging in various forms of advocacy when working with disadvantaged groups or individuals to reform social institutions or policies.

CRITICAL CONFLICT RESOLUTION FACILITATION AND TRAINING

Critical facilitation can be done between oppressed groups and their oppressors or within an oppressed group alone. Kelman (2002) has conducted interactive problem-solving workshops between groups with different levels of societal power. In his model of unofficial diplomacy, Kelman links the problem-solving sessions with the larger political negotiation process to bring the individual changes undergone by workshop participants to the larger political stage in order to change the social structure. Critical theory can inform this process as facilitators provide content observations and illuminate blind-spots for participants (potentially educating them as to unaddressed social justice concerns), though their primary role is safeguarding the process itself.

Truth and reconciliation commissions are another model for facilitating a forum between societal underdogs and elites to address social injustice. For example, in North Carolina the Greensboro Truth and Reconciliation Commission entered the societal discourse around race relations in the United States. They conducted an investigation of a shooting by Ku Klux Klan members on November 3, 1979, examining evidence, conducting interviews, and making recommendations for change as a result of the incident (Brown and others, 2006; Zucker, 2007). Facilitating community discussions and public interviews (in addition to reviewing written evidence) resulted in a community dialogue and a report that gave a new historical account of the incident for the community (Brown and others, 2006; Zucker, 2007).

Curle, on the other hand, has conducted seminars for the oppressed alone, designed to raise their awareness of structural inequalities and discuss strategies for nonviolent means to resist that oppression (Avruch, 2002; Curle, 1995). These trainings consist of instruction in skills such as mediation, facilitation, negotiation, general communication, organizing, and nonviolent action, but they also impart the principles of nonviolence, promote empathy, and emphasize compassion for others as a core value (Curle, 1995). The facilitator is not a neutral but an activist who enters the dispute between a community group and the established social structure as a supporter of the group (Avruch, 2002). The Dutch Reform Church, in conjunction with Cape Town University's Centre for Intergroup Studies, has used this workshop model in South Africa to shift South Africans away from the policy of apartheid (Curle, 1995).

CRITICAL CONFLICT RESOLUTION EDUCATION

Conflict resolution education is used to teach students in kindergarten through twelfth grade conflict resolution skills and participatory democracy (Hedeen, 2005). As schools are a microcosm for society, they can also constitute an excellent forum for educating students about social injustice, its expressions, and ways of resisting injustice in one's personal life (Bettman and Moore, 1994; Townley, 1994). Such is the goal of Freire's problem-posing education (1997). Raines (2004) and Tidwell (2004) illustrate how poignant conflict resolution education can be in developing or war-torn countries, where the effects of oppression and injustice are acute. Critical conflict resolution education goes beyond traditional conflict resolution education models by helping students see personal manifestations of oppression in their lives, discuss means of resisting them, and consider plans for doing so (Freire, 1997). For instance, instead of discussing racism generally and teaching students to be "colorblind," an antiracist education teaches students to see their racial privilege or internalized oppression and deliberately act against its overt and covert manifestations in their lives, altering racist social structures within their purview (Derman-Sparks and Phillips, 1997).

Critical higher education can be used by conflict resolution programs to bring critical theory and practice to curricula, furnish a venue for students to develop their critical practice skills, link classroom learning to real world *praxis* via service learning, and provide a rationale for a program's institutional practice to match its social justice mandate (Bettman and Moore, 1994; Galper, 1980; Gil, 1998; Knupfer, 1995; Scanlon and Longres, 2001; Wells, 2003). Various university conflict resolution programs have included courses addressing oppression as part of their curricula (such as the Women, Trauma, Leadership, and Peacebuilding class at Eastern Mennonite University; n.d.) or support students in taking such classes through affiliated university programs (such as the Race and Civil Rights Law class at the University of Denver; n.d.). The School for International Training has even created a master's degree program dedicated to educating students in conducting social justice work with conflict resolution skills (the Social Justice in Intercultural Relations program, n.d.).

Scholarship in higher education has another role to play in researching the process and outcomes of critical practice, improving practice and demonstrating effectiveness. Critical research can be used to build theory and practice, support political agendas, make the concerns of oppressed groups more visible, communicate societal concerns to a broader audience, and develop the analytic capacity of critical researchers and oppressed people (Galper, 1980; Kincheloe and McLaren, 2000; Scanlon and Longres, 2001). Many individual conflict resolution scholars have conducted this kind of research. George Mason University (n.d.) has even sponsored a publication that focuses on social justice scholarship (*Social Justice*). One conflict resolution program that has explicitly committed itself to social justice work is the International Center for Cooperation and Conflict Resolution (ICCCR) at Teacher's College in Columbia University (n.d.). The founder, Morton Deutsch (2006), believes that oppression is a root cause of most serious conflicts and thinks that conflict resolution can be facilitated when oppressed parties in conflict enhance their power and oppressor party power is suppressed. The ICCCR program has a stated mission to embrace social justice work and work against oppression in teaching and scholarship. They further this mission by creating scholarly conferences to discuss oppression and injustice, support student scholarship with social justice awards, and ultimately educate many soon-to-be teachers on principles and techniques that foster critical conflict resolution education in the classroom.

Conclusion

Conflict resolution practice and theory emerging from a critical framework point the profession of conflict resolution in a new and important direction: resisting an unjust status quo. Conflict resolution can be enriched with more attention placed on power analyses, power balancing, and the attainment of sustainable resolutions that resist social injustice and oppression. The skills used by conflict resolution practitioners (such as mediation, negotiation, facilitation, training, and education) could be effectively employed to confront societal oppression in alignment with critical theory, as illustrated by the examples in this article. Critical conflict resolution certainly has its limitations, but it can complement other forms of conflict resolution, addressing conflicts with underlying social justice concerns using techniques appropriate to those concerns. As such, critical theory and practice fill a specific niche in the field of conflict resolution. The critical theoretical framework should coexist with other theoretical orientations within the pluralistic profession of conflict resolution, adding to healthy discussion and debate in the field. Critical theory does not limit but broadens the field of conflict resolution. Conflict resolution practitioners and scholars can only benefit from the ideas and practices that it brings.

References

Alinsky, S. *Rules for Radicals: A Practical Primer for Realistic Radicals.* New York: Random House, 1971.

American Arbitration Association, American Bar Association, and Association for Conflict Resolution. *Model Standards of Conduct for Mediators,* 2005, retrieved Apr. 10, 2007 (http://www.acrnet.org/pdfs/ModelStandardsofConductforMediatorsfinal05.pdf).

Association for Conflict Resolution. "Frequently Asked Questions." *Official Website,* n.d., retrieved Jan. 6, 2007 (http://www.acrnet.org/about/CR-FAQ.htm).

Avruch, K. *Culture and Conflict Resolution* (3rd printing). Washington, DC: United States Institute of Peace Press, 2002.

Bettman, E. H., and Moore, P. "Conflict Resolution Programs and Social Justice." Education and Urban Society, 1994, 27(1), 11–21.

Brock-Utne, B. "Feminist Perspectives on Peace." In P. Smoker, R. Davies, and B. Munske (eds.), *A Reader in Peace Studies.* Oxford: Pergamon Press, 1990.

Brown, C., and others. *Greensboro Truth and Reconciliation Commission Report: Executive Summary.* Greensboro, NC: Greensboro Truth and Reconciliation Commission, 2006.

Burton, J. W. "Conflict Resolution as Political Philosophy." In D. J. D. Sandle and H. Van Der Werwe (eds.), *Conflict Resolution Theory and Practice.* New York: Manchester University Press, 1996.

Bush, R. A. B., and Folger, J. P. *The Promise of Mediation: Responding to Conflict Through Empowerment and Recognition.* San Francisco: Jossey-Bass, 1994.

Chambon, A. S., Irving, A., and Epstein, L. "Foucault's Approach: Making the Familiar Visible." In A. S. Chambon, A. Irving, and L. Epstein (eds.), *Reading Foucault for Social Work.* New York: Columbia University Press, 1999.

Chatterjee, P. *Approaches to the Welfare State.* Washington, D.C.: National Association of Social Workers, 1996.

Collins, R. *Three Sociological Traditions.* New York: Oxford University Press, 1985.

Columbia University. *International Center for Cooperation and Conflict Resolution,* n.d., retrieved Feb. 9, 2008 (http://www.tc.columbia.edu/ICCCR/centerMission.html).

Cornell University. *Legal Information Institute,* n.d., retrieved Apr. 10, 2007 (http://www.law.cornell.edu/wex/index.php/Critical_legal_theory).

Cotter, A., Monk, G., and Winslade, J. "A Narrative Approach to the Practice of Mediation." *Negotiation Journal,* 1998, *14*(1), 21–42.

Curle, A. *Another Way: Positive Response to Contemporary Violence.* Oxford: Jon Carpenter, 1995.

Derman-Sparks, L., and Phillips, C. B. *Teaching/Learning Anti-Racism: A Developmental Approach.* New York: Teacher's College Press, 1997.

Deutsch, M. "A Framework for Thinking About Oppression and Its Change." *Social Justice Research,* 2006, 19(1), 7–41.

Eastern Mennonite University. *Graduate Program Course Descriptions,* n.d., retrieved Feb. 9, 2008 (https://www.emu.edu/cjp/curdes.html).

Eide, A. "Dialogue and Confrontation in Europe." *Journal of Conflict Resolution,* 1972, *16*(4), 511–522.

Foucault, M. "The Subject and Power." In P. Rubinow and N. Rose (eds.), *The Essential Foucault.* New York: New Press, 1994a.

Foucault, M. "Truth and Power." In P. Rubinow and N. Rose (eds.), *The Essential Foucault.* New York: New Press, 1994b.

Freire, P. *Pedagogy of the Oppressed* (20th anniversary ed.). New York: Continuum, 1997.

Galper, J. *The Politics of Social Services.* Upper Saddle River, NJ: Prentice-Hall, 1975.

Galper, J. "Editorial: Social Work and the Left." *Journal of Sociology and Social Welfare,* 1976, *4*(2), 164–165.

Galper, J. *Social Work Practice: A Radical Perspective.* Upper Saddle River, NJ: Prentice-Hall, 1980.

Galtung, J. "Violence, Peace, and Peace Research." *Journal of Peace Research,* 1969, 6(3), 167–191.

Galtung, J. *Conflict Transformation by Peaceful Means: The Transcend Method, Participant's and Trainer's Manual,* 2000, retrieved Apr. 10, 2007. United Nations Disaster Management Training Programme (http://www.transcend.org/pctrcluj2004/TRANSCEND_manual.pdf).

George Mason University. *Social Justice,* n.d., accessed February 9, 2008 (http://journals.gmu.edu/index.php/socialjustice).

Gil, D. G. *Confronting Injustice and Oppression: Concepts and Strategies for Social Workers.* New York: Columbia University Press, 1998.

Hedeen, T. "Dialogue and Democracy, Community and Capacity: Lessons for Conflict Resolution Education from Montessori, Dewy, and Freire." *Conflict Resolution Quarterly,* 2005, *23*(2), 185–202.

Heyworth, E. "'Town'/'Gown' and Community Relations: Case Studies of Social Empowerment." In P. Harries-Jones (ed.), *Making Knowledge Count: Advocacy and Social Science.* Buffalo, NY: McGill-Queens University Press, 1991.

Kelman, H. C. "Interactive Problem-Solving: Informal Mediation by the Scholar-Practitioner." In J. Bercovitch (ed.), *Studies in International Mediation.* New York: Palgrave Macmillan, 2002.

Kent, G. "The Application of Peace Studies." *Journal of Conflict Resolution,* 1971, *15*(1) 47–53.

Kincheloe, J. L., and McLaren, P. "Rethinking Critical Theory and Qualitative Research." In N. K. Denzin and Y. S. Lincoln (eds.), *Handbook of Qualitative Research* (2nd ed.). Thousand Oaks, CA: Sage, 2000.

King, M. L. "Letter from a Birmingham Jail." In J. J. Fahey and R. Armstrong (eds.), *A Peace Reader: Essential Readings on War, Justice, Non-Violence, and World Order.* Mahwah, NJ: Paulist Press, 1992.

Knupfer, A. M. "Conflict Resolution or 'Convict Revolution'? The Problematics of Critical Pedagogy in the Classroom." *Urban Education,* 1995, *30*(2), 219–239.

Kritek, P. B. *Negotiating at an Uneven Table: Developing Moral Courage in Resolving Our Conflicts.* San Francisco: Jossey-Bass, 2002.

Lederach, J. P. *Preparing for Peace: Conflict Transformation Across Cultures.* Syracuse, NY: Syracuse University Press, 1995.

Longres, J. F. "Minority Groups: An Interest Group Perspective." *Social Work,* Jan. 1982, pp. 7–14.

Martin, A. S. "Working Paper 15: The Contribution of Critical Theory to New Thinking on Peacekeeping: Some Lessons from MINURSO," 2005, retrieved Apr. 10, 2007. Centre for Conflict Resolution, Department of Peace Studies, University of Bradford (http://www.brad.ac.uk/acad/confres/papers/pdfs/CCR15.pdf).

Marx, K., and Engels, F. *The Communist Manifesto.* In Marx/Engels Selected Works, Vol. 1. Moscow: Progress, 1969. [Originally published 1848]

Marx, K., and Engels, F. "Materialism and the Theory of Ideology." In R. Collins (ed.), *Three Sociological Traditions: Selected Readings.* New York: Oxford University Press, 1985.

McWhirter, B. T., and McWhirter, E. H. "Grounding Clinical Training and Supervision in an Empowerment Model." In E. Aldarondo (ed.), *Advancing Social Justice Through Clinical Practice*. Mahwah, NJ: Erlbaum, 2007.

National Association of Social Workers. *Code of Ethics*, 1999, retrieved Jan. 3, 2008 (http://www.socialworkers.org/pubs/code/code.asp).

O'Brien, C. "Integrated Community Development/Conflict Resolution Strategies as 'Peace Building Potential' in South Africa and Northern Ireland." *Community Development Journal*, 2005, *42*(1), 114–130.

Payne, M. "From Radical to Critical Perspectives." In *Modern Social Work Theory* (3rd ed.). Chicago: Lyceum, 2005.

Piven, F. F. *Challenging Authority: How Ordinary People Change America*. New York: Littlefield, 2006.

Piven, F. F., and Cloward, R. A. *Poor People's Movements: Why They Succeed, How They Fail*. New York: Vintage, 1979.

Quille, M. M. "Working Papers: A Response to Recent Critiques of Conflict Resolution: Is Critical Theory the Answer?" 2000, retrieved Apr. 10, 2007. Copenhagen Peace Research Institute (http://www.ciaonet.org/wps/qum01/).

Raines, S. "International Education and Conflict: Empowering Individuals, Transforming Societies, and Making Waves—An Interview with Jane Benbow from CARE." *Conflict Resolution Quarterly*, 2004, *21*(4), 483–490.

Rapoport, A. "Can Peace Be Applied?" *Journal of Conflict Resolution*, 1970, 14(2), 277–286.

Reardon, B. "Feminist Concepts of Peace and Security." In P. Smoker, R. Davies, and B. Munske (eds.), *A Reader in Peace Studies*. Oxford: Pergamon Press, 1990.

Rifken, J., Millen, J., and Cobb, S. "Toward a New Discourse for Mediation: A Critique of Neutrality." *Mediation Quarterly*, 1991, *9*(2), 151–163.

Roy, B. "Radical Psychiatry: An Approach to Personal and Political Change." In E. Aldarondo (ed.), *Advancing Social Justice Through Clinical Practice*. Mahwah, NJ: Erlbaum, 2007.

Scanlon, E., and Longres, J. F. "Social Justice and the Research Curriculum." *Journal of Social Work Education*, 2001, *37*(3), 447–463.

Schneider, R. L., and Lester, L. *Social Work Advocacy: A New Framework for Action*. Stamford, CT.: Brooks/Cole, 2001.

School for International Training. *Master of Arts in Social Justice in Intercultural Relations*, n.d., retrieved Feb. 9, 2008 (http://www.sit.edu/graduate/mair/index.html).

Spencer, M. "Advocating Peace." In P. Harries-Jones (ed.), *Making Knowledge Count: Advocacy and Social Science*. Montreal: McGill-Queens University Press, 1991.

Stohl, M., and Chamberlain, M. "Alternative Futures for Peace Research." *Journal of Conflict Resolution*, 1972, *16*(4), 523–530.

Tidwell, A. "Conflict, Peace, and Education: A Tangled Web." *Conflict Resolution Quarterly*, 2004, *21*(4), 463–470.

Townley, A. "Introduction: Conflict Resolution, Diversity, and Social Justice." *Education and Urban Society*, 1994, *27*(1), 5–10.

University of Denver. *Conflict Resolution Institute: Courses*, n.d., retrieved Feb. 9, 2008 (http://www.du.edu/con-res/grad_program/courses.html).

Ward, I. *An Introduction to Critical Legal Theory*. London: Cavendish, 1998.

Wells, C. V. "Service Learning and Problem-Based Learning in a Conflict Resolution Class." *Teaching in Psychology*, 2003, *30*(3), 260–263.

Winslade, J., and Monk, G. *Narrative Mediation: A New Approach to Conflict Resolution*. San Francisco: Jossey-Bass, 2001.

Zucker, A. *Greensboro: Closer to the Truth*. (Film). U.S. 2007.

Narrative Mediation

John Winslade and Gerald Monk

John Winslade is a professor at California State University, San Bernardino. He is the co-author of *Narrative Mediation: A New Approach to Conflict Resolution* (2000), *Practicing Narrative Mediation: Loosening the Grip of Conflict* (2008) and *When Stories Clash* (2012). He has also co-authored five other books on narrative therapy. His book with Mike Williams is titled *Safe and Peaceful Schools: Addressing Conflict and Eliminating Violence* (forthcoming). He edits *Explorations: An E-Journal of Narrative Practice* and is a board member of *The Journal of Conflictology, The International Journal of Narrative Therapy and Community Work, The Journal of Systemic Therapies*, and, formerly, *Conflict Resolution Quarterly*. His articles have appeared in *The Negotiation Journal, Conflict Resolution Quarterly, Family Process*, and many other places. He has taught workshops on narrative mediation and narrative therapy in North America, Australasia, Europe, Asia, and the Middle East.

Gerald Monk completed his PhD at the University of Waikato, New Zealand. He is the director of the Marriage and Family Therapy Program in the Department of Counseling and School Psychology. He is a practicing licensed marriage and family therapist. His research and teaching interests include Narrative–Affective therapy, narrative mediation and conflict resolution, constructionist and discursive theories, restorative practice, and mental health recovery.

Winslade and Monk introduce a model of mediation that breaks from the problem-solving approach to mediation in Epoch Two. A narrative approach takes as its starting point that people organize their experiences, including their conflicts, in story form. Narratives used to describe themselves and others are the building blocks of conflict stories. Narrative mediators focus on how conflict stories create reality, rather than how they represent reality. In other words, narrative experts focus on how stories perpetuate and create rather than represent some objective truth of the conflict. This shifting away of seeking an independent truth is a hallmark of Epoch Three. Narrative mediators create room for alternative stories by destabilizing *totalizing descriptions* and looking for opportunities to build trust. Techniques such as *externalization*—which separates people from the problem, mapping the effects of the conflict on all participants, and identifying competing cultural norms (dominant narratives)—provide opportunities for solution-bound narratives. Unlike earlier models of mediation, narrative mediation requires practitioners to engage in self-reflection, considering, for example, how their view of gender roles might influence the outcome. Narrative mediation, consistent with Epoch Three, also seeks to include the voices of multiple parties involved in the conflict, even if these individuals are not the ones who initially brought the conflict to mediation.

Questions to consider: Where do our stories about the world come from? What kinds of discursive assumptions do we have about what is culturally appropriate or acceptable in society (i.e., in relationship to race, class, gender, ethnicity, sexuality, ability, etc.)? How can understanding our own stories help us to see how we perpetuate conflict?

Narrative Mediation: What Is It?

John Winslade and Gerald Monk

The universe is transformation: our life is what our thoughts make it.

(Marcus Aurelius Antoninus, "Meditations")

Healing is a matter of time, but it is sometimes also a matter of opportunity.

(Hippocrates, "Precepts")

Greg wanted the custody of the children to be decided in the family court. "I'm sick of the bloody arguments," he said. "She keeps changing her bloody mind. One day she's all understanding and wanting me to be involved and the next day she's trying to keep me from having a say. I've had enough! I can't see how this mediation is going to make any difference. I don't want to have to rework this issue for one more day. She's made up her mind. It's like talking to a frigging brick wall. How are you going to make any difference? This mess has been going on for months!"

For those who have been involved in divorce mediation, such a scenario will not be unfamiliar. It presents many challenges for a mediator to start to work with. In this book we introduce you to how we would approach the process of mediation in such a situation. We think that the model we are proposing is significantly different from other approaches to mediation, particularly the commonly espoused problem-solving model of mediation.[1] We call our approach narrative to signify some of the ways in which we conceptualize mediation and also to link it to the work of other people who use this metaphor to describe their work.

To start, we tell you a story. It is the story of a mediation between Greg and Fiona. We usher you through this story to illustrate the approach we flesh out in the following chapters. This first chapter is like a snapshot; the more detailed moving picture comes later.

The story shows narrative mediation in action. This method has both a theoretical robustness and some creative ideas for practice to recommend it. The story provides an overview of some of the narrative moves used in mediating a conflict between Greg and Fiona. The challenges thrown up by this conflict are rich opportunities for demonstrating a range of mediation moves to help create preferred outcomes.

A Mediation Story

Greg was not enamored with the idea of mediation. (The comment at the beginning of this chapter is from his first meeting with the mediator.) He wanted a family court judge to put a stop to Fiona's "controlling and manipulative behavior." The judge would surely make a "sensible" decision and give Greg custody of the children. Greg was sure that the judge would understand his story.

Fiona had initiated the mediation. She had outlined to the mediator in a telephone conversation that she had interim custody of the three children and was highly motivated to avoid the agony of an expensive and lengthy court hearing. She did not think this ugly dispute was going to be solved by a judge.

Fiona was also sick of Greg's threats. She knew he would tell the mediator that she deserved to lose all the children, that she was to blame for the breakup of their marriage of fourteen years. Fiona was most upset about how Greg would run her down in front of her friends in their small rural community. He would tell her friends that she had no morals and that she had deceived him when she had an affair with Greg's friend three years previously.

Fiona and Greg had a well-developed problem-saturated narrative about the conflict.[2] Each described the other in unidimensional, fixed, and unyielding terms. Elements of this problem narrative had such a tangible and reified quality that both Fiona and Greg experienced their own storied account as the only true description of the events of the conflict.

THE STORYING PROCESS

The narrative perception is that people tend to organize their experiences in story form. The narrative metaphor draws attention to the ways in which we use stories to make sense of our lives and relationships.³ People grow up amid a multitude of competing narratives that help shape how they see themselves and others. They tell stories about themselves and about others. They act both out of and into these stories, shaping the direction of the ongoing plot as they do so. Descriptions of problems are typically told in narrative terms. Such problem narratives have often been rehearsed and elaborated over and over again by participants in a conflict.

Mediators who use a narrative orientation are interested in the constitutive properties of conflict stories. In other words, whether a story is factual or not matters little to the potential impact it has in someone's life. Our emphasis is on how the story operates to create reality rather than on whether it reports accurately on that reality. Stories therefore are not viewed as either true or false accounts of an objective "out there" reality. Such a view is not possible, because events cannot be known independently of the dominant narratives held by the knower. It is therefore more useful to concentrate on viewing stories as constructing the world rather than viewing the world as independently known and then described through stories.

Practitioners who use this approach are only too aware of the difficulties that arise when mediators seek an objective account of "what really happened" in order then to coach the parties into a more balanced way of looking at the problem. We would even expect such efforts to meet with resistance. From within a dispute it makes perfect sense for conflicted parties to "story" the conflict in their own terms. It is therefore more helpful for a mediator to validate explicitly the stories through which people experience the conflict and then to seek out the points where the story might incorporate some different perspectives.

Beginning the Mediation

Greg was mandated to attend at least one mediation session before the matter could be taken further in the family court. Although he was reluctant to attend, he still had a lot to say about his present circumstances and about his desire for custody of the children.

Greg had established his own courier company over recent years and described not having the time he would have liked to spend with his children and, now, his ex-wife, Fiona. He reflected back on these times with some regrets. Yet there was a great deal he was proud of. He was now a self-made man. He enjoyed a very good income and employed a growing fleet of drivers and a competent administrative staff to cater to the demands of his burgeoning business.

At first Greg was clear that his full commitment to his career and the establishment of a strong financial foundation were the best contributions he could have made to his family's development. He recollected clearly the financial struggles his parents had experienced in his early youth and the shame his father had suffered in barely managing to look after the basic needs of the family. Greg did not want to put his family through the money worries of his childhood. Indeed, Fiona had enjoyed a financially comfortable life with Greg in recent years and, while married, had needed to work only part-time, so she was able to follow interests outside of the family.

Greg and Fiona's children—Frank (fifteen) Jessie (eleven), and Thomas (six)—were receiving a high-quality education at a private school and had had some wonderful vacations with their mother in the last few years. Greg had missed most of these vacations because of the demands made on his time by work pressures. Clearly he regretted missing out on so much of the children's childhood. Earlier in the marriage he had wished that he was more nurturing toward Fiona, but now he was bitter about how she was behaving toward him. Greg was against the separation that Fiona had instigated some seven months before. Although he was still angry at her betrayal and the agitation she had caused him, he still loved her, he said.

Greg explained that it had taken time to build up his business. But now that it was virtually running itself, he imagined he could devote more time to the children, even if he couldn't be with Fiona. In fact, he saw that it was now his right to help shape the children's moral development.

Following his separation from Fiona, Greg had become reinvolved in a Christian fellowship from which he had been disengaged since his teens. He was keen to imbue a strong Christian presence into the children's lives. Greg explained that Fiona was now spending significant amounts of time socializing with friends and, in his view, was not providing the quality of care he thought the children deserved.

Greg was also agitated about the implications for his business of a matrimonial settlement that was still to be finalized through Greg's and Fiona's lawyers. Greg did not think Fiona was entitled to half of their assets. He felt it had been due to his own efforts that the business had gone so well. He recognized that legally he would very likely have to pay out a significant share to Fiona, but he wanted to minimize the size of this payout in order to maintain business solvency.

Greg was certainly unwilling to give up the family home. Fiona had moved into a two-bedroom apartment with Frank, Jessie, and Thomas. Greg, however, wanted the children to live with him in the family home. For her part, Fiona was convinced that the children were better off with her.

OPENING UP SPACE IN A TIGHTLY WOVEN STORY

Judgment and accusation are typically woven so tightly around the participants in a conflict that there does not seem to be any space for other descriptions of what has taken place or what could take place. We refer to these descriptions as totalizing descriptions; that is, they sum up a complex situation in one description that purports to give a total picture of the situation or of a person in it.[4] Totalizing descriptions of the conflict and of the conflict's protagonists tend to become highly evolved before the mediator has an opportunity to be part of the conversation.

One of the major tasks of a mediator is to destabilize the totalizing descriptions of conflict so as to undermine the rigid and negative motivations that the conflicted parties ascribe to each other. A variety of strategies can be employed by a mediator to loosen these negative attributions. These strategies help to create a context from which a preferred story line can be developed. They may include the following:

- Building trust in the mediator and in the mediation process
- Developing externalizing conversations
- Mapping the effects of the problem on the person
- Deconstructing the dominant story lines
- Developing shared meanings about the conflict and its solutions

These strategies are elaborated in considerable detail in the following chapters. However, here we briefly introduce them in relation to the scenario presented earlier, to give you the flavor of the narrative mediation process.

BUILDING THE RELATIONSHIP IN MEDIATION

Building trust with each of the disputing parties is crucial to the successful outcome of any mediation. When people feel hurt by the actions of another, they tend to rework aspects of the conflict story to reinforce their own sense of injustice, betrayal, victimization, or mistreatment. The mediator can use the narrative metaphor to convey to each of the parties that the mediator has grasped the depth of their distress, without appearing to collude with each party's problem-saturated descriptions of the other.

Mediators are interested in employing strategies that will take some of the intensity out of the conflict and destabilize it to the point where alternative stories can be considered. Careful, respectful listening is a key part of this process. Respect is demonstrated through taking seriously someone's story and avoiding making assumptions about underlying deficit in the person. The starting assumption of the narrative approach is that it is likely that everyone is doing their best to deal with the conflict with the resources they have at hand.

EXTERNALIZING CONVERSATIONS

Externalizing conversations are one of the most powerful methods that narrative practitioners can use to help disputing parties disidentify with the problem story and begin to develop shared meanings, understandings, and solutions.[5] Externalizing conversations reverse the common logic in both popular and academic psychology that increasingly focuses explanations for events inside the person. Externalizing conversations focus attention on the relational domain. As mediators externalize a problem, they speak about it as if it were an external object or person exerting an influence on the parties but they do not identify it closely with one party or the other.

In the first meeting with Greg, it was helpful for the mediator to prepare for an externalizing conversation with Greg by identifying some of the dominant themes in Greg's account of the problem. Certainly distrust, betrayal, and neglect featured prominently in Greg's descriptions of what was happening to him in his relationship with Fiona. The mediator could then speak of these themes as if they are the problem, rather than identifying Greg or Fiona as the problem.

The mediator asked Greg to identify what he thought were some of the central difficulties that had led to the current conflict over the custody of the children. After pondering the mediator's request briefly, Greg said, "Fiona has caused me a great deal of grief."

As is typical of parties caught in a prolonged conflict, Greg stayed with an internalizing, blaming description of Fiona. The grief he was experiencing was storied as originating from within Fiona, either as a deliberate desire to hurt him or as a result of her character. Externalizing conversations help separate the problem from the person and open space for a perspective in which blame and shame become less significant. Mediators who explore the use of externalizing conversations need not be disheartened by the blaming responses of the parties to one another despite the efforts of the mediator to externalize the problem. Careful listening by the mediator along with curiosity and enthusiastic persistence are useful in reconstructing problem narratives in less blaming terms.

The mediator next asked Greg, "If we could name this account of the difficulties you have experienced with Fiona 'a great deal of grief caused by distrust, betrayal, agitation, and neglect,' would that come close?" Greg wasn't exactly sure but he thought this description was close enough for now.

In interactions with Greg, the mediator often referred to the dispute over custody of the children as "this conflict" or "this betrayal," "this distrust" or "this neglect," or "this grief." The externalizing descriptions used depended on the direction of the conversation. Staying with the externalization of relational themes that underpinned Greg's blame of Fiona created an atmosphere in which Greg could focus on the effects of the conflict on his life and on the children. This helped him to avoid focusing on the character flaws and inadequacies he might have otherwise emphasized about Fiona.

MAPPING THE EFFECTS OF THE CONFLICT HISTORY ON DISPUTING PARTIES

Fuller descriptions of what is going on give the mediator much more information about how individuals construct problem issues. In the case of Greg and Fiona, the mediator explored the effects of the problem-saturated story in order to gain a richer description of the parties' different understandings of the conflict.[6] The mediator paid particular attention to fleshing out the history of this account of the problem. The ebb and flow of the conflict could then be storied from its origins in an externalized fashion to help the parties understand the impact that the evolution of the conflict had had on them.

A historical account allows for a time orientation to emerge. This time orientation offers an enriched perspective. The rhythms and patterns of the conflict are more clearly perceived by each of the parties as they gain clarity about how the conflict is changing and possibly escalating. Naming when the conflict began and tracing how it developed provide openings for the mediator to inquire about experiences that stand outside the conflict.

The mediator asked Greg, "When did you first became aware of the problems around custody of the children?" Greg stated that the problems started when he objected to Fiona's "declining ability to care for the children." One of the children had mentioned that their mother had gone out one night with a girlfriend and left Frank, the oldest child, in charge. She hadn't come home until midnight. Greg reported being furious on hearing about what he described as a "serious lapse" in her parenting. He now doubted her ability to provide consistent quality care for the children. Greg also reported that he worried about the children not getting an appropriate spiritual education. He added that he would be taking the children to church and Sunday school if the children were in his care.

The inclusion of *relative influence questions* or mapping-the-effects questions often builds momentum and volition within the parties. These questions map the effects of the conflict on each person associated with it. They assist the parties to come to grips with how much the conflict has cost them in both personal and material terms.

The mediator asked Greg how the conflict had been affecting his well-being. Greg reported that he was living with additional stress in his life. He was worried about the legal costs of gaining custody of the children and how he would fare in the pending court hearing. He said that his sleep patterns were disrupted and he had not been eating regular meals. He expressed concern about the toll it was all taking on his physical and emotional well-being. He was feeling desperately lonely and was painfully aware that he was not in a psychological space to develop a relationship with anybody else. The matrimonial property issues were weighing heavily on him.

But the effects of the conflict were not just on Greg and Fiona. The mediator wanted Greg to include in his story of the problem an account of the impact of the conflict on the children. There is value in helping disputing parties see how a conflict spills over into other domains in their own and other people's lives.

The mediator asked Greg, "What effect is the growing lack of trust with Fiona having on the children?"

"I haven't got the faintest idea," Greg said slowly but thoughtfully. "I am seeing so little of the children right now that I don't really know what shape they are in."

Greg was initially reluctant to consider seriously how the conflict had been touching the children's lives. After further discussion, it became clear to him that the children had been suffering as a result of the escalating dispute between him and Fiona. He was concerned about this. The lack of trust between Greg and Fiona was troubling the children, although at this point Greg was holding Fiona completely responsible for the conflict.

Jessie, the middle child, seemed to be suffering the most. Her teacher had reported that Jessie's grades had been deteriorating and she appeared to be mildly depressed. It seemed that the negative effects of the conflict were growing. The mediator asked Greg if he thought the lack of trust and grief were going to do further damage to himself and the children given the direction in which the conflict was moving. Greg stated that he thought the damage could get worse but it could be averted if the family court judge were to rule in Greg's favor soon. Even as he said this, Greg recognized that a ruling on custody was many months away.

In the course of such an inquiry into the effects of a problem on the people involved, a story develops about the functions of the conflict in everyone's lives. After sufficiently mapping these effects, the mediator asked Greg whether he would like to do something to change the direction of the conflict. These same lines of inquiry were followed with Fiona as well.

The mediator asked Greg, "Are you willing to continue adjusting to the growing deterioration of trust while waiting for a judge to take action, or are you interested in doing some damage control by building some trust in the meantime?" Greg was not sure what he could do, because it depended to a large extent on what Fiona did. He stated, however, that he would certainly be willing to do the best he could on his side to halt any further erosion of trust.

The significance of inviting the parties to make a judgment about the effects of the problem is elucidated in Chapter Seven.

CONSTRUCTING SOLUTION-BOUND NARRATIVES

It is significant for a mediator when one of the parties clearly states that he or she does not want to participate in escalating the conflict. This decision can open the door to a very different conversation. The mediator was now able to ask Greg if there had been any brief periods when there were interactions with Fiona in which he thought trust was building rather than diminishing. This move in narrative mediation is based on the notion that people in dispute are likely to have had experiences that were not completely dominated by the history of the conflict.[7]

In this initial session it was possible to begin to *coauthor* with Greg an alternative, non-problem-bound narrative that could serve as the rudimentary stage of a resolution to the problem. Greg could recall a few instances when his interactions with Fiona were not filled with angst. Although initially it was a struggle for him to remember, he recalled how Fiona and he had calmly discussed plans for Jessie's birthday. Greg described how a month earlier he had managed to spend a cordial and at times friendly evening with Fiona at Jessie's party.

Narrative mediators put effort into tracking non-problem-bound interactions. Through a series of questions about these interactions, the mediator and Greg were beginning to assemble some alternative descriptions of Greg's relationship with Fiona that were not completely dominated by lack of trust and bad feeling. Greg was beginning to open the door to building trust in his parenting relationship with Fiona. He did not need to put everything on hold while he waited for a decision from a family court judge. He was able to recall a number of other examples of collaborative and cooperative interchanges within recent months.

In their conversations thus far, Greg and the mediator had made the following progress:

- Greg was gaining a fuller appreciation of the toll the conflict was having on him and his family.
- He and the mediator were coauthoring an alternative account of Greg and Fiona working together.
- Greg was much more engaged in the mediation process and was beginning to recognize that establishing a cooperative parenting relationship with Fiona was necessary.

Fiona's Account

A separate meeting was arranged with Fiona. The mediator asked her to express her views on the present difficulties and to provide a brief overview of the history of the conflict with Greg.

Fiona was adamant that her marriage was over. She described many years of feeling empty and alone in the marriage. She felt that Greg had been consistently emotionally unavailable for long periods. Even a short while after marrying, Fiona had noticed a change in Greg. She remembered that he had been very attentive, available, and loving when they had lived together. All that had seemed to change after they got married. Fiona described Greg as losing himself in his work. He would be gone early in the morning and would often return late in the evening. He would be exhausted and spend little time with the children, even though he cared about them. All of this discussion supported a view of the negative effects on Fiona of Greg's single-minded focus on being a successful material provider.

Fiona indicated that she was completely responsible for attending to the children's psychological and emotional needs. She would attend to their distress, deal with their disappointments and conflicts, and delight in their successes. She granted that Greg did his best to play with the children and attend school functions, but he was usually unavailable. Fiona claimed that Greg would often lose his patience with the children and become short-tempered and somewhat aggressive with them.

It is useful for the mediator to store away such commentary because it provides a rich background picture in which some of the dominant cultural patterns that have influenced the direction and shape of the conflict can later be identified.

An assumption of narrative mediation is that conflict is produced within competing cultural norms. The mediator was therefore interested in eliciting from Fiona some of the dominant cultural norms that had had an impact on her. The mediator asked Fiona to discuss some of her ideas about marriage and what she had hoped for in her relationship and in the family she and Greg had developed.

> Fiona believed that in the early part of her marriage both she and Greg had expected that Fiona would be the homemaker and take charge of the domestic duties. She said they had never really negotiated this but had found themselves caught up in patterns that had been modeled by their parents. By adopting a curious and naive posture, the mediator helped Fiona to name how in both her and Greg's families of origin the women were primarily responsible for the psychological support of their husbands and children. Featured were traditional gendered patterns for the division of labor in which the male was responsible for the primary income and the female was responsible for the care of the home and the raising of the children.
>
> The mediator asked Fiona what her attitude was toward these cultural imperatives. She felt resentful about her predicament and wished that she had been more assertive with Greg about what she wanted. She had dedicated herself to being a good mother and homemaker. She had done her best to be responsive and caring toward Greg, but she felt she had gotten little in return other than temporary financial security. Now that too was gone. She did not have a career and she wished that she had insisted on support from Greg to commence some studies. She felt betrayed by Greg's "neglect of the family's psychological needs." Fiona was now immediately faced with minimal income. She would get a meager financial benefit from the state and she could supplement this income with her part-time work.
>
> Fiona felt entitled to at least half of the business assets because of the sacrifices she had made in raising the children and taking care of Greg's needs in the home. Yet she also felt guilty about the extra pressures this would put on Greg to find some way of keeping his business while dividing his assets in half to pay Fiona her share of the matrimonial property. This was an issue she would have to face.
>
> Fiona was clear that Greg was in no position to have custody of the children. Currently he had the children in his care every second weekend and set aside one afternoon per week to spend time with them after school. In Fiona's view, the children did not want to live with their father, though she recognized that Jessie had a stronger psychological tie with Greg. Fiona thought that Jessie felt responsible for providing some care and company for her father. Jessie had said to Fiona that she was worried about her Dad living all alone and that he needed somebody to look after him. Fiona was strongly against splitting up the custodial care of the children.

As Fiona told her story she began to get a clearer understanding of some of the dominant cultural messages that had affected her while she was married to Greg. It was important for her to identify these messages because it subsequently assisted her to be less dogged by guilt and self-blame for ending the marriage. By linking the gendered themes of servitude and submission implicit in Fiona's problem-saturated narrative, the mediator helped her to recognize that she was much more vulnerable to verbal attacks from Greg because of her dominant feelings of guilt and self-doubt.

During this meeting, the mediator asked Fiona what guilt and self-blame had done to her when the marriage had begun to unravel. Fiona responded that guilt and self-blame had been extremely costly for her. However, she had also spent long periods wondering whether she should try to repair the damage done to her relationship with Greg. This had left her feeling confused and had led her to give inconsistent messages to him about where their relationship stood. Sometimes, in an effort to alleviate the guilt, she had conveyed to Greg that there was still some hope for their relationship. At other times she was very clear that she could not return to the habitual pattern of relating that had characterized so much of their relationship. It had been too costly for her.

This interview with Fiona achieved a number of narrative mediation purposes:

- The effects of the problem narrative on her life were storied.
- Descriptions of a preferred future parenting relationship with Greg were explored.
- Preconceived notions about marriage and relationship that had been problematic for Fiona were identified.
- The features of the cultural context that had caught her in a particular pattern of relating to Greg were also identified. She could see how this pattern undermined her own sense of confidence and well-being. She could also see how this pattern created confusion and disruption for Greg.

DISASSEMBLING CULTURAL PRESCRIPTIONS

Fiona had been positioned (not so much by Greg as by conventional cultural discourse) as the domestic server and social-emotional caregiver of the family. Throughout her marriage she had felt obliged to take complete care of the children's psychological well-being and had assumed that this was her primary role in life. She now realized that over the years this role had taken its toll. The moral weight of it was particularly burdensome, because there was no sign that Greg would be relieving her of this responsibility.

Cultural norms invoke particular patterns or styles of relating that are enacted in repetitive ways. The mediator, using a narrative orientation, focuses on those cultural constraints that limit the possibilities available to individuals to address their concerns. Engaging carefully in a conversation about preferred experiences that lie outside the domain of the problem opens up new discursive or cultural possibilities.[8] These openings can lead to a resolution of the conflict.

Narrative mediation is not merely a set of techniques that can be clipped onto existing mediation models. This approach invites mediators to think very carefully about how their own constructions of the mediation process can significantly influence the outcome. The mediator in this conflict needed to be aware of his own gendered constructions about marriage and relationship, and he needed to consider how his own beliefs might contribute to shaping the conversation. Dominant cultural story lines are likely to influence the kinds of questions the mediator asks and how he hears and understands the parties' concerns. For example, if the mediator has fixed ideas about the kinds of roles men and women should play in a marriage, at some subtle level these views will have an impact on the mediation. We argue that neutrality and impartiality are severely constrained by the cultural location of the mediator.

Many mediation researchers suggest that the mediator should attend to the psychological relationships and to procedural or process matters and be less involved in the substantive or content aspects of any dispute.[9] For example, in the preceding scenario, many mediators would stress the importance of building a strong relational connection with the parties in early mediation interchanges and establishing appropriate procedural guidelines.

Yet there is also significant variation in how mediators respond to relational, process, and substantive issues because of the influence of their theoretical persuasions. For example, some mediators working with family conflict perform as advocates for children. They become keenly involved in substantive issues, particularly when children's needs have been neglected.[10] From this perspective, mediators are directly involved in the content discussions of the mediation. Other mediation researchers suggest that it is not appropriate for mediators to influence the parties directly in shaping content matters.[11]

We do not believe that the separation of process and content issues is as simple as it can be made to sound. Process issues shape the content that can arise, and any process will privilege some content issues over others. In practice, we argue, relationship, process, and content issues are all interwoven in the very fabric of mediation.

NAMING DOMINANT DISCOURSES

Because narrative mediators are interested in tracking the background narratives and identifying the themes that underpin the conflict, it is useful to record the dominant themes. Such recordings will of course be affected by the discursive themes that have an impact on the mediator. In the first session with Fiona, for example, the mediator noted the following background discursive themes that appeared to be a feature of her relationship with Greg:

- A wife should be submissive to the needs of her husband.
- A wife should gain her sense of pleasure and satisfaction through the achievements of her husband.
- A woman is responsible for the social and emotional needs of her husband and children.
- A woman should put aside her own career aspirations.

It seemed that Fiona was still heavily influenced by these discursive influences. However, mapping their effects on her sharpened her sense of the cost that these cultural prescriptions were exacting from her sense of well-being. She was clear too that she did not have to keep subjecting herself to these cultural norms or continue to seek fulfillment through being a dutiful wife and partner. This knowledge had assisted her decision to create a life independent of Greg. The clarity she was gaining from the early mediation session was enabling her to be more consistent with Greg about her intentions.

A DECONSTRUCTIVE CONVERSATION WITH GREG

The mediator met individually with both Greg and Fiona one more time before a joint session was held. Greg was not keen to meet with Fiona until he felt better prepared. From the mediator's perspective, there was potential value in strengthening Greg's degree of engagement in the mediation. The mediator also wanted an opportunity to understand further Greg's perspectives on the problem.

Before this second session with Greg, the mediator wrote down some of the discursive themes from the first session. The mediator saw Greg as being strongly positioned by a "head of the household discourse" that invited Greg into the position of making executive decisions—in this case, about what was required to resolve the conflict. In addition, in his understanding of Christianity, Greg saw himself as the appropriate moral educator for the children.

Greg felt entitled to be the custodial caregiver for the children. (We discuss how such entitlements are built from a discursive perspective in Chapter Four.) His sense of entitlement was founded on what he identified as Fiona's betrayal of her marriage vows and the damage he perceived the divorce would do to the children. In passing he did suggest that he would accept joint custody if it was not possible to have sole custody. He believed, however, that Fiona's unwillingness to try to rebuild their relationship was evidence of her lack of moral fiber. From the mediator's perspective, Greg was strongly positioned by a fundamentalist patriarchal stance.

This discursive imperative often invokes a rigid position in a custodial conflict. In the second session with Greg, the mediator explored with him other possible discursive imperatives that were influencing his view of what he was entitled to. They identified the following background discourses:

- Men contribute to the family by being primary income earners.
- The man is the head of the household and should take charge when the family is threatened.
- A good male provider is a good income earner.
- A woman who leaves her husband has betrayed the family. She loses her right to have any say over the welfare of the children. She has breached her contract.

- A Christian life is superior to an agnostic life. A practicing Christian is a better parent than a nonbeliever.

The mediator then went on to explore with Greg the effects of the statement, "A good male provider is a good income earner." The mediator developed an externalizing conversation in order to name the effects of this particular discourse on Greg, Fiona, and the children.

The mediator asked Greg whether he felt burdened by "being a good provider," and to what extent he had felt morally obliged to make so many work sacrifices. Greg described feeling the full weight of this responsibility and how it persuaded him into a quest to provide for Fiona and the children in a manner that he might have only dreamed about as a child.

The mediator then asked a relative influence question: "Greg, what have been the effects on you of feeling the full moral weight of responsibility for being a generous and successful provider?"

Greg responded, "I think I have done a great job in providing security for the family. I also feel genuinely proud of what I have accomplished in my work life, but I do have regrets. You know, I have sacrificed a lot, but I now wonder whether it was all worth it."

The mediator asked Greg to elaborate (a simple use of *narrative curiosity*).[12] Greg responded, "Well, I missed out on some of the most special times in the children's growing up, including vacation time. Their childhoods are almost half over and I'm only now beginning to realize the painful consequences of being so preoccupied with work commitments."

The mediator asked Greg about other costs of the "man is the provider" discourse. Greg had been suffering from high blood pressure and regular migraine headaches. He thought that these physical ailments were effects of the physical demands he had placed on himself. The stress of fighting for the custody of the children was currently exacerbating some of these physical symptoms.

Such questions helped "unpack," or *deconstruct,* some of the discursive content in Greg's story of Fiona's "betrayal." He had done his best to meet the demands of the dominant discourse. Fiona's initiative to separate from him and her rejection of the authority of this discourse appeared to discount this effort. The mediator's questions helped crystallize for Greg the role that being a good provider had played in this sense of betrayal, as well as its effects on his health.

Greg stated a wish to be freed from the discursive dictate to work slavishly at being a successful provider. He was already moderating his work to give him more quality time with the children and for his church activities. We would describe this wish as an expression of a desire to reposition himself within the provider discourse. However, the patriarchal discourse still had a very strong influence over him. The mediator did not want to be too directive in exploring the discursive underpinnings of Greg's identity as a father, for fear of coming across as intrusive or judgmental. Therefore, the mediator sought to acknowledge Greg's commitment to being a better parent. However, Greg's certainty about his custodial rights still provided little opportunity for creating leverage in the mediation. For significant movement to take place in the custodial dispute, Greg would also need to loosen his certainties about his role as the executive decision maker.

A DECONSTRUCTIVE CONVERSATION
WITH FIONA

When the mediator met with Fiona again, they continued to develop the deconstructive conversation they had begun in their first meeting. Here two parts of that conversation are highlighted.

The mediator asked Fiona what she needed in preparation for the joint session with Greg. She said she wanted to shore up her ability to manage guilt and to limit the effects of self-blame. The mediator asked Fiona a relative influence question about her growing ability to resist guilt and self-blame. She responded that increasingly she wanted to reposition herself as a woman making her way in the world independently of her husband. While Greg had continued to subscribe to traditional discursive prescriptions in the marriage, Fiona had over time clearly revised her own understanding of what it meant to be in partnership. Her current view was very different from what it had been when she began the relationship.

The mediator then asked Fiona what had influenced her to change her thinking. Fiona identified some alternative discourses that were emerging influences in her identity. At the end of the second session, she was clearly more comfortable with the following discursive themes:

- Addressing the other person's emotional and psychological needs should be reciprocal in a partnership.
- A woman has a right to develop her own career aspirations within a marriage.
- A male partner should take on a more equitable role in taking care of the psychological needs of the children.
- A female partner should have an equal role in the making of decisions in the home.

This kind of discursive analysis maps out the territory from which ways out of the conflict can be found. As we live, we "perform meaning" around such statements. We also offer one another positions from which to relate. The statements that embody dominant or alternative discourses are not compulsory requirements for living, however. As we weave stories around them, they come to express the realities of the relations between us.

In this case, there were some clear discrepancies between the discursive themes from which Greg and Fiona were operating. No amount of negotiation on substantive issues, or even negotiation on the basis of underlying interests, was going to shift that discrepancy. What was needed was a set of discursive statements in which both parties could feel included. Then some compelling stories would need to be woven around those themes before a way forward could be found in the conflict.

INTRODUCING THE CHILDREN'S VOICES

One of the options in a situation like this, where two competing stories were casting the two protagonists, Greg and Fiona, into conflict with each other, was to widen the conversation and include other voices. Other voices would alter the dynamics; they would call forth new responses so that Greg and Fiona would not simply respond to each other's voices (and each other's discursive positions).

In this case, further perspectives could be introduced by involving Greg and Fiona's children in the decision-making process. Frank, Jessie, and Thomas were all old enough to have their own perspectives on the kind of caregiving plan their parents could devise. Although Greg initially placed little weight on the children's views, he was willing to consent to the children being interviewed to determine their interest in where they might receive custodial care. The mediator's hunch was that introducing the children into the conversation could make it possible for Greg to review his claims to executive authority.

The mediator interviewed the children both separately and together. He paid particular attention to the use of *relative influence questions* to explore the children's reactions to the idea of living with either their father or mother or both at different times. In response to the mediator's careful questions, the children disclosed their preference for living with their mother, despite having to live in more cramped conditions, although Jessie acknowledged that she wanted also to live with her father, primarily because she felt responsible for monitoring his well-being. She was the only female child and seemed influenced by the story that girls and women are responsible for looking after brothers, fathers, and children. But if she were to consider her own preference, she wanted the status quo.

This is an instance in which the mediator's own values are present in the conversational moves. The mediator did not support the position taken by Greg that he should have an executive role in deciding where the children would live. The mediator saw the children as having a legitimate say in decisions about their future. He wanted them to have an opportunity to tell their father and mother, in an unthreatening context, their views about their care. He contracted with the children that they did not have to answer any questions they did not want to answer.

This stance is not a neutral one. It contradicts the dominant legal discourse that still sees children as chattel of their parents who are not expected to have a voice of their own.

THE FAMILY MEETING

Greg, Fiona, and the children all attended the next session. The mediator invited the children to speak about their own views on their caregiving arrangements. It was clearly difficult for Jessie to talk. She did not want her father to think she was abandoning him. The mediator supported Jessie's desire not to say anything while Frank and Thomas made their views clear to their father. They spoke frankly about their wish to keep the caregiving arrangements the same.

One of the tasks of mediation is to create contexts in which the participants in a conflict have opportunities to reflect on and examine their positions. This needs to be done in a fashion that does not create defensiveness and guardedness in the participants. Providing a context within the mediation where the children could speak about their desires and wishes was one such context. It enabled the parents to examine their views and reposition themselves in relation to the children's views as well as in relation to each other.

The mediator asked Greg to make meaning out of what the children had said. What had he heard them say and what did it mean to him? It became obvious to Greg, perhaps for the first time, that his children had clear ideas about what they wanted that were in contrast to his own. Again, the mediator inquired about the significance of this information. Greg recognized that to insist on his plans and make the children do something to which they were vigorously opposed would begin to alienate them from him. He began to rethink his role in the family.

This was a *unique outcome* in the conflict story.[13] It was the beginning of Greg's repositioning himself in relation to the custody dispute. Inviting the children into the mediation process proved to be significant. They stepped out of the position of being objects of their parents' discourse. As the parents made room in the conversation for the children's voices, their own positions were altered, both in relation to the children and in relation to each other. As Greg in particular revised his position about what he wanted for the children, it became possible to start to build a caregiving consensus between him and Fiona.

MOVING TOWARD CONSENSUS

In two subsequent sessions, Fiona became more flexible in her dealings with Greg as he softened his formerly authoritative stance. The mediator exercised his curiosity about the details of their ideas about caregiving arrangements. This led them to develop greater fluidity in these arrangements, particularly in relation to holiday plans for the children.

Greg was now willing to entertain some challenges to his patriarchal ideas about parental and marital roles. This was evident in his revisions of his relationship with the children. He was now less insistent and less sure that having the children live with him was the right option. Frank's and Thomas's comments had hit Greg hard. The boys had spoken eloquently about their wishes, and Frank had also explained that Jessie felt torn about wanting to live with Greg because of her feelings of responsibility for him. Greg was ready to hear these comments and clearly was revising what he thought should happen.

In addition, he was now less focused on blaming Fiona for the pain she had caused him and was more concerned about bringing this stressful conflict to a close. He agreed with the mediator's comment that Greg seemed less in need of controlling the caregiving arrangements, and he added that a lot of the tension and struggle he had been feeling for months was beginning to subside.

In the last session with Greg and Fiona, the mediator noticed a lightness in their voices as they talked about planning a surprise birthday party for Frank. Trust was building in their parenting relationship. Negotiating the caregiving arrangements for the children now seemed much more straightforward. Greg accepted that Fiona would continue as the primary caregiver but he would become more involved in the children's day-to-day lives. It was arranged that on the week-end the children were with Fiona, Greg would pick up Thomas and Jessie and take them to church. Frank and Jessie often wanted time with their friends on the weekends. Sometimes this meant they would not be with Fiona or Greg on one of the weekend nights. Greg was now much more accommodating of these requests.

HOLDING TO THE PREFERRED STORY

Fiona and Greg were now beginning to disengage from their totalizing descriptions of the other as hurtful and destructive. They were developing more understanding of what it meant to move from a couple relationship to a parenting one. In other words, they were developing a different story about their relationship. It was the mediator's concern to keep asking questions to help them elaborate this story.

In response to these questions, Greg was certainly able to distance himself more from his earlier struggles to control the outcome of the battle for custody of the children. He had been able to hear, perhaps for the first time, the wishes of his children, which were separate from what he desired for them. He was also beginning to realize that part of his fight for the custody of the children was his attempt to punish Fiona.

Fiona, for her part, was willing to be much more empathetic toward Greg as she saw him beginning to shift away from the authoritative, controlling stance he had demonstrated earlier. Although some mediators might conclude that the work was now done, a further session would prove to be an important investment in settling the somewhat fragile negotiations.

Many mediators prize the sweet taste of success when helping parties resolve a long-standing acrimonious conflict. It is therefore disheartening for a mediator to find his or her hard work unraveling when the conflicting parties return to the earlier interactional pattern that had escalated the original conflict. The narrative perspective makes sense of this backsliding by seeing it as a possible outcome of the competition between stories. The story of conflict has sufficient pull to upset the fledgling new story until the new story is knitted fully into the fabric of the participants' lives. For this reason, it is preferable in a mediation to spend time finding ways to strengthen the solution-bound narratives that emerge when greater understanding is achieved. It can take only one or two negative encounters to reactivate problem-saturated narratives.

A follow-up session with Greg and Fiona took place three weeks after the meeting with the children. Both appeared comfortable and reasonably relaxed. Although they reported that there had been no major disagreements about the caregiving arrangements over the last three weeks, they were both on tenterhooks about the matrimonial property settlement meeting that was scheduled for the following week. They were to meet together with their respective lawyers.

The mediator asked Greg and Fiona to reflect on the last six weeks and identify what they were particularly pleased about in their dealings with each other. Both commented that they appeared to be showing much more respect toward each other when they needed to discuss matters related to the children. They both continued to worry about Jessie because her school work was still deteriorating. What was different now was that they could support each other rather than blame each other for Jessie's difficulties. They both visited Jessie's teacher to discuss their concerns. They also reported that Frank's surprise birthday party had been a great success. Although Fiona had virtually organized it on her own, Greg had paid for the catering. They felt that they had both contributed but in different ways, and no bitter interactions followed.

The following interactional sequence took place.

> *Mediator:* I have to say that I am quite surprised by the way you are being with one another given how six weeks ago you had trouble discussing things without getting into a major disagreement. Can you see how I could be surprised?
>
> *Fiona:* I think I am the one who is most surprised about how well we are getting along. However, I am really worried about how we are going to get on dealing with the matrimonial property issues. We might find that everything is going to come crashing down around our ears. Still, Greg, I feel your whole attitude has changed.
>
> *Greg:* Yeah, I am worried about the money issues that are inevitably going to be tough issues to work through.

THICKENING THE PLOT

It was quite understandable for Greg and Fiona to turn to the difficulties they were about to face in the next week. A degree of trust had developed in the mediation sessions that provided safety for them to talk about these difficult issues that would otherwise be too upsetting to discuss on their own. Although they were ready to focus on the matrimonial property issues, the mediator wanted to stay with reflecting on the changes Greg and Fiona were making in their relationship. He felt that this discussion would give more fullness to the positive parenting narrative they were establishing for themselves and their children. "Thickening the plot" of the preferred narratives of a parenting partnership, would, the mediator believed, serve them both well in managing the difficult matrimonial property issues.[14]

> *Mediator:* I can appreciate that you want to discuss the implications for your parenting relationship given the financial issues you want to address. However, my hunch is that if you can get clearer about your abilities to work through problems together, this may better prepare you to negotiate your way through some of the specific financial issues that are coming up next week. Are you interested in taking a few minutes to reflect on what you have been able to achieve to date, and on some of the reasons for this, before discussing the matrimonial property issues?

The mediator wanted to stay with a curious and inquiring stance about Greg and Fiona's desired relational abilities. He believed that this approach would give further substance and strength to their cooperative parenting narrative. He needed to be respectfully persistent with this aim, but only with their consent. He did not want to take over as a knowing expert the delineation of what they were permitted to talk about, and thereby diminish their knowledge. He wanted, however, to state his preference for the kind of conversation that he believed would most support the growth of the alternative story. So he stated his interest and asked their permission to follow it. This approach is in line with the narrative stance called *coauthoring*.[15] Greg and Fiona agreed to follow the mediator's line of inquiry.

Next, the mediator focused on a narrative cluster of questions called *unique account questions*.[16] These questions are designed to help people identify how they were able to achieve their successes. This line of questioning added more richness and depth to the co-parenting narratives.

> *Mediator:* How do you make sense of the fact that you are both able to work so well together? You made a success of Frank's birthday, you are working together to address Jessie's schooling difficulties and depression, and you have been following a caregiving plan for the children that you developed yourselves.
>
> *Greg:* Well, I think I let go of trying to make things go in a direction that I wanted but that didn't seem to fit for the kids. I think I just listened to what the kids had to say and what they wanted.
>
> *Fiona:* I think we are starting to find a way of liking one another as parents even though there are still some big wounds there.

These interactions helped to name some of the relational strengths that were emerging. Specifically, Greg's response provided an opportunity for him to acknowledge his ability to listen to others' points of view even when they were not what he wanted to hear. Fiona's response demonstrated a willingness to let go of her susceptibility to the story that she had betrayed Greg, and to let go of her resentment over the years that he was unavailable to help with the parenting of the children. She was now able to concentrate on what was happening in the present parenting relationship. Further interactions followed that storied Greg's ability to listen and be attentive, and fleshed out in more detail Fiona's ability to be more trusting of Greg's motives.

The mediator asked Fiona and Greg what it said about them that they were developing a parenting partnership with attentive listening, growing trust, and diminishing bad feelings. This question was seeking a description of personal and relational qualities. It asked them to explore their experience and bring forth aspects of their character that previously had been unstoried. In response to such questions, favored events can be gathered together and storied into a robust account of cooperation. These questions are often difficult to answer but they are worth pursuing because of the potential for relational identity reconstruction they offer. Greg and Fiona were shifting from being an angry, feuding couple with few resources for solving their parenting issues, to being parents living separately who could make wise choices about what their children required. After some thought, Fiona was able to make the following statement:

> I think I am a quite trusting and forgiving person deep down and I am also beginning to appreciate that Greg sincerely believed that the way he was being a father of the children in our marriage was motivated by his best intentions. It has helped me see another side of him that I couldn't see before. However, too much has happened to want to try again. I guess that is just the way it is.

Greg followed shortly with his own summary of how he saw himself:

> Well, all I can say is that it has been a painful experience that I never want to repeat. I've learned a lot going through this and I can't say I am fully there yet. I have been really knocked around by this whole issue. However, I think I am a better man for it. I would like to think that I have the ability to put my family first, and under the circumstances I think I have taken a pretty unselfish view of things. I know that the financial settlement issues will hit me hard, but they have to be faced, and I now say the sooner the better so I can pick up my life again and go on.

STORYING THE FUTURE

These statements were enormously important because they were to help Greg and Fiona construct a positive foundation from which to tackle some of the more difficult issues they were about to face. I asked them whether they had learned some strategies that would help them deal with the challenging matrimonial property issues. Greg thought they had moved their relationship into a parenting and business partnership and, because they had built a greater degree of trust, he was not anticipating major problems with the property settlement. Already he was preparing to work with Fiona so that she would receive a just share of their assets. Greg wanted Fiona to be fairly resourced so that she could purchase her own home, one that would be much more appropriate for the children. Fiona, for her part, was going into the deliberations with the confidence that she was seeking a just share of their joint assets, and she was going to take considerable care in the way this would be handled.

The mediator then inquired further about how the changes they were now making were going to be kept intact. He was interested in what rescue plans they had devised, or planned to devise, to help them hold onto the progress they had made, in the event of any difficulties arising in the asset negotiation.

This question invited Greg and Fiona to reflect on future possibilities and to plan how to handle future difficult issues, at least in principle. *Unique possibility questions* prepare the way for the parties who were formally in conflict to reflect on the strategies, techniques, and problem-solving abilities they are putting in place.[17] Fiona and Greg were thoroughly involved in this process. A new chapter in their coparenting relationship was about to unfold.

This is also the end of the first chapter. No doubt this chapter has raised many questions about the narrative approach to mediation. We have made many allusions without providing full explanations. Our purpose has been to whet your appetite. The story we have told serves an introductory purpose for this book. We want it to convey a flavor rather than amount to complete coverage. In the next chapter we explain how a narrative approach is built on assumptions different from those that underlie the problem-solving approach. We then turn to a theoretical review of narrative mediation that underpins all of the important moves and strategies taken up in the mediation process. Later we speak more about the practice aspects of crafting a narrative conversation.

Notes

1. Moore, C., *The Mediation Process: Practical Strategies for Resolving Conflict* (San Francisco: Jossey-Bass, 1996); Fisher, R., and Ury, W., *Getting to Yes: Negotiating Agreement Without Giving In* (Boston: Houghton Mifflin, 1981).

2. White, M., and Epston, D., *Narrative Means to Therapeutic Ends* (New York: Norton, 1991); Monk, G., Winslade, J., Crocket, K, and Epston, D., *Narrative Therapy in Practice: The Archaeology of Hope* (San Francisco: Jossey-Bass, 1997); Freedman, J., and Combs, G., *Narrative Therapy: The Social Construction of Preferred Realities* (New York: Norton, 1996).

3. Bruner, E., "Ethnography as Narrative," in V. Turner and E. Bruner (eds.), *The Anthropology of Experience* (Chicago: University of Illinois Press, 1986).

4. Winslade, J., and Monk, G., *Narrative Counseling in Schools* (Thousand Oaks, Calif.: Corwin Press, 1999).

5. White, M., "The Externalizing of the Problem," *Dulwich Centre Newsletter,* 1989, special edition, pp. 3–21.

6. White, M., "The Process of Questioning: A Therapy of Literary Merit?" in M. White, *Selected Papers* (Adelaide, Australia: Dulwich Centre Publications, 1989).

7. White and Epston, *Narrative Means to Therapeutic Ends*; Monk, Winslade, Crocket, and Epston, *Narrative Therapy in Practice;* Freedman and Combs, *Narrative Therapy;* Dickerson, V., and Zimmerman, J., *If Problems Talked: Narrative Therapy in Action* (New York: Guilford Press, 1996).

8. White, M., "Deconstruction and Therapy," in D. Epston and M. White (eds.), *Experience, Contradiction, Narrative and Imagination* (Adelaide, Australia: Dulwich Centre Publications 1992); Fairclough, N., *Discourse and Social Change* (Cambridge, England: Polity Press, 1992); Weedon, C., *Feminist Practice and Poststructuralist Theory* (Oxford, England: Blackwell, 1987).

9. Moore, *The Mediation Process.*

10. Coogler, O. J., *Structured Mediation in Divorce Settlement* (San Francisco: New Lexington Press, 1978); Saposnek, D. T., *Mediating Child Custody Disputes: A Systematic Guide for Family Therapists, Court Counselors,* Attorneys, and Judges (San Francisco: Jossey-Bass, 1983).

11. Stulberg, J., *Citizen Dispute Settlement: A Mediator's Manual* (Tallahassee: Supreme Court of Florida, 1981).

12. Amunsden.J., Stewart, K, and Valentine, L,, "Temptations of Power and Certainty," *Journal of Marital and Family Therapy,* 1993, *19*(2), 111–123; Hoffman, L., "A

Reflexive Stance for Family Therapy," in S. McNamee and K. Gergen (eds.), *Therapy as Social Construction* (Thousand Oaks, CA: Sage, 1992); Anderson, H., and Goolishian, H., "The Client Is the Expert: A Not-Knowing Approach to Therapy," in S. McNamee and K. Gergen (eds.), *Therapy as Social Construction* (Thousand Oaks, CA: Sage, 1992).

13. White and Epston, *Narrative Means to Therapeutic Ends*; Monk, Winslade, Crocket, and Epston, *Narrative Therapy in Practice*; Freedman and Combs, *Narrative Therapy*; Dickerson and Zimmerman, *If Problems Talked*.

14. White, M., *Narratives of Therapists Lives* (Adelaide, Australia: Dulwich Centre Publications, 1997).

15. Epston, D., and White, M., "Consulting Your Consultants," in D. Epston and M. White (eds.), *Experience, Contradiction, Narrative and Imagination* (Adelaide, Australia: Dulwich Centre Publications, 1992).

16. White, "The Process of Questioning."

17. White, "The Process of Questioning."

Radical Care

Shawn Ginwright

Shawn Ginwright is a leading national expert on African American youth, youth activism, and youth development. He is an associate professor of education in the Africana Studies Department and a senior research associate for the César E. Chávez Institute for Public Policy at San Francisco State University. In 1989, Ginwright founded Leadership Excellence Inc., an innovative youth development agency located in Oakland, California, that trains African American youth to address pressing social and community problems. He is the co-founder of Flourish Agenda, a social impact company that supports schools and community organizations building well-being and healthy school climates. In 2011, he was awarded the prestigious Fulbright Senior Specialist Award from the State Department for his outstanding research and work with urban youth. He has advised the Ford Foundation, Spencer Foundation, and the Heinz Endowments on philanthropic strategies to support young people in urban communities. He received his PhD from the University of California, Berkeley. His research examines the ways in which youth in urban communities navigate through the constraints of poverty and struggle to create equality and justice in their schools and communities.

Ginwright offers a model of conflict intervention that differs from the problem-solving workshops, mediations, and transitional justice practices that define Epoch Two. Rather than formulating an intervention program, he embeds himself fully in the community he serves, as well as the social and economic constraints faced by Oakland youth.

Instead of trying to upend structural injustices directly, he helps youth navigate the challenging terrain of their own lives, including racist teachers, the shame of being homeless, and distrust of the police. He knows if he pushes directly against the structure (taking on the police, teachers, etc.), the structure will only push back. Instead, he provides a home and safe place where they can be heard. In this open discursive space, the young adults can reflect and consider their options without denying the realities they face. Through a deeply caring and consistent presence, Ginwright helps them gently shift their own sense of self-worth and identify where they have agency. This deep caring is a response to hopelessness and helps the young people develop the resilience necessary to take on the larger injustices in their lives. Because their trauma results not from a single act of violence, but rather from exposure to ongoing, life-threatening situations, deep interpersonal relationships can help prevent youth from internalizing the violence around them. Ginwright's radical care approach considers caring about the individual *as* caring about the collective.

Questions to consider: What makes this approach to radical care "political?" What is the role of social capital in shifting the meanings that youth have about themselves? How might embedding oneself in a community long-term create a different result than short-term interventions?

Fostering Caring Relationships for Social Justice

Shawn Ginwright

I have always loved autumn in Oakland. Waking up to see yellow beams of sunshine peering through my bedroom window is always a hint that the day will be blessed with warm breezes that stretch out into a golden lazy afternoon. Walking outside my home in East Oakland, I can hear the birds chirping, and sometimes I can smell freshly cut grass from my neighbor's home, which reminds me of how little time I seem to have to tend to my own overgrown yard.

It was nearly 70 degrees, and it was only 10:00 a.m., and as on most days, my calendar was full. I had several meetings to attend and a visit to a young person's home, and I had to prepare for a youth discussion group for Saturday morning. So I excused myself for taking more time than usual to get to the Leadership Excellence youth center in downtown Oakland.

When I arrived at work, my day began rather uneventfully. I read my e-mails, combed through the mail, and checked my voice mail. I found it strange that Mikayla, one of the youth, had left an urgent message for me to give her a call over the weekend. But before I could complete listening to the other messages, my cell phone rang. Mikayla's worried and tired voice was on the other end. When she arrived at the youth center about 30 minutes later, she was visibly upset. Immediately, Lisa, a long-term Leadership Excellence employee, stopped working to talk to her and find out what had happened.

It turns out that late Saturday night she and a friend had been driving around with a few guys they knew from school. Even though they really didn't know the guy driving the car, they had seen him around the neighborhood. She explained that they had just left a party in North Oakland when they decided to get a late night bite from Kwik Way's Burgers. When they pulled into the parking lot at Kwik Way's Burgers, they noticed that their driver was staring at someone in a car parked in the lot. Not thinking much of it, Mikayla and Rena exited the car to use the bathroom and purchase their food. Upon returning to the back seat of the car, they saw their driver hop out and swiftly walk to the driver's side of the other car in the parking lot. They watched as he pulled a gun from his jacket, pointed the gun, and shot the driver in the head at near point-blank range. He ran back to the car, where Mikayla and Rena were sitting in the backseat in shock, and quickly sped away before anyone could see what had happened. As Mikayla and Rena were yelling at him, he pulled the car over, looked at them in the backseat, and said, "I know where you live, so you better not say nothing to anyone . . . now get out!" That's when Mikayla called me, because she didn't know exactly what to do. Going to the police could get her killed and put her family in jeopardy. However, not being able to tell anyone made her physically sick. So she simply reached out for help in a dark situation.

We embraced Mikayla, with compassion and love, and created a space for her to share her fears and concerns without judgment and telling her what she needed to do. We knew that if she went to the police she could be in danger. Despite the fact that she witnessed what happened and knew who was involved, being labeled a snitch was a death sentence in Oakland. Recently there had been several shootings involving youth witnesses to crimes. Perhaps the most significant thing we could do for her at the time was to provide a safe place to listen.

This chapter highlights how care can foster activism for young people who experience trauma in their communities. Through in-depth interviews of three youth and participant observations of young people who participated in an afterschool program for 2 years with Leadership Excellence, I illustrate, through the grounded experiences of young people, the ways that urban issues such as violence and institutional failure prevent young people from healing from traumatic events. Often trauma and the inability to heal from it are significant barriers to academic success, civic participation, and general health and well-being. The trauma caused by unimaginable choices, however, can be healed. This chapter examines how caring relationships, political consciousness, and action all contribute to healing and well-being for youth who experience trauma in their communities.

Trauma, in this sense, is not simply a single act of violence, but more often ongoing exposure to life threatening experiences. The term *posttraumatic stress disorder* (PTSD) is commonly used to diagnose and describe individuals who have witnessed violence, such as riots, gang shootings, torture, or bombings. However, the term fails to capture the nuance and complexity of the ongoing trauma that urban youth experience. This is largely because the prefix *post* suggests that the traumatic events are in the past and because the focus is almost entirely on events rather than environments. A broader understanding of trauma captures not only the event, but also the community's response and how violence is treated in the general public (Washington, 2007).

For example, one of the most significant difficulties black youth experience is the way in which trauma in black communities is treated by the general public.

Embedded in newspapers and in evening news accounts of violence in urban black communities is the notion that violence in black communities is entirely the fault of the people in the neighborhood. Johnson (1995) argues that crime statistics and research tends to reflect and reaffirm racist notions that black communities, and therefore black people, are more violent than whites. Victims of violence events are framed by the media in such a way as to suggest that they deserve their fate. Rather than discussing how years of disinvestment in black communities has created joblessness, for example, the general public asks, "Where is the tragedy?"

> The tragedy of homicides among Blacks is negated in this suggested framework of crime and violence. Violence becomes the word that both subsumes one event (the tragedy of the victim's death) and qualifies another action (a brutal homicide). In addition, this framework defines the actors as potential menaces to society, thereby undermining any sympathy when lives are taken by an act of violence. As a result, the public feels a macabre sense of relief when it is reported that the "menaces" kill each other. Death framed as violence begs the question, "Where is the tragedy?" This framework leaves no room to mourn a family member lost to a brutal death. On an even more insidious level, the "violent" framing of African American homicide incriminates both the assassin and the deceased. Looking at death only through a lens of violence generates silence around the issue of this death as loss. Thus, the tragedy and overall impact of death felt by surviving African American adolescents is hidden by mainstream society's inability and unwillingness to deal with the issue of death or with the brutal way most Black adolescents encounter death. . . . In this harsh light and harsher silence stands the African American adolescent whose friend or loved one was gunned down. (p. 219)

Without a more critical understanding of the root causes of truama, black youth internalize these feelings and blame only themselves or their communities for their conditions. These feelings often are barriers to action. Caring relationships, however, can confront hopelessness and foster beliefs about justice among young people. These caring relationships are not simply about trust, dependence, and mutual expectations. Rather, they are political acts that encourage youth to heal from trauma by confronting injustice and oppression in their lives. Care builds hope, political consciousness, and the willingness to act on behalf of the common good. Care in this sense says, "Because I care about black people, I care about you," and it views each person as vital to a collective struggle for liberation. But young people must heal before they can act.

Care as A Political Act in Black Community Life

Often in black communities, beliefs about care, healing, and justice are found in the confines of the church. Sometimes, however, ideas about care, healing, and justice can be found in some aspects of civic life. Sullivan noted, "In cities ravaged by alcohol, cocaine, heroin addictions, and the nexus of the HIV/AIDS pandemic, networks of care, support, and counseling are some of the strongest, most vibrant, and most visible civic infrastructures existing in poor communities and neighborhoods" (1997, p. 1). The destruction of a healthy political infrastructure in black communities across America has in many ways threatened modes of care and justice that historically have played an important role in black social networks and activism. Increasingly, neighborhood-based organizations in black communities have come to recognize the role of care, healing, and justice in developing young people as well as fostering strong, vibrant community life.

Care has become particularly important, given that the state, which once provided basic social services, has failed to address these issues in black communities (Wacquant, 1998). In response to the state's neglect of facilitating basic social welfare, some community organizations have come to serve as a buffer to mitigate what Wacquant (2001) refers to as the "penal state"—the omnipresent influence of state institutions such as police, schools, and prisons that in concert encroach upon urban life through surveillance, zero-tolerance policies, and imprisonment in the name of public safety. Rather than building mutual trust, democratic participation, and community building, Wacquant argues, the penal state threatens the vitality of networks of care in black communities. Scholars have argued that growing poverty, crime, and violence, as well as the state's diminishing role in providing basic social services, has resulted in new forms of social capital in urban black neighborhoods (Dance, 2002). These new forms of social capital are much less concerned about how social networks are fostered and sustained through membership to civic and social organizations and much more focused on how "humane investments" of care contribute in healing and justice among African American youth (p. 84). Caring is one important aspect of social relationships between youth and adults. These caring relationships make possible the achievement of certain ends that would not be attainable (Dance, 2002).

Care among black youth, however, is more than simply trusting relationships and mutual expectations and bonds between individuals. Rather, care within black communities and among youth is viewed as a collective and individual responsibility. The emphasis of care in black communities is on cultural, communal, and political solidarity in addition to interpersonal relationships (Thompson, 1995). Thompson notes that care means "promoting cultural integrity, communal and individual survival, spiritual growth, and political change under oppressive conditions" (p. 29). In communities ravaged by violence, crime, and poverty, care is perhaps one of the most revolutionary antidotes to urban trauma, because it ultimately facilitates healing and a passion of justice. Without caring relationships people make the pain personal—the three Ps, which can hinder their capacity to transform the very conditions that created it. Care within the black community is as much a political act as it is a personal gesture: It requires that relationships prepare black youth to confront racism and view their personal trauma as a result of systemic social problems.

For example, the capacity for African American youth to develop a political understanding of racism can promote wellness and healthy development (Ward,

2000; Watts, Williams, & Jagers, 2002). Janie Ward (2000) notes that "addressing racism in an open and forthright manner is essential to building psychological health among African American youth" (p. 58), who have been failed by schools, social supports, and traditional youth development programming. In the context of economic decay, political isolation, and urban violence, care is cultivated through ties with adult community members and facilitated by building collective interests through political racial consciousness among black youth. Care in this context moves beyond coping and surviving and encourages black youth to thrive and flourish as they transform community conditions.

This way of conceptualizing care also builds from prior treatments of social capital that focus on the ways in which mutual trust facilitates community action (Ginwright & Cammarota, 2007). Building from Sampson and Raudenbush's (1999) discussion of collective efficacy, which highlights how linkages of trust and willingness act on behalf of the common good, ideas about care and social capital conjoined point to the ways in which trust and political consciousness translate into community action.

Leadership Excellence: Building Activism through Care

From Telegraph Avenue in downtown Oakland, it would be easy to miss the Leadership Excellence office, flanked by a beauty shop to the left and a Chinese takeout to the right. There are no large signs, posters, or billboards that announce the organization's precise location, only a glass door marked "1736 Telegraph" and a small black marquee next to a call box that lists three tenants in the building—AMN Architecture, first floor; Tagagi Engineering, second floor; Leadership Excellence, third floor. Entering the small foyer of the building, visitors can sometimes smell the chemicals coming from the beauty shop or the fried vegetables from the Chinese takeout next door, and sometimes the unpleasant smell of both at the same time. The loud, rickety elevator creeps and pulls its way up to the third-floor opening to a large, bright, loftlike space. The hardwood floors and red brick walls give the space a warm, welcoming feeling, despite the high, warehouselike ceilings and expansive 2,000 square feet of space. There are numerous bright, colorfully painted banners promoting the organization's programs that line the walls—"Oakland Freedom Schools," "Leadership Excellence, Educating Youth for Social Change," "Drop Squad." The space feels so large probably because there are no walls, mostly cubicles that divide the employees' work spaces. The large windows welcome ample sunlight into each cubicle, where photographs of youth from past summer camps, school activities, or overnight retreats can be viewed.

Toward the rear of the building there is a meeting area labeled "The Spot," which serves as both a youth lounge and a conference room. There are brightly colored plastic stackable chairs; several red, green, and blue beanbags; and two covered couches, all circling a colorful rug in the center of the room. The four walls were carefully hand painted in a mural that depicts a story of youth challenges in Oakland, each wall with a different story that ends with a vibrant depiction of black youth rising up, breaking the chains that kept them down.

Around 3 o'clock, streams of young people flow into the office and provoke conversations with staff members. Any work that requires a computer needs to be completed by 3:00 because after that, the loud chatter and laughter of young people is usually too distracting for a focus on paperwork. Besides, the youth always find a way to use the staff's computers to log on to their MySpace pages. No one really minds this, of course. In fact, the youth are explicitly told by staff, "This is your space," which sometimes means that after 3:00 the office is filled with hip-hop music, blaring from small computer speakers. Around 4:00 the energy settles down, and youth work on homework or attend one of the after-school workshops held in The Spot.

Most of the young people at Leadership Excellence (LE) describe the organization as being a family. Perhaps this is because Nedra, my wife and the codirector of the organization, views our work as an extension of our own family. In fact, the young people refer to Nedra as "Mamma Ned" and often call me "Babba Shawn." My role, for the most part, is to build a sustainable organization; Nedra's job is to make sure that I do it in a way that does not jeopardize our integrity. In fact, Nedra and I debate, and sometimes argue, about which funding sources to pursue and how to use funds to expand LE's work. These debates are sometimes the material of an after-school discussion topic. I might say to the youth, "Okay, y'all, we can apply for a $100,000 grant but it will come from the Philip Morris Tobacco Company. Now let's discuss the pros and cons of this opportunity." Nedra might glare at me for raising the issue to the youth, but know that I am right to do so. Our arguments, debates, and disagreements are all from a place of love, respect, and care, which is perhaps why Mikayla and other young people describe LE as a family.

Mikayla and Mamma Ned

Mikayla is a large girl with soft eyes and an old soul. Despite her cheerful spirit and youthful appearance, she has seen more than most 15-year-olds in Oakland, which probably explains why she is so self-confident. She was born in Tulare, California, and spent most of her early childhood years in Sacramento. At the age of 11, she moved to Oakland and has lived here ever since. Throughout Mikayla's life, her mother and her half-sister, Tatiana, have played prominent roles in shaping who she is today. She sees her mother as her best friend, and Tatiana, who is 9 years older than Mikayla, has been like a second mother to her. Mikayla's mother instilled in her the need to "speak your mind" and the need to be proactive, because "if you don't do it for yourself, nobody's going to do it for you."

Mikayla explains that being a part of LE is like being in a family. Her relationships with the adults, as well as the political education, have contributed to her activism:

You can't describe it. It's like one of those heartfelt things that you have no words for because it's like my family. If anything ever happened to me or I needed somebody to talk to, I could always come here. I started coming to Leadership Excellence, my sister got me into it and I was shy, didn't say very much. Now I'm the person that always has something to say, and they made me think about a lot of political stuff that I wouldn't have thought of if I wasn't in the program. They made me aware that I can make a change and act and not just accept things the way they are. It's kinda like . . . I'm in a family.

Since she can remember, Mikayla and her mother have never really had a home for a long period of time and frequently were homeless. This is largely because of her mother's substance abuse and alcoholism, which at times have required that Mikayla care for her mother. "Sometimes, she would just sleep all day and never get around to paying rent so we are always looking for a place to stay. Sometimes we would just sleep in our car, but when it gets too cold, I would have to call my sister, a friend, or somebody and ask them if we could stay with them."

Not having a stable place to live contributed to her lack of interest in school, which was exacerbated because she found the curriculum to be uninteresting and not applicable to her life. She explained that her teachers would routinely discriminate against her and other black students in her classes. For example, she had a teacher who gave all minority students grades of C or below. She also had teachers who believed that African Americans were lazy and didn't give needed help even though she asked for it. Consequently, she skipped a lot of school and eventually dropped out at the age of 15. She also often talks openly about racism she sees from the police. Mikayla dosen't trust teachers, police, or any authority figure. Most of her interactions with authority figures have been negative. For example, she witnessed police officers beating several of her friends directly in front of her.

The other day one of my friends was being questioned by the police near my house. He was just standing there with his hands in his pockets, and the police officer was like, "Get your hands out of your pockets!" He said it twice. My friend told the officer, "Why do I have to get my hands out of my pockets, I'm just standing here watching what's going on." So the next thing I know, the police officer pulls out his gun and puts it to his neck and then puts it to his head. The officer said, "Uh . . . get your, get your hands out your pocket." So he pushed him up against the car, put handcuffs on him, broke his wrists in the scuffle! He was just standing there, with his hands in his pockets not doing anything!

Over time, encounters like this have eroded Mikayla's trust in police and, like many youth in Oakland, she has little faith or trust that the police will protect and serve her or that teachers care about her. Which is why Mikayla came to LE, rather than the police, to share what she had seen on Saturday night.

Mikayla first became involved with LE at the age of 14. Tatiana, her older sister, who was studying social work, was an intern for LE and arranged for Mikayla to attend Camp Akili—one of the organization's summer programs.

While Mikayla enjoyed the camp experience and the opportunity to get away from home, she also expressed that she felt like she had joined a supportive community of peers and adults where she could be herself and learn about social issues.

The close and supportive relationships Mikayla developed with staff and other youth at LE has had a tremendously positive impact on her life. She recalled a time when Nedra came to her house, without notice, after Mikayla had dropped out of school and stopped going to LE's programs. "Mamma Ned" is a 30-something, petite sistah-girl who speaks the truth and her mind with frank eloquence—a straight shooter, no room for bullshit. Her truth speaking has frequently made me, as her husband, nervous because I know that the truth is not always what folks want to hear. Somehow, however, her honesty is rarely misconstrued by others, and just like medicine, they might not want it, but her honesty is precisely what they need to hear. As with so many other relationships Nedra had developed over the years, she went further with Mikayla. Mikayla's absence prompted Nedra to speak to Mikayla's mother and visit Mikayla at her home unannounced. Mikayla commented:

> When Nedra popped up at my house, I did not expect her to be there. It was like the afternoon and I was still in my pajamas! She sat down with me and my mom and she told me that she was disappointed in me because I had dropped out of school. Now no one really ever said that to me before and it hit me hard! I didn't want to be a disappointment to anyone, especially Momma Ned, after all she had done for me! Nedra was saying that I needed to get back in school and I knew she was right. Sometimes it just takes the right person to tell you what you already know. So I got back in school and eventually graduated but I really felt that LE was there for me.

Mikayla has a great deal of respect for the young adult volunteers because LE offers so much comfort and support to her. For example, when she was homeless, she stayed with female volunteers or she sometimes would sleep in the LE office and use the showers at the YMCA a few blocks away. "If I hadn't been in Leadership Excellence, I would have never graduated from high school . . . I would probably have some kids or something like that." Mikayla feels a unique bond with other youth participants because they have all endured a lot of pain in their lives, and they have all supported her when she has needed them.

While care is formed by interpersonal connections, collective responsibility to improve community conditions is a common theme in LE's relationships with black youth. After Mikayla graduated from high school, Nedra hired her to help coordinate one of the organization's after-school youth-led programs. At 17, Mikayla is responsible for recruiting and organizing other youth to political awareness workshops on Saturday mornings.

> Having the ownership of the program makes me feel like I have a purpose for what was going on in the community. It gives me a sense of family and being a part of someplace where I could go where my ideas

were respected. This never happens in school because I remember asking questions or I would say things in class at school and I was always
shot down. But I feel that my ideas about how to improve the community, for example, are respected at LE. I feel really nurtured by everyone
there.

Mikayla recalls one activity during a Saturday morning political education program where she learned a great deal about how to think and act in political ways:

> We were discussing a lot of issues that we [black youth] deal with here
> in Oakland. Typical stuff like crime, violence, drugs, police—stuff like
> that. Then we were asked, "If money was not an issue to address any of
> these issues what would you do?" I remember feeling like, are we ballin'
> or something like that? You know, the facilitator said that money is no
> object, we can do whatever we want to change the condition we want
> to take on in the community! It gave me a whole new way of thinking
> about stuff. There were no limits placed on who you are, where you are
> going, or what you want to do. So many things came out of that conver-
> sation because there were no limits placed on what we could imagine!

These rich conversations provided fertile ground for youth to develop a political
understanding about juvenile justice, racism, poverty, and how these social issues
shape their lives and communities. Through political education sessions, LE youth
discuss the root causes of problems in their communities and strategize about how
issues can be addressed. Collective responsibility to the broader black community
is a critical component of LE's caring relationship with youth. Slogans such as
"One life, one love, one people" or "I am because we are" and "I am my brother's/
sister's keeper" are commonly found in newsletters and on T-shirts, which reinforce the idea of a common collective struggle. LE adults often say that one central
purpose of the organization is to provide black youth with a "knowledge of self"
in order for them to be better equipped to address social and community issues.
Caring relationships are given meaning in collective struggle by creating a collective responsibility among black youth.

Mikayla finds meaning in relationships with adults at LE. These relationships
help build optimism and hope. Despite what she witnessed on Saturday night
being traumatic, there is a way to make it better. Such relationships, as Thompson
observes, are driven by the urgency to "alert young people to the various threats
to their survival and flourishing" (1995, p. 33), in order to carve pathways back
to peace and well-being. As we sat on the couch, listening intensely to Mikayla,
she continued to cry and explained that she wanted to go to the police but she
was also fearful of what could happen to her, and perhaps her mother or sisters, if
the perpetrator found out. We sat silently, without knowing exactly what to do or
say. Lisa stood up from the couch and walked toward the door, turned around,
and sat in a chair next to the couch. She brought her hands together and interlaced
her fingers and, with a confused look, said, "Maybe I can call the police watch
hotline. I can report it, but it would be anonymous." Mikayla looked up from
staring at the floor. Her eyes were still moist. She said softly, "You think so?"

While Lisa's call to the police never led to an arrest, the space for us to sit with her provided Mikayla a way to resolve what seemed to be an irreconcilable choice. Reflecting on that conversation, she commented, "They somehow don't make things seem like it's the end of the world when something happens, they make us feel like that there is always a way to make it better."

Mikayla's experiences with LE illustrates two points. First, trauma is not always conceptualized as a single tragic event, but can viewed as long-term exposure to dangerous situations, such as witnessing a murder. Sometimes trauma may stem from sociocultural environmental factors like distrust of the police and exposure to racist teachers or less obvious forms of trauma such as shame from being homeless and the psychic energy required to hide it from peers. For Mikayla, these experiences exact a toll on her overall well-being. Second, relationships among black youth in urban communities requires that adults transgress the traditional boundaries of trust between individuals by placing collective responsibility at the center of meaningful relationships. "We need to do whatever is possible to support youth with self-transformation," Nedra asserts frequently in staff meetings. "These relationships make us more than another after-school program because when I say to our youth, 'I know your grandmother or your momma,' they respect that I can say it and mean it; I really know their personal struggles. I think this gives us more trust because we are like extended family to these young folks."

These close relationships, however, are not without challenges. I recall a difficult group session that I was leading with both youth and adult volunteers. During that time in my life, I was having difficulty balancing care of my newborn child, raising money for LE, and transitioning to a new career as an assistant professor. As a result of these personal pressures, I could not focus on the training that I was conducting. I was unaware that many of the youth in the group had noticed my level of stress when one young person asked me, "What's wrong?" Until that point, I believed that my role as an adult community leader, founder, and executive director was to be a role model to young people by showing them a "trouble free" adult. In response to her question, I immediately put on the adult, "problem free" face and responded that there was nothing wrong with me. After they continued to probe me about why I seemed so stressed out, I finally confessed my troubles. I began describing my fears of not having raised enough money to keep the doors open. I told them how these financial issues would affect my family and new child. I also expressed my thoughts about leaving the organization altogether. After my emotional confession to the group, I was concerned that I had transgressed the boundaries of the adult professional role by violating the unspoken rule that you should separate your personal life from professional activities, but to my surprise, several youth responded, "Hey, man, you got problems just like me!" or "I thought you had life all figured out, that's cool that you got issues to deal with." Redefining my role as an adult partner contributed to an unanticipated outcome: I learned that when I made myself vulnerable, the young people could support me by listening just as I had listened to them. My vulnerability actually deepened their respect for me because I was honest with them about something as important as my own life. I am not advocating that all youth development professionals make their personal lives available to the young people with whom they work. The lesson I draw from this experience is that trust is also a collective phenomenon and as we care for youth in moments of our own vulnerability, they care for us as well.

Kevin's Rebound

While vulnerability is sometimes scary, risky, and uncomfortable, it frequently is a pathway to strong and meaningful relationships with young people. Perhaps no one knows this better than Kevin, a 20-year-old brotha with shoulder-length red-tinted locks who is constantly being torn between life in the streets and peace of mind. It is not his fake gold front teeth, baggy pants, and white T-shirt that have earned him respect in his East Oakland neighborhood, but rather his charisma, style, and intelligence. Kevin's sister had become concerned about his involvement in drug sales, crime, and petty theft, and that led her to call LE and inquire about how we could support Kevin. "I was falling really deep into the streets and digging a hole that I knew I could not get out! I felt like I was trapped and stuck getting deeper and deeper into the streets." Kevin grew up in East Oakland and as a child would look up to the older teens on his block. He was enamored by the "O.G.s" (original gangsters) on his block and saw them as strong male role models:

> When I was younger, the O.G.s would be out there on the block holdin' down. They would look like strong, powerful men. I grew up without a father and was raised by my grandma, my momma, and my sister. As I grew up, I felt like I needed to be around some men. I started hanging out with them because I need to learn how to be a man. When I was 14 or 15, I started to notice their nice cars and they always had money and girls with them. So I was like, "How can I get like that?" I remember when I would ask them for a dollar, and they would give me 5 or 10. As a youngster that's a lot of money!

Like many young men in Oakland, Kevin wanted only the glamour of street life, not the danger. In fact, he admitted that when he started hanging out, he didn't really know that violence, running from the police, and watching over your back was a part of selling drugs. Shortly after he began to hang out with groups of older teens, he experienced firsthand the danger that comes with selling drugs. He recalled the first time he held a gun, that "it was heavier than I thought it would be," but he quickly got used to wearing baggy clothing to conceal the gun when he needed to carry it.

> My niggas was always out on the block selling, grinding, trying to make some money. I had to really earn my respect with everyone. I don't want to go into detail about what I did but I had to do a lot and go through a lot. It was like an initiation, a fraternity or something. But

when I got in, it was like no turning back! I just focused my mind and molded myself into a gangsta.

But gangsta life turned out to be a tragedy for Kevin. He and his best friend, Amir, would often go to parties in East Oakland and shout out the name of their block, seeking respect and perhaps recognition from other folks at the party.

The night of May 8, 2004, began like any other Saturday night. Kevin gathered with his friends and heard about a party in nearby Richmond. As at many other parties, there was plenty to smoke and drink. They weren't really concerned that the party was on another turf. Kevin commented about hanging out with his friends: "When we all get together, we really don't give a fuck about anything!" When the young lady who invited them told them to "stay inside and keep the door closed because the niggas in Richmond don't like cats from Oakland," they really didn't pay her much attention. During the party, it wasn't long before other guys from the neighborhood attempted to crash the party and were quickly turned away by the host. Later that night, after everyone had left, Kevin was playing dominoes in the kitchen. The apartment was small and hot so his friend Amir kept opening the door to cool off. Amir had taken off his shirt and was standing in the open door when he was hit with bullets.

> All I heard were the gunshots outside—*bap, bap, bap, bap* . . . My first thought was, Are they trying to scare us or something? So I just kept on playing dominoes. When I looked up, Amir came running into the house. As he ran in, I could tell something scared him because he scanned the room and looked around for someone, and then he ran straight to me. As he came to me, I grabbed him and I looked down and saw all the blood. That's when I knew he had been shot. I was shocked and I didn't know what to do! What was I suppose to do? We called the ambulance and they came about 30 to 45 minutes after we called. During this time, Amir was laying on the floor trying so hard to live. His eyes were still wide open, but he was grunting and trying to hold on. When the ambulance arrived, one nurse put her gloves on and put her finger in one of the bullet holes, I guess to try to stop the bleeding. Blood was everywhere, man. As she was trying to stop his bleeding, I remember this clearly, the police rushed in the door and grabbed everybody including the nurse and pushed all of us into the back room! As I turned around to look back at Amir, I saw him panic because his chest was going in and out real fast. The police started to snap pictures of him, you know, homicide pictures of his body, but he was still alive!

The trauma of witnessing what had occurred to his friend Amir was more than Kevin could take. Anger, rage, sadness, and confusion all swirled inside of him with no place to go.

> I started trippin' out—I cannot even describe what I felt, it's something you gotta experience for yourself to understand, so I blew up with rage. They arrested everyone but took me to jail because I didn't have any

identification. I remember just sitting there thinking, Is he dead or
alive? I sort of knew he was dead.

Oftentimes traumatic events like the one Kevin experienced go undiagnosed and
ultimately contribute to even greater distrust, resentment, and anger. After spending 2 days in jail, Kevin learned that he was a suspect in the murder of his own
best friend! Despite the fact that there was no evidence to suggest that he should
be a suspect, he now has a permanent record that indicates that he was a suspect
in a murder investigation. Without his having a meaningful and productive outlet
to describe and heal from what happened, Kevin's frustration and anger turned
into numbness.

> I try to put that shit behind me but every time I go and try to get a job,
> that "suspect to murder" pops up even though I had nothing to do with
> it. Everytime it happens, it reminds me of the whole ordeal again. It
> pisses me off because it reminds me of what the police did, you know
> how they flipped his body over and took homicide pictures of him
> when he was still alive! I just didn't feel anything, I just felt numb. I
> just felt stuck in the middle. I didn't feel good about anything, or bad.
> I just felt stuck and I didn't give a fuck about anything!

Events such as these often result in unresolved rage, aggression, depression, and
fatalism (Poussaint & Alexander, 2000). Few educational and youth development
researchers have considered the ways in which trauma shapes both the educational
and youth development experiences (Obidah, et al., 2004). Traumatic events like
the one Kevin experienced have an impact on individual well-being, but there are
also social, political, and moral implications that reverberate throughout the
broader community. Amir was a son, a brother, and a uncle, whose loss will be
mourned by those who knew him, but mostly ignored in the media. Local concerns about safety and crime will continue to shape home values and thus educational quality in neighborhoods and residents will demand that their milquetoast
leaders provide greater safety. More important, however, are the existential questions Kevin and others will struggle with in trying to make meaning out of profound loss. Unfortunately, these forms of trauma have become normalized,
perversely usual, in black urban communities where death and dying have become
so common that some youth tell their teachers what they want to wear to their
own funerals.

Violence of this sort poses a serious threat to social bonds, relationships,
belonging, and sense of purpose. West suggests that the most profound result of
violence is a "numbing detachment from others and a self-destructive disposition
toward the world" (1993, p. 14). The impact of violence in communities has led
many researchers to reframe how they look at violence, moving away from restric-
tive beliefs about maladaptive behavior toward a more broad conceptualization
that considers the ecological terrain (the social, economic, political, and cultural
environment) in which violence occurs (Brooks-Gunn et al., 1993; Garbarino,
1995; Garbarino & Abramowitz, 1992). While there is substantial evidence to

suggest that "violence destroys the underlying interrelatedness and interdependence not only of its perpetrators and victims, but of the community at large" (Ward, 1995, p. 4), we understand very little about the redemptive process that restores these mutual ties and relationships. Restoring relationships, trust, care, and hope contributes to the healing process and is an important precondition for social action (Piven & Cloward, 1979).

In Johnson's examination of black youths grappling with death in a classroom setting, she argues for the need to "make connections between the day-to-day realities of students' lives and the day-to-day process of teaching and learning that takes place in urban public schools across the United States" (1995, p. 217). After realizing the profound impact of homicide on the lives of young people in her community, she came to understand the ways in which social marginalization and oppression create and sustain urban trauma. In connecting students' real-life experiences to classroom practices she describes a healing process that integrates issues of power, history, self-identity, and the possibility of collective agency and struggle.

Enacting Radical Care

Traditional modes of care in black communities have always been central to sustaining black life and affirming black identity in the context of brutal racism. Without these modes of care, hope, possibility and meaning give way to profound meaninglessness and hopelessness, which pose a serious threat to black life. These modes of care function as buffers, as cultural armor, that have created and sustained community life and "ways of life and struggle that embodied values of service and sacrifice, love and care, discipline and excellence" (West, 1993, p. 15). Such views of care were defined not simply by compassion, but also by communal survival: community members would support one another through personal hardships such as death, illness, or lack of shelter. There are few community spaces, however, for black youth to heal from the type of trauma experienced by Mikayla and Kevin. Schools are ill prepared to engage young people in a healing process. Often schools actually *breed* violence through draconian rules and a fetish for control, containment, and punishment. Churches often are overly resistant to urban black youth culture. After years of trial and error, we learned at LE that youth rarely want or need to be talked at, but want to be listened to without judgment, which of course is very difficult when you deeply care about someone.

Amir's death occurred shortly after Kevin started hanging out at the LE youth center. Fortunately he had a community of caring adults, peers, and what Noguera calls a "humane environment" in which to talk about the incident and there was a process that allowed him to openly grieve, heal, and hope again for a better way of life. After about a month, he was given a part-time administrative job sorting mail, copying, and running errands for the staff. In 2001, I stepped down from the executive director position, because of my other demands at the university, and Dereca Blackmon, a 30-something, Stanford-educated, gritty, streetwise sistah, took the helm of the agency in June 2002. For some reason, Dereca immediately bonded with Kevin and took it upon herself to support him through his healing process.

Dereca explained, "I am always drawn to the most challenging young people, the ones that everyone else cannot, or will not, deal with." Kevin was no exception; he had dropped out of high school a couple of years before he came to LE. When young people walk into Dereca's office at LE, she is always happy to see them and welcomes them with a hug and smile. In fact, hugging and embracing is an important ritual in LE's culture. Dereca explains:

> I am always excited to see the young folks come in. Good to see you man . . . howz you momma? We are all excited; we hug them and give them much love. Where else are they going to get that feeling of belonging, like really being honored for just walking through the door? Where else are they going to get that feeling of being celebrated for just being who they are? You don't get it at home, not at school, not on the streets, really. And they so much want that good *feelin'*. Like Neal, he is rejected everywhere else, but here he's a legend! Where else do youth get to feel like a legend!

Neal is a young man who had been an outcast in so many places not only because he is openly gay, but also because of his appearance. He is tall, with light skin, bright red hair, and freckles. Despite his being ridiculed everywhere else, the young people in LE saw him as a part of the family. This was reinforced by staff, who celebrated Neal when he would show up to programs after school, because of his outlandish personality and vibrant energy. Neal, and all youth, are always greeted with a hug. This is largely because central to the organizational philosophy is that black youth are rarely embraced by adults, or by one another, in ways that convey care, compassion, and love. In the harsh reality of urban life, tough fronts and postures are required to navigate violence and potentially life-threatening situations (Dance, 2002). These postures, however, are also walls that inhibit the healing process, and when young people embrace each other the tough exteriors melt away and the youth can be at ease. It is through touch and embrace that deep and meaningful relationships begin with connections from the soul.

More important than a single embrace, however, was the caring environment fostered at LE. Kevin started participating in a black male support group called Brotha's Keeper, where 10–15 young men from 14 to 25 years old would meet every Thursday night to talk about issues ranging from loss to academic success. The support group gave Kevin an opportunity to grapple with not only the loss of Amir but also the rage and numbness Kevin was experiencing. Connecting to other youth and young adults who experienced similar trauma provided Kevin a rare space in which to heal. He commented:

> The only way I would deal with this stuff before I came here was to drink. But that would make me real evil. All the rage would just come out to such an extent that my partners would tell me I need to stop

drinking. I really didn't know how to deal with this trauma. I don't know about getting a psychologist or something like that, cuz if I go see a psychologist, how they gone tell me 'bout something they never been through. The group of brotha's really helped me see what happened and deal with it differently. We talked about all types of little things that would keep my mind off of the streets. One time I got up and told a story about what happened, with Amir. The energy in the room was cool so everybody in the room was getting up to tell their stories so I kinda got a chance to let out some of my emotions. Everybody was emotional, so you know what I'm saying? I got to tell my story and just based off the energy in the room, I got a chance to let out my feelings.

These types of experiences were critical to Kevin's healing process. By being in a safe environment, he felt safe enough to listen to other young men's stories but also he felt the security to share his own. These environments are not easy to create. In fact, many of the young men had come from rival turfs. The leader of the young men's group, however, had taken time to prepare each participant by taking him away on a retreat to build a sense of trust and community. The investment in time and energy during the retreat created trust and respect whereby young people could be vulnerable to openly share.

Every day when Kevin entered the office, he would check in with Dereca to have a casual conversation or to get her advice about something. Dereca commented, "I would always check in with Kevin and say, What's up? We just talk about stuff, going on in his family, or on his block, his future or whatever." If he missed a day or so, she would ask him, "Why weren't you here yesterday, where were you?" She might add, "We missed you; we needed you to help set up the room for the meeting." For Kevin, the environment was a welcome change from what he experienced on the streets. On the block, he always had to be suspicious of everyone's actions.

Kevin developed a greater sense of belonging and connection, to Dereca and to the entire LE community of adults and other youth. He stated, "The people here trust me with everything, I feel like it is another kind of family because I feel like I belong here."

On one occasion, the young people decided that they wanted to paint a mural in the youth section of the office and had contacted a well-known local artist to train the youth in how to paint a mural and to work with them to create a mural that would convey the values and principles of the LE community. Kevin worked with the artist, K-Dub, for hours on the mural. His hard work was rewarded when K-Dub painted a portrait of Kevin, in the center of the mural, to represent a positive image of black male youth in the city. When K-Dub included Kevin in the mural, it also transformed how Kevin began to see himself. Kevin declared, "Man, the mural really made me feel like I was significant around here, like I mattered."

Belonging to the LE community was an important part of Kevin's healing process. His connections with other youth and young adults who shared a common experience provided powerful bonds that led to new, positive forms of community life. These strong, rich community connections are highly political. Ward argued that "the parenting of a black child is a political act. The psychological survival of a Black child largely depends on the Black family's ability to endure racial and economic discrimination and to negotiate conflicting and multiple roles and demands" (2000, p. 51). Similarly, relationships with youth are strengthened by honest and sometimes harsh discussions with adults about the conditions of black people. Building critical consciousness, or the capacity to understand how social, systemic, and structural issues shape day-to-day life, is an important component in building caring relationships. These conversations force young people to confront their own responsibilities as well as understand how to confront racial and economic oppression. These conversations are pivotal in moving from beliefs about care as simply compassion, to more radical ideas about care that foster critical consciousness and encourage changes in behavior. Kevin recalls one conversation he had with Dereca that illustrates this point:

> I'll never forget what she told me. I remember she said that basically what we want to do while y'all are here at LE is tell you that you have been lied to by society. What we see out there in the streets is not the truth. But we think that all there is to life is the block and partying. But she said that was what society wanted us to do, keep us docile slaves or whatever so they could do whatever they want to our communities, sell us stuff that's not good for us. All the while, we're just blind to everything going on. No one ever said anything to me before like that. So that's what really started making me real close to Dereca.

These conversations are significant because they not only establish care between two people, but also signify a broader caring about the well-being of black people. It is in this context that care is both intimate and political, individual and communal. Care, in this sense, allows young people to see themselves in a broader context of justice and liberation. Dereca noted, "We care about youth, because we love black people; and because we love black people, we care so much about youth." This mutual understanding and expectation that care, love, and well-being are intimately tied to achieving justice and liberation deepens the relationships between adults and among youth at LE. Dereca gave an example:

> One day Kevin found a way to go to the roof of the building at LE and he was feeding some birds bread. I guess someone saw him up there and called the police and told the police that a black man was going to jump from the building or something. Next thing I know there are five police cars out front; 10 police officers rush into the office asking how to get to the roof because there is a dangerous man up there. I calmly told them that he was a youth in our program and was on the roof feeding the birds. They demanded to go to the rooftop, but I went with them cuz I knew they would probably beat Kevin's ass if I was not there watching them.

Dereca's actions signified care about Kevin as an individual young person; further, it prompted a more radical form of care that was informed by a political awareness of how police treated black males in Oakland. This required that she use her adult authority to intervene and buffer any problems that might ensue from Kevin being another target for Oakland police. Care as a political act conveys the idea that individuals belong to a broader community, and any threat to the individual is a threat to the community. The strong sense of belonging, coupled with a radical form of caring, a form that is both personal and political, creates a fabric of trust and expectation that foster a sense of common struggle among youth and adults. Radical care can be seen everywhere in the organization. LE's slogans, such as "One life, one love, one people"; "I am because we are"; and "I am my brother's/ sister's keeper," reinforce the idea of collective struggle. LE adults often say that one central purpose of the organization is to provide black youth with a "knowledge of self" in order for them to be better equipped to address social and community issues. By creating a collective black youth identity that is connected to politically charged issues in Oakland, black youth develop politicized racial identities. Gregory noted that collective identities are "formed and reformed through struggles in which the winning of identification/the articulation of collective needs, interests, and commitments is itself a key stake in the exercise of domination and resistance" (1998, p. 18).

The Soft Side of Revolution, Care, and Rebuilding Community Life

Care is facilitated by building critical consciousness among black youth and providing opportunities and space for political expression and engagement. For example, ongoing police misconduct in Oakland in March 2003 prompted the chief of police, the mayor, and a local congresswoman to convene a town hall meeting to learn more about the community's experience with police misconduct. Dereca was asked to attend to represent Oakland's youth. Upon arriving at the meeting, she realized that no young people had been invited and believed that it was important for the officials to hear from youth themselves. She called from her cell phone several LE participants and asked them to come down to City Hall and tell them what was happening with black youth in Oakland.

> When I got to the meeting, it was the usual cast of characters, the mayor, congresswoman Barbara Lee, and the chief of police. We were there to talk about youth but there were no youth at the table. So I called a few youth who were hanging out at the LE center and asked them to come and represent and speak their mind to these so-called leaders. When they arrived, they got on the open mic and blew everyone away.

When Kevin approached the microphone, everyone immediately focused on how he dressed. His baggy jeans, oversized "hoody" sweatshirt, tennis shoes, and shoulder-length locks seemed to typify the urban uniform for young black males in Oakland. Although this style of dress is common among urban youth, black young males who dress in this way are often labeled as thugs and troublemakers by the police and often targeted for surveillance and searches. Kevin commented about his experience with the police:

> I just want to be real with y'all. When I am out there I feel like a target for the police. People see me, and look at the way I dress, and treat me like less than a man, less than human! I feel like a target for self-destruction! Sometimes I feel like giving up, fuck it! But I am a wise person, you cannot judge me by the way I look because I know what wisdom is inside me and I just need the opportunity for you to see me for who I am.

By providing meaningful opportunities to give voice to black youth and articulate their feelings about the police, LE challenges the problem-driven discourse about black youth in public policy and recasts black youth as key civic partners in community-change efforts. Equally important is the mutual trust that developed between Dereca and Kevin. Because LE creates a space in which black youth can be heard, and recasts black youth as political actors, Kevin pushed himself to live up to the positive political expectation that LE staff holds of him.

> They [LE adults] see stuff that you don't see in yourself, and they try to bring it out of you. They see me as an activist or something, and I'm not political like that. But when Dereca lets me speak my mind to folks like the mayor and political people, it makes you want to live up to that image, you know.

Care is created between LE youth and adults through mutual trust and reciprocity. That is, the adults have the expectation that black youth will engage in political affairs, and in turn black youth conceptualize civic and community change as a responsibility. By creating forums, participating in campaigns for youth funding, and other civic activities, LE challenges politically disabling discourse about black youth in Oakland as a threat to neighborhood safety. Care is created and sustained through opportunities in which black youth are viewed as legitimate political actors. The expectation that LE adults have about black youth reconstitutes images of black youth, no longer seen as a civic problem but as community activists, and LE youth reciprocate by viewing community engagement as a responsibility. Care also involves creating a collective racial and cultural identity among black youth that provides them with a unified understanding of their plight in American society. This is important, given the entrenched ways in which black youth in urban communities have been socialized to view each other through fragmented, often adversarial neighborhood identities (East Oakland versus West Oakland). LE's strategy to create a unified racial identity among black youth helps them develop identities that mitigate neighborhood turf conflicts.

The rich and meaningful relationships Kevin had developed at LE had contributed to new consciousness about his own life and gave him a sense of purpose. The meeting at City Hall Kevin had attended was broadcast on C-SPAN and was seen by thousands of people throughout the country. After learning about the significance of his comments and his newfound activist identity, Kevin became more eager to learn all he could so that he could be a better advocate for other black youth in Oakland. But he had not completed high school and never received his GED. Dereca had been nudging Kevin to enroll in a program, but her constant encouragement to get his GED only reminded him of what he had not accomplished.

Dereca continued to push him about his future plans. Despite being deeply committed to social justice, and having begun to organize his own block, he still had not completed school. She told him that he had to get his GED; everything he was doing was good, but without his education, he eventually would turn back to the streets. Kevin never did well in school, nor did he really see the need to get his GED, which made their conversation tense. Shortly after, Kevin stopped coming to work. He stopped participating in the programs and disappeared from the LE community entirely. Dereca feared that she had pushed him away by pressing him so hard about getting his GED. She lamented:

> He just stopped coming to work. I didn't see or hear from Kevin in nearly 3 months. This is after talking to him almost every day. I was hysterical, asking everyone if they know what was going on with him. I didn't know if he was alive or what. I talked to some of his friends here and they told me that they see him sometimes but he seemed distant, and he really didn't have much to say to them. What did I say to push him away? Why didn't he call or come around? Deep inside I was tore up because I knew I had pushed him away. After about 3 months, I was sitting right here at my desk in my office and he just showed up out of nowhere. I just burst into tears when I saw him. I asked, "Where have you been? Why didn't you call? What is going on with you?" I cried and hugged him even though I was so upset. He said to me, "I thought a lot about what you said and I wanted to do more with my life." He pulled out a picture of himself in his graduation cap holding his GED diploma and said, "Look, it's me!" I just cried and I still have the picture. He had been going to school the entire time, working on his GED. Then he told me, "And I also got my driver's license." We hugged and cried together. Then I hit him and told him, "Don't you ever do that to me again—you could have called me and told me what you were doing."

Janelle Dance (2002) encourages us to think more seriously about what she calls "the power of humane investments," the investments in young people's lives that require that we see in them more than they see in themselves. These investments build relationships that raise expectations about the possibilities in young people's lives. Dereca's investments in Kevin and Nedra's investment in Mikayla illustrate that one of the first steps in the healing process is to care more radically about black youth. This means that we ask not so much what we can do for black youth, but more important, how relationships can recalibrate what black youth can do for themselves.

One of the undertheorized aspects of social capital is the conceptualization of hope and its impact on community, educational, and civic life among black youth. Both Mikayla and Kevin demonstrate the ways in which radical care departs from traditional ideas about care by placing a greater focus on the impact of trauma and the collective process required to heal from it. By focusing on relationships and dimensions of community change, radical care serves as an important community and social resource for youth. Care is facilitated by intergenerational advocacy that challenges negative concepts about black youth and is developed by building a collective racial and cultural identity and sustained by understanding personal challenges as political issues. Healthy relationships are fundamental prerequisites for radical care between youth and adults. If care is given meaning through relationships between individuals, radical care is formed in community.

Social Media

Manuel Castells

Manuel Castells received his PhD in sociology at the University of Paris (the Sorbonne). At the young age of twenty-four, he began teaching in France and, eventually, found his way to the University of California, Berkeley, where he taught sociology and urban planning. Today, he teaches at the University of Southern California's Annenberg School for Communication and Journalism. His work continues to look at urban sociology, internet studies, social movements, and political economy. He coined the term "Fourth World" to refer to populations excluded from global society. He tends to see the Information Age as a positive change for society.

Castells addresses the importance of social media in the 2011 Arab Spring uprisings. People are challenging the structure of nation-states and other institutions of oppression through rebellions often coordinated largely online. Castells argues that the grievances existed apart from social media. Political blogs developed critical thinking which was then coordinated and mobilized largely through Twitter and Facebook as well as YouTube. These platforms appealed largely to the protestors under the age of thirty, who are arguably as, if not more, familiar with virtual communities than actual ones.

Uprisings are often led by the young, and this generation has access to a whole new host of tools not available to their predecessors. They are connected not only with their friends, relatives, and fellow citizens, but they also can swap ideas and inspiration with neighboring countries. The explosion of social media reflects more than simply a change in communication; it reflects a shift away from the old institutions and their norms. While militaries can squash rebellions, they will likely be unable to do little more than slightly delay the new networks and pathways between people altering societies worldwide.

Questions to consider: How might social media use impact the conflict landscape? What are the benefits and limitations of its use? Do you see social media as a tool for peacebuilding, mobilization and/or a vehicle for hate and radicalization?

Dignity, Violence, Geopolitics: The Arab Uprisings[1]

Manuel Castells

> The Arab world is today witnessing the birth of a new world, which tyrants and unjust rulers strive to oppose. But in the end, this new world will inevitably emerge. . . . Our oppressed people have revolted, declaring the emergence of a new dawn in which the sovereignty of the people, and their invincible will, will prevail. The people have decided to break free and walk in the footsteps of civilized free people of the world.
>
> Tawakkol Karman, statement on the occasion of receiving the 2011 Nobel Peace Prize for her work on peace and justice in Yemen and among Arab women at large.[2]

In the wake of the Tunisian and Egyptian revolutions, Days of Rage (*Yourn al-Ghadab*) surged across the Arab world in 2011: January 7 in Algeria, January 12 in Lebanon, January 14 in Jordan, January 17 in Mauritania, January 17 in Sudan, January 17 in Oman, January 27 in Yemen, February 14 in Bahrain, February 17 in Libya, February 18 in Kuwait, February 20 in Morocco, February 26 in the Western Sahara, March 11 in Saudi Arabia, March 18 in Syria. In a few instances (Saudi Arabia, Lebanon, Kuwait and the United Arab Emirates, where little happened in fact), the protest fizzled out for a variety of causes.[3] In others, uprisings were quelled by a mixture of repression and concession from the regimes (Morocco, Jordan, Algeria, Oman), although the ashes of the movements are still hot and could be rekindled at any moment. In Bahrain, a Saudi Arabia-backed savage repression crushed in blood a massive, peaceful movement largely made out of the Shia population in the "Bloody Thursday" of February 17. In Yemen, Libya and Syria, initially peaceful movements were met with utmost violence from the dictatorships, degenerating in civil wars that transformed these countries into battlefields where geopolitical contenders fought to assert their influence. Indeed, foreign direct military intervention was decisive in Libya and foreign geopolitical influence became an essential factor in the evolution of the Syrian uprising. These various movements emerged from causes specific to each country, and evolved according to the conditions of their contexts and to the idiosyncrasies of each revolt. However, they were all spontaneous uprisings stimulated by the hope inspired by the success of the Tunisian and Egyptian revolutions, conveyed by images and messages arriving from the Internet and from Arab satellite television networks. Without any doubt, the spark of indignation and hope that was born in Tunisia and had brought down the Mubarak regime, bringing in a democratic Tunisia and a proto-democratic Egypt, extended quickly to other Arab countries, following the same model: calls on the Internet, networking in cyberspace and calls to occupy urban space to put pressure on the government to resign and open a process of democratization, from the Pearl Roundabout in Bahrain to "Change Square" in Saana, or squares in Casablanca and Amman. States all over the Arab world reacted in different ways, from slight liberalization to bloody repression, out of fear of losing power. The interaction between the protests and the regimes depended on internal and geopolitical conditions.

To be sure, there were deep-seated grievances among a population that had been submitted to political oppression and kept in dire economic conditions for decades, without a chance to claim their rights under the threat of arbitrary violence from the state.[4] Furthermore, the majority of these countries' populations were composed of people under 30 years of age, many of them relatively educated, and most of them unemployed or underemployed. These youth were familiar with the use of digital communication networks, as the penetration of mobile phones exceeded 100 percent in half of the Arab countries, with most others over the 50 percent mark, and many in the urban centers had some form of access to social media (Howard 2011). Moreover, they felt daily humiliation in their lives, void of opportunities in their society and participation in their polity. They were ready to rise for their dignity, a more potent motivation than anything else. Some had done so in the last decade, only to be met with violence, imprisonment and often death. Then, the spark of outrage and the light of hope came to them simultaneously. The hope was provided by other Arab youth, like themselves, who had risen up in other countries, particularly in Egypt, known in the Arab cultural imagination as *urn al-dunya* ("mother of the world"). The spark resulted from specific events in each country: self-immolations and symbolic martyrdoms as a form of protest, images of police torture and beatings of peaceful demonstrators, assassinations of human rights advocates and popular bloggers. These were no Islamists, or leftist revolutionaries, although anyone with a project to change society eventually participated in the movement. Initially they were of a middle class background,[5] albeit usually an impoverished middle class, and many were women. They were later joined by poor people hit by inflation and unable to buy their daily food staples as a result of policies of economic liberalization and the subjugation of their countries to increased food prices in the world market.[6] Dignity and bread were the original drivers of most movements, together with housing demands in the case of Algeria. But asking for bread meant actually to reverse economic policies, and to end corruption as a way of governance. The assertion of dignity became a cry for democracy. Thus all movements became political movements, asking for democratic reforms.

The evolution of each movement largely depended on the reaction of the state. When governments showed some semblance of accommodation to their demands, and hinted at political liberalization, movements were channeled into a process of democratization of the state within the limits of maintaining the essence of elite domination. Thus King Abdullah II in Jordan sacked his prime minister and dismissed his cabinet (the target of the protest against economic policies), establishing mechanisms of consultation with citizens, particularly with representatives of the Bedouin tribes. King Mohammed VI of Morocco proposed a few democratizing amendments in the Constitution, including a transfer of the power to appoint members of parliament to the prime minister. The amendments were approved by referendum in July 2011 with 98.5 percent voting in favor. He also freed dozens of political prisoners and held new elections on November 25, 2011 that saw the victory of Islamist candidates (most of them moderate), as in all other free elections held in the Arab world in recent years.

However, when the regimes resisted the demands for political reform and resorted to sheer repression, the movements shifted from reform to revolution and engaged in a process of overthrowing the dictatorships. In such process, the interplay of internal factionalism and geopolitical influences led to bloody civil wars whose differential outcome is redefining the politics of the Arab world in the coming years.

A Digital Revolution?

As in Tunisia and as in Egypt, most of the Arab uprisings started with organization, debate and calls to rise up on the Internet, and continued and formed in the urban space. Thus, Internet networks provided a space of autonomy from where the movements emerged under different forms and with different results depending on their social context. As in all of the other cases of social movements I studied in this volume, there is also a raging debate in the media and in academia about the precise role of digital networks in these movements. Fortunately, in the case of the Arab uprisings, we can rely on a rigorous assessment of their role on the basis of social science research, thanks to the work that Philip Howard, Muhammad Hussain and their collaborators have been conducting on this matter for some time. I will summarize here their main findings because I think they have put to rest a meaningless debate about the causal role of social media on social movement. Of course technology does not determine social movements or for that matter any social behavior. But Internet and mobile phone networks are not simply tools, but organizational forms, cultural expressions and specific platforms for political autonomy. Let's look at the evidence collected and theorized by Howard, Hussain and their team.

First of all, in his book *The Digital Origins of Dictatorship and Democracy: Information Technology and Political Islam* (2011), written before the Arab uprisings, Philip Howard, on the basis of a comparative analysis of 75 countries, either Muslim or with significant Muslim populations, finds that, while framed by a number of contextual factors, the diffusion and use of ICTs favor democratization, strengthen democracy and increase civic involvement and autonomy of the civil society, paving the way for the democratization of state and also for challenges to dictatorships. Furthermore, involvement of civic young Muslims was favored by Internet use. He wrote; "Countries where civil society and journalism made active use of the new information technologies subsequently experience a radical democratic transition or significant solidification of their democratic institutions"

(2011; 200). Particularly significant, before the Arab Spring, was the transformation of social involvement in Egypt and Bahrain with the help of ICT diffusion. In a stream of research conducted in 2011 and 2012 after the Arab uprisings, Howard and Hussain, using a series of quantitative and qualitative indicators, probed a multi-causal, statistical model of the processes and outcomes of the Arab uprisings by using fuzzy logic (Hussain and Howard 2012). They found that the extensive use of digital networks by a predominantly young population of demonstrators had a significant effect on the intensity and power of these movements, starting with a very active debate on social and political demands in the social media *before* the demonstrations' onset. In their words:

> Digital media had a causal role in the Arab Spring in that they provided the fundamental infrastructure of a social movement unlike the others that have emerged in recent years in these countries. In the first few weeks of protest in each country, the generation of people in the streets—and its leadership—was clearly not interested in the three major models of political Islam. . . . Instead, these mostly cosmopolitan and younger generations of mobilizers felt disenfranchised by their political systems, saw vast losses in the poor management of national economies and development, and most importantly, a consistent and widely shared narrative of common grievances—a narrative which they learned about from each other and co-wrote on the digital spaces of political writing and venting on blogs, videos shared on Facebook and Twitter, and comment board discussions on international news sites like Al Jazeera and the BBC.

The Arab Spring is historically unique because it is the first set of political upheavals in which all of these things [alienation from the state, consensus among the population in the protest, defence of the movement by the international public opinion] were digitally mediated . . . It is true that Facebook and Twitter did not cause revolutions, but it is silly to ignore the fact that the careful and strategic uses of digital media to network regional publics, along with international support networks, have empowered activists in new ways that have led to some of the largest protests this decade in Iran, the temporary lifting of the Egyptian blockade on Gaza, and the popular movements that ended the decades long rule of Mubarak and Ben Ali. Digital media had a causal role in the Arab Spring in the sense that it provided the very infrastructure that created deep communication ties and organizational capacity in groups of activists before the major protests took place, and while street protests were being formalized. Indeed, it was because of those well-developed, digital networks, that civic leaders so successfully activated such large numbers of people to protest.

In every single case, the inciting incidents of the Arab Spring were digitally mediated in some way. Information infrastructure, in the form of mobile phones, personal computers, and social media were part of the causal story we must tell about the Arab Spring. People were inspired to protest for many different, and always personal reasons. Information technologies mediated that inspiration, such that the revolutions followed each other by a few weeks and had notably similar patterns. Certainly there were different political outcomes, but that does not diminish the important role of digital media in the Arab Spring. But even more importantly, this investigation has illustrated that countries that don't have a civil society equipped with digital scaffolding are much less likely to experience popular movements for democracy—an observation we are able to make only by accounting for the constellation of causal variables that existed before the street protests began, not simply the short-term uses of digital technologies during the short period of political upheaval.

In my words: the Arab uprisings were spontaneous processes of mobilization that emerged from calls from the Internet and wireless communication networks on the basis of the pre-existing social networks, both digital and face-to-face, that existed in the society. By and large, they were not mediated by formal political organizations, which had been decimated by repression and were not trusted by most of the young, active participants that spearheaded the movements. Digital networks and occupation of the urban space, in close interaction, provided the platform for autonomous organization and deliberation on which the uprisings were based, and created the resilience that was necessary for the movements to withstand ferocious assaults from state violence until the moment that, in some cases, out of a self-defence instinct, they became a counter-state.

There was another meaningful effect of the movements' presence on the Internet networks that has been pointed out to me by Maytha Alhassen: artistic political creativity. The movements, particularly in Syria, were supported by the innovative graphic design of avatar images, mini-documentaries, YouTube web series (such as Beeshu), vlogs, photographic montages and the like. The power of images, and creative narrative-activated emotions, both mobilizing and soothing, created a virtual environment of art and meaning on which the activists of the movement could rely to connect with the youth population at large, thus changing culture as a tool of changing politics.

Political blogs, in the time before the uprisings, were essential in creating, in many countries, a political culture of debate and activism that contributed to the critical thinking and rebellious attitudes of a young generation that was ready to revolt in the streets. The Arab uprisings were born at the dawn of the explosion of the digital age in the Arab world, albeit with different levels of diffusion of these communication technologies in various countries. Even in countries with low levels of Internet access, the core of activists that, as a network, networked the movement and the movement with their nation and the world, was organized and deliberated on the social networking sites. From that protected space, extensive mobile phone networks reached out to society at large. And because society was ready to receive certain messages about bread and dignity, people were moved and—ultimately—became a movement.

Notes

1. This chapter largely relies on the contribution of information, data gathering and advice of journalist and scholar Maytha Alhassen. For her own analysis of the Arab uprisings, see Alhassen, Maytha and Ahmed Shihab-Eldin (eds.). (2012) *Demanding Dignity: Young Voices from the Arab Revolutions.* White Cloud Press, Ashland, OR.

2. http://www.democracynow.org/2011/12/13/the_arab_people_have_woken_up

3. The context of each country partly explains the cases in which protests were limited in 2011 (still to be seen in the future). Thus, in Lebanon and Algeria, the memory of atrocious civil wars had a paralyzing effect, although active protests did take place in Algeria, and were reproduced in January 2012. In Iraq, the painful period of war, occupation, civil war and lingering terrorism left the population exhausted and yearning for peace. In Saudi Arabia, the limited protest that took place on March 11 was largely confined to the Shia minority in the Eastern part of the country, and so its movement was isolated from the Sunni majority, and easily repressed by an effective security apparatus. The most significant social movement in Saudi Arabia was the women's campaign for their right to drive, a movement still in process, with the potential of extending to other women's rights. In the United Arab Emirates, the fact that most residents are not citizens, and most citizens enjoy affluent subsidized lives creates a context in which the lack of liberty does not necessarily appear as a burden to the citizens, and is a factor of intimidation for the immigrants.

4. For a discussion on Arab dictatorships, see Marzouki (2004); Schlumberger (2007).

5. For the social background of Syrian activists, as well as a firsthand account of the uprising, see the excellent analysis by Mohja Kahf: http://www.jadaliyya.com/pages/index/4274/the-syrian-revolution-on-four-packs-a-day.

6. For the impact of the rise of food prices in the world on the social situation of the Arab countries (they import more food than any other region in the world), see: http://www.economist.com/node/21550328?fsrc=scn/tw/te/ar/letthemeatbaklava.

References and Sources

Council of Foreign Affairs. (2011) *The New Arab Revolts: What Happened, What It Means, and What Comes Next.* Council of Foreign Affairs, New York.

Howard, P. (2011) *The Digital Origins of Dictatorship and Democracy. Information Technology and Political Islam.* Oxford University Press, Oxford.

Hussain, M. M. and Howard, P. (2012) *Democracy's Fourth Wave? Information Technology and the Fuzzy Causes of the Arab Spring,* unpublished paper presented to the meeting of the International Studies Association, San Diego, April 1–4.

Marzouki, M. (2004) *Le mal arabe. Entre dictatures et integrisme: la democratic interdite.* L'Harmattan, Paris.

Noland, M. (2011) *The Arab Economies in a Changing World.* Peter G. Peterson Institute for International Economics, Washington, DC.

Schlumberger, O. (2007) *Debating Arab Authoritarianism: Dynamics and Durability in Nondemocratic Regimes.* Stanford University Press, Stanford, CA.

Upending Normative Processes

Michael Gardner

Michael Gardner worked for years as a police officer in Cincinnati, Ohio. After six years, he found himself in a negative loop, feeling trapped in a world of good guys and bad guys. He credits a neuro-linguistic programming (NLP) seminar for changing his life. The program taught him how to have control over feelings through a process called *anchoring*. He began shareing the concepts with his police partner. The two of them began experimenting with the tools in their own work. Using pattern interrupts and other techniques to diffuse hostile confrontations, the two officers found themselves tapped into an approach that was transforming their interactions in tense situations.

To really put these techniques to the test, the two policemen elected to take the toughest calls in order to explore some innovative approaches. Gardner explains that domestic violence calls tend to be some of the most dangerous to police because of the elevated emotions and close ties between the conflicting parties. A woman, for example, might pull a knife on the police to protect her abusive husband from arrest. Rather than simply increasing force to quell these violent outbreaks, the two experimented with language (verbal and nonverbal) during interventions. Through techniques of distraction, confusion, humor, shifting tones, and irony, they were often able to throw enraged couples off track. Their techniques proved so effective that these two eventually trained many other police. Furthermore, a number of the fighting couples made up during their interventions.

This article challenges the notion that big problems simply require more force. Skilled practitioners can upend dangerous storylines in mediation settings as John Winslade describes in his piece on Narrative Mediation, as well as in the midst of violence. Gardner points out how little training police receive in verbal techniques, even though these techniques not only help protect those in crisis, they also can protect the police. This piece suggests we need to train conflict resolution practitioners, in all levels of practice, to explore the power of language and humor during interventions. To see examples of how such techniques can be employed in international conflicts, see additional stories in Mark Andreas' book, *Sweet Fruit from the Bitter Tree.*

Questions to consider: If police are only trained to use force, how might this affect their ability to manage even simple altercations? If this kind of training became a standard for the police, how might this affect who is attracted to the police force? What other professions could benefit from this kind of training?

The Dork Police
Further Adventures of Flex Cop

Michael Gardner

Everyone in the field knows that the most dangerous part of police work is handling domestic disputes. Roughly one third of the police officer assaults and killings in this country occur during domestic disputes. A cop may go in to arrest the attacker and suddenly the spouse turns on him with the frying pan when she sees he's making an arrest. There's no telling who may be a problem, and people are much more likely to fight to defend their homes against intruders.

A lot of the calls we got on night shift were domestic violence runs. Cops hate making domestic runs because they're so dangerous, but for research purposes my partner and I asked other cops, "Do you mind if we start taking over your domestic runs so we can experiment with defusing hostile situations?" Of course we got no objections.

Traditionally, police officers are limited to only four choices for controlling situations—visual and verbal persuasion, chemical irritant, impact weapon, and deadly force. In training, most emphasis was on weaponry defense, without nearly enough on visual and verbal defense. My partner and I saw the need to stretch our flexibility to hundreds of choices in this uncharted territory.

The traditional approach in police work for a domestic run was to show up at an apartment and bang on the door using a raid-type knock with the police night stick, BAM BAM BAM BAM! I even hate it when the UPS or mail carrier bangs on my door to give me something I *want*, so I tried to imagine how someone already in emotional distress would be angered even more with a raid-type bang on their door. To be less intrusive and confrontational we started showing up and doing the "shave and haircut" knock, a very light "Rap ta-ta tap tap, tap tap." Even if the people inside didn't catch on to the jingle, it was a less invasive knock, and its association with a harmless advertisement was more to relax *us* than the people inside. It kept us at a condition orange—alert, but not the red of alarmed. We would even joke sometimes going into an apartment, "Hey let's be condition purple." What we were really saying was, "Hey let's not get red, because if we go in there red, we're going to have a fight."

The usual question police were trained to ask when entering a home was, "What's the problem here?" Well, if you enter after a loud raid-type knock and ask them, "What's the problem here?" They'll give you a problem, usually several. They may tell you their problems from twenty years ago.

Instead we'd ask something like, "What have you decided to do between the time you called us and the time we got here?" That put them in solution mode. Other times we'd ask people to step out into the hallway so they wouldn't feel the need to defend their turf. We also purposely wore our hats when we approached, so when we did enter their house or apartment we could take them off as a sign of respect.

My partner and I became known to our fellow officers as the Dork Police, because no one knew what crazy thing we were going to do next. They were equally amazed at our success in nonviolent control of tense situations. We experimented daily with ways of startling subjects into confusion in order to interrupt their dangerous mental patterns and provide a space for something more positive.

For example, we would sometimes approach potentially dangerous domestic disputes with our jackets purposely buttoned improperly, or with our caps pulled down so our ears stuck out. Other times we'd say "no" while nodding our heads up and down. Unless the combatants were too intoxicated or high to observe this odd behavior, they stopped, at least temporarily. They couldn't help responding to what they saw. Then it was hard for them to pick up their fight where they had left off.

Sometimes we'd walk into a shouting match between a couple, and we'd just run over and switch the channel on the TV set. If one of them said, "Hey, what the hell are you doing?" We'd say cheerfully, "Hey, you're not going to listen to us anyway, so we're going to watch some TV."

All we were trying to do was get them to refocus out of their anger and onto something else. We would do anything to create a change. Once that was accomplished, we'd offer suggestions for where couples could go for longer-term help.

Using humor was particularly useful when performing routine, uncomfortable tasks like patting down or frisking a suspect. While maintaining physical control, we would like to say, "You don't have any hand grenades, swords, or bazookas hidden on you, do you?" Subjects generally laughed it off. Now and then, one would disclose that he had a knife or razor.

When couples were screaming at each other we'd start sniffing and shouting out. "Oh, do you smell gas? Where's your stove? There must be a burner on!" While the fight was temporarily stopped, my partner and I would go to the kitchen and pretend to check the stove for gas leaks. After a few minutes of sniffing the stove and kitchen area, we would advise the people that everything was OK, then ask "What else can we help you with?" The response was amazing. Often they said, "Nothing, officer . . . " If the argument did begin again, all my partner and I had to do was to sniff with a concerned look on our faces. With this pattern interruption, the subjects' personal fighting became secondary to the threat of a gas explosion in their home. They may even start getting an unconscious connection of, *Every time I start getting nasty there's danger, maybe 1 should try something else.*

Other times, we would enter a residence and be greeted by someone standing in a fighting position and shouting, "You two think you can take me? Come on!" We would mirror his stance, but hold our palms up instead of making fists, saying, "No way. We heard how tough you are. We can't beat you, we'd have to call ten more guys in here." If that statement had any effect, we would follow up with, "Why don't we talk first, then you can kick our butts." On several occasions the potentially violent subject changed his mind. And if he didn't respond to our initial statement, that signaled us to try something else. Initially it was hard for us to give this kind of "pull" statement when a violent subject "pushed" us verbally. We instinctively wanted to "push" back with an "attack" statement. Yet the patience of our "pull" statement always minimized the force of our arrest.

One time we had a husband and wife close to killing each other. They were shouting countless obscenities at each other, and their hand gestures were disjointed and out of sync with the tone and tempo of their verbal language. I remembered the metaphor of an orchestra conductor—when people talk in rhythm with their gestures it tends to be good venting; letting their anger come out verbally rather than physically. But when their gestures are short, choppy, stab-like motions, disconnected from their language, it is likely that they're about to explode physically. This couple was actually making verbal threats like, "I'm going to kill you, you son of a bitch!" "You're dead, mother-fucker!"

In a flash I said, "In all my years of police work, I've never seen somebody able to express their anger like you can! I appreciate that, because sometimes things really piss me off and I wish I could express my anger like you are!" I was empathizing with them to bring their attention to me and to the importance of what they were feeling, and away from a fight.

Another time we came into an argument with the woman yelling and screaming at her husband. I said to her, "I bet you don't talk to the mailman this way, do you?"

"What? Of course not!"

"And I bet you don't talk to your car mechanic that way, do you?"

"No, of course not!"

"Well the reason you talk to your husband like that is obviously because you care a whole lot more about what he says than what the mailman or the mechanic says."

"Yeah, well I guess so."

My questions first took her attention away from her emotions and what she was mad about. Then I offered her a new meaning for her outburst—it was because she *cared* about her husband. After about 15–20 minutes of me telling them how frustrated I was at not being able to express my feelings the way they could, they started counseling me. Soon it was apparent by the way they were sitting next to each other and looking at each other that they were eager to be left alone. I think we reframed their anger toward each other to such an extent that they wanted us gone so they could make up!

Once we came into a heated dispute and I said to the man, "Hey, you don't work for the city, do you?"

"NO!"

"That car out there with the lights on, that's not your car, is it?"

"NO!"

"You don't want us here, do you?"

"NO!"

"You'll be happy when we leave here, won't you?"

"Fuck yeah!"

This way I matched him and let him express himself. He was in the mood to disagree, so I started with questions all of which let him say "No." Then I shifted to a "Yes" question, leading him to a more positive place and getting his explicit agreement that when we left he'd be happy. It might sound like a small thing, but it made a huge difference. Now we were on the same page and he was more relaxed—no longer disagreeing with everything we said.

We'd also do a thing I called "word salad." I never did it in a disrespectful way, but when people get violent they're behaving worse than childish. Sometimes I'd say, "What you're saying here sounds like a phonological ambiguity to me, so rather than jeopardize any other litigation circumstances why don't you just take a walk and let things cool off?"

They got so confused by the first part of my sentence, they would jump on the first thing that made sense, usually responding. "I'll just take a walk and cool off a bit."

I'd say, "Great, I appreciate that."

Often we would use many of these different tactics one after the other, until we found what worked. By systematically attempting to stop violence by using our appearance or words, we put ourselves in a position where we would be much more justified—both emotionally and legally—if we ended up having to resort to a higher degree of force. Yet in all these experiments on permanent night shift, and during my thirty-year police career, I never fired my gun. I had to use mace on a person only once, simply because the man was so intoxicated I couldn't communicate with him. We had tried many things, but he just wasn't there because of the alcohol. He had a little paring knife that he wouldn't drop. Technically I could have shot him, but I had been relaxed and aware enough to keep a table between us, so I was able to subdue him with the mace. As amazing as these techniques were for defusing violence in the moment, our biggest success was that we stopped getting return calls from the places we visited. Before we started using these techniques, it was common to get calls from the same location two or three times a night. Sometimes my partner and I would spend 15 or 30 minutes out on a call, and we'd get in trouble from our supervisor because he wanted us in and out. If they didn't straighten up right away he wanted us to simply arrest them. But we knew we could save time in the long run by coming to a peaceful resolution.

Probably our most interesting encounter came in June of 1984. My partner and I were patrolling our beat on a Saturday afternoon, when the dispatcher's voice crackled over our radio:

"Car 405, Car 405, respond to 755 East McMillan Street, reference a man with a gun. The only description we have is he's male, black, and his last name is

Large. He threatened to kill a person and stated he would kill the police. Car 405."

We replied, "Car 405, OK."

Our sergeant came on the air with, "Car 422, advise Car 405 to wait for my arrival before they approach the address. I'll respond with a taser gun."

Unfortunately for us, my partner and I happened to be on the one-way McMillan Street heading for that very address when the dispatch came out. Other police units were coming over the air advising that they would also respond. Since we were so close already, we parked near the location and advised our dispatcher that we were on the scene. Needless to say, our adrenaline was pumping. We often got calls where the details sounded frightening, but this one was different. We were afraid. As we approached an alley between two buildings, we observed a man in an army coat arguing with a woman. Without thinking, I blurted out, "Anyone here order a *large* pizza?"

The male subject turned and looked at me with a puzzled expression. Even my partner was looking at me funny. I could see the man's hands were empty. He said, "My name is Large."

With that we knew who he was. We quickly handcuffed him and put him in the back seat of our car. Fortunately, he did not have a gun—something we did not know until after we had him under control. It turned out that he was a walk-away mental patient from the Veteran's Hospital Psychiatric Unit. He had been walking around threatening to kill people, hoping to force the police to kill him. Who knows what might have happened if Mr. Large hadn't been caught off guard. I sincerely believe that on this particular day the flexibility that I'd learned saved the life of a mentally disturbed veteran—and perhaps my life as well.

My partner, himself a Vietnam veteran, was able to chat with Mr. Large on the way to the Veteran's Hospital. Upon our arrival, the hospital staff was shocked that we didn't have to struggle with Mr. Large. I can't thank the people enough who taught me how to use these skills. Even though we may have been justified legally with some tactical force, we could never have lived with ourselves if we had hurt Mr. Large.

Unfortunately, it's very difficult to measure what *doesn't* happen, but I can say confidently that I was involved in hundreds of peaceful resolutions that would have ended up in arrests or fights had we used traditional police procedure. Ever since my eyes were opened to what is possible, I've been studying and researching how police officers everywhere can increase their choices by using visual and verbal persuasion to prevent, or at least minimize, their use of force in violent situations. Believe me, police officers all over this country need new tools for accomplishing their duties. They are hungry for positive education that will enhance their control over themselves and others. No group of professionals needs flexibility more than police officers.

Participatory Action Research (PAR)

Michelle Fine and María Elena Torre

Michelle Fine is a distinguished professor of critical psychology, women's studies, American studies, and urban education at the Graduate Center of the City University of New York (CUNY). Her primary research interest is the study of social injustice: when injustice appears as fair or deserved, when it is resisted, and how it is negotiated by those who pay the most serious price for social inequities. She studies these issues in public high schools, prisons, and with youth in urban communities, using both qualitative and quantitative methods. She received her PhD in social psychology from the Teachers College of Columbia University.

María Elena Torre is a research scientist as well as the director and co-founder of the Public Science Project at CUNY. For the past fifteen years, she has been engaged in critical participatory action research projects nationally and internationally with schools, prisons, and community-based organizations, seeking to further social justice. Her work introduced the concept of "participatory contact zones," and she continues to be interested in how democratic methodologies, radical inclusion, and notions of solidarity impact scientific inquiry. Before becoming director of the Public Science Project, Torre was chair of Education Studies at Eugene Lang College, the New School for Liberal Arts. She received the American Psychological Association Division 35 Adolescent Girls Task Force Emerging Scientist and the Spencer Fellowship in Social Justice and Social Development in Educational Studies, and she is on the national board of the National Latino/a Education Research and Policy Project and What Kids Can Do.

This article discusses two research studies co-created, executed, and produced by the populations being studied. The first concerns a racially integrated high school with an enormous achievement gap between races, and the second examines the college education received in a women's maximum-security prison. The projects sought to discover how society produced the marginalization of certain groups as well as how privilege is created and protected. For these researchers, PAR is about identifying where and how change can occur.

The argument for including participants in the studies is several-fold; insiders have access to community knowledge often not visible or accessible to outsiders. By including them in the design of the study, the teams can ensure access to the best "contact zones." Additionally, fully recognizing the co-construction of knowledge requires acknowledging power relations in the production of knowledge. This means more than just bringing different groups to the project, but must also offer them the skills to be equal producers of knowledge (interviewing, research, etc.). In these studies, the participants received the training necessary to enable them to be significant and astute contributors to the project. This training addressed power imbalances created by differences in skills and also ensured that participants would receive benefits from their participation. Finally, if researchers study a group as a means of arguing the population is overlooked and/or undervalued, the most significant and direct way of communicating this sense of their value is to include them.

This study also provides an example of how statistical analyses can look in Epoch Three. While quantitative studies often become associated with Epoch One positivistic approaches to knowledge, Torre and Fine provide a stellar example of how quantitative studies can spawn from research projects that are participatory as well as reflexive.

Questions to consider: How might PAR help address some of the limitations and challenges of ethnographic approaches used in Epoch Two? Might the solutions generated from any studies last longer with such high-level participation of involved parties? What other conflicts might benefit from this kind of approach versus more top-down approaches to conflict?

Re-membering Exclusions

Participatory Action Research in Public Institutions

Michelle Fine and María Elena Torre

Introduction

As the global empire (Hardt and Negri, 2003) realigns within and beyond the United States, we confront the question of method. To what extent are social science methods theoretically and politically "of use" within/against neoliberal consolidation? And for those of us committed to social justice studies, how do these global and local shifts in power affect how we design and engage our work? In this essay, we take up the practice of participatory action research (PAR) (Fals-Borda, 1979; Freire, 1982; Torre et al., 2001; Fine et al., 2001) as a methodological strategy that can reveal the complex workings of power within institutions and re-member the bodies of social and political exclusion (Chang, 2001; Eng and Han, 2002; Christianse, 2003; see also Opotow, 2002). We write this essay as an open letter to researchers committed to inquiry within public institutions; those who still believe that these institutions, while perhaps hijacked at the moment, represent contested sites that must be reclaimed as democratic public spaces for all.

In PAR within public institutions, the very men, women and youth of poverty and/or color who have too often paid the greatest price within the neoliberal State have the opportunity to critically reframe the large and local questions of social justice. As a collective of researchers, including historically marginalized and privileged collaborators, PAR projects aim to reveal the complex fissures and inequities in systems that represent themselves as rational, just and coherent while at the same time burying the exclusions and suffocating the ghosts. Locally and globally, PAR pricks what Eng and Han call "psychic amnesia," offering us a method for critical work within communities and institutions, revealing the fractures of power and restoring images of "what could be."

In this essay we explore questions of epistemology and method burrowed within two PAR projects in public institutions: a series of racially integrated suburban public schools and a women's maximum security prison. Both institutions are woven tightly into the fabric of America's exclusions. Racially integrated schools are, ideologically, the site onto which America's fantasy of racial justice is projected, but on the ground, these schools walk a precarious line between racial/ethnic/class access and resegregation within (Orfield, 2003). Prisons, far more explicitly, are the spaces to which the excluded are sent in America, over 2,000,000 strong, exiled to invisibility. In each of these two projects we were invited to investigate a particular institutional concern about educational justice: Why does the "achievement gap" persist in racially integrated high schools? and What are the effects of college in prison? In each context we created only one condition of engagement: a participatory research team of youth and prisoners, respectively, who would be "trained" in research methods, and then participate fully as partners in conceptualizing the questions to be asked, the theories to be developed, the "variables" to be examined, the methods to be engaged, the interpretations to be crafted, and the products to be produced.

By drawing on these two projects, we do not mean to equate prisons and schools. Prisons are explicitly about State control; schools are much more complex settings of social reproduction and radical possibility (Weis and Fine, 2003). However, both are under State pressure to serve State interests, dependent on State dollars, and in the grip of a "control society" in which ideologies of safety and justice are undermined by practices of surveillance and outcomes of inequity (Deleuze, 1990; Cole, 2000). Both prisoners and students of color have been inscribed, in the national imagination and scholarly literatures, as lacking, deficient, disposable and barely worth public investment. In both projects our research would contend with politics, ideologies and an already churning discursive pot of (mis)representations (Farr and Moscovici, 1984). We recognize the paradoxes of participatory research when power is always present in the socio-political theatre of the public sector, within institutional arrangements (Powell, 1996) and within the praxis of social research (Foucault, 1977). We nevertheless consider social research to be a tool of democratic engagement in ongoing struggles for social justice (Martin-Baro, 1994; Anand et al., 2002).

March 1996–December 2001

Sitting around a table in the Learning Center in New York State's maximum security prison for women, with tea, coffee, papers, carried in black backpacks stuffed with data and prison bags (clear plastic for "security reasons"), lavender scarves and green uniforms, eyes watching, clocks ticking, stolen hugs. It's 11 o'clock.

We are the research team, meeting every other week for four years, seven prisoners, three graduate students from the Graduate Center, one from Harvard, and Michelle (see Fine et al., 2001). Our research team was a space for critical inquiry where we walked past barbed wire fences, through our racialized and classed histories, between biographies filled with too much violence and too little hope, and biographies lined with too much privilege and too little critique. We were, at once, a team of semifictional coherence, and, on the ground, a group of women living very different lives, defined in part by class, race and ethnic differences. Half of us could go home at night; half of us were "home." Many of us brought personal histories of violence against women to our work, while all of us worried about violence against, and sometimes by, women. Some of us had long-standing experience in social movements for social justice; others barely survived on the outside. Some of us were White, Jewish, Latina, Caribbean and African-American, some mixed. Most of us were from the mainland of this country, a few born outside the borders of the United States. The most obvious divide among us was free or imprisoned, but the other tattoos and scars on our souls weave through our work, worries, writings and our many communities. Usually these differences enriched us. Sometimes they distinguished us. At moments they separated us. We understood ourselves to carry knowledge and consciousness determined, at once, by where we come from, and shaped by who we choose to be, alone, and then twice a month, together (Hartsock, 1983; Harding, 1987; Smith, 1999).

March 2002

We work with a set of school districts from 11 inner ring integrated suburbs in the New York metropolitan area, as well as two urban districts. The full group of youth researchers have, thus far, met for two "youth research camp" retreats where they have become familiar with both the quantitative and qualitative features of the research. The first youth research camp of 36 high school students and 12 "first generation" college students, from across racial, ethnic and class lines, from special education to AP, from the wealthy suburbs to inner city, came together to design a survey that would not look like a test; a survey to be distributed to 7,000 youth in 13 school districts in NJ and NY. They insist that the survey include cartoons, open ended questions, their photos, names (as designers!) and that no question leaves respondents feeling like a failure.

At the camps, students in "special education" and students in "advanced placement" work alongside students from schools that refuse to label students. All import distinct, compelling and significant perspectives to the questions of class, race, ethnicity and opportunity in public education. The research is designed to answer four questions: How do students, across racial, ethnic, class and academic levels, view their opportunities, motives and the "achievement gap" in schools and in the nation? Where do youth perceive issues of racial, educational and social (in)justice in school and community? How well prepared are students across racial, ethnic groups and academic track for college postgraduation? What are the sites of racial, ethnic and class based possibilities – where are the spots for educational justice and opportunity in school and community?

And now, in this essay, we query aloud about undertaking theoretically rich, politically provocative, critical PAR for justice within public institutions; collectively crafted research designed toward democratic inquiry and progressive policy change (see Cochran-Smith and Lytle for parallel discussion of participatory work in schools, 1993). We track questions we have confronted on how to best design and undertake critical participatory action research, in institutions, with co-researchers who sit in some of the most vulnerable seats in the nation. Shedding the discursive cloak of institutional coherence and justice, PAR reveals the fractures, hypocrisies and inequities that constitute the public institutions of contemporary American life and, at the same time, helps us imagine radical possibilities for "what could be."

Moves of theory and method in participatory research

In both the prison and the schools, we have designed for a theoretical and methodological glide between wide angle analyses of socio-political structures and deep, upclose analyses of lives and relations (see Alford, 1998; Hitchcock, 1999; Weis and Fine, 2003). By committing to participatory methods, we recognize from the start that knowledge is located, produced, silenced and amplified in varied sites within an institution; that the dominant story told about institutional life is but one story and typically told from the "top," and that critical understandings of power and inequity, while usually buried, are essential to the democratic resuscitation of public institutions.

We undertake PAR to unravel the ideological weave and material conditions that produce a sense of coherence in these institutions and naturalize resultant inequalities. We seek to document how privilege and disadvantage constitute public institutions; we assess how inequalities grow embodied and legitimated within the bodies of corrections officers, school boards, educators, communities, students, prisoners, and those of us who witness. And we stretch to find those spaces in which the magic of social possibility and resistance survives (Weis and Fine, 2003). We write on key strategic moments of design, theory, method and ethics in PAR, as we aspire toward research of meaning in very hard times.

Designing for Democratic Participation

Historically, PAR developed out of the rich soil of critical, community knowledge held by "insiders" to community life. As those insiders sat at the bottom of social arrangements, they witnessed the holes in the ideological stories told, the practices engaged, and the contradictions that sustain stratification (DuBois, 1935; Lewin, 1951; Deutsch, 1974; Fals-Borda, 1979; Freiere, 1982; Collins, 1991; Martin-Baro, 1994; Greene, 1995; Hurtado, 1996; Smith, 1999).

We take seriously such insider knowledge which then forces us to trouble traditional notions of "whose knowledge counts." In the prison and the schools, we brought a commitment to create participatory research collectives into institutions in what Gloria Anzaldua would call borderlands: "Borders are set up to define the places that are safe and unsafe, to distinguish us from them. . . . A borderland is a vague undetermined place created by the emotional residue of an unnatural boundary. It is in a constant state of transition. The prohibited and forbidden are its inhabitants." (Anzaldua, 1999, p. 3). Drawing as well from Mary Louise Pratt's (1991) writings on "contact zones," we sought: "social spaces where disparate cultures meet, clash, and grapple with each other, often in highly asymmetrical relations of power" (Pratt, 1991, p. 4). Framing the space of our research as a contact zone pushed us toward a more textured understanding of human interaction across power differences, extending our collective theorizing beyond simplified binaries such as insider/outsider, oppressor/oppressed, to examine the activity of the space between, of Anzaldua's borderlands. A "contact perspective" highlights the interactive and improvisational elements of encounters across power differences, emphasizing how "subjects are constituted in and by their relations to each other . . . in terms of copresence, interaction, [and] interlocking understandings and practices" (Pratt, 1991, p. 5). Further, in theorizing our PAR collectives as contact zones, we recognize the co-construction not only of subjects but of knowledge and research, which forces us to explicitly address power relationships and analyze places of disjuncture within our team. This analysis holds the potential to reveal the radical possibilities of PAR for social imagination and critical knowledge production, as these sites often provide new understandings that each of us, as situated individuals (insiders, outsiders), would not likely come to on our own (Torre et al., 2001).

We therefore worked to create research collectives of very differently positioned researchers in both the prison and the schools (the Critical Gap Project), creating a montage of insiders and outsiders to institutional life. As political theorist Nancy Fraser (1990) would argue, we believe it is disingenuous to invite co-researchers to the table without equipping them (and us) with shared skills, knowledge and language for full participation. By recognizing the divisions and inequities wrought by social stratification, we carved out spaces to create an "us" struggling against the tides of separation and essentialism, so we built research teams by teaching first in the theory and methods of PAR and critical theory.

In the Critical Gap project, for instance, our initial task was to build a diverse community of high school researchers from urban and suburban communities, traversing zip codes, housing stock, racial and ethnic boxes, languages, families, sexualities, Advanced Placement and special education, athletes, students with disabilities, boys and girls. At the first research camp, a two day overnight at St. Peter's College in Jersey City, youth participated in "methods training," learning the nuances of interview, focus group and survey design. To begin, we had to deconstruct what a "researcher" looks like. Sati, a youth researcher from the South Bronx, sketched, and then disrobed, the balding white guy "scientist" (Figure 1).

In the prison, the building of a research collective involved the delicate knitting together of insiders and outsiders—graduate and undergraduate students

"Is this what a scientist looks like?" by Sati Singelton

interested in social (in)justice. Some in prison, some free. Together we circled, addressed, avoided and confronted with outrage, tears and theory, the enormous inequities with respect to power and freedom that sat around our table; that saturated our biographies; that threatened to predict our futures (see Torre et al., 2001). The dynamics of power, participation and humiliation in prison are raw, shocking and sometimes horrifying. Our research collective was by no means immune. Judy Clark, one of the prisoner researchers, reflects on our PAR process:

> One of the values of qualitative research is to challenge the traditional power relation between those who do the research and the object of the research, through a participatory process. But the realities and dynamics of prison, as the social context of this project, also affects the quality of work and the participation of the prisoner researchers in stated and unstated ways. As prisoners, we are always bounded by roles and rules of a closed institution. Some argue that we are in prison to be punished; others would argue, to be corrected. But in any case, we are essentially objects who must be controlled. On the other hand, we are striving to take responsibility for our lives, to become active, responsible subjects. This conflict of roles and expectations plays itself out in our roles as researchers in this project.

It was through such diverse and divergent experiences and standpoints that our research questions, methods, analyses and "products" were shaped, influenced and invented. We purposely created research collectives where varied perspectives could be aired, challenged and thoughtfully discussed—without the imposition of "making nice" or reaching unanimous agreement. When tensions emerged among the team, rather than ignoring or silencing them through consensus, we sought meaning in the friction. For instance, we analyzed the way our local tensions mirrored larger political dynamics of the institution. This doubled research practice calls for both micro and macro levels of analysis, as it explicitly recognizes power relationships and situates the work in a social historical context.

Critical Theorizing: Reframing the "Question"

As PAR moves forward, the first collective task involves the explicit reappraisal of the given question—in this case, "What causes the achievement gap?" and "Is college in prison a worthwhile social investment?" At the catalytic intersection of insider and outsider knowledge grows a critical reframing of the presenting question. By definition, PAR designs review the "problem" with an eye toward complexity, politics, social psychology and structure and away from simple victim-blaming explanations. By troubling dominant conceptions, PAR insists that researchers historicize, contextualize and fracture the "common sense" story.

To illustrate: In the prison study, the question we were invited to investigate asked, simply, what are the costs and benefits to society of college in prison?

Without the benefit of history, we would not have known that in 1994 there were 350 college-in-prison programs and in 1995 that number dropped to eight. In 1994, federal Pell grants were still available to all persons in the United States. But in 1995, President Clinton signed the Violent Crime Acts, which disallowed the use of Pell grants (federal dollars) for prisoners. With a national mood of "get tough on crime," punishment replaced rehabilitation as the explicit purpose of prison. The women in prison lived this history. They could narrate the shift in national opinion and prison policy as sophisticated archivists of carceral history.

Together we muddled through layers of history and politics in order to broadly theorize the impact of college in prison on the women, their children, their post-release outcomes, crime levels, the prison environment, the economy and the "tax burden". We learned that funding for public education and for prisons have been inversely correlated in New York State; just as dollars moved out of schools and into prisons, so too did young bodies of poverty and color move out of buildings with books into buildings with bars. We studied together the racial politics of who is arrested, who enjoys "alternative sentencing," who ends up in prison, who has access to quality secondary or higher education in and out of prison; and the extent to which state dollars flow to support prisons over higher education (see Gangi et al., 1998). We had to grapple with the fact that men of color are more likely to be in prison in New York State than in the State University system; that "downstate's crime is upstate's economy"; that most prisoners in New York State come from seven or eight communities in New York City, have extraordinarily low literacy rates, are disproportionately undereducated, are African-American and Latino; the fact that New York State now spends more on prisons than on college; that women are the fastest growing prison population; that federal financial assistance for college is shifting nationally from "need" to "merit" (Gangi et al., 1998).

We could have plucked our research out of history and asked a narrow, psychological question, like how is the self-esteem or personal efficacy of individual women affected by college classes in prison? And we would likely have produced positive results. But with a PAR design we were obligated (and honored) to join the policy debate and political struggle of prisoners' rights—in this case, the debate and struggle around the survival and restoration of college in prison. A "simple" and neat research design addressing the psychological impact on individuals involved in college would, by omission of the larger context, trivialize the sociopolitical relations that have saturated the growth of the prison industrial complex and shriveled the rehabilitative possibilities within prisons. We would have erased the historic offering and then withholding of Pell grants. We would have obfuscated the tragic state of public schooling in poor neighborhoods that produces, in part, the substantial prison population. A tight and narrow opening for inquiry gives vast license for institutional mis-rememberings of exclusions. Hard questions are exiled to the terrain of the unstudiable, fading from social consciousness. PAR, in contrast, is situated in local and national struggles and matures in long, difficult conversations among and between insiders and outsiders. Participatory action researchers design their work to provoke, theoretically and politically, a strategic widening of the analytic lens of social research.

Surfacing Counter Stories

As PAR widens the lens of analysis, it also surfaces a series of counter stories or social explanations that challenge dominant laminations of social arrangements. Insiders, particularly those who have watched an institution operate from the "bottom," know all too well the stories told about why the institution works for society and why they are failing. They know all too well how the institution insures its success (and their failure). Engaged outsiders can join the task by asking the naive questions about "what is" and importing critical perspectives about "what could be." In other areas these "outsiders" [insiders] can speak and get a hearing for counter stories. At the webbed intersections of PAR work, contestations of the dominant story, what might be called counter stories (Harris et al., 2001) frame the design and levitate in the analysis.

To illustrate: In the Critical Gap project, we examined the "achievement gap" initially as a problem of "race," ethnicity and class. The dominant explanation holds that students' race, ethnicity and class predict academic engagement, motivation, connection to school, preparedness for college. With an n of 3,799 quantitative responses to the survey items about engagement, motivation and achievement and narrative qualitative responses to questions such as, "What was the most powerful thing a teacher ever said to you, positive or negative?" or "Describe your best (worst) possible school experience," we were able to determine that for every item studied, race/ethnicity/class, indeed, predicted well and consistently.

To widen the analytic lens, however, and decenter this dominant explanation, we asked students to help us explain the observed race/ethnicity/class differences. They escorted us to an alternative explanation: tracking in suburban high schools. We extended the analysis then to examine how "track" affects student outcomes. Tracking, or leveling, designates those well established and hard to undo structural practices by which schools organize students' differential and racialized access to rigor. Students in the top track report significantly higher levels of access to rigor, qualified educators, rich curriculum and a smoother route to college entrance. And in these "integrated districts," 50 years after *Brown v Board of Education*, over 60% of White and Asian-American students in these schools are in the top tracks, while fewer than 40% of African-Americans, Latinos and Afro-Caribbeans are. These discrepancies hold even for students with college-educated parents (Mickelson, 2002; Orfield, 2002). We found that academic track predicts all of these quantitative and qualitative outcomes, better than race/ethnicity. In multiple regression and discursive analyses, track was a stronger predictor of academic engagement, motivation, aspirations for college and sense of personal agency than race/ethnicity (Wells and Serna, 1996; Oakes et al. 1997).

Within and across segregated and desegregated schools, race and ethnicity covary systematically with access to academic rigor. In fact, both within and across public schools—due to inequitable financing, the uneven distribution of teacher quality, persistent segregation and tracking within desegregated schools—African-American and Latino students have the least access to quality educators, state funding and academic rigor. Students across groups acknowledge these disparities, and they despair. At our second research camp, Emily, a biracial youth researcher, drew a portrait of "what it feels like to be the only, or one of the few Black kids in an honors class." She titled the sketch "Hunting Bison."

Insiders like Emily know well the systematic covariation of race, ethnicity and track. They witness how structural covariates are grafted onto demographics: how they are built, justified, internalized and secured. And so it is the explicit decoupling of covariates that critical participatory research must undertake. Had we not investigated questions of tracking (and other structures of stratification within and across schools) we too would have produced data that confirm a "gap" predicated largely on race/ethnicity "differences." PAR projects must be designed strategically to decouple covariates; to challenge inequities represented as "natural." Toward this end, when we analyze youth experiences in school, we produce analyses by race/ethnicity, by track placement and by parental educational status. We were distressed to see that even for those youth with college-educated parents, race/ethnicity still overdetermined track placement. Indeed, we have found that 74% of Asian-American students, 65% of White students, and 43% of African-American students and 35% of Latino students with college-educated parents are placed in top tracks. One might argue that the very desegregated schools born out of struggle to narrow the gap are actually contributing to a downward mobility of middle income African-American and Latino families.

The academic "achievement gap" is overpredicted. The confounding of race, ethnicity, class with few opportunities/inequitable resources is a political and

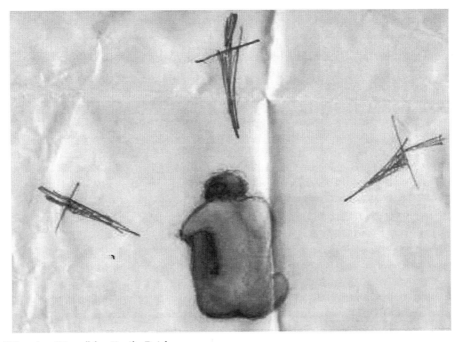

"Hunting Bison" by Emily Brisbane

moral problem for civic society. This is also a significant and underacknowledged threat to the validity of social research on "race," ethnicity and academic achievement. PAR kept us from naively replicating—and confirming—the dominant explanation.

Revealing the Production of Privilege

PAR designs are not only dedicated to revealing the gross effects of institutional inequity on those deprived; they can also reveal how institutions produce and protect privilege. Inside researchers know where to find pockets of exclusion and how to "out" the institutional secrets about power and privilege (Mills, 1959; Scott, 1990). In our work in schools, we were particularly interested in how class (middle and upper) and race (White) privilege consistently transform into "merit" (Burns, 2003). So we asked the students. We ran focus groups and conducted individual interviews with varied samples of students, including those students who were considered "high achievers" (predominantly White and middle/upper middle class). We asked these students to talk to us about how their teachers and families support their academic success.

The youth were quite forthcoming in enumerating the tutors, Occupational Therapy, psychotherapy, Physical Therapy, PSAT prep/SAT prep, chemistry tutors, Ritalin, learning disabilities that would permit extended time on standardized tests, writing camps, letters of recommendations from family friends, using "legacy" (referred to by some students as "White people's Affirmative Action") to get into college, having mothers write/edit essays or bibliographies, parents who called Guidance Counselors to make sure they were placed in the "top classes." The students revealed that they enjoy these supports individually, quietly, confidentially and consistently throughout their class fraction. They reminded us that these supports were purchased using private dollars, secured using private connections and acquired and maintained secretly (Newmann, 1990; Ogbu, 1990; Oxley, 1990; Pittman, 2001). Some of the more privileged students on the research team alerted us to this reservoir of evidence on academic steroids that elite families pump into their children so they appear meritorious (Burns, 2003).

By revealing how privatized supports convert private privilege into public merit, the PAR youth researchers were able to reframe what appears to be a race/ethnicity "deficit" as largely a question of covertly sustained privilege and institutional collusion. With insiders, we were able to document the increasing privatization of development. As a collective of insiders and outsiders, we have been able to work productively with schools and school districts to help them offer comparable supports to poor and working class students who are wholly dependent on, and trusting of, the public sphere for access to college.

Methodologically and ethically, we came to the realization that it is essential to study not only those who are "disadvantaged" but the full stratified formation within which "privilege" is acquired and protected. Indeed, we know now that it is most important to pierce the opaque walls of "privacy" for behind those walls lie the keys to how institutions seamlessly benefit those in power (see also Billig, 1995; Fine and Burns, 2003; Burns, 2003). This is, perhaps, the most theoretically and politically generative as well as potentially threatening aspect of PAR.

A Menu of Designs

We sketch below a series of possible design frameworks that may be useful to consider in participatory work on social (in)justice (see Bhabha, 1990; Farmer, 1992; Twine, 2000; Winant, 2003). Please note that these frameworks can be used with qualitative and/or quantitative methods and data. They share, at base, a commitment to reframing questions of theory, policy and politics from within institutional and community sites of contestation:

- Full compositional analyses: PAR designs pull for multiple perspectives within the same institution, organized through an analysis of questions of power. Such designs enable a mapping of the full community (see Fine and Weis, 1998) or institution (as in the schools) to document the aggregate view and the ideological representation of the whole. Full compositional analyses allow us to view the site through a lens of coherence and integrity. Though these full analyses often reproduce dominant representations, they nevertheless allow readers to grasp the familiar frame before the research ventures into more fractured analyses. Then . . .
- First fracturing analyses: Participatory researchers can identify the first fracturing analysis to produce an interior analysis of the institution/community through lines of "difference" and power. These analyses destabilize the representation of institutional coherence, integrity and stability; activating, typically, the first challenge to "well established facts" (Law and Mol, 2003). Drawing on the schools project, this involves disaggregating full-school data by race/ethnicity and class; or mapping who is in prison and who enjoys alternatives to sentencing (Gangi et al., 1998). Then . . .
- Contrastive/counter analyses: While the first fracturing analysis interrupts representations of coherence, this call for counter analyses presses the move to destabilize further. That is, in these analyses, we juxtapose the principle fracture lines with other lines of challenging analysis. In the prison study, we offer up perspectives from college students, dropouts and corrections officers to yield not only the ways in which they corroborate each other, but the spaces in which their analyses dynamically challenge each other. By placing these varied analyses adjacent to each other, we reveal the many competing stories that can be told about and within institutional life and power (Lather, 1991; see Bowen and Bok, 1998 for an excellent example). Ironically, these comparative analyses reveal where fault lines can be found, where mobilization can begin and where radical change is possible. And/ or . . .

- Local excavation: To determine the angles for contrastive or counter analyses, we have, in our work, identified a set of institutional corners or buried, dusty and marginal spots in which the institutional pulse has a resistant, rebellious or distinctive tempo (Guishard et al., 2003; Roberts, 2003), e.g., college in prison. The methods for levitating these spots may include:
- outlier analyses: seeking the outliers, the strange, prohibited and transgressive "cases" to understand how margins are created and defined in the institution; to reveal how outliers actually represent the institution/community by exposing the souls who must be purged.
- analyses of privilege: be sure to trouble who/what is advantaged, as well as who/what is considered disadvantage, and theorize the relations between lives of privilege and deprivation (see Cookson and Persell, 1985; Burns, 2003).
- splintering analyses: resist consensus as the driving force behind analysis and seek occasions to reveal dissensus, that is, varied perspectives on the same "finding" (Torre et al., 2003).
- Policy-in-practice analyses: This design strategy seeks to trace how obviously related, and seemingly remote social policies shape local contexts, group identities and individual lives. It is easy to write up institutional stories as thick, local qualitative descriptions, without revealing the spider webs of power that connect institutional and individual lives to larger social formations. And yet to not draw these lines for readers render them invisible and collude in obfuscating the structural conditions that undergird social inequities. Thus, when we engage in policy-in-practice analyses we, for instance, assess the extent to which particular policies (e.g., educational finance inequities or zero tolerance or no child left behind) affect youth outcomes.

In the prison study, we found ourselves tracing how seemingly remote policy changes in, for instance, deinstitutionalization of persons with mental health problems, parole practices and urban housing gentrification, have affected who is in prison, how long they stay and who returns. In the aftermath of de-institutionalization, and the acute loss of affordable housing, the numbers of low-income urban men and women swelled within rapidly expanding prison walls. Parole was harder to attain, "tough on crime" policies were passed and the prison economy and privatization flourished.

While causality remains to be determined, the linkages between who was deinstitutionalized and the rise (upwards of 50% of prisoners have mental health diagnoses) in mentally ill prisoners deserves attention. So, too, given that more than half of prisoners are released to homeless shelters, it comes as little surprise that approximately two thirds are reincarcerated within three years (Torre et al., 2001). And all the while, private prison stocks continue to rise.

It seems clear that researchers, as public intellectuals, are among the few who might dare to visibilize the strings that attach political and moral conditions with individual lives. Illuminating these strings, like re-membering exclusions, is precisely the task of theory, and therefore must be taken up by method.

- Revealing sites for possibility: As part of our theoretical and ethical commitment, we create designs that will document those spaces, relations, practices, subversive or explicit engagements in which possibility flourishes, democratic principles of justice whisper, or critique gets a hearing. Our commitment to revealing sites for possibility derives not only from a theoretical desire to review "what is" and "what could be" but also from an ethical belief that critical researchers have an obligation not simply to dislodge the dominant discourse but to help readers/audience imagine where the spaces for resistance, agency, and possibility lie. We craft research that aims toward Lather's "catalytic validity"; research that aims to provoke thought and action.

Ethical Quandaries of Deep Participation

"Is speaking the unspeakable possible? . . . Bearing official witness within a legitimate organization provides at least the assurance that there will be a witness to one"s witnessing; that one will encounter an ear with the duty to listen. But the question remains open as to whether telling and hearing are possible in everyday social encounters" (Apfelbaum, 2002, p. 26).

Filled with pleasures and challenge, participatory work within institutions, with low-power voices in the majority, trembles with ethical questions and dangers easily avoided in more traditional, distanced epistemologies. Initially we—those of us from the Graduate Center—established basic ground rules for working together. But almost immediately the larger collective we accumulated a series of ethical principles, necessary for our local work, including and extending well beyond the APA guidelines. We write in pencil as the negotiation of power and positionality is an active and ongoing practice among the team. Below we enumerate a set of these ethical moments that routinely occur within PAR.

We preface this section with an acknowledgement that PAR itself represents an ethical and epistemological stance that recognizes the power and knowledge of insiders; the strength of inside–outside collaborations; the generative power of difference and the urgency of critical work for democratic public institutions. While PAR will, undoubtedly, lift up ethical concerns typically detoured by more distanced methods, we would argue that much social research is, today, conducted on, despite and often against the knowledge and best interests of people who suffer most under current social arrangements. A new epistemological frame and set of commitments is needed for those of us concerned with the knotty relation of social science and social justice. PAR offers a flickering light for such work. Always riddled with the dialectics of power, the potential for co-optation and the likelihood of subversion, PAR nevertheless situates research at the heart of social struggle.

To begin with a simple, yet profound, ethical bump we consistently face is the challenge posed by questions of confidentiality and anonymity within institution-based PAR. The task, of course, is not as straightforward as altering the names and the demographics, because everyone in an institution knows everyone else. When we suggested the use of pseudonyms for the women in prison, for instance, most of the women rejected this offer. Having been denied the right to represent themselves for too many years, most wanted to use their real names in our publications.

In contrast, within the schools, when we would interview youth in a focus group, there might be only one African-American or Latino "high achiever" in the group. Whether or not we changed his/her name, everyone would know who s/he was. Our ability to promise these students anonymity was undermined by the systematic lack of students of color in the high achieving tracks. We could change the names so that no one outside the institution would know, but most within the institution knew the players well.

In addition to negotiating the ethics of local visibility, PAR designs within institutions must contend with local vulnerabilities. We try, always, to build in ways to anticipate varied responses to the work; to avoid the misinterpretation of empirical materials; to prevent the misuse of findings, and to counter any potential for the punishment of inside researchers for daring to speak truth to power. Researching critically from within, we therefore developed a finely tuned set of surveillance checks. In the prison, one prisoner per research session took on the role of the superintendent and the Department of Corrections, to anticipate any adverse reactions to our work. This does not mean we designed toward conformity or away from contentious issues. It means simply that we were ever vigilant, never insulated, thoroughly immersed in and ever resistant to, the authoritarian assertion of a single dominant voice. We were extremely conscientious about being in touch with administrators, beyond merely seeking permission. Prison administrators were and remain the gatekeepers to changes in policy and practice. PAR relies on co-researchers, many of whom are profound critics, a number of whom are most vulnerable. Those who dare to speak from within run an enormous risk of retribution. Therein lies the danger of speaking.

November 2002, Just Post-release of the Prison Report

Phone call: "Michelle, all of the prisoners who were on the research team are being interrogated, their cells searched, their papers, writings and poetry taken. Some are being threatened with being sent to another facility; others are being told they may go to SHU (the Solitary Housing Unit). Can you help us figure out why they are being singled out?"

As with speaking, within participatory work across differences, we confront ethical questions of witnessing. In the schools, a methodological feature of the PAR youth researcher work includes participant observations in each others' schools. In the Fall of 2002, a group of Lower East Side high school seniors, primarily poor and working class, educated at a very fine, but severely under-resourced small school in NYC, visited one of the more privileged schools in the research consortium. Well-rehearsed in their "researcher identities," this group had chosen to research finance inequity in NY State. The two districts—in New York City and wealthy Westchester suburbs—receive approximately $7000 per child and over $15 000, respectively.

As juniors they had traveled to several wealthy Westchester communities and documented differential access to computers, books, libraries, AP classes, etc. Faced with obvious inequities they were disturbed that "there's like no minorities in those top classes." Seeing privilege up close, however, was not merely an academic exercise. All too familiar with racist representations of "them," on the visits they confronted what they could not know: the striking material and intellectual capital accumulated through privilege.

Sitting on green grass waiting for their train back to the city, students expressed amazement at the differences between their own school and the large suburban complex they had spent the day visiting. "Did you see the auditorium? Okay, our auditorium looks like . . . [crap] compared to that one." "Because they have money, they could actually have a darkroom that they can do photography in," another exclaimed. Others focused on the library, "They have a lot of books!" "It"s like a regular library." "The computers!" One student highlighted the difference in access to technology within the classroom and its effect on student learning: "I went to [a science class where] a girl gave a presentation about abortion. She had slides to show everyone [on a slide projector and a computer] . . . when we had that in our school we just did a poster." Several, having also visited science classes, followed-up with remarks on the "real" science laboratories: the laboratory equipment, the sinks in the rooms, the materials for experiments.

As seniors, this same group visited another Westchester high school. Now adrenalin-filled with the terror and excitement of their own college application processes, these young people toured the building with a sense of awe, depression and disgust. Nikaury mumbled, "This school is college." Jose continued the conversation, "They already take psychology and advanced math and English." Emily nailed it, "We"re going to compete with these students when we get to college?" A confrontation with profoundly unjust social arrangements provoked a psychological glide from outrage to shame; a rainbow of emotions spilled onto the sidewalks, and consumed the air on the train ride back home. We have had to build in processes before, during and after such visits so that students can document inequity without losing their souls, spirits or their sense of hope.

Finally, we comment upon another lurking danger of PAR about which we worry collectively: publishing strong critiques of public institutions at a time when the public sphere is fundamentally under siege. At the present historic moment, any public critique of public institutions runs the risk of being appropriated by the Right, furthering the deprivation of those already oppressed by social arrangements. We worry about this in particular with respect to the integrated public schools, for too many are eager to shoplift critical research in an aggressive campaign against desegregation or racial justice in education. But prisoners' rights are equally under attack. And so we move forward with delicacy and commitments for a resuscitated, not stripped, public sphere.

But Is It Generalizable?

If, as we have argued, PAR yields multiple interpretations of social institutions, reveals broad-based contradictions and power-driven fissures in institutional life, and disrupts the ideology of consensus, then psychology's methodological commitments to inter-rater reliability, expert validity and generalizability are radically challenged. Indeed, PAR rejects traditional commitments to researcher distance, external expertise, consensus and scientific agreement (Harding, 1993). With democratic (de)construction of context and method, participatory social research incites thick, moral questions for which there is no neutral territory. Conceptions of "expert validity" and inter-rater reliability are unsettled. Who can validate a construct? Who must agree—or who should be kept out of the room—in order for high levels of inter-rater reliability to be reached?

On the other hand, we would argue that with PAR, construct validity is vitally enhanced. Sturdy, grounded local meanings are generated and negotiated in conversation between insiders and outsiders; and then confirmed empirically on the ground. So too catalytic validity (Lather, 1990) is strengthened by the deep, ongoing immersion of research praxis within local contexts and struggles.

Qualitative researchers have typically dodged questions about validity and generalizability, as if they were irrelevant to our work: too narrow; too positivist; too essentialist. Yet, committed to policy, practice, theory and politics, we are keenly interested in how our findings resonate in other sites. Thus, we offer the notion of theoretical generalizability: the extent to which specific, well-developed theoretical analyses, relations and patterns of institutional life effectively migrate from one site of study to other social locations. When we speak throughout the United States about our research with schools, prisons and low-income communities, we find audiences who resonate to the sense that poor and working class youth are regarded as disposable; schools are recognized as sites for perverse reproduction and at the same time extraordinary resistance; sites of possibility are documented even within oppressive contexts like prisons. It is from the global head-nods and requests to co-publish, from urban New York City to rural New Zealand, farms in Maine, death row in San Quentin prison, Aboriginal struggles in Australia, that we offer the notion of theoretical generalizability (see Laws and Mol, 2003).

Urgency: An Obligation to Act

PAR takes theory, practice, politics and action seriously. The research community is diverse and, by definition, grounded in local politics. The investigation is rigorous. The analysis promises to be kaleidoscopic, oscillating and bold—a response to the mis-rememberings of exclusion, the psychic amnesia that haunts America. Counter explanations will percolate, and dominant discourses may stutter or at least share the bias with competing explanations (Hurtado, 2003). But PAR insists on action, in the form of policy, practice, organizational change and or social movements. Toward this end, we try to design research to reveal spots of possibility, extraordinary spaces where democratic practice could does take place (Eisenhart, 2001; Weis and Fine, 2003).

We end with urgency because that is where PAR begins. Rooted in the "soil of discontent" (Roberts, 2003), PAR projects are radical strategies generated in response to oppressive conditions of struggle (Fals-Borda, 1979). Having imported PAR into public institutional work, we are now humbled by the risks involved because public institutions will serve to reproduce existing class and race relations unless they are intentionally interrupted and realigned. As Beverly Tatum (1999) explains, racism is like the moving walkway in the airport. You do not need to do a thing for it to keep rolling forward. To stop it, to interrupt, requires intentionality. PAR is intentional.

In the prison project, we have produced many reports and documents; met with legislators and representatives from the Governor's office; solicited conservative and radical "endorsers"; created a website from which the full report could be downloaded; and published and distributed widely community organizing brochures, in English and Spanish, for our friends and allies in community based and advocacy organizations.

So, too, in the school-based work, we are preparing, with youth and educators, ways to present the material back to schools; and to create power points and graffiti museums filled with quotes from students about school racial/ethnic relations. Some youth are creating activist brochures on school financing, others on tracking. Together we will write articles for teen magazines, scholarly journals, policy white papers, materials for educators, and produce a theatre in the round: "Echoes: Youth Perspectives on Brown then and now."

We do not believe, for a moment, that social injustice is a "cognitive" problem, but we do believe that social research, in collaboration with social movements within and beyond public institutions, can prick the "psychic amnesia" that has infected America.

Acknowledgments

Funding for these projects comes from: Leslie Glass Foundation, Open Society Institute, Rockefeller Foundation and Spencer Foundation. A preliminary version of this paper was presented at the Qualitative Inquiry Conference, University of Georgia, January 2003. We appreciate critical commentary from Susan Opotow, Martin Packer and many others.

Appendix A

The 1980s and 1990s, in the United States, were decades of substantial public and political outcry about crime, and about criminals. During these years, stiffer penalties were enforced for crimes, prisons were built at unprecedented rates, parole was tougher to achieve, "three strikes and you"re out" bills were passed, and college was no longer publicly funded for women and men in prison. Indeed, with the signing of the Violent Crime Control and Law Enforcement Act, President Bill Clinton stopped the flow of all federal dollars, which had enabled women and men in prison to attend college (Pell grants). It was then up to the states, simply, to finalize the closing of most prison based college programs around the nation. At Bedford Hills Correctional Facility, a vibrant college program had been coordinated by Mercy College for over 15 years. In 1995, this program, like over 340 others nationwide, was closed. This decision provoked a sea of disappointment, despair and outrage from the women at Bedford Hills who had been actively engaged in higher education and in GED ABE preparation. And yet, within months, a group of inmates met with the Superintendent and, later, an active community volunteer, and soon they, with a consortium of colleges and universities, committed to reestablishing college within the prison.

The design of the college was conceptualized through pillars of strong, ongoing participation by the prison administration, staff, the inmates, faculty and volunteers. Students, in particular, are expected to "give back" in any number of ways. They teach, mentor, pay the equivalent of a month"s wages for tuition, give back while in prison and demonstrate high levels of community engagement once they are released (see Fine et al., 2001). These women have, for the most part, spent the better (or worst) part of their lives under the thumbs of poverty, racism and men: 80% carry scars of childhood sexual abuse, terrible educational biographies, tough family and community backgrounds, long lists of social and personal betrayals. For these women, growing back the capacity to join a community, engage with a community, give back, and trust are remarkable social and psychological accomplishments.

Thus, when Michelle was asked to conduct the empirical documentation of the impact of college on the women, the prison environment and the world outside the prison, it seemed all too obvious that a participatory design behind bars would be nearly impossible—and essential. Committed to a Participatory Action Research Design, our research team combined Graduate Center researchers (Michelle Fine, PI, María Elena Torre, Project Director, Melissa Rivera, Rosemarie A Roberts and Debora Upegui) and prison-based researchers (Kathy Boudin, Iris Bowen, Judith Clark, Aisha Elliot, Donna Hylton, Migdalia Martinez, "Missy," and Pamela Smart). Conducted over the course of three years, the research design required a quantitative analysis to assess the extent to which college reduced reincarceration rates (conducted by the New York State Department of Correctional Services) and affected the tax burden imposed on citizens of New York State for prisons (conducted in part by Former Commissioner of Corrections Michael Jacobson) and a qualitative analysis to determine the psychosocial effects of college on the women, prison environment, their children and their postrelease transitions (for full report see www.changingminds.ws or Torre et al., 2002).

The research was designed to answer four questions:

1) What are the personal and social effects of college in prison on students and their children?

2) What is the impact of the college experience on the safety and management of the prison environment?

3) What is the impact of the college experience on the transition home from prison?

4) What are the fiscal costs and benefits of providing college to women in prison, and what are the fiscal costs and benefits of withholding college from women in prison?

The methods include:

Archival analysis: review the records of the college program since inception (1997), tracking rates of persistence, women drafted (transferred to other prisons mid-sentence), dropout rates, racial and ethnic distribution, percent in precollege and college courses.

Inmate-initiated research on the impact of college, which consisted of one-on-one interviews of four to five women each by 15 inmates (n = 65 interviews by 15 inmates).

Focus group interviews with women at BHCF, selected on the basis of the women"s status in the program: drop out; ABE GED student; precollege students; first-time college students; adolescent children of women in college; college leaders mentors; women in the ESL class (n = 43).

Individual interviews with college graduates postrelease from prison (n = 20). Each interview was conducted at the Graduate Center, City University, and lasted anywhere from one to three hours.

Women were compensated $50 for participating in the interview.

Interviews with Correctional Administrators and Officers. In order to understand the impact of the college program on the prison environment, interviews with administrators and Correctional Officers would be essential (n = 5).

Focus group interviews and surveys of educators. In order to document the impact of the college program on educators and college communities, a focus group with college faculty (n = 20) was conducted by the research team in 1999. A survey was distributed in the year 2000 to faculty of the Spring 2000 semester. Two group discussions were held with the Presidents of the Consortium universities (focus groups, n = 20 faculty; seven Presidents or designees; survey, n = 20).

Quantitative recidivism study: tracking of women who attended college while in prison and a comparison group of women who did not attend college while in prison (n = 2 74 women in the college program and a comparison group of 2031 women who did not attend college).

Cost Benefit Analysis of the College Bound Program relying upon data from 2000 to 2001.

Appendix B

The Race, Ethnicity, Class and Opportunity Gap project involves a multiracial and ethnic Youth Leadership and Research Community to investigate how race, ethnicity, class and opportunity and outcomes are aligned in public schools, from the perspective of a broad range of youth. Finance equities and geographic segregation assure that most youths attend segregated and differentially financed schools (Darling-Hammond; Education Week, 7 January 2002; Mickelson; Oakes; Orfield; Stuart-Wells). Wealthier and whiter students are more likely to attend schools with higher per capita expenditures, teachers with better credentials, who receive higher salaries and hold more rigorous expectations (Anyon, 1997; Ferguson, 1998). From integrated suburban and urban high schools, perhaps as painfully, we learn that race, ethnicity and social class, even in the same school, overdetermine academic placement, opportunities and outcomes. The promise of integration has never been realized; the structural, systemic and institutional features of the "gap" need to be examined even—or maybe particularly—within those schools in which integration presumably thrives. It is our hope that suburban and urban communities beginning to confront questions of why the gap persists can more effectively pursue strategies for how to narrow the gap, once they understand causes, consequences and potential remedies from the perspective of youth. It is our sense, further, that youth deserve a public and scholarly forum for analyzing and organizing around the "gap." Over two years, this Research Community will produce scholarship, reports for policy makers, brochures/newsletters/cultural products for community/popular education and materials for educators representing the range of views that youth hold about race ethnic inequities in opportunities and outcomes.

These 36 students (who are working with support teachers in their home schools) were trained over the course of the Spring and Summer 2002, and helped to design and interpret data from:

- A survey distributed across districts (n = 3799 ninth and twelfth graders, stratified by geography, race, ethnicity and academic history).
- An interview schedule used with a sample of recent graduates from four districts, who were tracked into college, work, military, prison or home, depending on their circumstances.
- A focus group format used in four districts with distinct groups of students (students at the academic "top," "middle" and "bottom" of their schools), gathering their views of race, ethnicity and opportunity in the country and in their schools.
- An observational/interview protocol for cross-visitation of each others' schools.

References

Alford, R. R. 1998: *The craft of inquiry: theories, methods, evidence.* Oxford University Press.

Anand, B., Fine, M., Perkins, T. and Surrey, D. 2002: *Keeping the struggle alive: studying desegregation in our town.* New York: Teachers College Press.

Anzaldua, G. 1999: Borderlands/La Frontera. San Francisco: Aunt Lute Publishers.

Anyon, J. 1997: *Ghetto schooling: a political economy of urban educational reform*. New York: Teachers College Press.

Apfelbaum, E. 2001: The dread: an essay on communication across cultural boundaries. *International Journal of Critical Psychology* 4, 19–34.

Bhaba, H. editor. 1990: *Nation and narration*. Routledge: New York.

Bhavnani, K. K. 1994: Tracing the contours: feminist research and objectivity. In Afshar, H. and Maynard, M., editors, *The dynamics of "race" and gender: some feminist interventions*. London: Taylor & Francis.

Billig, M. 1995: *Banal nationalism*. London: Sage Publications.

Bourdieu, P. 1999: *Acts of resistance: against the tyranny of the market*. New York: New Press.

Bowen, W. G. and Bok, D. 1998: *The shape of the river: long-term consequences of considering race in college and university admissions*. New Jersey: Princeton University Press.

Bowles, S. and Gintis, H. 1976: *Schooling in capitalist America: educational reform and the contradictions of economic life*. New York: Basic Books.

Brydon-Miller, M. 2001: Participatory action research: psychology and social change. In Tolman, D. L. and Brydon-Miller, M., editors, *From subjects to subjectivities: a handbook of interpretive and participatory methods*. New York: NYU Press.

Burns, A. 2003: Analyzing privilege: reflections on innocence and meritocracy. Unpublished master's thesis. New York: City University of New York, Graduate Center.

Carney, S. 2001: Analysing master narratives and counter stories in legal settings: cases of maternal failure to protect. *International Journal of Critical Psychology* 4, 61–76.

Chataway, C. J., 2001: Negotiating the observer-observed relationship: participatory action research. In Tolman, D. L. and Brydon-Miller, M., editors, *From subjects to subjectivities: a handbook of interpretive and participatory methods*. New York: NYU Press, 239–55.

Cheng, A. A. 2001: *The melancholy of race: psychoanalysis, assimilation, and hidden grief*. New York: Oxford University Press.

Christianse, Y. 2003: Passing away: the unspeakable (losses) of postapartheid South Africa. In Eng, D. and Kazanjian, D., editors, *Loss: the politics of mourning*. Berkeley, CA: University of California Press, 372–96.

Cochran-Smith, M. and Lytle, S., editors. 1993: *Inside/outside: teacher research and knowledge*. New York: Teachers College Press.

Cole, D. 2000: *No equal justice: race and class in the American criminal justice system*. New York: New Press.

Collins, P. H. 1991: *Black feminist thought: knowledge, consciousness, and the politics of empowerment*. New York: Routledge.

Cookson, P. and Persell, C. 1985: *Preparing for power: America's elite boarding schools*. New York: Basic Books.

Crenshaw, K. 1995: Mapping the margins: inter-sectionality, identity politics, and violence against women of colour. In Crenshaw, K., Gotanda, N., Peller, G. and Thomas, K., editors, *Critical race theory: the key writings that formed the movement*. New York: New Press, 357–83.

Darling-Hammond, L. 2002: *Apartheid in American education: how opportunity is rationed to children of color in the United States. Racial Profiling and Punishment in the U.S. Public Schools*. Oakland: Applied Research Center, 39–44.

Deleuze, G. 1990: Postscript on societies of control. *L'Autre Journal* 1, May.

Deutsch, M. 1974: Awakening the sense of injustice. In Lerner, M. and Ross, M., editors, *The question for justice: myth, reality, ideal*. Toronto: Holt, Rinehart and Winston.

DuBois, W. E. B. 1935: Does the Negro need separate schools? *Journal of Negro Education* 4, 328–35.

Ed Week. 2003: Quality counts. 7 January 2003. Eisenhart, M. 2001: Educational ethnography past, present and future: ideas to think with. *Educational Researcher* 30, 8, 16–27.

Eng, D. and Kazanjian, D., editors. 2003: *Loss: the politics of mourning*. Berkeley, CA: University of California Press.

Eng, D. and Han, S. 2003: A dialogue on racial melancholia. In Eng, D. and Kazanjian, D., editors, *Loss: the politics of mourning*. Berkeley, CA: University of California Press, 343–72.

Fallis, R. and Opotow, S. 2002: Are students failing school or are schools failing students? Class cutting in high school. In Daiute, C. and Fine, M., editors, Youth perspectives on violence and injustice. *Journal of Social Issues*. Special volume.

Fals-Borda, O. 1979: Investigating the reality in order to transform it: the Colombian experience. *Dialectical Anthropology* 4, 33–55.

Fanon, F. 1952: *Black skin, white masks*. Paris (1952). 1967: New York: Grove.

Farmer, P. 1997: On suffering and structural violence: a view from below. In Kleinman, D., editor, *Social suffering*. Berkeley: University of California Press.

Farmer, P. 2001: *Infections and inequalities*. Berkeley: University of California Press.

Farr, R. and Moscovici, S., editors. 1984: *Social representations*. Cambridge, UK: Cambridge University Press.

Ferguson, R. 2001: A diagnostic analysis of black-white GPA disparities in Shaker Heights, Ohio. In *Brookings Papers on Education Policy*. Washington DC: Brookings Institute.

Fine, M. and Somerville, J. 1998: *Small schools, big imaginations*. Chicago: Cross City Campaign for Urban School Reform.

Fine, M. and Powell, L. 2001: Small schools as an anti-racist intervention. Racial profiling and punishment in U.S. public schools. *ARC Research Report* October, 45–50.

Fine, M. and Burns, A. 2003: Class notes: toward a critical psychology of class and schooling. *Journal of Social Issues* 59.

Fine, M., Weis, L., Weseen, S and Wong, L. 1999: For whom? Qualitative research, representations and social responsibilities. In Denzin, N. and Lincoln, Y., editors. *Handbook of qualitative research*, second edition. Beverly Hills: Sage Publication, 107–31.

Fine, M., Torre, M. E., Boudin, K., Bowen, I., Clark, J., Hylton, D., Martinez, M., Missy, Rivera, M., Roberts, R.A., Smart, P. and Upegui, D. 2001: *Changing minds: the impact of college in a maximum security prison*. New York: The Graduate School and University Center, City University of New York.

Foucault, M. 1977: *Discipline and punish: the birth of the prison*. New York: Pantheon. Fraser, N. 1990: Rethinking the public sphere: a contribution to the critique of actually existing democracy. *Social Text* 25/26, 56–80.

Freire, P. 1982: Creating alternative research methods. Learning to do it by doing it. In Hall, B., Gillette, A. and Tandon, R., editors, *Creating knowledge: a monopoly*. New Delhi: Society for Participatory Research in Asia, 29–37.

Gangi, R., Schiraldi, V. and Ziedenberg, J. 1998: *New York State of mind: higher education and prison funding in the Empire State 1988–1998*. Washington DC: The Justice Policy Institute.

Gramsci, A. 1971: *Selections from prison notebooks*. New York: International.

Greene, M. 1995: *Releasing the imagination: essays on education, the arts, and social change*. San Francisco: Jossey-Bass.

Guha, R. and Spivak, G. C., editors. 1988: *Selected subaltern studies.* New York: Oxford University Press.

Guishard, M., Fine, M., Doyle, C., Jackson, J., Roberts, R., Singleton, S., Staten, T. and Webb, A. 2003: As long as I got breath, I'll fight: participatory action research for educational justice. Massachusetts: Harvard Family Research Project.

Habermas, J. 1971: Knowledge and human interests. Boston: Beacon Press.

Hall, B. 1993: Introduction. In Park, P., Brydon- Miller, M., Hall, B. and Jackson, T., editors, *Voices of change: participatory action research in the United States and Canada.* Westport, CT: Bergin & Garvey, xiii–xxii.

Harding, S. 1987: Introduction: Is there a feminist method? In Harding, S., editor, *Feminism and methodology.* Bloomington, IN: Indiana University Press, 1–14.

Harding, S. 1993: Rethinking standpoint epistemology: What is "strong objectivity"? In Alcoff, L. and Potter, E., editors, *Feminist epistemologies.* New York: Routledge, 49–82.

Harris, A., Carney, S. and Fine, M. 2001: Counter work: introduction to "under the covers: theorizing the politics of counter stories." *International Journal of critical Psychology* 4, 6–18.

Hartstock, N. C. M. 1983: *Money, sex, and power: toward a feminist historical materialism.* New York: Longman.

Hitchcock, P. 1999: *Oscillate wildly.* Minneapolis: University of Minnesota Press.

Hooks, B. 1984: *Feminist theory from margin to center.* Boston: South End Press.

Hurtado, A. 1996: *The color of privilege: three blasphemies on race and feminism.* Ann Arbor, MI: University of Michigan Press.

Hurtado, A. 2003: *Chicana feminisms.* New York: New York University Press.

Kidder, L. and Fine, M. 1997: Qualitative inquiry in psychology: a radical tradition. In Fox, D. and Prilletensky, I., editors, *Critical psychology.* London: Sage Publications.

Kvale, S. 1996: *InterViews: an introduction to qualitative research interviewing.* Thousand Oaks, CA: Sage.

Ladson-Billings, G. 2000: Racialized discourses and ethnic epistemologies. In Denzin, N.K. and Lincoln, Y.S., editors, *Handbook of qualitative research,* second edition. Thousand Oaks, CA: Sage, 257–77.

Lareau, A. 1989: *Home advantage: social class and parental intervention in elementary education.* Philadelphia: Temple University Press.

Lather, P. 1991: *Getting smart: feminist research and pedagogy with/in the postmodern.* New York: Routledge.

Law, J. and Mol, A. 2003: *Situating technoscience: an inquiry into spatialities.* Center for Science Studies, Lancaster University.

Lewin, K. 1951: *Field theory in social science: selected theoretical papers.* New York: Harper.

Lykes, M. B. 2001: Activist participatory research and the arts with rural Maya women: interculturality and situated meaning making. In Tolman, D.L. and Brydon-Miller, M., editors, *From subjects to subjectivities: a handbook of interpretive and participatory methods.* New York: NYU Press, 183–99.

Marable, M. 1999: *Black leadership.* New York: Penguin Books.

Marlin-Baró, I. 1994: *Writings for a liberation psychology.* Cambridge, MA: Harvard University Press.

Massey, D. and Denton, N. 1993: *American apartheid.* Cambridge, MA: Harvard University Press.

Matsuda, M. 1995: Looking to the bottom: critical legal studies and reparations. In Crenshaw, K., Gotanda, N., Peller, G. and Thomas, K., editors, *Critical race theory: the key writings that formed the movement.* New York: New Press, 63–79.

Mickelson, R. 2001: Subverting Swann: first and second generation segregation in the Charlotte-Mecklenburg schools. *American Educational Research Journal* 38, 215–252.

Mills, C.W. 1959: *The sociological imagination*. London: Oxford University Press.

Oakes, J., Wells, A., Yonezawa, S. and Ray, K. 1997: Equity lessons from detracking schools. In Hargreaves, A., editor, *Rethinking educational change with heart and mind*. Alexandria, VA: ASCD, 43–72.

Ogbu, J. 1990: Overcoming racial barriers to access. In Goodlad, J. and Keating, P., editors, *Access to knowledge*. New York: College Entrance Exam Board.

Opotow, S. 2002: Psychology of impunity and injustice: implications for social reconciliation. In Bassiouni, M.C., editor, *Post conflict justice*. Ardsley, NY: Transnational Publishers.

Orfield, G., Eaton, S. and the Harvard Project on School Desegregation. 1996: *Dismantling desegregation*. New York: The New Press.

Oxley, D. 1990: An analysis of house systems in New York City neighborhood high schools. Monograph, June.

Pittman, K. 2001: Youth today. The cost of being certain. International Youth Foundation Search Site.

Powell, L. 1996: The achievement knot. In Fine, M., Powell, L., Weis, L. and Wong, L.M., editors, *Off white*. New York: Routledge, 312.

Pratt, M.L. 1991: *Arts of the contact zone*. Modern Language Association, New York. Profession 33–40.

Roberts, R. 2003: Domination and resistance: embodied in movement. Unpublished doctoral dissertation in social personality psychology, The Graduate Center, CUNY.

Rubin, L. 1976: *Worlds of pain: Life in the working class family*. New York: Basic Books.

Scott, J. 1990: *Domination and the art of resistance: hidden transcripts*. New Haven: Yale University Press.

Smith, L. T. 1999: *Decolonizing methodologies: research and indigenous peoples*. London: Zed Books.

Stack, C. 1974: *All our kin: strategies for survival in a Black community*. New York: Harper and Row.

Tatum, B. 1999: *Why do all the Black kids sit together? And other conversations about race*. New York: Basic Books.

Torre, M. E., Fine, M., Boudin, K., Bowen, I., Clark, J., Hylton, D., Martinez, M., Roberts, R. A., Rivera, M., Smart, P. and Upegui, D. 2001: A space for co-constructing counter stories under surveillance. *International Journal of Critical Psychology* 4, 149–66.

Twine, F. 2000: Racial ideologies and racial methodologies. In Twine, F. and Warren, J., editors, *Racing research, researching race*. New York: NYU Press, 1–34.

Wasley, P., Fine, M., King, S. and Powell, L. 2000: *Small schools, great strides: the Bank Street Study of Chicago Small School Reform*. New York: Bank Street College.

Weis, L. and Fine, M. 2003: *Silenced voices, extraordinary conversations*. New York: Teachers College Press.

Weisenfeld, E. 1999: *The researcher's place in qualitative inquiries: un-fulfilled promises?* 1999 Caracas, Venezuela: 27th Interamerican Congress of Psychology.

Wells, A. and Serna, I. 1996: The politics of culture: understanding local political resistance to detracking in racially mixed schools. *Harvard Educational Review* 66, 93–118.

Wilson, W. J. 1996: *When work disappears: the world of the new urban poor*. New York: Knopf Publishers.

Winant, H. 2003: *The world is a ghetto*. New York: Basic Books.

Decolonizing Peace

Victoria Fontan

Victoria Fontan is a Professor of Peace and Conflict Studies and the Chair of the Division of Social Sciences and Humanities at the American University of Afghanistan. She is also a visiting professor at the Western Institute of Technology and Higher Education (ITESO), Guadalajara, Mexico; at the Institut Supérieur des Techniques de Développement, Kalehe, République Démocratique du Congo; and the University of Duhok, Iraq.

She has conducted research in Burma, Colombia, DR Congo, Kashmir, Somalia, Syria, Yemen, and others. Her original academic specializations have been twofold, first, critical terrorism studies from a peace studies perspective, focusing on the role of humiliation in relation to the emergence of insurgencies, mostly in a Middle Eastern context, and second, post-liberal peace studies, from a decolonial perspective. She now focuses on diverse aspects of human security.

Prior to her appointment to Afghanistan, she coordinated the establishment of the quality framework for HPass, the LinkedIn-type platform for humanitarian workers and volunteers. Fontan received her PhD in Peace and Development Studies from the University of Limerick, Ireland, and has a doctorate in education specializing in mediation from the Universidad De La Salle in Costa Rica.

In this semi-autographical writing, Fontan transgresses academic speak while bringing to bare critical questions about the peacebuilding industrial paradigm. Alongside critical perspectives such as Oliver Richmond's critique of liberal peace, Fontan's article questions the epistemological basis of peace as a theory, a practice, and a discipline. Foregrounding stories of human trafficking victims and slave labor, the article makes visible what is normally hidden from conversations about the practices of professionals and organizations operating in "the field." Official narratives that position the North as responsible for the rescuing or saving of the so-called Other, who are so often framed as the problem to be solved, are resisted through this representation of the lived experience of those most affected by neo-liberal peacebuilding strategies.

Questions to consider: "What is 'indigenous'?" and "What is 'universal'?" What are the dangers of Northern standards being imposed, while Northerners also contribute to corruption practices? What relationships of power are reproduced as a result, and how can peacebuilders de-colonize these approaches and shift the discourse to one that makes the invisible visible?

The Case for Decolonizing Peace

Victoria Fontan

In the past few years, rape in Eastern Congo has been the object of intense media coverage. This has contributed to the assistance and treatment of thousands of women and girls, taken from the front lines into safe houses in different urban centers of the region.[12] While the exact number of victims is difficult to gather, UN officials have referred to the Democratic Republic of Congo (DR Congo) as the "worst place in the world in terms of sexual violence."[1] There is one aspect of sexual violence, however, that the UN mission in DR Congo would rather abstain from mentioning: the rape of children and internally trafficked young women by some of its mission members within the towns of Bukavu, Goma and Uvira.[2] According to Congolese law, sexual intercourse involving children amounts to rape.[3] Yet, peacekeepers regularly pay for sex with children and women in and around some nightclubs and hotels in Kivu Province of DR Congo. While the aforementioned UN narrative paints sexual violence in DR Congo as a problem to be solved by the intervention of a benevolent savior, one may well consider the presence of this "savior" as a contributor of the current insecurity in DR Congo.

Amidst the controversy about Greg Mortensen's *Three Cups of Tea*, it is important to question, not only the motives and good intentions of self-proclaimed peacebuilders, but the systemic structures that allow for human rights abuses, embezzlement, and corruption to take place as part of peace missions.[4] Are those abuses the product of "a few bad apples," an exception to the rule, as each probe reluctantly carried out tends to tell us, or are the epistemological foundations of peace missions themselves responsible? Has our understanding of peace become the barrel within which anyone can fall over the edge of corruption, embezzlement, and even sexual abuse? A few months ago, I caught myself on the edge of corruption. Arriving to Rwanda without my office having arranged a Congolese visa for my foreseen three weeks stay in Bukavu, I immediately panicked at the idea of not being able to complete my mission there, anticipating a bad review from our project evaluators and a disappointed donor at a simple logistical mistake. I entertained the idea of attempting to bribe a border official to enter the country. I thought that to carry out my "peace"-related mission, the ends would justify the means. Understanding peace as an end, an objective, an outcome, is exactly what has precipitated many others to venture over the edge.

Using decolonizing research methods and critical pedagogy, this chapter will question the epistemological structure of peace as we know, practice, and teach it, as well as the implications of our thoughts and actions on the daily lives of the populations we are supposed to serve. By way of an illustration, I will take a close look at the resurgence of human trafficking in post-conflict areas, and will question how and why, in spite of an array of international legal instruments, internal UN policies and lessons learned, it is still one of the most widely practiced forms of abuse worldwide. This will lead me to question the epistemological basis of peace, as a theory, a practice, and a discipline. Finally, this chapter will make the case for a different approach to peace, one that does not rely on "benevolence" or any other colonial narrative that serves the social and economic interests of a complacent ruling elite. Decolonizing peace calls for an introspection of all aspects of the peace industry, the transcending of a structural elite toward the formation and facilitation of endogenously sustainable communities of peace processes. It brings parts of the invisible to the forefront. It involves the dismantling of "official" narratives, asserting the first person and subjective experiences of all those involved as visible and relevant.[5]

Huda and Sajeeda

In the spring of 2003, as the U.S.-led coalitions infamous de-Baathification program dismantled all law enforcement, legislative, and military Iraqi institutions, organized crime in Iraq was given a free hand to resume its pre-war activities, and extended its scope.[6] Sisters-in-law Huda and Sajeeda were abducted by armed men on a September morning while they were cleaning their front porch.[7] They were drugged, beaten into submission, and sold off to a pimp. A few days after their abduction, they were given fake passports and driven with their new "owner" through the Syrian-Iraqi border. Since borders were not protected by the coalition, not being a strategic priority in the "building" of a new Iraq, they were unable to alert any official at any point.[8] Upon reaching Damascus airport, they mistakenly thought that customs officials were going to help them. They pleaded for help to whoever was willing to listen to them. Their hope for salvation was crushed after money was exchanged between their pimp and officials, and they were subjected to a severe beating for trying to escape. Upon reaching Yemen, they started working in a hotel with another 180 Iraqi women and girls. The youngest among them was 11 years old. After a few weeks, they managed to contact their mother, and mother-in-law, Aisha, and asked her to organize their rescue. Aisha went to the Iraqi authorities, to no avail. She then tried the coalition, and was given a sympathetic ear by a U.S. sergeant on duty. While he could not enforce any legal provision to have them freed, he assisted her in putting pressure on the Yemeni embassy for their police to take action. By then, I had alerted Amnesty International of their case as well. This combination of efforts led to their hotel being raided by the Yemeni police in April 2004. All women were put in buses, and taken to Sanaa airport. They thought that this was the end of their ordeal, only to realize that they were left at the airport with no passports or money, trapped in a country whose authorities, or well-intentioned international NGOs, were unable and unwilling to offer any assistance outside of their budgetary scope. Most women settled for having their pimp marry them off, for a large sum of money, with the hope of returning to Iraq at a later date. Others made a deal according to which they would return to Iraq and work for their pimp in a brothel. Huda and Sajeeda were among these. As soon as they reached Baghdad, they escaped and returned home. While Hudas parents welcomed her with open arms, Sajeeda was threatened to death by her brother if she did not accept to divorce her husband and return to the family home, to be kept there under lock and key for the rest of her life, as her abduction alone was thought to have tarnished her family honor. She disappeared shortly after her return home and has not been seen since.

As far as Amnesty International was concerned, it had done its job by raising awareness of a heart-breaking issue. After all, there was no line on their sophisticated, London-elaborated budget for the repatriation of trafficked persons or their protection if/once they had returned home. Maybe a string of other agencies ought to have picked up on it, but a lack of co-ordination made this impossible. Still, this story, at the tip of the human trafficking iceberg, could have been carefully packaged to ensure a continuous flow of individual donations to their London-based office.

Moreover, while organizations such as Amnesty International have never made their yearly operational costs thoroughly transparent, the percentage of donations that actually benefit people on the grounds of their awareness campaigns is thought to be less than 20 percent at best.[9]

Human Trafficking and International Law

While commiserating on the desertion of Huda, Sajeeda, and their companions, one may feel consoled to know that International Law does protect what it refers to as "victims" of human trafficking. The ordeal of Huda and Sajeeda falls within the remit of the Palermo "Trafficking Protocol" of 2000, as part of the Convention against Transnational Organized Crime.[10] Human trafficking is defined as:

> 42(a) the recruitment, transportation, transfer, harboring or receipt of persons, by means of the threat or use of force or other forms of coercion, of abduction, of fraud, of deception, of the abuse of power or of a position of vulnerability or of the giving or receiving of payments or benefits to achieve the consent of a person having control over another person, for the purpose of exploitation. Exploitation shall include, at a minimum, the exploitation of the prostitution of others or other forms

of sexual exploitation, forced labour or services, slavery or practices similar to slavery, servitude or the removal of organs;

> 42(b) The consent of a victim of trafficking in persons to the intended exploitation set forth in subparagraph (a) of this article shall be irrelevant where any of the means set forth in subparagraph (a) have been used.[11]

While they were trafficked out of Iraq, Huda and Sajeeda were supposed to be protected by the 1st Protocol of the Geneva Convention, Article 75, as they were to be the "object of special respect and [. . .] protected in particular against rape, forced prostitution and any other form of indecent assault."[12] Even though the U.S. government never ratified the convention, it was and is still supposed to abide by it according to customary law when it is occupying a country.

Since full sovereignty was handed over to the Iraqi Transitional Government on June 28, 2004, the case of Huda and Sajeeda fell under the remit of the aforementioned Geneva Convention. Yet they were let down at many stages during their ordeal. The borders that they were forced to cross were not safe. They were not helped by the Iraqi police anti-trafficking unit, which, when I interviewed them, had decided that they had eloped with a pair of "lovers."[13] Their mother, and mother in law, Aisha, did not benefit from any institutionalized structure within the U.S.-led coalition to help find her daughters. Instead, she relied on the goodwill and heart of a U.S. soldier, who could equally have turned her away when she came to him for help. When they returned, Huda and Sajeeda were not afforded the protection of a safe house, where they could stay until their families decided to take them in. Rather, it is more than likely that Sajeeda either returned to the claws of sexual slavery, or was the victim of an honor killing. To this day, she has not reappeared. International law provides a hopeful response to the issue of human trafficking, yet in effect, fails to ensure the safety of human beings. From this perspective, we can see the wisdom of linguist Alfred Korzybski's famous phrase: 'the map is not the territory.'[14]

Abu Baker, Buk, and Koran

Human trafficking is not only limited to sexual slavery, it can also take the form of forced domestic labor, forced labor, reproductive slavery, etc.[15] According to a UN estimate, human trafficking touches 2.5 million people worldwide, and the annual profit it generates amounts to approximately US$ 31.6 billion.[16] In post-Saddam Iraq, human trafficking has recently reached a new height, in the form of forced domestic labor. Brought in with democracy and peace is a new fashion among the Iraqi elite Middle Class, the "ownership" of a house slave, or two. Should a shop be successful, having a Bangladeshi serving its customers is considered the height of refinement and the envy of one's neighbors. Asian migrant workers now fill the streets of Iraqi Kurdistan in Northern Iraq, as street sweepers, garbage collectors, painters, laborers, etc. They have also started appearing as domestic laborers for NGO workers and the international media. Meet Abu

Baker, another piece of Korzybski's "territory." Abu Baker is a Bangladeshi Sunni Muslim migrant who works in a hotel rented by one of the leading news wire agencies in the western world. For the last year, he has been working between 12 and 14 hours per day, cleaning the 12 rooms of this small hotel, and handling the guests' laundry and cooking, when possible. He came in from Saudi Arabia to Iraq, as he was told that working conditions in Baghdad were better, and since his arrival, his passport has been withheld. He is supposed to be paid $200 per month, but since he is expected to reimburse his employer for the airfare that brought him to Iraq, he never gets to see his wages. He is constantly hungry, sleeps very little, has no vacations or days off, no health-care, and sleeps on the hotel's kitchen floor.[17] In 2011, Iraqi legislation was enacted to "protect" people like Abu Baker. It has decided to no longer grant visas for migrant workers, although it is going back and forth on its decision.[18] Will this decision have any impact on his daily life? Will it help him at all?

Next door to Abu Baker's hotel are Buk and Koran, two migrants from Nepal, working in a house occupied by an Iraqi security company. They each earn $500 per month, $300 of which is transferred directly to a bank account in Nepal.[19] They assist one another in the villa's daily chores. They have a separate living area outside the kitchen, with bunk beds. They eat as much as they need and have one day off per week. Their employer did not give in to their recruitment agency's request to have their airfare reimbursed, so their salaries are not "taxed" for reimbursement each month through debt bondage. Their passports are in their possession, and until the governments decision to no longer grant visas for migrant workers, they thought that they would benefit from a free return ticket home for 10 days of vacations per year. While the Iraqi government is going back and forth on this decision, should it be maintained, how will it affect both them and Abu Baker? This depends only on the good will of their employer. Given the slavery situation in which Abu Baker finds himself, it is likely that his employer will force him to work until he no longer can, either falling gravely ill or dying on the job. For Buk and Koran, this means that they will be compelled to work without a vacation until they decide to go home for good.

In both cases, workers are trapped in Iraq, to different degrees. When many workers like Buk and Koran decide to return home, the "pool" of available workers in the country will decrease, opening the door to further abuse from employers. It is likely that "workers" will become more expensive to "acquire," and that "visas" will have to be paid for handsomely, resulting in a higher risk of debt bondage. For instance, since there will be less availability of new "blood," it is likely that "owners" will seek to keep their staff at any cost, preventing them from having any contact with the outside world which might lead them to better employment opportunities elsewhere. At the time of writing, the Iraqi government has indicated that it may lift its visa ban and begin "charging" between $500 and $1000 per visa. This amount would undoubtedly be re-paid by workers on the long run.[20]

The foreign journalists that live in Abu Baker's hotel do not seem to take notice of the living conditions of the man serving them on a daily basis. They are busy completing their daily tasks, championing press freedom and Iraq's new-found democracy, despite staying in a hotel where freedom only exists for the chosen few. This contradiction is worth more than mentioning. It forces us to acknowledge the fragmentation and limitations existing within post-conflict settings, whose deeply flawed peace paradigm only caters for a fraction of the populations is it supposed to reach. Within this paradigm, there is a hierarchy of human beings, values, origins, and ethnicity. This paradigm values the map above the territory, and, through a familiar religious narrative, rewards the chosen few for their best behavior, while promising the wretched that there is a place ready for them, peace heaven, should they behave in a way that will not upset the current social order. Abu Baker, be consoled, for you will be rewarded a hundred times when justice finally breaks out alongside sustainable peace, on judgment day. A few peace and conflict scholars have chosen to define this paradigm as "liberal peace", the linear, mechanistic building of peace as an aggregation of parts built through a liberal framework.

The Liberal Peace Paradigm

The critique of liberal peace questions the fragmentations, inconsistencies, and priorities regimenting post-conflict environments. It asks why some individuals are worth more than others, and who benefits from a peace whose expression is as industrial as its promotion is idealistic. A probing of liberal peace asks why Huda, Sajeeda, and Abu Baker are left behind while billions of dollars are poured into post-conflict areas on the basis of their "vulnerability." Oliver P. Richmond in *The Transformation of Peace* has provided reflections on the liberal peace model, which he understands as the universal, neo-colonial, state-building model applied indiscriminately in post-conflict missions after the Cold War. According to this model, salvation and sustainable peace in post-conflict situations are based on the construction of state mechanisms through the promotion of good governance, free market, law enforcement institutions, and human rights.[21]

The neo-colonial flavor associated with this enterprise relates to the idea that Northern-educated, seasoned "democrats" will be deployed to educate locals on the values that they ought to embrace and be grateful for. An illustration of this would be my own story: the deployment of an inexperienced, 25 year old French democratization officer to a small village in Bosnia Herzegovina, where only her passport credentials, her nationality, and birth-rights, endowed her with the privilege to "empower" women, youth, and politicians often twice her age, with no prior experience. This situation, Richmond suggests, often leads to the local rejection of or resistance to perceived neo-colonial institutions and models, as well as the resurgence of conflicts in many parts of the world.

Of importance to liberal peace is the fragmentation and prioritization of certain domains over others. Often, these priorities are dictated by the Northern capitals that these state-building enterprises emanate from, and at times create some extreme examples of the disconnect between what is considered policy priorities and some of the values these missions are supposed to champion or protect. An illustration of this would be the latest scandal involving Washington, DC–based security company Dyncorps, regarding a cable between an Afghan and a U.S. diplomat who discuss the purchase of dancing boys, *Bacha Bazi,* for Afghan policemen in exchange for their assiduous participation in a police-training program.[22] In the early 2000s, this same company was also involved in a human trafficking scandal in Bosnia Herzegovina, where it was supporting the United Nations International Police Task-Force.[23] Over a period of months, a Dyncorps employee collected information on the buying, selling, rape, and murder of women as well as children as young as 12 years of age.[24]

To this day, Dyncorps continues to be contracted by the U.S. Department of state in Iraq, Afghanistan, Sudan, and other places where the liberal peace paradigm is being applied.[25] In light of this, Mary Anderson's "Do No Harm" essay raises the question of a Hippocratic Oath for peace missions personnel, since, as international actors in times of conflict do become part of the conflict itself, an epistemological distance is called for.[26] Is this enough? More importantly, are peace workers aware of the contradictions and shortcomings that their presence represents? A Hippocratic Oath places the responsibility of success onto the shoulders of peace workers, while a critique of the liberal peace paradigm implies that the system itself is bound to fail. Peace mission personnel are not benevolent physicians at the side of a sick nation, society, etc. This narrative encourages challenges to peace to be seen as a sickness, an ailment to be cured, and in so doing may actually promote the renewal of an elitist system complacent to a neo-colonial power structure. Is the system bound to fail or re-create the same social order? Development efforts and their shortcomings are a constant reminder of this conundrum.

Indeed, Dambysa Moyo and William Easterly have deconstructed the logistical arm of liberal peace, development, and international assistance with great eloquence. In her book, *Dead Aid,* Moyo describes the systematic dependency of African nations toward the industry of international aid.[27] She contends that aid as a development model cannot function or be sustainable in the long term, as it creates a pattern of reliance on foreign economies and upholds the power structures of local elites. From her perspective, there is no incentive for sustainability in relation to aid, since it creates jobs in the North, and maintains a socio-political status quo in the South. In *The White Man's Burden,* William Easterly articulates the perspective that aid is not only an industry, but also a neo-colonial arm of Northern powers working to keep the greater South in a cycle of dependency and despair, while simultaneously granting themselves a moral self-righteousness for helping the worlds poor and pulling them out of "darkness."[28] His main argument condemns the vision of planning, or "planners" based in Northern capitals, masterminding operations to save Africans from themselves, while seldom understanding what needs, realities, and initiatives are endogenous to those environments. Easterly advocates for the morphing of planners into "searchers," who already do exist, and instead of applying one-size-fits-all solutions to Africa's woes, identify and customize actions according to local realities. Both Moyo and Easterly emphasize the fact that the billions of dollars spent to supposedly alleviate poverty seldom reach the people that desperately need it, and instead feed the egos and budgets of international NGOs and their idealist, Ivy-League-trained, "white" aid-workers.[29] Scores of articles have been written on the legitimate channeling of funds that make the aid community a business and an industry. Two illustrations come to mind.

The first one refers to a USAID-sponsored project I was asked to evaluate and monitor in 2005.[30] This project was designed to organize the first three elections of the new Iraqi electoral cycle from a logistical and voter outreach perspective, and to support the drafting of the provisional Iraqi constitution. Out of the $155 million allocated by USAID for this project, an estimated $100 million was directly allocated to contracting companies for their services, primarily to ensure the security of the aid workers involved in these various projects.[31] The actual funding delivered to communities for voter outreach or electoral document circulation was a fraction of this initial budget. Equally, the funds allocated to our evaluation project were minimally allocated to deploying field monitors around Iraq to assess the impact of the programs initiated by the USAID partners. Since we were not allowed to leave the safety of the International Zone inside Baghdad, more commonly known as the Green Zone, it made sense to allocate a strong budget for field research. This was not the case. Almost every dollar, from our transportation exclusively on American carriers to our daily spending at the local Subway franchise of the Green Zone, channeled our budget, spending money/per Diem, and salary back to Northern-based economic interests. This particular case presents more than an anecdote, it demonstrates the spending re-cycling of aid money, rarely channeled outside Northern business or NGO interests.[32]

The second illustration is an NGO I visited in Congo (DRC). The organization had been working to help rape survivors for the last 10 years. It then realized that, throughout this period, less than 20% of the funding raised in Belgium, where its Headquarters are based, actually reached the women it was supposed to help, despite following all applicable laws. Is peace as much an industry as any other? Is "peace" geared toward giving our Northern peace and conflict studies graduates careers *and* a good conscience?

The Field beyond Right and Wrong

Common to all these critiques of the peace-building world, whether it pertains to the discourse of liberal peace, international aid, or the planners' perspective, is a narrative of responsibility to save the greater South from itself, to bring it to "our" Northern level and standards—economically, politically, culturally, and legally.[33] The tools: democracy, state-building, good governance, transparency, accountability, human rights, and rule of law, are often lagging behind in our own Northern environments, i.e., Guantanamo Bay Detention Centre, Oil for Food scandal, etc., yet are presented to our Southern Other as their salvation, totems to the altar of their forced modernization.[34] In fact, as pointed out by Easterly, the past rhetoric of colonization vividly matches that of the main United Nations documents today.[35] The liberal evangelization of the 21st century is similar, in its narrative, to its religious counterpart of previous centuries.

This realization is what makes me, as a "practitioner," question the foundations of my discipline. What am I to say to my students from the global South when they deplore the fact that most of the theories we teach emanate from the greater North, using them, the South, the "Other," as mere case studies, as the problem to be solved? What am I to answer to well-intentioned colleagues when they come back from years of dedication to the "field" burned out and disillusioned? What advice am I to give my students who ache to go to the "field" to make a difference in the world? With "field," of course, comes the Orientalist characterization of the "Other" from the greater South.[36] In the same way that evangelization presented the glorious map of heavenly life as an ultimate reward, the liberal peace evangelists present the map of a magnificently just social order to the populations they so benevolently "help," while quietly earning money for it and maintaining a social status quo within the territory.

Sufi poet Rumi wrote: "Out beyond ideas of wrong-doing and right-doing, there is a field. I'll meet you there."[37] I do not want this reflection to take one side in relation to the impact, or not, of peace missions: other colleagues have already carried this out beautifully.[38] Rather, I wish for it to transcend a too obvious polarization that may have been generated by alternative voices in the field. I am aware of the dedication of my peers, of the positive impact of some projects on the ground, of the hope that some of our actions might bring: "success," "development," "relief," or at least a modicum of comfort and kindness in an overwhelmingly uncomfortable and unkind world, both to "us," and also "them." I also know that the road to peace mission hell, embodied by the resurgence of the Afghan *Bacha Bazi*, is paved with good intentions, and materialized by the rule of law, in this case, Afghan police reform. What I am challenging here is the assumption that the liberal peace model is what the "Other" needs, the assumption that any model that suits our good intentions is needed. I want the lessons learned to matter, so that children, women, and men, no longer suffer the consequences of our recurring mistakes. One does not need to break lives to make peace, for it then only represents a victor's peace. Finally, I also want to question the commonly expressed assumption that malpractices are exceptions to the norm. What is it, within the system, which transforms the exception into the norm?

No Solutions

At the University for Peace (UPEACE), I co-teach the foundation course in peace and conflict studies. I have been doing so since I arrived at the institution, and the content of my teaching, as well as my methodology, has changed drastically in the last few years. The main factor responsible for my different approach has been the diversity of our student population. Teaching peace and conflict studies in a Northern institution, where a strong percentage of the student body is homogenous, does not challenge the system within which one evolves at all. After all, this teaching will endow its privileged elite to go and save the world after they graduate. When I arrived at UPEACE, the base of my teaching was peace and conflict studies classics.[39] After a couple of years repeating the same models, I became increasingly aware that the majority of our students, from the greater South, were weary of both the theories and case studies utilized in the course. As mentioned earlier, they were being "studied" with a Northern eye. Some felt that they were being objectified, while others questioned their place within a university setting where they, the majority, perceived themselves as a minority. Were the conflict resolution mechanisms that we were teaching applicable to individual or collective settings? Where was the place for alternative conflict resolution mechanisms outside the rhetoric of "indigenous" traditions? Where does the universal finish and the indigenous start? Why would the Rwandan *Gacaca* practice, or the Hawaiian *Ho'ponopono* process, be considered by our literature as "indigenous," while Fisher and Ury be understood as universal?[40] At the same time, questioning the liberal peace paradigm raised some frustrations within parts of the Northern student population. The critique of liberal peace, it seems, was challenging the dreams and also the forming identity of some.

One specific interaction embodied this conundrum. After my first lecture, which deconstructed some of the Northern assumptions of peace and conflict studies, one British student was particularly upset. He emphatically let me know that just about every argument of my lecture had profoundly irritated him. His reaction was understandable: he was fresh out of his undergraduate studies, with little practical experience. He was too young in our "field" to be critical of the liberal peace narrative. At the same time, he was also enrolled in a graduate school where he ought to have expected to be intellectually challenged.[41] A deconstruction of the liberal peace paradigm had just touched his idealism at its core. If liberal peace was the expression of the status quo, and the aid paradigm an industry geared to maintain this status quo, where were his good intentions going to fit? In a meeting subsequently held, he expressed that he was reconsidering his decision to stay at UPEACE. He said that he had just spent an enormous amount of money to be given the tools that he would need to make the world a better place. Being told that there was no universal tool to alleviate the world suffering was just too much for him to take. He asked if he would be spending the rest of the year in his particular program, International Peace Studies, deconstructing liberal peace. I replied that at the beginning of the year, yes, we would deconstruct a great deal of theories and practices. However, after this initial phase, we were also going to explore some pathways toward post-liberal peace, decolonizing peace, as well as to offer alternative proposals to this conflicting paradigm. I also reminded him that, no, I had no universal tools to propose to him. In fact, a transcending of the universalism of liberal peace was the only certainty that I could propose to him. Peace, in the program, was going to be seen primarily as a process. We were not going to make a "peacebuilder" out of him. No community is an empty shell, nor does it need a fresh graduate to come and "build" peace from scratch. Rather, we

876 EPOCH THREE—RESEARCH METHODOLOGIES

were going to train him to facilitate peace as a process, if anything. Still, if he insisted on being labeled, he would leave the program as a peace-facilitator, or a vector of peace formation.[42] This, I contended, was the only intellectually honest label that I had to propose. A few days later, he switched to our law program. The map had more appeal than the territory. He now works for NATO.

Liberal Peace and its Enabling Great Caveat

The tools, little handbooks on, steps to, and paraphernalia of liberal peace, are legion. Peace, on paper, is a very straightforward matter. With a careful mix of good governance, rule of law, accountability, democracy, transparency, and multi-track diplomacy, a country can be sustainably transformed for the better. In fact, after reading these books, one with no field experience might get the impression that peacebuilding is like assembling a car, and that fixing a country and its people is a viable possibility. Since the 1960s, the greatest caveat, the safety net of liberal peace, has existed in the form of a false dichotomy between negative and positive peace.[43] We are told, and are still teaching, that, yes, harmonious peace is difficult to achieve, and that while negative peace, the absence of war, can be engineered mechanically, positive peace, or the fairy tale of happily-ever-after co-existence, remains complicated to achieve, yet attainable. We are told that positive peace takes years to foster, that it is no easy task, but that our good intentions, in the end, will prevail. While useful in its time, the cob-web-made safety net of positive peace still absolves us from questioning our entire paradigm. It enables us to retreat behind its safety when everything else fails, in the same way that Dyncorps' repeated scandals will be understood to be the exception to the rule. How often have we heard that, after trying everything, it was just impossible, within this or that failed state, this corrupt political culture, or amidst that reality of vicious/ atavistic ethnic hatred, to do anything more for "those" people, the "Other," who are not like us, do not understand our peaceful values?[44] How dishonest can we be to even assume that our mechanical actions bear no responsibility in the situations that we too often flee, evacuate from, or abandon?[45] In every such situation, there are people, civilians, including children, who will not survive our liberal peace paradigm, who will die because of it.[46] Regardless of the relevance of positive peace at the time, its obsolescence now makes it the enabler of our failures. We cannot but transcend it.

The Peace Universalism

Where does this paradigm emanate from? We may all agree that while we look into the transitions between stages of peacekeeping, peace making, and peace building, we are not looking at a strict linear progression. We may also be aware of the complexities existing within these classifications. For instance, we know that within one particular case, each of the stages mentioned above might be present at the same time. One case very obvious to me in relation to this is the situation of post-Saddam Iraq between 2004 and 2006. During this time, while a democratization process was taking place, generally classified as "peace building," many parts of the country were experiencing acts of ethnic cleansing, more related to the sphere of peace keeping.[47] The merging *of* all occurrences, and their complexities, can be seen to account for the failure of liberal peace in post-Saddam Iraq. We are still telling our student population that these models are the best we can offer them. Indeed they are. These models emanate from a paradigm that has been dominating our thinking for hundreds of years: Cartesian thinking.

In *The Turning Point*, Fritjof Capra analyses the key evolutions of Western/European thinking between the years 1500 and 1700.[48] While before 1500, the dominant view of the world combined both mind and matter in organic, collectivist and ethics-based communities, the arrival of the Scientific Revolution by way of the seminal works of Copernicus, Galileo, and Descartes, privileged a vision of the world as a machine to be tamed, controlled and engineered.[49] This vision of the world as a machine prevails today in our daily lives, e.g., the separation of academic departments within one university structure, or the prioritization of specific objectives within peace missions, at times privileging state building over basic human rights, as was the case with the lack of interest in countering human trafficking in 2003–2005 post-Saddam Iraq. While the Scientific Revolution was extremely useful at the time, and still is now, the separation of humanity from its environment, spirituality, and ethics, has brought a lack of equilibrium that is now culminating in, to name only a few impending catastrophes, climate change and nuclear disaster.

In *The Structure of Scientific Revolutions*, Thomas Kuhn argues that scientific evolution is not the result of a gradual process, but of revolutionary changes affecting the way we conceptualize the world as a whole, our social paradigm.[50] The Cartesian revolution, separating mind and matter, did transform our daily lives into compartmentalized settings, where one wears different hats at different times of the day, and where one's fragmented vision of the world transpires in one's actions. It is thus possible for a person to work in a peace mission during the day, and have a sex slave waiting for him/her to return home at night.[51] True, we can all reach post-conflict environments thanks to the technological advances of modern science. Yet, it is also modernity at its core, in its sheer methodical ruthlessness, which engineered and executed the Jewish Holocaust, validated colonization, and now fuels neo-colonialism.[52] At stake in this debate is not whether modernity is needed or not, rather, it is how the reliance on hard sciences as a paradigm, a model on which our lives are based, have brought disequilibrium to humanity. The word "humanity" is a very conscious choice as applied to this text. While the Cartesian thinking of "I think therefore I am" emanates from Europe, it is the paradigm that it has created that has permeated throughout the world, culminating in globalization and the universalism of peace studies.

Thus, when I see that to be a successful academic in an African university, one has to be educated in a Northern-based institution, and return as the prodigal son or daughter with these unfaltering credentials, I also deplore the pervasiveness of this neo-colonial model. Where is the space for academic creativity and innovation, if there is only one paradigm that dominates the thinking of elites worldwide? Recently, I was assisting in the development of a syllabus on good governance for a university in Eastern Congo. My colleague, a brilliant and resourceful professor, gave me an appalling first draft of his curriculum, listing governance models of the European Union, the World Bank, United Nations, etc. When I asked him how this would fit in Eastern Congo, he realized that his curriculum could be offered as part of any generic program anywhere in the world. When I asked how his region fared, was organized, and administered itself before colonization, he wondered if he could base his work on a traditional governance model to be applied to today's realities, mitigating all influences to fit his environment.

We are not calling for a return to the basics, to the proverbial "cave," but are merely looking into what governance could possibly mean in a contemporary Congolese context. Are some lessons learned from the past useful for our future? To date, very few models supersede the "indigenous" label that the imperialist Northern academia grants any of its competitors. Cartesian thinking as a paradigm, indeed, emanated from the West, and condemned all other paradigms to the "indigenous" label. This also alludes to the universalism of the liberal peace paradigm. Not only is peace administered as a mechanical remedy to conflict, its main precepts are also understood to be universal.

Decolonizing Peace

The case for decolonizing peace comes from the realization that the same paradigm that was invoked for colonization is now serving to channel neo-colonial liberal peace efforts worldwide. Decolonizing peace calls for a holistic, systemic approach to peace, the processes that represent it, and the ethics and values that it embodies. Decolonizing peace means harmonizing the map and the territory, bringing the invisible to our understanding and living of the visible. It calls for mitigation between localized social fabrics and values of peace, it also questions the idea of imposed change at any cost, usually that of a peaceful process. Contrary to colonial discourses, which once invoked that Africa as a whole was there to be discovered, conquered, and built from scratch, the narrative of decolonizing peace asserts that peace already exists at the local level, and that it does not need to be built according to values and understandings of a foreign environment.

Is there universality in ethics, human rights, and a culture of peace? Decolonizing peace does not call for a discarding of human rights or values of peace for the sake of cultural relativism. It does not call for a return to a basic order of patriarchal exploitation, for instance.[53] It questions the political and neo-colonial motives that are being pushed through the championing of certain "universal" values. When the map is no longer pitted against the territory, sustainability is not to be engineered, doctored, or re-invented: it is intrinsic to decolonizing peace. The role of the "peacebuilder" comes to be heavily challenged under the guise of decolonizing peace. The Northern-white-ivy-league educated expert and its elite-Southern-born-Northern-educated counterpart are asked to reflect on the compartmentalization of what they have understood to be an end justifying all means.

Decolonizing peace requires a paradigm shift that enables its practitioner to see initiatives through a different set of lenses and to employ a different array of what are no longer "tools" but understandings of what can be facilitated, strengthened, and enabled to flourish on the "ground." This paradigm shift transcends the power dimensions of social orders, it also evolves outside of the left-right political spectrum, for politics also kill the sustainability of any decolonized initiatives, as Nobel Prize winner and Indigenous leader Rigoberta Menchu's case would illustrate.[54] Of importance is the idea that peace becomes a decolonizing agent, but not a decolonized finality. It evolves within the complexity of a live adaptive system; it is always in motion, as a process. It goes through cycles, vanishes to re-emerge in another form, according to the bifurcation point that it takes through its constant adaptation and re-invention. It cannot be controlled, since it is a complex adaptive system.

A Different Lens

Wishful thinking or parallel reality; what does decolonizing peace look like? The paradigm shift that decolonizing peace represents is also in the eye of the beholder. It is not for this book, therefore, to convince anyone of its relevance. As mentioned earlier, an internationally funded NGO focusing on rape survivors realized that its activities were mainly benefiting a handful of elite employees both in Belgium and DR Congo. As less than 20% of its donations from Belgium actually reached rape survivors, they decided to re-evaluate their liberal peace activities of capacity building, women and youth empowerment, legal aid, and financial support to hospitals, to strengthening local initiatives.

The issue of rape in the DRC has been prominent in the international scene for some years. Thousands of women have been helped as a result of numerous campaigns. They have gained access to much needed surgeries, medication, and psychological assistance. In some cases, they have been given a new lease on life, and the issue of rape in war has gained much more exposure internationally. None of this much-needed assistance deserves to be questioned, yet, is it sustainable on the long run? There is one town in the Southern Kivu region of DRC where all this assistance is gathered: Panzi. Due to the concentrated media and academic coverage of this particular town, almost 100% of all medical services given to female rape survivors are provided there, neglecting the development of similarly relevant infrastructures elsewhere in the region.[55] Moreover, most reports focus on female victims, neglecting the equal prominence of sexual violence targeting men, hence the unavailability of treatment for male rape survivors.

Taking these parameters into account, alongside many more, the Belgian NGO decided to alter all its activities two years ago. It changed its local staff into a locally educated, gender-equal, and ethnically diverse team, and suspended all its liberal peace programs. It now focuses on logistically and financially supporting diverse homegrown initiatives and NGOs working on minimal, locally gathered funding, solely with local staff. Its headquarters have been transformed into a half-way house for survivors and local NGO workers to meet and work toward medical assistance, legal help, small business initiatives training, and very importantly, the emerging of a network of survivors to help one another once they return to their home environments.

The organization is also helping local hospitals and clinics so that survivors do not need to travel all the way to Panzi to benefit from medical treatment, thus provoking less of a negative impact both socially and family-wise. The treatment of men remains an issue, but has become part of the organization's agenda. No international "expert" has been detached from the Belgium headquarters to decide what its priorities ought to be. Rather, a local manager reports to Belgium. The idea behind this thinking is that the existence of local NGOs cannot depend on international money. Rather, those NGOs are based on a strong social fabric of mutual trust, resilience, belonging, and values of care. Money certainly helps for those values to blossom, but could never engineer them. A different set of lenses on part of this Belgium organization, coming from a paradigm shift regarding their own role and standing, made a difference to a resilient community, and fostered its sustainability. This bears the hallmarks of a decolonizing process, where an equal space exists for all.

Decolonizing Methodologies: Teaching and Writing to Transgress

It will not have escaped you, the reader, that this book is written with a semi-autobiographical tone, also placing other individuals at the forefront of the overall narrative. We are often told that individuals cannot be singled out, exposed, because they need to be "protected." Those individuals are moved from being seen in their humanity to being labeled as objects of our "independent" ethical research.[56] All individuals portrayed in this book except Mrs. C. pleaded with me to make their lives visible. From their perspective, they do not need "protecting": they want their ordeals to illustrate our failures as benevolent "peace builders." They seek to make us accountable in light of our own fiascoes. They want to matter. How can I, as a peace and conflict studies professor, training a little army of "peace builders" detach myself from the failures and crimes of our peace industry? An autobiographical style is also a statement of my own responsibility as a practitioner. It may be seen as a transgression from more conventional academic writing, yet it is a chosen stylistic transgression toward empowerment, awareness, and action.

The choice of the territory over the map stems from the epistemology of decolonizing peace. The individual is no longer portrayed as the problem, the exception to the beautiful rule on paper; rather, he or she represents the call for accountability in peace missions, theory, and teaching. The individual warrants the decolonizing of all, a reappraisal of peace as a process rather than a mere end. This also stems from the choice to teach and research peace and conflict studies from the perspective of critical and engaged pedagogy.[57] In teaching for and through decolonizing peace, there can be no boundary between the "subject" and "object," no barrier separating the researcher and the researched. In terms of research methods, all "material" for this book was gathered using Linda Tuhiwai Smith's decolonizing methodologies.[58] Stemming from the realization that conventional research methods can no longer be seen as an independent, clinical tool for data collection, a decolonizing methodology re-appropriates control over the formation of knowledge and one's understanding of their own reality. It becomes a dialogical process between all involved, stems from being more than participating, and does not rely on pre-established keywords and categories. Teaching, researching, and writing to transgress liberal peace becomes the process of decolonizing peace.

Conclusion

As I reflect on decolonizing peace, one of my former students has just been hired as a protection officer for an NGO in South Sudan. She is street-smart, under 25 years old, and full of ideals and energy. She has been working with me on this emerging paradigm for some time. Still, I wonder how many of my students will eventually be driven over the edge by the liberal peace system in the long run. As I set off to continue researching the abuse of local populations in DR Congo by MINUSCO staff, I hope to also remain in this parallel universe, not to be coerced into accepting the unacceptable.

Amidst former allegations of human rights abuses and sexual slavery, the UN mission to DRC was re-named as MINUSCO in 2010.[59] All controversy has been relegated to the past, with the assault, rape, and enslavement of women and children by UN staff and soldiers no longer tolerated as part of this new and improved mission and mandate. True, appearances are slightly more presentable. UN vehicles are no longer parked in front of nightclubs in and around Bukavu. When they do not use civilian cars, peacekeepers now send in their *petits,* errand boys, to bring them the children that they will safely rape in the confines of their environments.[60] Then they will build a mosque or a church to make it all even, to thank the local communities for having given them their pound of flesh. All is a little more difficult to track down, but still very real.

Where does this leave us as "practitioners"? Huda, Sajeeda and Abu Baker remain at the mercy of our good conscience, our willingness to search our own souls. Still, we can no longer say that there is no other way to approach peace. A parallel world exists: we have to acknowledge it and evolve according to its needs, even if this makes a part of us redundant.

Notes

1. Interview with Jean-Jacques Purusi, Mamas for Africa, Bukavu, April 22nd 2011.

2. Gettelman, J. (2011). "Rapes are again reported in Eastern Congo." *The New York Times*. New York.

3. Un-attributable interviews with two local NGO workers, Bukavu; one hotel owner, Uvira; one lawyer, Goma; one nightclub owner, Goma; Several visits to nightclubs in Bukavu, Goma and Uvira witnessing international personnel interactions with minors. See also: Caplan, G. (2012) "Peacekeepers gone wild: How much more abuse will the UN ignore in Congo?" *The Globe and Mail*, available online: http://www.theglobeandmail.-com/news/politics/second-reading/peacekeepers-gone-wild-how-much-more-abusewill-the-un-ignore-in-congo/article4462151/

4. Interview with Professor Jean-Claude Mubalama Zibona, Catholic University of Bukavu, April 21, 2011, referring to law #06/018 of July 20, 2006, articles 167-170-171bis-174c. 16 Kristof, N. D. (2011). "'Three Cups of Tea,' Spilled." *The New York Times*. New York.

5. A methodological discussion of both style and research can be found at the end of this chapter.

6. Fontan, V. (2008). *Voices from Post-Saddam Iraq: Living with Terrorism, Insurgency and New Forms of Tyranny*. Westport, CT, Praeger Security International. This de-Baathi-fication program, inspired from post–World War II de-Nazification was the first step toward liberal/orthodox peace-building in post-Saddam Iraq in 2003.

7. For a fuller account of Huda and Sajeeda's ordeal, see my original article: Firmo-Fontan, V. (2004). Abducted, beaten and sold into prostitution: two women's story from an Iraq in turmoil. *The Independent*. London.

8. For an interestingly prioritized nation-building/democratization narrative at the time, see Dawisha, A. I. and K. Dawisha (2003). "How to Build a Democratic Iraq." *Foreign Affairs* 82(2).

9. While the overhead expenses of Amnesty International USA account for 4.2% of their annual budget, their financial score is one of the lowest in terms of the actual funds that directly benefit people, excluding infrastructure, per diems, luxury accommodation for their staff, high salaries, etc. See: http://www.charitynavigator.org/index.cfm?bay = se-arch.summaryfiorgid = 3294; accessed on February 10th, 2012. For a discussion on the high valedictory payment of Amnesty International's former Secretary general Irene Khan, see: http://www.civilsociety.co.uk/finance/news/content/8390/charity_commission_has_no_jurisdiction_over_board_members_payment_from_amnesty; accessed on February 10th, 2012.

10. It is questionable that Human Trafficking only falls within the remit of organized crime, since it is undeniable that the presence of peace operations and peace-keepers in post-conflict settings increases the demand for sexual services. See: Firmo-Fontan, V. (2003). Responses to Human Trafficking: from the Balkans to Afghanistan. *The Political Economy of New Slavery*. C. Van den Anker. London, Palgrave. This "parking" of the issue within the remit of Organized Crime absolves peace operations from being probed as to whether they are ensuring any structural basis for human rights abuses in UN missions.

11. United Nations (2000). United Nations Convention against Transnational Organized Crime and its Protocols. United Nations. Palermo, Italy, Annex II, pp. 42–43.

12. See http://www.icrc.org/ihl.nsf/7c4d08d9b287a42141256739003e636b/f6c8b9-fee14a77fdc125641e0052b079; accessed on April 24th 2011.

13. Fontan, V. (2008). *Voices from Post-Saddam Iraq: Living with Terrorism, Insurgency and New Forms of Tyranny.* Westport, CT, Praeger Security International.

14. Korzybski, A. (1931). "A Non-Aristotelian System and its Necessity for Rigour in Mathematics and Physics." *American Association for the Advancement of Science, Science and Sanity Commission.* New Orleans.

15. Bales, A. and R. Soodalter (2009). *The Slave Next Door: Human Trafficking and Slavery in America Today.* Berkeley, University of California Press.

16. Centre, U. N. (2008) "UN-backed container exhibit spotlights plight of sex trafficked victims." *UN News Service.*

17. What Abu Baker should have known before arriving is that his hotel belongs to and is managed by Shi'ite Muslims. Amidst the animosity between Sunni and Shi'ite Muslims, exacerbated by the US invasion of the country, it is likely that Abu Baker's treatment at the hands of his management is influenced by his religious identity.

18. Interview with Abdul Karim, liaison with Baghdad immigration office, April 2011.

19. Skype interview with Buk and Koran, April 26th, 2011.

20. Interview with Abdul Karim, liaison with Baghdad immigration office, April 2011.

21. Richmond, O. (2007). *The Transformation of Peace.* London, Palgrave Macmillan.

22. Nova Lomax, J. (2010). "WikiLeaks: Texas Company Helped Pimp Little Boys to Stoned Afghan Cops." *Houston Press.* Houston; the cable can be assessed on http://www.guardian.co.uk/world/us-embassy-cables-documents/213720; accessed on March 9th, 2011. Dancing boys in Afghanistan, referred to as Bacha Bazi, are sold or abducted from their families to become the sex slaves of notables, powerful political and religious figures. This human rights abuse was documented in a Public Broadcasting Service documentary: http://www.pbs.org/wgbh/pages/frontline/dancingboys/; accessed on March 11th 2012.

23. Bolkovac, K. and C. Lynn (2011). *The Whistleblower: Sex Trafficking, Military Contractors and One Woman's Fight for Justice.* London, Palgrave Macmillan; Firmo-Fontan, V. (2003). Responses to Human Trafficking: from the Balkans to Afghanistan. *The Political Economy of New Slavery.* C. Van den Anker. London, Palgrave.

24. Bolkovac, K. and C. Lynn (2011). *The Whistleblower: Sex Trafficking, Military Contractors and One Woman's Fight for Justice.* London, Palgrave Macmillan.

25. See http://www.dyn-intl.com/; accessed on March 10th, 2011.

26. Anderson, M. B. (1999*). Do No Harm: How Aid can Support Peace—Or War.* Boulder, Lynne Rienner Publishers.

27. Moyo, D. (2010). *Dead Aid. Why Aid Makes Things Worse and How There is Another Way for Africa.* New York, Farrar, Straus and Giroux.

28. Easterly, W. (2006). *The White Man's Burden: Why the West's Efforts to Aid the Rest have Done So Much Ill and So Little Good.* London, Penguin Press.

29. White here refers to a paradigm of social whiteness. For a discussion on the whiteness paradigm and the "worship" of whiteness for economic, social, and political aims, see Painter, N. I. (2010). *The History of White People.* New York, Norton.

30. Brandstetter, R. H. and V. C. Fontan (2005). Final Report for Political Process Assistance Review. *Monitoring and Evaluation Performance Program, Phase II (MEPP II).*

I. International Business & Technical Consultants. Washington, D.C., United States Agency for International Development.

31. Ibid.

32. Keen, D. (2008). *Complex Emergencies*. Cambridge, Polity., specifically Chapter 6.

33. For a legal and international law debate on humanitarian intervention, see Kennedy, D. (2004). *The Dark Sides of Virtue: reassessing international humanitarianism*. Princeton, Princeton University Press.

34. Caplan, G. (2009). "Obama and Africa—A Major Disappointment." *The Nation*. New York.

35. Easterly, W. (2006). *The White Man's Burden: Why the West's Efforts to Aid the Rest have Done So Much Ill and So Little Good*. London, Penguin Press; see also Hochschild, A. (1999). *King Leopold's Ghost: A story of greed, terror, and heroism in colonial Africa*. Boston, Mariner Books.

36. Richmond, O. (2007). *The Transformation of Peace*. London, Palgrave, Macmillan.

37. Rumi, J. a.-D., C. Barks, et al. (1995). *The Essential Rumi*. San Francisco, Harper, p. 36.

38. Maren, M. (1997). *The Road to Hell: the ravaging effects of foreign aid and international charity*. New York, The Free Press; Rieff, D. (2002). *A Bed for the Night: humanitarianism in crisis*. New York, Simon and Schuster Paperbacks.

39. Fisher, R., W. Ury, et al. (1991). *Getting to Yes: Negotiating Agreement Without Giving In*. London, Penguin Books; Pruitt, D., J. Rubin, et al. (2003). *Social Conflict: Escalation, Stalemate and Settlement*. New York, McGraw-Hill Humanities.

40. For a dialogue on the local/indigenous and universal, see: Castro, A. P. and K. Ettenger (1996). Indigenous Knowledge and Conflict Management: Exploring Local Perspectives and Mechanisms for Dealing with Community Forestry Disputes. *Community Forestry Unit*. U. N. F. a. A. Organization. Rome, United Nations Food and Agriculture Organization. See also MacGinty, R. (2010). Gilding the lily? International support for indigenous and traditional peacebuilding. *Palgrave Advances in Peacebuilding: Critical Developments and Approaches*. O. Richmond. Basingstoke, Palgrave Macmillan. It is worth noting that ever since Getting to Yes, Rubin, Pruitt & Kim, there have been many critical voices both on the theory and pedagogy of the conflict resolution field, even from within the "Northern" scholars and practitioners' crowds. However, the basis of teaching negotiation often remains the same, while multicultural and gender aspects are provided as an addition and not a basis. For some very relevant critiques, see: Honeyman, C., J. Coben, et al., Eds. (2009). *Rethinking Negotiation Teaching: Innovations and Context and Culture*. Saint Paul, CreateSpace., and Honeyman, C., J. Coben, et al., Eds. (2010). *Venturing Beyond the Classroom*. Saint Paul, CreateSpace.

41. Easterly, W. (2006). *The White Man's Burden: Why the West's Efforts to Aid the Rest have Done So Much Ill and So Little Good*. London, Penguin Press.

42. Richmond, O. (2012). *Failed Statebuilding Versus Peace Formation*. Manchester, Manchester University.

43. Galtung, J. (1969). "Violence, Peace and Peace Research." *Journal of Peace Research* 6(3): 167–191.

44. For a vivid analysis of this particular narrative applied to Rwanda, Somalia and Bosnia-Herzegovina, see: Rieff, D. (2002). *A Bed for the Night: humanitarianism in crisis*. New York, Simon and Schuster Paperbacks., Maren, M. (1997). *The Road to Hell: the ravaging effects of foreign aid and international charity*. New York, The Free Press., and Caplan, G. (2008). The Betrayal of Africa. Toronto, Groundwood.

45. For an excellent debate on the issue, see Caplan, G. (2008). *The Betrayal of Africa*. Toronto, Groundwood.

46. For an illustration of how the liberal peace paradigm directly costs civilian lives, see chapter five of my Iraq book: Fontan, V. (2008). *Voices from Post-Saddam Iraq: Living with Terrorism, Insurgency and New Forms of Tyranny*. Westport, CT, Praeger Security International.

47. Ibid.

48. Capra, F. (1982). *The Turning Point: Science, Society and the Rising Culture*. New York, Bantam Books.

49. Ibid.

50. Kuhn, T. (1996). *The Structure of Scientific Revolutions*. Chicago, University of Chicago Press.

51. Bolkovac, K. and C. Lynn (2011). *The Whistleblower: Sex Trafficking, Military Contractors and One Woman's Fight for Justice*. London, Palgrave Macmillan.

52. Bauman, Z. (2001). *Modernity and the Holocaust*. Ithaca, Cornell University Press.

53. Achebe's novel *Things Fall Apart*, for instance, illustrates the deeply rooted patriarchal issues of pre-colonial Nigeria. This argument in no way means to return to an idealized antique order of social inequalities. Achebe, C. (1994). *Things Fall Apart*. London, Anchor Books.

54. While bringing indigenous issues at the forefront of the social debates both in Guatemala and worldwide, Menchu's presidential bid in 2007 and 2011 only gathered 3% of votes, signifying a shift in popular support among indigenous communities that saw her being co-opted by an institutional/elitist power-base.

55. Gettleman, J. (2007). Rape Epidemic Raises Trauma of Congo War. *The New York Times*. New York.; Initiative, H. H. (2010). "Now, The World is Without Me": An Investigation of Sexual Violence in Eastern Democratic Republic of Congo. Cambridge, Harvard University.

56. Israel, M. and I. Hay (2006). Research Ethics for Social Scientists. London, Sage.

57. Kincheloe, J. and P. McLaren (2007). *Critical Pedagogy: Where are we now?* New York, Peter Lang.; Hooks, B. (1994*). Teaching to Transgress*. New York, Routledge.

58. Tuhiwai Smith, L. (2008). *Decolonizing Methodologies: Research and Indigenous Peoples*. New York, Zed Books.

59. On former MONUC abuses, see: Lynch, C. (2004). "U.N. Sexual Abuse Alleged in Congo." *The New York Times*. New York.

60. Interview with Dr. Jean-Jacques Purusi Sadiki, Bukavu, April 24, 2011.

End of Epoch Questions

Questions for Discussion

- What event shifted the field yet again?
- What distinguishes Epoch Three from the prior two Epochs?
- What disciplines are now added to the field of conflict resolution?
- Imagine what some of the tensions might be between Epoch Three and the prior two Epochs. What conversations might be difficult?
- Discuss an Epoch Three intervention for the opioid crisis or North Korea's nuclear threat. What might this look like?
- Could Epoch Three praxis be included in strategies and approaches of the prior Epochs without discounting them? If so, how?
- What Epoch do you see represented most often in the news?

Final Activities Idea

- Research events about global conflicts hosted by universities, think tanks, or government institutions and see if you can identify which Epoch's discourse will likely predominate during the event.
- Role-play: Select a conflict to discuss. Have students break into groups of three. Each picks an Epoch. The students need to create a plan to respond to the conflict, each advocating for their own Epoch's approach. See what a comprehensive plan could include.

Bibliography

Akinyoade, Demola. "Developing Grounded Theory in Peace and Conflict Research." PhD diss., Peace and Conflict Studies Program, Institute of African Studies, University of Ibadan, Nigeria, 2018.

Allport, Gordon W. *The Nature of Prejudice*. Unabridged, 25th anniversary ed. Reading, MA: Addison-Wesley, 1979.

Avruch, Kevin. "Frames for Culture and Conflict Resolution." In *Culture and Conflict Resolution*, 52–57. Washington, DC: United States Institute of Peace, 1998.

Barash, David and Charles Webel. "The Individual Level." In *Peace and Conflict Studies*, 119–43. Thousand Oaks, CA: SAGE, 2002.

Brams, Steven J. "Theory of Moves." *American Scientist* 81 (November–December 1993): 562–70.

Brown, Juanita, David Isaacs, World Café Community, Peter Senge, and Margaret J. Wheatley. "Beginning the Conversation: An Invitation to the World Café." In *The World Café: Shaping Our Futures Through Conversations That Matter*, 1–11. San Francisco, CA: Berrett-Koehler Publishers, 2005.

———. "The World Café Hosting Guide." In *The World Café: Shaping Our Futures Through Conversations That Matter*, 162–73. San Francisco, CA: Berrett-Koehler Publishers, 2005.

Burgess, Heidi and Guy M. Burgess. "What Are Intractable Conflicts?" Beyond Intractability: Knowledge Base & Conflict Fundamentals. Last modified November 2003. https://www.beyondintractability.org/essay/meaning-intractability.

Burton, John. "Needs Theory." In *Violence Explained: The Sources of Conflict, Violence and Crime and Their Prevention*, 32–40. New York: Manchester University Press, 1997.

Castells, Manuel. "Dignity, Violence and Geopolitics: The Arab Uprisings." In *Networks of Outrage and Hope: Social Movements in the Internet Age*, 93–113. Cambridge: Polity, 2015.

Chayes, Antonia Handler and the Program on Negotiation at Harvard Law School. "Introduction." In *Imagine Coexistence: Restoring Humanity after Violent Ethnic Conflict*, xviii–xxii. San Francisco, CA: Jossey-Bass, 2003.

Cheldelin, Sandra I. and Maneshka Eliatamby. "Challenging the Dominant Narrative." In *Women Waging War and Peace: International Perspectives of Women's Roles in Conflict and Post-Conflict Reconstruction*. New York: Continuum International Publishing Group, 2011.

Cobb, Sara B. "Introduction." In *Speaking of Violence: The Politics and Poetics of Narrative in Conflict Resolution*, 3–19. New York: Oxford University Press, 2013.

Collier, Paul. "Economic Causes of Civil Conflict and Their Implications for Policy." In *Leashing the Dogs of War: Conflict Management in a Divided World*, 197–218. Washington, DC: United States Institute of Peace, 2007.

Curle, Adam. "Mediation." In *The Middle: Non-Official Mediation in Violent Situations*, 9–20. New York: St. Martin's Press, 1986.

Dwyer, Leslie. "A Politics of Silences: Violence, Memory and Treacherous Speech in Post-1965 Bali." In *Genocide: Truth, Memory, and Representation*, edited by Alexander Hinton and Kevin Lewis O'Neill, 113–46. Durham, NC: Duke University Press, 2009.

Enloe, Cynthia. "Gender Makes the World Go Round." In *Bananas, Beaches and Bases: Making Feminist Sense of International Politics*, 1–18. Berkeley, CA: University of California Press, 2014.

Enns, Diane. "When Victims Become Killers." In *The Violence of Victimhood*, 37–62. State College, PA: Penn State Press, 2012.

Esty, Daniel C., Jack A. Goldstone, Ted Robert Gurr, Barbara Harff, Pamela T. Surko, Alan N. Unger, and Robert Chen. "The State Failure Project: Early Warning Research for U.S. Foreign Policy Planning." Presented at *Failed States and International Security: Causes, Prospects, and Consequences*. Purdue University, West Lafayette, February 25–27, 1998. Web access: http://www.comm.ucsb.edu/faculty/mstohl/failed_states/1998/pape rs/gurr.html.

Everett, Jim A. C. "Intergroup Contact Theory: Past, Present, and Future." In *The Inquisitive Mind* 17. Last modified 2013. http://www.in-mind.org/article/intergroup-contact-theory-past-present-and-future.

Federman, Sarah. "Genocide Studies and Corporate Social Responsibility: The Contemporary Case of the French National Railways (SNCF)." *Genocide Studies and Prevention* 11, no. 2 (2017): 13–35.

Fine, Michelle and María Elena Torre. "Re-Membering Exclusions: Participatory Action Research in Public Institutions." *Qualitative Research in Psychology* 1, no. 1 (2004): 15–37.

Fisher, Roger and Daniel Shapiro. "Emotions Are Powerful, Always Present and Hard to Handle." In *Beyond Reason: Using Emotions as You Negotiate*, 3–14. New York: Penguin, 2005.

Fontan, Victoria. "The Case for Decolonizing Peace." In *Decolonizing Peace*. Lake Oswego, OR: Dignity Press, 2012.

Galtung, Johan. "Violence, Peace and Peace Research." *Journal of Peace Research* 6, no. 3 (1969) 167–91.

Gardner, Michael. "The Dork Police." In *Sweet Fruit from the Bitter Tree: 61 Stories of Creative & Compassionate Ways out of Conflict*, edited by Mark Andreas, 85–92. Boulder, CO: Real People Press, 2011.

Ginwright, Shawn A. "Fostering Caring Relationships for Social Justice." In *Black Youth Rising: Activism and Radical Healing in Urban America*, 53–76. New York: Teachers College Press, 2010.

Gopin, Marc. "Religion as an Aid and a Hindrance to Postconflict Coexistence Work." In *Imagine Coexistence: Restoring Humanity After Violent Ethnic Conflict*, edited by Antonia Chayes and Martha Minow, 252–66. San Francisco, CA: Jossey-Bass, 2003.

Hansen, Toran. "Critical Conflict Resolution Theory and Practice." *Conflict Resolution Quarterly* 25, no. 4 (March 2008): 403–27.

Hoey, Brian A. "A Simple Introduction to the Practice of Ethnography and Guide to Ethnographic Fieldnotes." West Virginia: Bepress; Marshall University Digital Scholar, June (2014).

Institute for Economics and Peace, Visions of Humanity. "Global Peace Index." Last modified 2017. http://visionofhumanity.org/indexes/global-peace-index/.

———. "Global Terrorism Index." Last modified 2017. http://visionofhumanity.org/indexes/terrorism-index/.

Irmer, Cynthia and Daniel Druckman. "Explaining Negotiation Outcomes: Process or Context?" *Negotiation and Conflict Management Research* 2, no. 3 (2009): 209–35.

Jabri, Vivienne. "Introduction: Conflict Analysis Reconsidered." In *Discourses on Violence: Conflict Analysis Reconsidered*, 1–28. New York: Manchester University Press, 1996.

Kelman, Herbert C. "Interactive Problem Solving as a Tool for Second Track Diplomacy." In *Second Track Citizens Diplomacy: Concepts and Techniques for Conflict*, 81–106. Lanham, MD: Rowman & Littlefield, 2002.

Kriesberg, Louis. "Identity Issues." In *Beyond Intractability*, edited by Guy Burgess and Heidi Burgess. Conflict Information Consortium, University of Colorado, Boulder. Last modified July 2003. http://www.beyondintractability.org/essay/identity-issues.

Lederach, John Paul. "An Integrated Model for Peacebuilding." In *Building Peace: Sustainable Reconciliation in Divided Societies*, 73–87. Washington, DC: United States Institute of Peace, 1997.

McClellan, Jeffrey L. "Marrying Positive Psychology to Mediation: Using Appreciative Inquiry and Solution-Focused Counseling to Improve the Process." *Dispute Resolution Journal* 62, no. 4 (2007): 29–35.

Monk, Gerald and John Winslade. *When Stories Clash: Addressing Conflict with Narrative Mediation*. Chagrin Falls, OH: Taos Institute Publications, 2012.

Nelson, Hilde Lindemann. "Reclaiming Moral Agency." In *Damaged Identities, Narrative Repair*, 1–35. Ithaca, NY: Cornell University Press, 2001.

Nordstrom, Carolyn. "Prologue." In *Shadows of War: Violence, Power, and International Profiteering in the Twenty-First Century*. Berkeley, CA: University of California Press, 2004.

Payne, Leigh A. "Contentious Coexistence." In *Unsettling Accounts: Neither Truth nor Reconciliation in Confessions of State Violence*, 279–92. Durham, NC: Duke University Press, 2008.

Pearce, Barnette and Stephen Littlejohn. "The Problem of Moral Conflict." In *Moral Conflict When Social Worlds Collide*, 48–81. Thousand Oaks, CA: Sage, 1997.

Rotberg, Robert I. and Dennis Thompson. "Truth Commissions and the Provision of Truth, Justice and Reconciliation." In *Truth v. Justice: The Morality of Truth Commissions*, 3–21. Princeton, NJ: Princeton University Press, 2010.

Sander, Frank E. A. "Alternative Methods of Dispute Resolution: An Overview." *University of Florida Law Review* 37 (1985): 1–18.

Sharp, Gene. "Facing Acute Conflict." In *Waging Nonviolent Struggle: 20th Century Practice and 21st Century Potential*, 13–24. Manchester, NH: Extended Horizons: 2005.

Vallacher, Robin R., Peter T. Coleman, Andrzej Nowak, Lan Bui-Wrzosinska. "Rethinking Intractable Conflict: The Perspective of Dynamical Systems." *American Psychologist* 65, no. 4 (2010): 262–78.

Volkan, Vamık D. "Large-Group Psychodynamics and Massive Violence." *Ciência & Saúde Coletiva*, 11, no. 2 (2006): 303–14.

Wertheim, Edward. "Negotiations and Resolving Conflicts: An Overview." College of Business Administration: Northeastern University, 2002.

Winslade, John and Gerald Monk. "Narrative Mediation: What Is It?" In *Narrative Mediation: A New Approach to Conflict Resolution*, 1–31. San Francisco, CA: Jossey-Bass, 2000.

Index

Page references for figures are italicized.